Comments on the first edition of *Scottish Education* included:

'The most comprehensive treatment ever of education in Scotland.'

Peter Scott, *Scottish Affairs*

'Extraordinarily good value . . . a vast assembly of impressive material.'

David Eastwood, *Times Educational Supplement Scotland*

'No end of authoritative material . . . The editors . . . deserve high admiration for an enormous labour of love.'

Dick Louden, *The Herald*

'*Scottish Education* is magnificently modest. It is never oversold . . . It is . . . a new platform, a new provocation. Others [who] will take up the challenge in their deliberations and practices . . . have much to emulate.'

David Hamilton, *Scottish Educational Review*

'This book tells us comprehensively how Scottish education works. It also sets a research agenda for the future.'

Sheena Erskine, *International Review of Education*

Comments on the second edition of *Scottish Education* included:

'A text that is authoritative yet accessible, scholarly yet provocative, definitive yet iconoclastic.'

Frank Pignatelli, *Times Educational Supplement Scotland*

'Excellent and admirably succinct . . . We are indebted to the hard working editors and authors. I am now much better informed, if a tad exhausted, by my reading of this important book.'

Sally Brown, *Scottish Educational Review*

Comments on the third edition of *Scottish Education* included:

'There are numerous chapters where the level of analysis is impressively high, which are models of lucidity, perceptive and stimulating, and well (in some cases, elegantly) written.'

Gordon Kirk, *Times Educational Supplement Scotland*

'A compendium which provides a compleat overview of the Scottish Education system. In all, this is a book even bigger than the sum of its parts.'

Cate Watson, *Education in the North*

'This third edition is an impressive and informative volume . . . a useful mix of "insider" practitioner perspectives with external "outsider" perspectives from academic researchers, journalists and a sprinkling of politicians and officials.'

Jean Barr, *British Journal of Educational Studies*

'As an account of Scottish education today, for anyone involved in or merely interested in education, this is an invaluable and unique source of information.'

Liz Clark, *Scottish Educational Review*

The first edition was awarded a Special Commendation in the National Library of Scotland/Saltire Society Research Book of the Year Award 1999.

SCOTTISH EDUCATION
FOURTH EDITION: REFERENDUM

Edited by T. G. K. Bryce, W. M. Humes, D. Gillies
and A. Kennedy

Section editing by
Julie Allan
Tom Bryce
Ian Finlay
Donald Gillies
Walter Humes
Aileen Kennedy
Ian Menter
Ian Smith

EDINBURGH
University Press

© in this edition Edinburgh University Press, 2013

Copyright in the individual contributions is retained by the authors

First edition published 1999
Second edition published 2003
Third edition published 2008

Reprinted 2014

Edinburgh University Press Ltd
22 George Square, Edinburgh EH8 9LF
www.euppublishing.com

Typeset in 10 on 12pt Ehrhardt by
Servis Filmsetting Ltd, Stockport, Cheshire, and
printed and bound in the UK by Charlesworth Press, Wakefield

A CIP record for this book is available from the British Library

ISBN 978 0 7486 4582 4 (paperback)
ISBN 978 0 7486 7810 5 (webready PDF)
ISBN 978 0 7486 7812 9 (epub)

The right of the contributors to be identified as authors
of this work has been asserted in accordance with the
Copyright, Designs and Patents Act 1988.

Front cover photos, left and bottom, and rear cover photo, top right: courtesy Alamy.
Front cover photo, right: courtesy Simon Price, Firstpix.

Contents

The Contributors

Julie Allan is Professor of Equity and Inclusion at the University of Birmingham and Visiting Professor at the University of Borås, Sweden.

Robert Anderson is Professor Emeritus of History, University of Edinburgh. He has written extensively on the history of education, in Scotland and elsewhere. His most recent books are *Education and the Scottish People, 1750–1918* (1995), *European Universities from the Enlightenment to 1914* (2004) and *British Universities Past and Present* (2006).

Rowena Arshad is Head of Moray House School of Education and Co-Director of the Centre for Education for Racial Equality in Scotland, University of Edinburgh.

Will Barlow is a Teacher of Drama within a local authority in the west coast of Scotland and a Doctoral student at the University of Strathclyde.

David Bell is Professor of Economics at the University of Stirling and at the Institute for the Study of Labor, Bonn.

Gert Biesta is Professor of Educational Theory and Policy at the University of Luxembourg.

Keir Bloomer is Chair of the Tapestry Partnership, Chair of the Court of Queen Margaret University and Chair of the School Reform Commission. He was formerly Chief Executive and Director of Education of Clackmannanshire Council.

Bill Boyd is an independent literacy consultant. A former English Teacher and DHT, he was an Education Manager at Learning and Teaching Scotland (now Education Scotland) during the development of Curriculum for Excellence.

Anne Bradley is Associate Tutor for PGDE, Secondary, Business Education at University of Glasgow School of Education; SQA Principal Assessor for Intermediate 1 and 2 Administration; and CPD Training Consultant for Business Education subjects.

Bob Brewer is a Lecturer in the Institute of Sport, Physical Education and Health Sciences at the University of Edinburgh.

Karen Bryce is Principal Teacher of Home Economics at Lochend Community High School in Glasgow.

Tom Bryce is Emeritus Professor of Education, University of Strathclyde in Glasgow. A former Vice-Dean for Research, his interests are principally concerned with Scottish teacher education and with science education, much of his research output being published in the *International Journal of Science Education*.

Richard Buchan is Head Teacher at Garrowhill Primary School, Glasgow.

Douglas Buchanan is a Lecturer at the Moray House School of Education, University of Edinburgh.

Alison Cameron is a Quality Improvement Manager in Learning and Leisure Services, North Lanarkshire Council.

Pete Cannell is Depute Director (Learning, Teaching and Curriculum) at the Open University in Scotland.

Roy Canning is a Senior Lecturer in the School of Education, University of Stirling.

Mike Carroll is PGDE Programme Leader and Programme Leader for the Masters in Professional Learning and Enquiry at the School of Education, University of Glasgow.

Claire Cassidy is a Senior Lecturer in the School of Education at the University of Strathclyde.

John Cavanagh, a teacher of Technical Education, has occupied several senior-level posts in Scottish schools. He is currently head teacher of his second secondary school. A doctoral graduate of the University of Glasgow, John was recently Chairman of the Educational Colloquium of the Universities of Glasgow, Strathclyde and West of Scotland.

Graham Connelly is senior lecturer in the Glasgow School of Social Work and is a researcher in the Centre for Excellence for Looked After Children in Scotland (CELCIS) at the University of Strathclyde.

James C. Conroy is Professor of Religious and Philosophical Education and Dean for European Engagement and Strategy at the University of Glasgow.

Amanda Corrigan is a Senior Teaching Fellow in the School of Education at the University of Strathclyde.

Stephen P. Day is a Lecturer in Education in the School of Education at the University of the West of Scotland.

Robert Doherty is a Lecturer in Education and Coordinator of Concurrent Education and programme leader for the Bachelor of Technological Education Programme in the School of Education, University of Glasgow.

Valerie Drew is a Lecturer in Professional Education in the School of Education, University of Stirling.

Sue Ellis is Reader in Education at the University of Strathclyde.

John Field is Professor of Lifelong Learning and Director of Research in the School of Education, University of Stirling.

Tony Finn is the Chief Executive at the General Teaching Council for Scotland.

Larry Flanagan is General Secretary of the Educational Institute of Scotland and a member of both the STUC and TUC General Councils.

Andy Furlong AcSS is Professor of Social Inclusion and Education and Director of Research in the School of Education, University of Glasgow.

Hugh Gallagher is a Lecturer in the School of Education at the University of Strathclyde.

Bill Gatherer, who died in 2009, was an HMI and Chief Adviser in Lothian.

Donald Gillies is Professor of Education Policy at York St John University. From 2005 to 2012 he was Lecturer, and then Senior Lecturer, in Educational Studies at the University of Strathclyde. He is the compiler of *A Brief Critical Dictionary of Education*, a free online resource available at www.dictionaryofeducation.co.uk

Donald Gray is a Senior Lecturer and Director of Research and Interdisciplinarity in the School of Education, University of Aberdeen.

Sotiria Grek is a Lecturer in Social Policy at the School of Social and Political Science, University of Edinburgh.

Deirdre Grogan is a Senior Lecturer in the School of Education at the University of Strathclyde.

Tom Hamilton is Director of Education and Professional Learning at the General Teaching Council for Scotland. Qualified in both Primary and Secondary, Tom was a

Principal Teacher of English then worked in a variety of roles in teacher education before joining the GTCS, where he is now involved in developing, promoting and implementing the Council's educational policies.

Linda Harris is a Lecturer in the School of Education at the University of Strathclyde.

George Head is Senior Lecturer in Inclusive Education at the University of Glasgow.

Allan Hewitt is a Senior Lecturer in the School of Psychological Sciences and Health, University of Strathclyde.

Peter Higgins is Professor of Outdoor and Environmental Education at the Moray House School of Education, University of Edinburgh.

Cathy Howieson is a Senior Research Fellow in the Centre for Educational Sociology at the University of Edinburgh.

Moira Hulme is Lecturer in Educational Research in the School of Education, University of Glasgow.

Ian Hulse is a Teacher of Mathematics at Menzieshill High School, Dundee.

Walter Humes is a Visiting Professor of Education at the University of Stirling. Prior to retirement in 2010 he held professorships at the universities of Aberdeen, Strathclyde and the West of Scotland.

Simon Jennings is the Director of Strategy and Policy at the University of Strathclyde and was previously Deputy Director (Policy) at Universities Scotland.

Aileen Kennedy is a Senior Lecturer in the School of Education at the University of Strathclyde.

George Kerevan is a freelance journalist and broadcaster. He was formerly associate editor of *The Scotsman* and, in an earlier incarnation, an academic economist.

Vic Lally is a Professor of Education at the University of Glasgow. He is Director of the Interdisciplinary Group for Research and Teaching in STEM Education and the Interdisciplinary Group for Science, Education, Technologies and Learning (ISETL).

Alastair Lavery is Chair of the Sustainable Development Education Network and former Head of Education for RSPB Scotland.

Don Ledingham is Executive Director of Services for People, East Lothian Council; and Director of Education and Children's Services, Midlothian Council.

Helen E. Lees is Research Fellow in the Laboratory for Educational Theory in the School of Education, University of Stirling. She is founding Editor-in-Chief of *Other Education*, the online open-access journal of educational alternatives: www.othereducation.org

Clare McAlister is a Teaching Fellow and the PGDE Geography Coordinator in the School of Education at the University of Strathclyde.

Diarmuid McAuliffe is a Lecturer and Subject Leader for Art and Design Education, in the School of Education, University of the West of Scotland.

John MacBeath OBE is Professor Emeritus at the University of Cambridge and Projects Director of the Commonwealth Education Centre.

Chris McIlroy worked for twenty years as a primary teacher and head teacher in Glasgow. Until he retired in 2011, he had responsibilities for seven years as a chief inspector in HMIE. He is currently leading an extended course for primary classroom teachers in Glasgow and working with the School of Education, University of Strathclyde.

Janis McIntyre is an Educational Developer in the Centre for Lifelong Learning, University of Liverpool.

Tommy MacKay is Director of Psychology Consultancy Services and Visiting Professor of Autism Studies at the University of Strathclyde.

Stephen J. McKinney is a Senior Lecturer in the School of Education, University of Glasgow.

David J. McLaren is a Senior Lecturer in the School of Education at the University of Strathclyde.

Effie Maclellan is Research Professor of Education in the School of Education, University of Strathclyde.

Neil McLennan is Acting Service Manager (Education, Culture and Sport) for Aberdeen City Council. He has served as President of both the Scottish Association of Teachers of History and the Enterprise Practitioners' Association. Currently he chairs the Royal Society of Edinburgh, Young Academy of Scotland Curriculum for Excellence Working Group.

Kenneth MacMillan is a Physics teacher and Acting Principal Teacher of Pastoral Care in Jordanhill School in Glasgow.

Marie-Jeanne McNaughton is a Senior Lecturer in the School of Education, Faculty of Humanities and Social Sciences at the University of Strathclyde.

Henry Maitles is Professor of Education and interim Head of School in the School of Education at the University of the West of Scotland.

Rob Mark is currently Reader and Head of Lifelong Learning at the University of Strathclyde, Glasgow.

Joan Martlew is Course Leader of the BA Childhood Practice degree and Lecturer in the School of Education, University of Strathclyde.

Ian Menter is Professor of Teacher Education and Director of Professional Programmes in the Department of Education at the University of Oxford.

James Miller is Director, Open University in Scotland.

Ian Milligan is a Senior Lecturer in the School of Applied Social Sciences at the University of Strathclyde and international lead for the Centre for Excellence for Looked after Children in Scotland (CELCIS).

Lio Moscardini is a Senior Lecturer in the School of Education, University of Strathclyde.

Robert Munro is an international e-learning consultant who was formerly Reader in ICT at the University of Strathclyde.

Anton Muscatelli is Principal and Vice-Chancellor of the University of Glasgow. His fields of research interest are monetary economics, including central bank independence and EMU, fiscal policy and macroeconomics.

Robbie Nicol is a Senior Lecturer and Programme Director of Outdoor, Environmental and Sustainability Education at the Moray House School of Education, University of Edinburgh.

Liz Niven is a Scottish poet and editor. She facilitates creative writing sessions in Educational Authorities and National Institutions across Scotland. She has participated in literary and language festivals in Europe, Scandinavia and China. www.lizniven.com

Graeme Nixon, formerly a Principal Teacher of RMPS, is a Lecturer at the University of Aberdeen's School of Education. Apart from teacher education in RME/RMPS for primary and secondary sectors, he has a number of teaching and research interests. He recently gained a doctorate in which he explores the reasons for the emergence of philosophy in RME.

Vincent Oates is a Lecturer in History in the School of Education at the University of Strathclyde.

Michael Osborne is Professor of Adult and Lifelong Learning, Director of the Centre for Research and Development in Adult and Lifelong Learning and Co-director of the PASCAL Observatory, School of Education, University of Glasgow.

Fran Payne is an Emeritus Senior Research Fellow in the School of Education, University of Aberdeen. She was President of SERA from 2003 to 2005.

Monica Porciani trained as a teacher of Biology and after a number of years working as a Public Health Specialist is now an Associate Lecturer for Health and Wellbeing at the School of Education, University of Strathclyde.

Mark Priestley is Professor of Education in the School of Education at the University of Stirling, where he is Director of the Curriculum and Pedagogy research programme. His main research interests concern the school curriculum, and especially the processes of curricular change.

Eileen Prior is the Executive Director at SPTC, the national membership organisation for parent groups in Scottish schools, based in Edinburgh.

Jackie Ravet is a Senior Lecturer and Director of Research Culture and Support in the School of Education, University of Aberdeen.

Morag Redford is a Senior Teaching Fellow and Director of Professional Education in the School of Education, University of Stirling.

Brian Reid retired as Associate Dean and Head of Division of Business and Computer Education in the Faculty of Education at the University of Strathclyde in 2008. He is currently a Principal Examiner with the University of Cambridge Local Examinations Syndicate.

Lesley Reid is a Senior Lecturer and Director of the PGDE (Primary) Programme at the Moray House School of Education, University of Edinburgh.

Sheila Riddell is Professor and the founding Director of the Centre for Research in Education, Inclusion and Diversity at the Moray House School of Education, University of Edinburgh.

Alasdair Roberts is a full-time writer in retirement from Aberdeen University's School of Education.

Boyd Robertson is Professor and Principal of Sabhal Mòr Ostaig, the National Centre for Gaelic Language and Culture, and one of the colleges of the University of the Highlands and Islands.

Janys M. Scott QC is a member of the Faculty of Advocates and the author of *Education Law in Scotland*.

Sheila Semple is an Associate in the Centre for Educational Sociology, University of Edinburgh.

Daniela Sime is a Senior Lecturer in the School of Applied Social Sciences at the University of Strathclyde. Her major research studies have focused on the experiences of migrant children, the impact of child poverty on children's education and improvement of service delivery for families.

Frances Simpson has been a Lecturer in Environmental Education in initial teacher education at both Strathclyde University and the University of the West of Scotland for a number of years and now works freelance.

Christine Sinclair is a Lecturer in E-learning at the Moray House School of Education, University of Edinburgh. She previously worked in educational development in three other Scottish universities.

Ian Smith is a Professor of Education at the University of the West of Scotland, where he was Head and Dean of the School of Education from 2000 to 2009.

Raymond Soltysek is a Lecturer in the School of Education at the University of Strathclyde, and is presently writing a behaviour management book aimed at early career professionals for SAGE publications.

Ernie Spencer is an Honorary Senior Research Fellow in the School of Education, University of Glasgow.

Craig Thomson's work and writing is focused on tourism and education. He has worked in education in the post-school sector in Scotland, England and internationally, including thirteen years as CEO/principal level in Scotland's college sector.

Dan Tierney is a Reader in Language Education at the University of Strathclyde.

Deirdre Torrance is Director of the Masters in Educational Leadership and Management and Director of the Certificate in Developing Educational Leadership and Learning in the Moray House School of Education, University of Edinburgh. Her PhD was entitled *Distributed Leadership in Scottish Primary Schools: Myth or Actualities?*

Rob van Krieken retired as Project Manager in SQA's Policy & New Products team in 2013.

David Wallace is Senior Lecturer in Community Education in the School of Applied Social Sciences, University of Strathclyde.

Malcolm Wilson is a Lecturer in Childhood Practice at Reid Kerr College, Paisley.

I

INTRODUCTION AND OVERVIEW

1

An Introduction to *Scottish Education, Fourth Edition: Referendum*

Tom Bryce and Walter Humes

This book provides an informed and critical account of contemporary education in Scotland, treating each of the main sectors (pre-school, primary, secondary, further, adult and higher education) in depth. The text tries to explain in detail 'how it all works' and, to do so, four important perspectives are also examined critically – the historical, the cultural, the political and the socio-economic. Each of the chapters was commissioned from specialists who have drawn upon up-to-date research and contemporary analysis to give fresh insights into educational developments in the period leading up to the referendum of 2014, when the Scottish populace will determine whether or not to opt for political independence from the rest of the UK. The text combines 'insider' perspectives, where material has been written by educationists with first-hand experience of their own organisations or fields of influence, and 'outsider' perspectives, where researchers and analysts have provided reflective commentary on a range of related topics. All of the contributors were asked to combine concise description with critical analysis – to give, in addition to basic information, an outline of the more contentious debates among the professionals concerned with each area. The balance of description to critique varies across the chapters, it being rather more difficult for 'insiders' to be as detached as 'outsiders'. Conversely the knowledge and insight which the 'insiders' have brought to the text is substantial and, in some respects, cannot be matched by the 'outsiders'. What is contained in this text is what Scottish educators think about their own educational system; the writers have revealed its strengths and its weaknesses, their pride in it and their concerns for it. They have endeavoured to 'tell it as it is', in contrast to the rhetorical prose so prevalent in much of the documentation issued by agencies in association with modern governments.

THE FIRST EDITION: 1999

SE1 Scottish Education	1999	Eds Bryce & Humes
SE2 Scottish Education: Post-devolution	2003	Eds Bryce & Humes
SE3 Scottish Education: Beyond Devolution	2008	Eds Bryce & Humes
SE4 Scottish Education: Referendum	2013	Eds Bryce, Humes, Gillies & Kennedy

The first edition of *Scottish Education* was published to coincide with the end of the millennium and the re-instatement of the Scottish Parliament in 1999. The editors reasoned that an understanding of education at that time, appropriately contextualised, would be important to the evolution of educational policy and practice in the future. The main target audience was both trainee and experienced teachers engaged in professional development. Sharing the broad spectrum of thinking which relates to policy and action is an important step in becoming an effective teacher or in extending one's field of influence and competence. Understanding the distinctive features of education in Scotland was considered important. That said, not everything about Scottish education is distinctive. Rather, an attempt was made to provide a wide range of material which would allow others to make their own judgements as to what is unique; what is similar but different; and what is indeed comparable to practices elsewhere in the UK, in Europe and beyond. In the final analysis, it would be for the reader to weigh things up and form judgements in the light of the evidence.

Pleasingly, the first edition was well received by both academics and students. Reviewers in many journals commended the authors for their informed and well-researched accounts: the content was both authoritative and critical in setting out what matters to educators. Student teachers and postgraduates (teachers and other professionals pursuing higher degrees as part of their continuing professional development) alike welcomed the accessibility that the text brought. A considerable amount of relevant material had been covered in one volume, pleasing students and education course directors alike. It was heartening also to learn how many others – researchers, organisations, individuals in central and local government, journalists and even some politicians – found the text to be a useful source of essential information.

THE SECOND EDITION: 2003

SE1 Scottish Education	1999	Eds Bryce & Humes
SE2 Scottish Education: Post-devolution	2003	Eds Bryce & Humes
SE3 Scottish Education: Beyond Devolution	2008	Eds Bryce & Humes
SE4 Scottish Education: Referendum	2013	Eds Bryce, Humes, Gillies & Kennedy

Four years on, a second edition was judged to be required and *Scottish Education: Post-devolution* was published in 2003. The first years of the Scottish Parliament had witnessed more changes than predicted, many but not all of them deriving from the operations of the Parliament itself. New departments of central government had introduced reform and local government continued to evolve, despite fears that centralisation of educational control might quickly result. Key bodies had changed or merged. Important initiatives had been brought about through the passing of the Parliament's first Act in 2000 (fittingly an Education Act). Primary, secondary and tertiary education had all encountered major shifts, particularly secondary and further education, with the implementation of National Qualifications (known initially as Higher Still). Universities had struggled with ever-increasing student numbers and related financial difficulties. Scottish education had survived its worst ever catastrophe with the Scottish Qualifications Authority exam debacle of 2000. The second edition reflected education post-devolution, tracking the effects of new parliamentary thinking and organisational change and brought everything up to date. Crucial gaps were filled and nine new topics were added in response to helpful feedback from readers. Some forty-two new authors were involved, many of the original team having changed field or retired.

The second edition continued to enjoy the popular and critical acclaim of its predecessor. Students and teachers, as well as reviewers and colleagues who work in teacher education throughout Scotland, said that the text was a unique source of vital information and ideas, helpful to their study and work, not least by what it locates in one accessible volume. Like their forerunners in the first edition, the authors of the 2003 *Post-devolution* edition had produced authoritative material and sharp reflective commentary. Along with commendation came an expectation that there should be future editions; that a book of this kind, updated as required, would be required from time to time to ensure shared understandings and common concerns throughout the profession.

THE THIRD EDITION: 2008

SE1 Scottish Education	1999	Eds Bryce & Humes
SE2 Scottish Education: Post-devolution	2003	Eds Bryce & Humes
SE3 Scottish Education: Beyond Devolution	2008	Eds Bryce & Humes
SE4 Scottish Education: Referendum	2013	Eds Bryce, Humes, Gillies & Kennedy

Five years on, the third edition, *Scottish Education: Beyond Devolution*, was published in 2008, the title signalling that the coverage concerned educational thinking and practice firmly contextualised in the by then familiar setting of devolved government – indeed with debate about independence on the increase (more of which later). The rapid developments in education between 2003 and 2008 could not be put down simply to devolution *per se*. The Labour/Liberal Democrat coalition which lasted until May 2007 continued to recognise the financial pressures on (post-school) students and adhered to its commitments to student support (for example, through not introducing top-up fees), though the consequences for the institutions themselves were demanding and rather complex. The school sector saw the beginnings of major curricular change with Curriculum for Excellence offering greater prospects for flexibility and 'bottom-up' initiatives to shift the system away from the constraining effects of 5–14. Some teachers became enthused and helped to bring about fast-changing developments, particularly in the primary sector; others awaited persuasion and change, such was the legacy of years of an *over*-specification of content and targets. Both primary and secondary schools had worked with new legislation concerned with learning support and, throughout both sectors, there was increasing recognition of the real benefits of formative assessment, a matter that sat (and continues to sit) uncomfortably alongside formal grading and the domination of the later stages of schooling by examinations and certification. As the third edition was going to print, the promised consultation on the upper school curriculum and assessment had just begun.

Significant political change was heralded, however, by the elections of May 2007, returning an SNP minority government under the leadership of Alex Salmond. In education, some changes were immediately signalled, such as a reduction in class sizes, beginning with the early years of primary school, and the abolition of the graduate endowment tax. A 're-branding' of the political framework took place in the autumn of 2007 when the new administration changed 'Scottish Executive' to 'Scottish Government'. (The word 'Executive' is still the legal term to be used in relation to parliamentary bills for that term featured in the legislation that set up the Scottish Parliament.) It was thought that other, more significant, changes would be predicated upon successful financial management at national level, particularly in the lead-up to the proposed referendum on independence which, at that time, was set to take place in 2010. It was anticipated that the government would not shift significantly on many matters of educational policy, but it was hoped that the consultation on examinations and certification would result in speedy, firm direction for the future of the upper secondary stages of schooling (which it did not).

Thus the commissioning of the authors for the third edition of *Scottish Education* took place during a period marked both by complex change and by hesitant expectations on several fronts. There is never a time when something like education stands still, permitting it to be thoughtfully described as 'in place': there is always a need for its fast-evolving complexity to be critiqued in order that participating professionals, and other stakeholders, can regain focus and, hopefully, impetus. Some forty new authors were commissioned for the third edition, testimony to the extent of change among personnel in schools, universities and government organisations. A few topics were dropped and/or relocated and combined differently, and three new topics were added: Citizenship Education; the Social Sciences in the Secondary Curriculum; and Multi-Agency Working. There was also a new, final section devoted to the future of education in Scotland.

As did the first two editions, SE3 received positive commendations from pre-service student teachers, from teachers studying for post-initial qualifications and degrees, and from reviewers in academic journals. It was pleasing to see that *Scottish Education* had become so established, an essential source text or guide to the educational system, spelling things out through critical appraisals of what goes on.

THE FOURTH EDITION: 2013

SE1 Scottish Education	1999	Eds Bryce & Humes
SE2 Scottish Education: Post-devolution	2003	Eds Bryce & Humes
SE3 Scottish Education: Beyond Devolution	2008	Eds Bryce & Humes
SE4 Scottish Education: Referendum	2013	Eds Bryce, Humes, Gillies & Kennedy

Not long after the publication of SE3 in 2008, the financial crisis affecting all of the developed world economies began with the calamities in banking. Public-sector pay freezes were quickly put in place in Scotland, as elsewhere in the UK, directly affecting the income of teachers and lecturers, and restricted budgets throughout the sector began to affect staffing, services and commitments. Scotland's economy was managed well by the SNP minority administration and the education sector fared no worse than in the other parts of the UK. Nevertheless, financial difficulties everywhere have continued to the present day, with little sign of improvement. During these years, a variety of different problems arose in education, not all caused directly by economics, though the financial ones have been the most challenging. Universities, largely driven by cost considerations (but also with an eye to the state of research and what particular institutions chose to prioritise), one by one took decisions to restructure themselves and to reduce their staffing, particularly in education. Details aside for the present, redundancies and non-replacement of lecturers resulted in consequence. There was a massive loss of experience and expertise across the seven institutions concerned with initial teacher education: faculties of education were reduced to 'schools' within larger structures. In further education, similar retrenchment took place and college mergers were accelerated as a result. At the time of writing, plans were in place to reduce Scotland's forty-one colleges to twenty-eight in number. In local authorities, restructuring led to the loss of many of the staff supporting teachers in various capacities, with reduced budgets necessitating shared arrangements across schools. Schools themselves have had to endure significant budget constraints and losses in staffing, particularly auxiliary staff in various categories.

Politically, the national election in 2011 resulted in a sweeping victory for the SNP under Alex Salmond due in part, no doubt, to his commanding leadership in difficult times and to perceptions of government prudence in the preceding four years. Clearly, the electorate considered that public services had been administered competently. Educationally, the new Cabinet Secretary, Michael Russell, had several significant matters to contend with. The fallout of the UK government's 2010 Browne Report into the funding of higher education (with universities raising fees dramatically and students being required to repay loans at the cost of borrowing to government) led to significant differences between Scotland and the rest of the UK. With regard to the school curriculum, the national consultation on assessment and certification saw government setting a timescale for the replacement of Standard Grade and Intermediate 1 and 2 Awards by National Awards at levels 4 and 5, though that proved to be difficult for many authorities and schools. It was coupled with the continuing slow implementation of Curriculum for Excellence in secondary schools and protracted debates about the specifications offered in respect of curriculum content and delays in consequence. How long a 'broad general education' should last in secondary schools (one, two or three years, three being the preference of government) became a matter of serious debate for it determines when National level 4 and 5 courses should commence.

Thus the commissioning of authors for a fourth edition of *Scottish Education* took place at a time of even greater challenges for all involved in education. Political machinations ensued between the Scottish SNP administration and the Conservative/Liberal Democrat Coalition government of the UK formed in 2010, regarding the date for the long-promised referendum on independence. At the time of writing, 2014 looked like the probable date, hence the choice of subtitle for this book. More than sixty new authors were required, once more reflecting how many of the previous editions' writers had departed from their posts throughout the various sectors, not least from university faculties/schools of education (for the reasons described above). The book's layout is similar to that of SE3, except that organisational and management issues affecting primary and secondary schools have been put together in one section (V). A number of new topics have been included, with chapters entitled Learning in Scottish Schools (6), Alternative Forms of Schooling (12), Education and the Law (17), Sustainable Development Education (31), The Scottish Approach to School Improvement (41), From Adult Learning to Lifelong Learning in Scotland (84), Poverty and Schooling in Scotland (92), The Funding of Scottish Education (105) and an additional chapter on The 3–18 Curriculum in Scotland (3). Two of the chapters are unaltered from SE3. One deals with the history of Scottish education up to 1980 (Chapter 22) and did not need updating. The other is Chapter 104 by Bill Gatherer on Scottish teachers. Sadly, Bill died not long after the publication of SE3. He was a highly respected figure in educational circles and the chapter has been enjoyed by many. Editors should not identify preferences but, unashamedly, this was a favourite of Bryce and Humes who have fond memories of the man's erudition and wit. The chapter has been included here, with the permission of his family, as a tribute to his contribution to education in Scotland.

Some aspects of the structure of the text will be self-evident from the section titles; however, certain emphases merit explicit comment and these are provided in the preface to each section (located at the start of the respective sections, as they were for SE3). All educationists share a professional shorthand, well known by the profusion of abbreviations and acronyms, and Scotland is no different from elsewhere in Europe. We have endeavoured to have these spelled out within each chapter where they are first encountered – for example, Education Scotland (ES) – but an additional glossary of terms and abbreviations has been supplied at the end of the volume. This lists all of the items found in the text and it is included in addition to the conventional index.

The final section of the book, 'The Future', has been included to provide focused thinking about several dimensions of Scottish education: the future of schools, colleges and universities, together with the funding of education, and an exploration of the tensions between local and central government, set against the European perspective. The chapters each consider the challenges and difficulties immediately ahead of us. In their very different ways, the writers say what has to be tackled and how the problems should be conceptualised. The final chapter, written by the editors, gives our own view of current affairs, not least what might happen in education depending on the outcome of the referendum. One way or the other, there will be implications for any future editions of this book.

REQUESTS MADE TO AUTHORS

We asked contributors to maintain the tone and quality of previous editions, requiring them to give a clear account of current provision but also to have an eye to the future. Among other recommendations, we asked that:

- Chapters should take account of recent research findings relevant to the topic.
- Reference should be made to recent policy initiatives and their implementation to date.
- Where there are areas of debate or controversy these should be explained and analysed.
- Chapters should not be simply descriptive but should offer a sharp, critical perspective on key issues.
- End of chapter references should be limited to ten. These should direct the interested reader to key texts should they require further material.
- Chapters should be of 5,000 words (the main chapters) or 2,500 words (notably the subject/ curriculum chapters, but also several others).
- In the case of the secondary curriculum chapters, authors should comment, where possible, on the effects of the faculty structures which had been imposed and the progress of any interdisciplinary developments as part of Curriculum for Excellence.
- The text should be readable by a wide audience but without over-simplification of complex issues: the over-use of professional jargon should be avoided wherever possible. The readership would consist mainly of student teachers and teachers undertaking various forms of continuing professional development, but the text would also be consulted by a wide range of researchers, administrators and policy makers.

CONFLICTING PERSPECTIVES

As before, it should be recognised that with so many contributing authors there are some conflicts and a few tensions evident in the text itself: it would be unreasonable to expect complete consistency of view and interpretation from everyone. In some instances the editors do not share the line taken by the author, nor would we expect to do so. Many issues in education are highly contestable and a healthy system requires vigorous debate. The individual writers were certainly encouraged to express their own reasoned position for the stances they take.

SECTIONS AND SECTION EDITING

Like the first three editions, this volume would not have seen the light of day had it not been for the good efforts of those friends and colleagues who shared the editing with diligence, patience and care, in some cases taking material from rough first draft, through several revisions, to the final published version contained in the text. Three of the section editors have now worked with us over two editions – Aileen Kennedy, Julie Allan and Ian Menter. Several were new to the task – Ian Smith, Ian Finlay and Donald Gillies. They tackled the work with energy and flair and, to them all, we express our sincere personal gratitude. The sections are:

I	Introduction and Overview	*The Editors*
II	Policy and Provision in Scottish Education	*Ian Smith*
III	The Administration and Control of Scottish Education	*Tom Bryce & Walter Humes*
IV	The Historical and Cultural Context of Scottish Education	*Walter Humes*
V	Management and Organisation in Schools	*Donald Gillies & Aileen Kennedy*
VI	Curriculum: Early Years and Primary	*Aileen Kennedy*
VII	Curriculum: Secondary	*Donald Gillies*
VIII	Assessment, Certification and Achievements	*Tom Bryce*
IX	Further and Higher Education	*Ian Finlay*
X	Challenges and Responses: Education for All?	*Julie Allan*
XI	Scottish Teachers, Teacher Education and Professionalism	*Ian Menter*
XII	Future	*The Editors*

ACKNOWLEDGEMENTS

While we have endeavoured to provide a *fourth* definitive text on Scottish education, we have done so in recognition of the very considerable contributions by numerous researchers over many decades. Scholarly writing about Scottish education did not begin with the opening of the new Scottish Parliament in 1999: it was alive well before that but until the 1970s much of it was uncritical and reflected the official views of policy makers. This volume provides a range of perspectives, informed by evidence, analysis and interpretation: it includes new contributions not only by experienced Scottish writers but also by younger academics and practitioners who are less well known. We are indebted to all of them for accepting the invitation to contribute to this latest edition.

Many others are due our thanks. Vivienne Watson helped to set up the database of individuals involved in the project, making it possible for us to keep on top of the extensive communications required. The library staff at the Jordanhill campus of the University of Strathclyde (prior to the closure of that campus) were extremely helpful in tracking down references and resolving problems we met in our own research and writing. Tom Malone created the cover for this and the earlier editions. His good efforts have sustained a recognisable brand. Our sincere gratitude goes to Anna Stevenson for her highly efficient and unfailingly courteous copyediting. We must also thank staff at Edinburgh University Press, in particular Nicola Ramsey. Her support throughout the production of the four editions has been steady and encouraging. Eddie Clark, EUP's managing desk editor, dealt professionally with all the final production details. There are others without whose help the book would not have been produced but formal acknowledgement must stop somewhere. As we concluded our acknowledgements for previous editions, we should like to thank the many pupils, students, teachers and colleagues who have, over the years, taught us about Scottish education and for whom this book might be seen as an expression of gratitude.

FINALLY

It will be apparent that the general editorship has changed from two to four individuals. We have both retired from full-time employment, but were fortunate in persuading Donald Gillies and Aileen Kennedy to share in the task of producing SE4 – a prudent piece of long-term planning.

II

POLICY AND PROVISION IN SCOTTISH EDUCATION

This section gives an overview of the whole field of Scottish education and contains introductory chapters for each of the four main sectors: primary, secondary, further education (FE) and higher education (HE). It is more than merely descriptive, with each of the authors outlining the contentious issues in their own field. The opening chapter (2) contains up-to-date data and trends in pupil/student and teacher numbers for each of the sectors of Scottish education, together with contextualised commentary on relevant policy initiatives. It notes the relative structural stability of the primary and secondary sectors as well as the extent of mainstreaming associated with the current provision of additional support needs. The focus of government policy upon the pre-school and early years is outlined, along with changes in the provisions taking place in further and higher education.

Chapter 3 is the first of several chapters dealing with Curriculum for Excellence (CfE), here explaining the main themes of this new development for the whole curriculum from 3 to 18; setting its present, evolving nature into recent historical context and pointing to research that 'raises important and uncomfortable questions about how policy makers might frame policy to facilitate teacher agency in curriculum-making, rather than seeking to control implementation processes or outcomes'. This chapter should be read first before the chapter in Section VI dealing with CfE in primary schools (42) and the corresponding chapter in Section VII dealing with CfE in secondary schools (50). Chapter 4 sets out the philosophy and practice of primary education and does so by reflecting on the philosophical links between and across three key educational reforms, in chronological order: The Primary Memorandum; the 5–14 Curriculum; and the current Curriculum for Excellence. The author notes the resonance between CfE and the Primary Memorandum of 1965. Those who wish to focus upon primary schooling should read this chapter prior to those in Section VI. Chapter 5 looks at Scottish secondary schools, considering the senses in which they may still be said to be 'comprehensive' in character, despite the variety of pressures to change over the last twenty-five years, and the very real developments that have occurred, especially in curriculum and pedagogy. Nevertheless, the extent of the stability and consistency in secondary provision is the striking feature of education in Scotland. The reader who is focusing upon secondary schooling should read this chapter prior to those in Section VII. Chapter 6 analyses the topic of learning and considers the main pedagogies that are encountered in modern Scottish classrooms. It looks critically at teaching approaches intended to make pupil learning more active, an important dimension to CfE.

Scotland's FE colleges provide post-school education. They have been run independently of local authorities since 1993 (the year of 'incorporation') on the basis of a block grant from the Scottish Funding Council and are quite diversified. Chapter 7 provides an introduction to the FE sector; analyses the development of the sector running up to the watershed year of 2012 when colleges faced up to the reform agenda instigated by government proposals for 'regionalisation'; and emphasises the very significant blurring of the FE/HE divide. The character and provision of tertiary education in Scotland is described in Chapter 8. Scottish universities have had to face up to very serious pressures in the last decade, not least financial ones, and the chapter analyses the extent to which traditional academic values are under threat as institutions change to position themselves globally.

Following these seven chapters are two that contextualise the statutory provision of education in Scotland. Chapter 9 looks at the policy process itself, highlighting changes in the years of devolved government and, in particular, the period following the May 2011 election to the Scottish Parliament. It explains (and questions) official versions of the policy agenda and explores the roles of the various stakeholders in negotiating change. Chapter 10 looks at how education has been dealt with in the political sphere and how educational issues are viewed and understood by politicians. It scrutinises the party political thinking behind recent and current policy initiatives, not least the priorities of the SNP in government, as well as the present domination of all political debate by economic imperatives. The chapter speculates about what might change in education depending on the result of the referendum on independence, a question that will be revisited in the final section of the book. Scotland has a small but not insignificant private school sector (dealing with some 4 per cent of the pupil population) and this, and its influence, is described in Chapter 11. The part played by the Scottish Council of Independent Schools in helping to represent the independent sector with some seventy schools is acknowledged. In the chapter that follows this (12) the distinction is drawn between alternative forms of education and alternative schools. While there are relatively few of the latter, Scotland has had its share of activists concerned to develop truly different forms of education, alternatives concerned with freedom, creativity, space to explore (literally and spiritually), the development of community and the promotion of individual autonomy. Home schooling is given particular attention. The section ends with an analysis of the distinctiveness of Scottish education. This chapter (13) endeavours to get behind the myths and traditional claims made about education in Scotland; it contextualises distinctiveness at a time of debate and decision making about devolution and/or independence.

2

Educational Provision: An Overview

Ian Smith

INTRODUCTION: STRUCTURE AND SECTORS

During the last quarter of the twentieth century, public discussion on Scottish educational provision would often centre initially on the period of compulsory education from age 5 to 16. This was provided by Scottish local authorities through the primary school sector until age 11 and the secondary school sector from age 12. However, twenty-first-century discussion of Scottish educational provision may more quickly include the significant contributions of other sectors, including pre-school provision, special education, post-school provision involving further education colleges and universities, and community education. (As will be discussed, new terms have been developed to describe provision in pre-school, special and community education.) Changes in the position of these other sectors within the overall Scottish educational structure have been more marked and complex in recent years, when compared to the comparative structural stabilities of the primary and secondary sectors (at least since the introduction of comprehensive secondary schools from the 1960s). There has been an increasing emphasis upon the importance of pre-school education and major expansion of provision in this sector. Particularly significant changes have taken place in recent years in special education, with developing philosophies of approach in this area. Further and higher education have been required to engage with complex issues on the nature of provision and organisational structure. More broadly, Scottish administrations have placed a greater emphasis on 'Lifelong Learning', defined as the overall learning activities undertaken by the Scottish population from age 16 onwards. This chapter will reflect the relative structural stabilities of sectors within Scottish educational provision by initially covering primary and secondary school provision before moving to other sectors. On the other hand, as will be mentioned subsequently, there has been much emphasis in recent Scottish Government policy on establishing approaches that cross the divisions between sectors. In particular, Curriculum for Excellence (CfE) is progressing curriculum development for ages 3–18, covering aspects of the pre-school, primary, secondary and further education sectors (see www.curriculumforexcellencescotland.gov.uk).

Scottish educational provision is largely a state-funded service. The vast majority of primary and secondary schooling is provided by Scottish local authorities (of which there are currently thirty-two). While independent schools can report very high levels of pupil attainment and school leaver entry to higher education, the size of this sector is limited. In 2011, only 31,425 pupils attended independent schools in Scotland, just over 4 per cent of all Scottish pupils. (Broader private sector involvement in pre-school education is more complex, as will be discussed later.) While Scottish universities and further education colleges can draw upon other funding sources, both sectors rely heavily for core funding upon public money received through the Scottish Funding Council (the SFC, created in 2005 by a merger of the previously separate Scottish Higher Education Funding Council and Scottish Further Education Funding Council). In 2009–10, higher education institutions had an overall income of £2,783 million, with public money providing £1,084 million (39 per cent) of this directly from SFC grants, and making other contributions to the 23 per cent from tuition fees and educational contracts, and the 21 per cent from research grants. Further education colleges had an overall income of £749 million, with public money providing £548 million (73 per cent) of this directly from SFC grants, and making other contributions to the 15 per cent from tuition fees and educational contracts, and the 0.3 per cent from research grants. In total, the SFC distributed £1,891.1 million in 2009–10, £707.5 million to colleges and £1,183.6 million to higher education institutions (these figures including capital funding). Finally, although both the publicly funded primary and secondary school sectors include 15 per cent of schools that are Roman Catholic denominational, these are managed by the local authorities, with certain rights for the Roman Catholic Church embedded in statute, for example regarding approval of teachers.

This chapter is concerned with the overall structure of provision between various sectors of education, including relevant statistics that illustrate the development of trends within this structure. Broader policy implications of overall provision will certainly be considered, but the chapter is not primarily concerned with the details of the delivery of provision within the various sectors of education. Such details are taken forward throughout the rest of this volume. Statistics quoted are principally from Scottish Government sources. Statistics for current and recent provision largely refer either to session 2011–12, 2010–11 or 2009–10 (the most recent full sets available at the time of writing vary depending on the aspect of educational provision). School statistics generally refer to publicly funded schools, although relevant independent school figures are also included. The references at the end of this chapter include further guidance on statistical sources to be accessed.

PRIMARY SCHOOL PROVISION

In 2011, there were 366,429 pupils in 2,081 publicly funded primary schools in Scotland. An additional 10,893 pupils were in fifty-four independent primary schools. Pupil projections for the first quarter of the twenty-first century indicate a primary school sector that has been declining in size but will increase again on a scale likely to be manageable. The number of pupils in publicly funded primary schools is projected to rise to 389,100 in 2020.

Scottish primary schools are relatively small, certainly compared to the general size of secondary schools. In 2011, the average size of publicly funded primary schools was 176 pupils. This means that the size of these primary school staffing complements is also relatively small. In 2011, the average number of teachers in primary schools was 11. Issues of primary–secondary transition are complex, and the size of primary schools may well be entirely appropriate to local social needs. However, differences in size between primary and secondary schools are part of the context for pupils' experiences of primary–secondary transition. Similarly, given the extent to which primary school staffing complements are smaller than those of secondary schools, it may be questioned whether Scottish policy discussion on school leadership and management distinguishes sufficiently between the two sectors.

For example, collegial approaches may be more readily applicable and easily achieved in primary schools.

In total, there were 22,851 teachers in publicly funded primary schools in 2011. The vast majority of these teachers were generalist classroom teachers, who may teach all aspects of the curriculum to their pupils. Only 1,156 teachers identified their main activity as more specialist (these were either teachers of art and design, music or physical education, or teachers working in support for learning and additional support needs). These figures indicate the current context for any future debate about the further development of specialist teaching in primary schools, for example by generalist primary teachers achieving specialist professional recognition through continuing professional development, or by primary/secondary specialists emerging as part of general developments in primary–secondary transition.

In publicly funded primary schools, the pupil/teacher ratio fell continuously from 2000, dropping from 19.0 in 2000 to 15.7 in 2008, then rose to 15.8 in 2009 and 2010, and to 16.0 in 2011. While there has been some reduction in average primary class sizes during this period, this has been relatively limited. Average primary class sizes for all classes moved from 24.4 in 2000 to 22.5 in 2009 and 2010, but rose again to 22.7 in 2011. For independent schools, the last full Scottish Government census on such matters was for 2009. In that year, the average size of independent primary schools was 194 pupils, with an average class size across all stages of 18.1 and a pupil/teacher ratio of 12.5.

Class sizes in the first three years of primary (P1–P3) in publicly funded schools have been of particular political significance. The SNP election manifesto in 2007 had included a commitment to reduce class sizes in P1–P3 to a maximum of eighteen 'as quickly as possible'. Soon after this election, Fiona Hyslop, the SNP Cabinet Secretary for Education and Lifelong Learning, called for flexibility on this target, and was immediately accused by the Labour opposition of broken promises. Some attempt was made to adopt a target of 20 per cent of P1–P3 classes at the eighteen maximum. In October 2010, the SNP government introduced a legal limit of twenty-five for P1 with effect from the 2011–12 school session. Michael Russell, Fiona Hyslop's successor, described this as a 'stepping stone' towards the target of the eighteen maximum in P1–P3. Certainly, regarding P1, 12.8 per cent of pupils were in classes exceeding twenty-five in 2010, but only 1 per cent in 2011. On the other hand, the proportion at eighteen or lower was 30 per cent in 2010, but 29 per cent in 2011. The proportion of P1–P3 in classes of eighteen or fewer (including classes of thirty-six covered by two teachers) was 12.7 per cent in 2006, 21.6 per cent in 2010, but 20.2 per cent in 2011. Political debate about class sizes in P1–P3 continues.

A description of the Scottish primary school sector may suggest a relatively stable and self-contained part of national education provision. However, there are complexities to this. The primary school system faces constant challenges in taking forward assessment and curriculum change, especially within the recent national programme on Assessment is for Learning and the current programme on CfE. Beyond this, there are deeper issues in the relationship between primary provision and the adjacent sectors of pre-school education and secondary education. The connection with pre-school education will be explored later in this chapter. The challenges and complexities of primary–secondary transition have been the focus of much thought within Scotland over a number of years, with issues at best partially resolved (see Boyd, 2005 and West et al., 2010 for fuller recent analyses). Some local authorities, such as Glasgow City Council, have formalised a new relationship between primary and secondary schools through the establishment of learning communities. A learning community comprises a secondary school and its associated primary schools. One of the relevant headteachers, not necessarily the secondary headteacher, is appointed as the overall 'principal' of the learning community. On teaching links, the General Teaching Council Scotland (GTCS) produced a Framework for Professional Recognition/ Registration (GTCS, 2007, www.gtcs.org.uk/professional-development/professional-recognition.aspx) which offers new possibilities for teaching across the primary/secondary sectors, including for primary teachers to work in the early years of secondary. More widely, as already discussed, CfE aims for a more coherent progression of learning and teaching from primary to secondary within the overall 3–18 context. However, this general area remains a challenge for the twenty-first-century Scottish system. For example, the learning community approach has not been adopted universally across Scottish local authorities. New teaching qualifications that cross the traditional primary/secondary divide have not yet been established in Scottish initial teacher education.

SECONDARY SCHOOL PROVISION

In 2011, there were 297,109 pupils in 367 publicly funded secondary schools in Scotland. An additional 18,795 pupils were in sixty independent secondary schools. Pupil projections for the first quarter of the twenty-first century indicate a secondary school sector that has been declining in size, and will continue to decline, but on a scale likely to be manageable, before showing some slight increase in size. The number of pupils in publicly funded secondary schools is projected to decrease to 269,100 in 2017, before rising from 2018 to reach 282,300 by 2020.

Scottish secondary school pupils attend schools that are significantly larger, on average, than their primary schools. In 2011, the average size of publicly funded secondary schools was 810. This means that the size of secondary school staffing complements significantly exceeds the primary school equivalents. The average number of teachers in these secondary schools in 2011 was sixty-six. These primary/secondary size differences have already been highlighted as potentially relevant for primary–secondary transition, and for approaches to leadership and management between the two sectors. The average size of independent secondary schools in 2009 was 329 pupils, and the pupil/teacher ratio was 8.3.

In total, there were 24,241 teachers in publicly funded secondary schools in 2011. The pupil/teacher ratio in secondary schools fell from 2000, dropping from 13.0 in 2000 to 11.6 in 2007. The ratio then rose again, reaching 12.3 in 2011. A ratio as low as this had already been achieved in the early 1990s; for example, the ratio was 12.2 in 1990. However, when compared with higher education where student/staff ratios in many disciplines and institutions may well have risen significantly during the same period, this underlying stability, or improvement until very recently, in pupil/teacher ratios can be presented positively as an indication of public resource commitment to the secondary sector.

In 2010–11, 93 per cent of S4 pupils in publicly funded secondary schools gained awards in both English and Maths at Scottish Credit and Qualifications Framework (SCQF) level 3 (e.g. Standard Grade Foundation) or better. However, improvements in S4–S6 attainment over recent years can be described as relatively modest. In 2005-6, the proportion of S4 pupils gaining awards in both English and Maths at SCQF level 3 already stood at 91 per cent, and the 2010–11 figure of 93 per cent is identical to the 2008–9 and 2009–10 figures. In 2005–6, 34 per cent of S4 pupils gained five or more Standard Grades at Credit level or equivalent (SCQF level 5), but this proportion had already exceeded 30 per cent in 1998–9 and only rose to 35 per cent in 2008–9, 36 per cent in 2009–10, remaining at 36 per cent in 2010–11. In 2005–6, by the end of S5, 21 per cent of the previous year's S4 year group attained three or more awards at SCQF level 6 (Higher) or better. This proportion had been 23 per cent in both 2003–4 and 2004–5. The figure returned to 23 per cent in 2008–9, then rose to 25 per cent in 2009–10 and 26 per cent in 2010–11. In 2005–6, by the end of S6, 19 per cent of the S4 year group from two years previously attained five or more awards at SCQF level 6 (Higher) or better. This proportion had been 20 per cent in 2003–4 and 19 per cent in 2004–5. This figure rose to 21 per cent in 2008–9, 22 per cent in 2009–10 and just under 24 per cent in 2010–11. In 2005–6, 12 per cent obtained at least one award at SCQF level 7 (Advanced Higher), the same proportion as both 2003–4 and 2004–5. This proportion rose to 14 per cent in 2008–9, 15 per cent in 2009–10 and just under 16 per cent in 2010–11. Across all of these statistics, 2010–11 attainment ranges no higher than 2–4 per cent above levels previously achieved in 2005–6 or earlier, suggesting there may be an underlying plateau in Scottish secondary public examination attainment levels.

Staying-on rates of pupils in publicly funded secondary schools also appear to have generally plateaued for much of the period since the late 1990s, only rising recently, presumably as more young people remain at school while the economic recession reduces their prospects of immediate employment. In 2000, 68.1 per cent of all pupils from the relevant earlier S3 cohort remained at school post-Christmas in S5, and 44.9 per cent of this cohort remained in school for S6. In 2008–9, 67 per cent from the relevant earlier S4 cohort remained at school post-Christmas in S5 and 45 per cent of the S4 cohort remained in school for S6. With the impact of recession, these proportions rose to 72 per cent and 50 per cent in 2009–10 and 75 per cent and 54 per cent in 2010–11. There is also evidence of underlying plateauing on entry to both further and higher education, with recent rises again linked to economic recession. The proportion of publicly funded school leavers entering full-time further or higher education first reached 50 per cent in 1999–2000 (32 per cent entering higher education and 19 per cent entering further education), and ranged between 50 per cent and 52 per cent from 2000–1 to 2004–5 (during these years, higher education entry ranged between 29 per cent and 32 per cent, and further education entry ranged between 20 per cent and 21 per cent). Certainly, by 2008–9, the proportion was 61.9 per cent, rising to 62.8 per cent in 2009–10 and 62.9 per cent in 2010–11. The proportion entering higher education was 34.9 per cent in 2008–9, 35.7 per cent in 2009–10 and 35.8 per cent in 2010–11. The proportion entering full-time further education was 27 per cent in 2008–9, 27.1 per cent in 2009–10 and 27.1 per cent in 2010–11. However, the main increase came between 2007–8 and 2008–9, as the proportion entering full-time further and higher education rose from 55.9 per cent (31.1 per cent higher education and 24.8 per cent further education) to 61.9 per cent. This coincided with those entering employment dropping from 25.3 per cent to 18.4 per cent, which would indicate that the rise in entry to further and higher education in 2008–9 can be linked to the onset of economic recession, and, of course, entry has largely plateaued since then.

This statistical analysis may suggest that public examination results, with consequent rates of entry to higher and further education, have essentially plateaued at a level consistent with underlying cohort attainment capacity relative to existing public examination standards, and with underlying cohort aspirations to continue in education (subject to some recent distortion because of economic recession). This raises interesting issues about how public policy debate should now proceed, especially if some may question the appropriateness of continuously targeting ongoing increases in upper secondary levels of attainment and the proportion of school leavers entering higher education. However, it can be argued that further increases can be delivered if relative underachievement in areas of deprivation is addressed, and this should be the focus of policy. For example, the Scottish Government has analysed school leaver qualifications in relation to the Scottish Index of Multiple Deprivation (SIMD), which uses a range of indicators to measure relative deprivation on a geographical basis across Scotland. Among 2010–11 leavers, only 8.5 per cent of the 'most deprived' leavers achieved five awards at SCQF level 6 (Higher) or better as their highest qualifications attained, compared to 52.9 per cent of the 'least deprived'.

The preceding analysis is based upon pupil attainment in publicly funded secondary schools. Certainly, levels of attainment are proportionately higher in independent schools. For example, of the 3,172 independent school leavers in 2008–9, 83 per cent entered higher education and 7 per cent entered full-time further education. However, because of the relatively small numbers involved, the inclusion of independent school leavers only raised the proportion of all school leavers entering higher and further education that year from 61.9 per cent to 63.5 per cent (with higher education entrants now comprising 37.6 per cent of the overall cohort, but further education entrants only comprising 25.9 per cent). Such statistical adjustments are not significant enough to alter the analysis of relevant public policy issues already presented.

As with the primary school sector, a description of the Scottish secondary school system may suggest a sector that has a relatively stable place within national educational provision. Again, however, there are complexities to this, in addition to the points about attainment levels and leaver destinations already discussed. Internally, the secondary system has to engage constantly with assessment and curriculum change. As well as national developments that also affect primary schools, such as progression within CfE from second level (to the end of P7) to third and fourth levels (S1–S3), secondary schools have to address specific issues such as those relating to the development and implementation of the new National 4 and 5 courses and assessments to replace the current Standard Grades (General and Credit) and Intermediates. However, perhaps more fundamentally, secondary schools face a continuing twenty-first-century debate about the place of their traditionally subject-based curriculum within overall Scottish educational provision. For example, if there is an effective limit to the proportion of school leavers who see entry to higher education as the next step in their personal and career development, will the secondary school system have to move even further beyond the subject-based curriculum than currently envisaged by CfE, with its greater emphasis on cross-disciplinary learning and teaching? Will engagement with vocational education, however this is defined, also have to move further than the current proposals under CfE, which include continuing development of 'Skills for Work' courses and collaboration with further education colleges?

PROVISION FOR ADDITIONAL SUPPORT NEEDS

Discussion of the role of special schools within overall Scottish educational provision has to be placed in the current context of the broader approach to additional support for learning (ASL) and additional support needs (ASN) (see Hamill and Clark, 2005 for a fuller treatment of this approach). Terminology in this area has developed continuously since the 1970s, and the careful and sensitive use of language is particularly important in this aspect of educational provision. Following the publication of the then Scottish Executive Education Department (SEED) Report *Moving Forward! Additional Support for Learning* (SEED 2003, www.scotland.gov.uk/Resource/Doc/47021/0023972.pdf), and the Education (Additional Support for Learning) (Scotland) Act 2004 (www.legislation.gov.uk/asp/2004/4/contents), policy and practice is based upon the overarching concept of additional support needs. This progresses the commitment to mainstream inclusion contained in the Standards in Scotland's Schools etc. Act 2000. Pupils who would formerly have been identified with 'special educational needs' are now more positively described as entitled to 'additional support for learning'. Official statistics moved from reporting on the 'Record of Needs' for pupils with special educational needs to reporting on the Co-ordinated Support Plan (CSP) targeting the additional support needs of young people receiving coordinated support. This will be developed from the Individual Educational Plan (IEP) which these pupils generally have. The 2004 Act was supplemented by the Additional Support for Learning (Scotland) Act 2009 (www.legislation.gov.uk/asp/2009/7/contents). This Act strengthens the rights of children with additional support needs, particularly on out-of-area placing requests by their parents, and on the position of looked-after children.

At the time of the introduction of the 2004 Act, the number of pupils in publicly funded special schools was projected by the then Scottish Executive to fall in line with the anticipated decrease in the number of children of school age, but also to account for the potential impact of mainstreaming of pupils with additional support needs. From a total of 7,100 in 2005, the number of pupils in publicly funded special schools was projected to fall to 5,200 in 2024. However, the numbers of pupils in publicly funded special schools fell to 6,673 in 2009, but rose again to 6,800 in 2010 and 6,973 in 2011. Currently, the Scottish Government is projecting a fall to 6,700 in 2020. In 2011, there were also 650 pupils in independent special schools.

More widely, in 2005, 34,577 pupils in publicly funded schools (4.8 per cent of all pupils) had a Record of Needs or IEP. Of these pupils, 27,540 (80 per cent) were in mainstream schools. They made up 3.9 per cent of mainstream school pupils. In 2011, 98,523 pupils (14.7 per cent of all pupils) had an additional support need recorded. Of these, 91,550 (93 per cent) were in mainstream schools. They made up 13.8 per cent of mainstream pupils. In addition to these pupils in publicly funded schools, in 2009, 417 pupils (1.4 per cent of all pupils) in independent primary and secondary schools had a CSP, Record of Needs or IEP.

Inclusion brings challenges for mainstream staff, and such statistics place the scale of inclusion in context. Policies based upon positive responses to additional support needs will clearly be central to the continuing development of educational provision in twenty-first-century Scotland.

PROVISION FOR EARLY YEARS EDUCATION AND CHILDCARE

Pre-school provision has developed significantly in recent years, and this is reflected in some complexity in the language used for this sector. Traditionally, the term nursery education, or even nursery schooling, may have been used specifically to refer to education for 3–4-year-olds. Then, the terms pre-school education or early education may have been adopted, on some occasions referring to the 3–4 age range, on others to the under-3s also. At other times, the term pre-school or early years care is used, referring to provision for 0–4-year-olds which is less formally educational. Most specialists will now stress the integration of early years education and childcare, particularly around the concept of learning.

The internal complexity of the early years education and childcare sector, in comparison to the structural coherence of the primary and secondary sectors, can be seen when current provision is summarised. From 2002, part-time pre-school education (normally five two-and-a-half-hour sessions per week for thirty-three weeks each year) was provided free for 3- and 4-year-old children in Scotland, should their parents wish it. This was subsequently increased to 475 hours' entitlement per annum (equivalent to thirty-eight weeks at twelve-and-a-half hours). Although *The Early Years Framework* (Scottish Government, 2008) proposed that this would increase to 570 hours in August 2010, this did not happen, but in March 2012 the First Minister pledged legislation to increase provision to over 600 hours for every 3- and 4-year-old 'as well as the most vulnerable 2-year-olds'. Education authorities provide pre-school education places in their own nursery classes and schools and also in partner settings such as playgroups and private nurseries. In September 2011, 29,510 children were registered for the ante-pre-school year (3-year-olds), 56,720 children were registered for the pre-school year (4-year-olds), with the combined figure comprising 99.5 per cent of those eligible. In January 2010, of the 2,762 centres providing pre-school education consistent with the 3–18 CfE, 2,615 were local authority or partnership. In December 2010, of the 2,464 nurseries registered with the Care Inspectorate, 60 per cent were local authority, 31 per cent were private and 9 per cent were not-for-profit. There were 5,529 active childminders in December 2010, 100 per cent private, and in November 2010, 28,000 children were attending childminders.

The involvement of private provision indicates that, while free part-time early years provision has expanded greatly, parents continue to face challenges in accessing and funding wider early years education and childcare in twenty-first-century Scotland. Costs of private provision are significant and continue to rise. For example, a Daycare Trust survey of February 2011 indicated that parents in Scotland spent an average of £5,178 per annum for twenty-five hours' nursery care per week for a child under 2, and £4,664 for the equivalent childminder care.

The complexities of this sector are also reflected in the staffing position within pre-school provision. In 2006, the then Scottish Executive completed a *National Review of the Early Years and Childcare Workforce: Report and Consultation* (Scottish Executive, 2006, www.scotland.gov.uk/Resource/Doc/135643/0033618.pdf). In its remit and approach, this Review focused on the relevant groups of workers to be registered with the Scottish Social Services Council (SSSC), i.e. those in early years care and learning, out-of-school care and playwork, and childminders. On the other hand, teachers working in early years settings were not part of the Review. Only some of the staff working in the pre-school sector are fully registered schoolteachers. For session 2009–10, of the 9,230 whole-time equivalent (WTE) staff providing pre-school education in local authority and partnership centres, there were 1,613 WTE GTCS-registered teachers (17 per cent of the WTE workforce). The Report's proposals, such as moving to degree qualifications for 'lead practitioners' and Higher National Diplomas (SCQF level 8) for practitioners, would still have left staffing of this sector much less clear than its primary school neighbour. The twenty-first-century Scottish 'Early Years and Childcare' workforce would still not become an all-graduate profession. Subsequent Scottish Executive and Scottish Government responses required all centres to be led by managers with SCQF level 9 qualifications from 2011, with programmes provided by September 2008 based on the Standard for Childhood Practice (QAA Scotland, 2007, www.qaa.ac.uk/Publications/InformationAndGuidance/Documents/earlyYears.pdf), and registration with the SSSC from November 2010. Practitioners had to be registered from September 2011, and must have qualifications at SCQF level 7 (such as SVQ 3 or HNC), although earlier qualifications would be accepted and this requirement remains short of the 2006 SCQF level 8 recommendation. In January 2010, 13 per cent of the childcare workforce had degrees; 15 per cent of the childcare workforce were managers, two-thirds of whom had qualifications equating to SCQF level 8 or 9; and 74 per cent of the childcare workforce had childcare SVQ 3 or above, equivalent to HNC and therefore SCQF level 7. However, while this figure was 87 per cent in the public sector, it was only 69 per cent in the private sector and 59 per cent in the voluntary sector. Of 5,560 active childmind-ers in Scotland, only 27 per cent had childcare SVQ 3 or above.

On the other hand, the Scottish Government continues to work at the development of the sector. *The Early Years Framework* emphasises the importance of a coherent approach from pre-birth to 8 years old, including especially a multi-agency approach from 0–3 involving health, education and social work, and based on the child-centred and multi-agency approach of *Getting it Right for Every Child* (GIRFEC) (Scottish Executive, 2005, www.scotland. gov.uk/Resource/Doc/54357/0013270.pdf). *Early Years Framework – Progress So Far* (Scottish Government, 2011, www.scotland.gov.uk/Publications/2011/01/13114328/0) continues to support and report progress on such approaches, including a shift in invest-ment in early years from crisis management to early intervention and prevention.

FURTHER AND HIGHER EDUCATION PROVISION

Further Education

Although publicly funded, Scotland's further education (FE) colleges have been independ-ent bodies since 1993 (except that education authority control was retained for the two col-leges in Orkney and Shetland). At the time of writing, there are forty-one further education colleges in Scotland. The colleges deliver a range of provision, including vocational and non-vocational courses at FE level (i.e. at SCQF level 6 or below), and courses at higher education (HE) level (mainly HNC and HND, i.e. SCQF levels 7 and 8). In 2009–10, Scotland's then forty-three SFC-funded FE colleges employed 11,751 teaching staff (4,813 full-time and 6,938 part-time).

FE college figures refer to enrolments on each separate course taken, and therefore may be higher than the total number of students in the system. In 2009–10, there were 438,522 enrolments for courses in FE colleges, equating to 347,336 students. Of total FE college activity, 72 per cent was at FE level, and 28 per cent was at HE level. At FE level, there were 48,365 full-time and 267,777 part-time students. The majority of enrolments at FE level are for vocational courses, which prepare students for employment or a profession, or enhance the skills of those already working. Between 2008–9 and 2009–10, there was an 11.2 per cent decline in the number of part-time FE students. However, there was an 8 per cent increase in full-time students, leading to a 1.5 per cent increase in FE activity at colleges. Although there was a significant decline in part-time FE students between 2008–9 and 2009–10, numbers of these students had generally risen from 2004–5 to 2008–9 (although the 301,692 part-time FE students in 2008–9 was slightly less than the 309,762 of 2007–8, this was still higher than any other total since 2001–2). The full-time FE total for 2009–10 was the highest in the period from 2001–2.

The overall number of HE students in Scotland has continued to increase in recent years, but this increase has been in the higher education institutions (HEIs) rather than the FE colleges. Between 2004–5 and 2009–10, total HE student numbers in Scotland rose by 6.4 per cent (from 270,260 to 287,565). HEIs saw an increase of 9 per cent (from 217,945 to

237,765). FE colleges saw a 4.8 per cent decline (from 52,315 to 49,800). However, numbers in colleges have been rising again from the low of 47,700 in 2007–8, and the overall decline since 2004–5 can be attributed to a decline in part-time students (from 26,690 to 21,160), with full-time numbers rising from 25,625 to 28,640.

While the Scottish FE sector faces challenges in maintaining and developing its provision in twenty-first-century Scotland, this is more likely to involve constantly adjusting to increasingly complex requirements, rather than simply 'downsizing' in response to declining demand for its provision. For example, the sector faces particular challenges following the Scottish Government's *Putting Learners at the Centre: Delivering our Ambitions for Post-16 Education* (Scottish Government, 2011). In the context of considering the full range of post-16 education and training, including both further and higher education, one particular emphasis of the Scottish Government is on 'regionalisation' of the college sector. While this does not necessarily imply only full merger, but can also include other forms of collaboration such as federations, it seems likely that a 'series of mergers, over time, to create regional colleges of scale' is the most likely outcome for the sector (see Scottish Government, 2011, p. 45). The Scottish Government is talking specifically of thirteen college regions. A recent example of a merger took place in September 2010, with Central College, Glasgow merging with Glasgow Metropolitan College and Glasgow College of Nautical Studies to form City of Glasgow College.

Higher Education

In 2009–10, there were 237,765 HE students at Scottish HEIs, of whom 162,970 were full-time and 74,795 part-time. The nineteen HEIs, members of Universities Scotland, comprise Scotland's fourteen campus-based universities, the University of the Highlands and Islands (UHI), the Open University in Scotland, the Scottish Agricultural College (SAC), Glasgow School of Art and the Royal Conservatoire of Scotland. All HEIs are self-governing, although in receipt of public funding through the SFC. The 2009–10 total includes the 16,855 Open University students in Scotland.

Higher education comprises three main levels: sub-degree (principally HNC, HND), first degree and postgraduate. HEIs generally will be more concerned with first degree and postgraduate work, and the universities almost exclusively so. Sub-degree work is more likely at FE colleges. In 2009–10, 15.7 per cent of students in HEIs were at sub-degree level, 61.2 per cent at first degree level and 23.1 per cent at postgraduate level. In 2009–10, HE in Scotland saw a record level of students, 287,565 (a 2.8 per cent increase since 2008–9), and entrants, 147,465. First degree numbers were up from 137,720 in 2008–9 to 146,175 in 2009–10, an increase of 6.1 per cent. The number of students in HEIs was up by 2.8 per cent, from 231,260 to 237,765, comprising 82.7 per cent of all Scottish HE. The number of HE students in colleges was also up by 3 per cent, from 48,355 to 49,800, comprising 17.3 per cent of all Scottish HE.

However, this conceals evidence of a plateauing in entry from Scotland to HE. The Scottish Age Participation Index (API) for a given year is an estimate of the proportion of 17-year-olds in the population who can be expected to enter HE (with a focus on full-time within the UK) for the first time before their 21st birthday. There have been changes to the national statistical method of calculating the API introduced since the third edition of *Scottish Education*, and national publications now apply these retrospectively to earlier figures. Based on most recent publications, the index was around 50 per cent at the beginning of the twenty-first century, having reached 50.2 per cent in 2000–1. However, the index then declined, reaching 42.2 per cent in 2007–8, although there was some recovery to 43.0 per cent in 2008–9 and 44.3 per cent in 2009–10. These statistics reflect the earlier discussion on plateauing of entry to higher education in relation to secondary school leavers. While the number of Scottish students in 2009–10 was up 3.1 per cent since 2007–8, this total was still lower than any figure between 2003–4 and 2006–7, having fallen by 3.6 per cent in 2007–8 alone.

Overall growth in student numbers can be associated with recruitment from outwith Scotland. The number of students from the rest of the UK in 2009–10 had risen 6.6 per cent since 2007–8, and the number of students from outside the UK had risen 19.8 per cent (with a 26.9 per cent increase in EU students). Since 2000–1, the number of students entering HE in Scotland from outwith Scotland continued to grow, from 18,155 (13.8 per cent of entrants) in 2000–1 to 34,970 (23.7 per cent of entrants) in 2009–10. In contrast, Scottish domiciled entrants declined from 86.2 per cent in 2000–1 to 76.3 per cent in 2009–10. Of the total number of HE students in Scottish HEIs and HE colleges in 2009–10, 75 per cent were from Scotland, 10.3 per cent from the rest of the UK, 5.6 per cent from the rest of the EU, 0.5 per cent from non-EU Europe and 8.5 per cent from beyond Europe.

Issues also persist on the wider access aspects of entry to HE from Scotland. Using the SIMD, the API can be analysed to compare participation from 'deprived' areas (the 20 per cent lowest ranked on the SIMD) and 'non-deprived' areas in Scotland. In 2001–2, the API for deprived areas was 26 per cent, compared to 48.5 per cent for non-deprived areas (a gap of 22.5 per cent). The API for deprived areas dropped to 22.8 per cent in 2003–4, a gap of 23.2 per cent with the non-deprived areas. Although the API for deprived areas then recovered somewhat, reaching 26.2 per cent in 2009–10, the gap for that year with the non-deprived areas was still 22.6 per cent. In other words, over a nine-year period, there has been no significant overall improvement in the API for deprived areas, nor significant narrowing of the gap with non-deprived areas. Such issues remain a priority for the Scottish Government's policies within *Putting Learners at the Centre*. There also appear to remain challenges in recruiting from lifelong learners beyond the API target cohorts. For example, the number of HE enrolments aged 30–60 decreased by 1,745 (2.2 per cent) between 2008–9 and 2009–10.

On the other hand, the success of Scottish HE in producing graduates required by twenty-first-century Scotland's economy and society seems clear. Of the 2009–10 graduates from Scottish HEIs, 78.6 per cent of all those in permanent employment after qualifying were employed in Scotland, with this figure rising to 90.3 per cent for Scots graduates (i.e. those whose pre-study domicile was Scotland). Of the overall Scottish labour force, the proportion of those aged 25–64 in employment who are graduates has increased steadily, for example from 21.6 per cent in 2004 to 25.1 per cent in 2008 to 27.5 per cent in 2010.

PROVISION FOR LIFELONG LEARNING, COMMUNITY LEARNING AND DEVELOPMENT

Lifelong Learning

In 2003, the Scottish Executive produced *Life Through Learning; Learning Through Life* (The Lifelong Learning Strategy for Scotland) (Scottish Executive, 2003, www.scotland. gov.uk/Resource/Doc/47032/0028819.pdf). This defined Lifelong Learning as being about 'personal fulfilment and enterprise; employability and adaptability; active citizenship and social inclusion'. Principally in the post-compulsory context, Lifelong Learning is seen to encompass 'the whole range of learning: formal and informal learning, workplace learning, and the skills, knowledge, attitudes and behaviours that people acquire in day-to-day experiences' (ibid., p. 7). Such definitions seem broadly consistent with academic conceptualisations of the learning society, for example as summarised by Lyn Tett, who identifies three relevant models of the learning society: learning for work; learning for citizenship; learning for democracy (Tett, 2010, p. 35, drawing upon Ranson, S., *Inside the Learning Society*, London: Cassel Education, 1998). Of course, it may be suggested that policy detail focuses heavily on 'learning for work'. For example, the Scottish Executive emphasised in its Lifelong Learning vision 'the best possible match between the learning opportunities open to people and the skills, knowledge, aptitudes and behaviour which will strengthen Scotland's economy and society' (Scottish Executive, 2003, p. 6).

Indeed, Scottish Government policy has increasingly linked the language of Lifelong Learning with the language of lifelong skills. In *Skills for Scotland: A Lifelong Skills Strategy* (Scottish Government, 2007), skills are defined as encompassing the capabilities acquired from education, training, practice or experience, and the 'behaviours, attitudes and personal attributes that make individuals more effective in contexts such as education and training, employment and social engagement' (p. 55). This required a focus on individual development and 'economic pull', such as 'improving the utilisation of skills in the workplace' (p. 5). There was also significant stress on the learning that takes place in the workplace, 'often informally', and a call to stop 'distinguishing between Earners and Learners' (p. 32) and to encourage employee learning (p. 33). Such themes were revisited in *Skills for Scotland: Accelerating the Recovery and Increasing Sustainable Economic Growth* (Scottish Government, 2010, www.scotland.gov.uk/Resource/Doc/326739/0105315.pdf). This repeats 'empowering people' as a priority theme, but also 'supporting employers' within a vision 'for a successful, globally competitive economy' (p. 6).

Some evidence for the extent of work-related learning can be found in the 2010 Scottish Employers Skill Survey (SESS) (Scottish Government Social Research, 2011, www.scotland.gov.uk/Resource/Doc/344028/0114449.pdf), which surveyed a sample of Scottish employers. This covers job-related training for the previous twelve months, but focuses on off-the-job training, i.e. training conducted away from an employee's immediate workstation. Such training could include full-time or part-time courses, correspondence or distance learning, or health and safety training (which may of course be statutory). On-the-job training, carried out at the employee's immediate workstation, may be less formal, for example including mentoring or 'buddying'. The survey found that only 38 per cent of all employees received off-the-job training funded or arranged by their employer (the figure for 2008 was 43 per cent). Of employers, 39 per cent provided no training to employees, 11 per cent provided off-the-job training only, 15 per cent provided on-the-job training only and 34 per cent provided a mixture of both types of training. The total providing some form of funded or arranged training (61 per cent) was less than in 2008 (65 per cent).

In addition to this somewhat inconsistent wider employer funded or arranged training, significant numbers also engage in specific publicly supported training programmes. As *Putting Learners at the Centre* emphasises, these include: Get Ready for Work, Scottish Government spend in 2010–11 £27m, 9,500 places allocated for 2011–12; Training for Work, Scottish Government spend in 2010–11 £12m, 5,000 places allocated for 2011–12; Modern Apprenticeships, Scottish Government spend in 2010–11 £69m, with funding to support 25,000 individuals in 2011–12; Individual Learning Accounts (ILAs), Scottish Government spend in 2010–11 £12m, with 40,000 awards estimated in 2011–12.

Community Learning and Development (CLD)

As with Lifelong Learning, the conceptualisation of 'Community Learning and Development' (CLD) requires consideration. From 2002, this term was adopted by the Scottish Executive to replace the former term 'community education'. In *Working and Learning Together to Build Stronger Communities* (Communities Scotland and Scottish Executive, 2004, www. scotland.gov.uk/Resource/Doc/47210/0028730.pdf), the national priorities for CLD were identified as 'achievement through learning for adults; achievement through learning for young people; achievement through building community capacity'. These were linked to 'closing the opportunity gap, achieving social justice and encouraging community regeneration' (pp. 1–2). Policy commitment to such approaches has been sustained by the Scottish Government. There was a joint statement by Scottish Government and the Convention of Scottish Local Authorities (COSLA) in 2008 entitled *Building on 'Working and Learning Together to Build Stronger Communities': The Role of Community Learning and Development (CLD) in Delivering Change* (COSLA and Scottish Government, 2008, www.scotland.gov. uk/Resource/Doc/920/0116795.pdf). This statement reaffirmed commitment to the three national priorities of the 2004 document, and also gave particular stress to adult literacy and numeracy, youth work and partnership, including with the third sector. In 2009, Scottish Government and COSLA produced *Community – Scottish Community Empowerment Action Plan – Celebrating Success: Inspiring Change* (Scottish Government and COSLA, 2009, www.scotland.gov.uk/Resource/Doc/264771/0079288.pdf), again re-emphasising themes from the 2004 document such as community capacity building. The Scottish Government has also shown a policy commitment to developing the CLD workforce. A Standards Council for Community Learning and Development for Scotland was set up in 2009 to develop, and establish an approvals structure for, qualifications, courses and professional development of the workforce (see Tett, 2010, p. 28). In implementing *Putting Learners at the Centre*, the Scottish Government has specifically committed to issuing new guidance on how CLD should contribute. Some CLD specialists are moving to a preference for the term community learning and participation, rather than community learning and development, reflecting their identification with the more positive tone of 'participation' (for example, see the emphasis on youth participation in Chapter 5 of Tett, 2010).

Not in Employment, Education or Training (NEET)

A particular concern for the Scottish Government in the broader context of post-compulsory provision is the number of 16–19-year-olds Not in Employment, Education or Training (NEET). The NEET proportion in Scotland had not changed significantly in any year between 1996 and 2005, fluctuating between 13 per cent and 15 per cent, with a figure of 37,000 (14.2 per cent) in 2005. At that time, reducing the NEET proportion was one of the then Scottish Executive's Closing the Opportunity Gap targets, with *More Choices, More Chances* (Scottish Executive, 2006, www.scotland.gov.uk/Resource/Doc/129456/0030812.pdf) containing a thirty-nine-point action plan to be delivered by central and local government and other partners from the public, voluntary and private sectors. The NEET proportion did decline between 2006 and 2008, reaching 12.4 per cent in 2006, 12.2 per cent in 2007 and 11.8 per cent in 2008. However, the proportion rose again to 13.7 per cent in both 2009 and 2010. In April 2012, the Scottish Government confirmed its commitment to Opportunities for All, which guarantees a place in education or training for all 16–19-year-olds. This is linked to the Scottish Government's *Youth Employment Strategy*, an 'all-Scotland ranging approach to supporting young people toward and into work' (Scottish Government, 2012, p. 19).

CONCLUSION: TWENTY-FIRST-CENTURY CHALLENGES

As indicated in the introduction to this chapter, the structurally most stable parts of Scottish educational provision remain the primary and secondary school sectors. However, even these sectors face significant challenges as Scottish education moves further forward in the twenty-first century. The relationship between the primary school sector and the adjacent early years and secondary school sectors continues to require specific consideration. Transition from the primary to the secondary school remains a particular issue. Within the secondary sector, the underlying challenge is judging whether CfE will sufficiently reform the current subject-based curriculum and assessment which may have reached some kind of systemic limit in overall levels of attainment, especially for progression to higher education, and in meeting young people's aspirations outwith higher education, particularly in areas of multiple deprivation.

Other sectors face challenges which may be even more directly structural. The fullest, most inclusive response to additional support needs may have reduced the role of special schools but has increased the demands on mainstream school staff. Policy on early years education and childcare must address the extent of free provision and the cost implications for parents if they have to move beyond free provision; and the nature of the workforce, especially levels of qualification, status and pay relative to schoolteachers. For higher education, there are challenges on whether recruitment from within Scotland has plateaued, unless wider access from school leavers and lifelong learners from areas of multiple deprivation is achieved, or whether further growth will depend on recruitment from beyond Scotland. Further education faces the challenges of regionalisation, and the need to clarify its role in a complex set of potential relationships, including partnerships with secondary schools, HEIs and employers. Lifelong Learning and CLD present a particular challenge for the Scottish Government to give substance to its broader aspirations in these areas.

REFERENCES

Boyd, B. (2005) *CPD: Primary–Secondary Transition – An introduction to the issues.* Paisley: Hodder Gibson.

Hamill, P. and K. Clark (2005) *CPD: Additional Support Needs – An introduction to ASN from Nursery to Secondary.* Paisley: Hodder Gibson.

Scottish Government (2007) *Skills for Scotland: A Lifelong Skills Strategy.* Edinburgh: Scottish Government. Online at www.scotland.gov.uk/Resource/doc/197204/0052752.pdf

Scottish Government (2008) *The Early Years Framework.* Edinburgh: Scottish Government. Online at www.scotland.gov.uk/resource/Doc/257007/0076309.pdf

Scottish Government (2011) *Putting Learners at the Centre: Delivering our Ambitions for Post-16 Education.* Edinburgh: Scottish Government. Online at www.scotland.gov.uk/Publications/2011/09/15103949/0

Scottish Government (2012) *Scotland's Youth Employment Strategy.* Edinburgh: Scottish Government.

Online   at   www.employabilityinscotland.com/sites/default/files/articles/5737/Youth%20
Employment%20Strategy.pdf

Tett, L. (2010) *Community Education, Learning and Development* (3rd edn). Edinburgh: Dunedin
Academic Press.

West, P., H. Sweeting and R. Young (2010) 'Transition matters: pupils' experiences of the primary–
secondary school transition in the West of Scotland and consequences for well-being and attainment', *Research Papers in Education*, 25 (1): 21–50.

Websites

Scottish Funding Council, especially statistics, at www.sfc.ac.uk
Scottish Government statistics at www.scotland.gov.uk/Topics/Statistics

3

The 3–18 Curriculum in Scottish Education

Mark Priestley

Scotland's Curriculum for Excellence (CfE) has attracted attention around the world. Its structuring around the notion of four capacities appears to be innovative and radical. The emphasis on active forms of learning and interdisciplinary learning appears to encapsulate pedagogical and curricular principles beloved of progressive educators. And its emphasis on engaging teachers as professional developers of the curriculum and as agents of change appears to offer considerable potential for achieving its oft-stated goal of delivering transformational change. However, there is a need to cast a critical eye over these apparent features of the new curriculum. This chapter offers a critical analysis of the current Scottish curriculum. The chapter first provides an overview of CfE. This is followed by a brief summary of the historical development of the 3–18 curriculum in Scotland. After setting the scene in this fashion, it then addresses the issues outlined in the first paragraph above. It concludes by offering some reflections on the current and likely future development of the 3–18 curriculum.

CURRICULUM FOR EXCELLENCE

CfE is significant in that it is the first systematic attempt to unify what had previously been disparate strands in Scottish curriculum policy. It brings under one roof early years education, primary and secondary schooling, and post-compulsory education (at least in schools and further education (FE) colleges, but arguably also permeating discourses in universities). The discourses of the new curriculum are also influencing developments in related spheres such as community education and social care. Thus in this sense at least, CfE represents a major educational reform initiative.

Curriculum Structure

CfE was launched in 2004, when the then Scottish Executive published a paper titled *A Curriculum for Excellence: The Curriculum Review Group* (see Education Scotland, 2011, for all official publications related to CfE), following the 2002 National Debate on Education. There are several significant features of this document. The central ideas of CfE are described in terms of values, purposes and principles. Instead of adopting a traditional 'aims and objectives' model of curriculum, CfE starts from a statement of 'the values upon which . . . the curriculum should be based' (p. 8). The words that are inscribed on the mace of the Scottish Parliament – wisdom, justice, compassion and integrity – are invoked and it is argued that both personal development and social responsibility depend on awareness not only 'of the values on which Scottish society is based' (p. 11) but also of 'diverse cultures and beliefs' (p. 11). In relation to purposes – a softer term than either aims or objectives – there is a clear statement of the importance of promoting four key capacities. The curriculum stated that all young people should become:

- successful learners;
- confident individuals;
- responsible citizens;
- effective contributors. (p. 12)

These capacities have been subject to little in the way of critical interrogation, tending to become broad slogans. More useful as over-arching purposes of education are the descriptor statements that accompany them; these provide considerable potential as a starting point for curriculum planning. This issue will be revisited in the final section of the chapter.

The 2004 discussion paper did not offer much in the way of extended justification for either its terminology or its recommendations. In this sense it should be regarded as a broad framework or discussion document, designed to form the basis of subsequent policy development, rather than as an extended rationale. Such development was initially slow to follow, but the pace has subsequently increased. The publication of *A Curriculum for Excellence* was accompanied by the *Ministerial Response* (Education Scotland, 2011), which set out future directions for the new curriculum in a more concrete manner than did the review document. This latter paper established, for instance, that the curriculum would be articulated as 'clear statements of the outcomes which each young person should aspire to achieve' (p. 4). Moreover, the response hinted that subjects would continue to be the basis of the curriculum. In 2006, *A Curriculum for Excellence: Progress and Proposals* (Education Scotland, 2011) started to add meat to these curricular bones, in particular emphasising the importance of engagement by teachers, the centrality of learning and teaching, and the unification of the curriculum from 3 to 18. This document outlined a series of six sequential levels, establishing the principle that 'expectations will be described in terms of experiences as well as broad significant outcomes' and that these would be 'designed to reflect the Four Capacities' (p. 12). Significantly, it was proposed at this stage that experiences and outcomes would be structured using the following areas:

- Health and Wellbeing;
- Languages;
- Mathematics;
- Science;
- Social Studies;
- Expressive Arts;
- Technologies;
- Religious and Moral Education.

Further guidance has emerged more quickly since 2006. This includes the *Building the Curriculum* series, for example, which has provided additional guidance on the eight curricular categories outlined above, the early years curriculum and assessment. These documents have been criticised for their lack of clarity and focus, and as a result were followed in

2010 by summary documents intended to provide an at-a-glance overview of key principles and concepts.

Another significant set of documentation has been the publication since 2007 of the experiences and outcomes (Es & Os) in each of eight curricular areas (Education Scotland, 2011). The writers of the Es & Os sought to combine within simple statements, set out in hierarchical levels, both the expected outcomes of learning and the experiences through which the outcomes might be achieved. The following examples from Science give a flavour of these.

> By contributing to experiments and investigations, I can develop my understanding of models of matter and can apply this to changes of state and the energy involved as they occur in nature. [SCN 2-05a]

> Through research on how animals communicate, I can explain how sound vibrations are carried by waves through air, water and other media. [SCN 2-11a] (Education Scotland, 2011)

Key Themes in Curriculum for Excellence

CfE exhibits a number of features that its proponents claim to be new, innovative and distinctive. The main themes are outlined briefly here, and will be explored more critically in the final section of the chapter. A major theme is flexibility. The new curriculum explicitly states that schools will be freed up to develop content and pedagogy to meet local needs, and to provide for the needs of individual learners. There has been a stated aim that the curriculum would be 'decluttered' (Education Scotland, 2011), thereby reducing content and limiting the necessity for teachers to transmit content. The Es & Os reflect such aspirations, framing knowledge in a more generic and less content-specific manner than was the case previously, and affirming the importance of skills development. Teachers have been explicitly positioned in this process as agents of change, drawing upon the arguably successful experience of engaging practitioners in pedagogical development during the pilot phases of the earlier Assessment is for Learning (AifL) programme (see Hutchinson and Hayward, 2005).

A second major theme concerns pedagogy. Indeed, it has been suggested that the key change sought by CfE lies in the development of new approaches to learning and teaching. Within these new approaches, learners are required to become more responsible for their own learning. Active learning is promoted by the new curriculum, although there is often little clarity about what this means in practice (it is regularly construed rather narrowly as kinaesthetic learning – see Chapter 49 for further discussion). In many local authorities, active learning has been developed using established approaches such as cooperative learning, which have come to complement, or in some cases replace, more traditional forms of didactic teaching, and the commonplace worksheet-based learning that developed through the 1980s and 1990s. Such social forms of learning extend to some extent the notion of active learning, but it is fair to say that more explicit work is needed in this respect, especially in terms of developing the notion of 'active' around concepts such as metacognition and intrinsic motivation.

A third theme relates to the organisation of knowledge. There are various cross-curricular themes – literacy, numeracy and citizenship, for instance – which are seen as the responsibility of all teachers. In many secondary schools, the systematic development of less fragmented provision of subjects in the years S1 to S3 (now known as the phase of broad, general education) is emerging. This development is explicitly framed to broaden the curriculum at this stage without the need for pupils to see fifteen or more subject teachers in a week, and to facilitate the making of cross-curricular linkages. Thus, for example, many schools are establishing fully integrated or modular (e.g. one teacher, three subjects) models for the social subjects and science. Other interdisciplinary approaches have become popular in secondary schools, notably the rich-task approach first developed in Queensland, where typically different subjects come together to constitute an event, for example an Africa-themed week. Such work often involves citizenship or global citizenship. The development of interdisciplinary approaches has been generally been well received in primary schools, which have experience of working in thematic ways. However, some of the development in secondary schools is more problematic (Priestley and Minty, 2012). There is a general lack of knowledge and understanding of theory relating to interdisciplinary approaches, and many initiatives have been tokenistic (to meet the requirements of CfE) and contrived (for example shoehorning subjects into a preconceived theme rather than selecting content to meet clearly defined curricular purposes). In some secondary schools, CfE as a whole has been framed within a set period of time each week (e.g. a double period), with the normal business of the school carrying on as usual for the remainder of the week. Furthermore, in the majority of secondary schools, there has been little attempt to change existing timetable structures; and the ubiquitous thirty-period week/fifty-three minute period is a major hindrance to developing interdisciplinary approaches and active pedagogies.

A fourth theme concerns the extension of CfE into age ranges not previously covered by national curriculum guidance. In many cases, this policy evolution reflects existing trends in practice. The formation of the early level brings together pre-school centres and primary schools, hitherto separate institutions governed by different guidance, and arguably quite different culturally and educationally. There is now an expectation that practitioners from a diverse range of pre-school centres will work with and in similar ways to primary school teachers. While this has been welcomed by many practitioners who have long called for greater integration, it is also challenging, given the previously very different ways of working, underpinning philosophies and educational backgrounds experienced by these two groups of practitioners. Another area where CfE formalises and builds upon existing practices in cross-sectoral working relates to the transition between secondary education and FE. FE colleges, like schools, are developing approaches to implement CfE, both for their more traditional students (post-16) and for increasing numbers of pre-16 school pupils who follow courses in college as part of collaborative school–college arrangements. Early anecdotal evidence suggests that many colleges are coping with the demands of CfE better than their secondary school counterparts. This can be largely attributed to the existence of mechanisms in colleges for cross-disciplinary working, continuous assessment and moderation and the development of core skills; recent experience of such activity is less well developed in secondary schools.

A final theme is assessment. New qualifications have been developed to replace the existing level 4 (Standard Grade General or Intermediate 1) and level 5 (Standard Grade Credit or Intermediate 2) with single qualifications. The new qualifications have been designed to meet the needs of CfE, containing for example a large continuous, school-based assessment component (in the case of the new National 4 qualification, this is to be assessed 100 per cent internally, and will not be graded). Levels 3 (continuation of Access qualifications, but discontinuation of Standard Grade Foundation), level 6 (Higher) and level 7 (Advanced Higher) will remain essentially unchanged. Many teachers have criticised what they see as the late arrival of these qualifications in relation to the new curriculum, complaining that they will not know what to teach until they know what is to be assessed. To some extent, such anxieties are understandable; secondary teachers are judged according to their success in raising attainment, and a lack of clarity in terms of qualifications is a serious concern for many. It remains to be seen whether the revised qualifications will reduce pressures to teach to the test, as is claimed; it may be that continued use of attainment data by local authorities, school managers and inspectors as a proxy measure of school and teacher effectiveness will militate against this.

Assessment is also a concern for primary teachers and within the early stages of secondary school. It has become increasingly clear since 2010 that assessment against the Es & Os will be a major feature of teachers' work within CfE. Significantly, early documentation demonstrated a sensitivity towards the dangers of assessment driving the curriculum, however subsequent developments reveal a shift in emphasis, making clear an expectation that the Es & Os are assessment standards. This has been exacerbated by the decision in many local authorities not only to assess against each E & O, but also to utilise a three-category scale within each level: (1) *Developing*; (2) *Consolidating*; and (3) *Secure* (Priestley and Minty, 2012). Such developments reveal a continued preoccupation with assessment, recording and reporting, which potentially both increases teacher workload and limits the aspirational scope of CfE to broaden education through school-based innovation.

At the time of writing, work on implementing the curriculum is ongoing; schools nationally were required to implement the new curriculum up to and including S1 by the end of the 2010–11 school year.

THE SCOTTISH CURRICULUM – HISTORICAL TRENDS

It is a well known axiom in Scottish education that primary schools teach children, whereas secondary schools teach subjects. There is some truth in this statement, as will be revealed through a brief summary of the historical development of the curriculum in Scotland, although as with any such witticism, if taken literally it can obscure important issues. This section briefly focuses on the primary and secondary curricula to illustrate the historical trajectories that have led to CfE. Lack of space precludes discussion of other areas such as early years.

The Primary Curriculum

The defining moment for the primary school curriculum occurred with what has come to be known as the *Primary Memorandum* (1965). This document laid down some of the defining principles of the primary school. These include child-centredness, active participation by pupils in their own learning, experiential learning, a thematic or interdisciplinary approach to the curriculum and teachers' active reflection on their work (see Cassidy, 2008). The *Memorandum* is often described as a sharp break with tradition, but according to Paterson (2003) this is not the case; it is better seen as a reaffirmation of trends that had been emerging since at least the 1930s. Moreover, unlike in England where progressive education was seen as being relatively unstructured, in Scotland the progressivism of the *Memorandum* was tempered by strongly entrenched notions of structure, hierarchy and the relative positioning of the teacher and the child. Its implementation reflected notions of schooling as the socialisation of 'children into responsible adulthood' (Paterson, 2003, p. 127). As such it represented a pragmatic mix of progressivism and conservatism, and a statement of evolutionary development rather than a radical step change.

Further change came in the 1980s, due in part to inspectorate criticisms of a narrow basic skills focus in primary schools (Cassidy, 2008), alongside increasing interest on the behalf of government to extend control and accountability into the domain of schooling. The result was the 5–14 Curriculum (for example, articulated in *The Structure and Balance of the Curriculum*), first introduced, following heated debate about the 'Englishing' of the curriculum, in 1991. The 5–14 Curriculum did represent a number of changes to the work of primary schools, reflecting the influence of the New Right in British politics. This is especially evident in the introduction of an outcome-based model, organised into sequential levels. This development introduced an overtly technicist element to schooling, allowing assessment to be specified against the curriculum outcomes. The curriculum was framed as guidelines rather than prescription, but in practice primary schools fell into line in implementing it. For the first time primary schools had to work to fixed time allocations. National tests (ostensibly to be used only as a back-up to teachers' professional judgement and available from a centralised bank) came to be utilised as the main yardstick for pupil attainment, and local authorities were able to collate attainment data from them, used subsequently as a proxy measure for school effectiveness. According to Cassidy (2008), 5–14 exerted a number of detrimental effects on primary education, including a recourse to rigid timetabling structures, curricular fragmentation and an over-focus on assessment, especially national testing. It is likely that this has contributed to a process of deprofessionalisation in primary schools, and to the development of a culture of accountability and performativity, which has subsequently limited capacity for school-based curriculum development.

The Secondary Curriculum

The evolution of the secondary curriculum exhibits a number of commonalities with its primary counterpart, but also a distinctive set of trends that explain the sharp differences in philosophy between the two sectors. Much of the development of secondary schooling was defined by the debate for the abolition of the selective senior/junior secondary system and the establishment of the comprehensive system. This debate occurred from the 1930s onwards, and widespread development of comprehensive schools became a reality following the election of a Labour government in 1964 and the parallel development of comprehensive education elsewhere in the UK. According to Paterson (2003), this was not simply a case of Scotland following England – indeed Scotland comprehensivised more thoroughly than England, reflecting the gathering momentum of popular support for such a move, fuelled by public and political debate over the previous three decades. The new comprehensive schools were characterised by a persistence of subject hierarchies. There followed a debate about whether academic subjects were suitable for all pupils – something that was to re-emerge in each subsequent curriculum reform. Such questions were tackled by the Munn and Dunning Reports, both published in 1977. The former dealt explicitly with the curriculum, eventually reaffirming the status quo, setting out a 'Hirstian subject-based curriculum with a nod in the direction of cross-curricular courses, but only for the less able' (Boyd, 1997, p. 60). After some debate and some pilot work, the proposals from Munn and Dunning were put into practice in a Development Programme, commencing in 1982, and including the establishment of the long-lasting Standard Grade qualifications. The secondary curriculum has remained substantially unchanged since this period, although a number of subsequent developments are worthy of mention.

First, while 5–14 – intended to bridge the primary–secondary transition – did not have a major effect on secondary schools (with the possible exception of Maths and English where national testing became the norm), it did reignite the subjects vs interdisciplinary debate, for example through its grouping of the social subjects into a common strand as part of the Environmental Science curriculum. It is however fair to say that such discourses did not greatly impact upon practice, with, for instance, the identified problem of fragmentation in S1 and S2 being addressed through subject rotations rather than integrated curriculum design.

Second, there was lively debate, exemplified by the 1992 Howie Report, about the place of vocational subjects in the senior curriculum. Howie's suggestion of a twin-track academic/vocational curriculum was rejected, but the debate, combined with development of vocational (SCOTVEC) modules and influence of the Technical and Vocational Education Initiative programme at this time, meant that the issue of narrowness in the curriculum continued to be widely acknowledged. This ultimately proved to be a contributory factor in the subsequent development of Higher Still. During this period, secondary education continued to be defined by the end point of external exams in academic subjects: the structure of the lower secondary courses has been driven by pupil choices and competition between departments for these pupils; and teacher effectiveness has been largely judged by attainment statistics – the ubiquitous Standard Tables and Charts (STACS) data. As with primary schools, a continual focus on attainment has led to a culture of performativity, often driven by perverse incentives. One example of this is the increasing tendency for students doing Higher courses (SCQF level 6) to be relegated to Intermediate 2 (SCQF level 5) even when they already have the equivalent Standard Grade Credit qualification (in 2009, nearly 6,000 pupils with an existing qualification in Standard Grade Credit English sat Intermediate 2 English – see Priestley et al., 2012). This is often justified as being in the student's best interest and is certainly helpful to the school in terms of boosting the proportion of students passing Higher.

CRITICAL ISSUES IN THE SCOTTISH CURRICULUM

The above discussion suggests that there are a number of critical issues that require further analysis. To some extent this is a challenging task: there has been no systematic funded research programme for CfE – in contrast to earlier curricular development. This has been exacerbated by a decline in research funding generally within the universities, meaning that rigorous empirical evidence is hard to come by. There are a number of key questions, which will be addressed in this final part of the chapter. First, one might ask whether CfE is indeed as original, innovative and radical in principle as some might claim; or is it more typical of other contemporary curriculum developments across the world? Second, one might pose the question of whether CfE is original, innovative and radical in terms of its position in the recent (and not so recent) history of curriculum development in Scotland. Third, it is interesting to examine the model, and associated educational policies that give shape to CfE, inquiring into issues of internal coherence, and whether or not the new curriculum takes account of curricular theory in forming a conceptual frame for educational practices. Finally, a critical observer might question whether the aspirational goals of CfE are realisable in practice, and whether the initiative will lead to lasting and meaningful changes in practices in Scottish schools and other educational centres.

CFE: AN ORIGINAL CONCEPT?

While CfE is widely seen as being distinctive, a look at parallel development from around the world suggests otherwise. There has been recent worldwide development of similar new models of national curriculum. The New Zealand Curriculum and recent changes to England's national curriculum (pre-2010 election, which has of course heralded another seismic shift) provide parallel examples of this emergence of a set of common trends in curriculum prescription. As in Scotland, the architects state that they provide both central guidance for schools (thus ensuring the maintenance of national standards), and sufficient flexibility for schools and teachers to take account of local needs in designing programmes of education. Thus they seek to combine what is claimed to be the best features of top-down and bottom-up approaches to curriculum planning. Such curricula are characterised by various common features, notably a structural basis in outcomes sequenced into linear levels, and a focus on generic competencies or capacities instead of a detailed specification of knowledge/content. As such, they have been criticised for stripping knowledge out of the curriculum (Young, 2009).

The outcomes tend to be predicated on what students are able to experience in their learning and/or do as a result of such learning. The following examples from the science curriculum in New Zealand (Ministry of Education, 2010) and CfE (Education Scotland, 2011) illustrate the similarities as well as a difference that seems to be idiosyncratic in Scotland – an enhanced focus on experience within the statement:

> Students will recognise that there are life processes common to all living things and that these occur in different ways. (Level 4, Life Processes, New Zealand Science Curriculum)

> I can sample and identify living things from different habitats to compare their biodiversity and can suggest reasons for their distribution. (SCN 3-01a, CfE)

Linked to the stripping out of knowledge/content from curricular outcomes is the framing of the new curricula around generic capacities or core/key competencies. The pre-2010 development in England posited three of Scotland's four capacities as its curricular aims, omitting Effective Contributors. New Zealand has adopted slightly different language in its key competencies, although the generic tone is similar: Thinking; Using Language, Symbols and Texts; Managing Self; Relating to Others; and Participating and Contributing.

CFE: BACK TO THE FUTURE?

If CfE is not terribly distinctive in worldwide terms, it is perhaps distinctive in terms of being a new and radical development within Scotland. It is clear from the above section that CfE is indicative of new trends in the specification of curriculum – a recourse to new types of outcome, and a shift to genericism in terms of specifying knowledge/content. In terms of pedagogy, it is widely claimed that CfE is taking Scotland in new pedagogical directions. It is certainly true that Scotland has witnessed the development over the last ten years of much pedagogical innovation. These include cooperative forms of learning, and formative assessment. However, two points must be made here. First, such changes were starting to happen anyway (for example under the influence of AifL). Thus, as with previous milestones such as the *Primary Memorandum*, there is a case for arguing that the policy is to some extent an affirmation of emerging forms of practice. And further, such pedagogical innovations are not new – cooperative learning, for instance, was developed in the 1970s and has been widely used across the world since then.

There is, then, an argument that CfE represents, or at least heralds, fairly radical shifts in some elements of teachers' practice. But it is debatable whether it heralds a similarly radical shift in policy intention. For example, Brown and Munn (1985) identified five main features of the 1982 Development Programme for S3 and S4 curriculum and assessment:

1. School-based curriculum development by teachers.
2. Assessment as an integral part of teaching and learning.
3. New qualifications.
4. New ways of defining and organising knowledge (for example interdisciplinary and multi-disciplinary approaches).
5. A research programme to support and inform development.

It is interesting to note the similarity of these features with CfE (with the obvious exception of the research programme, which has been manifestly absent from CfE). Moreover, similar rhetoric was evident in other policies such as the *Primary Memorandum* (see Paterson, 2003; Cassidy, 2008). One might make the case that CfE is a shift in lexicon more than a shift in substance.

CFE: A COHERENT MODEL?

CfE has been criticised for a lack of coherence in its underpinning model. Priestley and Humes (2010) have suggested that the architects of CfE have largely ignored a significant body of curriculum theory. The result, in their view, is a mix-and-match curriculum; a combination of a process curriculum (based upon the articulation of broad educational goals and processes or methods that are fit for purpose) and an outcomes curriculum (framed around the tight specification of large numbers of predetermined objectives). They claim that these models are incompatible. CfE, they suggest, offers two conflicting starting points for curriculum development: the big ideas encapsulated in the four capacities and their underpinning statements offer long-term goals for the curriculum, in line with the notion of a process curriculum; the Es & Os offer more short-term, instrumental objectives for curriculum development that are more in tune with the outcomes model. According to Priestley and Humes, this is a problem because it offers conflicting starting points for school-based curriculum development, with the danger that schools will choose the easier option of auditing current practice against the Es & Os, making minimal changes where necessary, and losing sight of the big ideas. Subsequent empirical evidence suggests that these dangers are real, and that the audit approach is the predominant starting point of school-based curriculum development (see, for example, Priestley and Minty, 2012).

CFE: THEORY INTO PRACTICE

The big question is whether CfE will lead to a transformational change in Scottish education. Recent research from two projects (see, for example, Priestley and Minty, 2012; Priestley et al., 2012) suggests that the big ideas underpinning CfE are widely welcomed by the teaching profession. Survey data from one local authority (Priestley and Minty, 2012) clearly indicate that this is the case across the profession – primary as well as secondary, experienced teachers and new entrants to the profession, school leaders and non-promoted colleagues. And yet the data also show a considerable level of discontent with the process of implementation. Such research illustrates the conscientiousness of Scottish teachers, but also the very real difficulties they often face in enacting their practice.

Part of the difficulty lies in the issue discussed above – the lack of coherence in the policy itself, its widely perceived vagueness (Priestley and Minty, 2012) and the lack of a clearly articulated process for development. The research suggests that many teachers have struggled to make sense of the new curriculum, a situation exacerbated by a lack of time and resources at a point when education services are facing serious cuts. A tension-ridden policy landscape also forms part of the problem. Teachers are expected to be agents of change in implementing CfE, but such decisions and subsequent actions are often fraught with danger. Innovation is a risky business in the culture of accountability that is the lived experience of teachers in modern schools. The hazards of adversely affecting attainment are simply too great for many, and the clear imperative is to play safe. These pragmatic issues are thus clearly significant in shaping teacher agency (see Priestley et al., 2012).

A second issue lies in capacity – of teachers, local authorities and other agencies such as universities – to engage in school-based curriculum development. This is partly due to the erosion of teacher professionalism and the disappearance in recent years of particular types of craft knowledge (for instance around assessment and moderation), as a result of the extension of central control over education over the last two decades. A related issue is the socialisation of teachers into the discourses of accountability. Research (Priestley and Minty, 2012) strongly suggests that teachers' responses to the new curriculum are framed to a large extent around the need to assess, record and report. As such, responses such as these to the challenges posed by CfE are necessarily circumscribed – the teachers participating in one of the research projects often lacked a sufficiently broad repertoire for manoeuvre to be able to respond in a flexible, agentic manner to the complex situations in which they found themselves (Priestley et al., 2012). In both projects, there was significant evidence that many teachers face daily dilemmas, as a culture of accountability leads them to make decisions that are in tension with their fundamental values as professionals. It is significant that teachers who were able to strongly express their educational values were also able to articulate a clear vision for CfE. This was especially the case where strong collegial relationships existed, and where teachers were not working in isolation.

This research raises important and uncomfortable questions about how policy makers might frame policy to facilitate teacher agency in curriculum making, rather than seeking to control implementation processes or outcomes. It raises important questions about how school leaders might shape their schools to be places where teachers are able to contribute to the development of a good education, through school-based curriculum development that is focused on the needs of students rather than on the performance of the school. This, in conclusion, suggests that it is one thing for policy to frame teachers as agents of change. It is quite another to enable this to actually happen in the practices that make up their everyday lives.

REFERENCES

Boyd, B. (1997) 'The statutory years of secondary education: Change and progress', in M. M. Clark and P. Munn (eds), *Education in Scotland: Policy and Practice from Pre-school to Secondary*. London: Routledge.

Brown, S. and P. Munn (1985) *The Changing Face of Education 14 to 16: Curriculum and Assessment.* Windsor: NFER.

Cassidy, C. (2008) 'Scottish primary education: Philosophy and practice', in T. G. K. Bryce and W. M. Humes (eds), *Scottish Education, Third Edition: Beyond Devolution.* Edinburgh: Edinburgh University Press.

Education Scotland (2011) *Understanding the Curriculum.* Online at www.ltscotland.org.uk/under-standingthecurriculum/index.asp (This website includes direct links to all of the CfE documentation cited in the chapter.)

Hutchinson, C. and L. Hayward (2005) 'The journey so far: assessment for learning in Scotland', *The Curriculum Journal*, 16 (2): 225–48.

Ministry of Education (2010) *Science Curriculum Achievement Aims and Objectives.* Online at http://nzcurriculum.tki.org.nz/Curriculum-documents/The-New-Zealand-Curriculum/Learning-areas/Science/Science-curriculum-achievement-aims-and-objectives

Paterson, L. (2003) *Scottish Education in the Twentieth Century.* Edinburgh: Edinburgh University Press.

Priestley, M. and W. Humes (2010) 'The development of Scotland's Curriculum for Excellence: Amnesia and déjà vu', *Oxford Review of Education*, 36 (3): 345–61.

Priestley, M., S. Robinson and G. Biesta (2012) 'Teacher agency, performativity and curriculum change: Reinventing the teacher in the Scottish Curriculum for Excellence?', in B. Jeffrey and G. Troman (eds), *Performativity across UK Education: Ethnographic Cases of its Effects, Agency and Reconstructions.* Painswick: E&E Publishing.

Priestley, M. and S. Minty (2012) *Developing Curriculum for Excellence: Summary of Research Findings from a Scottish Local Authority.* Stirling: University of Stirling.

Young, M. (2009) *Alternative Educational Futures for a Knowledge Society. Socialism and Education.* Online at http://socialismandeducation.wordpress.com/2009/12/06/alternative-educational-futures-for-a-knowledge-society

4

Scottish Primary Education: Philosophy and Practice

Claire Cassidy

This chapter considers three reforms in Scottish primary education since the 1960s rather than attempting to give a complete account of its history. There have been many influences on Scottish education, and Paterson (2003) offers a comprehensive analysis of the political and historical shaping of Scotland's educational system in the twentieth century. This chapter reflects on the philosophical links between and across three key Scottish educational reforms in our most recent past: *A Curriculum for Excellence* (Scottish Executive, 2004), the 5–14 Curriculum (see *The Structure and Balance of the Curriculum*, SOED, 1993 and LTS, 2000) and *Primary Education in Scotland* (SED, 1965), commonly known as the Primary Memorandum.

Scotland is currently working through a period of curricular reform that began in 2004 with *A Curriculum for Excellence* (Scottish Executive, 2004). The document, *A Curriculum for Excellence* (ACfE), grew out of the 2002 National Debate on Education, a Scottish Executive consultation exercise open to pupils, parents, teachers, employers and others with an interest in education. The debate was designed to explore the state of school education in Scotland. It revealed that, while there was perceived value in much of Scottish education, there was also a need and desire for improvement. Consequently, a Curriculum Review Group was established in 2003 'to identify the purposes of education 3 to 18 and principles for the design of the curriculum' (Scottish Executive, 2004, p. 7). The Group was charged with taking into account developing technologies and future demands and patterns of work in the global context, while also maintaining a view of children's development and the role of adults working with children in a range of educational settings. Ironically, the result was a document not far removed from the educational reform of 1965, *Primary Education in Scotland* (SED, 1965).

THE PRIMARY CURRICULUM

Primary Education Scotland (SED, 1965) was designed to share best principles and practice at both a philosophical and a pedagogical level. Teachers, administrators and others with responsibility for primary education were urged by William Ross, the then Secretary of State for Scotland, to use the *Primary Memorandum* to 'stimulate thought and constant reappraisal of our own work' (SED, 1965, p. iii). From the outset, the *Memorandum* declares

the need to focus on active participation of children in their own learning and the role of
the child at the centre of learning. This was far from a new notion and had strong parallels
with Jean-Jacques Rousseau's *Emile, or Education* written some 200 years previously. While
Emile gave a fictitious and hypothetical account of how one might educate a child from birth
to manhood (manhood being key, as this was a subset of adulthood), the impact of the text
in its own time, and subsequently 250 years later in Scotland, cannot be ignored. While at
the time of publication the book was popular enough with those parents in the privileged
classes to merit two translations of the text into English within six months of its initial
publication (see Darling, 2000), the influence of Rousseau's philosophy was more widely
felt and experienced in Scotland nearly fifty years ago, carrying something of a legacy to
this day. For Rousseau, freedom, not power, was the greatest good; and this ability to do as
one desires, being his fundamental maxim, applied to childhood: 'all the rules of education
spring from it' (Rousseau, *Emile, or Education*, London: J. M. Dent & Sons, 1948, p. 48).
Here, Rousseau directs us to the child at the centre, the child who learns from experience. It
is in this work that Rousseau advocates setting contexts and circumstances under which and
through which Emile may be educated. Situations are controlled, established or manipulated in order that Emile achieve the objectives of the lesson. There is no rote learning, but
full – and often radical – experiential learning. Over time, Rousseau's Romantic conception
of children and childhood, one where children were regarded as innocent and different from
adults, had great impact on the ways in which children are treated in education and society
more widely (Cassidy, 2007; Darling, 2000). The authors of the *Primary Memorandum* were
clearly influenced by this child-centred philosophy.

Coupled to the notion of learning through experience was stage maturation theory as
espoused by followers of Piaget. This developmental psychology saw children progress
through stages of intellectual maturity. Much of the *Memorandum* was allied to the idea that
children progress their abilities at specific stages according to age. The advice for teachers
was that they 'must appreciate the stages through which the child is passing in his development towards adulthood, and attempt to provide for him the environment, experiences and
guidance which will stimulate progress along natural lines' (SED, 1965, p. 3).

It was held that teachers should pay due attention to the natural development of the child
and that timing was all-important in the teaching of content. There are echoes here of *Emile*,
since Rousseau also held that children progressed through recognisable stages of development. Children, claimed Rousseau, should not be treated like forced fruit but should be
educated for life. While acknowledging the role of the child's environment and the need for
education to recognise it, the *Memorandum* saw the goal of education as being one that must
'concern itself with fostering in him [the child] the qualities, skills and attitudes which will
make him useful to society and adaptable to the kind of environment in which he will live
as an adult' (ibid., p. 17).

It was important that children were furnished with the tools to investigate for themselves, and that they would be encouraged to find answers to the questions they set themselves. Following not only from Rousseau, but also from Dewey, the *Memorandum* was clear
that children learn best when motivated by the area of study and that, therefore, learning
and, by implication, teaching should be developed from interest. The authors eschewed
the practice of a subject-based curriculum in favour of purposeful activities that would be
more meaningful to the child as a consequence of being responsive to his interests. Not
by accident is the first chapter of the *Memorandum* centred on 'The Child'. Step by step,
the chapter sets out considerations with regard to the child: growth and development; the

primary-school years; the needs of the child; the need for security; the need for guidance; the need for freedom; the need to understand; and the need for the 'real' and the 'concrete'. Each section explicates the key factors in relation to the child and his education, clearly highlighting values underpinned by the philosophies of Rousseau and Dewey. Teachers are guided towards supporting the child with advice on how best to think of children's development. The text takes this further to consider the child's environment. The global and societal environment is considered before reflection on the school environment and how it engenders positive learning experiences. These learning experiences, while initiated by the child, are facilitated by the staff of the school, and the *Memorandum* explores the roles of the headteacher, the class teacher, the specialist teacher and the ancillary staff in the child's education. The school is seen not simply as a place where children are put to be acted upon, but as a whole environment where an ethos is generated that is sympathetic to children's interests and, therefore, to their learning.

The *Memorandum* discusses a range of methods and organisational approaches considered to be conducive to child-centred learning – all this with a view to creating meaningful learning experiences for 'backward, able and gifted pupils', as these children would also 'grow up to be citizens of the future' (SED, 1965, p. 53). These meaningful learning experiences would occur by virtue of a curriculum influenced by the 1956 Schools (Scotland) Code, which set out the key aspects for instruction. The *Memorandum* expanded upon the Code's designated areas of spoken and written English, arithmetic, music, art and handwork, nature study, physical education, geography, history and – for girls – needlework, to create more open and versatile opportunities for teachers to create links across the subject areas. The *Memorandum*'s authors recognised the limitations of the Code and put extra emphasis on a more holistic approach that was more relevant for pupils without generating an overloaded curriculum. Integration of curricular subjects was viewed as essential. There was a place in environmental studies – the new collective term for arithmetic, history, geography and science – to find applications for language and mathematics skills, and teachers were urged to do so. Drama and music could also come together, and art and craft would be a merger of handwork and needlework that would be available for boys as well as girls. Further, time allocations were not seen to be helpful, and it was not anticipated that each child would have the same experiences in every class in every school; it was for headteachers and their staff to decide what best suited their children in their contexts in judging what to include in the curriculum, which now revolved around the main headings of Language Arts, Environmental Studies, Art and Craft Activities, Music, Physical Education, Health Education, Handwriting, Gaelic and Modern Languages. However, this was, in some ways, an ideal.

The 1980 HMI report *Learning and Teaching in Primary 4 and Primary 7* (Edinburgh: SED) surveyed 152 schools (6 per cent of the primary schools in Scotland), where 'They evaluated what teachers were doing and assessed what pupils were achieving' (ibid., p. 5). The survey took account of what was happening in P4 and P7, the rationale being that, by P4, children could read and count, and that P7 was the year before children migrated to secondary school. The survey showed that, far from the possibilities presented by the *Memorandum* to engage in a wide range of activities through a range of curricular areas, teachers were themselves constricting the learning of pupils by 'concentrating on a very narrow span of activity' (ibid., p. 46) with a determined focus on 'basic skills' to the detriment of other learning opportunities, 'with such conviction that it requires to be examined as a fundamental issue' (ibid., p. 46). It was not the curriculum that was failing pupils but, the report asserted, teachers' attitudes. The report went on to conclude that there was 'the need to preserve breadth in the curriculum; and the importance of maintaining and supporting a teaching force of quality and imagination' (ibid., p. 55).

5–14

It was this that the 5–14 programme worked to address. To anyone who has been teaching in a Scottish primary school since 1991, the 1965 curricular areas will not be new. In fact, for at least twenty years in Scotland, teachers very much held to the areas suggested above, but, under 5–14, in an arguably more prescriptive manner. The consultation paper *Curriculum and Assessment in Scotland: A Policy for the 90s* was issued in 1987 (Edinburgh: SOED) and heralded the advent of the 5–14 programme, addressing what was identified by the Secretary of State as 'a need for clearer definition of the content and objectives of the curriculum; the establishment of satisfactory assessment policies in all schools; and better communication between schools and parents, including reporting on pupils' progress' (SOED, 1993, *The Structure and Balance of the Curriculum*, Edinburgh: SOED, p. 1).

Following the review of the existing curricular advice by the Scottish Consultative Council on the Curriculum, guidelines covering curriculum and assessment were set for children aged between 5 and 14. Between 1989 and 1993, proposals relating to curriculum content and programmes of study were scrutinised and developed under six key areas: English Language, Mathematics, Environmental Studies, Expressive Arts, Religious and Moral Education, and Personal and Social Development, with Gaelic and Modern Languages coming later. There were also groups considering Assessment and Testing, and Developing the Whole Curriculum. Like the *Primary Memorandum*, the subject areas incorporated subgroups of subjects: for example, Expressive Arts comprised art, music, drama and physical education, while Environmental Studies was a composite of science, history and geography (later known as social subjects, science and technology); but different headings were used, such as People in the Past; People in Place, Earth and Space; and Living Things and the Processes of Life. Also, just as the *Memorandum* advocated working from children's knowledge, experience and interests to create learning opportunities for society's future citizens, the authors of the 5–14 programme saw the task of education as satisfying 'the needs of the individual and society and to promote the development of knowledge and understanding, practical skills, attitudes and values' (ibid., p. 3).

Interestingly, the document *The Structure and Balance of the Curriculum* was revised in 2000 (Learning and Teaching Scotland, 2000, *The Structure and Balance of the Curriculum*, Edinburgh: Scottish Executive) to take account of what had been recognised as good practice and successful under the terms set out by Her Majesty's Inspectorate of Education; but the focus remained on equipping children with the necessary skills, knowledge and attitudes that would lead to 'a personally rewarding life, productive employment and active citizenship' (ibid., p. 3). This document directs teachers to a 'structured continuum of learning' (ibid., p. 4) for their pupils and retains the Piagetian notion of learning through stages. While the *Memorandum* was open-ended, and teachers and headteachers had liberty to make use of the curriculum to fit contexts in which they found themselves and their pupils, the 5–14 programme did not work in the same way.

The programme laid out the governing principles of the 5–14 Curriculum: breadth, balance, coherence, continuity and progression. However, the application of these principles was much more rigid in practice than in theory. The philosophy behind the programme was such that it should allow for integration and cross-curricular opportunities while building upon children's experiences, all the while ensuring that there was a comprehensive range of curricular areas to learn about and to draw from. In practice, what tended to happen was that there was much focus on the balance of the curriculum.

The *Memorandum* had shied away from setting timetables, since this was seen as inflexible and led to rigid timetabling that would be too closely related to the teaching of discrete subjects as opposed to curriculum integration; it would ultimately lead to children disengaging with the topic under investigation, since neither their individual needs nor their interests would be taken into account. Significantly, in an attempt to ensure provision for a range of learning experiences and the attainment of high standards, the 5–14 programme recommended appropriate time allocations. A minimum time allocation for each curricular component was recommended for each of the five areas in an attempt to protect parts of the curriculum other than Language and Mathematics, following the earlier criticisms that these two areas dominated classroom practices. Mathematics and Language were each allotted 15 per cent of the timetable, with the Expressive Arts sharing 15 per cent. Environmental Studies was given 25 per cent of the timetable, and Religious and Moral Education had 10 per cent. There was provision for 20 per cent flexibility time which schools were allowed to use for an emphasis of their own choosing, such as whole-school activities, pastoral care or cross-curricular activities. It is important to note that the 5–14 Guidelines and its recommended time allocations very quickly became viewed not as guidelines, but as mandatory strictures that were fully enforced across the primary school sector.

Having taught in the primary sector throughout the 1990s, personal experience and observation indicate that these strictures were little challenged, and some staff found that they had to undertake exactly what the *Memorandum*'s authors had asserted as negative practice: the following of rigid timetables where children experienced, for example, art lessons at one o'clock every Thursday afternoon and similar regimentation for other areas, with headteachers counting up hours on timetables to ensure that the recommended time allocation was being met. Consequently, the curriculum became more and more fragmented, with class teachers teaching the curriculum in discrete subjects with limited evidence of cross-curricular activities or integrated approaches to learning, despite the principle of coherence which was originally designed to facilitate the linkages between one area of knowledge and skills and another. This was contrary to the stated intentions of the 5–14 programme. The guiding principles of breadth, balance and coherence were intended to go hand in hand with continuity and progression, and these latter two aims were supposed to work for the benefit of individual children.

ATTAINMENT AND ASSESSMENT

Continuity meant that teachers would try to build on children's previous experiences while also taking into account their abilities and attainment. Progression, similarly, allowed children to work towards goals that were set within the guidelines. The programme put in place a set of five attainment levels, ranging from level A through to level E, with a later addition of a sixth level, level F, to account for, and to allow provision for, more able children. It was intended that children would progress through each level, beginning at level A, following a programme of study set out under specific strands within each curricular area. For instance, within the English Language document, children would experience Reading, and within this there would be several related strands that ran across the levels: for example, reading for information, reading for enjoyment, reading to reflect the writer's ideas and craft, and so on. This allowed teachers a common language to share with colleagues and parents. Children would be expected to attain certain levels at certain stages throughout their primary school career and into the second year of their secondary schooling. This again mirrored the Piagetian stage theory found in the *Primary Memorandum*; the Scottish primary curriculum has found it difficult, impossible even, to move away from this notion. In order to progress from one level to the next, teachers would monitor and assess performance against the criteria set out in the strands.

Should teachers consider a child to have completed and grasped the work within the strand pertaining to a specific level, they would move on to the next. In maths and language, however, there were National Tests that children had to pass in order to progress to the next level. While the progressivism of the *Memorandum* denounced formal testing, particularly in the early years, in favour of observation or diagnostic testing, the 5–14 programme lauded it as good practice. What resulted was exactly what the *Memorandum* warned against: teachers limiting their content to 'teach to the test', or that the time-consuming activity would provide no more information on the children's learning than what the teacher had already observed in everyday teaching and interaction. While it was not intended that children be seen to pass or fail these tests, what often happened in practice was that children were made very aware of their attainment levels, and pressure was exerted on them and on teachers to ensure that each child was on the 'correct' level for his or her stage. This often resulted in teachers 'helping' the children to pass tests at the expense of their understanding, ability or readiness to move to the next level. There was an initial protest from teachers and parents over the tests and their implementation, but this was relatively short-lived. Simpson (2006) offers a critical discussion of the events that precipitated the National Tests and revisits the alliance forged between teachers, parents and the unions in their initial fight against National Testing. The 5–14 National Tests were later replaced by National Assessments, which are, to all intents and purposes, the same thing as National Tests but under a new and different name to reflect the work initiated in 2002 by the Assessment is for Learning (AifL) development (see Chapter 75).

Assessment is for Learning was published in 2002 and was a joint development by the (then) Scottish Executive Education Department (SEED), the Scottish Qualifications Authority and Learning and Teaching Scotland (LTS). Between 2004 and 2007, teachers were introduced to AifL with a view to aiding communication with pupils and parents and to supporting them in their assessment practices on both a formative and a summative level. The AifL programme encompassed three key areas: Assessment for Learning, Assessment as Learning and Assessment of Learning. Through a website, teachers were provided with opportunities to share good assessment practice. They were given an assessment toolkit, a research library and opportunities to meet at events to discuss assessment theory and practice; there was also a virtual space where teachers, policy makers and researchers could come together to reflect on assessment. With perhaps the exception of the formal National Assessments that seem little improved from the National Tests in terms of actual practice, the philosophy of assessment in Scottish primary schools appears now to be more positive in its approach to supporting teachers' assessment practices. This is true in the sense that teachers employ more formative assessment strategies in their teaching than may be implied by the summative National Assessments. The principles of AifL are now embedded in the CfE with *Building the Curriculum 5* (Scottish Government, 2011). This document outlines the principles and frameworks for assessment and makes comment on teachers' continuing professional development to ensure consistency of approach and quality in assessment. An online National Assessment Resource is also available to support practitioners in developing a common understanding of assessment and in sharing good assessment practice (www. educationscotland.gov.uk/learningteachingandassessment/assessment/supportmaterials/ nar/index.asp).

CURRICULUM FOR EXCELLENCE

The four capacities – 'successful learners', 'confident individuals', 'responsible citizens' and 'effective contributors' – are exactly what is hoped for in *A Curriculum for Excellence* (Scottish Executive, 2004). This document aims to 'establish clear values, purposes and principles for education from 3 to 18 in Scotland' (Scottish Executive, 2004, p. 3). It is worth noting that the original title, *A Curriculum for Excellence*, has now changed to *Curriculum for Excellence*. It is not clear why, or when exactly, this changed but in losing the '*A*', the implication is that this *is* the curriculum that will ensure excellence rather than being one of several that *might*.

CfE evolved from five National Priorities for Education that grew out of the National Debate on Education. The National Priorities of Achievement and Attainment, Framework for Learning, Inclusion and Equality, Values and Citizenship, and Learning for Life were pulled together to create cohesion across the ages and stages when children are expected to undertake some form of education or formal schooling. It was anticipated that these five priorities could be targeted through the four capacities that CfE aims to foster. What is perhaps worth querying is just whose values 'our' values are that are being espoused, since the document clearly states that 'It is one of the prime purposes of education to make our young people aware of the values on which Scottish society is based . . . Young people therefore need to learn about and develop these values' (ibid., p. 11).

While there undoubtedly was some agreement in the National Debate over the positive aspects of the curriculum as it stood under the 5–14 programme and the need for some revision or rethinking, it is a large claim to make that all Scots share the same values, and yet a further jump to suggest that children should be made to learn and develop these values. It is not in doubt that those with an interest in Scottish education will want the best for Scotland's children; however, the move to so explicitly state the teaching of values required of children was new. The values of the authors, though, are apparent in the document's rhetoric throughout, with many phrases open to accusations of ambiguity and interpretation, such as 'To enhance opportunities and allow greater personalisation of learning' (ibid., p. 15), or that the curriculum 'must be inclusive, be a stimulus for personal achievement and, through the broadening of pupils' experience of the world, be an encouragement towards informed and responsible citizenship' (ibid., p. 11). Perhaps this was the intention; in order to engage people in the reform, there was a need to spark dialogue to facilitate the new curriculum's development.

CfE retains something of the focus on experiential learning as promoted in the *Memorandum* while also maintaining a notion of stage development. What has been addressed, so far, in this reform is a move away from the 5–14 tendency to discrete subjects; and again teachers are being urged to develop cross-curricular approaches and an integrated curriculum through the principle of relevance and purpose. The principles for curriculum design hold onto the notions of breadth, progression and coherence, but these are now enhanced by once more suggesting that there should be enjoyment and challenge for children – and indubitably for teachers – while also offering personalisation and choice. Indeed, it appears that planning more responsively to accommodate children's interests is welcomed by many teachers, particularly in the early years. There is an explicit desire that children be encouraged to learn in a range of meaningful contexts rather than the rigid attainment levels previously advocated. The contexts being proposed are still, however, subject-specific: expressive arts, health and wellbeing, languages, mathematics, religious and moral education, sciences, social studies and technologies, with the suggestion that schools be allowed to decide for themselves how they organise learning. The stages are perhaps broader than those created under 5–14 but the experiences and outcomes, framed by the prefix 'I can . . .', are somewhat vague. Indeed, where 5–14 was very explicit, CfE remains rather oblique in terms of progression through the stages.

One danger is that teachers, especially those who undertook their initial teacher education (ITE) throughout the 1990s and into the early 2000s, will have found it difficult to move away from the pattern and rigid structure of 5–14, and that learning across the curriculum through integrated planning and implementation becomes contrived. Those designing CfE perhaps missed a huge opportunity to overhaul and rethink what happens in Scotland's schools under the guise of curriculum. The curriculum in Scotland at the beginning of the twenty-first century could have fallen under headings such as Creativity or Thinking or Problem Solving, if headings were needed at all. Perhaps an approach such as this might have encouraged teachers to think beyond curricular areas and make stronger integrated links that would enable them to move away from what Paterson calls 'the peculiarly Scottish version of child-centredness' (Paterson, 2003, p. 116), where controls and freedoms of children come into conflict. Such a move away from a direct curricular focus may have been a more appropriate way of viewing the new curriculum, since there is emphasis not just on formal content but on the overall ethos within the school and preparation for life as citizens in Scotland.

The recurring theme in the *Primary Memorandum*, the 5–14 programme and CfE is that of citizenship and future participation in the world of work as a citizen. None of the texts actually define just what a citizen *is*, but they all aspire to make citizens of Scotland's children. It is important and significant to note that nowhere is the child viewed as a citizen already; all references are anticipatory. In fact, in writing about children as future citizens, it would be impossible for a curriculum to be written for children *qua* children; this would require a very different philosophy resulting in potentially very different practices. What is clear, though, is that teachers are not clear about what citizenship means (Akhtar, 2008) and that when examined, the political dimension of citizenship appears to be missing from what teachers do under CfE (Biesta, 2008). In light of an SNP administration and a drive to promote Scottish studies more comprehensively under CfE, it seems peculiar that teachers and/or authors of curriculum documentation avoid this aspect of children's learning.

It is a further concern that teachers are no clearer about the other 'capacities' and what it means to be an 'effective contributor', 'successful learner' or 'confident individual'. The documentation fails to clarify this, resulting in trite mantra-type use of the phrases with children not being any clearer than their teachers. Perhaps it is acceptable that everyone interprets these notions differently but one might hope for some common understanding upon which the curriculum is implemented. Indeed, the language of these four capacities has disappeared from the experiences and outcomes outlined for the curricular areas. This has resulted in children being awarded stickers and certificates for being, for example, an effective contributor, with no idea of what this means.

March 2007 saw the first of sixteen 'roadshows' concerned with CfE organised by LTS. During these roadshows, teachers, headteachers, local-authority education personnel, members of the CfE writing team and other stakeholders within education were invited to engage with the first draft of the learning outcomes to have been produced; these related to science. The worries emerging from these early discussions appeared to be that the core skills within language and mathematics would be lost, and requests were expressed for more structure and a desire to know what *exactly* teachers would be expected to do. Interestingly, and perhaps in contrast to the dilemma of needing to know exactly what teachers were expected to implement, general discussion among some of those present suggested disappointment that what they were being presented with was nothing new and that they had anticipated innovation. Additionally, there were concerns from those attending the roadshows about increased workload and the difficulties in gaining an overview to avoid duplication in either the topics covered or the learning and teaching approaches used to meet the curriculum. Communication would become vital within schools and across the transition stages of pre-5 to primary and primary to secondary (with the additional possibility of the transition to further education for some children who cross the sector divide to undertake either academic or vocational qualifications). While the philosophy of teacher autonomy and opportunities to be creative were generally welcomed it appears that many teachers, though not all, are still doing as they did under 5–14, thereby, perhaps, imposing restrictions on themselves and their practice. In some ways CfE has not moved far from 5–14 as teachers consider there has been a lack of guidance about what they should cover. Perhaps, though, in making these criticisms there is a danger one overlooks that under 5–14 there was scope for integration and cross-curricular topics; that there was good practice. Indeed, the message is clear: teachers are seen as 'agents of change' but they demand structure, support and some form of 'meaningful engagement' in order that they do not simply resort to familiar old practices (Priestley, 2010, p. 34), or to prevent CfE from being perceived as promoting vagueness through autonomy rather than affording autonomy through vagueness.

The change in ethos might have proven difficult if one had read the language within CfE documentation carefully. During its inception, there was an expressed need for 'decluttering' the curriculum. It was not clear what was meant by this, and there was concern that specific subject areas would disappear but that the time teachers spent face-to-face with children would remain the same. The notion of decluttering disappeared after initial discussions about the need for curriculum reform. There was also a steady shift from softer language used initially, such as 'possible', 'may' or 'might', to words with more force such as 'must', 'should', 'will' and 'need'.

CHANGING ETHOS

In many respects, CfE resonates soundly with the 1965 *Primary Memorandum*. In fact, were today's ITE students encouraged to read the *Memorandum*, they would find that there is little difference in the stated philosophy of Scottish education in 1965 from that of today. Had 5–14 not ignored the very positive but now much neglected *Education 10–14 in Scotland* (Dundee: Consultative Committee on the Curriculum (CCC), 1986), the development from the *Memorandum* need not have taken as long as it has to reach the principles and philosophy of CfE. The 10–14 document built very much on the progressive Deweyian tradition of pupil experience being essential to learning. The curriculum design for this programme used helpful phrases that will be recognisable in the ethos and principles of CfE, for instance, 'learning to learn', 'physical development and wellbeing', 'social competence through active involvement in school life and activity', 'living together in a community and a society' and so on (CCC, 1986, p. 47). Further, the document called for greater continuity and liaison between primary and secondary schools. It also had as its axiom that 'a young person's experience of education should be coherent, continuous and progressive' (ibid., p. 5) and that, if these characteristics were missing, there needed to be 'sound educational reasons for their absence' (ibid., p. 5).

Conventionally, there has been an acknowledgement that teacher–pupil relationships are different in the two sectors, with children in the primary sector being taught by the one teacher throughout the year but with secondary pupils experiencing a range of adult input. There has been a marked change in this in the twenty-seven years since 10–14 was published, however. Nowadays, children in the primary classroom engage with a range of adults – visiting specialist teachers, community workers, learning-support assistants, parents, classroom assistants and so on. There is also an inclusion policy where all children are welcomed into classes and attempts are made to cater for individual needs. Teachers now take greater account of children's varying degrees of social and cultural capital and use these to help shape their approaches to learning and teaching. Of course, this is the ideal, which is not always realised fully in practice.

Certainly, teachers have begun to work in new ways, ways that require liaison with integrated services and the wider community. The school has come to play a bigger role in communities and vice versa. Catering for children's individual needs, though, may be the most difficult aim to meet in the coming years. While teachers may embrace the new curriculum and all of the approaches to learning and teaching that its architects espouse, social deprivation, poor parenting and a lack of resources for schools and those working with children will make this challenging. The UNICEF reports *The State of the World's Children* (www.unicef. org/sowc/) and *An Overview of Child Well-being in Rich Countries* (www.unicef.org/media/ files/ChildPovertyReport.pdf) show just how impoverished Scottish children are compared to children in the other wealthy, developed countries. Teachers and those working with them must battle hard to meet the philosophies or principles underpinning CfE; they work to help children learn and learn for themselves, but what needs further consideration is that to create any kind of meaningful educational reform, commitment is required and not solely from those working in schools. The political agenda will, as ever, impact on school practices and policies. The SNP took control of the Scottish Parliament in 2007 promising smaller class sizes starting in the infant stages; this might have been one of the first steps towards effecting change and reform in Scottish primary classrooms. This promise, however, was not fulfilled perhaps because of resistance from local authorities to its implementation. With a recent majority government this may yet happen.

What would resonate for anyone reading the *Primary Memorandum* is the call from Graham Donaldson in his 2010 review of teacher education, *Teaching Scotland's Future*, that in order to achieve a curriculum for excellence, the teachers most committed to children's learning are those who are academically able and imaginative. Soon after Donaldson's report, in 2011, came Gerry McCormac's review of teacher employment in Scotland, *Advancing Professionalism in Teaching*. In his opening comments McCormac sees both reports as working complementarily and states that these will 'have the potential to develop and strengthen teaching in Scotland while improving outcomes for children and young people' (2011, p. iii).

McCormac also uses the language of commitment and creativity in addressing the future of Scottish education. Both reports suggest a change in ethos for teachers where greater collaboration, stronger continuing professional development, practitioner researchers and changes in ITE are prominent. Undoubtedly, these, allied to the proposed changes in teachers' conditions (McCormac, 2011), will have a bearing, perhaps more than the curriculum itself, on the philosophy of and practice in Scottish primary schools.

REFERENCES

Akhtar, S. (2008) 'The implementation of education for citizenship in Scotland: recommendation of approaches for effective practice', *Improving Schools*, 11 (1): 33–48.

Biesta, G. (2008) 'What kind of citizenship? What kind of democracy? Citizenship education and the Scottish Curriculum for Excellence', *Scottish Educational Review*, 40 (2): 38–52.

Cassidy, C. (2007) *Thinking Children*. London: Continuum.

Darling, J. (2000) *How We See Children: The Legacy of Rousseau's Emile*. Aberdeen: University of Aberdeen, Centre for Educational Research.

Paterson, L. (2003) *Scottish Education in the Twentieth Century*. Edinburgh: Edinburgh University Press.

Priestley, M. (2010) 'Curriculum for Excellence: transformational change or business as usual?', *Scottish Educational Review*, 42 (1): 23–36.

Scottish Education Department (1965) *Primary Education in Scotland*. Edinburgh: HMSO.

Scottish Executive (2004) *A Curriculum for Excellence*. Edinburgh: Scottish Executive.

Scottish Government (2011) *Building the Curriculum 5: A Framework for Assessment*. Edinburgh: Scottish Government.

Simpson, M. (2006) *Assessment*. Edinburgh: Dunedin Academic Press.

5

Scottish Secondary Education: Philosophy and Practice

Tom Bryce and Walter Humes

In previous editions of this book, in 1999, 2003 and 2008, the chapter corresponding to this one characterised Scottish secondary education as being fairly uniform in nature across the country, the vast majority of the pupil population (some 95 per cent) attending state comprehensive schools. We also argued that the curriculum was dominated by the traditional subjects taught separately by specialist teachers and that the upper years had more influence upon what is taught in the lower years than did the primary school years that precede them. In 2013, fourteen years after the first edition, these features remain dominant: secondary schools continue to perform their traditional roles, 'delivering' a curriculum that is initially broad and general, then rapidly becomes more specialised through subject choices focused on what young people will tackle subsequently in further or higher education or on entry to the world of work. At the time of writing, curriculum debate centres on whether specialising should be delayed until S4 (the so-called 3 + 3 Curriculum for Excellence (CfE) model for the six secondary years) or should remain with the more traditional model with subject choice commencing in S3 (the 2 + 2 + 2 model). The latter is favoured by those who believe 'that pupils start to lose focus by the end of S2; they are ready to move on, to choose the subjects where they're likely to achieve and concentrate their efforts on areas that will help towards their future careers', in the words of one headteacher writing in the *Times Educational Supplement Scotland* (*TESS*) of 24 February 2012. Members of the general public typically reason that secondary education should help young people to make choices suited to their varied aptitudes and that good prospects are linked to natural ability. Sociologists argue about how pupils' destinations are strongly governed by their social background. Educators stress access and flexibility, with Paterson emphasising how comprehensives have successfully widened achievements (Paterson, 2003). However, at a time of dysfunctional capitalism, with massive unemployment in the young – even among some of those who are well-qualified – educational reckoning about how the secondary curriculum facilitates opportunity and success may seem somewhat irrelevant.

This is not to say that no changes have occurred in post-primary education. Indeed, the visitor to any secondary school today would be struck by several things, not least the number of adults other than the class teacher working in classrooms (e.g. classroom assistants, learning support specialists); the amount of learning and teaching involving group activities; the increased movement of pupils in and out of schools (at further education (FE) colleges, work placements and so forth); and the growing number of coordinated, inter-subject activities, sometimes with whole-school learning events. Also noteworthy is the sheer amount of 'bureaucracy' and regulation that patently invades the lives of pupils and teachers, the seemingly necessary paperwork being seen as a drudge, as for those who work in other professions. Most of the educational changes have come in the wake of national initiatives and programmes intended to widen access to courses suited to pupils' needs and to make learning more challenging across the ability range. Conspicuously, they all accompany the drive for efficiency and higher rates of attainment, a kind of pervasive 'philosophy' which means that everyone, not least teachers, must do better at what they have always been doing: practice is determined by success rates, for which schools and teachers are held accountable. This chapter sets out the main constancies to secondary schooling and contextualises the changes that are taking place at the present time.

COMPREHENSIVE EDUCATION?

The uniformity of secondary, comprehensive provision can be viewed in at least three ways: as an expression of social unity tied up with Scottish identity; as a reflection of democracy and communal solidarity (schools should serve their neighbourhoods); and as a demonstration that opportunities to succeed should be available to all. Social unity is usually interpreted as applying to class, gender and ethnic background but it is notable in Scotland that it does not apply to religion, where the principle of divided education has been accepted and endorsed in law since 1918. In west central Scotland in particular there is widespread provision for children to attend separate Catholic primary and secondary schools. These exist alongside non-denominational schools. Other chapters in this volume provide detail of this significant aspect of Scottish education (see Chapters 27 and 93 in particular).

Historically, it is well documented that secondary education was class-based and elitist up until the 1930s. It only became a statutory right in 1936. The idea of formal schooling being a sorting device or, in the words of the psychologist Sir Godfrey Thomson, 'a succession of sieves, sorting out pupils into different kinds' (quoted in Paterson, 1983), continued in the period after the Second World War when the junior/senior secondary system became formalised. The authors of this chapter went to senior secondary schools following their successful passes in the qualifying examinations at the end of their primary schooling. In the 1950s, some 35 per cent of the secondary school population in Scotland gained similar admission to senior secondary schools. In England during the same period only 20 per cent of pupils gained places at grammar schools (the equivalent of Scottish senior secondary schools). Thus Scotland could claim to be relatively democratic in its provision. Furthermore, in small towns and rural communities, where numbers could not justify the creation of separate schools, 'omnibus' schools catered for the full ability range but with strictly demarcated courses for those who 'passed' and 'failed' the qualifying examination. Official claims that junior and senior secondary schools were accorded parity of esteem were never convincing and sociological evidence indicated that there was a strong social class factor in selection. Despite the Scottish Advisory Council on Education's recommendation in 1947 that a comprehensive system, together with a common curriculum core and a common examination, should be put in place, it was not until 1965 that the Scottish Education Department formally decided to implement such a system.

The development of comprehensive education within secondary schools since then has been rather uneven, certainly during the years of the Conservative government (1979–97) where there were instances of policy change consistent with the concept of social unity (e.g. 'mainstreaming') but rather more where policy change was designed to counter it (e.g. parental choice). To an extent what pupils encounter in secondary schools varies with the relative affluence or poverty of the neighbourhood setting and in the conurbations of the central belt there is probably more variation amongst schools than elsewhere in the country. The parental choice legislation of the 1980s served to manipulate the intake of individual schools, such are the powerful perceptions of the curricula on offer and of the potential behavioural contagion of pupils in particular areas. The Labour–Liberal Democrat coalitions following the re-establishment of the Scottish Parliament in 1999, and the Scottish National administrations since 2007, have brought about no major changes to the structure of schools, though considerable efforts have been made to construct new buildings (and in quite a number of cases to effect mergers between schools where pupil numbers have fallen); to alter how they are managed through changes to the personnel and promotion structure involved; and to bring greater coherence to the curriculum and to qualifications obtainable by the end of the secondary years. During this period, we have also seen a greater devolution of (financial) management to headteachers from local authorities.

Over the last twenty years or so, there have been efforts of differing kinds to modify secondary school education, to depart from the 'one size fits all' approach. These have included the development of the National Qualifications (NQ) framework, covering both traditional academic subjects and vocational subjects, with increasing flexibility of attendance at school and college; the varied ways in which additional support needs are catered for; and the several specialisms available in some schools. However, Scotland has stopped well short of the level of diversity in England and it is fair to say that the 'Scottish comprehensive principle' has been subject to adjustment but not in ways that undermine its fundamental tenets. Indeed it received considerable public endorsement during the National Debate of 2002 which preceded the CfE programme. What can be said is that there is now greater awareness of the elusiveness of equality as a social and moral principle. 'Equal' treatment may not mean 'the same' treatment (equality of *process*) as in the case of children with disabilities. Nor is equality of *access* to educational provision enough to guarantee desired educational benefits for all. And despite the proliferation of qualification levels, few if any would claim that we have achieved equality of *outcome*. A more credible claim might be that we are trying to operate on the basis of equality of *consideration* for all pupils – a form of equality that recognises differences (of needs, interests and abilities) among pupils and tries to make appropriate, and fair, provision accordingly. The grounds for differential provision must, however, be adequately justified if adherence to a (modified) version of the comprehensive principle is to remain credible. Against this background, what evidence is there about the success of current Scottish secondary education?

AN OFFICIAL OVERVIEW

The report from Her Majesty's Inspectorate of Education (HMIE) entitled *Improving Scottish Education: A Report by HMIE on Inspection and Review 2005–2008* is the second of its kind, a substantial review containing major sections on each of seven sectors: Pre-school; Primary; Secondary; Special; College; Community learning and development; Prison learning, skills and employability; and a distinct section covering child protection services (HMIE, 2009). In his overall commentary, Graham Donaldson, Her Majesty's Senior Chief Inspector, states that inspection evidence shows that previously reported strengths have been maintained, and that 'since then, further aspects have moved to positions of strength and Scottish education in general is showing steady improvement' (p. 1). He does add that 'a number of significant problems remain and the need for further and faster improvement has grown'. Commendation is paid to the broadening of achievement emphasised in schools and the preparation that pupils receive in respect of positive post-school destinations. The strengths evident to inspectors are explicitly put down to the professional commitment and competence of Scottish teachers. Throughout the 108 pages of the report, there are numerous points of amplification to this, attesting to successful features of schools and colleges. However, in documenting some of the weaker points, inspectors consider the current attainment profile to be uneven, and that progress between mid-primary and well into secondary is not as hoped for in many cases. Difficulties in literacy and numeracy are of concern, as they were in the previous 2002–5 report, and it is hoped that Curriculum for Excellence developments will bring about improvements. There are variations within and between schools in respect of the quality of learning and teaching, and HMIE believe that self-evaluation, though improving across the country, has further to go.

With respect to the secondary sector in particular, pupil achievements in national examinations are said to be of continuing strength, and there have been notable improvements in respect of other awards (in youth achievement, Prince's Trust, community sport and dance, for example). Summary ratings of the quality of attainment rise as pupils move through school and HMIE judge pupils' overall attainment in secondary to be satisfactory or better in about 80 per cent of schools. The inspectors note however that in the Trends in International Maths and Science (TIMSS) survey of 2007, S2 Scottish performance had declined since 2003. In the Programme for International Student Assessment (PISA) 2006 survey of 15-year-olds, Scottish pupils performed better than the averages in reading, mathematics and science for the sixty-five Organisation for Economic Cooperation and Development (OECD) member states, but several other countries had overtaken Scotland and had significantly higher averages (in the case of science: Canada, Finland, Japan and New Zealand; in the case of maths: these four countries plus Australia, Korea, Netherlands and Switzerland; and in the case of reading: Canada, Finland, Ireland, Korea and New Zealand).

Commenting later, in 2012, the new head of PISA, Michael Davidson, stated that 'Scotland's scores for reading and maths show a declining performance over 10 years, but most of that decline has been at the bottom end of the ability spectrum' (*TESS*, 24 February, 2012). He considered that the highest-performing countries on measures overall, Finland and Canada, owe their performance to coping better with social diversity. Interestingly, where pupils perceive there to be a poor disciplinary climate in their school, their performance is lower. Where they judge the quality of pupil–teacher relationships to be poor, it has a much bigger impact on performance than in other countries. The Scottish Government has now decided not to participate in PISA and TIMSS.

According to the HMIE report, pupils' secondary learning experiences themselves are rated satisfactory or better for some 94 per cent of the school population. The Assessment is for Learning initiative (see Chapter 74) has enhanced the repertoire of teaching and learning approaches used by teachers. The previous report had highlighted that leadership, though strong, needed to be promoted at all levels in the management of schools. The 2009 report expresses the view that the appointment of business managers has 'significantly increased leadership capacity' (p. 13), 'allowing other senior managers to focus most of their attention on educational improvement' (p. 51), something we will comment upon later, and that the introduction of curriculum leader posts (such as in 'teaching and learning') is helping to improve quality assurance with respect to what takes place in classrooms. Secondary leadership was judged overall to be 'very good' or 'excellent' in nearly half of schools (p. 14) in the period reviewed.

The HMIE report notes that almost all schools enjoy positive partnerships with parents, school boards/school councils and the wider community: 'stakeholder satisfaction' is regarded as a continuing strength of secondary schools. Many are becoming proactive in seeking out effective new partnerships, though these tend not to be in community learning and development. Internally, staff are commended for the quality of the pastoral care they provide and, in almost all schools, young people feel that relationships with teachers are constructive and encouraging.

SOME RESERVATIONS

All this, of course, is the official narrative of the strengths and limitations of Scotland's secondary schools, written by officials who have responsibility for inspection and maintaining standards. It is based on evidence gathered from hundreds of schools across the country and needs to be given appropriate weight. However, the fact remains that, for a significant minority of pupils (estimates vary but a figure around 20 per cent is often given), their experience of schooling is disappointing, resulting in sporadic attendance, social alienation and poor levels of attainment. They represent the biggest challenge, both in terms of improving their literacy and numeracy and in terms of encouraging a more positive attitude to the benefits of learning.

In the 2007 OECD report *Quality and Equity of Schooling in Scotland* it was stated that 'In Scotland, who you are is far more important than what school you attend . . . the school system as a whole is not strong enough to make this not matter.' This comment made uncomfortable reading for education professionals brought up to believe in Scotland's commitment to equality of opportunity. Citing the OECD report in 2011, Graham Donaldson, former Senior Chief Inspector and author of *Teaching Scotland's Future*, listed a number of major challenges that are still resisting the best efforts of policy makers and teachers:

- the widening achievement gap from about Primary 5 onwards;
- marked social differences in basic attainment;
- declining student engagement and interest (especially in early secondary);
- marked gaps in Scottish Qualifications Authority (SQA) attainment;
- staying on rates that have ceased to grow;
- wide regional variations in post-compulsory participation;
- a worrying, comparatively high level of young people not in education, employment or training. (Donaldson, 2011, p. 18)

This last point is a source of particular concern, especially at a time of high unemployment when skill levels are vitally important in the competition to obtain jobs. In 2006, the Scottish Government produced a document entitled *More Choices, More Chances: A Strategy to Reduce the Proportion of Young People not in Employment, Education or Training in Scotland* (Scottish Government, 2007). Partnerships were established across the country, involving local authorities, schools and FE colleges, local businesses, the voluntary sector and Skills Development Scotland. A great deal of effort went into the programme but it was overtaken by the fallout from the economic crisis of 2008, the effects of which are still being felt. Another strategy document, *16+ Learning Choices*, appeared in 2010, guarantee-ing an offer of a place in post-16 learning for every young person who wanted it. But unless there is a prospect of a real job at the end of the learning experience it is difficult to prevent cynicism setting in. In 2011, a special *TESS* report entitled 'Struggle goes on to avoid a "lost generation"' (3 June 2011) presented an account of continuing efforts to address the problem of poorly qualified and unemployed young people. An important message for sec-ondary schools was that many employers were not looking for job-specific skills but general 'employability' skills, such as timekeeping, reliability, social competence, and basic literacy and numeracy. Examples of what schools do offer will be given in the next section. For youngsters from homes where there is little or no history of regular employment, and where dependence on the benefits system is seen as 'normal', inculcating employability skills is far from easy, particularly if there is a record of poor attendance. As each new initiative is launched, without any change in the underlying economic situation, the law of diminishing returns sets in. There are limits to what education and training can achieve in the absence of a healthy economy with real prospects of growth.

CONFLICTING PERCEPTIONS?

HMIE observations about leadership were mentioned earlier, and in particular reference was made to the appointment of business managers (sometimes called support services managers). This development has arisen from the policy of devolved school management which, in effect, is principally concerned with the shifting of financial responsibility from local authority to school level. It should be noted that business managers are not qualified teachers though they are sometimes members of the senior management team (SMT) in a secondary school. Unless sensitively handled, this can produce tensions rather than affording welcome relief to hard-pressed senior teaching staff more concerned with the educational aspects of school improvement than with accountancy and finance. Much depends on the personalities involved and the ability of staff with different types of expertise to respect each other's contribution to the effective and efficient functioning of the school. Another potential source of tension can arise from the different perspectives of headteachers and inspectors. Inspectors are under political pressure to give particular attention to pupil attainment, as reflected in examination results. It is well known, however, that such results are strongly influenced by, though not wholly dependent on, the social composition of the pupil intake. Some headteachers feel that the broader aspects of a school's performance (relationships, welfare, ethos) are not given sufficient weight and, in particular, that the highest rating for leadership will only be awarded if a school scores well on conventional academic criteria, regardless of how well it is addressing wider social factors that may affect pupil attainment. It has been alleged that such conflicting perceptions relate to the differing experiences of inspectors and the senior staff of a school. In the case of secondary schools, inspectors tend to be recruited from experienced principal subject teachers. Hence, the allegation is that few current members of the inspectorate possess credibility in relation to the full range of responsibilities that headteachers are expected to fulfil.

In schools serving socially disadvantaged areas, the daily pressures often make it dif-ficult for staff to think strategically about change and innovation. Immediate demands may have to be given priority over the kind of careful planning that new initiatives, such as Curriculum for Excellence, really require. Outside observers should, therefore, be cau-tious when forming judgements, particularly where a school's social environment harbours widespread deprivation and unemployment. The 'poverty of aspiration' that prevails in the worst of settings is a source of stress for many teachers and there are limits to what even the best efforts of senior management can achieve.

A CONTESTED CURRICULUM

We said in the introduction to this chapter that the subject-centredness of Scotland's secondary schools is of long standing and curricular influences tend to be top-down. What goes on in S1 is determined more by what goes on in S5 than by what goes on in P7, despite the significant recent efforts to improve continuity in the devising of Curriculum for Excellence. The majority of subjects leading to NQs in secondary schools (detailed in Section VII) are still based upon the eight curricular modes identified by the Munn Report in the 1970s and most predate the shift to comprehensive education, stemming as they did from the senior (but not the junior) secondaries that preceded the change. One of the main criticisms of schools by the rebellious R. F. Mackenzie (see Chapter 13) was that

> conventional education . . . lacked coherence in being too subject-centred and had no rationale that linked it in a grand design that would fire the imagination . . . and free children from the rigidity of a curriculum dominated by the need for exams. (Murphy, 1998, pp. 158–9)

This comment resonates to the present day. While Mackenzie would have rejoiced in devolution in 1999 and in the election success of a majority SNP government in 2011, he would surely have been disappointed to see so little change to the curriculum of secondary schools during the past few decades. We might usefully remember that his favourite quotation was from Ghandi: 'The thing I fear the most is the hard heartedness of the educated' (according to Murphy, 1998, p. 153). Have educationalists cared too little about young people and their personal development, construing secondary education in a largely instrumental way, teaching subjects only to equip pupils with enough 'knowledge' to prepare them for jobs and service to the economy? This question highlights the contested nature of the secondary curriculum and the challenge to conventional thinking, particularly from a wider perspective which takes a broad, liberal, humanistic view of the aims of education.

Academic vs Vocational Emphases

While Higher Still brought more vocational elements into the S5/S6 curriculum, and with them a wider range of capabilities to be developed, much of the curriculum has remained largely academic since 2000 (the year of the first new National Qualifications exam diet). Intermediate 1 and 2 courses were successfully introduced and expanded but the majority of them have been in the traditional school subject areas. The new National courses at levels 4 and 5 follow suit (see Chapter 74). It should be noted that there are areas where the vocational emphasis is on the increase, notably 'Skills for Work'. This term refers to those courses undertaken in S3 and S4 that try to develop in young people knowledge and skills relevant to employment. The courses are built around generic skills needed for employment rather than those required for specific vocational qualifications, though they are linked to particular areas of work, such as hospitality, hairdressing, construction crafts, agriculture, etc.; and they do provide progression routes into further education. Following two years of piloting, these have been running since 2007–8 and give pupils some experience of the areas in question through work placements (often half a day per week) and part-time attendance at a further education college through a local partnership arrangement. Prior to the launch of the National level 4 and 5 courses, the majority of the Skills for Work programmes led to Intermediate 1 or 2 qualifications. Information about Skills for Work is available from both the SQA and the Education Scotland (Learning and Teaching Scotland) websites; see respectively at: www.sqa.org.uk/sqa/5951.html and www.educationscotland.gov.uk/ nationalqualifications/about/skillsforwork.asp

The upper years of secondary for some pupils can therefore mean timetables that combine traditional NQ subjects and Skills for Work courses, providing a more varied educational experience. This departure from the traditional academic diet varies across schools and the catchment areas being served – the more 'academic' the school, the fewer the Skills for Work courses in S3 and S4. The individuals involved remain formally as pupils of the school, rather than being seen as students of the FE college concerned. HMIE (2009), referred to earlier, note that, in respect of curriculum improvement,

> Skills for Work courses have provided substantial numbers of young people with relevant learning experiences. Some schools are moving towards a greater emphasis on planning for learning which takes place beyond the classroom, as part of their broad view of the curriculum. (HMIE, 2009, p. 9)

In the Schools of Ambition initiative, schools were given additional funds and support to bring about 'transformational improvement' through CfE. HMIE (2010) records some of the lessons learned from the twenty schools involved in the first tranche. Over half of them demonstrated improvement on a range of indicators, many of them having made changes to their curriculum. They offered more choice and flexibility in pupil studies, not least in vocational activities as well as sport and creative arts pursuits. According to HMIE:

> Some were able to create specialist teaching areas, for example in hairdressing or construction, within existing school accommodation. These developments led to greater enthusiasm for learning. Some schools promoted young people's engagement in school and community events. Others enabled young people to work with business partners in a range of projects, for example growing and selling organic vegetables. Many young people, including those in need of more choices and chances, successfully developed skills in enterprise and sustainability and gained a better awareness of the world of work. (HMIE, 2010, p. 3)

Clearly, then, secondary schools can modify what and how they teach in the interest of pupil engagement – given additional funds, support and encouragement. Staff would be required to take seriously the flexibility afforded by CfE and to carry parents with them in departing from tradition (see Chapter 3).

Interdisciplinarity

Where subject departments collaborate to mount activities and events (including concerts and dramatic performances, charity events, eco-school activities, local community involvements, outdoor enterprises, foreign exchanges, etc.), pupils regularly attest to their enjoyment and benefits. Indeed they frequently stand out as memorable parts of school life. HMIE have noted the impact that they have on learning, particularly in respect of improving pupils' confidence and maturity. With regard to CfE, Education Scotland (see Chapter 19) has pressed for more content-focused collaboration and interdisciplinary teaching:

> Interdisciplinary learning enables teachers and learners to make connections across learning through exploring clear and relevant links across the curriculum. It supports the use and application of what has been taught and learned in new and different ways. It provides opportunities for deepening learning, for example through answering big questions, exploring an issue, solving problems or completing a final project. (See Understanding the Curriculum at www.education-scotland.gov.uk/)

To date, however, one would have to admit to a mixed picture across secondary schools. Very many school departments hang on to their subject territories, often resorting to time-table rotations rather than finding ways of bringing about integration meaningfully. The SNP government's intention to promote Scottish Studies as a required cross-disciplinary component of the curriculum may encourage greater flexibility. Where successful inter-disciplinary work does take place, it is often thanks to the energy and enthusiasm of a member of staff, rather than to systems and structures that might facilitate it. Restructuring secondary school staffing did however figure in the 2001 McCrone Agreement (*A Teaching Profession for the 21st Century*). Salary levels throughout Scotland became determined there-after within a new flatter structure of promoted posts through a 'job-sizing exercise' – the underlying thinking being that the salaries of promoted individuals should be dependent on the size of the responsibility of their post. Structural changes to the departments of second-ary schools often resulted in the creation of *faculties*, bringing together a number of subjects under the responsibility of one faculty head with claims of coherence or 'cognateness' among the subjects so gathered. Thus, for example, faculties of Science have been created in many schools, often at the point when a principal teacher (PT) of one of the sciences has retired, the head of faculty assuming responsibility for all those duties that the previous PTs of Biology, Chemistry and Physics discharged. In some cases, Mathematics is also part of such a structure. Other faculties combine Physical Education and Home Economics; some couple Technology with Home Economics; some group English, Modern Languages and Drama, and so on.

Views on the success of this significant change to the landscape of secondary schools have continued to be varied, more often than not negative, certainly among practitioners. The lack of positive reactions from the classroom since this was instigated across many authori-ties is striking. And there seem to be few at management level within schools who would champion the advantages accruing from the flatter structure now evident (with a secondary school having several depute headteachers, and half a dozen faculty heads, rather than say fifteen principal teachers of subjects). Many teachers regard that aspect of McCrone as having been little more than a money-saving exercise.

CHANGES TO HOW TEACHERS WORK? THE MCCORMAC REVIEW

In 2011, the Scottish Government instigated a review of the Teachers' Agreement which had been reached following the McCrone enquiry. The review group, chaired by Professor McCormac of Stirling University, was asked to consider how professionalism in teaching might be enhanced (and acknowledging the challenging financial climate). The group took evidence from primary and secondary teachers, representatives of their local authority employers and other bodies. With respect to the secondary sector, concerns were expressed to the review team about the overall reduction in the number of promoted posts, reducing the potential for career progression, with a sizeable minority wishing to see the re-introduction of assistant headteacher and principal teacher positions where they had been removed. The McCormac Review (see Scottish Government, 2011) nevertheless concluded that the present structure of management in secondary schools should be retained. It also recommended that there be no change to the amount of class-contact time for teachers (855 hours annually), nor to the thirty-five-hour working week. However, it did stipulate that more flexibility was needed to allow teachers to carry out collegiate work and that class contact should be managed over a longer timescale. The report also called for a revitalisation of professional development but did not say that the annual thirty-five-hour allocation (which had emerged ten years previously from the McCrone Agreement) should be changed. Clearly, deliberations about workload did not take into account the findings from research that show how much time Scottish teachers actually spend on essential activities. For example, investigations conducted by staff at Glasgow University recently concluded that 'teachers worked 45 hours per week on average and found it difficult to reduce their work to fit within a regular 35 hour pattern' (McPhee and Patrick, 2009, p. 86). The McCormac Report also recommended discontinuing the Chartered Teacher scheme (which was aimed at rewarding experienced classroom teachers who did not wish to apply for management posts) and stated that teachers should 'normally remain' on the school premises during the working day. Teachers' pay was deemed to be at an 'acceptable' level.

The General Teaching Council for Scotland (GTCS) was 'broadly supportive' of most of the recommendations but not that regarding Chartered Teachers. The reaction from the Educational Institute of Scotland (EIS) to the review was critical, interpreting its substance to be threatening to the working conditions of teachers. In the words of the then General Secretary:

> the report weakens key contractual protections introduced in the 2001 agreement and strengthens managerialist, as opposed to collegiate, approaches. Under the guise of 'flexibility', even greater burdens and controls are proposed for teachers who will have to rely on the benevolence of the headteacher to spare them from excessive workload. The proposals to reconfigure working time will not be well-received and, if implemented, would require a clock-watching approach that sits uncomfortably with enhanced professionalism. (Ronnie Smith, speaking on BBC News on 14 September 2011)

Thus the proposed excising of Annex E of the Teachers' Agreement, which lists routine duties that should *not* be carried out by teachers, was taken negatively by the workforce. Unsurprisingly, politicians, of all parties, tended to side with McCormac, being somewhat blind to the realities of school management and insensitive to what teachers can or should be asked to do at a time of retrenchment and pay freezes, and when the number of people working in education in Scotland had fallen by 9,000 (for the year 2011, according to the Office for National Statistics).

School Leaders Scotland (SLS, formerly the Headteachers' Association of Scotland) regarded the recommendations of the McCormac Review as 'not hugely controversial' (SLS, 2011). Rather predictably, the review of the McCrone job-sizing agreement was particularly welcomed by secondary headteachers, as was the support for their continued delegated powers, not least in budget management. SLS approved of the advice concerning continuing professional development (CPD), especially the proposed changes to more flexible applications of the working week and the working year, and sided with McCormac in moving against the Chartered Teacher Scheme. Senior teachers being able to 'move around' as part of their own planned CPD was endorsed, providing it did not result in 'musical chairs'.

Five months later, after fairly heated public and professional debate about the McCormac proposals to Scottish Government, and speaking to the *TESS* on the eve of his retirement in February 2012, Ronnie Smith wished that the McCormac proposals would not be implemented. He considered that there was little in them to assure teachers that they would be better placed to manage their workloads. Indeed, he believed that in the decade between McCrone and McCormac, 'we have moved in a negative direction. The underpinning principle of collegiate working is becoming progressively weaker and that's contributing to a decline in the general atmosphere and industrial relations in schools' (*TESS*, 17 February 2012).

Another report submitted to Scottish Government in 2011 was concerned with devolved school management (DSM) and written by a group chaired by David Cameron, former Director of Children's Services for Stirling. The main recommendation was that the national guidelines on DSM should be revised by the Convention of Scottish Local Authorities (COSLA) to give headteachers 'more meaningful control' (a task to be completed by the spring of 2012). Both David Cameron and John Stodter (General Secretary of the Association of Directors of Education in Scotland) have emphasised the inconsistency in approaches to DSM across the country. However, concerns have also been expressed that giving more power to schools could lead to greater fragmentation in the services provided by local authorities. Writing in the *TESS* of 14 October 2011, Stodter stated: 'Satisfaction with DSM schemes seems to be greatest when there is a combination of optimum devolvement; maximum flexibility across budgets; and corporate and inclusive working between heads and council officers based on transparency and confident leadership.' It remains to be seen whether the new guidelines will, in fact, accord with these sentiments and make any significant change to the management mechanisms that operate in secondary schools.

THE FUTURE OF SECONDARY EDUCATION

It was suggested at the beginning of this chapter that there had been a high level of continuity and stability in the form and content of Scottish secondary education in the decade following devolution. That is not to say that provision was static, but it is to suggest that the examination system – albeit one that has been subject to various changes – serves to constrain the degree of innovation that is possible. This conservatism is reinforced by the strong allegiance of most secondary teachers to their subject specialism and their stout defence of traditional time allocations on school timetables. CfE is intended to make it easier to innovate. All teachers are expected to contribute to the drive to improve standards of literacy and numeracy, and cross-curricular themes such as health and wellbeing and citizenship feature more prominently in pupils' experience. A wider range of pedagogic approaches is employed, with less emphasis on traditional didactic teaching and more on methods that encourage active and independent learning. Moreover, the recommendations of the McCormac Report on teacher employment, if fully implemented, will allow for staff to be deployed more flexibly in support of schools' development plans and strategic priorities. It is too early to say whether these intentions will be realised or whether the structures and established practices of secondary schools will prove resistant to significant reform. Early indications suggest that while some schools have responded well to the challenges of CfE, many are finding it hard to adjust to changed expectations (see, for example, Priestley and Humes, 2010; Priestley and Minty, 2012). For this reason, it is vitally important that the impact of CfE should be subject to rigorous, independent evaluation over, say, a five-year period. What would not be helpful, in terms of understanding the drivers of curricular change and teacher agency, would be an 'in house' evaluation carried out by ES. Staff within that organisation (and its predecessor bodies, HMIE and LTS) were closely involved in the development of CfE and so could not be regarded as sufficiently detached from the implementation process. They would be seen as having a vested interest in presenting a favourable view of the programme. What is needed is a substantial body of objective evidence, drawn from a wide range of schools, and subject to careful, dispassionate analysis by researchers with no axe to grind.

In contemplating the future, there are also bigger, longer-term issues to consider. How well are schools adapting to the massive technological changes that are taking place in society? There have been complaints by employers that school leavers often lack the necessary IT skills to function effectively in a work environment. The number of school students studying for exam qualifications in computing has actually dropped in recent years despite extensive out-of-school use of technology in all its forms. If this trend were to continue, it could lead to a dangerous gap between the learning environments inside and outside schools. The risk would be that schools could come to be seen as archaic institutions, failing to respond quickly and effectively enough to the pace of change accepted elsewhere in society. That, in turn, could lead to a loss of trust by parents and perhaps open the door for private sector incursions into education, in the form of commercial agencies which claimed to offer something more modern, relevant and attractive to young people. To education 'insiders', these comments may seem removed from the current situation and unduly alarmist. They are not intended to devalue in any way the excellent work undertaken daily by dedicated teachers up and down the country. However, the important point is that the efforts of individual teachers and schools need to be seen against the backdrop of powerful global forces which have the potential to overtake traditional practices, rendering them obsolete (see Chapter 106). The heavily bureaucratic nature of Scottish education makes it slow to respond to such challenges.

Early in 2012, a Commission on School Reform, set up by two 'independent' think tanks, Reform Scotland and the Centre for Scottish Public Policy, and chaired by Keir Bloomer, one of the authors of the original CfE document, was given the following task:

- to form a fair and objective view of Scotland's educational performance compared with what is provided elsewhere;
- to consider the challenges Scottish education is likely to face in the next 50 years and how likely it is to meet those challenges;
- to identify any problems with the current school system in Scotland and to try to analyse the root causes of them;
- to develop proposals that will enable young people, whatever their background, to fulfil their potential and meet the unprecedented challenges of the modern world. (www.reformscotland. com)

An invitation to submit evidence by 30 April 2012 was issued. However, although many members of the commission could be regarded as 'mainstream' educationists, the launch of the initiative was not well received. An adviser to the commission urged schools to move away from what he called the 'bog standard' model of comprehensive education and suggested that there was a culture of complacency within the system. This view was immediately rejected by the Cabinet Secretary for Education and Lifelong Learning, Michael Russell, and by representatives of teachers' unions. The phrase 'bog standard' may have been ill-chosen but the hostile reaction that it provoked demonstrates the power of existing bureaucratic structures. It could be interpreted as defensive resistance to anything that might require a more open, imaginative exploration of future options. It is entirely understandable that professionals should wish to defend those cherished values associated with the Scottish educational tradition (democracy, equality, social unity) but they also have a responsibility to assess whether the rhetoric of those values is matched by the reality of the student experience. A failure to adapt in the face of evidence that suggests the need for more radical reforms than CfE could, in the longer term, lead to what has sometimes been called the 'meltdown' scenario – escalating disenchantment by key stakeholders (pupils, parents, employers, politicians), teacher flight as the job becomes more and more difficult, and an open market of providers of very varying quality. Although state schooling has served Scotland well since it was introduced in 1872, there is no certainty that it will continue in its present form indefinitely. This may be particularly true of secondary schools. It is in everyone's interests to keep an open mind about possible future scenarios and to frame the debate in relation to the big issues of our time – globalisation, demographic movements, environmental sustainability, public ethics and economic uncertainty.

REFERENCES

Donaldson, G. (2011) *Teaching Scotland's Future: Report of a Review of Teacher Education in Scotland*. Edinburgh: Scottish Government. Online at www.scotland.gov.uk/Publications/2011/01/13092132/0

Her Majesty's Inspectorate of Education (2009) *Improving Scottish Education: A Report by HMIE on Inspection and Review 2005–2008*. Edinburgh: HMIE.

Her Majesty's Inspectorate of Education (2010) *Lessons Learned from the Schools of Ambition Initiative*. Edinburgh: HMIE.

McPhee, A. D. and F. Patrick (2009) '"The pupils will suffer if we don't work": teacher professionalism and reactions to policy change in Scotland', *Scottish Educational Review*, 41 (1): 86–96.

Murphy, P. A. (1998) *The Life of R. F. Mackenzie: A Prophet Without Honour*. Edinburgh: John Donald.

Organisation for Economic Cooperation and Development (2007) *Quality and Equity of Schooling in Scotland*. Brussels: OECD. Online at www.oecd.org/edu/reviews/nationalpolicies

Paterson, H. (1983) 'Incubus and ideology: The development of secondary schooling in Scotland, 1900–1939', in W. M. Humes and H. M. Paterson (eds), *Scottish Culture and Scottish Education, 1800–1980*. Edinburgh: John Donald.

Paterson, L. (2003) *Scottish Education in the Twentieth Century*. Edinburgh: Edinburgh University Press.

Priestley, M. and W. Humes (2010) 'The development of Scotland's Curriculum for Excellence: Amnesia and déjà vu', *Oxford Review of Education*, 36 (3): 345–61.

Priestley, M. and S. Minty (2012) *Developing Curriculum for Excellence: Summary of Findings from Research Undertaken in a Scottish Local Authority*. Stirling: University of Stirling.

Scottish Government (2001) *A Teaching Profession for the 21st Century: Agreement Reached Following Recommendations made in the McCrone Report*. Edinburgh: Scottish Government. Online at www.scotland.gov.uk/Publications/2001/01/7959/File-1

Scottish Government (2007) *More Choices, More Chances: A Strategy to Reduce the Proportion of Young People not in Employment, Education or Training in Scotland*. Edinburgh: Scottish Government.

Scottish Government (2011) *Advancing Professionalism in Scottish Teaching: Report of the Review of Teacher Employment in Scotland* (the McCormac Report). Edinburgh: Scottish Government.

School Leaders Scotland (2011) 'Advancing professionalism in teaching: The McCormac Review', in *Leaders. School Leaders Scotland Annual Review and Conference Guide*. Online at www.sls-scotland.org.uk/

6

Learning in Scottish Schools

Tom Bryce

This chapter will explore how learning can be conceived and must be distinguished from the teaching that purports to bring it about. The topic is a very large one and only the cognitive dimensions will figure here – thus attitudinal learning and skill acquisition in schools have been set aside. All teachers hope that the learning of their students will be meaningful to them and so the main pedagogies currently encountered in Scottish classrooms are scrutinised in the light of that intent (the pursuit of *meaning*). Active forms of learning, collaboration and discussion amongst pupils are much encouraged in the Scottish curriculum and the chapter considers some recent research on how these may be managed and what can be achieved. The chapter also looks at some of the approaches that have been advanced by enthusiasts as alternatives to traditional teaching methods. Findings from recent advances in neuroscience are used to comment on these and on important issues like gender differences and giftedness. The effectiveness of strategies that try to address learning styles and (so-called) multiple intelligences are examined from the same perspective.

THE CONCEPT OF LEARNING

The real point to teaching is that it should bring about learning, and the public has quite reasonable expectations that a significant amount of learning is taking place in schools. Leaving aside what should be learned (set out in the curriculum chapters of sections VI and VII) and the achievements and qualifications with which pupils leave schools (explored in Chapter 77), it is rather difficult to capture the amount and, more importantly, the quality of the actual *learning* that takes place in classrooms. We can portray aspects of *teaching* fairly easily. The methods that are used routinely by teachers can be described; the dynamics – or not – of schoolroom instruction can be revealed. But, when it comes to saying what is happening in the minds of learners, inferences are required to convey what we think is going on – and this is as true for observers as it is for the practitioners directly concerned. So much of learning is *mental* and therefore not directly observable. Pupils may be taught 'this' when in fact they learn 'something else', even where the words for 'this' and 'something else' are identical, with classroom discussion moving along on an assumption of mutual understanding that can so easily be unfounded. A young child, for example, might echo his teacher by saying, for example, that *the Earth is round*, but if his teacher does not realise that, at this point, this particular child is envisaging a flat, disc-shaped island in a dark blue sea, their conversations are likely to go amiss and subsequent, connected understandings will fail. The child has *not* learned that the Earth is round, even though he may say it is. Or, turning to numeracy skills for a different example, pupils may be trained to calculate in primary arithmetic and become rather good at formulaic exercises using memorised tables. But should they fail to see where and when these algorithms can be applied to real-world problems, their *mathematical* learning will not have been successful; they can't do maths. Perhaps that learning was sacrificed in favour of getting *the right answers* concerning the number facts? (We now realise that instruction only works when the tasks in which pupils are trained truly *problematise* the mathematics; where the learners are allowed to work out for themselves methods to complete the tasks; and where structured discussion requires pupils to routinely explain their thinking processes.)

Generalising these ideas, we have to concede that we are essentially *theorising* when we try to represent those understandings that we think are taking place and the abilities that we believe are developing (or not) on a day-to-day basis. The language and vocabulary of this theorising is familiar to anyone who thinks about learning, pertinent questions being:

- Is the learning *deep* or superficial? Has it had any *impact*? Can students *use* their learning?
- Does that learning *transfer* beyond the illustrations used in the lessons? Or, was it just *rote* learning?
- How *meaningful* and long-lasting will the learning be? Will these ideas stick in students' *memories*?
- Is the learning real and *authentic*?
- Fundamentally, what *motivates* young people to grasp ideas the way teachers do and realise their importance?

This last point concedes that very many questions about learning boil down to questions about motivation and interest.

WHAT HAS BEEN LEARNED ABOUT LEARNING?

Turning to research on learning, it may be useful at this point to summarise what is known about the psychology of school learning, for psychologists and educators agree, in broad terms, about how learning takes place, or at least under what conditions it occurs effectively. Adopting the now prevalent *constructivist* approach to learning, a brief summary of what has been learned about learning would be that:

1. Learning requires active involvement (people learn by constructing meanings on the basis of what they already know) and is primarily social in the everyday settings where people think and work together (*social-constructivism*)
2. Learners need to see the relevance and use of what they are learning in the activities in which they participate in the classroom
3. Learners benefit significantly by learning how to monitor their own learning and become familiar at working with feedback designed to take their learning forward; that is, when they get *feedforward* from their teachers
4. The focus of learning should be upon general principles and problem-solving strategies, rather than upon isolated factual detail
5. Partial understandings and misconceptions ought to be openly discussed and inconsistencies resolved as learning proceeds
6. Motivation to learn grows from working with motivated, expert teachers who are able to work alongside learners with a wide range of interests and capabilities.

See, for example, Ausubel (2000); Cohen, Manion, Morrison and Wyse (2010).

Some of the recent curricular initiatives led by Scottish Government (or its agencies) do reflect these points, though with varying degrees of consistency and impact upon practitioners. The whole thrust on more *active learning* which is embodied in the emphasis Curriculum for Excellence (CfE) places upon *challenge* and *interest* most certainly relates to points (1) and (2). Furthermore, the intention to *declutter* the curriculum in the move from 5–14 to CfE is consistent with points (4) and (5). The push for *collaborative learning* among pupils is evidently underpinned by (1), (5) and (6) and the largely successful movement Assessment is for Learning (AifL) explicitly follows from (3) (and is examined in detail in Chapter 75).

A number of rather different initiatives instigated by some enthusiastic teachers, and/or promoted by commercial programme developers, also connect with these points – notably so-called *brain-based*, or *neuro-scientific*, approaches, or pedagogies said to be aligned with personal *styles of learning*, in particular to points (1), (2), (3) and (6). As we shall see, claims for the effectiveness of some of these 'fashionable' pedagogies are largely exaggerated. That said, there is no reason to suppose that the numbers of Scottish teachers who incline to these approaches to teaching are any different, proportionally, from those in other parts of the UK; perhaps in even smaller numbers, given the natural conservatism of the teaching profession in Scotland.

Whether 'mainstream' or 'fashionable', pedagogies that try to make pupils genuinely active in their learning are consistent with constructivism. The terms are not completely interchangeable, however, for constructivism is essentially 'mental', and some forms of activity, even when visibly dynamic, with pupils not left as passive receptors of information, may not lead to them being able to use their current state of understanding to grasp new ideas. Activity makes meaningful learning more likely; it does not guarantee it and rote methods are very much less likely to promote meaningful learning. Since many teachers tend to eschew 'theory' and abstract terminology, perhaps the official thrust upon active learning has proved to be tactically wiser than urging teachers to be constructivist in the formal discourse regarding curriculum and instruction.

Nevertheless, and before we look further at some of these pedagogies, there is no getting away from the fact that some learning is an *individual* affair, no matter the amount of apparent activity. Pupils listen to teachers; they read texts and worksheets; they watch TV and recorded materials; they often work on their own with (usually well-)developed schemes of activity, many commercially produced; and they carry out practical work. Though almost always with the guidance of their teachers, pupils typically make some sense of new material on their own, despite the conventional view that pupils are told what to think and do. Didacticism is frequently characterised very negatively for reasons that we need to consider carefully. Clearly, on the other hand, much learning is social in the sense that working alongside others means that clarification, influence and stimulation arises from shared activity; the interpersonal context drives the learning that is taking place for many pupils. And, not to be neglected, some learning is incidental as far as individuals are concerned; they did not plan or expect to learn something, but it came about, either by virtue of the teacher's clever interjections during instruction or by peers' comments and reactions in the course of shared work and discussion.

Let us look now at the approaches that are in favour with teachers in Scotland, first one that figures in many primary classrooms involving a blend of individual and group work and which is much in tune with constructivism.

STORYLINE: A POWERFUL PEDAGOGY FOUND IN MANY PRIMARY SCHOOLS

Storyline is a child-centred, topic-based pedagogical approach where pupils are encouraged to devise a setting, invent characters and evolve a story with incidents and events in which these characters figure. The human element ensures that feelings, values and morals are integral to the classroom activities typically managed by the teacher and tailored to the children's inventions and the models they make. The tasks and artefacts usually vary, there being much scope for differentiation by ability. However, the ongoing 'story' enables the teacher to maintain a connecting 'line' and manage the class as a whole. The approach, which is popular in many Scandinavian countries as well as in its native Scotland, has been theorised in several ways, with Piagetian constructivism, Deweyian experiential learning and Vygotskian notions of language all figuring strongly (see Bell et al., 2007). MacBeath crisply captures the approach as one designed to

> enthuse and engage children in learning by making connections with the external world of their lived reality and the inner world of their creative imagination . . . it is called *storyline* because all learning is a form of narrative quest for deeper meaning. (MacBeath, in Bell et al., 2007, p. 17)

In Scotland, many educators see the Storyline approach as consistent with the curriculum advice advanced in the *Primary Memorandum* of 1965 and somewhat at variance with the subject or disciplinary emphasis of the 5–14 Guidelines which dominated the 1990s and early 2000s. Noting the centrality of shared learning and reflective learning, MacBeath observes that Storyline takes constructivism one stage further, 'exemplifying the interplay of doing and knowing, showing how children are able to construct new worlds, engaging the enactive in concert with the symbolic' (p. 18). Reflective learning occurs when children want to learn and it is important to recognise the fun and support that enthusiastic teachers give when working with Storyline; the affective dimension is vital. Many practitioners dedicated to Storyline attest to the fun they had themselves when they learned about the approach through the very active forms of continuing professional development (CPD) organised by the originators, Fred Rendell (alas deceased), Steve Bell and Sallie Harkness. Teachers who wanted to learn how to teach with Storyline went through the methodology itself: sleeves up, model making, bringing their stories alive and so on. The theoretical aspects (mentioned above) were very secondary to the real acquisition of skills and knowhow. With the shift from the 5–14 Curriculum to CfE, the focus upon more active forms of learning and explicitly *integrated* subject matter, Storyline has come into its own again (though it never went away in Scandinavia).

GROUPWORK

The term 'groupwork' covers a multitude of approaches used by both primary and secondary teachers, including Storyline. The SPRinG project funded by the UK Teaching and Learning Research Programme (TLRP) provides advice to teachers regarding the management of groups. Six key points to guide the planning of groupwork can be found in TLRP (2007a). These include advice about the number of groups that seems to work well in typical classrooms, group size (four to six pupils often seems best) and group composition, whether based on same or mixed ability, friendship, personality and working style, integrating those with particular needs or not, etc. Many Scottish practitioners would not be surprised to read that 'the best form of mixing is probably putting high and middle ability pupils and low and middle ability pupils together' (TLRP, 2007a). Additionally, the report stresses that groupwork is at its best when it enables pupils to think and talk together, explicitly about their understandings, and encourages them to question each other and share ideas. It also notes that social skills in pupils need to be developed first before communication skills such as taking turns at talk; active listening, questioning and explaining; summarising and persuading each other; and agreeing to group decision making. Subsequent attention to the learning of problem-solving skills is then possible. Both primary and secondary Scottish teachers use groupwork extensively, increasing the demands on pupils and upping the challenges as progress is made. Arguably, however, much more sharing of the advances made and the weaknesses still prevalent could be made between the two sectors in the interests of better pedagogy overall. Looking at the dynamic aspects of groupwork takes us to what is commonly referred to as *collaborative learning*.

COLLABORATIVE LEARNING

In recent years in Scotland, there have been a number of authority-wide CPD initiatives focusing on how teachers manage the work of small groups; on how pupils can learn to collaborate or cooperate with each other in the course of their learning; and on how discussion can be made more effective. Perhaps the most popular model of cooperative learning stems from the original North American work in the 1980s and 1990s by Johnson and others (described in Johnson, Johnson and Holubec (1998); see also the meta-analysis of its effectiveness in Johnson, Johnson and Stanne, 2000). This model is known as Learning Together and has five characteristic components. It would be fair to say that very many Scottish teachers, whether knowingly or not, do manage their pupil groups with some adherence to these features, namely that in their teaching there is:

- positive interdependence (pupils need each other as they work and discuss issues – mutual goals are arranged);
- individual accountability (the teacher ensures that individuals do not 'float');
- face-to-face interactions (under various arrangements – pairing, sharing, etc.);
- social skills (good manners and thoughtfulness are emphasised);
- group processing (with the teacher assigning essential tasks).

In some situations, the first of these requires considerable skill – and where discipline is wanting, unrelenting patience and effort – on behalf of the teaching staff to make progress. Recent research in Scotland by Stephen Day with science classes in S2 indicate the gains that can be made by determined staff who focus upon using cooperative learning to advance pupils' learning and develop scientific literacy. In the action research reported in Day and Bryce (2011 and 2012), three academic sessions figured in the work where the focus was upon the handling of controversial topic discussion (socio-scientific issues which have been prioritised in CfE science and crop up especially in the Topical Science strand). Conforming closely to the Learning Together model, the teachers devised tasks where:

1. pupils had to carry out activities and book/internet-based research, both of which were required to find answers to challenging questions (in this case about global warming);
2. individuals were encouraged to explain and account for their reasoning to each other and to the teacher, sharing their views in open discussion within their groups;

3. the teacher pressed for steps to be completed efficiently and ensured participation by all, asking questions as appropriate and directing pupil activity where required;
4. the noise level within groups was held at a reasonable level to enable all groups to work in parallel without disrupting each other;
5. groups were required to report to each other on the completion of particular steps, turns being taken for individuals to act as spokesperson, with completed diagrams/findings/conclusions displayed appropriately in the laboratory/on computers;
6. the teacher ensured that alternative views on contentious aspects were aired clearly in accord with pupils' scientific knowledge as then understood (and left unresolved if necessary).

Full details of the findings of this research are given in Day and Bryce (2011 and 2012) but some of the main findings are worth noting here.

Cooperative learning proved useful in effecting a shift in the pattern of typical exchanges within science classroom discourse away from teacher-to-pupil (traditional teacher dominated discourse which is *didactic*) towards pupil-to-pupil and pupil-to-teacher interactions. However, the majority of these interactions indicated that more work needs to be done to slow down the interaction and to infuse more higher-order thinking questions into the mix. A possible reason for the high proportion of fast exchanges was that the pupils were young and unfamiliar with both the cooperative learning approach being used in the science context and with the style of teaching adopted by their science teachers. (A questionnaire finding indicated that some 73 per cent agreed that these lessons were different from normal.) However, as teachers became more comfortable with the cooperative learning approach and the materials used, the proportion of slow interactions increased. The pupils noticed that their teachers 'had taken a step back'. There had been a palpable sense of apathy regarding school science (not confined to lower-ability pupils) across the S2 cohort in the first round of the action research which was not present in the second or third round cohorts.

The data certainly indicated that 'discussion lessons' can have an influence on pupils' opinions and attitudes towards issues such as climate change and global warming. Somewhat worryingly, 55 per cent of S2 pupils felt that they were not able to express their own opinions in the climate change and global warming discussion lessons. When asked why this was the case in follow-up interviews, the pupils reported a number of reasons. Some felt that their views differed from the majority of the class and did not want to stand out. Others did not feel comfortable expressing their opinions in a group where they did not know the other members well enough. Some said they did not feel that their view would be given proper consideration by other members of the group or by the teacher, which suggests that teachers need to get the classroom ethos right for these types of lesson before pupils will feel confident enough to offer their own opinions. Overall, we concluded that greater use of cooperative learning as part of the teacher's everyday practice should help foster greater social cohesion within the class which might in turn lead to pupils feeling more comfortable in expressing their views more openly.

In another strand to this research we compared the views of the science and the humanities teachers in that school regarding their use of discussion and what they thought it usefully achieved. Teachers of English, Religious and Moral Education, History and Geography as well as the science teachers were interviewed individually. There were detectable differences. The science teachers' emphasis upon discussion tended to stress social skills, communication skills and listening, thus providing practice for democratic citizenship (*discussion as an educational outcome*); whereas the humanities teachers' emphasis was on reasoning skills and the exposure of pupils to multiple perspectives, thus conceiving of discussion more as open-ended inquiry (*discussion as a method of instruction*). We have no reason to believe that the school in question was untypical of Scottish comprehensives. Before turning to other, 'alternative' pedagogies, it might be useful to contextualise them in a particular way, by outlining what recent research on the human brain has to say about learning.

MODERN NEUROSCIENCE AND MESSAGES FOR THE CLASSROOM?

Given the recent and rapid advances in the medical sciences, not least the variety of ways in which the human brain's workings can be scanned and monitored, there is growing interest in what neuroscience may offer to teachers. Unfortunately, there is rather more over-blown enthusiasm in the extrapolations of what scientists can say to teachers than recent research actually offers. Few texts speak plainly but without exaggeration to practitioners, exceptions being Geake (2009), TLRP (2007b) and Hall (2005). With regard to abilities, intelligence(s) and learning styles, in many cases neuroscientists have been able to overturn or at least qualify some of the common assumptions of the last few decades. Before looking at these, first consider the question of gender differences and comparisons between more talented and less able pupils.

The Intellectual Development of Boys and Girls

With advancing technologies, brain differences between men and women are known to be *greater* than previously understood, some of them affecting behaviour in unexpected ways. Women's brains are now known to be better interlinked with more parts involved in specific tasks, men's thinking taking place in more focused areas. Brain-imaging techniques reveal that different anatomical regions of the brain mature differentially in childhood, and typically by several years, for example, favouring earlier development in girls for those areas that handle verbal fluency, handwriting and face recognition; favouring earlier development in boys for those areas that handle spatial and mechanical reasoning and visual targeting (see detail and sources in Bryce and Blown, 2007). At face value, these might suggest that gender differences would be apparent in the development of children's understanding of commonly encountered phenomena in their pre-school and school years; in what children acquire by way of general knowledge. Learning of this kind has the potential to relate to the scientific and other ideas they are taught in schools, either directly (in which case there might be conflicts with ideas prevailing in their local ethnic groups and communities), or indirectly through the influences of role models and expectations that are sometimes held differently for boys and girls.

Our own research, using data about children's grasp of basic astronomy, shows clearly that gender does *not* however play an important part in such basic thinking. Boys' and girls' development and intuitive understandings are similar. This is important since significantly changed patterns of achievement in formal school learning have nevertheless been evident among boys and girls over recent decades, and these tell us about worldwide cultural change and improved professional expectations (and, arguably, account for what teachers have been able to do through more equitable instruction). The extent to which girls have overtaken boys in regard to achievements and the gender differences apparent in interests and attitudes in school, particularly in science, is reviewed in Bryce and Blown (2007) and across the wider range of achievements in Chapter 92 of this book. To make the point about gender differences more forcefully, there has been a reversal of educational disadvantage from female to male in recent years (just when there are declining proportions of male teachers – not just in Scotland, but worldwide).

Gifted Individuals

The neurological evidence to date, according to Geake (2009), does indicate that the observed differences between academically gifted (or talented) pupils and their less able counterparts are indeed apparent from brain scanning technology. Differences are detectable in the thickness and density of the neurons of the cortex. In one study, for example, 'the frontal cortices of the high IQ group were thinner when the children were young, but then grew rapidly so that when the gifted children reached adolescence, their frontal cortices were significantly thicker than average' (Geake, 2009, p. 82). Importantly, however, Geake is at pains to say that in drawing out implications educationally, it is crucial to note that, despite these anatomical/structural differences, 'the basic functioning of a gifted brain *when learning* is the same for all brains . . . Thus it is an unfortunate edu-myth that gifted children can teach themselves' (Geake, 2009, p. 83, emphasis added). He goes on to argue that they need guidance and encouragement like any other children, hence advocating that educational programmes for the gifted should include:

- setting tasks with high working memory demands, e.g. tasks with multiple components which require extensive information selection;
- reducing the quantity of small tasks, e.g. repetitive basic examples;
- using challenging tests to evaluate prior knowledge (gifted children, like all children, learn extensively outside of school);
- designing assessment tasks with the higher-order Bloom's taxonomies of analysis and synthesis;
- using above-age learning materials;
- offering lessons on topics beyond the regular curriculum. (Geake, 2009, p. 84)

This naturally takes us to the question of how intelligence itself is viewed.

Abilities and Intelligences

During the later decades of the twentieth century, it was (and probably still is) common to regard people as having *multiple* intelligences, rather than a certain level of *general* intelligence. Howard Gardner's original (1983) model of multiple intelligences (MI) splits human cognition into seven intelligences (linguistic, logical-mathematical, musical, bodily-kinaesthetic, spatial, interpersonal and intra-personal), postulating that people have a unique blend of these intelligences. Naturally these have had great appeal to educators, for the model implies that we need to attend to all intelligences during schooling. This has provided justification for increased variety and flexibility in the curriculum (see Gardner, 1999 and Smith, 2008). The evidence from neuroscience research, however, according to Geake (2009), is not supportive: 'the more sober reality is that cognitive abilities tend to be correlated within an individual; hence, the increasing numbers of teachers' reports about not observing any long-term impact of applying MI theory in their classrooms' (Geake, 2009, p. 79).

This means that the neuroscience is in line with earlier statistical research which revealed the inter-correlations among the various subtests of IQ measures. In his discussion of the multiple intelligence argument, Geake widens the debate, noting that: 'With a couple of updates of terminology, Gardner's MI is Plato's curriculum' (Geake, 2009, p. 78). And emphatically that:

> as worthy as such a curriculum might be, does this imply that our brains process the specialized information of these subject areas completely separately from each other? No . . . There are not multiple intelligences so much as there are multiple applications of general intelligence to various endeavours. (Geake, 2009, p. 78)

This is not hair-splitting, though in practice it perhaps turns on whether Gardner's theory is used to justify *restricting* what pupils get access to in order to promote their learning, or whether it is used to *broaden* what they need to tackle in order to promote their learning. School learning both reflects and contributes to individual cognitive differences and so, thinking of the typical Scottish school curriculum, the traditional stress has been on breadth rather than specialisation. CfE, however, enables schools to be more flexible in the curriculum that is offered to pupils and so a more restricted curriculum for some pupils might be an operational consequence of flexibility. How much variation will result when CfE beds down is difficult to forecast.

With regard to factors that determine human intelligence and age-old debates about nature *or* nurture, nature *and* nurture, nature *via* nurture, and so forth, behavioural geneticists such as Plomin have shown that (perhaps counter-intuitively) while there is certainly a significant genetic influence upon human intelligence, and environmental influences do significantly shape it, the heritable genetic contribution actually *increases* with age (see, for example, Plomin, 1994). That is, while environmental influences, including schooling, can give children more skills and knowledge, and therefore contribute to observable differences between individuals, learning also 'increases genetic influence by reducing random environmental effects. That is, learning enables us to reach our genetically mediated ceilings' (Geake, 2009, p. 89). Or, in the words of Ridley (2003), 'The older you grow, the less your family background predicts your IQ and the better your genes predict it' (p. 91).

Learning Styles

A major review and analysis of research into learning styles was conducted in the early 2000s by TLRP, south of the border. The findings were overall critical of what had been up until then a wide promotion of the idea that learners vary significantly in their preferred style of learning (there being very many ways of categorising these styles). In their recommendations, Coffield et al. concluded that pupils are more likely to gain from being trained in how to learn and develop themselves rather than in being assigned to a particular learning style: 'One of the main aims of encouraging a metacognitive approach is to enable learners to choose the most appropriate learning strategy from a wide range of options to fit the particular task in hand . . .' (Coffield et al., 2004, p. 132). Regarding one line of thought about learning styles, TLRP (2007b) refers to a recent investigation into the effectiveness of different learning styles taking up the notion that learners might have visual (V), auditory (A) or kinaesthetic (K) preferences. The TLRP reviewers noted that 'this study showed no benefit from having material presented in one's preferred learning style', concluding that:

> attempts to focus on learning styles were 'wasted effort'. Of course, this does not detract from the general value for all learners when teachers present learning materials using a full range of forms and different media. Such an approach can engage the learner and support their learning processes in many different ways, but the existing research does not support labelling children in terms of a particular learning style.

Scottish practitioners, on the whole, have never been extreme on this matter.

Neuroscience Myths: Drinking Water and 'Exercising' the Brain

The drinking of water is sometimes argued to be conducive to better learning but research fails to substantiate this. The advice in TLRP (2007b) is that:

> encouraging children to drink water when they are thirsty may be a more sensible approach than constantly monitoring the amount of water they consume. Exercise and unusually hot weather are the exception to this rule, when there is evidence that children's own monitoring systems are less reliable and they should be encouraged to drink in order to avoid dehydration.

In some *brain gym* programmes, claims are made about physical exercise being a positive influence on brain organisation relevant to reading and writing. The mechanisms cited in support of this are *not* recognised by neuroscientists. Similarly, arguments about educationally 'feeding' the 'left' or 'right' brains of pupils by different kinds of instruction, or achieving all-round improvement by better balancing of the 'left' and 'right' brains, are without foundation neurologically – *accelerated learning* will not result. In any case, in the vast majority of human beings, the left and right hemispheres are naturally linked via a band of nerve fibres known as the corpus callosum; we cannot voluntarily create new neural pathways. TLRP (2007b) notes that:

> It is true that some tasks can be associated with extra activity that is predominantly in one hemisphere or the other. For example, language is considered to be left lateralised. However, no part of the brain is ever normally inactive in the sense that no blood flow is occurring. Furthermore, performance in most everyday tasks, including learning tasks, requires both hemispheres to work together in a sophisticated parallel fashion. The division of people into left-brained and right-brained takes the misunderstanding one stage further. There is no reliable evidence that such categorisation is helpful for teaching and learning.

It should be noted, however, that there has been, for perhaps a decade, an over-promotion of 'right brain thinking' in some Scottish CPD provider circles, essentially telling teachers that they have been missing out on an important pedagogy which plays up to intuitive, thoughtful and subjective thinking. Whatever the benefits of the non-verbal, varied and often interesting techniques used to widen a teacher's repertoire of educational methods, their use ought not to be rationalised through invalid appeals to science.

Finally

At the start of this chapter it was conceded that learning is difficult to grasp conceptually, despite us all having firm *personal* understandings of what we variously do and do not understand as individuals – and equally strong views that we *are* capable of learning (we simply need the right kind of help). By exploring some of the main pedagogical approaches that are evident in modern Scottish classrooms (and probably, for the most part, elsewhere in the UK), the discussion has dwelt on approaches that are now part of the central educational landscape (like the *activity* so important to young people's advancement) and the strategies that teachers adopt in increasing numbers (such as managing *cooperative learning* in groups). Exploring them critically has raised a number of related ideas and practical considerations. Necessarily, the discussion has also raised 'alternative' pedagogies, several originating in the work of particular teachers and programme enthusiasts – with some being doubted for their real efficacy. Usefully, at least in this writer's eyes, modern science has been able, and will continue to be able, to shed light on what is worth doing or needs to be better developed. Learning being what learning is, this chapter has, however, only scratched the surface of a very big topic.

REFERENCES

Ausubel, D. P. (2000) *The Acquisition and Retention of Knowledge*. Dordrecht: Kluwer Academic Publishers.

Bell, S., S. Harkness and G. White (eds) (2007) *Storyline. Past, Present & Future*. Glasgow: Enterprising Careers, University of Strathclyde.

Bryce, T. G. K. and E. J. Blown (2007) 'Gender effects in children's development and education', *International Journal of Science Education*, 29 (13): 1655–78.

Coffield, F., D. Moseley, E. Hall and K. Ecclestone (2004) *Learning Styles and Pedagogy in Post-16 Learning: A Systematic and Critical Review* (Report No. 041543). London: Learning and Skills Research Centre.

Cohen, L., L. Manion, K. Morrison and D. Wyse (2010) *A Guide to Teaching Practice* (revised 5th edn). London: Routledge.

Day, P. S. and T. G. K. Bryce (2011) 'Does the discussion of socio-scientific issues require a paradigm shift in science teachers' thinking?', *International Journal of Science Education*, 33 (12): 1675–702. DOI:10.1080/09500693.2010.519804.

Day, P. S. and T. G. K. Bryce (2012) 'The benefits of cooperative learning to socio-scientific discussion in secondary school science', *International Journal of Science Education*. DOI:10.1080/0950 0693.2011.642324.

Gardner, H. (1999) *Intelligence Reframed. Multiple intelligences for the 21st century*. New York: Basic Books.

Geake, J. G. (2009) *The Brain at School: Educational Neuroscience in the Classroom*. Maidenhead: Open University Press.

Hall, J. (2005) *Neuroscience and Education. A Review of the Contribution of Brain Science to Teaching and Learning*. SCRE Report No 121. Glasgow: The Scottish Council for Research in Education. Online at https://dspace.gla.ac.uk/bitstream/1905/623/1/121%255B1%255D.pdf

Johnson, D. W., R. T. Johnson and E. Holubec (1998) *Cooperation in the Classroom*. Boston, MA: Allyn and Bacon.

Johnson, D. W., R. T. Johnson and M. B. Stanne (2000) *Cooperative Learning Methods: A Meta-Analysis*. See Exhibit-B.pdf from www.tablelearning.com

Plomin, R. (1994) *Genetics and Experience: The Interplay Between Nature and Nurture.* Newbury Park, CA: Sage.

Ridley, M. (2003) *Nature via Nurture.* London: Harper Perennial.

Smith, M. (2008) *Howard Gardner, Multiple Intelligences and Education.* See at www.infed.org/think ers/gardner.htm

Teaching and Learning Research Programme (2007a) *Principles into Practice: A Teacher's Guide to Research Evidence on Teaching and Learning.* See at www.tlrp.org/pub/commentaries.html

Teaching and Learning Research Programme (2007b) *Neuroscience and Education: Issues and Opportunities.* Online at www.tlrp.org/pub/documents/Neuroscience%20Commentary%20 FINAL.pdf

7

Scottish Further Education

Craig Thomson

A WATERSHED FOR FURTHER EDUCATION

The second decade of the twenty-first century is a period of profound change for the college sector in Scotland. During 2012, the sector found itself at a watershed. A continuous period of development stretching back to the 1992 Further and Higher Education Act and the incorporation of colleges in 1993 was coming to an end and a programme of fundamental reform was getting under way. This chapter endeavours to provide a description of the sector as it reached this watershed. The future of the sector beyond the watershed is considered later in this volume in Chapter 107.

In describing developments during the two decades from 1993 to 2012, this chapter reflects on the main events and changes that shaped the sector. The institutional map and patterns of funding are described to provide a snapshot of a sector on the threshold of far-reaching change. Further texture is provided by way of description of core activities, key relationships and qualifications offered.

Description of the role of colleges and the range of their work is made difficult by the lack of agreed, clear and consistent terminology to indicate the diverse learning stages, sectors and locations involved and the institutional and funding arrangements that support these. To avoid confusion as this chapter unfolds, it is important to clarify how a number of key terms will be used. *Further education* (FE) is defined as any activity up to but not including HNC/HND level and includes National Certificate (NC) units, SVQ/ NVQ to level 3, Access courses, Scottish Baccalaureates and Highers. *Higher education* (HE) covers programmes at and above HNC/HND level and SVQ and NVQ level 4. Based on the Scottish Credit and Qualifications Framework (SCQF) the dividing line is between levels 6 and 7.

The principal institutional components of Scotland's education system are referred to as *colleges, universities* and *schools*. Community learning and development is taken as encompassing community education and community-based learning, irrespective of the provider. The term 'college sector' is employed to refer to the area of work that is the primary focus of the chapter and the principal home of FE in Scotland.

The reform agenda facing colleges at the start of the 2012–13 session was signalled by the publication in September 2011 of the pre-legislative paper *Putting Learners at the Centre* (PLC) (Scottish Government, 2011). This was put forward as a consultative paper with the period of consultation stretching through to the end of 2011. Further detail of the likely shape of the changes was provided in *College Regionalisation – Proposals for implementing*

Putting Learners at the Centre in November of that year (Scottish Funding Council, 2011). In parallel with these documents, change was also signalled by the announcement in August 2011 of a governance review of the sector which subsequently took on the name of its chair as the Griggs Review.

While issues relating to College Board performance were in focus as the Griggs Review took place during the second half of 2011, the main driver for Griggs was structure and, as such, it matched (and as it unfolded tended to overlap and duplicate) the wider reform agenda set out in PLC. The resulting regional shape of the sector (described in Chapter 107) was confirmed with the announcement at the end of June 2012 of Board Chairs for thirteen new college regions.

In summary, the reform agenda as initially set out in consultation documents encompassed:

- proposals for the reform of the full range of government-funded post-16 education in Scotland, including HE, FE, skills and community learning and development (this included and built on Curriculum for Excellence reforms);
- the Scottish Government's legislative intentions, which included a new duty on widening access to HE and a cap on the fees institutions can charge to students from elsewhere in the UK;
- the core purpose and role of the different types of post-16 education in Scotland;
- the principles upon which post-16 education should be based, relating to the provision of flexible, efficient learner journeys; widening access; aligning learning and skills with jobs and growth; maintaining Scotland's position as a leader in university research; fair and affordable student support; effective and sustainable delivery; simplifying funding and increasing income generation; and performance, governance and accountability; and
- the Scottish Government's commitment to the provision of a place in post-16 education and training for all 16–19-year-olds; modernising career services; and development of the apprenticeship programme.

Subsequently, in a parliamentary statement (Scottish Parliament, 2012), following consideration of the responses to the PLC consultation, while the main thrust of PLC remained, the strands of reform were refined (as described in Chapter 108).

The response of the sector to the proposed changes and the challenging change programme was largely positive. However, this was tempered by concerns about the pace of change and the implications of cuts in funding that had been announced in the 2011 September statement from the Cabinet Secretary for Finance. The 2012 Scottish Budget confirmed cuts for the three financial years of 2012–13, 2013–14 and 2014–15 of 7 per cent, 3 per cent and 5 per cent respectively. Added to the 10.3 per cent cut imposed in the 2011–12 academic year, this created a prospective period of decline in funding of over 25 per cent in cash terms and between 30 and 40 per cent in real terms for the first half of the second decade of the twenty-first century.

THE JOURNEY TO THE WATERSHED

The period from 1993 to 2012 was one in which colleges in Scotland changed and developed fundamentally. Over this period, the political context shifted as the government at Westminster changed from Conservative to Labour in 1997; as the Scottish Parliament was re-established in 1999; and as the Scottish Parliament moved from Labour to SNP dominance in 2007 and on to SNP control in 2011. In parallel with these developments, the economic and social context changed as the UK economy expanded, unemployment ebbed and flowed, and public spending, after falling back initially, rose into and through the 2000s. During 2010–11, this rise came to an end and austerity became the order of the day.

Reflecting on colleges' work over this period, a picture can be painted based on three phases. In the first (phase 1) between 1993 and 1998–99, colleges experienced a settling-in period after incorporation followed by a difficult period of funding decline. During phase 1, colleges can be argued to have been located on the margins of Scotland's education system with a low profile, low status and limited recognition. This was followed by a period (phase 2) in which the sector moved more into the mainstream with the emergence of what could be argued to be the 'decade of ambition' for colleges, a period characterised by growth and change. The second phase, in which the work of the college sector gained greater prominence and recognition, lasted until the 2010–11 academic year. This was followed by a period (phase 3) in which deep cuts began, the early stages of significant reform were signalled and other policy shifts, including relative changes in funding for colleges and universities, raised the spectre of a return to the margins.

Four events during phase 1 and the early stages of phase 2 defined the shape and nature of the college sector through to 2012. These were incorporation; political change at Westminster; the creation of an FE funding council; and the creation of the Scottish Parliament.

Incorporation in 1993 saw colleges leave local authority control and become corporate bodies. A Board with sixteen members was established for each college and became the statutory body and the formal employer for all staff. In effect, colleges moved from being administered bodies to managed ones with the role of the principal cast in a new light. Principals moved from 'head of service' roles to more demanding positions as academic leaders, accountable officers and chief executives. The second defining event of phase 1, the election of a Labour government at Westminster in 1997, led to significant and favourable changes in the political context within which colleges operated. This reversed the trend in the final years of the outgoing Conservative government in the mid-1990s which had seen the sector in the political wilderness facing rapidly declining levels of funding for each learner.

Third, on 1 January 1999, the Scottish Further Education Funding Council (SFEFC) was created as an intermediary body between the sector and government funders. SFEFC formally assumed its full range of duties and responsibilities on 1 July. Fourth, and also in July 1999, the impact of the Scottish parliamentary elections began to take effect, with responsibility for FE devolved from Westminster to Holyrood.

The injection of new funding at the start of phase 2 in the late 1990s had enabled colleges to move into the new decade and new millennium maintaining a strong underlying trend of growth and responding positively to Scottish Executive direction that they should extend and enhance their contribution to economic development; social inclusion; and the extension of access to HE.

During phase 2, colleges underwent significant shifts in their overall profile as businesses. Each individual institution contracted with the Scottish Funding Council (SFC), a merger of the SFEFC and the Scottish Higher Education Funding Council (see below), on an annual basis for delivery of a fixed volume of learning activity based on student units of measurement (SUMs). These were notional forty-hour units of learning with weightings being applied to reflect differing resource requirements for delivery (for example, between engineering and business studies). While the SFC remained the dominant source of income with colleges typically relying on this for between 65 and 75 per cent of their core finance, other income lines grew significantly. Training and consultancy carried out on a commercial basis provided an important income stream. as did contracts to support national volume training programmes, first with Scottish Enterprise and subsequently, as the administration of this funding changed, with Skills Development Scotland. This volume training activity related mainly to work carried out in support of Scottish Vocational Qualifications (SVQs) and Modern Apprenticeships.

Phase 2 saw another Further and Higher Education Act (in 2005), the main outcome of which was the merger of the separate funding councils covering FE and HE. Beyond this, the Act related mainly to the definition of eligibility for funding and a number of other housekeeping points.

In the early years of phase 2, cooperation between the SFC and the colleges resulted in a number of initiatives addressing a broad agenda of improvement with financial health as the main priority. Remedial action, support and self-driven development saw colleges largely achieve financial security by the 2005–6 target date agreed by the sector and the SFC, with problems persisting only for a small number of colleges. Details of these and other aspects of college funding and financial health and academic performance at the time can be found at www.sfc.ac.uk

As colleges moved towards phase 3, the positive performance of the majority (as reflected both in financial performance and in Her Majesty's Inspectorate (HMIE) quality reviews) began to reverse, with a rising number of colleges revealing weakened financial positions, largely as a result of the reduction in SFC grant.

More positively, in addition to funding directly associated with the volume of delivery, phase 2 saw a change in funding to support estates development. This had a very visible impact on colleges. During 2006–7 and 2007–8, for example, allocation of funds to capital developments were £88m (in each year). Part of capital funding was allocated on a per college basis with significant sums also going to specific projects such as rebuilds for North Glasgow, Clydebank and Telford colleges. As phase 3 began, despite projected severe cuts to budgets, this continued with funding of up to £200 million being identified for City of Glasgow College and a further £50 million for Inverness College.

THE DEVELOPED SHAPE OF THE SECTOR

Based on the devolved model created and developed in phase 1, individual colleges were able to work autonomously and make local and individual decisions about the range and focus of their work. They developed during phase 2 to provide a common core set of courses and services customised in relation to local need as defined by a range of factors including sociodemographic and economic factors, history and location. Some colleges grew to present a portfolio primarily linked to a specific group of industries; others defined their role more in relation to their social or community setting. However, all found common purpose and, to a considerable extent, the sector was defined by shared values and a shared mission. These were reflected both in the core courses and services provided by colleges and by their boundaries with and links to other sectors in Scotland's complex learning landscape.

Colleges proved adept at managing these boundaries by working creatively within complex networks based on a range of loose alliances and more formal partnerships with councils, local employers, the voluntary sector, schools, universities, chambers of commerce, community groups and other colleges. Nationally, the sector managed a variety of demanding relationships with an equally diverse set of organisations and initiatives.

Table 7.1   Overall funding

Main teaching and student support grants for colleges	2010–11 £m
Main teaching grant	402.7
Student support	83.9
Fee waiver	57.8
Strategic funds	28.1
Economic downturn	8.4
Total	580.9
College capital	109

Colleges were also active internationally with significant flows of international students and delivery of corporate contracts along with a small but meaningful contribution to international development contracts.

While the number of colleges remained roughly stable during phase 2, the sector's shape evolved and the size in terms of students served grew. These changes are reflected in three developments. First, mergers created three larger colleges in Glasgow, Forth Valley and Fife (Adam Smith). Second, at the margins, two micro colleges emerged – West Highland College and Argyll College. Third, the University of the Highlands and Islands (UHI) was created, acting as a single management and administration unit for the HE work carried out by colleges from Perth to the Western Isles, to Shetland.

A snapshot of the sector as the structural reform process began at the start of the 2012–13 session is captured in Table 7.1 and Table 7.2.

Table 7.1 shows the overall funding provided by SFC for colleges for the 2011–12 year. In addition to funding for teaching, this shows student support funds (FE bursary funds; FE discretionary funds; HE loans and childcare funds); a notional total to cover the fees of students who were entitled to fee-free provision; and two elements of short-term funding drawn from SFC strategic reserves and EU funding. College capital funding is also shown.

Table 7.2 provides a list of colleges at that time along with details of founding dates and the breakdown of funding for 2011–12 which illustrates variations in size with allocation varying by a factor of ten, for example, between James Watt College and the small Orkney College. The 2011–12 financial year was the last in which funding was allocated within this profile. From 2012–13, regional funding was introduced.

Six of the colleges listed in Table 7.2 were among the fourteen institutions joined together for HE provision as part of the UHI. Their funding was allocated from two separate pots by SFC. Funding listed is for FE which remained the concern of a local board while HE was administered and governed centrally by UHI with funding arrangements in line with other Higher Education Institutions (HEIs).

CORE AREAS OF WORK

Four core areas of activity illustrate the diverse work carried out by colleges as they moved into the period of reform.

- The first, which developed and grew in prominence over phase 2 and was a strong priority as phase 3 and reform began, is the development of colleges' work providing skills for the economy.

Table 7.2   Colleges in Scotland: snapshot at the watershed

	Main location(s)	Teaching and fee waiver (000s)	Capital maintenance (000s)
Aberdeen College	Aberdeen	25,372,684	1,111
Adam Smith College	Kirkcaldy, Glenrothes	22,224,254	921
Angus College	Arbroath	7,714,038	340
Anniesland College	Glasgow	8,873,135	399
Argyll College	Dispersed locations		
Ayr College	Ayr	9,815,468	449
Banff and Buchan College	Fraserburgh	7,620,953	331
Barony College	Dumfries	2,201,825	133
Borders College	Dispersed locations	6,913,356	309
Cardonald College	Glasgow	13,122,413	571
Carnegie College	Dunfermline, Rosyth.	9,861,162	448
City of Glasgow College	Glasgow	30,479,739	1,434
Clydebank College	Clydebank	10,490,018	465
Coatbridge College	Coatbridge	7,404,347	333
Cumbernauld College	Cumbernauld	6,312,966	303
Dumfries and Galloway College	Dumfries	8,168,601	346
Dundee College	Dundee	18,810,631	800
Edinburgh's Telford College	Edinburgh	20,737,756	888
Elmwood College	Cupar	5,648,271	264
Forth Valley College	Falkirk, Alloa, Stirling	19,932,877	871
Inverness College	Inverness	7,846,374	345
James Watt College	Greenock, Kilwinning, Largs	27,681,777	1,101
Jewel and Esk College	Dalkeith and Edinburgh	11,552,036	522
John Wheatley College	Glasgow	7,177,461	309
Kilmarnock College	Kilmarnock	9,847,790	430
Langside College	Rutherglen	9,588,426	425
Lews Castle College	Stornoway	2,397,848	124
Moray College	Elgin	5,328,942	245
Motherwell College	Motherwell	15,905,242	676
Newbattle Abbey College	Dalkeith	526,570	
North Glasgow College	Glasgow	8,361,207	396
North Highland College	Thurso	7,887,472	333
Oatridge College	Broxburn	2,692,740	157
Perth College	Perth	6,541,141	293
Reid Kerr College	Paisley	14,438,105	635
Sabhal Mòr Ostaig	Sleat, Skye	675,446	
Shetland College	Lerwick	1,636,655	102
South Lanarkshire College	East Kilbride	6,702,100	333
Stevenson College	Edinburgh	15,768,848	684
Stow College	Glasgow	7,431,248	377
West Highland College	Dispersed locations		
West Lothian College	Livingston	7,877,775	374

- Second, although in decline and open to question, informal learning based on a strong vocational focus remained a significant area of work.
- Third, and increasingly during phase 2, colleges acted as a point of integration between HE and FE.
- Last, colleges provided the point where many school-based learning experiences were extended and enhanced.

SKILLS AND ECONOMIC DEVELOPMENT

The work of colleges in support of economic development illustrates the complexity and fragmentation of Scotland's post-school system. Two national funding bodies, SFC and Skills Development Scotland (SDS), are centrally involved; two qualifications systems and philosophies are in use, with SVQs rubbing up against Skills for Work programmes, National Certificates (NCs) and Higher Nationals (HNs); and it can be argued that the location of responsibility for policy and strategy is unclear, locking critical elements of these in an unhelpful dance of ambiguity. While the creation of a joint SFC/SDS skills committee enabled an element of join-up, the need for joint committees and clarifications simply served to underline that agency overlap remained as the watershed was reached and reform began.

PLC highlighted the need for colleges to increase their focus on skills and economic development. However, rather than representing fresh thinking, it might be argued that this reflected an enduring theme for the college sector. The outcomes of the *Review of Scotland's Colleges* published by the Scottish Government in 2006 had been highly positive, with recognition of the way in which colleges 'contribute to economic growth and help tackle poverty and disadvantage by supporting learners in acquiring skills' and it was recognised that they had 'a key role to play in delivering the Executive's *Framework for Economic Development in Scotland* (Scottish Executive, 2006). As phase 2 drew to a close and the economy moved into recession, the government turned to the colleges with extra funding in 2009–10, recognising that 'Scotland's colleges have responded quickly and strongly to the challenges that communities across Scotland have faced during the economic downturn. They will make a significant contribution to Scotland's recovery' (Scottish Government, 2010a).

This contribution was based on the core, SFC-funded full-time and part-time programmes of colleges including Access and Core Skills programmes and those leading to vocationally focused National Certificate, Higher Nationals, professional certificates, degrees and other qualifications. It also benefited significantly from funding from SDS as part of their funding of national training programmes (NTPs). SDS provided funding to colleges and to other learning providers as part of an annual budget in three areas:

- *Get Ready for Work*: funding for skills training and work placements for people aged 16 to 19 who were finding it difficult to access training, learning and employment;
- *Training for Work*: support for those aged 18 or over who had been unemployed for some time;
- *Modern Apprenticeships* (MAs): open to those aged 16 or over working towards industry-recognised qualifications with part of the training taking place in the workplace and training providers, including colleges, supporting both practical and theoretical parts of the programmes.

INFORMAL LEARNING

In the second of the four core areas, the diversity of the work of colleges extended to the provision of less formal and often uncertificated programmes. During phase 1, the profile and nature of these courses was shaped by their history largely as local authority recreational provision. However, during phase 2, a more demanding approach to this provision was increasingly applied and courses with topics and titles such as 'Digital Photography', 'Introduction to the Internet' and 'Sign Language' provided a wide range of new skills and development opportunities for adults, with some remaining as ends in themselves, addressing a specific personal interest, while others acted as an important 'toe in the water', building confidence and opening points of access to learning, development and employment. The reform proposals in PLC indicated that these aspects of the work of the sector would shrink significantly as funding for non-recognised qualifications (NRQs) was cut and removed.

HIGHER EDUCATION

Towards the end of phase 2, in 2008–9, 48,300 higher education students pursued their studies in the college sector with colleges playing a central role in providing HE opportunities for school leavers. Scottish Government figures for 2008–9 underline this point (Scottish Government, 2010b). They are based on the Age Participation Index (API) which provides an estimate of 17-year-olds who will participate in HE for the first time before their twenty-first birthday (a projection based on entry to full-time HE in the UK). The figures reveal that the API for 2008–9 was 43 per cent, rising to 44.3 per cent for 2009–10 (Scottish Government, 2011). Making up this total in 2008–9 were 27.4 per cent moving to study in HEIs and 14.0 per cent pursuing advanced level studies in colleges (the balancing 1.6 per cent moved to study in other parts of the UK).

Figures for 2008–9 highlight that Scotland's much reported level of 'progression to university' in reality stood at only 27.4 per cent. It was the options and opportunities provided by colleges that brought this figure up to levels comparable with other parts of the EU and with Organisation for Economic Cooperation and Development (OECD) benchmarks.

Many HE courses in colleges act as an end in themselves as students complete higher vocational programmes at technician and senior technician levels, achieving Higher National Certificates and Diplomas. Others enable students to move on from HE in colleges to university-based programmes through a range of bilateral articulation links. These specify progression routes for (generally full-time) students moving on from HNC or HND to an appropriate point of entry to a degree course. Where the curricular fit is good, progression can be from HNC to year 2 of a degree or from HND to year 3. Where articulation is less exact, the point of progression is to an earlier stage of the degree programme. As relationships between the college and university sectors matured during phase 2, articulation arrangements were established based on collaborative and innovative curriculum design. In a number of cases this has involved the university leaving the delivery of years one and two to the college and a small number of colleges now offer degrees validated by partner universities.

The creation of such programmes has played a significant role in developing routes and points of access for non-traditional university entrants, and the college sector has been central to the widening of participation in HE. However, articulation has tended to be patchy and based on inter-institutional arrangements as opposed to systems and entitlements, a challenge picked up by PLC. While much has been made of Scotland's high levels of progression to HE, progression and achievement for many non-traditional learners articulating from colleges has remained stubbornly problematic, with limited progress in addressing the failings highlighted by Field (2004). Poor completion rates remain a problem and, for many, appropriate articulation links are often limited to programmes in the newer universities.

While much of the focus falls on full-time learners, a further important element of HE in colleges is the proportion of study that is part-time. Just under 50 per cent of college HE students study on a part-time basis (compared with around a third in the university sector). A large number of HE students in the college sector combine their studies with full-time jobs, creating positive and productive opportunities for the integration of the learning place and the workplace.

The shape and extent of HE in the college sector changed over phase 2, partly as a result of developing links between colleges and universities and also as a result of the change of status of some of the work (with UHI provision being reclassified from college to university). However, as the watershed was reached, colleges remained central to the development and delivery of HE in Scotland and a major element in an ongoing and lengthy debate into the nature, purpose, funding and location of HE (Gallacher, 2006).

WORK WITH SCHOOLS

During phase 2, colleges stretched the work of schools, dealing with issues from disaffected youth to support for advanced school qualifications. Increasingly, they were centrally involved in work to create an integrated set of learning opportunities in vocational education for school students with the development of Skills for Work programmes central to this. Many colleges had a long tradition of partnership with schools, supporting specific courses and clubs and extending the curriculum in areas outwith school capacity such as sociology and psychology. As phase 2 gave way to phase 3, significant funding cuts implemented from the start of 2011–12 academic year saw the extension of this work reversed. The number of school students attending college programmes in the college or in school was reduced and limited largely to those in or approaching the planned senior phase of Curriculum for Excellence (CfE).

ASSESSMENT AND CERTIFICATION

The range and development of qualifications offered are further, distinctive features of the college sector and the changes shaping its future. The dominant group of qualifications offered is drawn from the Scottish Qualifications Authority (SQA). These include National Qualifications, HNCs and HNDs, Personal Development Awards (PDAs), SVQs and awards for specialist courses. The majority of colleges also offer Highers mainly to adults although in some cases a significant Highers programme is offered as an extension of or alternative to study at school. Working with universities, as noted above, a small number of colleges also offer degrees validated by their partners. Courses are also offered leading to a wide range of professional qualifications awarded by bodies such as the Chartered Institute of Marketing and the Chartered Institute of Personnel and Development. Other qualifications are drawn from City and Guilds and a large number of bodies providing qualifications in specific vocational areas as diverse as food hygiene, non-destructive testing and gas safety.

The period leading up to the publication of PLC was one of change and development in college qualifications. Four changes were particularly significant: the review of Higher National qualifications; the further development of SCQF; changes in qualifications associated with CfE; and, as part of this, the development of Skills for Work qualifications.

The review of the main HE qualification offered by colleges, Higher Nationals, represented a critical development for the sector. Vocational relevance is a vital element of the credibility of this range of qualifications and prior to the review several areas of the curriculum had begun to lack currency. Review got under way in 1995 and was initially a slow and lengthy exercise. The two main factors that shaped the review were *relevance* and *desirability*, that is, ensuring that the content of qualifications remained current and that HNs continued to enjoy a high level of fit with other parts of the qualifications structure. The HN Review was also shaped significantly by the SCQF, described elsewhere in this volume.

Given the many points of cross-boundary interaction and integration that characterise the college sector, SCQF has been welcomed by colleges. Although its wider adoption as a practical tool has been slow and patchy, implementation has helped to clarify the work of colleges and to smooth transition to college courses; from FE to HE within colleges; and on from college courses to later stages of study elsewhere.

Very positively, SCQF has provided a framework within which colleges can align their courses and, where necessary, formally assign levels where courses are not certificated by others. More of a challenge, SCQF has helped to highlight fault lines in the qualification framework in Scotland. These are apparent at the point of transition from HN programmes to degrees and most evident at the interface between SVQs and other vocational qualifications at National Qualification and Higher National levels. It is at these points that current arrangements are characterised by low levels of credit transfer resulting in duplication of learning and assessment for many, particularly young learners in work-based programmes.

Also very positively, SCQF has created the anchor point for the introduction of CfE. While the focus of much early work on the development of CfE fell on schools, considerable preparatory work was also required by colleges (albeit later in the phased introduction of the reforms). In considering this, it is important to note that CfE is a curriculum as opposed to an assessment initiative. Indeed, one of the core drivers of the CfE reforms was to reduce the extent to which education in Scotland is driven by assessment for certificates. Central to this has been the introduction of a broader and deeper general education in the first three years of secondary school, developing the four key CfE capacities (successful learners, confident individuals, effective contributors and responsible citizens). In the phase most relevant to colleges, the senior phase, while the focus on the broad development of capacities remains, there is a move to a more segmented curriculum- and assessment-driven study.

The development of qualifications associated with CfE, led by SQA, has represented a shared agenda for schools and colleges. In part, colleges' interest has been to ensure appropriate preparation for and transition to college courses as, for example, new qualifications are developed and introduced to replace Standard Grade and Intermediate 1 and 2 with new qualifications (National 4 and National 5). Their interest has also extended to the review of Highers and Advanced Highers which, although largely the concern of schools, are also provided by many colleges. Colleges' interest has been most intense where the change programme has reached core elements of their provision and the delivery of NC courses. NCs include core, transferable and specific vocational skills and are SCQF level 6 qualifications (based on a combination of unlevelled units and units at levels 4, 5, 6 and 7 (a minimum of 50 per cent of the twelve units required for an NC must be at level 6).

A specific initiative that was one of the first strands of development of CfE saw this basket of qualifications extended with the introduction of Skills for Work (SfW) programmes. These are primarily provided for 14–16-year-old school students and focus on experiential learning and the development of generic employability skills linked to a particular vocational area. They also aim to develop an understanding of the workplace; to build confidence; and to develop core skills (Communication, Numeracy, Information Technology, Problem Solving, Working with Others). SfW courses at SCQF level 4 normally consist of three internally assessed forty-hour units. At levels 5 and 6 there are normally four units. Assessment can be carried out by way of observation, practical assignments, personal logs and short tests. While some courses are completed with the help of training providers or employers, the majority of SfW provision is based on school/college partnerships.

Earlier in this chapter, it was suggested that colleges could be viewed as being involved in a return to the margins of Scotland's education system. It can be argued that the central, cohering role of colleges in Scotland's qualifications landscape highlights the dangers of this. Colleges, with their wide range of partnerships and shared agendas in the delivery of qualifications, operate as a central element of education in Scotland, providing practical articulation between FE and HE; linking school and post-school studies; and providing connections between academic, vocational, professional and work-based programmes. Overall, the changes in the framework for assessment and certification described above have heightened the importance of this.

MOVING FORWARD FROM THE WATERSHED

At the watershed, the twin-track impact of funding cuts and reform presented colleges with a complex, challenging and, at times, confusing agenda for change. The implications of funding reductions for reform of structure, focus and operation were fundamental but, as the watershed passed, the debate around these tended to be fragmented with politicians and policy makers preferring to discuss each separately.

These discussions and developments stretched well into the 2012–13 academic year, with colleges performing the balancing act required to embrace change while sustaining business as usual for their learners. Colleges continued to work effectively with their wide and diverse range of students within a context made additionally challenging by the demands placed on it by a faltering economy and significant challenges to society including very high levels of youth unemployment.

As this turbulent environment changed and developed, questions remained about the rhetoric and the reality of PLC. In particular, the extent to which such a broad and deep set of reforms could be successfully addressed remained open to question. As the watershed was passed, significant structural and financial reform got under way. However, the steps to achieving many of the more fundamental and more difficult changes remained fuzzy. Two 'acid test' points in question at the time can be drawn from the full title of the reform exercise, i.e. *Putting Learners at the Centre: Delivering our Ambitions for Post-16 Education.*

1. *To what extent would learners indeed be put at the centre?*
That is, would PLC live up to its initial ambition of ushering in comprehensive change in the sector with a resultant move to more learner centred provision?

2. *To what extent would ambitions for post-16 education be delivered?*
That is, would a more joined up, simpler and more coherent post-16 landscape emerge (as opposed to simply achieving a structural and financial refit for one part of post-16 education, i.e. the colleges, while leaving post-16 work in schools, universities and other sectors largely untouched)?

These questions remained at the watershed as colleges started the 2012–13 academic year and the complex and ambitious reform agenda moved forward from consultation to implementation. The likely shape of the future into which they were heading is the subject of Chapter 107.

REFERENCES

Field, J. (2004) 'Articulation and credit transfer in Scotland: taking the academic highroad or a sideways step in a ghetto?', *Journal of Access Policy and Practice*, 1 (2): 85–99.

Gallacher, J. (2006) 'Blurring the boundaries or creating diversity? The contribution of the further education colleges to higher education in Scotland', *Journal of Further and Higher Education*, 30 (1): 43–58.

Scottish Executive (2006) *Review of Scotland's Colleges: Unlocking Opportunity: The Difference Scotland's Colleges Make to Learners, the Economy and Wider Society*. Edinburgh: Scottish Executive.

Scottish Funding Council (2011) *College Regionalisation – Proposals for Implementing Putting Learners at the Centre*. Edinburgh: Scottish Funding Council.

Scottish Funding Council/Skills Development Scotland (2012*) Joint Skills Committee Newsletter No: 2/12*. Edinburgh: Scottish Funding Council.

Scottish Government (2010a) *Skills for Scotland: Accelerating the Recovery and Increasing Sustainable Economic Growth*. Edinburgh: Scottish Government.

Scottish Government (2010b) *Statistics Publication Notice: Lifelong Learning Series: Age Participation Index for Scotland 2008–09*. Online at www.scotland.gov.uk/Publications/2010/08/25161104/8

Scottish Government (2011) *Putting Learners at the Centre – Delivering our Ambitions for Post-16 Education*. Edinburgh: Scottish Government.

Scottish Parliament (2012) *Official Report Debate Contributions: Meeting of the Parliament 29 February 2012*. Edinburgh: Scottish Parliament.

8

Scottish Higher Education: Character and Provision

Walter Humes

Universities are often thought of as stable and traditional institutions, with a strong attachment to their conventions and rituals, and highly resistant to change. In fact, in recent years they have been required to respond to a series of external and internal pressures which have combined to alter their character in significant ways. There are conflicting views on whether these changes have been advantageous or harmful, some seeing them as a necessary response to political and economic realities (Barnett, 2005), others regarding them as symptomatic of the dominance of trends that threaten the integrity of academic values (Collini, 2012). It has been a time of turbulence which has provoked lively debate about the aims and functions of higher education (HE), not only in Scotland but in the UK as a whole and internationally. The leading universities now wish to position themselves as global institutions, recruiting distinguished academics from other countries and striving for excellence in teaching and research. At the time of writing, Scotland has five universities in the top 200 in the world (Edinburgh, St Andrews, Glasgow, Aberdeen and Dundee), as measured by league tables based on a range of criteria. For a nation of its size, this represents a significant achievement, but with countries such as China and India making a huge investment in higher education, the situation could change rapidly. It is against this background that any attempt to understand recent developments must be undertaken.

SCALE AND FUNDING

Among the key drivers of change have been the rapidly expanding scale of operations and the level of funding required to sustain a greatly enlarged system. Paterson (2003) draws a distinction between, on the one hand, the 1960s and 1970s, which he characterises as a period of 'expansion', and, on the other hand, the 1980s and 1990s, which he describes as the beginning of a period of 'mass higher education'. The number of full-time undergraduate students rose from 52,315 in 1970 to 143,913 in 2000 (Paterson, 2003, p. 165). By 2010, the total number of students in higher education in Scotland (including postgraduates, those studying part time and those undertaking sub-degree level courses) had reached 287,565 (Scottish Government, 2011a). It should be noted that these figures include higher education courses taught in some further education (FE) colleges: as will be shown below, articulation between the FE and HE sector, allowing for transfer to degree-level work, is a growing trend. The Higher Education Statistics Agency (HESA) compiles figures for the whole of the UK, giving detailed breakdowns by age, gender, school (state/independent), level of study, mode of study (part/full time), place of origin (home/overseas) and socio-economic status (www.hesa.ac.uk).

This allows some comparisons to be drawn, principally that the proportion of young people entering higher education in Scotland has tended to be high compared with other parts of the UK. In 2000–1 and 2001–2 it exceeded 50 per cent by the age of 21, a doubling of the rate in just over a decade. This compared with 35 per cent in England in the same period. The Scottish figure has, however, dropped somewhat since the high point at the start of the century (though applications for entry into higher education in 2012 suggest the beginning of another upturn, with a 4 per cent increase from the previous year). In 2009–10 it was 44.3 per cent, with significantly more females than males starting HE courses (a gap of 10.4 per cent). Concerns about student debt and uncertainty about obtaining graduate-level employment are possible reasons for the decline during the first decade post-devolution. This may be a particular issue for potential students from socially disadvantaged areas where the Age Participation Index (API) is consistently and substantially lower than for more affluent areas. In 2009–10 the API for deprived areas was 26.2 per cent (Scottish Government, 2011b). This inequality is a source of concern and, as will be seen, has influenced some recent policy initiatives.

Another area of concern is the comparatively high drop-out rate – that is, the proportion of students who do not continue beyond their first year. Although the overall rate has been falling in Scotland, at 9.4 per cent for 2010–11 it compared unfavourably with 8.4 per cent for England in the same period. There are, however, significant variations between institutions, ranging from less than 2 per cent at St Andrews to over 20 per cent at West of Scotland, which may be related to entrance standards and quite different portfolios of courses. West of Scotland also has a high proportion of part-time and mature students who often have to balance study alongside family commitments and employment. The student profile of institutions can vary quite considerably, with some recruiting heavily from the local community while others have a much wider geographical reach.

Rapid expansion inevitably placed strains on the system, evident in the need for new buildings and equipment, an increase in academic staff and the replacement of informal modes of decision making with formal management structures. Above all, it required a massive injection of public funds which depended on the relative strength of the national economy. In times of economic growth, governments of different complexions have been willing to provide the necessary resources, but in times of economic recession, universities, in common with other public services, have had their budgets squeezed. Furthermore, increased public funding has led to greater demands for accountability: universities have had to justify their existence in terms of their identifiable contribution to skills development, technological advance and knowledge transfer, which seeks to establish productive links between the academic world and the world of business. The Scottish Funding Council (SFC) is the body that allocates grants to higher education institutions. It has seven strategic priorities: employability and skills; access, inclusion and progression; knowledge exchange; specialism and diversity; collaboration; world-class research; and effective colleges and universities (SFC, 2009). Grants come in two forms: General Grants for teaching and research, and Horizon Funding for strategic initiatives. In 2010–11 the awards to Scottish institutions totalled £1.13 billion under the General Fund and £12.5 million under the Horizon Fund. Funding issues became particularly sensitive in 2010–11. A decision of the Westminster government to allow English universities to charge students up to £9,000 in annual fees put the spotlight on the Scottish situation, where students were not charged fees. Universities became concerned that a funding gap would place Scotland at a serious disadvantage, making it hard to maintain quality. In 2010, a government paper setting out various options, *Building a Smarter Future: Towards a Sustainable Scottish Solution for the Future of Higher Education*, was published, but it stopped short of offering a clear way forward. Following extensive public debate, the Scottish Government allocated additional funds to universities but held firm on the policy of not charging fees to Scottish-domiciled students. Universities could, however, charge fees to students coming from the rest of the UK (RUK). This has led to the anomaly of fees being chargeable to RUK students but not to students from elsewhere within the European Union, which is prohibited under EU agreements. Unsurprisingly, applications from EU students to Scottish universities have increased but applications to English universities have fallen. It is likely that this question will have to be revisited before long. A much fuller account of funding issues is given in Chapter 15.

In 2011, the Scottish Government published a paper entitled *Putting Learners at the Centre: Delivering our Ambitions for post-16 Education*. As the title indicates, the document extends beyond universities and higher education, reinforcing a trend towards the blurring of the divide between FE and HE, and emphasising the importance of flexible routes from the former to the latter. Of particular interest were the proposals to encourage universities to broaden their approach to selection, aiming to attract more students from socially disadvantaged backgrounds. A Widening Access Outcome Agreement was proposed which would carry the risk of financial penalties for universities that do not manage to reach their targets. It was also recommended that universities should be placed under a statutory duty to seek and recruit able pupils from schools that normally do not send many of their youngsters to higher education. It later emerged that Universities Scotland, in a collective response to the paper, opposed the proposals on the grounds that they would not resolve long-standing problems of inequality in higher education. Their submission stated:

> We believe further progress on widening access to university is a system-wide challenge in which universities have an important role but which is fundamentally reliant on early years and school-level action to ensure that learners from challenged backgrounds are able to realise their full potential. (*Herald*, 1 March 2012, p. 4)

Despite these arguments, the Cabinet Secretary for Education, Michael Russell, announced his intention to press ahead with the reforms. He also proposed that advanced technical apprenticeships, equivalent to degree-level work, should form part of the post-16 strategy, again indicating that FE and HE should be seen as a continuum, not strictly demarcated sectors.

INSTITUTIONS: HISTORY, DIVERSITY AND CULTURE

The HE sector in Scotland consists of nineteen institutions (fifteen universities, the Open University in Scotland, Glasgow School of Art, the Royal Conservatoire of Scotland (previously called the Royal Scottish Academy of Music and Drama), and the Scottish Agricultural College). Edinburgh College of Art was a separate institution until August 2011 when it merged with the University of Edinburgh. As noted above, a significant proportion of work at HE level is also offered in some FE colleges, often as part of an arrangement that allows students to transfer to degree courses at universities. Provision of this sort offers an important route for those students from 'non-traditional' backgrounds who may have left school with limited qualifications but who wish to re-enter education at a later stage.

Of the fifteen universities, four are 'ancient', dating from the fifteenth and sixteenth centuries (St Andrews, Glasgow, Aberdeen and Edinburgh). The prestige of these institutions is reflected in their architecture (buildings represent an important symbolic statement), in their many distinguished graduates, and in the significant sources of income that they enjoy from endowments and donations. Following the Robbins Report of 1963, which began a massive expansion of higher education across the United Kingdom, another four universities were created, three of these developing from existing institutions. Both Strathclyde in Glasgow and Heriot-Watt in Edinburgh had strong prior histories, particularly in the fields of science, engineering and technology. Queen's College, Dundee, which became Dundee University, had been an integral part of St Andrews University before gaining independent status. One entirely new university (Stirling) was established, initially with an emphasis on liberal arts but gradually acquiring a broader portfolio of courses. A further phase of expansion took place three decades later, leading to a group often referred to as the 'post-1992' universities: Robert Gordon (Aberdeen), Glasgow Caledonian, Edinburgh Napier, Abertay (Dundee), West of Scotland (formerly the University of Paisley), Queen Margaret (Edinburgh). All of these post-1992 universities developed from existing colleges and central institutions (the Scottish equivalent of English polytechnics). Starting in the same period, teacher education, which until then had taken place in specialist colleges of education, was gradually merged with the university sector: for example, Jordanhill College became part of Strathclyde University, and Moray House joined with Edinburgh University. The University of the Highlands and Islands (UHI), granted full university status in 2011, deserves particular mention. It consists of a partnership of thirteen colleges and research institutions covering a wide area in the north of Scotland, supported by fifty learning centres designed to make higher education available to students in remote areas.

All of these universities have a collective voice through Universities Scotland and receive public funding from the SFC. However, it would be hard to maintain that they all enjoy equal status. Their reputations depend on a number of factors: standards of admission and competition for places; the quality of teaching and research, as measured by the Quality Assurance Agency and the Research Excellence Framework; their ability to attract and retain leading academics; the percentage of students gaining 'good' degrees (first class or upper second) and securing employment in graduate occupations; the number of students pursuing postgraduate courses; the facilities available to staff and students (accommodation, libraries, laboratories, information technology, etc.). Universities have different 'missions', some aiming for academic excellence in traditional disciplines and professions (medicine, the law, religion), others defining themselves more in relation to the needs of commerce and industry, producing graduates with technical, entrepreneurial and managerial skills. It is not a uniform picture, however, and the profile of a university may show strengths in certain fields without being able to reproduce that quality across all subject areas. Moreover, as new areas of knowledge gain importance, universities develop courses in response to demand: for example, the field of business and management education has expanded from modest beginnings to become one of the most popular areas of study for both undergraduates and postgraduates.

The different priorities of universities are reflected in the fact that some have chosen to align themselves with 'mission groups' representing particular interests. Thus Glasgow and

Edinburgh are both members of the Russell Group, which represents twenty-four leading UK universities that are 'committed to maintaining the very best research, an outstanding learning and teaching experience and unrivalled links with business and the public sector' (www.russellgroup.ac.uk). One Scottish university, St Andrews, is a member of a smaller group of 'research-intensive' universities, the 1994 Group, which was formed partly in response to the granting of university status to former polytechnics, suggesting a strategic positioning within a rapidly changing sector.

Yet another grouping, consisting of twenty-six universities, which prefers to call itself a 'think tank' rather than a mission group, is Million+. Three Scottish universities (Abertay, Edinburgh Napier and West of Scotland) are members. Million+ sees itself as 'being at the forefront of the political debate about the role and contribution of the universities to the economy and society' (www.millionplus.ac.uk). A fourth grouping is University Alliance which currently has twenty-three 'business engaged' universities, including one in Scotland, Glasgow Caledonian. It is claimed that 'Alliance universities have innovation and enterprise running through everything they do and deliver' (www.university-alliance.ac.uk). Interestingly, Glasgow Caledonian switched from Million+ to University Alliance in 2010, with the principal explaining that the reason was a desire to join major business-focused universities at a time when the collective impact of institutions with common interests was crucial.

This highlights the fact that those universities that see merit in belonging to one of the groupings – and it should be noted that a number of Scottish universities do not belong to any of them (Aberdeen, Dundee, Heriot-Watt, Queen Margaret, Robert Gordon, Stirling and Strathclyde) – consider that membership enables them to have a public voice and to make representations to government and the funding councils. At the same time, their very existence raises questions about the coherence and unity of the higher education sector as a whole. Evidence of what the present writer has called 'tribalism' and 'competitive branding' (Humes, 2010) suggests that institutional diversity has now reached the point where it is very difficult to develop policy that can apply equally to all universities.

There is, however, one important respect in which all universities have been moving in the same direction, albeit to varying degrees. Starting in the 1980s, there was growing pressure for all public sector organisations to develop modes of operation that had been employed for many years in the private sector. This process has been described in various ways, often using terms such as managerialism, marketisation, performativity and account-ability. Mechanisms for monitoring targets, quality and staff performance are now standard practice, as well as tighter financial control and a sharper focus on measurable output. The older culture which allowed for a considerable measure of relative autonomy, professional judgement and self-regulation – implying a high degree of trust – has been replaced by one that requires clear evidence of achievement and value.

This shift is manifest in various ways. The relationship between academic departments and 'service' departments has changed significantly, with the former having to submit to the bureaucratic requirements of the latter. Central directives from departments of finance, planning, human resources, recruitment, marketing and public relations limit the degree of autonomy that academic departments once enjoyed. A much more 'corporate' approach to management has developed, reflected in a proliferation of policy documents and strategic plans, promoted by an expanding cadre of senior staff at vice-principal level, each with a specific managerial remit. All this has changed the culture of universities, some more than others, and has led to a degree of discontent among academic staff who feel that their efforts in teaching and research represent the 'core' work of universities, and that the ascendancy of what they regard as a bureaucratic mindset has undermined the true purpose of higher education. For example, it was reported in 2012 that a survey of staff at Glasgow Caledonian University found that less than 20 per cent considered that the senior management team were doing a good job. As will be shown below, the disjunction between the academic and managerial priorities has at times provoked public disputes which in 2011 led to the setting up of a committee to review the governance of Scottish higher education.

TEACHING, RESEARCH AND KNOWLEDGE EXCHANGE

The main activities of universities can be described under three headings. First, there is the teaching of students across a wide range of disciplines and using a variety of methods: as part of this, the quality of students' learning is regularly assessed. It is expected that the content of teaching will draw on the latest knowledge in the relevant field. The standard of teaching is subject to scrutiny on a UK-wide basis by the Quality Assurance Agency (QAA) which defines its function as 'safeguarding the public interest in the sound standards of higher education qualifications [and] informing and encouraging improvement in the management and quality of higher education' (www.qaa.ac.uk). QAA has a Scottish office in Glasgow. Parity of standards between universities, it is claimed, is maintained through a system of external examining, whereby academics from one university monitor the work of students in other institutions. The Higher Education Academy (HEA), another UK-wide agency, which has an office in Edinburgh, is also concerned to develop and improve teaching and learning: it strives to do this by 'recognising and rewarding excellent teaching, bringing together people and resources to share best practice, and by helping to influence, shape and implement policy' (www.heacademy.ac.uk).

The second area of activity is research. Universities are expected to generate new knowledge, advancing understanding in the disciplines they teach. The new knowledge may be 'pure', concerned with theories and principles that alter the way in which problems are framed or issues conceptualised, or it may be 'applied', having implications for the way in which practices in a wide range of fields (medicine, engineering, economics, government, law, etc.) are carried out. Funding from research comes from a variety of sources but the most prestigious awards, which attract strong competition, are made by the various UK Research Councils. The quality of research is assessed against national and international standards on a UK-wide basis through the Research Assessment Exercise (carried out in 2008) and the Research Excellence Framework (planned for 2014). Academic staff have come under increasing pressure to secure research grants and publish the findings of their work in leading academic journals. This has led some critics to argue that teaching is in danger of being undervalued. It used to be the tradition in Scotland that teaching of first-year classes would be undertaken by a professor, on the grounds that they deserved to hear leading scholars in the discipline. This is less common now, as senior staff are often recruited principally for their research expertise and may have very limited teaching commitments. Other critics argue that the heavy emphasis on research undermines the role of universities as democratic institutions, lessening their contribution to the public good (Bailey and Freedman, 2011).

The third area of activity, knowledge exchange (sometimes called knowledge transfer), has gained in significance in recent years as government wishes to see economic benefit from the large investment in higher education, and universities wish to demonstrate that they are not remote ivory towers but are engaged with the wider community. According to Universities Scotland

> Knowledge exchange is the process by which knowledge, expertise and skilled people move between research in universities and their user communities to contribute to economic development, effectiveness of public services and policy, and quality of life. This can range from setting up a new company to exploit the results of research, through advising government departments or charities on policy, to exhibitions, lectures or performances for the general public (www. universities-scotland.ac.uk).

The same organisation claims that £337 million was earned through knowledge exchange activity in 2008–9, that 3,315 staff were employed in companies spun out from Scottish universities, that 314 research contracts worth £9.4 million were secured with small and medium-sized enterprises, and that £7.8 million was earned from consultancy services. Significant legal and contractual issues, involving patents and intellectual property rights, arise from this kind of activity. Commercial companies are understandably concerned with the confidentiality of new products or processes and this can come into conflict with traditional academic impulses to make new knowledge available in the public domain as soon as possible. Furthermore, tricky ethical questions can arise when dealing with companies working in sensitive fields, such as pharmaceuticals, oil exploration or renewable energy. It is fair to say that while knowledge exchange has been energetically promoted by government and university senior management – both seeing it as a source of additional revenue as well as evidence of social engagement – some academics remain uneasy about what it means for the aims and values of universities. Moreover, in some fields, such as education, government funding of research, which might help to inform policy decisions, has actually declined, with a seeming preference for 'in-house' studies carried out by civil servants or limited surveys conducted by market research organisations. This raises questions about the objectivity of the 'knowledge' that is generated. Critics of knowledge exchange see it as the commodification and commercialisation of knowledge, which they fear may run the risk of compromising the role of the academy as a guardian of truth. It is perhaps no accident that the vogue for knowledge exchange has occurred at a time when the very concept of truth has come under attack from post-modern critiques.

THE GOVERNANCE OF SCOTTISH HIGHER EDUCATION

Throughout 2011, universities were constantly in the news, particularly in relation to the vexed question of student fees. The decision by the UK government to allow universities in England and Wales to charge annual fees of up to £9,000 raised challenging issues for the funding of Scottish universities: the details of these are discussed in Chapter 15. In addition, however, there was a series of press reports about other matters which, cumulatively, raised questions about the management and direction of Scottish universities. Proposals to close courses and departments at several universities provoked strong protests. The level of principals' salaries attracted criticism, as did the amount spent on the refurbishment of their residences at two universities. There was an allegation of cronyism in a professorial appointment at a post-1992 university. At another post-1992 university there was an embarrassing dispute between the Court and the former principal. The award of some honorary degrees also attracted adverse comment. More generally, as has been noted, there was felt to be a serious gap between the corporate culture embraced by senior management and the values of academics engaged in teaching and research.

Against this background, the Cabinet Secretary for Education and Lifelong Learning, Michael Russell, set up a review of the governance of Scottish higher education institutions in June 2011, with a particular focus on transparency, effectiveness and democratic accountability. The review group was chaired by Professor Ferdinand von Prondzynski, Principal of Robert Gordon University. There were four other members: Terry Brotherstone, a nominee of the Scottish Trades Union Congress; Alan Simpson, chair of Court at the University of Stirling; the Rector of Edinburgh University, Iain Macwhirter, a journalist; and the President of the National Union of Students Scotland, Robin Parker. The remit of the group had three main strands: to consider whether current institutional governance arrangements in the higher education sector in Scotland deliver an appropriate level of democratic accountability given the level of public funding institutions receive; to identify and examine proposals for change that observe the benefits of an autonomous sector but also consider the importance of full transparency; and to assess the effectiveness of management and governance, the clarity of strategic purpose and its efficient implementation.

In some ways the group was given an impossible task, having only six months to gather evidence and come up with recommendations. Submissions were received from a number of interested parties, both individuals and institutions, including staff and student organisations and Universities Scotland, the body representing the collective interests of Principals. In addition, a number of people (including the present writer) were interviewed and their comments helped to inform the deliberations of the committee. The report appeared in January 2012 and set its recommendations against the background of massive expansion of the sector, the distinctive Scottish educational tradition (as articulated in George Davie's celebrated book of 1961, *The Democratic Intellect*) and concerns about the effects of managerialism and corporate culture on academic values (Scottish Government, 2012). The major recommendation was that the Scottish Parliament should 'enact a statute for Scotland's higher education sector setting out the key principles of governance and management'. There followed a series of more detailed recommendations relating to: the role of university principals and of governing bodies and academic boards; statutory protection of academic freedom; the need for rigorous self-evaluation by governing bodies of their effectiveness in guiding institutional strategy and performance; the appointment and remuneration of principals, and the election of chairs of governing bodies; and mechanisms to ensure that concerns of staff can be independently investigated. In general, the recommendations were designed to ensure greater democratic involvement of all relevant stakeholders.

In the course of their enquiry, the committee members found that relatively little independent research had been undertaken in relation to the governance and management of Scottish higher education. The report pointed out that if future policy is to be genuinely 'evidence-informed' the research base needs to be strengthened. Accordingly, it recommended that the Scottish Government should 'instruct' the SFC to establish a Centre for Higher Education Research in a suitable institutional setting. This could serve as an important resource for future strategic decisions about the form and function of the sector.

At the time of writing it is expected that the report will form the basis of new legislation to be brought before the Scottish Parliament. It is anticipated, however, that some of its more radical proposals will be watered down as a result of private lobbying by powerful players (e.g. existing university principals) who may feel that the recommended changes go too far, too soon. Whatever finally emerges, it is fair to predict that higher education issues

will remain on the policy agenda for some time to come. In the final section, some consideration will be given to the form those issues might take.

BEYOND DEVOLUTION

Although Scottish school education had enjoyed a high degree of autonomy prior to the
establishment of the Scottish Parliament in 1999, that had been less true of higher education. Until the early 1990s, when there were still only eight Scottish universities, funding
had come from a UK body, the Universities Funding Council. With the expansion of the
sector through the creation of additional post-1992 universities, a new framework was
needed and this was given substance in the Further and Higher Education (Scotland) Act
of 1992. Funding now came from the Scottish Higher Education Funding Council (later
to become the Scottish Funding Council following merger with a similar body responsible
for further education funding). The scene was set for the development of greater diversity
within the HE sector in the UK, a process made easier by the devolution settlement. Wider
cultural developments meant that there was a public appetite for Scotland's universities to
assert their distinctiveness. With the success of the SNP in the elections of 2007 and 2011,
and the promise of an independence referendum in 2014, that trend may well continue.
There will, however, be both difficult practical problems and serious strategic challenges to
be negotiated.

The most immediate will be the sustainability of current funding provisions, particularly
given the disparity between the Scottish and the English arrangements on student fees.
If there is no improvement in economic prospects, it is doubtful if the present position
can be maintained without the risk of Scottish institutions finding themselves at a serious
disadvantage. This could have a negative effect on staff recruitment and success rates in
securing research grants. If there is a perception that Scottish universities are under-funded
compared with institutions elsewhere, this could reduce their attractiveness as research col-
laborators. It was noted at the start that the leading universities want to be regarded as global
institutions, with strong networks connecting them to research teams working in similar
fields elsewhere. Both for reasons of history and national pride, it is unlikely that Scotland's
Russell Group universities (Glasgow and Edinburgh) and others high in international
rankings (currently St Andrews, Aberdeen and Dundee) would be allowed to slip, but what
might happen is that a two-tier system of funding could develop, with some institutions
being funded principally for teaching, while others would be funded for both teaching and
research. It is already the case that there are large disparities in the research income of different universities and the result of the Research Excellence Framework in 2014 may make
the task of sharper differentiation easier. The effect may be mitigated slightly by extending
the policy of research 'pooling' whereby expertise in particular disciplines – particularly
expensive disciplines such as physics – is drawn from several Scottish universities and
allocated resources as a unit. Research collaboration across several institutions may become
much more common, particularly for smaller institutions which are unable to sustain
leading-edge research across a range of disciplines.

If the referendum on independence supports the notion of Scotland separating from
the UK, there would be a need to review a number of existing structural and institutional
arrangements. As explained above, the assessment of teaching and research quality is currently carried out by agencies that cover the whole of the UK. There are clearly benefits
in being able to compare standards across a significant number of universities. Likewise,

having comparative statistical data (such as that provided by HESA), and a UK-wide clearing house for applications (such as that provided by UCAS, the Universities and Colleges Admissions Service), has many administrative advantages. Dismantling these arrangements and setting up purely Scottish equivalents would be costly and bureaucratic, and might lead to a narrow, inward-looking attitude. So far, there is no indication of how the Scottish Government might deal with these matters. The universities themselves are likely to want to maintain existing systems which seem to be working well, with perhaps some reforms to take account of the changed political context.

The issues raised in the Von Prondzynski Report provide a good basis for a more extended debate about the future shape of Scottish higher education. There is inevitably a tension between short-term pragmatism – the need to respond to immediate pressures, particularly financial pressures – and the importance of a broader philosophical vision of aims and values, informed by historical understanding and cultural aspiration. There have been calls for a fuller enquiry on the scale of the Robbins Report of 1963 which sought to address both sets of issues in a substantial main document, supported by five appendices containing statistical information and research data. It is probably optimistic to expect anything like that at a time when political and constitutional arguments about Scotland's future are dominating public discourse. However, it is safe to predict that, after the results of the referendum on independence are known, whatever the outcome, the shape and direction of the higher education system will continue to be a focus for robust exchanges about national identity, institutional mission, economic value and intellectual purpose.

REFERENCES

Bailey, M. and D. Freedman (eds) (2011) *The Assault on Universities: A Manifesto for Resistance.* London: Pluto Press.

Barnett, R. (2005) *Reshaping the University: New Relationships between Research, Scholarship and Teaching.* Maidenhead: Society for Research into Higher Education & Open University Press.

Collini, S. (2012) *What are Universities for?* London: Penguin.

Humes, W. M. (2010) 'Tribalism and competitive branding in (Scottish) higher education', *Scottish Educational Review* 42 (2): 3–18.

Paterson, L. (2003) *Scottish Education in the Twentieth Century.* Edinburgh: Edinburgh University Press.

Scottish Funding Council (2009) 'Corporate Plan 2009–12'. Edinburgh: Scottish Funding Council.

Scottish Government (2011a) *Higher Education Students and Qualifiers at Scottish Institutions.* Edinburgh: Scottish Government.

Scottish Government (2011b) *Age Participation Index for Scotland 2009–10.* Edinburgh: Scottish Government.

Scottish Government (2012) *Report of the Review of Higher Education Governance in Scotland* (the von Prondzynski Report). Edinburgh: Scottish Government.

9

Policy Making in Scottish Education

Walter Humes

This chapter seeks to offer a description and analysis of the policy process in Scottish education, taking account of both continuity and change in the post-devolution period, and of the
new political landscape following the May 2011 election to the Scottish Parliament. It aims
to explain, but also to question, official versions of what happens and to highlight the roles
of different stakeholders in shaping the policy agenda. Purely 'rational' descriptions, which
present policy as a logical and linear process, involving successive stages of development and
implementation are, it will be argued, inadequate to account for the complex and sometimes
messy nature of policy negotiation. Consideration will be given to the roles of politicians;
officials in central and local government; national curriculum and assessment organisations;
teachers' professional bodies; academic researchers; and a range of interest and pressure
groups (e.g. parents) in the shaping of policy. The extent to which Scottish education can be
regarded as a relatively autonomous policy area, unaffected by developments elsewhere in
the United Kingdom, will also feature in the discussion that follows. Examples of particular
policies to illustrate the general argument will be offered.

OVERVIEW

One of the consistent features of Scottish politics, both pre- and post-devolution, has
been the importance attached to education by all parties and general agreement about its
significance for civil society. Education is seen as a vital component of Scottish identity, representing not only a means of personal fulfilment for individuals, but also an expression of
those social values often summed up in the phrase 'the democratic intellect'. As devolution
approached in 1999, much was made of the aspiration to make Scottish education even more
responsive to these principles. The Scottish Parliament was to be characterised by openness
in its development of policies, public scrutiny by parliamentary committees and a desire
to encourage participation by the wider community. The first major piece of legislation,
the Standards in Scotland's Schools etc. Act of 2000, was preceded by perhaps the most
extensive consultation exercise ever undertaken. Soon after, there was a National Debate on
the purposes of Scottish education designed to canvass opinion on future policy. This was
characterised, in the previous edition of this book, as a period of 'early promise'. It was suggested, however, that initial enthusiasm for democratic engagement diminished as the need
to reach closure and determine action, and the impossibility of satisfying all stakeholders,
became apparent. There was thus a 'retreat' to more traditional forms of exercising power,

most apparent in the response to the Curriculum Review Group's report of 2004 which led to Curriculum for Excellence (CfE), which will be discussed below. However, although the style of educational policy making may have varied in the post-devolution period, what has remained constant has been a belief that education must remain high on the policy agenda. This has been strengthened by the importance attached to knowledge and skills in relation to economic growth, and by international comparisons of educational achievement which show that, while Scotland is performing reasonably well, there is certainly scope for improvement.

In formal terms, policy is initiated and taken forward at a political level by the Scottish Government, led by the First Minister. This may involve introducing new legislation (or amending existing legislation) but it may be sufficient to promote policies through circulars and memoranda issued to local authorities and schools, or through financial incentives attached to particular initiatives. Traditionally, schools and local authorities in Scotland have looked to the centre to take a lead in educational matters. Until the 2007 election, there were two separate departments responsible for different sectors of education, each headed by a Minister – one dealing principally with schools, the other principally with post-school education and training. Since 2007, under successive SNP administrations, there has been a single department of Education and Lifelong Learning, headed by a Cabinet Secretary supported by initially two and later three Education Ministers. A feature of political life is the frequency with which leadership changes: for example, between 1999 and 2007, under Labour/Liberal Democrat coalitions, there were no fewer than five politicians in charge (Sam Galbraith, Jack McConnell, Cathy Jamieson, Peter Peacock and Hugh Henry). Of these, only Peter Peacock held the post for some time (2003–6). Post-1997, the turnover of SNP Cabinet Secretaries for Education has been less frequent (Fiona Hyslop 2007–9, Michael Russell, 2009–present), though there have been frequent changes at ministerial level. This raises issues of policy continuity and here politicians rely on the advice given by officials, principally senior civil servants. Also important in this respect are members of Her Majesty's Inspectorate of Education (HMIE – see Chapter 20): they too are civil servants, normally recruited from the ranks of the teaching profession, but until 2011 they operated as a separate Executive Agency (in 2011 HMIE and Learning and Teaching Scotland were reconstituted as a single organisation, Education Scotland – see below).

The relationship between these three groups – politicians, officials and inspectors – has varied over the years and can be analysed in terms of their relative power at different periods. For example, following the examination crisis of 2000, when there was a failure to release accurate and timely results to a significant minority of candidates, the role of the inspectorate was redefined and HMIEs were physically relocated at some distance from Victoria Quay in Edinburgh, the headquarters for civil servants. Arguably this strengthened the role of officials and, for a time, weakened the professional input of inspectors, though more recent events suggest that the inspectorate has managed to reposition itself quite successfully, and has regained some of its former authority. The decision to set up Education Scotland might be seen as evidence of this, with former HMIE staff seeming to take the lead in shaping the direction of the new body and the former Senior Chief Inspector (Bill Maxwell) confirmed as the permanent head of the new body in January 2012. It would be misleading to represent the relationship between politicians, officials and inspectors as a constant power play, with each trying to gain advantage over the others, but there can certainly be tensions, deriving from competing loyalties, differential access to information and questions of accountability. These can surface when parliamentary committees conduct enquiries into aspects of policy. The committees give backbench Members of the Scottish Parliament a chance to call Ministers and civil servants to account – as well as to hear evidence from outsiders – and sensitivities about who should be held responsible for particular actions can arise. For detailed accounts of educational proceedings in the Scottish Parliament, see the reports by Redford (2005–present) in *Scottish Educational Review*.

THE POLICY COMMUNITY

As Scottish education has expanded, a process that has been continuous since the 1960s, there has been increasing dependence on agencies outside the central political machine to ensure that policies are developed and implemented. These Non-Departmental Public Bodies (NDPBs) include the Scottish Funding Council (SFC), responsible for the allocation of resources to further and higher education, the Scottish Qualifications Authority (SQA), which runs the examination system, the General Teaching Council for Scotland (GTCS), which controls entry to the teaching profession, and (until 2011) Learning and Teaching Scotland (LTS), the advisory body on the curriculum 3–18. These organisations are not all constituted in the same way. For example, LTS had a Board of Directors and Advisory Council appointed by the Scottish Government, from which it received substantial funding, whereas the GTCS is self-funding (through registration fees paid by teachers) and has a majority of elected teacher representatives on its Council. Nevertheless, all of these bodies see their role as working in partnership with central government and do not have a track record of taking an independent line. They work 'with the grain' of official policy and their cooperation ensures that their senior officers are regarded as members of the 'policy community', which has been defined as 'the community of individuals who [matter], and . . . the forum in which the interests of groups [are] represented, reconciled or rebuffed' (McPherson and Raab, 1988, p. 433). This leads to a sharing of the 'assumptive world' of officialdom and a disinclination to call the rules of the game into question. That is not to say that all of these bodies enjoy equal power and influence or that there is consistency over time. For example, in the evolution of CfE the influence of the inspectorate was manifestly greater than that of the national curriculum body, LTS (partly because LTS was going through a process of internal restructuring when CfE was initiated), despite the latter having formal responsibility for developing the initiative. A similar degree of inspectorate influence was evident in an earlier reform, Higher Still. Power may be retained at the centre even though responsibility is devolved to other agencies.

Two key agencies within the policy community are in an interesting transitional stage, and merit particular comment. The remit of Education Scotland, which only came into being in 2011, has been defined by government as:

- leading and supporting the implementation of Curriculum for Excellence;
- increasing the capacity for self-evaluation and self-improvement amongst education providers and practitioners;
- promoting high quality professional learning and leadership;
- identifying and stimulating innovation, sharing successful approaches widely with others;
- providing independent external evaluations of the quality of educational provision at individual provider, local authority and partners, and national levels;
- supporting the development and implementation of policy at national level.

This is a substantial set of responsibilities and some concern has been expressed about the danger of Education Scotland becoming too powerful and exerting too much central direction over local authorities and schools; in effect, acting as an arm of the Scottish Government. Such a large body, combining the functions of inspection, curriculum reform and professional development, could – the critics claim – create an ethos and culture that was essentially bureaucratic and out of touch with what is happening in classrooms. Others suggest that, provided the new organisation works in genuine partnership with schools and local authorities, it could help to bring about significant change. Structural reform on its own rarely produces all the benefits that its proponents claim: much depends on relationships, trust and commitment to values that gain the willing assent of practitioners.

The GTCS is another organisation settling into a new role which may involve some repositioning within the policy community. In April 2012, it changed from being an advisory NDPB to a fully independent, self-regulatory body under the Public Services Reform (General Teaching Council for Scotland) Order 2011. The new Council is smaller than its predecessor (thirty-seven members instead of fifty) but still with a majority of elected teacher representatives), though its broad areas of responsibility – setting and maintaining standards and codes of conduct for teachers, supporting staff at various stages of their career, conducting enquiries into allegations of teacher misconduct and, if necessary, removing their names from the register – remain largely unaltered. The decision to grant the Council full independent status might be interpreted as evidence that its record since it was established in 1965 means that it can be relied upon to cooperate with government and other agencies, without any risk of embarrassing public dissent. In this sense, GTCS is very much part of the educational establishment, a safe player within the policy community.

There are other interest and pressure groups that are routinely consulted on policy matters and that sometimes adopt a more campaigning stance on particular issues, though it is generally expressed in measured terms. These include the Convention of Scottish Local Authorities (COSLA), the collective voice of Scotland's thirty-two councils; the Educational Institute of Scotland (EIS), the largest teachers' union; and the Scottish Parent Teacher Council (SPTC). Groups representing particular professional interests, such as the Association of Directors of Education in Scotland (ADES), and primary and secondary headteachers' associations, also usually respond to policy proposals. Although these various groups may diverge on specific issues, they all tend to share the 'received wisdom' about policy making in Scottish education: that it is based on partnership, consensus and consultation, and that the stewardship of those entrusted with formulating, developing and implementing policies is unproblematic.

Even before devolution in 1999, this view was subject to increasing critical scrutiny (see Humes, 1986; McPherson and Raab, 1988) and, if anything, scepticism has increased in the post-devolution period. The self-perceptions of members of the policy community have been challenged by commentators who have drawn attention to a number of ways in which the 'received wisdom' has been maintained: the use of patronage in appointing people to serve on committees and working groups; the role of the inspectorate in managing consent; the way in which research is commissioned and used to justify policies; and the use of confidentiality in controlling the release of information. Two concepts are particularly helpful in understanding these methods. The first is *narrative privilege*, which refers to the capacity of members of the policy community to compose, codify and disseminate the official version of events. The Scottish Government and NDPBs enjoy considerable power in the writing of minutes, reports, newsletters and other documents. Their voices are heard and listened to much more frequently than those of other stakeholders and it is not surprising that they tell a story that, in the main, reflects well on themselves. They manage to do this through the *power of discourse*, the skilful use of language in promoting the ideas that shape and frame the policy agenda which teachers are expected to follow. Thus, at the present time, concepts such as standards, improvement, excellence, citizenship, wellbeing, ambition, achievement, skills and outcomes are the currency of professional discussions. As will be shown shortly, not all policies, or the language used to justify them, can claim to be evidence-informed.

In attempting to explain educational policy making in Scotland, nothing has been said so far about education elsewhere in the United Kingdom. This should not be surprising since, even before devolution, education was seen (along with the law and the established church) as one of the distinctive features of Scottish cultural identity, with its own historical traditions, ensuring that its institutional structures would be allowed to develop autonomously. Thus, although studies of educational policy making in England (Ball, 2008; Whitty, 2002) are of some interest in relation to the theoretical concepts they employ – for example, Ball's work on discourse has helped to inform the present chapter – the specific cases they consider reflect a different set of policy priorities. Rather more important, in terms of understanding the changing dynamics of Scottish educational policy, is an awareness of the way in which devolution has altered the overall framework of central and local government (see Keating, 2005; McConnell, 2004). As Scotland moves towards a referendum on independence, these configurations are likely to continue to evolve.

EVIDENCE-INFORMED POLICY

Politicians now often claim that they seek to develop policies that are 'evidence-based' or, more modestly, 'evidence-informed'. By this they mean that, instead of deriving policy prescriptions from some rigid ideological position, they proceed pragmatically by taking account of data that have a firm basis in research. Within the Scottish Government, for example, there is an Analytical Services Division, whose purpose is described on its website as: 'To help the Scottish Government and thereby the wider public sector make decisions based on high quality evidence and analysis to deliver the right outcomes, and to deploy appropriate analytical resources to achieve this'. Towards this end, staff in Analytical Services conduct in-house research and also commission academics and others to carry out studies, the findings of which feed into the policy-making process.

All this sounds very reasonable and any sensible government should certainly take account of the evidence that is available before launching a new initiative. What happens in practice, however, does not always conform to the official account of the process. The processes of commissioning and awarding government research contracts are tightly controlled, with the topics determined by existing strategic plans. There is, therefore, very little scope for 'blue sky' research which does not start from current assumptions. Moreover, a report in the *Times Educational Supplement Scotland* (*TESS*) (Hepburn, 2011), entitled 'Mind the gap: the gulf between policy and research', suggested that contact between the research community and government officials had declined in recent years, and figures for investment in research also showed a decline. Projects commissioned by the Scottish Government dropped from twenty-eight in 2008–9 to ten in 2011–12. There are at least two possible explanations for this. One is that government expected the Applied Educational Research Scheme (AERS), a £2 million programme that ran from 2004 to 2009, to lead to a self-sustaining research infrastructure less dependent on government funding. Another is that there is now a preference for 'hard', quantitative research, much of which can be conducted in-house by civil servants rather than the 'soft', qualitative research which has tended to be the preferred methodology among academics.

At the same time, government has made more use of commercial market research organisations for surveys of various kinds. These are regarded by some academics as 'quick and dirty' exercises which lack depth but, from a government perspective, they provide a convenient basis for reaching policy decisions. The harsh reality is that politicians usually want simple answers to complex problems, often within a very tight timescale, so that they can announce their plans in a headline-grabbing way. What Murray Edelman has called 'policy spectacle' is often as important as the substance of reforms (Edelman, 1988). Serious academics resist over-simplification and try to reflect the complexities of their findings in carefully qualified conclusions. At the same time, they are under pressure from their universities to secure income from research contracts, particularly for projects where 'impact' can be demonstrated. Academic advancement now generally depends on a strong track record in such income generation and policy relevance. If their findings are perceived by politicians and civil servants to be pointing in an unwelcome direction, they may find themselves under pressure to modify their reports. Should they resist, their chances of securing future contracts may be diminished. In extreme cases, this can lead to policy-informed 'evidence' rather than evidence-informed policy.

An example of a policy that was not evidence-informed was the commitment of the SNP, in the run-up to the 2007 election to the Scottish Parliament, to reduce the number of pupils in the first three years of primary school from twenty-five to eighteen. This was an extremely popular proposal, appealing equally to teachers and parents: smaller class sizes seemed to offer the prospect of more individual attention to pupils and make the task of classroom management easier for teachers. However, the research evidence about the educational benefits of smaller classes was, at best, ambivalent, with a number of studies suggesting that improved outcomes could not be guaranteed and that teacher quality was more important than class size. Moreover, insufficient attention had been given to the logistical and cost implications, in terms of ensuring adequate accommodation and being able to afford increased staffing. A concordat between the Scottish Government and local authorities, which enabled the latter to use funding flexibly, without having to 'ring fence' resources for particular areas, such as education, exacerbated the problem. Eventually the policy had to be dropped, an about-turn that was particularly embarrassing as initial teacher education (ITE) intakes had been increased with the specific aim of enabling class size reductions: many newly qualified teachers were subsequently unable to obtain permanent posts.

CURRICULUM FOR EXCELLENCE

Since 2004, CfE has been at the centre of the reform agenda in Scottish education. It sets out the values, purposes and principles for education from 3 to 18 in Scotland. The original document that initiated the programme – there have since been numerous follow-up documents as the proposals have been developed and refined – was produced by a Curriculum Review Group, whose members were appointed on the patronage model which had been a feature of Scottish policy making since the 1960s and which had been subject to critical analysis by Humes and by McPherson and Raab in the texts cited above. Very soon after it appeared, the report was endorsed in its entirety by the Scottish Executive: it was never subjected to parliamentary scrutiny or public consultation. It quickly became accepted within the wider policy community and the four key 'capacities' that it recommended – successful learners, confident individuals, responsible citizens, effective contributors – soon became a kind of mantra to which ritual obeisance had to be paid. This was achieved through the power of discourse – a simple message, repeated often – and the careful exercise of narrative privilege which allowed those promoting the policy to have their voice heard in the arenas that more or less guaranteed endorsement by teacher educators, local authorities and senior figures in NDPBs. The process might be described as a kind of discursive capture, whereby alternative views of the form the curriculum might take were never allowed to surface. In fact, even now, although a number of articles about particular aspects of CfE have appeared, there is very little in the way of serious critical analysis of the thinking behind the programme – Gillies (2006), and Priestley and Humes (2010) are exceptions – though occasionally letters from disenchanted teachers do appear in the press. One described CfE as 'the most ill-conceived, ill thought-out, ill-described ragbag of empty verbiage and feel-good platitudes that I have encountered in 27 years of teaching' (*The Herald Society*, 10 July 2007, p. 11). Perhaps more damagingly, Carole Ford, a former headteacher of Kilmarnock Academy, and also a former president of School Leaders Scotland, has complained about 'the gulf in opinion between the educational establishment and the professionals on the ground' with regard to the success of the initiative (Ford, 2011). She cites 'poor management' and 'poor communication' as features of the way the development was promoted and poses the question: 'Where is the solid evidential and intellectual basis for CfE developments?' Questioning the recommended approaches to literacy and numeracy, and to interdisciplinary learning, as well as doubting the wisdom of giving so much weight to 'confident individuals' as one of the key capacities, she claims that 'much of CfE runs counter to teachers' experience, training and intuition'.

It will be some time before the success of CfE can be properly evaluated but teacher resistance could well have a negative effect on the outcome. A key feature of the reform has been an acknowledgement that more curricular flexibility is required. There is, however, a degree of ambivalence on the part of some teachers who seek the reassurance of clear specification while, at the same time, claim to desire more scope for professional judgement. What is actually taking place in the name of CfE developments offers rich territory for research. Significantly, however, one of the complaints reported in the *TESS* article about research and policy cited above was the dearth of independent studies relating to CfE. This could leave the way open for one of the unsatisfactory features of pre-devolution 'evaluations' to resurface – namely that they might be carried out by some of those who were responsible for the introduction of the policy, thus seriously compromising the objectivity of the findings.

COMMISSIONING REPORTS AS A BASIS FOR POLICY

It is common for politicians to commission advisory reports which, it is claimed, are used to inform policy decisions. The motives for this can be varied, ranging from a genuine desire to tackle an issue that clearly needs attention, to a cynical manoeuvre to delay action while giving the illusion that something is happening. In recent years, several important reports have been produced, the policy implications of which are still being worked through. Two of these will be considered here, not so much in terms of their substance (which will be addressed in other chapters, notably 96, 97, 98 and 102) but more in terms of what they reveal about the policy process.

The Donaldson Report, *Teaching Scotland's Future*, published in January 2011, was a review of teacher education. Its remit was 'To consider the best arrangements for the full continuum of teacher education in primary and secondary schools in Scotland'. Thus it covered not only initial teacher education but also induction and professional development, and the relationship between these three stages. Unusually, a single person, Graham Donaldson, who had recently retired as Her Majesty's Senior Chief Inspector of Education, was given the responsibility of producing the report, though he had the assistance of two 'professional advisers' and the support of a small 'reference group', consisting mainly of teachers and headteachers, which met five times between March and December 2010. When Donaldson was appointed, one observer remarked that it was an example of 'insider dealing' since his previous role had made him very much part of the educational establishment. Perhaps for this reason, care was taken to give full opportunity for a wide range of views to be heard. All seven universities providing teacher education were visited, as well as nine local authorities. A call for evidence was issued, which produced ninety-nine submissions, most of which were analysed by a market research organisation, George Street Research. In addition, a widely publicised teacher survey was launched, which led to 2,381 responses. A literature review was commissioned 'to understand the contribution that teacher education can make to the quality and effectiveness of the educational experience and wider personal development of young people, drawing on effective practice in Scotland and elsewhere'. There were also numerous meetings with individuals and stakeholder groups, including parents and pupils, at various stages of the process. The main recommendations of the report – about teacher quality, the form and content of qualifications, and partnership between universities, local authorities, schools, the General Teaching Council for Scotland and other agencies – were generally well received, though some tricky issues, such as whether there should be a reduction in the number of universities offering teacher education courses, were left unresolved. To take forward the recommendation about the need to develop strengthened models of partnership, a National Partnership Group was established in August 2011, with three subgroups each with a particular remit: one looked at the early phase of professional development; the second at career-long professional learning; and the third at professional learning for leadership. The work of these groups was completed in June 2012.

The second report to be considered here received a less positive reception. This was the McCormac Review of the 2001 agreement on teachers' pay and conditions. The review commenced in January 2011 and reported in September 2011 in a document entitled *Advancing Professionalism in Teaching: the Report of the Review of Teacher Employment in Scotland*. Its remit was 'to review the current arrangements for teacher employment in Scotland and make recommendations designed to secure improved educational outcomes for our children and young people'. Among the questions to be considered were whether the intended benefits of the 2001 settlement were being delivered and whether the restructuring of promoted posts (including the creation of the new post of Chartered Teacher) was suited to the requirements of CfE. This time a seven-person committee, chaired by Professor Gerry McCormac, Principal and Vice-Chancellor of Stirling University, was charged with the task of making recommendations. Professor McCormac had previously worked in Northern Ireland so could not be considered a Scottish 'insider'. However the other members included Graham Donaldson (presumably justified on the grounds that there were issues arising from his review of teacher education that might bear on the remit of the McCormac Review). There were also a secondary headteacher, a retired primary headteacher (who was also a former

President of the EIS, the largest teachers' union), a local authority chief executive (who had worked in education earlier in her career), a lawyer (perhaps to advise on contractual issues) and a well-known journalist and economic commentator.

The McCormac recommendations proposed control of the number and grade of promoted posts in schools, no increase in teachers' class contact time but greater flexibility in the use of non-contact time, and the ending of the Chartered Teacher scheme, which was felt not to have produced measurable benefits. This last recommendation has been subject to strong criticism, not only from chartered teachers themselves, but also from those who felt that some headteachers had shown a lack of imagination in the deployment of chartered teachers, and that local authorities were principally motivated by a desire to reduce salary costs. Another area of criticism was a perceived reduction in teachers' conditions of service, implying a lack of trust in their professional commitment. At the time of writing, some of these concerns are still the subject of debate but the Cabinet Secretary for Education and Lifelong Learning announced in February 2012 that the Chartered Teacher scheme would be discontinued. However, he stated that the Scottish Government was strongly committed to improved professional learning opportunities for teachers, supporting the vision of a masters-level profession.

One of the striking features of these and other similar reports in education is the way in which they bring to the surface various manifestations of professional and bureaucratic self-interest. Despite the frequent invocation of reassuring rhetoric that learners should always come first, if existing power bases are threatened all sorts of arguments are advanced in the interests of damage limitation. Against this background, it is perhaps not surprising that politicians sometimes grow impatient and decide to press ahead with their own proposals (even if it does involve undermining their claims to be genuinely consultative in their approach).

FROM INTENTION TO IMPLEMENTATION

Whatever the origins and intentions of educational policies, in the final analysis their success or failure depends on the expertise and commitment of individual teachers across the country. Communicating with practitioners at all levels involves the efforts of a wider range of people than those who might be regarded as central players within the policy community. Here the role of development officers, staff tutors and in-service trainers is important. All major programmes of reform depend on substantial input from 'intermediate' staff of this kind, often seconded from local education authorities on temporary or part-time contracts, who produce materials and explain and promote approved policies to groups of teachers throughout Scotland.

It is at this point that the complex nature of policy implementation becomes particularly apparent. To ensure the success of new policies, it is necessary to win the hearts and minds of teachers. This depends on several factors. Those seeking to promote the new ideas require not only energy and enthusiasm, but also a capacity to engage in discussion of principles with professionals who may have challenging questions to pose. It is not enough to be able to deal with the 'How?' of implementation: a capacity to answer 'Why?' questions is also necessary. Some reports of staff development events accompanying CfE suggested that those promoting the programme were comfortable addressing operational issues but less comfortable dealing with points that required engagement with the philosophical basis of the reform. Another factor is that levels of awareness of and receptiveness to reform proposals among teachers and schools will vary. A 'successful' school with strong leadership and good staff morale is more likely to be willing to take new ideas on board than one where these features are lacking. Where resistance is encountered, the 'intermediate' staff do not have an easy task as their power is limited. While they can convey concerns at local level back to the central agencies, they cannot guarantee that there will be an adequate response. Thus they occupy a somewhat ambivalent position, trying to satisfy two audiences – policy makers at national level, who expect them to drive the changes forward, and teachers at local level, who expect them to understand pressures and constraints.

There are some grounds for thinking that the infrastructure to support innovation has been weakened in recent years. Local authorities, facing budget constraints, have had to cut back on traditional forms of continuing professional development (CPD), particularly where these were provided by external agencies and required staff cover. The group of professionals, formerly known as advisers, but now more commonly called quality improvement officers, have had their role redefined, focusing on raising standards and school improvement, rather than professional support for teachers. The Association of Educational Development and Improvements Professionals in Scotland (AEDIPS), which represents the collective interests of this group, has been much concerned with their ambivalent position within the Scottish educational system. The universities too have tended to disengage from involvement in CPD as pressures for staff to engage in research that will generate income and lead to published output have increased. This process has been reinforced by the tendency of some local authorities to regard university providers as 'over-theoretical' in their approach, leading them to favour more 'practical' (and cheaper) in-house inputs. Unless the Chartered Teacher scheme is replaced with an alternative that attracts university involvement, the trend towards limited and under-conceptualised CPD will continue.

It may be tempting for policy makers to think that once they have proposed and refined their ideas following consultation, and commissioned supporting resources and materials, that the recommended changes will be duly translated into practice. The experience of all the major reform programmes of recent years suggests that that assumption is over-optimistic. Teacher resistance, overt or (more commonly) covert, can thwart official intentions. To attribute this entirely to professional conservatism would, however, be mistaken. Some of the proposed reforms have been under-conceptualised, lacking a firm basis in evidence and theory, while others have been affected by reconfigurations elsewhere in the educational system (e.g. changing relationships between civil servants, inspectors and agencies responsible for managing changes in curriculum and assessment). Reviewing the history of policy initiatives would provide salutary lessons for all the major stakeholders.

CONCLUSION

The policy-making process in Scottish education resists simple explanation for several reasons. First, it takes place within a political context that has been subject to considerable recent change and is still evolving. Second, it is strongly influenced – and often constrained – by powerful bureaucratic and professional groups that are motivated both by a genuine wish to bring about improvements and by a desire to maintain their own strategic position in the system. Third, the official discourse in which policy debate is encouraged, and the narrative privilege which certain key players enjoy, sets boundaries to the kind of dialogue that takes place. Fourth, at every stage of the policy process – initiation, development, implementation, evaluation – unexpected events can occur (such as restructuring, changes of personnel or financial constraints) which may disrupt the original intentions of the reform. All of this means that no single model of policy is sufficient to explain what happens and that the need for careful analysis and critical scrutiny, using a range of methodological approaches, remains undiminished.

REFERENCES

Ball, S. J. (2008) *The Education Debate*. Bristol: Policy Press.

Edelman, M. (1988) *Constructing the Political Spectacle*. Chicago, IL: Chicago University Press.

Ford, C. (2011) 'The trouble and truth about Curriculum for Excellence', *Times Educational Supplement Scotland*, 2245 (16 December), 35–6.

Gillies, D. (2006) 'A Curriculum for Excellence: A question of values', *Scottish Educational Review*, 38 (1): 25–36.

Hepburn, H. (2011) 'Mind the gap: The growing gulf between policy and research', *Times Educational Supplement Scotland*, 2244 (9 December),12–15.

Humes, W. (1986) *The Leadership Class in Scottish Education*. Edinburgh: John Donald.

Keating, M. (2005) *The Government of Scotland: Public Policy Making after Devolution*. Edinburgh: Edinburgh University Press.

McConnell, A. (2004) *Scottish Local Government*. Edinburgh: Edinburgh University Press.

McPherson, A. and C. D. Raab (1988) *Governing Education: A Sociology of Policy since 1945*. Edinburgh: Edinburgh University Press.

Priestley, M. and W. Humes (2010) 'The development of Scotland's Curriculum for Excellence: Amnesia and déjà vu', *Oxford Review of Education* 36 (3): 345–61.

Redford, M. (2005 present) 'Education in the Scottish Parliament', *Scottish Educational Review*, vol. 38 onwards.

Whitty, G. (2002) *Making Sense of Education Policy*. London: Paul Chapman.

10

The Politics of Scottish Education

Donald Gillies

The education system is essentially political. Founded, developed and operated under the control of politicians, it could not be otherwise. Yet education in its fullest human sense is boundless and unrestricted and, in a major way, in this contradictory intersection of the state and the individual, of the public and the private, of the controlled and the free, lies the source of the political debate and conflict that surrounds education. On the one hand are the unavoidable imperatives of a complex and elaborate system, its aims, functions and administrative demands, while on the other hand are the profoundly philosophical, contested but universal issues of human freedom, development and fulfilment.

The fact that every living human develops, that to be human is to be social, that to be social is to communicate and that, as John Dewey (1916) attested, all communication is educative, means that education in its broadest sense is of the essence of humanity and thus open to all the myriad interpretations and speculations of the inquiring mind. It is only to be expected, therefore, that education should be subject to debate and dispute since it deals with the great fundamentals of any examined life.

It should not be forgotten that while the education system is political, this political link with education is not unproblematic. One need only consider some of the arguments about state involvement in early years and childcare to encounter very thorny and complicated issues about the respective rights, entitlements and responsibilities of the state, the family and the individual. It is also worth reflecting on the relative youth of the concept of universal state education when considered against the long ages of human existence. For most of the human beings who have lived on this planet, the idea that education should be the domain of the state or of politics would not be one with which they were familiar nor one they probably ever even considered.

The education system is thus born of politics. While many involved with, and even employed within, the state system may profess a lack of interest or concern with things political, it is most certainly true that politics is interested in them.

POLITICS

Although closely related, the concepts of government and politics can be clearly distinguished. While government can be understood as the institutional framework of rule in a state, politics deals with all the processes and behaviours, of individuals and groups, their beliefs and values, which contribute to, and contest around, that controlling and organising function. Equally important to consider, however, are the ideas of Edelman (1985; 1988) who reminds us that politics is a 'spectacle' and that what the governed experience most of the time is not political events themselves, but language about political events, so that in a sense political language is political reality. These insights help us to understand the power of perception, impression and image in politics so that what is seen or understood to be the case is of as much importance as what is demonstrably the case. To the American politician Joe Kennedy is attributed the cynical apotheosis of this conception: 'It's not who you are but what people think you are that matters'. Public awareness of this has been sharpened in recent times with the recognition of the key role of 'spin' in politics, where governments and other political figures and groups seek to manage information purposively to portray themselves, their policies and their actions to the public in a favourable light. While the emphasis on this form of perception management has not been as marked in the Scottish political scene as elsewhere, it is a factor and it is one which, when exposed, can stimulate voter distaste and contempt. To be effective, therefore, the operation of 'spin' must remain undetected publicly, and there is no doubt that politicians and their officials are becoming much more adept at using 'spin' in increasingly subtle and imperceptible ways.

A further point to note is that for those politicians who view electoral success as a chief priority, the timescale of educational change is ill-suited to their needs. There are clear tensions between the educational sector, including its officials, academics and researchers, and the political sector because of the mismatch between the perceived needs and goals of the politician who works in a four-year electoral cycle and requires results within that period, and the world of professional education which sees education in a different light and recognises that quick-fix, short-term policies are never sufficient to address its complexity and variety.

The politics of Scottish education, as considered in this chapter, is about how education has been dealt with in the political sphere and how educational issues in Scotland are viewed, and understood, by politicians and their parties. This last point is worth stressing: the political system in Scotland has become a party political system to all intents and purposes, and most parties have adopted a rigid univocal approach so that individual, independent political voices have largely disappeared from the scene, leaving much of the debate to be conducted at the level of official party spokespersons. In the early years of the Parliament, much was also made of openness in terms of public consultation and popular involvement even at pre-legislative stages, but that, too, has tended to fade as the Parliament has settled into a more traditional role. Politics practised locally or informally is not the subject of this chapter but that does not mean that it is unimportant. There have been some interesting developments in Scotland in recent times which have demonstrated the potential power of extra-parliamentary politics. However, this chapter deals with politics at national level and at formal parliamentary level.

POLITICAL ROOTS IN SCOTTISH EDUCATION

From the first recorded education Act of 1496, through the educational restructuring of the Reformation and the great mass education programme of the Victorian age, education in Scotland has had a particular political edge. After all, James IV's Act was designed primarily to aid the national administration of justice, and the *First Book of Discipline*, while essentially about promoting literacy to enable mass Bible-reading and Christian salvation, also makes much of education, the school in every parish, as 'for the profite of the Commonwealth'.

The Act of 1872 which saw universal schooling fully applied also arose from concerns about national morals and the quality of the working population. Education for individual fulfilment is a relatively modern concept and, historically, educational change has largely reflected political priorities on the social and economic fronts. Indeed, it is interesting to re-read some of the Westminster debate that preceded the educational change of the 1870s: for some, the education of the working class was essential to remove the threat to vested interests of being overrun by this ignorant mob; for others, any extension of education to the mob was itself a danger because they feared, presciently as it transpired, that universal education would lead to future democratic pressures that would sweep the old aristocracy out of significant power. In the early days, however, elitist opinion had to be placated and several proponents of the state system were at pains to stress how minimal the education on offer would be. It was presented as offering no threat to the ruling class. It is also worth noting the importance of the economic rationale for mass schooling. Concern at Britain's place in the economic firmament clearly stimulated some of the drive to universal state education. W. E. Forster, the Liberal MP who introduced the education bill for England and Wales in 1870, argued that the system was needed to secure Britain's economic future: 'we can make up for the fewness of our numbers by the quality of our intellect' (quoted in Ball, 2008, p. 65). As will be seen, the economic purpose of education has come to dominate in more recent times too.

It should also be acknowledged, as Foucault (1977) argues, that the introduction of a national education system can be read as a part of an overall drive towards discipline and social control. While many figures behind the move to mass education seemed motivated by philanthropy and altruism, there is undoubtedly another perspective which sees its development in less noble terms and more as a way of controlling and managing society. The very fact that physical violence – in the form of corporal punishment – was at the heart of the system for more than a century is compelling evidence of that role, and its removal does not mean that 'socialisation' has disappeared as a purpose of schooling. The ever more elaborate assessment regime also points to this aspect of schooling: sorting, sifting, approving, disapproving, selecting, rejecting.

Yet the political struggle in Scottish education over the last two hundred years could equally be read in a positive light as the story of the persistent challenge of a liberal agenda, championing the rights and representing the outlook of the masses, matched against the stratified, hierarchical political ideology of a traditional, conservative elite. Over many decades, more and more political and educational rights were won for the disenfranchised and powerless, first in the breakthrough of the 1870s, and later in twentieth-century developments that saw free, equal access to primary and secondary education finally enshrined for all.

However, Humes (1986) suggests that detailed analysis would reveal much stronger counter-evidence of authoritarianism and deep-seated conservatism exercised by elites within the system. Paterson (2003) also argues that even the educational programmes of left-wing, campaigning radicals such as James Maxton (1885–1946) were relatively mild, in the sense that most political pressure was about this opening up of the education system for all, rather than about fundamental change to the nature and content of the system itself. The late-Victorian radicals were engaged in a struggle about equal access and meritocratic opportunity rather than about challenging the nature of the curriculum and any cultural or capitalist bias therein. The progressive educational movement of the 1960s and 1970s, the emancipatory educational programme of Freire, the deschooling agenda of

Illich, the Summerhill alternative of R. F. Mackenzie, for example, found few supportive protagonists within Scottish politics. Paterson (2003, p. 5) identifies the 'conundrum' of mass systems of education as being how to reconcile this emphasis on democracy, in terms of equal access, with the systemic requirements for selection. For Scotland, this has never been satisfactorily answered: equality has been clumsily addressed by offering a rigidly academic curriculum for all, which has undervalued and discriminated against the vocational. In recent times, the attempt to rebalance this has been through an inadequate equalising system of universal certification, which has brought its own paradoxes such as extended written examinations in even the most physical and manual of curriculum areas. Nevertheless, it may be that the current economic crisis and the problem of funding mass higher education may lead to a social realignment so that other post-school destinations become more popular and attractive, thus loosening the deadly grip of academic certification on the upper secondary school.

Even in terms of structure, the position in Scotland is not as uniformly comprehensive as one might be led to believe. The continued existence of a small, but significant, independent sector in Scottish schooling, particularly so in the capital city, is testimony in part to this lack of drive for structural equality. The settled role for denominational schooling within the system, and the odd status of the one remaining grant-aided school, is further tribute to a lack of appetite for ideological purity. Probably not since the ending of the junior–senior secondary divide, and the demise of selective and grant-aided schools, has there been a major ideological struggle in the politics of Scottish education. Only the political unrest about national tests, where the teaching profession, politicians and parents were able to unite around a common cause, has ever approached anything on that scale. Since devolution, the most heated educational debate centred on the repeal of legislation which had sought to curtail the ways in which the topic of homosexuality could be dealt with in schools. The resulting furore, though brief, had not been anticipated by government and demonstrated a highly unusual depth of feeling on an educational issue in Scottish public life.

THE SCOTTISH POLITICAL LANDSCAPE

The fact that the church, the law and education remained distinctly Scottish after the Union of 1707 no doubt gave a particular political edge to these aspects of Scottish nationhood. Paterson (2000) probes the particular role of education in shaping a sense of Scottish identity and, ultimately, of relative autonomy. At a simple level, one could note with interest how many Scottish parliamentarians have come from the legal and education professions, and how many important figures have been 'children of the manse'. It is no coincidence that so many, shaped in these distinctively Scottish institutions, should have become politically active and significant.

Prior to the transfer of devolved powers in 1999, the central government of Scottish education was controlled by the Westminster Parliament in London. Political control was exercised through the Scottish Office, headed by the Secretary of State for Scotland, a Westminster MP, with responsibility for civil service administration handled by the Scottish Office Education and Industry Department. Following devolution, education was removed from Westminster control and is now a function of the Scottish Government. Since 2007, the SNP has had parliamentary control, first as a minority government and then, since 2011, with an overall majority. Indeed, it was they who renamed themselves the Scottish Government, as opposed to the Scottish Executive, which had been the term used in the early years of devolution. It has been one of Glasgow City Council's more petty challenges to SNP rule that it still refuses to use the new term.

In terms of education, therefore, political responsibility is now held by the SNP Cabinet Secretary for Education and Lifelong Learning, who is supported by three ministers. These members of the Scottish Parliament (MSPs) direct civil service activity which is now run through one of the directorates of the Scottish Government – Learning and Justice. The Parliament also has a small committee of MSPs, with members drawn from various parties, whose role is to scrutinise the government's conduct of educational matters. The parliamentary committee overseeing education has gone through various guises, the current version being the Education and Culture Committee. While this new committee structure was seen as a major improvement over the relatively weak system of parliamentary scrutiny at Westminster, the lack of a committee dedicated solely to education has brought some criticism. It should be remembered, however, that while the Scottish Government has national responsibility for education, the duty to provide school education falls on the thirty-two local authorities in Scotland. Again, they have public servants administering local education, under the political direction of locally elected councillors.

From 1997 and the election of New Labour at Westminster, and through the early years of devolution and the Labour–Liberal Democrat coalition in the Holyrood parliament, there was a considerable turnover of ministers with responsibility for education. Between 1997 and 2002, there were five different politicians in charge but with the appointment of Peter Peacock, who remained for five years, at last came some stability and a degree of authority. His sure-footed and inclusive style brought some calmness to the educational world and also ensured that what changes were introduced came with broad support and acceptance. The SNP government has also had some stability with just two Cabinet Secretaries in their periods in office: first Fiona Hyslop and then Michael Russell, who had been a very effective opposition spokesperson in the early years of the Parliament.

Not surprisingly, political attitudes to education very much reflect the ideological standpoint of the parties. For Labour, so dominant in Scottish post-war political life, education has been the battleground on which much of its fight for equality and social justice has been fought. Viewed from the perspective of its long history, Labour has been very successful in bringing its vision of educational egalitarianism to fruition. The pressure against elitism in education and the demand that educational opportunity be open to all has seen its practical application, in Scotland, in terms of the comprehensive system which brought all state schooling on to the same level. While successes of this sort have been marked, the hope that education could solve social ills such as deprivation and disadvantage has not materialised. Labour still puts its trust in this vision but, although educational success has emancipated the lives of many individuals, as a whole society remains as polarised in socio-economic terms as ever. While there have been some directed programmes of 'affirmative action' such as early intervention schemes and nurture groups, the universal application of other policy initiatives such as free nursery provision has actually had the effect of widening the gulf between the performances of children from advantaged and disadvantaged backgrounds. In recent times, Labour has focused on skills for the knowledge economy and on boosting attainment levels to bring Scotland up the 'league table' in international comparisons. While losing much of its radical socialist agenda, Labour retains its trade union links and a rhetoric that opposes inequality and privilege in education.

The Conservative Party has had a mercurial relationship with the state educational sector over many years. For significant stretches of the post-war period it seemed to be involved in a long losing struggle to withstand wider societal changes as they affected schools. Opposed to the comprehensive reforms, it supported the retention of selection in schools, preferred traditional to progressive educational methods and has been consistent in its sympathy with the independent school sector. In its dealings with state education, its outlook has been marked by its suspicion of 'big' government involvement at both national and local levels. It broke up the regional authorities into smaller local authorities, although at least part of this was also inspired by the view that the bigger regions, largely under opposition party control, had previously been effective in blocking or at least diluting central Conservative government initiatives. However, in recent times this general policy outlook is clearly evident in the party's support for continued devolution of powers to headteachers and individual schools. Its most active days were during the years of Margaret Thatcher's premiership when new right ideology came to the fore. As part of its concerted restructuring of, or attack on, the public sector, it encouraged schools to opt out of local authority control, while at the same time seeking to rein in the profession's autonomy by increasing systems of accountability, including setting out curriculum guidelines and new national assessment systems. Although resistant to devolution, the party never promoted any move to end the distinctiveness of Scottish education, even although during its later years in power in the 1990s it was accused by trade unions and political opponents of pursuing policies leading to the 'anglicisation' of Scottish education. This Thatcherite period of ideological hyperactivity ended in electoral wipe-out when all Conservative MPs in Scotland were defeated in the 1997 election and, since that time, the party has tended to be less ambitious and has tempered the ideological zeal of its policy plans. If Conservative and Labour ideologies can be distinguished by the relative weights given to the concepts of liberty and equality, this can best be represented in Conservative support for less political control over schools and Labour's more actively involved role. Nevertheless, the opposite is true in its dealings with the teaching profession: Labour has traditionally tried to operate in partnership with the profession whereas Conservatives, particularly on the neo-liberal right, have been suspicious of what they see as the profession's self-serving agenda, and have sought to loosen their powers.

For most of the past century, the Liberal Democrat Party, in its various forms, has had little opportunity to put any of its educational ideals into practice. Despite continued traditional support in rural Scotland and the occasional by-election success during the early days of the Social Democratic Party (SDP), it was the arrival of proportional representation, long a party policy shibboleth, that eventually brought it into coalition power with Labour in the first two Scottish parliamentary administrations. Long-standing liberal concerns certainly appeared to put it in sympathy with Labour's traditional focus on equality in education. Nevertheless, the decision in 2010 of its UK party to enter an alliance with the Conservatives at Westminster, and in so doing to abandon many of its manifesto pledges, has proved to be electorally disastrous for the party in Scotland. In the 2011 elections, they lost even their traditional strongholds and were reduced to a parliamentary rump.

For the SNP, the key political issue, indeed its raison d'être, is the nation's constitutional status, and over many years the party could not be said to have had an ideological line that shaped its educational thinking. In the wake of the devolution setback of 1979, the party began to adopt a more left-of-centre position on most social issues and this led to considerable resistance to the Thatcherite model of educational provision. This move towards a complete political portfolio, as opposed to a mere commitment to independence and vague defence of things Scottish, led to a greater degree of clarity in its political vision for education. However, it could not be said to have promoted anything distinctively different from the general centre-left consensus dominating educational politics in Scotland. Its recent manifesto committed it to removing financial burdens on students, to reducing class sizes, to high standards, to addressing some of the concerns for the lowest attaining pupils and to early years provision. Its governance of education has been somewhat uneven, however. Some of this was self-inflicted, as it failed both to honour many of its 2007 election promises and to stem the mismanaged recruitment of student teachers, huge numbers of whom were left jobless when the promised class-size restructuring failed to materialise. Some has been unfortunate: they inherited Curriculum for Excellence just at the point of implementation, when the ideas, generally supported, actually met the reality of the classroom and teachers' daily lives. Nevertheless, that has been compounded by remarkable political vagueness and inertia in relation to finalising the assessment arrangements for the upper secondary. This has distressed considerably that increasingly significant section of the teaching population who operate an assessment-led approach to their work, and has fuelled a vocal reaction to this perceived lack of leadership. The SNP also had to face a growing economic crisis, not of their making, which has fundamentally undermined any hopes of developing the public sector, including education, and seems set to persist for much of this decade.

Of the other parties, the Greens present a manifesto that is distinctive in its rejection of the attainment agenda and its commitment to promoting the 'whole child'. The Greens also took the radical position of committing themselves to integrate denominational schools into a single non-denominational sector. Even the socialist parties did not commit themselves to such a position but instead aimed for this through negotiation and encouragement. Obviously, as one would expect, the party agenda for schools includes much about the environment and global perspectives on green issues.

The parties on the far left in Scottish politics have almost vanished electorally as a result of scandals, infighting and imprisonment. Their absence means a very different political outlook is largely unvoiced, paradoxically at a time of economic upheaval when a socialist alternative might well have found a receptive electoral audience.

With a few exceptions, there is a fair level of agreement across the political spectrum about the priorities in education. Humanist, vocational and social purposes of education are all given varying degrees of emphasis in a broad consensus but, overall, it has to be said that profound questions of aims and purpose in state provision have largely been abandoned and most political debate now centres on managerial, performative and administrative concerns rather than on any clash of fundamental values. For critics, there is much ammunition whether in the lack of energy with which narrowing the attainment gap is being addressed, or in the stress on materialism that continues to smother the broader educational claims about values and moral imperatives.

CURRENT POLITICAL DEBATE

While the system of proportional representation brought to parliament in 2003 a broad range of opinions from a wide array of political viewpoints, since 2007 it has become a two-horse race between the SNP and Labour. This narrowing of the parliamentary spectrum has served to diminish the liveliness and plurality of political debate. The magisterial parliamentary dominance of Alex Salmond has also led the opposition parties to appear even more enfeebled and, following his crushing electoral victory in 2011, all the other party leaders tendered their resignations, so leaving him almost unchallenged at Holyrood for months. Salmond's consummate political skill has rarely been applied to the educational field – somewhat surprisingly, given its importance as a devolved responsibility. His most noteworthy intervention came in his forthright commitment to free higher education for all ('The rocks will melt with the sun before I allow tuition fees to be imposed on Scottish students – upfront or backdoor'). Whether or not that can be sustained financially in the current economic trough remains to be seen, but at a time when England moved to crippling rates of university tuition fees, it was a bold restatement of educational principles.

Otherwise, the SNP has been notably cautious in its educational programme, but this can be attributed to the general political consensus about the thrust of Scottish education that currently exists. That need not be a criticism: after all, the National Debate of 2002 produced a picture of general popular satisfaction with the education system and no great evidence of any desire with the nation for radical restructuring or redirection. In addition, the joint approach that brought together the teacher unions, the Convention of Scottish Local Authorities (COSLA) and Holyrood under the umbrella of the McCrone Agreement of 2001, established a strongly interlinked style in the politics of Scottish education which on the one hand has brought stability but, on the other hand, has drawn criticism from those who see the relationship as too 'cosy' and monolithic. Some tension has developed since, and COSLA's submission to the 2011 McCormac Review could be seen as a considerable move away from any sense of unity with the teacher unions.

Current political debate is dominated by an economic focus that is reflected in education systems across the developed world and heavily promoted by the increasingly powerful Organisation for Economic Cooperation and Development (OECD) (Gillies, 2011). Influenced by human capital theory, this outlook sees educational provision as an investment that repays the individual in terms of future material rewards and the state in terms of creating an economically productive member. Educational funding is only justified if it can be seen to have an economic impact. This has huge implications for the arts and social sciences, and positively distasteful possibilities were it to be applied to the field of additional support needs where, thus far, fortunately, the rights of the child and less questionable values still prevail. Academic attainment thus becomes the priority because this is how individuals' economic potential is measured and how the state can secure its financial future. The more noble aims of schooling, the idea of personal growth, fulfilment and the more abundant life, have all been sidelined, only emerging blandly in introductions to policy documents before the real educational agenda is addressed.

How schools are understood and conceptualised politically has increasingly been reshaped by private-sector discourse. Part of this is a legacy from radical Thatcherism but part too is from this economic educational focus so that schools are seen as servants of business and so encouraged to ape their 'betters'. This can be seen in the emphasis in political debate on such issues as quality, on performance indicators, on leadership and in the prevalence of such terms as targets, stakeholders, delivery and excellence, which are all drawn from quality management discourse. Politicians find this paradigm entrancing because it purports to measure what the education system does and is capable of, and thus provides the data and statistics around which political argument and rhetoric can be woven.

Schools are still seen, however, as sites for social engineering. This is no longer in the sense of the 1960s' dream of comprehensivisation leading to a more equal society with increasing social mobility. Rather it is in the sense that schools are where perceived social ills have to be righted: schools are now expected to address a long list of troubling social issues such as drug abuse, sexual health, physical fitness, diet, obesity, wellbeing, citizenship, respect, behaviour, racism and social cohesion.

FUTURE TRENDS

Compared to some of the key debates of the latter half of the twentieth century, current edu-cational debate within Scottish politics could be seen to be fairly subdued. Major political surgery in terms of education has not been a recent feature in Scotland, with the approach being one much more of tweaking and revision, and so there has been little evidence of any great political polarities. As far as the school sector has been concerned, even the most significant development such as that around the new 3–18 curriculum has had the approval of the broad consensus in Scottish politics, although tensions have risen recently around assessment. There seems no good reason to suggest that the future will be marked by any great degree of change to this ethos, but it is clear that CfE will continue to be problematic for government in its relations with the teaching profession, at least in the short term. Were teachers' unease to spread to the general public, and to parents and caregivers in particular, then the situation would certainly become much more heavily charged and much more treacherous for those politicians held responsible.

Nevertheless, the apparently unquestioning consensus about the words on the mace of the Scottish Parliament – Wisdom, Justice, Compassion, Integrity – as somehow repre-sentative of 'national values', and so supposedly fundamental to the curriculum, and the generally uncritical acceptance of the four 'capacities' of the 3–18 curriculum – successful learners, confident individuals, effective contributors and responsible citizens – could be seen as typical of the level at which political debate and thinking operates as far as education is concerned. Again, there are no signs that any politically radical alternative viewpoint is likely to emerge in the near future.

There is little evidence of any political swing away from continued sympathy with the neo-liberal ideas that currently influence conceptions of the public sector, view the purpose of education as subordinate to the knowledge economy and hence stress academic attain-ment and related certification. Future political debate seems much more likely, therefore, to centre on means to improve or achieve in these areas, rather than about the value and force of such ends in the first place.

In this regard, it is highly likely that there will continue to be a move away from a public-sector ideology that viewed its concerns as those of the citizen and the good of society towards a paradigm that focuses instead on the concepts of consumers and private gain. This may be seen as rather surprising given the received wisdom about Scotland's stronger sense of community values. Many politicians appear to see their position and power as dependent on promoting and protecting the private interests and advantage of individuals as opposed to focusing on collective needs.

In similar terms, the view of the education system as servant to the economy seems to be politically entrenched also. Despite the more noble sentiments of the definition of the purpose of education in the Standards in Scotland's Schools etc. Act of 2000 – 'directed to the development of the child's personality, talents and mental and physical abilities to their fullest potential' – in practice the discourse has much more focused on schools' roles in pre-paring young people to be active and enterprising contributors to the knowledge economy. Much more is made of skills than education, and the commitment to Lifelong Learning seems more about training for changing employment patterns than about the development of the individual in any deeper sense.

This economic imperative also demands sifting by assessment and all political parties seem keen to keep focusing on raising standards and on academic attainment as the main measure of schools. While some attention has been paid recently to the poorest performing 20 per cent of the pupil population in terms of academic qualifications, no major party has shown any likelihood of adopting the radical agenda required to address the fundamental socio-economic inequalities that trigger educational disadvantage. Schools have instead been seen rather fancifully as places where social disadvantage can be overcome, where equal opportunities for all exist, rather than, as the evidence still suggests stubbornly, as places where broader societal inequalities are played out and reproduced.

At the tertiary level, the situation is less settled. The problems created by the increasingly marketised sector in England will continue to beset the Scottish university system. While the tuition fee problem has been partly addressed by Scottish Government funding decisions, this has been at the expense of the college sector and it is hard to see how current student population levels can be sustained in the long run. Free education was easy to champion when less than 10 per cent of young people went to university; when that figure is nearer to 50 per cent it becomes significantly harder. Tightening budgets have put pressure on university courses that have no obvious economic benefit, and administrators have been much more enthusiastic about subject areas that attract lucrative research grants and that have the potential to generate income through patents and spin-out companies. Universities that position themselves as autonomous agents in a global education market are less enamoured of political direction. Issues around widening access are largely unwelcomed, for example, because they are perceived as restricting the sector's independence and have the potential to affect status, which has all but become the primary focus of some institutions.

The resiting of the centre of educational power in Edinburgh following devolution has perhaps led to some degree of strain with local government control of education, and even more so since the SNP government has forced councils into freezing council taxes, thereby limiting their room for local manoeuvre. Despite this apparent centralising tendency, as far as political control of education is concerned the SNP government has not adopted a prescriptive approach. Indeed, some councils have bemoaned what is seen as a lack of national leadership, particularly in relation to the implementation of CfE, where many different models have been developed across Scotland's thirty-two councils. The SNP government, however, has interfered heavily in relation to rural school closures and this has again limited councils' control.

There are voices that question the continued role and powers of local authorities regarding education: on the one hand from those who want to see powers further devolved to schools, communities and parents, and on the other from those who wish to see power move in the other direction, away from the thirty-two separate authorities either to some form of return to regionalisation or indeed to more unitary national oversight. As pressures on public finance increase, it would seem likely that some adjustment will emerge, if only because of the economies of scale that could be achieved. The political Right are certainly enthusiastic about ending council control and to promote independent schools as have been developed in the 'free school' initiative in Sweden and England. However, there is little sign of right-wing politicians getting anywhere close to power in Scotland and so such a development must be considered unlikely. Given that the state system developed in the 1870s partly to address the fragmented, uneven, splintered picture of schooling identified by the Argyll Commission of 1867, it would seem perverse to risk a return to that sort of national position.

As one of the key devolved areas, education will continue to be of supreme political importance even if, as has been suggested, any major break in the broad political consensus on the state system seems unlikely. The constitutional question – as to whether or not

Scotland should become an independent state – which will continue to be central to Scottish political debate may seem to have limited relevance to the education system. Having always been separate in UK terms, the Scottish education system, to all intents and purposes, is, and has always been, independent. Nevertheless, the scale of the education budget is such that the economics of the independence question are hugely significant. While the governance of education may not be much affected by Scotland's constitutional future, its future financing is much more open to debate and dispute. It seems certain that it will be these sorts of fiscal arguments, rather than educational issues, that will determine the outcome of the referendum when it comes.

REFERENCES

Ball, S. J. (2008) *The Education Debate*. Bristol: Policy Press.

Dewey, J. (1916) *Democracy and Education*. New York: Macmillan.

Edelman, M. (1985) *The Symbolic Uses of Politics*. Urbana and Chicago, IL: University of Illinois Press.

Edelman, M. (1988) *Constructing the Political Spectacle*. Chicago, IL: University of Chicago Press.

Foucault, M. (1977) *Discipline and Punish*. London: Penguin.

Gillies, D. (2011) 'State education as high-yield investment: Human Capital Theory in European policy discourse', *Journal of Pedagogy*, 2 (2): 224–45.

Humes, W. (1986) *The Leadership Class in Scottish Education*. Edinburgh: John Donald.

Paterson, L. (2000) *Education and the Scottish Parliament*. Edinburgh: Dunedin Academic Press.

Paterson, L. (2003) *Scottish Education in the Twentieth Century*. Edinburgh: Edinburgh University Press.

11

The Independent Sector

Alasdair Roberts

There is something very separate-sounding about an independent 'sector' within Scottish education, but that degree of separation is quite modern. It arises from a time not so many years ago – well into the 1970s – when fee-paying day schools were grant-aided by central government and accessible to middle-income families. Local authority schools also provided opportunities for upward social mobility in exchange for very low fees (Muriel Spark's education at Gillespie's a high-profile example) until the advent of comprehensive secondary education made it impossible for them to continue as selective institutions. Assisted places were introduced in 1980 to provide an alternative form of government support, widening access to private schools while fees rose steadily, but there has been no form of grant aid since 1997.

The Scottish Council of Independent Schools (SCIS) has helped to establish the reality of a separate sector on behalf of more than seventy schools. It represents this varied interest group, providing annual facts and figures for government, press and the wider world. The number of pupils educated privately in Scotland is only 4.7 per cent of the total (compared with about 7 per cent for England). However only seven of Scotland's thirty-two education authorities have more pupils than the total attending SCIS schools. SCIS may be seen as performing a similar role to that of a local authority. Information is disseminated, partnerships are encouraged and guidance provided for governors, headteachers and staff. The organisation's own continuing professional development programmes were responsible for more than a hundred workshops, seminars and conferences in 2010. Increasingly there is structure to the sector.

At the start of session 2011–12, 31,425 pupils attended SCIS schools. This represents surprising stability in difficult economic conditions – the banking crisis was expected to impact directly on private schooling – at a time when state school rolls have been in decline. The number of secondary students at private schools rose slightly from the previous year, although there was a 7 per cent fall in P1 intake despite recent investment in nursery provision. The reason is partly demographic, but parents may also be saving their money for secondary education. Boarding numbers were on a par with previous years at 3,575, helped by a high proportion of international passport holders. Gordonstoun in Moray takes in a third of its boarders from forty nationalities overseas. The oil industry has added the International School (formerly the American School, now in new premises) to private provision in the Aberdeen area. The High School of Dundee is that city's sole recipient of fees at secondary level, but Perthshire has Morrison's Academy, Ardvreck (a rare Scottish prep school), Strathallan, Kilgraston, Craigclowan and Glenalmond – the last of these founded with the support of William Ewart Gladstone. Sharing a similar environment, nearby Dollar Academy is the world's oldest co-educational boarding school. However independent schools are mainly a feature of the central belt, with Stirling's Beaconhurst between the two cities of Edinburgh and Glasgow.

The High School of Glasgow was founded for cathedral choirboys in 1124, so it is by some way Scotland's oldest independent school – although three changes of site in later times have made the connection a tenuous one. Closure of the Boys' High by the local authority in 1976 led to a successful fight for survival. The co-educational senior school now occupies a new building on land owned by the Glasgow High School Club at Anniesland, while the junior one serves a largely local clientele at Bearsden to the north-west of the city. The Glasgow Academy has always been fully independent but Kelvinside Academy (at half its size) was grant-aided until this ceased to be possible. Both now accept girls, as do Hutchesons' Grammar School and the Jesuit foundation St Aloysius. Jordanhill has had a controversial modern history since it ceased to be a demonstration school for teacher training. Now funded by the Scottish Government, it charges no fees despite being independent of the local authority.

THE EDINBURGH ELEPHANT

'Under the comprehensive ethos, fee-paying schools are the elephant in the room which everyone can see but few educationalists will address' (Raymond Ross, 'Auld Reekie's private past', *Times Educational Supplement*, 30 September 2011). Although primary school numbers have declined over half a century, 24.7 per cent of secondary students in the city are still educated in fee-paying institutions. With the Parliament in what is now more evidently Scotland's capital, it is appropriate to ask why one teenager in four is being educated outwith the state system. The explanation is largely historical – though most enquiries to SCIS about choice of school are from 'first-time buyers' with no expressed interest in the history of institutions.

The town's grammar school or high school taught the culture of Greece and Rome and their languages, forming a basis for the eighteenth-century Scottish Enlightenment. As the Royal High School (moved to the top of the New Town) it was challenged from the 1820s by the Edinburgh Academy in a classical rivalry which encompassed architecture as well as curriculum. Fettes College, a late foundation which soon became known as 'the Eton of Scotland', was equally committed to Latin and Greek and won many scholarships to Oxford and Cambridge. However the answer to the question 'Why so many?' lies mainly in changes to the city's 'hospital' schools. (Similar rescue centres for needy children were founded by the Hutcheson brothers in Glasgow and Robert Gordon in Aberdeen.) Modelled on London's Bluecoat School, George Heriot's Hospital for 'poor fatherless boys' was opened in 1659. The modern school maintains that charitable focus through bursaries although its pupil intake is greatly changed. Heriot's striking architecture, celebrating the founder Jinglin' Geordie's generosity, served as a stimulus to the founders of other schools to come.

Other hospitals were mainly run by the Merchant Company of Edinburgh – the first, for girls, the result of a seventeenth-century legacy by Mary Erskine. Boys admitted to George Watson's Hospital in 1741 and after were next to benefit from years of boarding in a similar institution whose numbers were slow to reach three figures. As at neighbouring Heriot's, the hospital prepared pupils for craft apprenticeships although a few 'likely scholars' went on to university by way of the High School. John Watson and Daniel Stewart also left money for hospital schools in nineteenth-century Edinburgh, but when the charitable bequest of Provost William Fettes became available the result was a very different kind of boarding institution. In 1869, an Endowed Hospitals (Scotland) Bill was presented at Westminster as part of legislation to make state-funded education available for all on both sides of the border. Merchant Company endowments were liable to be redirected to general public education until a delegation went south to lobby the Lord Advocate. A 'permissive' clause was added which allowed the Company to make its own arrangements, and these followed with remarkable speed.

Parents were quick to spot an opportunity when prospectuses were circulated for low-cost boys' and girls' day schools. By the end of September 1870, 3,300 pupils were crammed into the hospital buildings founded by Mary Erskine and George Watson which looked south over the Meadows. The city's many small private schools lost out. As one of the 300 teachers who fruitlessly petitioned Parliament put it, the change did

> much more to cheapen the highest secondary education to those who needed no cheapening than to render it accessible to people in humble life . . . £10 a year for a girl, and £6 for a boy, are sums that cannot be paid by working people.

The uproar delayed attempts to take Heriot's along the same route, by which time the legality of proceedings to do with the Fettes Foundation was being questioned by Duncan McLaren, Edinburgh's Radical MP: 'When is this transfer from poor to rich to stop?' It was already accomplished. Thenceforward large day schools accounted for much of the city's private education. They occupied the middle of a hierarchy linked to the level of fees. 'What school did you go to?' became a very Edinburgh question.

INNOVATION IN EDINBURGH

Varying traditions made for distinctiveness, expressed in customs and esprit de corps, but innovation also featured strongly – not least in relation to the women's movement. Co-education was always the norm in Scotland's scattered towns and parishes, but in cities secondary education for girls developed through single-sex schools. Known from their locations as Queen Street and George Square, Edinburgh's two Merchant Company girls' schools (opened in 1870 and the following year) were staffed by men in the early decades as a mark of their serious purpose. Although Latin results in the Leaving Certificate lagged behind those of boys, the academic emphasis was much the same and university education followed on. Separate from what was then reserved for men, in 1886 St George's Training College started to prepare the first female secondary teachers in Scotland. Pioneering head-mistresses received their inspiration there at a time when Moray House was only for elementary teachers. Cranley School developed an integrated curriculum in which laboratory work proved beneficial to future women doctors, although scholarly St George's High School resisted physical science along with domestic science. St Trinnean's, under another Training College head, was 'the school where they did what they liked' – not in the wild way caricatured by Ronald Searle but through a progressive emphasis on self-organised work. It is worth adding that only in Scotland's fee-paying girls' schools was corporal punishment unknown.

Classical boys' schools maintained the tradition of humane letters, but during the Victorian era both High School and Academy lost pupils to a third force in the New Town. The Edinburgh Institution limited optional Latin to two hours a day with the rest of what was later called a 'cafeteria' curriculum given over to subjects of greater relevance to the business world such as modern languages, mathematics and drawing. There was a six-year course on offer but most only attended for their last year or two of schooling, and they did so in such numbers as to make the Institution one of Edinburgh's largest schools. A flexible approach meant that a pupil might be in the fifth class for English and the third for mathematics. What most impressed visitors was the emphasis on science, with chemistry experiments conducted by groups under the supervision of a master who had studied under Bunsen at Heidelberg. The Institution ('possibly the best school in Scotland') barely survived the Merchant Company challenge before it rose again between the wars as Melville College.

The Edinburgh Academy was also a failing school (according to its chronicler Magnus Magnusson) that was turned round by a rector who came from teaching at Loretto School in Musselburgh. There he had been enthused by the progressive ideas of Hely Hutchinson Almond. A statue of a boy in shorts and open-necked shirt celebrates Almond's commitment to fresh air and exercise: there was no childhood obesity there. Compulsory games spread from Loretto to other schools which acquired the spacious playing fields that most visibly mark them out as different today. Success at rugby, destined to become the defining sport for boys' schools, was fully achieved at Loretto. Seven Old Lorettonians were selected for one Oxford XV, and both captains in another Varsity match learned to scrimmage on Loretto's pitches beside the River Esk. Almond was the innovator who persuaded his boys (with some difficulty) to pass before they were tackled.

Team games apart (the head still played for the school cricket eleven as a white-bearded veteran), Loretto was a school where pupils exercised a responsibility that came close to self-government. When Almond was away from Musselburgh he left the head boy in charge: calling this a prefect system hardly does justice to what was transmitted to the Academy, and also to Melville by another Loretto master. The rest, including girls' schools, followed. Almond was always seeking ways to break down barriers between pupils and teachers, and his ideas were shared with the boys before being published as *Sermons by a Lay Head-Master*. Modern emphasis on curriculum and assessment would have been dismissed by him as mere 'information', trailing behind character, physique, intelligence and manners as the objects of education. A final general point on private school influence finds Loretto an exception for casting ties and caps aside. School uniforms were a stigma of hospital charity to the Victorians but that changed in the twentieth century. During the inter-war period it became a punishable offence to wear an unbuttoned blazer or walk out without regulation headgear. Uniforms, though less precisely defined, nowadays tend to be seen as good for any school.

INTO CO-EDUCATION

Private schools for young ladies offered 'accomplishments' like music and modern languages – never Latin, or maths for that matter. They gave way to small girls' schools in private houses emphasising family atmosphere. High post-war demand kept them in business but during the final third of last century it became clear that the time for small single-sex schools had passed. The 1970s saw a shift in the direction of co-education, in the west with 'Hutchie' (Hutchesons' Grammar) and the High School of Glasgow though not yet the two academies. In Edinburgh, George Watson's Ladies' College moved to the boys' school en bloc; Heriot's opened its impressive doors to girls at all levels; and Fettes set a cautious example of sixth form admissions. The Edinburgh Academy is the latest school to have followed that beginning with a second step, after consultation with parents, into full co-education. St Margaret's expanded on Edinburgh's South Side while other girls' schools merged or closed, helping the expansion, but then it also proved too small for the modern world. A St Meg's head laid some of the blame on rush-hour traffic, with parents looking for a single 'drop off' for their sons and daughters.

As a particular example common to three cities, convent education came to an end in Aberdeen, Edinburgh and Glasgow. Kilgraston near Perth was opened by Sisters of the Sacred Heart but today it flourishes as a girls' school (50 per cent more boarders in recent years) without any talk of Catholic ethos. Academic results are excellent, so that high numbers should not be attributed merely to its development as an equestrian centre. In November 2011, Kilgraston won Independent School of the Year, a UK award. St Margaret's in Aberdeen is presented rather fully as 'the only remaining school in the North of Scotland that caters exclusively to girls' education in primary and secondary departments', while old hockey rivals Albyn went through the process of taking in boys. This began at S1, and full co-education has only just been achieved. Glasgow's Craigholme School continues to supply a demand for what was once available through Park School and Laurel Bank. Edinburgh offers a choice of single-sex education in two forms. The campuses of merged Stewart's-Melville and Mary Erskine a mile apart are used flexibly to educate primary stage boys and girls together, then separately during five years of adolescence before coming together again for sixth year studies. The arrangement, which was certainly not planned from the start, now operates as Erskine Stewart's Melville Schools. Meanwhile stand-alone St George's – which once took pride in being smaller than the Merchant Company schools – faces the future confidently thanks to 1,000 girls aged 2 to 18. On the gender question, and with Albyn still all-girl then at the top, it is worth recording that three of the top four places for Advanced Higher success (percentage-wise) in 2010 included the Aberdeen school along with Kilgraston and St George's.

Merchiston, on the southern edge of Edinburgh, still thrives as a single-sex school for boys, with increased numbers of day scholars joining the boarders in class. Scotland's top A-Level results were achieved there in 2009. Merchiston's management team consider they are dealing with a niche market. Kilts were always an alternative form of uniform in Scottish schools of this kind, and not only in pipe bands leading cadets to camp. It is therefore surprising to find school tartans devised for girls, co-ed as well as single-sex, who wear them pleated or as plaid skirts. St Meg's may have misjudged in allowing pupils to choose their own tartans as a permitted alternative to uniform green. For girls and boys (the latter no longer forced into teenage shorts) berets and caps have gone the way of hats for adults. The ethos-building value of uniform is recognised at St George's, but this school with its age-old commitment to female education lets final-year students attend in smart street clothes. Power-dressing in business and the professions no doubt lies ahead.

CURRICULUM AND EXAMINATIONS

In terms of curriculum development the top levels of the 5–14 programme were implemented sooner in private all-through schools than in state schools seeking to bridge the primary–secondary gap. The early secondary years do not distinguish greatly between private and public, either in subjects covered or in the smaller class size which is often seen as the main reason for paying fees. Advantage is however taken of opportunities to use secondary subject teachers (and facilities) in art, music and physical education for the benefit of primary children. The main differences are to be found in upper secondary classes. Higher than average numbers in sixth year (or two-year sixth form for those on an English syllabus) make for a wider choice of subjects.

Mindful of the market, the managers of fine old buildings like the Edinburgh Academy have invested in state-of-the-art science centres. As early as the 1988 St George's centenary the school's first scientist-headmistress announced that, although many young people were avoiding the subject, her pupils were going 'in the opposite direction to the national trend: more pupils are now taking the sciences than taking the arts, and next year Physics is the most popular A-Level subject.' It may be noted in passing that this highly academic school has never allocated class places or ended the summer term with a prize-giving ceremony. During the last five years, independent schools have matched or bettered the national rise in take up of maths and science. St Leonards hosts a Techno Challenge Day for Fife schools: 'The pupils have a fantastic time taking part in a variety of activities which range from using their maths skills to solve problems to using hands-on skills to design and build rockets' (*Sunday Times*, 18 September 2011).

A remarkably wide-ranging approach to learning is to be found at the Steiner School in Edinburgh. It is the oldest of four in Scotland, with Waldorf an alternative label. Self-consciously different (always co-educational, never in uniform, eurhythmics instead of rugby) it trains its own teachers for an approach to children's learning which has needed to change surprisingly little in seventy years. Natural materials such as wood find favour at kindergarten, formal skills like reading are postponed to age six or seven, and electronic screens are kept in check. No early television and no computers until the end of Lower School at fourteen do not seem to hamper the development of eager learners. The Steiner system (a thousand schools worldwide) encourages imagination through art, craft, drama and stories. The 'soft skills' otherwise described as emotional intelligence are valued alongside analytical learning. Substantial time set aside at all levels for Main Lessons – topics such as astronomy or architecture studied in four-week blocks – might be expected to lower examination pass rates. In fact the Steiner School's 2011 Higher passes at A–C were among Scotland's best at 95.7 per cent.

Although league tables comparing examination success are common south of the border, SCIS schools – and Scottish education in general – have resisted them. As with those for local authorities, private school results appear in alphabetical order. Within the independent sector comparison is made difficult by the fact that a substantial minority (boarding schools in particular) work towards English A-Level. The two-year International Baccalaureate – there is no other qualification on offer at St Leonards Upper Sixth – adds a further complication, but overall comparisons can be made. Higher passes are achieved by 90 per cent at those independent schools that present pupils for them and 77 per cent for Scotland as a whole. More important (in terms of the university entry which these exams are mainly about) 49.6 per cent of private school students achieved Grade A in their 2011 S5 Higher results compared with 26.05 per cent in all schools. Advanced Higher (in its tenth year and thought to be more demanding than A-Level) provides a common target for both sectors in the last year of education. Private schools have improved their success in this qualification by 20 per cent over the last three years and the latest figures show their Advanced Higher pass rate to be 90.9 per cent (with 47 per cent at Grade A) compared with 79.4 per cent overall. This contributed largely to independent school results which *The Sunday Times* for 18 September 2011 described as 'little short of sensational'. Schools and SCIS are trying to persuade higher education authorities to acknowledge Advanced Higher more fully.

For many years the effect of 'creaming' able children from state schools into fee-paying ones has called into question the comparing of results. There can be no question about the unfairness of the comparison, although the differences between city districts may have even greater effects. Independent schools are not restricted to a catchment area in the way that neighbourhood schools generally are. Furthermore, where there is sufficient demand (waiting lists implied) they are able to select through entrance tests. Hutchesons' Grammar School, named by *The Sunday Times* for 13 November 2011 as Scotland's Independent School of the Year, accepts 150 out of 250 applicants at the start of secondary education. Presentation policies also vary, but there is no reason to suppose that Glenalmond was unusual in obtaining a rise in A-Level results in that year (notably in A* grades) while presenting the entire age group. The exam success of independent schools may be partly explained by the social class of parents. Beyond any parent effect, however, the positive outcomes due to private education's dedication to achievement can scarcely be doubted.

BEYOND THE CLASSROOM

Parents do not choose a school on the basis of its examination results. A 'State of the Nation' survey reported by *The Scotsman* some years ago (30 April and 4 May 2001) found that the three main reasons given for choosing to pay fees were a higher standard of education, individual attention in smaller classes and the opportunity for pupils to realise their full potential. Annual SCIS surveys have confirmed this on a regular basis. Other perceived advantages like exam results, a wider curriculum and better discipline come well behind, while bringing up the rear are better facilities and – dull phrase for happy times – extra-curricular activities. These last are now being described as 'co-curricular' for the way they are thought to complement classroom work. However that may be, offering a choice of twenty sporting activities or filling public concert halls to showcase musical talent demonstrates how serious these schools are about building confidence and helping pupils to 'realise their full potential'. Public speaking in preparation for success in adult life is an obvious one. When 400 teenagers gathered at Dundee in August 2011 for the World Schools Debating Championships, members of the Scotland team were all privately educated.

'Beyond the classroom' is one way of describing these activities, although basic school trips involving large numbers at all ages must count for more than a few seniors climbing mountains in Greenland. Belhaven Hill at Dunbar brings East Lothian beaches into the life of the school; Clifton Hall (outside Edinburgh at Newbridge) makes a feature of 'outdoor classrooms'. But travel to remote places can be useful, as when help is given to African villagers. Reports of interesting expeditions help in the increasingly important area of marketing. The school magazines which began by reaching out to former pupils are now colourful productions directed, at least in part, towards parents and potential parents. A final point of comparison may be made. Some time ago state school teachers withdrew from out-of-school activities in search of better pay and conditions. That situation no longer obtains, but their private school opposite numbers are probably more committed to putting in extra hours after the bell. Sometimes they are paid above the national salary scales in recognition of that voluntary effort.

COSTS OF PRIVATE EDUCATION

According to SCIS director John Edward, 'The financial climate is an enormous challenge for families, teachers and schools – but one that, to date, our sector has met with confidence, pragmatism and innovation' (*Sunday Times*, 18 September 2011). Fees for session 2011–12 averaged £3,318 a term for senior day school students and £8,693 for boarders, having risen by just under the rate of inflation. In contrast to the current debate about fees in higher education, transparency is a feature of school prospectuses – and also of websites which now include video clips. The SCIS (to whom around 1,000 telephone inquiries about choice of school are made each year) also has a website which makes it easy for parents to compare what is provided apart from tuition: some schools include textbooks in the price but only give jotters to juniors. Most of them offer 'sibling discounts' when more than one member of a family is on the roll. Every effort is made to ease the burden, and direct debit allows fees to be spread over the session. Financial advisers report, however, that few parents take advantage of schemes designed to spread the cost over a longer period. The great majority appear to pay out of income, although the contribution of grandparents is an unknown quantity.

Schools originally endowed for the relief of family hardship have always responded to a sudden reduction in home circumstances, perhaps due to the death of a parent. Bursaries have also been available for armed forces families and for teachers, but substantial sums of money are now being made available to parents who cannot afford full fees. Means-tested bursaries are increasingly on offer, and at schools of very different sizes. There are five free places at 300-pupil Cargilfield ('Scotland's first prep school') with a further nine pupils having their fees reduced. At the other end of the spectrum Hutchesons' Grammar with 1,500 on the roll assists 10 per cent of its secondary entrants. Overall the sums made available to families through scholarships and bursaries have risen from £12.5 million in 2005 to £35 million in 2011. Perhaps Duncan McLaren's question – 'When is this transfer from poor to rich to stop?' – is being answered at last.

Some of that money was formerly bequeathed for the children of fathers in occupations which have since declined, such as farming or mining. Recent changes by the Office of the Scottish Charity Regulator (OSCR) have made it easier to redirect funds more generally, but the remarkable rise of recent years stems from questions raised at Westminster about the tax-reduced charitable status accorded to independent schools. The Charities and Trustee Investment (Scotland) Act of 2005 set in motion a process by which OSCR is investigating 'public benefit' in the private sector. Twelve schools have now met criteria which are mainly to do with widening access. Much of the money previously reserved for scholarships (awarded on the basis of an entrance test) is now being channelled into means-tested bursaries. The latest to pass were Hutchesons' Grammar, Lomond School in Helensburgh, Merchiston and St Leonards after a two-year consultation process. Former Director of SCIS Judith Sischy pointed out in the last edition that 'taking into account the savings to the public purse of educating 31,500 children, the independent sector in Scotland estimates that it saves the country over 35 times as much as it receives in financial benefits . . .' (Sischy, 2008, p. 93).

INDEPENDENT SCHOOLS AND SCOTTISH EDUCATION

Each school has to secure its own future, although working within the SCIS structure helps. As economic conditions point towards a double dip recession, the sector's current success may possibly become harder to sustain. Independent schools are always liable to close or merge. That would not necessarily mean a decline in private education: the merging of pupils must explain why closing St Margaret's in Edinburgh did not register as a fall in overall numbers. For reasons to do with pupil: teacher ratio and capital investment the cost of educating a pupil in the independent sector is high, although size makes this less of a factor. George Watson's put its new sports centre swimming pool on hold for a while but it is now under construction. All-through city day schools like Watson's are better positioned for whatever may lie ahead than small ones in more isolated settings.

Prior to the 1999 general election 29 per cent of Scots wanted private education banned compared with 19 per cent in England. Since then fee-paying has become less of a political issue, with opinion polls showing lower levels of public hostility. New Labour values and the decline of the Labour Party in Scotland have combined to make it harder to sustain a case for abolition. Many SNP-voting Scots live in areas served by small-town comprehensives where there is no example of private education. That would largely explain why many parents say they would not consider sending their children to a private school. However a greater number of Scottish parents now tell pollsters that they would make use of the independent sector if they could afford it. Widening access should strengthen that attitude.

There is more support for parental choice than at any time since John Highet's *A School of One's Choice* appeared in 1969. No scholar followed up that broad sociological study of fee-paying in Scotland, and the independent sector has also been reticent on its own behalf. Now, however, there is a new feeling of outward-looking confidence. Private school facilities such as sports centres, playing fields and even specialist subject-teaching are increasingly being made available to others. Independent schools are represented on the Scottish Qualifications Authority Advisory Council, Curriculum for Excellence Management Board, the Scottish Teachers' Superannuation Scheme and the General Teaching Council. There is respect in both directions for headteachers and staff who are seen as fellow-professionals, sharing good practice for the benefit of all. The title of the latest SCIS report makes this explicit: 'Commitment, Contribution, Collaboration'.

REFERENCES

Almond, Hely Hutchinson (1886) *Sermons by a Lay Head-Master*. Edinburgh: n.p.
Highet, J. (1969) *A School of One's Choice: A Sociological Study of the Fee-paying Schools of Scotland*. London: Blackie.
Magnusson, M. (1974) *The Clacken and the Slate: The Story of the Edinburgh Academy, 1824–1974*. London: Collins.
Roberts, A. (2007, 2010) *Crème de la Crème: Girls' Schools of Edinburgh*. London: Steve Savage.
Roberts, A. (2009) *Ties that Bind: Boys' Schools of Edinburgh*. London: Steve Savage.
Sischy, J. (2008) 'The independent sector', in T. G. K. Bryce and W. M. Humes (eds), *Scottish Education, Third Edition: Beyond Devolution*. Edinburgh: Edinburgh University Press, pp. 90–7.
The Scotsman, 30 April and 4 May 2001.
The Sunday Times, 18 September 2011.

Website

Scottish Council of Independent Schools at http://scis.org.uk/schools

12

Alternative Forms of Schooling

Helen E. Lees

Scotland, provincial Scotland, is outwith the current of modern [educational] experiment.

A. S. Neill, 1936, p. 22

The title of this chapter is apt. It highlights the status of much alternative education in the context of Scottish education as a whole. For, alternative education – here defined as along a spectrum from radical to complementary and comprising various practices that can be close to or very different from a standard model school education – is often seen as an alternative to such schooling. This perception determines its status as marginal and other, in ways that are detrimental educationally across all forms of practice. In Scotland, if alternative education is seen as marginal it keeps it away, I suggest, from being able to inform mainstream practice, yet it has a role to play there. For instance it has much to offer an understanding of Curriculum for Excellence (CfE) that is still to be appreciated. Ironically, seeing alternative education as an alternative form of schooling is an educational mistake. Why?

NO ALTERNATIVE FORM

First from the perspective of alternative education: when radically alternative, it does not see itself either as an alternative to schooling, nor as a form, as the chapter title innocently suggests. It sees itself as education in its own right. This is without any necessary reference or conceptual juxtaposition to a school or schooling. Semantic bickering it seems, perhaps, but the consequences of not problematising the chapter title's construction allows sub-standard perceptions and sometimes difficult outcomes for education that is alternative. Also, radical alternative education that functions without coercive elements and prioritises emotional freedoms, as can be found in democratic schooling (e.g. A. S. Neill, 1968) and autonomous home education (e.g. Thomas and Pattison, 2007), enjoys a formlessness of practice contrasting strongly with the mostly predictable established structure and strictures of schooled experience. These structures and strictures are seen as such from the viewpoint of an alternative field of education: uniforms, compulsory lesson attendance and little choice in content, pace and nature of the curriculum are seen from this perspective as negative educational features and not helpful. The alternative perspective is interested in addressing issues of the curriculum in other ways and certainly freer ways. Their view is that substantial freedoms in education are more radically responsive and responsible to individuals but also more naturally in tune with what it means to be human (a question still to be answered . . .), rather than what it means to be socially and politically constituted. For instance, choosing what one learns, and when, is a natural feature for a student in a radically alternative educational setting.

Scottish schooling, as occurring with a standardised model – as much of the rest of this book inevitably discusses – is educational anathema to many 'alternative forms of schooling'. The differences between worlds of practice can be educationally profound. Whether the practice is radically different, as mentioned above briefly, or merely complementary to standard model school attendance, such as with Polish classes at the weekend or Forest School sessions (discussed below), the practice functions in ways different to a Scottish school. Alternatives – but especially radical alternatives – get away from a normal concept of schooling and the education we have all come to expect from schooling in a standard model, wherever and whenever they can. They believe they can do better. They delight in being different and perhaps for sound educational reasons. These reasons are perhaps those that make alternative education an educational field strongly characterised by reports of joy and personal and interpersonal ease (Lees, 2011; Stronach and Piper, 2008). From this perspective of joy, the traumas of standard or mainstream model schooling look substantial. A distain and dislike of such schooling offerings can be a strong feature of much alternative education discourse. This is often informed initially by accounts of bad personal experiences caused by encounters with schooling, which then develops into a wider perspective of the social and political as requiring another and different way forward.

So alternative education in Scotland can be seen as not just complementary, adjunct or alternative but a domain of its own, functioning on its own terms, with its own conversations and which can justifiably demand to be seen on its own terms. It is certainly operating far from the 'deep conservatism of the Scottish teaching profession' that Humes identifies (Humes, 2011, p. 67).

A CONCEPT OF OTHERNESS

To see alternative education in Scotland as an alternative form of schooling is one error that Scottish educational studies can make. The second is to underestimate the importance that alternative practice can have for providing educational options with regard to the right of a parent to educate their child or children in line with their own views, as supported by the 1948 United Nations *Universal Declaration of Human Rights*. If Scottish parents have no concept of alternatives to standard model schooling; if they have never considered their legal right to home educate as an option; if they persistently believe that children need to go to school by law; if they do not know about other ways for education to happen, then how can they ask schools to consider alternative practice? How can parents follow what they really want in the way of education for their children?

Also, and importantly, at the level of the key providers of most access to educational experiences: when alternatives to schooling are seen as just that – mere alternatives – does it mean that Scottish teachers are automatically not trained meaningfully for and with alternative practices but only for one educational type of provision, which is standard Scottish schooling? Even if academic lip-service is paid to alternative practice with a video about Summerhill or a brief introduction to the concept of home education, then left to one side, is this enough to suggest that education is diverse in modality of theory and practice so that teachers can be fully informed about what education is or might be? So far, the concept of otherness, reflected either in part or profoundly in the practice I now move to discuss, has been neglected and underestimated for its possible benefits in Scottish educational studies, it seems.

THE BENEFITS OF ALTERNATIVE PRACTICE FOR THE SCOTTISH MAINSTREAM?

In Scotland it is possible to imagine that a fundamental deep rethink of a Scottish educational world might bear fruit for initiatives such as the interestingly and promisingly different CfE. This initiative is said to have been broadly welcomed by teachers but is suffering from constraints because teachers do not feel they have enough agency. Sedimented structural schooling issues are showing themselves to be insufficiently responsive and flexible to the alternative approach that CfE offers schools (see Priestley, Chapter 3). Of course, a fundamental deep rethink looks the same as saying 'aims to engage teachers in thinking from first principles', as the Scottish Executive suggested in 2006 can be done by teachers through the CfE, as outlined in their document *A Curriculum for Excellence: Progress and Proposals*. The trouble is that the first principles the Scottish Executive identify may be ones that come only from a conceptual conflation of education with standard school practices and exclude alternative educational thinking. This is a Scottish educational mistake, especially given signs that Scotland is a potential world leader with a curriculum that, at least on paper, takes a bold and educationally important alternative approach.

So I suggest that the distinctive history of the Scottish form of education (see Humes and Bryce, Chapter 13) and a national pride in its 'supposed superiority' (see Anderson, Chapter 22), as found in achievements of a standard-school model (tests and assessment oriented), may be working against new Scottish interests. Nevertheless, the landscape of perspectives and visions of education in Scotland is changing. One of the drivers for this is technology. Where previously it was necessary to travel to and then enter a school building to meet teachers, now teaching can and does come in many different ways to a child through electronic devices. At the very least, this can trouble the necessity of schooling in the sense of physically going to a school at all, as Macbeath points out in the context of Highland and Island children receiving lesson work as mp3 downloads (see MacBeath, Chapter 107). Indeed, a situation in the not-too-distant future where all Scottish children have friends who go to school and friends who do not – at least for part of the time via flexi-schooling options – is possible.

THE *SIGN* OF THE ALTERNATIVE

As has been perhaps apparent in the above introduction, what an 'alternative form of schooling' actually is, is not only thorny as an issue, but complicated. In order to simplify matters a cursory spectrum was introduced, from radical to complementary, to include the experience of education that can seem sometimes close to schooled experience but also is or becomes spontaneously and without question utterly formless. But this is a conceptual construct to help the discussion rather than a truth statement: for alternative education to be alternative it must not and ought not to be pinned down like a butterfly, to a particular truth of what it is because this truth is always up for continual renegotiation in line with the views of its stakeholders. Practitioners of such education are in charge and can change such education. This fundamentally includes the children in the equation of decision making.

In terms of the complexity of alternatives for educational studies, one example is semantic or semiotic: 'Alternative Education Provision' can be used as a term in England and elsewhere, such as America, for state-organised, funded provision for children who are not being served in standard schools because of exclusion, ill health and other reasons. Such English schools are alternative education provision set up by local authorities, schools, community and voluntary organisations. These cater for young people for whom standard schooling is a failing scenario. In Scotland this is not different. For example, the term 'Alternative Education Support Centre' is used for a state-funded special school based in Kennoway, Fife.

Just because radically different styles of educational practice also use the label 'alternative' does not mean, of course, that state-funded education of whatever kind cannot itself be alternative to something. But in this sharing of the word amongst various domains and styles of practice is the crux of what it means for Scotland and Scottish education to take part in alternatives. A lack of conceptual access especially, to what radical alternatives of theory and practice might mean for Scottish education, and furthermore a dearth of examples (see below) is a limitation on the imagination for possibilities. The practice as outlined below that does exist in Scotland offers a window on options that can be identified as educational signs. Scottish educational studies requires new signs for its educational landscape in order for Scotland to form an enriched educational vocabulary. These signs or goods and the shop window that displays them on Scottish terms (rather than borrowing from American practice, for instance) is currently rather bare and for development.

To say the least, Scotland is currently not overwhelmed by progressive educational ventures. Such ventures would visibly, verbally and emotionally eschew a standardised schooling model where uniform is expected, where there is no use of first names for teachers, where students are often unquestionably obliged to do as staff tell them, where attendance at particular lessons at particular times is compulsory, a regularly repeated curriculum holds sway and so on. Only a small history of once vibrant experimental schooling, functioning without some or all of these elements, exists to show now how little actual schooling diversity at a modality (forms of theory and practice) level there is in Scotland.

A HISTORY OF OTHER-WISE EDUCATION IN SCOTLAND

Schools

> All I have done has been to prove that a school doesn't need to be a school. And my objection to
> Scots schools is that they are schools.
>
> A. S. Neill, 1936, p. 26

For non-standardised school education in the form of a school (defined here in a rudimentary way as a building with students and staff in attendance for the sake of education), there have been historically a small number of radical alternative schools in Scotland. I would list amongst them three genuinely radical alternative schools that practised a fundamentally different philosophy and theory of education than was to be found in the schools that surrounded them: Kilquhanity in Galloway, near Castle Douglas (1940–97), the Barns Hostel School in Peeblesshire (1940–53) and Braehead School in Buckhaven, Fife (1957–68). I define their status as genuinely alternative in the radical sense, by virtue of the nature of the organisation and management of the schools as either fully democratic in line with the philosophy of educational progressives such as A. S. Neill (quoted throughout this chapter), a Scot from Angus, who founded and ran the famous Summerhill School in Suffolk, England. Neill believed in emotional freedom above learning facts and figures (Neill, 1968). The first two of these Scottish schools mentioned above can be seen as also fully in line with the theory and practice of other progressive educationists such as Homer Lane, who ran a democratically organised school in Dorset, England, called the Little Commonwealth and who was an inspiration for A. S. Neill and others such as W. B. Curry, a headmaster of the progressive Dartington School in Devon, England.

Kilquhanity School was set up for students between the ages of 5 and 18 by John and Morag Aitkenhead. It ran a farm and had a regular democratically organised meeting to adjudicate issues and problems and organise the running of the school, including the 'daily work'. The children did household chores on a daily basis and this was seen as a part of their education in guiding them towards a sense of community and responsibility for self and others (Aitkenhead, 1962). Distinct from Summerhill School, run by A. S. Neill (see above), Kilquhanity expected children, once they had signed up to a particular set of lessons, to turn up regularly. This was seen by John Aitkenhead as appropriate, given that a teacher commits to a student. He saw non-attendance to lessons where commitment had been indicated by a child as antithetical to educational progress (Aitkenhead, 1962).

The Barns Hostel School was run by David Wills. This school was established by the Edinburgh Society of Friends (Quakers) for boys who had emotional difficulties that meant wartime evacuation into families was a problem. Wills ran the school along democratic lines and had the full support of the school's proprietors for his direction of the nature of the environment. He wrote books (*The Barns Experiment* and *Throw Away Thy Rod*) outlining his theory, practice and approaches. These qualify him to be thought of as a Scottish educational theorist-author of alternative practice, in the same vein as A. S. Neill and John Aitkenhead. Both Kilquhanity and the Barns Hostel School are what, it is suggested here, fall into the category of radical alternative schools in Scotland.

R. F. Mackenzie's headship of the Braehead School (1957–68) was a very unusual experiment in bringing the kinds of belief in non-coercion and non-punishment of children that worked well for Neill, Lane, Wills, the Aitkenheads, Curry and others, to a state-funded and state-managed school (Humes, 2011). Mackenzie was a man who considered that such radically alternative ways of educating ought to be accessible to children who came from families for whom private school fees, such as at Kilquhanity, were out of the question. The school was not run along fully radical alternative lines as with the other two schools mentioned, but there were strong threads of democratic management and child autonomy introduced into and affecting the school day. Mackenzie also felt that outward bound activities in the Scottish countryside were vitally educationally important for the children he served in the mining community of Buckhaven.

Home Education

> You cannot write about education and think only of schools.
>
> A. S. Neill, 1936, p. 75

Home education in Scotland has a history that is, of course, as long as educational history in Scotland. Nevertheless what is available as written documentation in the public domain on this subject is extremely limited. For the sake of this chapter it was not possible to find (at the time of writing) a single academic document discussing home education in Scotland as a focus. It may be that this is the first attempt to publish any form of history. It may also be the first public writing in an academic context on the subject of home education in Scotland. If these claims are indeed valid, this is a strange and startling educational situation and one telling of the response of Scottish educationists to alternatives. As mentioned before, they have previously been largely ignored in Scottish educational studies. Elsewhere in the English speaking world, the literature on home education is extremely extensive (see www. indiana.edu/~homeeduc/index.html).

What is perhaps most interesting for Scottish educational studies is the fundamental lack of strong differentiation in Scottish home education to practice in England. The only strong difference in practice in either country is the legal need for families choosing to home educate in Scotland to gain permission from the local council to withdraw their child from a school. The homogeny of home education practice (including issues and concerns) around the world is a political indicator of the position of this form of education as extra-national. This highlights the very distinctiveness of the creation of Scottish school education as nationally oriented (Humes and Bryce, Chapter 13) but also shows that not all education in Scotland is coloured by the blue and white flag. An educational situation escaping and able to escape the constraints and demands of national interests is, of course, both at one and the same time a release from any state failures regarding education and an area of interesting problematisation with regard to democratic social and community initiatives.

In Scotland, as in other areas of the UK, home education has been historically – since 1980 when it became clear that numbers of home educators were on the increase – a topic of public and private contestation between parents practising within the law and officials, often operating without proper conceptual knowledge of that law. Guidelines were published in December 2007 (Scottish Government, 2007), following a lengthy conversation with home educators and their representative organisations such as Scottish based Schoolhouse and the UK organisation Education Otherwise, who claimed they were not being adequately consulted. These guidelines are (rightfully) careful to state: 'This revised guidance has been developed following consultation with interested parties.'(Scottish Government, 2007, p. 2) because previous versions were deemed by practitioners to be outwith an appropriate framework. The purpose of such a document is to assist families and local authorities in navigating a relationship that spans the territory of state educational law and the private home: a territory that is usually only encountered in school settings when there are substantial problems, requiring parents to be answerable to outside agencies. It is perhaps for this reason, amongst others outside of the remit of this chapter, that home education is often and erroneously conflated with safeguarding concerns such as parental abuse of children. This conflation occurred with much controversy during the Badman Review of Elective Home Education in England (see Lees, 2011, for an overview of the debacle) and remains an ongoing aggravation in Scottish home education circles. It occurs because of substantial ignorance about home education that is common around the world.

CURRENT ALTERNATIVE PRACTICE IN SCOTLAND

> If education is learning then Scotland is educated, but if education is creation then Scotland is uneducated.
>
> A. S. Neill, 1936, p. 11

At present the most significant form of an alternative to (standard) schooling in Scotland is home education. Numbers of home-educating families and the children involved are difficult to gauge as there is no compulsion in law on families to signify to local authorities that their children are not attending a school, if those children have never been registered for school attendance. In 2009, the Scottish Government estimated in *A National Statistics Publication for Scotland: Children Educated Outwith School* that around 755 children in Scotland were being home educated (0.1 per cent of the population). This is an underestimation because it only captures a figure of children who are known to the local authorities, having been removed from a school by their parents or having been declared, or otherwise noticed. The real figure is likely to be much more than this and possibly much more than double because many parents interested in home education never register their children for schooling, there being no legal obligation to do so. Conroy highlights the situation in the UK regarding a rise in numbers of home educators with the following: 'Recent estimates in Britain suggest that the numbers in home education have grown from somewhere between 10,000 and 20,000 in 1998 to something in excess of 150,000 in 2007' (Conroy, 2010, p. 330). There is no reason to believe that Scotland is different in following such a pattern.

Apart from not knowing how many home educators there are in Scotland, the nature of the home education that takes place is also hard to define. What is clear is that home education is comprised of many styles and occurs for a number of reasons: from a reaction to severe peer bullying and/or school-based teaching failures, to philosophical aspirations relating to lifestyle. Furthermore, adopting home education practice for a family can be life-changing, for instance ushering in new ways of relating to the world and society that are said to be more holistic and environmentally aware (see, for example, Lees, 2011 and its links to other relevant literature on this matter). One of the very surprising things about some home education practice known as autonomous style home education – where children decide for themselves, at their own pace, how and what to learn – is that it is successful, through use of spontaneous conversations and the everyday as a cultural apprenticeship, for learning resulting in effective educational outcomes in line with and even potentially exceeding schooling provision (Thomas and Pattison, 2007). Without a teacher, children pick things up naturally in ways that challenge a notion of having to learn from books and teachers at regular and set times.

Other kinds of radical alternative educational activity in Scotland are happening in small-scale and emergent ways. Kilquhanity has been reopened since 2006 as a 'Children's Village', having been bought by a Japanese educationist called Shinichiro Hori who is an admirer and supporter of the work of A. S. Neill. Children from Japan-based democratic schools owned and run by Hori come over to Galloway for part of the year to learn from practical construction hands-on 'doing' tasks in project weeks, study English as a foreign language, follow an 'integrated studies' curriculum and participate in UK cultural events and usually access local artists, musicians and dancers for instruction. In 2012, local families near Kilquhanity approached Andrew Pyle, the co-head, with a view to exploring the reopening of the school if appropriate financial support could be found.

In the way of non-state-funded and non-state-organised alternative community language education activity little is known. In a 2001 article in the *International Journal of Inclusive Educational Researcher*, McPake and Powney put a dearth of research down to 'a lack of commitment throughout Scottish society to issues affecting minority ethnic groups' (5 (2–3): 155). There is a similar Scottish pattern with regard to home educators. The same lack of interest in genuinely engaging with otherness can also be seen in attitudes to traveller education, which operates according to mindsets that are not mainstream. However, recent revised guidelines on traveller education at least show a genuine attempt at sensitivity to difference in its approach, even if this does not always translate into school practices.

In the Camphill school communities of Aberdeen, 'vulnerable' children between the ages of 5 and 16, 'many with learning disabilities', go to a school that has therapeutic features, inspired by the thought of Rudolf Steiner. In Edinburgh a Steiner school has been established since 1939 for students aged 6–18 (including a kindergarten for children 3½ to 5). The school uses a curriculum that claims to integrate the arts with science and address different learning styles to develop the whole person. There are other Steiner schools in Glasgow, Moray and Aberdeen. The total number of students in these schools is approximately 500.

In 1994, a group of school students used Room 13 in Caol Primary School, Fort William, to establish and self-manage their own art studio. This has now grown in the UK and around the world with similar studios known as the Room 13 Network, including a further six studios in schools in other parts of Scotland. Room 13 studios have an artist in residence and are run democratically between the students and managed like a business, independently of adult interference or direction.

Also active in Scotland are a number of educational or child-focused activities that feature the forest and the outdoors as learning environment, tool and subject matter. In a recently opened (2007) nature kindergarten in Whistlebrae, near Braco in Perth and Kinross, children spend most of the day outdoors, where the curriculum is based on nature. For older children also, Forest Schools run activities that are mostly experiential sessions or residentials, chiefly attended by students from standard model schooling. These Forest Schools represent a relatively new conceptual setting for learning. Seen as a complement to the usual indoor desk-based style, they are organised by practitioners as an active regular introduction to woodland, often over extended periods.

There are no doubt other alternative education initiatives that fall somehow along a spectrum of radical to complementary practice. I have focused on education for children and young people. However, altogether these initiatives are relatively rare in Scotland compared to the standard model schooling experience for Scottish people of school age. They are beacons in the Scottish landscape for how education can be done in very different ways.

CONCLUSION

This brief overview offers a window onto 'alternative forms of schooling' in Scotland. Those inverted commas refer back to comments at the start of the chapter, where I commented on the slight irony of the chapter title. It gives a flavour of some of the activity that takes place. It also highlights how little of it there is, compared to the hegemony of mainstream schooling activity as educational activity, where the number of standard school students is currently just under 700,000. The shibboleth of the school as Education with a capital 'E' in Scotland is significant. What is clear is that this is not the only opinion or experience on offer but that the concept of otherness is lacking as something of value and for attention. What is also the case is that education is being practised in Scotland in ways that differ greatly from classroom structures that are commonly cemented in everyday consciousness. These forms of learning are not essentially new but they are a radical departure for a Scottish mentality of adhering to the educational norm and they challenge perceptions of educational possibilities in numerous ways which perhaps now have found their moment. The national CfE has many features that are commonly found in educational alternatives: creativity; space to explore; community and cohesion; autonomy and so on. By paying more attention to the diverse, experimental, open, creative and autonomous styles of learning, being and becoming that alternative education practice and theory offers, Scottish schools can only benefit in their own interpretation of what CfE can actually mean in all its possibilities for practice and outcome. The alternative outsider ought to be invited in from the cold into the educational house for a conversation by the mainstream fire.

ACKNOWLEDGEMENTS

Thanks for support with this chapter to Andrew Pyle of Kilquhanity School, Iris Harrison, Walter Humes, Ian Smith and Greg Mannion.

REFERENCES

Aitkenhead, J. (1962) 'Kilquhanity House, Castle Douglas, Scotland', in H. A. T. Child (ed.), *The Independent Progressive School*. London: Hutchinson.

Conroy, J. (2010) 'The state, parenting, and the populist energies of anxiety', *Educational Theory*, 60 (3): 325–40.

Humes, W. (2011) 'R. F. Mackenzie's "Manifesto for the Educational Revolution", *Scottish Educational Review*, 43 (2): 54–70.

Lees, H. E. (2011) 'The gateless gate of home education discovery: What happens to the self of adults upon discovery of the possibility and possibilities of an educational alternative?' Unpublished PhD thesis, University of Birmingham. Online at http://etheses.Bham.Ac.Uk/1570/

Neill, A. S. (1936) *Is Scotland Educated?* London: Routledge.

Neill, A. S. (1968) *Summerhill*. Harmondsworth: Penguin.

Scottish Government (2007) *Home Education Guidance*. Edinburgh: Scottish Government.

Stronach, I. and H. Piper (2008) 'Can liberal education make a comeback? The case of "relational touch" at Summerhill school', *American Educational Research Journal*, 45 (1): 6–37.

Thomas, A. and H. Pattison (2007) *How Children Learn at Home*. London: Continuum.

13

The Distinctiveness of Scottish Education

Walter Humes and Tom Bryce

Education has traditionally been identified as one of the three institutions that mark the social and cultural life of Scotland as distinctive, especially when compared to England (the other two being the law and the church). With the establishment of a Scottish parliament in 1999, and particularly after the election of a minority SNP administration in 2007, followed by a clear SNP victory in 2011, a new focus for the political identity of Scotland has been created. The promise of a referendum on independence in 2014 has meant that the status of Scotland as a nation is at the forefront of constitutional debate. Throughout the post-devolution period education has been high on the agenda of all parties and there has been much reflection on the particular contribution that the educational system has made and continues to make to national life. This chapter attempts to address this issue in a number of ways. It first looks at one influential account of the Scottish educational tradition, before going on to examine its formal distinctiveness as reflected in key educational institutions. It then attempts to uncover the values and principles that underlie the formal structures, noting the views of critics of the dominant Scottish tradition. Finally, it considers possible future directions, taking account both of developments elsewhere in the UK and of international pressures which make it difficult for educational systems to diverge markedly from global trends.

A useful reference point for the discussion that follows can be found in James Scotland's two-volume history of Scottish education, published in 1969. In his final chapter, Scotland attempted to define the Scottish tradition in education. He summed up his interpretation in six propositions which, he suggested, encapsulated the essence of Scottish attitudes towards education:

- Education is, and always has been, of paramount importance in any community.
- Every child should have the right to all the education of which he is capable.
- Such education should be provided as economically and systematically as possible.
- The training of the intellect should take priority over all other facets of the pupil's personality.
- Experiment is to be attempted only with the greatest caution.
- The most important person in the school, no matter what theorists say, is not the pupil but the (inadequately rewarded) teacher. (Scotland, 1969, p. 275)

Much has changed in the period since this list was drawn up and a few of the items no longer seem persuasive, but some at least (the first three?) would still receive widespread endorsement. And although the pride that Scottish people traditionally have had in the quality of their educational system is now held less confidently, belief in the importance of education, its value both for the individual and for society as a whole, remains unshaken. Thousands of Scots, many from modest backgrounds, can testify to the power of education to enrich (in some cases, transform) their lives, and even those who have not themselves done particularly well at school are often anxious that their own children should take advantage of the improved opportunities now open to them. However, the historian Rab Houston inserts a note of caution when he suggests that behind the ideal of egalitarianism invoked by writers on Scottish education from the Reformation onwards 'lay both a firmly elitist version of meritocracy and a socially conservative vision of a limited mass education as a civilizing and pacifying force' (Houston, 2008, p. 64).

These attitudes, whether laudatory or qualified, help to ensure that the position of education in the national consciousness remains strong. Moreover, belief in the worth and purpose of education is linked to the sense of national identity which is regularly invoked to draw attention to the differences between Scottish and English society. This takes the form of a story or 'myth', shaped by history but not always supported by historical evidence, to the effect that Scotland is less class-conscious than England; that ability and achievement, not rank, should determine success in the world; that public (rather than private) institutions should be the means of trying to bring about the good society; and that, even where merit does justify differential rewards, there are certain basic respects – arising from the common humanity of all men and women – in which human beings deserve equal consideration and treatment. Taken together, these features can be summed up in the phrase used by George Davie for the title of his famous book, *The Democratic Intellect* (1961). To describe the democratic intellect as constituting a 'myth' is not to dismiss it as untrue. Gray, McPherson and Raffe make the point that a myth is a narrative that people tell themselves for two reasons – 'first, to explain the world and, second, to celebrate identity and to express values' (*Reconstructions of Secondary Education*, London: Routledge, 1983, p. 39). The extent to which the values are actually achieved in practice is a matter for analysis and interpretation. So too is the question of who promotes the myth and who benefits from it. These are crucial issues that will be revisited later in the chapter.

At this point, however, it is necessary to ground the discussion in some factual information about those features of the day-to-day workings of the Scottish educational system which mark it out as distinctive. How are the differences between Scottish and English education reflected in the experiences of pupils, teachers and parents? What is the significance of these differences? And how do they connect with broader questions of consciousness, identity and values?

FORMAL DISTINCTIVENESS

Perhaps the most potent expression of the distinctiveness of Scottish education is the separate legislative framework which sets out the nature of provision and the agencies responsible for its delivery. Chapter 17 provides full detail of Scottish law as it pertains to education but some preliminary points may be noted here. Legislation is now framed by the Scottish Government and formal responsibility for the system as a whole rests with the First Minister. Prior to devolution, Scottish legislation often (but not always) post-dated statutory provision in England, but it did not always follow an identical pattern. A clear example was the legislation relating to parental choice of school enshrined in the Education Act of 1980 (England and Wales) and the Education (Scotland) Act of 1981. Legislative differences were also evident in the arrangements for school boards in Scotland compared to governing bodies in England, devolved school management in Scotland compared to local financial management in England, and the circumstances that required the opening and maintenance of a Record of Needs for children requiring special educational provision in Scotland compared to the Statement of Needs in England. Subsequent amendments to all of these provisions did not lead to greater uniformity in Scottish and English practice.

One of the first Acts of the Scottish Parliament was the Standards in Scotland's Schools etc. Act 2000. It introduced a new school improvement framework, one part of which set out five national priorities for education under the following headings: achievement and attainment; framework for learning; inclusion and equality; values and citizenship; learning for life. The emphasis on inclusion and equality has been a consistent feature of policy throughout the post-devolution period. Provision for pupils with disabilities and additional support needs has been improved, partly through better diagnosis and programmes catering for diverse requirements of individual pupils. The role of learning support teachers and classroom assistants, working in conjunction with classroom teachers, has also been important. While it was left to schools and authorities to implement the national priorities, the legislative framework required them to formulate improvement and development plans accordingly. This can be seen as a familiar Scottish combination of firm central direction of policy alongside delegation of responsibility for implementation to local government in the interests of democratic accountability.

Evidence of Scottish distinctiveness can be seen in the separate institutional apparatus that maintains the system. There is one national examination body, the Scottish Qualifications Authority (SQA), whereas in the rest of the UK there are several examination boards, ostensibly serving different parts of the country though schools are not confined to entering candidates in the board located in their geographical area. Other important bodies expressive of the separate character of the Scottish system include Education Scotland (ES), which since 2011 has had full responsibility for work previously carried out by two predecessor bodies (Learning and Teaching Scotland and Her Majesty's Inspectorate of Education) and the General Teaching Council for Scotland (GTCS). ES advises the First Minister on all matters relating to the curriculum as they affect the age range 3–18 and has a particular responsibility for leading and supporting the implementation of Curriculum for Excellence (CfE). Unlike in England, there is no formally prescribed national curriculum though, in practice, most schools follow closely the recommendations contained in national documents such as those deriving from CfE. Other areas of activity for which ES has responsibility include: evaluating the quality of educational provision at school, local authority and national levels; encouraging innovation, particularly in the use of educational technology; increasing the system's capacity for self-evaluation and self-improvement; and promoting high-quality professional learning and leadership.

The GTCS, established by statute in 1965, is the body that controls entry to the profession, accredits initial training courses for teachers and has responsibility for assessing whether probationary teachers can proceed to full registration. In April 2012, GTCS changed from being an advisory Non-Departmental Public Body (NDPB) to a fully independent, self-regulatory body under the Public Services Reform (General Teaching Council for Scotland) Order 2011. Among its main areas of activity are setting standards and codes of conduct for teachers, reviewing the training appropriate to teachers, providing opportunities for professional development, and conducting enquiries where there are concerns about teacher competence or misconduct. The GTCS's existence is testimony to the relative status of teaching as a profession in Scotland, compared to England. An English GTC was not established until 1998, with powers that were significantly weaker than those enjoyed by the GTC in Scotland, and only lasted until March 2012, following a decision by the UK Conservative–Liberal Democrat coalition to abolish it.

The way in which the institutional apparatus of Scottish education functions helps to explain a somewhat ironic feature of the system. Although the educational workforce consistently exhibits anti-Conservative tendencies (in a party-political sense), the process of educational advancement nonetheless reflects a kind of determined conservatism. Scotland has never been extreme with its educational innovations: the Scottish approach has always been to integrate innovation firmly into traditional approaches. This is consistent with James Scotland's observation that a feature of the Scottish tradition is that 'experiment is to be attempted only with the greatest caution'. National bodies such as ES and the SQA operate as bureaucracies with established ways of doing things and a concern to ensure that safeguards are built into the system. Most developments are rooted in existing practice, though the rhetoric of CfE has sometimes shifted uneasily between claims that it is a radical reform and assurances that many teachers already teach in ways that are consistent with its recommendations. Key agents of change are members of the inspectorate, a small but powerful group (now part of ES but previously a separate executive agency), who seek to identify and disseminate 'good practice'. Through the exercise of their very considerable informal power, inspectors influence not only the work of schools and the policies of local authorities but also those teacher educators who contribute to educational reform. For major initiatives, the coordinated efforts of all these groups are important and the small size of Scotland is often seen as an advantage in this respect. People tend to know each other and a consensus is perhaps easier to reach than it would be in a larger, more anonymous system. This consensus is often presented as a distinctive and positive feature of Scottish education but it has a downside as well. It can lead to complacency and a failure to question existing practice in the fundamental way that may be needed. The 'practice-driven' approach to curriculum development helps to explain the relative conservatism identified by James Scotland.

Provisions for the testing of pupils have also been different north and south of the border. The Conservative government of the 1990s under John Major tried to put national testing in place in Scotland as it did in England and Wales but considerable resistance from parents, teaching unions and local authorities (particularly Strathclyde Region) resulted in different legislation being enacted in Scotland. As described elsewhere in this volume (Chapter 77), up to 2004 teachers carried out national testing at times of their choosing to check their classroom assessment judgements, and did so by drawing upon available national item-bank test materials. There was, therefore, no centralised capacity to assemble data such as had been used for league tables in England and Wales. Forms of national assessment endeavour to fulfil two purposes, one being accountability and the other being the checking of individual pupil progress. In Scotland, the first of these has been pursued through national monitoring exercises, originally the Assessment of Achievement Programme (AAP) from 1983 until 2004, then the Scottish Survey of Achievement (SSA) from 2005 until 2010, now replaced by the Scottish Survey of Literacy and Numeracy (SSLN) from 2011. The second purpose was pursued by national testing, then superseded by the Assessment is for Learning (AifL) movement, the latter emphatically recognising that the close monitoring of individual pupils can only be done usefully in the classroom. Significantly, however, AifL was dropped from official documentation in session 2010–11 (see Chapter 74).

An important feature of Scottish education for which claims are made in respect of distinctiveness is the breadth of the curriculum available to pupils in schools, and it would be fair to say that all the national programmes – Standard Grade, 5–14, Higher Still and now CfE – have preserved breadth of study. The replacement of Standard Grade and Intermediate courses by National level 4 and 5 awards has not diminished that breadth. CfE was still in the process of implementation as this volume was going to press. As Chapters 3, 41 and 49 indicate, from the primary and secondary perspectives, it is predicated on a recognition that greater diversity and flexibility should be encouraged – to a much greater extent than heretofore – within nationally prescribed guidelines. The principles of challenge, enjoyment, personalisation, choice and relevance imply that curriculum balance is being construed in terms of individual children rather than in terms of time allocation for subjects. While it remains to be seen just how, and how extensively, teachers seize the opportunities afforded to them, the potential for difference from England's more prescribed curriculum is quite significant. The early progress in primary schools does seem encouraging.

Compared with the school system, the formal distinctiveness of Scotland's universities is less clear cut. For most of the twentieth century Scottish universities were seen primarily as United Kingdom institutions and the body responsible for their funding – originally the University Grants Committee (later the University Funding Council) – was accountable to the Department of Education and Science (DES) in London. This position was reviewed from time to time but the consistent message from Scottish University Principals was that they were against the Scottish Office taking over responsibility. Part of the explanation was a desire to retain international standing and a fear that the Scottish Office might try to interfere with academic freedom. These attitudes began to change in the 1980s when, following a major financial exercise involving severe cutbacks, in which there was a feeling that the UGC's understanding of, and sympathy for, the Scottish dimension was deficient, demands for the establishment of a separate Scottish subcommittee of the UGC were voiced. These were initially rejected but the climate had altered and it was only a matter of time before the funding arrangements were revised. In 1992, the Scottish Higher Education Funding Council (SHEFC) became responsible for distributing grants for teaching, research and associated activities in all Scottish higher education institutions. In 2005, SHEFC was replaced by the Scottish Funding Council under the provisions of the Further and Higher Education (Scotland) Act which brought together funding arrangements for both further education colleges and universities. Matters relating to quality assurance in universities, however, continue to be administered on a UK-wide basis under the direction of the Quality Assurance Agency (QAA), a body established in 1997. Similarly, research is assessed on a UK-wide basis – the next assessment is due in 2014 – with the results having important implications for the funding of universities (though the detailed allocation of funds is decided by each country's funding council). During 2011, Scottish universities came under public scrutiny following debates about student fees, cutbacks on staffing, the threatened closure of courses and concerns about a serious divide between management and academic staff. This led to review of the governance arrangements and a report recommended changes designed to increase democracy and accountability (see Chapter 8 on the Prondzynski Report). One commentator's reading of this period of turbulence in the system – in particular its implications for the distinctive Scottishness of higher education – will be referred to in the next section.

Teacher education in Scotland is now part of the university sector – previously there were separate colleges of education – but the distinctive character of provision remains strong. Whereas in England the Office for Standards in Education (Ofsted) and the Teaching Agency (previously the Training and Development Agency for Schools) exercise considerable control over matters of supply, funding and curriculum content, these agencies have no counterparts in Scotland. Here a partnership model operates, strengthened by the recommendations of the 2010 Donaldson Report, involving university schools of education, Scottish Government, local authorities and the GTCS. That is not to say that there is complete satisfaction with the system – critics complain that the prevailing model of teacher education is too conformist – but there is certainly no desire to follow the English pattern.

UNDERLYING VALUES

The extent to which the various manifestations of formal distinctiveness embody a particularly Scottish vision of the nature and purpose of education is a matter of continuing analysis and debate. G. E. Davie (in *The Democratic Intellect*) argued that the special character of Scotland's educational system has been progressively weakened by a process of assimilation to English norms, notwithstanding the separate legislative framework. According to Davie, the Scottish university curriculum, with an emphasis on curricular breadth and philosophical enquiry, was steadily weakened during the nineteenth century by a narrow English empiricism that led to specialisation and fragmentation of knowledge. This process was aided by the introduction of English-style examinations and the appointment of English candidates to key university chairs in Scotland. Secondary schools were required to adapt to the changes in order to prepare candidates for university entrance and so the Anglicising tendencies gradually entered the whole system. One manifestation of the trend was the disparagement of Scots and Gaelic as legitimate forms of language for learning. A re-statement and updating of Davie's analysis was offered by A. L. Walker in his highly polemical study *The Revival of the Democratic Intellect* (Edinburgh: Polygon, 1994).

The pessimism of Davie and Walker would now be challenged. One observer, writing in 1997 about attitudes to Scots and Gaelic, says that 'the age of hostility is past'. Similarly, it is possible to point to the development of curricular materials with a strong Scottish flavour across a range of subjects in primary and secondary schools. Scottish history is now well established as a field of study in schools and universities, and the use of Scottish texts in drama and literature courses is widespread. In 2011, the Scottish Government announced its intention to make the teaching of Scottish Studies compulsory for all secondary pupils. Although this provoked some hostility from critics who feared that it represented an attempt to politicise the curriculum in favour of the SNP's independence agenda, it attracted strong support from a wide cross-section of academics, artists, writers and poets. Add to this the wider cultural renaissance in Scotland, which includes art, music and media, and the argument that Scottish society and Scottish education are dominated by English values and institutions seems hard to sustain.

There is, moreover, some evidence of greater confidence in asserting the separate and distinctive character of Scottish higher education. Following the report on university governance referred to above, Iain Macwhirter, a leading journalist and former Rector of Edinburgh University, published an article entitled 'Scotland's universities are of and for the people' (*The Herald*, 2 February 2012). He wrote: 'Scotland's universities should be seen as engines of social and cultural improvement – not just for the benefit of the individual but for society as a whole.' Taking issue with the reshaping of universities in corporate, market-driven directions, he questioned some of the economic assumptions about the purposes of higher education which had come to dominate debate in England. The principle of not charging tuition fees to Scottish students, he argued, was an important expression of Davie's 'democratic intellect'. Universities should not become finishing schools for the well off. Nor should they be run as private businesses, paying disproportionate salaries to their Principals. Their governing bodies should be opened up to election by staff, students and the wider community, with democratically elected chairs.

It is, however, not a simple either/or issue, with the 'purity' of Scottish values being set against the 'contamination' from south of the border. A significant number of Scots feel themselves to be both Scottish and British (and in some cases European as well) and they want the next generation to enjoy the freedom to enter different cultural worlds. They certainly want Scottish identity and culture to be given proper recognition within the curriculum but they also want their children to be able to cope with the globalisation of knowledge. The international character of many areas of learning and the employment markets associated with them (e.g. technology, computing, economics, banking, law, government) is now recognised. These are cross-national trends that cannot be resisted. To the extent that any educational system must try to prepare young people for the future, Scotland cannot afford to construct a curriculum on the basis of romantic retreat to an imagined golden age of the past. Scottish distinctiveness has to be shaped and redefined in a way that is compatible with the realities of the modern world.

Furthermore, self-confidence about one's own national identity should not be incompatible with tolerance of diversity in other people. That is a mark of cultural maturity. A useful first step would be recognition of the diversity inside Scotland itself. There has always been considerable cultural variation within Scotland – between Highlands and Lowlands, Edinburgh and Glasgow, cities and rural communities, Catholics and Protestants. This diversity has sometimes been submerged in a standardised and idealised model of Scottish life which, with staggering improbability, manages to combine elements of Knox, Burns, Hampden, Red Clydeside and a kailyard version of community life. Stripping away these internal mythologies may serve to counteract the easy recourse to demonising the English. Blaming England for Scotland's ills prevents the hard thinking that is needed now that Scotland has assumed greater responsibility for its own affairs. And if independence were to become a reality, the scope for excuses and attributing blame to others would be further diminished.

CRITICS OF THE SCOTTISH TRADITION

One way of extending the demythologising process is to examine what critics of the Scottish educational tradition have had to say. The accounts of that tradition that receive greatest attention and that help to shape popular consciousness tend to be those that are written by members of the educational establishment. It is not surprising that interpretations coming from such sources should give more prominence to the achievements of the system, rather than its shortcomings. However, there is a counter-tradition – albeit a minor one – of radical twentieth-century criticism which casts interesting light on the cherished principles invoked by officials. It is an interpretation, moreover, that raises important questions about the relation between schooling, society and values.

One early critic was Patrick Geddes (1854–1932), a botanist and environmentalist, who described elementary and secondary schools as 'prisons for body and mind' whose main function was to serve the needs not of children, but of 'text-book perpetrators' and 'examination-machine bureaucrats' (quoted in P. Boardman, *Patrick Geddes: Maker of the Future*, Chapel Hill, NC, 1944, pp. 269, 266). Underlying this criticism was a profound awareness of the ways in which schooling, the provision of which was intended to open up opportunities, could become an oppressive institutional apparatus for stifling genuine interest in children. Geddes was a keen advocate of getting children out of the classroom and encouraging them to discover things for themselves: his advocacy led to the introduction of nature study in primary schools. A similar philosophy was evident in the writings of A. S. Neill (1883–1973) who became a key figure in the progressive movement, attracting enthusiasm and notoriety in almost equal measure for his school, Summerhill. Neill left Scotland because he disagreed fundamentally with the emphasis on discipline and authority, and the centrality of the teacher rather than the pupil. Strongly influenced by Freudian psychology, he based his school on the principle of freedom and saw modern society as hostile to individuality and creativity. Summerhill continues to the present day (currently under the headship of Zoe Readhead, Neill's daughter) having defeated the (then) Department for Education and Employment when it tried to close the Suffolk school following an inspection report. The 2007 High Court ruling was described by one observer, Libby Purves, as acknowledging that 'the school's duty was not to the nation but the child'. Neill was an important influence on John Aitkenhead (1910–98) who founded Kilquhanity House, a small experimental school, in south-west Scotland during the Second World War. Aitkenhead was a pacifist and a nationalist whose founding motto for his school was 'Liberty, Equality and Inefficiency'. Standardisation and regulation were anathema to him and there was a delightful amateurish quality about the way he operated. This meant, among other things, that the financial position of the school was always extremely precarious. There was a strong emphasis on the creative arts – painting, music, theatre, woodwork and crafts – which reflected a belief that the real aim of education was not to pass exams or impose discipline but to nourish the human spirit. Like Neill, Aitkenhead was not afraid to talk of the promotion of happiness as a guiding principle in his approach to children. 'Happiness' is a word that is rarely found in official statements about educational policy – the dominant discourse is one of standards, targets, and outcomes. Kilquhanity closed in 1997, the year before Aitkenhead's death, but it attracted the interest and support of the progressive Japanese educator, Shin-ichiro Hori (himself influenced by Neill), and it was reopened in 2009, offering satellite provision for a progressive group of Japanese schools. However, it is not currently registered as a school in Scotland.

Yet another critic, R. F. Mackenzie (1910–87) tried, ultimately unsuccessfully, to establish a regime within the state system which challenged traditional ideas on curriculum content and pupil learning. His efforts led to his suspension and subsequent dismissal as head of a comprehensive school in Aberdeen. In retirement he wrote a 'Manifesto for the Educational Revolution' which, though inspiring and visionary, was never likely to overturn the powerful structures and practices of mainstream Scottish education (Humes, 2011). Like Neill, Mackenzie saw attitudes to schooling as symptomatic of wider social attitudes: 'The crisis in Scottish schools is a crisis in Scottish life . . . Scotland's schools are at the centre of Scotland's perplexity, one of its main causes' (*The Unbowed Head*, Edinburgh: EUSPB, 1977, p. 6). He believed that for many Scottish youngsters the experience of schooling was largely negative. They were given few opportunities to explore and enjoy learning in creative ways that connected with life outside school; they were constantly reminded of their inadequacies and failures; and they were ill-equipped to meet the challenges they would face as adults. These deficiencies, Mackenzie believed, helped to explain the cultural malaise from which he felt Scotland suffered – a malaise evident in a lack of drive and initiative, a passivity in the face of officialdom and an impoverished sense of life's possibilities. It is a bleak picture of institutional failure and missed opportunities. Harry Reid, in his foreword to Peter Murphy's biography of R. F. Mackenzie, reflects on what he would have made of the Scottish Parliament and of education in particular. Mackenzie would certainly [be] 'teaching, always teaching us to reject the mendacious and the meretricious, to discard the conventional, to reject the divisive and – above all – to be kind, and to think well and think big' (Murphy, 1998, p. vi).

The current generation of teachers and headteachers would certainly disagree with the critics and claim that modern schools are much less oppressive places where pupil achievements are celebrated and the richness of learning in all its forms is recognised and encouraged. That may be so – though it would be a matter for debate – but it does not diminish the responsibility to confront past practices and to reflect on their significance for the present and future. The value attached to schooling in Scotland makes it doubly important to consider its wider social impact and here the need to confront uncomfortable truths remains strong. In a statement that resonates powerfully with the critics, the historian T. C. Smout comments:

> It is in the history of the school more than in any other aspect of recent social history that the key lies to some of the more depressing aspects of modern Scotland. If there are in this country too many people who fear what is new, believe the difficult to be impossible, draw back from responsibility, and afford established authority and tradition an exaggerated respect, we can reasonably look for an explanation in the institutions that moulded them. (Smout, 1986, p. 229)

Even if the radical educational philosophies of Geddes, Neill, Aitkenhead and Mackenzie are not accepted, it is possible to recognise the validity of what Smout is saying about Scottish society. The situation may be improving as the referendum approaches, but it is a slow process. Resistance to change in working practices, reluctance to take on new challenges, unwillingness to accept leadership roles, reticence in the face of professional and bureaucratic authority – these are still recognisable features of life in Scotland. They are by no means universal but they are sufficiently widespread to have attracted the attention of social commentators. In the Thatcher years they led to the phrase 'dependency culture' being coined, a concept that implied an expectation that the state would provide when personal responsibility failed. Under New Labour an attempt was made to address the problems associated with passivity and defeatism through an emphasis on civic involvement, entrepreneurship and creativity – all designed to reduce dependence on state benefits and encourage people, particularly young people, to become active citizens, contributing not only to personal advancement and the economic life of the country but also to attitude sets in families and communities. This strand of policy has been continued under minority and majority SNP administrations following their electoral successes in 2007 and 2011.

The Scottish Parliament certainly has the potential to promote significant economic, social and cultural reform. For that to happen on the scale that is needed, however, would require a major transformation encompassing not only education but a wide range of other public and private services as well. The capacity of children to benefit from schooling is profoundly affected by issues of housing, employment, poverty and health. It is in the interconnection of these forces that solutions to the sort of cultural defects that Smout describes must be found. A major test of the Scottish Parliament, therefore, has to be its success in tackling these problems in an innovative and coordinated way – in other words, in showing that 'joined up government' can make a difference. Prior to the reorganisation of local government in 1996 some of the larger regions (notably Strathclyde and Lothian) tried to coordinate social strategy on a multi-disciplinary basis but, with the fragmentation of services involved in the creation of thirty-two councils, some ground was lost. The importance of developing policies that locate educational provision in the context of broader social issues is, however, now well understood by both politicians and professionals. Integrated community schools, serving as focal points for a range of services, not just schooling, were promoted strongly in the immediate post-devolution period, but inter-professional working has proved difficult to operate and effective integration of services is more of an aspiration than a reality. The squeeze on local authority budgets means that simply maintaining existing provision now takes priority.

COMPETING INTERPRETATIONS

In earlier sections of this chapter a contrast has been drawn between celebratory interpretations of the Scottish educational tradition (such as James Scotland's) and critical interpretations (such as R. F. Mackenzie's). To polarise these inevitably over-simplifies the forces at work, not least by failing to take account of the particular circumstances at any given time in the evolution of the tradition. Lindsay Paterson has claimed that an analysis of the ways in which Scottish education has been subject to reform suggests that a highly complex blend of traditional and radical thinking can be detected at various points in recent educational history (Paterson, 1996). He argues that it is misleading to interpret the development of Scottish education in terms of a crude dichotomy between control and liberation. Depending on the circumstances of the time, different educational philosophies were mobilised in a variety of ways. Referring to the introduction of comprehensive education, he states that 'the single act of abolishing selection [was] a real victory for progressive educational thought' and that its radical effect can be seen 'in the slow revolution it has brought about in the educational aspirations of the whole community'. Significantly, however, the switch to comprehensivisation was not a peculiarly Scottish development, though it is often claimed that comprehensive schools had their roots in the old 'omnibus' schools found in small towns and rural communities in Scotland. This claim ignores the extent of selection and streaming within omnibus schools. Nevertheless, evidence from public consultation as part of the National Debate on the future of Scottish education carried out in 2002 indicates continuing support for the comprehensive principle, however defined.

Paterson's analysis highlights the 'negotiated' character of Scotland's educational distinctiveness; that is, the extent to which cherished principles – expressive of 'the myth' – have to be redefined in response to changing social and economic pressures. Here there are some very interesting tensions. At one level, the establishment of a devolved government and the possibility of complete independence in the foreseeable future, points in the direction of a more robust assertion of Scottish distinctiveness in education (as in other fields). At the same time, however, Scotland – like England – is subject to global pressures that are tending to push educational systems in similar directions. These global pressures are political, economic, cultural and technological in character. They involve international comparisons of educational attainment on a range of measures; analyses of future requirements in terms of workforce planning and skill needs; interpretations of the impact on educational systems of migration within Europe and from further afield; the expectations of multinational companies in respect of infrastructure support and human resources; and, above all, the shift from an economy based principally on heavy industry requiring limited education in the workforce to one that is knowledge-based and requires high levels of basic skills, regular retraining and flexibility. If Scotland wishes to be taken seriously on the international stage it cannot afford to ignore these trends. Its educational system has to respond to them and this may involve adjusting and redefining aspects of its educational tradition. The hard task is to negotiate this process skilfully, taking account of external realities while remaining true to values and principles that have important social, cultural and historical resonance.

Raffe (2004) has tackled the question of Scottish education's distinctiveness from five different perspectives, each of which, he argues, 'incorporates a different concept of education and different criteria of distinctiveness. These perspectives and concepts are often implicit, but they may yield different conclusions on the distinctiveness of Scottish education'. His five perspectives focus on (1) 'the shaping myth, values and traditions of the education system'; (2) 'the "societal logic" and the political economy of education'; (3) 'policy discourse and strategy'; (4) 'the "administrative system" of education – its institutions, formal curricula, regulatory arrangements, etc'; and (5) 'the social relations, processes and outcomes of education'.

On several of these, Raffe's arguments are similar to what has been suggested in this chapter. This is particularly so in respect of (1) where he reasons that the persuasive effects of tradition probably embellish the extent of distinctiveness which Scotland attributes to itself. With respect to the social and economic dimensions of education (2), Raffe's view is that many of the influences on the Scottish and English systems are rather similar. This is not surprising since both are subject to the same global pressures. On (3), Raffe largely agrees with our own view of the strength of support for comprehensive state education and inclusivity in Scottish educational policies and discourse and the greater enthusiasm in England for the discourse of New Public Management which emphasises targets, strategic planning and accountability. The expansion of Academies, Trust, Foundation and Faith schools in England, operating outwith the local authority system, reinforces this point: there has been no demand for anything similar in Scotland. 'Administrative' distinctiveness (4) is conceded to be strong for the most part, but Raffe questions whether the differences matter as much as we often like to think. He observes that overseas commentators tend to be rather more aware of the *similarities* between Scottish and English education. With regard to (5) Raffe limits his discussion to three categories of outcomes (participation, attainment and equality) but concludes that comparative data are insufficient to draw firm conclusions about Scottish distinctiveness.

Raffe also weighs up the extent of the distinctiveness thrown up by these five perspectives, arguing that (1) shows the greatest and (2) shows the least, but stresses that these perspectives (and the others) are not different answers to the same question; they constitute different interpretations of the meaning of distinctiveness. On the question of whether education in Scotland is becoming more or less distinctive with the passage of time, Raffe recognises how little there is by way of researched data to draw upon for argument. He suspects, however, that the net effect of this is for writers to exaggerate Scottish distinctiveness somewhat.

Assessments of how devolution has affected the distinctiveness of Scottish education offer varying emphases. Thus Arnott (2005), writing before the SNP assumed power, suggested that Labour administrations chose 'to pursue a largely conservative agenda which [was] shaped by the myths and traditions associated with the social democratic consensus'

(p. 257). At the same time, she noted that there were elements of both convergence and divergence in educational policy between Scotland and England. Given the global pressures deriving from economics, technology and the requirements of the labour market, it is not surprising that many countries are adapting their educational systems in similar ways, while trying to explain and justify the changes in terms that resonate with familiar discourse. Arnott and Menter (2007) suggest that neo-liberalism, in the form of New Public Management, has influenced educational policies in both countries but stress that 'while globalization may be a convergent force, nationalism is (and always has been) a divergent force. In the new settlement since devolution, it is important to Scotland, if not to England . . . to "carve its own furrow"' (Arnott and Menter, 2007, p. 261). In another paper, Arnott and Ozga (2010) argue that 'nationalism – as an idea – is being used as a discursive resource in policy-making by the new Scottish government' (Arnott and Ozga, 2010, p. 347), promoting a sense of national identity (e.g. through the emphasis on citizenship education). At the same time, the international emphasis on competitiveness, skill development and employability tends to limit the scope for national distinctiveness. A slightly different emphasis is offered by Ozga and Lingard:

> For the most part, devolution seems to have enabled the continuation of Scottish distinctiveness, while simultaneously beginning to open up some of its more traditional aspects including, perhaps, the academic bias and the caution about experimentation . . . It may also have enabled change in the traditionally rather hierarchical nature of schools and of the teaching profession (p. 74).

All this helps to bear out Paterson's point about the complexity and malleability of traditions. The story of the distinctiveness of Scotland's educational tradition can be told in more than one version. New 'myths' can replace the old ones and the task of deconstruction is never-ending. What can be said is that the claims made for the quality of Scottish education, past and present, have been substantial and that they have sometimes led to an unjustifiable degree of complacency. The value attached to education, both by policy makers and by ordinary Scots, remains high but the ideals expressed in the official discourse need to be constantly tested against the realities as experienced by pupils, teachers, parents and employers. As the Scottish Parliament continues to grapple with these challenges, Scottish education needs both its advocates and its critics.

REFERENCES

Arnott, M. (2005) 'Devolution, territorial politics and the politics of education', in G. Mooney and G. Scott (eds), *Exploring Social Policy in the 'New' Scotland*. Bristol: Policy Press, pp. 239–61.

Arnott, M. and I. Menter (2007) 'The same but different? Post-devolution regulation and control in Scotland and England', *European Educational Research Journal*, 6 (3): 250–65.

Arnott, M. and J. Ozga (2010) 'Education and nationalism: The discourse of educational policy in Scotland', *Discourse: Studies in the Cultural Politics of Education*, 31 (3): 335–50.

Davie, G. E. (1961) *The Democratic Intellect*. Edinburgh: Edinburgh University Press.

Houston, R. (2008) *Scotland: A Very Short Introduction*. Oxford: Oxford University Press.

Humes, W. (2011) 'R. F. Mackenzie's "Manifesto for the Educational Revolution"', *Scottish Educational Review*, 43 (1): 56–72.

Murphy, P. A. (1998) *The Life of R.F. MacKenzie: A Prophet Without Honour*. Edinburgh: John Donald Publishers Ltd.

Ozga, J. and B. Lingard (2007) 'Globalisation, education policy and politics', in B. Lingard and J. Ozga, *The RoutledgeFalmer Reader in Education Policy and Politics*. London: RoutledgeFalmer, pp. 65–82.

Paterson, L. (1996) 'Liberation or control: What are the Scottish education traditions of the twentieth century?', in T. M. Devine and R. J. Finlay (eds), *Scotland in the 20th Century*. Edinburgh: Edinburgh University Press, pp. 230–49.

Raffe, D. (2004) 'How distinctive is Scottish education? Five perspectives on distinctiveness', *Scottish Affairs*, 49: 50–72.

Scotland, J. (1969) *The History of Scottish Education*, vol. 2. London: University of London Press.

Smout, T. C. (1986) *A Century of the Scottish People 1830–1950*. London: Collins.

III

THE ADMINISTRATION AND CONTROL OF SCOTTISH EDUCATION

The chapters in this section look at how education is controlled in Scotland. Six chapters deal with the key administrative functions of parliament and government, both nationally and locally, and how bodies like Her Majesty's Inspectorate of Education (HMIE), Learning and Teaching Scotland (LTS) – these now combined as Education Scotland (ES) – and local authorities operate to manage the system. Two further chapters examine, respectively, the legal framework of education and the views of parents.

The opening chapter (14) analyses the political administration at national level during the third session of the Scottish Parliament (2007–11) and comments on the initial work of the SNP majority administration in the fourth session (2011–16). It describes the implementation of policy decisions by civil servants, non-governmental bodies and local authorities, exploring the continuities and changes during this period, in particular the effects of the Concordat Agreement between the Convention of Local Authorities (COSLA) and the Scottish Government. That agreement distanced policies from their implementation through the formulation of outcome agreements, a move which has not been without controversy, not least for its effects upon the size of the teaching workforce. The chapter also notes the effects of parliamentary petitions and government priorities.

The chapter following this (15) focuses on higher education policy and funding, noting how, following the Browne Review, the 'seismic changes' in student finance and fees south of the border required Scottish Ministers to reappraise how the Scottish higher education system should be funded. It notes increasing tensions between the universities and the government and the decisive outcome of the Spending Review in 2011. The workings of the Scottish Funding Council (SFC) are described, exposing the thorny fee comparisons between different groups of students at Scottish universities depending on their country of origin. The chapter also sets out how teaching and research are funded and looks at matters of governance.

Scotland has long depended upon its local authorities for the frontline administration of schools. Local government structure has undergone several reorganisations but the provision of essential services (such as education) has required continuity of mandatory operations at local level: these are described in Chapter 16, as are the challenges in carrying them out satisfactorily during a period of economic stringency. Present forms of local governance are discussed in this context. The author then speculates on possible future models, from increased central government control of schools, through shared service agreements at local level, joint committee or lead authority models, to various 'third party' alternatives.

As earlier chapters in Section II have indicated, the Scottish educational system is quite distinctive and therefore Scottish law provides its administrative framework, the enactment of policy being guided by parliamentary acts and regulations. Where necessary, courts are sometimes required to interpret the law. Chapter 17 has been written by a QC specialising in the application of the law to education and succinctly describes the legal obligations and duties falling to local authorities, teachers, pupils and parents. It deals also with the legal dimensions to placing requests, exclusions, additional support needs and equal opportunities. The conduct of teachers must conform to legislation, of course, and the chapter briefly looks at their statutory duties and necessary obligations. For those readers who wish to pursue the particulars of legal acts, precedents and the like, this chapter (unlike others in the volume) has a full set of footnotes identifying the sources of legislation.

Teachers have for a decade been familiar with the operations of the body responsible for developing and supporting the curriculum. Equally, they have long been used to the efforts of the inspectorate to scrutinise the work of schools, including the quality of teaching and learning, the educational environment and the pastoral support for pupils. The two bodies concerned, LTS and HMIE, have operated very differently and merit the separate, detailed examinations given to them in Chapters 19 and 20, respectively. As indicated above, the decision to bring these bodies together to form ES was taken in 2011. Chapter 19 tracks the operations of LTS, its funding by Scottish Government to cover all aspects of the curriculum including support for relevant information and communications technology (ICT). It is noted that, in its early years, there was a perception that it was a somewhat 'compliant project delivery vehicle for government'. With changes in management and pressures to drive forward Curriculum for Excellence in the second half-decade of its existence, LTS operated differently, though not to everyone's satisfaction, as the author explains. The development of GLOW, the national education intranet, is also considered in this chapter.

With regard to HMIE, whose work originated in 1840, the writer of Chapter 20 also focuses upon the first decade of this century. The introduction of 'inspection cycles' for primary and secondary schools, the development and use of quality indicators, and the partnership between HMIE and schools which was instigated to further the 'improvement agenda' for schools are each analysed. Inspection reports have been made clearer and more accessible (if a little formulaic) during the past decade and these also figure in the discussion. The strengths and achievements of the Scottish inspectorate are set out, acknowledging the importance of teacher development with regard to advancing Curriculum for Excellence.

The final chapter (21) in Section III examines the parental dimension to education in Scotland: the various ways in which parents have been involved with schools, not least the long-established Parent Teacher Associations (PTAs) and the establishment in 2006 of Parent Councils (PCs) to be independent of both school and local authority control. The author writes from her position as Executive Director of the Scottish Parent Teacher Council (SPTC). That body remains a key organisation with respect to education and is justifiably looked to as the voice of parents. It devotes much of its energy to supporting local parent groups across the country, correctly pointing out that children whose parents are actively involved in their education do better at school. In so arguing, the chapter looks at the research concerned with parental involvement and examines how that involvement actually works in Scotland and what influence parents might have in the near future, particularly should local government evolve in any of the ways signalled at the conclusions of Chapter 16.

14

The Political Administration of Scottish Education, 2007–12

Morag Redford

The 2007 elections for the Scottish Parliament brought a minority political administration led by the SNP and the renaming of the Scottish Executive as the Scottish Government. The SNP came into political power with an aim to make Scotland 'smarter', to 'expand opportunities for Scots to succeed from nurture through life long learning ensuring higher and more widely shared achievements' (Scottish Government, 2007). This chapter presents an analysis of the political administration of Scottish education in the third session of the Parliament and concludes with an introduction to the work of the administration in the fourth session of the Parliament. The records of the Education and Lifelong Learning and Culture Committee (ELLC) of the Parliament reveal a government that continued key developments from the previous administration, such as Curriculum for Excellence (CfE), but introduced a new relationship with the Convention of Local Authorities (COSLA) that disturbed the balance of power between local authorities, teaching unions and central government. The changes in the balance of power combined with the overt SNP agenda of skills and employability strongly influenced the work of the administration in this period.

The SNP government introduced immediate changes to the roles and responsibilities of the Scottish cabinet. Fiona Hyslop was appointed to the new post of Cabinet Secretary of Education and Lifelong Learning with Maureen Watt as the Minister for Schools and Skills and Adam Ingram as the Minister for Children and Early Years. Adam Ingram held his post throughout the parliamentary session, Maureen Watt was replaced by Keith Brown in February 2009 and Fiona Hyslop by Michael Russell in December 2009. The political administration of education was supported by civil servants working in three directorates in 2007: the Schools Directorate, the Children and Young People Directorate and the Lifelong Learning Directorate. In 2008 the directorates were renamed as Schools; Children, Young People and Social Care; and Lifelong Learning. These changes reflected the government priorities in education at that time. There were further changes to the management of education with internal civil service reform in 2010, after which education was split between the Learning Directorate, which took responsibility for all school-based learning and national qualifications, and the Employability, Skills and Lifelong Learning Directorate, which held responsibility for post-16 education and skills. The number of ministerial changes, with the related movement of civil servants between the directorates, is likely to have affected the continuity of policy development and implementation for the first few years of the SNP government.

In the Parliament all areas of education – further and higher education, Lifelong Learning, schools, pre-school care and skills – fell within the remit of the ELLC, a new committee covering education, Lifelong Learning and Culture. For the period of the third parliament (2007–11), Karen Whitefield (Labour) was the Convener, with Rob Gibson (SNP) as the Deputy Convener to June 2008 and Kenneth Gibson (SNP) from June 2008 to March 2011. The legislation introduced during this parliament was:

1. the Graduate Endowment Abolition (Scotland) Bill, which received Royal Assent on 4 April 2008;
2. the Education (Additional Support for Learning) (Scotland) Bill, a bill to amend the law in relation to placing requests of children and young people with additional support needs in respect of arrangements between local authorities: this received Royal Assent on 25 June 2009;
3. the Public Services Reform (Scotland) Bill, which simplified and reframed some public bodies, including the establishment of Social Care and Social Work Improvement Scotland which took some scrutiny functions from HMIE: this bill received Royal Assent on 28 April 2010;
4. the Schools (Consultation) (Scotland) Bill, which was introduced to provide for a Ministerial call-in in relation to the closure of rural schools: it received Royal Assent on 2 January 2010;
5. the Children's Hearings (Scotland) Bill, which restated and amended the law relating to children's hearings and received Royal Assent on 6 January 2011.

Scottish education in this period was led politically by government policies, administered through parliament and the civil service, but the implementation of policy and legislation was the responsibility of local authorities and three non-departmental public bodies funded directly by the government: Her Majesty's Inspectorate of Education (HMIE), Learning and Teaching Scotland (LTS) and the Scottish Qualifications Authority (SQA). The role of HMIE was to promote quality and attainment in nursery, primary, secondary and college education in Scotland through independent evaluation. Graham Donaldson was Senior Chief Inspector of Education and led the organisation until his retirement in February 2009 when Bill Maxwell returned to the inspectorate from Wales to take up the post of Senior Chief Inspector. LTS worked in partnership with the government and local authorities to develop the curriculum and promote learning and teaching, in particular the use of information and communications technology (ICT) through the development of GLOW, an online resource for school communities. The chief executive of LTS during this period was Bernard McLeary. These responsibilities were confirmed following a government review in 2010 with the announcement that the core remit of LTS would be curriculum, assessment, GLOW and ICT. However this was overtaken in October 2010 when the Cabinet Secretary for Education announced the creation of a new education agency for Scotland, to combine the work of LTS, HMIE, the National Continuing Professional Development (CPD) Team and the Positive Behaviour Team. Bill Maxwell was appointed transitional chief executive of Education Scotland, which came into being on 1 July 2011, and was confirmed in the post in January 2012. The creation of Education Scotland left the SQA as the only freestanding non-government public body working with school education. The SQA is the national body responsible for the development, accreditation, assessment and certification of qualifications other than degrees, and was led throughout this period by Janet Brown who had moved to that post from Scottish Enterprise. The Scottish Funding Council (SFC) also sits as a non-government public body and contributes to the funding of teaching and research in Scotland's forty-one colleges and nineteen higher education institutions (HEIs). Mark Batho moved from the Lifelong Learning Directorate in the civil service to become chief executive of the SFC in 2008. The nineteen HEIs are supported by Universities Scotland, which is the collective voice of the university principals.

In this administrative structure, nursery, primary and secondary education were managed separately by each of the thirty-two local authorities. The authorities reported directly to the government on their activities but negotiations in relation to annual budgets, new legislation and government initiatives were led by COSLA, as the national voice for local government. COSLA and the government, along with representatives of the teaching unions, formed the Scottish Negotiating Committee for Teachers (SNCT), which negotiated the pay and conditions of service for teachers. During this period the Educational Institute of Scotland (EIS) and the Scottish Secondary Teachers Association (SSTA) were the principal unions to represent teachers. School Leaders Scotland represented senior leaders in secondary schools and the Association of Heads and Deputies Scotland school leaders in primary and special schools, with the Association of Directors of Education Scotland (ADES) representing local authority management in education. The General Teaching Council for Scotland (GTCS) was the professional regulatory body with the responsibility for teaching standards in Scotland. Tony Finn was the Chief Executive of the GTCS during the period of the parliament, during which time the organisation worked closely with the government in the move towards independent status, following legislation passed in 2009 to enable the GTCS to become an independent, profession-led body in April 2012.

All of these organisations took an active role in the discussion and development of education policy in this session of parliament, contributing papers and evidence to the ELLC. The education agenda for the parliament was presented to the ELLC by Fiona Hyslop, the Cabinet Secretary for Education and Lifelong Learning at her first meeting with the committee in June 2007. She spoke about developments in the following areas: early intervention; supporting vulnerable children and families; improving the learning experience in school; developing skills and Lifelong Learning ; and promoting excellence and innovation. The work towards this agenda across the period of the administration was influenced by three key areas affecting education policy and legislation: the impact of the Concordat Agreement between the government and local authorities, the influence of the parliamentary petition system on policy and legislation, and the determination of the minority administration to implement SNP education policies.

THE CONCORDAT AGREEMENT

The underlying thread to all the debates the ELLC held with government ministers was the concordat agreement between COSLA and the government. This innovative agreement was key to the relationship between the minority SNP administration and COSLA, which itself was strongly influenced by Labour-led local authorities. The concordat agreement created distance between government policies and the enactment of those policies in schools through agreed outcomes. Previous administrations had depended upon separate negotiations and agreements for each development or change to the education system. The concordat established one agreement at the start of the parliamentary term, with separate outcomes agreed between each authority and the government in return for the continuation of traditional funding formulas. This reduced some 'ring-fenced' or direct funding of specific initiatives, and gave local authorities greater freedom to set budgets to suit local contingencies. The initial impact of this change was that local authorities reduced the funds that had been ring-fenced for work with specific groups of children and young people. Many of these projects were delivered in partnership with charities for children with additional support needs and a number of long-standing projects ended across Scotland. It also meant that the government had to negotiate some of their manifesto policies such as the introduction of reduced class sizes through the concordat agreement. The scrutiny role of the ELLC on the education budget was limited by the agreement as the government had no control over the budget allocation that the local authorities gave to any of the initiatives they introduced. The Cabinet Secretary and civil servants responded to any questions about funding for specific initiatives with the stock reply: 'we have put sufficient resources into the local government settlement . . .' (Redford, 2009a, p. 111). The ELLC challenged government ministers and civil servants repeatedly in relation to the funding given to specific education developments and in 2009–10 undertook a scoping exercise on the local authority funding of Education and Children's Services. During their investigation Colin MacLean, who led the Directorate for Schools, reported to the committee that the detail of service delivery was a matter for individual councils. He described to the committee the way in which the concordat and single outcome agreements with each local authority had replaced the use of ring-fenced funding to pursue policy objectives and explained that ring-fenced funding had never been more than 5 per cent of funding for local authority education. The evidence from COSLA demonstrated the acceptance between the Scottish Government and COSLA that the concordat agreement was part of an ongoing development in the relationship between local and national government. Barbara Lindsay for COSLA put it this way:

> During the discussions on the 2007 settlement, it was clear that there was an appetite to develop that relationship further, alongside the resource negotiations. That led to the concordat, which covered the financial settlement, as well as aspects of the relationship. The concordat set out the framework for the relationship and the resources that were available to local government. (Redford, 2010, p. 92)

The concordat had particular impact on the numbers of teachers employed during this period. For while government policies recommended the use of early retirement offers and the reduced use of supply teaching posts to ensure that posts were available for newly qualified teachers, local authorities were free to make their own staffing decisions. Ken Macintosh, a Labour MSP, was particularly concerned about the mismatch in numbers recruited to teacher training and the posts available: 'it seems daft to recruit into the profession and then disappoint even more teachers at the end of their probationary year' (Redford, 2009a, p. 111). The Scottish Government established a Teacher Education Working Group in 2008 to investigate teacher workforce planning, which was chaired by Joe Di Paulo of COSLA. The working group commended the teacher induction scheme in enhancing the quality of teachers coming into the school system but drew attention to the variation in the employment formulas for teachers across local authorities. The outcome of the review was that COSLA would work closely with the government on a six-year projection of teacher numbers, but the number of teachers unable to find employment after their induction year became a major political issue in 2009 and Fiona Hyslop made dramatic reductions in the number of places available in teacher training, in particular on one-year postgraduate courses. At the same time 100 extra teachers were funded to support the introduction of CfE and continue to work towards the SNP policy of smaller class sizes. The balancing act between class sizes and teacher employment continued through to the autumn of 2010 when Michael Russell, as Cabinet Secretary, urged local authorities not to look to retiring teachers as an opportunity to save money but to recruit recently qualified teachers to fill those posts. The ELLC debated with Michael Russell the number of teachers required in Scotland: he asserted that the suggested figure of 53,000 teachers was 'essentially arbitrary and, indeed, we now know that it was unsustainable at the best of times' (Redford, 2010, p. 94). In the discussion he looked to the review of teacher education which the government had commissioned Graham Donaldson, retired Senior Chief Inspector of Education, to undertake. He also indicated at that meeting that the government was open to discussion about teachers' working terms and conditions through the SNCT. The committee reviewing teacher education in Scotland was commissioned in November 2009, began taking evidence in February 2010 and reported in December 2010. The report of the review, *Teaching Scotland's Future*, was published in January 2011 with the government accepting in principle the majority of the recommendations. The government commissioned Gerry McCormac, Principal of the University of Stirling, to chair a review of teacher employment in January 2011. The report of the commission was published as *Advancing Professionalism in Teaching* in September 2011, during the fourth session of the Parliament.

THE INFLUENCE OF PARLIAMENTARY PETITIONS

The period 2007–11 saw skilful use of the parliamentary petitions system to bring a range of education issues to the attention of the ELLC. Petitions offered a way to raise concerns directly with the Parliament and influence policy development. Four petitions had particular influence on the work of the ELLC and legislation passed during this parliament: Class Sizes (PE 1046); Rural Schools (Closure) (PE872); Children's Services (Special Needs) (PE853); and Autistic Spectrum Disorder (PE1213). The first of these, PE1046, was submitted by Ronnie Smith (General Secretary) on behalf of the EIS to the previous parliament. It called on the Parliament to support significant reductions in class sizes in Scottish publicly funded schools during the lifetime of the next Scottish Parliament. This petition was signed by almost 80,000 people and framed the ELLC discussions on class sizes throughout the third parliament. The debates on this issue ran alongside the struggles of the government to reconcile their manifesto commitment to reduce class sizes in P1 to P3 to a maximum of eighteen, with the different ways in which each local authority worked with the funding for teachers and available space in schools. In June 2010, the government reached an agreement with COSLA that 20 per cent of P1 to P3 pupils across Scotland would be in classes with eighteen pupils or fewer by August 2010. But in September 2010, the government attempted to regain the impetus towards their original manifesto commitment through the introduction of regulations which limited P1 class sizes to twenty-five from autumn 2010. This was announced at the same time as a review, led by David Cameron, then president of ADES, of the existing mechanisms to control class sizes. The review recommended that legislation should be used to set an upper limit for class sizes but also that the legislation should recognise that the size of pupil groups related to the learning activities they were involved in. The government did not introduce legislation in this parliament relating to class sizes.

Petition PE 872 against the closure of rural schools had first been lodged with the Parliament in 2005 and related to an earlier petition, PE 342, against the closure of six schools in Argyll in 2001. The SNP began their administration with a manifesto commitment of legislative presumption against the closure of rural schools and introduced the Schools (Consultation) (Scotland) Bill to provide for an automatic ministerial call-in for the proposed closure of any rural school. The consultation processes for this bill illustrate the way in which the petitions system, the ELLC and the government worked together to introduce legislation to address an issue of concern to the public. This included a series of ten public meetings around the country, workshops with pupils and parents, and a series of meetings with ADES, COSLA and the Scottish Rural Schools Network. The responses from the consultation informed the draft bill which was considered by the ELLC and then debated in parliament. Petition PE 872 was only closed by the ELLC in 2009 once the legislation had been passed by the Parliament.

The Education (Additional Support for Learning) (Scotland) Bill was also directly informed by petition. The work of the ELLC on this bill related to petition PE 853 on Children's Services (Special Needs), which was also first lodged in 2005. This legislation was proposed to clarify specific operational aspects of the 2004 Act, in particular the jurisdiction of the additional support needs tribunal and the right of parents to make out-of-area placing requests for children with coordinated support plans. As Adam Ingram, then the Minister for Children and Early Years, described it:

> The bill amends the 2004 act in light of the reports by Her Majesty's Inspectorate of Education, the Court of Session rulings, the annual reports from the president of the additional support needs tribunals for Scotland, stakeholders' views and informed observations in light of practice. (Redford, 2009a, p.115)

The reform of the 2004 Additional Needs (Scotland) Act demonstrates the way in which the use of petitions could force further investigation and bring changes to legislation. However, not all petitions were as influential. Petition PE 1213, on the assessment, diagnosis and support available in the education system for children with autistic spectrum disorder, was considered at the same time as the ELLC were working on the Education (Additional Support for Learning) (Scotland) Bill. The ELLC consulted stakeholders to explore the issues and agreed to keep the issues of autism and the support for children on the autistic spectrum under review but took no action on the petition and closed it in December 2009. They returned to the issue of support for people on the autistic spectrum when they considered a private member's bill introduced by Hugh O'Donnell, MSP in 2010. He described the bill as 'an equalising bill that seeks to address the levels of institutional and indirect discrimination that are faced by people with autism in accessing mainstream or person-centred services' (Redford, 2010, p. 99). The government argued against the bill as they were working with partners to develop a strategy through an autism reference group. Rachel Sunderland reported to the ELLC on behalf of the Learning Directorate that the legislative framework was in place through the 2004 and 2009 Additional Support for Learning (Scotland) Acts, and added that on a policy level both the existing and previous administrations did not wish to list specific groups of children. The committee chose not to support the bill which fell when considered by Parliament in January 2011.

SNP EDUCATION POLICIES

The education policies of the SNP administration focused particularly on schools through class sizes and rural schools as illustrated above. They introduced a pilot of free schools meals for children in P1–P3 in the first year of the Parliament and continued the work of the previous administration in relation to the development of the school estate and CfE. SNP policies were against the use of public finance initiatives to fund the schools' building programme but the administration took considerable time to introduce a new funding mechanism. The funding mechanism was moved to sit with the Scottish Futures Trust only in 2011. The work on the development of CfE continued throughout the Parliament and the debates concerning CfE in the ELLC echoed the questions in the press and amongst teachers and parents about the timescale for the implementation of the new curriculum and what was viewed as a slow rate of progress in many secondary schools. The Cabinet Secretary and civil servants from the curriculum division of the Learning Directorate reported regularly to the ELLC on the progress of CfE and from 2008 there was a joint team from the curriculum division of the Learning Directorate and COSLA working together to support local authorities. It was at this time that ADES expressed concern about the pace of change and the lack of definition about CfE. When members of the ELLC questioned David Cameron (ADES), the local authority representative on the management group for CfE, he said that he felt that the members of the management group (civil servants, HMIE, LTS and SQA) were constrained by their working relationships with the government. In this remark David Cameron hinted at an issue that greatly concerned all of those involved with the implementation of CfE in schools: namely, that no one on the CfE management group would speak out about the challenges schools were facing with the implementation of CfE because the majority of the group were directly, or indirectly, government employees. The point that David Cameron made to the ELLC indicated to the committee that there were concerns in the group about the pace of the development but that the management group would continue to follow the government timeline for implementation.

The administration had greater success with some of their other education policies which sat outside the direct influence of COSLA. The Public Services Reform (Scotland) Bill followed from development work in the previous Parliament and created a new non-departmental public body, Social Care and Social Work Improvement Scotland, which has since become known as SCSWIS. This new body took some of the existing responsibilities for inspection and care to provide the capacity for simpler joint inspections. In relation to children and young people the new body integrated the HMIE responsibility, for inspecting child protection and integrated children's services, with the related responsibilities of the Scottish Commission for the Regulation of Care and the Social Work Inspection Agency. One of the first actions of the SNP administration was the creation of another new non-departmental agency called Skills Scotland. This was a formed through a partnership between Highlands and Islands Enterprise (HIE), Learndirect Scotland, Careers Scotland, Scottish Enterprise and the government. The aim was to create a body with responsibility for skills and training linked to employability, a thread which ran through much of the political activity in this parliament.

This emphasis on skills and training was part of the agenda the Cabinet Secretary set for the Joint Future Thinking Taskforce on Universities which was established in 2007 and chaired by Sir Muir Russell, then Principal of the University of Glasgow but previously a civil servant and Permanent Secretary to the Scottish Executive. The remit of the taskforce was to consider the contribution the universities could make over a period of twenty years to the Scottish economy, culture, society and the political priorities of the Scottish Government. The taskforce recommended that the universities could become a key economic sector through the creation of a more flexible funding scheme to provide new opportunities for university-led developments. As Fiona Hyslop put it, 'universities must clearly demonstrate that in return for the substantial public funding that they receive, that Government-funded activities are aligned with the Government's purpose' (Redford, 2009b, p. 100). There was much concern in the second half of this parliament about the need for flexibility in the funding for higher and further education as institutions in England were free to charge higher student fees up to £9,000 per annum, while the Scottish Government retained its commitment to charge no fees for Scottish students on undergraduate programmes. This issue was investigated by an advisory group in 2008 which included representatives from Universities Scotland, the SFC and the Scottish Government. The group reached the conclusion that the funding of higher education had grown in a similar way between Scotland and England until that point and made no recommendations in relation to the fee discrepancy with England, Wales and Northern Ireland. The university sector was particularly concerned about the impact of higher fees in England which would fund posts and developments in a way that universities in Scotland, without access to similar student fees, would be unable to compete against. The administration was adamant in its determination not to introduce student fees and to reduce student debt. One of the first pieces of legislation the Cabinet Secretary for Education introduced in 2007 was to abolish the graduate endowment fee. The Graduate Endowment Abolition (Scotland) Bill was a manifesto commitment from the SNP and argued for on the basis that it would reduce student debt for most students in Scotland by more than £2,000.

The work of the Parliament and the ELLC during this period addressed a wide range of issues related to children's services and Lifelong Learning . Other matters that were considered included the Children's Hearings (Scotland) Bill and an Offender Learning Project which was established to look at offender learning across Scotland, with the aim of providing a more streamlined and improved service for offenders in custody, adult offenders and ex-offenders in the community. The ELLC also addressed legislation relating to individual learning accounts, the funding structure of the Scottish Agricultural College, the protection of children, nutritional advice in schools, student loans and legislation under which the Edinburgh School of Art became part of the University of Edinburgh and the Royal Scottish Academy of Dramatic Art was renamed as the Royal Conservatoire of Scotland. The committee received annual reports from HMIE and Scotland's Commissioner for Children and Young People. The first Commissioner, Kathleen Marshall, demitted office in May 2009 and Tam Baillie was appointed as Commissioner. Members of the ELLC knew Tam Baillie well from his previous work with Barnardo's in Scotland in the course of which he had often given evidence to the committee. On his first visit to the committee as Commissioner he outlined the three areas he intended to work on during his time in office: the United Nations Convention on the Rights of the Child, the involvement of children and young people, and discrimination. He described how he wished to consult and contact young people through the education system and new technology, which he introduced through a consultation process called 'A Right Blether'.

The 2007–11 parliament ended with two key developments for Scottish education: the publication of *Teaching Scotland's Future* (Scottish Government, 2011) and the formation of Education Scotland. The fifty recommendations in *Teaching Scotland's Future* will impact on the structure of teacher education, relationships between universities and local authorities, and the way in which professional development opportunities are available for teachers and education leaders throughout their careers. The 2007–11 administration accepted the majority of the recommendations and left office in May 2011 with the promise of a national partnership group, to be jointly chaired by government, ADES and the universities, to develop the recommendations for implementation by August 2012.

Education Scotland was formally established as an organisation just into the start of the 2011–16 administration, following an election that produced an SNP majority administration with Michael Russell continuing as Cabinet Secretary for Education and Lifelong Learning. In his press statement about Education Scotland, Michael Russell talked about the important role the organisation would play 'in achieving our aspirations for Scottish education'. He also looked forward 'to working with Bill [Maxwell] and his team to further improve Scottish education and the life chances of each and every learner in Scotland' (Scottish Government, 2011). This comment illustrates the success of the 2007–11 administration, the first SNP government, in embedding their political connections and aspirations with a small group of key players and organisations at the centre of Scottish education. As noted above, Bill Maxwell worked with HMIE, spent some time in Wales and was then appointed Senior Chief Inspector of HMIE and acting Chief Executive of Education Scotland: he was subsequently confirmed in the substantive post. Graham Donaldson retired as Senior Chief Inspector only to be immediately charged with undertaking a review of teacher education in Scotland. The government also worked with individuals who had moved between the civil service and other organisations: Mark Batho in the SFC and Sir Muir Russell in the University of Glasgow. They worked closely with David Cameron in his role at ADES and following his retirement as Director of Education and Children's Services with Stirling Council. In the same way as the administration established connections and worked across education networks in Scotland, they skilfully commissioned Gerry McCormac, then recently appointed Principal of the University of Stirling, new to Scotland and not part of the group of key players in Scottish education, to lead the review into teacher employment. Similarly, the administration successfully established close working relationships with COSLA through the concordat agreement which pulled local authorities directly into the government's education agenda. This was seen most successfully in the spring of 2011 when the strength of that partnership saw through agreement at the SNCT in relation to changes to teachers' working conditions. The challenge that faced the 2011–16 administration was to work with COSLA and the teaching unions in the implementation of the recommendations of the report of the McCormac Review into teacher employment. The headline issues of additional support needs and rural schools had helped the SNP maintain a positive education profile with the general public during their minority administration. In the first year of their majority administration, the SNP had to work hard as a political party to retain public confidence through the next stage of the implementation of CfE while continuing to address rural schools, additional support needs and a new education agenda.

AN SNP MAJORITY ADMINISTRATION

Michael Russell set out the education agenda for the new administration in his opening remarks to the first education debate of the 2011–16 parliament on 16 June 2011. He announced a Commission on the Delivery of Rural Education; the development of a Change Fund to create new family centres; emphasis on literacy and language learning in CfE; continued support of modern apprenticeships and a review of university governance (Scottish Government, 2011). This agenda focused on the areas of education where SNP policy was being developed through specially created working parties and commissions rather than through the committee structure of the parliament. This included the government's response to *Teaching Scotland's Future* which was taken forward through the work of a National Partnership Group in 2011–12; and their response to the report *Advancing Professionalism in Teaching* which was worked on with the SNCT in the spring of 2012. In this way Michael Russell created space between the government and the recommendations in both those reports. In fact he responded directly to only one of the recommendations in *Advancing Professionalism in Teaching* but took from the date of publication of the report in September 2011 until February 2012 to agree with the recommendation to close the Chartered Teacher scheme. The use of working groups and long response times meant that teacher disquiet about this recommendation was no longer at the forefront of media attention when the final announcement was made.

The main political focus of the government was CfE and it remained the education story politically and in the press throughout the first year of this administration. It permeated the work of the Parliament through questions and debates, caused the ELLC to seek evidence about the actions of East Renfrewshire Council which was the only council to delay the implementation of the new exam structures for one year, and received more press coverage than any other education topic. The SNP administration used every opportunity to publicise the funding that was put into CfE, as Alec Salmond did on a visit to the newly built Carnegie Primary School in Dunfermline at the start of the school year in August 2011:

> This year the Scottish Government is also investing more than £17 million to support the second year of the Curriculum for Excellence, which has been introduced across the country to help raise standards by making learning and teaching more relevant, engaging, inspiring and connected. (Salmond, 2011)

The use of the First Minister, the most well-known and politically astute SNP MSP, illustrates the importance of the success of CfE to this administration – an administration that, despite a majority in parliament, chose to develop education policies at a distance through working groups, the SNCT and the concordat agreement. The direct involvement of representatives from across the education workforce in the NPG appears a democratic development but it also leaves the education workforce with the responsibility for implementing Michael Russell's vision for Scottish education: to improve attainment and realise his ambition for all of Scotland's children and young people.

REFERENCES

Redford, M. (2009a) 'Education in the Scottish Parliament', *Scottish Educational Review*, 41 (1): 109–25.

Redford, M. (2009b) 'Education in the Scottish Parliament', *Scottish Educational Review*, 41 (2): 99–109.

Redford, M. (2010) 'Education in the Scottish Parliament', *Scottish Educational Review*, 42 (2): 89–103.

Redford, M. (2011a) 'Education in the Scottish Parliament', *Scottish Educational Review*, 43 (1): 86–105.

Redford, M. (2011b) 'Education in the Scottish Parliament', *Scottish Educational Review*, 43 (2): 91–4.

Russell, M. (2011) *Education Debate: Taking Scotland Forward*. Online at: www.scotland.gov.uk/News/Speeches/Education-16-06-11

Salmond, A. (2011) *First Minister Welcomes Pupils Back to School*. Online at: www.scotland.gov.uk/News/Releases/2011/08/17114125

Scottish Government (2007) *Principles and Priorities: The Government's Programme for Scotland*. Online at: www.scotland.gov.uk/Publications/2007/09/05093403/0

Scottish Government (2011) *News Release: Education Scotland*. Online at: www.scotland.gov.uk/News/Releases/2011/07/01114648

15

Scottish Higher Education: Policy and Funding

Simon Jennings

A CHANGED CONTEXT

Since 2010, the political and financial context for higher education in Scotland has fundamentally changed. There had been incremental change in the period since devolution as successive administrations at Holyrood pursued policies that differentiated Scotland from England, such as the abolition of upfront fees and the introduction of the Graduate Endowment by the Labour and Liberal Democratic coalition following the 1999 Cubie Report, or the minority SNP administration's abolition of the Graduate Endowment in 2008. However, in a context where significant numbers of students move between the devolved regions of the UK, seismic changes in the student finance and fees regime in England has required Scottish Ministers to undertake a major reappraisal of the funding of the Scottish higher education system and introduce radical and, at times, controversial new policies.

Critical to the recent radical change to higher education policy and funding in Scotland were the October 2010 report of the independent review of higher education and student finance in England – otherwise known as the Browne Review (Lord Browne of Madingley, 2010) – and the historic election of a majority SNP government for Scotland in May 2011. The Browne Review was established in 2009 by the then Labour government led by Gordon Brown. Chaired by former BP Chief Executive Baron Browne of Madingley, the review was to consider widening participation alongside student funding and report to the government in advance of the 2010 election. At its launch Labour peer Lord Mandelson indicated that the Review would consider the 'balance of contributions to universities by taxpayers, students, graduates and employers' in the pursuit of 'excellence'. Amidst some controversy, the review did not report until five months after the election and therefore submitted its findings to the recently formed Conservative and Liberal Democratic coalition. The report's recommendations to abolish the English £3,290 fee cap, substantially withdraw public funding, devolve fee-setting powers to universities and set no upper limit on the fees institutions could charge represented a radical market-led proposal for the future of higher education in England.

In responding to the Review's recommendations the UK government diverged from the system Browne proposed by setting an absolute fee cap of £9,000 per annum and requiring a range of bursary and related spend to be approved by the Office of Fair Access if an institution planned to charge more than £6,000 a year. Whilst these modifications placed some constraints on the market for higher education in England and an average fee of £7,881 was eventually to emerge, the reforms begged two critical policy questions for Scotland: how would Scotland match the estimated 10 per cent additional funding which would flow to English universities as a consequence of these changes; and, in light of the existing £1,820 fee charged to students from the rest of the UK, how would the potential increased demand from students elsewhere in the UK be managed?

Seeking answers to these questions and under pressure from universities, the Scottish Government established a Joint Technical Working Group with Universities Scotland as part of its *Building a Smarter Scotland* consultation, published in December 2010. The remit of this joint group was to 'consider the size of the likely gap in funding between north and south of the border which may be opening up, and comment on the possible effect of some of the funding solutions in this paper in terms of helping to close that gap' (Scottish Government, 2011). Working when the average fee level in England was still unknown, the group modelled various potential fee levels and concluded that the funding gap was in the range of £97m to £263m, with the exact figure depending on the final average fee in England. The group also explored options to raise funds including a graduate tax, one-off fixed contributions of up to £6,500 payable on graduation, increasing fees charged to students from the rest of the UK, the potential to increase funding from philanthropic and business sources, and efficiency savings.

Published in February 2011, the figures in the joint report shaped the UK pre-election debate around higher education and influenced political parties' manifesto commitments. The report also led to occasionally fractious relations between universities and the Scottish Government as the two drew differing conclusions about the likely scale of the funding challenge facing Scotland. In the run-up to the May election all political parties in Scotland with the exception of the Scottish Conservative and Unionist Party adopted positions that contrasted starkly with the market-led system in England and promised that Scottish students would not pay fees up front, nor pay a contribution toward tuition costs on graduation. Most strident in this debate was the SNP, with First Minister Alex Salmond quoting Robert Burns in declaring that 'rocks will melt wi' the sun before I allow tuition fees to be imposed on Scottish students'.

Following the SNP's return to government with a surprise parliamentary majority in May 2011, ministers moved quickly to introduce draft legislation that would devolve to universities fee-setting powers for students resident in the rest of the UK, capped at the English limit of £9,000. Amidst widespread concern about both the disparity and complexity of fees and funding arrangements facing applicants across the UK, this was undoubtedly regarded as a controversial move. It is this move that has led to such fundamental change in the sector and may yet alter the nature of the sector's relationship with government.

The September 2011 Spending Review announcement indicated that, in addition to fees charged to the rest of UK students, the remainder of the funding gap would be met by a combination of efficiency savings of £26m per annum and a cash uplift in government funding for the sector totalling £327m over three years. In a context where the Scottish Government faces 'real terms' decreases in funding and other sectors face reductions in funding, this uplift represents a significant public investment in free education and in Scotland's universities. However, the commitment may well have strings attached given that a review of the sector will bring forward a new legislative framework over the course of 2012 and could see significant change to the regulation of the sector.

THE SHAPE OF THE SECTOR

Higher education in Scotland may mean one of two things. The first defines the sector by level, that is academic activity at or equivalent to the first year of undergraduate study. The second definition focuses on institutions and defines the scope of the sector on the basis of the nineteen higher education institutions (HEIs) in Scotland. This group of nineteen includes Scotland's fifteen universities: the four 'ancients' dating from the fifteenth and sixteenth centuries (Aberdeen, Edinburgh, Glasgow and St Andrews), four awarded university title in the 1960s (Dundee, Heriot-Watt, Stirling and Strathclyde) and seven awarded university status since 1992 (Abertay, Edinburgh Napier, Glasgow Caledonian, Queen Margaret, Robert Gordon, the University of the Highlands and Islands and the University of the West of Scotland). The four remaining HEIs are the Glasgow School of Art, the Open University in Scotland, the Royal Conservatoire of Scotland and the Scottish Agricultural College. Whilst these institutions have in common an eligibility for funding from the Scottish Funding Council (SFC), membership of a common representative body (Universities Scotland) and provide 99 per cent of Scottish first degree enrolments (the 20 per cent of higher education enrolments provided by Scottish colleges being primarily at Higher National level), they are a diverse group of institutions. Across the sector, turnovers range from under £20m to well over £600m, student bodies vary in size from under 1,000 to over 22,000, the percentage of total income each receives from the SFC extends from under 30 to over 65 per cent, and individual HEIs vary in their mission and in the scale of their research activities. The term 'universities' is used to refer to this group of nineteen institutions in the text below.

The SFC was established by a 2005 Act of the Scottish Parliament and, in budgetary terms (£2.2bn), is the largest non-departmental public body (NDPB) in Scotland. The Act specifies that the Council should secure 'coherent provision by the fundable bodies (as a whole)' and ensure that such provision is of 'a high quality'. Whilst Scotland's universities enjoy and vigorously defend a considerably greater level of autonomy than many across Europe, the Council, and the Minister from whom it receives an annual letter of direction, exert a significant influence and can effectively constrain their autonomy by attaching legally binding conditions to SFC funding. However, universities have enjoyed considerable success in their efforts to expand income from other sources and SFC grant funding comprises only 39 per cent of the sector's total income.

Universities generate non-governmental revenue from a range of sources other than the SFC, including international and postgraduate tuition fees, research contracts, residences and catering activity, intellectual property and, in a growing number of cases, endowment and philanthropic income. However, the vast majority of such funding is either ring-fenced for delivery of a specific activity or service, or constrained by a donor's wishes, and is consumed in meeting the costs associated with that activity, with little contributing to core costs. Indeed, some charities and public bodies look to contract with universities on the basis that work will be undertaken at cost and, were they to contract on a commercial or profit-driven basis, universities would secure significantly less income from this source.

Despite the ring-fenced nature of non-SFC income, the sector's declining reliance on Scottish Government funding is a trend that would appear set to continue. Whilst the generous 2011 Spending Review settlement represents a significant cash increase in funding from the Scottish Government, the fees collected from students from elsewhere in the UK will become a significant additional source of non-governmental income. In addition, universities' efforts to expand international student numbers, be it in Scotland or by means of establishing campuses overseas to deliver education in-country, is likely to further increase the proportion of income generated independent of the SFC. Despite this trend, universities' single biggest funder will remain the SFC. The quality of the education and research they undertake, as well as the equipment and infrastructure that underpin them, are critically dependent on this source.

TEACHING FUNDING

Delivery of undergraduate teaching accounts for approximately a quarter of the funding that the SFC distributes to the sector but, in line with the diversity of individual universities' missions, the relative scale of this activity varies by institution. This funding is provided to institutions on the basis of an allocation of a number of 'funded places' (expressed as full-time equivalents). An individual university's allocation of places will be spread across six (until 2012–13 there were thirteen) funding subject groups, with places in each group funded to a total 'unit of resource' per annum that ranges from £16,734 (for clinical subjects) down to £5,278. Postgraduate funded places are allocated by the SFC on the same basis, albeit in lower total numbers, however, institutions are free to charge additional fees to UK and EU students for such provision. International students from outwith the EU are not eligible for SFC-funded places at either undergraduate or postgraduate level, with institutions free to set their own fees for such students.

Prior to academic year 2012–13 these funded places were allocated for universities to fund universities' admission of students from the UK and EU member states. The fee element for Scottish and EU students was met by the Student Awards Agency for Scotland (SAAS) and UK students from outwith Scotland were personally liable for meeting the fee element, albeit with the support of means-tested contributions to these costs for some and income-contingent low-interest government loans for all. However, the move to deregulate universities and permit them to charge fees of up to £9,000 to students from the rest of the UK (currently circa 23,000 students, or 17 per cent of the UK undergraduate population studying in Scotland) has changed this situation. Allocations of undergraduate funded places from 2012–13 will now relate only to students ordinarily resident in Scotland and to students from EU member states, for whom SAAS will continue to meet the fee element. However, there will be no funded places or other per capita SFC funding for students from the rest of the UK (except in relation to clinical subjects where the cost of delivery exceeds the £9,000 fee cap) and institutions will set and collect fees of up to £9,000 per annum from such students. As is the case for rest-of-UK students choosing to study in their own UK nation, income-contingent loans will be available to meet the cost of these fees.

This changed situation with respect to students from the rest of the UK means that there will now effectively be three distinct categories of undergraduate student, each with distinct fee arrangements. These are summarised in Table 15.1.

With significant numbers of students from the rest of the UK historically being concentrated in a small number of institutions (most notably the University of St Andrews and the University of Edinburgh), the effect of these changes on individual universities and their SFC grant for teaching will vary as will their opportunity to generate income from fees. As in England, the market for higher education is untested and applicants' behaviour cannot be readily predicted. Nevertheless, the early indications from Universities and Colleges

Table 15.1   Fee arrangements for undergraduate students

Undergraduate student group	Scottish & non-UK EU	Rest of UK	Non-EU international students
Fee arrangements	Set and paid by Scottish Government	Set by individual universities. Upper limit of £9,000 per annum for 2012–13.	Set by individual universities. No upper limit.

Admission System (UCAS) applications data available at the time of writing suggest that the proportion of applicants applying to universities based in other nations around the UK remains constant.

Looking to the future, a major consideration for politicians, civil servants and the Scottish economy as a whole will be the proportion of its young people to whom Scotland offers an education leading to a first degree qualification. In 2000, the UK was ranked third amongst Organisation for Economic Cooperation and Development (OECD) nations for the percentage of young people it was educating to degree level, a position supported by the Blair government's target that 50 per cent of young people participate in higher education. However, the most recent OECD data demonstrate the global push to expand higher education provision in an effort to secure the economic benefits associated with high-value graduate jobs. The UK is now ranked fifteenth in this table, below the mean for OECD nations. The capacity of Scotland's higher education system to provide sufficient opportunities to meet the aspirations of its young people and maintain Scotland's competitiveness in the global economy appears likely to become a defining issue in future. This is not just the case for Scotland. The challenge of global competitiveness is recognised across the UK and the reforms to student finance in England were, in part, intended to facilitate an expansion of student numbers.

TEACHING POLICY AND QUALITY ASSURANCE

The SFC has no formal role in determining the detail of specific subject provision at universities, nor the length or nature of such courses, except in relation to controlled subjects such as Medicine, Veterinary Science and Teacher Education, where the availability of work placements means the Scottish Government exercises a control on overall numbers. This means that, whilst funded places are allocated between different funding subject groups, universities can apply to the SFC for resource transfers between different subjects in a system that permits universities to ensure their provision is relevant and can respond to changing patterns of demand from both students and employers. However, on behalf of the Scottish Government, the SFC does operate a policy of 'consolidation limits' which imposes a fine on institutions if they under- or over-recruit students beyond a tolerance band (currently 10 per cent of their total number of funded places), thereby enabling the government to control overall student support costs (i.e. maintenance loans and grants funding) funded through the Student Support Agency Scotland.

Whilst not responsible for determining the detail of subject teaching at individual institutions, the SFC does have statutory duty to secure the 'coherent provision by the fundable bodies (as a whole)' of a high quality of fundable further education and fundable higher education. The role of the Council in securing 'coherent provision' across universities and colleges has increasingly been understood to relate to the social, cultural and, most particularly, economic role Scotland ascribes to its universities – a subject of particular interest to Ministers. The requirement to secure quality is delivered on the SFC's behalf by the UK's Quality Assurance Agency (QAA) via a dedicated Scottish Office. QAA Scotland's role is to develop and operate quality assurance and enhancement arrangements which reflect the needs of higher education in Scotland. In so doing it reports to the QAA Scotland Committee which takes overall responsibility for the Agency's work in Scotland.

Since 2003–04, QAA Scotland has operated a system of 'Enhancement-Led Institutional Review' (ELIR). Introduced as a 'lighter touch' alternative to the previous bureaucratic system which assessed individual departments, it failed to secure the full confidence of the academic community and could not satisfactorily accommodate the diverse range of academic views about how to best identify and assess teaching quality. The ELIR approach, by contrast, operates at the level of the institution as a whole and a university's delivery within an individual subject area is assessed only exceptionally. The focus of the ELIR process is to review the approach universities take to improve the student learning experience, as well as to assess an institution's ability to ensure the academic standards of its awards and to manage the quality of the learning opportunities on offer to its students. ELIR reviews are carried out by a team of six reviewers which comprise one student reviewer, one international reviewer, three senior UK-based academic reviewers and one coordinating reviewer. Detailed and summary findings are produced by the review team on the conclusion of its assessment visit and made publicly available on the QAA's website.

RESEARCH FUNDING AND POLICY

Approximately 25 per cent of SFC funding currently supports research activity. As with teaching, the SFC does not determine what research universities should undertake and the proportion of individual institutions' funding allocations dedicated to research varies in relation to their mission. The award of research funding is concentrated in individual departments through a policy of research selectivity underpinned by a funding formula which has increasingly directed research funds to those departments where research has been assessed to be of the highest in the UK-wide Research Assessment Exercise (RAE).

The RAE is a periodic assessment of research across all universities which has been renamed as the 'Research Excellence Framework' (REF) in advance of its 2014 iteration. The RAE and REF are jointly managed by the four higher education funding councils in the UK (responsible for England, Northern Ireland, Scotland and Wales, respectively). The process requires universities to make a submission for each department that they wish to be assessed. These submissions include a narrative element but also details of the unit's staffing complement, its researchers' most significant publications, details of research income secured and doctoral training activity. For the 2014 REF submissions will additionally require universities to demonstrate the 'impact' of their research on wider society. Whilst this additional requirement is in keeping with increased government interest in universities' outputs and their contribution to the economy, the move has attracted some controversy. Some suggest it may compromise notions of academic freedom, others query the practicality of measuring 'impact' in a manner that is fair, impartial and makes defensible relative judgements between different kinds of impact.

Since 1990, the results of the RAE have been used to allocate the four UK Funding Councils' research funding on the basis of independent assessment of departmental research output and the award of a quality judgement on a five-point (and latterly four-point) scale. Following each iteration of the RAE, in 1992, 1996, 2001 and 2008, the distribution of research funds has increasingly been weighted towards departments scoring the highest ratings. In line with explicit instruction from the Cabinet Secretary, the SFC's indicative allocations to universities for 2012–13 take this trend further, with funding to be made available only to those departments that secured one of the top two ratings in RAE 2008, with the funding weighted very significantly in favour (a 3:1 ratio) of those departments achieving the highest possible score in RAE 2008.

The widespread acceptance of the need for selectivity in research funding allocations, as well as the increasing extent to which the RAE has determined funding allocations and the consequent influence it has, have had significant impacts on the academy, not all of which are adjudged to be positive. Many argue that the process encourages researchers to pursue research in areas that might be regarded as mainstream, that is published in specific journals and that receives financial support from established and prestigious sources and is therefore more readily recognised in the RAE's peer assessment process. Whilst it is suggested that the introduction of the 'impact' assessment may have some effect on these perceived weaknesses of the process, this remains to be seen. Whatever the behavioural effect of the 2014 changes (if any) it remains clear that the REF, like the RAE before it, will represent a critical focus for funders and institutions. It seems equally clear that the policy of research concentration is likely to continue.

Scotland's pursuit of research excellence and the concentration of funding in highly rated departments is distinct from that of the rest of the UK in one important way. Whilst the primary focus in other nations, most notably England, has been to focus research funding within specific institutions, Scotland's initiative in 'research pooling' has taken an alternative approach. The policy has created collaborative 'research pools' which draw on Scotland's universities as a whole to bring together highly rated researchers in the same subject field in order to create 'critical mass', with the intention of providing Scotland with research teams as large, if not larger than, those in departments in the world's largest research-intensive universities. Based on initial indications from the 2008 RAE and from research pools' success in attracting leading staff, students and external research grants, the initiative is regarded to be a significant success, one that has attracted interest from researchers and policy makers from around the world. The success and recognition of research pools, particularly in relation to their ability to attract overseas funding, has led to Scottish ministers focusing resource on them in terms of additional funding to attract PhD students and to support bids for European Framework funding.

Closely related to the research endeavours of Scotland's universities and the REF 'impact' agenda is the 'knowledge transfer' or 'knowledge exchange' activities of universities, with a particular focus on their contribution to the Scottish Government's overarching aim of creating sustainable economic growth. Such activity has, since 2002, been supported by means of the SFC's Knowledge Transfer Grant, a funding stream that totalled £1.6m in 2011–12. This funding not only assists universities in involvement with business, but also contributes to public engagement and cultural outreach activity which seeks to interest the public at large in the findings of the research undertaken in universities.

Just as Scottish universities have sought to collaborate in research pooling, they have worked together in a variety of ways in order to maximise their levels of knowledge exchange and have been encouraged to do so by both the SFC and the Scottish Government. Whilst a number of the research pools pursue their own knowledge exchange activities on behalf of participating members, there are also pan-Scotland initiatives including a single point of contact for small and medium-sized enterprises (known as 'Interface'), a single online source for licensing opportunities (www.universitytechnology.com) and a set of standard contracts for collaborative work with business. The Scottish Government appears to be seeking still greater collaborative activity in this area and, to the consternation of many in the sector, has asked the SFC to pursue the development of a single knowledge exchange office for all Scottish universities.

GOVERNANCE AND ACCOUNTABILITY

Universities are independent legal entities that enjoy charitable status and are governed by the legal persona of a Governing Body, sometimes known as the university 'Court'. The universities are fiercely protective of their autonomous status and, in light of studies linking the autonomy of a country's universities to their success (e.g. Aghion, 2010), wary of potential erosion of this which would hand greater control to ministers or the SFC. The sector's readiness to leap to the defence of its autonomy, and staff and student equation of this autonomy with a lack of accountability, can be seen in the highly politicised media debate on the topic which led up to the 2011 Scottish elections and, in turn, to the July 2011 announcement of a review of higher education governance. Published in February 2012 (Scottish Government, 2012) and containing a number of recommendations the sector may well regard as controversial, the review will provide the backdrop for debates about governance and autonomy over the next twelve to eighteen months (at the time of writing the government had yet to make a formal response to the recommendations).

University managers would argue their institutions are highly attuned to government priorities and their autonomous status is balanced by an extensive range of accountabilities. Scottish Ministers use their powers to direct the SFC, directions that are reflected in the Council's Conditions of Grant with which institutions must comply. Universities are required to submit a strategic planning document to the SFC which sets out the teaching, research and resource management plans for the institution for a period of four years. In addition, the SFC has responsibility for making sure that institutions have appropriate mechanisms for financial management, for preparing their accounts, and for ensuring that they use public funds in a manner consistent with the purposes for which they have been allocated. In order to effect this, the SFC requires that all institutions comply with the requirements of the UK Combined Code on Corporate Governance, in so far as they relate to the higher education sector, particularly in relation to internal control, audit and the publication of accounts, all of which are subject to a financial memorandum between the SFC and each university.

In addition to these documented lines of accountability, university governing bodies must also appoint a principal as chief accounting officer for the use of SFC grant and establish an audit committee to oversee the arrangements for internal and external audit. The Scottish Parliament also has recourse to summon the designated accountable officer to provide evidence to parliament in relation to financial regularity and propriety. Should the SFC determine that a university is in breach of its conditions of grant and has used public funds inappropriately, the Council has the ultimate sanction of suspending a university's grant funding temporarily or permanently and to demand the repayment of such funds. Universities are also subject to oversight and are accountable for their actions through the statutory powers vested in the Office of the Scottish Charities Regulator (OSCR), the

Office of the Scottish Information Commissioner (OSIC), the Scottish Public Services
Ombudsman (SPSO) and the Auditor General for Scotland. Beyond this, universities
are responsible to other funders for the delivery of services they provide, be it research,
consultancy or education in return for fee-paying postgraduate and international students.
Nevertheless, what is referred to as the 'democratic accountability' of Scottish universities
remains a matter of debate.

THE FUTURE FOR HIGHER EDUCATION POLICY AND FUNDING IN SCOTLAND

The Scottish Government's policy on tuition fees has introduced a regime for the funding
of undergraduate education which is in direct opposition to the market system that will
operate in England from 2012–13. The medium- and long-term stability of the current
arrangements will, in large part, be determined by what happens in the political arena. Any
change in the UK government that saw a move away from the current market arrangements
may well require a change in the current Scottish fees regime for rest-of-UK students but,
even if the UK's current arrangements persist, the continued high level of demand for
undergraduate education combined with the pressure on public finances are likely to see the
funding of higher education remain an area of media and political debate.

More immediately, the Scottish Government will bring forward legislation relating to
the sector in 2013. This will build on a process of consultation which began in December
2010 and continued throughout 2011. It will also incorporate the government's response to
the review of governance. Key areas where change may be likely include additional ministerial powers to force institutional mergers; legislative targets and penalties intended to widen
participation amongst the most deprived socio-economic groups; legislative requirements
relating to the progression of students from Higher National qualifications; and potential
changes intended to increase the democratic accountability of universities' governing
bodies. With many of these areas already the subject of heated debate, the immediate policy
environment in which Scotland's universities operate looks likely to remain contentious,
with the potential for significant impact on universities' operations.

In the medium term the most fundamental policy questions lie in the area of constitutional
reform. Research currently remains a reserved matter and Scotland outperforms other areas
of the UK in winning competitively awarded research funding from the UK-wide Research
Councils when compared to Scotland's share of the UK population. The future treatment
of such reserved matters (including the regulation of many professions founded on graduate
and postgraduate qualifications) will be of significance in any enhanced devolution settlement. In the case of a move to a full independence, then continued access to EC Framework
Programme and European Research Council funding will be issues of critical concern to
Scottish universities as will Scotland's visa regime and the fee regime for students from
the rest of the EU. Non-UK citizens of EU member states currently enjoy the same state
support as Scottish students and do not pay fees for undergraduate study at Scottish universities. One school of thought suggests that a future independent Scotland with membership
of the EU would be required to offer English, Welsh and Northern Irish students equivalent
treatment, with potentially profound pressures on demand assuming fees of up to £9,000
continue to apply in these students' home countries. Whatever the outcome of the constitutional debate, it seems likely that change may be the one constant in the policy and funding
of Scotland's universities.

REFERENCES

Aghion, P., M. Dewatripont, C. Hoxby, A. Mas-Colell and A. Sapir (2010) 'The governance and performance of universities: evidence from Europe and the US', *Economic Policy*, 25 (61): 7–59.

Lord Browne of Madingley (2010) *Independent Review into Higher Education Funding and Student Finance*. See at http://webarchive.nationalarchives.gov.uk/+/hereview.independent.gov.uk/hereview/Scottish Government (2005) 'Further and Higher Education (Scotland) Act 2005'. See at www.legislation.gov.uk/asp/2005/6/pdfs/asp_20050006_en.pdf

Scottish Government (2011) 'Short Life Technical Working Group'. See at www.scotland.gov.uk/Topics/Education/UniversitiesColleges/16640/stakeholdergroups/ShortlifeWorkingGroup

Scottish Government (2012) *Report of the Review of Higher Education Governance in Scotland*. Edinburgh: Scottish Government. Online at www.scotland.gov.uk?Resource/0038/00386780.pdf

16

The Local Governance of Education

Don Ledingham

Despite a range of local government reorganisations since 1926, a constant feature of educational provision has been the role of the local authority (in whatever guise) in the governance and operational responsibility for schooling within its boundaries. The place of the 'education authority' to set policy, allocate budgets and scrutinise performance has been sacrosanct. Locally elected members and senior officers have held sway over education with a constancy that few other aspects of public service delivery can match. Yet over the last few years we have begun to see forces at work that have the potential to undermine and destabilise that comfort zone with critical consequences – unless radical steps are taken to redesign the 'taken for granted' modus operandi. In recognition of this state of flux this chapter will attempt to describe the current obligations facing education authorities; consider the forces for change that are challenging this status quo; and finally describe some of the emerging models in this new world and explore how these might evolve in practice.

CURRENT OBLIGATIONS FOR EDUCATION AUTHORITIES

An interesting fact to be drawn from the Standards in Scotland's Schools etc., Act 2000 is that there is no difference between the local authority and the education authority, i.e. they are one and the same thing. This feature is worthy of note given some of the alternatives to be considered later in this chapter. The Act sets out the following key obligations for education authorities:

Duty of Education Authority in Providing School Education
Where school education is provided to a child or young person it shall be the duty of the authority to secure that the education is directed to the development of the personality, talents and mental and physical abilities of the child or young person to their fullest potential.
Education Authority's Annual Statement of Improvement Objectives
The education authority, after consulting such bodies as appear to the authority to be representative of teachers and parents within their area and of persons, other than teachers, prepare and publish a statement setting objectives.
Raising Standards
An education authority shall endeavour to secure improvement in the quality of school education that is provided in the schools managed by them; and officers shall exercise their functions in relation to such provision with a view to raising standards of education.
School Development Plans

For the purpose of securing improvement in the quality of education an education authority will ensure that there is a school development plan prepared by the school.

Review of School Performance

An education authority is required to publish, as respects quality of education provided, measures and standards of performance for the schools managed by that authority. In addition the education authority shall review the quality of education which the school provides; and if, having regard to the measures and standards of performance relevant to the school, it concludes in any such review that the school is not performing satisfactorily, it shall take such steps as appear to them to be requisite to remedy the matter.

Delegation Schemes

An education authority must devise a scheme for delegating to the headteacher of a school that share of the authority's budget for a financial year which is available for allocation to individual schools. The expectation is that education authorities will devolve as much of their budget as possible to schools.

The education authority may also delegate other management functions in relation to the school as is deemed appropriate.

Requirement that Education be Provided in Mainstream Schools

There is an assumption that all children will have right to be educated in mainstream schools unless their needs are so extreme as to make that impossible to deliver.

Additional Support for Learning

Each education authority must make adequate and efficient provision for the needs of each such child or young person, and must have in place arrangements for ensuring that the additional support being provided remains adequate to meet those needs (ASL Act 2004).

The following are some of the other major responsibilities for education authorities set out in the 2000 Act:

- school boards;
- home education;
- pre-school education;
- home-to-school transport;
- education of children unable to attend school;
- rights of appeal against exclusion;
- placing requests/appeals;
- grants; clothing, etc.

As can be seen from the above, the range of obligations facing an education authority is wide-ranging. However, it is possible to tease these responsibilities out into three broad areas: (1) the provision of education; (2) managing school performance; and (3) additional support for learning.

CURRENT GOVERNANCE MODEL

In order to deliver the above obligations most councils delegate the responsibilities to an Education Committee who oversee budget, policy and scrutiny matters relating to education. The Committee is composed of elected members and three church representatives and is chaired by an Education Convener, who will be a member of the ruling political administration. The Education Committee will consider reports prepared on its behalf by officers of the council and will approve or reject recommendations as they deem appropriate. The key element to be borne in mind in the current structure is that schools and officers are accountable to locally elected members. It is important to emphasise this element given some of the alternative models that might potentially come in to replace the current system.

Each education authority will have identified a range of political objectives relating to education and these will vary according to local administrations and their manifesto pledges. These objectives will have a significant influence upon the reports coming forward to the Education Committee but beyond those reports it could be argued that 80–90 per cent of the daily business in schools runs without reference to local political mandate.

This reflects the realities that, in addition to the broad political objectives, schools and education authorities are obliged to conform to national legislative and curricular guidance on educational and support for learning provision and also adhere to the nationally and locally negotiated agreements with teachers' unions. Finally, the expectations of Her Majesty's Inspectorate of Education – now in its new guise of Education Scotland – which are set out in evaluation guidance in the form of a report entitled 'How Good is our School?' has a very significant effect on the limited degree of variation seen between one authority and another. The consequence of these combined influences is that there exists a high degree of uniformity in the nature of education provision throughout Scotland. Before exploring alternatives to the current governance model it might be best to describe the forces at work that are so undermining the current system.

THE ECONOMIC AND SOCIAL CONTEXT

At the core of the pressures for change is the global recession that can be traced back to the financial crash of 2008. For the first time in living memory public service budgets in general, and education budgets in particular, are experiencing reductions in real terms, so much so that it is predicted that local authority budgets will not return to previous levels until 2027. For officers and elected members who have become used to annual budget growth this has been a dramatic change in circumstances, as previously they had become conditioned to driving policy and improvement agendas through allocating budgets and resources. Rather than making decisions about where 'new money' is to be spent, the locus is now upon where existing resources can be withdrawn or reduced. The language of 'efficiency' and 'best value' has come to permeate local government and new mindsets have had to be adopted. Nevertheless, the expectations of the general public and the workforce probably continue to exceed the capacity of the system – and certainly lag behind any acceptance that change must happen. It is within this very challenging environment that elected members and officers must lead their working lives – trying to meet the expectations of their constituents and employees while managing ever-reducing budgets. The reality of the current situation is that we are only beginning to enter this new world and it is for that reason that some of the system changes that will be necessary are at a nascent stage at the time of writing.

The recession brings with it other social consequences that impact upon educational delivery and will make additional demands upon the system. Record levels of youth unemployment for the 16–24 age range present a real challenge to schools who have long taken it for granted that their work is done simply by providing the young person with the necessary passports via qualifications to make their way in the world. Added to that uncomfortable truth is the impact upon the economically disadvantaged as UK politicians seek to tackle what is perceived to be a dependency culture. Welfare reform resulting in changes to housing benefits, child allowances and a raft of other measures will reduce the available income in non-working households. There exist strong correlations to prove that such circumstances directly result in increases in drug and alcohol abuse, incidents of child neglect and abuse, and domestic violence, all of which lead to negative educational outcomes for children brought up in such environments. This factor was a key feature of the Organisation for Economic Cooperation and Development (OECD) Report on the Quality and Equity of Scottish Education (2007) which highlighted the fact that the outcomes for economically disadvantaged children were worse in Scotland than in most other countries in the world when compared with their more advantaged peers in the same country. The challenge facing schools and local authorities will be to enable such children to overcome the impact of poverty and show resilience to match the outcomes of their peers, as is the case in some other countries. The consequences of social inequality in Scotland are likely to lead to increased demands upon social services with larger numbers of children being taken into the care of the council and increased demands upon behaviour and learning support in schools. It is against this backdrop that local authorities will have to examine their role and make decisions that will shape school education over the next twenty years.

Aside from the financial and social challenges there is another factor that has the potential to influence the local governance of education. Decisions to establish national Police and Fire Services demonstrate the appetite of the Scottish Parliament to centralise services at a national level. Arguments about improved efficiency and capacity could just as easily be made in relation to education with a national service linked through some form of local accountability, as will be the case in the new Police and Fire Services – although operational control will lie at the national level.

It could be argued that the failure of local authorities to establish any really significant shared models of service delivery could compel the government to decide that more radical action requires to be taken if the efficiencies of partnership working are to be derived – as is claimed to be the case in the national Police and Fire reforms.

Paradoxically, running parallel to the dilemma of local or national control is a growing trend towards community or neighbourhood delivery of services. The Scottish Government has championed community planning aligned to the achievement of national outcomes in a Single Outcome Agreement with community planning partners including representatives from local authorities, the police, health authorities, the voluntary sector and other key agencies who are involved in enabling better outcomes such as those for children and young people. As the community planning agenda becomes more embedded there is a growing realisation that a 'one size fits all' approach does not meet the needs of very diverse communities within a single geographical council area. Such an insight is leading to the establishment of locality or neighbourhood plans, where responsibility and budgets are devolved to those who live and work in that area. Such a direction of travel presents challenges to both elected members and officers who have tended to see policy development and operational management to be uniform across their area of responsibility, whereas the future will require a much more 'hands-off' and enabling approach rather than any 'command and control' model of practice.

Local authorities could therefore see themselves as facing two opposing forces, with the potential of their being cast adrift in the middle ground between national and community-focused agendas. It is against this uncertain and challenging backdrop that some possible scenarios for the governance of education in Scotland will now be mapped out.

ALTERNATIVE GOVERNANCE MODELS

National Governance of Education

This scenario depends upon a national decision to remove the responsibility for education from local authority control. In much the same way as has occurred with the National Police and Fire Service reform overall strategy, policy development and some forms of operational delivery would be drawn into the centre and managed nationally on behalf of the Scottish Government. The senior accountable officer would be answerable to the Cabinet Secretary with responsibility for education and would have oversight of educational delivery at local level – possibly aligned with health board areas or some other geographic split that did not match current council boundaries. Inevitably these areas would have managers who would be overseen by the senior accountable officer for delivering national policy. The bottom line here is that a large number of directors, heads of service and service managers would no longer be required, as their role to support local educational delivery would be declared redundant.

A key challenge facing the national service would be to identify the budget contribution of each local authority, and this could either be removed at source by reducing pro-rata the grant awarded to individual local authorities by the Scottish Government, or by requiring authorities to directly fund the service – as is currently the case with police and fire. However, this will not be as easy as it might appear, as the way services to schools such as catering, janitorial services, music instruction, repairs and maintenance are provided is not uniform across Scotland. Deciding, therefore, what is within the scope or outside the scope of the budget would be fraught with all sorts of problems. Inevitably, this would lead to disputes between local authorities and the Scottish Government about the level of funding and local variations over the current budget allocation. Nevertheless, this is a route that other countries such as New Zealand have managed to tread in the past and formulae can be created and applied to overcome such disparities over a reasonable transition period.

Common policies on diverse topics such as bullying, reading programmes, staffing formulae, school design, class arrangements, pupil support structures and devolved school budgets could be set at a national level and implemented within every school in Scotland. This contrasts with current practice where all of the above are currently within the remit of the local authority. In a similar fashion arrangements for supporting children with additional needs for learning could be standardised across the country at a time when the potential for differences in funding could lead to quite significant disparities of support. It is interesting to note at the time of writing that this disparity of funding is providing a real challenge to emerging national Fire Service provision – as would undoubtedly prove the case with a national education provision.

If such drawing of power into the centre were to come to fruition the whole notion of local accountability – a strength of the current system – would be at risk. Taking heed of the current direction of travel in the emerging national police and fire services, it is likely that accountability will lie with a national board and some form of local scrutiny through councils – but the councils will not have any locus in operational matters. One could imagine a scenario where the local area education manager, who is managed by the national body, is called to deliver a report on education within a council area – but with no reference to local political priorities as would be the case at present.

Shared Service Governance Models

If we accept that the 'nationalisation' of education exists at one end of the continuum from current governance models, what might be the models that reduce management expenditure but maintain local accountability and influence over policy and budget? At the heart of these alternatives is the notion that councils would have to work together to establish a delivery model that oversees their political imperatives but at a substantially lower cost than is currently the case. There are three governance arrangements that could be adopted to achieve this model of delivery:

- *Joint Committee*: Representatives from each authority;
- Lead Authority (a form of public-public partnership): Appointing one or other of the partner authorities to lead on the delivery of the service;
- *Joint Board or other Third Party Employing Organisation (e.g. Company Limited by Guarantee)*: Establishing a new organisation to be wholly owned and controlled by the councils, as either a not-for-profit or a for-profit organisation.

Joint Committee Model

The Joint Committee is a joint body set up, by agreement, to discharge some agreed functions on behalf of two or more authorities. Functions cannot be delegated to a Joint Committee in cases where representatives from outwith the participating local authorities are given voting rights. Joint Committees are not corporate bodies, which means they do not have their own legal identity, they cannot enforce contracts and they cannot employ staff. They can, however, operate as a new shared entity, which would be hosted by one or other authority but provide service to both. The service would deliver the policies set by the Joint Committee. Elected members who sit on Joint Committees must act in the best interests of the Joint Committee, but in practice this can sometimes be difficult to achieve and representatives need to be ready to declare potential conflicts of interest as required.

Joint Committees are probably the most common form of formalised joint working between local authorities, attesting to the growing strength of authorities seeking to work in partnership by agreeing a mechanism for making joint progress on some shared priorities. However, anecdotal evidence would suggest that in practice individual partners' self-interests can sometimes dominate Joint Committee decision making (more likely to occur when one partner is clearly more powerful than the other) and implementation of joint decisions across both the participating organisations can sometimes be problematic. In practice, it is sometimes the case that the Joint Committee does not have the necessary clout to ensure that joint decisions are implemented with equal vigour by both partners.

Joint Committees can become vulnerable to unpicking in times of financial pressure. Were Joint Committee arrangements an assured means for progressing joint working, we should see many more examples of shared services in Scotland than we do at present. The fact that we do not (as yet) indicates that perhaps something more substantial than Joint Committee governance is needed if we are successfully to derive step-change benefits, including savings, from sharing education services.

Lead Authority Model

The Lead Authority and Joint Committee approaches are relatively closely related in that both are 'internal' governance solutions that do not require changing the staffing arrangements of the participating authorities. The Lead Authority option is simpler, however, in that it does not require a new decision-making forum to be established. This option depends on a formal transfer of Authority A's budget (and staffing) for a service into Authority B which then assumes responsibility for delivery of that service across a wider geography. If the circumstances are right, this can be a good way to make progress on a shared service agenda.

Specific challenges can arise under this choice of governance where the delivery priorities or methods or the culture of Authority A do not match those of Authority B. Unless all aspects of shared delivery are captured and formalised in fine detail in the working arrangements agreed, evidence from the UK would suggest that the Lead Authority arrangement may not be able to respond flexibly enough or quickly enough to both authorities' emerging priorities. In practice, a sense of 'winners and losers' may sometimes emerge in relation to which of the two partners has greater strategic control and ownership of the duty being discharged (as distinct from agreed delegation of operational delivery).

A particular risk may also arise when too much political and official time and effort is spent deciding, formalising and delivering only the shared delivery priorities across both authorities in each service area, leaving vulnerable the client authority's capacity to prioritise and deliver services that are not explicitly captured by the Lead Authority agreement.

The Lead Authority model usefully allows for a start to be made between two authorities who may, in the future, wish to move in a gradual way towards greater sharing. However, there are concerns about how the Lead Authority model could secure local democratic accountability equally well in both authorities or how it could, in practice, promote greater innovation, efficiency and effectiveness in operational delivery.

Third Party Organisations – An Outline

Setting up third party entities for delivery of an activity or function is common across both the public and private sectors. There are two principal forms of third party governance available (discounting from the start any notion of privatisation from consideration). These are:

- *Joint Board*: established through application to Scottish Ministers;
- *Social Organisation*: established through forming a not-for-profit social enterprise organisation, such as a Company Limited by Guarantee (CLG) or a Community Interest Company (CiC).

Both types would involve setting up a corporate body, which would establish a *commercial organisation* that could:

1. employ staff (as many or few as desired);
2. enter into contracts with other organisations, if wished;
3. require to be audited;
4. grow its own distinctive organisational culture and identity;
5. deliver shared operational support services.

A Joint Board is set up through application to Scottish Ministers in an order-making process involving the Scottish Parliament, whereas the other two types can be set up directly by the councils themselves in a process that is wholly controlled by the councils. A Joint Board may be restricted in regard to who can sit on the Board. The membership of a Joint Board must consist of elected members from the constituent councils, along with church representatives. Joint Boards can of course avail themselves of external advice as required. The other two types would allow the councils, if they wished, to expand the core membership to include additional advisory and/or voting representation from, for example, parents, trades unions or the local business community.

The Commercial Organisation types (Limited Liability Partnership and Company Limited by Share Capital) are profit-driven, whereas the other two are not. The Social Organisation types (CLG and CiC) can, however, be set up to generate *surplus* for annual re-investment, and in that sense would share some of the operational behaviours found in a Commercial Organisation (e.g. incentivising staff and management performance around lean delivery of essential functions and processes). Some forms of Social Organisation (the CLG forms, but not the CiC) can gain charitable status whereas the other two types cannot.

Advantages and Disadvantages of the Third Party Organisation Types

Joint Board

The major advantage of the Joint Board is the high positive public recognition of the role of a Board in regulating aspects of public life. It has worked successfully in a number of vital and prominent areas, including health and policing. (However, it is also fair to add that that success is recognised from within the traditional 'business as usual' mould – and it is precisely business as usual that is coming under pressure in every aspect of public service delivery in the current financial climate.)

A disadvantage is that it requires councils to cede an element of control to Scottish Ministers in agreeing the content of a potential Order, and to the Scottish Parliament in enacting the Order through a prescribed legislative process. The latter process requires that if a change of any content is requested by the authorities during the course of the application, then the entire legislative amendment process begins again from scratch.

Joint Boards must consist solely of elected members of the constituent councils, which of course provides for highly assured local democratic accountability. (There is a specific additional statutory requirement for Education that three church representatives sit on councils' Education Committees or other equivalent decision-making fora.) Elected members can and do strengthen their own hand by drawing onto the Board some additional expertise and perspectives in an advisory capacity. If councils wished to pursue a Joint Board for shared education and children's services, they may wish to consider the composition of both voting and advisory board membership so as to provide the Board as a whole with stronger overall scrutiny and challenge of the operational body, or to draw in new voices from the community in a way that is highly consistent with councils' values for strong and effective localism.

A Third Party Social Organisation

The typical underlying argument for choosing a third party organisation is that the service area in question is sufficiently distinctive, large or important that it requires a more structured, professional and/or productive organisational status than is possible as a Directorate within the authority. In general, setting up a third party entity is the most appropriate choice when

- the service is already performing well but new external or internal factors have arisen that put a premium on revising the underlying delivery model; and/or
- the service cannot improve to the extent required or innovate sufficiently within its current decision-making and performance management environment; and/or
- the service is sufficiently specialised and/or large to require a separate entity (e.g. police); and/or
- there is clear recognition amongst those who are accountable for the service that they can exercise that accountability more decisively when there is a formal split between themselves as the owner and those who are responsible for delivery (the operational body).

Outline Benefits to be Realised from Third Party Organisations

The net benefit for the owning organisation(s) should be to create a third entity that is both more clearly defined than an in-house Directorate (for example, as a consequence of the detailed specification work needed for entering into a contract-type arrangement) and is easier to manage and control.

At its best, this arrangement promises the councils strategic control of – and clear accountability for – outputs and outcomes, releasing the third party organisation to get on with the operational delivery. The arrangement potentially empowers the councils with well-defined sanctions should they need to take corrective action against the operational body, and it gives them both the evidence and the tools they need to hold the operational body strongly to task. From the other side of the relationship, at its best the arrangement provides the new organisation with the imperative to secure significantly better performance and operational improvement than would be possible under the status quo, by using the opportunity of sharing to innovate. While improvement is of course a prerequisite for all manner of arrangements in delivering public services, the third party arrangement provides that the Managing Director would be held responsible to the shared service board for delivering required outputs and outcomes, within a contract-style financial reporting regime.

Of course, the phrase 'at its best' is deliberate since the success of the arrangement depends on how well it is implemented. The arrangement needs to be closely designed around realising the benefits sought of it, and needs to be monitored and evaluated against its successes (or failures) in so doing over an agreed period of time. To realise the benefits, the operational criteria that drive the new organisation's business plans need to derive logically from the benefits sought when setting up the new entity, and need to be testable over time against agreed key performance indicators.

Outline Risks of Third Party Organisations

Third party organisations carry key generic risks for councils. The most prominent of these are:

- Third party organisations are driven by contract, or contract-like agreements. However, contractual terms can be hard to vary en route (unless some deliberate wriggle room is built into the contract), or can only be altered in certain formally prescribed ways. In the case of Joint Boards especially, the latter requirement could emerge as a disadvantage.

- Third party organisations need sufficient and smart scrutiny arrangements by the authorities who remain accountable for the services provided. It is essential that the councils retain sufficient capacity to effectively challenge as well as support the new body. Opposing roles of commissioner and supplier must be well matched in expertise and authority if the relationship is to start out – and remain – healthy and vigorous in its ambition to deliver step-change improvement. There is a risk that the transfer of staff into a third organisation may denude the authorities of the skills needed to ensure the contract relationship does not become one-sided.

NEXT STEPS

It will be interesting to reflect upon this chapter ten years hence. As with any attempt to look into the future the likelihood is that the fevered imaginings of the writer rarely come to fruition and the actual outcome is a much more graduated and finessed version of current events than has been set out in this chapter. Nevertheless, the general consensus is that change is on the horizon: more devolution of power to schools and headteachers; a change to funding mechanisms to schools and the associated role for local authorities; and an associated change to the role of local authorities in setting policy.

No one reckons that there will be wholesale changes along the lines that were experienced in 1995 when the most recent local government reorganisation took place, primarily due to the fact that any externally driven change requires the government to pick up the tab for the change process. This is where a comparison between what has happened in England over the last twenty-five years or so can prove useful. It is unlikely that Scotland will follow the English model in terms of the final outcome, e.g. academies, trust schools, and so on, but rather it might follow the change strategy. It seems that one of the main means adopted in England has actually depended more upon repealing legislation as opposed to the starting point being the creation of new legislation. That is not to say that new legislation will not be necessary but the starting point could be to consider which pillars of the existing system could be pulled away, which in itself might lead to radical change. This is certainly what happened in England in the 1988 Education Reform Act, which saw a range of powers for local authorities being removed and either passed down to schools and their governors, or passed upwards to the government. Over the next twenty-three years those twin directions of travel were inexorable. This is most recently evidenced in the (England and Wales) 2011 Education Act, which further repealed the duties of local authorities. In that period the government has not had to legislate for change in the organisational structure in local authorities, but rather by changing the responsibilities of local authorities it created an environment where the local authorities had to adapt themselves to their changing role.

So what might be the duties currently undertaken by Scottish local authorities which, if removed, might lead to the most significant change?

Three of the four duties outlined in the Standards in Scotland's Schools etc. Act (2000), if removed, might result in dramatic change to the education system in Scotland. The first duty is the role of the local authority in relation to school improvement. If this were removed it would be a fundamental shift in practice and would transform at a stroke the role of the local authority. The second associated duty that could be removed is that regarding school development planning, which would remove the obligation of the school to take account of the local authority's statement of educational objectives. The third and last duty that could be removed is that relating to the delegation of budgets to schools. This presupposes that the delegation scheme is devised by the authority. However, if this were removed it could be replaced by a national scheme of delegation which is simply overseen by the authority.

All of these suggestions must be read in the knowledge that no substantive alteration to the governance role of local authorities in education has taken place in the last eighty-six years: this is a system that has successfully resisted change. Nevertheless, the forces acting against the status quo mean that we are on the threshold of what might be considered to be a key tipping point in Scottish education – and one from which there will be no return.

17

Education and the Law

Janys M. Scott QC

Scotland has, and has always had, its own distinctive system of school education. The law provides the administrative framework for education. The basic structure is now to be found in the Education (Scotland) Act 1980 although this Act has been much amended since 1980. The Scottish Parliament has passed no fewer than nine statutes principally concerned with school education. It has also made numerous regulations. The courts are occasionally called upon to interpret and apply the law. The following is a brief guide, rather than a comprehensive statement.

THE SCOTTISH MINISTERS AND EDUCATION AUTHORITIES

Oversight of education was devolved to the Scottish Ministers by the Scotland Act 1998. The Scottish Ministers have the responsibility of securing improvements in the quality of school education and setting national priorities in education.[1] They are advised by Her Majesty's Inspectors of Education.[2] The Scottish Minsters have the power to pass regulations prescribing the detail of how education should be provided. It is, however, a feature of education law that government has on the whole preferred to issue guidance, rather than pass regulations. While regulations must be obeyed, guidance may be departed from if there is good reason not to follow it.

Public education in Scotland is managed by councils operating as education authorities. Scottish legislation refers to a school where education is provided by an education authority as a 'public school', as opposed to a private school under independent management. Every education authority has a duty to secure that there is made for its area adequate and efficient provision of school education.[3] 'School education' means progressive education appropriate to the requirement of pupils, regard being had to the age, ability and aptitude of such pupils. It includes activities of a kind suitable for pupils who are under school age and the teaching of Gaelic in Gaelic-speaking areas. As part of the duty to secure provision of school education, an education authority should secure for pupils the provision of adequate facilities for social, cultural and recreative activities and for physical education and training. Psychological services should also be maintained

---

[1] Standards in Scotland's Schools etc. Act 2000, sections 3 and 4.
[2] Education (Scotland) Act 1980, section 66.
[3] 1980 Act, section 1.

to advise parents and teachers on appropriate methods of education for children with additional support needs.[4]

An education authority is generally expected to provide school education free of charge.[5] Pupils provided with free education must also receive free books, writing materials, stationery, mathematical instruments, practice material and any other article necessary to take full advantage of education.[6] The authority may provide clothing for activities such as physical exercise.[7] Where ordinary clothing is necessary to allow a pupil to take advantage of education this must be provided.[8] The authority should make such arrangements as it thinks necessary for pupils' transport to school.[9] Food and drink may be provided in school, in which case it must be provided free of charge to pupils whose parents are in receipt of certain benefits. The availability of school lunches should be promoted.[10] Education authorities are required by law to observe certain nutritional requirements.[11] A teacher has no right to inflict corporal punishment on a pupil, but physical restraint to avert danger of physical injury or danger to property will not be treated as corporal punishment.[12]

Although there is, in effect, a national curriculum, which schools are expected to follow, the curriculum is not prescribed by law. There are some rules on the content of education, but these appear to reflect preoccupations of legislators at various points of time. Schools are required to continue religious observance and instruction, unless a local referendum permits discontinuance.[13] All public schools must be open to pupils of all denominations and any parent may withdraw a child from religious instruction and observance.[14] In 2000, a ban on the intentional promotion of homosexuality in schools was repealed and a positive duty imposed on education authorities to have regard to the value of a stable family life in a child's development and the need to ensure that the content of instruction is appropriate, having regard to the age, understanding and stage of development of each child.[15] The Scottish Ministers may issue guidance about sex education.[16] Somewhat archaically, education authorities are required to:

> ensure that care is taken to develop in pupils . . . reasonable and responsible social attitudes and relationships, to cultivate . . . consideration for others, and to encourage . . . the practice of good manners, good attitudes to work, initiative and self reliance and habits of personal hygiene and cleanliness.[17]

There is a relatively recent requirement that education authorities should endeavour to secure that schools are 'health promoting' by providing activities and an environment and

---

[4] 1980 Act, section 4.
[5] 1980 Act, section 3.
[6] 1980 Act, section 11(1).
[7] 1980 Act, section 11(2).
[8] 1980 Act, section 54.
[9] 1980 Act, section 51.
[10] 1980 Act, section 53A to 53B; amended by Education (School Meals) (Scotland) Act 2003.
[11] 1980 Act, sections 56A to 56E; Nutritional Requirements for Food and Drink in Schools (Scotland) Regulations 2008, SSI 2008/265.
[12] 2000 Act, section 16.
[13] 1980 Act, section 8.
[14] 1980 Act, section 9.
[15] Ethical Standards in Public Life etc. (Scotland) Act 2000, sections 34 and 35.
[16] 2000 Act, section 56.
[17] Schools General (Scotland) Regulations 1975, SI 1975/1135, regulation 11.

facilities which promote the physical, social, mental and emotional health and wellbeing of pupils.[18] Pupils should be encouraged and assisted to take advantage of facilities for medical and dental treatment in school.[19] They should have access to careers advice.[20]

PUBLIC SCHOOLS

In public schools,[21] free nursery education must be provided for children broadly between the ages of 3 and 5, for twelve-and-a-half hours per week, over thirty-eight weeks of the year. Nursery education may be provided for other pre-school age children.[22] Parents do not have to send children to nursery school.

Parents do, however, have to provide education for children once they are of school age. A child will be of school age on the commencement date (usually the first day of the new school year) immediately following his or her fifth birthday. A child may start primary school at the age of 4, provided he or she attains the age of 5 before a particular date, usually at about the end of February.[23] Younger children may be admitted to primary school at the discretion of the education authority if the education provided is suited to the age, ability and aptitude of the child.[24] Primary education is designed to meet the needs of pupils up to the age of 12.[25] A primary one class taught by a single teacher is generally limited to twenty-five pupils. Primary two and primary three classes may contain thirty pupils.[26] There is no legislative restriction on the size of upper primary classes, but teachers' contracts do not require them to teach more than thirty-three in a single year group class and composite classes containing pupils from more than one year group are limited to twenty-five.[27] Numbers in a class may be further limited by the size of the room in which pupils are being taught.[28]

Secondary education caters for children who have attained the age of 12.[29] Subject to the size of the room, the number of pupils in a class is limited by teachers' contracts to thirty-three in the first two years, and after that to thirty, save for practical classes where the limit is twenty. A child ceases to be of school age at about the age of 16 and may leave school at the beginning of the Christmas holiday or at the end of May, depending when his or her birthday falls. A pupil who attains the school leaving age does not have to leave school. A pupil over the school leaving age who has not attained the age of 18 is treated as a 'young person' and as such generally exercises his or her own decisions in relation to education, rather than having decisions taken by parents.

Denominational schools are public schools that have a link with a church or religious

[18] 2000 Act, section 2A, inserted by Schools (Health Promotion and Nutrition) (Scotland) Act 2007.
[19] National Health Service (Scotland) Act 1978, section 39(3).
[20] Employment and Training Act 1973, section 8.
[21] That is, schools managed by education authorities.
[22] 1980 Act, section 1(1A) to (1C), Provision of School Education for Children under School Age (Prescribed Children) (Scotland) Order 2002, SSI 2002/90.
[23] 1980 Act, section 32.
[24] 2000 Act, section 38.
[25] 1980 Act, section 135(2)(a).
[26] Education (Lower Primary Class Sizes) (Scotland) Regulations 1999, SI 1999/1080, as amended by SSI 2010/326.
[27] SNCT Conditions of Service.
[28] Schools General (Scotland) Regulations 1975, SI 1975/1135, regulation 8.
[29] 1980 Act, section 135(2)(b).

body. The existence of such schools is deeply rooted in Scottish history, particularly in the case of the Roman Catholic community. These schools transferred to the control of education authorities after 1918,[30] or were established later as religious foundations and transferred to the public system.[31] An education authority has the power itself to establish denominational schools.[32] The education authority controls the curriculum and appoints staff, but teachers must be approved as regards religious belief and character by representatives of the church or religious body in whose interests the school is conducted. The time set apart for religious instruction or observance should be maintained. There should be an unpaid supervisor of religious instruction.[33]

If an education authority proposes to close a public school, or to effect other material changes in the provision of education, it must follow a procedure prescribed by law.[34] It must prepare a statement indicating the educational benefits of the proposal and a paper setting out the details of what is proposed. It must then consult with persons including the parent council of the school, the parents, the pupils, the staff and any trade union representing staff, and the community council. Her Majesty's Inspectors of Education should be asked for a report on the proposal. A public meeting should be held. The education authority should then prepare a consultation report. Special considerations apply to the closure of rural schools, where the authority must consider whether there is a viable alternative to closure, the likely effect on the community if the proposal is implemented and the effect on the travelling arrangements for pupils. The Scottish Ministers may call in a closure proposal if it appears that the education authority may have failed to comply with the requirements of the Act or failed to take account of a material consideration relevant to the decision to implement the proposal. If a call-in notice is issued, then the authority requires the consent of the Scottish Ministers to proceed. Changes affecting the provision of education in denominational schools will generally require the consent of the Scottish Ministers.[35]

EDUCATION OTHER THAN IN PUBLIC SCHOOLS

Parents may choose to send their children to a private independent school. These schools are required to register with the Registrar of Independent Schools in Scotland. An application for registration will only be granted if the Scottish Ministers are satisfied that efficient and suitable education will be provided and that the welfare of pupils will be adequately safeguarded and promoted. The proprietor and teachers must be proper persons to act as such and the premises must be suitable.[36]

There is one mainstream school in Scotland that is neither managed by an education authority, nor an independent school. Jordanhill School receives direct grant aid from the Scottish Ministers[37] and the reasons for this are historical.

Children may be educated at home by their parents, in which event there is no require-

---

[30] Education (Scotland) Act 1918, section 18.
[31] 1980 Act, section 16.
[32] 1980 Act, section 17(2).
[33] 1980 Act, section 21.
[34] Schools (Consultation) (Scotland) Act 2010.
[35] 1980 Act, sections 22C and 22D.
[36] 1980 Act, sections 98 to 103B, as amended by School Education (Ministerial Powers and Independent Schools) (Scotland) Act 2004.
[37] 1980 Act, section 73.

ment to follow any particular curriculum or undertake any form of assessment of progress. If a child has attended public school, the consent of the education authority is required before the child may be withdrawn from school.[38] No consent is required for home education of a child who has not attended public school, or who has finished primary education but not commenced secondary education. An education authority has no duty to monitor home education, but if it becomes aware that a child is not receiving education suitable to age, ability and aptitude then notice should be served on the parent requiring information about the education being provided. Continued failure could result in an attendance notice requiring the child to attend a particular school.[39]

PARENTS

Parents have a statutory duty to provide efficient education suitable to the age, ability and aptitude of their children either by causing them to attend a public school regularly or by other means.[40] If a child who has attended a public school subsequently fails without reasonable excuse to attend, the parent may be committing an offence.[41] No offence is committed if a child would be required to walk an unreasonable distance to school. For children under the age of 8 the 'walking distance' is two miles and for children of 8 and over it is three miles. Beyond those distances education authorities should provide transport. If the child attends a particular school as a result of a placing request by the parent, then the parent is responsible for getting the child to school whatever the distance. Where a child is unwell the parent does not have to send the child to school, although the education authority may seek a medical examination. Other circumstances may also provide a reasonable excuse,[42] but unreported bullying has been held not to exonerate a parent from sending a child to school.[43] There is controversy about the criminal liability of a parent who is not aware that the child is not at school. On one view such a parent could not be prosecuted.[44] A child who fails to attend school regularly without reasonable excuse may be referred to the children's hearing for consideration of compulsory measures of supervision.[45]

The corollary is the general statutory principle that, so far as compatible with the provision of suitable instruction and training and the avoidance of unreasonable public expenditure, pupils are to be educated in accordance with the wishes of their parents.[46] This does not, however, mean that parental wishes must in all cases prevail, as there will generally be other factors to consider.[47]

When the Education (Scotland) Act 1980 refers to a 'parent' this includes a mother and a father, provided she or he has parental responsibilities and parental rights or the

---

[38] 1980 Act, section 35(1).
[39] 1980 Act, sections 36 to 41.
[40] 1980 Act, section 30.
[41] 1980 Act, section 35.
[42] 1980 Act, section 42.
[43] *Montgomery* v. *Cumming* 1999 SCCR 178.
[44] *O'Hagan* v. *Rea* 2001 SCCR 178 *cf. Barnfather* v. *Islington Education Authority* [2003] EWHC 418 (Admin), [2003] 1 WLR 2318.
[45] Children (Scotland) Act 1995, section 52(2)(h), to be repealed and replaced by Children's Hearings (Scotland) Act 2011, section 67(2)(o).
[46] 1980 Act, section 28.
[47] *Harvey* v. *Strathclyde Regional Council* 1989 SLT 612, HL.

responsibility to maintain the child. In practice all parents are likely to fall within this defini-tion (unless the child has, for example, been adopted). Both parents remain responsible for the child's education, even if separated and even if the child lives with one and not the other. A step-parent who has accepted the child as a member of his or her family will be liable to maintain the child and so is treated as a 'parent' for the purposes of the child's education. A person who is actually looking after the child, such as a foster parent, should also be treated as a 'parent'. Parents have a right of access to the educational records of their children.[48]

The Scottish Schools (Parental Involvement) Act 2006 establishes two bodies to encour-age parental involvement in schools.[49] Each public school has a 'parent forum' which is simply a collective term for all the parents of pupils in attendance at the school (other than a nursery school or class). A parent forum may be represented by a parent council. There is no statutory blueprint for a parent council, but membership is restricted to parents and persons co–opted by the parent council. In the case of a denominational school, the council must co–opt at least one member nominated by the church or body with which the school is associated. A parent council is required to support the endeavours of those managing the school in the exercise of their statutory functions.[50]

PUPILS

Education authorities have a duty to provide schools. Parents have a duty to provide edu-cation. Until comparatively recently there was no express recognition of the right of the child to receive education. Section 1 of the Standards in Scotland's Schools etc. Act 2000 now states the right of every child of school age to be provided with school education by or by virtue of arrangements made, or entered into, by an education authority. Article 2 of the First Protocol to the European Convention on Human Rights gives a child the right not to be denied education. The weak negative formulation in the Convention has been interpreted by the European Court of Human Rights as a positive right for persons to avail themselves of the existing means of instruction provided by the state[51] but does not confer the right to attend any particular school.[52] The domestic formulation of the child's right to education is positive, and reflects article 28 of the United Nations Convention on the Rights of the Child.

Section 2 of the Standards in Scotland's Schools etc. Act 2000 is also self-consciously modelled on the United Nations Convention on the Rights of the Child. An education authority is required to secure that education is directed to the development of the person-ality, talents, and mental and physical abilities of the child or young person to their fullest potential,[53] reflecting the right of the child in terms of article 29 of the United Nations Convention. In carrying out this duty, an education authority is required to have due regard, so far as reasonably practicable, to the views of the child or young person in deci-sions that significantly affect him or her, taking account of the child or young person's age

---

[48] Education (Disability Strategies and Pupils' Educational Records) (Scotland) Act 2002, section 5; Pupils' Educational Records (Scotland) Regulations 2003, SSI 2003/581.
[49] Scottish Schools (Parental Involvement) Act 2006, section 5.
[50] 2006 Act, section 8.
[51] *Belgium Linguistics Case (No 2)* (1968) 1 EHRR 252.
[52] *Ali* v. *Head Teachers and Governors of Lord Grey School* [2006] UKHL 14; *R (on the application of SB)* v. *Denbigh High School Governors* [2006] UKHL 15.
[53] 2000 Act, section 2(1).

and maturity.[54] This is consistent with the right of the child capable of forming views to express those views freely found in article 12 of the United Nations Convention.

The statutory structure of education law is gradually being amended to give effect to the rights of children. Education authorities should give pupils the opportunity to make their views known when preparing annual statements of improvement objectives.[55] Pupils should be consulted in relation to school development plans.[56] There are provisions for consulting pupils of a suitable age and maturity in respect of school closures or other significant changes that may affect them in respect of the structure of educational provision.[57] If a medical examination is required in connection with the child's education then it is a precondition of the examination that consent is given by the child, if he or she has sufficient understanding to give consent.[58] Children may ask to see their own pupil records, provided they have a general understanding of what it means to exercise this right.[59]

Children attain capacity to take decisions in relation to their own affairs at the age of 16.[60] This is broadly reflected in legislation relating to education. Young persons over the school leaving age exercise their own rights to make placing requests and appeal against exclusion from school, in place of their parents.[61]

PLACING IN SCHOOLS

Pupils are deemed to belong to the area in which their parents are ordinarily resident.[62] Each education authority will have general arrangements for placing children in their area in public schools. These arrangements should be published or otherwise made available.[63] As a matter of practice, education authorities will delineate a particular 'catchment area' for each school so that pupils living in that area will generally attend that school. Education authorities in Scotland do not practise academic selection of pupils. There is a legal requirement to publish information about schools, including basic general information about schools in the area, information relating to a particular school and supplementary information about arrangements for placing children in schools.[64] Information about a particular school is usually presented in the form of a school handbook and updated annually.

Parents are entitled to make a placing request for their child to attend a school other than the one in which the child would be placed under the authority's general arrangements.[65] The authority must have guidelines that it undertakes to follow in the event that more placing requests are received than there are places in a particular school.[66] The authority is entitled to reserve places for children moving into the area. Subject to this, the authority

[54] 2000 Act, section 2(2).
[55] 2000 Act, section 5.
[56] 2000 Act, section 6.
[57] Schools (Consultation) (Scotland) Act 2010, section 2 and schedule 2.
[58] 1980 Act, section 131A.
[59] Data Protection Act 1998, sections 7, 8, 9A and 66.
[60] Age of Legal Capacity (Scotland) Act 1991, section 1.
[61] 1980 Act, section 28G.
[62] 1980 Act, section 23(3).
[63] 1980 Act, section 28B.
[64] Education (School and Placing Information) (Scotland) Regulations 2012, SSI 2012/130.
[65] 1980 Act, section 28A, amended by School Education (Amendment) (Scotland) Act 2002 to ensure placing requests may be made for primary one for a child under five .
[66] 1980 Act, section 28B.

is only entitled to refuse a placing request on one or more of a number of grounds. The grounds include having to employ an additional teacher or extend the school accommodation, or if the capacity of the school would be exceeded. A placing request may also be refused if admitting the child would be seriously detrimental to order and discipline or to the educational wellbeing of pupils.[67]

If the authority refuses the request the parent may appeal to an appeal committee.[68] This is a committee set up and maintained by the education authority.[69] Appeals should be dealt with promptly, and in accordance with rules of procedure.[70] The committee may confirm the decision of the education authority if satisfied that one or more of the grounds for refusal exists or exist, and that it is in all the circumstances appropriate to do so.[71] If decisions by the education authority, or the appeal committee, are not taken within prescribed time limits they are deemed to have been refused,[72] so that parents may proceed to the next step in the appeal process.

A parent whose appeal is refused by the appeal committee may appeal to the sheriff by way of a summary application.[73] The sheriff will hear evidence in private and may confirm refusal of the placing request if, on the evidence at the time of the hearing, one or more of the grounds for refusal exists or exist and that it is in all the circumstances appropriate to confirm the refusal. The sheriff's decision is final, which means there can be no further appeal. If, however, the sheriff has exceeded his powers by, for example, misconstruing the legislation or trespassing into matters of policy that are for the education authority, the Court of Session may intervene in a petition for judicial review.[74]

EXCLUSION FROM SCHOOL

An education authority should not exclude a pupil from school unless the parent refuses or fails to comply, or allows the pupil to comply, with the rules, regulations or disciplinary requirements of the school. A pupil whose continued attendance would be likely to be seriously detrimental to order and discipline in the school or the educational wellbeing of pupils there may also be excluded.[75] There is a prescribed procedure for exclusion. On the day that a decision is taken to exclude the pupil the parent must be told, orally or in writing, of the decision and given a date within seven days of the date following the decision, where the headteacher, other teacher, or official of the education authority will be available to discuss the decision. If the pupil is not readmitted within seven days, or if the parent has not indicated that there will be no appeal, then there must be written notice to the parent of the reasons for the exclusion, any conditions for readmission and of the right to appeal.[76]

---

[67] 1980 Act, section 28A.
[68] 1980 Act, section 28C.
[69] 1980 Act, section 28D and schedule A1.
[70] Education (Appeal Committee Procedures) (Scotland) Regulations 1982, SI 1982/1736.
[71] 1980 Act, section 28E.
[72] Education (Placing in Schools Etc – Deemed Decisions) (Scotland) Regulations 1982, SI 1982/1733.
[73] 1980 Act, section 28F.
[74] See, for example, *Dundee City Council, Petrs* 1999 Fam LR 13, *Aberdeen City Council* v. *Wokoma* 2002 SC 352.
[75] Schools General (Scotland) Regulations 1975, SI 1975/1135, regulation 4.
[76] SI 1975/1135 regulation 4A.

A parent may appeal against exclusion and a young person over the school leaving age may appeal in place of the parent. A child under the school leaving age may also appeal if he or she has legal capacity.[77] The test of legal capacity is whether a child has a general understanding of what it means to instruct a solicitor, with a presumption that a child of 12 or more will have such an understanding.[78] The legislation makes no provision for a conflict between the actions of a child and those of a parent in relation to an appeal.

An appeal against exclusion should be made to the appeal committee.[79] The rules of procedure are the same as for placing requests.[80] If the appeal is not determined expeditiously it will be deemed to have been refused.[81] Further appeal lies to the sheriff. There have been a number of conflicting approaches to appeal but, since a decision on judicial review in the Court of Session in 2004, the law on how a sheriff should approach an exclusion appeal has become more settled. The sheriff requires to be satisfied that the decision to exclude the pupil was justified in all the circumstances of the case. This means the court should look at the factual basis for the exclusion.[82]

ADDITIONAL SUPPORT FOR LEARNING

A pupil has additional support needs where, for whatever reason, he or she is, or is likely to be, unable without the provision of additional support to benefit from school education. The statutory provision for such children is found in the Education (Additional Support for Learning) (Scotland) Act 2004.[83] Additional support in relation to children at school is provision which is additional to, or otherwise different from, the educational provision made generally by the education authority for pupils of the same age.[84] Every education authority should make adequate and efficient provision for such additional support as is required by the individual child or young person, and should also make appropriate arrangements for keeping the needs and adequacy of the support under review.[85]

Special schools and special classes exist to provide education specially suited to the additional support needs of children or young persons selected for attendance there by reason of their needs.[86] Education for pupils with additional support needs should, however, where possible, be provided in mainstream schools.[87] Only where mainstream education would not be suited to the ability or aptitude of the child, or would be incompatible with the provision of efficient education for other children, or would result in incurring unreasonable public expenditure, should a child be educated in a special school.

Certain children qualify for a co-ordinated support plan. These are children whose

---

[77] 2000 Act, section 41.
[78] Age of Legal Capacity (Scotland) Act 1991, section 2(4A) and (4B).
[79] 1980 Act, section 28H.
[80] Education (Appeal Committee Procedures) (Scotland) Regulations 1982, SI 1982/1736.
[81] Education (Placing in Schools Etc – Deemed Decisions) (Scotland) Regulations 1982, SI 1982/1733 regulation 5.
[82] *Glasgow City Council, Petitioners* 2004 SLT 61, approving *Wallace* v. *City of Dundee Council* 2000 SLT (Sh Ct) 60, followed in *F* v. *City of Glasgow Council* 2004 SLT (Sh Ct) 123 and *S* v. *City of Glasgow Council* 2004 SLT (Sh Ct) 128.
[83] As amended by the Education (Additional Support for Learning) (Scotland) Act 2009.
[84] 2004 Act, section 1.
[85] 2004 Act, section 4.
[86] 2004 Act, section 29(1).
[87] 2000 Act, section 15.

support needs are likely to have a significant adverse effect on their school education or whose needs arise from multiple factors which, taken together, would have such an effect. No support plan is required unless the needs are likely to continue for over a year, the education authority is responsible for the pupil's education and significant additional support will be needed from more than one source, whether within the local authority or by another agency as well as the education authority.[88] A co-ordinated support plan will set out the factor or factors from which the pupil's additional support needs arise, the educational objectives to be achieved taking account of those factors, the additional support required and the persons by whom the support should be provided.[89] It will also nominate the school the pupil is to attend. The 2004 Act makes provision for assessment and examination of pupils with a view to identifying those who have additional support needs and those who require a co-ordinated support plan.

Disputes relating to co-ordinated support plans may be referred to the Additional Support Needs Tribunal.[90] This is an expert tribunal composed of a legally qualified convenor and two other members. A president, appointed by the Scottish Ministers, is responsible for administration. The Additional Support Needs Tribunal operates in accordance with rules of procedure,[91] the overriding objective of which is to enable the tribunal, with the assistance of parties, to deal with references fairly and justly. Proceedings should be informal and flexible and avoid delay, in so far as is compatible with proper consideration of the issues. The tribunal may confirm or overturn the decision of an education authority in respect of the need for a co-ordinated support plan or the contents of the plan, or require the education authority to prepare a plan or review a plan or to amend its contents. The tribunal may also require the authority to rectify a failure to provide, or make arrangements for provision of, additional support identified in the plan.[92] An appeal lies on a point of law to the Court of Session.[93]

Where a child has additional support needs there are separate provisions for placing requests.[94] A placing request may be refused on the same general grounds as those that apply to children who do not have additional support needs, but in the case of children with such needs a placing request may be made specifying a special school. This may be a school under the management of the authority, or it may be an independent special school in Scotland, or elsewhere in the United Kingdom, provided the managers are prepared to admit the child. If the specified school is not a public school, the education authority may refuse the request if they are able to make provision for the additional support needs of the child in a school other than the specified school, they have offered the child a place at the other school and if it is not reasonable, having regard to the respective suitability and cost of the two schools, to place the child in the special school. Appeals in respect of refusal of a place at a special school are referred to the Additional Support Needs Tribunal, as are refusals for children with a co-ordinated support plan.

---

[88] 2004 Act, section 2.
[89] 2004 Act, section 9; see also Additional Support for Learning (Co-ordinated Support Plan) (Scotland) Amendment Regulations 2005, SSI 2005/518.
[90] 2004 Act section 17 and schedule 1.
[91] Additional Support Needs Tribunals for Scotland (Practice and Procedure) Rules 2006, SSI 2006/88.
[92] 2004 Act, section 19.
[93] 2004 Act, section 21.
[94] 2004 Act, section 22 and schedule 2.

EQUAL OPPORTUNITIES

The Equality Act 2010 applies in certain respects to schools in Scotland. This Act protects particular characteristics, including disability, pregnancy and maternity, race, religion and belief, sex and sexual orientation.[95] If a person treats another less favourably because of a protected characteristic, this constitutes discrimination.[96] It is also discrimination to apply a provision, criterion or practice which puts a person with a protected characteristic at a disadvantage when compared to someone who does not have that characteristic, if this is not a proportionate means of achieving a legitimate aim.[97]

This Act bears upon education authorities, independent schools and grant-aided schools. The body responsible for a school must not discriminate against a person in its admission arrangements, the way in which it provides education, or gives access to a benefit, facility or service, or by excluding a pupil or subjecting a pupil to any other detriment.[98] However, these measures do not apply to anything done in connection with the curriculum.[99] With regard to religion or belief, these provisions do not apply to denominational schools, nor to anything done in connection with acts of worship or other religious observance organised by or on behalf of a school (whether or not forming part of the curriculum).[100] A body responsible for a school must not harass a pupil. Harassment occurs when a pupil is subjected to unwanted conduct related to a protected characteristic that has the purpose or effect of violating the pupil's dignity or creating an intimidating, hostile, degrading, humiliating or offensive environment for him or her.[101] A responsible body will be held responsible for discrimination or harassment by its employees unless it has taken all reasonable steps to prevent such behaviour.[102] Claims relating to contravention of the Equality Act 2010 are generally heard in the sheriff court.[103]

The Equality Act 2010 makes significant changes for pupils with disabilities. Before the 2010 Act came into force it was not discrimination to impose sanctions on a disabled pupil if the sanctions would have applied to a pupil who was not disabled who behaved as the disabled pupil had done. Now if a disabled pupil behaves in a particular way in consequence of his or her disability and as a result is treated less favourably, that is discrimination, unless the person accused of the discrimination can justify what he or she has done by showing that it was a proportionate means of achieving a legitimate aim.[104] The Act also imposes a duty to make reasonable adjustments in certain respects to avoid disadvantage to persons who are disabled.[105] There is a new duty to take such steps as are reasonable to provide auxiliary aids and services to pupils who would, but for such aids and services, be put at a substantial disadvantage in comparison to pupils who are not disabled.[106] This duty came into force on

---

[95] Equality Act 2010, section 4.
[96] 2010 Act, section 13.
[97] 2010 Act, section 19.
[98] 2010 Act, section 85.
[99] 2010 Act, section 89(2).
[100] 2010 Act, section 89(12) and schedule 11, paragraphs 5 and 6.
[101] 2010 Act, section 26 and 85(3).
[102] 2010 Act, section 109.
[103] 2010 Act, section 114, save in relation to disability discrimination, where claims are to the Additional Support Needs Tribunal.
[104] 2010 Act, section 15.
[105] 2010 Act, section 20.
[106] 2010 Act, sections 20, 98 and schedule 13, paragraph 2.

1 September 2012. Complaints about disability discrimination in schools should be made to the Additional Support Needs Tribunal.[107]

In addition to duties under the Equality Act, bodies responsible for schools are required to prepare accessibility strategies designed to increase the extent to which disabled pupils can participate in the curriculum, and improve the physical environment of schools to assist pupils with disability to take advantage of education and associated services.[108]

CLAIMS AGAINST TEACHERS AND EDUCATION AUTHORITIES

It is not generally possible to sue an education authority for failure to carry out a statutory duty.[109] If an authority does not comply with its statutory duties a complaint may be made to the Scottish Ministers who may order the authority to discharge its duty.[110] Education authorities are also vulnerable to complaints to the Scottish Public Services Ombudsman, if injustice or hardship has been suffered in consequence of maladministration.[111] The Ombudsman cannot investigate the giving of instruction, whether secular or religious, the curriculum or discipline in an educational establishment under the management of an education authority. Where no other appeal or review is possible, decisions of education authorities may be subject to judicial review by the Court of Session.

Teachers are, however, vulnerable to actions for damages, and education authorities and managers of independent schools may be liable in respect of the actions of their employees.[112] Teachers owe a common law duty of care to pupils. The standard of such care is sometimes seen as equivalent to the care that would be afforded by a reasonable parent.[113] The role of a teacher is in most cases more complex than that of a parent and the more modern test rests on the standard of a professional person.[114] A professional person who fails to act as a member of that profession with ordinary skill would do if exercising ordinary care is open to an accusation of negligence.[115] Such allegations may arise if a pupil is injured at school. Pupils injured as a result of bullying at school have made claims, but most of such claims have failed, mostly because it is difficult to show that injury has been caused by failure on the part of teachers.[116] Negligent failure to address a pupil's educational needs may give rise to a claim in damages, as where an educational psychologist negligently failed to diagnose a pupil's dyslexia, resulting in a failure to address her problems,[117] but such claims are rare.

---

[107] 2010 Act, section 116 and schedule 17, paragraphs 7 to 12.
[108] Education (Disability Strategies and Pupils' Educational Records) (Scotland) Act 2002, sections 1 to 3.
[109] *X (Minors)* v. *Bedfordshire County Council* [1995] 2 AC 633, HL.
[110] 1980 Act, section 70.
[111] Scottish Public Services Ombudsman Act 2002.
[112] *Phelps* v. *Hillingdon London Borough Council* [2001] 2 AC 619, HL.
[113] For example *Gow* v. *Glasgow Education Authority* 1922 SC 260.
[114] *Beaumont* v. *Surrey County Council* (1968) 66 LGR 580; *McPherson* v. *Perth and Kinross Council*, Lord Eassie, 26 January 2001, unreported.
[115] *Hunter* v. *Hanley* 1955 SC 200.
[116] See *Bradford-Smart* v. *West Sussex County Council* [2002] EWCA Civ 7, [2002] ELR 139.
[117] *Phelps* v. *Hillingdon London Borough Council* [2001] 2 AC 619, HL.

FUTURE LEGISLATION?

The law relating to education is now set out in a patchwork of legislation. Some of the language of the Education (Scotland) Act 1980 has a distinctly archaic ring. There is a degree of overlap and confusion in the law as a whole. A new, unified Education Act for Scotland is long overdue. Such an Act would however be a mammoth task. There are unlikely to be resources for such an overhaul of the law. Further, there may be distinct drawbacks. The quality of legislation emerging from the Scottish Parliament has on occasion left much to be desired. There have been regular complaints from the courts struggling to construe and apply new law. It will not serve the interests of schools, teachers and pupils to be regulated by new measures if these prove difficult to understand and put into effect. Further, Scottish education currently enjoys considerable independence. New and comprehensive legislation may be more prescriptive, constraining educators in ways that are traditionally foreign to Scotland. This may not be an improvement.

18

Local Authority Support

Alison Cameron

'Local authority support' takes many forms: local authorities direct and enable the work of schools and nursery centres in virtually every respect, from making sure buildings are fit for purpose to organising transport, from regulating the budget to employing and managing staff. The main focus of this chapter, however, is the nature of the support provided by a group of people employed neither as frontline staff nor in the direct management of schools, but rather occupying a middle ground in the business of delivering an education service at local authority level. Previous chapters in earlier editions of this book (*Educational Development Services, SE 1999, 2003, 2008*) have charted the history of this aspect of local authority support. Variously referred to as 'advisory', 'educational development' and, most recently, 'quality improvement' services, not surprisingly their role has grown and developed over the past fifty years in response to changing educational demands. Broadly speaking, however, the function of staff employed in this capacity has been to support and also to challenge schools and centres in respect of their main function as learning and teaching organisations. A brief history of key episodes in the emergence and shaping of this service may first be useful in order to understand what it is that quality improvement services across the country have contributed to the delivery of education in Scotland, and what the implications may be, in these straitened times, of reducing or removing them. It will be argued here that their role has never been more essential, or better aligned with the needs of schools and nurseries, as they attempt to meet the aspirations and demands of Curriculum for Excellence.

EARLY DAYS

From the 1960s, when subject specialists were first brought out of secondary schools to organise cross-authority events, the introduction of successive curricular reforms saw a new tranche of 'staff tutors' and 'advisers' brought in to help teachers negotiate their way through the changes. At secondary level, those appointed were usually effective and innovative former principal teachers with credibility in their subject area, whilst primary advisers, typically former headteachers, fulfilled a more generalist function, able to provide not only curriculum and staff development, but also management advice to their former colleagues.

By the late 1970s, 'advisory services' were well established. Depending on size, education authorities could count on teams of primary and secondary advisers, and at least one special needs and pre-5 adviser. Across Scotland, this allowed the cross-fertilisation of ideas and practice, and support networks of local authority advisers were formed to influence the development of the curriculum nationally, enabling the sharing of expertise across a range of specialist areas. In the 'them and us' of education authority and schools, advisers were first and foremost seen as teachers, still in touch with learning and teaching, still passionate advocates of their subject disciplines, and despite some grumps and groans about individual personalities, viewed as friends rather than foes. They had left the classroom, true, but had not gone so far as to cross the rubicon that divides those who teach children from those who manage a service.

Any service involved in neither direct delivery nor line management, however, is liable to be called into question when local authorities restructure or need to cut budgets. Succeeding years saw a variety of measures introduced both locally and nationally to create a more accountable and less idiosyncratic service, and one that would therefore be less vulnerable when the chips were down. These periods of review and reform have inevitably reflected changing preoccupations locally and nationally, and what follows charts the process whereby 'advisers' morphed into 'quality improvement officers', in line with a new 'continuous improvement' agenda being driven forward nationally.

There was undoubtedly a need to introduce more rigour and accountability into a service that ran the risk of not keeping pace with the changing needs of schools, and also, it has to be said, of being something of a law unto itself. The first restructuring of the advisory service in Strathclyde Region in the early 1990s, for example, reflected the realisation that the pace of educational change needed a continuous transfusion of new blood into the service, and a large number of practising teachers were seconded to supplement the existing permanent cohort of advisers. The second, which took place prior to local government reorganisation (1996), was an attempt to impose the principles of the market economy. Schools were given credits with which they could buy services (centralised or in-house staff development, curriculum development or management consultancy) delivered by members of the (renamed) 'educational development service', as required by their clients. Not only did this challenge the balance of power – advisers were used to determining both their own and schools' priorities, albeit in a benevolent, largesse-distributing sort of way – but it made it clear that the prime task of an adviser was to serve schools, rather than to carry out the many administrative functions (short of direct management of schools) that tended to fall their way. It also attempted to make service provision to schools more equitable, encouraging less proactive establishments to take advantage of the service on offer and others to become more self-reliant. Perhaps most significantly, it may have helped preserve a service that was in danger of disappearing altogether by delivering a hard reality check: advisers/development officers were not there as of right, and would not continue to exist unless their services were perceived as valuable by schools and centres.

Despite the inevitable upset to those delivering the service (the old title of 'adviser' carried a prestige and a status that 'development officer' did not), the Strathclyde restructuring may be seen to have set in motion a necessary transition from an unwieldy, permanent, secondary-dominated, subject-focused service to a more flexible and needs-related model which stood a better chance of surviving local government reorganisation in April 1996. This created thirty-two unitary authorities where in terms of educational provision there had previously been twelve 'local' providers (nine regional and three island authorities) and the implications for educational development services were profound. The smaller unitary authorities could not afford the same level of provision, and at the very point where cooperation and a sharing of services might have been sensible, there was an equal and opposite pressure to go it alone.

When the dust settled, a very uneven picture emerged across Scotland. Factors of geography, size, past history, funding base and political will influenced whether and/or in what degree a development service was built into the new structures. The results of a survey carried out by the then Association of Educational Advisers in Scotland (AEAS) in August 1997 showed that some councils had retained large advisory teams with subject-specific remits, while others had no educational development service staff as such. The 1997 survey showed educational development services in Scotland comprising anything from three to ten individuals whose remits ranged widely across subject specialisms and age ranges, and included any number of authority-wide responsibilities. There was much to do. The advent of the 'Excellence Fund' (later 'Action Fund') in 1997 did release additional funding for government priorities, but although new staff were seconded to develop specific initiatives, through time, as project funding was withdrawn or mainstreamed, the small number of permanent staff took on an increasing range of cross-authority responsibilities.

FROM DEVELOPMENT TO IMPROVEMENT

A parallel theme emerging in local authorities was the gradual refocusing of the work of advisers on the performance monitoring and quality assurance duties detailed in the Standards in Scotland's Schools Etc. Act 2000. This placed a statutory duty on education authorities to 'secure improvement in the quality of school education which is provided in the schools managed by them . . . with a view to raising standards of education'. The protracted negotiations over pay and conditions for teachers which culminated in February 2001 in the McCrone settlement, *A Teaching Profession for the 21st Century*, subsequently formalised this trend, although it was over a year before the Scottish Negotiating Committee for Teachers (SNCT) finally published its 'Salaries and Conditions of Service Agreement for Education Advisers' (Circular SNCT/12). This agreement introduced national salary scales which broke the unofficial link with teachers' pay. It also included a directive that the title of 'Adviser' or 'Educational Development Officer' would change to that of 'Quality Improvement Officer' (QIO) with effect from August 2002. For the first time, duties for members of educational development (now to be 'improvement') services were set down nationally, as follows:
  Quality Improvement Officers will require to

- analyse and use performance information to challenge schools to improve;
- ensure that local authority (and national) priority areas and targets are taken forward appropriately by schools;
- draw on the knowledge of schools to support and inform strategic planning and policy development.

                                            (Circular SNCT/12, April 2002)

While the circular contained limited reference to a traditional 'development' role, it was significant that none of the three broad duties listed above referred to the traditional work of advisers: curricular and staff development. Instead, they related closely to the now-statutory duty of the authority to secure school improvement, and were couched in terms of national and authority rather than school priorities. Circular SNCT/12 had a major impact on the role of local authority advisers/development officers. Traditionally regarded as essentially still teachers, with a subject or sector specialism to offer, and performing an advocacy role

for schools, the newly styled Quality Improvement Officers were now to be seen as regulators of standards and quality and as agents of the authority. A new mantra, 'challenge and
support', slid into vogue, although the national emphasis on school improvement effectively
meant that 'support' took a back seat. Over the next few years, those previously known as
advisers became recast as QIOs with responsibilities for improvement planning, performance review and pastoral support for nurseries and schools, usually on an area basis. In many
authorities, the subject or sector specialism was also brought into play, with an authority-
wide functional responsibility added as a third aspect of the QIO's remit. Although local
authorities differ in the way that they organise and deploy staff, and in some cases have
assimilated or rebadged the role in the course of restructurings, this tripartite remit remains
broadly typical of the kinds of duties that QIOs perform at the time of writing. (Note that
while the term 'QIO' is used throughout this chapter to refer to all those working in a
'support and challenge' capacity, in some authorities those employed as 'service managers'
or 'education officers' may carry out broadly the same functions.)

SNCT/12 did not bring the matter to a close: not everyone was happy. Applying the
McCrone pay rise to QIOs would virtually remove the differential between their salaries
and 'third tier' managers within council structures, and this had been resisted. Removing it,
however, caused recruitment problems, undermining the ability of QIOs to be perceived as
being sufficiently credible to perform the quality assurance role with colleagues in schools.
A leader in the *Times Educational Supplement Scotland* (*TESS*, 15 March 2002) reflected the
dilemma at the heart of the 'betwixt and between' status of advisers, and also the lukewarm
support accorded them by their professional body:

> Yet at issue remains the future role of advisers. It will have to be settled over the next two years
> through the post-McCrone job-sizing exercise. Advisers say they are teachers, which is as impor-
> tant in how they want to be perceived by classroom colleagues as in how their pay is calculated.
> The employers see them as part of the quality control apparatus.
>
> Before too long all advisers may find themselves on the bottom rung of education directorates.
> That at least would stop them being at the EIS's mercy.

In the event, as the new QIOs prepared to bring a legal challenge and the stand-off rumbled
on, a new salary scale emerged which restored QIO salary scales to where they had been in
relation to teachers, solving the problem of recruitment and retention, but failing to resolve
the erosion of pay differential with third tier officers. SNCT/32 (March 2004) delineated
three categories of post: Quality Improvement Officer (QIO), Education Support Officer
(ESO) (to include 'Staff Development Officer', 'Curricular Development Officer' and 'Staff
Tutor') and Quality Improvement Manager (QIM), someone who manages QIOs and
ESOs. SNCT/32 further specified the work of QIOs/QIMs in performing the challenge
role demanded of local authorities. They should, for example, 'apply procedures associ-
ated with HMIE inspection of schools, including those associated with Follow Through
Reports'.

Although one of the eleven responsibilities specified was 'identify good effective practice,
including classroom practice' and another was 'identify and promote staff development
opportunities within the improvement agenda' (two traditional roles for advisers in their
support capacity), the remainder of the points related to taking on a quasi-HMIE role,
albeit at authority level. The language used throughout was redolent of a 'quality assurance'
as opposed to a developmental role in bringing about improvement, with 'improvement'

appearing to be the kind that is measurable against given indicators and achievable by the application and monitoring of externally agreed systems and processes. By contrast, the job description for ESOs, on a lower salary scale, was couched in terms of the craft of learning and teaching as opposed to the measurement of quantifiable outcomes. The job outline was less mechanistic and hierarchical, the language much more suggestive of personal contact and support. And so SNCT/32 to an extent removed any existing ambiguities inherent in the role of adviser, by stipulating that the newly styled QIO would focus on 'challenge', leaving the role of 'support' to staff at a lower grade, often seconded rather than permanent, and paid considerably less.

By effectively hijacking and conscripting its members to a national improvement agenda, the McCrone outcome safeguarded it at local level, not only for tasks associated with the HMIE inspection process and local versions of quality assurance activities, but also for developing educational policy and practice in other respects. Two surveys carried out in 2005 on behalf of the Association of Educational Development and Improvement Professionals in Scotland (AEDIPS) by Brian Boyd and Fiona Norris, as recorded in *From Development to Improvement, a Step too Far?*, revealed that while virtually all respondees now had a quality improvement aspect to their remit, other tasks were being fitted in, as predicted, 'around the margins'. While in some authorities there did appear to be a division of labour with QIOs performing the quality assurance role and ESOs (often seconded) taking forward continuing professional development (CPD) and curriculum development, more typically the generic quality assurance role was combined with a range of pastoral and curricular duties, tied in with lead responsibilities for local and national initiatives, leading even then to some virtuoso plate-spinning. The redefinition of the local authority support role as essentially one of preparing schools at local level for HMIE inspection was examined in the AEDIPS research. Boyd and Norris questioned the duplication of effort and uneasy relationship of quality improvement officers to HMIE and inspection processes, and the amount of time spent on them; and the relationship between school self-evaluation and the activities of QIOs and HMIE. They asked whether national inspection was necessary 'when so much support and challenge is offered by local authority staff', and suggested that one option would be to have a greater separation of roles, with 'development' being the task of advisers and 'inspection' the role of HMIE. They drew attention, significantly, to the apparent confusion that existed between the concept of 'improvement' and that of 'inspection', and flagged up the danger of spending so much time on inspection-related activities when all the research evidence pointed to the need for a collaborative approach to school improvement 'both internally within schools and among all players in the school improvement game'. In asking, 'Can the new manifestation of the traditional advisory service perform both a developmental and an improvement function?' they concluded that 'the evidence from the surveys suggests that they continued to try to do so, but that this was at a cost'.

CURRENT CHALLENGES

Ironically enough, the tensions and the questions flagged up by Boyd and Norris in 2006 have largely been resolved. Succeeding years have seen a number of developments that might, indeed should, have rationalised and stabilised the position of those involved in local authority support for some years to come: QIOs, despite the somewhat anachronistic title, have surely come into their own. There are three major reasons for this. The first relates to the relationship with HM Inspectors, and the now more acknowledged role of

QIOs in relation to the school improvement agenda. The second relates to CfE and the critical role of QIOs in interpreting, developing and translating into practice the new national agenda. And the third is the cumulative scope and scale of the responsibilities which local authorities have been expected to undertake over the years, many of which are managed by QIOs. We need to consider each of these three areas in turn in order to gain a fuller picture of the responsibilities and tasks now undertaken by those employed as QIOs, and to understand the urgency of engaging at a strategic level with the problem of how the quality of Scottish education can be maintained and further developed through this period of immense change, if, as seems likely, the support structures on which it currently depends are further eroded.

The Evolving Nature of the Improvement Agenda

The statutory responsibility placed on education authorities by the 2000 Act has meant QIOs working at local level to the improvement agenda set by HMIE, using the quality indicators set out in *How Good is Our School?* and *Child at the Centre* as benchmarks against which performance of schools and centres may be judged. At times this has created a tension in their relationships with schools, particularly where local quality assurance protocols and working practices mirrored those of HMIE too closely. Conversely, schools and centres have often appreciated the support given by link officers and subject specialists in preparing them for the arrival of the dreaded 'box' presaging an inspection visit: working alongside colleagues on potential areas of weakness beforehand, mediating the post-inspection feedback with inspectors and then providing the training, guidance and support to see them (in most cases) 'signed off' on a return visit.

Successive reviews of the inspection process, however, have led to an inspection regime that looks and feels very different. This has been due to a number of factors: the 2007 Crerar Review certainly pointed the way to a leaner, more proportionate inspection regime, but there was also a growing sense that inspections, *per se*, did not improve schools, and an increasingly negative perception of the way in which visits were conducted. Perhaps a further influence has been the continually changing learning and teaching landscape ushered in by CfE, making the business of delivering categorical, nationally benchmarked judgements altogether more precarious. On the one hand the new regime is no less rigorous, with ever more exhaustive and exacting standards against which classroom practice and curriculum design will be weighed and measured set out progressively via 'advice notes'. The *manner* of inspection, however, has changed markedly, with inspection teams walking the new talk of 'professional dialogue' and 'collegiality', including school and local authority staff in the process and placing more weight on the school's own 'capacity for continuous improvement'. Feedback, while still accompanied by grades, comes in the form of a letter to parents, with performance less subject to public scrutiny.

There has also been a sea change in the way in which HM Inspectors, now part of Education Scotland, the new national support and challenge agency, have embraced a developmental agenda. It is very much to be welcomed, given their previous ambivalence towards CfE, that HM Inspectors now appear to be its strongest advocates and taskmasters. With the current Cabinet Secretary committing Education Scotland to offering assistance to any school or authority 'needing support' in working to CfE deadlines, inspectors have extended their activities to include offering assistance in promoting and clarifying the national agenda. Prior to assuming agency status in 2001, when they were removed from policy making, HMIE had played a lead role in curriculum development in their specialist roles. In more recent times, it nevertheless represents a curious volte-face which Boyd and Norris, reflecting in 2006 on whether QIOs would not be better to stick to development and leave the inspectorate to focus on the 'improvement' side of things, could scarcely have envisaged.

There are distinct implications for local authority support in all of this. Greater transparency on the part of HM Inspectors has led to improved partnership working with local authority staff, and with CfE developments sweeping away all the old certainties and placing creativity and innovation at the heart of learning, everyone is learning on the hoof. Few folk – and this may include HM Inspectors – have ready-made answers to offer schools. The 'them and us' of HM Inspectors and schools/nurseries, of QIOs and schools/nurseries, of HM Inspectors and QIOs, has not disappeared, but the rules of engagement have changed, with relationships more collegiate, dialogue more reciprocal. The debate about whether challenge or support is the more legitimate activity for either party seems increasingly irrelevant, or has at least come full circle.

With the inspectorate operating on reduced resources, the more proportionate approach to inspection visits has meant a correspondingly greater expectation that local authorities will know their schools very well and will be actively involved in building capacity for improvement. QIOs already monitor, evaluate, support and challenge the schools and nurseries for which they have responsibility, assisting with the improvement planning and reporting cycle, providing advice and guidance on a wide range of issues, identifying and disseminating good practice, encouraging pace and challenge in learning, reviewing the tracking and targeting of students, stimulating creativity and innovation, encouraging multi-agency working and taking the lead on a range of national and authority developments. Now, in virtually all cases, they also have formal responsibility for follow-through visits after inspections and the production of reports, leading to a significant increase in workload.

Curriculum for Excellence

If properly supported through to full implementation, CfE will bring about radical transformation of Scottish education, changes which are necessary to prepare young people for the challenges and uncertainties they are likely to face in the future. Given that they will need not only knowledge but the skills to apply their knowledge in ways we can only try to imagine, we need in a very short space of time to work together to turn the supertanker that is Scottish education around from a knowledge-driven, largely conformist curriculum to a skills-driven, explicitly personalised one. Possibly because we are on a change trajectory which by its very nature defies centralised prescription and control, or because the changes are so all-encompassing that there has been insufficient time to think them through, authorities and schools are charged with 'responding to local needs' (or, as some would say, 'working it out for themselves'). Within broad national parameters, the responsibility for devising programmes of study and developing approaches to learning, teaching and assessment now lies with individual class teachers and heads of establishment, with local authorities assuming responsibility for providing support, managing the pace of change and assuring the quality of provision. The model has much to commend it. We should be encouraging the autonomy, creativity and self-determination in staff that we want to develop in our young people, and a strong theme running through CfE is that one size does not fit all. However, expecting a teaching force previously constrained by central direction to wholeheartedly embrace a change programme with much of the small print missing is perhaps overly optimistic.

With the curriculum now defined as 'the totality of experiences which are planned for children and young people through their education, wherever they are being educated' (*Building the Curriculum 3*), the need for local authority intervention in the form of reassurance, guidance and challenge to staff in the frontline has never been more pressing. And as the changes bite and deadlines for meeting aspects of the reform programme loom large, local authorities find themselves responsible for transforming aspiration into reality as never before. In promising teachers 'more autonomy and professional responsibility', *Building the Curriculum 5: A Framework for Assessment* (2011) explicitly charges local authorities with responsibility for setting up arrangements for assessment and moderation of standards reached by young people against the CfE experiences and outcomes, and for ensuring consistency in teachers' judgements and the application of standards. This 'make it so' approach to carving out national policy and practice is philosophically in tune with CfE, as is the reliance on teachers' professional judgements as they work together to build up an understanding, for themselves and by stages, of what 'breadth, challenge and application' in learning really means. It will, however, take years. In the meantime, with standards as yet undefined, HM Inspectors rightly still expecting to find pace, challenge and rigour when they visit, and no national test results to fall back on, everyone is edgy. Just as staff are coming to terms with planning learning and assessing and tracking progress against the experiences and outcomes of the broad general education (3–15), a new set of national qualifications is being launched for the senior phase of learning. In such circumstances, the role of QIOs in mediating these changes at local authority level, working with subject specialists, running training courses and overseeing the production of new course materials, is critical to their success.

The broadly 'hands-off' approach to managing change is, to be fair, accompanied by support materials available via the Education Scotland and Scottish Qualifications Authority (SQA) websites, and an increasing willingness on the part of HM Inspectors to offer support. However this cannot of itself address the gulf between aspiration and current practice. While teachers have shown a remarkable degree of resilience and adaptability, many are finding the pace and scale of the changes overwhelming. It is in this context that a knowledge of schools and individuals, trusting relationships built up over time, well-established support networks and strong leadership at local level makes all the difference. Local authority support is vital if Curriculum for Excellence is to become properly embedded in our schools and centres. 'Maintaining frontline services' is critical, but it is disingenuous to suppose that we can remove the support structure, without the pieces falling through the middle.

Raised Expectations

To turn the screw even further, the years of plenty and a strong developmental agenda underpinned by ring-fenced funding from central government (in recent years replaced by Scottish Government's Single Outcome approach) has meant that the scope and scale of local authority involvement in training, support and development around 'added value' initiatives of one kind or another has been substantial. Add to this the raft of legislative measures which schools, centres and local authorities have had to comply with over the past decade in relation to the children's services agenda, *Getting it Right for Every Child* (GIRFEC), additional support needs, equality duties, parental involvement and health promotion, and we have a hefty list of statutory duties to fulfil, let alone the extraordinary change agenda outlined above.

Pastoral responsibility for a number of schools and centres – engaging with the wider life of the school, helping to develop learning and teaching, ensuring that learners' needs are being met, representing the authority on interview panels and supporting headteachers and heads of centres in their leadership role – is hugely rewarding. It can also be very time-consuming, especially when crises arise, or when dealing with a range of complex issues regarding young people and their families. As parental expectations have risen over the years in response to a greater awareness of rights, and with many families under pressure of one kind or another, responding to parental complaints can at times reach unmanageable proportions.

WHERE TO NEXT?

It is unfortunately, therefore, in the context of a significantly extended quality improve-ment role, an extraordinary change agenda and heightened expectations on every front, that the numbers of those employed in this local authority 'support and challenge' capacity has already been substantially reduced. An article in *TESS* (13 May 2011) headed 'A downward spiral if quality officers are cut?' recorded a 25 per cent drop in the number of quality improvement posts across the country as a whole, from 355 in 2009 to 266 in 2011. As coun-cils set out their 'efficiencies' measures for 2013–16, no longer able to protect even frontline services, it is inevitable that many more posts will go. AEDIPS, which had provided vital networking and professional support for those employed in an advisory/improvement capacity across Scotland, has shut up shop, yet another victim of these recessionary times. A sad notice on its homepage (www.aedips.org.uk), posted September 2012, reads, 'Goodbye and thank you for your support.' With authorities no longer willing or able to release either office-bearers to organise or members to attend its programme of conferences and issues seminars, the decision had been taken to close down operations, the reason given as follows:

> Over recent years the situation in which our members and associates work has become ever more difficult. Local authority teams have shrunk, remits have altered (never reduced) and recruitment has almost dried up. Many people engaged in quality improvement, support and development have found themselves stretched almost to breaking point.

The notice to members ends with the hope that at some point in the future, 'circumstances will improve' and it will be possible to form a new association to take up where the old one left off.

The necessity for leadership at all levels to address the serious question of how we can work differently has been mooted and is clearly being discussed at senior levels, but so far nothing very much has emerged beyond desultory attempts to 'share services', which arguably may result in spreading an already depleted service even thinner. No one seems to be able to suggest what it is we will stop doing, because all of it is important. Education directorates are understandably too absorbed in achieving the required bottom line on the balance sheet to be able to take the longer view, but ultimately we cannot continue to soldier on, expecting more and more from fewer and fewer people. The worrying thing is that with all education, community and partnership services being cut back – nationally, at local authority level, in the further education sector and now in schools – the potential to 'pass the parcel' of responsibility for curriculum development, leadership development, quality assurance, not to mention the plethora of responsibilities described above, is also rapidly disappearing. The crunch point has not yet come, but at the time of writing, it seems a case of 'when?' rather than 'if?'

At both national and local level, the understanding of how we can best support schools has already changed. HM Inspectors recognise that in the McKinsey 'good to great' trajectory of improvement (*How the World's Most Improved School Systems Keep Getting Better*) we are now at a place where the improvement can no longer be achieved by the application of prescription. The work of David Hargreaves, Michael Fullan and Richard Elmore, amongst others, has shown that achieving consistently high standards can only be managed by getting better at sharing within and across schools and systems, and by developing leadership capacity within the teaching profession as a whole. At local level, the enthusiasm created in recent years by various different models of 'teacher learning communities', where teachers support one another in developing classroom practice, is testament to the success of this approach. No one is advocating a top-down, highly controlled model for CfE, and there is a recognition that too much central interference, whether nationally or at local level, may actually inhibit schools from developing a greater degree of self-determination and initiative. In an interesting article on School Improvement written for SOLACE (December 2010), Leora Cruddas reflects on the paradigm shift from seeing school improvement as top-down, centrally driven and focused on individual organisations, to accepting the need, as Hargreaves and others would argue, to build the capacity of the system for improvement. While endorsing the need for a new discourse around improvement, she argues that a local authority role is more important than ever in creating 'a sustainable and coherent self-improving system', and in holding schools to account on behalf of the community.

In the meantime, what is most at stake is equity for all learners. CfE is predicated on unleashing the energy and innovation and creativity of all teachers and learners, and has already achieved some very encouraging results. Arguably, however, the gap between the early adopters and those who find change difficult is widening, as teachers retrench in the face of too many things changing all at once. Not everyone, particularly some subject specialists in secondary schools who are anxious about an approach that seems to value skills over content, has bought into the vision. Strong leadership may be critical, but as yet there is inconsistency across systems in the ability of leadership to enact the changes needed. And building the capacity for a more devolved, more mature and more self-determining system, encouraging leaders to take responsibility for their own destiny, for using self-evaluation to get better, for example in the form of learning rounds (as opposed to relying on external feedback) or teacher learning communities (as opposed to expert-delivered CPD) does not happen by itself. Staff need support to get from where they currently are to where they need to be.

For many involved in education in Scotland, there has never been a time with greater potential to 'get it right'. If CfE, despite the doomsayers, is to be the vehicle for achieving a major breakthrough in improving the learning experiences and the life chances of young people, the stakes are very high. As education directorates struggle with the unenviable task of offering up savings without damaging frontline services, quality improvement services are an obvious target. Elected members question the expenditure on what they view as highly paid officers, who are not directly accountable to them and whose role is difficult to comprehend. But arguably, the very diffuseness of the role is both a weakness (in terms of vulnerability and perhaps also accountability) and a strength. In his article, *Leading without Power*, published in ASPECT's journal *Improvement* (Spring 2009), David Cameron, the former Director of Children's Services for Stirling, discusses the potential for marginalisation of QIOs now that schools are seen as the agents of change in taking forward CfE. Reflecting on increasingly complex problems faced by young people, and their entitlements to an education that will adequately prepare them for an uncertain future, he acknowledges that 'not all schools will have the capacity to make the changes that are required', and goes on to describe QIOs' 'unique position to provide support and direction' through 'influence and persuasion', rooted in 'belief, knowledge and understanding' in this period of extraordinary change.

It is time to stop and think. In the face of a continuous improvement culture, rights-led legislation and CfE, we have built up a complex support system, locally and nationally. We are in the middle of an ambitious reform programme, now being driven at the rate of knots after a faltering start. Every part of the education system is being affected, and every member of staff is in danger of feeling, to a greater or lesser extent, de-skilled. Local authority support mechanisms may appear dispensable, and in time, may be so, but for now they are an integral part of the ecosystem that is Scottish education. In a keynote address delivered at the Scottish Learning Festival in 2012, Matthew Taylor referred to the need to balance the benefits of individualism, with a central driving vision, and a sense of shared purpose, citing the current direction of educational policy in England as an example of where this can get badly out of kilter. We have a very different system here, but we need networks of people, centrally, locally and in schools, to pull things together, releasing staff from the restrictions of the past, encouraging innovation and creative solutions, directing and pacing the delivery of the central vision, Curriculum for Excellence. What we can offer children is braver, bolder, and more attuned to what we need for the twenty-first century than ever before. We cannot afford at this critical stage to let things fall apart, because the centre cannot hold.

REFERENCES

Boyd, B. and F. Norris (2006) 'From development to improvement, a step too far? The evolving contribution of Quality Improvement Officers to the school improvement agenda in Scottish local authorities', *Scottish Educational Review*, 38 (2): 213–24.

Cameron, D. (2009) 'Leading without power', in Improvement, ASPECT.

Cruddas, L. (2010) 'School improvement', in *The 'Big Society': Next Practice and Public Service Futures*, ed. R. Tuddenham. London: Solace Foundation Imprint.

Elmore, R. (2008) 'Leadership as the practice of improvement', in B. Pont, D. Nusche and D. Hopkins (eds), *Improving School Leadership, 2*. Paris: OECD.

Fullan, M. (2005) *Leadership and Sustainability*. New York: Corwin Press.

Hargreaves. D. (2010) *Creating a Self-improving School System*. Nottingham: National College for Leadership of Schools and Children's Services.

19

National Curriculum Support: From LTS to Education Scotland

Bill Boyd

BACKGROUND

The history of Learning and Teaching Scotland (LTS) and its place in Scottish education is a brief one, coinciding almost exactly with the first decade of the new millennium. Formed on 1 July 2000 as the main organisation to develop and support the curriculum, and to promote the application of information and communications technology (ICT) in schools on behalf of the Scottish Executive, as it was then called, LTS began as it finished with the forced merger of two organisations that wanted to remain independent – the Dundee-based Scottish Consultative Council on the Curriculum (SCCC) and its Glaswegian ed-tech counterpart, the Scottish Council for Educational Technology (SCET).

Over the term of its existence, LTS was responsible for producing a wide range of publications as well as providing advice, support, resources and staff development aimed at enhancing the quality of learning and teaching in schools and early years settings. It played a significant part in the initial thinking behind Curriculum for Excellence (CfE) and a less significant role in determining its final structure. LTS also played a leading role in major developments in the use of ICT to support learning and teaching in schools – starting and finishing with a better reputation in this regard than with respect to the curriculum which was supposed to be its core function. It facilitated national and area networks and was the principal organiser of educational conferences, including major national events such as the highly successful annual Scottish Learning Festival – originally called the Scottish Education and Teaching with Technology Conference (SETT).

To be effective, LTS needed to work alongside the Scottish Government, Her Majesty's Inspectorate of Education (HMIE) and the Scottish Qualifications Authority (SQA) – the established triumvirate of Scottish education – as well as the Association of Directors of Education in Scotland (ADES), local authorities, schools and other educational establishments and organisations, including NHS Education for Scotland, and it increasingly became a focus for working with education authorities to assist them in delivering their responsibilities under government initiatives. The activities of LTS were almost entirely funded by the Scottish Government, with a turnover at its height in excess of £20 million per annum (not including the £37.5m GLOW project which was funded separately). LTS also had at its peak a core staff of 200 which was supplemented by a team of curriculum and educational technology specialists who were largely seconded from schools, local authorities and other partner organisations, to ensure that the work of the organisation was reflecting current good practice, as well as maintaining credibility and the respect of the wider education community.

Following the reviews of SCCC and SCET, a Merger Action Group, set up in mid-1999 within the Scottish Executive Education Department (SEED), proposed to Ministers the scope of work to be undertaken by a merged organisation. It recommended that the new body should cover all aspects of the curriculum delivered in the school and pre-school sectors, including provision for additional support needs. As this covered a number of areas, such as Higher Still, which were also delivered by the Further and Higher Education sectors, then the new merged body would be required to work with other relevant bodies to ensure coherent support across the spectrum. Similarly, terms of the work inherited from SCET, the recommendation was that LTS should have the primary role to provide advice and support to Ministers in relation to the use of ICT in education as a whole, a role that in reality was never realised beyond pre-school and school education. However, there was no reference to a 'principal' or 'primary' advisory role in the Management Statement and Financial Memorandum which specified the key objectives for LTS. Nor was there such a reference in relation to the curriculum, and thus it differed from its predecessor the SCCC, where the Council had been termed 'the principal advisory body for the Minister'.

The governance of the new body was considered by the Merger Action Group to be one of the most important issues to be addressed. In particular, there was a need to establish a clear relationship between the management of LTS, and the then Scottish Executive (rebranding to 'Scottish Government' only happened after the elections in 2007). The Group suggested a small non-executive Board of around eight members, appointed by Ministers, and a Council of around twenty members, also appointed by Ministers. The Council would carry out consultations, and offer advice to the Scottish Executive. In the event, these features were reflected in the final structure, with an 'Advisory Council' chaired by the Chair of the Board – an anomalous feature not mentioned in the 2001 Management Statement – though by 2006 the Council members were appointed 'in liaison with' Ministers, not by them, a subtle but important difference.

JULY 2000–JUNE 2004

The early years in the life of LTS coincided with those of a fledgling Scottish Parliament and an unprecedented level of investment in Scottish education, so in terms of funding – especially when viewed retrospectively – it really was the best of times. However, by an unfortunate coincidence, the crisis that was to hit SQA in the autumn of 2000, when more than 17,000 young people received incorrect or incomplete examination results, meant that Ministers were determined not to keep a non-departmental public body (NDPB) at such arm's length in future, setting the tone and the context within which LTS would operate during the time of its existence. It was also a period of immediate internal conflict at LTS. The fact that the organisation had been born of a merger between two existing bodies resulted in a great deal of energy being diverted towards internal matters such as pay, grading and conditions. That LTS was also responsible for some considerable achievements during this early period is tribute to the quality and professionalism of most of its staff who were operating within the constraints of what was still in many respects a dysfunctional organisation. Furthermore, this was the period when significant developments in Early

Years Education, Health Promoting Schools and the National Priorities for education were either led by, or were at least heavily influenced by, the new body.

The most notable example was the location in LTS in 2001–02 of the Assessment is for Learning (AifL) programme, aimed at improving the understanding of the relationship between learning and assessment in Scottish classrooms (see Chapter 74). The groundwork had been done by research groups in SEED, and was then developed through teams working with all of the thirty-two local authorities. In each authority a number of schools engaged actively in a programme of research and development topics, working on key issues such as formative assessment, personal learning plans and their management, gathering and interpreting evidence, local moderation and reporting to parents. This was an action-based approach, aiming to support and sustain the development of professional knowledge and to build, through partnership, self-sustaining authority-based systems. By March 2006, over 1,000 schools were involved and the model of engagement still stands as one of the best examples in recent times of introducing new ideas and working practices into Scottish schools. Unfortunately, lessons were not learned and the model was not replicated when it came to the much more radical call for change that was to be CfE.

The implementation and modification of the 5–14 Curriculum had been a dominant feature of the previous decade, and LTS continued where the SCCC had left off, the immediate priorities being the completion of a review and then revision of the troublesome national guidelines for Environmental Studies, along with work in Health Education, ICT and on the structure and balance of the curriculum. For the post-14 stage, LTS continued working with SQA – to develop Higher Still (now National Qualifications) support materials – as well as the Higher Still Development Unit (HSDU), the Scottish Further Education Unit (SFEU), local authorities and others. Then, almost overnight, in December 2000, LTS was given full responsibility for the HSDU, which was renamed the National Qualifications Support Team. LTS continued its working relationship with SQA and the SFEU, producing dozens of titles in the National Qualifications Curriculum Support series (and distributing them to every school in Scotland from its distribution centre in Dundee), as well as managing and developing the NQ Online website. Launched in September 2002, NQ Online provided access to online interactive materials, and reflected the growing shift from print-based to web-based support for teachers and schools.

At the same time, SCET's largely malfunctioning and commercially unviable software development and ICT training functions were being replaced by the much broader – and publicly funded – National Grid for Learning (Scotland). It was a period of massive growth in the education budget and a time when LTS was seen by many to be leading significant technological change in the public education system in Scotland. The National Grid for Learning (Scotland) had been launched in 1998 following an English consultation paper *Connecting the Learning Society* (DfEE, 1997), and had three main aims in relation to ICT in education: to improve and extend the ICT infrastructure; to run staff development programmes and provide training for teachers, educationalists, librarians and community development staff; and to provide high-quality digital resources suitable for the Scottish educational context.

Between 1999 and 2006, £160 million was provided by SEED to local authorities to support ICT infrastructure developments, and over £50 million was allocated to central projects, most of which were managed by LTS and dominated its ICT programme. Many continued after the National Grid for Learning funding ended, some becoming part of the Scottish Schools Digital Network (SSDN), later known as GLOW, the national intranet for which LTS was also handed responsibility. As a result, LTS was now beginning to provide a fully integrated online service for Scottish education, including four major websites (Early Years Online, 5–14 Online, NQ Online and ICT for Communities). Additional websites were supported by funding from other divisions within SEED, although their insistence on discrete web areas for every separate funding stream, no matter how small, led to a huge number of 'websites within the website', a format that made little sense to external visitors simply looking for information or advice. Nevertheless, a report in 2005 on the impact of ICT initiatives (Condie et al., 2005) cites the LTS website as a key source of information to schools and LTS itself claimed over 1.1 million visitors to the website as early as the last quarter of 2006.

In addition, through the publication of the award-winning *Connected* magazine, email bulletins, online news and events, and other publications, significant energy was being put into community development and to disseminating information relating to ICT in education. The annual SETT show, attended by more than 4,000 delegates in 2004, continued to expand as the Scottish Learning Festival, attracting over 7,000 visitors at its peak in 2009. Through its 'Heads Together' and 'ICT Masterclass' initiatives, LTS could also claim to have made significant efforts to raise the awareness of headteachers and improve leadership at all levels in the use of ICT in the classroom, and the organisation's commitment to the innovative use of technology saw the introduction, in 2006, of the Consolarium, an initiative designed to examine the benefits of games-based learning in the classroom. Working directly with teachers and young people, the project had an immediate impact and demonstrated that in terms of ICT at least, LTS had the capacity to be a leading player in the digital revolution that was transforming education across the globe.

The organisation of the functions of the new LTS generally reflected the balance of that of its predecessors, still broadly split between 'Curriculum' and 'Resources', though from 2002 onwards LTS adopted a more strategic approach, prudently aligning its array of projects with government initiatives. Thus, from 2002 to 2005, the dominant theme was a focus on the government's National Priorities (Scottish Executive, 2000). From 2005 onwards, there was a shift to reflect the expectations of Ambitious, Excellent Schools, and, simultaneously, the slowly emerging concept of CfE.

The main criterion for success for LTS at this time was its continued support from SEED, which needed a financially viable organisation to provide support for new initiatives, some of which were requested at very short notice by Ministers in response to the social, political and economic pressures of the day. In return, the organisation was expected to produce annual reports on time, avoid giving its sponsoring divisions problems and implement good governance procedures. SEED did not explicitly assess whether meeting these requirements had any effect on the quality of the organisation's output, or examine the impact of LTS on the education system. Indeed it might have been awkward to query its impact, given that the bulk of activity was initiated by SEED, and, in many cases, micromanaged by it. One consequence was a lack of any real pressure on LTS to stand back from its role and assess the effectiveness of the organisation, or the appropriateness of its functions.

What was separately detectable during this period was an uncertainty about the contribution that LTS was making to the strategic development of learning and teaching in Scotland. If the members of the senior management of LTS were aware of this, it was not obvious. There was a degree of private dissatisfaction among, for example, some heads of educational services in local authorities, middle managers and others within LTS, and with some civil servants at SEED, but this did not manifest itself at Board level. On the surface, LTS appeared to manage major SEED developments and initiatives effectively, judged by the fact that projects were signed off and funding continued to flow. It delivered significant events, such as the high-profile Scottish Learning Festival, and provided a range of curriculum, technical and other support for schools, which many schools and teachers clearly found useful. At a national and political level, therefore, LTS did not present a threat.

Arguably, the organisation was viewed at this time as a helpful and harmless agency which did not challenge pedagogical thinking, nor have major cost implications for local authorities (unlike those of the SQA, for example, all LTS services were provided free at the point of use). Any internal inadequacies could therefore be ignored, but for those whose expectations were that LTS would be the driving force for innovation, creativity and change in Scottish education, these were extremely frustrating times. It appeared that the character of the organisation was being established as a largely risk-averse and compliant project delivery vehicle for government, a character that would ultimately lead many to question its very existence, and that potentially would make it an easy target for abolition when the public finances came under close scrutiny following the Scottish Government elections in May 2007.

JUNE 2004–JULY 2008

LTS was entering a new phase, heralded by the retirement of the CEO and the appointment of a new leader with the reputation of having a strong management style. The immediate effect was a new injection of energy and dynamism that had previously been lacking in the organisation, and initially it looked like LTS could at last be focused on leading the changes in Scottish education identified as necessary in the National Debate of 2002. The sale of the LTS HQ, the former convent which had been SCET's office in the affluent West End of Glasgow, was also regarded as a symbolic marker of change, and the move to a new central Glasgow office, co-located with the SQA, provided the opportunity to bring what had been until then a largely conservative organisation into the twenty-first century (and for the next few years the opportunity for some to speculate that a merger with the former examination board was being planned). However, it takes more than 'hot-desking' and open-plan design to change deep-seated cultures and the move only provided short-term cover from the systemic organisational problems that had been inherited from the previous regime. Disquiet over staff pay and conditions rumbled on, as building the LTS corporate brand increasingly took precedence over building the curriculum.

In the context of SEED's Ambitious, Excellent Schools agenda announced in 2004, LTS moved to simplify the description and management of its operations by grouping the 120-plus individual projects for which it was now responsible into more coherent 'programmes' of work. These groupings would be the subject of much debate in the coming months and years as the organisation tried to second-guess what might emerge from the mist surrounding CfE, and what its role would be in relation to the biggest single review of Scottish education ever undertaken. In the meantime, another revised remit for LTS, agreed with Ministers in 2005–06 had as its main requirements that LTS would:

- support the implementation of national developments in education, including reviewing and refreshing the curriculum, to ensure Scotland is at the cutting edge in the use of ICT in delivering high quality support for teaching and learning;

- provide guidance, leadership and support to education authorities and schools to help implement educational policy and promote innovation;
- drawing on evidence from research and external evaluation, provide sound, coherent advice to Ministers on support for continuous improvement in Scottish education;
- systematically evaluate the impact of all aspects of its work across the education system.

Effectively, the main differences between the new remit, 'the objects' in the Memorandum and Articles of 2000 and the Strategic Priorities of 2000–5 were a support rather than an initiating role for curriculum review; a proactive role in relationships with local authorities; a re-emphasis of the importance of research if LTS was to provide a base for authoritative advice; and an explicit requirement to evaluate the impact of its work.

By spring 2007, the latest version of the LTS programme structure had five headings for the grouping of projects: Building Capacity, Excellence for All, Curriculum and Assessment, ICT and GLOW. This attempt to group such a large number of diverse projects on the curriculum side of the organisation into three distinct programmes (the first three on the list of five) was, however, largely undermined by micromanagement practices at SEED and business managers within LTS with little or no experience of education. The latter group, which should have been focused on facilitating the work of the education staff within the organisation, more often than not were creating bureaucratic hurdles which contributed little to organisational effectiveness and impacted negatively on the external perceptions of LTS as an organisation fit to lead a major overhaul of the curriculum.

LTS had been given a commission from SEED to take forward Phase 2 of CfE. In practical terms, this required within a year: the preparation of coherent 3–18 guidance in all specified curriculum areas; the production of a communications strategy for the educational community; support for all staff involved in the delivery of CfE; and advice on national staff development, tasks for which a weak and disorganised curriculum directorate within LTS was quite ill-prepared. In the event, and largely through the efforts and commitment of a relatively small number of professionals (many of them secondees from schools and other establishments), the government's request for curriculum frameworks in each of the eight identified curriculum areas was met by the required deadline, but by this time the LTS role in the development of the new curriculum was reduced to 'fleshing out' a structure that had been predetermined elsewhere.

Reactions to the publication of the 'experiences and outcomes' within each of the curriculum areas of CfE – essentially the blueprint for the new curriculum – were mixed, some regarding them as inspirational while others claimed that they were too vague and called for more detail. Many would argue that, in itself, the division of the curriculum into the eight curriculum 'areas' that define CfE, more or less reflecting the subject department structure in secondary schools – which had remained unchallenged for decades – provided a barrier to progress. It ensured that national qualifications would continue to dominate learning and teaching practices in the secondary sector, and did little to bring closer the vision of an integrated curriculum from 3 to 18 described in the original report of the Curriculum Review Group in November 2004.

LTS, in an attempt to meet the requirements of its revised remit and in response to accusations of a lack of responsiveness, had by now instituted annual consultations with stakeholders, involving meetings with representatives of local authorities and a wide range of organisations, including teaching unions. Feedback from these consultations was used in meetings with SEED when discussing the forward programme of SEED funding, and for developing the LTS Annual Plan. The consultation process and other sources of comment, such as that from seminars and conferences, provided positive feedback as well as suggestions for improvement. Some were not new and included: too many teachers and other authority staff not using LTS regularly for advice and information; a lack of awareness of much of LTS's activity and support services; a shortage of sources of reliable research in relation to best learning and teaching practice; the need to provide a coordinating role between and across authorities; the need to mitigate the effect of the loss of subject advisers; and requests to assign LTS officers to particular authorities.

The pleas for better links with authorities, which had been made to SCCC and SCET in the past, were perhaps more urgent and real following the reorganisation of local government into thirty-two smaller authorities. Given the increased pressure upon these smaller authorities to implement government initiatives, meet targets, demonstrate best practice and be prepared for external inspection, perhaps this was not surprising. Fortunately, with a change in senior management at LTS from mid-2004 onwards, and a new Chief Executive with first-hand knowledge of local authority management, it was an appropriate point to shift focus. LTS over the first few years of its life had demonstrated its ability to handle SEED project demands effectively. Now it also had to work in closer partnership with local authorities and teachers, demonstrating an ability to meet the needs of its 'real customers', while at the same time facilitating national developments and evaluating their impact. In September 2005, formal Partnership Agreements were drawn up between LTS and the Association of Directors of Education in Scotland (ADES), the Convention of Scottish Local Authorities (CoSLA) and HMIE, to promote complementary working.

Thus LTS, having reorganised its structure and had a major revision of its remit which made the support of education authorities explicit, moved to position itself as a more proactive organisation, able to take a lead strategic role in supporting authorities to deliver the national priorities and key initiatives. At the same time, it appointed six Area Advisers to provide direct, focused support to education authorities, their schools and services. As a result, and within the new partnership arrangements, LTS and ADES developed over 2006–07 a programme of national seminars for Directors of Education and their senior colleagues, on aspects of self-evaluation and other priorities. LTS began supporting a number of inter-authority consortia, designed to deliver a range of shared priority developments in areas such as CfE, leadership development, continuing professional development, management information systems, implementation of additional support needs legislation and quality assurance generally.

This attempt at repositioning proved to be popular, but its success was limited by the organisation's apparent inability to shift resources quickly enough into new areas of work. There were still many more people working on individual projects and responding to the demands of their separate fundholders at SEED than there were operating as part of the LTS 'support team'. The organisation also found it increasingly difficult to recruit and retain staff as it continued with a pay and grading system that was not aligned with post-McCrone teaching salaries or those of senior staff in local authorities.

GLOW

While LTS struggled to maintain a significant role in curriculum development, plans to develop the world's first national education intranet were coming to fruition, when GLOW (originally the Scottish Schools Digital Network) went live in September 2007. As early as 2002, during the National Grid for Learning (Scotland) programme, some staff within LTS, SEED and the local authorities had started discussing a national vision for ICT in schools. It appeared at the time that there were at least three things that needed to be done. First of all there was a need to provide some basic services, funded nationally, to every student and every teacher in the country (at the time some local authorities had extensive ICT services whilst others had none). Second, there was a view that these services should be web-based, to enable access anywhere, and at any time, on any connected device. Third, it was agreed that there should be a shift from centrally provided content to an approach that would make tools available to support collaborative working and communities of practice. Over the course of the next couple of years a specification was drawn up by LTS, the Scottish Government, local authority and school staff, for what was to become GLOW, the national schools intranet and the national local authority interconnect. In 2005, following a rigorous European procurement exercise, the GLOW Intranet contract was awarded to the specialised education technology company RM Education.

Almost immediately the GLOW project was attracting attention and winning admiration from around the world. However, domestically – as a result of local authority legacy systems and lack of local capacity – GLOW was very slow to take off and was a national intranet in name only until well into the initial contract. To make matters worse, the core technology within GLOW was not refreshed quickly enough and for users who had become used to the internet the experience was often slow and frustrating. This led to some warranted criticism and provided the opportunity for a small but vociferous number of IT-literate and hyper-connected individuals to suggest that there was no need for a national system, and that schools should simply provide open wireless access to the plethora of free tools available on the world wide web. In response the Education Secretary, under significant financial pressure in an economic recession, elected to cancel the procurement of 'GLOW 2' until a full review had been undertaken. (See also Conlon, 2008.)

JULY 2008–JULY 2011

Following the election of the SNP minority government in 2007, LTS was anticipating a review of its functions and operations as part of the government's manifesto promise of a clearer, simpler and more efficient public sector. This process was announced in January 2008, with some organisations such as the SQA escaping untouched, whilst others were abolished without a review. For LTS, focused on meeting the Scottish Government's timetable for completion of the frameworks for CfE, it was a long period of uncertainty, as the much-promised review failed to materialise, and the organisation was left in limbo for twenty months until October 2009. In the end LTS survived, apparently intact, with yet another revised remit:

- to keep the 3–18 curriculum under review and provide advice and support, including quality assured resources, on the 3–18 curriculum to Ministers and the education system;
- to provide advice and support to Ministers and the education system on assessment to support learning, with support from SQA as appropriate, and to work with SQA to ensure the availability of quality assured resources to support assessment;
- to provide advice and support to Ministers and the education system on the use of ICT to support education, to establish and maintain technology standards for education, to ensure practitioners have easy online access to advice and support, including digital resources and

to manage the provision of the national ICT infrastructure to support education, currently GLOW, the LTS Online Service and the local authority Interconnect.

This final iteration of LTS's role and purpose in Scottish education, with the emphasis on 'reporting to Ministers', bears all the linguistic contortions of a document written by committee – which it almost certainly was – and perhaps gives some indication of what was to follow less than a year later. Having secured their new remit on 8 October 2009, LTS senior management and staff were taken by surprise on 14 October 2010 when the Education Secretary announced that the organisation was to be merged with HMIE to form a new support body – initially named the Scottish Education Quality and Improvement Agency (SEQIA) but rebranded as Education Scotland by the time it eventually launched in July 2011.

It was difficult for neutral observers to conclude anything other than that LTS had been 'taken over' by HMIE (dubbed in the past as the key players in 'the leadership class in Scottish education' (Humes, 1968), a title with which the organisation itself would almost certainly have been comfortable), whose inspectors would continue to be appointed by the Privy Council and be referred to as 'Her Majesty's' inspectors. The fact that LTS had been shedding staff at an alarming rate in the months leading up to the merger also led many to believe that the merger was simply a cost-cutting exercise, but given that the first annual budget for the new organisation was in the region of £32m (hardly a massive saving when compared to the combined budget in the previous year for LTS and HMIE of just over £38m and in the context of the overall budget for education), it is an argument that is hard to sustain.

Ministers insisted that the move was curriculum driven, and that Education Scotland would provide both the challenge and the support necessary for authorities and schools to move towards full implementation of CfE. Whether it is possible for a single national organisation to perform such a dual role would be the subject of close scrutiny in the years to come.

REFERENCES

Condie, R., R. Munro, D. Muir and R. Collins (2005) *The Impact of ICT Initiatives in Scottish Schools: Phase 3*: Final Report. University of Strathclyde, Glasgow: QIE Centre.

Conlon, T. (2008) 'The dark side of Glow: Balancing the discourse', *Scottish Educational Review*, 40 (2): 64–75.

Department for Education and Employment (1997) *Connecting the Learning Society: National Grid for Learning*. London: Department for Education and Employment.

Humes, W. M. (1986) *The Leadership Class in Scottish Education*. Edinburgh: John Donald Publishers.

Ross, H. (1999) 'The Scottish Consultative Council on the Curriculum (SCCC)', in T. G. K. Bryce and W. M. Humes (eds), *Scottish Education*. Edinburgh: Edinburgh University Press.

Scottish Executive (2000) 'The Education (National Priorities) (Scotland) Order 2000.

Scottish Statutory Instrument 2000 No. 443'. Edinburgh: The Stationery Office.

Scottish Executive (2004) *A Curriculum for Excellence*. The Curriculum Review Group. Edinburgh: Scottish Executive.

Scottish Government (2004) 'Evaluation of the Masterclass Initiative'. See at www.scotland.gov.uk/ Publications/2004/09/19963/43202

20

HMIE as an Executive Agency, 2001–11

Chris McIlroy

Since its inception in 1840, the role of Her Majesty's Inspectorate and its place in Scottish education have been heavily influenced by the educational politics of the times. Political events and policies have changed the position of the inspectorate over time in relation to government, the civil service, other national agencies and the education professions (Bone, 1968). The politics of education, in its broadest sense incorporating the educational, social and economic ambition of the times and embodying the interests and views of education professionals, employers, parents, the general public and the media, has also shaped the emphasis placed on different purposes of inspection during different periods.

As a result there has been variation in national policy on the weight given to public assurance and accountability, particularly in relation to schools, which is the focus of this chapter. This affects the frequency of inspections; the nature of reports to parents about the quality of their local schools; the extent to which the context of a school is taken into account during an inspection; policy advice to civil servants and Ministers; support for national curriculum development; and the promotion of good practice and improvement. In some periods, inspection gives primacy to evaluation, accountability and compliance with government policies. At other times, increased stress is placed on professional dialogue, improvement advice and support; space for schools to innovate; and the development of positive relationships between inspectors and teachers. The recent decade has seen significant swings in emphasis.

Early in the decade, in 2001, following the examination crisis of 2000 and concerns over the Higher Still development, Her Majesty's Inspectorate of Education (HMIE) was established as an executive agency of Scottish Government. The new agency was designed to create a distance between HMIE and the government and civil service, and to reduce its role in direct leadership of national developments so that the risk that it could end up 'inspecting its own advice' in evaluating developments was minimised. The change was symbolised in the movement of HMIE headquarters out of Victoria Quay and in a decision that members of HMIE would no longer chair national committees. Symbolic changes proved less powerful than the agency's strength within Scottish education, its usefulness as a key source of evidence and advice with a guardianship of the 'folk memory' of educational change and practice. Throughout the first decade of the twenty-first century, these strengths combined with confident and skilful leadership ensured that HMIE continued to remain highly influential across Scottish education.

However, the decade also saw the development of an increasingly febrile politics of education as Ministers and other politicians in the new Scottish Parliament and its committees began to play a more confident and assertive role in exercising their power. The politics of education became more intense, quixotic and parochial. The tradition of Ministers of education spending one day a week in Scotland (with the balance in Westminster) was replaced by full-time teams of education Minsters in Holyrood with personal and local networks of advice and feedback on education. Public scrutiny of education was magnified through the work of Scottish parliamentary committees and a dramatic increase in media attention. The Parliament provided fuel for news stories at a Scottish level and media became more active and influential in lobbying on educational issues. Within the Parliament a broad consensus on most policies for Scottish education coexisted with political point-scoring and Ministers' idiosyncratic views on aspects of education, often emphasising topical but relatively peripheral matters and sometimes constraining coherent educational development.

An archetypal example of the new politics of Scottish education at the end of the period was the sudden announcement, in 2010, of a further major change to the status of HMIE sending a seismic shudder through the executive agency. Its functions were to be included within a new 'improvement agency' alongside those of Learning and Teaching Scotland (LTS) and elements of Scottish Government. This marked a 'U turn' from the 2001 intentions to clarify functions and increase checks and balances across the powerful 'players' in Scottish education. Some of the resulting issues will be discussed in the context of the new agency in the final section of this chapter.

SCHOOL INSPECTION IN 2001

At the beginning of the period, inspection programmes were based on a recurring inspection cycle with a high level of consistency in the process of inspection. Before 2001, politicians, parent groups and the media had unearthed examples of schools that had not been inspected for over twenty-five years, embarrassing HMIE's claim that inspection provided satisfactory assurance to parents and the public. In England, the Office for Standards in Education (OFSTED) had introduced a four-yearly cycle of school inspections, which was at the high-frequency extreme and left insufficient time for school improvement between inspections. However, in an increasingly politicised climate, the infrequency of inspection of some schools in Scotland exposed HMIE to legitimate criticisms of weaknesses in public assurance. A 'generational cycle' had therefore been introduced in 2001 to guarantee a minimum entitlement to inspection: each primary school would be inspected within seven years (the time that it takes for a 'generation' of children to move through primary school) and similarly each secondary school would be inspected over six years.

This cycle reflected a reasonable compromise between recognising the importance of public assurance and allowing schools time for improvement between inspections. It provided a stable context over the decade in which inspection approaches could shift emphasis towards improvement. It also enabled sufficient resources to be allocated to each inspection to ensure that inspectors could understand the school and experience a good sample of its activities. Nevertheless, the generational cycle was tight in terms of HMI staffing.

The inspection model of that time involved rating thirteen or fourteen quality indicators in every primary and secondary school. This tended to lead to a similar set of activities in every inspection: consistency was valued over customisation and responsiveness. The teaching profession saw the quality indicator ratings or grades as 'high stakes', and debates about the grading for 'leadership' were personalised and could dominate an inspection and reduce its impact on improvement. Many in the education community saw being 'held to account' and 'compliance with government policies' as prominent features of inspection. Evaluation was emphasised over advice, dialogue and support. The inspector's priority was to get the evaluations right; it was for the school and the education authority to take forward the improvement agenda. As at national level, there was a caution, unwarranted at the school level, against giving advice or direction to avoid 'inspecting your own advice' at the time of follow-through inspection. One of the key quality indicators against which standards of attainment were judged took no account of the socio-economic context of the school (*How good is our school?*, SOEID, 1996).

Within this inspection model, individual inspectors did their utmost to make inspection work well for a school and continued to provide good advice and support. Establishing rapport with educators, understanding how they work, making judgements about the strengths and potential improvements in learners' experiences, sharing the wider experience of practice that inspectors bring and using dialogue honestly and sensitively to discuss improvement are enduring features of the work of high-quality inspectors in any inspection model. However, policy and approaches to inspection are important because they enable and support, or alternatively constrain, the ability of inspection teams in achieving an inspection that is regarded as fair, provides sound evidence and public assurance, and leads to improvement for learners.

CHANGES TO SCHOOL INSPECTION: A RADICAL CHANGE IN APPROACH

A new Senior Chief Inspector (SCI) was appointed towards the end of 2002. He had a very different vision of inspection as a partnership, between school and inspectors, harnessed towards an improvement agenda. Inspection should combine the key roles of providing assurance, promoting good practice and building a school's capacity to improve, towards the aim of promoting improvements for learners. By 2006, with his senior management team (the present writer was a member of that team) he had designed an inspection model that started with the school's own account of its self-evaluation and journey towards improvement. Professional dialogue, including more time for exchanges with teachers, was stressed as a vital way of understanding a school and assisting improvement. Inspections would be conducted with staff ('inspecting with rather than to'), show respect for their knowledge and views, seek to inspire teachers and celebrate their good practice by publishing examples of good practice in each report. A major programme of staff development was introduced for all inspectors to make them aware of the impact of the tone and manner of an inspection on staff perceptions and their motivation towards improvement.

A welcome feature of the approach was much greater responsiveness to the particular needs and context of a school. Space to be more responsive was created partly by reducing the number of quality indicators to a core of five. It was also facilitated by inspectors 'disengaging' from gathering evidence when they had sufficient evidence for their evaluations. They could then agree with the headteacher a shift towards improvement activity. The new approach reduced, but did not end, the emphasis on grading. The quality indicator rating for leadership was helpfully replaced by a written comment and made less personal by taking account of the effectiveness of all levels of leadership within a staff team. Community Learning and Development (CLD) inspectors joined secondary school inspection teams to gain a better view of the contribution of the partnership with CLD services and the school to supporting learning and community.

In developing the new approach to inspection, HMIE also took account of contemporary political developments. The Scottish Government introduced a new National Performance Framework to show how public services were performing, a very worthy idea but one that was never followed through with sufficient rigour to establish its use by the public. The framework included three of the quality indicators used in school inspections, raising their profile in inspection. Reflecting reviews and restructuring of inspection and regulation in the south, the Scottish Government asked Professor Lorne Crerar in June 2006 to review the inspection and regulation of public services in Scotland. The Scottish Government's response to the review left intact HMIE's role in inspecting education. It stressed the need for inspection to build on self-evaluation, to lead to minimum intrusion to service delivery, to reduce bureaucracy surrounding inspection, to have a focus on the views of service users, and to be proportionate. Inspection reports should provide clear and accessible assurance to users.

These developments and recommendations sat easily with the grain of internal thinking about inspection and were built into the new model. Almost all of the advanced paperwork requested for inspection was discontinued. Proportionality was introduced first by matching follow-through to the findings of inspection and was later developed by the switch from evaluative activity to support during some inspections. Reports would now be written for the parental audience and the more detailed inspection notes would be shared with the headteacher.

Taken as a set, the changes constituted a fundamental and positive reorientation of the approach to inspection. They repositioned inspection away from 'reading the meter' and 'finger wagging' towards a partnership activity designed to promote dialogue, good practice and improvement. Feedback from the education community and surveys from professional associations on the approach in practice was extremely positive. The new approaches to inspection positioned HMIE very well as a constructive and supportive partner working with teachers and others in the education community to achieve improvement. They retained a frequency and transparency in reporting, which met the needs of parents and the public and, necessarily, inspectors remained able to report without fear or favour where required.

In the spring of 2008, a storm of media publicity and political interest in the stress of inspection followed the tragic death after an inspection of Irene Hogg, the headteacher of Glendinning Terrace Primary School. The death was a huge loss for Irene's family, friends and the school community. The inspection team and education authority staff involved were also significantly distressed. The Sheriff at the Fatal Accident Inquiry made no recommendations for changes to inspection or criticism of the inspection team, as reflected in the *Times Educational Supplement Scotland* (*TESS*) headline 'Inspection Vindicated'. This very sad event reinforced the importance of the direction of travel already taken with changes to inspection.

CHANGES TO SCHOOL INSPECTION: FURTHER CHANGES

A new SCI was appointed early in 2010. The ink had hardly dried on the new inspection model when a new Cabinet Secretary for education, Michael Russell, was appointed. He was not fully convinced that changes in inspection were yet sufficient to make it more supportive for teachers. After a meeting attended by the Cabinet Secretary and a range of stakeholders, the SCI initiated a review of the school inspection framework supported by a public consultation on the proposals. The public consultation was a useful way of gaining public endorsement and was astute in providing evidence that could bring stability to inspection programmes, in case of further proposals for change within the new politics of education.

The most significant change emerging from these proposals was a major reduction in the resource allocated to general inspection with an aim to reduce the number of general inspections from 400 to around 240 by 2013. This reduction was to be accompanied by a shift towards proportionality. Over the latter part of the decade, ideas of proportionate inspection programmes based on 'intelligence' or 'risk' were increasingly driving policy for the inspection and regulation of public services, including education across Europe. The notion of a cycle or minimum entitlement to assurance and improvement through inspection was challenged by this shift in policy. 'Proportionate' approaches are based on the principle of directing more resources to those schools where the need is greater.

Applying the principle in education is not straightforward because it involves value judgements about where finite resources are most needed and best used. One obvious priority for inspection, which commands general support, is the need to inspect schools that are achieving poorly and where children's education is at most risk. But there are other worthy claims. A significant proportion of Scottish schools achieve well but many remain steady at that level and are at risk of continuing to underachieve for some of their learners. If Scotland is to improve its overall achievement, then inspection of this group of schools is an important way of stimulating improvement from 'good to great'. There is also a powerful case for inspecting the most effective schools, particularly those that have addressed successfully difficult issues such as the impact of social disadvantage on achievement. Inspection helps in understanding their success, disseminating ideas across the system, motivating their continued progress and encouraging their engagement in system-level improvement.

A further problem with applying proportionality to individual schools is that good intelligence is needed to make sensible decisions in directing resources. Currently, in Scotland, we lack sound evidence on which to base such decisions. We no longer have nationally comparable data on children's achievements before S4 as a source of intelligence about learners' outcomes from our schools. Our education authorities vary considerably in the extent to which they gather user views of their schools. They also vary considerably in their knowledge of the quality of education in their schools, and their Quality Improvement Officers (a key source of intelligence) were reduced across Scotland by around a quarter between 2009 and 2011. This makes it difficult to rely on education authority intelligence in a number of authorities in highlighting schools for possible inspection. The decision to introduce proportionality at a time of rapidly reducing resources and in the absence of sound data was premature. Despite the public rhetoric of proportionality, reality dawned as the edge of the chasm appeared. In planning the general inspection programme for 2011–12, only forty schools (one in six) were to be nominated from discussions between District Inspectors and Education Authorities, a very modest step towards proportionality. The pursuit of responsiveness during inspection continues to provide a more effective way of meeting the needs of schools.

The review proposed a further set of changes in inspection. For example, a move away from inspecting four subject departments in secondary schools was recommended with the time redeployed to observe learning and teaching more generally and reflect the focus on literacy, numeracy, and health and wellbeing within Curriculum for Excellence (CfE). Subject departments in secondary schools would be inspected through separate visits but

would no longer be reported on publicly as part of a school report, marking a further dilution of an aspect of direct public assurance.

A proposal to develop 'clearer, more accessible reports' or letters to parents continued
previous aspirations. A pilot was promised to determine whether quality indicator grades
should continue to be published in reports to parents. Views were invited on extending
parental involvement in the inspection process, for example at the planning stage, but
parents responding to the consultation did not see this as bringing much additional value to
an inspection. A new idea was to involve a senior member of school staff in some class visits
with inspectors. This positive step went with the grain of openness and sharing expertise
in self-evaluation developed by HMIE over recent years through, for example, the involvement of teachers and headteachers in inspections as 'associate assessors'. There was an
attempt to reduce the notice of inspection even further as the period before an inspection
can be a stressful time for staff and because parents are anxious that inspectors observe the
school as it normally works. However, there are currently practical limits on how far this can
be taken because of the need to carry out and analyse surveys of the views of staff, parents
and learners.

THE IMPACT OF THE CHANGES TO INSPECTION BY 2011

Although there has been much continuity in the core of good inspection practice over
recent decades, inspections in 2011 were very different from inspections in 2001. Feedback
from those involved is increasingly positive. There are a few exceptions where an inspection is perceived as negative but these are less frequent than in the past. More generally,
class teachers continue to feel that they receive insufficient focus and feedback during
inspections.

By 2011, almost all inspections were successful in promoting a partnership approach
firmly focused on improvement. The starting point of an inspection is now in the hands
of the school to explain its context, its self-evaluation and its track record in improvement.
Feedback on inspections is increasingly positive about the use of self-evaluation in shaping
inspections: it is a customised, responsive inspection. Professional dialogue plays a key role
in inspection, and is valued by the teaching profession. The tone is positive and collaborative. Evidence gathering is focused on collecting just sufficient evidence to understand the
school and its strengths and development needs and justify the public report. There is a
clear focus on good practice and improvement. The changes in tone and in the partnership
approach to inspection focused on improvement over this period represent a very significant
achievement.

Questions remain about whether more recent changes, accelerated by resource reductions, have significantly weakened the assurance provided by inspection to the public.
School inspections are less frequent, reports are less transparently evaluative and, in electronic form, are less accessible to some parents. Issues of frequency and transparency will
be discussed in the final section.

NOTABLE CHANGES IN OTHER AREAS OF THE WORK OF HMIE

This period saw numerous developments in the wider work of HMIE. Over the decade,
greater priority was given to promoting good practice and effective innovation. Thematic
reports, such as the *Learning Together* series, and published reports on schools and colleges

increasingly described and praised examples of good practice observed in inspections. *Journey to Excellence* won numerous plaudits as a pioneering online resource that made a huge library of good practice, commentary and research available to practitioners at the click of a mouse. The focus on involving learners in their education was sharpened. Health and nutrition inspectors were introduced to inspection teams, strengthening the health promotion agenda, and inspections of psychological services were introduced.

Deaths resulting from child abuse across the United Kingdom, and a series of inquiries into the failure of children's services in preventing them, led to political and media calls for improvement and inspection. In Scotland, the First Minister asked Graham Donaldson to lead in developing arrangements with social work, social care, the police and health agencies to inspect services for children. The inspection of child protection services involving multi-disciplinary teams of inspectors was a new, complex and challenging task for HMIE. It was carried out impressively. The new child protection inspections combined innovation with rigour and earned high respect in Scotland and beyond for stimulating significant improvements in children's services. Illustrating the fast pace of political change over this period, HMIE's lead role in inspecting child protection was passed towards the end of the period to the Care Inspectorate (SCSWIS – a new agency combining the Care Commission and the Social Work Inspection Agency) as part of the Scottish Government's response to the Crerar Review.

The introduction of *Improving Scottish Education* reports as a periodic independent and comprehensive public evaluation of Scottish education was a major development. These reports and others such as *Teaching Scotland's Children* on progress in implementing the teachers' agreement since 2001 evaluated key aspects of government policy. Some politicians and civil servants regarded them with apprehension as they could be used to hold aspects of their policies to account and fuel political and media debates at Scottish election times. Many also recognised the value of a strong independent inspectorate presenting evidence and evaluations publicly. This is a healthy role for an inspectorate to play in a mature democracy and it was used with responsibility and a concern to report fairly and accurately what the evidence showed.

The inspection of the education functions of local authorities (INEA) had established a more consistent standard across authorities in the processes of councils' management of education. Successive cycles of INEA were adding less value and councils were raising issues about the time and bureaucracy of inspections from different agencies. INEA was replaced by new arrangements for all relevant inspectorates and regulators to pool their evidence of the quality of each local council's services in an annual 'Shared Risk Assessment'. In education, a new approach to evaluation was introduced where some education authorities worked in partnership with HMIE on 'validated self-evaluation' of aspects of their education functions. The Schools (Consultation) (Scotland) Act 2010 increased the responsibilities of HMIE in cases of school reorganisation, such as amalgamations and closures, to provide advice to Scottish Ministers on consultation processes and the anticipated 'educational benefit' of changes.

The leadership of CfE over this period tested the effectiveness of post-2001 arrangements for leading curriculum reform in Scotland. Following the decisions of 2001, HMIE could not lead this development. Although inspectors remained highly influential in providing professional advice and feedback on its progress, the leadership of the partners working on CfE fell to senior civil servants in Scottish government, some of whom contributed ably alongside others who found it difficult to make an impact. Education Ministers of different parties reinterpreted what CfE 'is about' in terms of their personal agendas to stress at different points, for example, curriculum choice, excellence, early years, skills, interdisciplinary learning, learning and teaching approaches, innovation, modern languages, physical education, and Scottish history and literature. This made consistent development and communication of the key ideas of CfE difficult, and highlighted the question of an appropriate level of political (particularly ministerial) intervention in forming curriculum advice, as against the right of political parties and their manifestos to influence its broad shape.

Moreover, this ambitious programme of curriculum reform aimed to engage staff in the process of curriculum development to encourage greater professional responsibility and local flexibility and variation in curriculum. Developing these approaches successfully across a range of education sectors, and in a way that engaged over 50,000 teachers and other professionals rather than through traditional research, development and dissemination of curriculum advice, was highly challenging and ambitious. It ran into trouble.

In response, during autumn 2010, the SCI offered to the Cabinet Secretary to send in the cavalry. He announced a pause in inspections in local authority secondary, secondary special and all-through schools and reductions to primary inspections until January 2011. Inspectors were deployed to work with education authorities and national agencies to support the progress of CfE, particularly in secondary schools, and to increase their preparedness for introducing new qualifications. Activities utilised inspectors' evaluation skills and credibility: in turn many developed their own skills in professional dialogue in supporting improvement. A variety of activities was designed to respond to the needs of individual schools based on their self-evaluation. They included visits to schools and departments, curriculum area conferences within and across authorities, and meetings and workshops with groups of staff in schools and authorities. The evaluations of these activities were very positive indeed (though later evaluations about their impact on classrooms, away from the events, were less so). They worked very effectively in stimulating a real sense of urgency and progress with CfE in secondary schools.

LOOKING FORWARD: THE NEW IMPROVEMENT AGENCY, QUESTIONS AND CHALLENGES

On 14 October 2010 the Cabinet Secretary announced 'a new Scottish Education Quality and Improvement Agency', which emerged on 1 July 2011 as 'Education Scotland'. Key aspects of its remit include leading and supporting the implementation of CfE; increasing capacity for self-evaluation; promoting high quality professional learning and leadership; identifying and stimulating innovation; providing independent external evaluations of the quality of educational provision at all levels; and supporting the development and implementation of policy at national level.

The new agency would bring together LTS, HMIE and very small parts of the education department within Scottish Government. Although the changes were presented as not financially driven, the economic tide of stringency quickly led to severe reductions in staffing in the period following the announcement of the new agency, outweighing any potential benefits from synergies in aspects of work. There was a very significant loss of the amount and range of experience and expertise to support both curriculum and inspection. Significant reductions in staffing were made in LTS by December 2011. By this time the complement of HM Inspectors was cut by almost a third, with further reductions planned.

Some reductions in available capacity will have short-term implications for support to CfE. Others are likely to impede the quality of specialist policy advice, aspect reports and influence on features of Scottish education through development work and inspection in the longer term. The secondary inspection team has been particularly depleted, leaving precarious gaps in its expertise in a number of subject areas. The agency will grapple with a number of crucial questions and challenges. Three critical issues are:

Curriculum Review, Advice and Support

The history of Scottish curriculum agencies has been one of peaks of success during major development programmes followed by long troughs when it struggles to find a role and is viewed by many in schools and authorities as ineffective. To address this it is important that the curriculum dimension is prominent in the new agency. Yet, the Education Scotland remit refers only to *implementation* of CfE. Why is there no reference to the previous responsibilities of LTS for curriculum review, development and support? And, under 'matching' arrangements, senior posts in Education Scotland are likely to be filled almost entirely by staff from HMIE. How will this impact on the focus and effectiveness of curriculum review, development and support in the coming years?

The new agency provides an opportunity for a radical improvement in the national strategy for curriculum review, development and support. A later chapter of this book (Chapter 41) questions the effectiveness of national agencies and education authorities in working with schools to present a coherent and steady picture of change and avoid requiring them to consider too many fragmented and specific developments. The account of the strategic management of curriculum change in this chapter reinforces that case. Some curriculum functions need to remain at national level, including establishing a clear curriculum vision and reviewing evidence of the connections between curriculum practice and outcomes for learners. CfE currently provides a vision for the curriculum that needs to be communicated more effectively and consistently, harnessed with other developments to meet Scotland's major challenges to:

- improve achievement at a faster pace;
- close the gap between high and low achievers linked to social background so that 'who you are' matters less to chances of educational success;
- improve the higher-order skills and understanding of our young people to equip them for a changing world; and
- reduce the variation in the quality of teaching and achievement in different classes.

That requires Scotland to build a new consensus on managing curriculum and educational change more strategically and effectively and to hold fast to that.

As part of a strategy, it requires a shift in the centre of gravity for curriculum development and evaluation to teachers, schools and groups of schools, alongside a greater role for education authorities in stimulating and evaluating curriculum change. Approaches to teacher engagement in CfE and to teacher development in *Teaching Scotland's Future* are sides of the same coin. They rightly stress teacher development as the key to curriculum and educational change and require significant changes in our approach to professional development in Scotland, with more focus on local development and local support mechanisms, and on the role and responsibilities of the classroom teacher.

Inspection

Inspection models have major strengths as a result of the development work over the last decade. Two key challenges facing inspection are the frequency of inspection and the transparency in reporting: both are important to schools' accountability to parents and the public.

Parents and politicians want inspectors to tell them that their local school is working well, and to stimulate quick action if not. An important role for inspectors is also to be advocates on behalf of children where the quality of their educational experiences can be improved. New approaches to inspection mean that they are potentially powerful in improving practice. These are all facilitated where inspections are not too widely spaced. Much tighter staffing will exacerbate reductions already planned in the number of schools inspected and will widen the gap between inspections, and could reduce their overall impact on improvement. The percentage of primary schools inspected in 2011–12 will be 57 per cent of the number two years earlier. Previous levels of assurance will be extremely difficult to restore. Will any entitlement to a maximum number of years between inspections be guaranteed? Will parental and public concerns reignite, particularly where a long gap between inspections is followed by a critical inspection report?

The reduced emphasis on relying on ratings for transparency in published reports is welcome. It brings with it a responsibility to present clear judgements in straightforward language. The clarity of evaluation has been blurred in recent reports. Bland statements such as, 'We think your children are motivated and keen to learn' (it would be unusual in a large school if it was all children, to the same degree, in all classes and all aspects of the curriculum) and occasional contradictions are features of the new 'letters to parents'. The necessary move to be supportive to teachers must not impede inspectors from making and reporting judgements clearly. What sense does a parent make of these two statements from the same report?

> Across the primary classes, staff are now addressing significant weaknesses in children's skills in areas of English and mathematics.

> . . . following recent improvements to learning approaches, most children are now developing their basic literacy and numeracy skills well.

Clarity of Role and Purpose

Successful agencies generally have very clear purposes and functions and are well focused on their particular contribution. The creation of the new agency, Education Scotland, reintroduced a greater potential for role confusion and loss of focus than during any period since the 1960s, when Senior Chief Inspector Brunton set up agencies separate from HMI with responsibility for curriculum, inspection and qualifications to ensure a clear focus on distinct functions. The remit of Education Scotland is wide-ranging and currently needs more clarity about how the differing aspects of the remit are emphasised, interact and draw on the strengths of the agency in its roles in inspection, curriculum advice, support and innovation.

An important example of a potentially serious conflict in function relates to the role of the Chief Executive as senior professional adviser with direct access to Ministers. The

SCI was responsible for providing independent, evaluative evidence based on inspections, and advice on the success and progress of government educational policies. Yet the Chief Executive of Education Scotland now has responsibility for *leading* the implementation of CfE. Who will be held to account if progress is poor? Is it the Chief Executive for his leadership? Is it Ministers and policy makers in Scottish Government? More generally, to combine responsibility for advice on education with the responsibility for evaluating it in the single post of Chief Executive is deeply flawed. One proposed 'solution', to allocate responsibility for independent evaluation to a Chief Inspector, will not resolve this issue because the Chief Executive cannot delegate accountability for this work to a member of staff. Moreover, every individual inspector making evaluations during an inspection will face a tension between a collective responsibility to lead CfE and to evaluate it. What will the impact be of these arrangements on national publications such as *Improving Scottish Education*, and more generally on the independence of HMIE in evaluations during inspection, which was a strength of Scottish education? There are important and thorny questions here for the new agency.

The new agency is in an early stage of transition and it is far too early to say how successful it will be. At the time of writing, staff are currently experiencing its extended, debilitating and painful birth as it continues to develop internal structures, posts and functions. It is important to Scottish education, and everyone involved in that enterprise will want it to work and to make a major impact. There are high levels of expectancy and it needs some quick successes. Its urgent priority must be to become more outward-focused and successful in supporting CfE in authorities and establishments. That will gain it the time needed for deeper thinking around its developing role and clarity of purpose.

REFERENCES

Bone, T. R. (1968) *School Inspection in Scotland 1840–1966*. Edinburgh: Scottish Council for Research in Education.

Her Majesty's Inspectorate of Education (2011) *HMIE Response to School Inspection Framework Review*. Edinburgh: HMIE. See at www.hmie.gov.uk

Scottish Government (2007) *Report of the Independent Review of Regulation, Audit, Inspection and Complaints Handling of Public Services in Scotland* (The Crerar Review). Online at www.scotland.gov.uk/Publications/2007/09/25120506

Scottish Office Education and Industry Department (1996; 2002) *How Good Is Our School?* Edinburgh: Scottish Government.

21

The Parent Dimension in Education

Eileen Prior

Parental involvement is a term that is used frequently but means many different things to different people. This chapter will look at what structures are currently in place in Scotland regarding parental involvement, why parental involvement is increasingly recognised as important and the different forms it takes. It will also give a perspective on current parental contributions and consider what may lie ahead.

WHERE ARE WE NOW?

Perhaps the most useful place to start is with a reflection on the current position. The Scottish Schools (Parental Involvement) Act 2006 paints the backdrop: the legislation created the possibility of a parent council (PC) in every school in the country as a means of involving the parents of all children at a school (termed the parent forum) in the life of the establishment. This Act took forward a notion of parental involvement able to be tracked back to the Local Government (Scotland) Act 1973 which created school councils – the first parent bodies to be specified in legislation. Based on what would now be called a cluster or learning community, school councils brought together parents, teachers and local authority and gave the views of parents recognition. Under the 2006 Act, the parent forum (i.e. all parents with children at the school) was given the right to have a PC, a right that is currently exercised in the majority of schools. The legislation was deliberately non-prescriptive in how the PC is to become reality – that is up to the parents to decide – and so it may be by election, nomination or simply an open door to any parent who wishes to take part.

This is not the only area in which the legislation is non-prescriptive. In fact it is simpler to list those aspects that are defined:

- The PC must be chaired by a parent of a child at the school.
- The headteacher has a right and a duty to attend PC meetings.
- The parent forum has a right to be involved in the appointment of senior management at the school (although what that should look like is not defined).
- Local authorities are obliged to provide support to PCs (although the nature of that support is not specified).
- While the PC is a parent body, it may coopt individuals to membership who are not parents.
- In denominational schools, the church has a right to representation on the PC.
- The PC may call itself any name it chooses, for example 'Friends of . . . '.

In essence, the 2006 Act establishes PCs as independent of both school and local authority, with the freedom and flexibility to work in whichever way they see fit. They are constituted voluntary bodies, although a small number choose to register as charities. The guidance produced by government places an emphasis on the PC as a representative body for the parent forum, encouraging partnership with the school and local authority to promote parental involvement and pursue areas of interest to parents.

Alongside PCs, schools in Scotland may also have a Parent Teacher Association (PTA) or similar body. PTAs have a long history in our schools going back to the 1920s, primarily as bodies that bring together staff and parents, organising fundraising and social events and generally building community within a school. Like PCs, PTAs are independent of school and local authority and are constituted voluntary bodies. The arrival of PCs on the scene has had a significant impact on the number of individual PTAs: over the years, many PTAs have merged into the PC as a subcommittee. The reasons are straightforward: more often than not, both bodies were fishing in the same small pool, drawing on the same group of parents who are willing and able to engage. Moreover, there is financial advantage as both groups require public liability insurance if they are organising events: as one body, one insurance policy suffices. The reference to insurance moves this overview nicely onto the question of national bodies.

The longest-standing national parent body is the Scottish Parent Teacher Council (SPTC) which was formed in 1948 (see SPTC, 1998) and, despite the usual travails endured by voluntary organisations, has been successful in sustaining its original purpose of serving parent groups and promoting partnerships between schools and parents. The advent of PCs was a significant one for SPTC: having identified the need for the new groups to have public liability insurance, SPTC quickly met this need by providing low-cost insurance wrapped up with a range of member benefits. As a charity, the organisation relies on its membership fees as its only significant source of income. SPTC's membership increased exponentially with the introduction of the 2006 Act and the creation of PCs, as did its financial stability and its influence across the sector: with more than 2,000 parent group members, SPTC built an increasingly confident voice in all matters relating to parents and education. Although physically a very small organisation (with just a handful of part-time staff), SPTC punched above its weight in terms of its influence. This can be attributed to the energy and enthusiasm of a small cohort of volunteer directors (both parents and teachers) who were tireless in their support of the organisation, and particularly to Judith Gillespie who was initially convener and then SPTC's first Development Manager, a post she held for many years until she retired in 2010.

While membership numbers have dropped a little over the years, SPTC remains a key organisation for those wishing to hear a parent perspective. Its independence from government, especially financial independence, is keenly protected by its directors, a mix of parents and teachers. As a result, SPTC is regularly asked to be involved in working groups and committees run by a wide range of stakeholders in education, asked to speak at events and to comment upon draft policy relating to education and families. The media also routinely refer to SPTC for comment on parental and educational issues. With PCs and PTAs as members, SPTC provides information and support both to parent groups and to individual parents. In some cases, local authorities pay directly for all of their PCs to be SPTC members, thus ensuring PCs have insurance cover for their various activities. In addition, as well as operating telephone and email helplines which are well used by parents the length and breadth of the country, SPTC publishes a wide range of leaflets on relevant topics, releases a regular newsletter, and also has a website with information and resources for parents (www.sptc.info). Perhaps its most significant contribution to supporting the engagement of parents is its programme of information sessions around the country. Since 2010, the organisation has focused its energies on developing and delivering a range of such sessions for parent groups – increasingly through employment of sessional staff – to help them understand how PCs can work and to develop strategies for productive involvement with their children's school.

The last part of the parental involvement jigsaw is a body that was also part of the Parental Involvement legislation of 2006. Within the Act, the government committed to develop a national parents' body that would take forward the 'parents as educators' agenda (see below). The result was the National Parent Forum Scotland (NPFS), which was formed by the government in 2009. The Forum is intended to comprise one parent from each local authority area, nominated or selected by parent councils or the local authority. The body's purpose is to provide parent councils, in fact all parents, with an opportunity to discuss and raise educational issues at a national level. Members of the NPFS have been invited to participate in many significant decision- and policy-making bodies in Scottish education. Their role is to give a parental perspective on the big issues facing the education system in the twenty-first century. The advent of the NPFS represented a sea change in the government's approach to engagement with parents: parents have the opportunity now to be at the policy-making table, instead of reacting to what flows from it. Created, funded and serviced by the government – which can open doors and facilitate much – the NPFS has the potential to play a valuable role in ensuring the parent perspective is heard in important places. However, for parent volunteers (and each member of the NPFS is a volunteer in just the same way as PC members) the level of commitment possible is necessarily limited and variable. The NPFS is therefore faced with many of the same problems of commitment, consistency and momentum as every PC. Parental involvement is constantly challenged by these same issues. The overarching question, of course, is why is it important?

WHY PARENTAL INVOLVEMENT?

Historically, there has been substantial resistance in some quarters to any parental involvement that went beyond that of willing supporter at home. This resistance from some teachers and those who manage education reflected the widely held view that parents are focused only on their own children and that only the sharp-elbowed middle classes are moved to be active, in order to promote their own agenda. Combined with the conceit of all professions that 'we know best' and fear of criticism, the seed of active parental involvement for many years fell on stony ground in Scotland. However, we have moved from a point where parents were given a duty to ensure their child was educated (the 1872 Education Act) to one where a child's attendance is not enough – legislation is now in place to support parents to be involved, too. What has brought us here? In truth, there is probably no one thing that has created this changed situation, but rather a combination of factors that has led to the present form of parental involvement.

The first of these is the research that began to emerge in the last quarter of the twentieth century and which spoke of the influence of parental involvement in the attainment of young people. The 1980 Education Act – which created School Boards, the precursor to PCs – was the first parliamentary acknowledgement of that growing realisation: children whose parents are actively involved in their education do better at school. It was becoming clear that children were being substantially disadvantaged in their schooling by factors including poverty and socio-economic standing, and that parental expectation and involvement also play very significant roles in educational outcomes. One need only look at the regularly produced league tables in the Scottish media which show a strong correlation between exam results and postcodes to understand the reality of this.

Parenting, and engagement of parents, therefore began to appear on policy documents as a way of addressing the issue of young people who were at best not achieving their potential, and at worst leaving school with no qualifications and no prospect of gainful employment or training – the NEET (not in employment, education or training) group. Ultimately, the emerging policy imperative around parental involvement is about impacting on outcomes, both educational and social, and reflects a growing understanding of the inter-relationship and interdependency of home and school when it comes to young people's learning.

Early research into parental involvement was undertaken by Macbeth in Scotland and Bastiani in England (see Macbeth, 1989; Bastiani, 1987). More recently, the most significant figure in this area of academic work is Desforges (see Desforges and Abouchaar, 2003), whose analysis of the research up to that date led to the conclusion that there are two quite distinct types of parental involvement: the spontaneous engagement of parents because they are motivated to do so, and the interventions by professionals designed specifically to engage parents in their child's education or school. While the first category is well researched (though generally in the United States) the second is backed primarily by anecdotal evidence.

What Desforges demonstrates, however, is that spontaneous parental involvement is not about to make radical changes to outcomes for the NEET group of youngsters any time soon. He shows that parents are more likely to be involved with their child's school if:

- they are middle to upper class;
- the mother has been successful in higher or further education;
- there is no deprivation, no significant ill health (particularly mental health) and both parents are together;
- the child is in his or her early years at school;
- the child is showing high levels of attainment;
- the child is skilled in mediating between home and school – in other words is playing a part in managing that relationship;
- the family is white and/or from a western cultural background.

Should we be surprised by any of this? The parents who are likely to become engaged spontaneously with their child's education are also likely to become engaged with sporting, cultural and other interests because they often have the capacity, confidence, wherewithal and drive to do so. This contrasts sharply with those families who live in poverty, who have health or social issues, where the parents' own experience of school may not have been happy or where there simply is not the capacity to take on the added role as partner educator. The challenge, however, is that although parental engagement with education is generally associated with good outcomes for young people, there continues to be significant debate about what is meant by engagement and how the dynamics of that process lead to better outcomes (see Feinstein et al., 2006; Hills and Stewart, 2005).

Parents have always been, and will always be, advocates for their own children. For most young people, the requirement to have parents as advocates diminishes as they grow and determine their own direction. However, it is worth highlighting the groups of young people who do not fit this general rule: young people with disabilities who continue to need extensive parental engagement with the education system to ensure their needs are met; young people who are in care for whatever reason and rarely have an adult who is passionately involved with their upbringing, and so have no one in the role of advocate in their education. These two groups of young people share something with the NEET group: positive educational outcomes and positive destinations are in short supply. Desforges cites 'at-home good parenting' as having a significant positive effect on children's achievements

> when all other factors bearing on pupil attainment are taken out of the equation, parental involvement . . . has a large and positive effect on the outcomes of schooling. This effect is bigger than that of schooling itself. Research consistently shows that what parents do with their children at home is far more important to their achievement than their social class or level of education. It would seem that if the parenting involvement practices of most working class parents could be raised to the levels of the best working class parents in these terms, very significant advances in school achievement might reasonably be expected. (Desforges and Abouchaar, 2003, p. 87)

If we are to accept this principle of 'at-home good parenting' as being of central importance to attainment at school, we have to be mindful that children from many different backgrounds benefit from a good home, and conversely recognise that poor parenting exists in both affluent and deprived homes. It must be added that Cuthbert and Hatch (2008) argue that nearly all parents have positive general aspirations for their children. Mongon and Chapman (2012) take the debate around the known benefits of parental involvement further:

> it has been an act of faith for many school and children's service leaders to believe that *a closer connection with families* would lead to better outcomes for young people. The evidence is more tenuous. *'Spontaneous' parental involvement* (in crude terms, a 'good home') is associated with positive outcome. In contrast, the evidence from *'enhanced' parental involvement* (in crude terms, programmes to involve parents) is at best inconclusive albeit showing high levels of appreciation from the adults involved.

The introduction of the concept of parent forums and PCs in Scotland can therefore be seen as a response to the evidence outlined by Desforges: these are deliberate strategies to engage all parents at a school based on that act of faith identified by Mongon and Chapman. It is indeed a leap of faith, placing on parents an expectation that they step beyond their traditional role as advocates for their own children and take on a role of involvement with their child's school and, potentially, the country's educational policy.

It is worth noting that the mode of parental involvement we are now pursuing in Scotland is in marked contrast to the previous system of School Boards, which gave parents a quasi-management role within schools, attracting as a result those parents who were able and willing to take on the workload and challenges of such a role. It was the eventual realisation that School Boards were ineffective in engaging a wide range of parents – and therefore (possibly) impacting on educational outcomes – that led to their demise.

One final perspective informs debate about parental involvement: the parent as consumer. Without doubt a massive change has taken place in our culture in recent years as the age of the consumer has arrived. Every walk of life is now subject to the influence of the market, including public services from health to police and, increasingly, education. The advent of the internet has also has a substantial impact, supporting the rise of the consumer:

we no longer simply seek and take advice from a professional, we check it out on the web and join forums where we share information, views and knowledge.

Parent as consumer is perhaps best exemplified in the use of placing requests. While most will elect to send their child to the local school, parents have a right to request a placement outside their catchment area. The right to make a placing request is generally exercised by parents who believe the quality of education offered by another school is significantly better than their own (generally based on attainment league tables) or parents of children with additional support needs who want their child to attend a specialist school. Placing requests are a bone of contention for both parents and schools: the process is not straightforward and there are differences in the protocols for these two groups of children. Another aspect of consumerism, discussed in Chapter 12, is home schooling.

Parents have increasingly woken up to the reality that they, on behalf of their children, are consumers of the education service and so they have the right to question and, if they need to, challenge what is happening in their child's school or classroom, and indeed to opt for a school they believe is better. PCs give parents a sound platform to take forward their concerns and issues around the workings of a school or the education of their child. This creates tensions and challenges. Parents are simultaneously partners with their child's teacher(s) in his or her education; consumers of the service and therefore free to be critical; and also potentially involved in decision making and policy making at a local and wider level. To wear all of these hats presents significant challenges.

Education is no different from many other public services, however: while consumer engagement may be encouraged, the people who work in the service may embrace or obstruct it depending on their personal perspective. The result is a patchwork where the parent as consumer is not guaranteed a welcome.

HOW IS PARENTAL INVOLVEMENT WORKING IN SCOTLAND?

The policy framework is in place; the mechanisms for delivering parental involvement are established. However, the question that must be answered is this: is it working? If PCs and PTAs are now the primary formal mechanisms for parental involvement, are they living up to expectations and delivering greater parental involvement with the educational structures and, perhaps, leading onto greater parental engagement with the education of their children? PCs have now been operational since 2006. Designed with a light touch so that each parent body had the flexibility to address the issues concerning them and their school, the outcome has been predictably variable.

The non-prescriptive approach adopted in the legislation, while laudable in its objective of enabling flexibility, has left the door open to confusion as to the rights and responsibilities of PCs among parents themselves, school management and local authorities – and a tendency to cherry-pick the elements that appeal or are easy, and leave the rest to one side. The patchwork and sometimes haphazard nature of implementation can, in part, be put down to the nature of the parent body: parents (and therefore the PC) are a fluid group of individuals who come and go with little or no warning as families move house and their children change school, and as other roles and responsibilities become more pressing. In blunt terms the personnel is deeply unstable: not only do parents move around, they also face the constant challenge of juggling their various commitments at home and at work. Even with the best will in the world, parents who find their shifts have changed or their health has deteriorated will feel under pressure and their ability to maintain school involvement will be squeezed.

Many PCs, therefore, struggle to sustain themselves: information that was given to the initial set of parent council members back in 2006 (a substantial ring binder containing a DVD and printed guidance, called *Parents as Partners*) has now largely been lost as people have moved on and information has been mislaid. The task of keeping PCs working effectively, let alone developing, has been likened to that of painting the Forth Road Bridge. The government did refresh and reissue guidance for PCs once again in 2011: a welcome move, particularly as all material is now online.

A further factor influencing PC effectiveness has been the level of support enjoyed by PCs as they have evolved. While each local authority is charged with providing support to help the parent groups function, in reality this has been wildly different across the country. Parent Officers, who were charged with helping PCs to find their feet, have often found their role has changed over the years, so that they are now responsible for many other areas of work (for example, home schooling, school refusers, continuing professional development and so on) and parental involvement is now a very small part of their role. This is a practical example of how the initial energy committed to supporting PCs has been dissipated, but lying behind this is a more fundamental issue: the level of commitment within the local authority to parental involvement. The notion of parents as partners, much less consumers, who have the right to be heard and to have their views taken into account, is as yet in its infancy in many areas of Scotland. In truth, as indicated earlier, there is a long history of resistance to parental involvement in our schools. While headteachers and local authorities have been happy to accept the money raised by parent groups, a significant number are less happy to share information and some measure of power with the parent body. Information flow is often seen as a one-way process – towards parents – with a marked reluctance to hear, and act upon, those views from parents that come back up the chain. This is evidenced by the way in which PCs are, in some areas, left to their own devices, information flow to the parent body is restricted and tightly managed, and leaders at local authority and school level work to contain the operations of the PC to areas such as fundraising and social activities. Even where the local authority has a positive outlook on parental involvement, the individual head teacher is in a position of substantial power as to the freedom or otherwise of the parent body to participate in decision making in a school.

Putting these potential barriers to one side, probably the greatest challenges facing PCs – even in areas where they have a supportive partnership with school and local authority – is one of fully embracing the potential of the role. Broadly, the operational areas for a PC can be seen as falling into the following areas: school matters; communication; learning; social and fundraising; campaigning.

School Matters

School matters encompass the work a PC does with the senior management team and local authority around areas such as school budgets; development plan; policies such as bullying or school uniform; recruitment of headteacher and senior staff; local authority consultations; and school inspections. From the start of session 2011–12, a new inspection regime was introduced by Education Scotland which is designed to engage the parent body more in the process of school inspection. Probably the most significant change is the provision of the Record of Inspection Findings (RIF) to the chair of the PC at the same time as it goes to the local authority and headteacher. It previously was given only to the latter (though was available to others through a Freedom of Information request). This is a confidential document which the chair – ideally jointly with the headteacher – is expected to consider and use to lead discussions with the PC and the parent forum. In particular, this needs to be linked to the school development plan. For the PC chair, this is both an opportunity and a threat: he or she has to make a judgement as to how the key principles of the inspection findings are shared with the PC and the wider parent forum, without compromising the confidentiality of the information received in the RIF and while being a robust protector of the parental interest.

Communication

Communication is a critical role for the PC: the body is a conduit between the parent forum (i.e. all parents or carers of children at the school) and the senior management team and local authority. Information should flow through the PC to and from parents, the SMT and the local authority. In reality, this is an issue most PCs have grappled with, with greater or lesser success, since they were formed. Engaging with parents who have busy lives, substantial other commitments and/or a lack of confidence in dealing with a school (particularly a secondary school) is both relentless and challenging, and PCs need a lot of support to achieve this effectively.

Learning

Educational involvement is the area that sits more comfortably with the traditional view of parental involvement (i.e. supporting the learning of one's own child). The emphasis on parents as partners in education gained momentum with the advent of Curriculum for Excellence (CfE). Taking a cue from the Parental Involvement legislation, CfE explicitly identifies parents as key and critical partners in their children's education. Any adult volunteering for a role in a school is of course likely to be captured within the terms of the Protection of Vulnerable Groups (Scotland) Act 2007 (PVG), which was enacted in 2011. PVG requires qualifying adults to join the PVG membership scheme, a sometimes unwelcome and sadly cumbersome process. The substantive difference to the proposition is that parents – and indeed other willing members of the community – have the opportunity to get involved in the teaching and learning at school as well as at home. This could be in demonstrating a specific craft or skill, leading an outdoor activity or supporting learning in a classroom. Once again, this pushes out the boundaries of parental involvement by bringing them more actively into the learning at school, building on the well-established role of parent helper but taking it much further.

Social and Fundraising

Another traditional role of parents is as fundraisers and organisers of social activities. The former is an increasingly important role: many parent bodies (both PTA and PC) raise thousands of pounds from parents and the local community to support the work of the school – money that is often used to purchase items that may increasingly be seen as core rather than additional, such as IT resources, interactive white boards, gym and play equipment. This is, of course, a matter of some concern to parents who are aware they are playing a part in widening the gap between schools: while in certain areas parents may work hard to raise just a few hundred pounds each year, some parent bodies fund their school to the tune of tens of thousands of pounds. The social aspect is also very important: often the school acts as the hub of the community and so social activities are one of the forms of glue that hold communities together, especially at primary schools and in rural areas.

Campaigning

Campaigning is a role that parents have been very adept at over the years, whether in relation to their own school, the policies of their local authority or indeed of the government of the day. The only thing that is certain about parents who join together to campaign is that they are both unpredictable and a force to be reckoned with. They are also very often successful in the long term. The examples are legion: from the mass parental rejection of Conservative Education Secretary Michael Forsyth's plans to introduce national tests in the early 1990s, where parents chose to opt out of the regime of testing at each stage of the 5–14 curriculum, forcing a climbdown on compulsory testing; to the Renfrewshire parents who, in 2011, unanimously rejected their local authority's plans to bring non-teaching staff into the classroom to instruct children during teacher non-contact time, again forcing a climbdown. The threat of school closure is a further example of an issue that, time after time, brings parents out on the streets. The power of parents is therefore not to be taken lightly; it should not be assumed that they will simply kowtow to the latest government policy or thinking. This unpredictability is certainly one of the factors that the educational establishment finds difficult when dealing with the parent body.

The leap of faith is still being made. Among advocates of parental involvement, the arguments are straightforward: through proactive engagement with parents, schools have the potential to gain substantially from engaging with the wider community, access all sorts of resources it would not otherwise and become a true community hub.

THE FUTURE

With their focus on parents as partners in children's education, the combination of CfE and the Parental Involvement Act is promising but challenging. However, the difference between rhetoric and reality remains. As for expectations of gains being made in pupil attainment as a result of greater parental involvement, there remains little firm evidence. During 2011, there was a government consultation on the School Handbook, a document which surprisingly is enshrined in legislation (the 1980 Act) but which very many parents will be largely unaware of. While ostensibly about the handbook – what it should contain and how it should be shared with parents – the consultation in reality highlighted the frustrations of parents in relation to home/school communication as a whole. The year 2012 saw the government bring forward revised guidance on school handbooks, with the aim of enabling greater parental input on content and format. In the background, also, is a sense that the existing system of education services delivered by thirty-two local authorities – specifically the cost, duplication and variation that is inevitably part of this – should be addressed. There is a groundswell of opinion that the delivery mechanism for education services should be revised. We are beginning to see new models emerge, in the shape of shared services between two or more local authorities and proposals from one authority for greater parental and community involvement in planning and direction at a cluster level. There are many potential directions in which the service may move: one wonders just how great a part parental opinion will play in shaping the future governance of education, should these ideas come to reality.

REFERENCES

Bastiani, J. (1987) *Parents and Teachers: Perspectives on Home–School Relations.* Windsor: NFER-Nelson.

Cuthbert, C. D. and R. Hatch (2008) 'Educational aspiration and attainment amongst young people in deprived communities'. Online at www.crfr.ac.uk/spa2009/Cuthbert%20C,%20Hatch%20R%20-%20Educational%20aspiration%20and%20attainment%20amongst%20young%20people%20in%20deprived%20communities.pdf

Desforges, C. and A. Abouchaar (2003) 'The impact of parental involvement, parental support and family education on pupil achievement and adjustment: A literature review'. Research Report No 433. London: DfES.

Feinstein, L., R. Sabates, T. M. Anderson, A. Sorhaindo and C. Hammond (2006) 'What are the effects of education on health?' OECD Copenhagen Symposium on Measuring the Effects of Education on Health and Civic Engagement. Online at www.oecd.org/dataoecd/15/18/37425753.pdf

Hills, J. and K. Stewart (eds) (2005) *A More Equal Society? New Labour, Poverty, Inequality and Exclusion.* Bristol: Policy Press.

Macbeth, A. (1985) *Involving Parents: Effective Parent–Teacher Relations.* Oxford: Heinemann.

Mongon, D. and C. Chapman (2012) *High-Leverage Leadership: Improving Outcomes in Educational Settings.* London: Routledge.

Scottish Parent Teacher Council (1998) *50th Anniversary of the Scottish Parent Teacher Council 1948–1998.* Edinburgh: Scottish Parent Teacher Council.

IV

THE HISTORICAL AND CULTURAL CONTEXT OF SCOTTISH EDUCATION

This section brings together a number of contributions that offer insights into the historical and contemporary cultural context of Scottish education. Two chapters set the historical background. Chapter 22 provides a broad overview of the evolution of the Scottish educational system, including the significance attached to the parish school in the years following the Reformation; the challenges thrown up by the industrial revolution and responses to them; the increasing role of the state, leading to the Education (Scotland) Act of 1872; and the gradual provision of mass secondary education in the twentieth century, first in an elite, selective system and then, from 1965 onwards, in an all-through comprehensive system for 11–18-year-olds. Chapter 23 focuses on the more recent past, taking as its starting point the significant ideological shift represented by the ascendancy of the New Right at UK level, signalled by the election of a Conservative government in 1979. Although there was considerable resistance to Thatcherism in Scotland, various reforms in curriculum, assessment and school management were introduced. The outcomes of schooling were expected to be geared to the needs of the economy and the world of work. The rights of parents were strengthened and teachers became subject to tighter regimes of control. With the re-establishment of a Scottish Parliament in 1999, however, the distinctiveness of Scottish education from that of the rest of the UK was reasserted. Although post-devolution Scottish administrations, whether Labour–Liberal Democrat coalitions (until 2007) or SNP (2007 to the present), have retained some of the reforming discourse of the preceding decades, they have been keen to pursue a very different agenda from that south of the border.

Four chapters explore important aspects of national identity. Chapter 24 examines the complex interplay of forces (literary, political, intellectual) which fed into the nationalist movement in the twentieth century, raising challenging questions about the relationship between 'Scottishness' and 'Britishness'. The particular contribution of mass education to this process is an important part of the story. The role of language in shaping identity and expressing cultural values is discussed in Chapters 25 and 26, the former dealing with Gaelic, the latter with Scots. In the past, both have been subject to marginalisation and even attempts to eradicate their use in education, but the climate is now more positive. Chapter 25 describes the range of efforts, at all levels of education, to preserve and extend the use of Gaelic, including the development of new resources aimed at both learners and native speakers. The celebration of the rich variety of accents, dialects and vocabulary in the Scots language is outlined in Chapter 26 and it is noted that, although there is still scope for development (e.g. in the training of teachers), progress has been made both in terms of the use of Scots in the classroom and in the texts that feature on the curriculum. Religion is another vital aspect of cultural identity and in Chapter 27 the distinctive character of the Catholic community in Scotland, recognised through the provision within the state sector of denominational primary and secondary schools, is explained. Understanding the historical reasons for this arrangement, and the controversy that it sometimes provokes, is essential to a proper appreciation of the Scottish educational system, particularly in the west of Scotland.

The days when schooling prepared youngsters for clear pathways into the world of work, through apprenticeships or other forms of training, are long past. Economic conditions are uncertain, employment opportunities volatile and subject to rapid change, sometimes leading to a mismatch between qualifications and job requirements. Chapter 28 looks at the changing nature of employment from the perspective of different groups: early school leavers who are vulnerable to unemployment; graduates who find that the labour market has changed and may have to adjust their expectations; and the 'missing middle' of moderately qualified young people who are often forgotten in policy proposals. The link between education and employment is part of the debate about social inequality, a recurring theme for governments of all political persuasions. Chapter 29 looks at the various schemes that have been made to improve access to higher education for both young and mature students from socially disadvantaged backgrounds. These encounter problems relating to entrance qualifications, cultural awareness and internal university structures. There are some good examples of support mechanisms and outreach schemes, linked to schools in deprived areas but, even where universities succeed in attracting 'non-traditional' students, the drop-out rate can be high, indicating that retention remains an unresolved issue.

The final two chapters address topics that feature strongly on the current policy agenda. One of the key 'capacities' of Curriculum for Excellence (CfE) is 'responsible citizenship', and Chapter 30 explores the various dimensions of citizenship education. It argues that the model of citizenship that is presented in CfE documents is more individual and collective, more social than political, and more inclined to favour sameness rather than difference. While the aim of promoting citizenship is laudable, it is suggested, a deeper analysis of what this might mean for democratic processes is required. Finally, Chapter 31 traces the growing importance of sustainable development education, noting the challenges it presents in requiring an interdisciplinary approach to social and economic issues, and its inevitable encounter with sensitive political issues. It is argued that the topic needs to be viewed not simply in terms of the content of the curriculum, but should include the campus environment and the wider community of which the school forms a part. The landscape of Scotland is well suited to a serious exploration of global concerns, including renewable energy and environmental protection.

22

The History of Scottish Education, pre-1980

Robert Anderson

Scottish education has been characterised by a peculiar awareness of its own history. Since 1707, its distinctness has been a mark of national identity to be defended against assimilation with England, and its supposed superiority has been a point of national pride. Two achievements were especially notable: the early arrival of universal or near-universal literacy, and a precociously developed university system; on these was founded the 'democratic' myth of Scottish education, later expressed in the literary and popular image of the 'lad o' pairts', the boy of modest social origins from a rural or small-town background climbing the educational ladder to such professions as the ministry, schoolteaching or the civil service. Like other national myths, this idealises reality but has a core of truth, though most historians would agree that it represented an individualist form of meritocracy, rather than reflecting a classless society. For all the virtues of the rural parish school, the chief features of modern Scottish education were created in the few decades following the Education (Scotland) Act 1872, and as a pioneering urban and industrial country Scotland was deeply marked by the class divisions of the nineteenth century. The 1872 Act was a political and administrative landmark, but (as we shall see) the basic task of schooling the new working class had already been largely overcome, and the increased intervention of the state was not so much a reaction against the previous dominance of religion and the churches, but rather a modernised and secular form of an ideal of 'national' and public education, aimed at imposing cultural uniformity, which can be traced to the Reformation, if not before, and which is itself a strong constituent of the Scottish tradition.

THE PARISH SCHOOL AND LITERACY

The leaders of the Scottish Reformation had an unusually clear vision of the role of education in creating a godly society. The First Book of Discipline of 1560 sketched out an articulated educational structure, from parish school to university, and aimed at providing basic religious instruction and literacy in each parish. Achieving this was the work of several generations, but it is today generally agreed that by the end of the seventeenth century the network of parish schools was largely complete in the lowlands, though not in the highlands. The Act of 1696 passed by the Scottish Parliament, which was strengthened in 1803 and remained the legal basis of the parish schools until 1872, consolidated this structure. The landowners (heritors) were obliged to build a schoolhouse and to pay a salary to a schoolmaster, which was supplemented by the fees paid by parents; ministers and presbyteries were responsible for the quality of education and the testing of schoolmasters. This was a statutory system, but one run by the church and the local notables rather than the state.

Schooling did not become compulsory until 1872, and attendance in the early modern period depended partly on the perceived advantages of education (which were greater for boys than girls) and partly on the pressure of landowners, ministers and community opinion. Attendance was clearly not universal, and recent studies of literacy have challenged the traditional optimistic picture. Houston (1985, pp. 56–62) estimates male literacy (defined as the ability to write a signature rather than a mark) at 65 per cent in the lowlands in the mid-eighteenth century, and female at no more than 25–30 per cent. This put the Scottish lowlands among the more literate areas of Europe, but it was not a unique achievement. As elsewhere, literacy varied regionally (the borders and east central Scotland being the most advanced), was higher in towns than in the countryside, and was correlated with occupation and prosperity, reaching artisans, small merchants or farmers before labourers, miners, factory workers or crofters.

It is very likely that the early stages of the industrial revolution, with the accompanying phenomena of urbanisation and migration from the highlands and Ireland, worsened overall rates of literacy. But exact figures are lacking until the official registration of marriages was introduced in 1855. At that time, 89 per cent of men and 77 per cent of women could sign the registers – compared with 70 per cent and 59 per cent respectively in England. But signature evidence may underestimate the basic ability to read, for writing was taught as a separate skill, with higher fees, and many children, especially girls, did not advance beyond reading. Taken as a whole, the evidence on literacy suggests that by 1800 Scottish lowland communities had made the fundamental transition to written culture. Illiteracy survived but was stigmatised and deplored by the church and the secular authorities, and the ability to read was broad enough to support the beginnings of a tradition of working-class self-education and self-improvement.

None of this applied to the highlands, where attempts to create schools suffered from adverse economic and geographical conditions, the slow penetration of the church's basic parochial organisation and the resistance of an oral Gaelic culture. After 1715, and even more after 1745, church and state combined to enforce loyalty and orthodoxy, and it was axiomatic that this must be through the medium of English. Parish schools were supplemented by those of the Society in Scotland for Propagating Christian Knowledge, founded in 1709, but the refusal to teach in Gaelic (except initially as an aid to learning English) created a formidable cultural barrier between family and school. Nevertheless, by the early nineteenth century, conditions in the more prosperous parts of the highlands and islands were not so different from the lowlands, though usually with scantier resources, and illiteracy was being driven into its last redoubts in the Western Isles.

A notable feature of the parish school was its connection with the universities. Schoolmasters were expected to have some university experience, and they taught enough Latin to allow boys to pass directly into university classes. This system had evolved to encourage the recruitment of ministers, and there were bursaries to give promising pupils financial support. This was the origin of the tradition of the 'lad o' pairts', and though in practice most such boys came from the middle ranks – the sons of ministers, farmers and artisans – rather than the really poor, the educational opportunities offered in the countryside made Scotland unusual.

BURGH SCHOOLS AND UNIVERSITIES

The parish school legislation did not apply in burghs. It was normal for royal burghs to maintain burgh schools, whose existence can be traced back into the Middle Ages. Originally these were grammar schools, teaching Latin with an eye to the universities, but town councils began to appoint additional teachers for modern and commercial subjects, and by the late eighteenth century there was a move to consolidate the various schools in an 'academy', usually housed in impressive new buildings. The expanding middle class of the towns was thus well catered for, and outside the big cities the burgh schools and academies were open to both sexes, an unusual feature at the time. But town councils had no statutory duty to provide education for the mass of the population, and most basic education in the towns was given by private teachers. Although Scotland has a strong tradition of public education, private schools once had a vital role, in rural areas as well as in the towns, being squeezed out only in the nineteenth century by competition from churches and charitable bodies as well as the state. These schools have been underestimated as they left few traces in historical records. They ranged from the 'dame school' where a woman taught reading to young children in her own home, through the 'private adventure' school which at its best could give the same sort of education as a parish school, to expensive boarding and day schools in the cities, training boys for the university or a commercial career, or 'young ladies' in the accomplishments expected of a middle-class bride.

The vigorous state of urban education by 1800 reflected the prosperity of the age of improvement, as did the striking success of the universities, of which Scotland had five. Three were founded in the fifteenth century (St Andrews, Glasgow and King's College Aberdeen), and two after the Reformation (Edinburgh and Marischal College Aberdeen), but the Reformation did not change their fundamental character, as inward-looking institutions teaching arts and theology, whose core task was the training of the clergy. The political and religious upheavals of the seventeenth century were damaging, but after 1700 the universities embarked on a notable revival culminating in the age of the Enlightenment, when Scotland was for a time in the van of European thought. The lecture-based curriculum had a broadly philosophical approach embracing modern subjects like science and economics, and directly expressed enlightened ideals of politeness, improvement and virtue. The universities could thus offer a liberal education to the social elite, while simultaneously developing professional training, especially at Edinburgh, in law and medicine. Medical education was especially important in securing the universities' reputation and in attracting students, as was to remain the case in the nineteenth century. Socially, the fact that all the universities except St Andrews were situated in large towns kept them in touch with contemporary demands and made them accessible to the new commercial and professional classes; the sons of the aristocracy and gentry, no longer sent abroad to universities like Leyden, rubbed shoulders with a more modest and traditional contingent aiming at the ministry or schoolteaching.

THE INDUSTRIAL REVOLUTION AND MASS EDUCATION

By the end of the eighteenth century Scots were aware of the distinctive character of their educational system, and already saw it as a point of superiority over England. But it had evolved within a predominantly agrarian society, dominated by its traditional elites, and committed to religious uniformity. Industrialisation, the appearance of modern class divisions, the rise of political democracy and the growth of religious pluralism posed formidable challenges and required far-reaching adaptations. The working of the Scottish system had not been affected by the union of 1707, but the practical and political response to industrialisation was inevitably similar in Scotland and England, and required legislation that brought them closer together.

The problems of educating the new urban working class were first tackled around 1810, initially by philanthropists advocating the 'Lancasterian' method of monitorial instruction, but mainly by the church. Supporting schools became a standard activity for church congregations, and there were many religiously inspired committees and societies that promoted special types of school – infant schools, schools in the highlands, schools for girls, schools for the 'ragged' children of the streets, evening schools for factory workers. These activities were coordinated locally by the church's presbyteries, and nationally by the General Assembly's influential Education Committee. But hopes of a continuing partnership between church and state were shattered by the Disruption of 1843, after which the Church of Scotland was a minority church. Shortly afterwards, in 1846, state aid to education (which had started in the 1830s with building grants, and was supervised from 1840 by a Scottish inspectorate) was reorganised to give annual grants to schools that followed the state's curricular 'Code'. The grant system encouraged the professional training of teachers through the 'pupil-teacher' system of apprenticeship, linked with the 'normal' or training colleges run by the churches. In dispensing its grants, the state did not discriminate between denominations. The new Free Church threw itself into an ambitious educational programme, while Episcopalians and Roman Catholics concentrated on providing for their own adherents. The growth of Catholic schools, especially in Glasgow and the west, was fuelled by Irish immigration, and state support was especially important because of the poverty of the Catholic community. The Catholic system also had distinctive cultural features such as teaching by religious orders, and separate boys' and girls' schools.

There thus developed a dual system: the statutory parish schools, still limited to rural parishes, and a very diverse sector of denominational and voluntary but state-aided schools. Attempts to merge the two systems and achieve a more rational use of resources preoccupied politicians for many years, but always foundered on the rocks of party-political and religious dissension. The 1872 Act was thus a considerable achievement. It created a 'state' system by giving control of most schools to an elected school board in each burgh and parish, and persuaded the presbyterian churches to hand over their schools to the boards. This contrasted with the situation in England and Wales, where the Education Act 1870 inaugurated a bitter rivalry between board and church schools, requiring further legislation in 1902 and 1944.

The 1872 Act created two new agencies which, in different forms, were to share the direction of education thereafter. The school boards gave new scope to local opinion. They were elected by a form of proportional representation, and the franchise included women if they were independent property holders; women could also be members of the board, and made a distinctive contribution in the larger towns. School boards lasted until the Education (Scotland) Act 1918, when they were replaced by ad hoc education authorities on a county basis; only in 1929 was education transferred to the all-purpose local authorities. The second creation of 1872 was the Scotch Education Department (SED: not renamed Scottish until 1918). From 1885, the SED was attached to the new Scottish Office, and its early secretaries Henry Craik (1885–1904) and John Struthers (1904–23) turned it into a powerful bureaucracy, giving Scotland a more centralised and uniform state system than England.

The balance between central and local control was weighted from the start towards the SED, since school boards and local authorities, despite their rating powers, still depended on state grants and had to meet the conditions laid down centrally.

BEFORE AND AFTER THE EDUCATION ACT 1872

The creation of state systems of popular education was a general feature of the nineteenth century, related to broader movements of democratisation (the franchise was extended to urban workers in 1867), to the needs of a developing economy and to the rise of the nation-state and national rivalries. Legislation reflected the desire of the state to control a vital agency of citizenship and national efficiency, as much as to promote mass literacy. In fact both school attendance and literacy were already at a high level in Scotland, as the reports of the Argyll Commission in 1867–8 revealed. The practical significance of the 1872 Act was that it established common standards and filled the gaps that the voluntary system had been unable to reach.

The first gap was between men and women. In 1870, 90 per cent of bridegrooms could sign their names, but only 80 per cent of brides. The idea that girls needed a less complete schooling than boys lingered, but in the mid-nineteenth century there had been a growth of separate schools for girls, which probably helped to accelerate female literacy. It was associated with the rise of the woman teacher, and although it was well after 1872 before women outnumbered men in the profession, the training colleges offered women a significant path to independence and social mobility. After 1872 school boards usually abolished the small girls' schools, and mixed education became the norm. By 1900, when formal literacy was virtually complete, there was only one point between men (98 per cent) and women (97 per cent), and girls stayed slightly longer at school than boys (Anderson, 1995, pp. 234, 305).

A second gap was within the working class. Under the voluntary system, skilled and 'respectable' workers, who could afford to pay the standard school fee of about threepence a week, had access to schools of reasonable quality, and their children could stay long enough to master the basics, as did nearly all children in the rural lowlands. But the urban poor usually had access only to inferior schools, charging a penny a week or giving a charitable free education. In factory and mining districts, and in the big cities, child labour was a major disincentive to education. Factory legislation, as well as compulsory schooling, progressively removed this obstacle, and though school fees were not abolished until 1890, school boards offered an education of equal quality to all their constituents. The huge urban schools that remain the symbol of the Victorian era in education became part of the homogeneous working-class experience which had evolved by 1900.

A third gap was between lowlands and highlands. The Argyll report revealed the poverty and backwardness of education in the Western Isles, Skye and some mainland districts, though these conditions were by now untypical of the highlands as a whole. For some years highland school boards were to struggle with inadequate resources, but the problems were overcome within a generation. Part of the price was a further retreat of Gaelic. The 1872 Act has often been blamed for this, and it is true that official policy made only minor concessions to the language; but there was nothing new in this, for highland educational initiatives had always insisted on the primacy of English. It was not until after 1945 that serious efforts were made to promote bilingualism.

A fourth gap, which the 1872 Act did not remedy, was the situation of Catholic schools. Illiteracy persisted in the Catholic community, and helped make the western counties a problem area. The religious settlement of 1872 was not accepted by Catholics or Episcopalians, and they continued to receive direct state grants, which covered running costs but not capital expenditure. The Episcopalian schools stagnated and eventually withered away, but the Catholic sector expanded, from sixty-five schools in 1872 to 226 in 1918; about an eighth of all Scottish children were in Catholic schools. Lack of resources meant that schools were under-equipped, teachers poorly paid, and secondary education underdeveloped. This was increasingly felt as an injustice, and the 1918 Act transferred Roman Catholic schools to the education authorities, to be supported on the same financial basis as other schools, with safeguards for religious instruction and the denominational affiliation of teachers. Protected and promoted by the hierarchy, often in alliance with the new Labour electorate, Catholic schools soon acquired an entrenched position in the public system (see Chapter 25).

The 1872 Act made education compulsory from 5 to 13, raised to 14 in 1883. But this was theoretical, as children could leave earlier if they had mastered the 'three Rs'. From 1901, however, 14 was enforced as the effective leaving age, and by then the elementary curriculum included subjects like history, geography, elementary science, physical training and some semi-vocational elements: woodwork for boys, cookery and 'domestic economy' for girls. Once every child passed through the school, governments also saw its value as an agency of social welfare: school meals and medical inspection were put on a statutory basis in 1908. The daily routines of the elementary school were not to change fundamentally thereafter until the 1960s.

THE REMODELLING OF ELITE EDUCATION

While elementary education developed on its own lines, having an essentially working-class character which contrasted with the lack of sharp social differentiation in the old parish schools, secondary schools and universities were remodelled to meet the needs of the expanding middle class for professional qualifications and examination credentials. The movement for university reform began early, and was often controversial. There were royal commissions of inquiry in 1826 and 1876, and reforming Acts of Parliament in 1858 and 1889, which overhauled both constitutions and curricula. In the early nineteenth century the universities had no entrance examination, and although there was a recommended curriculum, many students stayed for only a year or two, chose which lectures to attend and took no examinations – formal graduation had become the exception. But this no longer suited the needs of the age, and the outcome of reform by the 1890s was a standardised pattern of graduation, with the arts curriculum offering a choice between three-year Ordinary and four-year Honours degrees. Specialised courses, including separate faculties of science, replaced the old MA curriculum with its compulsory Latin, Greek and philosophy. The typical age of entry rose from 15 or 16, as it still was in the 1860s, to 17 or 18, and free entry gave way to an entrance examination equivalent to the school Leaving Certificate introduced by the SED in 1888. These changes were only possible because secondary schools had been reformed and given an extended academic curriculum.

A 'secondary' system (the term itself appeared only in the 1860s) was constructed from disparate elements. The 1872 Act transferred the burgh schools to school boards, but otherwise did little for secondary education. Resources were found instead from endowments, and in the 1870s and 1880s many older endowed schools, including the former residential 'hospitals' like George Heriot's in Edinburgh, were modernised. Further gaps were filled by 'higher grade' schools, founded by school boards as extensions of elementary schools, especially in Glasgow. In 1892, the first state grants for secondary education appeared (ten years earlier than in England), and were used to build up schools in smaller towns as well as to strengthen existing ones. The result was that although schools differed in prestige and legal status, they formed an effective national network able to prepare both for the universities and for business careers. The Argyll Commission in the 1860s had identified fifty-nine public secondary schools with 14,879 pupils. By 1912, there were 249, with 38,312 pupils (19,611 boys and 18,701 girls). Of these 143 gave a full five-year course, and 106 a three-year or 'intermediate' one; 171 of the schools charged no fees (R. D. Anderson, *Education and Opportunity in Victorian Scotland: Schools and Universities* Clarendon Press, Oxford, 1983, pp. 134, 243–6). This pattern was to change little until the 1940s.

Two points were especially significant. First, though Scotland was not a pioneer in university education for women – because of legal obstacles, their admission was delayed until 1892 – mixed secondary education became firmly established, at least outside Edinburgh, Glasgow and Aberdeen, where high schools and endowed schools remained single-sex. Middle-class parents now had as good a choice of education for their daughters as for their sons, and this was reflected in the percentage of women students at the universities, which was high by contemporary standards: 23 per cent by 1914, rising to 34 per cent in the 1920s, though it fell again in the 1930s to 26 to 27 per cent.

Second, the schools served a wide social range. The road to the university now lay only through the secondary school, but analysis of the social origins of university students suggests that opportunities for mobility were not narrowed. Although Scotland had a few English-style 'public schools', like Fettes College, and some exclusive day schools, like Edinburgh Academy and its equivalents in Glasgow (see Chapter 9), the Scottish middle class was generally content to use its local schools. At the other end of the social scale, accessibility was wide because many secondary schools charged no fees, and bursaries were fairly widely available. Transfer from elementary to secondary schools around the age of 12 became an accepted if still limited phenomenon. The 1918 Act required education authorities to make free secondary education available to all, though they could and did retain fee-paying in designated schools.

THE TWENTIETH CENTURY: TOWARDS AN INTEGRATED SYSTEM

By 1900, the extension of the elementary curriculum and the increasing number of children staying at school after age 12 raised the question of relations between the two sectors. The SED was now using the term 'primary' for the early stages of education, but the underlying social conception was still that true secondary education was only for an academically gifted minority, and it was official policy (formalised in 1903) to draw a sharp distinction between secondary and advanced elementary education. A 'qualifying examination' at 12 identified the exceptional talents who might climb the educational ladder (a favourite image of the time), but the majority stayed on in the primary school and took 'supplementary courses'. After leaving school, they were encouraged to attend evening 'continuation' classes, mostly vocational. The reforming mood created by the First World War raised hopes of an end to this dualism, especially as the 1918 Act proposed raising the leaving age from 14 to 15. But financial crisis suspended this provision – and also plans for compulsory continuation classes for adolescents – and the SED resisted pressures for 'secondary education for all', continuing to insist that the different types of course should be rigidly separate. Its controversial regulations of 1923 renamed the supplementary courses 'advanced divisions', but these were denied secondary status, and most had only a two-year curriculum.

In practice the inter-war years saw a blurring of the distinction between courses. In smaller towns, both types were given in 'omnibus' schools which took all older children, and elsewhere the authorities usually grouped advanced education in 'central' schools, replacing all-age schools with a redistribution at age 12 (the 'clean cut'). The Education Act 1936 proposed raising the leaving age to 15 in 1939, and although this was postponed because of the war (until 1947) the SED finally accepted that all post-primary courses should be called secondary, divided where necessary between 'senior' (five-year) and 'junior' (three-year) schools. This system was consolidated and developed in the 1940s. Most senior secondary schools were old-established secondaries, with superior buildings, equipment and staffing, while junior secondaries were either former central schools or new foundations. All-age primary schools finally disappeared except in remote rural areas. Thus apart from places served by bilateral omnibus schools, Scotland now had a selective secondary system based on the 'twelve-plus' examination, given new scientific authority by the intelligence testing developed in the 1930s.

Secondary schools were the most dynamic sector of Scottish education between the wars: numbers rose to about 90,000 by 1939. But low birth rates and the collapse of traditional industries had a generally negative and depressing effect. Despite a few initiatives like the creation of the Scottish Council for Research in Education in 1928, official thinking remained conservative. There was, for example, no vigorous promotion of scientific and technical education, of a kind that might have helped revive the Scottish economy. The Second World War changed this, directly by underlining the importance of science and advanced education, indirectly by creating long-term social aspirations that broke the fetters of the selective system. Even for the political left, selection seemed acceptable after the war as an expression of equality of opportunity, and the more idealistic vision expressed in the 1947 report of the Scottish Advisory Council on Education was rejected by the SED. But the breaking down of the old industrial economy, with its relatively small elite and its mass working class, undermined the assumption that academic education and examination qualifications could be reserved for a quarter or a third of the population. There was also a fundamental change in the career expectations of women. Thus by the 1960s, there was an increasing demand to stay on at school, and to gain qualifications which the junior secondaries were unable to offer. One response was the introduction of the Scottish Certificate of Education in 1962, with a Higher Grade which was less university-oriented than the old Leaving Certificate, and a new Ordinary Grade offering a wider range of subjects for fourth-year pupils.

These pressures paved the way for the eventual raising of the leaving age to 16 in 1973, and more immediately for the abolition of selection in 1965, a policy which aroused some controversy at the time, but which soon achieved wide acceptance, as it failed to do in England. The pattern of mixed, six-year comprehensives was almost universal in Scotland. Difficulties arose chiefly in the cities, where it meant the end of the remaining fee-paying schools, and where residential segregation strongly influenced the character and achievement of schools. A further consequence of the policy, also concentrated in the cities, was the withdrawal of the state's direct grants to old-established endowed schools, which now passed with their middle-class clientele into the independent sector.

The organisation of secondary schooling and its relation with primary schools was the most politically sensitive issue in Scottish education for much of the twentieth century. But primary education had its own revolution after 1945. An expanding birth rate, and the shift of the population from central districts to suburbs and new towns, required a massive programme of new building and teacher training. So did the introduction of more child-centred educational methods, and the SED's Memorandum *Primary Education in Scotland* of 1965 gave these official sanction.

Expansion was also marked at the post-secondary level. Government policy after 1945 accepted the need for more students in both traditional universities and technical colleges, and the Robbins Report of 1963 only endorsed a trend already well under way. A new university opened at Stirling, and Strathclyde and Heriot-Watt universities were created from existing advanced technical colleges. Technical colleges had their roots in the nineteenth century, and the leading ones had been financed directly by the SED as 'central institutions' since 1900. Now full-time and degree-level work was encouraged, and local technical and adult education were combined in a network of 'further education' colleges. The old teacher-training colleges, renamed colleges of education in 1958, were also encouraged to expand their remit and award degrees. By 1980, therefore, the concept of a 'tertiary' education of which traditional universities were only one part was well accepted, and it attracted more than 15 per cent of the age group; but the general extension of university status remained in the future.

CONCLUSION

The growth of secondary and higher education since 1945 can be seen as the latest stage in a continual expansion of education, and of its place in the lives of individuals, which began in the mid-nineteenth century and shows no sign of coming to an end. At its outset most working-class children, if they attended school at all, left at 10 or 11, while middle-class children, apart from a small minority who went to the universities, left at 14 or 15. By 1980, the age of leaving full-time education, though still conditioned by social class, ranged from 16 to 22 or more. In responding to the problems created by the industrial revolution, Scotland was given a good start by its tradition of national education and by a cultural disposition, with religious, political and social roots, to value educational achievement. But as other countries caught up, Scotland ceased to be so exceptional, though some indicators (notably the rate of participation in higher education) remained very favourable. Many historians would argue that while the system promoted meritocracy, and allowed individual Scots to move upwards into both Scottish and British elites, the education offered to the ordinary child was less impressive. The structure of schooling that developed after 1872 reflected class divisions in Scotland, much as elsewhere, and twentieth-century progress towards greater equality of opportunity, though perhaps made smoother by an idealised conception of the educational past, had still to contend with social inequalities which the formal integration of educational institutions achieved by 1980 could not itself remove.

REFERENCES

Anderson, R. D. (1995) *Education and the Scottish People, 1750–1918.* Oxford: Oxford University Press.
Gray, J., A. McPherson and D. Raffe (1983) *Reconstructions of Secondary Education: Theory, Myth and Practice since the War.* London: Routledge.

Houston, R. A. (1985) *Scottish Literacy and the Scottish Identity: Illiteracy and Society in Scotland and Northern England, 1600–1800.* Cambridge: Cambridge University Press.

Humes, W. and H. Paterson (eds) (1982) *Scottish Culture and Scottish Education, 1800–1980.* Edinburgh: John Donald.

Scotland, J. (1969) *The History of Scottish Education*, 2 vols. London: University of London Press.

Withrington, D. J. (1988) 'Schooling, literacy and society', in T. M. Devine and R. Mitchison (eds), *People and Society in Scotland. I. 1760–1830.* Edinburgh: John Donald.

23

The History of Scottish Education, 1980 to the Present Day

Donald Gillies

While the picking of a year from which to start a historical overview inevitably does some violence to the nature of time and of human activity, 1980 does represent a useful departure point for a modern history of Scottish education. In this chapter, the focus will be narrowed to a history of compulsory schooling over the years since. The year before, 1979, had witnessed two major political developments which were to have lasting effects both for Scottish society and for educational governance. The first of these was the Referendum of March 1979 which brought failure to a devolution campaign that had been in progress since the SNP breakthrough at the two Westminster elections of 1974. The second was the victory of the Conservatives under Margaret Thatcher in the general election of June 1979. This would be the first of four successive election victories, representing an unbroken spell of government of nearly eighteen years for that party. Yet this unparalleled period of Unionist power would, perversely, play a significant role in the revival of the devolution campaign, a revival that would result in victory in the referendum of 1997, just months after the defeat of the Conservatives at the national polls. The Conservative government, however, cannot simply be seen as a mere interlude between two devolution campaigns. It was a government of extraordinary ideological commitment and its devotion to monetarism initially, to neo-liberal policy generally, and to an unflinching sense of British sovereignty, fundamentally and irrevocably transformed the United Kingdom in terms of both its economic structure and its political outlook.

CONSERVATIVES IN GOVERNMENT: BEFORE THE DELUGE

From the perspective of twenty-first-century Scotland, 1980 does seem both distant and quaint in relation to education: a time before radical Thatcherism had taken hold; a time of no systematic assessment in primary school or the early stages of secondary; a time of 'non-certificate' classes'; a time when continuing professional development (CPD) was an unrecognisable and random combination of letters; and, of course, a time when the voice of the Lochgelly could still be heard in the land.

   The first Conservative administration passed two education Acts and brought forward arrangements for new courses and assessment systems for S3 and S4. These had been in abeyance since the Munn Committee and the Dunning Committee had reported in

1977. The former recommended a broad curriculum in line with Paul Hirst's theory of knowledge disciplines – probably the last time a curriculum development would rely on philosophical ideas, as opposed to 'best practice'. The latter introduced Standard Grade qualifications at three levels: Credit, General and Foundation, with the admirable intention that all young people would be certificated for what they could do and had achieved, rather than judged, harshly and negatively, in relation to academic qualifications expressly designed for the few. The development of these new courses required a significant amount of work on the part of the teaching profession and, for some, a fundamental challenge to elitist values. The understandable desire by government to achieve full implementation quickly, led to considerable strain with teachers whose sense of grievance in respect of pay levels and conditions of service was increasingly audible. Teachers made highly effective use of 'action short of a strike' as part of the growing dispute and, by withdrawing from development work in relation to Standard Grade, they delayed its full introduction for the best part of a decade.

As far as legislation is concerned, the Education (Scotland) Act 1980 was a disparate and wide-ranging document running to 137 sections. The Education (Scotland) Act 1981 can, by contrast, be seen to represent much more of developing Conservative educational thinking. The emphasis on consumer rights which so defined the Conservative Party of that era – the right to buy council houses for the first time, for example – is given due prominence. The first provision of the Act was to establish the right of a parent to request an education authority to place their child in a specified school within the authority, this placing request only to be denied under very specific circumstances. The other main ideological aspect of this Act was the establishment of the assisted places scheme, which allowed parents to seek government assistance in paying school fees in the private sector. Less ideological, but much more significant in the long run, was the third main provision of the Act which required local authorities to make specific arrangements for children deemed to have special educational needs and, for those who fell under a particular definition of these, to open a Record, specifying the nature of their needs and related special provision. During this period, the use of corporal punishment in Scottish schools finally came to an end, although only after a parental appeal to the European Court of Human Rights. While some local authorities had already moved to end the practice, it must seen as something of a national embarrassment to have required external pressure to stop the systematic beating of children (Paterson, 2003, pp. 122–3).

EDUCATION AND EMPLOYMENT

A central aspect of government thinking in the early 1980s was to seek to establish a much more direct linkage between school and the world of work, a development that has grown over the decades since, as the economic purposes of schooling became more and more dominant in politics, and the notion of the knowledge economy has taken deep root. Part of the initial impetus was an implicit recognition of the seismic effects of the government's monetarist policies which had devastated state industry and vastly increased unemployment (Devine, 2006, p. 591 ff.). Thus were born various initiatives such as the Youth Opportunities Programme, the Manpower Services Commission and the creation of the Technical and Vocational Education Initiative which funded, particularly within deprived areas, various projects in schools, provided they had a vocational purpose. In a similar vein, government also established the Scottish Vocational Education Council (SCOTVEC) to provide courses for those 16–18-year-olds not going on to higher education. Many such youngsters remained at school simply because there was no employment outside and these courses aimed to provide meaningful education. Their long-term significance was probably most evident in their design: in modular form, with stated learning outcomes, wholly internally assessed and focusing much more on skills and competencies than on knowledge or understanding

THE TEACHERS' DISPUTE

The teachers' dispute straddled the first two Conservative administrations. Ably led by some impressive figures such as John Pollock of the Educational Institute of Scotland (EIS), the dominant trade union, the teachers managed to win public support, in levels rarely seen since, for their long-running pay claim. A series of one-day national strikes, accompanied by the boycotting of curriculum development work, extra-curricular activity and exam marking, was given a real edge by the targeted withdrawal of labour in schools in Conservative-held constituencies, particularly those of ministers such as that of George Younger, the Secretary of State for Scotland, in Ayr. Massive disruption could be created, and real pressure put on these politicians, for little cost, as teachers nationally contributed to a fund to compensate local teachers for loss of earnings. Government refused to budge, however, until the arrival of Malcolm Rifkind as Scottish Secretary. He appeared to accede to union demands, setting up an inquiry to look into the matter. The Main Committee reported in 1986, proposing limits on the amount of time worked, simplifying and improving the pay structure, and creating the new post of senior teacher, the first of several faltering attempts to seek to reward more handsomely teachers for their teaching, rather than for their administrative, management or perceived leadership qualities.

Thus, the dispute was settled, prior to the 1987 general election. Given the crushing of the miners' dispute, it was a relatively successful outcome for the teacher unions, even although it marked the start of a tradition of selling hard-won conditions of service for short-term financial gain. Government, having targeted union power elsewhere in the economy, would not be so accommodating again and, indeed, drew many strategic lessons from the conflict. One was to seek to open a gulf between senior management and teaching staff. One of the strengths of the teachers' side had been the solidarity across management structures, but government now sought, first by boosting senior management salaries, and second through devolved management of schools, to privilege headteachers, a move that succeeded very quickly, evidenced by the emergence of new representative bodies for heads, thus drawing them away from what were to become increasingly rank-and-file unions.

CURRICULUM CHANGE

One of the interesting features of the broad coalition that comprises the Conservative party is the way in which this can manifest itself in quite strikingly polar ways from time to time. The curriculum, as a field of political contestation, is a case in point. On the one hand, the libertarian wing of the Conservative party in the early 1980s, represented by such as Keith Joseph, the prophet of monetarism or, to others, the 'Mad Monk', strongly resisted moves towards a 'national' curriculum in England, arguing instead for individual freedom and local decision making. On the other hand, what could now be seen as the more neo-conservative wing, represented by such as Kenneth Baker, argued, and won, the case for stipulating in very explicit terms what each school pupil should study, for how long and, in many cases, through the medium of which specified teaching methods.

In Scotland, the move towards increased curricular prescription in P1–S2 education was not simply political. Her Majesty's Inspectorate (HMI) (SED, 1980) had already reported on the somewhat patchy implementation of the *Primary Memorandum* in the years since 1965. Therefore, while there might be a political drive to see named curricular elements taught, there was also an equity issue about children's mixed experiences. Inspectors found that some schools had a narrow curriculum, some a broad and imaginative mix, but others even had limited engagement with the core fundamentals of language and mathematics. While professional autonomy in relation to curriculum, pedagogy and assessment might be seen by teachers as defining issues, it is clear that the abuse of this autonomy represents a challenge to democracy. The democratic control of state education would be pointless were it not to seek, at least, to shape and influence the decision making of key professionals, aiming to ensure that all youngsters experience the education to which they are entitled.

With the development of the 5–14 programme from 1987, government sought to exert control over curriculum structure, progression, time allocation and assessment. The perceived problems of primary–secondary transition had exercised a previous committee (Education 10–14 in Scotland) and by extending curriculum guidelines to S2, this new report sought to address this issue. The curriculum was to be arranged in five curricular areas and each was allocated a recommended percentage of the available teaching time. These were later revised, as were the original five attainment levels (A–E), with a sixth level, F, added after pressure from parents and teachers.

Parents and teachers also combined effectively to campaign against the system of national tests introduced for P4 and P7. Some teachers refused to implement the tests and many parents withdrew their children from school on test days. Eventually, following the 1992 election, the government relented and testing was left to teachers' judgements as to when a pupil was ready to be tested at a particular level.

There were also further calls for revision to the upper secondary curriculum. More young people were staying on at school and, for many, Highers were not appropriate courses. In 1990, the Howie Committee was set up to make recommendations which they duly did two years later, advocating separate academic and vocational pathways. The report was never acted upon and, instead, with Higher Still, the government initiated a new programme retaining Highers, adding Advanced Highers for S6 and introducing Access and Intermediate courses as progression from Standard Grade, for those for whom Higher level demands were unsuitable. Teachers complained again about speedy implementation with limited resources and delays were conceded by government so that it was not until the new century dawned that the S5/6 reforms were established nationally.

By this stage, there were already concerns about the lack of coherence in the curriculum through its various stages and, at secondary, some concerns about the suitability of Standard Grade as preparation for Higher for some pupils in some subjects. Schools, with local authority support, began to adapt the new Intermediate courses for S3 and S4 pupils, even although they had been designed for a more mature, independent S5/6 learner. At primary, concerns grew regarding the 'cluttered' nature of the curriculum areas, their numerous strands and attainment targets, and the increasing demands made of schools to address various social concerns such as education on drugs, alcohol, sexual issues, diet, health, racism, multiculturalism, tolerance, respect and even teeth-brushing.

In 2002, the then Scottish Executive launched a national debate on education, followed by the establishment of a review group to take forward the key messages that emerged. The result was A Curriculum for Excellence (CfE) – proposals for a 3–18 curriculum centred not on content or process but on purposes. The curriculum was to aim to develop all young people as successful learners, confident individuals, responsible citizens and effective contributors. Unusually, given previous experience with curriculum proposals, this document was endorsed in its entirety by the ministerial team without being subject to any further political or professional consultation or debate. The relative simplicity of the proposals was somewhat complicated by the sudden, unheralded emergence of eight curriculum areas, around which the curriculum was to be structured. Given that decluttering the curriculum was one of the motivations behind the CfE development, moving from five to eight curriculum areas in P1–S2 did seem surprising. Any hopes that clarity might be retained were soon abandoned when the assessment details were finally produced: masses of documentation, listing the 'experiences and outcomes' expected in each curricular area at each of the four levels of attainment within the programme. Thus, a curriculum designed to focus on broad outcomes became immersed in the detail of content and assessment minutiae. The examination arrangements for upper secondary remained obscure and uncertain for some time. This could be viewed as apt since the increasing demand for qualifications from youngsters, parents, higher education institutions and employers has meant that education, in its broadest sense, effectively ends in S3 in Scottish schools, after which a programme of mass, detailed certification and assessment takes over. The dominance of assessment in S4 and S5 in particular too often reduces the educational experience of young people to test-driven activity. CfE may well, in effect, remain a 3–15 programme, with 16–18 devoted to the old favourites of rushed preparation for examinations, stressed examinations diets and anxious anticipation of examination results.

The integrity of the Scottish examinations system had been badly undermined in 2000 when the Scottish Qualifications Authority (SQA) – formed from the merger of the Scottish Examination Board with SCOTVEC – failed to produce accurate results for thousands of candidates (Paterson, 2000). While there were resultant casualties at the SQA, the main focus of reaction proved to be HMI. Their independent judgement was said to have been compromised, having been tasked with both promoting the Higher Still reforms and also evaluating the success of their implementation. Critics argued that they should have raised concerns about the likelihood of resultant certification problems. HMI was reformed to become more distant from government, being turned into an executive agency before being merged with Learning and Teaching Scotland (LTS) in 2011 to become Education Scotland.

The last thirty years of curriculum reform in Scotland cannot be summarised easily. Where any discernible trajectory can be defined at all, snake-like and tortuous would fail to capture its labyrinthine convolutions. Yet some common features can be identified: detailed curricular guidelines, however prescriptive their status, now encompass the whole lifespan of compulsory education. Indeed, they even reach into the pre-birth period, with advice being issued about the potential educational impact of expectant mothers' behaviour on the unborn child (LTS, 2010). There is undoubtedly now much more explicit and comprehensive political guidance in relation to the curriculum than ever before. With that has come much more accountability, with teachers, establishments and local authorities being held liable for the complete range of learners' educational experiences.

Assessment too has developed exponentially. All children, pupils and students can now expect to have the full range of their educational activities assessed regularly and repeatedly in both formal and informal contexts, and in a much more nationally uniform manner.

Again, such assessment data can be, and is, used to hold educational staff increasingly to account.

Finally, there can be observed in relation to curriculum a gradual, if by no means uninterrupted, transition from a focus on content, factual knowledge and disciplinary integrity to a modern curricular context that has a greater focus on skills, competencies and integrated or cross-curricular approaches.

GOVERNANCE

The way in which state education is managed, controlled and administered has undergone significant change in the last three decades. The most striking has undoubtedly been the (re)establishment of a Scottish Parliament and so the return of the seat of power from Westminster to Edinburgh. Education, as one of the key devolved portfolios, undoubtedly attracts much more political attention than before, although the central machinery of government – the ministerial–civil service nexus – has essentially remained unaltered.

In the devolution era, the central administration of education in Scotland has been marked by relative moderation, during the first two Labour–Liberal Democrat coalitions and continuing into the two SNP governments since. There has been little structural change to the system, in contrast to the situation in many developed countries where there has been considerable adjustment of, and retreat from, the notion of comprehensive state provision. England has experienced some fundamental reforms, most of which are market-oriented, but even bastions of welfare democracy such as Sweden have embarked on a neo-liberal programme of deregulation, promoting the development of 'free schools' – independent, privately run, profit-making enterprises. The three main companies financing this development are all owned by private equity firms, one of which is actually based in Denmark (Ball and Olmedo Reinoso, 2011). In this new landscape, the notion of a 'state' system is profoundly compromised. Thus, while activists of both Right and Left may decry the lack of change in Scotland, simply maintaining a comprehensive state system, coupled with a political rejection of charging fees for tertiary education, can be seen, in international terms, to represent a quite radical position, albeit by default.

Devolution has certainly reduced the pressure on Scottish education to follow the English route into quasi-markets and fragmentation. Yet this has been more to do with the eclipse of the Conservative party than with constitutional arrangements. During the late 1980s and particularly during the period when Michael Forsyth was a significant figure in the Scottish Office, there was a considerable political push to reconfigure, and reduce, the state system. As has been seen, the Assisted Places Scheme boosted the independent sector, and there was also a drive to encourage other schools to 'opt out' of local authority control. This was given added momentum by the powers given to the new School Boards so that groups of committed parents could wield much greater power than in the past, and by the devolved school management initiative that sought to give more powers to headteachers. While some of this stemmed from Conservative ideology which instinctively opposes 'big' government, some also stemmed from a political desire to undermine regional authority control in Scotland – at that time very much under Labour domination. The big regional authorities had served as considerable barriers to the Conservative party's attempts to pursue their agenda. Not surprisingly perhaps, the Conservatives soon abolished them and their district council relatives altogether, replacing them by the current system of thirty-two local authorities in 1995.

Both the Assisted Places Scheme and the ability to opt out of local authority control were immediately abolished following the catastrophic Conservative collapse in Scotland and the election of the New Labour government in 1997. Further legislative changes altered the nature of parental involvement, as school boards were replaced by parent councils with a much less divisive role. As for children and young people, their rights and responsibilities have increased steadily over the decades. The UN Convention on the Rights of the Child (1989) and the Children (Scotland) Act (1995) clarified children's rights and the associated rights and responsibilities of parents. The Standards in Scotland's Schools etc. Act (2000) also stressed the need for local authorities to take into account the views of children and young people in matters concerning their education, and made it legally binding for headteachers to report on how they had consulted with pupils regarding the school development plan and involved them in decisions about the everyday running of the school. In addition, the growth of bodies and charities promoting children's views and rights over recent decades has been notable and this has been matched by political developments such as the appointment of a Commissioner for Children and Young People in Scotland.

Under the SNP administrations, councils have been given a degree of latitude in relation to educational provision in return for an agreement to freeze council taxes. While this has given respite to taxpayers locally, it has meant continuing pressures on local authority budgets, with inevitable cuts and retrenchment. In terms of its national policy initiatives, the SNP has been challenged strongly by some local authorities, particularly Labour-led Glasgow, a position further entrenched by the failure of the SNP to make any real headway in Glasgow in the 2012 local government elections.

THE RISE OF PRIVATE-SECTOR CULTURE

Since 1980, one feature of the governance of the education system has been political attraction of the private sector. The Thatcherite position was one of considerable antipathy to the public sector, in terms of both its scale and its nature. Most of the major public utilities were sold off so that there was a departure from any active state participation within the energy, transport or industrial sectors. While state education largely survived, private-sector involvement was encouraged and quasi-markets established in such areas as resources, construction and maintenance, all under the umbrella of New Public Management. Local authorities reduced their direct involvement in these areas, instead being required to offer them for outside tender. The most controversial of these were the complicated schemes to finance new capital spending. Local authorities could no longer borrow to finance school building programmes and, instead, the Conservative government introduced the Public Private Partnership scheme, amended by New Labour as the Private Finance Initiative. Both of these approaches encourage private capital outlay twinned with leaseback arrangements so that local authorities are effectively renting their own educational premises. Some of these schemes have attracted harsh criticism, the amounts being repaid considered to be inordinate. Even insiders referred, somewhat ill-advisedly, to the sums on offer as 'rich pickings' (*The Lawyer*, 3 July 2006). The SNP government had promised to provide an alternative, less burdensome model and eventually it established the Scottish Futures Trust, designed to achieve just that. Its Schools for the Future programme claims to be 20 per cent cheaper than the previous models (Scottish Futures Trust, 2011). As the previous models offered returns that would have embarrassed a protection racketeer, this may not represent a great deal for the public purse either.

As well as these structural changes, there has been a very pronounced move toward private-sector practices and discourse within education. Managerialism has been a significant aspect within education for more than twenty-five years now. This outlook argues that educational outcomes – a contested term, it should be stressed – can be much improved simply through better management, thus screening out a whole number of key issues such as the impact of socio-economic factors, for example. Local authorities have adopted a number of models from the private sector, such as total quality management, so that educational discourse now becomes replete with previously incongruous terms such as client, customer and delivery. Criticism has been directed at the inappropriateness of such concepts for the field of education, and at the way in which educational activity, experiences and outcomes become crudely simplified and misrepresented simply in order to become susceptible to the prevailing quantitative model of targets and performance indicators (Humes, 2000). The inspectorate has also promoted the use of business models through their highly influential self-evaluation packages for educational establishments, such as *How Good is Our School?* and *Journey to Excellence*. The mixed evidence of the effectiveness of this managerial and performativity culture has now transformed into a much sharper focus on leadership to provide the key to school improvement. The development of the Scottish Qualification for Headship can be seen as part of this trend which both sees headteachers more as chief executive officers than educational professionals and requires of them proven evidence of technical managerial skills.

Perhaps because the 'standards debate' has been less shrill in Scotland, there has been little evidence of managers from outside the education field being imported to run schools or local authority portfolios, as has been widespread in England. Nevertheless, the merging of education with other local authority services such as health and social work into Children's Services departments can mean that key officials involved in running multi-million-pound education budgets may have had no direct professional experience of schools and other relevant establishments.

INCLUSION

While Thatcherism fundamentally reconfigured the context within which the education system operates, the most significant change in the nature of teaching has undoubtedly come around through the emergence of inclusion as a key political and social priority. There are essentially two strands to this: one is a broad international movement to end segregated schooling for children with support needs, drawing its impetus from the Salamanca Agreement of 1994. This has been supplemented by a political drive, very prominent in the early years of the New Labour administration, to encourage the inclusion of a whole range of disparate groups across society who had previously suffered marginalisation or discrimination, or who had, indeed, opted to withdraw. Some of these developments, particularly in relation to support for learning, have been buttressed by landmark legislation. The Standards in Scotland's Schools etc. Act (2000) established mainstream education as the default position for all children, except in very specific circumstances. The Additional Support for Learning Act (2004) broadened the concept of additional support needs to include a wide range of circumstances, from the relatively minor and temporary to the much more severe and permanent. The Record of Needs was removed to be replaced by a Coordinated Support Plan.

Concern about inclusion also led to an expansion of nursery provision and the emergence of nurture groups in some primary schools. In cultural terms, Gaelic medium education has expanded hugely in the last thirty years and, although prospects for the language remain hazardous, at least the education system is now attempting to right some of its past wrongs in relation to the language. The changing population of Scotland and new patterns of migration have also had an impact on the inclusion agenda: schools across the country have become much more multi-cultural and multi-ethnic, the last survey suggesting that 138 different home languages were spoken by Scotland's school population.

The inclusion agenda has radically altered educational establishments and the nature of the teaching process. Effective professionals now must be far more adaptable and understanding, and have a more developed pedagogical philosophy and associated skill set. Unfortunately, there is no sign yet of this having any significant impact on the attainment gap in Scottish schools. Children from advantaged backgrounds continue to outperform the rest of society from the earliest recorded stages onwards: Scotland's unequal society merely becomes reproduced in educational terms.

Inclusion is not universal, however. Elite exclusion has rarely been highlighted or challenged so that across the UK a small, but unduly influential and powerful, class of the very wealthy and privileged continue to attend their own private schools and favoured universities, operate in their own exclusive circles, employ each other in a range of capacities and exist in a gated world quite removed from what the rest of the country would understand as society. In a country ruled by a hereditary monarchy and with an unelected House of Lords perhaps that should not be too surprising. It must, nevertheless, be somewhat galling for minority ethnic groups, asylum seekers, migrants and others to be told repeatedly, by representatives of this closeted elite, that they must 'integrate'.

TEACHERS

The world of the teacher has changed in other ways. It is now an all-graduate profession, but also less elitist. The salary enhancements and additional promotion opportunities solely reserved for honours graduates have gone, as have the deferential titles of school 'master' and 'mistress'. Gender issues remain: female headteachers, inspectors or directors of education are not the rarities they once were, but they are still not in numbers one might expect, given their dominance of the profession. In 1956, 84 per cent of primary teachers were female and 42 per cent of secondary teachers (Paterson, 2003); in the most recent census these figures now stand at 92 per cent for primaries and 61 per cent for secondaries. While 85 per cent of primary headteachers are female, for secondary the figure is a mere 29 per cent (Scottish Government, 2009).

The status of the teaching profession has also evolved over the last thirty years and the public no longer views it in the same respectful way. This could be seen as part of a much more fundamental social change in relation to equality and as a reflection of the general loss of public trust in government and the professions. In some ways also, the profession has acted to dilute its own elevated position: during the 1980s the EIS affiliated with the Scottish Trades Union Congress (STUC) as part of what could be seen as general movement to stress its links with workers and the general population. Teachers, therefore, tended to position themselves with other public-sector workers rather than as a distinct, privileged group.

Teachers' conditions of service have also changed. Some of these have been traded willingly for financial gain while others have come around through government action.

The McCrone Agreement of 2001 was a highly significant development, again created by a political reaction to growing professional disquiet about both pay and workload. This agreement gave a significant boost to pay, set out teachers' duties clearly, introduced statutory professional development, established the Chartered Teachers scheme and put probation and induction for new teachers on a proper footing. The costs involved were considerable and as the economic situation worsened it was little surprise when the McCormac Review of 2011 reconsidered some of these issues.

A long-running campaign over the last decade to address teacher workload concerns by reducing class sizes did find political support, particularly from the SNP. In government, however, they failed to act initially – the costs and logistics being daunting – although they finally moved to cap P1 at twenty-five.

SECURITY, LITIGATION AND RISK AVERSION

Loss of trust in government and the professions has led to the public nowadays being much more willing to seek legal redress for deemed wrongs. Within education, this has ranged from such issues as allegations around lack of educational support and lack of action on bullying behaviour, and in relation to injuries and even deaths. Local authorities have responded in a number of ways but a key strategy has been to limit risk as far as possible. Councils have been wary about organising or supporting any activities where there might be a risk to participants and those seeking to organise activities, particularly off-site, have found themselves having to complete voluminous documentations and to carry out risk assessments, often with the effect of having organisers simply abandon the activity as too administratively burdensome.

One of the understandable responses to the Dunblane Massacre of 1996 was for schools to become much more secure and for the screening of those working with young people to be intensified. Access to schools became much more difficult for everyone, and vetting restrictions often made it harder for schools to organise events involving adult volunteers. Concern has been raised about the subsequent increased use of CCTV surveillance, electronic scanning and biometrics in schools, with questions asked about privacy, proportionality and intrusiveness (Bryce et al., 2010).

CONCLUSIONS

In the three decades covered by this overview, Scottish education has experienced significant change and yet the casual observer entering a school today would find much that is familiar. Technological, political, economic, social and administrative developments have all served to remould the modern educational experience. However, the basic interactions between teachers and learners, between schools and parents and guardians, between staff and local authorities, and between the various arms of government are fundamental constants that have altered little in essentials. Curriculum, pedagogy and assessment have all been subject to adjustment and reform over the years but the central work of schooling goes on with the same key ingredients as before: teachers, learners, resources; perspiration, frustration, imagination, inspiration; and, perhaps just at times, but for the fortunate sufficiently often to motivate and fulfil, exhilaration.

REFERENCES

Ball, S. and A. Olmedo Reinoso (2011) 'Global networks and education policy; new actors, new spaces, new networks'. Paper presented at the European Conference on Educational Research, Berlin, Germany.

Bryce, T., M. Nellis, A. Corrigan, H. Gallagher, P. Lee and H. Sercombe (2010) 'Biometric surveillance in schools: cause for concern or case for curriculum?', *Scottish Educational Review*, 42 (1): 3–22.

Devine, T. (2006) *The Scottish Nation 1707–2007*. London: Penguin Books.

Humes, W. (2000) 'The discourses of educational management', *Journal of Educational Enquiry*, 1 (1): 35–53.

Learning and Teaching Scotland (2010) *Pre-birth to Three: Positive Outcomes for Scotland's Children and Families*. Glasgow: Learning and Teaching Scotland.

Paterson, L. (2000) *Crisis in the Classroom*. Edinburgh: Mainstream.

Paterson, L. (2003) *Scottish Education in the Twentieth Century*. Edinburgh: Edinburgh University Press.

Scottish Education Department (1980) *Learning and Teaching in Primary 4 and Primary 7*. Edinburgh: SED.

Scottish Futures Trust (2011) *Business Plan 2011/12*. Edinburgh: Scottish Futures Trust.

Scottish Government (2009) *Teachers in Scotland, 2009*. Edinburgh: Scottish Government. Online at www.scotland.gov.uk/Resource/Doc/293703/0090773.pdf

24

Shared Destiny: National Identity, Culture and Education in Modern Scotland

George Kerevan

Education, in its widest sense, concerns the transmission of received cultural values. When those values are in rapid change, or contested, the educational system is affected. Scotland during the twentieth century underwent a profound shift in national identity, from loyal and active partner in an imperial union to the rediscovery of a sense of separate – perhaps, eventually, independent – nationhood. It is impossible to understand the modern Scottish education system without placing it in this specific historical context.

This chapter will give a brief historical outline of the interplay between culture, education and changing national identity in creating modern Scotland. We will examine three distinct phases. First, the profound impact, in the inter-war era, of Modernism and its local manifestation in the Scottish Renaissance, which led to the emergence of a new 'non-tartan' sense of national identity, to the formation of the SNP and to agitation for the education system to give greater priority to teaching the vernacular. The second phase, covering the end of Empire, the Cold War and the de-industrialisation of the 1970s, saw the emergence of a more politically assertive Scotland and calls for devolution. This coincided (not accidentally) with new, popular forms of cultural expression (such as folk songs) and with the massive expansion of higher education. This phase ended with the failed devolution referendum of 1979. A third cycle began with the election of Margaret Thatcher when political impotence north of the border coincided with a veritable explosion in cultural life, and with the transformation of the education system at the behest of a service economy and globalisation. The net result was a further decline of 'Britishness' in Scotland and the election of a devolved parliament in 1999. As we shall also see, many of the intellectuals involved in this history were simultaneously influential in the worlds of culture, politics and education – a particularly Scottish phenomenon.

MODERNISM, THE SCOTTISH RENAISSANCE AND A NEW SENSE OF NATIONAL IDENTITY

Nationalism is the myth of a shared destiny. Such myths have to be manufactured. Contemporary political nationalism in the shape of the SNP (founded in 1934) grew directly out of a domestic response to Modernism in the 1920s, the so-called Scottish Renaissance. These cultural and political changes also led to distinct educational developments – a greater formal treatment of Scottish literature and history in schools and universities, for instance. Many of the personalities involved in the development of Scottish Modernism were also involved in the creation of the SNP.

This is not the place for a detailed examination of that complicated cultural, social and indeed political movement known as Modernism. In shorthand, Modernism marked a sharp break with Victorian-era bourgeois cultural practice, values and motifs in Europe and North America. Among the driving forces were increased urbanisation and the move to large-scale mass production techniques in the late-nineteenth century, which transformed social relations in all classes; the carnage of the Great War, which undermined Victorian optimism; the rise of Marxism and Social Darwinism, which challenged the existing social order; and the emergence with Einstein of relativistic physics, which suggested a universe far less predictable than the mechanistic notions of its Newtonian predecessor.

It is hardly surprising that Scotland was affected by the rise of Modernism. The 1890s saw a massive immigration into the west of Scotland from Ireland and the highlands, and the transformation of Clydeside into a global industrial powerhouse. In 1900, just one Glasgow engineering company, Beardmore's, employed 40,000 workers. Industrial unrest and class conflict soon followed. The new (and Home Rule) Independent Labour Party (ILP) would recruit a third of its members in the west of Scotland. The Great War was followed by the slump of 1921, which pitched Clydeside into economic crisis until the Second World War. The moment was ripe to challenge the old order, especially as the Versailles peace settlement had created a plethora of new, innovative small states in Europe.

In Scotland, the cultural questioning of the old order – referred to as the 'Scottish Renaissance' – centred on the iconoclastic ideas of the poet, critic and left-wing nationalist Christopher Grieve, writing under the pseudonym Hugh MacDiarmid. Throughout the inter-war period, Grieve produced an endless series of influential and knowingly controversial articles on Scottish and European literature, the best-known examples being published in the *Scottish Education Journal*, still Scotland's main publication for the teaching profession.

The Scottish Renaissance covered a vast agenda, from the (abortive) revitalisation of the Scots vernacular as an avant-garde literary language, a serious attempt to examine contemporary life; the fictional re-imagining of the highlands (as an antidote to Victorian romanticism); and, new for Scotland, the importance of women writers. Apart from Grieve, key participants in the Early Modern Movement included Edwin and Willa Muir, Lewis Grassic Gibbon, Neil M. Gunn, Naomi Mitchison, Catherine Carswell and Sydney Goodsir Smith.

The influence of Modernism in Scotland was far more than a literary phenomenon – a point often ignored. It was felt in new directions in music (F. G. Scott, Erik Chisholm, Ronald Centre), painting (the Colourists, William Johnstone, William Gillies), documentary cinema (John Grierson) and powerfully in architecture (Robert Matthew, Robert Hurd, Alan Reiach, Basil Spence). The Modern Movement took institutional form in 1936 with the creation of the Saltire Society to 'restore the country to its proper place as a creative force in Europe'. The society was to become a driving force in promoting modern architecture in Scotland, effectively changing Scotland's built environment.

With the passage of time, the literature and political thought of the Scottish Renaissance has come in for criticism, even in nationalist circles. There are occasional hints of anti-Englishness and Scots racial superiority (dangerous always, but especially as the spectre of Nazism loomed in the 1930s). From a contemporary view, the classic texts rarely challenge conventional masculine stereotypes. On the other hand, no one can really fault the internationalism of the Scottish Modernists. And the novels of Catherine Carswell and Naomi Mitchison – especially *We Have Been Warned* (1935), which tackles rape and abortion – represent the first significant feminist writing in Scotland. Whatever its faults and limitations, if there is a model of nationalism seeking to be universal rather than parochial, it lies in the Scottish Renaissance.

Grieve's endeavours, no matter how idiosyncratic or provocative, inspired a generation of writers and artists to seek a fresh, distinctively Scottish view of the world free from the couthy kailyard (cabbage patch) and Celtic Twilight visions of the Victorian era. At the same time, in the words of Tom Normand (2000):

> The commitment to an independent Scottish nation was, in this period, predicated upon a belief in the viability and validity of an authentic Scottish culture, the recovery of which might be fulfilled only through the restoration of a national status in the form of self-government.

As in Ireland, writers and poets were to play a significant role in the birth of political nationalism in Scotland. They include Grieve himself (a founder of the National Party of Scotland in 1928 and an SNP candidate in 1950), Compton Mackenzie and the poet Douglas Young (SNP leader from 1942 to 1945). Leading Modernists in other fields also became nationalists, including the architects Robert Hurt (though English) and Robert Matthew (after breaking with Labour).

How did Modernism impact on education? The Scottish Renaissance, while ultimately a prime mover in transforming the raison d'être, cultural role and syllabus of Scottish education, took a generation to make its impact felt – not until the 1960s. Indeed, it would not be until the 1990s that Scottish schoolchildren would be officially encouraged to express themselves in the vernacular. This lengthy gestation is explained by the time it takes for any intellectual movement to influence popular culture and the political establishment. But we can say with reasonable certainty that the Scottish Renaissance set much of the intellectual agenda in education reform for the next half century.

Consider the emphasis the Scottish Renaissance put on the study of native Scottish history as an aid to national regeneration. Modernists, early nationalists and ILP left-wingers united in their vision of an egalitarian, proto-democratic Scotland (perhaps mythical) that had been subverted by Union and Empire. Before 1939, history of any kind did not figure as a subject in the Scottish Certificate of Education, never mind Scottish history. In the whole of Scotland there were only eleven posts for specialist history teachers. After 1945, history became a subject in both the Higher and Lower grades, though only four questions out of twenty-eight in the 1948 Higher referred to Scottish history. But at last Scottish secondary pupils were learning about their country's past and with it a new sense of national identity. It would be 1962 before there was a completely Scottish section in the Leaving Certificate history exam.

Why was Modernism ultimately so influential in Scotland? In part, its internationalism, abstraction and cultural interconnectedness appealed to intellectuals brought up in the more generalist and theoretical discourse of the ancient Scottish universities (as opposed to Oxbridge). In part, it arrived at the right historical moment for those seeking a break with an older, conservative Scotland that had already appropriated Burns and tartanry for its cultural legitimacy. In part, Marxism as a contemporary competitor to Modernism had limited roots in Scotland. Above all, a political project of national cultural and economic regeneration – for once the term 'modernisation' is appropriate – had a unique resonance during a period of economic decline to which the Imperial Parliament in London had no obvious answer.

POPULAR CULTURE AND RESISTANCE IN THE ERA OF MASS EDUCATION

It would be a while, however, before the old Unionist edifice crumbled. In the 1955 general election, the Conservative and Unionist Party in Scotland won an absolute majority of the votes cast. It was the high water mark of Unionism north of the border, based on an electoral alliance between the Protestant skilled working class (soon to be made obsolete by de-industrialisation and mass production) and a middle class temporarily seduced by the collective 'Britishness' of World War II.

Thereafter came the recession of 1957 which graphically revealed the backwardness of British industry and its narrow educational infrastructure. The next thirty years saw (in a rush) the death of the old Clydeside industries and with it the loss of indigenous Scottish business ownership; mass emigration and the building of new towns such as Cumbernauld and East Kilbride; the collective entry of women into the labour force; and, with comprehensive education and university expansion, the birth of a youth culture.

These dramatic economic and social changes were accompanied by a new development – the rise of popular culture, and one that suddenly developed a distinct Scottish face to reinforce the intellectual front opened by Grieve and the Scottish Modernists. Of course, there had always been mass popular entertainment – from the 1930s on the Scots developed a passion for cinema. But it was the arrival in 1957 of Scottish Television Ltd, the first commercial station in Scotland, that transformed things.

Scottish Television was the brainchild of Roy Thomson, a Scots-Canadian entrepreneur and newspaper owner who had returned to the land of his ancestors and (to the horror of the Edinburgh establishment) bought the staid *Scotsman* newspaper and put news on the front page instead of ads. Thomson seized the chance to launch commercial television in Scotland, famously calling it 'a licence to print money'. But Thomson was neither a boor nor someone who pandered to the lowest common denominator. Rather, he decided to compete with the BBC by offering a local television channel that deliberately reflected Scottish life rather than metropolitan values and preoccupations. Suddenly Scots could hear the news read with a local rather than an RP accent. As well as American westerns, viewers could watch John Grierson present the best documentaries. The BBC had to reply in kind to keep audiences and thus the most potent cultural medium of the twentieth century became a platform for rediscovering and reinforcing Scottish national identity. One early and highly popular television drama series from BBC Scotland was *This Man Craig*, starring John Cairney, based on the life of a Scottish comprehensive school (then a new phenomenon).

The unfolding economic crisis shifted Scotland to the political left and revived the SNP and Home Rule movement. As the Cold War deepened, mass protests were mounted against the arrival of American nuclear submarines in the Holy Loch in 1961. These mass mobilisations, the entry of a new generation of young people into politics and the rise of youth culture in general helped initiate an indigenous folk song movement in Scotland. The key figure involved was an ex-Communist Party member, intellectual and Scottish nationalist, Hamish Henderson. The new folk groups were soon regulars on Thomson's Scottish Television. At the height of the movement in 1960s there were over 100 folk clubs.

The movement made a conscious link with more traditional Scottish folk music, adding to the growing sense of a revival in Scottish identity. The folk movement, with its national-ist and political undercurrents, also went straight into Scottish schools. Two of its main progenitors, Morris Blythman and Norman Buchan, were teachers. Blythman set up a folk club when teaching at Allan Glen's in Glasgow, and Buchan followed suit at Rutherglen Academy. Out of the folk revival came, in 1969, what was to become Scotland's unofficial national anthem, 'O Flower of Scotland', written by Roy Williamson of the Corries:

> Those days are past now
> And in the past they must remain
> But we can still rise now
> And be the nation again . . .

The bittersweet quality of this lyric reflects the rapid industrial decline at the end of the 1960s, which led to the occupation of Upper Clyde Shipbuilders (UCS) in 1971. Led by Jimmy Reid (like Hamish Henderson, a Communist who later gravitated to the SNP), the work-in became the focus of a plan to rejuvenate the entire Scottish economy. On 18 August 1971 a third of Scottish industrial workers joined a general strike in support of UCS – the first political strike in Scotland since 1926. UCS was seen as a popular victory against London indifference. Together with the discovery of North Sea oil, it provided Scotland with a rare sense that change was possible, and led directly to the 1979 devolution referendum.

Meanwhile, the rapid expansion of university education (an economic imperative) created the infrastructure for an equally massive growth in Scottish academic studies, par-ticularly the emergence of truly Scottish national historiography that rejected (in the words of Tom Devine) the traditional narrative 'of defective and inadequate development'. Among the new wave of historians were Archie Duncan, Ranald Nicholson, Gordon Donaldson, William Ferguson and T. C. Smout. For the first time, emerging Scottish national identity had a written history to identify with.

As regards school education, the influence of the new nationalism *per se* was strangely limited. Nationalists, socialists and radicals were all at one with the times in supporting comprehensivisation (which began in 1965), a wider curriculum and the end to traditional authoritarian discipline and rote learning in the Scottish classroom – a revolution in itself. But beyond that consensus there was little original thinking. One of the most important nationalist texts from the 1970s, *The Radical Approach* (1976), dedicated to examining policy in an independent Scotland, is devoid of any discussion of education at all. It has chapters on health, housing, industrial relations and environmental policy, but nothing on schools. The highly influential, pro-devolution *Red Paper on Scotland* (1975), edited by Gordon Brown with contributions by socialist and nationalist intellectuals including Vince Cable, Jim Sillars and Robin Cook, was similarly challenged. Only one out of its twenty-seven chapters covers education (and this seems to point in the direction of the Soviet edu-cational model). The reason for this policy lacuna is easy to spot: nationalists and socialists in the 1970s were preoccupied with questions of the economy. For the SNP, the successful slogan was 'It's Scotland's oil'.

It has recently become commonplace to dismiss the 1960s and 1970s as a passage when Scotland 'missed' or participated only to a modest degree in Western modernity and political radicalisation. According to the historian Richard Finlay, 'the swinging sixties passed Scotland by' (Findlay, 2004, p. 292). Even at the time Tom Nairn could write (in 1970) about a clerical and authoritarian Scotland, 'I see that Scottish Nationalism now has the benediction of our annual General Assembly of Crows . . . As far as I'm concerned, Scotland will be reborn the day the last minister is strangled with the last copy of the Sunday Post' (Nairn, 1970).

This analysis is open to challenge. First, the global impact of Scottish intellectuals in this period on the shift in sexual and moral norms in the West (favouring individual freedom and expression) is extraordinary. In many ways this was the result of Scottish intellectuals being caught in the cultural nexus between a conservative, religious culture and the radical agenda of the Scottish Renaissance – and perhaps the glacial pace at which the Scottish Modern Movement was altering domestic society.

Glasgow-born avant-garde novelist Alexander Trocchi had an international reputation and influence in the 1950s and 1960s. Trocchi's essay 'Invisible insurrection of a million minds' was published in the Scottish journal *New Saltire* in 1962 and subsequently as 'Technique du Coup du Monde' in *Internationale Situationniste*. In it he proposed a 'spontaneous university' as a cultural force. His ideas were to help shape the student movement later in the decade, though more on the Continent than in the UK. Trocchi spoke at the highly influential Edinburgh Writers Festival in 1962, which gathered together the cream of the world's avant-garde and radical novelists. There he claimed sodomy as a basis for his writing, doubtless for effect. Famously, MacDiarmid (never used to being upstaged) denounced him as 'cosmopolitan scum'. Then there is R. D. Laing, the radical psychologist and psychiatrist (or 'anti psychiatrist') who challenged received wisdom by arguing that most mental illness is a social and political construct by an authoritarian capitalist society. Like Trocchi, Laing had a famously liberal attitude to recreational drug taking. We might also mention A. S. Neill and his disciple John Aitkenhead (another Scottish nationalist) and their contribution to a child-centred, 'progressive' educational philosophy. Neill was strongly influenced by Freud and Reich and their views on Victorian sexual repression. It can be argued that Trocchi, Laing and Neill were all exiles from Scotland but that is to miss an important point. Each reacted to what they perceived as a repressed traditional Scottish culture. As such, they were part of a wider national awakening that began with the Scottish Renaissance. Their collective impact on the rest of the world in the 1960s (especially educational philosophy) was to give modern Scotland a significant independent voice.

As for the assertion that Scotland's youth failed to rebel, that is also wrong. In the autumn of 1974, a majority of Scotland's young teachers – many just out of university and heavily influenced by the tide of unrest unleashed by the Paris events of May 1968 – launched a spontaneous wave of unofficial strikes that would keep disrupting schools for the entire academic year. They were led by the self-styled Rank & File Teacher group, itself heavily influenced by members of the Trotskyist Socialist Workers Party and International Marxist Group. The leadership of the official teaching unions, caught off guard, initially opposed the actions but were forced to adopt a more militant stance in order to retain credibility. Ostensibly, the movement sought a £15 a week pay rise, but in essence it was a protest at the conservative boundaries of Scottish education and the subordinate role afforded junior teachers, especially women. It was also an implicit critical response to the rapid expansion of education and higher education as a tool of industrial policy, just like May '68 in Paris. Local Action Committees organised strikes, street activities, demonstrations and even an occupation of the offices of the Educational Institute of Scotland (EIS), the main Scottish teachers' union. The revolt ended in a significant pay settlement but it also transformed the internal culture of the Scottish teaching profession. The Rank & File group continued to campaign around a very wide range of issues – women's and gay rights, against the use of corporal punishment in schools and for the right of school pupils to organise.

We might ask, as did the new wave of historians, why a 250-year-old Unionist identity imploded so quickly in the twenty years between 1955 and 1975? One answer comes from Professor Colin Kidd, formerly of Glasgow University. He argues (Kidd, 1993) that the Scots interpretation of Britishness should not be read as their acceptance of a 'pan-Britannic national identity'. Rather the emergent Scottish middle class believed firmly that an English-style political order and bourgeois values were central to modernising 'backward', feudal Scotland and held that view until World War II. As soon as Britain became associated with decline, in the mid-twentieth century, and as soon as Scottish civil society mobilised to defend its imperilled economic interests, it was probably inevitable that Scots would redefine themselves.

However, despite the new sense of Scottish identity, opposition to London and the youth revolt, the 1970s were to end in a conservative reaction. In 1979 Scotland voted by a major-ity of 52 per cent to 48 for a devolved assembly. But as less than 40 per cent of registered voters had said yes, the proposal was vetoed by Westminster. At the subsequent general election, the SNP received an electoral drubbing while the rest of Britain voted in Margaret Thatcher.

THATCHER'S CHILDREN

After the failure of the first devolution referendum, a superficial reading of events might have led to the conclusion that the Scottish Question would recede into history. In fact, the opposite occurred. With local politics in a vacuum, Scotland's intelligentsia and artis-tic community were now to go beyond devolution and embrace an outright nationalist stance.

The period from 1979 to the second devolution referendum in 1997 saw an extraordinary outburst of creative energy in the arts in Scotland, especially in theatre. While Scotland had always maintained a lively theatrical tradition in music hall and pantomime – where, indeed, the vernacular speech and a working-class Scottish identity were perpetuated – circumstances combined to limit domestic playwriting. Famously, George Gregory Smith's sympathetic study of Scottish literature in 1919 remarked that dramatic writing in Scotland was as scarce as the 'owls and snakes of Iceland'. This began to change with James Bridie (Henry Mavor) in the 1920s and 1930s – though never close to Grieve, Bridie's darker works can be seen as part of the Modernist impulse. Bridie went on to help found the College of Drama in Glasgow in 1950 (forerunner of the Royal Conservatoire of Scotland). The 1960s brought the avant-garde Traverse Theatre in Edinburgh as a cockpit for new Scottish writing and an influential harbinger of the international youth counter-culture. But it was not until the 1970s, as mass protest combined with popular culture, that a new theatrical tradition emerged with a very Scottish identity. Playwrights such as Donald Campbell, Roddy McMillan and Bill Bryden used the Scots vernacular to reach out to a new audience with plays of contemporary relevance (in a sense completing Grieve's original project). Above all, the work of John McGrath and the 7:84 Theatre caught the mood of the times with *The Cheviot, the Stag and the Black, Black Oil* in 1973, a neo-nationalist history of Scotland portrayed (with great exaggeration) as a colony first of England and then of America. McGrath reached back into the Scots' music-hall tradition for his nonrealist approach, eschewing London realism, and paved the way for a distinctively Scottish contemporary theatre in the decades to come.

However, the full cultural impact of this new Scottish theatre did not emerge until the era of Thatcherism, when it became the voice for rejecting free-market values and (in the confusion after the failed 1979 referendum) a veritable political opposition in its own right. The mood also affected literature. A new generation of writers emerged including James Kelman, Alasdair Gray, Liz Lochhead, Tom Leonard and (in Gaelic) Aonghas MacNeacail. These writers were to achieve international prominence with works such as Irvine Welsh's *Trainspotting* (1993), Alan Warner's *Morvern Callar* (1995), Gray's *Poor Things* (1992) and Kelman's *How Late It Was, How Late* (1994). Gray and Lochhead used their prominence to argue for independence, though neither joined the SNP. The writing of this generation of novelists is infused with a visceral hostility to Thatcherite values, frequently exploring the plight of the dispossessed parts of Scottish society. Their use of Scots working-class dialect and colourful expletives marked a final victory of the vernacular movement. More important, Scottish contemporary literature had imagined a new national identity into being.

The distinctive and self-confident Scottish cultural production of the period is most noted in two globally competitive genres, rock music and science fiction. Despite a slow start, Scottish rock first drew attention in the 1970s with the Average White Band, Nazareth, Alex Harvey and the Bay City Rollers. The Thatcherite 1980s saw the floodgates open with Simple Minds, Maggie Reilly, Annie Lennox, Hue and Cry, and Primal Scream. The 1990s and beyond saw Scottish performers continue to achieve critical and commercial success internationally, with the likes of Franz Ferdinand, Biffy Clyro, KT Tunstall and Idlewild. A stern Christopher Grieve would have been appalled, but he couldn't deny that the kailyard had been well and truly left behind.

As far back as the 1950s, Scotland had its own science fiction magazine, *Nebula*, published in Glasgow – an indication of the fixation the urban west of Scotland had with American popular culture. It comes as no surprise that the writers of the Scottish Renaissance, in their desire to break with the past, experimented with science fiction, or at least speculative fiction, e.g. Naomi Mitchison's feminist *Memoirs of a Spacewoman* (1962). But Scottish science fiction did not go into stellar orbit till the 1980s and 1990s with the work of Iain M. Banks and Ken MacLeod. Both went to Greenock High School and are left-wing nationalists. In a sense, their writings can be considered the culmination of the Scottish Literary Renaissance project – radical, stylish and mythic. If there is a common theme running through the novels of Banks and MacLeod (and of Scottish science fiction as a whole) it concerns the issues and frictions that arise between coloniser and colonised, and between races of different values and types of society. It is not too far-fetched to see in this a reflection of Scotland and Scottish culture trying to reassert itself with the UK, and as part of a wider world.

It was not long before politics followed in the wake of this cultural revolution. Scotland's pro-devolution groups, including the main churches (but not the SNP) joined together to form the Scottish Constitutional Convention, which held its first meeting on 30 March 1989. After New Labour's election victory in 1997, a second devolution referendum passed with a decisive 74 per cent of the popular vote. The devolved Scottish Parliament met for the first time in 1999. On the wall of its new building is a quote from Alasdair Gray (though he attributes it to someone else): 'Work as if you live in the early days of a better nation'.

It is worth asking why Scottish intellectuals in this period adopted not just an over-whelmingly nationalist stance, but also a fiercely collectivist one in an era when libertarian and free-market values were predominant? This dominant social democratic viewpoint would have major implications for education in a devolved Scotland, such as the SNP government's costly decision to reject university tuition fees.

One wing of European Modernism, reflecting the horrors of industrialisation and World War I, rejected the mechanical and perhaps totalitarian certainties that underlay French Enlightenment thinking. But Scottish Modernists, because of their education in a more humanist tradition of the Enlightenment found in Scotland, retained the view that social progress was not only possible but desirable. That vision was given concrete political form in the project to build an independent Scottish nation. But it had a wider cultural echo in the idea that society has a moral purpose that trumps naked self-interest.

SCOTLAND'S INTELLECTUALS AND THE UNIVERSITIES

The link between nationalism, culture and education lies in the intellectual. Modern materialist theories give intellectuals a primary role in developing national identity. A core argument advanced by Benedict Anderson (1983), Ernest Gellner and Tom Nairn (applied specifically to Scotland) is that national allegiance is invented as a mobilising force to aid 'modernisation', i.e. capitalist industrialisation. This invented nationality is necessary to mobilise popular support for the new state against internal and external enemies, and against old allegiances – feudal, religious, political or cultural. The intelligentsia plays a crucial role in forming and disseminating the ideas and national myths that create allegiance to this new state. As we have outlined above, this model fits Scotland well. For Nairn, the modern nationalist movement is a response to the need for Scotland to break out of British imperial decline.

The radicals of the Scottish Renaissance offered a challenge to the orthodox thinkers of what we might call the Scottish Establishment, or (to invent a term) Empire Intellectuals such as Walter Scott or, later, John Buchan. This is not to denigrate the art or sophistication of the Imperial Intellectuals. Their work portrayed the Scots as an equal partner in a grand Imperial adventure with England and the other English-speaking peoples, to 'civilise' the world. Late-nineteenth-century calls for administrative devolution or even Scottish dominion status (on a par with Canada) were not at variance with this idea. Indeed, one wing of the early nationalist movement, led by the Tory Earl of Montrose, remained wedded to the concept. But in this Imperial myth, Scotland was an ancient, savage land (populated, no doubt, by tartan-wearing noble savages); while latter-day Scots were Imperial adventurers, like Buchan's fictional heroes David Crawfurd (in *Prester John*) and Richard Hannay (in *The Thirty-Nine Steps*).

The certainties of the Empire Intellectuals imploded with the Great Depression and the disintegration of the British Empire. But their domination of the ancient universities and professions meant their brand of cultural orthodoxy remained strong even in the 1950s. As a result, Scottish nationalism – cultural and political – emerged mainly from intellectuals outside the university system. The leading figures of the Scottish Renaissance were from a classic petty bourgeois background, often itinerant, and finding marginal employment where they could in order to fund their writing. Christopher Grieve was a sometime journalist, Edwin Muir a factory worker, Neil Gunn a customs officer and Grassic Gibbon a clerk.

However, that is not to say the nationalist ferment was absent inside Scotland's universities. Glasgow University in particular was to play a central role in the creation of the SNP.

In September 1927, Glasgow University Student Nationalist Association (GUSNA) was formed by ex-members of the Labour Club. The membership card gave GUSNA's aims as 'securing self-government' and 'advancing the ideals of Scottish culture within and without the University'. The moving spirit in GUSNA was John MacCormick, a gifted orator trained in the famous Glasgow University Union weekly debates, and a leading figure in the history of Scottish nationalism. Using GUSNA as his base, MacCormick convinced the disparate nationalist and Home Rule organisations to merge into the National Party of Scotland (the SNP's direct predecessor) in early 1928.

But the influence of GUSNA did not end there. MacCormick and GUSNA took immediate advantage of two peculiarities of university government to propel the infant nationalist movement onto the national political stage – the rectorship and the fact that the four ancient Scottish universities combined to form a Westminster parliamentary constituency with an MP elected by all their graduates.

In 1928, MacCormick and GUSNA promoted the candidacy of R. B. Cunninghame Graham – a left-wing former Liberal MP and early Scottish nationalist – for Lord Rector of the university, the chair of the university's governing body and also the students' official representative. The charismatic Cunninghame Graham came within sixty-six votes of beating Stanley Baldwin, then Prime Minister. At the next rectorial election, in 1931, the GUSNA candidate, the novelist Compton Mackenzie, actually won, defeating Oswald Mosley (then the darling of the left). Both elections received widespread publicity outside Glasgow University, putting political nationalism, as an independent force, on the map for the first time.

While the results of university rectorial elections undoubtedly had relevance in Scotland, they hardly mattered when it came to Westminster politics. But elections and by-elections to the Combined Scottish Universities parliamentary seat in the House of Commons certainly did. Between 1918 and 1950 (when such seats were abolished) the four universities, voting as a single, multi-member constituency, were entitled to elect three MPs using the single transferable vote system (or first past the post in by-elections). The electors consisted of all existing university graduates (who also retained their ordinary vote), meaning the electorate represented a serious cross-section of Scottish middle-class opinion.

In January 1936, there was a sensational by-election in the Scottish Universities constituency when the National Government tried to find a seat for former Prime Minister Ramsay MacDonald, who had been defeated at the general election the previous year. The SNP candidate, Andrew Dewar Gibb, then Regius Professor of Law at Glasgow University, came a good second, taking 31 per cent of the poll. Gibb was leader of the SNP, from 1936 to 1940.

During the 1940s and early 1950s, the infant SNP was torn by internal strife. At this nadir, student activists in GUSNA were once again to put Scottish nationalism in the headlines. In October 1950, John MacCormick, who had quit the SNP to lead the cross-party Covenant movement seeking Home Rule, was elected Lord Rector of Glasgow University. Then on Christmas Day 1950 a group of GUSNA members led by Ian Hamilton – who would later become a Queen's Counsel – famously removed the Stone of Destiny from Westminster Abbey.

Student politics played a significant (and often underestimated) role in the formation of the SNP and modern Scottish nationalism. More so, certainly, than student politics ever played in English politics (except, perhaps, for the 'King and country' debate at Oxford in 1936). In this regard, the dynamic in Scotland looks more European than is the case for England, where trades unions, English country houses and London clubs served as traditional political nerve centres. Perhaps this Scottish exceptionalism can be explained by the location of three of the four ancient universities (particularly Glasgow) in major urban centres; by the more central role played by Scottish universities in educating the middle-class professions; and by the relative social importance of the ancient Scottish universities as institutions inside a small nation.

However, when all is said and done, academic debate inside Scotland's official university system was not the primary vehicle for forging a new national identity. That required the emergence of what the Italian Marxist philosopher Antonio Gramsci termed 'organic intel-lectuals'; i.e. a new group of writers, artists, historians and theoreticians with close popular connections to the new political movement. Only at a later stage, from the 1970s, when the independence issue became dominated by the question of Scotland's economic viability, did Scottish university academics become involved as academics. By then, no one doubted that Scotland was indeed a nation.

CONCLUSION

The election in 1999 of a devolved Scottish Parliament (with control over education) did not blunt the rise of political nationalism as some had predicted. A minority SNP govern-ment was returned in 2007, followed by a majority nationalist administration in 2011. The Cabinet Secretary for Education in the majority SNP government was Michael Russell, a writer, novelist, film maker and fluent Gaelic speaker; and thus very much a product of the Scottish Renaissance.

The devolution era saw the creation of new state-funded cultural institutions: Creative Scotland, the national arts agency, and in 2006 the National Theatre of Scotland, which scored an instant international reputation with a play about the Iraq War, *Black Watch*.

In education, the devolution period since 1999 has seen a significant divergence in the education systems of Scotland and the rest of the UK, particularly England. South of the border the process of dismantling the comprehensive system which began under New Labour has gathered pace with the Conservative–Liberal Democrat coalition elected in 2010. At secondary level, stand-alone and often tacitly selective academy schools and faith schools are replacing the traditional local authority comprehensives. At university level, student tuition fees are now mandatory. North of the border, the social democratic ethos that infuses the new sense of Scottish national identity has worked to retain the comprehen-sive approach and free university education.

The issue here is not which approach is correct but that this (growing) divergence has its roots in the distinctive cultural and political shifts that have taken place in Scotland since the 1920s. Whether or not Scotland ultimately opts for complete independence, it seems unlikely these shifts will be reversed. Or that Scotland's national approach to educational philosophy or management will cease to be influenced by its new sense of nationhood.

REFERENCES

Anderson, B. (1983) *Imagined Communities: Reflections on the Origin and Spread of Nationalism.* London: Verso.
Finlay, R. (2004) *Modern Scotland 1914–2000.* London: Profile Books.
Kidd, C. (1993) *Subverting Scotland's Past: Scottish Whig Historians and the Creation of an Anglo-British Identity.* Cambridge: Cambridge University Press.

Nairn, T. (1970) 'The three dreams of Scottish Nationalism', in K. Miller (ed.), *Memoirs of a Modern Scotland*. London: Faber and Faber.

Normand, T. (2000) *The Modern Scot: Modernism and Nationalism in Scottish Art 1928–1955*. Farnham: Ashgate Publishing.

25

Gaelic Education

Boyd Robertson

Gaelic is the longest-established of Scotland's languages. It was brought to Scotland by settlers from Ireland in the fifth and sixth centuries AD. These immigrants, known to the Romans as *Scotti*, gave the country its name; their Celtic language penetrated almost every part of Scotland and became, for a brief period, the language of the Crown and of government. From the twelfth century onwards, the status of the language was eroded by anglicising influences from the south and it became increasingly marginalised.

Today, only 1.2 per cent of Scots speak Gaelic. These 58,652 Gaelic speakers are to be found mostly in the Western Isles and on the western fringes of the mainland but there are also significant communities of Gaelic speakers in urban centres such as Glasgow, Edinburgh and Inverness. The last thirty years have, however, seen a remarkable renaissance of the language and culture, reflected in the arts, the media, the socio-economic sphere and education.

PRE-SCHOOL EDUCATION

It is singularly appropriate to begin an overview of Gaelic education with the pre-school sector because this has been the seedbed for much of the regeneration and growth in Gaelic.

Increasing exposure to the English language and to Anglo–American cultural influences caused parents and Gaelic activists to become concerned about the detrimental effect this would have on young children's fluency in, and attitude towards, Gaelic. It was considered essential to counteract this trend by seeking to associate the minority language with positive and enjoyable experiences and this led in the late 1970s to the formation of the first Gaelic playgroups and to demands for children's programmes in Gaelic on television. A national association, Comhairle nan Sgoiltean Àraich (CNSA), was set up in 1982 to promote the development of Gaelic-medium playgroups. Despite being a voluntary sector provider with limited resources, CNSA worked wonders to begin with helping to set up a network of pre-school groups across Scotland. However, the introduction by the government of an entitlement to funded nursery education for 4-year-olds and subsequently for 3-year-olds led to a mushrooming of nursery school provision and a reduced role for CNSA. Over 800 children now attend sixty-six Gaelic nurseries, most of which are located in schools with Gaelic-medium streams. The government's official agency for the language, Bòrd na Gàidhlig, is developing a comprehensive new early years service in partnership with local authorities and the Parental Advisory Scheme and there are currently seventy 0–3 groups throughout the country.

PRIMARY EDUCATION

Provision for Gaelic in primary schools has been transformed in the last four decades. Before the reorganisation of local government in the 1970s, Gaelic had a minor role in the primary curriculum. Even in schools in strong Gaelic-speaking communities, the teaching medium was almost exclusively English, the home language of most of the pupils being reduced to the status of a subject to be studied.

The position of Gaelic changed radically in 1975 with the launch of a bilingual education project by the newly formed local authority for the Outer Hebrides, Comhairle nan Eilean. This initiative received government backing, with the Scottish Office jointly funding the first two phases of the project which sought to build on the home language of the majority of pupils and used Gaelic as a teaching and learning medium along with English. This was the first time that the use of Gaelic as a medium of instruction was officially sanctioned in state schools and represented a major advance for the language in education. There was a favourable parental response to the project initially but, by the early 1980s, concerns were being expressed about the level of fluency in Gaelic being attained by pupils in some schools after several years of bilingual schooling. Parents also voiced dissatisfaction with the progress being made by certain schools in implementing the bilingual scheme.

Doubts about the ability of bilingual models to deliver fluency in Gaelic comparable to that in English and a growing awareness of the erosion of the language amongst the school-age population made parents, educationalists and language activists realise that another approach was needed. Developments in Welsh and in other minority languages were studied and the findings suggested that use of the minority language as the medium of education had to be maximised to ensure language maintenance and transmission. The first Gaelic playgroups had demonstrated the viability of this approach and convinced parents that it should be continued in primary school.

Highland and Strathclyde Regional Councils responded to parental pressure for Gaelic-medium education and set up units in schools in Inverness and Glasgow in 1985. The success of these first units and the continuing spread of the playgroups fuelled demand for provision in other areas. By 2011–12, sixty-one schools and 2,418 pupils were engaged in Gaelic-medium education. Most schools are in the Highlands and Islands but there are several in non-Gaelic-speaking areas such as Aberdeen, Cumbernauld, Edinburgh, Kilmarnock and Stirling. Gaelic-medium units, or streams, as they came to be called, are generally located in local schools in which the majority of pupils are educated in English, but 1999 saw the beginning of a new phase in Gaelic-medium education with the opening of Scotland's first all-Gaelic school in Glasgow and the designation of five schools in the Outer Hebrides as Gaelic schools. The first purpose-built all-Gaelic school opened in Inverness in 2007. Edinburgh City Council eventually bowed to parental pressure to replace the Gaelic Unit at Tollcross with a wholly Gaelic school as from 2013 and Highland Council has approved the creation of dedicated Gaelic schools at Fort William and Portree.

In virtually all Gaelic-medium classes there is a mix of fluent speakers and learners. The proportions vary depending on the type of community the school serves. In rural, island schools, several of the pupils come from Gaelic-speaking homes while in urban, mainland schools, few pupils have that home background. Research shows that factors that influence parents to opt for Gaelic-medium education include maintenance and development of the mother tongue; restoration to a family of a language that has skipped a generation or two; acquisition of a second language; the perceived advantages of bilingualism; and access to Gaelic culture and heritage.

The Gaelic-medium curriculum adheres to the principles of the overarching Curriculum for Excellence which seeks to 'enable all children to develop their capacities as successful learners, confident individuals, responsible citizens and effective contributors to society'. The framework for Literacy and Gàidhlig is formulated along similar lines to that for English. It sets out 'broad descriptions of the range of learning opportunities which will contribute to the development of literacy' in the language and recognises that there are significant differences in the development of certain linguistic skills between English and Gaelic. This arises from the fact that Gaelic-medium education begins with a period of total language immersion.

Her Majesty's Inspectorate of Education (HMIE), in its 2011 report, 'Gaelic Education: Building on the successes, addressing the barriers', adjudged that the total immersion phase works best when it is continued until late in P3 or P4, giving children 'a secure foundation in the language' and a platform of transferable skills that could be readily applied to reading and writing in English. During this phase, the teacher uses Gaelic almost exclusively and the emphasis is on the development of listening and speaking skills. The focus on oral skills, which continues beyond the immersion phase, means that pupils in Gaelic-medium classes attain targets in these and in literacy skills in a different sequence and time frame from those in English-medium classes.

The overall aim of primary Gaelic-medium education is to give pupils equal fluency and literacy in Gaelic and English. It is left to the discretion of local authorities and schools how this should be achieved. The HMIE report found considerable variation in practice between authorities in the use made of English as a teaching medium beyond the total immersion phase. The balance between Gaelic and English can range from 60/40 through to 90/10 and parents are concerned that the weaker Gaelic model inhibits the development of fluency. There is a tendency for schools to introduce reading and writing in English in P3 and increase the weighting given to English in P6/7.

There is little doubt that Gaelic-medium education has been a success. Research into the attainments of pupils receiving Gaelic-medium primary education found that Gaelic-medium pupils often outperformed their English-medium peers even in English language (Johnstone, 1999). Similar results were reported in a more recent Edinburgh University study (O'Hanlon et al., 2010). A 2005 HMIE report, *Improving Achievement in Gaelic*, found that 'pupils in Gaelic-medium primary schools are generally attaining well', while the 2011 HMIE report claimed that Scotland has the potential to become 'an international model of best practice in the promotion of minority language communities across Europe'.

Gaelic features in the curriculum of primary schools in another two forms. In the Outer Hebrides, some schools that do not have Gaelic-medium units offer pupils a form of bilingual education developed from the earlier programme. Schools that have units also provide a measure of bilingual education to pupils outwith the unit. In other schools, Gaelic is taught as a second language for a short time each week by a specialist itinerant teacher or by a member of staff with the appropriate skills. This type of provision has been offered in schools in parts of Argyll and Perthshire, in Inverness and in areas such as Lochaber, Skye and Lochalsh, and Wester Ross for the best part of three decades, but it has been superseded by a model based on the Modern Languages in the Primary School scheme in which class teachers are given a period of tuition in the language to enable them to teach it at a basic level. A Bòrd na Gàidhlig survey in 2009 found 202 teachers engaged in providing around 5,500 pupils in upper primary classes with an introduction to the language through the Gaelic Learners in the Primary School (GLPS) initiative. A significant proportion of these are in the English-medium streams of schools that have Gaelic-medium units.

SECONDARY EDUCATION

The use of Gaelic as a medium of education in secondary schools has not kept pace with developments in the primary sector. The language was first used in the teaching of second-ary subjects in 1983 when Comhairle nan Eilean set up a pilot project as an extension to its primary bilingual programme. The two-year pilot involved two small secondary schools in Lewis, Lionel and Shawbost, and concentrated on the social subjects. Pupils responded positively to the use of their mother tongue and the pilot was deemed a success.

The first Gaelic-medium unit on the mainland opened at Hillpark Secondary in Glasgow in 1988. Further provision was established in 1992 in Millburn Academy, Inverness and Portree High School thus ensuring continuity of Gaelic-medium education for pupils of the three largest primary units. By 2011–12, Gaelic-medium education was operating in four-teen secondary schools. August 2006 saw the opening in Glasgow of the first all-through Gaelic-medium school in Scotland affording pupils education through the language from age 3 to 18.

The use of Gaelic as a medium in secondary is restricted to two or three subjects in most schools. Only three schools, Greenfaulds in Cumbernauld, Portree High and Sgoil Ghàidhlig Ghlaschu, offer a significant number of specialisms in Gaelic. History is the subject most widely taught through Gaelic. Candidates may elect to sit Gaelic versions of Standard Grade examinations in History, Geography, Mathematics and Modern Studies, and Higher Mathematics may be taken in Gaelic.

The development of Gaelic-medium education in secondary has been hampered by a number of factors. One of the most significant of these is the fragmented nature of the secondary curriculum with its specialist subject structure. To operate economically and effectively, this requires a substantial cohort of pupils in any one year. The typical primary school structure with one teacher per class lends itself more readily to a smaller cohort and the level of subsidy required is significantly less. It will be some considerable time before the Gaelic-medium year groups in most receiving secondaries reach the point of economic viability in a range of subjects. Attempts have been made to address this issue through dis-tance and blended learning but these have only been successful in particular subjects (such as Geography) and in certain circumstances.

Financial considerations were probably uppermost in influencing HMI to conclude in its 1994 report that 'the provision of Gaelic-medium secondary education in a number of subjects, determined by the vagaries of resource availability, is neither desirable nor feasible in the foreseeable future' (1.12). This recommendation, which contrasted with the report's commendation of Gaelic-medium primary education, was accepted by the then Conservative government and became Scottish Office policy. It provoked an indignant response from the Gaelic community which highlighted the absence of any educational rationale for the deci-sion, the disjunction it would cause in children's education and the illogicality and absurd-ity of abandoning a scheme in which so much had been invested. Happily, this policy was overturned by the incoming Labour government in 1997. Education Department officials were asked to consult local authorities about ways 'to support and extend Gaelic-medium teaching in specified subjects in the secondary curriculum'. It is somewhat ironic that the 2005 HMIE report lamented the fact that only 55 per cent of P7 pupils continue with Gaelic-medium education in S1 and acknowledged that 'There continue to be key weaknesses in the extent to which Gaelic-medium provision is systematically followed through from Primary to the Secondary stages'. The 2011 HMIE report reached a similar conclusion, saying that secondary 'does not provide for effective progression for young people learning through the medium of Gaelic' and pointing to instances of pupils not continuing with Gaelic-medium education beyond primary in some parts of the country.

Pupils in Gaelic-medium classes also study the language as a subject. They take the Gàidhlig course which is designed for fluent speakers and leads to certificate examinations at Standard Grade, Intermediate 1 and 2, Higher and Advanced Higher. In 2012, 173 candidates sat the Standard Grade exam, forty-five took Intermediate exams and 116 were presented for Higher. The fluent speakers' category includes pupils who have been in bilingual programmes in primary, and a small number who may not have had access to Gaelic-medium education and have had little or no exposure to the language in primary, but who come from Gaelic-speaking homes and begin formal study of the language in secondary.

A Gaelic (Learners) course leading to separate certificate examinations was instituted in 1962. This followed a campaign by prominent Gaelic teachers who highlighted the inequity of asking learners of Gaelic to sit the same examination as native speakers. The new course brought provision for pupils learning Gaelic broadly into line with that for pupils learning other modern languages.

Classification of pupils as learners or fluent speakers is a recurrent issue. The Scottish Qualifications Authority (SQA) Gaelic Assessment Panel produced revised guidance on categorisation in 2002 but the interpretation and implementation of the guidelines is sometimes challenged by parents. This usually arises where a school has adjudged a pupil to be a fluent speaker and parents feel that categorisation as a learner would improve the child's chances of success in certificate examinations.

Less than 10 per cent of state schools offer the Gaelic (Learners) option. Most of these are located in the Highlands and Islands. The number of schools has reduced through amalgamations and closures from forty to the mid-thirties and there have been regional fluctuations with expansion in the Inverness area and contraction in Glasgow. Four Glasgow schools have ceased to offer Gaelic in the recent past and there is now only one school where Gaelic is taught in a city with over 5,000 Gaelic speakers. Some schools in the independent sector occasionally present pupils for National Qualification examinations. The number of presentations for the Gaelic (Learners) exams in 2012 was 362 at Standard Grade, forty-three at Intermediate levels and 127 at Higher.

In schools in the Outer Hebrides, Skye and the West Highland mainland, it is council policy that all first- and second-year pupils study Gaelic and another modern language. In most other parts of Scotland, pupils typically have to choose between Gaelic and French, or Gaelic and German, from first year or take Gaelic as a second language option in second or third year. These option arrangements militate against a large uptake of the subject.

The teaching of Gaelic has changed radically in the last thirty years. Where it was once a subject of study and analysis with an approach not unlike the classical languages, it progressed through a stage where the emphasis was on vocabulary, grammar and structure using English as the medium of instruction, to a methodology today that aims to produce learners with communicative competence in the language and uses the target language extensively in the classroom.

In addition to the long-term courses outlined above, there are also short-term modular courses for both learners and fluent speakers. There are twenty-five National Certificate (NC) modules for learners which adhere closely to Modern Languages module specifications. There are only three units specifically designed for fluent speakers but any of the units on the SQA catalogue may be delivered and assessed through the medium of Gaelic.

SUPPORT STRUCTURES

Recent developments have been facilitated and sustained by the creation of enabling mechanisms and support structures. Chief among these has been the Scheme of Specific Grants for Gaelic Education initiated by the Conservative government in 1986. Under this scheme, local authorities submit project proposals to the Scottish Government and receive up to 75 per cent funding for approved projects. Grants are awarded for new or additional provision and authorities are expected to meet the full costs of initiatives after five years. The Scheme's initial budget of £250,000 had risen to £4.48 million in 2011–12. Authorities can bid for funding on an individual or collective basis, but the government expects authorities to allocate a proportion of total funding to collaborative projects.

The Scheme of Specific Grants and the impulse to collaborate created a need for coordinated action by local authorities and led to the formation of an inter-authority network. A structure, affording cooperation at political, managerial and curriculum development levels, was put in place by the three local authorities with the largest concentrations of Gaelic speakers – Highland and Strathclyde regional councils and Comhairle nan Eilean. Other authorities with Gaelic provision joined the network's Management Review Group which prioritised development proposals submitted by Primary, Secondary and Community Education Review Groups. This review process resulted in projects such as the production of maths and science schemes for primary schools, a learners' course for secondary schools and the creation of a database for modern Gaelic terminology. Although the inter-authority network made substantial progress in addressing the main areas of need, it was clear that a more permanent arrangement for the production of resources was required. This led to the establishment by the government of a national resource centre for Gaelic on Lewis in 1999. The new centre, Stòrlann, has delivered an extensive publishing programme but resources are still needed in most curricular areas.

National agencies such as the SQA and Education Scotland (ES) play significant roles in supporting Gaelic education. The SQA has a Gaelic Assessment Panel which nominates setters, examiners, moderators and markers for national examinations and provides advice on matters relating to syllabus and assessment. The panel has produced a revised and extended set of guidelines on Gaelic orthography which update and further exemplify the Gaelic Orthographic Conventions published in 1981 by the Scottish Examination Board. SQA and ES representatives participate in working parties which prepare subject guidelines and advice for national curriculum development programmes.

ES hosts a Gaelic Resource Bank, Stòras na Gàidhlig, that includes a thesaurus, terminology database, place name maps, songs and stories. The GLOW site has a virtual community, CPD Central, a facility for continuing professional development which is particularly helpful in the Gaelic context where many teachers are located in rural and islands schools and can feel isolated. There is also a Gàidhlig and Literacy GLOW Group. An online

Gaelic Resource Database developed by Comhairle nan Eilean Siar furnishes teachers with an informative catalogue of resources for use at all stages of the curriculum.

Teachers can access a bank of radio and television programmes designed for use in school. The main provider, the BBC, produces programmes on radio and television, which cater for learners and fluent speakers and address various stages within both primary and secondary. MG Alba, which administers an £11 million Gaelic Broadcasting Fund, sponsors Film G, an annual short film competition for schools, and is involved in other initiatives such as a website for learners of Gaelic of all ages, LearnGaelic.net

Language development bodies and other agencies also play a key role in bolstering and promoting Gaelic in education. The language development agency, Comunn na Gàidhlig (CnaG), played a vital role in community animation and in the development of many aspects of Gaelic education in the 1980s and 1990s and was instrumental in setting up Comann nam Pàrant (Nàiseanta), a national association of parents, which has branches in most places where there is Gaelic-medium education. In 2002, the then Scottish Executive established a national Gaelic agency, Bòrd na Gàidhlig, which took over many of the functions of CnaG, including the national coordinating role formerly undertaken by CnaG's education officer and now part of the remit of the Bòrd's education manager. The formation of an organisation for secondary teachers of Gaelic, CLAS, was one of the legacies of CnaG's education officer. Bòrd na Gàidhlig has set up an advisory national body for Gaelic education that brings together local authorities, universities, colleges and national education agencies and the Bòrd funds a range of projects and initiatives designed to develop Gaelic education.

TEACHER EDUCATION

Teacher training in Gaelic is currently concentrated in two teacher education institutions (TEIs) – the University of Strathclyde in Glasgow and Aberdeen University. Both offer some training in Gaelic within the BEd and Postgraduate Diploma in Education (Primary) (PGDE(P)) courses. There are Gaelic pathways in the BEd course which enable Gaelic-speaking students to receive tuition in linguistic skills and teaching methods. Periods of school experience in a Gaelic unit are built into the pathway and into the training of students on the PGDE(P) course. Most of the training in Gaelic is optional and outwith core elements of the course. The University of Glasgow has, in the past, made occasional provision for its Gaelic-speaking students.

Dissatisfaction continues to be voiced about the nature and extent of training provided for Gaelic-medium teachers. Surveys have shown that newly qualified teachers are highly critical of pre-service arrangements and feel inadequately prepared for the Gaelic-medium classroom with its additional demands and specialised requirements. The present situation where students receive no certification or formal qualification for Gaelic-medium teaching is deemed increasingly anomalous and was highlighted in a report published by the General Teaching Council for Scotland (GTCS) in 1999. The report, *Teaching in Gaelic-medium Education*, made a series of recommendations for change, including the development of a dual English-/Gaelic-medium route in BEd and PGDE courses which would confer a qualification to teach in either medium and be formally recognised by certification.

Pre-service training arrangements for secondary teachers of Gaelic are more established. Gaelic is one of the subject specialisms in which students undertaking the Postgraduate Diploma in Education (Secondary) course (PGDE(S)) can qualify and they receive training in Gaelic teaching methods as a core part of the course. Their training enables them to engage in teaching both the Gàidhlig and Gaelic (Learners) courses. There is, however, very little pre-service provision for trainee teachers of other subjects intending to teach their specialisms through the medium of Gaelic other than a generic module and a school placement at Strathclyde.

Most in-service training in Gaelic is organised and delivered at local authority and school level with occasional input from TEI staff. An t-Alltan, a large-scale event open to all Gaelic teachers, is organised annually by Stòrlann and there are training events as part of national curriculum development initiatives. Teachers wishing to convert from secondary to primary or to gain a qualification to teach another secondary subject can do so by means of a one-term Additional Teaching Qualification (ATQ) course at a TEI. Several teachers have entered Gaelic-medium teaching by this route and the ATQ has helped authorities address staffing shortages in particular places.

A number of steps have been taken to increase the supply of Gaelic-medium teachers. Recruitment drives have been mounted by Bòrd na Gàidhlig and the Scottish Funding Council (SFC) has funded places specifically for Gaelic-medium students at the universities of Aberdeen and Strathclyde. A PGDE(P) with Gaelic course developed by the University of Strathclyde has been available on a distance-learning basis to students at Lews Castle College and some other colleges of the University of the Highlands and Islands (UHI). Another UHI partner college, Sabhal Mòr Ostaig, collaborates with Aberdeen University to offer an MA (Hons) in Gaelic with Education and an in-service course, Streap, designed to equip qualified teachers with sufficient linguistic competence and confidence to transfer to the Gaelic-medium sector. These measures have helped to reduce the gap between supply and demand, particularly in the primary sector, but the throughput of trained personnel is still not sufficient to allow expansion of the Gaelic-medium service, especially in the secondary field.

A Gaelic-Medium Teachers' Action Group set up by the then Scottish Executive reported in 2005 and made a series of recommendations to improve procedures for the recruitment and retention of Gaelic-medium teachers. To help realise its objectives, it called for the appointment of a Gaelic Teacher Recruitment Officer, a post now hosted by Bòrd na Gàidhlig. In addition to liaising closely with schools, colleges and universities, the postholder also organises short courses for teachers who wish to develop their language skills with a view to teaching in the GLPS scheme or through the medium of Gaelic.

FURTHER AND HIGHER EDUCATION

The use of Gaelic as a medium of education extends into the tertiary sector and is, indeed, at its most comprehensive in one college. Sabhal Mòr Ostaig was founded in 1973 as a Gaelic College in the Sleat area of Skye. Initially, the College ran a programme of short courses in Gaelic language and culture but, ten years on, it embarked on full-time provision.

Today, the college, which has received government recognition as the National Centre for Gaelic Language and Culture, offers a range of certificate, diploma, degree and post-graduate courses in Gaelic language and culture. Some of these courses can be undertaken by distance learning. One such, An Cùrsa Inntrigidh, is designed to give students the language proficiency necessary to engage in study through the medium of Gaelic. All courses are delivered and assessed in Gaelic and the administration of the college is also conducted in Gaelic. Sabhal Mòr has considerably expanded its portfolio of short courses and over 800 students enlist annually for tuition in a variety of language and culture classes. The college campus houses a historical Gaelic dictionary project, Faclair na Gàidhlig, a Gaelic place names project, Ainmean Àiteachan na h-Alba, and a marketing and communications company, Cànan. Sabhal Mòr is also home to Tobar an Dualchais/the Kist o Riches, a large-scale project to digitise the extensive folklore and music archives of the School of Scottish Studies at Edinburgh University, the Gaelic Department of BBC Scotland and the Campbell Collection in Canna. These archives of folksong and folklore, tales and traditions are a treasury of Gaelic and Scots material ripe for exploitation in the Curriculum for Excellence.

The year 1997–8 saw the introduction of a full-time Gaelic immersion course at Sabhal Mòr. The first such immersion course, sponsored by CnaG, was piloted in Lochaber in 1995–6 by Inverness College and offered in a number of colleges the following session. While the effectiveness of learning a language through immersion is widely attested, provision remains confined to a handful of colleges.

Sabhal Mòr Ostaig, Lews Castle and other colleges in the north have joined forces to form the UHI, Britain's newest university. UHI, which is a federal, collegiate institution embracing thirteen academic partners, gained full university status in 2011. Sabhal Mòr Ostaig is the principal partner in UHI's Gaelic and Related Subjects Scheme in which Lews Castle College also participates.

Traditionally, students wishing to study Gaelic at university have had to go to Aberdeen, Edinburgh or Glasgow, each of which has a Celtic department. These three departments offer a range of undergraduate courses in Gaelic and Celtic Studies and students can take an Honours degree in Celtic or a joint Honours in Celtic and another subject. Celtic Studies encompasses the study of other Celtic languages, particularly Irish Gaelic and Welsh. Provision is made for those wanting to learn the language and Celtic Civilisation classes cater for those with an interest in cultural heritage. Postgraduate study opportunities are also available in the discipline. Following its merger with Jordanhill College, the University of Strathclyde introduced Gaelic Studies classes, and the Royal Conservatoire of Scotland in Glasgow offers a degree course in Scottish Music which has Gaelic language and Gaelic music components.

COMMUNITY EDUCATION

Time spent in school is but a fraction of the time spent in the home and the community, and the contribution of these domains to the education of the child is being recognised increasingly in the development of Gaelic education.

A number of local authorities arrange evening classes for parents who wish to learn Gaelic in order to assist, and keep in step with, the linguistic progress of their offspring. A website for parents and children engaged in Gaelic-medium education run by Stòrlann offers a homework helpline and various learning aids. Some authorities also provide language packs for parents who are not Gaelic speakers so that they can help their children with homework. Reinforcement of the language beyond the school is regarded as a vital part of the Gaelic-medium education strategy, especially for children from non-Gaelic-speaking homes, and a nationwide network of Gaelic youth clubs for children aged 5 to 12 was established by CnaG.

Another community initiative, Fèisean nan Gàidheal, seeks to reinforce the link between the language and the culture. A *fèis*, or festival, is typically a week-long event that offers children tuition in Gaelic and in a variety of Gaelic arts including drama, storytelling, song and music. The *fèis* movement began in Barra and has evolved into a national agency that assists with the organisation of forty-four separate *fèisean* in communities in, and beyond, the Highlands and Islands. Fèisean nan Gàidheal also provides a Gaelic theatre in education service to schools.

In addition to the classes for parents mentioned above, a number of agencies run classes and short courses for adult learners. The community education departments of local authorities and further education colleges continue to be the principal providers. Most of the classes are designed for beginners and follow an SQA modular scheme or have a less defined conversational format. University departments of continuing education also offer similar kinds of classes. Intensive short courses for learners are organised by a number of public and private agencies. Among their number are the orally based Ulpan classes modelled on the Hebrew courses for immigrants to Israel which were intended to help new citizens integrate quickly into society.

RESEARCH

Although a great deal of research has been conducted on linguistic, socio-linguistic, demographic and literary topics by university departments, agencies such as the Lèirsinn Research centre at Sabhal Mòr Ostaig and individuals such as Professor Kenneth MacKinnon, Gaelic education has not received the attention it warrants. There was, until lately, little available in published form.

The School of Education at Stirling University has been the locus for three important research projects into aspects of Gaelic education. The first of these was an evaluation of the Western Isles Bilingual Project, published in 1987. The findings were generally favourable to the project and supportive of the bilingual scheme. Professor Richard Johnstone's review of research, *Impact of Current Developments to Support the Gaelic Language*, published in 1994, gave a comprehensive account and perceptive analysis of developments in education and other fields of Gaelic activity. The third government-funded Stirling project was a three-year programme of research into the attainments of pupils in Gaelic-medium primary education in Scotland. The research, conducted in collaboration with the Scottish Council for Research in Education (SCRE) and Lèirsinn, and published in 1999, confirmed that pupils educated in Gaelic 'were not being disadvantaged in comparison with children educated through English' and were, in many instances, outperforming English-medium pupils, while also gaining the advantage of proficiency in two languages (Johnstone, 1999). These findings have been echoed in a 2010 study conducted by a team of researchers (O'Hanlon, McLeod and Paterson) from Edinburgh University.

Like Stirling, Lèirsinn has been involved in a number of research projects concerned with Gaelic education. The agency was commissioned to undertake a review and assessment of support and provision for Gaelic-medium education and produced two reports, *Teacher Training* and *The Critical Skills*, in 1996. More recently, Lèirsinn has investigated emergent identities in bilingual education and patterns of Gaelic speech in secondary education.

A major conference on Gaelic research, Rannsachadh na Gàidhlig, is held biennially in one of the universities with a Celtic or Gaelic department. Papers on linguistic, literary, educational and cultural topics are published in conference proceedings. Socio-linguistic research in Gaelic received a major boost in 2009 with the advent of the Soillse research network, a partnership of the universities of Aberdeen, Edinburgh, Glasgow and UHI. The Soillse programme, which has a £5.29m budget and is scheduled to run for five years, aims to increase research capacity in the language and focuses on Gaelic in education, policies for Gaelic and Gaelic as a community language.

PROSPECTS

It will be apparent from the foregoing review that substantial progress has been made in Gaelic education, particularly in the provision of Gaelic-medium pre-school and primary education. Buoyant and burgeoning as the Gaelic-medium development would appear to be, it is, nevertheless, a tender and fragile flower. This was graphically illustrated in 1996 when cutbacks in local authority funding led to a proposal to close a thriving Gaelic-medium unit in East Kilbride. A concerted campaign by parents and language agencies averted closure. This incident and other threats to the development of Gaelic-medium education, such as proposals to cap enrolment in the system in certain localities, led proponents to campaign for more recognition of the language and greater security of provision in education. The campaign led by CnaG produced the first tangible result when Gaelic was specified as one of the national priorities in the Standards in Scotland's Schools etc. Act 2000. The Act created a new statutory framework for schools' education and local authorities, and schools were required to plan, monitor and report on improvements in Gaelic education.

The establishment of the first government agency for the language, Bòrd na Gàidhlig, in 2002 was a further significant step towards conferring official recognition on the language. That process culminated in the passing of the Gaelic Language (Scotland) Act in 2005. The Act seeks to secure 'the status of Gaelic as an official language of Scotland' and to create the conditions for a sustainable future for the language by providing direction to Gaelic development activities through a strategic language planning approach. Under the Act, Bòrd na Gàidhlig became a statutory body with responsibility for advising the government on all matters relating to Gaelic language and culture. It is charged with the responsibility of devising a National Gaelic Language Plan that specifies strategies and priorities for future development. The first National Plan was published in 2007 and the second in 2012. The Act confers powers on the Bòrd to require public authorities in Scotland to produce language plans that should articulate with the National Plan.

The Act also requires Bòrd na Gàidhlig to prepare a National Education Strategy as part of the Plan. The Bòrd considers Gaelic-medium education to be the 'principal means by which new Gaelic speakers are created' and consequently 'will seek to increase the numbers in GME substantially while continuing to value and support other forms of Gaelic education such as Gaelic learner education . . . and Gaelic awareness'. One of the priorities identified in the plan is the recruitment of 'a confident, appropriately trained workforce'. The GTCS will be a key partner in this and will play a prominent part in delivering some of the main recommendations in the aforementioned Action Group Report, including expansion of new routes into Gaelic teaching and implementation of the GTC Report of 1999 on Gaelic-medium education.

While the growth in Gaelic-medium education in the past twenty-five years has been remarkable, significant challenges lie ahead. One of these will be to deliver the ambitious aim in the National Plan of doubling by 2017 the number of children entering Gaelic-medium education from a baseline of 400 in 2011–12. The growth experienced by the all-Gaelic schools in Glasgow and Inverness and the opening of similar schools in other centres of population will go some way towards that goal. However, these advances in urban areas have not been matched in rural areas of the Highlands and Islands. Indeed, requests by parents in communities in Skye, the Uists and Lewis and in Morar to establish dedicated Gaelic schools in these localities have been frustrated by local opposition, much of it orchestrated by strident anti-Gaelic elements in the wider community. The creation of Gaelic schools in dispersed rural areas remains more problematic than in urban centres and it is an issue which Bòrd na Gàidhlig will have to resolve in its engagement with local authorities during production of their language plans.

Good practice in maximising the use of the language as the vehicle of instruction needs to be more uniformly adopted if the target of attaining communicative competence in both languages by the end of primary school is to be achieved. While nursery education is now much better integrated with primary provision, properly planned progression across all sectors of Gaelic-medium education remains an aspiration. In particular, the issues around the primary/secondary interface that lead to a halving in the number of pupils following the Gaelic-medium curriculum in secondary have yet to be resolved. The planning process should be informed by the experience and expertise available in Wales and Ireland where similar problems have been encountered and addressed.

Access to the language and culture should not be confined to the Gaelic-medium sector. Over 90 per cent of secondary school children in Scotland are denied the opportunity to learn Gaelic in their local school. Research, attitudinal surveys, audience figures for learners' programmes on television and the uptake of learners' classes in continuing and higher education all suggest that there is considerable potential for the development of provision for learners within secondary schools. The National Plan recognises the need to expand Gaelic learning in the school, college and university sectors and in informal settings.

Celtic and Gaelic elements of Scottish heritage, life and culture continue to be neglected in Scottish schools and it is an indictment of the education system that so few pupils have any awareness of Celtic civilisation and Gaelic culture. A Working Group set up by the Scottish Government has recommended that Scottish Studies should be embedded in the curriculum and that a new qualification in the subject should be introduced. It is hoped this new initiative will be sufficiently cross-curricular and cross-sectoral to ensure that all pupils in Scotland are informed about the Gaelic element of their heritage at some stage of their schooling.

REFERENCES

Bòrd na Gàidhlig (2011) *The National Gaelic Language Plan 2012–17: Growth and Quality.* Inverness: Bòrd na Gàidhlig.

Curriculum for Excellence (2011) *Gaelic Excellence Group Report.* Glasgow: Education Scotland.

Her Majesty's Inspectorate of Education (2011) *Gaelic Education: Building on the Successes, Addressing the Barriers.* Livingston: Her Majesty's Inspectorate of Education.

Her Majesty's Inspectors of Schools (2005) *Improving Achievement in Gaelic.* Edinburgh: Scottish Office Education Department.

Johnstone, R. (1999) *The Attainments of Pupils Receiving Gaelic Medium Primary Education in Scotland.* Stirling: Scottish Centre for Information on Language Teaching and Research.

Nicolson, M. and M. MacIver (eds) (2003) *Gaelic Medium Education: Policy and Practice in Education 10.* Edinburgh: Dunedin Academic Press.

O'Hanlon, F., W. McLeod and L. Paterson (2010) *Gaelic-medium Education in Scotland: Choice and Attainment at the Primary and Early Secondary Stages.* Inverness: Bòrd na Gàidhlig.

Robertson, B. (2013) *Gaelic: The Gaelic language in education in the UK.* Leeuwarden: Mercator-Education.

26

The Scots Language in Education

Liz Niven

THE SCOTS LANGUAGE – ITS HISTORY AND DEVELOPMENT

Scots is an Indo-European language descended from a northern form of Anglo-Saxon. By the seventh century AD, this Germanic branch of the language had reached the south-east of what is now Scotland and by the eleventh century AD was firmly established across central and southern Scotland. In addition to such Anglo-Saxon vocabulary as *bairns*, *thrawn*, *bide* and *byre*, strong Scandinavian, French and Dutch influences can still be heard in words such as *lass*, *lug*, *lowse*, *braw*, *douce*, *fash*, *scone* and *redd*. Latin remains in, for example, *janitor* and *dux*; Irish and Scots Gaelic have provided further lexical items such as *ben*, *glen* and *strath*. Thus, as with the English language, contact with other countries and the legacy of loan words from several nations have contributed to the formation of the Scots language.

Much written Scots was produced in the late-fourteenth-century court of James IV by the King's commissioned poets and dramatists, and by the early sixteenth century Scots was developing as an all-purpose national language. This was the nearest Scots came to adopting a written standard, accepted on equal terms, with other European languages. However, English began to wield greater influence around the time of the Reformation in 1560 when the Geneva Bible was translated into English rather than Scots. Anglicisation increased, particularly among the Scots nobility, after the departure of James VI to London and the Union of the Crowns in 1603. Finally, after the Treaty of Union in 1707, English became the official language of government and of the court, even though Scots was almost universally spoken throughout lowland, central and north-east Scotland, and Gaelic in the Highlands and Islands.

CONTEMPORARY SCOTS

Contemporary spoken Scots embraces a wide variation in language on a continuum from Scottish Standard English to broad Scots. The possible range of pronunciation, vocabulary, grammar and idiom is extensive, and nuances can be so subtle that its speakers are often unaware that they are not actually speaking English. While examples of overt Scots might be demonstrated in vocabulary such as *aye* or *wee*, *kye* or *yowe*, covert Scots might be employed in the use of words such as *pinkie* or *outwith*. In some situations, words have different meanings in English than in Scots. For example, 'a chap at the door' or 'going for the messages' are common Scottish phrases with a different meaning when spoken by English speakers.

Similarly, grammatical constructions such as the use of the indefinite article and possessive pronoun ('I have the flu and I'm away to my bed' rather than 'I have flu and I am going to bed') are typically Scottish while the use of 'yous' as a second person plural pronoun emulates the 'vous' of French grammar. Yet these are often regarded as 'bad grammar' rather than examples of legitimate Scots. A good description of contemporary Scots is supplied in *Understanding Grammar in Scotland Today* (2009):

> Broadly speaking, we can argue that part of that history involves contact between two distinct language varieties – Broad Scots and standard Southern English – a contact that eventually created a third variety: Scottish English. Language users in Scotland can make use of any of these three varieties.

Frequently, speakers will codeswitch and shift between speech forms depending on their audience and purpose. The Scottish writer Andrew Greig succinctly expresses this in his novel *Electric Brae*:

> His accent was moving in and out of focus like his finger. Who are we? I wondered. We don't even speak consistently. We'll say 'yes' and 'aye' in the same conversation, alternate between 'know' and 'ken', 'bairn' and 'wean' and 'child' and not even know why. Even the old man did it, and I've lost half his tongue, the better half. We're a small country with blurry boundaries.

SCOTS – LANGUAGE OR DIALECT?

The Mercator-Education Dossier, *The Scots Language in Education in Scotland*, states:

> One of the greatest barriers to Scots being acknowledged as a distinct language in Scotland is its close proximity to English. As both are Germanic languages, from a common root and sharing much vocabulary, modern Scots tends to exist on a continuum with broad Scots at one end and Scottish Standard English (SSE) at the other. This situation is roughly similar to the continuum that exists in Dutch/German and Danish/Norwegian. No controversy exists with these languages in establishing whether they are dialects or languages.

The Scottish Language Dictionaries list ten dialect areas. All have their own particular pronunciation and dialect variations. For example, 'good' might be written and pronounced as *guid* or *geed* or *gweed*. Opinions vary widely as to whether an agreed written standard is desirable; some creative writers and readers fear a dilution in individuality while some language activists would prefer an agreed written language, not necessarily spoken by any particular region of the country. The argument as to whether Scots is a language or a dialect frequently provides a diversion from productive discussion about Scots language issues. However, several factors contribute to a widespread belief that Scots is indeed a language: it is widely spoken throughout Scotland; it has all the elements of a language (that is, accent, dialects, grammar, idiom); it has a clear geographical boundary within a nation state; and it has a centuries-old pedigree in literature. The only missing element is the lack of a standardised written form.

COMMON PERCEPTIONS OF SCOTS

The perception of Scots as an inferior version of English has led to its lack of official recognition, as well as confused and conflicting attitudes. Worryingly, it is often those who are themselves Scots speakers who perceive their voice as less acceptable. Various studies, mostly university based, have been conducted on attitudes towards Scots. When interviewed, a vast number of speakers refer to their speech as slang rather than Scots. The implications of these beliefs for Scottish national identity are considerable. In a study of Glasgow dialect it was noted that:

> To move into the realms of 'proper' speech holds national significance as well as class significance for the Scot. Even if the English dialect speaker takes lessons to perfect an RP accent, he will still be English. If the Scot does this, he may throw away more in the loss of an outward, recognisable national identity . . . both may disguise their regional origins but only one belies his national identity. Yet many Scots speakers continue to feel inferior about their voice thus perpetuating the phenomenon kent as The Scottish Cringe. (Janet Menzies, *An Investigation of Attitudes to Scots and Glasgow Dialect Among Secondary School Pupils*, p. 3: www.arts.gla.ac.uk/STELLA/STARN/lang/MENZIES/menzie1.htm)

OFFICIAL ATTITUDES

The gathering of accurate statistics has, until recent years, been unsatisfactory and inadequate. However, trial questions for the 2001 National Census revealed that there are at least 1.5 million Scots speakers while an Aberdeen University study (whose questions were more detailed, including prompts as to specific dialects of Scots) suggested a figure nearer 3 million. In 2010, a Scottish Government survey was conducted, entitled Public Attitudes towards the Scots Language. The findings revealed that:

- 55 per cent believe Scots should be taught in schools; 29 per cent do not.
- 56 per cent agree that Scots has educational benefits for children.
- 85 per cent say they speak Scots, 43 per cent 'a lot/fairly often'.
- 64 per cent agree that 'I don't really think of Scots as a language – it's more just a way of speaking'.
- 63 per cent disagree with the statement that Scots 'doesn't sound nice – it's slang'.
- 86 per cent agree that Scots is an important part of Scottish culture. (www.scotland.gov.uk/Publications/2010/01/06105123/0)

In response to the government survey, a National Survey of Teacher Attitudes to Scots Language in Curriculum for Excellence was compiled by the Education Sub-Committee of the Cross Party Group on the Scots language. Two hundred and six teachers and other education professionals responded to the survey. When asked, 'What place should Scots have in Curriculum for Excellence?', 72 per cent of primary respondents and 58 per cent of secondary agreed that it should be used across learning. Among education professionals, the survey demonstrated that a large majority believes Scots is an important part of Scottish culture (82 per cent primary, 76 per cent secondary). Further, 64 per cent of primary teachers were confident in teaching Scots, but only 44 per cent of secondary teachers were. There was some feeling amongst secondary schools that no additional help or support was needed and the current position should be maintained. Some secondary teachers are already comfortable with teaching Scots as part of their subject and felt individual teachers should have a choice about whether they use texts in Scots or not.

The National Census in 2011 introduced Scots into the Language section and a question was asked regarding whether an individual could 'Speak, Understand, Read or Write

English, Scottish Gaelic or Scots'. A further question asked, 'Do you use a language other than English at home?' with the invitation to 'Tick all that apply'. Although there would be individuals uncertain whether their language was Scots, the inclusion of Scots into the question, and alongside Gaelic, was a watershed moment. The confusion for some individuals accepting that their language was a form of Scots might have prevented an accurate statistical record from being formed. Figures are still being processed but the Census demonstrates an official approach by the government to collate statistics about the language.

At an anecdotal level, much more Scots across the continuum is heard at all levels of society both formal and informal. Scottish voices are evident in the media though their distinctiveness lies more often in their strong accents rather than in the use of vocabulary and grammar. Spoken Scots is heard in radio and television interviews conducted with the public although the voice of the interviewer tends to remain Scottish-accented English.

The formation of a Cross Party Group for Scots Language in the Parliament seemed to indicate positive support for the language at a national level. This group has compiled a Statement of Linguistic Rights for Scots. The Scottish Government also maintains a website outlining its support for the language, and in 2001 the United Kingdom government ratified the Charter for Minority Languages for Scots. Theoretically, this supports several practical conditions for Scots language in education, notably 'the provision of appropriate forms and means for the teaching and study of regional or minority languages at all appropriate stages'. Nevertheless, a parliamentary response stated in early 2002 that the Executive 'does not consider that any action is necessary to comply with the European Charter for Regional or Minority Languages' and 'has not formulated any policy on the numbers of speakers of Scots'. However, in November 2002, the Executive adopted the McGuigan Report which recommends increased support for Scots.

SCOTS IN EDUCATION – POLICY

Official attitudes have altered since an early schools inspector observed that Scots 'is not the language of educated people anywhere'. More recently, Her Majesty's Inspector of Schools' report on English in the series *Effective Learning and Teaching in Scottish Secondary Schools* (1992) stated that 'it should be the aim of English teaching throughout the secondary school to develop the capacity of every pupil to use, understand and appreciate the native language in its Scots and English forms'. The 1990s also saw some supportive statements about Scots in the curriculum in several 5–14 documents, primarily in English language. In the section devoted to Scottish culture, it stated:

> The first tasks of schools are therefore to enable pupils to be confident and creative in this language and to begin to develop notions of language diversity, within which pupils can appreciate the range of accents, dialects and languages they encounter. This will involve teachers in valuing pupils' spoken language, and introducing them to stories, poems and other texts which use dialect in a positive way.

Curriculum for Excellence (CfE) replaced the 5–14 National Guidelines, with phased implementation required by 2010. A reference to Scots language and literature in CfE appears in the Principles and Practice document and while positive and supportive it is not an extensive statement. Interestingly, the final draft of the experiences and outcomes for Literacy and English cut the explicit references to Scots language and texts in every outcome – making, according to Maureen Farrell, a teacher-education lecturer, 'the permeation of Scots Language and Literature throughout the curriculum of every school, a somewhat unlikely possibility'. There are no other references relating to Scots in the document's statements about literacy although Scotland's other indigenous language, Gaelic, is given consideration in parallel to English and Modern Languages.

Since the 2011 amalgamation of Her Majesty's Inspectorate of Education (HMIE) and Learning and Teaching Scotland (LTS) into the new body, Education Scotland, a series of five in-service days have been offered 'to support teachers who have little knowledge of teaching Scots'. It remains to be seen if this positive development will continue and begin to remedy the continuing situation whereby many Scottish teachers, families and pupils remain illiterate and lacking in confidence and knowledge about their own language. Writing and reading in Scots remain at a minimal level, and at the whim of an interested teacher or a supportive local authority. Retaining explicit references to Scots in the Literacy outcomes would have given a *heeze up* to the language as well as an indication to schools that there can be literacy in Scots.

Although there are positive statements, and information about the language in other areas of CfE, there is still an overall sense of the need to 'sell' its inclusion in the curriculum rather than treat it in the same way as English language is viewed. In 'Knowledge of Language', the entry heading for English lists, 'Parts of speech, punctuation, grammar and syntax', whereas Scots does not. Its heading summarises thus: 'An essential introduction to the Scots language with information on its history, dialects, its role in education and how to incorporate Scots into teaching across the curriculum'. While there is clearly now information and support for Scots in CfE, Scots still requires special treatment different from English. Perhaps similar listings of 'Parts of speech, punctuation, grammar and syntax' might be included in the next updated CfE, indicating that Scots has achieved parity with English language and does not require justification of its 'role in education'.

Scots language and literature have been included in the examination syllabus. Candidates are encouraged to 'write in Scots where appropriate' as part of their creative writing paper at Higher Level. (While there is no specific advice in the guidelines, it has always been possible to do this at Standard Grade.) In 1997, it was eventually agreed that the study of a Scottish text would be compulsory in the Higher Still curriculum. This directive was rescinded in 2005, although the report for that year does record that a significant number of texts chosen for assessment are Scottish texts. The latest advice for the Higher exams suggests that 'candidates should study at least one Scottish text, or in the case of poetry a group of short texts'. This does not have to be assessed and therefore may not really be binding in any meaningful way. It also need not be a text in Scots language. However, the Minister for Education announced in 2012 that there will again be a mandatory Scottish text at Higher Level. The introduction of an optional Scottish Language paper at Advanced Higher Level in 2000 allowed candidates to select from topics such as the use of Scots in contemporary literature, the difference between the Scots of young and old people, and the use of Scots in the media. The topic headings for this paper, Advanced Higher Language and Communication, continue to include the use of Scots in contemporary literature, but the topics on history and varieties of Scots have been amalgamated with English language.

A further question is now included on multiculturalism in contemporary Scotland, which allows candidates to comment on the government's linguistic policies or to analyse codeswitching and conversation among multilinguals in Scotland. However, in the ten years since the exam's inception, very few pupils have been presented for it. Teachers indicate that, apart from the usual school timetabling constraints, there is a general lack of knowledge and confidence about Scots language issues. Unless this situation is addressed, teachers are unlikely to begin presenting pupils for the Scottish language options at Advanced Higher Level.

SCOTS IN EDUCATION – PRACTICE

Policies, then, seem to be more positive, but in practice it would be fair to say that the experience of any individual child will depend very much on the teacher's attitude to the Scots language. In some primary schools the situation is similar to that described by Robert Tyson in *Scots Language: Its Place in Education* (Chapter 6, 'Scots language in the Classroom: Viewpoint 1', pp. 71–5) where Scots language and culture is an everyday feature of the whole school experience of the pupils. Across the country now, more teachers, particularly primary, are including Scots literature, celebrating St Andrew's Day, printing signs around the school in Scots as well as English, compiling local dictionaries of Scots. However, in many primary schools Scots features only in the study of poetry and prose and in some places that still means learning a poem for Burns night but seeing no other Scots throughout the year. Similarly, in secondary English departments, listening to, reading, writing and speaking in Scots are part of each day's experience in some classrooms, while next door there can be teachers who feel they have to 'get through' at least one Scottish text at Higher, and that is not necessarily one written in Scots. Some experienced teachers of Scots in secondary English are seeking new resources and approaches for direct use in the classroom and look forward to a situation where Scots is confidently established in the secondary curriculum.

Many teachers across Scotland have reported improvements in levels of attainment and attitude among their pupils as a direct result of building more Scots language into their programmes of study. In the 2010 Scots in Schools survey, responses to the question 'Are there any benefits to teaching Scots in schools?' indicated that 67 per cent felt that Scots valued the child's home language, 53 per cent thought that it engaged and motivated children and 46 per cent believed that it helped to produce confident individuals and responsible citizens, compared with just 1 per cent who felt there were no benefits and 6 per cent who felt that it caused confusion.

Teacher education institutions (TEIs), hampered by ever-shortening contact time with students, include some discussion about Scots within language and literature classes. Some students select Scots language as their area for specialist study and a few TEIs include lectures and suggest resources. However, as long as there is no compulsory study of Scots language and literature for all teachers in training, practitioners with limited knowledge about and confidence in these areas will continue to appear in the classroom, thus perpetuating the current anomalous situation.

SCOTS LITERATURE

One area where Scots is alive and vigorously kicking is in contemporary literature. As has been stated previously, Scotland has a rich literary heritage, much of it in Scots, and in the early part of the twentieth century, the so-called 'Scottish Renaissance' is well represented by poets such as Hugh MacDiarmid (who observed in 1958 that 'if Scottish writers use English, they must be content to play a very subordinate role') and prose writers like Nan

Shepherd and Lewis Grassic Gibbon (the latter of whom stated that Scots would 'adorn his meaning with a richness, a clarity and a conciseness impossible in orthodox English'). In the latter part of the twentieth and into the twenty-first century, a similar resurgence has been noted, resulting in a clear confidence in the way that writers use the languages of Scotland in whatever forms they choose, whether these languages are English, Scots, Gaelic, Punjabi or a mixture of these or any other languages heard in Scotland. Also there is renewed interest in and respect for writing in Scots. James Kelman's Booker Prize for *How Late It Was, How Late*, and the international reputation of *Trainspotting* by Irvine Welsh are two of the most obvious examples of this, but there is an increasing appetite by publishers, reviewers and translators outwith Scotland for Scots writing. Members of the Association for Scottish Literary Studies annually attend American Literature Conventions and report a healthy interest in Scottish writing. This can only have a positive effect on the perceptions of the Scottish people, especially young people.

EDUCATIONAL RESOURCES

The existence of suitable resources with which to teach Scots language and literature is crucial, especially since many teachers have not had specific or thorough training in these areas. Increased burdens of assessment have meant that teachers have less time to prepare new materials and therefore look to texts that have commercially or centrally produced worksheets for them. This has tended to favour texts in standard English and it is clear from the publishing experiences of the last twenty years that the production of curricular materials for Scots language is an ongoing problem. Commercial British publishers have been reluctant to produce materials for a relatively small market while the few Scottish publications emerging over the last twenty years have been faced with the dilemma of short print runs followed by out-of-print titles in a very short space of time. A major example of this short-sightedness can be seen in the 1996 model of *The Kist/A Chiste*, published collaboratively by LTS and commercial publishers Nelson Blackie. A richly produced anthology of Scots and Gaelic texts with two photocopiable worksheet booklets, a teachers' handbook and a complete set of audio tapes of all the texts, despite having been awarded the *TESS/Saltire Education* prize, have been allowed to go out of print. Only the anthology remains in print from Education Scotland, formerly LTS, Nelson Blackie having opted out. However, Education Scotland are currently digitising some of the resources.

Building on good resources and heightened awareness of Scots language issues raised in the early 1990s, to support the 5–14 programme, a new publisher emerged. The Itchy Coo project, in its first ten years from 2002 to 2011, working with Edinburgh-based Black & White Publishing, created a range of quality books in Scots, mostly for young readers and pre-school children. They also developed an outreach and education role, taking Scots into schools and libraries, and acted as advocates and consultants for the development of Scots language policies in different institutions and organisations, including local and national government. The outreach, education and advocacy parts of Itchy Coo ended in 2011. The publishing side of the project continues, and it is likely that two or three titles will be added to the list annually from 2012 onwards. The success of the project demonstrated that there is a great demand for books in Scots, and that children, young readers and adults would respond enthusiastically to material in Scots, especially if the production values of the books were as high as equivalent publications in English and other languages.

Another example of an out-of-print high-quality resource is the five-part Channel 4 series of programmes, *Haud Yer Tongue*, originally available on video tape and accompanied by a teacher's book of curricular activities. Also noteworthy is the TES/Saltire award-winning textbook, *Turnstones 1*, the first of a series for secondary English departments published by Hodder & Stoughton. It integrated Scots and English in poetry, prose and drama-related work as well as exercises in debating skills and formal language skills. One of the advantages of this series is that the work is in both Scots and English, which means it is a highly flexible resource. Like *The Kist*, *Turnstones* also addressed the issue of the lack of confidence that prevents some teachers from using Scots materials, since it provided a clear framework and extensive glossary, with teacher's notes available on an accompanying CD. Despite repeated requests from informed educationists all the above materials and initiatives have become unsupported and unobtainable.

The Association of Scottish Literary Studies, based at Glasgow University, has supported and published texts in Scots for many years. They state that they don't have a fixed policy on Scots language but simply see it as their duty to promote it at all times. They do always try to have at least one language paper in their annual conference and have published Scotnotes on a wide variety of Scots texts suitable for school use. They have also produced CDs and published John Corbett's *Understanding Grammar in Scotland Today* which is an excellent text book for teachers and pupils seeking an informative linguistic analysis of the language.

Scottish Language Dictionaries (SLD), government-funded by an annual £200,000, produces Scots dictionaries, classroom-related materials, interactive language activities, a grammar workbook and a website for education entitled the Scuil Wab. There is a dedicated Education Officer with a remit to maintain and develop resources and run workshops for staff and pupils. Education Scotland has provided support notes and bibliographies for Scots language elements of Higher Still English and Communication. Support from such bodies or the ring-fencing of funds for Scots language resources (paralleled in other countries with minority languages) would still seem to be necessary if the curriculum demands resources. A major factor in determining how much demand there actually is for Scots language teaching materials is the influence of the Scottish Government. This remains ambivalent in practice although there are increasingly supportive statements in documents. The Minister-led Scottish Studies Working Group has proposed the development of a national online resource, Studying Scotland, which will 'include exploration of the means of providing a greater focus on Scots'. It seems that public subsidy in some form will continue to be necessary for some time to come, if Scots language books are to be enabled to compete fairly in the marketplace against English language books with their vastly greater economies of scale.

CLASSROOM PRACTICE

How is this material used in the classroom? A typical starting point for many teachers in both primary and the early stages of secondary is to introduce poetry in Scots, often in the variety most familiar to the area. The focus is often on encouraging pupils to become more comfortable reading in Scots. Depending on their previous experience, some pupils will have already seen written Scots and may find it easier to read than English, while for others it will be unfamiliar.

Another typical lesson is to increase vocabulary using word banks and dictionaries. One of the most important points about this apparently very simple exercise is that it shows pupils that Scots words are actually words in their own right, not simply corruptions of English. Knowledge about language, grammar and linguistic concepts can all be taught through the medium of Scots. Opportunities for pupils to write in Scots would usually be offered, and, depending on the confidence and experience of pupils (and perhaps the teacher), this may take the form of a dialogue or short play.

Often the greatest challenge pupils find in writing Scots is how to spell it. Since there is no standardised version of Scots spelling, this can provoke anxiety in both teachers and pupils, as correct spelling is a cornerstone of learning to write. The use of a Scots dictionary can help, offering various spellings from which a pupil may choose the one nearest to the form of Scots he or she wishes to write. However, for some children the dictionary can be a hindrance, particularly if they are, perhaps for the first time, writing in their own 'voice', and teachers may wish to suggest that the pupil leaves the dictionary aside until he or she has written that voice in what seems the most appropriate way. In fact the process of writing in Scots, and the linguistic and cultural questions that arise from such lessons, provide opportunities for highly sophisticated language issues to be aired and discussed.

At later stages, models of increasing sophistication will be used and while poetry is still popular, there are increased opportunities for studying work in drama and prose. Prose fiction still tends to be represented by short stories, and it is an example of the increasingly established position of Scots in the curriculum that anthologies of short stories produced specifically for use in schools (such as the *Heinemann New Windmill Book of Scottish Short Stories*) now include a far greater proportion of stories in Scots than was the case even ten years ago.

SCOTS LITERATURE VERSUS SCOTS LANGUAGE?

However much user-friendly Scots material becomes available in classrooms and however many policy documents are produced supporting Scots, is it the case that, while Scots literature is acceptable in the classroom, Scots language is still barely tolerated? Scots is the first language of many pupils (and often the second language of many whose first language is other than English) and, informally, many teachers in both primary and secondary classrooms (of all subject areas) may speak Scots or use Scots vocabulary or grammatical constructions. But the prevailing perception of Scots as an 'inferior' version of English, fit perhaps for comedy programmes or the intimacy of family life but not for the serious, public face of language, means that very few would actually teach lessons in Scots, even when the lesson is about Scots. And it is still the case that pupils may be corrected if they speak Scots in the classroom, thus breaching linguistic rights outlined in the UK-ratified Charter for European Minority Languages.

> Since English is perceived as the most important of the languages of Scotland, some questions continue to raise their heads. Does encouraging pupils to become fluent in Scots in some way hamper their ability to communicate in English? Does time spent on Scots language activities mean less time available to teach them standard English? Research suggests that those who are fluent in their mother tongue and whose linguistic competences are developed in that language are more easily able to learn other languages.

This parallels the experience of other bilingual children in Scotland, those who are speakers of community languages such as Punjabi and Urdu. In fact, many of the conclusions of the authors of *Education of Minority Ethnic Groups in Scotland: A Review of Research* (Powney, McPake, Hall and Lyall, SCRE, 1998) could apply to those children who are Scots speakers.

> While many different languages are spoken by some pupils in Scotland, there is little research investigating the effects of bilingualism on learning. More attention has been paid to provision of English as a Second Language (ESL) than to providing opportunities for pupils to develop their skills in community languages. Bilingualism has been shown to have positive effects on children's educational development. However American research suggests that failure to develop children's skills in both languages can have detrimental effects. In the UK, bilingual education for Welsh and Gaelic speakers is well established but has never been a serious proposition for bilingual children from minority ethnic backgrounds. (p. 2)

Not only has Scots-medium education never been a serious proposition, but many parents and some teachers seem to feel that teaching pupils in their own language and about their own language will actually disadvantage them. The cultural and historical reasons why this is so have been discussed above.

PROSPECTS

It continues to be difficult to predict the future prospects for the Scots language in education. On the one hand it would seem to be optimistic given the re-establishment of a Scottish Parliament and its inclusion of a Cross Party Group for the language. However, in 2000, the Scottish Executive published its National Cultural Strategy in which support for Scots language and culture seemed lacklustre seen in the light of its highly supportive stance towards Gaelic culture. There continue to be major difficulties for Scots to become accepted at a formal level. Some consider that the lack of standardisation of the written language is a drawback and its non-inclusion in the judiciary or in parliamentary documents prevents its ratification by the European Charter of Minority Languages, which would give it greater status and protection.

A government response from the Minister for Skills and Learning, dated 29 November 2012, included the following statement:

> The Scots language is an integral part of Scotland's distinctive culture and heritage and the Scottish Government has taken a number of important steps to improve its use and status in a variety of settings, based on research evidence, with a particular focus on its place in education. The Scottish Government is making progress with a number of the recommendations of the Scots Language Working Group. Key responses were to establish a network of Scots Language Co-ordinators and to establish a new concept of 'Scottish Studies' in schools and progress is being made with both these recommendations. A number of the recommendations of the working group are not within the remit of the Scottish Government but they have been drawn to the attention of the relevant bodies. We also currently provide £70,000 per annum to the Scots Language Centre and £200,000 per annum to the Scottish Language Dictionaries.

The Ministerial Working Group on Scots Language published its report in November 2010. Among the key recommendations it lists is the development of a Scots language policy to be enshrined in an Act of Parliament. It also notes that development in the area of education requires the most urgent action because the lack of resources and priority for Scots in education 'endangers all recent progress'. The report records that CfE provides a promising environment for Scots but also suggests that there is now an opportunity for the development of a permanent dedicated Scots language bureau to meet the growing demand for training and resource development. The report calls for dedicated Scots language coordinators and an educational website, and indicates that regional dialect diversity should be integral to education policy. It also stipulates that Scots language should form part of all initial teacher education courses.

In August 2011, the Scottish Government set up a working group, convened by the Minister for Learning and Skills. The group's remit was to provide strategic advice and direction to support the development of Scottish Studies in schools. A distinct strand of learning focused on Scotland and incorporating Scottish history, literature, Scots and Gaelic languages, wider Scottish culture and Scottish current affairs was proposed. Pupils at all levels would have access to this subject, though the working group pointed out that the focus of this will avoid marginalisation of Scottish learning. As a result of this report, the Studying Scotland website is now under development.

The Goring Report on Scots Language and Literature in CfE was published in February 2010. It calls literature 'one of Scotland's finest indigenous arts', going on to say that 'a thriving literary culture is an important element in the wellbeing of the nation'. The report's main recommendations include the establishment of a Scottish Academy of Literature; a compulsory question at Higher; and the commissioning of a national policy for children's literature. The study of literature in Scots would seem, then, to be recognised as an 'important element' of the school curriculum, but the status and nourishment of the language as the medium of education is rarely referred to with such enthusiasm.

Working groups such as the current Scottish Studies group and the recent Ministerial Scots Language group indicate at least a willingness to recognise and discuss the language. Education Scotland has responded by offering a series of in-service days to teachers on the use of Scots as well as holding Learning about Scotland conferences, and the General Teaching Council for Scotland (GTCS), prompted by the Cross Party Scots Language Group, has awarded certificates to a number of teachers including Scots in their classroom teaching. However, it remains to be seen whether the recommendations of any of these groups will be backed by substantial financial support and steps taken to consolidate and develop resources and staff for schools and teacher training institutions.

Judging by the language's ability to survive in its rich diversity of forms across the country, despite centuries of difficulties and obstacles in both education and official circles, it might be accurate to predict its future prospects as being highly optimistic. Its greatest hope of survival might be in its proximity to the English language and thus its adaptability to contemporary needs. Greater public awareness of Scots in its twenty-first-century forms and clearer support from the Scots-speaking public might be required to bring about increased inclusion in education. However, this may well require more knowledge about Scots language in the curriculum to raise the status of the Scots language in the minds of Scots themselves.

In a typically democratic manner, the fate of Scots language will probably be decided by the Scottish people and not imposed from above. However, many educationalists and activists, aware of the implications of language repression, would prefer to see a more concerted structured approach with language maintenance and planning debated at a national level. It would seem that the Scottish Government, the Scottish education system, its teachers and pupils as well as the latter's parents are still uncertain as to how to proceed with their treatment of twenty-first-century Scots language. On the one hand, there is widespread support for the inclusion (though not necessarily compulsory) of Scots literature in the curriculum.

On the other hand, there is still unease about the encouragement of spoken Scots in education and in formal society. The puzzle remains: why is there such reluctance about the value or the consequences of 'allowing' a nation to hear and cultivate its own voice? Meanwhile, between 1.5 million and 3 million Scottish people continue to speak the language at some point on the linguistic continuum.

POSTSCRIPT

As this text was going to press (Spring 2013), Education Scotland sought applications for *Scots Language Coordinators* (twenty-three-month secondments). Coordinators will:

> work with the Scottish Government and other key organisations to establish a vision for the national development of the Scots language within Scottish education. Working with education authorities and schools, Co-ordinators will provide support in developing learning, teaching and assessment that provides progressive and coherent learning of the Scots languages across the four contexts of 3–18 learning.

REFERENCES

Corbett, J. (1997) *Language and Scottish Literature*. Edinburgh: Edinburgh University Press.

Corbett, J. and C. Kay (2009) *Understanding Grammar In Scotland Today*. Glasgow: ASLS.

Education Scotland (2009) *Curriculum for Excellence*. Edinburgh: Education Scotland.

Hodgart, J. (2010) 'Scots and the Curriculum for Excellence'. Paper for Scots Language Centre, Perth.

Kay, B. (1986) *Scots the Mither Tongue*, Darvel: Alloway Publishing.

McClure, J. D. (1988) *Why Scots Matters*. Edinburgh: Saltire Society.

Niven, L. (2002) *The Scots Language in Education in Scotland*. Lijourt: Mercator-Education: European Network for Regional or Minority Languages and Education.

Niven, L. and R. Jackson (eds) (1998) *Scots Language its Place in Education*. Newton Stewart: Watergaw.

Scottish Government (2010) *Public Attitudes Towards the Scots Language*. Online at www.scotland.gov.uk/Publications/2010/01/06105123/0

Scottish Office Education Department (1991) *5–14 National Guidelines English Language*. Edinburgh: Her Majesty's Stationery Office.

Websites

Dictionary of the Scots Language at www.dsl.ac.uk

Education Scotland at www.educationscotland.gov.uk

Scottish Government at www.scotland.gov.uk

Scottish Language Dictionaries at www.scotsdictionaries.org.uk

Scots Language Centre at www.scotslanguage.com

Scuil Wab at www.scuilwab.org.uk

27

Catholic Education in Scotland

Stephen J. McKinney

This chapter on Catholic education focuses on the contemporary position and continued existence of state-funded Catholic schools in Scotland. It begins by briefly exploring a variety of issues concerning the conceptualisation of the debate: explaining terminology; arguing that the debate concerning Catholic schools is not conducted within a cultural and historical vacuum; and that, within the discussion, the identification of various forms of *insider* status is imperative to understand fully the complexity and the limitations of the debate. The chapter then locates Catholic schools within a broader examination of the contemporary faith schools debate that has emerged in England and Wales. It continues by offering a brief sketch of the history of Catholic schools, discusses the contemporary rationale for Catholic schools as articulated by the Catholic Church and examines the current provision of Catholic schools and Catholic support systems. Finally, the chapter examines the contemporary challenges and opportunities that emerge from this debate concerning Catholic schools.

PRELIMINARY REMARKS

The history of Catholic schools and the associated histories of the Catholic Church and the Catholic community in Scotland are complex, and nomenclature can be ambiguous and confusing. For the purposes of this chapter, 'the Catholic Church' will refer to the Roman Catholic Church led by the Catholic hierarchy and also to the Scottish Catholic Church. The expression 'the Catholic community' will refer to all those who claim some form of link or allegiance to Catholicism in Scotland but who will have a wide variety of interpretations of Catholic identity that may consist of religious, national, cultural or even secular elements – or combinations of these elements. One of the interesting features of Catholic schools in Scotland is that, apart from sacramental and liturgical celebrations in Catholic churches, the Catholic school may be the main, if not the only, meeting point for the full range of the Catholic community.

An important feature of the discussion and study of Catholic schools in Scotland is the status of those engaged in this discussion. With one or two notable exceptions the majority of academics writing about Catholic schools in Scotland, certainly those supporting Catholic schools, come from, or have some association with, the Catholic community in Scotland (e.g. Fitzpatrick, McKinney, O'Hagan). This means that they have some form of insider status, and can be considered by others to share certain preconceived views, be uncritically supportive of Catholic schools and possibly defensive of the position of Catholic schools in Scottish education and society. On the other hand, these academics, motivated by their insider status, are probably the only academics with the impetus and interest to research Catholic schooling in Scotland in any depth and, by doing so, add to the body of knowledge concerning this topic – a topic that is highly relevant to Scottish education and society. There are signs that academics are becoming increasingly aware of the implications of this insider status and acknowledging that it does entail a particular perspective but they also recognise the advantages of this insider status. Arguably, some of the academics who are opposed to Catholic schools also have some form of insider status, coming from a particular educational, sociological or philosophical perspective that has its own internal dialogues or discourses, shared opinions and degrees of conformity to accepted norms of beliefs. Therefore the notions of insider status and insider views are useful in that they challenge us to be critically aware of our preconceived views and intellectual standpoint as we engage with the issues of Catholic schools in Scotland and faith schools in general.

The academic discussions of Catholic schooling in Scotland are only one element of the debate. The issues surrounding Catholic schools in Scotland are aired, like many debates concerning Scottish education, in a variety of arenas and are frequently the object of media attention and often presented as a 'controversial' issue in the popular press. Yet the debate touches on complex interconnected issues of religion, philosophy, education, culture and society that should not be trivialised or sensationalised. The academic approach, while following the media debate closely, has a responsibility to pose deeper questions and to engage with the complexity of issues that emerge from these questions and, where appropriate, challenge the media debate to engage at a deeper level.

CONTEMPORARY FAITH SCHOOLS IN SCOTLAND

Catholic schools are not unique to Scotland, because there are Catholic schools, constructed on similar lines, in England and in other Western English-speaking countries (such as Australia, Canada and New Zealand), though they may not all be fully state-funded. Catholic schools are uniquely placed in Scotland, however, because, with a few exceptions, they are the only form of state-funded faith schooling in Scotland. According to the Scottish Catholic Education Service (SCES) website, there are 370 Catholic state-funded schools in Scotland. There is also a Jewish primary school (Calderwood Lodge) and a small number of Episcopalian schools (McKinney, 2008a). Calderwood Lodge, however, is the only Jewish school in Scotland and the links between the Episcopalian schools and the Episcopalian Church appear tenuous, apart from small grants from the Church to support the provision of Religious Education. Arguably, these other forms of faith school, despite being constantly referred to as other examples of faith schooling in Scotland for the purposes of academic accuracy, seldom feature in the faith school debate in Scotland in any meaningful way. Ironically, the debate over the *possibility* of establishing a state-funded Muslim school in Glasgow has generated more interest and publicity in recent years.

The public and academic debates on state-funded faith schools in Scotland, then, have become focused, understandably, on Catholic schools. This focus on Catholic schools in Scotland contrasts with the focus in England and Wales, where the wider variety of state-funded faith schooling and the recent expansion and extension of faith schooling (though not without critical dissent from some politicians and educationalists) enables a more sophisticated and more complex academic engagement. The debate in England and Wales, for example, is not simply focused on one form of Christian faith schooling (and limited questions associated with issues such as divisiveness and sectarianism) but instead is focused on a variety of Christian faith schools (such as Church of England, Catholic, the Emmanuel Schools Foundation) and a variety of other faith schools (such as Jewish, Muslim and Sikh), and this religious and cultural diversity means that the debate does not easily lend itself to generalisations, categorisation and, importantly, stereotyping (see McKinney, 2008b, 2011 for a discussion of contemporary faith schools in the UK).

A BRIEF HISTORY OF CATHOLIC SCHOOLS IN SCOTLAND

No contemporary comprehensive history of Catholic schooling in Scotland has been published (the most comprehensive history is now outdated: Dealy (1945) *Catholic Schools in Scotland*, 1st edn. Washington, DC: The Catholic University of America Press), but specific features and stages of the history of Catholic schooling have been examined in some depth in selected articles in the *The Innes Review*. Some recent books have examined the role of religious orders and congregations in Catholic schools: O'Hagan (2006) and Kehoe (2010). The reader is referred to these articles and books, and to the chapters on Catholic education by Tom Fitzpatrick that have been published in previous editions of this volume (1999, 2003). These sources will provide further bibliographic details and detailed historical accounts and insights.

Contemporary Catholic schooling originates in the schools that were established for the small number of indigenous Scottish Catholics and the Irish Catholic immigrants who had settled in Scotland in the early nineteenth century. Indigenous Scottish Catholicism was increased greatly by the waves of immigration in the nineteenth and twentieth centuries that drew Irish, Italian, Lithuanian and Polish Catholics to Scotland, but the Irish (and those of Irish descent), the largest national-cultural group within Scottish Catholicism, provided the critical mass required to establish Catholic schools. The schools were initially established to educate the children within the Catholic-Christian faith and, presumably, where applicable, to preserve some form of Irish culture and identity. The Catholic school system grew throughout the nineteenth century, coming under considerable pressure as the numbers of Irish Catholic immigrants rose quite dramatically as a result of a series of potato famines in Ireland (1845–9).

A variety of forms of schooling, of varying quality, had emerged by the mid-nineteenth century, including other Church schools such as Episcopalian and Presbyterian. The reports from the Argyll Commission (1867–8) called for a state rationalisation of schooling throughout Scotland, and the 1872 Education (Scotland) Act was a milestone in this process. The Catholic community declined the invitation to be incorporated into the state, concerned that the Catholic ethos, right to appoint Catholic teachers and the Catholic religious instruction available in Catholic schools would be jeopardised. The Catholic schools continued to be independently funded by subscription but struggled to maintain adequate standards both in terms of resources and building infrastructure. The negotiations surrounding the 1918 Education (Scotland) Act brought the Catholic schools into the state system as fully state-funded and, ultimately, ensured that these rights were preserved. One of the effects of the 1918 Act was that the Catholic schools became part of the 'official' educational discourse in Scotland.

A number of Catholic religious orders and congregations (such as Jesuits, Marists and Notre Dame Sisters) had a key role in Catholic schooling throughout the late nineteenth century and much of the twentieth century, and, in the case of the Notre Dame Sisters, in the training of Catholic teachers. The Catholic schools continued to grow and develop throughout the twentieth century. Popular history regularly recounts the enormous contribution of Catholic schooling to the greater social mobility of the Catholic community, but it is important to emphasise that Catholic schools were only one of the contributors to this social mobility. Other socio-economic and historical factors are widely considered to have co-contributed: the (arguable) decline of structural sectarianism after the Second World War; the rise of the multinationals; free access to higher education; and the inauguration of comprehensive education. It may be difficult, therefore, to isolate the extent of the contribution of Catholic schools from these other factors. The numbers of Catholic schools, like non-denominational schools, experienced a post-war boom in the 1960s and 1970s, and the 1970s and 1980s were marked by the withdrawal of the religious orders and congregations from schooling and the recognition of the emerging importance of the 'lay' Catholic teacher. The 1990s and early 2000s were to witness the increased success of Catholic schools as measured by Her Majesty's Inspectorate of Education reports and the cruder indicators of the 'league tables'.

CONTEMPORARY RATIONALE FOR CATHOLIC SCHOOLS

The scope of Catholic education in Scotland, from a Catholic perspective, is quite broad and varied because it is rooted in the concept of Catholic education as a lifelong process, or journey, to Christian maturity, and includes formal and informal education and education of both children and adults in primary, secondary and tertiary modes (see documentation and statements on Catholic education posted on the Vatican and SCES websites). The attempt below to summarise the Catholic rationale for Catholic schools is problematic in that, like all such attempts, it is open to the criticism that it is based on theological clichés being substituted for the development of a distinctive philosophy of Catholic education. McLaughlin (1996) argues that Catholic documentation on education must be studied, not raided for theological sound bites. The reader is referred, then, to the following documents on the Vatican website for detailed explanations and development of this rationale (www.vatican.va/). The key document for the contemporary discussion is *Gravissimum Educationis* (*Christian Education*) (1965), followed by *The Catholic School* (1977); *Lay Catholics in Schools: Witnesses to Faith* (1982); *The Religious Dimension of Catholic Schools* (1988); *General Directory for Catechesis* (1997); *Catholic Schools on the Threshold of the Third Millennium* (1998); and *Educating Together in Catholic Schools* (2007). These primary sources can be augmented by secondary texts from some of the major writers on Catholic education: John Sullivan, Gerald Grace, James Arthur, Graham Rossiter and Tom Groome.

Catholic schools are perceived by the Roman Catholic Church to be a faith-formational approach to education and, where they exist, an integral component of the lifelong process of Christian formation. This Catholic formation is sometimes conceived as a dynamic relationship between evangelisation (call and recall to faith) and catechesis (deepening of faith). The Catholic Church states that the role of Catholic schools is to assist parents (the primary educators) to educate children in the Christian faith and to provide an effective general education that will enable the children to contribute actively to society as good citizens and as mature Christian men and women. Catholic schools provide a context for the pursuit of a synthesis of faith and reason and should engage with contemporary culture and life. The Catholic school aspires to be a Christian community – a community that is founded and operates on 'Gospel values' (values such as love, equality, compassion, inclusion), and these should be manifested in the daily activities of the school and in the mutually respectful relationships. The Catholic school aspires to be a community that has prayer and liturgical life at the heart of its daily operation. Religious Education in Catholic schools is considered to be rooted in this vision of faith formation and an important part of the primary and secondary school curricula. This education in Christian faith is constructed as an invitation and all documentation prohibits coercion or any suggestion of indoctrination.

CONTEMPORARY CATHOLIC SCHOOLS IN SCOTLAND AND CATHOLIC SUPPORT SYSTEMS

According to the 2001 census, 15.88 per cent of the population of Scotland identify themselves as Catholics. See Scottish Executive Statistics: Analysis of Religion in the 2001 Census, 2005, www.scotland.gov.uk/Publications/2005/02/20757/53568

There are fifty-three secondary, 313 primary and four additional support needs (ASN) state-funded Catholic schools in Scotland. There are also a small number of private Catholic schools, two in Glasgow and one in Perthshire. The state-funded Catholic schools, like all other state-funded mainstream schools, are comprehensive and co-educational (with the exception of Notre Dame High School for Girls in Glasgow). Approximately 120,000 children attend Catholic schools, accounting for 20 per cent of the overall school population. According to the Scottish Bishops' Report, which acknowledges that the following figures are approximates, '5% of Catholic students attend non-denominational state schools and around 10% of students in Catholic schools are not baptised Catholics' (Religion in Scotland's Schools, 2006, Report from Bishops' Conference of Scotland). Catholic schools tend to be located primarily in the post-industrial west central belt where many of the Irish immigrants and their descendants had worked and settled, but there are a small number of Catholic secondary and primary schools in Dundee, Perth and Edinburgh, and primary schools in Aberdeen, Inverness, parts of the Highlands and the Borders (for the full geographical extent of Catholic schools and regular updates, see the SCES website).

As part of the state school system, Catholic schools share equal access to local and centralised support systems. They have access, for example, to local authority curriculum advisors and are invited to send delegates to meetings for all new initiatives. The Catholic schools, however, have other tiers of support established to focus on the 'Catholic' aspects of Catholic schools or to review general educational initiatives and their implications for Catholic schooling. The Scottish Catholic Education Commission (CEC) sets national policy on all educational matters on behalf of the Catholic Bishops of Scotland. The creation of SCES (the operational arm of the CEC) and the appointment of Michael McGrath as full-time director in 2003 have had a significant impact on the profile and development of Catholic schooling in Scotland. SCES has created a mission statement and policy documents designed to enhance Catholic education (*A Charter for Catholic Schools in Scotland*, 2004; *Shining the Light of Christ in the Catholic School*, 2009). SCES has also led and overseen the creation of *Called to Love* (2008) (programme of relationships and moral education for Catholic secondary schools) and *Chaplaincy in Catholic Secondary Schools in Scotland* (2009), and provides a wide variety of resources on its website. In addition, SCES provides continuing professional development for Catholic teachers and supports the work of the Religious Education advisors employed by the Catholic Church and the organisations that represent the Catholic primary and secondary headteachers. Perhaps the most significant achievement has been the launch of the national syllabus for Religious Education in Catholic schools – *This is our Faith* (2011). This syllabus encompasses P1 to S3 and carries the endorsement of the Vatican. SCES has also consolidated and enhanced Catholic representation at various levels of local and central government. This is exemplified in the strategic and formalised participation in the development of the national curricular initiative Curriculum for Excellence (Religious Education Roman Catholic Schools). At the time of writing, SCES has forged a stronger working partnership with the Scottish Qualifications Authority (SQA). Internationally, SCES has been working collaboratively with partners in Catholic Education throughout Europe and hosted a meeting of the European Committee for Catholic Education in 2010.

The majority of Catholic teachers are trained in the School of Education, University of Glasgow, primarily following the traditional BEd (Hons), PGDE Secondary and PGDE Primary courses (for a fuller discussion of the history of Catholic teacher education in Scotland, see Fitzpatrick, 1999, 2003). The student intake on the initial teacher education (ITE) courses is not exclusively Catholic, but the main ITE courses are funded by the Scottish Funding Council for the training of teachers for the Catholic sector, and the School has a responsibility to undertake this task. Catholic teachers wishing to teach in the Catholic sector are able to acquire a qualification, but not approval, to teach in the Catholic sector. Approval of 'religious belief and character' (for all teachers) to teach in a Catholic school comes exclusively from the Bishops of Scotland and is separate from the function of the School.

CHALLENGES AND OPPORTUNITIES

In this section, the challenges and opportunities for Catholic schools in Scotland are examined using two lenses: (1) external and (2) internal challenges and opportunities. This is an artificial heuristic tool as there is considerable overlap between the two lenses, but the distinction is intended to draw out that there are debates and discourses about Catholic schools that are undertaken and engaged in through external forums and there are debates and discourses that are more relevant to the internal forum of the Catholic community and Catholic schools.

There are a number of external challenges and opportunities, but the discussion will focus on three key themes: the state funding of Catholic schools; Catholic schools as anachronistic; and, finally, Catholic schools perceived as divisive. First, the state funding of Catholic schools is one of the central issues in the Scottish faith school debate as well as the wider faith school debate and is often formulated as a question: why should the state fund faith schools? The state funding of Catholic schools in Scotland is an historical legacy from an accommodation for denominational schools that was available to all denominations, not just Catholics. Organisations such as the National Secular Society (see www.secularism.org.uk/) and the British and Scottish Humanist Societies (see: www.humanism.org.uk/home; www.humanism-scotland.org.uk/) oppose faith schools in Scotland (and the UK) and question if this legacy should be allowed to continue. Although they respect the right of freedom of religious expression and belief they argue that this should be consigned to the private sphere and should not impinge on the public sphere. They would also argue that the state should not fund any form of faith schools because the state and organised religion should be separate. The continuing existence of state-funded faith schools (whether Catholic, Church of England or Jewish) indicates that the state recognises the importance of faith in some forms of schooling, or, at least, is prepared to tolerate this form of schooling. Faith schools, therefore, are perceived to be an unwelcome and formal link between the state and religion by the secularists and the humanists.

Those who support state funding for faith schools use a number of counter- arguments. Catholic schools in Scotland are supported by members of the Catholic community who are taxpayers, and the state, rightly in their view, is supporting their choice of school education for their children. This is a choice that is increasingly being exercised by the wider community in Scotland, as anecdotal evidence suggests that more non-Catholic families seek to have their children admitted to Catholic schools. A further argument is that Catholic schools contribute to Scottish education and society because they are, arguably, successful academically and in terms of social environment and social capital; some Catholic schools could be regarded, like their counterparts in England, as exemplars of state schooling. In recent years, Catholic schools in Scotland have been validated and even celebrated by some public figures. Alex Salmond, the Scottish First Minister, delivered the annual Cardinal Winning lecture in February 2008 at the University of Glasgow. This lecture named after the late Cardinal, a staunch supporter of Catholic education, is used to highlight the value and contribution of Catholic schools to Scotland's Catholic community and the wider society. Mr Salmond used this opportunity to voice his own unequivocal support for Catholic schools. Some of those involved with Catholic schools perceived this support from a leading politician to be an historical precedent and some indication of the acceptance and inclusion of the Catholic community in twenty-first-century Scotland. Alternative interpretations suggest that this was an attempt to generate a wider appeal to Catholic voters. Nevertheless, the lecture remains greatly significant as it was a formal and highly publicised statement of political approval for Catholic schools, and approval that is expected to remain as long as Mr Salmond retains power.

A related argument to the question of state funding is whether Catholic schools are now anachronistic. In the late twentieth century, Catholic schools were considered by some to be anachronistic. This argument was initially linked to the historical aim of Catholic schools to aid the social mobility of the socially and economically disadvantaged Catholic community. This was perceived to be a worthwhile aim and the state could be commended for assisting in this process by continuing to fund Catholic schools. It has been argued that as the Catholic community has become more socially mobile and prosperous, Catholic schools may no longer be required. The counter-argument states, first, that aiding social mobility was only one of the aims of Catholic schools. Second, if social mobility has been achieved within the Catholic community, it has only been achieved by a certain percentage. Many Catholics still belong to the low-paid employed and the unemployed 'underclass' (See Netto et al., 2011). A more sophisticated version of this argument has emerged in recent years, stating that Catholic schools are an anachronism in the sense that they are unwelcome reminders of a shameful history of Christian sectarian conflict and divisiveness in Scotland. As Christianity and Christian influence on private and public life wanes and dies, it is argued, so too would this reminder of the past be best removed. This conflict, which requires further examination and analysis, is, arguably, balanced by the historical contribution of Christianity to Scottish culture and society. Further, there may have been a marked decline in the numbers of people actively affiliated to the mainstream Christian churches, but the announcement of the death or terminal decline of Christianity may be a little premature. The mainstream Christian churches, despite numerical decline, still exercise considerable influence in Scottish public life.

There is a popular argument that Catholic schools are divisive in the sense that they physically separate children in the same geographical location, on religious grounds, from an early age. There can be a perception held, especially by those outwith the Catholic community, that the school system in Scotland should be more uniform and children should be educated together within a local school context, although this argument has become somewhat obfuscated by the desire, and drive, for greater diversity in twenty-first-century Scottish schooling. The much-vaunted parental right of choice in schooling has been expanded by the introduction of a Gaelic school and of specialist schools for music, dance and sport. Should Catholic schools be viewed as divisive or as part of this increasing diversity? One strand of argumentation is that this separation could breed a separate religious and cultural identity and this leads to another common and related argument that separate Catholic schools cause or promote sectarianism. This will be discussed, in some depth, elsewhere in this volume (see Chapter 94).

Paralleling this discussion of external challenges and opportunities, there are also sets of internal challenges and opportunities. The discussion will focus on only three: the popularity of Catholic schools in the wider community and the implications for inclusion; the effects of mergers and closures; and the related challenge to maintain the option for the poor in Catholic schools.

As has been suggested, Catholic schools in Scotland have become more popular in the sense that increasing numbers of non-Catholic parents send their children to Catholic schools. From one perspective, this is a measure of the perceived success of Catholic schools, in terms of both academic achievement and the social environment of Catholic schools. From another perspective, increased numbers of non-Catholic children can be perceived as problematic for the Catholic schools as they strive to balance inclusion with the need to retain a Catholic identity and preserve a coherent atmosphere of Christian prayer and spirituality (Sullivan, 2001; Ryan, in McKinney, 2008b). In some parts of Glasgow, for example, Muslim parents, exercising their legal rights, are withdrawing their children from specifically Catholic forms of worship. This challenge for Catholic schools may be further compounded by the increasing number of children from the Catholic community whose family links with Catholic Christianity may be tenuous (as measured by falling church attendance), and whose understanding of the aims and practice of Christian life may be somewhat limited.

The rationalisation of schooling within many local authorities has entailed widespread audit of school rolls, often resulting in closures, mergers and, in some cases, joint campuses. The effect of closures and mergers is that the 'local' primary school may no longer be within walking distance. From the perspective of the Catholic Church, it could mean that there is no local primary school that is linked with the local Catholic parish. This may have implications for the maintenance of the social and spiritual capital of the Catholic school (built on close relations between school, parish and families) and for the preservation of Catholic schooling, and a Catholic presence, in the more socially deprived areas (see below). The controversy, often more anticipated than actual, of joint campuses has been the object of intense media attention which has distracted public attention from the economic expediency that has frequently led to their existence and the fact that some have existed for a number of years (e.g. Fox Covert in Edinburgh). The Catholic Church appears to have accepted a limited number of these campuses as economic and strategic necessities, but has taken steps to ensure the integrity of the Catholic education of the children attending such institutions.

One of the claims of the Vatican documentation on education, cited earlier, is that the Church has a mission to educate the poor. This is initially articulated in *Christian Education* (1965), section 9, as Catholic schools 'caring for the needs of those who are poor in the goods of this world or who are deprived of the assistance and affection of a family...' This idea is revisited in subsequent documents and *The Religious Dimension of Education in a Catholic School* (1988), sections 85–9, discusses a 'preferential option for the less fortunate' as part of the Christian ethic that should characterise Catholic schools. Some writers have perceived this 'preferential option for the poor' as a key feature of the historic mission of Catholic schools in Scotland and the wider UK, serving a community that was primarily at the lower end of the socio-economic scale (O'Hagan, 2006; Grace, 2002). As has been mentioned above, the 'preferential option for the poor' can be compromised by the closure, or merger, of Catholic schools, particularly in areas of urban deprivation. The Catholic Church, cooperating with the local authorities, has to share hard strategic decisions in the rationalisation of state-funded schooling in many areas, but especially in deprived urban areas. Will the mergers and closures in the less affluent areas, where church attendances are lower, have a proportionally more serious effect as the poor and the marginalised struggle to retain a Catholic identity, especially as these are often the areas where the local Catholic Church may have been closed, due to similar socio-economic considerations? Perhaps the Catholic Church constantly has to recall its own expressed aim to assist and educate the marginalised. Those responsible for the future of Catholic schools within the Catholic Church have to balance these profound theological aims with increasing political and economic pressures.

CONCLUDING REMARKS

At the time of writing, a number of important issues have come to the forefront. There is currently a heated debate about the Scottish Government's proposal to legalise same-sex marriages, opposed by the Catholic Church and other mainstream Christian churches. This is indicative of increasing liberalisation and subsequent state legalisation of new sexual mores – a process that clashes with the Christian position on sexuality that is taught in Catholic schools. A recurring issue is the requirement for approval to teach in a Catholic school. This can be interpreted as a form of positive discrimination or as another example of the divisiveness of Catholic schools. In a sense, it can ultimately depend on the perspective of the protagonist. Part of the reason the debate on Catholic schools in Scotland is fundamentally problematic is that it is undertaken against the backdrop of the uneasy coexistence between the secularist agenda of the separation of the state and religion and the twenty-first-century agenda of accommodation, if not celebration, of a multicultural, multiethnic and multireligious Scotland.

As Scottish society in the twenty-first century continues to engage in this debate about the existence and continued role of Catholic schools, there remain many complex internal and external challenges and opportunities concerning Catholic schools – some of which have been discussed above. It could be argued that if there were a wider variety of faith schools in Scotland, the debate would not be as focused on Catholic schools. Those opposed to Catholic schools would not be so easily suspected (and sometimes accused) of being anti-Catholic. Perhaps those opposed to Catholic schools should be more sensitive to this and frame their viewpoint within wider and more measured argumentation. Perhaps, equally, those who support Catholic schools should be wary of being perceived as over defensive, continue to be transparent about the aims, rationale and operation of Catholic schools, and be more willing to engage in wider debates concerning educational purposes and the unique blend of faith and reason within faith schools.

REFERENCES

Fitzpatrick, T. A. (1999, 2003) 'Catholic education in Scotland', in T. G. K. Bryce and W. M. Humes (eds), *Scottish Education*. Edinburgh: Edinburgh University Press.

Franchi, L. and S. J. McKinney (eds) (2011) *A Companion to Catholic Education*. Leominster: Gracewing.

Grace, G. (2002) *Catholic Schools, Mission, Markets and Morality*. London: Routledge.

Kehoe, S. K. (2010) *Creating a Scottish Church*. Manchester: Manchester University Press.

McKinney, S. J. (2008a) 'Catholic schools in Scotland and divisiveness', *Journal of Beliefs and Values*, 29 (2): 173–84.

McKinney, S. J. (ed.) (2008b) *Faith Schools in the 21st Century*. Edinburgh: Dunedin Academic Press.

McKinney, S. J. (2011) 'The contemporary faith school debate in the United Kingdom', *Education Today*, 61 (2): 11–18.

McLaughlin, T. (1996) 'The distinctiveness of Catholic education', in T. McLaughlin, J. O'Keefe and B. O'Keeffe (eds), *The Contemporary Catholic School*. London: Falmer Press.

Netto, G., F. Sosenko and G. Bramley (2011) *A Review of Poverty and Ethnicity in Scotland*. York: Joseph Rowntree Foundation.

O'Hagan, F. J. (2006) *The Contribution of the Religious Orders to Education in Glasgow during the period 1847–1918*. Lampeter: The Edwin Mellen Press.

Sullivan, J. (2001) *Catholic Education: Distinctive and Inclusive*. London: Kluwer.

Websites

Scottish Catholic Education Service (SCES) at www.sces.uk.com

The Innes Review at www.euppublishing.com/journal/inr (the best source of scholarly articles on the history of Catholic schooling in Scotland)

28

Education and Work

Andy Furlong

The worlds of education and work have always been closely linked. Education is tasked with preparing young people for a future in the labour force by equipping them with the hard skills required by employers in modern technologically advanced work contexts as well as the soft skills that may help them to manage careers and interact with clients and colleagues in the new, service dominated, economy. Through the system of qualifications and through processes of internal selectivity, education also filters human resources in ways that smooth the allocation of individuals to labour market positions characterised by unequal reward structures. Education has always played a significant role in the reproduction of inequalities and in the distribution of life chances: a role frequently legitimised by the dubious idea that educators are uniquely able to identify those individuals who are talented and motivated and are fully committed to promoting equal opportunities.

Since the 1980s, patterns of participation in education have changed significantly and young people's relationship with education systems has also been transformed. Young people in Scotland spend longer in educational environments and the qualifications they gain have a strong bearing on post-educational pathways. Labour market opportunities for young people have also been transformed and transitions from education to work have become more protracted and more complex. The current economic crisis is likely to accelerate changes already in train and may exacerbate existing inequalities. Within the new economy, it is important that we reach new understandings of the relationship between education and work and rethink some of the priorities for Scottish educational policy within the context of late modernity.

Under conditions of economic uncertainty and austerity, young people's relationship with education and work is changing in ways that call for more flexible and imaginative policy frameworks. It is increasingly important that Scottish educators have a clear awareness of the challenges young people must be prepared to meet and the skills that they will need to develop if they are to effectively navigate new complexities. The chapter begins by exploring changes in the relationship between education and work, focusing on the implications of extended patterns of participation, the delineation of transitions and the fragmentation of traditional opportunity structures. The following sections focus on the conditions encountered by early school leavers and those with relatively poor qualifications, the experiences of those graduating from tertiary education and, lastly, a group referred to as the 'missing middle' (Roberts, 2011): a group with mid-range qualifications who do not progress to higher education.

CHANGING NATURE OF YOUTH TRANSITIONS

In early discussions of education-to-work transitions, schools were clearly seen as environments where family-based perspectives on the world, often firmly embedded in social class-based assumptions and tradition, were largely reinforced resulting in a process of anticipatory socialisation within which young people were prepared for future patterns of labour force engagement that mirrored predominant patterns within a community. In Scottish schools, young people received clear messages relating to their future prospects in contexts where working-class failure and early leaving were almost taken for granted. In Scotland among those from working-class families, minimum age leaving was the norm and, depending on labour market conditions, early school leavers tended to make fairly rapid, linear transitions from school to unskilled and low-skill positions in manufacturing and service environments. For many of these minimum-aged school leavers, qualifications provided relatively few advantages in the labour market and young people had little incentive to invest in education. In these contexts, many young people from working-class families rejected education and looked forward to an early entry into the adult world of work.

The decline in the manufacturing industry and the collapse of the youth labour market during the 1970s and 1980s impacted both on opportunities for work as well as on educational experiences. In the emerging post-recession economy, opportunities for unqualified young people were scarce; the 'pull' of the labour market was slowly transformed into a 'push' into education as a means of avoiding unemployment and the alternative of unpopular government-sponsored training programmes which frequently failed to lead to employment. In this context, more young people began to remain in education beyond the minimum age and their lack of qualifications began to be seen as an impediment to successful transitions to work.

Beginning in the 1980s and continuing to the present day, one of the key trends in the Scottish labour market has been the loss of skilled, non-graduate jobs, along with an expansion of low-skill service-sector jobs at the bottom end of the labour market and of high-skill jobs in the knowledge sector at the top end. Sometimes referred to as a 'hollowing out' of the labour market, or an 'hourglass' economy, it is frequently argued that opportunities have become polarised into the 'lovely' and the 'lousy' (Goos and Manning, 2003). Indeed, recent evidence from the UK Labour Force Survey shows that over the last decade employment growth for males was concentrated in the three highest- and three lowest-paid occupations, while for women there was significant growth in public-sector professional occupations as well as in low-paid personal service occupations (Sissons, 2011).

The recent recession has had a negative impact on mid-level jobs while professional jobs have continued to grow. There has also been a post-recession growth of low-skill, low-wage occupations. For young people leaving education or planning educational careers, we have something approaching a 'winner takes all' situation: higher education has become the key to the high-wage economy, but in a context of increased competition in the graduate labour market, significant numbers of well-qualified young people will face disappointment. For those who do not progress to tertiary education, many will experience periods of unemployment, frequently protracted, and when they find employment they may be 'churned' between a series of insecure and low-paid jobs. The policy focus here is on the NEET group (those not in education, employment or training), with a priority being placed on encouraging those without jobs to reconnect with education or join a training programme, as promoted in Scotland under the policy framework of *More Choices, More Chances*.

In the new economy, young Scots are forced to negotiate complex opportunity structures in which old road maps may be of limited value. Modern contexts require resourcefulness, imagination and a willingness to explore alternative routes. In any cohort of educational leavers, around one in two young people will follow what have been described as non-linear pathways (Furlong et al., 2003): routes that involve frequent changes of direction, back-tracking and unusual experiential sequences. Whereas once young people made collective transitions in which they were able to identify others following similar pathways and map their own progress against that of their peers, today pathways are increasingly individual-ised and it is often difficult to identify and learn from others whose experiences are similar. This provides new challenges for educationalists and careers advisors who must help equip young people with different skill sets, facilitating the development of effective navigators who are able to read confusing signals and manage careers characterised by complexity and change.

EARLY LEAVERS

Whereas early school leaving in Scotland was once fairly common, today very few leave at the minimum age and most will participate in some form of post-compulsory education. In the mid-1980s, post-compulsory participation was still a minority experience with 43 per cent staying on beyond the age of 16 in 1985 (Scottish Government, 2009): by 2010–11, this had almost doubled with 83 per cent experiencing post-compulsory schooling (Scottish Government, 2010). There are a number of reasons for the change including stronger qualification profiles of 16 year olds as a result of curricular change, more positive attitudes towards education among groups who had previously rejected schooling as something that had limited relevance to their lives and a decline in opportunities for early school leavers.

While they have become a minority group, early school leavers face a particularly acute set of problems and are especially vulnerable to unemployment. Their vulnerability is not so much because of a shortage of low- skill, low-wage jobs to absorb them (such jobs have been increasing); it is mainly a consequence of employer preferences. The supply of labour available for low-skill work is reasonably plentiful and, for similar wage outlays, employers are able to attract well-qualified, customer-friendly workers with developed soft skills. This labour pool includes the growing number of students working to support their studies, graduates who require stop-gap employment while they attempt to penetrate the graduate labour market and older workers seeking jobs to fit around childcare responsibilities. Poorly qualified, inexperienced school leavers may find it hard to compete in this labour pool.

Changes in policy have seen the progressive removal of benefit entitlements and, despite extremely high levels of worklessness, unemployment has more or less become a redundant term. From a policy perspective, the priority has been to keep those below the age of 19 in education unless they have secured employment or training. In the current context, in which we are witnessing record levels of worklessness, there are many young people out of work who meet the usual definitions of unemployment, yet the term NEET is increasingly used in a wide range of countries to capture those who have not made transitions to the 'positive' destinations of education, employment or training. NEET is a controversial term, partly adopted for political reasons by governments who want to suggest that young people who are unemployed have 'chosen' to avoid the range of positive alternatives provided for them in education and training (Furlong, 2006). Thus youth unemployment is presented as an entirely avoidable consequence of the actions of young people themselves rather than a structural issue related to labour market demand. The NEET group is overwhelmingly comprised of young people who are available for work and actively seeking employment, although it also contains a range of others such as those with disabilities, the long-term sick, those with caring responsibilities and those simply taking time out to pursue other interests or develop skills in an informal context.

While the preferred terminology helps avoid direct discussion of youth unemployment, worklessness is a serious problem in contemporary Scotland. The young unemployed may find it difficult to build social and human capital in a period of their lives in which learning remains crucial to smooth transitions and to long-term prospects. Employers can be suspicious of those who have a history of worklessness and economists have argued that the experience of youth unemployment leaves 'scars' that adversely impact on patterns of labour market participation across the life course.

One of the major problems with the focus on the NEET group is that another vulnerable group, those constantly churned between poor-quality, insecure jobs are largely overlooked in policy terms. Many early leavers will secure jobs and avoid becoming NEET, but such jobs are frequently part-time and tend not to involve training or prospects of progression (Furlong et al., 2003). In many advanced societies there are great concerns about the growth of insecure and fragmented forms of employment among young people, but, with a concern about the more politically sensitive unemployment rate, there is little political action. Ulrich Beck (2000) has argued that the labour markets in advanced societies are undergoing a process of Brazilianisation, by which he means that they are coming to resemble countries like Brazil where opportunities are strongly polarised with large populations engaged in precarious forms of work. In the UK, similar observations have been made and it has been argued that employment trends demonstrate a continual increase in the size of the precarious sector (Standing, 2011).

As new entrants to the labour market who tend to lack human capital, early school leavers are well-represented among what Standing (2011) refers to as the 'Precariat'. There are no statistics on the number of young people in Scotland (or indeed the UK) who fall into this category, but a rough estimate derived from a vulnerable population suggests that in terms of size it is roughly equivalent to the number of people in the same age group who are unemployed (Furlong and Cartmel, 2004). In some other countries, such as Japan, statistics are collected in such a way as to be able to differentiate between those who are NEET and those in precarious positions, making to easier to monitor trends and target a vulnerable population. Among 16–18-year-olds in Scotland, the number of school leavers who are NEET stands at around 13 per cent, although among those who left school at the end of S4, the figure is much higher at 24 per cent (Scottish Government, 2010). Taken together with the number in precarious positions, perhaps one in two early leavers can be regarded as vulnerable.

For policy makers, the most straightforward way to 'solve' the NEET problem is to encourage young people to take up what are described as 'positive' options, such as education or training. In Scotland, *More Chances, More Choices* is designed to provide fresh options in education and training in order to reduce the NEET pool. In the long run, being NEET is expensive for the state in that young people affected are prone to further periods of unemployment across the lifespan: a study carried out on behalf of the Audit Commission estimated the lifetime cost of being NEET at in excess of £50,000. The problem is that where young people are pushed into situations that they would otherwise avoid, participation may be short-lived and outcomes can be negative. Increasing the school-leaving age to

18 or making benefits conditional upon participating in a training scheme is only likely to be effective when young people see personal value in these opportunities.

HIGHER EDUCATION AND THE NEW GRADUATE LABOUR MARKET

The expansion of higher education has seen it transformed from an elite to a mass experience. No longer the preserve of a small minority of young people from privileged backgrounds heading for professional and managerial careers, almost one in two young people in Scotland will experience some form of higher education. Yet expansion has been accompanied by the stratification of higher education, while the increased supply of graduates has led to a weakening of the links with the professional sector of the economy.

Organisationally, higher education is divided between a relatively well-funded, highly selective elite sector and a less selective set of institutions that tend to cater for less qualified students, often from poorer backgrounds. Higher education is also stratified in terms of subject areas with some studying courses that tend to provide smooth access to high-status careers (medicine and dentistry, for example), while others study courses without clear links to a career (English or history, for example) or courses with links to lower-status occupations that once recruited non-graduates (nursing or nutrition, for example).

Within institutions, especially within the elite institutions, there are also a range of other divisions that impact on the experience of education and which have implications for future patterns of occupational attainment. Divisions between students who live at home while studying and those who move away are important, as are the related divisions between those able to construct student-centred lifestyles and those living employment-focused lifestyles. The decision to remain at home while studying tends to be an economic decision and it is those from less affluent backgrounds who tend to stay at home for the duration of their studies. Home-based students tend to have a poorer educational experience, can feel isolated from their fellow students and are less likely to secure graduate-level employment on completion.

While the current funding regime in Scotland provides locally domiciled students with low-interest loans and exempts them from fees, few students are able to afford to move away from home to study without significant financial subsidies from their parents. Many students also need income from employment to help subsidise their studies, even if they remain in the parental home. While students can hold a part-time job without it impacting significantly on their academic work or on the broader student experience, some students have to work extremely long hours in order to survive financially. Working-class students tend to work the longest hours and frequently work such long hours that hours devoted to study become secondary to those allocated to employment. Aside from the negative impact of long working hours on academic attainment, heavy engagement in employment adversely affects the students' experience in ways that have implications for subsequent patterns of employment. In particular, social contact with more affluent peers is restricted, which can impede the sharing of knowledge about opportunities and prevent access to the middle-class networks that can smooth transitions to graduate careers. In terms of educational policy, higher education institutions have been described as inflexible and greedy, operating under an outmoded assumption that study can be prioritised over employment, and that students are able to limit and control the hours they work. In the US, where students tend to be extensively engaged in jobs, curriculum delivery is often more flexible and greater respect is accorded to individualised forms of engagement.

Although the term 'graduate labour market' still tends to be used in policy circles, in reality graduates enter a range of occupational sectors, some of which have only recently begun to recruit heavily from the graduate pool. Traditional graduate occupations in areas such as the professions and higher-level management track jobs recruit a minority, while many enter jobs on the new graduate labour market in fields such as hospitality and health-related professions. Moreover, many will work in sectors of the labour market dominated by those without higher education, and some will never enter the types of occupation that they might consider appropriate to someone with advanced qualifications. For significant numbers, the transition into secure positions where they might utilise some of their skills will be protracted and it is not uncommon for a graduate to remain in the part-time, 'temporary' job they held while in higher education for some time after they have completed their studies.

THE 'MISSING MIDDLE'

Falling in between early leavers and graduates from higher education is a group of people whose opportunities are increasingly limited and who tend to fall beneath the policy radar. Sometimes described as the 'missing middle', this heterogeneous group is largely comprised of moderately qualified young people, although it also includes well-qualified people who have decided not to progress to higher education as well as those who have completed upper secondary education while gaining little in the way of qualifications. This intermediary group is squeezed from above by graduates who have been unable to find a higher-level occupation and, following investment in extended education, hope to avoid a future in low-skill, insecure jobs. It has been argued convincingly that the focus on those qualified to enter higher education on the one hand, and those who are NEET on the other, render those with 'moderate qualifications' invisible in policy terms (Roberts, 2011).

This group has suffered badly through the effects of qualification inflation. Many of the types of jobs that would once have been open to those who had completed upper secondary education, such as clerical jobs, senior posts in a variety of sales occupations and junior managerial positions, are now part of the new graduate labour market and are clearly in demand by those exiting from higher education who hope that getting a low-level foothold in these occupations will open up possibilities for subsequent career progression.

The intermediate group in Scotland, as in the rest of the UK, tends to face greater difficulties than its counterparts in countries where there is a thriving manufacturing sector, such as Germany. In such countries, there are often more opportunities for apprenticeship training and skilled and technical employment which have provided a degree of protection for the intermediary groups. In Scotland, training opportunities for non-graduate labour are in relatively short supply and where they exist are subject to high levels of demand. Moreover, college courses that have been developed to meet the demand from young people for routes into skilled employment are often limited by the lack of practical placements that are required for higher-level accreditation. Partly as a result of these recent trends, there has been much discussion about how to address the needs of those in jobs without training (commonly referred to as JWT). Here the recent Nuffield Review of 16–19 education suggested that those in full-time employment who are not receiving, or do not possess, training to the standard of National Vocational Qualification 2 or beyond may well be placed in a situation where they cannot advance beyond routine poor-quality jobs (Roberts, 2011). Those in jobs without training tend to be concentrated in sales and elementary occupations and are often in temporary or casual forms of employment.

Of course in some countries vocational education is deeply embedded in the secondary curriculum where there may be clear academic and vocational streams. From an educational point of view, there is a strong rationale for developing a vocational pathway aimed at those with little interest or aptitude for the traditional academic curriculum and, in Scotland, the Technical and Vocational Education Initiative (TVEI) represented a somewhat short-lived attempt to implement a dual-track system in secondary schools. Vocational subjects may increase engagement and motivation and promote extended educational participation among groups who would otherwise make early exits from education. From a social justice perspective, there is downside: a dual system tends to constrain the potential for social mobility and may limit the aspirations of individuals who may otherwise have thrived in an academic environment.

While some of the 'missing middle' will receive training from their employers, some of which may be at a reasonably advanced level and of a good standard, much of the training provided for this group has been, under various guises, sponsored or delivered by government agencies. These forms of training are of variable quality and are frequently criticised by young people who can object to low training allowances, may lack confidence that training will lead to stable employment or may have little interest in training for a particular occupation. At the same time, those without work may have little option but to agree to participate in the forms of training offered.

CONCLUSIONS

Changes in the world of work pose a number of challenges for educationalists. The occupational landscape has changed significantly over the last couple of decades and continues to evolve in ways that lead to an erosion of traditional opportunities for young people. Certainly educational systems have also changed: both the upper secondary school and systems of higher education, in particular, have been forced to accommodate a more diverse student body with a different set of needs and expectations. While not denying the importance of the changes that have taken place, one might be tempted to argue that education systems have been expanded rather than transformed. Structures have changed little and the greater protraction of engagement with education has not resulted in a greater equality of opportunity.

The question that we must address concerns how we can best prepare young people for an occupational world that is increasingly precarious and unpredictable. How do we equip young people with relevant skills without simply fuelling qualification inflation or taking on a warehouse function to limit flow into the labour market in order to allow government to reduce the number of young people who are NEET? In contemporary contexts, young people will have to manage multiple job changes and are likely to be employed in occupations where a wide variety of skills is called for. Forms of careers education built on the assumption that young people can be prepared to enter stable occupational niches are no longer appropriate.

In the modern world, the important skill relates to the ability to navigate complex contexts, to present the self in an ever-changing variety of ways in order to gain access to opportunities as they arise. Beck (2000) has referred to these skills as the entrepreneurship of the self and has argued that individuals need to perform as a 'Me & Co', selling themselves creatively in constantly changing landscapes. The ability to imaginatively navigate seas of uncertainty is part of a skill set that educationalists need to nurture: and these are skills that are equally required by those heading for higher education as much as by those leaving school at the minimum age. Another important task for educationalists concerns their responsibility to promote social justice and to tackle inequalities. The growth in participation in post-compulsory education provides fresh opportunities to address inequalities and to help ensure that schools do not simply act as agents of social reproduction, helping families to pass on advantages between generations while blocking social mobility. Changing patterns of participation have not led to a reduction in social inequalities in Scotland, partly because schools, colleges and universities have allowed new patterns of stratification to emerge and have failed to put structures in place that prioritise the promotion of equal opportunities.

REFERENCES

Beck, U. (2000) *The Brave New World of Work*. Cambridge: Polity Press.

Furlong, A. (2006) 'Not a very NEET solution: Representing problematic labour market transitions among early school leavers', *Work, Employment and Society*, 20 (3): 553–69.

Furlong, A. and F. Cartmel (2004) *Vulnerable Young Men in Fragile Labour Markets*. York: York Publishing.

Furlong, A., F. Cartmel, A. Biggart, H. Sweeting and P. West (2003) *Youth Transitions: Patterns of Vulnerability and Processes of Social Inclusion*. Edinburgh: Scottish Executive.

Goos, M. and A. Manning (2003) *Lousy and Lovely Jobs: The Rising Polarization of Work in Britain*. London: London School of Economics, Centre for Economic Performance Working Paper.

Roberts, S. (2011) 'Beyond NEET and tidy pathways: Considering the "Missing Middle" of youth transitions', *Journal of Youth Studies*, 14 (1): 21–39.

Scottish Government (2009) *Change over Time in the Context, Outcomes and Inequalities in Secondary Schooling in Scotland, 1985–2005*. Edinburgh: Scottish Government. Online at www.scotland.gov.uk/Publications/2009/04/27160059/7

Scottish Government (2010) *Staying on Rates and Destinations of Leavers by Stage of Leaving*. Edinburgh: Scottish Government. Online at www.scotland.gov.uk/Publications/2010/11/30144422/3

Sissons, P. (2011) *The Hourglass and the Escalator: Labour Market Change and Mobility*. London: The Work Foundation.

Standing, G. (2011) *The Precariat: The New Dangerous Class*. London: Bloomsbury.

29

Access and Retention

Michael Osborne

GENESIS OF ACCESS

The formalisation of access to higher education (HE) in terms of discrete provision can be traced back to the late 1970s in Scotland when universities such as Glasgow in 1979 and Dundee in 1980 set up their own part-time courses for adults to provide entry to arts and social sciences degrees. It was almost another decade before a further development in the field of widening participation emerged in the form of the Scottish Wider Access Programme (SWAP) in 1988. SWAP was a national consortia-based initiative launched by the then Scottish Office Education Department (SOED), which involved collaboration between local authorities, further education (FE) colleges and universities with the aim of promoting 'wider access to vocationally relevant higher education' and 'to encourage the establishment of permanent arrangements to make easier, more effective progression from further to higher education'.

It was during these decades at the end of the twentieth century that access to HE first became a small but increasingly significant part of educational provision. The decision to promote something as systematic as SWAP stemmed from two main strands of thinking. First, initiatives were associated with improving opportunity for adults for reasons of social justice and equality of opportunity. Second, that access would be to areas with vocational relevance. This agenda is summarised in what became a second phase of SWAP in 1993, which spoke about the objective to 'identify and support new groups of students and in particular: the economically and socially disadvantaged; women wishing to make a career in engineering, the sciences and technology; members of ethnic minority groups; those with physical disabilities'.

The very earliest actions of the Scottish universities were a response in this part of the UK to the Department of Education and Science (DES) White Paper of 1978, *Higher Education into the 1990s*, which had predicted a decline in school leavers and had suggested that initiatives should be taken to create 'more systematic opportunities for recurrent education by mature students'. Another DES White Paper, *Meeting the Challenge*, published almost a decade later in 1987, provided further impetus for developing within higher education a focus on access, and can be seen as one of the immediate precursors for SWAP. However, local influences, particularly in the then Strathclyde Regional Council (SRC) in Glasgow, were also a powerful force. As Cooke (1995) has reported, SRC had developed in the 1970s a social strategy that targeted areas of particular social and economic deprivation for priority treatment, and amongst its strategies was the improvement of opportunity through increased adult education provision. In advance of SWAP in 1987, two FE colleges (Stow and Langside) and four higher education institutions (HEIs) – the Universities of Glasgow and Strathclyde, Glasgow College of Technology (now Glasgow Caledonian University) and Paisley College (now the University of the West of Scotland) – in the Strathclyde area formed a consortium within which the colleges would run courses in science and technology, with those who passed receiving guaranteed places in HE. The focus on science and engineering was a reflection not only of the particular interest of the partner institutions, but also of the particular object of the 1987 White Paper to increase recruitment to these subjects. These were amongst the first courses that provided formal-ised relationships between FE and HE, which are now routine within the Scottish system, albeit now in the form of articulation with transfer of credit. It was also in 1987 that similar arrangements were put into place between Cardonald College and the then Glasgow College in the areas of social science and business studies, the target population being adults in the area of Govan, a particularly deprived area of Glasgow.

The creation of SWAP was followed closely thereafter by an invitation from the Scottish Education Department to regional councils and HEIs to bid to create consortia to widen access, the pre-condition being that of collaboration, with evidence of employer support for initiatives being an added advantage. As a result four consortia were set up in the east, north and south of Scotland and mid-Scotland in April 1988. Very soon a set of courses was developed, mainly offered on a full-time basis at FE colleges with guaranteed entry upon completion to an HEI. In the first year of operation in 1989, 750 students had enrolled in the SWAP courses with 71 per cent successfully completing. Three years later, numbers of enrolments had almost tripled to 2,103.

Although still only a small proportion of all mature entrants to Scottish universities (around 4 per cent in 1991), this rapid development of provision for under-represented groups was a substantial achievement in such a short period. One of the reasons that provision was able to be offered so quickly and across a range of disciplines was that no new curriculum needed to be developed. SWAP courses were based on suites of existing modules drawn from the then SCOTVEC portfolio of courses. These modules with crite-rion-referenced continuous assessment and recognition as a nationally valid qualification were perceived to be suitable for the requirements of adult learners, many of whom would have been out of formal education for a considerable time. Furthermore, Access courses could be constructed around these modules in a flexible fashion to suit the requirements of HEIs. This was the rationale for the choice of this method of course construction. Critics have since argued that vocationally oriented provision with content and assessment modes quite different from those of qualifications traditionally used to prepare students for HE, and most importantly very different from those of HE provision itself, would inevitably be problematic.

It is very important to stress that in these early days of widening participation the emphasis was centred on adults, with a specific focus on under-represented groups, which in Scotland equated largely to those from lower socio-economic classes. That is not to say that those from ethnic minority groups, those in remote and rural locations, women and the disabled were ignored, but given the composition of the population of the country and the mismatch of its profile with those who entered HE, it is clear why socio–economic class was at the fore of initiatives. The second characteristic, as is already evident, was vocationalism and, in the early 1990s, provision soon extended from science and technology to teacher education and other professional areas.

There is little doubt the survival and expansion of many departments of education was due to their adult intake, and that includes departments in Scotland such at that in Stirling, as reported by Cope and Osborne (1993). This is just one example of how links with local colleges – in this case in particular with the then Clackmannan and Falkirk Colleges (now integrated as Forth Valley College), Cumbernauld College and Perth College – facilitated through the SWAP programme produced a significant number of mature graduates in a key profession. Developments that offered alternatives to the use of traditional qualifications, however, were contentious, and debates from the very early days of widening participation were often characterised within the rhetoric of 'standards', although much early research demonstrated that performance of those entering via Access routes was largely comparable to those entering from schools with conventional qualifications. A further and what seemed rather prosaic internal debate among advocates of widening participation centred around the distinction between 'access' and 'Access'. The lack of capitalisation in the term refers to making the system of higher education more accessible in a variety of ways, such as making it more flexible in terms of structure, and in a range of spatial and temporal modifications to its provision. This is distinct from the creation of programmes of study designed to provide a route to the existing configuration of HE provision. This was evident in the *Flexibility in Teaching and Learning Scheme* (FITLS), introduced in 1993 by the Scottish Higher Education Funding Council (SHEFC) and existing until 1995. FITLS specifically sought to encourage access from under-represented groups, particularly as designated by socio-economic class and ethnicity, and to develop greater flexibility in provision. Many projects were funded at the Scottish universities, including the creation of part-time awards at Certificate level for adults at the University of Glasgow (Turner, 1998) and the creation of an evening part-time degree programme and later a Summer Academic programme at the University of Stirling. Also at Stirling a work-based Access programme for employees was created through the Learning at Work programme.

Some twenty-five years since the first initiatives in Scotland, the scale of activity in the area of widening participation has increased considerably in line, to a large extent, with the expansion of the HE system as a whole. More significantly, the form that developments have taken has qualitatively changed. An observer who simply looked at the statistics of numbers of adults entering HE via the SWAP programme might conclude that there had been an early plateauing and even decline in this field of work. For example, if SWAPWest is considered, numbers peaked in 1992–3 when 1,063 students were enrolled. In 2010–11, the number was 797, and in the late 1990s it dipped below 600 (Anderson, 2007). This, however, ignores developments in other fields of widening participation, which put greater emphasis on accessibility rather than customised provision.

A range of concerns at both national and institutional level related to factors including economic competitiveness, demographic change and institutional survival from the late 1980s onwards have seen widening participation to HE become much more strongly embedded in policy debates. From being something on the margins advocated by a relatively small number of activists and supported by largely left-leaning regional authorities, it is now something that few, irrespective of political allegiance, would argue against (Osborne and Houston, 2012).

MOVING FROM THE MARGINS

The absorption of widening access into mainstream debate started with a series of reports across the UK in the late 1990s, notably the Dearing (and the linked Scottish variant of the Garrick Committee), Fryer and Kennedy Reports, which presented visions for the development of HE and FE within the framework of a learning society. Dearing put forward a socially inclusive and socially cohesive vision of such a learning society which would embrace people at all levels of achievement, envisaging the expansion of HE provision with particular emphasis on the sub-degree level, and reiterated the need to address the under-representation in HE of particular social groups. Garrick echoed these concerns in Scotland, recommending, for example, enhanced access routes into degree programmes for students in FE colleges, the diversification of provision and a new Scottish Qualifications Framework.

The new UK Labour government's vision of this learning society was subsequently described in a series of Green Papers published in 1998 in each of England, Scotland and Wales, including, in Scotland, *Opportunity Scotland* and *Opportunities for Everyone, A Strategic Framework for FE*. To a considerable extent the debates found in these Green Papers have a common precursor in the European Commission's White Paper of 1995, *Teaching and Learning: Towards the Learning Society*, which signalled a common set of challenges for education and training on the continent, including the impact of the information society, internationalisation, and advances in science and technology. These challenges were to be met by emphasising the merits of a broad base of knowledge and by building up employability.

It is instructive to reflect on some of the rhetoric of *Opportunity Scotland*, which adopted a similar perspective and argued that individuals would need to take personal responsibility to ensure their future employability, through updating their skills: 'People at all levels need to use learning opportunities to keep pace in the jobs market and to ensure that Scotland is equipped to compete in the global economy' (p. 4); 'People who update their skills and learn new ones will get better paid jobs and achieve more success in their chosen fields of work' (p. 28).

Opportunity Scotland also argued that 'involving adults in lifelong learning is our greatest challenge' (p. 8), because it highlighted their own perceived difficulties and barriers that related to personal circumstances or previous low attainment at school. Some adults 'simply never think about learning at all' (p. 8). To an extent, then, it would appear that the problem lies with adults themselves, and whilst factors other than the dispositional were acknowledged, subsequent developments have paid more attention to interventions at earlier ages where it is perceived that more traction is possible. The targeting of young people from deprived areas had already been a focus of attention by universities themselves with Special Entry Summer Schools; for example at the University of Dundee as early as 1993 such a programme was offered (Watt and Blicharski, 1997). And from the late 1990s until the present day, there has been a considerable shift of emphasis from adults as the target group of widening access to school leavers, and to even younger age groups on the basis that early awareness and aspiration-raising is more effective in reaching the lowest socio-economic groups, who are still disproportionally under-represented in HE. The inclusion of representative proportions of young people from all strata of society within HE has since become the major imperative of government.

Further, from the time of *Opportunity Scotland*, the wider conception of accessibility of

HE began to emerge, and arguably it is from this period that 'access' rather than 'Access' began to dominate. A number of specific policy initiatives were launched at this time, which gave particular weight to collaboration and systemic structural modifications. These included the encouragement of new forms of partnerships between educational providers, advice agencies and employers through the aegis of LearnDirect Scotland (launched in 2001) using information and communications technology (ICT) as an important vehicle to do so, and the establishment of a national qualifications framework based on Higher Still and the Scottish Credit Accumulation and Transfer (SCOTCAT) frameworks. FE colleges and HE institutions were funded from 2000 via a Widening Access Development Grant by their respective funding councils, the then SHEFC and the Scottish Further Education Funding Council (SFEFC), to promote wider access initiatives, including through part-time study. The Wider Access Development Grant comprised four strands, including development of the FE/HE interface; institutional development and coordination; regional forums of providers from different sectors (primarily FE and HE); and selective funding. These grants have been used to fund a variety of institutional and supra-institutional developments, including the establishment of four Wider Access Regional Forums (WARFs) and the Scottish Network for Access and Participation (SNAP), the work of which spanned both the further and higher sectors.

The creation of the regional access forums provided some stability for the SWAP consortia. The Scottish Office withdrew its funding in 1994, and there followed the removal of local authority funding in 1995 following the reorganisation of local authorities under the Local Government (Scotland) Act 1994. This led to a period of uncertainty for the consortia. In the west of Scotland an Access Forum was created, supported by HE institutions and FE colleges to allow continuing collaboration. This became the West of Scotland Access Consortium (SWAPWest) constituted as a registered charity. Similarly a SWAPNorth and SWAPEast were set up to cover the rest of Scotland and together these three consortia continued to provide access programmes within these regional partnerships arrangements. The establishment of regional access forums by the funding councils created a means to assure the continuing existence of SWAP.

In addition to these initiatives, a number of student support measures were announced by the Scottish Executive at the beginning of the twenty-first century. In its response to the Cubie Inquiry into Student Finance in 2000, the Scottish Executive stated very explicitly that the main aim of FE and HE in Scotland was now to widen access. The Executive's consultation document made a number of recommendations designed to target resources on the socially excluded. This included funding for childcare support worth £8m over two years (targeted at FE students); means-tested bursaries of up to £2,000 with a further £500 available in loans for poorer students (estimated at 30 per cent of the total student population); £10m of funding to support mature students, £2m of which was 'new' money (again estimated as helping up to 30 per cent of the student population); and the waiving of the student contribution to tuition fees.

A DISTINCT SCOTTISH FRAMEWORK FOR ACCESS

As Gallacher (2007) has reported, since devolution in Scotland, a certain amount of distinctiveness has emerged in relation to HE policy, and the Scottish Government has been able to exert its considerable autonomy in this sphere. This first became visible in a number of documents published during the early part of the first decade of the twenty-first century, including the Final Report of the *Inquiry into Lifelong Learning of the Scottish Parliament* in 2002, the Scottish Executive's lifelong learning strategy document, *Life through Learning – Learning through Life* of 2003 and its *Framework for Higher Education in Scotland* of the same year. From the time of the Parliament's report, HE has been considered in policy terms as part of a wider notion of lifelong learning that also encompasses FE, vocational education more widely and community learning. Within such a policy framework, one of the main tasks of HE would explicitly be about securing greater social justice for citizens of Scotland through the achievement of more equitable participation. These documents also put considerable emphasis on collaboration between sectors in attaining this goal, and particularly between HEIs and FE colleges. This was reflected in increasing attention being given to transition between the sectors through articulation between Higher National (HN) awards and undergraduate degree programmes. These sentiments could have been merely something of a wishlist without accompanying structural changes to the way in which the HE and FE were funded. However, with the creation of the Scottish Funding Council in 2005, which amalgamated the previous SHEFC and SFEFC, an integrated approach to strategic questions that affected both sectors came about. Furthermore, in the case of collaboration between the sectors the creation of the Scottish Credit and Qualifications Framework (SCQF) in 2001 offered a structure within which clear tariffs were established for provision at a series of levels. The SCQF brought together not only qualifications offered at HE level, but also the National Qualifications (NQs) of the Scottish Qualifications Authority (SQA) offered in schools, FE and by other providers, into one structure intended as a ladder of progression that crosses sectors.

A final important element within the overall strategy developed in this period relates to funding. Various premiums additional to core funding for teaching and research were introduced by the funding councils to both HE and FE, as well as specific grants in support of widening access. These were specifically targeted towards widening access, disabled students, part-time provision and FE/HE articulation. The Widening Access Premium was based on a metric related to numbers of students admitted to HE courses from postcodes where participation rates in higher education were less than half the national average. The additional requirements of disabled students were also recognised, and the specific focus on part-time students and the transition from FE to HE signalled the importance being accorded to structural flexibility. Funding was also made available from the funding councils to the four WARFs, again an illustration of the importance accorded to cross-sectoral flexibility. Finally, with regard to funding, there have been some incentives at an individual level such as the fee waiver for part-time undergraduate study for students from groups under-represented in higher education, including low-income groups and those on disabilities allowance. Perhaps the greatest funding incentive to those considering HE in Scotland has been the consistent policy of all governments in Scotland not to follow the rest of the UK, which has introduced fees for home undergraduate students. There is considerable evidence that the anticipation of debt is a particular deterrent for students from those groups targeted in widening access initiatives.

Overall it is therefore possible to observe a strong alignment by the mid-2000s between policy, structure and funding incentives. This was consolidated with an eye for the future in 2005, when the Scottish Funding Council (SFC) published *Learning for All*, the results of a SHEFC/SFEFC working party's review of widening access policy and strategy. This document articulated the priorities for widening access in both FE and HE for the following five years and beyond. Further it suggested that whilst some progress had been made in accessing FE and HE, it has been slow for individuals from the most deprived areas still unlikely to access HEIs. Collaboration at a regional level across sectors once more was at the fore, and the importance of early intervention and aspiration-raising within schools was highlighted.

> Regional collaboration matters. Many of the ways forward we suggest in the report rely on the wider access regional forums working effectively because some of the under-participation is concentrated in particular geographic areas and because many issues are best tackled by the HEIs, colleges and schools working together locally on aspiration raising, on transitions, on access courses. We need to broaden the forums' missions to include all post-compulsory education, to put them on a firmer footing and to enable them to contribute to the national campaign we advocate in this report. We note that not all of the widening access forums have been equally successful to date – we need to work to make sure they are in the future. (*Learning for All*, SFC, 2005)

This report importantly provided a structure within which all of those involved in widening participation would develop and implement widening-access action plans with regular re-assessments of progress, the sixth of which was published in 2012.

In the last ten years there have been changes in emphasis in the targeting of intervention, and in particular of funding. Notably from 2008–9, the SFC reconfigured the Widening Access Premium to a Widening Access Retention Premium (WARP), changing the focus from simply recruitment to improving the retention and progression of students from the most deprived areas, allocating £10m to this area. Arguably it is relatively easy to increase participation, less easy to widen it, but the hardest task is to ensure successful outcomes in HE, particularly given that staffing and support mechanisms have not expanded as rapidly as the numbers and diversity of students. At the same time, the SFC also put further emphasis on collaboration through a further allocation of £5m for work across the FE/HE interface in order to enhance articulation, address the problems of student transition across the sectors, and enhance existing links and develop new ones. It created six Articulation Hubs with an overall national coverage, with the aim of increasing opportunity for students to transfer from FE to HE with advanced standing for their HN qualification and also to aid the retention of these articulating students within HE. These hubs also play a role in creating some coherence between the offers made by FE and HE institutions in order that articulation can play a role in meeting perceived skill shortage. In the same year, 2008, the SFC signalled further the importance of this area of work by creating an Access and Inclusion Committee in order to raise the profile of widening participation. These developments represented a wish by the funding council to create an over-arching strategy for equality, access and retention that crossed sectors, incorporated actions at local, regional and national level, and was linked to outcomes and to the Scottish Government's own national performance targets for a 'wealthier and fairer', 'healthier', 'safer and stronger' and 'smarter' country. The integration of widening access funding within strategic concerns became more evident in funding terms from 2009–10 onwards. Funding for this area became one of seven elements of the SFC's larger Horizon Fund for Universities, a funding stream designed as a catalyst for change in ways described by the SFC as potentially groundbreaking, nationally and internationally.

FAST-TRACK TO 2012

In 2012, the sixth update on progress within *Learning for All* was published. The original report had proposed measures of success for widening access policies in 2005. These were that 'patterns of participation would be more even across different groups in society', that 'there would be more even demand for learning across all groups in society' and that 'all learners would achieve and have a good learning experience that enhances their life chances'. Specifically the quantified improvements that the government expected to see and which the SFC now reports on in updates are:

- increasing participation in HE from publicly-funded schools;
- increasing articulation from colleges to universities for those students with advanced standing;
- increasing the proportion of mature students from deprived backgrounds; and
- national improvement in retention levels at universities.

The sixth update of *Learning for All* provides extensive and very detailed data on all of the above indicators, reflecting priorities that have emerged in the last two decades. The shift in focus to include young people as well as adults is evident within this range of expected improvements. Certainly there has clearly been a significant increase amongst school leavers entering both FE colleges and HEIs. In the period 1993–4 to 2010–11, those entering HE have increased by nine percentage points (from 27 to 36 per cent), whilst those entering FE have increased by 12 percentage points (from 15 to 27 per cent) over the same timeframe. Very noticeable is that young women outstrip young men in terms of progression, especially to HE; in 2010–11, 40 per cent of female school leavers as against 32 per cent of their male counterparts entered the system.

However, when considering articulation from FE to HE, despite efforts over the last decade, numbers entering the second or third year of a degree with an HNC or HND were less in 2010–11 than in 2002–3. There was a notable dip from 2009–10 to 2010–11, which has been ascribed by the SFC to the heavy demand on university places in that year and 'lack of coherent planning of articulation places by universities'. The SFC has now announced that it expects that all lead universities in its Articulation Hubs 'to have in place systems that plan articulation numbers in partnership with key college partners and that guarantees places as part of efficient learner journeys'.

In the latest update the SFC uses the Scottish Index of Multiple Deprivation (SIMD) to classify deprivation, dividing Scotland into 6,505 data zones which are then ranked by deprivation within quintiles. Whether it is young people or mature students, the statistics show that the proportion of those entering universities from the most deprived areas continues to be less than that from less deprived areas, and does not represent the nature of the population as a whole. This proportion of entrants from each quintile has hardly changed in the last six years, with the most deprived gaining only a percentage point of the share and the least deprived losing just over a percentage point. In 2010–11, whilst 20 per cent of the population lived in each quintile, the least deprived quintile supplied 29.1 per cent of students to universities and the most deprived quintile only 11.6 per cent. In FE colleges, within which 45,700 of the 230,990 total students taking HE level courses were studying in 2010–11, there is very little difference in proportions across the quintiles. However, looking at the data in a little more detail, it is evident that there is an even greater skewing by type of university, with the ancient universities admitting only 7 per cent of their students from the most deprived quintile and 38 per cent from the least deprived. There are number of possible explanations for these differences, but the most compelling is simply that the numbers of applicants with the highest tariff bands in the school-leaving examinations that are required to enter the most selective of institutions is much lower in the most deprived areas. This in turn may be related to differential performance and opportunity at school level across the country. However, there is also some evidence on a UK-wide scale that in certain disciplines other factors are may be at play. For example, in medicine it has been shown that controlling for all other variables, school leavers from lower socio-economic groups with equivalent high tariffs are least likely to be admitted (Thomas et al., 2005). This points to entry being related to other personal characteristics in some selective disciplines when academic qualifications cannot distinguish candidates.

Information related to retention points to the necessity to consider access as but one stage in the student life-cycle. There is now considerable data published by the SFC on non-continuation rates for the year after entry for full-time first degree entrants to universities. In the latest year for which data are available, 2008–09, the overall rate in Scotland was 9.3 per cent. This rises to 14.8 per cent for mature entrants and 15.9 per cent for those from the most deprived quintile. The two strongest predictors of non-continuation are deprivation (measured using SIMD) and prior attainment (UCAS tariff). The fact that these percentages have been decreasing for all categories since 2004–5 may point to some impact of the focus of the SFC moving from access to retention in recent years.

CONCLUSION

In earlier work with a number of colleagues, we have argued that to understand and classify the various forms of provision that exist within the field of widening access, a somewhat more sophisticated typology than that used historically is needed. Initiatives extend across the student life-cycle, some starting with awareness-raising that the possibility of higher education is a realistic goal as early as in primary school. Such a perspective continues through a variety of means to secure admission to HE study, and support within HE for retention, employability and employment. A number of studies have sought to conceptualise and categorise initiatives, designed with the direct purpose of widening participation. A Universities Scotland (2001) report on access in Scottish HEIs described developments at that time in terms of how they addressed three issues affecting access and retention: *academic* (raising entry qualifications); *cultural* (raising awareness); and *internal* (changing institutional structures). In Murphy et al.'s (2002) study on widening participation in Scotland, work in this domain was classified as *in-reach*, focusing on individuals 'getting in' to HE, or *out-reach*, emphasising the staff of universities 'getting out' of the campus into the community to reach people under-represented in HE respectively. The in-house Access courses of universities started thirty years ago, as well as the Summer Schools for school leavers from deprived areas who have just missed the required tariff required for entry, are examples of in-reach. Out-reach refers to a range of partnerships with schools, communities and employers, and of course the links between FE colleges and HEIs that seek to 'get out' to under-represented groups and the socially excluded. A number of initiatives, however, can be categorised primarily neither as in-reach nor as out-reach, and have more to do with transformations and adjustments to the structure, administration and delivery of HE programmes: these are referred to in the same study broadly as *flexible* access initiatives. They are designed to make the curriculum more accessible through changes in its structure, and in form, place and timing of delivery. Provisions such as the use of Accreditation of Prior Learning (APL), Open and Distance Learning (ODL), Information and Communications Technology (ICT) and part-time or summer undergraduate provision come under the aegis of flexibility (Houston, McCune and Osborne, 2011).

This overview of more than three decades of access activity would suggest that most of the early forms of provision still exist, though they have not expanded significantly in absolute terms, and as a consequence since the system of HE has expanded considerably are less significant. The provision that can be classified as in-reach, the Access courses and Summer Schools for young people, are still a feature of the offerings of many Scottish universities. Links between FE colleges and HEIs through SWAP or via articulation arrangements through HN courses are a continuing feature of the system, but in terms of volume of activity, have in both cases plateaued, and indeed declined. Furthermore, particularly in the case of articulation with advanced standing, this is largely a feature of the post-1992 universities with scarcely any penetration into the ancients. As has been argued, there have been an acceleration of efforts to target the most deprived parts of society, and a particular focus on early intervention within the school years to increase awareness of what might be possible. This is the main manifestation of *out-reach* for Scottish universities. Many schemes have been supported through the WARFs, and there are many success stories. However the Access and Inclusion Committee of the SFC itself has acknowledged that despite a range of widening participation initiatives, the evidence suggests that these have failed to significantly affect participation in higher education by young people from the lowest socio-economic groups and from geographically isolated areas.

The biggest challenge still appears to be to create true flexibility within the system. The paucity of provision in either full-time or part-time mode offered at times and locations that suit the needs of adults, including via the use of ICT, and the lack of routes based on accreditation of learning achieved other than through formal qualifications, is evident despite notable exceptions including at the University of the West of Scotland (UWS), Glasgow Caledonian University (GCU) and the Open University in Scotland. For example, the long-standing Part-time Forum at UWS together with the Open University has recently been focusing on flexible study for higher level skills development of the workforce, and GCU through the Scottish Centre for Work-based Learning offers a BA by Learning Contract for individuals, linking learning at work to credit within an academic programme. There are also smatterings of accredited prior experiential learning in the system, but very much at the margins and only offered for limited amounts of credit at a small number of institutions. Despite having the vehicles in place such as the SCQF, few of the drivers have passed the test. In most areas associated with flexible provision there has been little progress and indeed in some activities a decline – for example, we see little evidence that the initiatives funded by FITLS in the 1990s have been sustained. The latest government Green Paper in 2011, *Building a Smarter Future: Towards a Sustainable Scottish Solution for the Future of Higher Education*, suggests that 'Current approaches to widening access to higher education in universities have not produced the step change in participation that we would have liked' (p. 13), and raises the question as to whether funding might be better diverted from universities and colleges to local authorities to work on raising aspirations in the early years of schooling. It is not obvious, however, that there exists systematic evidence that current work in aspiration-raising within schools has made a difference, given that over the last six years hardly a dent has been made in the most deprived quintile of school leavers. It is also clear that even though that they receive no direct funding to offer Access courses for adults, universities have done so very successfully for thirty years. With some funding incentives and a breakdown of the barriers relating to which institutions should be funded to do particular levels of work, there is potential for all sectors to do more.

REFERENCES

Anderson K. (2007) 'SWAPWest: Twenty years in the transition business', *Proceedings of Centre for Research and Lifelong Learning 4th Annual Conference: The Times, They are a-Changin', Researching Transitions in Lifelong Learning*, University of Stirling, 22–24 June, 2007.

Cooke, A. (1999) 'Opportunity Scotland: Lifelong learning and the Scottish universities', *Scottish Journal of Adult and Continuing Education*, 5 (2): 77–88.

Cope, P. and M. Osborne (1993) 'Access: Instrumentalism in action? A case study of access to secondary teacher training', *Journal of Access Studies*, 8 (2): 246–54.

Gallacher, J. (2007) *The Impact of Devolution on Higher Education in Scotland*. Glasgow: Centre for Research in Lifelong Learning.

Houston, M., V. McCune and M. Osborne (2011) *Flexible Learning and its Contribution to Widening Participation: A Synthesis of Research*. York: HEA.

Mullen, F. (2010) *Widening Access to Higher Education: Policy in Scotland*. Edinburgh: Scottish Parliament Information Centre.

Murphy, M., B. Morgan-Klein, M. Osborne and J. Gallacher (2002) *Widening Participation in Higher Education*. Glasgow: Scottish Executive.

Osborne, M. and M. Houston (2012) 'Universities and Lifelong Learning in the UK – Adults as losers, but who are the winners?', in H. Schuetze and M. Slowey (eds), *Higher Education and Lifelong Learners: International Perspectives on Change*. London: Routledge.

Turner, R. (1998) 'Making the rhetoric of lifelong learning a reality?' *Innovations in Education & Training International*, 35 (4): 302–9.

Scottish Funding Council (2005) *Learning for All*. Edinburgh: SFC

Thomas, L., H. May, H. Harrop, M. Houston, H. Knox, M. F. Lee, M. Osborne, H. Pudner and C. Trotman (2005) *From the Margins to the Mainstream*. London: UUK/SCOP

Watt, S. and J. Blicharski (1997) 'Beyond the barricades. Accessing and participating in higher education: a case study of the successful "graduates" from a Scottish Special Entry Summer School', *Journal of Access Studies*, 12 (2): 212–23.

30

Citizenship Education

Gert Biesta

Citizenship has recently moved to the centre of attention of politicians and policy makers in many countries around the world. The interest in citizenship partly stems from a concern for the quality of democratic processes and practices and the opportunities for citizens to participate actively, productively and critically in collective decision making. But there are also more pragmatic reasons, such as concerns about social stability and social cohesion and about the decline of pro-social and the rise of anti-social behaviour. The discourse on citizenship thus stretches in a number of directions that are not always compatible and sometimes actually in tension or conflict with each other (see Biesta, 2011). While many countries have longstanding traditions of civics or citizenship education, and while questions about citizenship and democracy have traditionally had a place in such subjects as history, geography and social studies, the increased attention for citizenship has led to a more explicit focus on the contribution education can make to the formation of citizens and the development of good citizenship. Although there are many similarities in the ways in which the question of citizenship education has been taken up in different countries, there are also important differences, particularly within Britain (see Andrews and Mycock, 2007).

In England, the decision was taken to make citizenship into a new compulsory subject for the national curriculum for secondary schools; in Scotland, however, citizenship has been considered as something that should permeate the whole curriculum rather than something that could or should be confined to a particular subject. The Scottish Curriculum for Excellence thus lists 'responsible citizenship' as one of the four capacities that it envisages all children and young people should develop. It depicts responsible citizens as individuals who have 'respect for others' and a 'commitment to participate responsibly in political, economic, social and cultural life' and who are able to 'develop knowledge and understanding of the world and Scotland's place in it; understand different beliefs and cultures; make informed choices and decisions; evaluate environmental, scientific and technological issues; [and] develop informed, ethical views of complex issues' (Scottish Executive, 2004, p. 12).

The discussion on citizenship education in Scotland received a new impetus as a result of the establishment of the Scottish Parliament in 1999 (see Munn and Arnott, 2009). Early on the Scottish Executive announced five national priorities for schools in Scotland, of which priority number 4 focused on values and citizenship. In 1999, the Scottish Executive and the Scottish Consultative Council on the Curriculum (later merged into Learning and Teaching Scotland which, in turn, became Education Scotland in 2011) set up a working group to focus on education for citizenship. The group produced a discussion and consultation paper in 2000 (LTS, 2000) and a more detailed paper 'for discussion and development' in 2002 (LTS, 2002). The then Minister for Education and Young People endorsed the latter paper 'as the basis for a national framework for education for citizenship from 3 to 18' (LTS, 2002, p. 2) and commended it 'for adoption and use in ways appropriate to local needs and circumstances' (ibid.). In 2003, Her Majesty's Inspectorate for Education (HMIE) published a follow-up document intended to assist schools in evaluating the quality and effectiveness of their provision for education for citizenship (HMIE, 2003). In 2004, the Scottish Executive published *A Curriculum for Excellence* (Scottish Executive, 2004) which, as mentioned, presented the capacity for responsible citizenship as one of the four purposes of the curriculum from 3–18 (Scottish Executive, 2004, p. 12). In 2006, HMIE published a 'portrait' of current practice in education for citizenship in Scottish schools and pre-school centres (HMIE, 2006a), followed by a similar report on provision in Scotland's colleges (HMIE, 2006b).

In this chapter I provide an analysis of the particular conception of citizenship that informs the approach to citizenship education in Curriculum for Excellence. I show that the Scottish approach has a tendency to focus on the individual rather than the collective; on the social more than on the political dimensions of citizenship; on social activity more than on political action; and on a community of sameness more than a community of difference. Against this background I then raise some questions about the content and form that citizenship education takes within Curriculum for Excellence, in order to highlight some of the potential limitations of the particular approach taken.

INDIVIDUAL MORE THAN COLLECTIVE

The individualistic take on citizenship and citizenship education is clearly exemplified in the 2002 *Education for Citizenship* document. It opens by saying that '[s]chools and other educational establishments have a central part to play in educating young people for life as active and responsible members of their communities' (LTS, 2002, p. 6), thus reiterating the idea that citizenship resides first and foremost in personal responsibility. The document depicts citizenship responsibility as the corollary of citizenship rights. Citizenship involves 'enjoying rights and exercising responsibilities' and these 'are reciprocal in many respects' (ibid., p. 8). The document emphasises that young people should be regarded 'as citizens of today rather than citizens in waiting', an idea that is linked to the *UN Convention on the Rights of the Child* which states that children 'are born with rights' (ibid.). The individualistic tendency is also clearly exemplified in the overall goal of citizenship education which 'should aim to develop capability for thoughtful and responsible participation in political, economic, social and cultural life', a capability that is considered to be rooted in '*knowledge and understanding*, in a range of *generic skills and competences*, including "core skills", and in a variety of *personal qualities and dispositions*' (ibid., p. 11; emphasis in original). The document seems to hint at a distinction between necessary and sufficient conditions for citizenship, arguing, for example, that 'being a capable citizen' is not just about possessing knowledge and skills but also about 'being able and willing to use knowledge and skills to make decisions and, where appropriate, take action' (ibid., p. 11). Similarly, 'effective citizenship' is not just about having the capacity and dispositions to be active, but is also about 'being able to take action and make things happen' (ibid.). Capability for citizenship is therefore said to depend on a number of literacies: social, economic, cultural and political. In doing so it pursues a common way of thinking about the possibilities of education for citizenship, namely one in which it is argued that education can work on (some of) the necessary conditions for citizenship, but, on its own, will never be sufficient for the development of effective and involved citizenship. This is why 'the contributions of formal education need to be seen alongside, and in interaction with, other influences' from, for example, 'parents, carers and the media and opportunities for community-based learning' (ibid., pp. 9–10).

While all this points towards a strong emphasis on individuals and on citizenship as an individual responsibility and capacity – something that is further exemplified by the strong emphasis on the development of values such as 'respect and care for people and a sense of social and environmental responsibility' (ibid., p. 11) – there are some other aspects of the 2002 *Education for Citizenship* document that point in a different direction. Most significant in this regard is a passage in which it is acknowledged that '[w]hilst all individuals share the rights and responsibilities of citizenship, regardless of status, knowledge or skill, it is clear that citizenship may be exercised with different degrees of effectiveness' (ibid., p. 9). This variety is attributed both to personal and to social circumstances. Here, the document refers, for example, to homelessness as a factor that may impede (young) people from exercising their citizenship rights, just as 'poverty and other forms of disadvantage' may impact on the capacity for effective citizenship. The document therefore concludes that it is in the interest both of individuals and of society as a whole 'that rights and responsibilities of citizenship are well understood, that young people develop the capability needed to function effectively as citizens in modern society' and '*that structures are provided to enable them to do so*' (ibid.; emphasis added). Within the 2002 *Education for Citizenship* document this is one of the few places where the possibility of a structural dimension of citizenship – and by implication a responsibility for citizenship that does *not* lie with the individual but rather with the state – is being considered. The general thrust of the document, however, is on the individual and his or her actions and responsibilities.

This line of thinking is continued in the *Curriculum for Excellence* document where 'responsible citizenship' figures as one of the four capacities that the curriculum from 3 to 18 should enable all children and young people to develop (Scottish Executive, 2004, p. 12). *Curriculum for Excellence* is explicit and upfront about the values that should inform education. It reminds its readers of the fact that the words 'wisdom, justice, compassion and integrity . . . are inscribed on the mace of the Scottish Parliament' and that these 'have helped to define values for our democracy' (ibid., p. 11). Hence it is seen as 'one of the prime purposes of education to make our young people aware of the values on which Scottish society is based and so help them to establish their own stances on matters of social justice and personal and collective responsibility' (ibid.). Therefore, young people 'need to learn about and develop these values' (ibid.). To achieve this, the curriculum 'should emphasise the rights and responsibilities of individuals and nations'; 'should help young people to understand diverse cultures and beliefs and support them in developing concern, tolerance, care and respect for themselves and others'; 'must promote a commitment to considered judgement and ethical action' and 'should give young people the confidence, attributes and capabilities to make valuable contributions to society' (ibid.). Although the *Curriculum for Excellence* document acknowledges what we might call the situated character of citizenship, its depiction as value-based, its articulation in terms of responsibility, respect and commitment to responsible participation, plus the fact that it is embedded in a capacity-based conception of education, all highlight the strong individualistic tendency in the conception of citizenship and citizenship education.

SOCIAL MORE THAN POLITICAL

Whereas the conception of citizenship as an individual capacity based upon the responsible action of individuals is clearly individualistic, and whereas the emphasis of the educational efforts on the development of knowledge, skills and dispositions has a strong focus on individuals and their traits and attributes also, this is mitigated within the Scottish approach by a strong emphasis on the need for experiential learning within the domain of citizenship. All documents agree that the best way to learn citizenship is, as it is put in the 2002 *Education for Citizenship* document, 'through experience and interaction with others' (LTS, 2002, p. 10). 'In short, learning about citizenship is best achieved by being an active citizen' (ibid.). This idea is one of the main reasons why the approach proposed in the document 'does not involve the creation of a new subject called "citizenship education"' (ibid., p. 16). Instead, the document takes the view 'that each young person's entitlement to education for citizenship can be secured through combinations of learning experiences set in the daily life of the school, discrete areas of the curriculum, cross-curricular experiences and activities involving links with the local community' (ibid.). The ethos of education for citizenship is therefore explicitly 'active' and 'participatory' and based on opportunities for 'active engagement' (ibid.). This view raises a crucial question, which is about the kind of communities and activities considered to be relevant for citizenship learning. What, in other words, is considered to be the domain for citizenship and, hence, for education for citizenship and citizenship learning?

Most documents denote this domain in broad terms. In the 2002 *Education for Citizenship* document the overall purpose of education for citizenship is defined as 'thoughtful and responsible participation in political, economic, social and cultural life' (LTS, 2002, p. 11; see also p. 3, p. 5). A similar phrase is used in *Curriculum for Excellence* and in the HMIE document (HMIE, 2006a). Whereas several of the documents include questions about the environment in their conception of the domain of citizenship, the HMIE document is the only document discussed in this chapter that makes mention of spiritual values alongside political, social and environmental values as the set of values that education for citizenship should seek to promote (see ibid., p. 3). A reference to religion is, however, remarkably absent in the documents.

The broad conception of the citizenship domain represents a clear choice on behalf of the authors of the 2002 *Education for Citizenship* document. The document starts from the assumption that everyone belongs to various types of community, 'both communities of place, from local to global, and communities of interest, rooted in common concern or purpose' (LTS, 2002, p. 8). Against this background, citizenship is said to involve 'enjoying rights and responsibilities in these various types of community' (ibid.). The document then adds that this way of seeing citizenship 'encompasses the specific idea of political participation by members of a democratic state' but it also includes 'the more general notion that citizenship embraces a range of participatory activities, not all overtly political, that affect the welfare of communities' (ibid.). Examples of the latter type of citizenship include 'voluntary work, personal engagement in local concerns such as neighbourhood watch schemes or parent-teacher associations, or general engagement in civic society' (ibid.).

Although the *Curriculum for Excellence* document is shorter and far more general than the *Education for Citizenship* paper, and although it does locate questions about citizenship within a wider political context, its articulation of the abilities involved in responsible citizenship lacks an explicit political and democratic dimension and is predominantly at the social end of the spectrum. Responsible citizens are depicted as individuals who have 'respect for others' and a 'commitment to participate responsibly in political, economic, social and cultural life', and who are able to 'develop knowledge and understanding of the world and Scotland's place in it; understand different beliefs and cultures; make informed choices and decisions; evaluate environmental, scientific and technological issues; [and] develop informed, ethical views of complex issues' (SE, 2004, p. 12). The emphasis on the social dimensions of citizenship is even more prominent in the HMIE *Education for Citizenship* document (HMIE, 2006a). Although some reference to democratic processes, the Scottish Youth Parliament and issues 'such as social justice and human rights' is made, citizenship is depicted predominantly in relation to society at large, with a strong emphasis on the involvement of pupils in decision making at school level and, to a lesser extent, the wider community. What is mostly lacking is a connection of citizenship with the political domain, in terms both of the 'scope' of citizenship and of the way in which relevant learning processes are understood and depicted.

SOCIAL ACTIVITY MORE THAN POLITICAL ACTION

Although the social dimension of citizenship and an emphasis on participation and active involvement are not unimportant for the development of citizenship knowledge and dispositions, and although an emphasis on the social dimensions of citizenship is definitely important for the preservation and maintenance of civil society, an almost exclusive emphasis on these aspects runs the risk that the political dimensions of citizenship, including an awareness of the limitations of personal responsibility for effective political action and change, remain invisible and become unattainable for children and young people. There is the danger, in other words, that citizenship becomes depoliticised and that, as a result, students are not sufficiently empowered to take effective political action in a way that goes beyond their immediate concerns and responsibilities.

There is a similar danger with regard to the third aspect of the Scottish approach: the strong emphasis on activity and active citizenship. The idea of active citizenship is important and significant, with regard both to understanding what citizenship is and entails and to citizenship learning. As I have argued elsewhere in more detail (see Biesta, 2011) the most significant citizenship learning that takes place in the lives of young people is the learning that follows from their actual experiences and their actual 'condition' of citizenship. These experiences, which are part of the lives they lead inside and outside of school, can be said to form the real citizenship curriculum for young people, which shows the crucial importance of opportunities for positive experiences with democratic action and decision making in all aspects of young people's lives. In this regard I could not agree more with the claim made in the 2002 *Education for Citizenship* document that 'young people learn most about citizenship by being active citizens' (LTS, 2002, p. 3). But the crucial question here is what young people's active citizenship actually entails.

This depends partly on the domain in which citizenship activity is exercised. But it also depends on the nature of the activity. In this regard it is important not to lose sight of the specific history of the idea of active citizenship, which was introduced by Conservative governments in the late 1980s and early 1990s as a way to let citizens take care of what used to be the responsibility of the government under welfare state conditions (see Faulks, 1998). While it is difficult to argue against active citizenship, it is important, therefore, to be precise about the nature of the activity and the domain in which the activity is exercised. Active citizenship in itself can operate at either the social or the political end of the citizenship spectrum and can therefore either contribute to politicisation and the development of political literacy, or be basically apolitical or non-political. Given the different views on the domain of citizenship, it is, therefore, not entirely clear how political and how enabling active citizenship within the Scottish context will be, although the tendency seems to be on a form of active citizenship located towards the social end of the citizenship spectrum.

A COMMUNITY OF SAMENESS MORE THAN A COMMUNITY OF DIFFERENCE

The fourth characteristic of the Scottish approach is its strong emphasis on community. It is, perhaps, significant that in the 2002 *Education for Citizenship* document the word 'community' is used seventy-six times and the word 'communities' thirty-one times, while the word 'democratic' is used nine times and the word 'democracy' only once. The point I wish to raise here is not about the fact that citizenship is depicted in relation to (local, and sometimes also global) communities, but concerns the particular way in which communities are conceived within the documents. In all documents, 'community' is used as an unproblematic notion and generally also as a positive one. The documents speak about young people and *their* communities, suggesting not only that it is clear what these communities are, but also that young people's membership of these communities is obvious and taken for granted. An important question, however, is what actually constitutes a community and what the difference might be between a social, a cultural and a political community.

There is a strong tendency within the literature on communities to think of them in terms of sameness, commonality and identity. This may be true for many cultural and, perhaps to a lesser extent, social communities – and it seems to be the conception of community implied in most of what the documents have to say about community. But whereas cultural and social communities may display a strong sense of commonality and sameness, this is not how we should understand *political* communities. One could argue – and many political philosophers have argued this point – that the very purpose of politics, and more specifically democratic politics, is to deal in one way or another with the fact of plurality, with the fact that individuals within society have different conceptions of the good life, different values and different ideas about what matters to them. Ultimately, political communities are therefore communities of plurality and difference, and it is precisely here that the difficulty of democratic politics is located. Whereas there is some awareness within the documents, particularly the earlier parts of the 2002 *Education for Citizenship* document, of the particular nature of political communities – most notably in the recognition of the plurality of perceptions of rights and responsibilities (see LTS, 2002, pp. 8–9) – the predominant conception of community in the documents is that of the community as a community of sameness (for a similar conclusion, see Ross and Munn, 2008).

THE CONTENT OF EDUCATION FOR CITIZENSHIP

If this gives us an indication of the ideas about citizenship that inform the Scottish approach, then the important question is how we might characterise this approach in order to understand the particular choices involved. To do this I make use of a typology developed by Westheimer and Kahne (2004) in their analysis of educational programmes for the promotion of democratic citizenship in the United States. Westheimer and Kahne make a distinction between three visions of citizenship – the *personally responsible citizen*; the *participatory citizen*; and the *justice-oriented citizen* – which they characterise in the following way.

The personally responsible citizen:

> acts responsibly in his or her community by, for example, picking up litter, giving blood, recycling, obeying laws, and staying out of debt. The personally responsible citizen contributes to food or clothing drives when asked and volunteers to help those less fortunate, whether in a soup kitchen or a senior centre. Programmes that seek to develop personally responsible citizens, attempt to build character and personal responsibility by emphasizing honesty, integrity, self-discipline, and hard work. (ibid., p. 241)

Participatory citizens are those:

> who actively participate in civic affairs and the social life of the community at the local, state, or national level. [. . .] Educational programs designed to support the development of participatory citizens focus on teaching students how government and community-based organizations work and training them to plan and participate in organized efforts to care for people in need or, for example, to guide school policies. Skills associated with such collective endeavours – such as how to run a meeting – are also viewed as important [. . .]. [P]roponents of participatory citizenship argue that civic participation transcends particular community problems or opportunities. It develops relationships, common understandings, trust and collective commitments [and thereby] adopts a broad notion of the political sphere. (ibid., pp. 2 41–2)

Justice-oriented citizenship – 'the perspective that is least commonly pursued' (ibid., p. 242) – is based on the claim 'that effective democratic citizens need opportunities to analyze and understand the interplay of social, economic and political forces' (ibid.). Westheimer and Kahne refer to this approach as 'justice-oriented' because advocates of this approach call explicit attention 'to matters of injustice and to the importance of pursing social justice' (ibid.):

> The vision of the justice-oriented citizen shares with the vision of the participatory citizen an emphasis on collective work related to the life and issues of the community. Its focus on responding to social problems and to structural critique makes it somewhat different, however [as it seeks] to prepare students to improve society by critically analyzing and addressing social issues and injustices. [. . .] These programmes are less likely to emphasize the need for charity and voluntarism as ends in themselves and more likely to teach about social movements and how to effect systemic change. (ibid.)

When we look at the Scottish approach to education for citizenship against this background, it is obvious that there are elements of all three orientations. This, as I have shown, is particularly the case in the 2002 *Education for Citizenship* document although already within that document we can see a shift towards an emphasis on personal responsibility. What emerges from the analysis, therefore, is that the conception of citizenship informing the Scottish approach is predominantly that of the personally responsible citizen. Within the documents there is also a strong emphasis on participation. Although this shifts the conception of citizenship towards a more participatory approach, I am inclined to understand this mainly in relation to the approach to educational processes aimed at promoting citizenship, rather than that they are central to the *conception* of citizenship pursued. It is, in other words, important to make a distinction between the conception of *citizenship* and the conception of citizenship *education* in the documents, and my suggestion is that the conception of citizenship veers more towards the personally responsible citizens, whereas participation is presented as a key dimension of how students can *become* such citizens. This is, of course, not all black and white, but I hope to have presented a sufficiently detailed reading to warrant this conclusion.

By mapping the Scottish approach onto the categories suggested by Westheimer and Kahne, it is possible to see that the Scottish approach represents a particular *choice* – which means that other options are possible. A crucial question here is whether the choice presented in the Scottish approach is the 'best' choice. Answering this question crucially depends on how one wishes education for citizenship to function and, most importantly, in what way and to what extent one wishes education for citizenship to contribute to a particular – democratic – configuration of society. At this point it is important to take into consideration Westheimer's and Kahne's observation that an emphasis on personal responsibility in citizenship is 'an inadequate response to the challenges of educating a democratic citizenry' (ibid.). The issue here is that 'the emphasis placed on individual character and behavior obscures the need for collective and public sector initiatives; that this emphasis distracts attention from analysis of the causes of social problems and from systematic solutions' and that 'voluntarism and kindness are put forward as ways of avoiding politics and policy' (ibid.). The main problem Westheimer and Kahne see is that whilst no one 'wants young people to lie, cheat, or steal' the values implied in the notion of the personally responsible citizen 'can be at odds with democratic goals' (ibid.). '[E]ven the widely accepted goals – fostering honesty, good neighborliness, and so on – are not *inherently* about democracy' (ibid; emphasis in original). To put it differently: while many of the values and traits enlisted in relation to the personally responsible citizen 'are desirable traits for people living in a community [. . .] they are not about democratic citizenship' (ibid.). And, even more strongly: 'To the extent that emphasis on these character traits detracts from other important democratic priorities, it may actually hinder rather than make possible democratic participation and change' (ibid.).

A too strong emphasis on personal responsibility, on individual capacities and abilities, and on personal values, dispositions and attitudes does not only run the risk of *depoliticising* citizenship by seeing it mainly as a personal and social phenomenon. It also runs the risk of not doing enough to empower young people as *political* actors who have an understanding of both the opportunities and the limitations of individual political action, and who are aware that real change – change that affects structures rather than operations within existing structures – often requires collective action and initiatives from other bodies, including the state. To quote Westheimer and Kahne once more: the individualistic conception of personally responsible citizenship rarely raises questions about 'corporate responsibility . . . or about ways that government policies can advance or hinder solutions to social problems' and therefore tends to ignore 'important influences such as social movements and government policy on efforts to improve society' (ibid., p. 244). An exclusive emphasis on personally responsible citizenship may therefore well be 'inadequate for advancing democracy' as there is 'nothing inherently *democratic* about personally responsible citizenship' and, perhaps even more importantly, 'undemocratic practices are sometimes associated with programs that rely exclusively on notions of personal responsibility' (ibid., p. 248; emphasis in original).

THE FORM OF EDUCATION FOR CITIZENSHIP

If this provides a perspective on what we might call the content of citizenship education, I wish to conclude with two observations about the particular form citizenship education takes in Curriculum for Excellence. I have shown that Scotland has chosen *not* to make citizenship into an additional subject on the curriculum but rather to position it as one of the four broad capacities that all educational activity from 3 to 18 should aim to promote and cultivate. In this sense the Scottish approach to curriculum is distinctively different from approaches taken in other countries as it neither specifies the particular content that children and young people should acquire through the curriculum nor prescribes how teachers should teach the curriculum – which leaves teachers with more space for agency than in more prescribed forms of curriculum planning and policy. Yet this is not without problems.

One obvious problem is that when citizenship is made a responsibility of everyone, it runs the risk of becoming the responsibility of nobody. Whether this is so is partly an empirical question that is beyond the scope of this chapter. A paper published by Cowan and McMurtry in 2009 – but reporting on a small-scale project conducted in 2004 – does indeed indicate that many schools were only just beginning to pay attention to the citizenship dimension across the curriculum, thus indicating that it is indeed a serious challenge how to make citizenship an integral part of the curriculum rather than something safely 'parked' within a particular curriculum subject. A more interesting – and in a sense more encouraging – perspective can be found in a study conducted by Maitles (2010). His detailed study of a single school does indeed show that a school-wide and curriculum-wide approach to citizenship is possible and that it also can have effects on students' values. What is also interesting about this particular study is its focus and emphasis on values that are more on the political than the social end of the spectrum, although they remain within a more individual than collective framing of the desirable outcomes of citizenship education.

A second problem that comes with the particular 'form' chosen in the Scottish approach is that of expertise. If citizenship education is seen as the responsibility of everyone one also needs to ask where particular expertise about citizenship and citizenship education might reside in a school. If there is no subject to teach it is unlikely that a school will appoint – or will even be able to appoint – someone who has particular expertise in the domain of citizenship and its pedagogy. So while all teachers can do their best to include a citizenship dimension into their own area of teaching, there is a real danger that this remains at a low and general level and actually reproduces everyday ideas about citizenship rather than promoting a thoughtful and informed approach to citizenship education. A recent study by Fotheringham (2010) did indeed reveal widely different interpretations of what citizenship is about amongst staff at a Scottish further education college. The Scottish approach, while laudable from one angle, does therefore raise important questions about the expertise necessary to support the promotion of responsible citizenship and thus about the general quality of the approach taken.

IN CONCLUSION

The Scottish approach to education for citizenship differs significantly from what is going on in many other countries around the world. To think of citizenship as something that should permeate the whole curriculum is an exciting prospect, rightly informed by the idea that the most significant learning in the domain of citizenship is experiential learning closely connected to young people's positive and negative experience with citizenship. The analysis of the documents that frame the Scottish approach to citizenship shows a tendency towards an individualistic and to a certain extent apolitical conception of citizenship that may not necessarily or automatically support the development of democratic processes and practices and a democratic disposition. The fact that citizenship is the responsibility of all raises the question of how schools can build capacity and expertise to sustain the important contribution they can make to the formation of truly democratic citizens.

REFERENCES

Andrews, R. and A. Mycock (2007) 'Citizenship education in the UK: Divergence within a multi-national State', *Citizenship Teaching and Learning*, 3 (1): 73–88.

Biesta, G. J. J. (2011) *Learning Democracy in School and Society: Education, Lifelong Learning and the Politics of Citizenship*. Rotterdam: Sense Publishers.

Cowan, E. M. and D. C. McMurtry (2009) 'The implementation of "Education for Citizenship" in schools in Scotland: a research report', *The Curriculum Journal*, 20 (1): 61–72.

Faulks, K. (1998) *Citizenship in Modern Britain*. Edinburgh: Edinburgh University Press.

Fotheringham, J. (2010) 'Making sense of citizenship at college in the context of Curriculum for Excellence'. Masters thesis for the award of Master in Technology-Enhanced Learning, University of Stirling.

Her Majesty's Inspectorate of Education (2003) *How Good is our School? Education for Citizenship*. Edinburgh: HMIE.

Her Majesty's Inspectorate of Education (2006a) *Education for Citizenship: A Portrait of Current Practice in Scottish Schools and Pre-School Centres*. Edinburgh: HMIE.

Her Majesty's Inspectorate of Education (2006b) *Citizenship in Scotland's Colleges. A Report by HM Inspectorate of Education for the Scottish Further and Higher Education Funding Council*. Edinburgh: HMIE.

Learning and Teaching Scotland (2000) *Education for Citizenship: A Paper for Discussion and Consultation*. Dundee: Learning and Teaching Scotland.

Learning and Teaching Scotland (2002) *Education for Citizenship: A Paper for Discussion and Development*. Dundee: Learning and Teaching Scotland.

Maitles, H. (2010) 'Citizenship initiatives and pupil values: A case study of one Scottish school's experience', *Educational Review*, 62 (4): 391–406.

Munn, P. and M. Arnott (2009) 'Citizenship in Scottish schools: The evolution of education for citizenship from the late twentieth century to the present', *History of Education*, 38 (3): 437–54.

Ross, H. and P. Munn (2008) 'Representing self-in-society: Education for citizenship and the social-subjects curriculum in Scotland', *Journal of Curriculum Studies*, 40 (2): 251–75.

Scottish Executive (2004) *A Curriculum for Excellence*. Edinburgh: Scottish Executive.

Westheimer, J. and J. Kahne (2004) 'What kind of citizen? The politics of educating for democracy', *American Educational Research Journal*, 41 (2): 237–69.

31

Sustainable Development Education

Peter Higgins and Alastair Lavery

The concept of sustainable development education (SDE) requires an understanding of the highly contested notion of 'sustainable development' (SD). This term was succinctly defined in *Our Common Future*, the Brundtland Report (1987), as 'development that meets the needs of the present without compromising the ability of future generations to meet their own needs'. While this definition has been both elaborated and critiqued, it has stood the test of time and is generally accepted to imply a human dimension, the concept of current and intergenerational social equity, as well as the preservation of earth systems and biodiversity.

At its simplest, 'sustainable development education' is about acquiring the knowledge and skills needed to take decisions that are compatible with sustainable development. The open-ended nature of SDE was stated in the Scottish Government statement on SDE in 2006, *Learning for our Future*, as follows:

> The purpose of sustainable development education is not to tell people what is important and what they should do, but to enable them to decide what is important to them, decide what they want to do about it, and equip them with the skills they need to do it.

More complete descriptions of SDE's definition and rationale began in the UK with *Education for Sustainable Development in the Schools Sector* (Panel for Education for Sustainable Development, 1998) and form the basis for those currently in use. In Scotland, early advocates of SDE promoted the use of the term employed here, 'sustainable development education', over the term used in the rest of the UK, 'education for sustainable development' (ESD). This was to emphasise that the purpose of SDE is to provide knowledge and skills to support decision making, not to dictate the instrumental nature and direction of the decisions, implied by education *for* sustainable development.

HISTORICAL BACKGROUND

The history of SDE in Scotland has been well documented in the series of reports discussed here and in summary analyses by Lavery and Smyth (2003) for the period up to 1999 and McNaughton (2007) for the period 1993–2007. This history is significant in both the Scottish response to this agenda and the Scottish influence in international development. Scotland made an early start in considering SDE, with a groundbreaking report by

Her Majesty's Inspectors of Schools, *Environmental Education*, in 1974. As a result of a combination of political indifference and major structural changes in the education system, this radical statement of the importance of what is now called SDE was not implemented. However, it was effective in two ways: in having influence on developing international thinking and in stimulating the grouping of teachers, teacher educators and academics that formed into the Scottish Environmental Education Council (SEEC) in 1997.

SEEC was the centre point for the next round of developments, involving capacity building and providing grassroots support for a growing number of schools, universities and colleges, experimenting with learning and teaching about the environment. It is worth noting that throughout this period the term 'environmental education' was used in a wider sense in Scotland than in many other education systems and was close to the current usage of SDE.

This period of development led, in 1990, to the formation of a government working group, chaired by John Smyth, to consider the need to implement SDE in all aspects of Scottish education. This widely participative group reported in 1993 with the influential *Learning for Life*, published by the Scottish Office in the immediate aftermath of the 1992 United Nations Earth Summit where, partly as a result of John Smyth's influence internationally, education was a central feature. Again because of political ambivalence and conflicting policy drivers, government response to *Learning for Life*, in a Scottish Office paper *A Scottish Strategy for Environmental Education*, was delayed until 1995. This was not a fully developed strategy, but recommended that a further advisory group be established to make new proposals for implementation. This group, the Education for Sustainable Development Group (ESDG), reported in 1999 in a paper entitled *The Learning Process* (Scottish Office, 1999), setting an agenda for the Scottish Parliament established that year.

Progress was again slow. In 2000, SEEC was disbanded following severe cuts in its government grant and SDE, seen in *Learning for Life* as a process involving all aspects of education, formal, informal and non-formal, became more fragmented. However, considerable grassroots support and action in all education sectors had been building throughout this period. The Sustainable Development Education Liaison Group (SDELG) was established by Learning and Teaching Scotland in this period to advise on SDE for schools and was successful in influencing the direction of the Scottish Government response to the United Nations Decade of Education for Sustainable Development 2005–14 (UNDESD) and the development of SDE in the review that led to Curriculum for Excellence (CfE). Through this period there have also been UK and international SDE-related teacher education initiatives, and the Scottish response to these has also been variable (Higgins and Kirk, 2009).

CURRICULAR CONTEXT

Sustainable development education is one of a group of curricular areas that emerged as claimants for a place in schools over a thirty-year period. The group includes, for example, citizenship, international education, financial education and outdoor education. They characteristically provide a new focus or context for teaching and learning across a range of traditional academic disciplines. They have been given a range of group titles, from 'adjectival' educations to cross-curricular themes, the current usage being interdisciplinary learning. SDE presents two distinct challenges to the curriculum: its interdisciplinarity and its political content:

- *Interdisciplinarity*: An interdisciplinary topic is difficult to place in a discipline-based curriculum. As this was one of the challenges CfE was designed to meet, SDE's accommodation into the curriculum is perhaps no surprise but is worth noting as an achievement.
- *Political content*: There is anecdotal evidence that SDE, and its partial precursors 'environmental' and 'development' education, met with political resistance in the 1980s and 1990s. The very significant changes in societal and political attitudes to sustainability have made SDE acceptable to schools, though contested topics, such as climate change, continue to make parts of the topic controversial, relevant and potentially interesting to learners.

THE CURRENT PLACE OF SDE

In 2008, the Scottish Government engaged with UNDESD by publishing a five-year action plan for SDE, *Learning for our Future*. This was followed in 2010 by the Scottish Government plan for the second half of the decade, *Learning for Change*. These set ambitious plans for SDE in three sectors: schools, universities and colleges, and communities.

The development of CfE within the timeframe of UNDESD has led to a full integration of SDE into the curriculum. Sustainable development themes are prominent in the 'experiences and outcomes' in many curriculum areas, particularly in Science, Social Studies and Technologies. For example, in Technologies one aim is to 'be capable of making reasoned choices relating to the environment, sustainable development and ethical, economic and cultural issues'. This aim is fully developed in the experiences and outcomes in the 'Technological Developments in Society' contexts.

In the senior stage of secondary school, the skills and content of the examination arrangements have been extensively revised at levels 4–7 (National – Advanced Higher) and the new syllabuses show a strengthening of sustainable development topics, again particularly in science and social subjects. For example, Higher Biology contains a unit 'Sustainability and Interdependence', covering the science of food production, of biodiversity and of interdependence in ecology.

Prior to the current round of curriculum review, most schools' work in SDE took place in interdisciplinary learning, often as informal or extra-curricular work. Most influential was Eco-Schools Scotland, with almost all schools registered and nearly 50 per cent having achieved its highest award, the Green Flag. Other initiatives, such as the John Muir Award and Rights Respecting Schools, have played a significant role in bringing a wider understanding of SDE to schools. However, as these are not curricular initiatives they are not available to all school pupils, and part of the challenge to schools in implementing CfE will be to bring the freshness of these and other SDE-related programmes into the framework provided by the new curriculum. In fact, it could be argued that the success of integration of SDE into mainstream schooling might be measured by this transition.

SDE IN SCHOOLS – CAMPUS AND COMMUNITY

Sustainable development education is not confined to the curriculum. It encompasses all aspects of a school's work and can be conveniently organised in terms of curriculum, campus and community. In schools, most recent progress has focused on curriculum. Though government and local authority targets on carbon following the Climate Change (Scotland) Act 2009 have given energy use in schools a renewed impetus, progress on sustainable aspects of school design has been patchy, due at least in part to the variable approaches of local authorities. Attention to the sustainable aspects of school grounds, covering outdoor teaching, play and biodiversity, have achieved prominence through a range of initiatives (see Chapter 68) but are at present under threat from cuts in support from government and its agencies.

A school is in essence a 'community of learners' – a wider community than often acknowledged – including pupils, teachers and support staff, and the totality of the schools external contacts. Learning through sustainable practices as well as the curriculum is core to a proper understanding of the concept of sustainability and this potentially has implications for all those who study or work there or who come into contact with the school. Further, as the centre of the local community, schools are recognised as places where young people develop knowledge and values that then engage their families and others. Whilst this is seen as a means of encouraging a broader community to adopt more sustainable behaviours, the effectiveness of such an approach is not clear and in need of research attention.

SDE IN HIGHER AND FURTHER EDUCATION

Higher and Further Education institutions in Scotland have a role in the general understanding of sustainable development related issues through their work in the main disciplinary areas, in climate and other forms of environmental change, in applied areas such as renewable energy and in more general overviews of sustainable development. As such they are a natural destination for school graduates with an interest and training in these areas, and UK universities and colleges have responded to the opportunities presented by SD and to the interest of applicants.

In the present context it is the role of Teacher Education Institutions (TEIs) in training teachers in SDE that is the most imminent concern. There is no current requirement for Scottish TEIs to include any detailed coverage of SD in their programmes, and those that do so include SDE as an option or as a part of another course. Without input into their training, the level of interest, knowledge and skills teacher graduates possess and are able to deploy in their teaching will always be a matter of chance.

SDE IN SCOTLAND IN A GLOBAL CONTEXT

In 1998 in Thessaloniki, UNESCO established an initiative 'Reorienting Teacher Education towards Sustainable Development'. Because of Scotland's early progress in SDE a representative from Moray House Institute of Education was invited to the initial meeting of ten TEIs, and this involvement has been maintained. The international network has now grown to over 200 colleges and TEIs and progress specifically in re-orienting teacher education in Scotland has been slow in comparison to many other countries.

In 2004, Learning and Teaching Scotland published a research report for the Sustainable Development Education Liaison Group, *Sustainable Development Education in England, Wales, Northern Ireland and Scotland* (LTS, 2004). This was followed by *Sustainable Development Education: An International Study* (LTS, 2006), describing progress in SDE in ten countries and across five continents. Both the reports identify areas of good practice in many other education systems that could be adopted in Scotland and provided a benchmark for developments here. A prominent theme was that developments in SDE could be adversely affected by withdrawal of funding or by change in government policy. Overall, the studies placed Scotland in the leading group in international comparisons. A recent UK-wide analysis for the UK National Commission for UNESCO noted that the 'absence of an overarching UK strategy for sustainable development that sets out a clear vision about the contribution learning can make to its goals is a major barrier to progress', but commended Scotland for leading recent developments within the UK (Martin et al., 2013). The conclusion of UNDESD in 2014 would be a suitable time for a further international review, but in terms of Scotland's status much will depend on the Scottish Government's continued support and the success of the revised GTCS professional standards.

FUTURE PROSPECTS

UNDESD has served as a stimulus for SDE, building upon both Scotland's rich tradition and the introduction of CfE. However, as 2014 approaches there is the potential for loss of momentum to occur. There are several aspects of policy practice that should reduce the likelihood of this:

1. Several Ministerial Advisory Groups were established in 2011 with relevant remits. Whilst the 'Scottish Studies' group had culture, history and language as part of its remit, the Scottish landscape also featured and this provides rich opportunities for helping students to understand issues central to climate change, biodiversity and community development (www.scotland. gov.uk/Topics/Education/Schools/curriculum/ACE/ScottishStudies). The remit of the 'One Planet Schools' Advisory Group was to explore the concept of SDE within the context of Curriculum for Excellence, and reflect the general thrust of *Learning for Change* (http:// www.scotland.gov.uk/Topics/Education/Schools/curriculum/ACE/OnePlanetSchools). This signalled the government's intent to help schools gradually reduce their use of resources and develop a values orientation that addresses sustainability through a whole-school approach integrating three equally important facets – Sustainable Development, Global Citizenship Education and Outdoor Learning (see also Chapter 68). The Ministerial Advisory Group report (titled *Learning for Sustainability*) was published in March 2013 Scottish Ministers accepted all thirty-one recommendations – almost in full. One key outcome is that the Scottish Government is establishing a 'Learning for Sustainability Implementation Group' to ensure that 'learning for sustainability' is integrated within the whole education system.
2. The end of the UNDESD in 2014 has stimulated discussion on means of maintaining the momentum of current SDE structures and groupings, and of ensuring that relevant initiatives (in mainstream schools, non-governmental organisations, further and higher education, government etc.) continue to be funded. One way other parts of the UK and other countries have addressed this is through establishing a UN-accredited 'Regional Centre of Expertise' (RCE) in ESD (http://rcescotland.org/). The proposal for a Scotland-wide RCE was accepted in December 2012 and it is clear that the Scottish Government will look to the RCE to take an important facilitating role in the 'Learning for Sustainability Implementation Group'.
3. The Scottish Government commitment to renewable energy and 'green employment' will mean that the technological and social aspects of SD will need to be considered in schools and institutes of further or higher education. Whilst this is essentially an instrumental outcome of other educational initiatives the pressure to meet renewables and other targets must act as a stimulus for SDE. For example, the government's economic strategy includes six strategic priorities, one of which is newly included – the 'Transition to a Low Carbon Economy' – and suggests that all of Scotland's demand for electricity should be met by renewables by 2020, and that a greener economy could support 130,000 jobs by 2020 (Scottish Government, 2011).

4. In December 2012 the GTCS published its revised 'Professional Standards' which will become part of a national framework for teachers' professional learning and development (http://www.gtcs.org.uk/standards/revised-professional-standards.aspx) (see Chapter 98). 'Learning for Sustainability' is embedded with the professional values, personal commitments and leadership aspects of the three new Professional Standards relating to Registration, Career-long Professional Learning and Leadership and Management, and every teacher and education professional will be expected to demonstrate learning for sustainability in their practice.

In the context of shrinking financial resources local authority support for SDE is becoming more limited, and maintaining momentum will require creativity. One approach being supported by Education Scotland is to build on the skills and experiences of teachers who have succeeded in enhancing SDE in their schools by encouraging them to act as mentors for staff in other schools, building peer-support and collaboration. This process relates closely to the *Learning for Change* Action Plans and the practitioner-to-practitioner support encouraged in the Donaldson Report, *Teaching Scotland's Future* (2010). Whilst such approaches are not national policy, the combined developments outlined in this section provide an excellent opportunity for Scotland to implement SDE fully within the whole education system and maintain its reputation internationally. However, much will depend on the degree of commitment of Scotland's government and education agencies to ensuring that, in the context of clear knowledge of the sustainability issues we face and twenty years after the publication of *Learning for Life*, SDE/Learning for Sustainability finally becomes a priority in Scottish education.

REFERENCES

N.b. A number of government reports are referred to in the text but are not cited as reference sources. These are easily traceable through the title, year and government source.

Higgins, P. and G. Kirk (2009) 'Sustainability Education in Scotland: The impact of national and international initiatives on teacher education and outdoor education', in B. Chalkley, M. Haigh and D. Higgitt (eds), *Education for Sustainable Development*. London: Routledge.

Lavery, A. and J. Smyth (2003) 'Developing Environmental Education, a review of a Scottish project: international and political influences', *Environmental Education Research*, 9 (3): 361–83.

Learning and Teaching Scotland (2004) *Sustainable Development Education in England, Wales, Northern Ireland and Scotland*. Glasgow: Learning and Teaching Scotland.

Learning and Teaching Scotland (2006) *Sustainable Development Education: and international study*. Glasgow: Learning and Teaching Scotland.

Martin, S., J. Dillon, P. Higgins, C. Peters and W. Scott (2013) 'Divergent Evolution in Education for Sustainable Development Policy in the United Kingdom: Current Status, Best Practice, and Opportunities for the Future', *Sustainability*, 5 (4): 1356–763.

McNaughton, M.-J. (2007) 'Sustainable development education in Scottish schools: The sleeping beauty syndrome', *Environmental Education Research*, 13 (5): 621–35.

Panel for Education for Sustainable Development (1998) *Education for Sustainable Development in the Schools Sector*. Reading: Council for Environmental Education.

Scottish Government (2011) *The Government Economic Strategy*. Edinburgh: Scottish Government.

V

MANAGEMENT AND ORGANISATION IN SCHOOLS

Section V considers issues relating to the management and organisation of schools across the stage spectrum, providing authoritative commentary on issues that pertain both to sector-specific and cross-sector contexts. Readers wishing to gain a more detailed picture of the wider context of schooling in Scotland should read the relevant chapters in Section II first.

In this section, Chapters 32 and 33 cover early years-specific issues, Chapter 33 dealing with childcare and early education, that is, policy and provision outwith the formal primary school context; and Chapter 33 dealing with early schooling. In Chapter 32, the Scottish context is considered in relation to policy directives emerging on a European stage where provision is arguably more advanced. It tackles contentious issues such as the structural divide between education and care, workforce qualifications and status, and the challenges of ensuring sustainable interventions that make a long-term difference to outcomes. Chapter 33, in focusing on early schooling, discusses the educational provision for 3–8-year-olds in Scotland and considers the impact of Curriculum for Excellence (CfE). It sets this analysis against the literature on how young children learn. Chapters 34 and 35 consider primary-specific issues, namely: leadership, management and organisation in primary schools (Chapter 34) and discipline, behaviour and ethos in primary schools (Chapter 35). The discussion in Chapter 34 provides insight into the roles and challenges of managing and leading in primary schools, with a particular focus on the concept of leadership for learning. In Chapter 35, behaviour in primary schools is discussed in relation to popular discourse, political pressure and classroom practice, providing an analysis of how the concepts of discipline, behaviour and ethos have changed over time. It usefully identifies gaps in research, but ends on an optimistic note in relation to the direction of travel in Scotland at this time. The transition between primary and secondary school is the focus of Chapter 36, and the author highlights the enduring nature of the challenges associated with this particular transition phase. Transition is considered in relation to both social and academic concerns, and attention is devoted to the potential ways in which schools and teachers might work towards addressing the challenges identified within a new curricular structure that arguably provides greater latitude for progress.

Chapter 37 is the secondary equivalent of Chapter 34 but here the focus is more on the development of the discourse in recent times as headteachers have moved from roles as administrators, through managers, to leaders, most recently within what are promoted as collegial settings. The chapter argues that rationalist models of headship have limited leverage and that a recognition of the importance of the 'spiritual' dimension to effective leadership needs to be embraced. Chapter 38 examines ethos and behaviour in secondary schools and should be read in the light of Chapter 35. The chapter notes some of the recent developments in Scottish schools in relation to the management of behaviour as the climate shifts from an emphasis on rules and sanctions to one where much more stress is laid on building relationships, on participation and on inclusion as the keys to setting and maintaining an effective climate for learning. Chapter 39 examines an emerging phenomenon in Scottish schools which relates to the effective management and deployment of school support assistants at classroom level. The focus in this chapter is on the primary sector but much of the discussion is of generic value. Chapter 40 examines some of the tensions and paradoxes in personal support and personal and social education that have surfaced in the wake of the McCrone Report and the implementation of CfE. This chapter would be worth reading alongside Chapter 60 which deals with health and wellbeing in the secondary school.

In the final chapter (Chapter 41) an overview is provided of the role of self-evaluation across the school sectors in Scotland and how this has developed historically. Given its close links to the inspection regime, it is best read in conjunction with Chapter 20 in Section III, and also Chapter 18 which outlines the role of local authority support in school development. Chapter 110 in Section XIII also gives an indication of how the concept of school self-evaluation has been exported from Scotland and how it sits within the European educational context.

32

Childcare and Early Education

Malcolm Wilson

This chapter outlines the emerging policy landscape and its impact on Scottish childcare services as they increasingly move towards an integrated model of service delivery based on holistic, multi-agency, evidence-based interventionist and preventative approaches. The Scottish approach seeks to reconcile core values of children's rights, universal outcomes and parental participation within a context of endemic child poverty and austerity in public spending. Key influences on the delivery of early years services, as well as national qualification systems for work in the early childhood field, will be explored. Future challenges for all professionals engaged in the delivery of early years services will be outlined.

KEY TERMS

For the purposes of this chapter, early years will be defined as pre-birth to 6 years old. Pre-school will be defined as the period pre-birth to 5 years. This broad definition of early years recognises the importance of pregnancy in influencing outcomes and that the transition into primary school is a critical period in children's lives. Early childhood education and care (ECEC) will be used to refer to Europe-wide early years services.

CHILDCARE PROVISION IN SCOTLAND

There are 2,615 local authority or partnership pre-school education providers in Scotland. Childcare Partnerships involve local authorities cooperating with private and voluntary providers, schools, employers, health boards, parents and others in planning and developing services. Local authorities support collaboration among the different sectors and commission private and voluntary pre-school centres to provide pre-school education and care. Scotland has 276 892 (5.47 per cent of the total population) children between 0 and 4 years of age (Source: 2011 Census) with approximately 20 per cent of children living below the low-income threshold (Scottish Government, 2009), which can affect not only their material wellbeing, but also their physical and emotional wellbeing. By the age of 3, a disadvantaged child's development is already up to a year behind that of their peers (Scottish Government, 2008). All 3- and 4-year-olds in Scotland are entitled to 475 hours of funded pre-school education over the school year. This usually means that a child is offered five sessions of education a week, of about two and a half hours each, throughout the school year. Alex Salmond, the Scottish First Minister and leader of the majority SNP administration, has stated that a Children's Bill will be introduced to Holyrood in 2013 that will include a 'statutory guarantee of over 600 hours of free nursery education for every Scottish 3 and 4 year old and for every looked after 2 year old in our land'. According to the Children (Scotland) Act 1995 Section 17 (6) a child or young person is 'looked after' by a local authority if he or she is: (1) provided with accommodation under Section 25 of the Act (voluntary agreement); (2) subject to a supervision requirement (by a children's hearing); (3) subject to an order, authorisation or warrant (such as a child protection order); or (4) subject to an order made by a court in another part of the UK.

Pre-school services in Scotland take a diverse range of organisational forms. Nursery schools and classes, run by local authority education departments, offer almost exclusively part-time education to 3- and 4-year-olds for the duration of the school year. Traditionally, these settings are staffed by qualified teachers and by child development officers with a lower level of qualification, where their 'client' has primarily been the child. Day nurseries, family learning centres and children's centres (various other titles are also used) are now also run by local authority education departments (although historically run by social work departments), and offer part-time or full-time care to children from 0 to 5 years, often for 50 weeks a year. These services are staffed by child development officers and usually led by managers with a Bachelor of Arts degree in Childhood Practice. Historically, for many of these services, the 'client' was primarily the parent or carer. Public provision of pre-school services is supplemented by private sector provision in the form of daycare services and by approximately 6,000 childminders, usually providing services within their home. The Care Inspectorate regulates all pre-school settings and inspects the quality of care provided. Where the pre-school setting belongs to, or is in partnership with, the local authority, Education Scotland and the Care Inspectorate inspect jointly.

Over the past fifteen years, increased political awareness of the benefits of quality childcare provision has contributed to greater cross-sector convergence in policy goals and the shape of services. There is currently a shared focus on partnership working with parents, integrated forms of multi-agency working and increasing examples of professional role convergence. However, some significant discrepancies between stated national and local policy aspirations and practice do exist, and it has been suggested that national legislation and policy concerning type of provision, access, funding and workforces have served to maintain the structural divide between education and care. In addition, while recent state pronouncements of extended childcare hours are to be welcomed, the scope of Scotland's early years provision continues to lag well behind models that have been developed in other parts of Europe. Scotland still has a significant distance to travel if it is to meet targets for providing an entitlement for full daycare for ECEC set by the European Commission in 2002.

THE EUROPEAN POLICY CONTEXT

Since the 1992 European Council Recommendations on childcare, ECEC has been a recurring topic on European policy agendas. Throughout the European Union (EU), there is a consensus on the need for additional and higher quality services, increasing integration of 'childcare' and 'early education', as well as enhanced training and status for a workforce whose members are seen as essential to quality provision. The European Commission maintains that ECEC has a crucial role to play in laying the foundations for improved competences of future EU citizens and developing a skilled workforce capable of contributing and adjusting to technological change. The EU has gathered evidence that participation in high-quality ECEC leads to significantly better attainment in international tests on basic skills, such as the Programme for International Student Assessment (PISA) and the Progress in International Reading Literacy Study (PIRLS); this can be equivalent to between one and two school years of progress. It has been noted that the impact of solid foundations in the early years are long-lasting: later learning is more effective and is more likely to continue for the duration of the child's life; risks of early school leaving are lessened; equitable educational outcomes are more likely; and the costs for society in terms of lost talent and of public spending on social, health and even justice systems are reduced. This understanding, that effective integrated early years services support children, not only in their future education but also in their assimilation into society, generating wellbeing and contributing to their employability, has become part of the default manifesto position of major political parties across the continent and beyond.

International research evidence that has drawn attention to the experience of high-quality early years services and its beneficial impact on disadvantaged children, including those from migrant and low-income backgrounds, has a particular resonance within debates in Scotland. The argument that it can help to lift children out of poverty and family dysfunction, and so contribute to wider governmental poverty reduction goals, has helped support the growth of a new, dynamic area of both national and local authority policy thinking space.

THE SCOTTISH POLICY CONTEXT

Since the establishment of the Scottish Parliament in 1999, a range of major policy initiatives have been launched by successive governments. Policy developments in Scottish childcare provision have followed the lead set by many of our European counterparts. Policies have been introduced that support the improvement of child health, social and educational outcomes and reducing related inequalities. Most policy documents refer to the body of evidence on the effectiveness of early childhood intervention and the economic argument for taking this approach. Key children's policies in Scotland include:

Overarching Policy

- Getting it Right for Every Child (2008)

Health Policy

- Health for All Children, 4th edition (2003)
- Early Years Framework (2008)
- *Equally Well* (2008)
- *Achieving our Potential* (2008)
- Better Health, Better Care (2007)

Education Policy

- Curriculum for Excellence (3–18 yrs) (2004)
- *Pre-Birth to Three: Positive Outcomes for Scotland's Children and Families* (2010)

The Scottish parliamentary debates fuelling the policy development process were typically framed within the UK government's arguably neo-liberal discourse which holds the individual parent or family responsible for the problems of inequality they endure, whether this is unemployment, poverty or 'failure' as a parent. Resulting policy solutions have stressed the need for improved parenting and the value of employment as the road out of poverty. However, such proposed solutions are not necessarily mutually consistent and may have served to undermine a wider Scottish vision of universal service provision.

A pivotal policy, the *Early Years Framework* (published by the Scottish Government in 2008), calls for a renewed focus on birth to 3 years as the period of a child's development that shapes future outcomes. It emphasises the increased need for developing parental skills, antenatal and postnatal support, and centre- and community-based services for young children. An important government research body, the Scottish Collaboration for Public Health Research and Policy (SCPHRP), maintains that a degree of targeting of services is both necessary and inevitable in order to identify pregnant women and infants at high social and developmental risk. SCPHRP has proposed a mixed, two-generation model on which this could be based. The model is intended to inform provision of a universal seamless continuum of care and support from pregnancy through to school entry, with the intensity of support graded according to need. This model is increasingly being used as a basis for realising the aspirations of the Early Years Framework in terms of developing detailed plans and strategies that will be necessary for its full implementation. The policy language being used here is interesting. A subtle but important tension exists between a universal continuum and a universal service, with resulting implications for future investment in children's services. Service providers are presented with the task of reconciling the complex, diverse and changing concerns of children during their early childhood within a continuum approach of delimited, targeted intervention. Such an approach is not necessarily consistent with ensuring universal access to the appropriate intervention at the point of most need. It has recently been suggested that Scotland has the potential to resolve this dilemma by adopting an 'active filtering' approach in which professionals and families together determine level of need with reference to standardised assessment tools (Wilson et al., 2008). In other words, we need an intelligent system for 'case-finding', an assessment of the level of child/family need and appropriate resource allocation, often called progressive universalism (Wilson, 2011).

HEALTH POLICY

The implementation of *Health for all Children* (published by the Scottish Government in 2003) across Scotland has resulted in a screening and surveillance programme that aims to target children and families most in need more effectively. The strategy is to classify children as low, medium or high risk by 6 to 8 weeks of age, after which there is no routine contact with those deemed to be low risk until the universal visual screening at 4 years of age (except for immunisation, when contact depends on the caregiver bringing the child). There is evidence from Glasgow that only half of high-risk children at the age of 1 year or older are identified by 4 months by health visitors (Wright et al., 2009). Risk factors embedded in adverse experiences during the first years of life have a huge influence on the future mental health of the child. In one long-term follow-up of children suffering abuse in the first years of life, 90 per cent had at least one psychiatric diagnosis by age 17.

Numerous interventions designed to impact on maternal and child health have been implemented in Scotland – including Triple P: positive parenting programmes – but very few have been evaluated robustly (see Geddes et al., 2010). Such preventive programmes offer intensive and structured home visiting, delivered by specially trained nurses (family nurses), from early pregnancy until the child is 2 years old. The aim is to improve pregnancy outcomes, child health and development and parents' economic self-sufficiency by encouraging young mothers to aspire to improving their lives by, for instance, finding work. The methods are based on theories of human ecology, self-efficacy and attachment, with much of the work focused on building strong relationships between the mother and family nurse to facilitate behaviour change and tackle the emotional problems that prevent some mothers and fathers caring well for their child. Three trials in the US in 1977, 1987 and 1994 produced strong evidence, consistently showing that the scheme led to improved prenatal health of mother and baby, fewer childhood injuries, fewer subsequent pregnancies and longer breaks between births, increased maternal employment and greater readiness for school. Researchers returned to children in the first trial when they reached 15 and found a 48 per cent reduction in child abuse and neglect, a 59 per cent reduction in arrests and a 90 per cent cut in numbers receiving supervision orders. Tentative, early positive research findings emerging in both Scotland and England suggest that it is increasingly likely that such an approach will form a cornerstone of Holyrood's early years policy in the future.

EDUCATION POLICY

Scottish Government education policy has focused on the issue of continuity of learning between the nation's varied early childhood services and school through developing new curriculum frameworks in the form of *Pre-Birth to Three: Positive Outcomes for Scotland's Children and Families* (published by Learning and Teaching Scotland in 2010) and *Curriculum for Excellence* (CfE) (published by the Scottish Executive in 2004). The establishment of an early level within CfE covering both pre-school and early primary (3–6 years) represented an historic shift in emphasis from previous approaches. The Scottish curriculum now treats both pre-school education and the early part of primary school as 'early education' and promotes similar kinds of learning in both settings (see also Chapter 33). It argues that active learning is crucial as the means by which children develop vital skills and knowledge and a positive attitude to learning. This has helped to fuel national debates about the roles and qualifications of different professionals working across Scotland's diverse early years services. Transforming a curriculum framework from paper into classroom practices that make a difference for children, especially in the early stage of primary school, is perhaps one of the most significant challenges currently facing the Scottish system. The process and issues are complex and the Scottish Government is supporting new specialist postgraduate early years teacher qualifications to help address these.

The evolution of both curriculum frameworks reflected political debates nationally and internationally (most notably in New Zealand) which identified a need for a clearer articulation between learning in schools and the social and economic needs beyond the school. Both Scottish documents suggest that learning and growing during the early childhood years should be seen as part of a continuum, linked to age, while also recognising that development will vary for individual children in unpredictable ways. The frameworks emphasise the holistic way children learn and grow, promote children's learning through the responsive and reciprocal relationships with people, places and things, and recognise the significance of the wider world of family and community. CfE is intended to deliver 'challenge and enjoyment, breadth, progression, depth, personalisation and choice, coherence and relevance'. Early years professionals have been set the challenge of realising this curricular vision by providing children with greater control and independence as well as opportunities for playful collaboration in their choice of activities and materials, promoting creative use of learning environments (including the outdoors), extension of skills, logical and creative thinking, and encouragement of a problem-solving approach. A number of local authorities have developed and issued guidance based on *Pre-Birth to Three: Positive Outcomes for Scotland's Children and Families* for directly managed and partner provided services.

INTEGRATED SERVICES

Greater integration amongst the range of professionals involved with families with young children is another key theme within the Early Years Framework. This recognises the benefits of integrated working in terms of providing children with a focused, better quality, more roundly informed and seamless experience. The need for collaborative working between different professional groups in the interests of children was well articulated in the report *For Scotland's Children* (published by the Scottish Executive in 2001). However, while integration of services for families with young children has been seen as highly desirable for a considerable period of time, it has proved more elusive to implement. This is in part due to most policy areas affecting children (including education, family law and social services), except for social security, having a long tradition of separate Scottish legislation (Bryant, 2006). In addition, service integration has had to address the issue of cross- and intra-regional differences in the co-location of services as well as competing understandings of integration at management and direct service levels. Historically, Scottish social care and health services have been organised in variable forms of coexistence or minimal cooperation involving services operating independently of one another, with no, or extremely limited, sharing of information or resources. Scotland has now moved towards greater coordination involving more professional commitment to relationships in which the health, social care and education professionals retain their individual autonomy but agree to some joint planning and coordination for a particular time-limited project or service, for example a child protection case conference or coordinated support planning meetings for children with additional support needs. These forms of collaboration involve high-intensity professional relationships in which the parties share resources and jointly plan and deliver particular services. This, however, remains some distance from integration in its fullest form, involving a complete merging of services to form a new entity (Horwath and Morrison, 2007). The evolution of multidisciplinary working relationships within early years services is, however, enshrined in the principles that underpin *Getting it Right for Every Child* (2008).

GETTING IT RIGHT FOR EVERY CHILD (GIRFEC)

The Children (Scotland) Act 1995 reflected a general policy trend towards a more preventive approach to children's services, through introducing the obligation on local authorities to provide targeted services for 'children in need' (Tisdall and Plows, 2007). Subsequent Scottish policy initiatives increasingly made links between children in special circumstances and the general child population, with regard to needs and services. This blending of generic and targeted policies has been exemplified in the promotion of the Integrated Assessment Framework, developed as part of GIRFEC (published by the Scottish Government in 2008). GIRFEC assisted the growth of the preventive approach by emphasising early identification of children at risk and the provision of services designed to avert or minimise such risk. The GIRFEC model assessment triangle and wellbeing indicators were developed to provide useful tools for all professionals to identify risk factors, as well as protective factors for individual children. The 'My World Triangle' assessment instrument is used to assess the strengths and pressures on a child's growth and development, from home and community life. This gives centrality to the child's perspective and provides a mental map that helps practitioners, children and families explore the child's ecology. Key areas of the child's development and circumstances can be highlighted under the headings 'How I grow and develop', 'What I need from people who look after me' and 'My wider world'. The tool allows for risks to be identified earlier, and aims to support the management of risk factors in a manner that is both proportionate and appropriate. Equally, the model facilitates the identification of cumulative concerns by the use of chronologies, information sharing and analysis. The 'Child's World' triangle supports professionals involved in key areas of a child's life to evidence their analysis and their decision making as well as to evaluate their planned intervention.

The reform in service operations enshrined in the GIRFEC approach was complex and far-reaching, depending not just on legislation but mainly on helping existing agencies to change systems, streamline processes, modernise services and work closely together to support practice change to the benefit of the child. The GIRFEC approach has been instrumental in promoting a new culture of integrated service provision in early years services by ensuring consistency of assessment across professional, sectoral and authority boundaries.

WORKFORCE QUALIFICATIONS

The qualifications and workplace settings of staff in early childhood centres are recognised as perhaps the most significant contributory factor towards achieving and maintaining high-quality services (Oberhuemer, 2011). Over the past decade, more coherent and consistent policies have evolved for both pre-service preparation and continuing professional development of early years practitioners. The establishment of the Scottish Social Services Council (SSSC) in April 2003 with the explicit aim to develop the regulation and registration of the early education and childcare workforce in Scotland, and the subsequent publication of the Standard for Childhood Practice (published by the Quality Assurance Agency for Higher Education in 2007), has arguably helped to strengthen the professional status of the early years workforce.

In 2008, the basic level qualification needed for work as a practitioner in early years settings, the Higher National Certificate (HNC) in Early Education and Childcare, was reviewed. The aim of the revised HNC was to provide an integrated course of knowledge, theory and practice to equip practitioners to work effectively in a wider range of childcare settings. Alongside the Scottish Vocational Qualification in Children's Care, Learning and Development, the HNC serves as the central gateway in to the profession for more than 74 per cent of the Scottish early years workforce. The qualification is designed to be flexible enough to meet the needs of employers throughout Scotland and to address emerging trends and issues for the sector.

The Standard for Childhood Practice (2007) led to the development of a degree qualification for early years managers and lead practitioners. This sought to take forward government policy goals for the early years workforce by strengthening leadership in the sector. The new leadership qualification is based on a vision of the manager/lead practitioner in the early years and childcare service who will lead and support the provision of high-quality and flexible early years and childcare services, work in partnership with families and communities, and collaborate with other agencies and other children's services. However, many staff, having undertaken degree studies in childhood practice, are finding that the educative nature of their role continues to be underacknowledged and that recognition as a professional appears more achievable if they move into related fields such as preparing the next generation of early years workers. In addition, pervasive differences in remuneration levels across the workforce have not adequately reflected the demands of changing management roles within the new graduate-led profession.

Managers and lead practitioners of early years services experience limited opportunities for extended professional development when compared with early years teacher colleagues holding honours degree-level qualifications that support access to a variety of postgraduate career development pathways. Recent moves by the Scottish Government to support the extension of the BA Childhood Practice award to honours level, as well as a new integrated Masters level qualification in early years pedagogy (within at least one Scottish university), are set to be notable future workforce developments. This reflects emerging trends in continuing professional development across the wider European early years workforce where qualification levels and competences of staff are currently being explored (Oberhuemer et al., 2010).

While this new coherence in workforce qualifications is broadly welcomed, improvements in the quality of service experienced by children have been blurred by controversy surrounding geographical variations in new deployment patterns of one professional group. The repeal of the Schools (Scotland) Code in 2002 revoked local authorities' previous statutory commitment to have a qualified teacher in every nursery school or class. Many local authorities used this regulatory anomaly – originally intended to increase flexibility and support developments in collaborative working – to achieve budgetary efficiencies through substitution of permanently employed teachers with less-qualified staff on lower salaries. This led to the situation in 2012 where 29 per cent of 3- and 4-year-olds in local authority nursery schools had no regular access to teachers. Since 2005, the number of nursery teachers employed by local authorities fell by 12 per cent from 1,702 to 1,496. Stirling, Angus, Argyll and Bute, Inverclyde, Western Isles and Moray local authority areas had fewer than 60 per cent of nursery children taught regularly by teachers, below a national average of 71.3 per cent. Increasingly, nursery teachers are being deployed as curriculum managers of teams of child development officers and childcare assistants across a range of early years settings, leaving many children without contact or with only marginal contact with a qualified teacher. Such a position conflicts with key findings from research into early years learning and quality issues which have identified teacher contact with children 'for a substantial proportion of time' as having the greatest impact on quality, being linked specifically with better outcomes in pre-reading and social development at age 5 (Sylva et al., 2004). It also contrasts markedly with European models; for example, in Sweden a move towards coherent administrative structures has been associated with a commitment to ensuring the quality and consistency of all early years provision through the staffing of all centres by qualified teachers.

CONCLUSION

It is important to recognise that issues of engagement with children and families and delivery of effective early years services are complex and that there is no single simple solution.

The consistent message that emerges from research is that complex issues need complex solutions and that policy makers need to look creatively at how they aim to move children out of challenging situations and combine holistic work with sustained funding for initiatives. There is a clear need, identified in research that has reviewed the impact of interventionist strategies, for models of policy implementation in the early years that support sustained work with children who have the most complex problems. Short-term work with these children and families has often led in the past to disillusionment and weariness with services and initiatives (Boag-Munroe and Evangelou, 2009). In order to ensure that early years services are best placed to continue to develop their work with those most in need, funding needs to be available to ensure that services are adequately staffed and resourced; that staff are retained to sustain relationships with children and families; and that staff are appropriately trained and supported for their work. One consistent message from those writers investigating how services work with young children is that integrated working practices are not yet operating in sufficiently holistic ways for children to benefit fully. Staff need professional development which will allow them to build up and sustain complex skill sets to allow them to work on the multiple issues they confront in everyday practice. It is clear from HMIE reviews that the best supported services are doing a great deal of effective work and creative thinking about how to develop their service in terms of impacts on those children and families who most need their support. A useful concept around which professional thinking might be organised is what Edwards (2005) calls 'relational agency': the knowledge of 'how to know who'. This may have a critical role to play in developing the kinds of strategies that ensure young children facing particular challenges are able to access the right balance of professional support that may be needed to help them demonstrate the necessary resilience to overcome the difficulties they face.

It is important to emphasise that the issue of childhood poverty and disadvantage are deeply embedded within the structural relations of Scottish and wider UK society. The delivery of best practice models of early years pedagogy and integrated professional working, on their own, may be marginalised by the impact of increasing disparities in the concentration of wealth. The Child Poverty Act (2010) has enshrined the pledge to eradicate child poverty in the UK by 2020, and successive subsequent Scottish governments have reiterated this commitment. In 2011, however, the Institute for Fiscal Studies forecast that relative child poverty throughout the UK will rise by 800,000 by 2020 as a result of current macroeconomic policies. The Child Poverty Action Group (CPAG) in Scotland believes almost 100,000 Scots children who were saved from poverty between 1998 and 2010 could soon be facing it again because of government austerity measures that include controversial changes to the benefits system. A key challenge facing the current political class is whether to address the fundamental issue of wealth redistribution that this poverty eradication goal is likely to require.

REFERENCES

Boag-Munroe, G. and M. Evangelou (2009) 'A systematic review of the literature on how hard-to-reach families might be engaged to reduce social exclusion', British Education Research Association (BERA) *Research Intelligence*, 108 (August): 22–3.

Edwards, A. (2005) 'Relational agency: Learning to be a resourceful practitioner', *International Journal of Educational Research*, 43 (3): 168–82.

Geddes, R., J. Frank and S. Haw (2010) *Interventions to Promote Early Child Development for Health*. Edinburgh: Scottish Collaboration for Public Health.

Oberhuemer, P. (2011) 'The early childhood education workforce in Europe between divergencies and emergencies', *International Journal of Childcare and Education Policy*, 5 (1): 55–63.

Oberhuemer, P., I. Schreyer and M. J. Neuman (2010) *Professionals in Early Childhood Education and Care Systems: European Profiles and Perspectives*. Opladen & Farmington Hills, MI: Barbara Budrich.

Sylva, K., E. C. Melhuish, P. Sammons, I. Siraj-Blatchford and B. Taggart (2004) *The Effective Provision of Pre-School Education (EPPE) Project: Findings from Pre-school to End of Key Stage 1*. London: DfES/Institute of Education, University of London.

Tisdall, K. and V. Plows (2007) *Children in Need: Examining its Use in Practice and Reflecting on its Currency for Proposed Policy Changes*. Edinburgh: Scottish Executive Education Department.

Wilson, P. (2011) 'Why invest in the pre-school years?', in W. Bird et al. (2011), *Thinking Ahead. Why we Need to Improve Children's Mental Health and Wellbeing*. London: Faculty of Public Health.

Wilson, P., J. Barbour, J. Furnivall, G. Connelly, G. Bryce, L. Phin and A. Stallard (2008) 'The work of health visitors and school nurses with children with emotional, behavioural and psychological problems: Findings from a Scottish Needs Assessment', *Journal of Advanced Nursing*, 61 (4): 445–55.

Wright, C. M., S. K. Jeffrey, M. K. Ross, L. Wallis and R. Wood (2009) 'Targeting health visitor care: Lessons from Starting Well', *Archives of Disease in Childhood*, 94: 23–7.

33

Early Schooling

Deirdre Grogan and Joan Martlew

In Scotland, the new Curriculum for Excellence (CfE) has attempted to ensure progression from the nursery curriculum and the first years of school by introducing one 'early' level, which covers children aged 3 to 6 years and encompasses the two contexts. This new approach attempts to take the best elements of the old pre-school 3–5 curriculum and develop it as a stronger element of the teaching and learning approach in the first years in primary school. The early level sets out experiences and outcomes within eight main subject areas in order to address progression in children's learning. These are Expressive Arts; Health and Wellbeing; Literacy and English (Gaelic Learners); Numeracy and Mathematics; Religious and Moral Education; Social Subjects; Science; and Technologies.

In Scotland, children begin compulsory schooling in the August nearest their fifth birthday, starting school between the age of 4 years 7 months and 5 years 5 months. All children in Scotland are entitled to nursery education from the age of 3; normally children attend five half days per week during school term times. A key current challenge for Scottish teachers is the changing philosophy and methodology of this new curriculum in relation to the primary school sector. The underpinning philosophy is based on the principles of active learning, increasing the ownership of children's choice and ensuring an appropriate level of challenge.

In other parts of the UK, active learning is part of the guidance on effective practice in the early years; for example in England this is promoted as an appropriate pedagogy in the early years Foundation Stage. The guidance for the Foundation Stage for children aged 3 to 7 years old in Wales refers to 'play/active learning' and 'active educational play' and argues that 'The value of play/active learning cannot be emphasised strongly enough' (*Play/active learning: Overview for 3- to 7-year olds*, Welsh Assembly Government, 2008, p. 7). Similarly, the Foundation Stage in Northern Ireland stresses the benefit of children being actively involved in their learning experiences. This chapter discusses the educational provision for 3–8-year-olds in early education in Scotland and considers the impact of this new curriculum.

THE ORGANISATION OF LEARNING

CfE has at its core seven key principles:

- challenge and enjoyment;
- breadth;

- progression;
- depth;
- personalisation and choice;
- coherence;
- relevance.

The key principles must be taken into account when planning learning experiences for all children and young people. They apply to the curriculum at an organisational level, in the classroom and in any other setting where children and young people are learners. The learning environment should allow children to take ownership of their own learning and to set their own challenges.

Play is considered to be an integral element of a high-quality provision for young children (Siraj-Blatchford and Sylva, 2004). Recent research provides evidence to suggest that play develops children's content knowledge across the curriculum and enhances the development of social skills, competencies and disposition to learn (Wood and Attfield, 2005).

While play is considered to be a vital component of an early years environment, many primary teachers are unsure of how to organise a play-based curriculum (Moyles, 2011). CfE in Scotland has introduced the term 'active learning', which is defined as:

> learning which engages and challenges children's thinking using real life and imaginary situations. It takes full advantage of opportunities for learning presented by: spontaneous play; planned, purposeful play; investigating and exploring; events and life experiences; focused learning and teaching; supported when necessary through sensitive intervention to extend or support learning. (Scottish Executive, 2007, p. 5).

Therefore, if active learning is defined as learning where the child or young person is responsible for initiating, planning and controlling his or her learning, these approaches are relevant at every stage within the primary school, not only in the nursery setting. Everyday practice should include the learners in planning experiments, testing hypotheses, discussing their ideas, establishing investigations, reviewing or revisiting their discoveries and undertaking creative work in the expressive arts.

However, the term 'active learning' can be interpreted differently by teachers. Martlew et al. (2011) found that play in some 'active learning' classrooms was peripheral, something that the children were engaged in during parts of the structure of the day rather than an integral element of the learning process. In order to develop this model of active learning teachers need a sound theoretical knowledge of how young children learn and the importance of an environment that promotes and supports the children's learning. Children need to be allowed to focus on their own learning and to become involved through motivating opportunities and experiences. Thus, the traditional classroom setting needs to be redesigned to afford children the freedom to make choices whilst still retaining the necessary balance between child-initiated, teacher-initiated and teacher-focused learning (Fisher, 2008).

The design of the learning environment promoting a play-based pedagogy could incorporate specific learning bays with a limited number of desks and chairs, children given responsibility for the design and resource allocation of specific areas, time allocated for consultation and reflecting on learning between the children and the teacher.

THE NATURE OF YOUNG CHILDREN'S LEARNING

Fisher (2008, p. 12) identifies the learning characteristics of young children as follows:

- Young children learn by being active.
- Young children learn by organising their own learning experiences.
- Young children learn by using language.
- Young children learn by interacting with others.

Therefore careful consideration needs to be given by the teacher not only to the organisation of the classroom or nursery environment itself but also to the organisation of the structure of the day. Although the pedagogical approach in the primary classroom is to some extent building on the play-based learning seen in the nursery setting, it should aim to mirror and extend this type of pedagogy to enable progression in the children's learning. On entry to nursery, children should be encouraged to self-register, make decisions about the organisation of their day through deciding when to have a snack, who to play with, and what resources and experiences they will explore. This type of approach should span the early level where the educator will carefully observe, support and extend the children's learning. The adults should employ a variety of strategies to develop the children's understanding and thinking.

An important factor in developing quality interaction is through sustained shared thinking (Siraj-Blatchford and Sylva, 2004) when the adult is with one or two children; this allows the adult to tune in to the children's thinking and to develop a deeper understanding. The importance of conversations and appropriate use of questions is crucial to develop a shared understanding of the child's intellectual process. The findings from this research indicate that children who engage in sustained shared conversations are more likely to do well in school and in life. Various strategies have been developed in order to support the adult's role in this interaction:

- tuning in;
- showing genuine interest;
- respecting children's own decisions and choices by inviting children to elaborate;
- recapping;
- offering the adult's own experience;
- clarifying ideas;
- suggesting;
- reminding;
- using encouragement to further thinking;
- offering an alternative viewpoint;
- speculating;
- reciprocating;
- asking open questions;
- modelling thinking. (Siraj-Blatchford and Sylva, 2004)

Thus essential features of quality interactions that lead to a higher level of engagement for the child are identified. Bruner (1990) suggests that the most sustained and productive conversations come from children working together. This encourages discussion and the development of ideas which are not 'dependent' on adult intervention. These findings emulate the work of Laevers (1994), who stated that children were more likely to be involved with their own learning if they were offered choices and ownership. He outlined a five-point scale (the Leuven Involvement Scale) for assessing the child's level of involvement and engagement using five categories: (1) low activity; (2) frequently interrupted activity; (3) mainly continuous activity; (4) continuous activity with intense moments; and (5) sustained intense activity.

Teachers working with children in the early stages of school must carefully consider the ways in which young children learn. Young children are actively trying to make sense of the world around them, each discovery or solution leading to the child formulating new threads of learning. Children are curious, capable and persistent learners and, if this is respected by teachers, they can reach new understandings through self-directed learning experiences.

THE DEVELOPMENTS OF THE EARLY LEVEL FOR THINKING CHILDREN

Traditionally within the Scottish education system there have been separate curriculum guidelines for nursery and primary schools. This resulted in major differences not only in the philosophies about how young children learn but also in pedagogies. The primary curriculum guidelines (or '5–14', as they became known) were introduced in the 1990s and contained broad statements of attainment outcomes within each strand of learning for each curricular area. Each strand had descriptors for each level A–E and children were tested at the appropriate level prior to moving on to the next level. This resulted in many teachers feeling that they were forced to 'teach to the test' and that the curriculum was becoming overcrowded. Packs were created to support teachers in the implementation of each level of the guidelines and the type of tasks within these packs were overwhelmingly written, worksheet-based and to be undertaken on one's own. Many teachers felt that the packs stifled their ability to shape the curriculum to meet the particular learning needs and interests of the pupils in their classes. Many also thought that the packs forced teachers into a particularly inactive pedagogy and that children's enjoyment of learning was being eroded.

One new and positive aspect of these 5–14 Guidelines was that they were developed to support the child's education from the first class in primary school into their second year of secondary education. It was felt that children would benefit from a clearer progression of their learning and indeed primary–secondary liaison became much stronger with many upper primary teachers and secondary teachers taking time to discuss children's next steps in their learning. At this time, some far-sighted education authorities saw the potential in viewing a child's education as a seamless process and so encouraged nursery staff to meet with primary early years teachers to discuss children's progress.

The first document designed to support the curriculum for children attending nursery was *Partners in Learning: 0–5 Curriculum Guidelines*, published by the then Scottish Office Education and Industry Department (SOEID) in 1994, a guide developed to assist with planning and reviewing the nursery curriculum within Strathclyde Region in Scotland. It identified five broad curricular bands: Language and Literacy; Mathematical; Expressive and Aesthetic; Environmental; and Personal and Social, with each of these broad bands broken into key areas. The key components were Learning Processes, Contexts and Content with special emphasis on the child at the centre. There was also recognition given to the role of the parent as the 'prime educator':

> Children learn through interaction with their environment and with the people in it. In nurseries
> and at home, adults and children form partnerships which support the children as they learn and

develop. Adults carry the responsibility for ensuring that, as far as they can, the environment in which the child learn is used effectively for learning and that the interaction and conversations which take place between adults and children increase the competence of the children as learners and help children to value themselves as persons. The central role is that of a partner in learning. (SOEID, 1994, p. 123)

This first document proposing nursery curriculum guidelines was followed by *Curriculum Framework 3–5*, published by the SOEID in 1999 and designed to support all nursery providers throughout Scotland. The guidelines were divided into key aspects with features of learning (outcomes) recorded for each area. Each key aspect was illustrated with examples from practice and supported with reflective questions. The curricular areas were similar to the primary curriculum except that mathematics was incorporated into environmental studies (Knowledge and Understanding of the World). Teachers used the guidelines to direct their planning and to assess the children's learning:

> Effective planning establishes clear goals for learning that are designed to match the needs and achievements of children. Planning, whether long or short term should leave the staff clear, confident and well-prepared for what they are trying to achieve in children's learning. (SOEID, 1999, p. 4)

This document provided teachers with a clear explanation of how young children learn and the power of play in contributing to this.

Children's transition from the nursery setting to the more traditional classroom environment within the primary school became a crucial aspect to be reviewed in order to ensure a smoother and more natural development in their experiences, thinking and learning. However the 5–14 curriculum guidelines, despite good intentions, were criticised by many teachers. Apart from the formal assessment practices that pressured children and overburdened teachers, many criticised the lack of a theoretical basis for the content of the levels. The lack of a focus on appropriate pedagogies was also deemed to be unsatisfactory and it became apparent that the curriculum in Scottish schools needed to be reviewed. A review group was established in 2004 to evaluate the existing curricula. The 2004 review of Scotland's school curriculum offered the potential for radical change in the education of young people, placing a greater emphasis on learners and learning than there had been previously. The outcome of this review was the development of the first single curriculum that allowed for more depth in terms of the children's learning and more space for teachers to make decision about the focus of their teaching. This curriculum was called Curriculum for Excellence and it addressed the learning and teaching of young people from 3 to 18. The current curriculum is now divided into curricular areas and has outcomes/experiences at each level which the child has to achieve over a period of time. This singular curriculum replaces both the 5–14 and the 3–5 curriculum guidelines. An early level has been introduced which specifically addresses the nursery stage but also includes the first class in primary, thus signifying a new dawn in continuity and progression in children's learning. The new curriculum, with its seven principles of pedagogy, aims to develop active, experiential learning for all learners, not just for young children. This new level allows staff from different establishments such as a nursery school and the infant department of a primary school to make joint plans to ensure clear development for the children. It also focuses on meeting the needs of the children, taking account of how young children learn. *Building the Curriculum* documents have been devised to support teachers in their thinking, in particular the implementation and the assessment of learning. Active learning is paramount in both nursery and primary settings, and teachers are now reflecting on their current practice in order to improve their approach to children's learning and development to relate to this new level. Her Majesty's Inspectorate of Education (HMIE), in their *Report on Inspection and Review 2002–2005*, identified this as a key theme for improvements in primary schools, stating 'the quality of pupils' learning experience is still too variable and too often lacks relevance, engagement and excitement' (p. 4). Questions have been included in the *Building the Curriculum 2* document to allow teachers to be reflective and to evaluate the opportunities planned for children's learning, and asking if children can revisit their own work in order to achieve depth of learning. This new level can only benefit children in their learning as children will be able to discuss their own development and, thanks to the joint methodology, to make links in their own discoveries.

The principles that provide the pedagogical basis for the new guidelines are as follows:

- depth;
- progression;
- personalisation and choice;
- challenge and enjoyment;
- continuity;
- breadth;
- coherence.

Once all Scottish teachers engage with these principles they will be ready to embrace the true philosophy of CfE. Engagement with only the experiences and outcomes will not result in real changes in Scottish education.

PLANNING FOR CHILDREN'S LEARNING

Responsive planning is common in the nursery environment in Scotland but has been less so in the formal school sector and is not supported by many of the planning frameworks commonly used in primary schools. *The Child at the Centre*, published by the Scottish Executive in 2007, places emphasis on the notion of the child being at the centre of the planning process and highlights clearly that learning should be relevant and meaningful to the child. The new curriculum, CfE, endorses this view of the child being actively engaged in his or her own learning by involving the child in the planning of this. Responsive planning closely links to the concept of the emergent curriculum; teachers need to be flexible and creative in their thinking in order to allow the children to direct their own learning. Through scaffolding the learning and developing effective interactions the child will be supported to make his or her own discoveries or to identify potential solutions to the initial hypotheses. Teachers within the nursery environment are accustomed to the children designing and developing the curriculum, however, some primary school teachers find this new method of planning a challenge (Martlew et al., 2011). The emphasis on planning for learning in the early stages has changed, with the focus now strongly related to active learning and a play-based pedagogy. *Building the Curriculum 2*, published by the Scottish Executive in 2007, indicates that the learner should be responsible for instigating, planning and managing his or her learning.

The focus on early learning being delivered through a more child-orientated method is also being given increasing emphasis with other parts of the United Kingdom and Europe promoting this shift. The Welsh Assembly Government highlights the importance of play as a vehicle for children's learning:

> children being active and involved in their learning. Children learn best through first-hand experiences . . . The purpose of play/active learning is that it motivates, stimulates and supports children in their development of skills, concepts, language acquisition/communication skills and concentration. It also provides opportunities for children to develop positive attitudes and to demonstrate awareness/use of recent learning, skills and competencies, and to consolidate learning. (Welsh Assembly Government, 2008, p. 54)

In Northern Ireland the revised curriculum for 4- to 5-year-old children (*The Enriched Curriculum*, 2000) emphasises the importance of a play-based curriculum which provides the children with high-quality learning experiences as opposed to the more formal adult-directed learning that preceded it.

Responsive planning has also been successfully implemented within Reggio Emilia pre-schools since the 1980s where the teacher is perceived as having an equal role with the child; both are viewed as learners. This is in line with the current policy direction as outlined in the *Donaldson Review of Teacher Education*, published by the Scottish Government in 2011, where teachers are seen as learners and enquirers. Within Reggio Emilia the initial planning phase focuses on the child sharing his or her interests and possible questions, known as 'verbal outpouring', with the teacher. The teacher supports the child or a small group of children in co-constructing their knowledge through the identified interests of the children using the environment as 'the third educator' (Malaguzzi, 1995).

This new pedagogical approach in Scotland has been welcomed by teachers in the early years; however, the development needs to be supported for those teachers who require clarity and additional guidance to help them implement responsive planning in the primary school classroom. Fisher's model (2008) clearly outlines the elements required for the successful implementation of responsive planning which teachers could use as the basis for developing their own pedagogical stance in relation to the balance of child-led and teacher-led learning experiences.

Moyles (2011) develops this further and describes 'three major concepts of play and playfulness that need to be explored when considering an appropriate pedagogy' (p. 21). She identifies these as Play, Playful Learning and Playful Teaching. She also stresses that time should be given so that children can evaluate and reflect on their learning. If these models are to be implemented successfully, teachers should plan on a weekly basis to ensure a balance of child-initiated, teacher-initiated and teacher-focused experiences. Modification of weekly plans in response to observations of children's learning and consultation meetings where children discuss and record their ideas will then drive the next week's learning experiences.

THE OBSERVATION AND ASSESSMENT OF YOUNG CHILDREN'S LEARNING

The importance of observing young children in order to gain an insight into their thinking and learning takes considerable organisation in terms of time and methods of recording or documentation. Teachers must ensure that time is allocated within their weekly planning to allow this important task to be undertaken. One method of documentation that is currently implemented within some nursery settings in Scotland is based on the Reggio Emilia approach; a method of recording children's involvement and learning using photographs, narrative and children's drawings (Malaguzzi, 1995). This method allows the teacher to review and analyse further in order to set appropriate next steps in a child's learning. Another development of documenting children's learning has been devised by Carr (2001) who refers to this method of documentation as a Learning Story. As the name suggests, this documentation contains both narrative and photographic evidence. Both methods allow children to comment on their own learning through revisiting evidence of their prior learning. This evidence could include photographs, examples of emergent writing, narratives of conversations with the child and paintings and/or drawings, allowing the teacher and the child the opportunity to retell the story of the learning. Although this method of documenting children's learning is well established within the nursery sector, it is not widely used currently within the primary school. The demands of CfE require a shift in recording of children's learning. *Building the Curriculum 5*, published by the Scottish Government in 2011, states that the child should have regular time to talk about his or her learning, and therefore traditional methods of assessment have little value as summative assessment material or test results cannot be revisited to develop a child's thinking or identify next steps in his or her learning.

> What must be clear from all this, is that the evaluation of effective learning and teaching cannot be reduced to a simple test or even a collection of individual test score (however robust these tests may be). At best tests demonstrate how well the pupils can make these. (Van Oers, 2003, p. 23)

Goouch (2008) suggests that teachers through their ongoing observations should engage and support young children and help them 'find meaning and sense in their play narratives' (p. 101). However, she states that the teachers must be confident and believe that cognitive development will occur without the need to 'hijack' the situation (Goouch, 2008, p. 101). This should impact on the quality of both teaching and learning within the classroom situation.

REFLECTIONS

In light of the recent changes in pedagogical approaches and curricular developments there is a requirement for those professionals working with children in the early years to reflect on their own pedagogical stance. All early years teachers have knowledge about how young children learn; they now need to consider how they use this knowledge and the impact that this will have on the organisation of the learning environment and the design of appropriate learning experiences. Early years teachers are aware that young children gain more in terms of knowledge and skills when the learning experiences take account of children's interests, therefore the teacher should ensure that this design allows children to take their own learning along exciting new threads. There is a current shift in the thinking of the role of the teacher; teachers need to be observers, responsive planners, scaffolders and extenders of children's learning.

There are, however, perennial questions to think about. How can teachers be supported with this shift in thinking in the delivery of the curriculum for young children? Are teachers given time to debate pedagogical issues with their professional partners (nursery or primary teachers)? Is there a need for specialist teachers within the early years to promote and develop this particular and vitally important stage in educational provision? As stated in *Building the Curriculum 5* (2011, p. 19), 'Learners do well when engaging fully in their learning, collaborating in planning and shaping and reviewing their progress.'

It has been recognised within Scotland that there is demand on early years teachers, in the context of the delivery of this new curriculum (CfE), and new specialist qualifications have been designed to help address this.

> Given the evidence on the potential benefits of having teachers with specific early years skills working in early years skills working in early years settings, the Scottish Government is committed to working with teacher educations to develop courses which will offer more specialised early years teaching skills. (Scottish Government, 2009)

Educational Institutions have responded to this initiative and have created a range of courses targeted at this area of development. The University of Edinburgh has a Froebel qualification in place and the Universities of Strathclyde and Aberdeen have an Early Years Teacher Specialism blended learning course, thus ensuring that the philosophical basis for effective learning and teaching can be showcased and shared with other colleagues and debated in a range of fora. Through this professional debate teachers will explore their own pedagogical processes and through this exploration will question and develop their own practice. This will result in deeper understanding of the child as a learner, and the creativity, competence and knowledge children bring to learning situations. The potential for Scottish education to be at the cutting edge depends on staff commitment, expertise and professional development in both nursery and primary. The vision and understanding of the importance of this developing pedagogy relies not only on the teachers involved in implementing this approach within the learning environment, but also on the management team within the setting understanding and putting mechanisms in place to support these developments.

Finally, teachers need to truly believe in this developing pedagogy, otherwise the danger may be that they resort to traditional teaching methodology. Teachers and school managers need to allow time to embed this child-centred pedagogy in order to see the long-term benefits to children's participation and engagement in their learning.

REFERENCES

Bruner, J. (1990) *Acts of Meaning*. Cambridge, MA and London: Harvard University Press.

Carr, M. (2001) *Assessment in Early Childhood Settings: Learning Stories*. London: Paul Chapman.

Fisher, J. (2008) *Starting from the Child? Teaching and Learning from 3–8* (3rd edn). Buckingham: Open University Press.

Goouch, K. (2008) 'Understanding playful pedagogies, play narratives and play spaces', *Early Years*, 28 (1): 93–102.

Laevers, F. (ed.) (1994) *Defining and Assessing Quality in Early Childhood Education*. Leuven: Leuven University Press.

Malaguzzi, L. (1995) 'History, ideas and basic philosophy: An interview with Lella Gandini', in C. Edwards, L. Gandini and G. Forman (eds), *The Hundred Languages of Children: The Reggio Emilia Approach to Early Childhood Education*. Greenwich, CN: Ablex.

Martlew, J., C. Stephen and J. Ellis (2011) 'Play in the primary school classroom? The experience of teachers supporting children's learning through a new pedagogy', *Early Years*, 31 (1): 71–83.

Moyles. J. (ed.) (2011) *Thinking about Play: Developing a Reflective Approach*. Maidenhead: Open University Press.

Scottish Executive (2007) *Building the Curriculum 2: Active Learning in the Early Years*. Edinburgh: Scottish Executive.

Siraj-Blatchford, I. and K. Sylva (2004) 'Researching pedagogy in English pre-schools', *British Educational Research Journal*, 30 (5): 713–30.

Van Oers, B. (2003) 'Learning resources in the context of play. Promoting effective learning in early childhood', *European Early Childhood Education Research Journal*, 11 (1): 7–26.

Wood, E. and J. Attfield (2005) *Play, Learning and the Early Childhood Curriculum* (2nd edn). London: Paul Chapman.

34

Leadership, Management and Organisation in the Primary School

Richard Buchan

Primary school leaders have a key role and indeed are ultimately accountable for ensuring the highest standards of learning and teaching in schools. Significantly, headteachers need to ensure that the leadership actions they take lead to improved and enhanced outcomes for all learners. Law and Glover (2000) support this view and extend it to include staff learning. They argue that 'the central task of educational leadership is fostering and then sustaining effective learning in both students and staff' (p. 161). The importance of leadership as a key determinant of improvements in children's learning has also been endorsed by the Donaldson Report (Donaldson, 2011) where leadership is rated the second most important influence after the quality of classroom teaching to securing successful and sustainable school improvement.

LEADERSHIP FOR LEARNING

The nature of education and the drive to ensure children's learning improves is what distinguishes educational leadership from that of corporate or commercial leadership. The leadership and management practice considered to be the most effective in schools has steadily evolved, influenced by a rapidly changing world and its implications for schools, along with the growth of a body of leadership and management literature. The research base has been highly influential in shaping leadership approaches adopted by leaders in primary schools.

The traditional 'heroic type' or single leader theory as a necessary prerequisite for effective leadership that will effect successful school improvement has been challenged in educational contexts. It could be argued that there are insufficient numbers of such charismatic leaders to fill all the vacant headteacher posts. These leaders may have been judged to be appropriate and effective in the past but are less relevant in a fast-changing world. In practice, there have been examples of 'superheads' recruited to turn around schools facing difficulties. They may well achieve improvements but this success can be short-lived, with the result that when they leave, the improvements in learning cannot be sustained. The shortcomings of the single person theory of effective leadership and the need for sustainable school improvement led to the evolution of different approaches that advocated less hierarchical organisational structures of leadership in schools and proposed greater sharing of leadership amongst staff.

The concept of distributed leadership is an approach that involves sharing out leadership across a school. It has gained prolific currency and is promoted throughout the educational leadership literature. Her Majesty's Inspectorate of Education (HMIE) (2007a) also commend this approach to change, encouraging a flattening out of the traditionally structured leadership hierarchy of schools. This shift is viewed as essential in the drive to raise standards and achieve high quality of learning, teaching and achievement. The document argues that 'the most effective organisations have strong leaders at every level' (2007a, p. 17). This approach to leadership is also encouraged by other influential researchers in the leadership literature field, such as Southworth (2005) who promotes learning-centred leadership approaches, where schools nurture many leaders who can influence improvements to the quality of learning and teaching in classrooms.

A major development in the twenty-first century is an enhanced focus on leadership for learning. In Scotland, HMIE published an influential document that promotes the wide adoption of a 'leadership for learning' approach and argues that 'leadership for learning is about initiating changes that improve the chances of all learners to achieve well and means putting learning and learners at the centre of the agenda and remain focused on that' (HMIE, 2007a, p. 50). However, some authors have highlighted the complexity of the term 'leadership for learning' and what exactly it means. MacBeath and Dempster (2009) point out that there is no firm definition of the term either nationally or internationally. They identify five principles that underpin leadership for learning: distributed leadership; a focus on learning; the creation of the conditions favourable for learning; the creation of a dialogue about leadership and learning; and the establishment of a shared sense of accountability.

The drivers for changes to leadership approaches discussed above have also strongly influenced leadership policy and practice for Scottish primary school headteachers. Changes to the promoted post structures in primary schools have served to support the idea of distributing leadership practices. In particular, the creation of a new leadership post of principal teacher in primary schools has offered opportunities for staff to take on leadership opportunities by leading whole school development activities and providing strategic direction to staff. This leadership post replaced the previous promoted post of senior teacher that was originally designed to encourage good primary practitioners to remain teaching in the classroom. The allocation of principal teacher posts is related to the pupil roll although primary headteachers do have influence over the promoted post structure within their own schools, giving them some control over the number and type of promoted posts within their own establishment.

The promotion of a collegial approach advocated by the McCrone Agreement in 2001 also encouraged a distributed leadership approach to school leadership. Time planned to focus on discussing teaching and learning as well as developing strong teamwork is in line with the principles of encouraging greater dialogue about learning and shared decision making amongst staff. Primary headteachers require to consult and obtain agreement with staff annually regarding the Working Time Agreement for the following school session. This sets out a plan for use of the collegiate hours over the session and is distributed amongst activities such as curriculum development, sharing good practice, planning, reporting to parents, and assessment and recording.

Harris (2010) highlights the limited number of studies that have explicitly explored the link between distributed leadership approaches and improving pupil learning in the classroom. However, whilst recognising the growing research evidence that suggests a stronger link between the two, she (p. 66) advises caution about adopting distributed leadership, indicating the limitations of the evidence base and argues that the concept is 'certainly not a panacea or a basis for reckless prescription'. Potential barriers to distributed leadership that may exist include the continuing belief in one leader and the reluctance of some leaders to let go and delegate leadership opportunities to other staff. Some other arguments against the concept in primary schools in practice include teaching staff perhaps believing that in taking on additional roles and responsibilities they are doing the job that senior leaders are paid to do. In addition, if staff are to take on board leadership opportunities, they may need to be released from classroom teaching commitments in order to undertake development work. This raises the challenge of securing teaching cover for the class and the potential disruption that may occur to pupil learning. Nevertheless, inspection teams in Scotland will expect to see evidence of unpromoted teachers engaged in leadership opportunities for the benefit of schools and improving learning.

IMPLEMENTING CURRICULUM FOR EXCELLENCE (CFE)

The moral imperative underpinning primary school leadership to achieve improved learning for all pupils, and the expectations that accompany it, has never been higher with the introduction of CfE and its aim to transform Scottish education for all learners from 3 to 18. CfE heralded the dawn of a massive change in Scottish education and is hailed as arguably one of the most significant educational change initiatives faced by primary leaders and staff in a generation. There exists a strong and collective commitment to inclusion amongst primary school leaders. However, leading staff to adopt appropriate teaching strategies to meet the learning needs of an increasingly diverse range of pupils arriving in schools remains a considerable challenge in practice. Undoubtedly, schools require sufficient resources in terms of support staff allocations in order to enable this desired outcome for learners to be met. In the context of a turbulent and restrictive economic environment and its accompanying efficiency-saving and budget cutbacks, schools may experience greater tensions between the ideals of inclusion and its practical realities. The transformational change required in primary schools to achieve the aims of CfE has clear implications for school leaders and how they lead and manage these changes, working with classroom practitioners to influence practice in order that outcomes for learners are enhanced. How change is led and managed will directly impact upon its successful introduction.

Given that changing classroom teaching practice can be challenging as well as a deeply personal experience for teachers, it is imperative that leaders pay considerable attention to fostering and maintaining a positive emotional climate for change within schools. There is a growing awareness that the interpersonal qualities in school leaders such as support, care, trust, participation, facilitation and whole staff consensus potentially offer more powerful ingredients for improving more sustainable outcomes for learners. Mulford and Silns (2005, p. 153) refer to some evidence in this regard, stating 'schools where the headteacher leadership was rated as more supportive and directed towards instructional excellence and school improvement and the school climate was seen in positive terms produced greater-than-expected improvements in student learning over time'.

Central to the success of this approach is the time leaders invest in building openness and trust with staff, through positive actions ensuring staff feel valued by celebrating their successes and reassuring them of their value to the school and making a positive impact upon pupil learning. The importance and influence of these interpersonal skills cannot be underestimated in terms of their impact upon change initiatives. Therefore, primary leaders require to pay close attention to the emotional context of the school.

The higher expectations of Scottish schools in general, and school leaders in particular, emanates from another source in the form of a self-evaluation framework that exists to support school leaders to evaluate their schools' practice across a whole range of quality indicators. The previous framework, published in 2003, was entitled *How Good is our School?* However, this was updated with the launch of CfE, and a suite of revised quality indicator descriptors were produced that shifted the focus from being effective to a drive for excellence, thus raising the bar and promoting higher expectations for all. School leaders are encouraged by HMIE to embark on a 'Journey to Excellence' with staff, pupils and the wider community. Thus, higher expectations were set out to encourage headteachers to lead schools to aspire to be as good as they could be. Central to this was securing high-quality outcomes for all learners. Of particular relevance to primary school headteachers are the four key leadership quality indicators included in the HMIE self-evaluation guide (HMIE, 2007b), expressing features of excellence in these leadership areas of leading and managing schools.

In leading school teams through the necessary CfE changes to practice, perhaps one of the greatest challenges for school leaders at present lies in the area of leading staff in the introduction of the new assessment framework. The expectation that children will have regular opportunities to engage in reflective discussion about their learning with a known adult is a commendable aspiration. It is hoped that through time, the challenges of providing such a rich and valuable level of personal support to learners in busy classrooms with large numbers of pupils can be fully achieved.

Whilst a broader range of assessment techniques is to be welcomed, particularly if they impact positively and lead to improvements in learning and higher standards overall, the vacuum left by the withdrawal of the national assessment bank has left many primary school headteachers with a significant void to fill. Losing the support of the set of national assessment results for each class has also led to concern for school leaders, raising questions about how to best track pupils' learning as well as evidencing that learners are making good levels of progress in schools.

Relying upon self- and peer assessment by pupils and on teacher judgements regarding progress in learning is likely to contain a large degree of subjectivity. Therefore, it could be argued that there will always be a need for some form of summative assessment. A number of assessment tools have been researched extensively across the UK as a whole and provide objective measures of expected levels of attainment for cohorts of pupils. The best instruments are diagnostic and offer rich data to be fed back to teachers who can adjust teaching approaches accordingly. As there is no national assessment test produced by the Scottish Government, primary headteachers throughout Scotland have researched and purchased a range of different assessment tools to measure progress in key skills of literacy and numeracy as appropriate to their own context. Standardised assessments offer an opportunity to measure how pupils have performed when compared to national benchmark data.

IMPROVING THE QUALITY OF LEARNING AND TEACHING

Of all the tasks facing primary headteachers, ensuring high standards of learning and teaching throughout a school surely rests high on the list of priorities. Sometimes there can be greater variation between the teaching practices in classrooms within one school than between two neighbouring schools. A major focus for primary school leaders, then, is to ensure consistency in standards of learning and teaching within schools. The principal means of achieving this lies in the quality assurance policy and procedures adopted by headteachers. Headteachers implement a plan to include a number of classroom visits to evaluate teaching practice and provide feedback for improvement. Samples of pupil work and teachers' planning will also be monitored and cohorts of pupils from classes will discuss their learning experiences with senior members of staff.

The Donaldson Report (2011) also underlines the task of improving the quality of learning and teaching as a top priority in order to achieve improved learning outcomes for pupils. A key leadership and management focus for primary heads is how to best support staff in schools to embrace change and adapt classroom teaching practices in order to fulfil the key purpose of ensuring enhanced learning for pupils. The implementation of CfE with its promotion of active learning approaches, the need for greater involvement of learners in their own learning and the teaching strategies inherent in the Assessment is for Learning framework all involve changes to teachers' practices and emphasise the continued need to focus on improving practitioners' knowledge, understanding and skills in classrooms to benefit learners.

There is no doubt that the success of any change initiative depends foremost upon teaching staff demonstrating commitment to change proposals and, crucially, trialling new approaches and embedding them into teaching practice. When teachers are fully involved in all change initiatives, and can view the benefits of changes for themselves and learners inside classrooms, it could be argued that there is a greater likelihood that the changes will be successfully adopted. This leadership approach to implementing change could potentially lead to more sustainable improvement. This leads to the significant issue of teacher professional learning. There is a connection between teachers' learning and children's learning. Given that CfE requires transformative change, it is imperative that consideration is given to this area. Issues surrounding teacher professional learning in Scotland are discussed in Chapter 97.

In 2011, the McCormac Report (Scottish Government, 2011) reviewed the effectiveness of teacher working practices and conditions as introduced by the McCrone Agreement in 2001. These arrangements did not have the intended impact upon pupil learning that was expected. In particular, the use of collegiate time to be undertaken at a time and place of the teacher's choosing came under criticism. The potential for greater teacher learning was lost here and the recommendation that non-class contact time is undertaken in school is welcomed by primary headteachers and could offer greater scope for staff to collaborate and learn together.

Leaders of primary schools need to demonstrate a strong commitment to learning themselves through their role as head or lead learners. The McCormac Report identifies the need for continued leadership training for headteachers throughout their careers. There have been recent calls to establish a school of educational leadership similar to the National School for Educational Leadership that was set up in England in 2000, although the practicalities of establishing such a college need to be considered. Other innovative techniques to develop the quality of leadership of existing headteachers can include participation in electronic learning communities and initiatives such as peer headteacher review established in local authorities. The opportunity of becoming an associate inspector with Education Scotland also provides excellent personal and professional development for headteacher practitioners. However, the web of informal networks of support that exist amongst primary headteacher colleagues and acquaintances is arguably one of the most powerful learning contexts for headteachers. These levels of support are helpful to reduce the feeling of isolation involved in the job and give headteachers the opportunity to share practice and learn from each other.

Finally, there is a need to ensure that teachers who aspire to headship also receive a high standard of development and learning geared to prepare them for leadership. The Scottish Qualification for Headship structure offers a high-quality training programme alongside other flexible routes for those staff interested in headship. There are concerns about insufficient numbers of future leaders coming forward to take up some primary headship posts. There is sometimes insufficient financial incentive for candidates to apply for headteacher posts with the resultant additional responsibilities they will carry. This requires to be addressed in order to attract the highest calibre of potential leadership applicants for the future.

ORGANISATION

A key task facing primary headteachers each session is the organisation of classes and staff. The staffing allocation is directly linked to the pupil roll and can therefore vary from session to session. There has been a gradual change in the structure of class sizes in the primary school and although the maximum class size of thirty-three pupils remains for pupils in P4 to P7 (including a maximum of twenty-five in composite classes), there have been a couple of more generous class size changes in the early stages in recent years. The rationale for these improvements stems from a focus on early intervention strategies where smaller classes are believed to be more effective in raising standards of attainment.

Classes in the first three years of primary were reduced to a maximum size of thirty several years ago. The recent legislative introduction of a maximum class size of twenty-five pupils in P1 is a welcome improvement, as it ought to lead to all pupils receiving greater levels of individual teaching input. This is vital in the crucial early stages of learning. In theory, children should be making greater progress in their learning when they are taught in a smaller class. However, it could be argued that the expected improvements in progress will not occur in a smaller class unless staff adapt their teaching styles to ensure greater levels of individual teaching support. This requires to be closely monitored by headteachers to ensure that a smaller class size impacts positively upon young learners. Otherwise the reduction in class size may appear to benefit teaching staff in terms of reduced workload rather than the pupils.

A possible unintended outcome of the changes to the structure of class sizes in primary schools is that it may require headteachers to reclassify more frequently as children move to the next stage in their primary education. This may lead to the creation of more composite classes. In schools where there is no tradition of creating composite classes, parents and carers can become anxious about their child being placed in one, mistakenly taking the view that their child may repeat the work of the younger pupils and not make sufficient progress in their learning. Primary headteachers need to reassure parents and allay fears through strong communication about the changes and how pupil progress is monitored. In reality, all primary classes are 'composites' as there is always a range of ability in any one class and teachers adapt their teaching styles to cater for the variety of learners' needs through employing an array of approaches to differentiation.

In many rural primary schools, headteachers have to manage the challenge of multi-stage composite classes. The rural primary headteacher's task of managing the learning and teaching of a multi-stage class alongside leadership and management responsibilities is a very tall order. A related organisational issue worth highlighting concerns the joint head-ships that exist in some primary schools, again usually located in rural areas of Scotland. This role certainly presents challenges in leading and managing two or more schools with potentially significant differences in ethos, pupils, parents and staff teams. Strong leader-ship and interpersonal skills must feature prominently in successful primary headships of this nature in order to achieve consistency and quality across schools.

Included in the staffing allocation to primary schools is a staffing quotient to give primary teachers a weekly entitlement of two and a half hours of non-class contact time. This change, introduced as part of the McCrone Agreement, was greeted positively by primary staff and put them on an equal footing with secondary colleagues. Primary headteachers wrestled with the issue of how the children spent this period of time. Ensuring that pupils received a high-quality learning experience was a driving force in making the decision of how to allocate the time. In the best practice, headteachers ensured that pupils received quality teaching in music, physical education, art and design, or drama. These may be cur-ricular areas where a school has been in the fortunate position of being able to capitalise on the skills and enthusiasm of particular members of staff. However, if teachers are required to focus solely on particular aspects of the curriculum then it is vital to plan ongoing training opportunities for individuals and the wider staff team to ensure that teaching staff do not become deskilled in other areas of the curriculum.

As well as teaching staff, primary headteachers are also responsible for leading and managing teams of support staff. This comprises teams of clerical assistants and pupil support assistants. The introduction of classroom assistants to primary schools following a successful pilot was an excellent enhancement to levels of primary staffing. Pupil support assistants reinforce and support classroom teaching. This includes direct supervision and targeted support for learners as well as the preparation of resources and supervision in the playground areas during breaks. With good quality support and training, these teams of pupil support assistants can make a valuable and significant difference to improving levels of attainment and learning for individuals and groups of pupils. This is particularly true in relation to pupils with additional support needs.

A final area of contention that can arise in relation to staffing is the recruitment and selection of teaching staff. It can be somewhat frustrating if a headteacher is not able to make choices about staff recruitment. Under compulsory transfer procedures, primary headteachers with teaching vacancies in their schools can be compelled to accept specific members of staff who have been declared surplus in other establishments. In attempting to raise standards of teaching and learning across a school, it is vital that headteachers are given the opportunity to appoint new members of staff on occasion. Being able to appoint staff through advertisements is preferable and can make a tremendous difference to leading change initiatives in a school. This is particularly relevant in schools with a long-standing, stable staff team where newly qualified teachers can bring refreshing ideas and influence the momentum for change in classroom practice.

Many primary schools in Scotland now work in conjunction with partner educational establishments in clusters of learning communities. This is particularly pertinent at times where pupils transfer between sectors. This arrangement can bring together a variety of educational establishments, including the associated secondary school, partner primary schools and pre-five establishments, and can include specialist schools. The key purpose of these joint-working partnerships is to improve communication and working practices in order to secure improved outcomes for all learners. Traditionally, barriers to smooth transitions between different sectors of a child's educational journey have sometimes existed. For instance, a 'fresh start' stance adopted by some P1 teachers and S1 staff created much frustration amongst early years and primary colleagues who considered that their knowledge and expertise of children's capabilities was not being taken into account in the next steps in a learner's educational journey. The joint working practices, alongside the CfE, offer a real opportunity to address and remove some of these historic barriers. (See Chapter 36 for more detailed discussion of primary–secondary transition.)

PARTNERSHIPS WITH PARENTS AND CARERS

Research studies often highlight a strong link between levels of parental involvement and levels of attainment achieved by pupils. Working with younger pupils, primary headteachers have traditionally played a significant role in promoting positive and productive partnerships with parents and carers throughout the seven years that pupils attend primary school.

The formal structure that exists to encourage parent involvement in primary schools emanates from the Scottish Schools (Parental Involvement) Act 2006 that was designed to promote greater parental involvement in children's learning and in the life of the school. This was an attempt to improve the previous School Board structure that was viewed as being rather too formal and was not considered to be parent-friendly. Primary headteachers now have a duty to attend all Parent Council meetings and to share information about the school and how parents can be actively involved in improving the school.

However, there have always been informal routes for parents to be involved in their children's education and primary school. For instance, the majority of primary schools have a group of parents and staff who work together to plan and organise a variety of fundraising and social events to benefit the school. Primary schools actively encourage parents to become involved in the life and work of the school through helping out on school trips, providing assistance within the classroom through supporting play activities in the early years or sharing expertise in classrooms and leading after-school clubs. Some headteachers provide weekly open surgeries as encouragement to raise concerns or issues about their child's education. Primary schools offer a range of curricular workshops to highlight learning programmes and provide guidance for parents about how to support their child's learning at home. In addition, parents are widely informed about the work of the school through regular communications and consultations from the headteacher. There can also be occasions when parents are encouraged to be actively involved in developing a school's improvement plan priorities in partnership with school staff.

CONCLUSION

This chapter has considered the leadership, management and organisation of primary schools in Scotland. In leading and managing primary schools on journeys to excellence and transforming the curriculum to make it fit for the twenty-first century, Scottish headteachers require to be relentlessly focused on ensuring that sustainable learning lies at the heart of all school practice and is promoted at all levels. Leadership for learning approaches may provide some positive outcomes through promoting greater staff involvement and ownership in change initiatives. The emerging shared leadership practices can also lead to enhanced pupil engagement and motivation in classroom learning. Arguably these approaches offer the potential for more sustainable improvement in practice.

The leadership styles adopted by headteachers are influential in encouraging staff to embrace change initiatives successfully. This is particularly significant given the changes necessary to implement the CfE. Overhauling a prescriptive curriculum that was embedded into primary school practice over a lengthy period continues to be a key leadership challenge in the forthcoming years. A focus on people and developing their skills and talents is central to successful approaches. This approach aligns well with the shift towards more participative forms of leadership such as distributed leadership widely promoted in the educational leadership literature.

A key issue in the discussion has highlighted the moral imperative of educational leadership to enhance pupil learning. The task of ensuring the highest standard and quality of teaching in classrooms and promoting consistency amongst all practitioners remains a top priority for leaders seeking to achieve improved learning for pupils. The need to ensure learning occurs is a recurring theme and extends to include the continued development of teaching and support staff as well as the continued learning of headteachers themselves.

Whilst there is much positive about the features, approaches and principles of CfE, several issues require to be addressed as the implementation gains momentum and more balanced and workable solutions reached. This is particularly pertinent in the context of the recommended assessment framework, and its successful implementation in classrooms will require strong leadership, direction and sustained effort from all practitioners. Thus, strong individual and collective leadership will be the key to realising the opportunities presented by CfE, ensuring it is fit for purpose and provides pupils with the skills they need to progress in the world.

REFERENCES

Donaldson, G. (2011) *Teaching Scotland's Future: Report of a Review of Teacher Education in Scotland.* Edinburgh: Scottish Government.

Harris, A. (2010) 'Distributed leadership', in T. Bush, L. Bell and D. Middlewood (eds), *The Principles of Educational Leadership and Management.* London: Sage.

Her Majesty's Inspectorate of Education (2006) *Journey to Excellence.* Edinburgh: Scottish Executive Education Department.

Her Majesty's Inspectorate of Education (2007a) *Leadership for Learning: The Challenges of Leading in a Time of Change.* Edinburgh: Scottish Executive Education Department.

Her Majesty's Inspectorate of Education (2007b) *How Good is Our School?* Edinburgh: Scottish Executive Education Department.

Law, S. and D. Glover (2000) *Educational Leadership and Learning, Practice, Policy and Research.* Buckingham: Open University Press.

McBeath, J. and N. Dempster (eds) (2009) *Connecting Leadership and Learning: Principles for Practice.* London: Routledge.

Mulford, B. and H. Silins (2005) 'Developing leadership for organizational learning', in M. Coles and G. Southworth, *Developing Leadership: Creating the Schools of Tomorrow.* Maidenhead: Open University Press.

Scottish Government (2011) *Advancing Professionalism in Teaching: The Report of the Review of Teacher Employment in Scotland.* Edinburgh: Scottish Government.

Southworth, G. (2005) 'Learning-centred leadership', in B. Davies, *The Essentials of School Leadership.* London: Paul Chapman Publishing and Corwin Press.

35

Discipline, Behaviour and Ethos in Primary Schools

Jackie Ravet

Concern over standards of behaviour in schools is, arguably, one of the key educational issues of our times. It has simmered near the top of the government agenda for decades, fuelling public debate and stimulating the ongoing quest for the causes of troublesome behaviour and effective approaches to discipline in the primary classroom. In Scotland, headteachers, teachers, support staff and pupils have been invited explicitly to add their voices to this debate, and to explore 'their experiences and perceptions of behaviour and discipline in schools' (Better Behaviour in Scottish Schools, 2004), by contributing to an ongoing series of national studies of behaviour in schools. The Scottish Government claims to be listening to the outcomes of these studies and is committed to the implementation of a range of initiatives to address participant concerns. The inclusion of pupils within this consultation reflects a powerful and relatively new dimension of Scottish educational policy that is currently undergoing considerable consolidation with the implementation of Curriculum for Excellence (CfE), Scotland's curricular framework for learning. The emphasis on child-centred practice and participation within this framework has the potential to transform radically the way that pupil behaviour is currently understood and approached, and will have important implications for all those involved in promoting positive behaviour in primary classrooms. It is likely to herald a dramatic shift in our expectations of the ethos of Scottish primary schools.

In this chapter, the links between the concepts of discipline, behaviour and ethos within the Scottish educational context will be examined. This analysis will begin with an historical overview that will highlight the evolution of these concepts over past decades. The focus will then shift to recent policy initiatives and their implementation to date. Areas of controversy associated with policy implementation will be highlighted in order to provide a critical perspective.

HISTORICAL CONTEXT

The way that terms such as discipline, behaviour and ethos are understood and addressed in primary schools is inextricably linked to historical and socio-cultural context, institutional context and, of course, the specific context of individual classrooms. There is therefore an inevitable disjunction between the way that these concepts are constructed theoretically and the myriad of ways in which they are interpreted in schools. They cannot, therefore, be treated as unitary concepts; this makes discussion of them problematic. Further, though it is useful for the purposes of this chapter to attempt to identify the broad trends that have, historically, shaped our understanding of discipline, behaviour and ethos, it would be a considerable over-simplification to suggest that there has been a neat, linear progression over past decades. The following overview should therefore be treated with a degree of caution, while noting that, inevitably, it is a construction and a selection.

Arguably, the notion of discipline that has dominated educational thinking until relatively recently has been broadly associated with the control and regulation of pupil behaviour by teachers in order to facilitate learning and socialisation. In the early twentieth century, this formulation was expressed as a harsh authoritarianism. Scottish schools at this time were highly formal places in which teachers transmitted knowledge didactically, and pupils were expected to be silent, still and learn – by rote where possible. Classes were large, authority was strict and control was maintained via rigid rules and routines enforced through the use of corporal punishments (Gavienas and White, 2003). Behaviour that flouted the rules or deviated from rigid teacher expectations was viewed as maladjustment and explained as a psychological or medical problem in the child, not as a problem linked in any way to school ethos, that is the general climate of a school – its atmosphere, relationships and practices and the values that underpin them. Thus, attitudes reflected the wider values and morals of Scottish society with its expectations of deference, respect and conformity to authority.

The cultural upheaval of the 1960s, however, gave rise to some considerable questioning of notions of power and authority within Scottish culture, and triggered a period of significant educational change. Policy was influenced by liberal writers such as Montessori and Froebel, and by the research of Jean Piaget. The result was a substantial softening of many of the harsher realities of classroom life as child-centred education became the new orthodoxy as set out in the landmark report *Primary Education in Scotland*, published in 1965. This report had a considerable impact on practice. For example, teachers were encouraged to make the school environment welcoming and stimulating, to adapt the curriculum to the needs and interests of primary-aged children, to grant pupils new freedom to learn through discovery and to create an ethos that was positive, warm and supportive. The report argued that these reforms would help pupils to take more responsibility for their behaviour in the classroom.

Corporal punishment was reviewed for the first time during this period, and its use gradually waned throughout the 1960s and 1970s until it was finally abolished in state schools in 1981. However, sanctions such as verbal reprimands, detention and lines continued to be common currency in primary schools and constituted the main approach to low-level indiscipline in the classroom. Referral to the headteacher and exclusions were generally reserved for more serious misdemeanours such as verbal abuse, aggression or violence, whilst pupils considered too difficult to manage were often moved to special schools or units for what became known as pupils with social, emotional and behavioural difficulties (SEBD). This categorisation has always been vague (Macleod and Munn, 2004) and became a catch-all label for pupils whom teachers perceived as challenging and resistant to help. The implication of the label at this time was that such pupils had a psycho-medical problem requiring specialist input that was beyond the reach and remit of teachers in mainstream schools.

Though the use of physical force was no longer sanctioned, the teacher's singular power to shape and determine pupil behaviour continued unabated despite the advent of child-centred education. Indeed, Piaget's theory of developmental sequentialism was used to justify the view that young pupils are largely dependent on the expert guidance and protection of teachers, and incapable, by virtue of their age and developmental stage, of acting as independent agents who might contribute to discussions about behaviour. Thus, teachers were constructed as nurturers and protectors whose power over pupils was fully legitimised by society. Further, pupils largely expected teachers to be in control.

Parents, however, began to have more involvement in education as a result of the new child-centred policies of the 1960s. Educators recognised that parents might act as a useful bridge between home and school and had the potential to reinforce learning and standards of behaviour at home. Research indicated that there were clear benefits for pupils in terms of improved attainment, attendance and behaviour (MacBeth et al., 1984). Thus, by the 1980s it had become axiomatic that parents were 'welcome' in schools and that this should be integral to primary school ethos. However, the parental role was generally limited. Subsequent research suggests that parent participation at this time was, and arguably still is, predicated on the tacit understanding that they must work for, not against, teachers and schools, and act as willing conduits for the standards, values and norms advocated by them, especially in matters of behaviour (Crozier and Reay, 2005). The minority of parents who tried to question teacher decisions on discipline had little real power to bring about change.

In the 1970s, a new wave of sociological researchers began to question who was setting the school discipline agenda and whose purposes it served beyond the classroom. It was argued that discipline in schools reflected the values and beliefs of dominant groups within wider society and might be viewed as a form of social control that reproduced class hierarchies and perpetuated social inequality. Research into the curriculum and the hidden curriculum, that is the way in which the curriculum is organised, taught and managed, explored their influence on pupil behaviour (e.g. Lacey, 1970). There was evidence that teacher attitudes and labelling shaped pupil identity via the 'self-fulfilling prophecy'. These findings heralded a growing discomfort with the child deficit model and the exclusion of pupils with SEBD to special schools. Many of these concerns were highlighted in the Pack Report (1977), an influential government enquiry into truancy and indiscipline in Scottish schools.

Throughout the 1980s, school effectiveness research appeared to confirm that the environment of the school could exacerbate, if not create, indiscipline. The ethos of the primary classroom therefore became a new focus for enquiries into the causes of pupil indiscipline, with the implication that teachers and schools could, and should, do something about it. In 1992, the Scottish Office acted upon this by distributing indicators to schools to enable them to review and evaluate the quality and effectiveness of school ethos. A significant feature of this new directive was the emphasis on prevention, rather than punishment, through the use of behaviourist approaches such as praise, points systems and other forms of reward for good behaviour. Supporting pupil self-esteem became an important aspect of school ethos. Positive, respectful relationships between teachers and pupils were also highlighted.

This initiative signalled a significant departure from the traditional approach to discipline outlined above, with its emphasis on problems in the child and reliance on punishments and sanctions. Within this new model, teachers were no longer constructed as the victims of pupil behaviour, but as the potential architects of discipline and indiscipline in the primary classroom. The then Scottish Office tried to support schools to address its new expectations throughout the 1990s via the Scottish School Ethos Network, the Promoting Positive Discipline Initiative, plus a plethora of teacher handbooks and resource packs designed to help schools bring about improvements in various aspects of ethos. It was hoped that these measures might also help to reduce rates of exclusion in primary schools in view of the sharp upturn that occurred in the mid-1990s.

Many teachers took advantage of these support mechanisms to improve their practice. However, the uptake of positive approaches was uneven across Scottish schools and also varied from classroom to classroom depending on the perspectives of individual teachers (Gavienas and White, 2003). This is linked to the problem, mentioned earlier, of the interpretation of definitions of discipline and behaviour. Thus, there was considerable variation in the way that policy was enacted, and little debate on the subject between or within schools. The result was a lack of a shared understanding of what, in practical terms, a positive school ethos meant, and how it could be created across the widely varying contexts, locations and catchments of Scottish schools (ibid.). Some teachers felt that the focus on prevention rather than punishment undermined their authority and made the enforcement of school standards difficult. Thus, in some schools the emphasis on sanctions continued. A survey of primary teachers conducted in 1997 revealed that low-level disruption such as talking, playing, wandering about and disturbing others were the behaviours of greatest concern to teachers at this time. Verbal abuse and violence were considered relatively rare, though bullying, for the first time, was considered to be a growing problem and tackling it became an educational priority in the late 1990s.

The association of good discipline with positive ethos and prevention therefore had a gradual evolution across Scottish primary schools. However, the impetus for change gathered pace with the emergence of new legislation on pupil rights. This legislation has changed the landscape of Scottish education dramatically. Its impact on notions of discipline, behaviour and ethos will now be considered,

CHILDREN'S RIGHTS AND DISCIPLINE IN THE PRIMARY SCHOOL

In 1989, the United Nations Convention on the Rights of the Child set out a framework for children's rights that included two articles (Articles 12 and 13) calling for the creation of better opportunities for children to voice their thoughts, opinions and concerns, and to participate in decision-making processes affecting their lives. In 1995, this document gained legal status in Scotland via the Children (Scotland) Act. This was followed by a host of further Acts and codes of practice that applied the spirit of the convention to the sphere of education. Importantly, this legislation was aligned to an emerging focus within Scottish educational policy on the inclusion of pupils with special needs within mainstream contexts, including pupils with SEBD. This rights-based, inclusive approach was set out in the Standards in Scotland's Schools etc. Act (2000).

Inclusive practice has since become the key organising principle for a new vision of schooling that places an unprecedented emphasis on learners' rights, especially learners with 'additional support needs'. This label has replaced special educational needs (SEN) within the Scottish educational lexicon, conveying a far broader construct that includes all pupils with disabilities, pupils with SEBD and other pupils struggling to engage with school life on either a temporary or a permanent basis. The legislation expresses the presumption that these pupils will be included in mainstream schools rather than being taught separately in special schools and units (except in exceptional circumstances) thereby reversing, in theory at least, decades of exclusionary practice. Pupils with additional support needs have also been given an entitlement to a say in decisions affecting their education that is explicitly enshrined in law. This means decisions about the curriculum, target setting, individualised educational plans (IEPs) and assessment, as well as matters of discipline. These same rights have also been extended to parents.

Decisions about such matters had traditionally been considered integral to teacher role and dependent on their specialist knowledge and expertise. The fact that they are, potentially at least, being opened up to pupils and parents represents a considerable shift in thinking about the forms of knowledge that should influence classroom practice and behaviour management. However, current research into pupil voice provides an evidence-based rationale for enhanced pupil involvement. Researchers in this field suggest that, contrary to traditional assumptions based on the Piagetian developmental model, primary pupils are quite capable of reflecting upon various aspects of their schooling and contributing their ideas, views and opinions to strategic decision-making processes in schools (Ravet, 2007). It is argued that pupil perspectives have the potential to redress the adult bias that has traditionally dominated educational thinking, and can ensure that decisions about school improvement are accurately focused on matters of direct concern and relevance to those they are meant to benefit – the pupils themselves.

What pupils repeatedly report is that problems within the teacher–pupil relationship and boredom with the curriculum are two fundamental causes of learning disengagement and low-level indiscipline in the primary classroom (ibid.). School - based enquiries into pupil involvement further reveal that where participation is genuine, as opposed to tokenistic, it can help pupils to develop the communication skills, social skills, metacognitive skills and problem-solving skills that underpin academic achievement and learning progress (ibid.). Participation is also associated with enhanced learning ownership, improved engagement and, importantly, better behaviour in the classroom (ibid.).

The relationship between behaviour, learning and ethos highlighted by research, and the principle of pupil involvement advanced by policy and legislation, were brought together in a landmark document, published by the Scottish Executive Education Department in 2001, entitled *Better Behaviour, Better Learning* (BBBL). This was launched in response to concerns about widespread indiscipline in Scottish schools. It states:

> discipline policy cannot, and should not, be separated from policy on learning and teaching – the two are inextricably linked. Children and young people are more likely to engage positively with education when careful consideration is given to their learning and teaching. (p. 8)

BBBL therefore emphasised the role of a positive learning environment in creating the conditions for positive discipline. It also highlighted the fundamental importance of positive and supportive relationships between pupils and teachers as a means of preventing indiscipline. Though the report acknowledged the continuing role of rules, rewards and sanctions in the classroom, it also recognised that causes of indiscipline are often many and varied and that pupils, teachers and parents must work together to explore specific problems and identify appropriate solutions. Partnership with pupils, parents and other agencies was therefore given considerable emphasis, and a range of new approaches to support participation and social justice in the classroom was recommended for trial across Scottish schools, such as restorative approaches, solution-oriented approaches, nurture approaches and approaches to emotional literacy. The report acknowledged explicitly the link between pupil participation and the reduced incidence of challenging behaviour (p. 33).

This document clearly signalled a radical departure from the idea of discipline as the imposition of extrinsic control. According to the Scottish Government, behaviour in

Scottish schools was now to be viewed essentially as a collaborative enterprise with its roots in positive relationships and positive learning. Subsequent policy developments, especially CfE, align with, and reinforce, the message of BBBL. CfE lies at the heart of the Scottish Government strategy to provide a broader, more flexible, child-centred and participatory curriculum that will foster a sense of pupil agency, involvement and control. It is proposed that this should have a positive impact on behaviour. However, issues of interpretation and enactment have been recurring themes throughout this chapter, and it has become clear that there is no necessary or direct link between policy edict and practice in schools. It might, therefore, be prudent to consider how schools have responded to policy, and to evaluate its impact.

PROMOTING POSITIVE BEHAVIOUR: IMPLEMENTATION AND IMPACT

In 2009, the Scottish Government published the latest report in a succession of three-yearly national surveys of behaviour in schools undertaken in consultation with school management, teachers, support staff and pupils. The report, entitled *Behaviour in Scottish Schools* (Munn et al., 2009), aimed to provide 'a clear and robust picture of positive and negative behaviour in publicly funded schools and of current policy and practice in relation to managing behaviour' (pp.1–2). A Scottish Government summary listed the key findings as follows:

- The overwhelming majority of staff saw all or most pupils as generally well-behaved.
- The most frequently encountered negative behaviour is low-level behaviour such as running in corridors and talking out of turn in class.
- Physical violence and aggression towards staff are very rare.
- Physical aggression between pupils is more common.
- Overall perceptions of behaviour including positive behaviour, low-level negative behaviour and serious indiscipline/violence have improved since [the previous survey in] 2006.
- The only behaviour which is consistently perceived as getting worse is pupils withdrawing from engagement in class.
- All schools use a multi-pronged approach to promoting positive behaviour and responding to negative behaviour.
- The overwhelming majority of staff are confident about promoting positive behaviour and dealing with negative behaviour and feel supported by senior staff.
- Local authorities have a key role in providing support and training to schools – they provide a strategic framework, help and advice, and access to specialist resources. (Scottish Government, 2010, p. 2)

Overall, this summary suggests that, whilst some problems still prevail, concerns about widespread indiscipline in Scottish schools are now largely unfounded, and that much good practice in schools had been triggered by the implementation of BBBL. On the surface, at least, its impact seems overwhelmingly positive. However, the full interim report reveals, in its minutiae, a rather more mixed and complex story than the summary above suggests. For reasons of space these complexities cannot be explored fully here. However, the feedback on participation is worthy of note. For example, the report indicates that though there is some evidence of more widespread use of participatory approaches across Scottish schools, the idea of pupil participation, arguably the foundation of BBBL, is still far from being embedded in school practice (Munn et al., 2009). The evidence indicates that teachers in the primary sector continue to prefer using the more traditional forms of behaviour inter-vention, such as rules and rewards, referral to senior staff and breaktime supervision (ibid., p. 40) rather than the newer, more pupil-centred, participatory approaches mentioned above. This is largely confirmed by pupil feedback. Pupils indicate that opportunities for participation are generally limited to pupil councils, which tend to be infrequent and tokenistic (ibid., p. 37). However, they acknowledge improved relationships and the caring, positive ethos in primary schools (ibid., p. 38). Thus, whilst behaviour may be slowly improving, the approaches used to achieve this could not yet be said to have departed sig-nificantly from the behaviourist approaches of the past.

CURRENT ISSUES

A number of issues emerge from BBBL and the wider policy and legislative context of behaviour in Scottish primary schools. Some of these issues will now be discussed briefly.

First, it seems clear that a fundamental problem for educational change in Scotland is the ubiquitous gap between theory and practice, referred to in the literature as the 'implementa-tion gap' (Supovitz, 2008 in Priestley, 2010, p. 25). This is amply illustrated in the historical overview and evaluation above. This implementation gap arises from a tendency for factors such as prevailing school values, priorities, structures and constraints, and the personal beliefs and practices of individual teachers, to mediate policy and in so doing 'mutate' it (ibid.). Priestley proposes that these factors have diluted the implementation and impact of CfE. Arguably, they may explain the continuing default to more traditional approaches to discipline in schools compared to the newer, more pupil-centred and participatory approaches advanced in BBBL.

Perhaps this is not surprising. The inherent logic of these approaches asks that the meaning of discipline and indiscipline now be *negotiated* with pupils, parents and support agencies, rather than being prescribed and imposed by teachers or policy makers. CfE has amplified this demand significantly. This suggests the need for two important develop-ments in schools:

- a shift from the behaviourist perspective where the focus is on a deficit view of the child and extrinsic behaviour management, to a social constructivist perspective where the focus is on environmental as well as child factors, and the development of personal meanings through active participation;
- a form of power-sharing with pupils (and parents) that permits entry into decision-making and facilitates genuine ownership of discipline processes.

These developments are necessary underpinnings for a radical revision of the meaning of discipline in our primary schools. However, both require teachers to renegotiate their roles, work dialogically with pupils and parents, accommodate multiple, and possibly conflict-ing, perspectives, and accept a degree of relaxation of teacher control. Some teachers may well feel fearful of, and disempowered by, the dramatic transformation of teacher identity implied by this way of working. They may resist it altogether or opt for more superficial forms of partnership that pose less of a threat to their traditional roles. Teachers may also struggle to see the value of such changes whilst under pressure from the competing and con-tradictory policy agenda on attainment. These contradictory demands create significant ten-sions and confusion for teachers which are rarely discussed or resolved. Pupils and parents may also fail to take up their entitlement to participation, either because they lack the means or motivation to do so, or because they continue to view discipline as the responsibility of the teacher and school. All of these factors have serious implications for the genuine implementation of the participatory approach to discipline now being advocated.

Policy makers and school managers therefore have a central role to play in nurturing the relationships and roles, and creating the structures and processes that will enable teachers, pupils and parents to work together in partnership on matters of discipline. This in turn requires school management that values and prioritises partnership and demonstrates this commitment via the quality of its own actions. Arguably, emotional literacy and distributed leadership are essential components of the transformation required at staff level to meet the partnership agenda. The Scottish Government appears to be initiating change at this level by prioritising the development of positive relationships, social and emotional wellbeing and positive behaviour for staff as well as pupils (Scottish Government, 2010).

However, even if teachers take up the call to participation, a second problem relates to how successfully they 'enable' pupil involvement in order that they might meet their participatory potential. This is by no means a straightforward matter. The issue of enablement is a key theme within current research into pupil voice and addresses the complexity inherent in inviting primary-aged pupils into discussions and decisions about their learning and behaviour (Ravet, 2007). This research touches on matters of mobilisation, presentation, ethics and communication, and how these can make a crucial difference to the quality and depth of collaboration achieved in the classroom. Ethics is of particular importance, since teachers are not used to treating pupil contributions with the confidentiality automatically extended to adults, and frequently speak for, over and instead of pupils, rather than *with* them, without being aware of it (ibid.). Teachers may also be unprepared to treat pupil contributions seriously and act upon them where appropriate, especially those of pupils labelled as SEBD. Such selectivity subverts the participatory ideal and, of course, undermines inclusion.

Enabling collaboration with parents is arguably no less problematic. Research suggests that partnership with parents has always been predicated on the assumption that they will work for, not against, school and teacher agendas and priorities (Crozier and Reay, 2005). Parents who fail in this respect can be viewed as threatening and difficult, and may be excluded from sensitive discussions on behaviour. Schools therefore have much to do to ensure that the welcome extended to parents goes beyond the purely rhetorical, and that the ethos of partnership is robust enough to accommodate parental challenge. This implies an awareness of the role of emotional literacy mentioned above, and of how power, language and cultural differentials within the teacher/parent relationship can undermine the quality of partnership and the capacity for genuine negotiation. Without this awareness, parental involvement is likely to remain tokenistic. Interestingly, parents are not consulted as part of the interim reports on behaviour in schools. This possibly reflects their marginal status, despite the admonitions of BBBL.

A third matter concerns the link between behaviour and learning within current policy and its implications for behaviour management. It might be argued that these links are currently drawn somewhat vaguely. There is therefore a need for greater clarity as to how teachers might be expected to transform their pedagogy in order to promote learning for all, especially with regard to pupils with SEBD. Head (2007) argues that a clearer policy emphasis on better learning as a fundamental prerequisite for better behaviour would be helpful, rather than the other way around as implied by the title of *Better Behaviour, Better Learning*. He argues that this might facilitate a reconceptualisation of SEBD as, primarily, a 'learning difficulty rather than a behaviour difficulty' (ibid., p. 73), and place discipline matters squarely within the sphere of teaching and the responsibility of teachers. This, Head proposes, would bring the links between teaching and behaviour into sharper relief and clarify the need for what he refers to as a 'mediational' style of teaching, that is an approach in which teachers actively engage pupils in metacognitive discussions about their behaviour and learning that involve reflection, analysis, problem solving, monitoring and evaluation. Importantly, the aim of such dialogues would be to re-establish learning engagement rather than to explicitly 'fix' poor behaviour (ibid., p. 1). The concept of behaviour 'management' would become far less significant within this learning-focused framework. More attention will need to be given to alternative pedagogies such as this if the links between teaching, learning and behaviour promoted in Scottish policy are to be enacted effectively across primary schools.

CONCLUSION

Over the past ten years, the Scottish Government has initiated a substantial, and arguably radical, programme of reform and development with the aim of promoting positive, participatory approaches to discipline across Scottish schools. At the heart of this programme lies an emphasis on improving behaviour by improving relationships between teachers and pupils, by enhancing the quality of teaching and learning, and by fostering pupil and parent participation in matters of discipline. CfE has further reinforced the message that a positive, nurturing and pupil-centred school ethos is fundamental to pupil happiness and progress, and underpins better behaviour and better learning. These initiatives reflect the broader and more holistic understanding of discipline in schools that has emerged in recent years.

To date, there is clearly room for cautious optimism regarding the influence of these policies on pupil behaviour. Munn et al.'s report (2009) indicates that although there is still evidence of low-level disruption, perceptions of behaviour have generally become more positive since the introduction of BBBL. More serious behaviours, such as violence and aggression toward others, continue to be perceived as rare. Government statistics also show that the numbers of pupil exclusions have been gradually falling since 2006. For example, there were 30,211 cases of exclusion in 2009–10 compared to 33,917 in 2008–9 – a drop of 11 per cent (Scottish Government *Statistical Bulletin: Summary Statistics for Schools in Scotland*, 2011). However, the 2009 interim report suggests that this positive trend has not been achieved by the implementation of new participatory approaches. These have yet to make their mark. Rather, improvements in behaviour and recent reductions in exclusions are attributable to traditional approaches used in the context of the more positive learning environment, relationships and ethos reported across Scottish primary schools.

If, as the Scottish Government claims, the principle of participation lies at the heart of better behaviour and better learning, it seems clear that more must be done to help teachers and support staff make sense of the many complexities of the participatory approaches to discipline. Indeed, for the future, it will be important that cultural, institutional and individual barriers to participation are identified and addressed in order to challenge traditional thinking, stimulate restructuring and facilitate a deeper transformation of ethos, behaviour and discipline in schools. Links between behaviour and learning and their implications for pedagogy will require further research, wider dissemination and effective implementation. If these needs can be acknowledged, and the appropriate funding and support put in place, the promise of *Better Behaviour, Better Learning* may yet be fully realised.

REFERENCES

Crozier, G. and D. Reay (2005) *Activating Participation: Parents and Teachers Working Together towards Partnership*. Stoke-on-Trent: Trentham.

Gavienas, E. and G. White (2003) 'Ethos, management and discipline in the primary school', in T. G. K. Bryce and W. M. Humes (eds), *Scottish Education, Second Edition: Post Devolution*. Edinburgh: Edinburgh University Press.

Head, G. (2007) *Better Learning, Better Behaviour*. Edinburgh: Dunedin Academic Press.

Lacey, C. (1970) *Hightown Grammar*. Manchester: Manchester University Press.

MacBeth, A., T. Corner, S. Nisbet, A. Nisbet, D. Ryan and D. Strachan (1984) *The Child Between: A Report on School–Family Relations in Countries of the European Community*. Brussels: European Commission.

Macleod, G. and P. Munn (2004) 'Social, emotional and behavioural difficulties: A different kind of special educational need?', *Scottish Educational Review*, 36 (2): 169–77.

Munn, P., S. Sharp, G. Lloyd, G. MacLeod, G. McCluskey, J. Brown and L. Hamilton (2009) *Behaviour in Scottish Schools 2009*. Edinburgh: University of Edinburgh. Online at www.scotland.gov.uk/Publications/2009/11/20101438/0

Priestley, M. (2010) 'Curriculum for Excellence: transformational change or business as usual?', *Scottish Educational Review*, 42 (1): 23–36.

Ravet, J. (2007) *Are We Listening? Making Sense of Classroom Behaviour with Pupils and Parents*. Stoke-on Trent: Trentham.

Scottish Government (2010) *Building Curriculum for Excellence Through Positive Relationships & Behaviour*. Online at www.scotland.gov.uk/Publications/2010/06/25112828/2

36

Primary–Secondary Transition

Amanda Corrigan

More corridors. More floors. More teachers. More subjects.

Lewis, age 11

In Scotland the transition between primary school and secondary school has tradition-ally been a major landmark in a child's life. Between 11 and 12 years of age the majority of Scottish children experience a transition that requires a physical move to a new school environment where new people, new expectations and new practices have all to be negoti-ated. The move from primary to secondary school is also a challenge for educators who have debated a range of issues consistently across a number of generations. This chapter will look at this key stage in the education system as both a social transition and an academic transi-tion and will highlight recurring themes.

THE HISTORICAL CONTEXT

To understand current issues in primary–secondary transition it is useful to consider the historical context. The 1901 Education (Scotland) Act raised the compulsory school leaving age from 13 to 14 years of age. With the introduction in 1903 of supplementary courses for those aged 12 to 14, the notion of 'promotion' to secondary education was established (McIntosh, 1949). By 1946, in response to the Education (Scotland) Act 1945, the Advisory Council on Education in Scotland recommended that the transition from primary to sec-ondary education should no longer be considered as promotion, but rather as a transfer (Scottish Education Department, 1946). The implications of the term promotion – an upgrade, moving on to something better – had a lasting impact on the education system that, for some, has been difficult to extinguish fully.

By the time of the publication of the *Primary Memorandum* in 1965, educators were being encouraged to see the primary phase of the education system as a stage in its own right, not as a preparation phase for secondary school. This forward-thinking report suggested that the primary school be treated as a separate entity to the secondary school and that the sectors should not be seen as part of a continuum. While written to promote primary educators' use of child-centred approaches, which at that time bore little resemblance to learners' experi-ences of secondary education, the idea of continuum would become a recurring theme for educators over the coming decades.

The delineation of primary and secondary schools as separate entities continues today for the most part. An aspirational report in 1986, Education 10–14, was designed to address the disconnection between the primary and secondary sectors. This report, which was never implemented because of political reasons, promoted a coherent, continuous and progressive education for children moving between sectors and rejected the notion of a 'fresh start' in the first year of the secondary school (Consultative Committee on the Curriculum, 1986). The idea of a 'middle school' teacher specialising in education 10–14 was mooted with a call to the then colleges of education (now all incorporated in universities) to consider a special qualification for teachers teaching at this stage. This concept moved beyond sectors to focus on what was best for the learner, but even at the time of publication the authors themselves acknowledged the barriers to these ideas that were created by tradition, systems and attitudes.

It was not until the 1990s that the national 5–14 Guidelines identified a defined set of levels and learning outcomes for pupils from P1 to S2 which encouraged teachers across the sectors to consider continuity and progression through the curriculum as a set of defined targets. Children in primary school worked within a framework that would, at least theoretically, be consistent as they moved on to secondary school. Teachers, for the first time, could see the progression expected as children moved beyond the primary school but, importantly, secondary school teachers had access to a curriculum that showed what primary teachers were expected to cover in terms of content. Not without its problems and defined as a curriculum that was too restrictive, the National 5–14 Guidelines started to be replaced by Curriculum for Excellence 3–18 in 2007. While designed to provide a coherent curriculum for all young people aged 3–18, and with successful transition between stages and establishments a key priority, the impact of this new curriculum on the primary–secondary transition experience has yet to be seen.

A SOCIAL TRANSITION

The social transition that takes place during the move from primary to secondary school is a major event for most children. Despite advice from as early as 1946 that schools should take deliberate steps to minimise the impact of this move (Scottish Education Department, 1946), most pupils approach the move to secondary school with a mixture of anticipation and apprehension. For many pupils the key features of the transition revolve around practical considerations. Children who may lose classmates as they leave one school have the opportunity to meet many new classmates in their new school. A new journey to an unfamiliar building becomes part of daily school life. A plethora of new staff will be encountered in this new setting and, for the first time, a timetable has to be followed independently. These considerations, coupled with local stories and myths about what happens in secondary school, can make the move a daunting prospect for pupils.

Over the decades, secondary schools have made great strides in the level of support and range of opportunities available to promote smooth social transition. Transition programmes can now run through the whole of the P7 year, with some schools organising transition tasters in P6 or earlier. Visits from secondary staff, and sometimes pupils, to the primary school allow primary pupils to hear about what happens in the secondary school and to better understand the expectations that will be placed on them as they become secondary school pupils. Opportunities to visit the secondary school are always popular and provide opportunities for primary pupils to meet new peers, get to know the building, meet staff in situ and partake in sample lessons. More recently a wider range of activities has

become more common. These are planned by secondary schools to enhance the social transition process for pupils and to help pupils create social networks before they move school.
Sports events, enterprise projects, interdisciplinary topics and collaborative tasks are some
of the many opportunities organised by secondary schools, sometimes in conjunction with
their associated primaries, to make best use of the time available while also embracing the
ethos of Curriculum for Excellence.

Although the transition to secondary school can be challenging, for most children this
is also an exciting time. However, additional support is often required to enable the social
transition of children who might be particularly vulnerable during major change like this.
Vulnerability can stem from a range of issues from additional support needs to children who
lack confidence, who have emotional or behavioural difficulties or who struggle to cope with
change. Local authorities and individual schools and clusters have a variety of arrangements
in place to provide sustained support for these children before, during and after the move
takes place. A range of key adults, including staff from both sectors, parents and guardians,
associated professionals and other agencies, work together to develop individual transition
support programmes to help these children get off to a successful start.

Despite the efforts of secondary schools to support students as they move between
sectors, there are innate differences between the social setting and expectations of the
primary school for a P7 pupil and the secondary school for an S1 pupil. In the seven-week
break between P7 and S1, pupils obviously and automatically lose their status as the oldest
children in the school. With this goes the high level of responsibility to which most P7
pupils are accustomed. Pupils in P7 often have a range of civic duties within the primary
school community. These can include anything from managing ICT facilities at school
events to running a school enterprise company. In the primary school this responsibility
usually comes with age rather than merit, most schools working hard to ensure all P7 pupils
are involved in the wide range of extra-curricular opportunities available. In secondary
schools these opportunities vanish for many pupils in S1.

Pupils leaving primary school have worked daily with a small number of staff who
know them, and often their families, very well. Pupils move to secondary school where
each teacher they work with has responsibility for the learning and development of large
numbers of other pupils across a wide age range. Pupils at primary school have had regular
opportunities to share their feelings, emotions and experiences with usually one main
teacher and their classmates through activities like Check In and Circle Time. In response
to Journey to Excellence: Part 3 (HM Inspectorate of Education, 2007), secondary schools
are required to meet the emotional and social needs of learners, particularly during the
transition phase, but this will not usually be with one teacher whom the child sees daily and
who knows the child well. This level of support can often be provided only where there is
an identified and genuine need.

Moving to a new school with new people, to a new community with a new ethos, is a giant
step. The efforts invested by schools have seen many successes as the majority of pupils
adapt quickly to life in the secondary school. However, the social transition is only part of
the transition experience. In 2006, Her Majesty's Inspectorate of Education found pastoral
arrangements during transition to be of a high standard, but highlighted serious concerns
about continuity and progression in learning (HM Inspectorate of Education, 2006).

AN ACADEMIC TRANSITION

While social transition issues are often viewed as the most important aspect of the move to secondary school by the pupils involved, it is the pupils' academic progress that is the single biggest recurring issue for educators. Generations of educators and researchers have highlighted the lack of academic progress made by pupils as they move between sectors, and the way to address this lack of progress prompts regular debate. Unfortunately, the impact of this debate on practice has, to date, been fairly limited and debate itself is often only the result of the publication of a new national or international study of performance at this stage.

While in recent years successive curricula have been designed to promote continuity and progression in learning across the period of compulsory schooling continuity and progression across the primary and secondary sectors cannot be assured by producing directives, policies and new curriculum frameworks alone. Successive generations, governments and curricula have proved this to be true: as they changed, the problem persisted.

Where the 'fresh start' approach taken in secondary schools had often been blamed for a slump in pupil attainment as pupils moved between primary and secondary school, the Scottish Survey of Achievement of Mathematics in 2008 and of Reading and Writing in 2009 showed the slump in attainment starting as early as P6, with the sharpest decline occurring in the earliest years of secondary school. The new Scottish Survey of Literacy and Numeracy – which focused on numeracy in 2011 – suggests that primary schools have started to address this downturn in attainment in numeracy in the upper primary but this produced what appeared to be a larger slump in attainment in S1 and S2. The different rates of adoption of Curriculum for Excellence across the sectors may have exacerbated the 2011 figures but it is this decrease in attainment at the primary–secondary transition stage that has given persistent cause for concern for over sixty years. How to address the concern is less clear as the key issues are complicated and often multi-layered.

WORKING IN TWO SEPARATE SYSTEMS

It is important to remember that primary and secondary schools are separate entities. They have their own distinct ethos, their own rules and regulations and their own values. The General Teaching Council for Scotland (GTCS, 2012) acknowledged this difference recently when it highlighted different approaches to teaching and the different range of teaching skills that primary teachers have in its response to the debate around secondary principal teachers applying for primary headteacher posts.

Many teachers, regardless of their sector, have limited knowledge of the structures, principles and practices of a sector they have not worked in. Most teachers' experience of life in another sector comes down to irregular visits for meetings and events or, for many, their own experience in that sector as a pupil. Without knowing what happens in the school P7 pupils will move on to, or the school S1 pupils have just left, it is little wonder that teachers organise the transition process from the perspective that they know best. Continuity and progression are difficult to ensure with limited experience across the sector divide.

During most periods of a child's compulsory education their teachers have some knowledge of not only what came before and what will come after, but also how it was taught and the ways in which pupils learned. Primary school teachers in Scotland are educated to fulfil their duties with children aged 3–12 years so can build upon children's previous knowledge and academic experience across this age range. Secondary school teachers can do the same from 11 to 18 years as they understand progression through their subject. This leaves a disconnection for pupils moving between P7 and S1. P7 teachers often have limited knowledge of the principles and pedagogy underpinning learning experiences in the secondary school. Their ability to prepare their class for the academic expectations of the secondary school is limited as a result. While it is clear that it is not the function of the primary school to be a preparation phase for secondary school it may be useful for primary teachers to support their pupils in developing the skills and abilities that will be expected of them in the secondary school. S1 teachers on the other hand, even those who have spent time visiting primary schools, often have limited understanding of the philosophies underpinning learning in the primary classroom, and this is compounded by the fact that they may have children in their S1 class from a variety of P7 classes in a wide variety of schools. While teachers in the secondary school have been derided for decades for taking a 'fresh start' approach, their ability to understand the previous learning and experiences of all S1 children in their charge may seem, at times, an impossible expectation.

Most teachers in Scotland complete a four-year undergraduate programme in Education or undertake the Professional Graduate Diploma in Education (PGDE) after completing an undergraduate degree. Traditionally these courses segregated students into sectors from their earliest days on their chosen programme. Despite working on the same campus, and often within the same buildings, primary and secondary student teachers often did not meet and there was little if any opportunity to work together. Boyd (2005) suggested this segregation at the earliest phase of teacher education meant teachers entered the profession into separate sectors and regarded themselves as 'being quite different' (p. 33). It is possible that this separation at university exacerbated differences or, perhaps worse still, presented the sector divide as normality. In recent years, some universities have worked to provide opportunities for primary and secondary students, particularly on PGDE programmes, to work together in order to discuss educational matters and to share practice. New undergraduate programmes being devised in response to the Donaldson Report – Teaching Scotland's Future – will have the opportunity to do the same, with one university already offering secondary school placement experience for students on their undergraduate primary education programme.

Once teachers enter the profession, however, their opportunities to work with colleagues beyond their own sector can be non-existent. Even where universities work to encourage collaboration this may not be continued beyond the university phase of a teacher's education. The GTCS has some systems in place to enable teachers to transfer between sectors but this is an unusual course of action, while the aspirations of Education 10–14 to educate teachers with the skills, attitudes and insights to teach children across the primary–secondary divide seem a long way off (CCC, 1986).

THE QUEST FOR CONTINUOUS PROGRESS

Despite guidelines spanning the primary and secondary curriculum, concerns about continuity and progression in learning across the sectors are persistent. Finding ways to apportion blame for poor progress is often the first response to new studies highlighting old problems: the secondary schools are falling short in their ability to move the children's learning on, or primary schools' poor preparation has created shaky foundations on which to build any new knowledge, are both common and relentless responses.

In some local authorities and in some individual school clusters, groups of staff have been more proactive in taking responsibility for devising a coherent curriculum to enhance and satisfy national requirements across the primary–secondary transition. Some of these pro- grammes of work start as early as P6 and run until S2, allowing children entering secondary school to continue with common programmes of work and to have progress measured against a consistent set of standards. This approach offers an opportunity for staff to make decisions about curricular content, delivery and assessment at a local level. Boyd (2007) suggests that approaches like this can help practitioners get to the heart of the principles of the curriculum as well as helping teachers discuss different approaches to pedagogy. This teacher-led approach gives staff the responsibility and ownership for the programmes they develop.

One of the clusters involved in a Scottish Executive funded pilot project to improve primary–secondary transition embraced this ideal and went beyond focusing solely on devising programmes of work (Scottish Executive Social Research, 2007). The project created opportunities for staff across the primary and secondary sectors to come together in a social setting in the first instance. This opportunity was seen to be an important factor that created working relationships that addressed the feelings of apprehension expressed by some staff about working with staff from another sector. This 'soft start' led in successive months to staff carrying out peer observations across the sectors before coming together for the common purpose of sharing best practice. As well as producing a programme of work that promoted continuity and progression, other gains included primary staff receiving support for teaching elements of the primary mathematics curriculum while secondary teachers learned about the pedagogy used in the cluster primary schools. Staff in both sectors then used what they had learned to develop the delivery of their own teaching programmes.

Not all schools are in a position to undertake projects like this. Funding and the support of the school management team are often the catalysts for change; however, other issues such as having a multitude of associated primary schools from a variety of towns must also be taken into consideration. In some authorities more general programmes devised by writing groups are produced in the interests of continuity and progression. These are often distributed to teachers with no real discussion of principles or teaching approaches, which can lead to the individual interpretation of programmes by individual schools. What appears on paper to be a progressive, coherent learning experience in reality remains a learning experience taught by two different sectors with no real dialogue between those being asked to deliver the content. And so, the problems of continuity and progression to create a con- tinuum are never truly addressed.

Where cross-sector projects are not in place it is more regular for primary schools to provide packs of information to accompany pupils during their transition. Primary teachers are well placed to provide detailed information about each learner; as they work with their class across all subjects over a whole academic year evidence can be used from a variety of sources to provide a holistic picture of the child. However, the quality and the usefulness of the paperwork that is prepared for the transfer to secondary school have been called into question for over sixty years. Primary teachers have consistently been charged with overestimating the attainment of children in their class despite successive curricula being more prescriptive with a common language and common learning outcomes and targets. The quality of assessment evidence has been brought into question, with the Scottish Office Education and Industry Department (SOEID) (1997) suggesting that this concern was based on a lack of trust by teachers of judgements made outwith their own school. Decisions about what will be sent and what is useful is often a management decision. Teachers who create the data and teachers who are being asked to use it are seldom asked to speak together let alone make decisions about the kind of information that would be useful to aid continuity and progression. Information provided by one primary teacher is being sent to a school where a child will be taught by many teachers. Where the information is stored, who has access to the information and what teachers are expected to do with what they have been given can all affect the impact of the data being transferred during transition.

As a result of *Building the Curriculum 5* (Scottish Government, 2011), profiling has been developed as a means of students in P7 and S3 having a purpose for drawing together a range of evidence to demonstrate learning and achievement. Primarily produced for learners and their parents, the Scottish Government suggests that this information, because of the timing of the profiling, will also be useful to enhance transition between the primary school and secondary school and between S3 and S4. The information in the profile, it is suggested, will inform and support transition. While at the time of publication profiling is still an emerging theme of Curriculum for Excellence, it is difficult to see how this will enhance a learner's academic transition unless there is greater dialogue between the teachers involved in supporting learners in the creation of the profiles and the teachers who will receive the profiles. While the learner is central to this process, systems will have to be developed that give this new development every opportunity to be worthwhile and useful during the transition process; otherwise, this will be a new method of transferring data about students interpreted by each sector from their own perspective.

CONCLUSION

The pursuit by schools for a smooth and straightforward transition is laudable. Progress in supporting the social transition of pupils has been good, but while the need for coherence, continuity and progression in the curriculum during transition is obvious, how this can be achieved for all pupils across all subjects is less clear. Widening the scope of the curricular guidelines – 10–14, then 5–14, then 3–18 – has not so far been enough to address the issues identified. Since 1946, there have been recommendations by successive generations of educators that primary and secondary teachers meet to discuss the philosophies and principles of their own practice. However, this is not written into new curricular documents and more pressing educational issues tend to occupy the time and energy of teachers. Time should be created for teachers across the sectors to share their own expertise and to discuss how they conceptualise learning in their classroom (Boyd, 2005); this takes more than irregular school visits. Class teachers rather than school managers should be given autonomy in a supportive environment to discuss, observe, team teach and support their peers across the sector divide. Meaningful partnership has to be created. Teachers need to be given the opportunity to see themselves as part of the solution for an effective academic transition. An expectation of change and ways to measure that change need to be developed and adhered to. As the education system moves forward in the twenty-first century this could be the catalyst for change that creates real impact.

REFERENCES

Boyd, B. (2005) *Primary–Secondary Transitions – An Introduction to the Issues.* Paisley: Hodder Gibson.
Boyd, B. (2007) *The Learning Classroom – A Teacher's Guide from Primary to Secondary.* Paisley: Hodder Gibson.

Consultative Committee on the Curriculum (1986) *Education 10–14 in Scotland: Report of the Programme Directing Committee*. Dundee: Dundee College of Education.

General Teaching Council for Scotland (25 April 2012) 'GTC Scotland response to BBC Scotland story about the employment of secondary principal teachers as primary head teachers'. Online at www.teachingscotland.org.uk/education-in-scotland/primary-teaching/news-gtcs-response-to-bbc-scotland-employment-of-secondary-principal-teachers-as-primary-heads.aspx

McIntosh, D. M. (1949) *Promotion from Primary to Secondary Education*. London: University of London Press Ltd.

Scottish Education Department (1946) *Primary Education. A Report of the Advisory Council on Education in Scotland*. Edinburgh: Her Majesty's Stationery Office.

Scottish Education Department (1965) *Primary Education in Scotland (The Primary Memorandum)*. Edinburgh: Her Majesty's Stationery Office.

Scottish Executive Social Research (2007) *Evaluation of Pilots to Improve Primary and Secondary School Transitions*. Online at http://dera.ioe.ac.uk/7024/1/0044590.pdf

Scottish Government (2011) *Building the Curriculum 5: A Framework for Assessment*. Edinburgh: Scottish Government.

Scottish Office Education and Industry Department (1997) *Achieving Success in S1/S2. A Report on the Review of Provision in S1/S2 by HM Inspectors of Schools*. Edinburgh: SOEID.

37

Leadership, Management and Organisation in the Secondary School

John Cavanagh

A recurring theme when headteachers (HTs) congregate, apart from speculation about a suitable collective noun for the group, is lamentation, amongst more senior colleagues, about the loss of the autonomy they once enjoyed in the halcyon days when they were masters and commanders of *their* schools. There is a real sense view that the reduction in the autonomy of individual heads is genuine rather than imagined, despite a public and political view that HTs are free agents. This reduction in autonomy has come about, it is claimed, as the result of an increase in demands placed on schools and their HTs from beyond the school itself. There is a temptation in a chapter of this type to focus in on 'particular' examples – how individual initiatives have impacted on the techniques of service delivery, or on how particular policy shifts have been implemented in the face of professional reluctance from HTs. However these few pages will focus, instead, on the changing conceptions of the 'macro' nature of leadership, management and organisation of schools rather than on specific, tangible and named initiatives affecting headship at the level of the school – for example the implementation of Curriculum for Excellence (CfE). It will explore concepts that have come to the fore, attached themselves to school management discourse and then receded without having solved or reduced the complexity of school governance in ways that have garnered consensus across the community of interest. The chapter will conclude by pointing to difficulties and paradoxes in current understandings of the concepts in practice as well as the frequent collision of these with competing management paradigms and will suggest that a reconceptualisation of the problem of school governance may be required at an early opportunity. In so doing, the role, right and duty of the leader, manager or organiser in asserting his or her professional right to influence policy in light of developments taking place beyond the boundaries of the school will be scrutinised. It will seek to expose a climate in which the HT may be occupying, wittingly or otherwise, a context and administrative space that sits apart from the arena in which HTs could competently fulfil a more enhanced role of intellectual 'practitioner advocate' (Kogan, 1971) rather than that of a disciplined policy implementer. The concepts examined are administration, management (in adapted forms), leadership (again modified by qualifiers) and collegiality. These are selected as having emerged and receded (in this order over time) without having had much impact on the delivery of education and hence the quality of school output.

HEADTEACHERS AS EDUCATIONAL 'ADMINISTRATORS'

'Educational administration' emerged in post-war years in the university. Courses in school administration suddenly surfaced and an intellectual and theoretical edge to the 'running' of the school was identified and sharpened. Several think tanks and their journals emerged to support this academic activity. Highly significant was the inauguration of the British Educational Administration Society (BEAS) and the Commonwealth Council on Educational Administration (CCEA). BEAS was to become BEMAS – the British Educational Management and Administration Society – before becoming the British Educational Management, Leadership and Administration Society (BELMAS). Far from being interesting items of trivial general knowledge, these shifts in title match discursive shifts in emphasis and, in keeping with work elsewhere (Cavanagh, 2010), the naming of these gatherings of minds and thought are highly significant. The Kellogg Foundation also injected significant funds in the direction of bolstering academic activity in this area in a philanthropic effort to improve education. Educational administration became a serious theoretical space on the bookshelves and a much respected area of academic writing and activity.

An initial struggle arose from the tension between the definitions of administration and management; that the term 'administration' was the preferred term for higher-level tasks of a strategic nature while management referred to the more 'hands-on' delivery of the results of the administration (Hughes et al., 1985). It seems to be the case that the reverse is true in the United Kingdom whereby 'management' emerged as the more philosophical facet of the operation of the school. Suffice to say that at the intellectual level there emerged an interest in the tactical (theory-influenced) delivery of schooling to be distinguished from the tacit procedures where HTs were left to their own professional space and devices.

THE POLITICISATION OF EDUCATION

The reduction in individual HTs' control over their establishments is generally accepted and frequently linked to the increasing politicisation of education which itself is often located in, and aligned with, political interventions dating from the Great Debate speech given by James Callaghan at Ruskin College in 1976. The influence of the New Right (under the influence of Margaret Thatcher and her acolytes both north and south of the border) was obvious and critiqued in the 1980s. The ongoing political interest in the detail of school management/leadership was prominent in the speeches of Tony Blair and his New Labour colleagues. Political drivers of educational policy and process resurface presently where political interest in the detail of schooling can no longer be seen as being simply a partisan or ideological issue arising from a particular political vision. HTs can now no longer operate in isolation according to their own values and vision; education policy and national social policy are legitimate topics in the debating chamber at Westminster, and more locally, in Edinburgh. The question of whether or not HTs should have a more meaningful independence is not an easy one to answer and is, in a large part, a question for educational philosophy.

What we have therefore is the concatenation of two influences: a political space for (and interest in) headship, and an emerging academic trend the result of which was an increased and abiding interest in strategy in schooling for different reasons depending upon the motives and passions of different constituencies. Since the 1970s, therefore, the educational 'manager' has been faced with a lexicon to signify discursive shifts in how schools are run, these being increasingly influenced by the policy community which itself has (increasingly) come under the control of the political administration of the time and place.

However, the political focus and, in turn, individual HTs' obligations to the demands of their political masters (local and national) cannot be seen in isolation from the global phenomenon whereby education in most developed western democracies has become increasingly linked with economic prosperity. The World Bank (WB) and the Organisation for Economic Cooperation and Development (OECD) have been influential in shaping political approaches to education and promoting policy shifts now being imposed on educational policy and practice in the UK and (for the purposes of this chapter) in Scotland in particular. The shift towards an atmosphere of performativity is evident beyond the context of *Scottish Education* and equally discernible are the demands and effects this has had on the practice of leadership, management and organisation. For over almost five decades, the role of the HT in her or his school has been visited by key concepts which, it is claimed, when deployed will bring to bear improvement in how schools do what their political masters want them to do.

THE EMERGENCE OF DISCOURSES OF SCHOOL MANAGEMENT

A simple timeline can illustrate efforts directed at the modernisation of school governance from the 1980s until now. This modernisation can be aligned to an obvious political concern that schools deliver in return for the significant fiscal investment. Aside from direct political intervention by two Prime Ministers (the Great Debate speech by James Callaghan in 1976 and the singular intervention of Margaret Thatcher in the form of the Technical and Vocational Education Initiative (TVEI) in the early 1980s), there are examples of a more subtle and gradualist approach to promote the idea that educational underperformance can be 'managed', 'led' or 'organised' out of the system and society. The careful use of language and the revision of such language has represented a discursive attempt to shift the mood and attitudes of all teachers towards the idea that they are not only the solution to educational ills but perhaps the causes of them (Cavanagh, 2010). Freud described words as 'magical' and the language and words of school improvement can be seen to have been modified over time to influence the 'behaviour' of professionals.

THE EMERGENCE OF SCHOOL MANAGEMENT

When we look to the language of school 'direction' in the 1980s there is a recurrence of the term 'management'. Specifically, it was in the early 1980s that a key agency of the Scottish policy centre, Her Majesty's Inspectorate (HMI), published a report which introduced the term 'whole school management'. Underpinning this was the assumption that everyone in the school was a manager and everything could be managed. Furthermore, explicit in this argument was the idea that by being well managed schools would, as a direct consequence, deliver more and better. An attractive aspect of this understanding was helpful in beginning to break down a 'silo' and departmentalist mentality within secondary schools in terms of narrow 'subject' autonomy and isolation from a broader conception of the school as a critical social service. As the result of this report, elected members and officers in the then Strathclyde Regional Education Department (as an example) produced two local reports, *Managing Progress* (secondary education) and *Management Matters* (primary schools), which re-interpreted these into practice and policy statements for teachers. The time for management had come. HTs had become school managers and principal teachers (PTs) had become departmental managers. They started to 'manage' behaviour, professional learning, staff performance (or otherwise) and links between the school and its associated partners in social service.

However, against this came a reaction to a climate of managerialism, the idea that techniques of management transcend organisational peculiarities and contexts (imposing itself not only on education) which was to prove unpopular with teachers, HTs and professional organisations who argued that an ill-considered transfusion of the tenets of managerialism into public services, education in particular, was unworkable and inherently wrong. Despite attempts to reconstruct understandings of management by attaching qualifying adjectives to give us distributed management, shared management, consultative management and participative management (which undoubtedly has a place in organisations), these all become collocated (in people's minds) with managerialism. So, towards the mid-to-late 1980s there was a sufficient reaction against the term and its disciples to render it redundant in any campaign to encourage teachers to come together under the same model by which schools might be 'administered' in a particular way.

LEADERSHIP TO THE RESCUE?

There then emerged the preference for the language of 'leadership'. To draw more on the Freudian assertion that words affect people, it was the case that leadership was viewed as being less objectionable than management; the concept of school leadership had come of age and the language of 'management' receded. Senior management teams became senior leadership teams and principal teachers were relabelled as leaders of learning. Leadership was and is a softer term to the ear, it is *prima facie* less pejorative and it came to be the new orthodoxy. In 2000, the then Scottish Executive published a hefty document on leadership (SEED, 2000). This document regurgitated the notion that all problems could be led (rather than managed) to a solution, and that everyone should consider him or herself a leader. The discourse of leadership was better received than was the discourse of management but, as with management, the academic community had developed robust critiques of the arguments. Reid et al. (2004), at a time when the discourse of leadership itself was being reconsidered, pointed to the paradox that as everyone became leaders in schools the capacity for teachers to teach had inevitably become limited and compromised. Wright (2001) asserted that that while words may have changed, the motivation of these discursive moves remained the same – namely, the imposition of techniques by which teachers' work could be controlled at a distance by the policy community rather than by the local HT.

Notwithstanding this respected academic critique of centralist impositions of models of leadership programmes on, for example, schools, teachers and school leaders, and despite a change of government from the New Right to the Centre Left or Third Way under Tony Blair and New Labour in 1997 (Giddens, 1998), the attraction to leadership as the causal force for good or bad schools was to prove exceptionally powerful for the Blair government. Reflecting on this, Levacic (2005, p. 197) argued, convincingly, that this causal link was 'widely implied in policies, practice and research'. At the same time, Hatcher (2005, p. 253) was convinced that government saw 'heads as its agents [who could] establish an official orthodoxy with regard to the leadership and management of schools'.

An analysis of Tony Blair's speeches at the time point to a very firmly held view that the success of a school hinged in most significant ways on the leadership capacity of the HT and

Blair even took the trouble in a speech (coincidentally at Ruskin College) and in a summit at Downing Street to reinforce his views with HTs. His views were given expression in HMI and the Office for Standards in Education (OFSTED) inspections in the course of which many 'failing' schools were placed under 'special measures' and HTs removed from position; these moves have been more obvious in England and Wales than in Scotland. The simple problem? Underperforming schools were being badly led by the HT.

The leadership agenda had migrated across the border, and the policy community and politicians in Scotland were equally persuaded of its value. A variation emerged, however, by which the terms 'distributed' and 'distributive' leadership surfaced. This move signalled a wish to ensure and assure that all teachers had a role in leading their school – or the particular part of their school. This effort was in no small part directed at placating an uneasy trade union community and reassuring them that their professional perspectives would continue to be regarded and respected. While the term 'distributive' leadership continues to confuse, the idea of distributed leadership could be read in two ways. First, it could be unpacked attractively to mean a genuine attempt to further the aims of participative and consultative delivery of service across the school, aims surfacing in the epoch of management. From a cynical position, however, it could be read as an effort to blur the distinctions between layers in hierarchical models of management 'structures' for reasons of economy, control and 'modernisation' of teachers' contracts. This modernisation was to begin at the turn of the millennium following the commissioning of a review of the teachers' contract under the chairmanship of Professor Gavin McCrone (hereinafter McCrone or the McCrone Report).

THE COLLEGIATE TEACHER FOR THE TWENTY-FIRST CENTURY

A Teaching Profession for the 21st Century (the McCrone Report) was commissioned to review the pay and conditions of Scottish teachers. Interestingly and confusingly, though, the post-McCrone Agreement Report (*A Teaching Profession for the 21st Century Agreement*) and related activity gave rise to a further discursive shift which has prevailed until very recently. The language of leadership came to be supplemented (perhaps concealed) behind an emerging lexicon of 'collegiality'. As a model for school management this became the preferred option in Scotland but there is evidence that the emphasis on it is also receding, and the opportunity may exist for a reconceptualisation of the power and influence balances in schools at this time. The confusing aspect of collegiality is that it does not enjoy much exposure either within the main McCrone Report, the Agreement document arising from it or in the appendices supporting the detail of its arguments. It can be argued with the benefit of evidence that collegiality emerged in the wake, rather than as a direct result, of the McCrone Report. Collegiality as a concept (Cavanagh, 2010) occupied the spaces in the management/leadership debate as the umbrella body of Scottish local authorities (LAs), the Convention of Scottish Local Authorities (COSLA), sought to implement a pay solution with modernised and efficient working expectations and contracts. Put simply, collegiality was a by-product of McCrone rather than a central thread in his argument and recommendations. The 'terms of collegiality' – collegiality, collegial and collegiate (Cavanagh, 2010) – have come to represent a linguistic shift which further softens the language of management and renders the motivation of policy makers and senior implementation officers and politicians even less threatening than leadership, which in turn emerged from a reaction to management and managerialism.

The McCrone review was one of the most significant for two and a half decades. Its effects were probably the most far-reaching since the 1970s. It delivered a dubiously generous pay rise and reconfigured the role and identity of the teacher and the career teacher's career path. In addition, however, by happenstance or design, it delivered a potent model for taking control of the teacher's working day and for managing the teacher in order to manage the system and the welter of changes to be visited upon Scottish education over the decade to follow.

However, it is the immediate aftermath of the McCrone 'Agreement' that is of interest. It is from the work done to *implement* this agreement that the terms of collegiality emerge. There is no denying that the implications of McCrone implied cooperative or, more commonly, 'collaborative' working and the principles of collegiality, but the emergence of the terms of collegiality as key phrases and words used freely and daily (and with some comfort) by teachers follows from attendant documentation prepared by a COSLA sub-group called the Teachers Agreement Communications Team (TAC Team). 'School Leadership and Collegiality' (2004) was highly influential. This paper, which is poorly written and conceptually confused, manages to channel in the new discourse of collegiality. Thus from 2004 until 2010, we find the educational debate peppered with appeals and strategies for collegiate working. TAC 2004 offered guidance on the accurate expression of the teachers' Working Time Agreement (WTA) but significantly confused collegiality with leadership and management, succeeding in forming statements and making assertions that use these terms almost interchangeably. It is poorly referenced, leaves collegiality undefined philosophically and fails to recognise a significant practical and conceptual conundrum posed by collegiality as it is variously understood and applied. The conundrum is that in order to work in a non-anarchic way, collegiality has to be administered, managed and led, and 'controlled' very carefully.

The further 'side effect' of McCrone was the wholesale reconsideration of career and promotion structures, but the restructuring of management models within schools was about more than the cost of management. McCrone developments effectively reconstituted the duties of teachers by simplifying the career path.

The effect of the McCrone Report was to reconstruct theory and practice (directly or indirectly) in relation to school leadership, management and organisation. By altering ways of working and reconstructing career paths, McCrone confronted HTs with significant personnel issues at a time when it was also seeking to level a hierarchy and free the basic grade teacher to have much more influence on his or her working time. McCrone also created the space for discussion on shared responsibilities across the spectrum of promoted levels which was to be developed by COSLA into an abiding promotion of collegiality as a new paradigm of school 'direction'.

The implementation of the McCrone settlement encouraged LAs to reconfigure school management structures along the lines where managerialism as a 'cure-all' resurfaced for a time once again. The argument advanced regarding secondary schools was that it mattered not who was managing a particular curricular discipline in schools (secondary) and that management was a generic skill that transcended departmental boundaries (a discussion redolent of popular definitions of managerialism). A further result was a very inflexible definition of the contracted school week which demanded the crass adding up of numbers of hours to total 195 over an academic year. If by collegiality the documentation implied flexibility and professional influence, the WTA, which the above counting mechanism came to be called, confronted and affronted any notion of vocation and profession amongst many teachers. As it came with an attractive (in the short term) salary deal, the major professional organisations took the agreed steps to deliver the terms of the agreement and stripped schools of the capacity and the potential to be flexible and adaptive, two characteristics essential in what is in effect a chaotic environment about to be faced with a chaotic and unpredictable reconceptualisation of the curriculum, pedagogical approaches and assessment techniques. Current struggles in the implementation of a new curriculum and a revised examination structure have been exacerbated by the very lack of flexibility pre-existing the strict adherence to a thirty-five-hour-per-week contract.

In summary, therefore, the emergence of school management, from the new epoch of educational administration and from the politicisation of schooling, as an elixir to raise standards and expose underperformance, gave way to the language of leadership, a more acceptable discourse. Leadership, like management, could be shared. Whether or not the sharing was for the purpose of professional development and career opportunity or a ruse for adding to non-promoted teachers' workloads is a question that can be left hanging. The radical teacher settlement of 2001 chauffeured in a new discourse – that of collegiality – which at first glance is normatively agreeable, and allowed the restructuring of school management along lines that assumed (mistakenly) positive responses to collegiality. However, one might consider in this summary that the potential of the HT to deliver without having to broker a number of micro-political agreements has been severely limited. Schools are being managed and led with evidence of collegiate practice but the biggest problem is that leadership, management and organisation of the school is in urgent need of reinvention particularly at a time when change is so rapid, technology so influential and education (so crucial to the future prospects of young people and not just the economy) is in the process of changing beyond recognition.

NATIONAL AND LOCAL POLICY AND EDUCATIONAL LAW: THE HT'S ROLE?

Currently, the role of headteachers has been significantly diminished. Daily their signatures are important, their accountability absolute, but their capacity to effect significant change is much diminished. Perhaps this is correct and that today's community of HTs is suffering for the sins of its megalomaniac 'fathers' (we all remember at least one). There is the danger here, though, that if the capacity of the HT and his or her senior team is limited in terms of the changes they can advance and manage with others to conclusion, then the attractive notion of the HT as the leader of learning will be nothing other than hollow rhetoric. More recently, it seems that the key function of the HT is to deliver policy formulated elsewhere and to ensure that colleagues do not fall foul either of it or of legislation.

A more recent and sinister move, surfacing in some discussions as the result of the contraction of LA education departments because of budget control, is the relabelling of the HT as an 'officer of the council'. This identity is worrying from two perspectives. First, HTs can be seen to be increasingly out of school on 'council business'. This is undesirable for the most obvious of reasons. Second, the deconstruction of the term 'officer of the council' portends a situation where the individual professional voice of the headteacher, presumably refined (intellectually and in terms of confidence) over years of experience, may be silenced by the precedence of council policy over professional critique. The officer of the council is quite rightly a position defined by its potential and capacity to be a conduit of council policy. The role of the HT is something more than this, however, and may in fact have at its heart a right, and a duty to challenge policy from the Scottish policy centre of the LA. Unless HTs fight for this strategic element in their professional identity and contractual rights, it may be that they end up being monitors of other people's ideas, brokering fragile agreements with teachers-as-technicians and delivering an agenda potentially void of sound educational philosophy and brimming with untested fads and fashions of which there is no shortage. They may become a policing service for policy and law rather than creators of it.

THE SKILL OF THE LEADER/MANAGER OR ORGANISER

Effective headteachers are adept at managing the chaotic systems that schools comprise (chaos is properly defined by words such as untidiness, frenzy and unpredictability). Furthermore, HTs are where they are, in most cases, because they have had experience both within and beyond the school and classroom which has helped make them Jacks-of-all-trades: brokers of agreements; dreamers; deliverers; human resource managers; micro and macro politicians; and public relations officers, to name a fraction of their capacities. Increasingly, though, the climate and context in which they work is disallowing some of the more tacit skills and potential of HTs to surface in the face of increasingly centralised direction by their own masters. The autonomy of the HT is under threat, not in the sense of the selfish inconsiderate use of power, but as a prerequisite for initiative. With a nod to Stephen Ball (2003), the HT is struggling for his or her soul.

At the root of the struggle there are several problems. First, the political and operational managers do not properly understand the tensions and tasks faced daily by HTs (fewer and fewer HMIE and education officers have occupied the position). These groups cannot conceptualise the management of chaos and large communities of adults and children, and the transactional problems that can arise when the two groups mix. Second, the would-be critic of the HT would do well to shadow the work of one to witness, first hand, 'chaos-in-action' in order to appreciate to the complexity of the job. Third, HTs themselves as a group are losing confidence in the face of an onslaught of criticism (common in other professions too) and, finally, the community at large lacks an understanding of the distinctive peculiarity of teaching as a vocation/profession and of schools as places where people live and learn – not just work and earn. In summary, educational leadership has lost its identity and needs renovation both conceptually and practically.

AN EMERGING NEW PARADIGM

Houston (2009) acknowledges that the term 'spirituality' may seem 'soft' at best and out of place at worst in the world of educational management, but he goes on to defend what he clearly sees as an intellectual direction worth following and one commensurate with the series title of his book – The Soul of Educational Leadership. He takes time to distinguish very carefully his understanding of spirituality from anything approximating modern religion. Houston and his team place emphasis on the need to recognise the limitations of rational and logical approaches to solutions in crucially human contexts. Houston draws on Deal (1995) who, in deconstructing the management of a highly successful industrial project, concludes that the success was due in large part to ensuring that the task in hand was not more *rational* but more *meaningful* to all those involved; the solution lay in shared culture rather than in adherence to rules and regulations. Deal develops a discussion around the emergence of secular spiritualism across cultures. The paradigms shift, he claims, when rationality is found to be 'not working' and 'unable to explain or control behaviour in human organisations'. He develops his discussion to the point where he claims that 'in every organ-ised activity, it is important that people believe in what they are doing, share a common heritage and faith – and dream together'. In Deal's view faith replaces hope and prediction and in organisations, such as schools, the overriding purpose must be articulated clearly and embraced wholeheartedly by all concerned. Drawing comparison with the models of 'administration' discussed earlier, Deal would reject the view that belief and unqualified sense of shared purpose can be managed, led, administered (however collegiately) *into* the system by some formulaic artificial mechanism.

The fundamental prerequisite is a passionately shared sense of mission tied together with a common spirit of optimism. At this point it may be worth a pause to reflect upon the success or otherwise of major curricular reform in Scottish schools and to view the reality through Deal's lenses rather than those of a traditionally/historically 'socialised' policy maker and implementer.

A leadership founded on spiritual principles ensures that 'the crucial task of manage-ment involves the construction and maintenance of systems of shared meaning and culture' – culture being defined as 'symbolically shared and transmitted knowledge of what is, and what ought to be, symbolised in art and artifact'. In the context of organisations and schools or human institutions, the encouragement of 'shared symbols and symbolic activity' is 'able to build organic webbing across competing subcultures of [in the case of schools] teachers, students, parents and administrators'. Connection has to be made at the cultural/spiritual level. The same is true for the many subcultures in the school. The least articulate child can quickly express lack of understanding of purpose and the novice teacher can see 'box-ticking- for-its-own-sake' a mile off. It is the inability to properly engage with the subculture that erects the barrier to commonality and singularity of purpose.

However, in the context in which schools exist in groups – at the level of the nation or the region – the policy and rituals that inform and guide them must be derived in the same way. Diktat and fiat will never deliver a community of educational leaders who will share the symbol, the ritual and the vision. So we have a problem for three groups that should not be separate: those who lead the leaders, the leaders who set the policy climate, not for the followers, but for the community that walks at their shoulders. Having ignored the spiritual elements of organisations and culture we have established boundaries between groups and subcultures that are cemented by nothing but lack of understanding and bad communication.

WICKED PROBLEMS

At the heart of all that has been discussed above is what have been called 'wicked problems'. Grint (2005), in explaining change, classifies problems into three types: critical problems, which require decisive commanders; tame problems, which require linear and already prac-tised responses; and wicked problems, which resist easy responses, require the engagement of appropriate others and may involve inelegant, negotiated solutions.

Educational leaders and practitioners have never been good at jettisoning what they understand nor at thinking out of the box. HTs face conflict over wicked problems but their managers fail to appreciate this as do their colleagues and constituencies faced with the consequences of the problem. Adapting these typologies to the larger argument about school leadership, management and organisation above, we can see that the creation of a comprehensive model of school leadership is a wicked problem; it will never be solved. It cannot be 'commanded' out of existence, it cannot be 'managed' by rehearsed processes. It may depend upon a novel concatenation of people, resources and extremely creative thinking which lead to an ugly but workable solution. But wicked problems are explainable and explanations often placate reaction and intolerance. HTs are not good at failing or admitting powerlessness and are daily bedevilled by wicked problems. Those who hand policy down to HTs are not good at admitting weakness in the face of wicked problems. Wicked problems are wicked because old models do not work and individuals steeped in old models have great difficulty with new ones.

The arrival at a model for educational management is wicked and unsolvable. However, it is containable and improvable if managers at all levels inhabit a new paradigm of an understanding of culture and spirituality, and embrace and enjoy the challenge of the wicked problem; this can only be done if they communicate widely and talk 'with' rather than 'to' those whom they might consider subordinate.

Grint (2010) argued recently that the problems facing the (educational) 'leader' on a day-to-day basis require bricoleurs. Bricoleurs makes sense from a range of disparate things they might find lying around. Bricoleurs have the capacity to say yes when they see something rather than no. Their response to wicked problems is instinctively to ignore the rational and the tested solution. They share the problem and approach it with others equally confused but at least connected at the level of spirituality and optimism; to use Deal's term the bricoleur 'dances and dreams' in his or her community where the symbols and purposes and values and rituals of the community are unambiguously shared. The bricoleur starts to look for the solution in places where he or she senses energy at whatever location in the organisation.

May it be the case that we recognise, as educational managers, our own tacit capacity for bricolage? May it be the case that our masters themselves should recognise in us the capacity for bricolage-formed solutions to the wicked problems we encounter rather than seek to continually reinvent variations on a theme (a managerialist theme) that has never worked? If both levels in educational administration could do this and take their people forward with attention to the spiritual undercurrents of the task, we might solve two problems immediately: we will, in bricoleurs, have arrived at the oft-sought collective noun for headteachers, and we will have readjusted their thinking away from the need and wish for autonomy to the passion for bricolage where like-minded people can drive human organisations, with all their idiosyncrasies, forward to an unknown future which is developing exponentially.

REFERENCES

Ball, S. (2003) 'The teacher's soul and the terrors of performativity', *Journal of Education Policy*, 18 (2): 215–28.

Cavanagh, J. (2010) 'Managing collegiality: The discourse of collegiality in Scottish school leadership'. EdD dissertation, University of Glasgow. Online at http://theses.gla. ac.uk/2254/01/2010CavanaghEdD.pdf

Deal, T. (1995) 'Symbols and symbolic activity', in S. Bacharach and B. Mundell (eds) *Images of Schools: Structures and Roles in Organizational Behavior*. Thousand Oaks, CA: Corwin Press, pp. 108–36.

Giddens, A. (1998) *The Third Way: The Renewal of Social Democracy*. Cambridge: Polity Press.

Grint, K. (2005) 'Problems, problems, problems: The social construction of leadership', *Human Relations*, 58 (11): 1467–94.

Grint, K. (2010) 'Wicked problems and clumsy solutions: The role of leadership', in S. Brookes and K. Grint (eds), *The New Public Leadership Challenge*. Basingstoke: Palgrave Macmillan, pp. 169–86.

Hatcher, R. (2005) 'The distribution of leadership and power in schools', *British Journal of Sociology of Education*, 26 (2): 253–67.

Houston, P. (2009) 'Introduction', in P. Houston, A. Blankstein and R. Cole (eds), *Spirituality in Educational Leadership*. Thousand Oaks, CA: Sage.

Hughes, M. (1988) 'Leadership in professionally staffed organisations', in R. Glatter, M. Preedy, C. Riches and M. Masterton (eds), *Understanding School Management*. Milton Keynes: Open University Press, pp. 3–27.

Kogan, M. (1971) *The Politics of Education*. Harmondsworth: Penguin.

Levacic, R. (2005) 'Educational leadership as a causal factor: methodological issues in research on leadership effects', *Educational Management Administration & Leadership*, 33 (2): 197–210.

Reid, I., K. Brain and L. Boyes (2004) 'Teachers or learning leaders? Where have all the teachers gone? Gone to be leaders, everyone', *Educational Studies*, 30 (3): 251–64.

Scottish Executive Education Department (2000) *Improving Leadership in Scottish Schools*. Edinburgh: SEED/HMI.

Wright, N. (2001) 'Leadership, bastard leadership and managerialism', *Educational Management and Administration*, 29 (3): 275–90.

38

Ethos and Behaviour in Secondary Schools

Raymond Soltysek

RECENT CONTEXTS

Four days of rioting in major English cities in August 2011 threw into sharp focus society's concerns over the behaviour of British 'youth', provoking a debate about the state of society much of which centred on speculation about the existence of sections of the community that seemed not to share common values with the majority of citizens.

The response of government representatives was largely unanimous in its portrayal of the rioters as criminals operating outside the bounds of 'decency', and largely concentrated on the need for punishment which in some cases went beyond established judicial practices. The Justice Secretary, Ken Clarke, spoke of 'a feral underclass, cut off from the mainstream in everything but its materialism', while the Mayor of London, Boris Johnson, warned of sections of the society having 'an endless sense of entitlement'. The Prime Minister, David Cameron, told the House of Commons that anyone convicted of violent disorder should expect a prison sentence, in doing so arguably interfering with the independence of the judiciary.

The implication of politicians and commentators from what might be characterised generally but not exclusively as the political Right was that there exist in society dysfunctional groups who, because of a lack of moral values, ineffective parenting, poor education and inadequate socialisation, are incapable of engaging responsibly with the structures and systems of society.

The accuracy of such a characterisation of young people is not a matter for debate here, although it is fair to say that such a view tends to simplify the issues underlying the social unrest. Briefly, such issues included: a fatal shooting which acted as a lightning rod for local community anger at the way in which it was policed; an economic system responsible for several years of wage depression and inflation, exacerbating poverty and disadvantage; a government imposing economic policies responsible for community service cutbacks for which it could be argued it had no clear mandate; and the perceived unfairness of social and economic inequalities which resulted in a number of worldwide citizen protests, including the so-called 'Arab Dawn' and the Occupy movements.

Whatever the truth of the government's description of the rioters, however, the identification of a large minority of the young as socially, educationally and morally deficient undoubtedly struck a chord with a media skilled in sensationalising youth misbehaviour, including its occurrence in schools. Somewhat regrettably, it also strikes a chord with some teachers for whom the policy of inclusion in particular has had a deleterious effect on educational standards and behaviour in the classroom; a quick perusal of letters pages in newspapers or of teachers' online forums reveals a vocal and largely anonymous element who express views that echo that of the government, most especially the notion that there are 'feral' pupils beyond the control of teachers and consequently ill-suited for education in a mainstream setting.

Although Scottish cities avoided the unrest of 2011, it would be complacent to conclude that these social problems 'couldn't happen here', or to suggest that the subsequent negative perceptions of young people are uncommon north of the border. However, there is cause for optimism given the way in which the curriculum generally and behaviour support in particular have been dealt with by successive centre-left Scottish administrations who share a roughly similar view of education and of young people.

BEHAVIOUR, ETHOS AND CURRICULUM FOR EXCELLENCE

The socialisation of pupils has become a central plank of the new Curriculum for Excellence, with two of the four capacities – 'Responsible Citizens' and 'Effective Contributors' – expressly placing critical reflection, self-reliance, personal responsibility and collaboration at the heart of what and how pupils learn in school. It will be a matter for future research to determine the impact a curriculum with such social aims at its core has had on the behaviour of children and on society as a whole. There is already considerable evidence, however, that creating conditions that offer pupils opportunities to participate in decision-making processes, to think critically and to engage in meaningful debate enrich the learning process and chime well with the overall constructivist philosophy originating in the work of Piaget and Vygotsky which underpins much of the current thinking about best educational practice: for example, Boyd (2008) distils much of the theoretical debate and relevant evidence to propose 'ten principles of the learning classroom' which address specifically the Scottish context.

With regard to classroom ethos in particular, Scottish government support for behaviour management has been markedly coherent and increasingly more effective since the *Better Behaviour, Better Learning* (2001) report, commissioned by the Labour Education Minister of the time, Jack McConnell. It is this document that has driven provision for the past twelve years, expounding as it did an agenda of increased resources and training for behaviour management, increased curriculum flexibility to cater for the needs of all pupils but especially the most demotivated and disaffected, and increased awareness of all forms of pupil achievement in school, both academic and social. While it reported on the issue in the context of general public anxieties over pupil behaviour, it was informed by a more professional debate led by work of academics such as Munn (1999) that looked at the issue from a positive perspective, examining and celebrating efforts in schools around the country that were engaging with pupil behaviour in imaginative, strategic ways.

Better Behaviour, Better Learning was the foundation for a range of nationwide initiatives, strategies and resources. Most importantly, the 2004 *Better Behaviour in Scottish Schools; Policy Update* committed the government to major studies of behaviour in Scottish schools every three years, providing the most up-to-date data and rigorous analysis possible of behaviour issues in schools as perceived by teachers, managers, support staff and pupils.

The latest of these, *Behaviour in Scottish Schools* (2012), just published at the time of writing, paints a largely positive and improving picture of the ethos in Scottish secondary schools. For example, where comparisons between responses in the 2006 and 2009 studies were possible, secondary teachers reported improvements in all eleven surveyed positive behaviours, such as listening respectfully to others or following instructions; conversely, they reported a decrease in nine of the eleven surveyed low-level disruptive behaviours (such as latecoming or work avoidance) and an increase in only one (the inappropriate use of mobile phones). This significant increase in positive perception of pupils' low-level disruptive behaviour is reflected in the reports of secondary headteachers and support staff, and is mirrored in reports about such behaviour around the school generally. Thus, teachers feel pupils are behaving better in 2012 than they did in 2006 and 2009.

The survey indicates once more a number of conclusions that seem commonsensical.

1. *Pupils, on the whole, are well behaved*: 99 per cent of headteachers, 88 per cent of secondary teachers and 61 per cent of secondary school support staff noted pupils as 'generally well behaved' in all or most lessons, an improvement in all groups from the 2009 survey.
2. *Physical violence* is of course always a cause of considerable concern, but its occurrence *is very rare*. Only one out of 2,022 secondary teachers reported violence against them in the teaching week before completing the survey, although there has been an increase from 1 per cent to 3 per cent since 2009 of headteachers reporting physical aggression against them.
3. *General verbal abuse is more common*: 20 per cent of teachers and 27 per cent of support staff reported such behaviour in the week prior to survey; again, however, these figures represent a marked decrease since 2006, and the fact that headteachers noted an *increase* in this behaviour over the same period may suggest it is more often being reported to school management who then deal with it in ways that are reducing its occurrence in the classroom. This may also account for the *increase* in sexist abuse of staff reported by headteachers but the corresponding *decrease* in its incidence reported by teachers themselves. However, this needs further exploration.
4. *Pupil-on-pupil indiscipline is more common than indiscipline towards or involving staff*: 47 per cent of support staff reported having to deal with pupil-on-pupil physical violence in the week before completing the survey, and, while pupils generally report feeling safe at school, there are concerns about bullying. However, despite the use of mobile phones to bully pupils being a more common occurrence, there are once more significant improvements reported in this area in comparison with the 2009 survey.

Generally, then, large majorities of those who actually work in schools express a broad satisfaction with the ethos they encounter. Of course, this is again no reason for complacency, particularly with the comparatively more common incidence of pupil-on-pupil aggression, a phenomenon that can have disastrous consequences for the motivation, self-esteem and confidence of learners. However, the image is not one of schools being dominated by a 'feral underclass', despite the pronouncements of the politicians, the media and those on social networking sites.

This overall sense of cautious satisfaction and improvement is reinforced by exclusion figures for 2010–11, during which time the 21,685 exclusions from secondary schools represented a decrease of around 12 per cent on the previous year. Of course, some would suggest that a decrease in exclusions indicates not an improvement in behaviour, but a cynical attempt by local authorities to meet targets, insisting that schools avoid excluding pupils at all costs for public relations purposes. But as these figures coexist with an exhaustive survey that reports generally increased positivity about behaviour, such negative claims require further evidence if they are to be taken seriously.

This close attention to behaviour and ethos in schools in Scotland has also generated a range of local and national initiatives and policies which have placed these issues at the forefront of school development planning. In the 2012 survey, a majority of secondary teachers reported having been 'actively involved in policy development', while 98 per cent of headteachers reported that they had 'involved teachers in developing behaviour management strategies' (though the survey suggests that support staff were not similarly involved, and other sectors of the school community were even less frequently involved).

In addition, this focus on behaviour management as a key component of development planning has brought into schools high-quality resources and expertise. Notable amongst these is the Dealing with Disruption website developed by Edinburgh University and issued to all schools on CD which offers an integrated professional development package to support staff and pupils at all levels. It is also worth noting that the attention paid to behaviour management since 2001 has made experts such as Alan McLean (on motivation), John MacBeath and Pamela Munn (on positive behaviour management) and Geoff Moss and John Bailey (on assertive discipline) the educational equivalent of household names in schools. However, as in 2009, only 45 per cent of secondary teachers reported their behaviour management training as 'effective': this suggests that what is planned by development managers and what is on offer from training providers is not meeting the perceived needs of teachers.

BEHAVIOUR VS DISCIPLINE

It is perhaps telling that the title of this chapter is 'Ethos and Behaviour in Secondary Schools', when in the 2008 edition the equivalent contribution was titled 'Ethos and Discipline in the Secondary School'. There is an important distinction to be made between behaviour and discipline, and there are signs that awareness of this distinction is having a fruitful effect on secondary schools.

There has, of course, been much concern expressed about *indiscipline* in the classroom that is seen to be reinforced by the growing identification of children with social, emotional and behavioural difficulties (SEBD) as suffering from pathologies that are suitable cases for effective medical intervention, including the use of drugs. Munn (2008) writes of 'an ever-increasing litany of disorders', while Head (2007) describes this 'construction of the SEBD child' as characteristic of a behaviourist model that encourages a perception of the child as 'deficient', itself a barrier to inclusion. On the other hand, there is no doubt that work from the clinical psychiatric point of view on disorders such as attention deficit and hyperactive disorder and autism has provided a greater understanding of the relationship between child development, brain function and behaviour, and has pointed towards social and educational provision which can help ameliorate the effects of these conditions on the classroom and, more importantly of course, on the child.

However, in terms of ethos and behaviour management in schools, such issues are merely one end of the continuum. Not every child who misbehaves has an SEBD and not every child with an SEBD misbehaves. Indeed, issues around 'behaviour' are not limited to those who misbehave; just as important – perhaps more important, the author would argue – is how the majority of the school population interact on a day-to-day basis with the structures of the school and with their individual teachers.

In the past, such school arrangements for behaviour management were often called 'discipline policies' and consisted of bureaucratic procedures to be followed in the event of a pupil misbehaving. Such policies stipulated when punishment exercises were to be issued and what these exercises should consist of (frequently, mundane written tasks). They also defined the different roles and responsibilities of the class teacher, the principal teacher and the senior management team (SMT) in the system, establishing a hierarchy of powers that usually ended with the SMT's ability to exclude.

There is evidence of a shift in perception as to what a 'behaviour management policy' is. More and more, schools are putting into place systems that acknowledge that behaviour management is much more than the management of misbehaviour, and recognise that establishing an ethos in schools entails the management of the interaction between the school, the staff and the pupils in its entirety.

Put simply, if we ask 'What is behaviour management?' the reply is a tautologous 'the management of behaviour'. However, every pupil in a school constantly 'behaves' during a school day, and, as we have seen, most pupils are perceived to behave 'well'. Therefore, if we accept that behaviour management is concerned with the management of behaviour and that most behaviour is satisfactory, then what teachers should be concentrating on most of the time is managing that satisfactory behaviour.

The effect of doing so is to promote satisfactory behaviour in the classroom as a model. Just as we would praise, acknowledge or reward an outstanding pupil essay or drawing in order to exemplify best practice and establish what successful outcomes look like, we should do the same for behaviour. Spending time drawing attention to the satisfactory behaviour that we see from minute to minute in school, it is argued, helps children learn what acceptable behaviour is.

This is a fundamental principle of assertive discipline strategies which are more and more underpinning school behaviour management policies. Such strategies rest on the notion that pupils should be made aware of explicit expectations of acceptable behaviour, and then be encouraged to meet those expectations through explicit and consistent rewards for meeting them and sanctions for not meeting them. This is, of course, a system founded on behaviourist principles, which are looked on suspiciously by some educationalists, but at a practical level it has been adopted with wide success in many schools.

Such schools have developed sophisticated reward schemes; the 2012 survey describes them as one of the 'top three approaches' used in secondary schools. These may be based on 'merits' that can be awarded by individual teachers and tracked through computerised registration systems such as SEEMIS. Pupils are sometimes organised into 'houses' for which they can earn 'house points' that can translate into a range of rewards such as trips, social events such as discos, or activity days. Some schools have regular award 'ceremonies' that publicly celebrate 'good' behaviour.

It is probably fair to say that such systems depend on a foundation of classroom ethos. Many teachers have developed systems of individual and class-wide rewards, including positive stickers and badges; positive notes or 'praise postcards' sent home (an unusual experience for parents); special activities such as quizzes or games with prizes, earned for meeting behaviour targets; motivational visual measures of behaviour that set objectives, such as charts or 'marbles in a jar'; or tangible rewards such as pens or (becoming less common in a health-conscious environment) sweets. The clarification of expectation and the establishment of explicit routines and procedures (signals for attention, acceptable noise levels, etc.) creates a framework in which pupils have more opportunities to have acceptable behaviour recognised. In the past, 'good' children were often 'taken for granted': assertive discipline schemes are putting paid to such attitudes.

However, it is probable that teacher engagement with such reward systems is variable between schools or even within individual schools. For some teachers, rewarding pupils for acceptable behaviour has become part and parcel of the learning and teaching in their classes; for others, it may be seen simply as a bribe to keep children quiet, or a bureaucratic imposition.

Certainly, there is a great deal of current debate about the efficacy of rewards, with a body of opinion suggesting that a reliance on a reward culture builds dependence and discourages the development of intrinsic drivers – or what McLean (2008) terms 'motivational resilience' – to engage fully with learning and, consequently, to behave in an acceptable manner in the classroom. However, there is a general acceptance of the notion that *praise* that is honest, specific and genuine is a key factor in building confidence and motivation in pupils, which in turn has a positive effect on their behaviour. The teacher who praises often and genuinely is likely to have a productive, well-behaved, positive classroom, and, for such teachers, the assertive discipline catchphrase 'catch them being good' has become something of a mantra.

In dealing with unsatisfactory behaviour, assertive discipline techniques again stress the need for clarity and consistency. Reward-based strategies are sometimes perceived as 'soft' on misbehaviour, but the truly assertive approach demands that misbehaviour be addressed *each time* it occurs: that is, classroom teachers should be prepared to deal with misbehaviour at all times, and refuse to 'turn a blind eye'. Key to this strategy is a 'discipline hierarchy', and many schools have instituted such hierarchies as whole school policy. Consisting of a series of 'stages' that are explicitly communicated to the pupils (often through a notice on the classroom wall and in clear assertive statements by the teacher) and which make it clear to them what the consequences of misbehaviour will be, a typical discipline hierarchy may look like this:

> First occurrence: warning
> Second occurrence: final warning, name noted
> Third occurrence: move seat in class
> Fourth occurrence: stay behind after lesson
> Fifth occurrence: remove to another class/referral to management

What is noticeable is that more and more schools are rejecting written punishment exercises as an effective sanction; quite apart from the fact that many see using writing as a punishment as counter-productive to developing the literacy skills necessary for learning, such exercises often caused as many problems as they solved and were often not used consistently, effectively or, indeed, fairly.

The assertive discipline strategies becoming more common in schools stress that the *consistency* of sanction is far more effective than the *severity* of the sanction: that is, if a pupil knows that misbehaviour *will* earn a sanction, they will be less likely to behave that way, while in systems that are inconsistent, the pupil may decide to 'gamble'.

The assertive discipline model has obvious attractions for the school as an organisation because it is a simple 'input-output' model where effort put in to consistently clarifying expectations, consistently recognising acceptable behaviour to ensure its repetition and consistently sanctioning unacceptable behaviour to ensure its eradication results in a more productive classroom ethos.

However, many schools are beginning to recognise that building relationships with pupils requires more than such basic systems: it is highly doubtful that young people develop an intrinsic sense of social responsibility – or of right and wrong – based solely on being rewarded and punished, and yet it is this intrinsic sense that is one of the aspirations of Curriculum for Excellence. As a result, a battery of strategies designed to *include* pupils in the building of school ethos has been developed which offer them a more active part to play in the decisions that affect their day-to-day education; in this respect, advice and encouragement has been forthcoming from the Scottish Government through the *Practice for Positive Relationships* papers.

At a school level, most now have some form of mechanism that allows pupils to be consulted by or to influence decisions made by the school management: indeed, the Standards in Scotland's Schools etc. Act (2000) expressly charges school managers with a duty to 'consult the pupils in attendance at the school . . . and . . . seek to involve them . . . [in] decisions concerning the everyday running of the school'. While in primary schools this has been done in a range of imaginative ways utilising experiences with which the children are familiar – circle time, classroom discussion exercises – it is probably fair to say that the secondary approach has been to mimic adult structures through bodies such as pupil councils. The comprehensive Edinburgh University study Having a Say at School (HASAS) research project (2010) suggests mixed successes in the work of schools councils due to a number of factors including involvement in superficial aspects of school life (break times, school social functions, fundraising, and so on) rather than matters relating to teaching and learning, and a lack of funding; however, encouragingly, the main purpose for schools having pupil councils in the first place was noted as 'laboratories of democracy'. Rather interestingly, the report, commissioned by Children in Scotland, was accompanied by a comic book issued to all schools about aliens visiting Earth to investigate democracy by examining the work of schools councils, and lived up to its aspiration of according pupils a voice with the development of an interactive website. In addition, pupils are beginning to be involved more than ever before on substantive matters such as the appointment of staff and the design of the many new school buildings currently being developed.

This 'democratisation' can be seen at the personal as well as the organisational level, and pupils' ability to contribute to the development of relationships in the school is being recognised by a variety of strategies that give them a place at the centre of everyday interactions. Common among these strategies include buddy schemes, whereby senior school students 'mentor' younger pupils, particularly in first year; support schemes, in which trained seniors assist other pupils with homework or basic literacy and numeracy; or peer mediation schemes, where issues and conflicts between pupils are dealt with through structured discussion with trained pupils acting as mediators, thereby avoiding potential escalation and resulting punishment.

The 2012 survey notes that a 'wide range of different approaches are used in secondary schools to encourage positive behaviour', which suggests that a flexible, solutions-focused mentality is finding some currency. Linked to this is the fact that schools are also using newer strategies, such as restorative practices (RPs).

In the traditional model of discipline management, the key function was the apportionment of guilt; procedures attempted to find out what happened, who was to blame and what the appropriate punishment should be. RPs, developed from reparative and restorative justice strategies in the criminal justice system, adopt an inclusive approach that involves an investigation of any event in order to prevent its recurrence, and is, as such, a 'no blame' strategy. The key drivers of the restorative investigation include:

- What happened?
- Who has been affected and how?
- How can the harm be repaired?
- What has been learned to prevent it happening again?

The strength of such strategies is to allow the 'victim' to be central in any resolution of conflict arising in school, offering a powerful way to deal with issues such as bullying. Schools, in a highly structured and supportive environment and with the agreement of all concerned, can bring together the relevant parties involved (pupils, teachers, support staff, parents, and so on) to interrogate the circumstances of any conflict and find solutions that meet the needs of the 'victim', the 'perpetrator' and the institution.

RPs are relatively new in Scottish schools, and more extensive research will reveal their impact on school ethos: however, the *Restorative Practices in Three Scottish Councils* (2007) report into pilot schemes was rightly optimistic about the capacity of RPs to create a positive, inclusive and empowering ethos. It is fair to say that many schools are still experimenting with RPs, the contexts in which they are best used and their relationship with other aspects of behaviour management (Soltysek, 2011), but the trend is positive, with 88 per cent of schools reportedly using RPs in 2012, an increase of 13 per cent from 2009.

NON-GOVERNMENTAL INITIATIVES

The penetration of initiatives such as Charter Mark or Investors in People in the education sector has been pronounced, and there have been clear links drawn by Her Majesty's Inspectorate of Education in Scotland between the standards set out in such schemes and the quality indicators of *How Good Is Our School?* While encouraged to take part in these schemes – which largely, among other matters, provide a mechanism for the self-evaluation of educational establishments' development plans for staff improvement – their impact on increased pupil achievement, on staff morale and on school ethos is perhaps less clear to the layperson.

Other initiatives that are designed to be embedded in the classroom are arguably more worthy of mention in the context of school ethos. The Eco-Schools Project, involving over 98 per cent of local authority schools, is designed to promote whole school participation in environmental projects. From initiatives to improve the school environment itself (litter and recycling campaigns) to curricular projects (eco-gardens, healthy lifestyle promotion) most Scottish schoolchildren have had some experience of the interplay between environment and ethos; over 40 per cent of schools have achieved the highest award for environmental awareness, the Green Flag. However, it would seem from the 2006 study *Evaluation of Eco-Schools Scotland* that the picture is more positive in primary schools than in secondaries; the report comments, 'It appears that secondary pupils not only have to contend with the apathy of some of their peers, but also with a growing awareness of the more intractable nature of some of the environmental problems we all face.' However, this awareness may be a strength, as older pupils who become more aware of the socio-economic and political dimensions of environmental issues may also be more adept at challenging the vested interests that prevent environmental development; the popularity of the Fair Trade Schools scheme may be an indicator of a growing engagement with such issues.

The Rights Respecting Schools Award is another recent initiative that is beginning to have an important impact on the ethos in Scottish schools. Run by the United Nations

Children's Fund (UNICEF) UK, it offers schools an award-based programme to encourage the application of the United Nations Convention on the Rights of the Child to school development, policies and ethos. Some 20 per cent of schools are involved in the scheme. Anecdotally, pupils are energised by having an opportunity to be involved in developing the ethos of the school – the author visited a local secondary to interview some articulate, motivated pupils who had given an assembly presentation to their peers on bullying and the infringement of Human Rights – but the only objective evaluation comes from England. The 2010 evaluation undertaken by the Universities of Sussex and Brighton reported highly favourably on the scheme's effect on ethos across thirty-one schools, noting positive and improving relationships between staff and pupils and a sense of empowerment and corresponding responsibility on the part of the pupils.

CONCLUSIONS

Teaching has never been an 'easy' profession. Aristotle famously bemoaned the bad manners and lack of respect for their elders of Athenian youth, while in 876, a teacher at Malmesbury School, John Scotus, was murdered by his pupils who stabbed him to death, it is reported, with their pens. This is not to say that schoolchildren today are 'better' than their predecessors, but it is highly debatable that they are 'worse'.

What is clear is that the last decade or so has seen a shift of attitude in Scottish schools towards the management of young people's behaviour. It is now less about control and punishment and more about building relationships, collaboration, participation and inclusion. Schools take a much more strategic view of the issue, seeing the use of explicit and consistent systems as a means of creating a productive ethos that encourages responsibility. Stressing the need to recognise pupils' positive contributions to the school, there has been a growing emphasis on including young people in the decisions that are made about their education through curricular initiatives, solutions-focused approaches to dealing with problems and organisational arrangements that offer pupils a say in decision-making processes.

This changed attitude makes sense in a context of a new curriculum which gives importance to the development of social as well as academic or vocational skills, and the evidence from the available research and evaluations of projects give grounds for optimism about the future of the ethos of schools delivering Curriculum for Excellence.

REFERENCES

Boyd, B. (2008) *The Learning Classroom*. Paisley: Hodder Gibson.
Children in Scotland and Edinburgh University (2010) *Having a Say at School*. Online at www. havingasayatschool.org.uk/promoting.html
Head, G. (2007) *Better Learning, Better Behaviour*. Edinburgh: Dunedin Academic Press.
McLean, A. (2008) *Motivating Every Learner*. London: Sage.
Munn, P. (1999) *Promoting Positive Discipline: Whole School Approaches to Tackling Low Level Disruption*. Edinburgh: Moray House.
Munn, P. (2008) 'Ethos and discipline in the secondary school', in T. G. K. Bryce and W. M. Humes (eds), *Scottish Education, Third Edition: Beyond Devolution*. Edinburgh: Edinburgh University Press.
Scottish Executive (2000) *Standards in Scotland's Schools etc. Act*. Online at www.legislation.gov.uk/ asp/2000/6/contents

Scottish Executive (2006) *Practice for Positive Relationships, 'Positive about pupil participation'*. Online at www.scotland.gov.uk/Resource/Doc/182858/0051876.pdf

Scottish Executive (2007) *Restorative Practices in Three Scottish Councils*. Online at www.scotland.gov.uk/Resource/Doc/196078/0052553.pdf

Scottish Government (2011) *Schools Safety – School Exclusions, High Level Summary of Statistics Trend*. Online at www.scotland.gov.uk/Topics/Statistics/Browse/SchoolEducation/TrendSchoolExclusions

Scottish Government (2012) *Behaviour in Scottish Schools*. Online at www.scotland.gov.uk/Resource/0040/00403817.pdf

Soltysek, R. (2011) 'Confident application is key to behaviour management'. *Times Education Supplement Scotland*. Online at www.tes.co.uk/article.aspx?storycode=6076825

UNICEF (2010) *Evaluation Of UNICEF UK's Rights Respecting Schools Award*. Online at www.unicef.org.uk/Documents/EducationDocuments/RRSA_Evaluation_Report.pdf

University of Glasgow (2006) *SCRE Research Report No 124, Evaluation of Eco Schools Scotland*. Online at www.eric.ed.gov/ERICWebPortal/search/detailmini.jsp?_nfpb=true&_&ERICExtSearch_SearchValue_0=ED497546&ERICExtSearch_SearchType_0=no&accno=ED497546

39

Classroom Management: Working with School Support Assistants in the Primary Classroom

Mike Carroll and Deirdre Torrance

The role of the class teacher continues to evolve, responding to changing priorities and perceived needs. Despite historical reluctance on the part of teachers and their professional organisations to attribute management to the role of the teacher, on a practical level there is much that needs to be managed within the classroom context in relation to pupil ability, pupil needs and the people tasked with supporting the educational experience of pupils. In schools there are a range of adults who work either as 'teachers' or as 'support staff', including parent helpers. Support staff fall into five broad categories:

- learning support staff who work with teachers in the classroom, including classroom assistants, additional support needs (ASN) assistants, peripatetic specialists (for physical education, drama, music, and so on), English for Speakers of Other Languages (ESOL) teachers, etc.
- specialist and technical staff, including librarians, information and communications technology (ICT)/audio visual (AV) technicians, science technicians, food technology technicians, etc.
- pupil support/welfare staff, including youth workers (i.e. active break workers), attendance officers, school nurses, counsellors, etc.
- administrative staff, including administration and finance assistants, clerical assistants, team leaders (office), school support coordinators, etc.
- facilities staff, including catering staff, janitorial staff, cleaning staff, etc.

It is evident that support staff can either have direct or indirect contact with pupils. In this chapter we are primarily concerned with support staff who have direct contact with pupils and teachers situated in the classroom environment with the intention of supporting teaching and learning. Classroom assistant (CA) is the most widespread term adopted in Scottish schools to describe adults who are employed to work alongside teachers in classrooms, particularly providing support to pupils considered as having additional support needs; however, in this chapter we will use the term school support assistant (SSA).

The role of SSAs has also evolved in response to changes in expectations of the teacher's role. The SSAs' role has become increasingly complex, developing from an auxiliary role to that of supporting pupils' learning (Mistry et al., 2004). Furthermore, within a distributed perspective on leadership and management SSAs often find themselves encouraged to move into roles previously reserved for teachers or those with formal management positions, in particular relation to the public spaces of the school. Moreover, increased inter-agency working can result in boundary spanning, challenging established cultures (Stead et al., 2007). This carries with it implications for staff relationships and school practice.

This chapter first explores the changing role of teachers with regard to their relationship with SSAs in order to meet the increasingly diverse needs of learners. It goes on to explore the expectations for and challenges of the SSAs' role before examining some potential tensions between the roles of the class teacher and SSAs in order to suggest some recommendations for practice.

A CHANGING EDUCATIONAL LANDSCAPE

In Scotland, as in other parts of the UK, the role of the class teacher has changed considerably over the last twenty years. Workforce reform has prioritised the deployment of class teachers to concentrate on learning and teaching in an effort to improve standards by identifying activities to be undertaken by SSAs rather than teachers, so freeing up teachers' time to teach. Coterminous with workforce reform, an increased number of SSAs have been appointed to support the realignment and transformation of the educational landscape with respect to the structure and philosophy of special education (Moran and Abbott, 2002), resulting in the inclusion of pupils with ASNs in mainstream schools. Previously these pupils were effectively excluded from their local neighbourhood school by being educated in separate establishments, so-called 'special schools'. The move towards inclusive education represents a rejection of separation on the basis of perceived need, arguing that it is a form of 'educational apartheid'. The simple but nevertheless powerful underlying assumption of inclusive education is that all pupils have the right to be educated in their neighbourhood school and to receive the same educational opportunities as every other pupil of their age. As a consequence, the modern-day classroom in Scotland is one containing an increasingly diverse population of learners. The implication of this for schools is that they need to consider how they can provide equal opportunities for teaching and learning through the adaptation of an inclusive pedagogy to meet diverse needs. The policy of inclusion leads directly to the perceived need for additional in-class adult support for pupils with ASNs.

Input from SSAs for pupils who require additional support for their learning is also seen as being crucial as we move towards constructing more collaborative, active and interdisciplinary learning experiences, with pupils taking responsibility for 'planning and reflecting on their own learning, through formative assessment, self and peer evaluation, and personal learning planning' (Scottish Government, 2008, pp. 27–8). Blatchford et al. (2009) argue that SSAs have become an essential component of practice with regard to the integration of pupils who have barriers to their learning in mainstream schools. Consequently the growth in the number of SSAs can be linked to this changing educational landscape; however, we will argue that rather than more adults, we need more teachers in the classroom. The relief to teachers provided by an 'extra pair of hands' in the classroom should not be confused with effective education for pupils. If we are truly seeking inclusive education, with all pupils participating as members of the school community, then having another adult by a pupil's side, for all or part of the school day, may only serve to exacerbate rather than ameliorate the pupil's sense of exclusion, particularly if the adults who take on the primary burden for the successful inclusion of pupils into the mainstream are not adequately trained.

The changing classroom topography requires teachers to take responsibility for the supervision and ongoing mentoring of SSAs despite the fact that there has been scant recognition of the specific skills and personal aptitudes required for working with adults in the management of classroom support. Training for such responsibility does not form part of initial teacher education and there is little by way of in-service training (Blatchford et al., 2009). Experienced teachers previously accustomed to high levels of autonomy have had to adjust to the demands of team working in the support of pupil learning. It has been largely left to staff to form new understandings of what it means to work cooperatively and collaboratively.

More recently, a number of specific challenges have surfaced in relation to the teacher's changing role. Although many teachers have developed experience of, and skill for, the mentoring of newly qualified teachers, little consideration has been given to the different mentoring needs of SSAs. As various funding streams and government priorities have resulted in an array of SSAs' roles, fresh challenges have emerged in relation to managing the roles and responsibilities of SSAs with various remits. Care is required to balance role definition with pragmatic flexibility (Stead et al., 2007), avoiding either ambiguity or restrictive practice. As SSAs become increasingly skilled, the middle ground between the prescribed duties of SSAs and teachers provides a source of potential confusion and conflict as it is not always easy to neatly delineate between teaching and supporting. Increased expectations placed on support staff have also increased the complexity of their role.

What is being described is a move away from the teacher working in 'splendid professional isolation' in his or her own classroom to someone who is connected both within and beyond the classroom to a range of other adults who work as part of an extended classroom team seeking to meet the needs of pupils. Perversely the addition of SSAs, so creating extended classroom teams, adds to the responsibilities of class teachers as they are expected to supervise and support these adults.

TEACHER AS SUPERVISOR

Generally appointed without training, qualifications for, or experience in the role, SSAs generally learn on the job in response to contextual expectations. Beyond the induction phase, SSAs often receive little training (Stead et al., 2007) and commonly find their continuous professional development (CPD) needs are not adequately addressed (Blatchford et al., 2009). In addition, the role of SSAs is diverse and context-specific. Experience within and between schools can vary considerably, with SSAs being allocated to more than one classroom, working alongside different teachers, each with his or her own expectations and ways of working, as well as being tasked with administrative duties and supervision in the school's public spaces.

Meanwhile, teachers are more used to working with children than other adults whilst in the classroom. It is also unusual for teachers to think of themselves as having a supervisory role or to have the training to act in a supervisory capacity with respect to other adults in the classroom. Despite the fact that a range of adults enter the classroom to work alongside teachers, there is little by way of guidance as to their respective roles and responsibilities. Generally the responsibility for developing SSAs lies with the institutions in which they are placed. This will require a whole-school, team-led approach to mentoring aimed at providing support and training within schools. Arguably this will also need to be addressed at all levels of teacher development, from initial teacher training onwards; the Standard for

Initial Teacher Education states that student teachers should demonstrate competence that they can 'work effectively in co-operation with other professionals, staff and parents in order to promote learning' and 'demonstrate the ability to identify the ways in which additional support in the classroom can assist pupils' learning' (GTCS, 2006, p. 11).

For on-the-job orientation and training to have any meaningful impact, particularly in the absence of a whole-school approach, it becomes necessary for the class teacher to take on the role of 'mentor' in order to facilitate understanding of duties, tasks to be undertaken as well as the development of basic 'teaching skills'. Notwithstanding the fact that organising support and training for both teachers and SSAs is not unproblematic, the mentoring role of classroom teachers is made difficult by the fact that although the work of SSAs may be under the supervision of the class teacher this does not mean that the teacher is their line manager (Mistry et al., 2004). Line management of SSAs can be unclear in that they may interact with a number of classroom teachers and the school management team whilst taking direction from the Special Educational Needs Coordinator (SENCO). The issue here is not that the SSA interacts with several staff, indeed this fits well with the notions of collegial working and distributive leadership, but rather that a confused line management structure, which may reside outside any given school, is likely to lead to breakdowns in communication that will hinder attempts to provide staff development opportunities for SSAs including mentoring by teachers.

The 'supervisory role' of teachers is predicated upon two assumptions, namely that every teacher is able to lead and manage adults, and that he or she wishes to lead and manage adults. Popular discourse suggests that leadership should be integral to the role of every teacher without necessarily considering whether all teachers are capable of a leadership role or not. However, for some teachers, a leadership role does not come naturally and for others, it might never fully develop. Not all teachers have the confidence to lead colleagues and some may not have the necessary interpersonal skills. For others, personal or family circumstances mean that it is unrealistic to expect that they would undertake a leadership role. For others, their aspirations lie elsewhere. Perhaps it is unreasonable to conceive that all teachers can engage in leadership roles consistently throughout their career. For some teachers, taking on a leadership role is not considered part of their professional identity. Furthermore, the focus for teacher leadership and influence is predominantly related to the curriculum, teaching and learning, and assessment rather than to leading and managing adults. There is an additional tension inherent within the relationship between class teachers and SSAs which can lead to a dichotomised identity amongst SSAs. Within the classroom context the teacher holds the key role with position and authority conveyed to that role. Yet within the public spaces of the school SSAs can hold a key role with position and authority conveyed to them through the school's formal leaders. The leadership role of SSAs is often less obvious and less recognised than that of teaching staff. The leadership role SSAs play in the public spaces of the school is not generally reflected within their classroom role. Support staff can have a legitimised leadership role with respect to 'pupil care, welfare and/or personal concerns' when they are perceived as the expert in providing long-standing support for a high-tariff child. Beyond that, SSAs often have scant influence in their relationships with teachers. There is often lack of recognition that SSAs could play a significant leadership role of different but equal status. Furthermore, teachers do not perceive themselves to have a role in developing the leadership capacity of SSAs.

Leadership may not be perceived by teachers as an integral part of their role. Leadership can be perceived as an 'opt in' or 'add on'. Indeed, a small number of teachers may be resistant to engage in leadership roles. Teachers might be expected and encouraged to lead but they cannot be forced to do so. That means that staff goodwill can be withdrawn at any point, adding to the process of constant negotiation. National and local agreements on teacher workload can be as stifling as they are enabling. Although key, within such circumstances, maintaining positive relationships between staff is not easy. A careful balance needs to be maintained.

CROSSING THE BOUNDARY INTO TEACHING

School support assistants can provide an 'extra set of helping hands, eyes and ears' in and beyond the classroom by undertaking clerical work so enabling the teacher to spend more time on teaching (preparing materials for lessons, for example), putting up displays, supervising non-teaching activities taking place outwith the classroom (such as playground duty, cafeteria duty, etc.) as well as assisting with personal care. More recently, SSAs have begun to undertake more of a pedagogical role under the direction of the teacher. This can involve providing supervision in small-group settings, facilitating follow-up instruction (such as paired reading, practice of reading words and phonics), help with homework, supporting children in the development of their social skills through encouraging peer interaction, and the development of positive relationships and behaviour.

Teachers and SSAs can find it difficult to negotiate the boundaries between teaching and non-teaching roles, giving rise to a zone of uncertainty (Moran and Abbott, 2002) with some SSAs being judged to overstep the boundary into teaching. Teachers can be unclear as to the role of SSAs in the classroom as SSAs can work across several different members of staff all of whom will have slightly different expectations with respect to their role. In addition, some SSAs are employed to support individual pupils, usually someone with a significant barrier to their learning, whilst others function as general SSAs. In primary schools, SSAs tend to be used more flexibly in that they can support an individual pupil as well as moving between groups of pupils; however, SSAs in secondary schools are more likely to support individual pupils (Blatchford et al., 2009). The feature that they should all have in common is that the primary purpose of their work is to assist and support pupils' engagement with the learning process in cooperation with the classroom teacher.

IT'S GOOD TO TALK

Scheduled meetings, no matter how brief, provide space and time for communication between teachers and SSAs to take place. The nature of the talk that takes place will vary depending upon what needs to be accomplished but this can involve:

- planning talk during which the teacher outlines the objectives and learning intentions to be achieved;
- differentiation talk focused on identifying the different teaching strategies that are available to achieve the desired objectives, for particular groups and individuals, and what this means in terms of the respective roles and responsibilities of the teacher and the SSA;
- implementation talk focused on agreeing the actions that are necessary in order to implement the teacher's plan;
- review talk during which the teacher and the SSA will discuss whether targets have been met and what adjustments to future plans need to take place;

- social glue talk during which the relational context of the team is attended to through sharing personal information, views, feelings, and so on.

Finding opportunities to talk is a key concern as regular meetings are important to maintain rapport and communication and to discuss progress or problems. The extra pair of 'hands, eyes and ears' provided by SSAs is often not put to best use as there is insufficient time set aside for teachers and SSAs to plan their work together. Time scheduled for discussion, let alone planning, remains rare with collaboration between teachers and SSAs being largely informal and dependent upon the teacher. Communication is critical not only to ensure productive learning experiences for pupils but also to help create and support a productive work environment constructed upon mutually reinforcing professional relationships. The issue will always be one of when to meet. For some this will mean scheduling specific times each week to meet, such as at the start or the end of the school day, assuming the SSA is available. For others the reality may be that planning involves flexibility, linked to the commitments of both the teacher and the SSA. This may mean that all that is available are a few brief moments snatched prior to lessons or during 'quiet moments' within a lesson. The point is that it is worthwhile to persevere in identifying opportunities to sit down and talk.

Including SSAs in regular meetings should achieve two key goals. First, it will provide necessary support in developing the SSAs' understanding of the issues to be addressed with respect to individual pupils' progress. That the SSA is aware of the plan and what is involved in its implementation is likely to facilitate a more effective engagement with pupils. Second, addressing the relational context signals that the relationship between all those charged with providing productive learning experiences for pupils is one of mutual respect. Without a sense of respect participants are likely to remain closed to each other and consequently it will prove difficult to work collaboratively as SSAs in particular may feel excluded from the classroom team (Mistry et al., 2004).

Planning talk provides SSAs with information on the learning intentions and what this will mean in terms of their contribution during the course of a lesson, when and to whom they will provide support and the purpose of this interaction. As part of discussions on planning, teachers can work with SSAs to determine what is entailed in meeting individual education plans for those pupils who have them and what this means in terms of the level of support that is needed for these pupils. Taking this further, teachers can provide SSAs with knowledge as to the methods to be used to address particular aspects of learning as well as any modifications that may be required in terms of teaching and/or materials to be used. It is important not to assume that the SSA understands the conceptual framework that underpins teaching nor why teachers choose different strategies to teach different concepts. Providing the SSA with a clear explanation is essential if he or she is to be in a position to implement the plan effectively (Hauge and Barkie, 2006). Plans do not always work in the way that is intended, so incorporating a review of classroom activity and pupils' work will enable the classroom team to identify and implement adaptations to the curricular plan for individuals, so personalising the learning experience. This will ensure that all members of the classroom team are aware of every pupil's progress rather than allowing demarcation of responsibility for particular pupils, especially those with barriers to their learning, being assigned to one member of the team. Planning does not always remove issues with respect to appropriate pedagogical and social interactions between SSAs and pupils. Periodically it may be necessary, as part of the process of review, to take time to provide the SSA with insights as to how to alter his or her interactional matrix in order to improve its effectiveness in bringing about positive outcomes for pupils. It is crucial that the classroom team have an agreed protocol for intervention, particularly when the teacher identifies impediments to learning as they arise. Such protocols are critically important in order that the SSA does not 'lose face' in front of the pupils as this would only serve to undermine any future contribution that he or she has to make within the classroom. In addition to an intervention protocol it is essential that subsequent discussion aimed at remediation takes place in a private space (Hauge and Barkie, 2006) for the reason stated above.

EXCLUSION BY MISGUIDED GOOD INTENTIONS

Blatchford et al. (2007) indicate that teachers are generally positive about the contribution of SSAs in terms of:

- increased attention and support for learning (e.g., more one-to-one attention particularly for children with ASNs);
- increased teaching effectiveness (e.g., in terms of productive group work, utilisation of practical activities); and
- effective classroom management.

The presence of another adult in the classroom provides teachers with the possibility to hand over to the SSA pupils who are most demanding of a teacher's time, for example, lower-ability pupils, pupils with ASNs and those pupils with emotional and behavioural difficulties all of whom are likely to have complex needs; it is less common for SSAs to work with more able pupils. Blatchford et al. (2009, p. 683) state that this is another aspect of the changing educational landscape as prior to the growth in the number of SSAs teachers would have had responsibility and provided support for all the pupils in their classroom. As SSAs also provide general support for all pupils there can be some degree of overlap in the two main types of support provided by SSAs. The advantage of giving SSAs the 'neediest' pupils is that it frees up the teacher to focus his or her attention on the rest of the class in order to meet their needs. This can be easily rationalised as the most vulnerable pupils are being provided with individual support. Increasingly SSAs assigned to accompany pupils with specific barriers to their learning or to aid the teacher in a more general way are being asked not only to take on responsibility for meeting the disparate support needs of pupils but also to assume a pedagogical role (Blatchford et al., 2007). The inherent problem with the approach outlined above, however attractive it may appear to teachers, is that in deploying SSAs to help provide this support we are often assigning the least qualified staff to those pupils with the most complex learning needs. This may explain, in part, why the available evidence as to the impact of SSAs on academic attainment has been largely unconvincing (Blatchford et al., 2009).

The increased adult–student interaction provided for pupils with barriers to their learning is mostly from SSAs rather than teachers. In working to support pupils with ASNs and those with emotional and behavioural difficulties SSAs make a positive contribution to classroom management. This means that teachers spend less time on dealing with 'disruptions' within a lesson, giving them more time to spend providing individual attention to the rest of the class. One consequence of the proximity of SSAs is that supported pupils can end up having less, rather than more, contact with the class teacher, which can be exacerbated if SSAs periodically take pupils out of the classroom. Even when teachers and SSAs are working within the same classroom they may well be focusing their attention on different pupils and adopting, in the absence of coherent planning, different approaches to teaching and patterns of interaction. For instance, SSAs tend to be less mobile than teachers with a tendency to work in one location with their designated pupils; teachers are more fluid in their pattern of interaction, moving between whole class, group and individual interactions. Consequently SSAs do not provide additional support but alternative support (Blatchford et al., 2009); as such although the classroom may be inclusive thanks to the presence of diversity it can remain exclusive with respect to practice.

The proximity of SSAs can cause them to become 'overprotective', albeit out of misguided good intentions, leading to separation from classmates, dependency on adults and loss of personal control (Causton-Theoharis and Malmgren, 2005). SSAs can form very close relationships with pupils, particularly when compared to the relationships that teachers are able to develop given that they have a large number of pupil needs to address (Hauge and Barkie, 2006). Often pupils can be in constant contact with the SSAs during the course of the school day, during lessons and break times, so minimising the extent of contact with other pupils and teachers. SSAs can provide a 'connecting bridge' between the pupils they have responsibility for and the teacher (Mistry et al., 2004) so it is important for the teacher to understand this relationship in order to detect the emergence of 'nannying' (Moran and Abbott, 2002) with pupils seeking assistance only from the SSAs rather than from their peers or the class teacher. One aspect of 'nannying' is that the challenge of planned learning experiences can be diminished as the SSA completes the task rather than the pupil even in the absence of any request for assistance from the pupil with a view to enabling the pupil to 'keep up' with the rest of the class (Moran and Abbott, 2002). Another aspect of this is that pupils with barriers to their learning often have difficulty with social interaction (for example, misunderstanding social cues, not following social conventions of taking turns in talking, etc.). There are a number of ways in which the development of social skills can be compromised, such as removing pupils from the classroom environment, particularly when they are perceived as being disruptive; working with a pupil away from other pupils within the classroom, so reducing opportunities for peer interaction; isolating the pupil within the classroom on the grounds of accessibility; and providing incentives that reinforce social isolation (such as individual computer time). These fairly common practices serve to reduce the amount of time that pupils have available to interact with their peers in the classroom and they do nothing to alleviate any difficulties with social interaction these pupils may already have.

The practice during paired work of the SSA acting as the partner to the pupil rather than supporting peer interaction can reduce the possibility of social skill development as well as compromising the learning intentions underpinning collaborative work (Causton-Theoharis and Malmgren, 2005). Opportunities for peer interaction can be subverted by the asymmetrical power relationships between the SSA and pupils as all communication can go through the SSA, leading to the supported pupil being sidelined. Many SSAs, and teachers, view independence with adult support as a key goal of inclusion; in reality this may only exacerbate social isolation within an inclusive setting as the real goal is one of interdependence with peers and adults (Causton-Theoharis and Malmgren, 2005). The trap to be avoided is in assuming that because a SSA is available to a pupil, due to there being an identified barrier to learning, this need for support completes the possibilities for that pupil. That the pupil needs to be supported is not in question but it is important to encourage the pupil to contribute to decision making about how supports can be enacted within his or her context. This could involve making adjustments to the support provided by replacing some, or all, of the support from the SSA with that of support from peers. The SSA can be located outside the group whilst remaining available to intervene when needed so allowing the pupils to support each other.

CONCLUSION

There is a paucity of research exploring teachers' perceptions of their role in relation to developing the capabilities of SSAs or of SSAs' experience of the increasingly complex nature of their role as they move between the semi-private spaces of the classroom and the public spaces of the school. Nationally, as the role of teachers comes under review it seems an opportune time to reflect on where leadership sits in general within that role. More specifically, a clearer understanding of the nature of teacher leadership would be helpful, in relation to the organisation, supervision and ongoing mentoring constituting the classroom management of SSAs. Such understandings need to develop from the initial teacher education stages. It also seems an opportune time to consider a more sophisticated understanding of the complex role of many SSAs, along with the implications of that for school practice, and a career structure that recognises both the skills of and the contribution made by SSAs.

At local authority and school levels, a number of aspects might be worthy of further discussion, in an effort to build understandings for mutually supportive roles and to maximise the benefits of limited resources for supporting pupils' needs:

- role clarity for the different types of SSAs, along with expectations for and of the role;
- pre-appointment and ongoing training for SSAs together with structured career development and enhanced status;
- pre-appointment and ongoing training for teachers particularly in relation to mentoring and supervising SSAs;
- clarification of the line management of SSAs and performance review and development processes;
- open discussions about the challenges inherent in managing the various roles and responsibilities of SSAs and the need to balance role definition with flexibility;
- open discussions about the leadership role of SSAs and its implications for their role within the public spaces of the school and semi-private classroom environment;
- time available for joint planning and feedback;
- cover to minimise disruption to the timetabled support provided.

REFERENCES

Blatchford, P., A. Russell, P. Bassett, P. Brown and C. Martin (2007) 'The role and effects of teaching assistants in English primary schools (Years 4 to 6) 2000–2003. Results from the Class Size and Pupil–Adult Ratios (CSPAR) KS2 Project', *British Educational Research Journal*, 33 (1): 5–26.
Blatchford, P., P. Bassett, P. Brown and R. Webster (2009) 'The effect of support staff on pupil engagement and individual attention', *British Educational Research Journal*, 35 (5): 661–86.
Causton-Theoharis, J. and K. Malmgren (2005) 'Building bridges: Strategies to help paraprofessionals promote peer interaction', *Teaching Exceptional Children*, 37 (6): 18–24.
General Teaching Council of Scotland (GTCS) (2006) *Standard for Initial Teacher Education*. Edinburgh: GTCS. Online at www.gtcs.org.uk/web/FILES/the-standards/the-standard-for-initial-teacher-education.pdf

Hauge, J. M. and A. M. Barkie (2006) 'Develop collaborative special educator-paraprofessional teams: One para's view', *Intervention in School and Clinic*, 42 (1): 51–3.

Mistry, M., N. Burton and M. Brundrett (2004) 'Managing LSAs: An evaluation of the use of learning support assistants in an urban primary school', *School Leadership & Management*, 24 (2): 125–37.

Moran, A. and L. Abbott (2002) 'Developing inclusive schools: The pivotal role of teaching assistants in promoting inclusion in special and mainstream schools in Northern Ireland', *European Journal of Special Needs Education*, 17 (2): 161–73.

Schlapp, U., V. Wilson and J. Davidson (2001) *'An Extra Pair of Hands?' Evaluation of the Classroom Assistants Initiative. Interim Report. Report 104.* Edinburgh: Scottish Council for Educational Research.

Scottish Government (2008) *Curriculum for Excellence: Building the Curriculum 3: A Framework for Learning and Teaching.* Edinburgh: Scottish Government. Online at www.scotland.gov.uk/ Resource/Doc/226155/0061245.pdf

Stead, J., G. Lloyd, P. Munn, S. Riddell, J. Kane and G. MacLeod (2007) 'Supporting our most challenging pupils with our lowest status staff: Can additional staff in Scottish schools offer a distinctive kind of help?', *Scottish Educational Review*, 39 (2): 186–97.

40

Personal Support and PSE in the Secondary School

David J. McLaren

THE ORIGINS OF PERSONAL SUPPORT

The 2005 *National Review of Guidance* (SEED, 2005) introduced the term Personal Support to replace what had previously been known as Guidance. However, the term Personal Support has not yet been universally adopted. Guidance has become known throughout Scotland variously as Personal Support; Pupil Support; Pupil Support/Pastoral Care (PSPC) and, less commonly, Pastoral Care. To confuse matters even further, there are a quite a few schools that retain the term Guidance.

In itself, this plethora of terms associated with Pupil Support may seem innocuous enough – merely an indication of a system engaging in necessary change. However, when this is combined with a similar multiplicity of terms in the National Review relating to staff involved (for example, Key Staff; Designated Staff; Senior Personal Support Staff) and with the opposite problem in Curriculum for Excellence (that is, a general failure to recognise its specific contribution to capacities and curricular areas), it might be argued that there is a vagueness in terms of definition and understanding and, consequently, of practice. Some of this will be discussed later. However, in order to better understand where Personal Support is now, it is necessary to understand a little of where it came from.

Many would argue that the system of Guidance that existed up until the publication of the McCrone Agreement document (SEED, 2001a) originated in 1968 with the publication of the Scottish Education Department's (SED) paper *Guidance in Scottish Secondary Schools*. Schools had always been concerned with the welfare of their pupils but the move to comprehensive education in the 1960s was the first time that the education system as a whole had had to face up to the challenge of S1–S6 all-through secondary schooling. There had always been 'omnibus' schools in rural areas of Scotland, but throughout the country many large secondary schools were created which catered for a much wider ability range and socio-economic mix than ever before. The problem of how to accommodate pupil needs was as contentious then as it is now. Embedded in the notion of comprehensive education itself was the commitment to ensuring the best provision possible for the individual, meeting individual needs and recognising that pupil 'potential' was a much wider concept than academic achievement. The comprehensive schools ostensibly offered a wide and varied curriculum at the appropriate levels for all pupils. By encouraging a wider social mix, elitism and divisiveness would become things of the past and there would be a new emphasis on equality of opportunity. Social inclusion, it seems, is not a new idea.

The SED identified 'personal', 'vocational' and 'curricular' guidance. In 1968, 'personal' tended to mean discussing vital problems of the day (unlike its usage in Curriculum for Excellence as an umbrella term for the whole support process), while 'vocational' had to do with careers information and 'curricular' tended to focus on option choice at S2. Each pupil had the right to receive advice or help from a teacher who had 'a special and continuing responsibility for him' and, most importantly, Guidance was for all pupils, not only for those who had problems. The Guidance system might be organised vertically (for example, into house groups which many schools already had in some form or another) or horizontally (year groups), and staff would require training.

Four years later, in anticipation of the raising of the school-leaving age, a promoted post structure was introduced for dealing with increasing numbers of pupils who were required to stay on at school. It is highly significant that the promoted post structures in Guidance and 'subject' (introduced at the same time) were almost identical and that these parallel structures remained largely unchanged for some thirty years. However, there was still considerable confusion as to what exactly Guidance was all about, not least among newly appointed Guidance staff. By the mid-1970s, Her Majesty's Inspectors had become involved and, while they reiterated the importance of personal, curricular and vocational guidance for pupils, they stressed that, in addition to the specific responsibilities of promoted staff, all staff had responsibility in this area – a principle recently reiterated in the Curriculum for Excellence documentation. There was also a growing recognition in the 1970s and 1980s that the formal subject curriculum was insufficient preparation for the world outside school and that 'Social Education' classes were required to deal with such matters as relationships, health and work. Guidance staff, with their cross-curricular approach and concern for the whole pupil, were seen as appropriate staff to devise and deliver Social Education programmes, along with other staff.

By far the most important influence on the aims, objectives and practice of Guidance was the position paper *More Than Feelings of Concern* (SCCC, 1986). This was the first real attempt on a national scale to define aims and objectives for Guidance. It reinforced earlier messages about pupils being well known personally by one member of staff while reiterating the general staff responsibility for pupil welfare. It tried to identify the characteristics of a 'caring' school and it argued, above all, that guidance was more than just good intentions: it was, or ought to be, an active, ongoing process that required planning. It even provided objectives to aid such planning. This report was a seminal piece of work, not necessarily for its intellectual depth or its great vision, but for its practicability. It provided a major stepping-stone into the educational world of the 1990s and gave Guidance an enhanced status and a much surer footing on which to engage with important contemporary issues such as school ethos, quality and performance indicators, school effectiveness, profiling, inter-agency collaboration and education for personal and social development – issues that the 1968 paper could not be expected to envisage. In 1996, Her Majesty's Inspectorate (HMI) considered the objectives of *More than Feelings of Concern* 'as relevant today as they were 10 years ago'. HMI also reiterated the general responsibility of all staff for supporting pupils (HMI, 1996) but they were at pains to point out that such 'first-level' (normally unpromoted) staff were entitled to expect clear remits, responsibilities and line management – still a major issue today.

The McCrone Report and the *Agreement* document which followed it in 2001 (SEED, 2001a) challenged the thinking about Guidance, largely because it ignored it. The report takes a very traditional view of the teacher – one that is subject and classroom based, with Guidance/Personal Support being marginalised. McCrone had only two things to say in passing about Guidance. First, more unpromoted staff and Register teachers were to involve themselves in pastoral care. Second, there was a brief mention of the duties of a promoted member of staff referred to (but not discussed or rationalised) as principal teacher (PT) Pastoral/Guidance. The problem was that there was no indication of how Pupil Support/ Guidance might be structured in a new system. It seemed that Guidance was to have a broader base and no middle layer of management (that is, no Assistant Principal Teacher posts), and be managed by a small team of PTs. Inevitably, local authorities had to consider the possibility of full-time Guidance staff with increased caseloads, little or no subject com- mitment but perhaps a teaching commitment to Personal and Social Education. At the same time, the Scottish Executive Education Department's (SEED's) discipline 'task group' (SEED, 2001b) urged schools to consider merging their 'support' systems – normally Guidance, Learning Support and (where applicable) Behaviour Support. Most impor- tantly, it also recommended a comprehensive national review of the nature and purpose of Guidance and of the training of Guidance staff.

The publication of the resulting National Review document *Happy, Safe and Achieving their Potential, Report of the National Review of Guidance* (SEED, 2005), was much delayed, however. There was some suspicion that the delay was not accidental and that SEED had been reluctant to enter into the uncharted waters of the McCrone settlement, preferring instead to leave it to local authorities to work out the practicalities of Pupil Support struc- tures and responsibilities (which the local authorities duly did). Some local authorities increased the number of PT posts and some tried a more broad-based approach but there was a general expectation amongst practitioners that the Review document – one of the first under the new Curriculum for Excellence banner – would provide clarification. However, the report, which covered primary, secondary special education sectors and (ambitiously) 'partner agencies providing learning opportunities and support' (SEED, 2005, p. 10), was never going to be the prescriptive, directive kind of document of earlier decades. In common with similar reports in other areas such as social work and youth justice, a 'Standards' model was presented for all involved. Rather than tell schools how to organise themselves, most reports of this kind are determined at all costs to avoid what they see as prescription, preferring instead to issue a set of principles or guidelines, or 'Standards', that have to be met. The Review produced ten 'Standards for Personal Support' which schools might work towards, but it was up to local authorities and individual schools to work out the detail, although some exemplars of 'emerging' practice were included.

THE NATIONAL FRAMEWORK

The scene seemed set for the redefining of 'Guidance' as 'Personal Support' across three sectors and partner agencies, using the Standards as a framework . There was some criticism as to the operational utility of these Standards but work proceeded apace and for two years the Scottish Government funded working groups developing (and collating) good practice and various staff development materials were produced. However, without warning (or indeed, any consultation whatsoever), the following announcement appeared (briefly) on the Learning and Teaching Scotland (LTS) website in late 2009:

Autumn Update
There is a recognition of a change in policy direction in personal support from ten standards for personal support provided in 'Happy, Safe and Achieving their Potential' to a broader definition required to meet the commitment in *Building the Curriculum 3*.

Quite who was responsible for this apparently unilateral 'change in policy direction' was never explained (a feature not uncommon in Personal Support policy making). Many would argue that *Happy, Safe* had already broadened the definition of Guidance/Support rather beyond what was practicable but here there was to be an even broader understanding of support, from age 3 to 18 and possibly beyond, based on an 'Entitlement' (one of several) outlined in *Building the Curriculum 3* (Scottish Government, 2008). All children and young people were entitled to personal support to enable them to:

- review their learning and plan for next steps;
- gain access to learning activities which will meet their needs;
- plan for opportunities for personal achievement;
- prepare for changes and choices and be supported through changes and choices.

There is little that is controversial here. These principles have been around for decades in Guidance/Support work. The Entitlement continues in similar vein with exhortations about the necessity of ensuring that an adult knows pupils well, removing barriers, enrichment, care, welfare, achievement. This is equally uncontroversial but there was (and is) a feeling that wheels were being reinvented. The *Autumn Update* of 2009 created (another) policy group to 'support the delivery of the overarching strategic priorities of Early Intervention, Early Years, Health Inequalities and Anti-poverty Strategies' which would 'help deliver' key national outcomes for children and young people including the four capacities. Significantly, and arguably straining credibility to breaking point, it intended to 'draw together the full range of approaches and frameworks across 25 policy areas'.

At the time of writing, the Policy Group above has extended (although, arguably, not meaningfully developed) the 'Entitlement' and the twenty-five policy areas mentioned above into a 'National Framework for Support', which seems set to dominate the Personal Support agenda for the foreseeable future. Education Scotland indicates that the National Framework is 'for all practitioners and partners, in every setting, aiming to help in supporting learners from early years to positive, sustained destinations' (www.ltscotland.org. uk/supportinglearners/). Further, 'it also recognises the need for supporting learners from birth to 18+ and therefore aligns with the national frameworks currently in place for children's and young people's services in Scotland'. In fact, the policies referred to cover an age range from pre-birth to 25+ years of age.

Already it might be argued that such a framework attempts to do far too much, across too many sectors, and that any resulting policy or guidelines must inevitably be compromised in terms of their practical value in schools, particularly perhaps in the secondary sector where 'Guidance' had a strong established base and working practices – most of which are barely referred to at all in the new documentation in its attempts to be all things to all people. To date, as far as can be ascertained, all the information is contained in a website, presumably because hyperlinks allow easy access to other sources but also perhaps because any further 'change in policy direction' can be accommodated quickly and quietly. In as much as there is any workable policy at all in any of this, the Framework is divided into four major areas:

1. *Legislation and Policy*: this resembles a bibliography and is a list of reports and papers across a spectrum comprising, among others, education, health and social work (pre-birth *Positive Outcomes* to *Youth Work, 8–25*) which might be referred to for information and advice.

2. *Entitlement to Support*: the four headings from 'Entitlement' above are reiterated here (with the addition of 'pre-school centres and school working with partners'). Each of the headings is a gateway to further information but these are exceptionally brief and add little or nothing to the points outlined in the Entitlement.

3. *Targeted Support*: this section covers additional support needs, specific learning difficulties, highly able children and 'More Choice and More Chances' and has links to further documentation. In a few cases, there are links to some resource materials.

4. *Universal Support*: this covers potentially huge areas such as wellbeing, inclusion, equality, relationships, personal learning planning, achievement and the concept of the key professional. Again, there are links to numerous documents and classroom materials and these go off in many directions at the same time, but there is very little in the way of advice, information and help as to how a school might impose some kind of 'structure' on all of this. It is particularly unhelpful regarding the role of specialist staff, key professionals, first-level unpromoted staff and line managers – all issues that secondary school must grapple with, particularly given the re-emphasis on the responsibility of all staff for supporting pupils.

The National Framework, then, is intended 'for all practitioners and partners, in every setting'. It would appear to be an extremely large and disparate 'framework' with little holding it together and one whose inherent stability might therefore be at risk. As might be expected, it raises a number of issues, some of which will be considered later in the chapter.

WHAT IS INVOLVED IN PERSONAL SUPPORT?

What do Personal Support staff currently do in a secondary school? Attempting to outline all the functions is not for the faint-hearted but it is possible to give a very brief overview of some of the tasks currently undertaken by promoted staff and, increasingly, by unpromoted volunteer staff. The following is adapted from a local authority document detailing what it expected from its promoted Guidance staff, post McCrone:

> *S1/S2*: transition arrangements: liaison with primary staff and pupils, including visits; reception/induction of new intake; checking primary progress reports; disseminating information; making up new classes; arranging paired reading and buddy systems; pupil interviews; pupil monitoring, reports and parents' evenings; option choice programme;
> *S3/S4*: pupil interviews: coordinating and monitoring pastoral and discipline referrals; monitoring progress/problems in new courses; careers information, action plans; reporting to/meeting with parents; SQA presentation checks; post-16 induction; options programme; managing work experience;
> *S5/6*: school bursaries/pupil interviews; advice on study skills/decision-making; monitoring progress in post-16 courses; careers adviser; HE/FE application forms; university/college open days; visits from employers/FE/HE personnel; SQA presentation check; community involvement programme.

The list above can reveal only some of the many and varied activities involved in Pupil Support. Some of the duties are year-specific and some others (such as organising pupil councils) are more generic and apply across all year groups. In addition, Pupil Support staff spend an enormous amount of time dealing with matters relating to attendance (such as truancy and school refusal) and in communicating and meeting with parents on a regular basis. They are often dealing with pupils and families affected by issues relating to social deprivation, unemployment, family breakdown and poverty. It is important to point out that all teachers have to deal with these issues but Personal Support staff currently have a specific responsibility to support individual pupils affected by them and this will often involve working very closely with individual pupils and with partner agencies such as Social Work and Psychological Services and perhaps chairing the Joint Assessment Team in the school. Liaison with these agencies includes case conferences, pupil contracts, individual pupil support, action planning and target-setting, and all of these are crucial if a pupil is to benefit from a coherent inter-agency approach.

Pupil Support staff also require to liaise closely with other school staff in this respect. There is little point, for example, in Personal Support staff, psychological services and social work agreeing a strategy on behaviour management or learning targets if Personal Support staff do not involve subject staff in the issues and discuss with them how this strategy might operate in the classroom. While it is helpful that recent reports re-emphasise the involvement of all staff in supporting pupils, it seems equally clear that there is a need for specific staff to have specific responsibilities to ensure that this is delivered in a systematic, coherent and professional way and it is certainly the contention in this chapter (and in many local authorities) that this is best achieved by having a team of promoted (possibly full-time) Personal Support staff backed up by an extended first-level system across the school. One wonders how long we can continue having Personal Support delivered by staff who are still expected to be experts in and to deliver curricular areas.

In terms of 'structure', secondary schools still tend to opt for either a 'vertical' house-type system which includes pupils across the S1–S6 age range, or a 'horizontal' system of age and year groups, but an increasing number of schools are experimenting with 'flatter' and/or broader structures involving a larger number of staff such as tutor group teachers, register teachers, form tutors, first-level Personal Support tutors – the terminology varies across (and sometimes within) local authorities and the picture here is much less clear because these new structures have not had time to develop. This team of staff will meet their pupil groups on a regular (if sometimes fairly brief) basis and will often discuss whole-school, cross-curricular topics, as well as monitoring progress and attendance. There may still be promoted staff managing the system – perhaps principal teachers of Personal Support but not necessarily so. Line managers might be year heads, faculty heads or depute heads. Again, there are various versions of this type of approach to Personal Support and, inevitably, all of this raises a number of issues that have yet to be resolved. It seems likely that traditional structures will give way to this broader approach which, superficially at least, seems to involve more staff in supporting pupils. What is less clear is which staff will take specific responsibility for pupils in their care.

PERSONAL AND SOCIAL EDUCATION (PSE)

An early 5–14 document noted that what it called Personal and Social Development was 'essentially concerned with the development of life skills . . . All aspects of a child's experience at home, in school and outwith school contribute to PSD' (SOEID, 1993, p.1). Similarly, the Scottish Consultative Council on the Curriculum's (SCCC's) *Heart of the Matter* offered the view that education for personal and social development had to do with:

developing certain qualities and dispositions which will help them to make sense of an increasingly complex world and to respond in a pro-social way to the diversity of circumstances, systems and working environments they face in their lives. (SCCC, 1995, p. 1)

For some time, PSE suffered the same confusion over terminology/nomenclature as Pupil Support. Many documents referred to PSE in relation to the timetabled course in school. Others saw PSE as part of a wider programme across the school known as Education for Personal and Social Development (EPSD or sometimes just PSD). Health Education was often included and some documents referred to Personal, Social and Health Education (PSHE). The SQA referred to Personal Development. This uncertainty continued even at the highest levels until fairly recently. Many schools opted for timetabled PSE, usually one period per week, S1–S6, while others favoured a permeation model, where issues and topics were dealt with through subjects. Most schools covered topics such as health education, careers education, study skills, anti-bullying strategies, anti-racism, citizenship, enterprise education and many more. The classes were normally smaller than subject sections with a more active, learner-centred methodology.

There is absolutely no doubt that the school curriculum was and is under enormous pressure to accommodate the demands of every pressure group, political or otherwise. Every report appears to identify a new 'vital' area with which pupils must engage. Schools have often 'coped' with these in the PSE programme but it will be interesting to see how much pressure there will be to establish a stronger identity for some of these new priorities. At the moment, schools could be forgiven for thinking that everything is a priority. In terms of identity, however, PSE has now been subsumed under the 'Health and Wellbeing' aspect of Curriculum for Excellence, covering mental, emotional, social and physical wellbeing (see Chapter 60). This may well be a very positive move. For years, PSE, Health, Citizenship, Enterprise and various other elements were vying for recognition in an overcrowded curriculum. Her Majesty's Inspectorate of Education also had increasing concerns about the quality of PSE in schools. Theoretically, Curriculum for Excellence provides some major opportunities to address previous weaknesses in what has been considered a 'soft skills' area by:

- bringing together some of the more disparate elements under one heading and by designating this as a curricular area;
- providing experiences and outcomes;
- insisting that it is important enough to be one of three 'compulsory', cross-curricular areas, which will ensure schools take it seriously;
- re-emphasising the role of every teacher in the process.

There are some issues, however, that require further thought. First, PSE, like all cross-curricular areas, found it difficult in the past to establish an identity in a subject-dominated curriculum. A permeative (or embedded) curricular model is laudable, perhaps, but there is no doubt that it is a difficult way to organise a structured, coherent and progressive programme of meaningful activities. The same issue arises with Health and Wellbeing and will be a major (if not the major) challenge of the Curriculum for Excellence developments. Some schools opted for curricular PSE slots and there needs to be a new debate on how best to deliver and manage quality, coherent provision across the school in a way that avoids fragmentation and a patchwork of expectations and outcomes.

Second, the extended experiences and outcomes for Health and Wellbeing are heavily dominated by Health Education and Physical Education, the latter being a strong and clearly defined subject area in the traditional curriculum, and one wonders about the relative value that is likely to be given to other areas such as 'Interpersonal Skills' and 'Choices and Changes'.

Third, designation as a curricular area with experiences and outcomes raises yet again the question of whether 'personal and social' elements of a pupil's experience should be outcomes-driven in the first place. For many years, a pupil's personal and social development was regarded as more of a process than a subject or curricular area to be 'achieved'. The ongoing development of Curriculum for Excellence may well illustrate the need for further thinking about some of the above, not least in relation to the training and development needs of staff involved.

CURRENT ISSUES IN PUPIL SUPPORT/PSE

In a short chapter such as this, it is clearly impossible to discuss major issues in any great detail. There are simply too many of them. However, it is necessary to look in a little more detail at some of the more important ones that have emerged very recently.

Policy Issues

For Pupil Support, the arrival of the National Framework has been the culmination of six years of inconsistent and sometimes incoherent policy making. There have been at least three ongoing and parallel approaches to policy development – never designed to converge and with few bridges between them.

First, the 'Standards' approach resulted from the *National Review of Guidance* – a review that ignored HMIE's contribution to the debate and made virtually no mention of the good practice (and policies) developed over forty years in secondary schools. The ten Standards and their various subdivisions outlined in the Review were occasionally vague but certainly provided a clear framework within which schools and other agencies could work.

Second, while all this was being rolled out, a separate approach was being taken by the series of documents produced under the heading of *Building the Curriculum*. These contain only one reference to the importance of *Happy, Safe*, preferring instead to reintroduce the notion of 'Entitlements', last seen in the 1980s, replete with all the noble sentiments frequently associated with rights and entitlements. This was followed by the unexpected unilateral decision to drop the Standards model completely (while still maintaining that it was important), in favour of the National Framework. As for the Framework itself, this may appear to some as little more than a very lengthy series of unconnected mission statements with an appended bibliography.

Third, this situation has not been helped by HMIE's apparent decision to pursue a separate strand of thinking on 'Excellence' which is only partly related to any of the above and which uses its own terminology that is quite distinct from 'Standards' or 'Entitlements'. For example, Personal Support does not even appear as one of the ten Dimensions of Excellence (each of which is said to be a key process in a school). Instead, HMIE eventually uses terms such as 'Wellbeing and Respect' – but not directly related to Health and Wellbeing experiences and outcomes. Similarly, *How Good is our School? 3* (HMIE, 2007) introduces an unsuspecting public to the Quality Indicator of 'Care, Welfare and Development', under which three (and only three) Personal Support themes are listed and which seem to be mapped against no other Personal Support policy document – and vice versa.

Given all of the above, schools are entitled to wonder which policy is to be adopted. How it is to operate in a secondary school? For how long and to what end? In terms of self-evaluation, they are equally entitled to ask which yardsticks might be applied: Standards or Entitlements? The National Framework or *HGIOS 3*? The situation is far from satisfactory. On a wider level, it could be argued that many of the issues here stem from a flawed notion of curriculum development in the first place, where 'top down' and 'bottom up' have completely failed to meet and where teachers have not been involved as 'agents of change' (Priestley, 2010).

PSE/Health and Wellbeing

There are grounds for cautious optimism in this area. The incorporation of PSE into the Health and Wellbeing area is potentially a positive move for personal and social elements within the formal curriculum, although there are some issues still to be resolved. At the time of writing, it is noticeable that, while there appears to be little further development work in schools in relation to the National Framework, the opposite is the case with Health and Wellbeing. Considerable time and effort is being expended by organisations such as Education Scotland in developing Health and Wellbeing as a curricular area. Precisely because it is a curricular area with experiences and outcomes, it is easier to develop classroom resources, packs, kits and staff development opportunities than it is to develop practical guidelines in a National Framework with a theoretical target audience from conception to 25+ years of age.

It is to be hoped that Physical Education and Health topics do not dominate to the exclusion of other areas and this will be an issue of leadership and management. In a similar vein, it is less than clear how this (or any other) cross-curricular, permeating issue might be managed and led to ensure progression, coherence, depth, balance and other basics of curriculum theory. Indeed, any reference to structure and staff responsibilities is largely absent in the documentation across Health and Wellbeing and the National Framework. Bland terms such as 'key professionals', 'designated staff' and their potential responsibilities need further investigation. This is particularly relevant for Personal Support staff in secondary schools who had a significant role in the delivery and management of PSE prior to Curriculum for Excellence. Similarly, the continuing emphasis on the fact that Personal Support and Health and Wellbeing are the responsibility of all staff is over-simplistic and, unless there is some further consideration of roles and remits, it will become the responsibility of no one and pupils will slip through the net.

The National Framework

There are many issues relating to the National Framework but it can be argued that they all stem from one fundamental problem, namely, that the Framework tries to cover too many sectors and too wide an age range to be meaningful in any practical sense. The problem began with *Happy, Safe* attempting to cover primary, secondary, special education sectors and partner agencies. This was subsequently compounded by the Framework's attempt to include everyone from pre-birth to 25+ years of age, across every conceivable agency. This seems to be as impossible as it is undesirable and it is hardly surprising that, as a result, the Framework has difficulty with policy statements that provide guidelines and advice on Personal Support in secondary schools. Similarly, the failure to recognise the existence of different educational sectors, far from being a unifying, collaborative step, designed to increase multi-agency working, merely serves to underline the need to recognise the specific requirements of each sector. Although generic principles have a value, teachers in school require more from the policy makers. It is not helpful when policy makers use 'non-prescription' as an excuse for 'non–development' of guidelines.

For secondary schools, these issues have a particular resonance, given that Guidance has had thirty-five years in which to build fairly robust practical and theoretical frameworks, all of which could have been adapted and improved to accommodate Curriculum for Excellence. However, these were almost entirely ignored in an attempt to provide an all-embracing, all-through system without the realisation (currently considered to be heretical) that the best way to ensure quality all-through provision is to recognise the existence of and differences between sectors as a starting point, rather than to reinvent numerous wheels. Finally, if the intention was to emphasise the need for better multi-agency cooperation, there is already the *Getting it Right for Every Child* programme, the position of which in the National Framework is less than clear and which appears to be something of a separate entity altogether.

It is clear that there are significant and fundamental issues to be addressed in relation to the National Framework. Overall, if people are unclear about terms, definitions, structures, arguments and so on, they will inevitably be unclear about content, process and quality. The Scottish Government will doubtless argue that schools ought to be left to build their own structures within general policy statements and that headteachers are best placed to decide priorities and structures. Some headteachers may well agree, as more and more power comes their way. But in these days of multi-agency working and integrated approaches, Personal Support is too important to be left to develop in an ad hoc way, particularly if the reason for that is the absence of sector-appropriate advice and guidelines. Similarly, when provision becomes too variable it calls into question the whole concept of a local authority 'policy' on inclusion and, indeed, its very role as an education provider. One school's devolved power is another parent's postcode lottery – nowhere more so than in the field of Pupil Support. Failure to address the weaknesses in the National Framework will have serious consequences for secondary school provision and will only increase the feeling that the Framework is fatally weakened by a plethora of platitudes.

REFERENCES

Her Majesty's Inspectorate (1996) *Effective Learning and Teaching in Scottish Secondary Schools: Guidance.* Edinburgh: HMI.

Her Majesty's Inspectorate of Education (2004) *Personal Support for Pupils in Scottish Schools.* Edinburgh: HMIE.

Her Majesty's Inspectorate of Education (2007) *How Good is Our School? The Journey to Excellence. Part 3.* Edinburgh: HMIE.

Priestley, M. (2010) 'Curriculum for Excellence: Transformational change or business as usual?', *Scottish Educational Review*, 42 (1): 23–36.

Scottish Consultative Council on the Curriculum (1986) *More than Feelings of Concern.* Dundee: SCCC.

Scottish Consultative Council on the Curriculum (1995) *The Heart of the Matter.* Dundee: SCCC.

Scottish Executive Education Department (2001a) *A Teaching Profession for the 21st Century. Agreement Reached Following Recommendations made in the McCrone Report.* Edinburgh: SEED.

Scottish Executive Education Department (2001b) *Better Behaviour, Better Learning. Summary Report of the Discipline Task Group.* Edinburgh: SEED.

Scottish Executive Education Department (2005) *Happy, Safe and Achieving their Potential. A Standard of Support for Children and Young People in Scottish Schools. The Report of the National Review of Guidance.* Edinburgh: SEED

Scottish Government (2008) *Curriculum for Excellence. Building the Curriculum 3: A Framework for Learning and Teaching.* Edinburgh: Scottish Government.

Scottish Office Education and Industry Department (1993) *5–14 Guidelines: Personal and Social Development.* Edinburgh: HMSO.

Website

Education Scotland 'Supporting learners' at www.educationscotland.gov.uk/supportinglearners/

41

The Scottish Approach to School Improvement: Achievements and Limitations

Chris McIlroy

Scotland is often regarded as a world leader in improvement through self-evaluation in education, with many countries across the world adopting or adapting Scottish approaches. They often use *How Good is our School?* (SOEID, 1996; 2002), or related guides for other sectors of education, as a key component of their approach. The rationale for self-evaluation is straightforward, logical and powerful: if you know and understand the strengths and development needs in your current practice, you can use that understanding to give direction to improvement. Conversely, if you do not have a clear picture of your qualities and improvement needs, you are unlikely to concentrate on improving the right things in a way that suits your situation.

Self-evaluation also recognises and values the central role of those engaged in frontline services in improving their practice and the responsibility of professionals, individually and collectively, to reflect on the quality of their work and strive continuously to improve it. It therefore sits well with concepts such as the 'reflective practitioner', the 'extended professional' and 'increased devolution of responsibility and autonomy' for schools and teachers. These ideas are in harmony with the messages of *Teaching Scotland's Future*, the 2011 report reviewing the whole spectrum of teacher education (Scottish Government, 2011).

Inspection evidence over the last twenty years indicates that Scottish education is now much better at 'improvement through self-evaluation'. Successive *Improving Scottish Education* reports show increasing proportions of pre-school centres and schools achieving positive ratings during inspections in comparison with earlier data. Over the same period, evidence of the achievements of our learners as reflected, for example, in the Organisation for Economic Cooperation and Development (OECD) Programme for International Student Assessment (PISA) surveys shows that Scotland continues to perform well in reading, mathematics and science (OECD, 2009a). However, these surveys also show that our rate of improvement is relatively slow in comparison with other countries (see also Chapter 5).

This suggests an important paradox. At a time when Scotland is a world leader in improvement through self-evaluation and our schools seem to be getting better and better at it, standards and quality in Scottish schools are improving at a slower rate than in many other countries. Why is the 'leader of the pack' improving its own education system more slowly than many other countries? Either we have taken a wrong road to improvement through self-evaluation, or the way that we are going about it is not working as well as we think. It is time for a radical reappraisal of the effectiveness of the particular approach to improvement through self-evaluation that we have adopted in Scotland and disseminated across the world. This chapter provides an explanation for the paradox and suggests a way forward.

REVIEWING THE SELF-EVALUATION STORY

Developing the Quality Indicators

The story begins in 1985 when the Management of Education Resource Unit was set up within Her Majesty's Inspectorate of Schools (HMI). From the late 1980s onwards, HMI in Scotland used this unit in pioneering work on self-evaluation by developing sets of performance indicators and ethos indicators which were subsequently incorporated into quality indicators. Encouraged by warm responses to *Effective Secondary Schools* and *Effective Primary Schools* published in 1988 and 1989 respectively, inspectors at that time were increasingly confident that they could capture and describe the characteristics of quality across a range of aspects of educational provision. At this stage, the main driver for this development was the intention to improve consistency of judgements and benchmark standards across inspectors and inspections. This initial driver emphasised better consistency in public assurance over the promotion of improvements in learning or achievement.

Groups of inspectors identified and discussed features of practice which, in their collective professional judgement, were features of good-quality practice. They then wrote word pictures or 'illustrations' which summarised these features for aspects such as 'teaching', 'assessment', 'ethos' and 'leadership'. Their approach was analytical in breaking up 'quality' into a set of indicators, and was systematic in checking that 'the parts' captured the important elements of 'the whole'. Early work was carefully tested out with colleagues to determine whether their analysis had significant omissions and whether it had successfully captured 'what matters' in relation to quality.

Inspectors organised the word pictures to illustrate and separate out performance at different levels of quality, originally from 'unsatisfactory' to 'very good' and later from 'unsatisfactory' to 'excellent'. This would help the inspectorate to be more confident that when inspectors in one school described an area of practice as 'very good', they were recognising similar features and expecting similar standards as inspectors in another school. The indicators, supported by training activities that involved groups of inspectors discussing and using them in evaluating examples of practice, would help to ensure more consistent evaluations from school to school. As a result, inspectors would be more confident and evidence-based in distinguishing between, for example, 'very good' and 'good' practice.

Parallel benefits were seen in helping teachers to benchmark the quality of their practice, to answer the 'how good' question in self-evaluation. Quantitative data on aspects such as attainment or attendance can be used to assist benchmarking of some aspects of quality in education. The illustrations would now help to evaluate more qualitative aspects by allowing teachers to decide how closely their practice met a description at a particular level. Of course, this process will never be straightforward: it is impossible to capture entirely a complex aspect such as the quality of learning in a short description. Moreover, individual teachers may have different interpretations of what the words mean and will bring their differing experience to the table. Recognising these caveats, the indicators nevertheless marked a step forward in the discussion and evaluation of aspects of quality in education.

The original work developed sets of indicators at the level of both the individual classroom and the whole school. Subsequently these were merged into a single set of indicators for the whole school and, as a result, indicators specifically aimed at the class were never published. This decision was made for understandable reasons. There were advantages in streamlining the sets of indicators into a single set, replacing two evaluative tools with one, and stressing the commonality of many issues at classroom and whole-school levels. Later in this chapter, it will be argued that this decision was misguided. It limited the way that the indicators would be used in practice and their potential use in promoting improvement, with predominant attention given to whole-school issues. The combination of 'bottom-up' improvement activity in the classroom with whole-school development is a very potent force for improvement. This potential is weakened without a strong 'bottom-up' dimension.

Looking to a New Horizon: Awareness of the Potential Benefits

This was an exciting and visionary development, one that deservedly began to attract international admiration. Inspectors quickly perceived opportunities for wider benefits in the use of quality indicators than simply promoting consistency in inspections. There were opportunities to develop a common language across the profession to discuss quality and improvement; to encourage teachers to use the indicators in improving their own practice through self-evaluation; and to support 'openness' by using the same set of tools for both self-evaluation and inspection. Using the same indicators for self-evaluation and improvement would also expose the quality indicators to critical public scrutiny, a positive move and one that considerably enhanced their development and status.

Grasping these opportunities would be realised by publishing the quality indicators. This, in turn, led to the benefits of increasing involvement and sense of ownership by the profession in designing future editions of the indicators. Representatives of education authorities, policy civil servants and the teaching profession were actively consulted and involved in developing subsequent editions through extensive discussions and opportunities for comment. This approach to developing quality indicators enjoyed considerable success in establishing a professional consensus on features of quality, at first a consensus across inspectors and later a wider consensus across the profession. The aspiration of building a quality culture in Scotland seemed to be a prize within reach. Schools would be increasingly aware of their own strengths and weaknesses in practice, use this knowledge in planning their own improvements, be supported by education authorities in that process and periodically receive support and evaluation thorough inspection. Her Majesty's Inspectors had effectively transferred ownership for improvement through self-evaluation from inspectors to the wider education profession.

The indicators were not explicitly derived from research, although research influenced their development in two very useful ways. Research and development teams in 'school effectiveness' (see Mortimore, 1998) during that period were working in similar territory to those designing quality indicators. By identifying key characteristics of effective schools, researchers had a broad but significant influence on the indicator writers, and close partnership working with individual researchers also fostered constructive two-way influence on their development. For example, John MacBeath and others worked closely with HMI in developing support materials for self-evaluation and were closely involved in school effectiveness, then school improvement research. MacBeath and Mortimore collaborated on the *Improving School Effectiveness* project funded by the Scottish Office Education Department. In some areas the indicator writers' knowledge of specific research influenced the way that they described particular features of quality. For example, the influence of research can be clearly seen in indicators on 'leadership' and 'assessment'. However, many indicators were based on professional views, experiences, values and craft knowledge and some were based on contemporary policies or innovations in Scottish education.

Setting Sail: *How Good is our School?* is Published

Looking back over a decade later and with the benefit of hindsight, the first edition of *How Good is our School?* had limited success in communicating the breadth of the vision for improvement through self-evaluation. The foreword makes very clear references to improvement in 'standards and quality in education' and to 'raising achievement in our classrooms'. It sets this alongside other purposes for self-evaluation such as being able to respond to questions from parents and the public about the quality of education, supporting development planning and guiding the preparation of standards and quality reports at school level. School standard and quality reports would complement the national standards and quality reports, 'to help all Headteachers, all teachers and education authority officers move closer to answering the local question "How good is our school?"' The improvement purpose was unhelpfully submerged in a multiplicity of purposes.

In subsequent sections of *How Good is our School?* the improvement message remains obscure. For example, the response to the question 'What is school self-evaluation?' makes no reference to improvement as a key purpose: school self-evaluation is about asking ourselves, for example:

- How are we doing in this school?
- How are we doing in this classroom?
- How are we doing in this department?

Although in later sections, there are some references to identifying priorities and to taking action, the overwhelming emphasis is on 'How are we doing?' and 'How do we know?' Indeed, the entire fourth section, headed 'Self-evaluation: practical examples', deals only with numerous cases illustrating 'How do you know?', 'Some features you might look for' and 'Some ways of finding out'. It contains no examples of improvement.

It is important to recognise that inspectors are highly committed to improvement and one aim of this work was to promote improvement. However, this publication provided much more support towards knowing 'how good' quality is rather than how to improve provision and taking steps to achieve improvement. This emphasis was to shape later developments in the use of self-evaluation in practice and inhibit the most effective use of the indicators. It was a serious flaw in communicating an approach that could improve quality.

In the first decade or so of their use, inspectors and development officers familiarised schools with the indicators, their structure and their uses in benchmarking and supporting improvement. This was exciting pioneering work for HMI in Scotland and the response was to exceed expectations. Although the indicators were presented as *one way* of developing an organised approach to improvement through self-evaluation, their adoption and use quickly became established as the norm in Scottish schools. They spread to other countries and stimulated parallel developments in other sectors of Scottish education from pre-school to community learning and development services, psychological services and education authorities. HMI in Scotland became torchbearers for self-evaluation.

The desire to promote improvement through self-evaluation spread to developed education systems across the world. Visits, conferences and exchange of documents provided one source of communicating practice. Within Europe, the Socrates project from 1995 to 1997, *Evaluating Quality in School Education*, involving twelve countries of the European Union, provided a significant spur to sharing thinking and practice. The Standing International Conference of Inspectorates (SICI), with wide representation across Europe from those involved in administering and inspecting education, was influential in bringing together aspects of national arrangements through its regular focus on self-evaluation and improvement issues in education. Educational researchers and writers such as John MacBeath, Michael Barber and Michael Fullan were influential in developing international ideas on aspects of self-evaluation practice such as stakeholder involvement and the role of professional development and of communities of schools in achieving change at system as well as school level. Mainly, but not exclusively, in the United States, education managers were searching for reliable and fair 'value added' data that could be used to evaluate pupils' progress, to provide information on areas of strength and weakness in provision and, if required, to grade teachers and schools. It highlighted the tensions between data and professional judgement and between support and accountability in evaluation and self-evaluation, and the importance of a clear purpose so that data serves rather than drives the purpose.

The models in different countries that developed were and remain diverse. They vary with key factors in professional and political culture such as the views of teachers on their autonomy and responsibility to colleagues and managers; the roles of stakeholders in relation to schools; notions of trust, support, empowerment and accountability, monitoring and control; the focus on classroom teaching and school leadership; the use of evidence and 'critical friends'; the nature and frequency of inspection and its role in relation to self-evaluation; and expectations of impact at classroom, school or wider levels versus a perception of self-evaluation as an administrative exercise. The inspection profiles on the SICI website show the diversity of self-evaluation (and inspection) practice across Europe as well as some emerging common features. A study of recent developments in self-evaluation in Ireland and Iceland exemplifies this diversity. It contrasts the lack of impact of an externally shaped national initiative on self-evaluation in Ireland with a more participative capacity-building approach, which shows more promising impact on practice (see McNamara et al., 2011). Given such variations, it is important that each model is evaluated in terms of its impact on improvement of learner outcomes, the common purpose of self-evaluation across different systems. There is little evidence of such evaluation at present.

Stormy Seas: Experience of Using the Indicators in Practice in Scottish Schools

Meanwhile, back home, practical questions emerged. A frequent question from headteachers was 'How do we manage the use of all of these indicators to make judgements about the quality of our school?' A recurring question from inspectors during inspections was 'How do you know how good you are at x or y?' These two questions led to a developing concentration on *management*, *processes* and *evidence* with a clear focus on the 'how good are we?' question which encouraged teachers to benchmark or judge the quality of their practice against a description of standards. There was a correspondingly lighter emphasis on improvement processes which unfortunately reinforced a loss of clarity of purpose in using the indicators.

Responding to early experience related to these issues, *How Good is our School?* provided advice about *managing* the use of quality indicators based on a 'scan' of the school's quality across the set of indicators, supported by 'taking a closer look' at some aspects of provision. This combination of a 'scan' and 'taking a closer look' was also common in schools using the Guidelines for Review and Internal Development in Schools (GRIDS) in England and Wales. It became an established way of working with the indicators in many Scottish schools. The whole staff or groups of staff met together initially to scan the quality indicators, often allocating a quick intuitive level for each indicator in preparation for the school improvement plan. Frequently headteachers then set up working groups to take forward the priorities identified in the improvement plan and to take a closer look at a relevant subset of quality indicators. Although working groups were intended to increase staff engagement in self-evaluation, they very rarely grounded developments in classroom practice, more often directing attention to broad whole-school issues such as the development of resources or policies. Indeed, working groups often had the contrary effect of distancing improvement through self-evaluation from classroom practice.

The focus on *evidence* also prompted the growth of an industry in some schools, with headteachers often placing particular value on paper evidence that could be shown to inspectors when the school was inspected. Some schools gathered boxes, even filing cabinets of evidence related to each indicator or to a group of indicators. Unfortunately, the extent of evidence gathered was not always proportionate to the educational improvements achieved and it sometimes got in the way of seeing the big picture through the detail. In some schools excessive bureaucracy became another distraction hindering an active approach to improvement through self-evaluation.

Inspection reports were fulsome in their praise where they found a set of *processes* which produced a range of evidence about quality. This set of processes included scrutinising attainment data, commenting on teachers' plans, sampling pupils' work and observation by senior staff of learning and teaching (peer observation was at that time, and remains, rarer). As a result, these processes quickly became established features of 'good practice'. Schools were encouraged to organise their processes into an annual self-evaluation calendar with some processes featuring throughout the year and some in particular terms of the year. As schools became familiar with these processes, their ratings for self-evaluation during inspection improved. Inspection evidence shows that in some cases these processes did promote significant improvement. It also shows that in other cases they did not. Used well and followed by action, these processes have good potential to improve learning and achievement but unless they are followed by action, they are unlikely to lead anywhere. There was still a considerable way to go to achieve the right balance between processes and a focus on impact and outcomes.

The decision in 1996 to publish quality indicator ratings in the reports on all schools inspected made matters worse. It magnified the attention given to the levels awarded to a school rather than to what the staff were doing, and needed to do, to make improvements. It followed an internal debate within the inspectorate. One side of the debate was supported by the case for openness and transparency in reporting to parents and the public, arguing that ratings provided 'sharp evaluations' that could be readily understood by parents and the wider public and would encourage teachers to evaluate carefully the levels of quality demonstrated in their provision. These arguments chimed well with the political view of education of the times. They stressed external accountability and openness in the period following the Parent's Charter first introduced by John Major in England, with parallel changes in Scotland during Michael Forsyth's regime as Secretary of State.

Inspectors taking a contrary view argued that assigning a level created a spurious image of precise measurement that did not reflect the sophisticated thought processes of using a range of evidence to make holistic professional judgements about quality. They recognised that levels were useful in discussing and benchmarking where 'a school was at' in relation to a feature of quality, but cited regular cases where inspectors would differ about a level, particularly where evidence indicated that practice was 'on the cusp' between levels. It was better, therefore, to use levels in professional discussion rather than to publish them as precisely measured judgements. Words were a much sharper method of reporting strengths and weaknesses in educational practice and could capture the nuances of a judgement in a more useful way than reporting a level. For example, to say that 'the quality of teaching is good. It is particularly effective in the early primary stages. Improvements are needed to the teaching of reading in some upper primary classes' carries better information than to say 'the quality of teaching is good'. This argument was convincing but did not carry the day.

The decision was taken to publish the quality indicator levels in all inspections. The fears of those who opposed their publication were realised in practice. The grades became 'high stakes'. Many readers of inspection reports placed value on the ratings rather than the text to the extent that, at the extreme, the text was sometimes ignored. Increasing emphasis, debate and occasional friction in inspections about the quality indicator levels took attention away from dialogue about improvement. Schools increasingly saw the main purpose of self-evaluation as external accountability rather than improvement.

Over time, inspectors became more and more aware that the self-evaluation process had, at least to some degree, lost its way in many schools. The implementation of a laudable and soundly based vision for improvement was faced with a growing number and impact of perverse effects. Purposes had become muddled with too much emphasis attached to grading, and inspection sometimes reinforced this emphasis. In some schools, self-evaluation had become an end in itself. Staff would carry out evaluation processes diligently but with insufficient focus on taking the actions needed to win improvements in learning and achievement. In some cases, despite these processes, self-evaluation did not show that the school 'knew itself' (the acid test of a good self-evaluation). There were issues of excessive bureaucracy in some schools and a lack of direct engagement at the classroom level.

Shifting the Tiller

Public recognition that all was not well came in *Improving Scottish Education 2002–2005* and in the 2009 edition of *How Good is our School?*. The Senior Chief Inspector in his introduction to the 2009 edition made a much needed statement. He called for a much stronger emphasis on taking action for improvement:

> One important difference in the approach to self-evaluation in this edition of *How Good is our School?* is the increased focus on impact and outcomes particularly those outcomes for learners which are stated within Curriculum for Excellence. This reinforces the notion that self-evaluation is not an end in itself. It should lead to the maintenance of high standards, ongoing improvements in performance, targeted action on areas needing to be improved, and to continuous improvement in the pursuit of excellence.

The quality indicator for self-evaluation was revised to underline this stronger emphasis on improvement and retitled 'improvement through self-evaluation' to reinforce the message.

This redirection was necessary and helpful. It undoubtedly had some impact, but it was insufficient to turn the tanker round. Many of the perverse effects persisted in influencing the approach. Some inspectors continued to be impressed by a well-organised set of processes when rating the quality indicators. The result is that we cannot be sure whether our schools are genuinely getting better at improvement through self-evaluation or whether they are demonstrating the surface features of self-evaluation without changing their quality and impact. The tension between grading and improvement remained firmly lodged in practice, despite a helpful reduction in the number of quality indicators used in new inspection models. Using quality indicators to support improvement continued to be trumped by grading in the perception of many schools.

At the start of the second decade of the twenty-first century, the power of the initial vision, the engagement of the profession in developing a shared understanding of features of quality and the invaluable experience of self-evaluation in practice are deep-seated strengths of the Scottish approach. Three key problems need to be addressed to get the approach back on course to achieve its key improvement purpose.

- It is not addressing sufficiently the priorities for our education system as a whole.
- The implementation of our approach to improvement through self-evaluation has created perverse effects, sometimes reinforced by inspection, which are undermining the focus on improvement.
- The power of engagement of the class teacher, the most direct influence on quality and class-room practice, is neglected.

The final section of this chapter sets out changes needed to address these issues and to refocus the approach.

GETTING BACK ON COURSE: CHANGES NEEDED TO THE SCOTTISH APPROACH

Achieving a Better Alignment Between the Education System and Individual Schools

We know that Scottish education as a whole is improving relatively slowly from a solid base of achievement. At national level, our major challenge is to use Curriculum for Excellence to:

- improve achievement at a faster pace;
- close the gap so that 'who you are' matters less to chances of educational success (OECD, 2009b);
- improve the higher-order skills and understanding of young people to equip them for a changing world; and
- reduce the variation in the quality of teaching and achievement in different classes.

It is salutary to reflect that these challenges rarely appear as priorities in the improvement plans of individual schools. Yet if these are the major challenges for Scotland as a whole, they must also be challenges for many of its individual schools. The country as a whole will not address these challenges well unless they feature directly in improvement action in its classrooms and schools.

The explanation for this lack of alignment between the improvement priorities for the nation and for individual schools lies in the many competing interests that shape school improvement. National developments, education authority and cluster priorities are considered alongside the priorities emerging from the school's own self-evaluation. Schools then shape their annual improvement plan to address these competing interests and attempt to define a manageable number of priorities, taking account of their particular capacity for change. The process is pressured, the big picture can get lost in the detail and the time-frame is often too short to address difficult long-term issues. This raises the wider issue of the effectiveness of national agencies and education authorities in working with schools to present a coherent and steady picture of change and avoiding requiring them to consider too many fragmented and specific developments. It should be an aspiration for Scotland to achieve a new consensus in our political and educational leadership on more effective management of educational change.

More immediately achievable is to build in a requirement for all school improvement plans to consider the extent to which key national issues apply to their learners and how best to address improvements needed. The challenges to educational progress would then become recurring themes required for all schools to consider. Expectations of progress in addressing them will be realistically paced over an extended period so that annual progress is informed by a longer-term view of major change. This would result in a better alignment between school and national priorities.

Re-establishing Improvement as the Key Purpose in Using Quality Indicators

The organisation of quality indicators into levels had a significant influence on their use. The levels and illustrations were designed to help practitioners and inspectors to answer the 'how good' question about aspects of their practice. The 'how good' question is an important one. It is of particular interest to those who are concerned with assurance to the public or reassurance to school managers that standards in a school are sound. It is also important for all teachers to know whether their learners are progressing and achieving as well as comparable learners in other schools, and for parents to be reassured that this is the case. The more important question for the purpose of improvement is 'How can we make it better?' and within that context issues of grading are subsidiary.

Mortimore, in reflecting on his experience of the school effectiveness movement, highlights the importance of clarity of purpose: 'The key lesson from school-effectiveness research is that the ends must constantly be kept in sight in order to prevent any of the means from assuming importance *in their own right* and, thereby, distracting energy from the main task' (Mortimore, 1998, p. 176).

It is crucial to a system concerned with improvement to get this emphasis right. Benchmarking has a role and a value but it needs only to be an occasional or periodic activity and it is not an end; it is a means to an end. Improvement makes things better for learners: it is the regular business of practitioners, and teachers' energy should be primarily directed towards the improvement purpose. It would be a little harsh to say that this lesson had not been applied in Scotland because inspectors, headteachers and teachers derive their motivation from making improvements for learners. Separating the approach from the individuals, however, the quotation captures very well the distorting impact and unintended consequences of grading and other purposes on improvement through self-evaluation. For, as we have seen, in practice there was a drift in emphasis in Scottish schools towards evidence, processes and management of grading or benchmarking, sometimes at the expense of making improvements.

It is urgent to recreate an approach that reinvigorates the core purpose of improvement and achieves the right balance between means and ends. Schools need to redirect their energy towards *evidence* of improvement, *processes* of improvement and the *management* of improvement (with a corresponding reduction in emphasis on management and processes to gather evidence about levels). Schools need to put the grading issue in its proper place by using the quality indicator levels for periodic discussion about their standards and quality, and reflecting on how the quality of their work compares with the illustrations. They do this by comparing their uneven profile of strengths and development needs with level descriptors to reach a *broad* view of their quality. Levels are not precise measurements or calibrations. They are useful for the national collation of inspection evidence but their value to a school lies in identifying areas where practice is strong and where improvement is needed. This is much more important than deciding whether a level is exactly x or y.

Inspection also has a significant role in helping schools to achieve the right balance. The common purpose of inspectors and schools in promoting improvements is enhanced if professional dialogue throughout an inspection is mainly about the school's approach and its success in making improvements, rather than on discussion of quality indicator levels. On the other hand, the current practice of issuing forms that ask for quality indicator levels at the start of an inspection can set up an unhelpful early concentration on whether these levels are 'correct', with much evidence-gathering to justify the label attached to a level. Altering this practice would build on recent changes to inspection to emphasise and celebrate examples of improvement and success in learning and achievement.

A discussion of how the school benchmarks its quality should be a single inspection activity setting the inspectors' wide experience of practice in different schools alongside the in-depth knowledge of the school about its work and context. Quality indicator levels are a useful point of reference in this discussion which will lead to dialogue and reflection about standards where there are significant differences in view. The more important question remains whether the school is improving learning and achievement.

Inspection reports will best meet their important responsibility for public assurance by reporting their evaluations clearly and sharply in plain English *words* rather than *grades* or *numbers* for levels.

Revitalising the Role of the Teacher in Improvement through Self-evaluation

Variation in quality between classes in the same school remains an issue (OECD, 2007) and engaging each teacher in improving learning in his or her classroom is the most direct way to address this. Yet much work in improvement through self-evaluation currently focuses on the whole school rather than the classroom. With hindsight, the Scottish approach lost a major opportunity to engage class and subject teachers in direct reflection and improvement of what happens in their classes. The publication of *Teaching Scotland's Future*, with its stress on the professional role of the individual teacher in reflecting on and improving his or her classroom practice, reinforces arguments for increased focus on the classroom level.

Although common themes apply to the classroom and the school as a whole, there are also differences between the two in the context and in the level of detail at which ideas are applied. For example, class teachers reflecting on 'challenge' may talk about recent interactions or tasks set in their classroom, describe their learners' responses and comments, and think about whether their learners' thinking or skills were stretched and helped to progress, or whether they found them too easy. They may consider the steps that they can take in the immediate future to improve the level of challenge in their dialogue with learners or in the resources used, tasks set or independence required in tasks. At the classroom level, teachers often illustrate their discussion points with reference to individual pupils or groups or by citing examples of their work.

This tightness of focus will be unlikely in whole-school self-evaluation; the discussion is usually at a much more general level. In the case of 'challenge' it may lead to discussion of groups of pupils or aspects of the curriculum where challenge is successful or requires improvement. Perhaps as a result of the common focus on whole-school issues, teachers rarely use *How Good is our School?* to reflect on and improve the quality of their own classroom practice. Moreover, some whole-school indicators such as 'policy review and development' or 'staff sufficiency, recruitment and retention' are less directly relevant to the day-to-day purposes of the classroom teacher, and the breadth of indicators in *How Good is our School?* can take attention away from the key ideas that are most relevant to the classroom, broadly those about curriculum, learning and teaching, and assessment.

It is now time to re-emphasise the role of improvement through self-evaluation at the classroom level as well as at the whole-school level. This does not mean teachers working in isolation: effective schools function as collegiate teams, discussing and observing classroom practice together with a clear focus on improvement. It requires them to work together but prompts a necessary shift in emphasis towards practice in the classroom. Class and whole-school improvement will then be more effectively linked in both directions, so that classroom issues across a number of classes become whole-school priorities and school improvement priorities are grounded in the realities and priorities of the classroom. The author of this chapter is currently working on a project with class teachers in Glasgow to increase their focus on classroom improvement.

Achieving this will depend on developing in pre-service and in-service training the necessary ideas and skills to make improvement through self-evaluation work well. Such skills and ideas are developed to some extent in pre-service training through encouraging student teachers to think of themselves as 'reflective practitioners', though at that stage their limited experience and responsibility place a ceiling on their development. The skills and ideas are very unevenly developed in continuing professional development (CPD) for teachers. A priority for the professional development of all teachers should be developing those skills and understandings that contribute to improvement through self-evaluation in their own classroom and as part of the professional team responsible for quality at whole-school level. Action research, support materials and CPD will be important components of local support to make this happen.

FINAL THOUGHT: OTHER ROUTES TO IMPROVEMENT

Schools in other countries take different approaches to improvement and Scottish schools achieved improvement long before the onset of quality indicators. Some teachers tend to work intuitively, spotting and using a new idea or teaching approach that makes things better for learners. They may be inspired by a course, a role model, a peer observation or a response from learners to improve their practice. Many leaders have a 'built-in' vision for their own school, a clear image of what quality would look like for them, and communicate this to their colleagues. Local and national initiatives in curriculum or on aspects such as early intervention can lead to significant improvements. Analytic and systematic approaches can be highly effective routes to improvement, but they are not the only routes and they do not suit every team or situation equally. Some other countries have been more successful than Scotland at improvement achievement in recent years. The 'Scottish approach' offers a sound improvement through self-evaluation but we should value any route that takes us forward effectively.

REFERENCES

McNamara, G., J. O'Hara, P. Lisi and S. Davidsdotter (2011) 'Operationalising self-evaluation in schools: Experiences from Ireland and Iceland', *Irish Educational Studies*, 30 (1): 63–82.

Mortimore, P. (1998) *The Road to Improvement: Reflections on School Effectiveness*. Lisse; Exton, PA: Swets and Zeitlinger.

Organisation for Economic Cooperation and Development (2007) *Quality and Equity of Schooling in Scotland*. Online at www.oecd.org/dataoecd/59/22/40328315.pdf

Organisation for Economic Cooperation and Development (2009a) *PISA 2009 Results: Executive Summary*. Online at www.oecd.org/dataoecd/34/60/46619703.pdf

Organisation for Economic Cooperation and Development (2009b) *PISA 2009 Results: Overcoming Social Background: Equity in Learning Opportunities and Outcomes (Volume II)*. Online at www.oecd.org/document/24/0,3746,en_32252351_46584327_46609752_1_1_1_1,00.html

Scottish Government (2011) *Teaching Scotland's Future: Report of a Review of Teacher Education in Scotland*. Edinburgh: Scottish Government.

Scottish Office Education and Industry Department (1996; 2002) *How Good is our School?* Edinburgh: Scottish Government.

VI

CURRICULUM: EARLY YEARS AND PRIMARY

This section addresses the eight curriculum areas found in Scottish primary schools which, in alphabetic order, are: Expressive Arts (here described in Chapter 46); Health and Wellbeing (48); Languages (43 for Literacy and English, 44 for Modern Languages); Mathematics (47); Religious and Moral Education (49); Sciences; Social Studies; and Technologies (here all described in Chapter 45). The eight areas actually span a range of particular subjects as will be evident from a reading of these chapters. Prior to them, however, the section opens with a discussion of the whole curriculum, looking at its underlying principles, its overall structure and how that is translated into specific learning experiences for children. This chapter (42) should be read in conjunction with Chapters 3 and 4 in Section II which describe Curriculum for Excellence (CfE) more generally and trace its historical evolution from previous versions of the primary curriculum. Chapter 50 in Section VII provides a secondary perspective on the same topic. By 2011, all Scottish primary schools were expected to use CfE as the basis for practical planning of the learning experiences for pupils. The author notes that, as implementation continues, it is still difficult to judge whether or not the new curriculum is fulfilling its intended purposes.

The chapter following this (43) explains how there are frameworks in CfE relating to 'literacy' and to 'literacy and English' and the responsibilities of all teachers for these vital elements. Literacy now has a broader definition than heretofore and includes digital, visual and auditory texts. Figure 43.1 on page 459 sets out the frameworks in the familiar terms of *listening and talking*, *reading* and *writing*. Attention is paid to survey findings concerning children's attainment in literacy, and the chapter explores the wide range of issues implicated in children's competence in this area. Modern Languages in the Primary School (MLPS) are considered in Chapter 44. Their treatment has waxed and waned, with politicians every so often expressing embarrassment over Scottish (and English) pupils' seeming incompetence compared to their European counterparts, thereby trying to inject new impetus into developments in primary and secondary schools. Different emphases, indeed different rationales, have been given to language learning in the primary sector over the last five decades, most notably in recent times with the generalist primary classroom teacher taking responsibility for modern foreign language learning (along with everything else). The author expresses concern at the dangers for the educational system in not learning from past endeavours and paying insufficient attention to relevant research.

The writer of Chapter 45 records that 'Environmental Studies' was the umbrella term in the earlier 5–14 Curriculum used to group together the subject areas of science, the social subjects and technology. She traces the evolution of these into the separate curricular areas spelled out for CfE, noting the effects of various policy agendas of government for some of the emphases therein. It is argued that more of the changes here have been brought about by developments in pedagogy rather than curriculum content. The innovative approaches that contemporary primary teachers now use to teach in these curricular areas are described and the CfE principle of integrated learning is discussed in this context. Some of the subject matter, particularly in the sciences, has proved difficult for many primary teachers (as researchers and curricular developers repeatedly find) and the author connects the challenges posed by these particular subjects with the arguments raised in the Donaldson Report about the nature of future professional learning (see Chapter 98 in Section XI).

Expressive Arts is also a catch-all term, here embracing art, drama, music and dance, and in CfE they are grouped together. Chapter 46 sees them addressing the 'basic need for self-expression and creativity', noting how learning *in* the arts and learning *through* the arts can complement each other. This means that suitably flexible programmes in expressive arts devised by teachers help balance and round the learning of young people, allowing goals to be achieved. The chapter also addresses the wider cultural context of the arts in Scotland.

Mathematics is the subject of Chapter 47 and the idea of numeracy (or mathematical literacy) is looked at in depth. The analysis includes a scrutiny of the different ways in which the numerical skills of the pupil population are revealed (local/school measures reported by authorities; national surveys such as the 2011 Scottish Survey of Literacy and Numeracy; and international surveys like the 2007 Trends in International Mathematics and Science Study), all of which throw up concerns about what Scottish pupils can do numerically. The chapter examines what it means to teach mathematics, recognising that 'numeracy is both complex and critically important'. Suggestions are made as to the collaborations that should be now be made between Education Scotland, researchers and teachers themselves.

Given the poor health statistics of the population of Scotland, Health and Wellbeing has rightly gained a greater focus in the modern curriculum and much falls to teachers in both primary and secondary schools to improve the situation. The author of Chapter 48 (and also of Chapter 60 in Section VII) tracks the political imperatives shaping educational input, the changes in how health topics are tackled and the changing culture of schooling itself. Partnerships and collaborations across sectors and with parents are now seen as being crucial to progress. Methodologies recommended in CfE are consistent with the switch that the Chief Medical Officer has recently advocated in respect of health creation. Rather than dwelling on what people lack, we should take an 'asset-based approach' that builds on individuals' strengths, acknowledges the social setting and gives children confidence.

Religious and Moral Education (RME) is the subject of the last chapter (49) in this section. The author shows the approach currently taken in Scotland is fairly similar to that in many European countries. In a generation or so, there has been a significant shift away from one that emphasised Christian observance to an 'educational, non-confessional, belief sensitive, professionally delivered and philosophical RME' following the pivotal Millar Report of 1972: pupils now learn about the variety of religious (and non-religious) beliefs and the curriculum emphasises values such as honesty, justice, compassion and integrity. Effective RME, according to the writer, allows pupils to explore and develop their own sense of personal meaning and that places the subject at the heart of the primary curriculum. Taken together, the chapters in this section provide both an overview of the Scottish primary curriculum and a more focused insight into what goes on within specific curricular areas.

42

Curriculum for Excellence in the Primary School

Lesley Reid

The curriculum experienced by children in Scottish primary schools, Curriculum for Excellence (CfE), is part of a framework for learning that encompasses pupils from 3 to 18 years old. It evolved over the decade following a national debate on education in 2002 and included a lengthy period of consultation and development (see Chapter 3 for a more general discussion of CfE). The value base, guiding principles and educational aims of this aspirational curriculum policy are all articulated in official documentation. Learner entitlement in Scottish primary schools is described and pathways for progression established. This chapter considers the aims and value base of the curriculum, its structure and how it is translated into learning experiences for children in primary schools. It evaluates the theoretical base of the policy and issues emerging from its current implementation in Scottish primary schools.

The value base for CfE is tied to those egalitarian principles that are perceived to support Scottish democratic society: wisdom, justice, compassion and integrity. Education is characterised as a way for Scottish society to enact and develop these values through active citizenship. The identified universal societal positives are difficult to question; the school curriculum as a vehicle to achieve those ends through individual achievement perhaps more open to debate. What has been questioned (see Chapter 4) is whether it is possible to have true consensus about the meaning of such values in a pluralistic society; whether apparently commonsense understandings are really sense held in common. The individually located qualities of ambition and high aspiration in the rhetoric of the written curriculum are coupled with a social justice agenda driven by tolerance, care and respect for others. While these are all justifiable values, they can be seen as oppositional rather than complementary.

The principles that underpin CfE were arrived at through a rationale for change presented in the early policy documentation. Its predecessor, the 5–14 Curriculum, was perceived as content-heavy, fragmented and poorly linked to later educational experiences in secondary schools. During the last decade of the twentieth century, the relationships in the education system between curriculum, pedagogy and assessment had become imbalanced. Teaching in primary schools had become overly assessment-driven and this in turn influenced the way the 5–14 Curriculum was interpreted. Although the Assessment for Learning programme had done much to redress the balance between teaching and assessment, the national debate on education indicated that curricular reform was necessary to address the perceived deficits in the areas of content and integration. CfE principles emphasise coherence and progression alongside both breadth and depth of learning. Personalisation, choice and relevance to children's lives sit beside challenge and enjoyment in the new curriculum, at the expense of the balance and continuity that were core principles of the 5–14 Curriculum. CfE is therefore less content-driven than the previous primary curriculum and more focused on ensuring motivation for learning.

AIMS OF THE CURRICULUM

Policy makers also made the case for change to the Scottish curriculum as a necessary response to social and economic developments. Thus, the new curriculum was seen as playing an active role in ensuring Scotland's place in a global market economy. Preparing pupils to take on the mantle of contributing to future economic prosperity was presented as an important purpose of schooling. CfE has been criticised for this anticipatory focus (see Chapter 4). Rather than addressing the needs of children 'in the moment' the linking of curricular purpose to a national economic purpose can be perceived as politically instrumental.

Stated alongside this economic aim was a child-centred, personalised aim that established learner entitlement in relation to the new curriculum. A second purpose was identified for the curriculum of ensuring that all children developed the attributes, knowledge and skills they would need to flourish in life and learning. These attributes and skills are enshrined in four overarching capacities: children are expected to become successful learners, confident individuals, responsible citizens and effective contributors to society. Thus the economic and child-centred aims are supplemented by a more socially driven one that acknowledges the collective good through the concept of good citizenship. The aims of the curriculum are therefore collective, economic and societal as well as individualistic; as such, they are linked to rights, responsibilities and obligations.

The mix of values, articulated principles and desirable capacities within early CfE documentation can be seen as an attempt to make the 'hidden' curriculum in schools more visible. McCutcheon (1988) distinguishes between the formal policy curriculum (the intended curriculum) and the enacted curriculum (that which is actually delivered in classrooms). 'Hidden' aspects of the curriculum usually include the transmission by educators of values and beliefs (as well as knowledge) in the dialogic social context of the classroom. Curricular values and purposes that in the past in Scotland remained more implicit in curricular guidance are made explicit in CfE. Whether or not the articulated value base of the formal curriculum will therefore become more consensually shared through the enacted curriculum is uncertain. There has certainly been an effort on the part of policy makers to realise this aim – posters displaying the four capacities, for example, were distributed to be displayed in all Scottish schools; many staffrooms and classroom walls bore testament to this policy initiative. It seems unlikely that this open 'sharing' will eliminate completely the operation of what may be alternative values of a hidden curriculum. The extent to which the value base of the curriculum becomes consensual is likely to depend on the extent to which it resonates with the teachers who enact the curriculum in their classrooms.

PUPIL ENTITLEMENT

Within the formal curriculum framework for primary schools, pupils do have individual entitlements: they have a right to benefit from their education and to have their achievements valued. All young people have a right to cumulatively develop knowledge and skills that will prepare them for later life. The experiences planned for them should enable them also to develop the qualities of citizenship, enterprise and creativity and the four capacities outlined above. While the qualities of citizenship and enterprise can be included in the capacities of responsible citizenship and effective contribution, creativity is not an integral part of any of the other capacities, unless it is construed as part of being a successful learner. This can be seen as a significant omission; for some the ability to respond flexibly and creatively to challenge and change is an essential capacity for a twenty-first-century citizen. While creative skills are developed within individual discipline areas such as expressive arts, creativity is not given a weighting equivalent to that of the cross-cutting themes of citizenship or enterprise.

Within CfE, there are also pupil entitlements relating to the assessment of primary school pupils. Building on the research–informed progress achieved through the Assessment for Learning Programme in Scottish schools (2002–10), assessment is seen as something that should support learning, rather than simply measure it (see Chapter 75). Children therefore have an entitlement to experience formative assessment and receive feedback in a form that supports their learning. This in turn implies an entitlement for pupils to develop metacognitive capacity; to develop awareness of themselves as learners, as well as awareness of the learning itself. Alongside this formative assessment entitlement goes a right to personal support in response to individual need within a coherent curricular experience. The policy intention therefore is to realise the social justice agenda in a highly ipsative way, tailored to individual need.

THE STRUCTURE OF THE CURRICULUM

Once the underpinning values, principles and purposes of the curriculum had been established, a construction metaphor was adopted by policy makers in documentation that reinforced the idea that the curriculum was being developed through continued consultation. The process of curricular construction was explained in the *Building the Curriculum* series of documents, numbered 1–5, published between 2006 and 2011. The focus of each is outlined in Table 42.1:

CfE has emerged as a curricular edifice comprising many interlocking and interdependent components. This coherence can be perceived as a strength of the policy or, conversely, the resulting complexity can be seen as weakening the integrity of the whole, by making implementation confusing.

As the process of 'bedding in' the new curriculum took hold in primary schools (2005–12), greater attention was paid to the ways in which learning could be best encouraged and enabled. A structure emerged whereby learning was organised into curriculum

Table 42.1 *Building the Curriculum* documents

Year	Document	Focus
2006	*Building the Curriculum 1*	Outline of curriculum areas
2007	*Building the Curriculum 2*	Learning in early years
2008	*Building the Curriculum 3*	Key areas of knowledge and contexts for learning
2009	*Building the Curriculum 4*	Skills for learning, life and work
2011	*Building the Curriculum 5*	Assessment

areas and progression described through the identification of progressive experiences and outcomes in those areas. The traditional broad-based general Scottish education that ranges across subject disciplines therefore remains enshrined in the curriculum documentation. However, increased status is given to literacy, numeracy and health and wellbeing, which are seen as the responsibility of all teachers, across all sectors. The new status given to Health and Wellbeing as an identified curriculum area is a natural one for primary school teachers who have always adopted a holistic view of their responsibilities that includes pastoral as well as academic duties.

Learning in primary schools is not only experienced through study of the subject disciplines, but also through the other 'contexts for learning': through the ethos and life of the school; through interdisciplinary studies and through opportunities for wider achievement such as extra-curricular opportunities. For some, the identified contexts for learning appear to stretch the definition of the curriculum as the '*totality of planned experiences*' for young people. The claim that extra-curricular activities are contexts for learning that are simultaneously part of the curriculum is a little disingenuous. Similarly, to have progression in learning defined through tabulated experiences and outcomes while being expected to contextualise learning in interdisciplinary topics creates a very real challenge for Scottish teachers. While many welcome the pedagogical flexibility offered by this interlocking curricular architecture and praise the opportunities it provides for depth of learning, others are frustrated by its intricacy and lack of clarity.

Further building blocks have been added during the period of curriculum development that imply ever more complexity for teacher/planners. Global citizenship, sustainable development, international education, citizenship education and enterprise education are all branded as 'Learning across the Curriculum'. Additionally, creativity, outdoor and active learning, cooperative and collaborative learning and peer education are considered as 'Approaches to Learning'. The emergence of this rather bewildering array of curricular organisers has placed further demands on the role of teachers as planners and orchestrators of learning.

As a pragmatic response to this complexity, the primary organiser that is used by teachers to plan learning for children is the tabulated experiences and outcomes. They are arranged principally according to traditional subject areas of study covering arts, humanities and sciences (languages, mathematics, sciences, social studies, expressive arts, religious and moral education) with technologies, and health and wellbeing additionally identified subject areas that reflect societal and political agendas for change. It is likely is that applying a subject-centred base to primary education is a consequence of the creation of CfE as an educational continuum spanning both primary and secondary education.

The descriptions of each of the curricular areas reflect contemporary societal issues as well as political concerns in each field of study. For example, the description of languages includes both Gaelic and modern foreign languages, reflecting population migration during the new century as well as a national cultural revival. Mathematics stresses not only numeracy, but also the importance of problem solving and information handling. Social studies includes the inter-relationships between the local and global environments and human influences upon both.

The identification of literacy, numeracy, and health and wellbeing as the responsibility of all teachers reinforces the child-centred aims of the curriculum, alongside the political and societal ones. The prioritisation of health and wellbeing alongside literacy and numeracy also softens the subject-centredness of the CfE. It represents an innovative way of tackling

Table 42.2   Curricular levels

Level	Primary years	Pupil age (years)
Early	In pre-school and in P1	3–6
First	By end of P4 but earlier for some	8
Second	By end of P7 but earlier for some	11

personal and social education within the Scottish educational system and reflects social and political concerns about children's diet, exercise habits and emotional wellbeing that are well-publicised in the press and backed by longitudinal research of Scottish lifestyle (www. growingupinscotland.org).

The structural organisation and content of CfE is therefore seen as an instrument of potential societal as well as economic change by government.

PROGRESSION IN LEARNING

Although a curriculum for primary schools dominated by traditional subject boundaries can be seen as old-fashioned and dominated by secondary school structural demands, the identified curriculum areas are a convenient and easily recognisable device to support the progressive development of ideas, skills and ways of thinking. CfE therefore takes an epistemological organisational stance. Linking progression to 'ways of knowing' in traditional subject areas enables the 3–18 age span to be characterised in linear stages. For primary school pupils, these stages are defined in Table 42.2:

Although the level descriptors are presented as a linear progression linked to chronological school stages, these are not intended to place limits on children's progress; rather they represent typical progress expected. As can be seen in Table 42.2, the levels are deliberately broad-banded and represent children's progress over more than one school year. Opportunities for more rapid progress are explicitly stated according to individual ability and pace of learning. The bridging of pre-school and P1 by the early level allows for a 'settling out' of differing pre-school experiences. It allows for improved transition between the more active learning environment of pre-school settings and the more formal learning environment of the primary school. Similarly, transition between the primary and secondary stages of schooling is eased by a flexible approach to the upper and lower limits of attainment in primary schools. In primary schools in Scotland, these expectations for achievement are not tied to formal, externally imposed assessment points.

The tabulated descriptions of progression in learning within individual curriculum areas are described in terms of pupil engagement in activities (experiences) and the product of that engagement (outcomes). These outcomes are explained in terms of how the learning will be made visible; what the young person will be able to explain, apply or demonstrate. The coupling of learner engagement in an activity with its learning outcome is intrinsically coherent as a means of delineating steps of increasing difficulty. Curriculum principles are further reinforced through the aspirational, achievement-focused 'child speak' discourse adopted to describe the experiences and outcomes. For example, 'I can explain how different methods can be used to find the perimeter of an area of a simple 2D shape or volume of a simple 3D object' (MNU 2-11c). Every one of the proactive *I can* statements frames a personal challenge for children.

The coupling of the activity with the learning outcome also strengthens the focus within the curriculum on the active engagement of learners. Tasks and learning are portrayed as inseparable and learning as active. Children are thus framed in the discourse of the documents as active participants in the process of learning, co-constructors of learning or effective contributors to the learning process. The innovative use of the language of child-speak implies that the words of the experiences and outcomes will be shared with children, that teachers are therefore less privileged as gatekeepers of curriculum-content knowledge.

THE THEORETICAL BASE OF CURRICULUM FOR EXCELLENCE

The interplay between the tabulated experiences and outcomes of the curricular areas and the identified contexts for learning reveal the theoretical base of CfE. There is evidence to suggest that it draws not only on well-established curriculum theory but also appropriately on both learning theory and pedagogical theory. The emphasis on active learning, for example, stretches back historically to Dewey's curriculum theory work on experiential education in the early twentieth century, where he debated the relative importance of the acquisition of knowledge and skill and how they are co-constructed by teachers and pupils. However, active learning within CfE is not only concerned with Dewey's hands-on physical activity; it also emphasises active thinking approaches. Dewey's view therefore of the teacher as facilitator and guide in the active construction of knowledge is also influential.

The creation of an early level spanning the pre-school years and the first year of primary school has created more permeability between pre-school and primary teaching approaches. The phrase 'purposeful play' is used in *Building the Curriculum 2* to describe a learning context that provides opportunities for active learning in both primary and pre-school classes. Such contexts capitalise on Piagetian developmental theories but are also underpinned by the social constructivism of Bruner. While more focused and direct learning and teaching approaches are expected towards the end of P1, planned, purposeful play experiences in primary schools are seen as one way of easing the transition between the sectors for young children. So too are the expected opportunities for spontaneous and exploratory play in well-resourced environments. The theoretical roots of CfE in social constructivism and developmental psychology are clearly demonstrated in these approaches to learning.

The influences of Dewey, Piaget and Bruner on CfE can be situated alongside others in Illeris' analysis of learning theory. Illeris (2002) identifies a tension between the cognitive, the emotional and the social aspects of learning. For Illeris, the process of learning is an entity, where the various aspects are united into one whole:

> It combines a direct or mediated interaction between the individual and its material and social environment with an internal psychological process of acquisition. Thus learning always includes both an individual and a social element, the latter always reflecting societal conditions, so that the learning result has the character of an individual phenomenon which is always socially and societally marked. (p. 227)

Illeris' analysis draws upon not only the developmental psychology of Piaget and Kolb, but also the activity theories of Vygotsky, Engestrom and Bruner. Also included are contributions on collective learning from socialisation theorists. Central to Illeris' synthesis is the work of Wenger, whose concept of communities of practice combines the social and individual from a social perspective. The emphasis on learning experiences alongside learning outcomes in the subject descriptors of CfE indicates that it embraces a social and collective view of learning that transcends individual cognitive construction. Many of the descriptions of the learning experiences in CfE are premised upon social interaction. They involve pedagogies that necessarily include collaborative group work as well as individual cognitive 'work' in the classroom.

Thus the social is embedded in learning in Scottish primary schools at all levels: children learn in and out of classrooms in collaborative working groups; they experience a sense of the collective good through a carefully managed sense of school ethos. Schools are seen as creating communities of belonging and as being integral parts of wider locally based communities.

The inclusion within the experiences and outcomes of progression in the learning of attitudes alongside skills and knowledge further demonstrates CfE roots in both individual and social views of learning. The attitudes fostered may be concerned with individually located phenomena or with more socially mediated ones. Some experiences and outcomes carry Illeris' societal marking in an overtly political way. 'Green' environmental and sustainability issues, for example, figure prominently in the science curriculum, phrased in a way that is not politically neutral: 'I can investigate the use of and development of renewable and sustainable energy to gain an awareness of their growing importance in Scotland and beyond' (SCN 3-04b).

Within CfE, Illeris' social aspect of learning may be achieved through specified curriculum content as well as through pedagogical approaches adopted by teachers: 'Having selected a significant individual from the past, I can contribute to a discussion on the influence of their actions then and since' (SOC1-106a).

The ways in which the individual cognitive aspects of learning are achieved have undergone a paradigm shift in Scottish schools since the embedding into practice by teachers of formative assessment practices in the first decade of the twenty-first century. Underpinned by the pedagogical theoretical and experiential base developed by Black and Wiliam (1998) and integrated into CfE in *Building the Curriculum 5*, the social constructivist base of classroom pedagogy has been extended to include the development of metacognitive capacity in young learners. *Building the Curriculum 5* re-asserts the primary purpose of assessment in primary schools as being to support learning. This is placed within a wider assessment framework that avoids national testing at fixed points in a child's school career but focuses instead on both formative and summative assessment as an integral part of day-to-day activities in classrooms. The formative assessment principles developed by Black and Wiliam are interpreted to ensure that pupils are involved in the assessment process and develop an awareness of their own strengths and development needs as learners. Coherent theoretical links between curriculum, pedagogy and assessment are therefore emerging as a strength of current Scottish primary school education.

EMERGING ISSUES

By 2011, all Scottish primary schools were expected to use CfE as the basis of the learning experience provided for pupils. The complex planning task of using the tabulated experiences and outcomes in subject disciplines, alongside the identified contexts for learning and the learning across the curriculum themes of citizenship, sustainability and enterprise is now a reality for teachers. So too is the expectation that the approaches to learning that they adopted would involve creativity, outdoor education, and active and cooperative learning.

Perhaps not surprisingly, the combining of so many elements of curriculum design to create programmes of work for pupils has proved very demanding for teachers.

At this stage of implementation, it is very difficult to judge whether or not the new curriculum is meeting the purposes identified in early documentation. The wider economic and societal aims can only be realised over an extended timeframe as today's children grow into tomorrow's adults. The individual, child-centred ambitions of Curriculum for Excellence are more readily evaluated over a shorter timescale. There are signs that not all schools are embracing the freedom afforded by the deliberately broad-banded experiences and outcomes and the other interlocking curricular building blocks. Some schools and local authorities have felt the need to support teachers by detailing more prescriptive, smaller steps in learning for teachers to use when planning and tracking learning, particularly in the areas of languages and mathematics.

However, for primary schools that are engaging with curricular complexity, two principal issues have arisen in professional exchanges. These relate, first, to the creation of interdisciplinary learning experiences as contexts for learning for pupils and, second, to skill progression within the curriculum as a whole. The implementation of interdisciplinary learning contexts has led to professional dialogue about planning worthwhile learning experiences for children and has opened up spaces for creative teaching. Some primary schools have adopted more flexible timetabling arrangements and encouraged collaborative working across traditional age and stage groupings. This is evidenced in many case studies on the Education Scotland and GLOW websites and by innovative planning practices adopted in schools for topic work.

Interdisciplinary contexts for learning within CfE are seen as supported by an appropriate school ethos promoted by a strong sense of school community. The concepts of school ethos and community are intrinsically nebulous and much more difficult to define than curricular content or subject categories. They depend on human interaction and leadership and as such are relationally based. While this human interpretation of education is optimistic, it remains challenging for those charged with implementing it. It is tied to individual locations and the people who inhabit those spaces and places. As such, it may prove problematic on a national scale; individuality and context-dependent flexibility do not necessarily sit well with consistency of entitlement. However, the combination of interdisciplinary contexts for learning and themes across learning with traditional subject areas, supported by a positive school ethos, underpinned by a sense of community do offer Scottish teachers particular autonomy in curricular implementation.

Coping with the opportunity to teach in interdisciplinary ways while maintaining depth of learning has become a significant professional issue for Scottish primary school teachers. While planning cross-curricular projects has been an established part of the repertoire of primary school teachers since the 1960s, doing so while implementing the CfE principles of depth, coherence, personalisation, choice and relevance in interdisciplinary contexts requires the adoption of new pedagogies. The embedding of skill progression within and across the experiences and outcomes of the subject disciplines makes the tracking of progress complex. Many teachers are drawing upon prior experience of 'topic web' approaches to planning. While this may help them address the principles of coherence and relevance in learning, it may not allow them to address depth or progression of learning.

Perhaps as a response, there has been renewed interest in Storyline approaches to interdisciplinary learning since CfE became more embedded in practice (Bell et al., 2007).

This approach uses the benefits of a strong narrative line of topic development and elements from the creative arts to engage pupils (see Chapter 6). The emphasis on outdoor and active learning within the new curriculum has encouraged many teachers to develop learning experiences for pupils based in the environment local to the school that draw upon science, social studies, and health and wellbeing subject disciplines. Rapid improvements in electronic communication have facilitated investigation projects that draw on global issues. All of these developments indicate active engagement of the teaching profession with the professional issue of interdisciplinary learning.

The second important issue to emerge in professional debate has been the place of skills development, and in particular thinking skills, in the curriculum. This has arisen partly as a result of teacher concern over progression in learning and the need to reconcile breadth and depth of learning within the flexibility offered by CfE. Skills for learning and life are one of the curricular entitlements for all pupils but clear understanding of what exactly is meant by these skills is difficult to decipher in curricular advice.

Amidst the plethora of skills types described as necessary within *Building the Curriculum 4*, a triad of skill sets has emerged as helpful for teachers: cognitive skills, metacognitive skills and emotional literacy skills. The identification of higher-order critical thinking skills (applying, analysing, evaluating, creating) as important has enabled connections to be made by teachers with the hierarchical skills characterised by Bloom in his taxonomy for cognitive skills. Additionally the metacognitive skills fostered through formative assessment practices have extended teacher understanding of pupil personal learning skills development. Formative assessment approaches built into learning encourage the metacognitive awareness that is an important part of self-knowledge as a learner. Furthermore, the innovative approach to health and wellbeing within CfE has created an opportunity to include emotional literacy skills and the skills required for successful collaborative learning at the heart of Scottish education. The outcomes that relate to mental, emotional and social wellbeing and 'planning for choices and changes' can be achieved most readily through pedagogical approaches that are familiar to most primary school teachers. Organising learning in collaborative group contexts provides opportunities to develop awareness of relationships and the needs of others in line with the socially oriented theoretical base of the curriculum. All three types of skills development have sound roots in research literature and have the potential to help Scottish teachers make sense of the complex architecture of CfE and give them confidence to take advantage of the pedagogical flexibility it offers.

The relatively 'light touch' to curricular content within CfE can therefore be seen as allowing teachers to concentrate on enacting the curriculum in an authentic way, planning and implementing learning in engaging contexts. The perceived need for increased specification of learning in mathematics and literacy, however, indicates that ensuring consistent pupil progression in learning remains a continuing difficulty for teachers. While some are meeting the challenge of implementing a complex curricular framework of principles, capacities, outcomes, experiences, contexts and cross-cutting themes, others may not be coping as well with what can be perceived as an over-elaborate curricular architecture. National developments in assessment for primary schools have acknowledged this difficulty and have provided support for primary teachers during the period of curricular change. At the time of writing, therefore, the curriculum, teaching and assessment elements of the education system appear to be relatively in balance in Scottish primary education as teachers gradually take increasing responsibility for the continued building of a curriculum that appears to have solid theoretical foundations. The construction task is, however, a complex and demanding one; one that will require a highly skilled and knowledgeable teaching force in the years ahead.

REFERENCES

Bell, S., S. Harkness and G. White (eds) (2007) *Storyline Past, Present and Future*. Glasgow: Enterprising Careers.

Black, P. and D. Wiliam (1998) 'Assessment and classroom learning', *Assessment in Education*, 5 (1): 7–71.

Illeris, K. (2004) *The Three Dimensions of Learning*. Leicester: Niace Publications.

Krathwohl, D. R. (2002) 'A revision of Bloom's taxonomy: An overview', *Theory into Practice*, 41 (4): 212–18.

McCutcheon, G. (1988) 'Curriculum and work of teachers', in M. Apple and L. Beyer (eds), *The Curriculum, Problems, Politics and Possibilities*. New York: State University of New York Press, pp. 191–203.

Scottish Executive (2006) *Building the Curriculum 1: The Contribution of the Curricular Area*. Edinburgh: Scottish Executive.

Scottish Executive (2007) *Building the Curriculum 2: Active Learning in the Early Years*. Edinburgh: Scottish Executive.

Scottish Government (2008) *Building the Curriculum 3: A Framework for Learning and Teaching*. Edinburgh: Scottish Government.

Scottish Government (2009) *Building the Curriculum 4: Skills for Learning, Skills for Life and Skills for Work*. Edinburgh: Scottish Government.

Scottish Government (2011) *Building the Curriculum 5: A Framework for Assessment*. Edinburgh: Scottish Government.

43

Literacy and English

Sue Ellis

Literacy and English are key parts of 'Languages', one of eight curricular areas in Curriculum for Excellence (CfE). There are frameworks relating to 'Literacy' and to 'Literacy and English'. Each describes the curriculum in five levels: early (pre-school and P1); first (by the end of P4 or earlier); second (by the end of P7 or earlier); third (S1–S3) and fourth (S4–S6). The *Literacy and English* documents outline experiences and outcomes, and principles and practice, relating to early, primary and secondary English practitioners but another two documents, *Literacy: Experiences and Outcomes* and *Literacy Across Learning: Principles and Practice*, outline the responsibilities of every teacher in every subject area for literacy teaching. These documents all share a common framework (see Table 43.1).

The Experiences and Outcomes for *Enjoyment and Choice* emphasise the importance of providing opportunities for young people to make increasingly sophisticated choices; those for *Tools* outline the strategies, skills and knowledge required for pupils to become competent language and literacy users, and the Experiences and Outcomes for *Finding and Using Information*; *Understanding, Analysing and Evaluating*; and *Creating Texts* encourage progression in locating, using, producing and analysing spoken and written texts. By defining the curriculum through experiences as well as outcomes, CfE seeks to emphasise the coherence of progression through both the content and the contexts for learning, thereby promoting smoother transitions between the nursery, primary and secondary sectors.

CfE has widened the definition of literacy to explicitly include digital, visual and auditory texts. It celebrates Scotland's vibrant literary and linguistic heritage and its indigenous languages and dialects by promoting Gaelic, Scots and Scottish literature whilst recognising that the languages of Scotland also include the 138 home languages children bring to school (the top ten of which, in descending popularity, are: English, Polish, Punjabi, Urdu, Arabic,

Table 43.1   The English and Literacy and Literacy framework in CfE

Listening and talking	Reading	Writing
Enjoyment and choice	Enjoyment and choice	Enjoyment and choice
Tools for listening and talking	Tools for listening and talking	Tools for listening and talking
Finding and using information	Finding and using information	Finding and using information
Understanding, analysing and evaluating	Understanding, analysing and evaluating	
Creating texts		Creating texts

Cantonese, French, Gaelic, Bengali/Bengalis and German). The focus on Scotland's literary heritage and current reality presents some dilemmas. The publishers of modern Scottish authors are (often American-owned) international businesses, keen to maximise international distribution and profits. Thus J. K. Rowling wrote *Harry Potter* in Scotland, but it is not a distinctly Scottish text. To widen international appeal, Mairi Hedderwick's *Katie Morag* stories about life in a Scottish island community were changed; the original 'Grandpa' became a rather masculine 'Grannie Island' to placate US sensibilities about young girls visiting old men. Books with Scottish vocabulary, such as Teresa Breslin's popular novel *Divided City*, present comprehension challenges to the rest of the world, which limits their international reach and the author's influence outwith Scotland.

READING, WRITING, TALKING AND LISTENING

Almost all primary schools use commercially published schemes for teaching reading, phonics, grammar, handwriting and punctuation, and often writing too. Alongside this, CfE promotes cross-curricular links, flexible and integrated use of literacy, and literary projects such as whole-class novel studies. Within-class attainment grouping is common for teaching reading and, sometimes, writing. Class-setting for language is less common but does occur, sometimes involving similar-attainment but different-age groups working in one class. This simplifies teaching, but may not improve learning: it may impact negatively on the self-esteem and aspirations of those in lower sets; younger, able children may struggle socially when working with older pupils and it leaves the main class teacher unable to link ideas or to reinforce literacy skills through other curricular work, which is particularly important for struggling pupils.

CfE emphasises enjoyment and engagement, leading schools and local authorities to explore the possibilities of literature circles, paired reading and personal reading time in class. However, the quality and use of classroom libraries varies and there is a tendency to over-regulate activities, rather than creating the open, social spaces that Moss and McDonald (2004) indicate are necessary if pupils are to define themselves as readers/writers. In literature circles, teachers will often weaken pupil ownership by imposing roles and tasks that control the content and flow of discussion.

Non-fiction reading and writing are reinforced through topic work, with differentiated worksheets and tasks for those with literacy difficulties. Much writing is taught as a whole-class activity and desktop publishing is encouraged. Following international trends, most authorities adopt a broadly genre-based approach to non-fiction writing. Narrative writing is common, but children tend to retell stories heard elsewhere or describe personal experiences rather than invent stories. Children rarely choose their own writing topics, although the emphasis on writing for enjoyment is creating renewed interest in the pedagogies around 'writing journals' (Graham and Johnson, 2003).

MONITORING AND ASSESSMENT

The term 'achievement' (rather than 'attainment') is used to reflect the importance of broad success measures. The Assessment is for Learning initiative (AifL), instigated in 2002, promoted formative assessment strategies as procedural and conceptual scaffolds for teaching and it is standard practice for teachers to share learning objectives and success criteria at the start of language lessons. In some lessons, pupils often indicate their understanding or confidence to tackle a task with a show of 'traffic lights' (red/amber/green) or 'thumbs' (up/horizontal/down). Teachers encourage pupils to self-assess and peer-assess against predetermined success criteria. Teachers' feedback on writing often takes the form of 'two stars and a wish', indicating two things the pupil has done well and one improvement to make in future. These make the learning content and progression clear but can detract from intrinsic purpose in tasks and can promote a skills-and-strategy-based culture of performativity.

Local authorities collect summative data on reading and writing standards in their schools. The National Assessment Resource of contextualised observations and test-tasks was created by teachers and linked to CfE levels. Although these locate pupils on the CfE ladder of levels, they are not standardised and do not focus on elements of central importance to literacy development. Most local authorities and some schools buy standardised and semi-standardised tests because they need literacy data that is reliable, focused and age-specific. This introduces inequity; poorer local authorities and schools cannot afford the data available to richer ones.

Scotland takes part in the Programme for International Student Assessment (PISA) survey of achievement for literacy for 15-year-olds, but withdrew from the Progress in International Reading and Literacy Survey (PIRLS), which focused on primary pupils. In PISA (2009) Scotland ranked in the middle group of the Organisation for Economic Cooperation and Development (OECD) countries, significantly below Australia, Canada, Finland, Japan, Korea, New Zealand, Shanghai-China, Hong Kong-China and Singapore. Reading attainment remained static and 16 per cent of pupils performed below Level 2, the OECD baseline proficiency required for full participation in democratic society. The difference between the averages of the top and bottom attainment quartiles equates to 5.5 years of schooling. Scotland was also below the OECD average for reading for enjoyment; 47per cent of pupils 'read only to obtain the information they need' and 26 per cent agreed that 'reading is a waste of time'. Socio-economic status and gender strongly influence reading attainment.

The Scottish Survey of Literacy and Numeracy, an annual national survey, focused alternately on literacy and numeracy. The first CfE-aligned literacy survey was in 2012 and results are published on the Scottish Government's website. The 2009 survey (aligned to 5–14 Curriculum levels) reported strong effects of socio-economic status on literacy; that, in general, girls performed better than boys; that reading attainment at all stages remained static; and that the proportion of pupils attaining expected levels decreased through primary and into secondary, as did their confidence in their ability to read, write, talk and listen.

HISTORICAL CONTEXT

Three distinct curriculum policy phases have characterised Scotland's language and literacy teaching in the past sixty years. Between 1960 and 1989, curriculum advice was developed collaboratively by teachers, inspectors and teacher educators working for the Scottish Committee on Language Arts in the Primary School (SCOLA), reporting to the Committee on Primary Education. This promoted integrated methodologies such as Scottish Storyline (Bell and Harkness, 2006) but there were no mechanisms to ensure that recommendations were implemented; schools had complete autonomy over content and pedagogy and, despite a system supposedly founded on debate followed by consensus, there were wide differences in expectations and attainment.

The next policy phase, 1989–2004, addressed these problems of continuity, breadth, progression and compliance by providing curriculum guidelines (*The 5–14 English Language Guidelines*). These framed Her Majesty's Inspectorate of Education inspections, which ensured they were taken seriously. Literacy had a distinct 'slot' in the curriculum and an agreed progression of knowledge and skills. However, there was scant regard to cross-curricular contexts or overall coherence, and they led to serious curriculum overload. Language and literacy teaching became fragmented in a way that was never envisaged: schemes and worksheets (providing easy evidence of coverage and progression) replaced more integrated, responsive, active and interactive pedagogies. In forward planning, teachers mapped activities to attainment targets rather than identifying the priorities and contexts that would give the best learning payoff for pupils. The demand for coverage created time pressures and few opportunities for literacy to be social, relaxing, contextualised, purposeful or self-directed. Extended writing, spontaneous talk, responsive teaching and opportunities to link or revisit ideas were hard to accommodate. The Scottish Storyline method migrated to Scandinavia, where it thrived (see Chapter 6).

Under 5–14, there was more emphasis on equity and attainment and the variability between schools decreased. However, some learning environments were dysfunctional; they deskilled teachers and did not foster creativity or intellectual and emotional engagement. This, then, was the backdrop against which CfE was introduced in 2004.

ISSUES

At its heart, CfE recognises that literacy and literacy learning are socially and culturally mediated. It offers the potential to challenge the individualistic, skills-based models of literacy that divorce literacy learning from its context of use. This could drive new dialogues about literacy teaching in Scotland, and the world, by promoting curriculum designs and pedagogies framed explicitly by socio-cultural, ethnographic and critical-literacy perspectives. However, designing a curriculum that is meaningful, efficient and effective for specific communities requires access to research knowledge, and support in applying it. Specifically, it necessitates a shift from viewing literacy as a set of autonomous, culturally neutral skills to seeing it as socially and culturally situated practice (Street, 1984) and an understanding of how to create empowerment through critical literacy (Comber, 2010).

Engagement and empowerment through literacy is central to harnessing intrinsic motivation, particularly in pupils from low-literacy backgrounds, and to delivering CfE's overarching purpose, embodied in the four capacities (successful learners, confident individuals, responsible citizens and effective contributors). Although CfE hints at aspects related to pupils' agency as language and literacy users it does not directly ensure teachers empower pupils through literacy. For example, the 'Reading' experiences and outcomes identify choice as central to promoting enjoyment and engagement, but progression focuses on pupils' ability to *justify* choice rather than on how choice promotes agency and drives social and emotional empowerment. In 'Writing', choice is presented as the ability to address the needs of the audience rather than as central to understanding how writing fulfils intellectual and emotional needs, creates social agency and can be harnessed to effect change. The AifL strategies already mentioned, which actively promote performative assessment and technicist views of writing and do not set up the teacher to respond seriously to what each writer has to say, compound this. Yet only when writers see readers responding to *what* they have written (rather than *how*) will they find learning to write a positive, empowering process.

To be convinced that the effort of becoming literate is worthwhile, pupils, particularly those from low-literacy backgrounds, require repeated demonstrations that literacy can help them achieve things *they* want to achieve. Schools need help to prioritise and create social spaces away from the teacher in which pupils, particularly low-achieving pupils, can network in positive ways around books and writing and so create their own identities as readers and writers (Moss and McDonald, 2004). Although the writers of CfE took pains to ensure that the experiences and outcomes reflect 'active learning' (for example, they stress *making* notes, rather than the passivity implied by *taking* notes), there is insufficient emphasis on demonstrating the agency and power that mastery of literacy and language affords its users. Despite its emphasis on digital and other literacies, early interpretations of CfE reflect the fundamentally traditional understandings of becoming literate under 5–14 rather than the new literacies' more radical approach to harnessing literacy to pupils' own cultural practices and concerns, or identifying and challenging how texts position readers, writers and subject.

Scottish models of continuing professional development currently favour locally based, teacher-driven improvement and it is unclear how these new and radical perspectives on literacy and literacy learning, and other reliable research knowledge about what works, for whom, in what circumstances, will reach Scottish teachers and inform CfE implementation. The issue is systemic. Scotland's decentralised, 'bottom-up' approach to professional knowledge and lack of reliable attainment data contrasts with highly successful Canadian and Australian models which, though centralised, promote nuanced and evidence-based implementation (Levin, 2009).

Luke (2003), writing about the Australian literacy curriculum, distinguishes between schools that provide 'balanced programmes' and those with 'shopping-list programmes'. Balance requires schools to have 'thoughtfully exchanged information, audited their staff expertise, enlisted external help and critical friends . . . and balanced their program in relationship to what they know are the needs of the kids' (Luke, 2003, p. 79). It requires complex understandings of literacy learning as a decoding, semantic, pragmatic and critical endeavour. The first reaction of Scottish teachers was to create 'shopping lists' to ensure CfE compliance. In implementation, CfE needs to challenge the old 5–14, skills-based, autonomous model of literacy if it is to deliver a socially and culturally useful, coherent, intellectually demanding, transformative curriculum. It is early days in implementation and such major shifts in professional views need time. It may yet be possible for teachers to harness reliable research knowledge and create a curriculum that enacts the CfE capacities, rather than one that delivers the framework.

The published curriculum framework is only one aspect of a complex, dynamic picture of literacy education in Scotland; the implementation process is crucial in shaping what CfE could mean for literacy in the classroom. For early years and primary practitioners to steer the development of a proactive, assertive, coherent, nuanced, attuned curriculum, they undoubtedly need regular and better access to reliable research advice, to sophisticated understandings of what it means to be literate and to what matters about how literacy is 'lived' in school and community. They will need national discussions that are evidence-informed and systems that prompt them to attend to the literacy practices and beliefs of school communities and to research advice about bridging between these and schooled literacy.

REFERENCES

Bell, S. and S. Harkness (2006) *Storyline: Promoting Language Across the Curriculum*. Royston: United Kingdom Literacy Association.

Comber, B. (2010) 'Reading places', in K. Hall, U. Goswami, C. Harrison, S. Ellis and J. Soler (eds) *Interdisciplinary Perspectives on Learning to Read*. Abingdon: Routledge.

Graham, L. and A. R. Johnson (2003) *Children's Writing Journals* (Minibook 16). Royston: United Kingdom Literacy Association.

Levin, B. (2009) *How to Change 5000 Schools*. Toronto: University of Toronto Press.

Luke, A. (2003) 'Making literacy policy and practice with a difference: Generational change, professionalisation and literate futures', *Australian Journal of Language and Literacy*, 26 (3): 58–82.

Moss, G. and J. W. McDonald (2004) 'The borrowers: Library records as unobtrusive measures of children's reading preferences', *Journal of Research in Reading*, 27: 401–12.

Street, B. (1984) *Literacy in Theory and Practice*. Cambridge: Cambridge University Press.

44

Modern Languages in the Primary School

Dan Tierney

THE HISTORICAL AND LINGUISTIC CONTEXT

Previous experiments in teaching modern languages in primary schools (MLPS), normally French, German, Italian or Spanish, in the 1960s, in both Scotland (SED, 1969) and England (Burstall et al., 1974), were deemed to have failed. The main problems identified included the linguistic competence of teachers, inappropriate methodology for early learners and transition to secondary school. Consequently, MLPS disappeared from the educational landscape. Of course, any consideration of MLPS in the UK must also take account of another factor: in non-English-speaking countries, English is the dominant taught language and primary language learning may be seen as a first step in the study of English which will continue through secondary schooling. In most European countries, this will usually be based on the Council of Europe's Common European Framework (CEFR) (2007). In Scotland, it is difficult to predict which language a child may need in future. Given the growing importance of English in the 1980s, many continental countries were introducing English into their primary school curriculum. In 1989, the Scottish Education Department issued Circular 1178 in which the Secretary of State announced that he wanted to examine the case for beginning the study of a modern European language in primary school.

THE PILOT STAGE

Scotland reintroduced MLPS with the establishment of pilot projects in six 'clusters' involving the associated primary schools for six secondary schools in different parts of Scotland. These 'clusters' were to focus on either French or German in P6 and P7.

In 1990, a further six clusters were added to the pilot; these included one in Spanish and one in Italian and brought the number of French clusters to six and German clusters to four. The initial model was to involve the secondary specialists working in partnership with their primary colleagues. The plan was not to offer a general language awareness course but to extend the period a pupil would study a language from P6 to S4. Giovanazzi, Her Majesty's Inspector responsible at the time, described it as 'no mere softening up process' (Sharpe, 2001, p. 123). The project was evaluated by a research team from the University of Stirling. It looked at pupil attainment, mainly in a comparative study with pupils who had not been involved in the pilot, and the findings were mostly positive, although some concerns were identified such as different attitudes to writing and the inability of some pupils to manipulate language. The Scottish Office decided to extend the programme gradually to every primary school in Scotland: 'building on these foundations [i.e. the National and Regional Pilots], we now propose that all Scottish Primary Schools should offer teaching in a modern European language: French, German, Spanish or Italian' (Scottish Office Press Release, 1993).

A phased programme of training was rolled out across Scotland in November 1993. The Inspectorate explained the change from secondary specialist to the primary teacher was because of new ideas coming out of the pilot about the truly distinctive nature of the early start and therefore it was felt that primary class teachers were best placed to deliver modern languages in primary schools. Participating primary teachers were given a programme of training over a period of twenty-seven days, usually on a once-a-week basis. Clusters of schools entered training at the same time such that one teacher from each primary school in the cluster underwent the training during the same school session. Languages provision in the first year of secondary was considered, and where diversification was in existence then some teachers from some of the primary schools in the cluster would be trained in one language, and others in the other language.

By the year 2000, a total of 5,200 teachers had been trained across Scotland and thus almost all pupils in Scotland, at these stages, were being taught a foreign language.

THE EVALUATION AND EMERGING ISSUES

During the period 1996–8, Her Majesty's Inspectorate monitored the implementation of MLPS in forty-two schools nationally, and in 1999 published a report entitled *Standards and Quality in Primary and Secondary Schools 1994–1998: Modern Languages*. It identified the key strengths of the project as the 'enthusiasm and motivation of almost all pupils; high attainment by some very able pupils; examples of good or very good teaching in 85% of schools; and very good organisation of resources and classroom display' (Scottish Office Education and Industry Department, 1999). However, it also identified some perceived weaknesses in implementation, in pedagogy and in teacher education and, in order to address these, recommended that:

> the study of a modern language is included in the curriculum of all pupils in P6 and P7; time allocated to foreign languages is broadly consistent within and across schools; courses include elements of reading and writing; appropriate links are made with other curricular areas, particularly English language, and with the local secondary school; teachers record pupils' attainment; and appropriate time and support is provided for staff teaching languages to maintain their skills, prepare work and consult with other teachers. (Scottish Office Education and Industry Department, 1999)

The then Minister for Education set up a national group entitled the Action Group on Languages (AGL) to consider languages at both primary and secondary levels. In respect of MLPS, the AGL made a number of recommendations including an 'entitlement' to learn a language with students taking one and the same modern language at P6 and P7 for 75 minutes per week, amounting to approximately 100 hours at primary school. The 5–14 Guidelines (the curriculum framework that preceded CfE in Scotland) were also revised to take account of the primary experience. These set out what was expected in the four skill areas of listening, speaking, reading and writing. Some primary teachers complained about the 'goalposts being moved'. The pilot had been largely based on listening and speaking with an emphasis on games and language enjoyment. Some argued that it was becoming too serious and another part of the busy curriculum to be assessed.

The AGL also highlighted another issue which had been around since the generalisation of the project, the supply of primary language teachers through the pre-service route. In spite of Ministerial statements about the need for pre-service preparation, teacher education institutions (TEIs) had not moved to make a language a core part of the BEd degree. For a variety of reasons – promotions, illness, retirement and so on – some gaps appeared in the MLPS teaching force, and provision of language teaching was reduced in some schools. The recent review of teacher education in Scotland (Donaldson, 2011) recommended a new degree to replace the BEd and it might be the case that this increases the number of primary teachers with linguistic competence. Nevertheless, the problem of which language to study remains. Many future teachers at undergraduate level may understandably opt for the popular Spanish, only to find themselves in a school where French is taught.

Diversification emerged as an issue as the MLPS project evolved, since in some cases there was a mismatch of languages contrary to the Giovanazzi vision, and the recommendation of the AGL regarding one and the same language. In one large city authority, teachers were trained in one language. However, declining rolls meant that schools were closed and catchment areas redrawn. The consequence was that children were then going to a secondary school that did not offer the language taught in primary. In another authority, a new secondary headteacher decided to end diversified provision in S1 whereby pupils did one of two languages, French or Italian. Some primaries in the cluster had volunteered to train in Italian but were now required to retrain in French. In a third case, a school had an RAF base within its catchment area with children whose parents came from another base in England, having been taught either a different language or no language in primary school. In a fourth authority, some teachers were reluctant to train in German as it was only taught in one secondary and therefore French might be more attractive in the promotion stakes. Teachers move around, and of course, so do pupils.

Tierney (2009) found that in some cases there was again the problem of mismatch of languages between primary and secondary. Transition arrangements were not always good and in some cases the secondary knew little about the primary experience and adopted a fresh start approach. Thus pupils may have covered a significant amount of content in one language, only to find their secondary teacher going over the same ground. Tierney (2009) also found that pupils were mostly positive about their primary language experience but in terms of implementation there were gaps in provision in some schools or there was uneven provision in clusters. In 2010, the problem was again highlighted by Her Majesty's Inspectorate of Education (HMIE) at the Scottish Centre for Language Teaching's National Conference at which Dr Bill Maxwell, Senior Chief Inspector, revealed that HMIE were still finding schools where MLPS was not being offered.

CURRICULUM FOR EXCELLENCE

Curriculum for Excellence (CfE), probably in response to the difficulties of transition, proposed a shift away from a content-driven approach to MLPS. The fact that there is less prescription in terms of what to teach has been generally welcomed by primary teachers. There is a greater emphasis than before on how language works and on language skills. Pupils explore the sounds of language through songs and rhymes. They develop language strategies such as using gesture and eye contact. Under the strand entitled 'Knowledge about Language' there is a move away from the one-language approach in Modern Languages: experiences and outcomes as 'the pupils explore comparisons and connections between sound patterns in different languages' (Learning and Teaching Scotland, 2009, p. 4). Links with literacy are made much more explicit. There is also more emphasis on social, cultural and geographical aspects of the countries under study. The greater emphasis on the intercultural elements has allowed primary teachers to include festivals, customs, history and geography in their topic plans. Other primary teachers, who may have no foreign language, are also able to introduce cultural aspects through English. MLPS has become more of a language awareness programme, albeit maybe through the learning of one language, rather than the development of linguistic competence over a longer period. The advantage of this shift is, of course, that these skills are transferable even if a pupil changes language at S1. Crichton and Templeton (2010, p. 142) highlight how the focus is on depth rather than breadth and how this 'contrasts with the "scattergun" approach used by some in the primary sector, whose aim at present appears to be to cover a wide assortment of topic vocabulary with little regard for the underpinnings of the language'. This is a welcome move away from a 'noun pumping' approach and the pressure to cover what were previously traditional S1 or even S2 topics. CfE could have gone further and advocated partial competence in two languages, French with one of the other languages, German, Italian or Spanish. That would probably have addressed the continuity issue in most clusters as well as using those two languages as a means to develop generic language skills and awareness. Nevertheless, CfE represents a pragmatic response to one of the issues that has emerged, namely transition to secondary. Unfortunately, in practice, that still remains a major problem, as it has been historically. Some schools have gone for continuity in one language, others have gone for a dual-language experience and others have gone for a carousel model where children experience different languages over, for example, eight-week blocks. An additional issue, which is still evident, is that whereas some clusters have good joint planning, that is not universal and it is reported that in other clusters there are no meetings. The obvious consequence is the fresh start approach which has undermined linguistic progression for so long, although one might argue that other subjects have also suffered this approach.

In 2012, another national working group, the Languages Working Group, issued their report into the future of languages, 'Language Learning in Scotland: A 1 + 2 Approach'. In spite of the evidence that MLPS were not yet properly established with the P6 and P7 model, it advocated a start at P1 and two languages in primary school. In doing so it claimed that 'There is a considerable body of evidence which indicates that young children learn languages more easily than older learners' (p. 12). The research evidence is split on this and there is no consensus on whether younger is better.

The Languages Working Group also decided not to set up a 'hierarchy of languages' and although the main European languages are seen as important it also mentions Chinese, Portuguese, Arabic, Russian, Gaelic, Polish, Punjabi and Urdu. It leaves it to local authorities and schools to determine which additional languages to offer. The report recognises the problems of transition to date. However, it refers to clear progression from P1 through to S1, particularly in the second language. If which language is left to schools or even local authorities there remains the obvious problem of coherent continuity within clusters and across authority borders. It will require better planning than what has happened to date and pupils moving schools may face problems. The report also notes another key issue, the longstanding problem of teacher supply. It remains to be seen whether the Donaldson review

(2011) and new primary education programmes will address this well enough to meet the ambitious recommendations of the latest national report.

Historically, primary languages in an English-speaking country have not proved easy to implement. Many fine words and reports have been written. A lot of hard work and significant funding have been invested in recent initiatives. However, sufficient account may not have been taken of the research evidence and there is a grave danger of the mistakes of the past being repeated.

REFERENCES

Burstall, C., M. Jamieson, S. Cohen and M. Hargreaves (1974) *Primary French in the Balance.* Windsor: National Foundation for Educational Research in England and Wales.

Crichton, H. and B. Templeton (2010) 'Curriculum for Excellence: The way forward for primary languages in Scotland?', *The Language Learning Journal* 38 (2): 139–47.

Council of Europe (2007) *Common European Framework of Reference for Languages.* Cambridge: Cambridge University Press.

Donaldson, G. (2011) *Teaching Scotland's Future: Report of a Review of Teacher Education in Scotland.* Edinburgh: Scottish Government.

Learning and Teaching Scotland (2009) *A Curriculum for Excellence: Modern Languages.* Glasgow: Learning and Teaching Scotland.

Scottish Education Department (1989) *Circular 1178.* Edinburgh: SED.

Scottish Office Education and Industry Department (1999) *Standards and Quality. Primary and Secondary Schools 1994–98 In Modern Languages.* Edinburgh: Her Majesty's Stationery Office.

Sharpe, K. (2001) *Modern Foreign Languages in the Primary School.* London: Kogan Page.

Tierney, D. (2009) 'The pedagogy and implementation of modern languages in the primary school: Pupil attitudes and teachers' views'. Unpublished PhD thesis, University of Strathclyde.

45

Sciences, Social Studies and Technologies

Frances Simpson

'Environmental Studies' was an umbrella term used in the previous 5–14 Curriculum to group subject areas defined as those in which pupils 'learn about the world' – science, social subjects (History, Geography and Modern Studies) and technology. Whilst appearing in Curriculum for Excellence (CfE) as separate curricular areas they are grouped together in this chapter for historical and practical reasons.

CURRICULUM OVERVIEW

In CfE experiences and outcomes (LTS, 2009) sciences, social subjects and technologies are broken down into sections, and whilst initially appearing very different, they retain significant commonality in pedagogy and approach. Science no longer reflects the traditional Physics/Biology/Chemistry divisions but is arranged under five 'organisers' – Planet Earth; Forces, Electricity and Waves; Biological Systems; Materials; and Topical Science. Here an attempt has been made to incorporate biodiversity and sustainability with traditional science, and to link the areas of study to real-life situations. The changes are perhaps intended to reflect a more modern, popularised approach to science. The mix of scientific concepts, such as those represented by 'Planet Earth' and 'Materials' in particular, help to provide a more integrated view that is well suited to the primary arena where cross-curricular work has traditionally been valued and is now regarded as an essential feature of CfE. 'Topical Science' encourages teachers to pursue areas of current interest that may arise and to look at the history of science, an over-arching aim being to build scientific literacy from an early age.

'Social Studies' underpinned most cross-curricular topics of the pre 5–14 era. They sustain this role again in CfE and provide the basis for some excellent examples of integrated learning, but with the intention now of focusing on depth rather than breadth of coverage. The traditional divisions have been maintained: History, Geography and Modern Studies. 'People, Past Events and Societies' looks at Scottish history, exploring evidence, places and artefacts. 'People, Place and Environment' encourages exploration of the Scottish landscape, particularly the local area, including aspects such as food origins, weather and travel to help children to develop a sense of Scotland as a place to live, play and work. In the upper primary pupils are encouraged to compare Scotland with other places in the world. Finally, 'People, Society, Economy and Business' brings current issues into focus with aspects such as fair trade, community activities, discrimination, setting up in business, democracy, and rights and responsibilities, thereby providing a strong citizenship agenda.

'Technologies' reflects the current Scottish Government policy agenda (see, for example, Technologies Strategy Board Press Release, 2012), referring to a strong tradition of excellence and innovation in technological research and working to sustain the contribution of technology to economic prosperity. The 'purposes of learning' in this subject intend strong grounding in the real world and include aspects of global citizenship. The modern terminology – ' ethical decisions', 'informed producers and consumers' – is perhaps seeking to strike a chord with a future workforce from an early age and to appeal to the 'business' lobby. Children will be encouraged to explore how we use technology in everyday life and develop practical skills, undertaking activities based around a small business model. The inclusion of 'food and textiles', again tapping into popular culture, reflects the increasing media focus on fashion and cookery.

A recent push for children to learn not only how to become effective users of information and communications technology (ICT) but also to develop basic programming skills and begin to understand how ICT works is reflected in the final sections of this subject. Whilst 'Computing Science' addresses deeper theoretical and practical understanding of the development and application of hardware and software, 'ICT to enhance learning' provides a clear outline for developing the use of ICT throughout the curriculum, encouraging basic computer literacy. In many primary schools the paucity of good ICT equipment and effective networks still makes these areas difficult to address although recent developments such as the 'Raspberry' – an inexpensive gadget that provides programming facilities through a normal PC may open the door here.

PEDAGOGY

Encouraged by CfE, pedagogy in these subjects has moved away from traditional 'chalk and talk' approaches towards greater engagement with practical activities in the class and providing a degree of self-determination by pupils. These three areas all lend themselves to lively and interesting lesson structures and interdisciplinary study, and in the last few years dramatic changes have taken place in many schools as they have moved towards active learning strategies, with learning recorded on posters, mind-maps, models, wall displays and through ICT. 'Exploration' – an umbrella term for a range of activities including observation, questioning, discussion, research, experimentation, investigation, and trial and error – is used throughout CfE for these three subjects. Pupils are encouraged to identify questions and then seek answers. The investigative approach is promoted in science, mirroring that of traditional scientific work. This works well at primary level when teachers thoroughly understand the subject and are able to assist in solving some of the inherent problems of experimentation, such as designing and resourcing equipment.

A central principle of CfE is integrated learning which, as we learn more about how our brains work, seems a more effective way to present information, promote understanding, and develop skills and emotional engagement (Barnes, 2007 pp. 72–99). Strengthening links between subjects helps the learning to become deeper and firmly established. These subjects lend themselves easily to cross-curricular work, the inclusion of values education, citizenship and development of the four capacities. Care needs to be taken, however, that core subjects are not subverted to become dominated by language and expressive arts, as often happened in the topic studies of the pre 5–14 era. The task of the teacher is to select appropriate areas of study that have genuine links and to keep such an exploration manageable and effective in developing the required skills and knowledge. If, as is suggested by

CfE, the pupils are to have a decision-making role in directing the study, care must be taken to ensure effective progression and depth. Some schools are trying out pupil-led topic studies but find planning and assessment problematic. Approaches such as Storyline (Bell, Harkness and White, 2007 and see Chapter 6 here) can be used to assist in this process and help to ensure that essential skills, knowledge and understanding are taught, but within a flexible framework that also allows creative exploration of the topic.

These areas of study have always featured children working in small groups, mostly of mixed ability, with limited individual opportunities. 'Critical Skills', 'Cooperative Learning' and other current popular training programmes have all helped to encourage much more effective group work and enable children working in pairs, trios and larger groups to reach stated goals. Research has shown structured group work to be an effective means of enhancing learning (Howe et al., 2007). However, whilst this works well for most children, opportunities for challenging more able children must be actively sought or they may simply spend their time supporting less able peers and acting as teacher/mentor without moving their own learning forward.

The use of ICT has allowed increasingly sophisticated presentation of resources. Access to websites such as SCRAN, museums, art galleries and historical sites provide classroom experiences that could not be imagined twenty years ago. In keeping with the everyday experience and expectations of children, study in these areas can easily be made colourful, interesting and exciting and can become interactive through the use of such things as interactive whiteboards and personal response units. Extensive resources are available for all these subjects and perhaps the biggest problem is that of deciding which to use. However, teachers must also be aware of potential drawbacks such as information overload, political/ideological bias, age appropriateness, misinformation and distractions. Primary teachers continue to find and use real artefacts, objects and equipment to provide hands-on experiences that engage and motivate children to learn.

Outdoor learning is an important feature of science, social studies and technologies. Some of the richest lessons in these areas can come from outdoor exploration, and increasingly schools are developing their grounds to incorporate areas for gardening, pond-life, woodland and other habitats as well as for reflection and other learning activities. The recent strengthening of links between schools and science centres, outdoor education centres, museums and castles encourages visits away from the school campus, although the cost, management and risk assessment of such trips can present hurdles that deter some teachers.

ASSESSMENT

Assessment was highlighted in Her Majesty's Inspectorate of Education (HMIE) reports on social subjects (HMIE 2008a, p. 4) and on science (2008b, p. 25) as an area where improvement was needed. Issues identified included the lack of assessment that challenged pupils and involved them in review of their own learning; tracking and monitoring achievement consistently and using this to inform planning; a need for improved feedback to pupils; and finding out what children know before starting a new topic of work. Observation in a number of schools, and of the GLOW education website, would seem to indicate that most schools are tackling these issues, and examples of good practice are now starting to fill the NAR (National Assessment Resource), but many remain unsure of the way forward.

With the propensity for group work in these subjects, it can be difficult to assess individual achievement in any particular task. Although children are likely to be engaged in self- /peer assessment and are becoming much more adept at recognising whether or not they have achieved the intended learning, this can be influenced by peer pressure, honesty and pupil confidence. Identifying if all children are participating and learning in group situations can be difficult for a teacher. Current common practice for pupils to research (usually online) an aspect of their choice within a broader topic area, can lead to a free flow of information that can be correct, incorrect, age-inappropriate or difficult to interpret. Assessment of this work relies on teacher knowledge and expertise in the subject. If pupils have explored aspects with which the teacher is unfamiliar, misinformation and misunderstanding can be reinforced and shared with other pupils.

Sciences, social studies and technologies have not traditionally been subject to formal summative assessment in primary schools, with the exception of science which appears in the Trends in International Maths and Science Survey (TIMSS) (Scottish Government, 2009) and some PISA assessments. Teachers remain unsure of government and local authority expectations for summative assessment in these subject areas, and the focus, for the time being, remains primarily on literacy and numeracy.

DISCUSSION

Changes occurring in these three subjects have probably been brought about more by developments in pedagogy rather than curriculum content. Whilst CfE content may appear to have been thinned down, the lack of detail in the outcomes for these three subjects masks the fact that CfE is as crowded as its predecessor. Many schools are engaged in a process of breaking down the outcomes into a series of 'I can . . .' statements that resemble the 5–14 targets, which casts doubt on the value of reforming the curriculum in this way. Whilst teachers feel released from some of the strictures of 5–14, in many ways things have changed little and there are still problems of teacher confidence and competence, especially with regard to some aspects of Technologies and Science. The Science and Engineering Education Advisory Group Report (SEEAG 2012, p. 14) states that 'The limited knowledge and understanding in mathematics and science of primary teachers and the resulting lack of confidence are identified from data in the TIMSS 2007 report as a major cause for concern'.

The long-term lack of progress in improving teacher confidence and competence in these subjects may stem back to teacher education. Following the integration of initial teacher education (ITE) into universities, there has arguably been a steady move away from courses that have a strong, practical, subject-studies basis towards a more academic, theoretical approach. However, in the Donaldson Report into teacher education (Donaldson, 2010), subject knowledge was identified by qualified teachers as being the third most useful aspect of their ITE course, and in discussions 'many teachers felt that they needed a greater focus on subject knowledge' (p. 35). Donaldson acknowledged the difficulties for student primary teachers to develop subject knowledge and expertise and suggests that before commencing training, prospective students 'could reasonably be expected to develop and deepen their curriculum knowledge' (p. 37). This approach could bring significant changes if appropriate materials can be provided for online study and prospective students be persuaded to engage with them.

Many teachers – newly qualified to very experienced – at times learn just enough to stay one step ahead of pupils, particularly in social subjects, technology and science. This can be effective (though not desirable) – for example, learning about events in history, but for other aspects of the curriculum such as certain scientific concepts, geographical skills, technological processes, it can lead to misunderstanding and misinformation. Many concepts in science, in particular, are difficult to interpret without the support of a knowledgeable tutor/mentor and misconceptions are very common amongst primary and even some secondary teachers.

The Donaldson Report suggested that teacher education should be seen as a continuum from the pre-service stage throughout a teaching career. Taken as this wider view, there should be the opportunity for teachers to develop subject knowledge and expertise within the first few years of teaching but this requires subject expertise that already exists within the education system to be used effectively in support. Models of continuing professional development have changed rapidly in the last few years away from the one-off courses and events towards collegiate local meetings. Whilst this approach can work well for a number of areas, such as language and generic professional aspects, for social subjects, science and technology there may not always be appropriate expertise available and not all 'experts' in these subjects are good at interpreting the specific needs of teachers in the primary sector. The proposed reformation of four-year teacher education courses may well bring such expertise into the arena, as courses will include concurrent significant academic study outwith education alongside rigorous professional development for teaching. This may boost the number of primary teachers entering the profession with expertise in this group of subjects.

We are early in the process of substantial change in these areas and it will be some time before the difficulties can be overcome and the success of innovation measured. Despite serious concerns about science in particular, one cannot help but be optimistic that education in social studies, science and technology will be considerably improved in years to come.

REFERENCES

Barnes, J. (2007) *Cross-curricular Learning 3–14*. London: Paul Chapman Publishing.

Bell, S., S. Harkness and G. White (2007) *Storyline Past, Present and Future*. Glasgow: University of Strathclyde Continuing Education Centre.

Donaldson, G. (2010) *Teaching Scotland's Future: Report of a Review of Teacher Education in Scotland*. Edinburgh: Scottish Government Publications. Online at www.scotland.gov.uk/Publications/2011/01/13092132/0

Her Majesty's Inspectorate of Education (2008a) *Developing the Four Capacities through Social Subjects: Focusing on Successful Learners in Primary Schools*. Livingston: HMIE. Online at www.educationscotland.gov.uk/inspectionandreview/Images/dssps_tcm4-712875.pdf

Her Majesty's Inspectorate of Education (2008b) *Science – A Portrait of Current Practice in Scottish Schools*. Livingston: HMIE. Online at www.educationscotland.gov.uk/inspectionandreview/Images/HMIeScienceReport_tcm4-712879.pdf

Howe, C., A. Tolmie, A. Thurston, K. Topping, D. Christie, K. Livingstone, E. Jessiman and C. Donaldson (2007) 'Group work in elementary science: Towards organisational principles for supporting pupil learning', *Learning and Instruction*, 17 (5): 549–63.

Learning and Teaching Scotland (2009) *Curriculum for Excellence – Experiences and Outcomes*. Online at www.educationscotland.gov.uk/Images/all_experiences_outcomes_tcm4-539562.pdf

Scottish Government (2009) *Trends in International Maths and Science Survey (TIMSS) 2007 – Highlights From Scotland's Results*. Edinburgh: Scottish Government Publications. Online at www.scotland.gov.uk/Publications/2009/10/13150724/1

Science and Engineering Education Advisory Group (2012) *Supporting Scotland's STEM Education and Culture – Science and Engineering Education Advisory Group – Second Report*. Online at www. scotland.gov.uk/Publications/2012/02/4589

Technology Strategy Board (2012) '£20 million Government investment will stimulate growth-creating technology innovation'. Scottish Government press release (31 May 2012). Online at www.innovateuk.org/content/competition-announcements/20-million-government-investment -will-stimulate-gr.ashx

46

Expressive Arts Education

Marie-Jeanne McNaughton

Expressive Arts addresses the basic human need for self-expression and creativity. This has been increasingly recognised in Scotland in recent cultural and educational initiatives. Curriculum for Excellence (CfE) describes Expressive Arts within the Scottish curriculum as encompassing the areas of art, drama, music and dance. These play a significant part in the education of all primary school pupils and they fulfil a vital function in the development of young learners. The high level of active engagement and enjoyment experienced during good primary school Expressive Arts experiences facilitates learning within and beyond the curriculum (Wilson et al., 2008).

Across the arts areas, primary school pupils are offered a very wide and varied range of experiences, enabling them to communicate in a number of ways, for example orally, visually, kinaesthetically and through music. The collaborative nature of many arts activities enables learners to develop social skills though working cooperatively with others, often in creative, problem-solving situations. The arts can also offer primary school pupils many opportunities to be proactive and enterprising within meaningful and relevant contexts. In addition, they are viewed as being a way of allowing children to achieve success and of offering opportunities for teachers to teach in ways that are not always assessment-driven.

PRINCIPLES OF LEARNING IN EXPRESSIVE ARTS

There are two different but complementary aspects of Expressive Arts education (Deasy, 2002). On the one hand, there is learning *in* the arts, where it is proposed that subject-specific knowledge and concepts, skills, techniques and processes may be acquired progressively and systematically, leading to varying degrees of proficiency within each subject area. On the other hand there is learning *through* the arts. Here, the arts may be viewed as a way to enhance learning by reinforcing skills, allowing practical application and making cross-curricular links, and to enable learning by engaging children's imagination, encouraging creative responses and deepening understandings across traditional subject areas.

Learning in the Arts

The Scottish model of learning *in* the arts suggests that specific curricula should be designed to help learners to form ideas systematically, to work through and realise these ideas and to respond critically to their own work and that of others. However, there is a lack of research evidence that establishes, conclusively, the most beneficial ways of developing and delivering a systematic, progression-based arts curriculum in primary schools. This is indicative, perhaps, of the complex nature of the expressive arts. The many overlapping skills and concepts, together with the emotional/affective dimensions and the elusive nature of 'talent', do not match themselves to a rigidly objectives-based, cognition and skills model of progression. Nonetheless, CfE offers a three-level framework that encompasses learning in primary school Expressive Arts, outlining broad developmental stages in exploring, creating and presenting across the four arts areas.

Learning through the Arts

It is widely held that participation in the Expressive Arts can help primary school children to achieve education goals: literacy and numeracy skills can be enhanced through the arts; creativity is naturally developed through the arts; understanding of one's self and others expands with arts education. Harland et al. (2005) found that engagement in the arts can boost general academic performance, increasing knowledge and skills both within particular art forms and across subjects. They also found that creativity, imagination and thinking skills, communication skills, and personal and social development were enhanced, and there was evidence of an increase in the quality of the artistic responses. Both pupils and teachers reported a heightened sense of enjoyment, excitement and fulfilment while engaging in arts-based activities.

Flexible programmes of Expressive Arts, then, are important in balancing and rounding learning and for allowing for affective as well as cognitive responses. They provide children with opportunities to 'look round the back of things'; to explore why things happen; to look at what it feels like to be in situations outside their own physical and temporal reality; and to make real, meaningful responses to a range of questions, issues and experiences. This fits with the principles of CfE, which advocates more meaningful and 'joined-up' learning for all pupils.

EXPRESSIVE ARTS EDUCATION: THE SCOTTISH PRIMARY CURRICULUM

Two key studies, the first a literature review (McNaughton et al., 2005) and the second a review of practice (Wilson et al., 2005; 2008), commissioned by the Scottish Government, examined the provision for arts education across all sectors of Scottish education. The findings from these informed the development of Expressive Arts in CfE.

The consultation document, *Building the Curriculum 1: The Contribution of Curricular Areas* (2006), recognised the power of Expressive Arts to help learners to develop the four capacities of CfE. Specifically, in terms of primary education, it recognised that Expressive Arts can develop successful learners by helping children to express themselves, think innovatively, meet challenges positively and find imaginative solutions to problems. It can develop confident individuals by encouraging children to become more confident as they draw on their own ideas, experiences and feelings and express these through, for example, improvisation, sounds and images. Children can derive personal satisfaction from experiencing and taking part in the arts, and their self-discipline can be enhanced. The arts can encourage responsible citizenship by enabling young learners to explore and express their responses to personal and social issues, helping them to question and develop stances and views. Children can explore the importance of cultures, the arts and heritage in Scotland and in other societies, thus extending their valuing of cultural identities, which helps them to recognise the importance of the arts to the identities of nations. And, finally, the arts can help to develop effective contributors by offering powerful opportunities for learners to develop their creativity, work cooperatively and communicate with others, and show initiative, dependability, leadership and enterprise. Participation in the arts – individually, in groups or in communities – can also greatly enhance the quality of life in families, the school and the community.

In *Building the Curriculum 1*, teachers are encouraged to plan innovative and motivating arts experiences for their pupils and to provide opportunities that allow them to work in creative ways. There is an emphasis on enjoyment and the development of personal expression. It recommends that schools work in partnerships with artists and with the local communities and cultural organisations to 'enliven and enrich young people's learning and experience' (p. 7).

Building the Curriculum 3: A Framework for Teaching and Learning (2008) states that it is the responsibility of schools to bring the experiences and outcomes together and to plan programmes for learning. Teachers and curriculum planners are charged with ensuring that their Expressive Arts programmes adhere to and demonstrate the 'principles for curriculum design' (p. 32): challenge and enjoyment; breadth; progression; depth; personalisation and choice; coherence; relevance. At primary level, the arts should encompass a broad range of contexts to develop children's thinking and their personal, social and emotional growth. Children should be supported to become increasingly independent and should be offered many opportunities to work together cooperatively. Teachers should limit the use of low-level, repetitive tasks and, instead, should aim for higher-order tasks that demand individual and collaborative problem solving, creative responses and the application of specific arts-based knowledge and skills. To ensure depth, teachers should not move quickly from one area to the next but should spend time helping the children to see patterns and to make connections between aspects of learning: connecting their own experiences of the world with their own interests or future needs. It is important, too, that progression is built into the arts curriculum and that the children are able to evaluate the development of their knowledge and skills. Although there is little emphasis on summative assessment, teachers are required to be mindful of the quality of the children's responses.

The *Expressive Arts* experiences and outcomes (2011) document lists one common Expressive Arts outcome, 'Participation in Performances and Presentations', covering early level to level 2: 'I have experienced the energy and excitement of presenting/performing for audiences and being part of an audience for other people's presentations/performances' (EXA 0-01a / EXA 1-01a / EXA 2-01a, p. 2).

Within the four arts areas, Art comprises six sets of experiences and outcomes while the other three areas each comprise four sets. In all four areas there is an emphasis on the development of specific subject-related knowledge, skills and techniques. However, across the four areas, there is a common focus on the sharing and presentation of one's own work and an appreciation of the work of others, both one's peers and professional artists. Another common thread emphasises the expressing and communicating of ideas, thoughts and feelings through creative activities.

A cautionary note might be sounded in relation to the above-quoted statement relating to performance and presentation. This might be interpreted as placing emphasis on the 'end product' rather than the experience of the learning processes involved. In reality, many arts lessons for primary pupils will not have an explicit end product in terms of a painting, a play, a musical composition or a dance performance. For example, children may be engaged with the teacher in a 'living through' drama, where the engagement in and evaluation of the drama is both the process and the product, or they may take part in expressive or exploratory music, art or movement where the activity is an end in itself.

In 2012, as part of the research for this chapter, an extensive internet search of Scottish primary school websites revealed that almost all schools now include Expressive Arts within their curriculum statements. A common theme is the ability of the arts to develop artistic skills and to inspire creative responses across the curriculum. The change of focus in CfE, moving away from balancing aspects of the curriculum in terms of percentages of subject time towards a more meaningful integrated approach, appears to benefit the arts in primary schools. The increased emphasis on learning *through* the expressive arts offers opportunities for more holistic pedagogical approaches. Primary schools appear to recognise that pupils should be helped to experience, explore and experiment while further developing knowledge and specific skills to encourage their progress in the arts and to develop their powers of observation, personal response, critical analysis, evaluation and communication. However, Wilson et al. (2008) reported that many primary teachers did not feel equipped to plan and teach aspects of the arts. Core modules in Expressive Arts are offered on all Scottish initial teacher education courses. On the other hand, an internet search of continuing professional development (CPD) provision revealed limited ongoing specialist help and CPD opportunities to enable teachers to capitalise on the potential for the expressive arts. Perhaps this is the result of the current climate of financial austerity. The Education Scotland website offers pages with support materials and examples of practice. At the time of writing, these were fairly sparsely populated in terms of Expressive Arts exemplars of good practice in arts education in primary schools.

A particular challenge for the integration of Expressive Arts has occurred in primary schools because of the need to facilitate class teacher non-contact time (two and a half hours per week). This is often met by timetabling arts lessons to be taught by visiting or designated arts teachers. However, close collaboration between the class teacher and the arts teacher to ensure that arts lessons fit with ongoing cross-curricular themes can facilitate both learning in and learning through the arts.

THE ARTS, CULTURE AND CREATIVITY IN SCOTLAND

In 2010, the Scottish Government published *Education and the Arts, Culture and Creativity: An Action Plan*, directed at 'developing the role and impact of creativity within and across the curriculum' (p. 2). The report recognised the central role of arts education in helping to meet the aspirations of the National Performance Framework (www.scotland. gov.uk/Publications/2007/11/13092240/9) in which five strategic objectives are set out for Scotland to become 'wealthier and fairer, smarter, healthier, safer and stronger [and] greener'. Creative Scotland and Education Scotland are charged with developing four specific 'workstreams' to:

- develop a vision for, and understanding of, the importance of developing creative skills in children and young people, and their parents, and the application of creative learning and teaching;

- build capacity, skills and expertise of learning providers and creative professionals to support creative learning and teaching;
- share information and good practice, including applications of creative teaching;
- develop a strategic approach to pathways for the enthusiastic and talented across lifelong learning and into positive and sustained destinations beyond school.

Although these directives will have an impact on Expressive Arts education across the sectors, there are very specific implications for the arts in the primary curriculum: that schools should strive to ensure that Expressive Arts continues to hold a prominent place within the primary curriculum; that teachers' capacities and competence of teaching the arts should be a focus for CPD; and that schools should seek opportunities to develop meaningful and relevant links with a wide range of professional arts organisations and individuals.

In response to the Action Plan, an Expressive Arts Excellence Group was set up, comprising representatives from the Scottish Qualifications Authority, Her Majesty's Inspectorate of Education, expressive arts teachers and practitioners from national arts companies, arts institutions and local organisations. The group undertook a wide review of current arts provision and compiled a set of recommendations for future development of arts education. Its two aims were to find 'ways in which the school experience gave pupils skills development in the expressive arts alongside gaining knowledge', and to 'embed the use of the expressive arts as pathway to creative teaching across the curriculum' (p. 2). This group presented its recommendations in November 2011, a key one of which was that primary schools should develop more and better links with excellent creative partners such as Scottish Opera. While the value of partnerships is not in dispute, there are obviously financial implications for schools that have not been considered in the report.

To summarise, the outlook for the development of Expressive Arts in the primary curriculum looks positive. The Education and the Arts, Culture and Creativity action plan has moved the arts further up the educational agenda and CfE seems to be particularly conducive to the idea of the arts being central to balanced, progressive learning. Opportunities exist, but arts educational programmes that would fit with both local and national needs are still in the early stages of development. A start has been made within the plan on a Scotland-wide audit of good practice but what is also needed is more up-to-date research on the place and provision of Expressive Arts in Scottish schools. This would ensure that decisions about what constitutes good practice are sound and evidence-based.

REFERENCES

Deasy, R. (ed.) (2002) *Learning in the Arts and Student Academic and Social Development*. Washington, DC: Arts Education Partnership.

Education Scotland (2011) *A Curriculum for Excellence: Expressive Arts*. Online at www.ltscotland.org.uk/learningteachingandassessment/curriculumareas/expressivearts/index.asp

Harland, J., P. Lord, A. Stott, K. Kinder, E. Lamont and M. Ashworth (2005) *The Arts-Education Interface: A Mutual Learning Triangle?* Slough: National Foundation for Educational Research.

McNaughton, M. J., L. Mitchell and W. Eaton (2005) *A Curriculum for Excellence Review of Research Literature: Expressive Arts*. Glasgow: University of Strathclyde.

Scottish Government (2010) *Education and the Arts, Culture and Creativity: An Action Plan*. Online at www.scotland.gov.uk/Resource/Doc/920/0104516.pdf

Scottish Government (2011) *Expressive Arts Excellence Group Report*. Online at www.scotland.gov.uk/Resource/Doc/91982/0114473.pdf

Wilson, G., R. McDonald, C. Byrne, S. Ewing and M. Sheridan (2005) *Delivering the Arts in Scottish Schools.* Edinburgh: Scottish Executive Education Department.

Wilson, G., R. McDonald, C. Byrne, S. Ewing and M. Sheridan (2008) 'Dread and passion: Primary and secondary teachers' views on teaching the arts', *Curriculum Journal*, 19 (1): 37–53.

47

Mathematics

Effie Maclellan

POLICY AND ITS INFLUENCES

The current policy for Mathematics is both laudable and ambitious. Good numeracy skills, competent use of both arithmetical and mathematical processes, a sophisticated knowledge of the value of mathematics and the ability to reason and solve problems through mathematics are considered central to a mathematically skilled and highly numerate population. Such policy, like that for all curricular areas, is directed by Scottish Government Ministers who take advice from a range of stakeholders. Implementation of policy is devolved to Education Scotland, the national body established by the Cabinet Secretary, Michael Russell, in 2011. Education Scotland inherits the full range of functions formerly undertaken by Her Majesty's Inspectorate of Education (HMIE) and Learning and Teaching Scotland (LTS). It is responsible for supporting quality and improvement in learning and teaching from early years to adulthood, and for supporting continuing professional development (CPD) at national level. The Scottish Qualifications Authority (SQA) is instrumentally involved in the implementation of national education policy through designing and developing new qualifications, providing national assessment resources and administering national assessments. Within broad policy, schools and local authorities make fine-grained decisions as to how the Mathematics curriculum is to be enacted, with the professional autonomy of teachers being considered important to the full implementation of Curriculum for Excellence. While mastery of an outcome-based curriculum is considered important, such mastery is to service the more fundamental ideal of enabling people to be mathematically literate.

EXPERIENCES AND OUTCOMES

Curriculum for Excellence characterises its national guidance within each curricular area as experiences and outcomes. For early/primary Mathematics this is Information Handling (data and analysis; and ideas of chance and uncertainty); Shape, Position and Movement (properties of 2D shapes and 3D objects; and angle, symmetry and transformation) and by far the largest section, Number, Money and Measurement which is essentially Numeracy, in its widest definition of the term. While Numeracy was once upon a time considered to be little more than the computation of basic arithmetic and, thereby, a mere preliminary to the 'serious' business of Mathematics, it is accorded a fundamental place in Curriculum for Excellence. Numeracy (as well as Literacy) is to be monitored annually and nationally through the Scottish Survey of Literacy and Numeracy (SSLN) and its development is now an explicit part of secondary education contributing to Mathematics courses at Access 3 and National 4 and 5 levels, as well as being available in distinct units for adult learners.

MATHEMATICAL PERFORMANCE AND ASSESSMENT

Mathematical performance in Scottish primary education can be seen through three different lenses. At the 'local' level of class and school, assessment is understood as an integral part of learning and teaching and is informed by the values of Curriculum for Excellence; the purposes and principles of assessment; evidence for optimum timing and methods of assessment; quality assurance to both improve attainment and practise equitable assessment; the need for effective communication of learner progress; and the embedding of all of these dimensions into self- and school improvement. 'Local' assessment is therefore multidimensional and delicately nuanced. The complexity of this framework presents very considerable challenges to the coordination of assessment resources and procedures (which involves the SQA), continuing staff development in assessment practices (which at policy level is the preserve of Education Scotland) and local authority recommendations to improve learners' competence given that, nationally, there has been no overall improvement in Numeracy in recent years.

A second lens through which performance can be seen is the SSLN, a national sample-based survey which replaces the Scottish Survey of Achievement (SSA) to monitor performance at P4, P7 and S2. The last SSA to focus on Mathematics and Numeracy was in 2008 in which the trend identified in previous surveys persisted: strong attainment in the early years – between 85 per cent and 90 per cent of pupils having 'well-established' skills (meaning they correctly answered 65 per cent or more of the items), deteriorating through primary school such that by S2 only 30 per cent and 45 per cent respectively had 'well-established' skills. Consistent with evidence worldwide, higher levels of socio-economic deprivation correlated with lower levels of attainment. Interestingly, teachers' judgements of pupils' mathematical achievements were consistently higher than the SSA results.

The first SSLN was one of Numeracy in 2011 with initial results now available. Trends identified in previous Scottish surveys still obtain, though the Data Tables merit more detailed consideration than space in this chapter allows. For example, one interesting observation is that at each level, participants were more accurate in addition than in subtraction. This is consistent with findings that children often do not see subtraction as the inverse of addition, as adults do. The complexity of understanding inversion is detailed in *Key Understandings in Mathematics Learning* (Nunes, Bryant and Watson, 2009), a set of findings that could be exploited usefully by Education Scotland in their discharge of CPD. Survey participants for SSLN are selected randomly by the Scottish Government's Education Analytical Services to generate a representative sample. As well as gathering performance data on pencil-and-paper tasks and on interactive/practical tasks, the SSLN used questionnaires to solicit pupils' attitudes to, and experiences of, Numeracy; and teachers' implementation of the Mathematics experiences and outcomes. This information is to provide snapshots of achievement in Numeracy at specific points in time, allow comparisons over time and provide evidence from which resources are to be developed by Education Scotland. However, it will be important that such information and resources are translated coherently into workable practices. The whole point of using assessment to inform learning is to 'short-circuit the randomness and inefficiency of trial-and-error learning' (Sadler, 1989).

Expectations that assessment informs actual progress (rather than merely highlighting the progress needed) require that learners understand the level, goal or standard to be achieved (in other words have an understanding that approximates with that of the teacher), can calibrate their own performance against what is required and actively work to 'close the gap'. At the moment there is little evidence for what learners actually *do* with knowledge of their own performance. This is a serious gap, because subscribing to a constructivist view of learning (the rationale for what Curriculum for Excellence refers to as 'active learning') means that learners themselves are a definitive source of their own feedback and as such need to regulate their own learning (see Chapter 6). Teachers therefore need to operationalise practices that dispose learners to take responsibility for their own learning rather than misleading learners (and others) into believing that learning is the teacher's exclusive responsibility. The intention to learn, the deliberate direction of thought, the control of effort and attention, and actions to solve problems are necessary elements of active learning. In the context of assessment, the lack of attention paid to learners' self-regulation is a matter of concern.

The third lens through which performance can be viewed is an international one. The Trends in International Mathematics and Science Study (TIMMS), conducted in 2007, assessed performance of pupils in their fourth and eighth years of schooling. For the primary-aged pupils half of the assessed content focused on 'Number', which required knowledge and understanding of place value, representation of number, number relationships, number sense and computational fluency in the four operations. Summary finding showed Scottish pupils performing below (the TIMMS) average. However, there were methodological problems in constructing the Scottish sample. Nevertheless below-average performance resonates with the downward trend identified in the Scottish surveys. The Organisation for Economic Cooperation and Development's Programme for International Student Assessment (PISA) also collects data from Scottish pupils but uses only 15-year-olds, which is outwith the scope of this chapter. But on a positive note, PISA findings state that 'Scotland performs at a consistently very high standard' and that 'few countries can be said with confidence to outperform it in mathematics' (OECD, 2007).

WHAT IT MEANS TO TEACH MATHEMATICS

No one particular style of teaching is espoused in Curriculum for Excellence. All approaches have merit so long as they engage/involve learners actively in their own learning. *Learning Together: Mathematics*, published by HMIE in 2010, characterises teaching as 'strong' when there is:

- consistent sharing and discussion of the importance of real-life applications and relevance of Mathematics and Numeracy;
- use of open and searching questions and building on learners' response (whether these are 'right' or 'wrong');
- setting high expectations of achievement;
- optimum use of peer interaction and investigative, active approaches;
- explicit reference to key mathematical concepts;
- good use of information and communications technology (ICT);
- planning which takes account of learner progress, interests and preferences;
- involvement of learners to reflect on what they have learned and what their 'next steps' might be.

This level of generality in the guidance offered may not be appreciated by all teachers but it is appropriate given the limits of the collective knowledge-base on effective teaching generally and on Mathematics in particular. Although significant aspects of teachers' practice are documented to demonstrate its effects on learners (motivation, collaborative learning, ICT), we are still far from providing evidence-based descriptions of effective Mathematics teaching. We are, however, beginning to realise that skill efficiency and conceptual understanding are features identified across a wide range of studies as being critically important in mathematical learning (Hiebert and Grouws, 2007). A major obstacle to the development of reliable guidance as to what makes effective Mathematics teaching has been the lack of robust theorisation of classroom teaching, although powerful work on the pedagogy of learning is now being developed (Marton, 2007).

WHAT IS PROBLEMATIC?

There is one very significant, and entrenched, issue to be addressed in the effective delivery of Numeracy in the primary school. HMIE reports that teachers acknowledge their lack of confidence in teaching ratio and algebraic processes. Successive Scottish surveys have repeatedly reported a dip in performance from the middle of primary school onwards; evidenced by lack of understanding of common and decimal fractions, of ratio and proportion, of percentages and of the relationships between these numerical representations. Lack of confidence may be caused by a range of factors but there is robust evidence that underscores that lack of *understanding* contributes to lack of confidence. Thus a direct way in which to improve confidence is to improve knowledge, as the research on expertise testifies. A baseline for the improvement of Numeracy knowledge lies in recognising that there is not a smooth and continuous path from early addition and subtraction to multiplication and division. Nor does knowledge of whole number give way, automatically, to knowledge of rational number. Being able to operate confidently with decimal and common fractions, percentages, ratio and proportion requires a reconceptualisation of number itself, and this will happen spontaneously only for a minority of learners (Hiebert and Behr, 1988). Explicit teaching to replace the lingering use of simple additive strategies with more powerful multiplicative ones is required (Nunes et al., 2009). It goes without saying that for learners to develop this qualitatively more sophisticated knowledge, they need teachers who have both sound subject-matter knowledge and sophisticated pedagogical content knowledge to generate a coherent sequence of topics of instruction (including the ordering of tasks and exercises). It is this knowledge that underpins the teacher's contingent action to allow a teaching agenda to digress or to prevent a particular learner from getting into unrecoverable difficulty (Rowland, Huckstep and Thwaites, 2005).

Improving teachers' knowledge for the teaching of Number includes not only instrumental understanding of procedural effectiveness but also the development of understanding such that decimal and common fractions, percentages, ratio and proportion are not isolated topics acquired in a linear fashion but are an interconnected web in which the meaning of any one of these components triggers connections with the others. This is what is meant by reconceptualising Number, and teaching to support this reconceptualisation is much more difficult than was once thought. There is evidence to suggest that one way in which such reconceptualisation by primary teachers might be effected is through the vicarious or actual experiences of working with learners to understand their mathematical thinking in parallel with extending content knowledge (Philipp et al., 2007). Although not recognised in Scotland, the research on cognitively guided instruction (Carpenter et al., 1989) exemplifies how teachers' practices change to effect improvement in pupil mathematical learning when teachers study research-based knowledge about learners' mathematical thinking. However, such professional development would require powerful and synergistic relationships between Education Scotland and University Teacher Educators (including research-active ones) to provide effective evidence-based learning opportunities for teachers and to contribute to the knowledge-base of what constitutes effective teaching in Mathematics. Further, such professional development has to take place over extended time (to allow teachers' own active involvement in their own learning, without which the introduction of new initiatives has transitory and superficial influence) and be fully supported at both policy and administrative levels to achieve fidelity in its implementation (to secure the improvements in pupil learning).

In conclusion, there is now recognition that Numeracy is both complex and critically important. Curriculum for Excellence in respect of Mathematics may well be the crucible in which Scotland can regain some standing as having a high-class educational system. For this to happen there needs to be collaboration between Education Scotland, teachers and education researchers on projects around how Scottish schools currently operationalise the teaching of multiplicative reasoning. Different projects could start by looking at one of the constituent topics only, in order to build up knowledge of how particular teachers manage any one topic and of how this compares with documented studies and trialling intervention activities that have been successful elsewhere in improving learner achievement. Dissemination of these findings could then inform further inquiry.

REFERENCES

Carpenter, T., E. Fennema, P. Peterson, C. Chiang and M. Loef (1989) 'Using knowledge of children's mathematics thinking in classroom teaching: An experimental study', *American Educational Research Journal*, 26 (4): 499–531.

Hiebert, J. and M. Behr (1988) 'Introduction: Capturing the major themes', in J. Hiebert and M. Behr (eds), *Number Concepts and Operations in the Middle Grades*. Reston, VA: Lawrence Erlbaum Associates and the National Council of Teachers of Mathematics, pp. 1–18.

Hiebert, J. and D. Grouws (2007) 'The effects of classroom mathematics teaching on students' learning', in F. Lester (ed.) *Second Handbook of Research on Mathematics Teaching and Learning*. Reston, VA: National Council of Teachers of Mathematics, pp. 371–404.

Marton, F. (2007) 'Towards a pedagogical theory of learning', *British Journal of Educational Psychology, Monograph Series*. II (4): 19–30.

Nunes, T., P. Bryant and A. Watson (eds) (2009) *Key Understandings in Mathematics Learning*. London: Nuffield Foundation.

Organisation for Economic Cooperation and Development (2007) *Reviews of National Policies for Education – Quality and Equity of Schooling in Scotland (Complete Executive Summary)*. See at www.oecd.org/document/18/0,3746,en_2649_39263231_39744402_1_1_1_1,00.html

Philipp, R., R. Ambrose, L. Lamb, J. Sowder, B. Schappelle, L. Sowder and J. Chauvot (2007) 'Effects of early field experiences on the mathematical content knowledge and beliefs of prospective elementary school teachers: an experimental study', *Journal for Research in Mathematics Education*, 38 (5): 438–76.

Rowland, T., P. Huckstep and A. Thwaites (2005) 'Elementary teachers' mathematics subject knowledge: The knowledge quartet and the case of Naomi', *Journal of Mathematics Teacher Education*, 8 (3): 255–81. DOI: 10.1007/s10857-005-0853-5.

Sadler, D. (1989) 'Formative assessment and the design of instructional systems', *Instructional Science*, 18 (2): 119–44.

48

Health and Wellbeing in Primary Education

Monica Porciani

CHILD HEALTH IMPROVEMENT

In 2010, the Scottish Government announced that 64 per cent of P1 pupils had no obvious signs of dental decay, thus meeting the 2010 target of 60 per cent. The fact that a major public health target had been not only met but surpassed was a huge achievement for the public health partnership approach, which had begun a decade earlier. More importantly, as good oral health is also an indication of good general health in children, and is closely associated with improved diet, this announcement confirmed that the drive to lay the foundations of good health from the early years onwards was starting to make some progress. Furthermore, the government announced that the Childsmile Nursery and School Programme (www. child-smile.org.uk/professionals/index.aspx) would be funded as a key priority throughout Scotland, providing a holistic approach to tackling dental health inequalities.

In its commitment to improving the health of the nation, and that of children in particular, one of the key objectives of the Scottish Government over the past two decades has been to create a public health alliance between health and education. At a strategic level, setting targets for improving child health has established a set of shared goals and principles with a clear focus on delivering evidence-based services and approaches. The Scottish targets (see *Health Improvement Targets*, NHS Health Scotland, 2011–12) for improving specific outcomes for children include: a child healthy weight programme (preventing obesity), promoting oral health through the Childsmile programme and education aimed at protecting children from second-hand smoke.

In order to facilitate public health action and support decision making, the Scottish Public Health Observatory (ScotPHO) was created to provide easy access 'to clear and relevant health intelligence and statistics'. Its website provides a link to the most recent Community Health and Wellbeing Profiles (ScotPHO, 2010), with complementary profiles focusing on children and young people, showing the considerable variation that often exists between areas. As a consequence, all local authorities must now work in partnership with NHS health boards and provide a Three-Year Integrated Children's Services Plan. Plans must include evidence of monitoring and evaluation of the eight indicators of wellbeing to ensure that all children are: safe, nurtured, healthy, achieving, active, respected, responsible and included. These themes are now firmly embedded in Curriculum for Excellence (CfE), which has provided a new impetus to place health and wellbeing at the centre of school life and become a focus for whole-school learning. In order to understand how the current policy and curriculum framework is placed to deliver a step-change in health and wellbeing, it is important to look back briefly at how this has developed.

HEALTH-PROMOTING SCHOOLS

For the past 100 years, Scottish education has placed a high value on providing children with appropriate life skills for healthy living. The 'spic, span and sporty' type of approach was prevalent until the 1960s, where home economics and cooking skills (for girls), hygiene and physical education, or drill, as it was more commonly known, were all part and parcel of a traditional primary education. A recent international review of the evidence for health promotion in schools highlights that 'providing healthy food and social support at school is one method of improving attendance and enabling young people from disadvantaged backgrounds to benefit from the education provided' (St Leger et al., 2010, p. 3).

Scotland's decision to join The Health Behaviour in School-Aged Children (HBSC) Cross-National Study in 1986, an international collaboration with the World Health Organisation (WHO), demonstrated a strong commitment from the outset to invest in an evidence-based approach. Conducted every four years since 1990, it provides a wide range of health behaviour and lifestyle information on young people as they move from puberty into adolescence. More importantly, it also provides health intelligence at a strategic level to inform policy decisions and set targets for improving health.

In 1993, Scotland became a member of the European Network of Health Promoting Schools (ENHPS), which signalled a move away from traditional health education approaches focusing on single issues, such as smoking, physical activity and alcohol use, to one that embraced a more structural and organisational approach. This involved collaboration with external agencies, working with local communities and adopting whole-school policies to promote and protect health.

In 2002, the Scottish Executive announced that all schools in Scotland should become health-promoting by 2007. The Scottish Health Promoting Schools Unit (SHPSU) was then established to offer 'strategic and practical support' to embed health promotion into school life. In 2004, the SHPSU launched a National Framework document, *Being Well, Doing Well*, which laid the foundations for planning, implementation and evaluation. The key idea here was that 'in order to do well, pupils had to be well'. The framework helped to create a coherent approach by outlining six key characteristics for addressing health promotion in schools: leadership; ethos; partnership working; curriculum, learning and teaching; personal, social and health education programmes; and environment, resources and facilities. This brought together the 5–14 Guidelines for Personal and Social Development (PSD) and Health Education, guidelines that shared common goals, philosophy and teaching approaches. In order to assist schools in implementing *Being Well, Doing Well*, an award scheme was introduced, which allowed schools to become accredited.

Simultaneously, a programme of health improvement introduced three key health improvement strategies and set the foundations for a more sustained approach. In 2002, *Hungry for Success* paved the way to revitalising the provision of school meals, by setting and monitoring nutrient-based standards for school lunches. The Active Schools programme, introduced in 2003, provided practical help and funding to build capacity and offer a wider range of physical activities in an effort to encourage greater participation in physical activity and sport. Third, the *National Programme for Improving Mental Health and Well-being Action Plan 2003–2006* set the scene for promoting mental, emotional and social wellbeing in schools. Finally, this national drive to improve and sustain health promotion as a mainstay of school life was consolidated through the Schools (Health Promotion and Nutrition) (Scotland) Act 2007. This defining piece of legislation simply states that schools have a duty to promote the mental, emotional, social and physical health and wellbeing of all pupils.

CHANGING SCHOOL CULTURE

An exploration of effective practice in school health promotion conducted on behalf of the SHPSU in 2008 identified a number of key features including: strong leadership and management structures; the contribution that pupils can make when they are invited to become active participators; developing approaches that are innovative, creative and fun; and external partnerships with pupils, parents and the wider school community. A review of health promotion (St Leger et al., 2010) also identifies similar features and highlights the fact that holistic approaches that have a strong focus on mental and emotional wellbeing are essential to the process of immersing health promotion into the daily life of the school. Overall, the health-promoting school model introduced a cultural shift with healthy living being built into the school's culture. This reflects one of the ten dimensions in *The Journey to Excellence* (HMIE, 2007) where health promotion has to become an integral, embedded part of school life – 'a way of being' rather than something that is 'in addition' to everything else.

Perhaps the biggest cultural change for primary and nursery schools has been the development of a wide range of partnerships and collaborations, including those with parents. Schools that were considered to be 'more effective' placed greater emphasis on relationship-building, particularly with pupils. Regarding pupils as 'equals', and providing opportunities for pupils to become involved in decision making and partners in the planning process, has also helped to develop key life skills such as autonomy, teamwork and communication. This fresh approach places value on the contribution that young people have to offer in terms of their own health.

LEARNING, TEACHING AND CURRICULUM

CfE builds on the key characteristics of the health-promoting school, offering a new health and wellbeing framework designed to encourage learning and teaching approaches that help to develop life skills; allow for greater flexibility to meet pupils' needs and local circumstances (see Chapter 60 for more information on the health and wellbeing framework and documents). Wellbeing presents a positive concept of health and is a combination of feeling good and functioning well. Interestingly, the phrasing of the health and wellbeing statements has pleased early years practitioners, who prefer that they are written from a pupil's perspective. This articulates well with early years approaches, which are more consistently based on observation and planning in response to individual children's needs. However, this may be more challenging to implement in a primary classroom where pupil/teacher ratios are traditionally much higher.

The *Health and Wellbeing Principles and Practice* document identifies the roles and responsibilities of practitioners as well as a broad range of features that develop effective learning and teaching. These encourage practitioners to take account of the views of young people; to use active learning strategies that are both fun and challenging; and to use the outdoors and specialist expertise to build the school's capacity to deliver an agenda that helps young people adopt and maintain a healthy lifestyle. It also highlights the need to ensure that approaches are evidence-based and take 'account of research and successful practice in supporting the learning and development of young people, particularly in sensitive areas such as substance misuse' (Scottish Government, 2009).

Recent government policy recommends that substance misuse education should use interactive and interdisciplinary learning approaches across a range of curriculum areas. 'Curriculum for Excellence will provide new opportunities for schools to plan challenging interdisciplinary learning studies . . . This will ensure that they have a sustained impact' (Scottish Government, 2008, p. 18). This marks a significant shift in the delivery of substance misuse education, which was previously delivered as part of Personal, Social and Health Education classes (Stead et al., 2009). Two learning approaches which have been used successfully in health education, particularly for exploring more sensitive areas of the curriculum, are the Storyline approach and the Draw and Write technique developed by Noreen Wetton. Both methods encompass learning styles and experiential learning which can help pupils to use their 'own experiences' to explore feelings, emotions, relationships and peer pressure.

Whilst the health and wellbeing agenda is aspirational, offering new opportunities to develop creative approaches across learning, it is not without its challenges. It requires careful monitoring and evaluation to assess if there has been a consistent interpretation of the broad statements into meaningful experiences and outcomes for improved health and wellbeing. Additionally, for some schools the practical elements, particularly in relation to delivering practical food skills without proper facilities and trained staff, could be difficult. However, in many areas cluster approaches, which use the skills and expertise of secondary Home Economics teachers, can offer a solution.

IMPROVING OUTCOMES FOR CHILDREN

Deep concern remains that young people living in poverty are not showing the same level of health improvement as children living in more affluent circumstances. As such, the gap in health inequalities is actually widening in Scotland. Additionally, too many children are affected by parental drug and alcohol abuse which can result in a lack of parental care. *The Road to Recovery* (2008) identified that between 40,000 and 60,000 children are affected by parental drug use. Equally high numbers of children are also referred to the Scottish Children's Reporter Administration (SCRA) because of concerns about their welfare. In 2010–11 in Scotland, 33,710 children were referred to the SCRA on care and protection grounds (SCRA, 2011).

Furthermore, recent policy initiatives by the Scottish Government – *The Early Years Framework* (2008), *Getting it Right for Every Child* (2006) and *Equally Well* (2008) – have further focused attention on addressing the entrenched health inequalities and poor outcomes for children and young people. More importantly, CfE has recently added a new National Framework as part of pastoral care and pupil support (see Chapter 47) which shares a common set of goals and values. These broadly aim to ensure that children are central to planning and that they receive the right type of support when they need it. It now defines two types of support available: universal support, offered to all children and providing a key adult who has a holistic overview of their learning and personal development; and targeted support, which identifies when children have specific needs that require intervention.

The 2010 HBSC survey showed some interesting trends in pupils' lifestyle behaviours.

Encouragingly, daily consumption of sweets has decreased by a third and consumption of crisps and chips has halved. Confidence levels have not been so encouraging. Although confidence levels are higher for 11-year-olds than any other age group, they have fallen for the first time since 1994, particularly for girls, where the rate has fallen from 16 per cent to 11 per cent. Clearly as a key capacity for CfE, this is a complex issue that will require careful analysis and definition to ensure that simplistic measures, such as social confidence or being able to give a talk, are not routinely used.

In 2010, the Chief Medical Officer for Scotland identified that for many sectors of society the current approaches, which define people in terms of their problems and what they are lacking, are not working. He suggests that emerging evidence on adopting an 'asset-based' approach 'may provide the necessary step change in health creation' (Glasgow Centre for Population Health, 2011, p. 10). Emerging research on this approach defines it as one that is concerned with promoting the positive coping capacities, skills and knowledge, 'rather than on their needs, deficits and problems' (ibid., p.4). CfE is an 'asset-based' model and has placed health and wellbeing in a strong position to start redressing health inequalities and improving outcomes for children; building on the strengths of individuals; acknowledging the social context; using positive statements on what individuals can do; and building resilience and social capital. As such it has the potential to effect change if it is backed by appropriate resources and staff training, which develops a workforce who feel confident rather than overwhelmed by their new roles and responsibilities.

REFERENCES

Currie, C., K. Levin, J. Kirby, D. Currie, W. van der Sluijs and J. Inchley (2011) *Health Behaviour in School-aged Children: World Health Organisation Collaborative Cross-National Study (HBSC): Findings from the 2010 HBSC Survey Scotland*. Edinburgh: University of Edinburgh Child and Adolescent Health Research Unit.

Glasgow Centre for Population Health (2011) *Asset Based Approaches for Health Improvement: Redressing the Balance*. Briefing Paper 9, Concepts Series. Glasgow: Glasgow Centre for Population Health.

Scottish Government (2008) *The Road to Recovery: A New Approach to Tackling Scotland's Drug Problem*. Edinburgh: Scottish Government.

Scottish Government (2009) *Curriculum for Excellence. Health and Wellbeing across Learning: Responsibilities for All Principles and Practice*. Edinburgh: Scottish Government.

Stead, M., R. Stradling, M. MacNeil, A. M. MacKintosh, S. Minty, L. McDermott and D. Eadie (2009) 'Bridging the gap between evidence and practice: A multi-perspective examination of real world drug education', *Drugs: Education, Prevention and Policy*, 1 (20): 1–20.

St Leger, L., I. Young, C. Blanchard and M. Perry (2010) *Promoting Health in Schools from Evidence to Action*. Paris: International Union for Health Promotion and Education (IUHPE).

49

Religious and Moral Education

Graeme Nixon

EUROPEAN PERSPECTIVES

This chapter focuses on religious and moral education (RME) in Scottish primary schools. However, before going on to discuss the detail of the Scottish context, it is important to set developments within a wider international context. The European Forum for Teachers in Religious Education (EFTRE) has published reports from a number of European countries into the nature of religious education (RE) provision (as it is more typically called in Europe) and current issues within the subject in these countries (see www.eftre.net). A summary of EFTRE reports into developments in European RE reveals very similar trends, developments and issues across the participating countries:

1. the debate about a confessional or educational approach and the unpopularity of the confessional approach (Austria, Estonia);
2. the perceived need for religious literacy (Estonia, France), particularly in the face of religious extremism (Germany) and consumerism (Estonia);
3. the influence of political ideology, particularly in post-Soviet states (Estonia, Hungary), but also where there is a political will to teach citizenship and ethics (Belgium, France);
4. the sensitivity to diverse views, seen in the various manifestations of the conscience clause and the triggers for a non-confessional approach (Finland, Estonia, Austria, Denmark, Norway);
5. the emergence of an educational approach to the subject (Austria, Estonia, Hungary, Sweden);
6. increasingly philosophical content on ethics and science (Denmark, England and Wales, Sweden, Belgium);
7. the rejection of a multi-religious approach, favouring a single-faith approach to teaching about the religion or philosophy of the child (Finland).

The Scottish RME context is concerned with the first six developments above: the move to educational, non-confessional, belief-sensitive, professionally delivered and philosophical RME is very much in evidence and these trends have framed the trajectory of the evolution of the subject in Scotland since the pivotal Millar Report of 1972 (SED, 1972).

This analysis of European developments, while revealing that Scotland is conceivably well advanced in terms of the evolution of RME, also evidences similar trends and pressures across the developed countries of Europe. Such homogeneity of social climate may also counter the view that developments in Scotland are unique to the Scottish context. There are also a number of wider framings that are currently influencing RE across Europe, including increasing alignment with the United Nations, the European Union and the Council of Europe. The recommendations of these institutions for RE are synthesised in the *Toledo Guiding Principles on Teaching about Religion and Beliefs* (OSCE, 2007). To a degree, this and similar international studies into RE represent a process whereby RE is becoming internationalised. The Toledo paper, in describing the societal and international events that prompted such a publication, outlines the need to meet the challenges of the processes of migration, to avoid misconceptions about religion and belief resulting from ignorance and recent history (particularly the events of 11 September 2001) and to enhance international security through the development of tolerance. The core principles of the Toledo document are the right of everyone to freedom of speech and conscience, and that knowledge of religion and belief is foundational to combating prejudice and fostering community cohesion.

The design principles for RME curricula should therefore be informed by 'migration, environmental degradation, contacts with other cultures, new interpretations of Holy texts, scientific developments, as well as wars and conflicts' (ibid., p. 45). RME should foster freedom and offer knowledge and understanding of 'societal diversity' (ibid., p. 16) which includes religious and non-religious perspectives. The aim of Toledo is to deepen commitment to human rights principles. RME should be grounded in, and develop, the principle of 'multi-perspectivity' (ibid., p. 45) and curricula should be sensitive to religious and secular plurality, though certain beliefs may be privileged in light of their place in the cultural and religious lives of nations.

SCOTTISH RME

Within Curriculum for Excellence (CfE), the experiences and outcomes for RME and the related Principles and Practice paper (Scottish Government, 2009) unfortunately do not reference these international framings for the subject explicitly. Nevertheless, CfE guidance does aim to address many of these issues. For example, key aspects are imagined to be facilitating the recognition of the significance of religion in modern life; learning about and from religious and non-religious traditions as a means to developing in pupils their own perspectives on philosophical and ethical matters; recognising the existence of diversity and the challenges this can present; liaising with faith groups and other bodies in the development of curricular guidance and delivery; developing pro-social moral views and a disposition to enact them; and enhancing skills of discernment and criticality. RME in Scottish non-denominational primary schools has been identified as one of eight curricular areas within CfE. The emphasis placed on values, beliefs and critical thinking skills within CfE establishes RME, for many, as an important part of the curriculum. Perhaps no other subject has such an explicit role in cultivating the purported values of Scotland (honesty, justice, compassion and integrity) as does RME.

The maintenance of RME as a statutory area of the curriculum (Scottish Government, 1980; 2011) is also framed by the Education Act of 1872 in which Religious Instruction (as it was then called) persisted as a means by which the Protestant churches could be satisfied that the Christian ethos imagined by John Knox for Scottish schools could be safeguarded. Though this aim for RME and the social climate in which it was imagined no longer exist, RME has perhaps undergone a metamorphosis, as have society and spirituality, now meeting an ongoing, albeit altered, need for identity and meaning, as well as addressing changes in Scottish society. The other aspect worth mentioning of the legislation created in 1872 is the conscience clause whereby parents continue to have the right to withdraw their children from RME. To date there is no reliable evidence on the levels of withdrawal from the subject, beyond the well-attested withdrawal from RME of Jehovah's Witnesses. Despite the Scottish Humanist Society's publicising withdrawal letters for parents to use, and perhaps a climate where the 'new atheists' such as Richard Dawkins seem to offer a rallying banner for the secular lobby, withdrawal from RME remains small scale. Perhaps this is the result of the fact that modern RME, both in policy and in the vast majority of classrooms, is fundamentally unobjectionable. Where withdrawal does take place one can speculate about parents projecting their own experiences of RME onto their children; parental inexperience of modern RME; conflation of RME and Religious Observance (RO) in parental minds; or, in some cases, concerns that a multi-religious, philosophical approach may be a threat to familial commitment. That said, there may also be a minority of teachers in primary schools who, either through unfettered evangelism (religious or otherwise) or in assuming that nothing has changed, do need to recalibrate how they deliver RME.

APPROACHES TO TEACHING AND ASSESSING RME

Within current RME policy the 'Personal Search' approach continues to be seen as pivotal to effective RME. CfE imagines this approach as permeating RME, as opposed to existing as a separate curricular strand as it did within the 5–14 national guidelines for RME. According to Kincaid and McVeigh (2001) Personal Search is a method through which pupils can discover and develop their own beliefs and values, involving pupils in coming to their own conclusions by developing skills in critical thinking and evaluation. This process has four stages, though the following order does not necessarily have to be followed:

1. *Preparing the way*: In this stage the teacher provides the context, objectives and aims of the learning experience.
2. *Finding out*: In this stage pupils learn about religious ideas, festivals, stories and customs. This is 'designed to enable pupils to go beyond just finding out what other people believe. It involves pupils first of all entering into the thoughts and feelings of believers by allowing the symbols, artefacts, festivals and stories of their religions to work on their imaginations' (ibid., p. 20).
3. *Making connections*: In this stage the pupils are invited to compare and contrast the content of the learning experience with their own experiences, beliefs and values. The intention is to develop empathy and understanding but also to facilitate the pupil's own personal search for meaning.
4. *Thinking it over*: In this stage pupils reflect on the learning experience and should be provided with the opportunity to offer their own conclusions about the material engaged with.

The benefits of such an approach are that religious practices (and non-religious philosophical views) can be seen as universal responses to the human condition. When this is grasped pupils can develop not just a tolerance for the views of others but a deeper compassion and empathy and an appreciation of the reality of their peers as other centres of experience with universal concerns and questions. This approach goes well beyond pedagogy that develops a rote-based religious literacy which confuses RME with the retention of facts about the phenomena of religion. As such the learning is deeper, and pupils develop their moral imagination through a genuine encounter in the RME classroom. This can be further developed by teachers exploring the use of experiential approaches to the subject. This can include visits (real or virtual) to places of religious and spiritual significance, role play and the use of silence, reflection and mindfulness in pupils that may allow them to begin to grasp the silence that is at the heart of all religious traditions as found in prayer, mysticism and meditation.

RME provision in the primary school can involve discrete presentations or units of work on world religions. The CfE Principles and Practice paper, in attempting to declutter the curriculum, advocates that schools should study Christianity and a maximum of two other religious traditions. The arguments for the mandatory study of Christianity are presented in terms of cultural literacy. Issues around planning an RME curriculum should consider the range of religions studied and perhaps allow for comparison between Middle Eastern and Indian traditions. This rich comparison does not exist where pupils are only presented with the Abrahamic traditions (Judaism, Christianity and Islam).

An alternative to the discrete world religion approach is to study religions thematically, looking at festivals, traditions and beliefs across religions. Common themes, for example, include 'Festivals of light' or 'People who help us'. There are obvious benefits in allowing pupils to compare and contrast traditions, but teachers must be aware of crude equivalences being made that can distort an authentic understanding of religions or at worst be offensive to believers (for example, if we suggest that Mohammed is like Jesus for Muslims). A solid grasp of the subject area is essential.

Within CfE for RME, non-religious views are also to be considered. Though this guidance is obviously sensitive to the reality that around a third of Scots (Census 2001) claim to be non-religious, there is no sanctioning of the explicit study of traditions such as Humanism. Instead it is imagined that the non-religious views will be discussed in the context of the study of religious traditions. Arguably this is to misrepresent Humanism as simply the antonym of religion.

RME is well placed to be delivered through interdisciplinary approaches; it is, however, all too often studied in the context of only the six world religions as they currently exist. RME can also be delivered, for example, in the study of Scottish history (looking at Celtic and pre-historic religion and associated archaeology); ancient history (ancient Egypt should always include a discussion of life after death); literature (which should introduce pupils to the ideas of myth, symbolism and multi-layered texts); and social subjects (for example, studying a particular region and the indigenous and developing beliefs within it).

When it comes to the assessment of RME teachers should ask themselves a number of questions:

1. Are learners being given the opportunity to develop their own beliefs and values?
2. Are pupils learning *about* religion, morality and philosophy?
3. Are pupils learning *from* religion, morality and philosophy?

As with other curricular areas teachers should try to select key RME experiences and outcomes as a focus as well as selected relevant outcomes from other areas (health and wellbeing, literacy and social subjects should feature prominently). Matched to these experiences and outcomes should be learning intentions and success criteria. These should be generated and framed in terms of the skills to be developed or consolidated. Teachers should also have an idea about what the range of means will be by which pupils can evidence progress. In RME the aim is to assess not so much the pupils' beliefs as their ability to articulate and share their thoughts and to empathise with those of their peers. RME therefore represents a real opportunity and context in which to develop skills such as metacognition, discernment and criticality. A further aspect of the assessment cycle should be that teachers identify areas of development for both themselves and their pupils.

CONCLUSION

As previously stated, CfE arguably places RME at the heart of the curriculum. This represents a great opportunity to revisit the educational aims, credentials and importance of the subject. Victor Frankl (2004), who witnessed the horrors of Auschwitz, formulated the idea that people survive and flourish where they have a sense of meaning and are able to place themselves in a wider context. In a world that seems to be obsessed with the will to power and the will to sex, Frankl's idea of human flourishing existing in the will to meaning is worth revisiting. Effective RME, which allows pupils to explore and establish their own sense of meaning (whether religious or otherwise), becomes all the more important.

REFERENCES

Frankl, V. E. (2004) *Man's Search for Meaning*. London: Ryder.

Kincaid, M. and B. McVeigh (2001) *Effective Teaching of Religious and Moral Education: Personal Search*. Edinburgh: Learning and Teaching Scotland.

Office for Security and Cooperation in Europe (2007) *Toledo Guiding Principles on Teaching about Religion and Belief in Public Schools*. Warsaw: Office for Democratic Institutions and Human Rights.

Scottish Education Department (1972) *Moral and Religious Education in Scottish Schools* (the Millar Report). Edinburgh: HMSO.

Scottish Government (2009) *A Curriculum for Excellence, Experiences and Outcomes for RME*. Online at www.ltscotland.org.uk/learningteachingandassessment/curriculumareas/rme/nondenominational/eandos/index.asp

Scottish Government (2011) 'Curriculum for Excellence – Provision of Religious and Moral Education in Non-denominational Schools and Religious Education in Roman Catholic Schools, letter to headteachers of all schools'. Online at www.educationscotland.gov.uk/Images/rmerercletter_tcm4-650439.pdf

Scottish Office (1980) Education (Scotland) Act 1980. Online at www.legislation.gov.uk/ukpga/1980/44

VII

CURRICULUM: SECONDARY

This section gives an overview of all the curriculum subjects commonly encountered in Scottish secondary education today. In the immediate wake of the early Curriculum for Excellence (CfE) documents, it seemed that such an approach to the curriculum might have become obsolete but, in fact, the development has continued to be centred around 'curriculum areas' and the secondary school version of this is thus considered in this section. Given the nature of the new 3–18 Curriculum, it makes sense to read this section in the light of Sections V and VI and, indeed, Sections VIII and X. In addition, Chapter 5 in Section II provides a valuable review of philosophy and practice in secondary schools which helps set this coming section in context.

The individual subjects are presented alphabetically, following an opening chapter (Chapter 50) which deals with the impact and current position of CfE within the secondary school. This chapter also focuses on two aspects of CfE development – active learning and interdisciplinary learning – which have been somewhat troublesome for the teaching profession but which offer much educational potential. Many of the chapters that follow pick up these issues from the perspective of the particular subject area. Apart from the focus on specialist subjects, the section also covers a number of topics of particular curricular interest in the secondary school. Chapter 54 covers the issue of career education; Chapter 60 offers an overview of one of the 'cross-cutting' themes of CfE – health and wellbeing – not itself a curriculum subject, but a key current priority; Chapter 63 examines the role and potential of Information and Communications Technology (ICT); and Chapter 68 explores the place of outdoor education, an area of considerable growth and renewed interest, despite the thorny related issues of risk, and health and safety.

All of the curriculum areas are currently encountering considerable change, and chapter authors have had to deal very much with a developing field. The CfE programme has triggered significant change in relation to curriculum structure, content, pedagogy and assessment. In addition, the arrival of faculties within secondary schools has challenged traditional approaches to curriculum leadership and development. The current economic situation is also affecting schools in relation to available resources but may well have further repercussions for schools in terms of staffing and the breadth of curricular provision. What is presented, therefore, comprises a snapshot of a development that will continue to be in flux for some years yet.

For the expressive arts, CfE is presented in this section as being in sympathy with the prevailing pedagogy in these subject areas. For Art and Design (Chapter 51), the move towards more pupil-centred approaches is welcomed, for Music (Chapter 67) active involvement in composition is highlighted, while for Drama (Chapter 57) the opportunity for the creative exploration of pupils' own lives is stressed. In all cases, however, tensions are indicated in relation to assessment and to their positions as subjects of intrinsic worth or as merely a means towards other curricular goals such as the 'four capacities', or preparing young people for future economic roles. The new political and educational emphasis on health and wellbeing has positioned Physical Education somewhat differently in recent years, and Chapter 69 explores the implications of this, as well as the vaunted 'legacy' anticipated from the 2012 Olympics and 2014 Commonwealth Games.

For Languages, the place of literacy as a central curriculum theme and the responsibility of all teachers represents a considerable logistical and professional challenge but also denotes a heightened importance for the subject. Chapter 58 examines the way ahead for English teaching, marrying this pressing need for high standards of technical accuracy with the enrichment, and critical judgement, that come through engagement with literature. Chapter 65 notes the changing face of Modern Foreign Languages in secondary schools, including the decline in German provision but the growth of Spanish. The place of Gaelic is considered separately in Chapter 25 in Section IV. Like English, Mathematics faces a new curricular landscape because of the importance of numeracy as a cross-cutting priority. Chapter 64 identifies a number of challenges for the teaching of Mathematics in relation to both pedagogy and attainment.

In Chapter 71, the increased uptake in SQA presentations in Religious, Moral and Philosophical Studies is examined as part of current developments within RME as the subject establishes itself as a discrete CfE curriculum area but one shifting from a Christian-dominated approach to one that embraces more modern understandings and practices of 'spirituality'. The chapter deals with non-denominational provision, while Chapter 27 in Section IV looks at Catholic education in Scotland.

The chapters on the sciences encompass a number of pressing claims on the science curriculum, from the universities demanding higher levels of specialist knowledge, the political and economic desire for a more science-friendly workforce, to increased ethical and environmental concerns around scientific activity. These make choice of content, and related approaches, particularly problematic in the sciences. Chapter 72 argues that CfE offers the potential for a real engagement with the moral and environmental questions around science, but that this needs to be promoted explicitly if it is to become classroom reality. In Chapter 52, the philosophical underpinnings of Biology as a discipline are suggested as one way of making sense of all the competing demands that are currently serving to trouble the subject. In Chapter 55, the impact of budget restraint is identified as a key challenge for the sciences, and for Chemistry in particular, with the quality of laboratories, equipment, support staffing and resources all currently under pressure and serving to restrict teacher options and pupil experiences. In Chapter 70, the revision of curricular content and related pedagogical challenges for the sciences are highlighted, in this case in relation to Physics. As with all the sciences, there is concern about the ability of schools to maintain coherence in terms of progression and pedagogy, especially given the impact of SQA requirements in the upper secondary.

In Chapter 59, the challenge of 'green' and ethical concerns about the human impact on the environment, a growing focus for the sciences, is seen as a positive for continued pupil interest in Geography as a school subject. The renewed interest in Scottish history which came with devolution and the advent of SNP government has presented its own challenges for History as subject departments aim to ensure that young people engage with both the local and the global. Again, the backwash from SQA arrangements has considerable influence on the history curriculum as Chapter 61 outlines. Chapter 66 stresses the importance and value of Modern Studies as a means of encouraging political literacy – a key component of the democratic citizenship that CfE purports to uphold. The continued growth of the subjects of sociology, politics, psychology and philosophy is tracked in Chapter 73, and the role of the FE sector in this rightly acknowledged. Given the central place of Personalisation and Choice as a CfE principle, there is no doubt that schools need to keep looking at such issues of subject popularity and uptake as an important element in overall curricular provision.

Alignment with the CfE theme of Health and Wellbeing brings added bite to Home Economics provision, as Chapter 62 indicates, but only adds to the complexity of provision as departments negotiate their way through the vast number of different courses, options and interdisciplinary opportunities that are available. The costs of resources and equipment are a challenge in the current economic environment, and this affects the Technologies significantly. As with Home Economics, it is clear that for Computing there is a very difficult task for schools to keep up with technological change in society at large, as Chapter 56 shows, yet its importance to the economy is seen to be vital, as is the case with Business Education in Chapter 53. For Technology education, there are similar challenges but also questions around its overlap with Computing and with Art and Design. These make for difficult demarcation issues but also offer hope for genuine interdisciplinary potential, as Chapter 74 manifests.

All of these secondary subjects bear scars from protracted CfE implementation and the evolving nature of SQA requirements. These two are not always aligned and it is certain that adjustments will be made in the coming years. For example, it is unclear how CfE endorsements of collaborative learning, active learning and interdisciplinary learning sit within a system so thirled to individual assessment within single subject areas. The importance of SQA arrangements in influencing the secondary school curriculum cannot be overemphasised and unless, or until, these are revised further in the light of the ethos of CfE, curriculum subjects in secondary schools remain compromised in their efforts to embrace its spirit fully.

50

Curriculum for Excellence in the Secondary School

Valerie Drew

Secondary education in Scotland at the time of writing is in a state of flux and flow as the sector continues to develop and implement Curriculum for Excellence (CfE, Scottish Executive, 2004) across thirty-two local authorities. The pace and scope of change varies as educators, schools and local authorities work, both individually and collaboratively, to make sense of how this policy will enable them to provide a 'good' educational experience for every child and young person in their own contexts and settings. The full potential of CfE has yet to be realised and meantime offers particular challenges for the secondary sector with regard to structural and pedagogical implications.

The secondary curriculum encompasses the concluding phase of a young person's period of compulsory education (up to 16 years) plus a two-year post-compulsory phase (16–18 years) within the Scottish policy framework of lifelong learning. CfE engenders an explicit understanding of the contribution of lifewide learning which occurs in spaces and places beyond the confines of the classroom and school, for example through clubs, sports, interests, part-time work, engagement in further education and so on. The requirement to map a young person's attainment and wider achievements throughout his or her secondary education renders impending changes in assessment more complex. (See Section VIII: Assessment, Certification and Achievements.)

This chapter explores the development of CfE in the secondary curriculum from its origins in the National Debate on education in 2002 through the developing policy process with a focus on the values, purposes and principles and their pertinence to the secondary curriculum. It outlines some key features of CfE in secondary education through the broad general education and senior phase. Finally it considers some of the implications for pedagogy and learning promoted through the policy by examining the constructs of 'active learning' and 'interdisciplinary learning'.

THE NATIONAL DEBATE AND SECONDARY EDUCATION

The Scottish Executive initiated the National Debate on education in 2002, suggesting that whilst Scottish education displayed a number of strengths, there was a need to consider aspects for improvement to ensure that schools continued to offer young people a good educational experience that prepared them for life beyond school in the twenty-first century.

This debate, whilst not particularly 'well attended' (around 1,500 responses suggested to represent an estimated 20,000 people), has been taken into account in shaping the direction of future educational policy in Scotland with considerable repercussions for the secondary curriculum. The debate reiterated the seemingly widely held view of pride in the Scottish education system and indicated strong support for the inclusive nature of comprehensive education. However, it raised a number of concerns, including the lack of relevance of some learning; an over-emphasis on assessment; a perceived lack of choice; and an apparent lack of flexibility in its capacity to support the needs of all young people in preparing them for living and working beyond the period of compulsory education (SE, 2003). The latter point was raised despite recent changes in the post-16 curriculum when the Higher Still initiative was implemented to offer greater choice between academic and vocational courses.

CURRICULUM FOR EXCELLENCE

The introduction of CfE (SE, 2004) was a bold attempt to build on the strengths of Scottish education whilst introducing a radical new approach to prepare children and young people to address some of the challenges they would face beyond school in the twenty-first century. The policy set out the intention to develop a coherent curriculum, spanning the early years to the end of the secondary phase, for children and young people from 3 to 18 years. The initial publication in this burgeoning policy framework, entitled *A Curriculum for Excellence: The Curriculum Review Group* (SE, 2004), articulated the values, purposes and principles that would underpin the new curriculum. This was heralded by the policy makers as a new dawn for Scottish education, an opportunity to take account of global influences and to address some of the particular health, social and economic challenges facing Scotland. In an unprecedented move the Scottish Executive immediately endorsed the Review Group's report, accepting the recommendations in full and outlining a programme to address the implications. This meant that the teaching profession was not required to deliberate and debate the underpinning values, purposes and principles at this crucial early stage; consequently many secondary schools' initial engagement with the policy was at a fairly superficial level and as a result its full impact is still to be realised some ten years later. Perhaps it seemed that there was little to argue with: the policy articulated a set of worthy values, aspirational purposes and robust principles to underpin the development of a new curriculum planned to move Scottish education forward apace in order to address the challenges of the twenty-first century (SE, 2004). It was difficult to dispute values of wisdom, justice, compassion and integrity 'borrowed' from the engraving on the Mace in the Scottish Parliament as anything other than positive qualities to be developed in young people through their engagement in formal education. The aspiration 'to enable all young people to become successful learners, confident individuals, responsible citizens and effective contributors' or any combination of these helped give shape to 'our' responsibilities for the development of future generations. And, finally, the range of principles, old and new (challenge and enjoyment, breadth, progression, depth, personalisation and choice, coherence and relevance) were selected to inform curriculum planning in order to meet the needs of all children and young people. However the lack of (requirement for) professional debate at the time of publishing meant many of these elements remained relatively unchallenged. It was only later, when the implications of putting these into practice in devising the secondary curriculum began to disrupt some of the traditional structures, systems and subject boundaries, that there was a great deal of angst amongst the profession and some teachers felt they were lacking the appropriate knowledge, skills and capacity required to implement this new curriculum model.

The Scottish Executive Ministerial Response to the Review Group in 2004 provided some indication of the changes ahead in setting out a number of challenges for second-ary education. A call for clarity in expected outcomes was accompanied by a demand for renewed focus on literacy and numeracy across the curriculum. In addition, a 'reformed approach to education in S1–S3' was proposed to increase challenge and improve pupil motivation during early secondary education. This was an attempt to maintain pace and eradicate the perceived S2 'slump' so often lamented by Her Majesty's Inspectorate of Education (HMIE) and heralded one of the most significant changes ahead.

This call to envision new and revised curriculum architecture opened up possibilities for schools to imagine the curriculum differently. This was especially challenging in the design and administration of the secondary school timetable and marked a significant change to timetabling arrangements latterly designed to accommodate the number of subjects studied over the week. The Ministerial Response suggested creating longer periods of time to allow pupils to engage in more demanding extended learning activities that moved beyond and across traditional subject boundaries and required an increasing emphasis on pedagogies. Finally, the importance of the Skills for Work agenda was highlighted and followed up with a more focused and integrated strategy for schools and their partners, published some five years later (Scottish Government, 2009). (See further discussion below.)

Whilst work behind the scenes got underway with consultations to begin planning systems and structures for change, it was business as usual in many secondary schools. To inject some adrenalin into the system, the SE published *A Curriculum for Excellence: Progress and Proposals* (2006a) which reiterated key messages and articulated future direc-tions. In essence, all educators in every educational setting had the responsibility to develop the four capacities in each child and young person through a coherent 3–18 curriculum; and a number of cross-cutting themes, including enterprise, citizenship, health, creativity and problem solving, were to be embedded and developed coherently across the curriculum. It was proposed that this would be achieved through focus on pedagogy and learning and renewed consideration of the how of teaching, building on the relative success, mainly in primary schools, of the Scottish Assessment is for Learning programme. This would help to ensure that assessment during S1–S3 was 'integral' to teaching and learning.

The establishment of the curriculum areas was a defining moment for CfE (SE, 2006a). The curriculum from early years to the end of the secondary phase was structured around eight curriculum areas:

- Expressive Arts;
- Health and Wellbeing;
- Languages;
- Mathematics;
- Religious and Moral Education;
- Sciences;
- Social Studies;
- Technologies.

These areas were designed to offer opportunities for 'learning and the development of skills across a broad range of contexts' (SE, 2006a, p.15). However, these groupings represented little change from earlier curriculum models and seem to refute the claim that CfE has 'profound implications for what is learned' (SE, 2004, p. 3). A less ambitious statement, some two years on, claiming that curriculum areas and subjects would be 'refreshed and re-focused' (SE, 2006a, p. 10) appears to represent the sort of dampening down of ambition that led Priestley and Humes (2010, p. 358) to suggest that CfE 'runs the risk of promoting innovation without real change'.

The second phase of policy documentation with direct implications for those working across the secondary sector was published four years after the initial document. *Curriculum for Excellence, Building the Curriculum 3: A Framework for Learning and Teaching* (SG, 2008) provided some of the anxiously awaited detail to help educators imagine how the new curriculum might evolve and develop. This document promoted the wider understanding of curriculum (originally outlined in SE, 2006a) as:

> the totality of experiences which are planned for children and young people through their education, wherever they are being educated. It includes the ethos and life of the school as a community; curriculum areas and subjects; interdisciplinary learning; and opportunities for personal achievement. (SG, 2008, p. 14)

This recognition of curriculum as providing an educational rationale for the pupils' experience beyond that of subject disciplines necessitated secondary schools to consider how to incorporate some of the previously informal or extra-curricular experiences into the planned curriculum for every child and young person. This move has potential to address some of the inequities for the young people previously unable to access such opportunities. This document reiterated the need for change, calling on evidence from HMIE and the Organisation for Economic Cooperation and Development (OECD) to address, through strategies such as strengthening vocational education, the number of young people leaving secondary education with 'minimal or no qualifications'.

TRANSITIONS AND PHASES IN, THROUGH AND BEYOND THE SECONDARY CURRICULUM

An entitlement for all young people to experience a smooth transition throughout their 3–18 education demands attention to transition processes as young people prepare for, engage in and move on from secondary education. The transformation from a three-stage model (2+2+2) of secondary education encompassing S1/2, S3/4 and S5/6 into a two-phase model (3+3) was proposed to smooth this pathway. The revised model comprising a broad general education (S1–S3) and the senior phase (S4–S6) would ensure a more coherent educational experience for young people through the secondary curriculum. However, careful planning is required to ensure valid and reliable assessment of attainment and achievement throughout to ensure that individuals' needs are addressed as they progress through each phase.

The expectations for learning and development in the curriculum areas and associated skills for learning, life and work are set out in the experiences and outcomes (see www.educationscotland.gov.uk/myexperiencesandoutcomes/index.asp). The experiences and outcomes articulate the quality of the learning experience and what is to be achieved. A young person's progression in his or her education will be described through the experiences and outcomes against one of the six levels: from early, through first and second level to the end of P7 for most pupils; and from third and fourth levels with progression to qualifications in the senior phase for most secondary pupils. The introduction of broad levels was intended to be flexible to meet the needs of all pupils and thus ensure smooth transition from one level through to the next. (See *The 3–18 Curriculum in Scottish Education*, Chapter 3, for further information on curriculum levels.)

S1–S3 (Broad General Education)

CfE (SG, 2008) states that every child and young person is entitled to a period of broad general education extending from pre-school to the end of S3. This entitlement includes all the experiences and outcomes across all curriculum areas to and including the third level, although some young people will progress to the fourth level. This broad foundation will ensure young people experience a range of subjects from which they select options to study in more depth during the senior phase. Most importantly this broad experience will enable them to:

- achieve the highest possible levels of literacy and numeracy and cognitive skills;
- develop skills for life and skills for work;
- develop knowledge and understanding of society, the world and Scotland's place in it;
- experience challenge and success. (SG, 2008)

The planning of this broad general education is proving challenging to secondary schools. The removal of the Age and Stage Regulations for external assessment had resulted in some schools asking pupils to select options to study towards qualifications during S1, although most schools offered choice for specialism at the end of S2. Now schools are required to embed assessment in the broad general education phase as part of the learning process and to ensure recognition of wider achievement is included in this practice.

At the time of writing, this development is causing considerable consternation for teachers and schools as they begin to plan this phase of the secondary curriculum. The accountability of the attainment agenda has played a major role in shaping the first four years of the secondary curriculum as schools attempted to raise pupils' performance in high stakes examinations over recent years. The government suggests that this has resulted in a narrowing of curriculum as 'teaching to the test' has permeated professional pedagogical practices in some secondary schools. Even the Assessment is for Learning programme has been appropriated by many teachers in an attempt to improve examination results through concentrating mainly on techniques that would enhance cognitive understanding (a focus on product-orientated learning) rather than developing longer-term strategies to enhance pupils' capacity to learn (a focus on the processes of learning). The tensions between what teachers espouse – that there is too much focus and pressure on attainment in secondary schools – and what they practise, for example teaching to the test, will not radically change until they have more confidence in their ability to manage the risks involved in the new curriculum related to pupils' attainment and their own reputation.

The Senior Phase

The senior phase comprises young people in S4–S6 and includes 16- to 18-year-olds out of school, for example in colleges. Although young people can officially leave school at 16 years of age, increasing numbers choose to stay on at school through S5 and S6 and are now actively encouraged to do so until they have planned to move onto a 'positive and sustained destination' such as training, further education or employment (SG, 2008). The 16+ learning choices are designed to support planning and development of a coherent curriculum for all young people in the senior phase. During this phase it is expected that the young person will continue to develop the four capacities through a range of activities including, for example, service to school or community, work experience or sports coaching, as well as beginning to build their lifelong learning portfolio of qualifications. The Scottish Credit and Qualifications Framework (SCQF) sets out the criteria for skills and learning to be achieved from SCQF level 1 to SCQF level 7 to meet the needs of all young people during this phase. At or towards the end of their broad general education most pupils will be expected to choose subjects from the curriculum areas to study in more depth towards qualifications at National 4 and 5 (SCQF levels 4 and 5); they may then progress to Highers in S5 (SCQF level 6) and Advanced Highers or Scottish Baccalaureates in S6 (SCQF level 7). Some pupils in the senior phase will study for qualifications through partnerships with colleges, employers and other agencies. A number of curriculum models are currently being developed and trialled across schools and local authorities in order to ascertain which one provides young people with a smooth progression into the appropriate SCQF level. Models are being developed that allow young people to select different numbers of subjects to study in more depth at different stages. The system is designed to be flexible. For example, some schools are starting this process during the phase of broad general education to enable their students to undertake study for Highers over a two-year period; consequently the senior phase will not comprise a standard 3+3 model across schools and local authorities. (See Section VIII: Assessment, Certification and Achievements.)

Skills for learning, skills for life and skills for work

Notwithstanding the global phenomenon of rising youth unemployment, the Scottish Government proposes that prioritising skills development will help to bring about the 'transformational changes' required to improve young people's opportunities in life by providing them with the knowledge, skills and attributes to be flexible and adaptable lifelong learners. *Building the Curriculum 4: Skills for Learning, Skills for Life and Skills for Work* (SG, 2009) highlighted the entitlement of all children and young people to develop and apply skills in learning across all sectors from early years to the senior phase. These skills include:

- literacy, numeracy and associated thinking skills;
- skills for health and wellbeing, including personal learning planning, career management skills, working with others, leadership and physical coordination and movement skills;
- skills for enterprise and employability. (SG, 2009, p. 10)

These skills are embedded in the experiences and outcomes in an attempt to diminish the boundaries between academic and vocational education, and skills progression is signposted to enable educators to support young people in recognising and valuing their progress in this aspect of their education. The development of skills is the responsibility of all 'partners' working with children and young people across schools, colleges, universities, voluntary organisations, youth workers, employers and so on. The secondary school will be responsible for planning and mapping the development, application and progression of young people's skills from primary transition through their broad general education and senior phase which may take place in partnership with other post 16+ providers listed above. It will be challenging for secondary schools working across curriculum areas and providers to ensure successful integration and coherent progression of skills development for all young people.

IMPLICATIONS FOR PEDAGOGY AND LEARNING IN THE SECONDARY CURRICULUM

Active learning and interdisciplinary learning are promoted through *Building the Curriculum 4* (SG, 2009, p. 2) as a means of enabling young people 'to develop, demonstrate and apply a wide range of skills'. However, there is a lack of clarity surrounding the definition of these constructs in both the policy and the literature, which has resulted in some teachers struggling to make sense of these and a range of interpretations being enacted in practice.

Active learning

The discourse of 'active learning' promoted through CfE appears to be a means of developing the knowledge, skills and dispositions, including literacy and numeracy, considered necessary by the European Commission (2009) for lifelong learning to enable young people to address the social, political and economic challenges they will face in life beyond formal education. In this respect active learning is concerned with the skills of learning (process-orientated) rather than as a set of pedagogic strategies to enhance learning outcomes (product-oriented) which has implications for learning and teaching.

CfE fosters an implicit expectation that learners will engage in active lifelong learning through developing their capacities as: successful learners, confident individuals, responsible citizens and effective contributors. The only explicit definition, '[A]ctive learning is learning that engages and challenges children's thinking using real-life and imaginary situations', is found in *Curriculum for Excellence: Building the Curriculum 2: Active Learning in the Early Years* (SE, 2007, p. 5) where active learning is defined and justified in terms of engagement and challenge linked to conceptions of learning through play (ironic, perhaps, given the implicit understanding of developing skills for work). In subsequent policy documents related to secondary education there is an explicit acknowledgement that active learning approaches will 'encourage participation', 'build upon children's enthusiasm, inventiveness and creativity' and 'promote the development of logical and creative thinking and encourage a problem–solving approach' (SG, 2008, p. 30).

There is an assumption that educators understand the term and how to enact this concept in their practices: a notion reinforced by HMIE which singles out active learning as one of the elements for improvement in learning and teaching to enable schools to move from 'good to excellent' (HMIE, 2007: 2010). An exploration of the literature suggests that 'active learning' is used to cover any and all activities experienced in education, for example reading, writing, listening, discussing and problem solving; through individual, peer, collaborative and cooperative activities; and includes using resources inside and outside the classroom (Drew and Mackie, 2011). This lack of clarity creates opportunities for policy makers, academics and educators to define the concept to suit their own intentions and renders the concept hazy and often empty of meaning. Indeed, active learning is immediately problematic in that it appears to be placed in opposition to *passive* learning, a notion that seems intrinsically improbable if learning is defined as a change in behaviour, knowledge, understanding, skills, attitudes and/or values (Coffield, 2008; see also Chapter

6 of this book). Watkins et al. (2007, p. 71) offer a comprehensive framework which suggests that active learning encompasses three dimensions:

- Behavioural: the active employment and development of resources;
- Cognitive: active thought about experiences to make sense and so foster construction of knowledge;
- Social: active interaction with others on both a collaborative and resource driven basis.

The exploration of the literature on active learning indicates these dimensions are most frequently found in combination, although few definitions encompass all three dimensions (Drew & Mackie, 2011). In addition, the literature reveals an affective dimension (see for example Stephen et al., 2008) absent from this framework which encompasses factors such as pupil attitudes and values, intrinsic and extrinsic motivational factors, and pupil engagement. Drew and Mackie (2011) suggest that the addition of a fourth dimension – the affective dimension pertaining to a mindful disposition - would support the development of a more robust framework to explore this construct.

Not unsurprisingly Drew and Mackie's (2011) literature search revealed some apprehension concerning the implications of active learning in practice. There is a perception that implementing active learning might diminish the role of the teacher in the classroom; however, it seems to involve additional responsibilities as teachers are challenged to motivate, guide, facilitate, innovate, mentor, coach and collaborate. The lack of clarity in definition and understanding can lead to the employment of a range of techniques which may have short-term impact on pupil attainment rather than long-term impact on developing pupils' skills in metacognition. Some teachers alluded to factors such as lack of confidence, slower progress in curriculum, lack of time to develop strategies, loss of control and increased workload. There were also concerns regarding some pupils' ability or inclination to engage with certain approaches or their stated preference for teacher-led lessons. These perceptions have particular implications for the senior phase where teachers feel under pressure to cover the curriculum prior to examinations.

Interdisciplinary learning

Interdisciplinary learning (IDL) is one of the four contexts of CfE curriculum planning. It seems to present greater challenges for secondary schools where traditionally most pupil learning has taken place in discrete subject disciplines; consequently secondary teachers require space to collaborate with colleagues and/or partners from other disciplines to plan authentic IDL opportunities. There also appears to be some lack of clarity of understanding surrounding this construct. The Curriculum Review Group's use of the term 'cross-subject activity' (SE, 2004, p. 3) and its appeal for 'more teaching across and beyond traditional subject boundaries' (p. 16) may have led some educators and local policy makers to use the terms 'cross-curricular learning' and 'interdisciplinary learning' interchangeably. This has resulted in a multiplicity of practices being enacted in schools across Scotland. Later policy documents attempted to clarify this construct, stating:

> The curriculum needs to include space for learning beyond subject boundaries, so that learners can make connections between different areas of learning. Through interdisciplinary activities of this kind, young people can develop their organisational skills, creativity, teamwork and the

ability to apply their learning in new and challenging contexts. To be successful, these activities need to be well planned with a clear purpose and outcomes in mind. (SE, 2006a, p. 10)

This sentiment was reiterated in the first of the *Building the Curriculum* series (SE, 2006b, p. 3) which urged schools to be innovative and creative in planning for 'wider cross connections and interdisciplinary work'. This document suggested IDL was likely to 'involve both research and a strong element of presentation' (p. 17) and be 'challenging and motivating' (p. 40). In an attempt to further clarify the construct, Learning and Teaching Scotland produced a paper on IDL in 2010 which suggested there are two (sometimes overlapping) types of interdisciplinary learning:

> Learning planned to develop awareness and understanding of the connections and differences across subject areas and disciplines. This can be through the knowledge and skill content, the ways of working, thinking and arguing or the particular perspective of a subject or discipline. Using learning from different subjects and disciplines to explore a theme or an issue, meet a challenge, solve a problem or complete a final project. This can be achieved by providing a context that is real and relevant, to the learners, the school and its community. (www.ltscotland.org.uk)

This definition seems to incorporate the key elements of Repko's (2012) integrated definition:

> Interdisciplinary studies is a process of answering a question, solving a problem, or addressing a topic that is too broad or complex to be dealt with adequately by a single discipline and draws on the disciplines with the goal of integrating their insights to construct a more comprehensive understanding. (p. 12)

However, some current IDL practices in schools are based on themes such as energy or a particular country where each subject can plan the learning activities in relative isolation from others. This practice appears to conflate an interdisciplinary approach with a cross-curricular or multidisciplinary approach. A multidisciplinary approach refers to 'the placing side by side of insights from two or more disciplines' (p. 16). This approach often necessitates the researcher or pupil making the connections between the disciplines. This is in contrast to an authentic IDL experience where complex questions may be initiated from the pupils themselves, who look to the relevant disciplines (or subjects) to explore and develop answers to open questions.

The policy drivers for interdisciplinary education require learners to develop the skills required to explore the complex problems confronting society in the spaces in between disciplines. CfE alludes to this practice by identifying sustainable development and health promotion as examples of some of the complex problems facing Scotland today which might be addressed through this form of enquiring approach. However, there are inherent tensions between promoting IDL and planning a curriculum using fairly traditional curriculum areas. The reaffirmation of fairly traditional subject boundaries is at odds with the government's plea 'to include space for learning beyond subject boundaries, so that learners make connections between different areas of learning' (SE, 2006a, p. 10) and appears to restrict the potential of interdisciplinary learning in the secondary curriculum from the outset.

Building the Curriculum 3 (2008) suggested that IDL should be 'planned around clear purposes' (p. 21): some of the current ad hoc IDL development will prove problematic when schools attempt to map the young person's coherent experience across the curriculum.

An absence of focus on IDL during early discussions on summative assessment seems to have resulted in less attention being paid to the development of this context for learning since generally the current model of assessment does not embrace IDL. An exception to this is the Interdisciplinary Project, unique to the Scottish Baccalaureates, although these qualifications are only offered at SCQF level 7 (see www.sqa.org.uk/sqa/34638.1567. html). However, recent developments including the proposal for Scottish Studies and the exemplification of assessment of literacy and numeracy at National 3, 4 and 5 appear to be founded on an interdisciplinary approach.

'WHAT ARE WE GOING TO DO NOW?'

Her Majesty's Inspectorate of Education (2007, 2010) asks schools to envision the future through consideration of this question, although it is perhaps less concerned with imaginings of how things might be and more concerned with the practicalities of how schools intend to get 'there'. CfE is a model of educational reform that seeks to develop 'the imagined community the nation wishes to construct through schooling' as well as 'the skills and dispositions thought necessary to the so-called knowledge economy and globalization' (Rizvi and Lingard, 2010, p. 96). CfE opens spaces to articulate the values and enact the purposes and principles educators believe are important; in other words it provides opportunities for educators to be creative, to explore possibilities and to realise imaginings. Secondary schools and their partners must continue to engage in debate and deliberation about the purposes of education and how these are communicated to the young people in their care.

CfE offers educators space to enhance and develop the secondary curriculum to ensure Scotland continues to offer good education to prepare young people for the rapidly changing demands of the twenty-first century. The current economic, environmental and social global challenges require young people to be creative, flexible and adaptable; the secondary curriculum has an important role to play in ensuring they have the opportunities to develop the knowledge, skills, dispositions and resilience to lead healthy and sustainable lives and be able to deal with uncertainties and dilemmas ahead. The challenge for schools is not how to hold on to all of the practices that have served us well in the past but to continue to grapple with the challenges of developing a good secondary education fit for purpose in the twenty-first century.

REFERENCES

Coffield, F. (2008) *Just Suppose Teaching and Learning Became the First Priority*. London: Learning and Skills Network.

Drew, V. and L. Mackie (2011) 'Extending the constructs of active learning: Implications for teachers' pedagogy and practice', *The Curriculum Journal*, 22 (4): 451–67.

European Commission (2009) *Education and Training 2010 Work Programme: Assessment of Key Competences*. Brussels: European Commission. See at http://ec.europa.eu/dgs/education_culture

Her Majesty's Inspectorate of Education (2007, updated online 2010) *How Good is our School? The Journey to Excellence Part 1 and 2*. See at www.journeytoexcellence.org.uk/learningandteaching/improvementguide/promotionofactivelearning.asp

Priestley, M. and W. Humes (2010) 'The development of Scotland's Curriculum for Excellence: Amnesia and déjà vu', *Oxford Review of Education*, 36 (3): 345–61.

Repko, A. F. (2012) *Interdisciplinary Research Process and Theory* (2nd edn). London: Sage.

Rizvi, F. and B. Lingard (2010) *Globalizing Education Policy*. Abingdon: Routledge.

Scottish Executive (2003) *Educating for Excellence: Choice and Opportunity, the Executive's Response to the National Debate*. Edinburgh: Scottish Executive.

Scottish Executive (2004) *A Curriculum for Excellence: The Curriculum Review Group*. Edinburgh: Scottish Executive.

Scottish Executive (2006a) *A Curriculum for Excellence: Progress and Proposals*. Edinburgh: Scottish Executive.

Scottish Executive (2006b) *A Curriculum for Excellence: Building the Curriculum 3–18 (1): The Contribution of Curriculum Areas*. Edinburgh: Scottish Executive.

Scottish Government (2008) *Curriculum for Excellence: Building the Curriculum: A Framework for Learning and Teaching*. Edinburgh: Scottish Executive.

Scottish Government (2009) *Curriculum for Excellence: Building the Curriculum 4: Skills for Learning, Skills for Life and Skills for Work*. Edinburgh: Scottish Government.

Stephen, C., P. Cope, I. Oberski and P. Shand (2008) '"They should try to find out what the children like": Exploring engagement in learning', *Scottish Educational Review*, 40 (2): 17–28.

Watkins, C., E. Carnell and C. Lodge (2007) *Effective Learning in Classrooms*. London: Paul Chapman.

51

Art and Design Education

Diarmuid McAuliffe

This chapter draws on Marshall McLuhan's now infamous idiom 'the medium is the message' in order to help capture current Art and Design educational discourses and practices in Scottish secondary education. It then moves in part two to capture the many initiatives that are beginning to point so positively towards a new era for Scottish secondary Art and Design education – the growth in uptake in Higher Photography as illustrated in Table 51.1 is an example of one such initiative. Central to this observation is the realisation that if you change the medium you somehow change the message, thus allowing new discourses and new Art and Design practices to emerge.

THE MEDIUM IS THE MESSAGE: SECONDARY SCHOOL ART AND DESIGN EDUCATION NOW

Whilst there is a degree of turmoil south of the border, with political imperatives once more denigrating the subject of Art and Design and its infrastructure, in Scotland art education is in a relatively good place as it begins to draw in oxygen from the various subject-specific reforms currently under way as part of the roll-out of Curriculum for Excellence (CfE).

Table 51.1   Course entries and awards 2008–12
Art and Design

	2008	2009	2010	2011	2012
Adv Higher	1,413	1,544	1,602	1,583	1,415
Higher	6,991	7,232	7,239	7,192	7,019
S Grade	15,559	13,280	12,802	11,293	11,259
Int 2	5,648	6,264	6,653	7,047	7,126
Int 1	2,672	3,287	3,875	3,683	3,740
*Photography**					
Higher	537	768	947	1,153	1,495

SQA, 2012

* Photography is generally taught within the Art and Design department, although in some schools it is taught in other departments such as Computing and Design and Technology. Prior to 2011 it was known as Photography for the Media.

How and why we teach, learn and assess in Art and Design is currently under review and whilst there are still some with deeply felt reservations about the CfE programme, many teachers, it must be argued, at least within Art and Design, regard the process as a genuine opportunity for reflection and renewal.

For the highly motivated Art and Design teacher, the CfE reforms represent nothing more than a 'rubber-stamping' of what they themselves have always done well, and that is to teach the subject of Art and Design within the broad context of culture and society. For this sizable group of art teachers, a certain 'keep calm and carry on' attitude prevails towards their current pedagogical practice. However, there is still also a 'sizable other', whose practices remain outmoded and inflexible and do not serve the population well in preparing young people for life and work in the twenty-first century.

Learning must be at the centre of what is done in Art and Design and it is widely acknowledged now that for the subject to remain relevant in a twenty-first century school environment it must shift away from the teacher-led pedagogies of the past (the sizable other) that are overly didactic and product-led to a new pupil-centred, concept-based and process-led pedagogy that privileges the pupil voice and the world of ideas.

Today, deep and meaningful conversations concerning learning and the value of learning in and through art are occurring across the sector with words such as 'relevance' and 'context' finding their way into the lexicon of Scottish school Art and Design education – a lexicon that hitherto was largely dominated by such words as 'accuracy', the latter being at the core of Scotland's entrenched classroom practices of drawing and painting. The challenge, as Jerome Bruner sees it, is 'always to situate our knowledge in the living context' and within 'broader culture' (1995, p. 44); he suggests that simply demonstrating 'how to' and providing practice at doing so is not enough (p. 54) and has led to many art teachers in Scotland becoming mere technicians rather than leaders of learning. Studies of expertise, as Bruner argues, 'demonstrate that just learning how to perform skillfully [and accurately] does not get one to the same level of flexible skill as when one learns by a combination of practice and conceptual explanation . . .' (p. 54).

This time of 'renewal and opportunity' for Art and Design teachers in Scotland is also a time of imminent challenges. The question of subject leadership is beginning to emerge at a critical juncture in the subject's development as many experienced principal teachers of art now find themselves taking on wider faculty management roles and responsibilities as the traditional identity of 'principal teacher' is eroded or in some cases dropped altogether. The impending reduction in time spent studying the subject from the current two years of compulsory study to one coupled with fewer periods of art per week as we lose out to other areas of the curriculum such as health and wellbeing may result not only in a reduction of departmental staff, but in art departments becoming no longer able to provide the 'quality' that they have traditionally provided at National Qualifications (NQ) level.

Art departments that have done well in the past and have worked hard to build up their reputations are hugely concerned about the relinquishing of some of the assessment controls from a centralised Scottish Qualifications Authority (SQA) in favour of a greater blend of assessment methods, including internal assessment and regional moderation in the case of National 4. Teachers fear most that decentralisation will result in a lowering of grades for departments that have traditionally done well through the centralised assessment process.

There are also fears that too great an emphasis is being placed on the intellectual side of the subject at the expense of 'practical art skills'. What teachers should therefore be aspiring towards is what Atkinson and Dash (2005, p. xii) have called 'a critical based arts practice' which consists of a 'fusion of the practical with the critical whereby art practice is critical practice', where critical ideas are given visual form. External assessors' reports repeatedly refer to some of these tensions and outmoded practices still occurring in our art rooms. In a recent externals' report for the expressive unit within Standard Grade, it was noted that pupils encountered 'difficulties when faced with very poor and uninspiring groups of objects from which to work (for Standard Grade in 2011) (SQA, 2011). Similarly, encountering whole classes expressing the same or similar opinions in written work and in art work too is not that unusual as standardisation, though not prescribed, has nevertheless been inadvertently embedded in art education in Scotland to the extent that external examiners have called for urgent change in the way Art and Design is summatively assessed (Hepburn, 2011, p. 14).

Some art teachers, it must be argued, have for too long adhered slavishly to a set of practices promoted by the SQA in its annual exhibition and publication of exemplars. Similarly, the *Times Educational Supplement Scotland*, in its weekly publication of an artwork from a Scottish school, confirms these normative and largely mimetic practices that have come to represent Scottish school art. The pervading message that emerges from much of the work at NQ level, with the exception of design work and Advanced Higher work, is one of compliance to a set of 'past practices' and 'orthodoxies' (Atkinson, 2005) that privileges technical skills and teacher-led pedagogies at the expense of creativity and more pupil-led pedagogy that champions free expressive modes of thinking and making whereby the pupil voice is made audible. Similar issues are evident in the teaching of art history where often what pupils receive is a 'caricature' (Hughes, 2005, p. 35) relating to a standardised outline of art history.

It is now well recognised that Scotland has had an unhealthy obsession with summative assessment in Art and Design – a subject with a natural impulse for self- and continuous assessment. This obsession, or 'groupthink' culture, has slowly emerged over the decades and has simply discouraged creativity and risk-taking, these being the very 'oxygen' that is now required to develop and sustain progressive practices as promoted by CfE.

Encouragingly, formative assessment is now well on its way to becoming the dominant form of assessment in schools. However, the art produced in the middle years of schooling in particular continues to be 'end product' driven with little concern for the 'deep search' that CfE is seeking. For the vast majority of schools in Scotland the SQA manages, in a straightforward and relatively trouble-free way, the public examinations for Art and Design. Some schools, though, mostly private, choose the English A-Level route as it is considered less constraining and far less onerous in terms of assessment when compared with the SQA. The old adage 'if it's not assessed it will not happen' has been a definite feature of Scottish art education, particularly in the middle years of schooling, S3/4. Tied to this are teacher-led art pedagogies which must now be revised in favour of a more personalised and pupil-led pedagogy.

If, as McLuhan argues, 'the medium is the message' we then need to change the medium and adopt new ways of meaning-making that reflect the age we live in. This does not mean dispensing with paint and charcoal but rather calls for the end of 'procedural orthodoxies' that have determined school art in Scotland for the best part of a century.

CHANGING THE MEDIUM CHANGES THE MESSAGE: SCHOOL ART MOVES FORWARD

With the introduction of National 4/5 in 2013–14, replacing all previous courses in Art and Design, we are slowly seeing the emergence of a different learning environment. No longer can school art be just about the privileging of observational drawing over free expressive modes – a practice that served well in the training of engineers and craftsmen for Scotland's flourishing industries of the past. An art education today needs to equip young people to meet the challenges of the twenty-first century and be inquiry-led. And while we acknowledge that much has changed over time in art rooms up and down the country, change has not come nearly quick enough. School art remains largely disconnected from contemporary art practice and as such is retrospective in its outlook – one could date many of its practices to the nineteenth century. Why is this? Surely the 'medium' of the twenty-first century is different to that of the nineteenth? And if the medium was to change, surely the message too would change and what would that message mean to our young people attending their art class today?

Nevertheless, the most pressing concern for Art and Design teachers today is assessment. Assessment, it is proposed, will be more decentralised and with that, personalised, enquiry-based learning, a central tenet of CfE, will hopefully be assessed in a more meaningful way. 'Fit for purpose' assessment procedures currently being developed include a mix of formative and summative, the latter involving internal and local assessment along with regional moderation. The decentralisation of assessment, whilst a worry for some as earlier mentioned, will enable new and more diverse practices to emerge, leaving behind the often overly restrictive and standardised three A2-sized submissions that have been a distinguishing and limiting feature of Scottish Art and Design education for many a decade. Meaningful assessment methods are called for, and it is likely that assessment through learners' sketchbooks will be one feature of the process (Education Scotland, 2012a). New media-based submissions including film and animation along with the huge growth in the uptake in photography (see Table 51.1) at all levels will begin to push boundaries in terms of subject matter and personal response and will inevitably change 'the message' of school art in Scottish education.

The Assessment is for Learning strategy, or formative assessment as it is otherwise known, has been the most noticeable advancement in teaching and learning in Art and Design in recent years. It has been well received by teachers of Art and Design and has resulted in getting pupils to participate actively in the assessment of their own work. Learners are now encouraged to review their own learning and are involved in setting their own personal learning goals (Scottish Government, 2010). This represents a clear focus on the individual learner and his or her development and progress. It has also resulted in the teacher making explicit the learning intentions and success criteria at the start of a lesson, and this is now a commonplace feature of Art and Design teaching in Scotland. Much innovation is currently taking place in relation to the monitoring and reporting aspects of assessment with teachers working with increasing confidence with the experiences and outcomes of CfE. Teachers recognise the need for a coherent approach to learning, teaching and assessment as we move away from the grade-based assessment narrative towards that of 'developing', 'consolidating' or 'secure'. The ability of children and young people to apply learning in 'new and unfamiliar contexts' is a refreshingly apt measure of learning.

Questions foremost in the minds of all Scotland's Art and Design teachers are what does 'secure' look like, what evidence would be needed to show that a young person was 'secure' in his or her learning? Departments have been innovative in the ways in which they gather evidence of achievement and lots of dialogue about a shared understanding of standards is currently taking place. Note-taking by teachers of an individual's achievement is becoming commonplace, with many using digital cameras to record achievement as they assess a pupil's progression from developing, through consolidating, to secure. Evidence-gathering should accommodate the wide range of creative responses to tasks that pupils might have and should be based on what the pupils can 'say, write, make and do' (Education Scotland, 2012b).

The lack of exemplification in Art and Design has been contentious as the profession is left to its own professional judgement. Over-exemplification has been discouraged by central government and art teachers within local authorities are increasingly 'coming together' to discuss these matters. In the past this lack of exemplification was perceived as a 'vacuum' which would most certainly have been filled by willing 'consultants' but so far this so-called vacuum is not seen necessarily as a negative thing but rather is providing teachers with an opportunity to reflect deeply on the nature of what they teach. There are also signs that the value of not always knowing 'the outcome' has found favour and whilst teachers can determine what the learning objective might be, which is crucial, to determine the final outcome is often to cut short an individual's learning journey. The aspect of 'group learning', which is given much attention in CfE, raises many questions for teachers of Art and Design where the culture has traditionally been very much focused on individual learning. Art and Design will also no longer be hermetically sealed, as cross-curricular and interdisciplinary learning take root.

Alternative models of practice to mainstream art education provision do quietly exist in such forms as Room 13 (Gibb, 2011, p. 113), a social enterprise model of art education embedded in a number of primaries and one or two secondary schools in Scotland. Where this model exists, socially engaged and enquiry-based pedagogical practices flourish. Learners manage their own learning and have 'creative autonomy in determining the subject, media and direction of their work' (Adams et al., 2008, p. 11).

There is a growing desire within the Scottish Government and 'good art teachers' to foreground 'creativity' in all teaching and learning and increasingly this is happening as Standard Grades and Intermediates are replaced by National 4/5. However, at the time of writing 'teaching to the test' does still remain a feature of Scottish art education and creativity as an attribute has yet to be taken seriously.

CONCLUSION

Art and Design remains one of the most popular and successful subjects in the curriculum with consistently healthy uptake across all levels and, arguably, whilst teachers are facing real challenges there has never been a better time to be an art teacher in Scotland (see Table 51.1). Art teachers are having to think for themselves as the old certainties of the past with the SQA firmly in control and a principal teacher leading the subject can no longer be relied upon. However, there is still much to do in order to reach a point where learning is privileged over procedure and learning objectives are shared with pupils and displayed prominently within the art room alongside reference to the department's commitments to literacy and numeracy and to the wider school curriculum. There is no doubt that pupils are becoming more articulate about their learning, and learning is being organised in a variety of ways through whole-class teaching or in small groups. Ideas are being 'problematised' through 'rich tasks' and through enquiry-based approaches to learning. And art lessons may occasionally be occurring in another faculty or department away from the art department, or even beyond the school altogether, as schools seek greater learning opportunities through working across and beyond the curriculum where partnerships and entrepreneurship is encouraged.

Note: The terms 'Art' and 'Art and Design' are used interchangeably throughout this chapter.

REFERENCES

Adams, J., K. Worwood, D. Atkinson, P. Dash, S. Herne and T. Page (2008) *Teaching Through Contemporary Art: A Report on Innovative Practices in the Classroom.* London: TATE Publishing.

Atkinson, D. (2005) 'Approaching the future in school art education: Learning how to swim', in D. Atkinson and P. Dash (eds) *Social and Cultural Practices in Art Education.* Stoke on Trent: Trentham Books, pp. 21–30.

Bruner, J. (1995) *The Culture of Education.* Cambridge, MA: Harvard University Press.

Education Scotland (2012a) *Learning through Sketchbooks in Art and Design.* Online at www.ltscotland. org.uk/sharingpractice/l/learningthroughsketchbooksinartanddesign/intro.asp

Education Scotland (2012b) *Marks on the Landscape: Inspiring Creativity across the Curriculum.* Online at www.ltscotland.org.uk/marksonthelandscape/curriculum/artanddesign/assessment/index.asp

Gibb, C. (2011) 'Room 13 Art Studio', in F. Allen (ed.), *Education: Documents of Contemporary Art.* London: Whitechapel Gallery.

Hepburn, H. (2011) 'On your marks: How the SQA exam system works and what the assessors thought of this year's papers', *Times Educational Supplement Scotland* (4 November), 14.

Hughes, A. (2005) 'Don't judge pianists by their hair', in R. Hickman (ed.), *Critical Studies in Art & Design Education.* Bristol: Intellect.

McLuhan, M. (2002) *Understanding Media: The Extensions of Man.* London: Routledge.

Scottish Government (2010) *Building the Curriculum 5: A Framework for Assessment: Recognising Achievement, Profiling.* Edinburgh: Scottish Government.

Scottish Qualifications Authority (2011) *External Assessment Report, 2010.* Online at www.sqa.org.uk/files_ccc/EA_Report_ArtDesign_SG.pdf

Scottish Qualifications Authority (2012) *Statistics 2011.* Online at www.sqa.org.uk/sqa/57517.html

52

Biology Education

Stephen P. Day

Modern biology is an eclectic mix of subjects that evolved from traditional fields of botany, zoology, microbiology and physiology to newer areas such as molecular and cellular biology, to name but two. Biologists use a wide array of analytical techniques found in other disciplines to push the boundaries of knowledge. Nowhere is this interdisciplinary approach more evident than in biomedical science, where knowledge gains over the last decade have been substantial, advances being driven by the ability of modern biologists to learn, develop or adapt analytical techniques as required. Biology's diversity is educationally problematic, particularly within the context of curriculum design. Fairly considerable tensions exist between proponents of differing content areas as to what knowledge ought to be taught. In addition, consideration must also be given to the moral, ethical and social perspectives that impinge on the use of biological knowledge, as well as which methods and techniques should be introduced to pupils to allow them to experience the subject's practical side.

THE PHILOSOPHY OF BIOLOGY

Despite approving of T. H. Huxley's view of biology as 'a coherent subject with a coherent philosophy and . . . [providing] a firm basis for future study in a range of specialised disciplines', Slingsby (2006) has noted that, as biology has grown, the addition and removal of content to the biology curriculum has been haphazard and without regard to the effect these revisions have on the overall philosophy of the subject. According to Griffiths (2008), Biology's philosophy can be viewed from three distinct but related perspectives: (1) by looking to biology to test general theses within the philosophy of science; (2) by engaging with conceptual problems that arise within biology itself; and (3) by looking to biology for answers to distinctively philosophical questions in such fields as ethics, the philosophy of the mind and epistemology.

How biology education reflects these perspectives lies at the heart of tensions that exist within the biology curriculum in Scotland. For example, the Standard Grade Biology course rationale indicates that the course topics are derived from three general aspects: (1) the biological basis for life, encompassing the study of cells, growth in plants and inheritance, and of the mechanisms for continuity and change from generation to generation, as well as the processes necessary for survival of animals; (2) relationships, encompassing the study of ecology to provide a basis for understanding the interactions amongst organisms and their environments; and (3) application of biological principles in work, health and leisure activities, encompassing the study of biotechnology.

The Standard Grade Biology course aimed to contribute to pupils' general education through their involvement in the processes of scientific investigation. It was thought that through these processes, the development of attitudes and abilities such as objectivity and an analytical approach to tackling problems would be fostered. Furthermore, the subject aimed to provide pupils with a rational basis for considering many of the related issues affecting themselves and society. In practice, these intentions were eclipsed by content knowledge acquisition and the development of data analysis skills, which was reinforced through the examination focus on the elements of knowledge and understanding (KU) and problem solving (PS). The developing informed attitudes (DIA) element of the course effectively disappeared. The neglect of this ethical, moral and societal perspective of the philosophy of biology was also reflected in practice in the Intermediate 1 and 2, Higher Biology and Human Biology courses, and to a lesser extent the Advanced Higher. It might be said that these courses only attended to the general testing of theses in the biological context and engaging with conceptual problems that arise within biology perspectives. This has led to claims that the general emphasis in biology education lies towards ever-increasing specialisation without regard for the social, ethical and moral implication that biology might have in societal terms. As a consequence it fails to provide a holistic view of the subject and an adequate platform for pupils' development towards functional scientific literacy.

UPTAKE AND SUCCESS IN SECONDARY SCHOOL BIOLOGY

Biology emerged from humble beginnings in the mid-1960s to become, by 2010, the third most popular subject taken by pupils in Scotland (SQA, 2010) (see Table 52.1).

Table 52.1 shows that candidate numbers increased in all courses except for Standard Grade Biology. This decrease was related to the removal of the age and stage restrictions, resulting in more schools offering Intermediate courses in discrete sciences to S3 pupils instead of Standard Grade Science (which showed a dramatic decline in candidate numbers), coupled to the fact that pupils who struggled with Standard Grade Biology were being switched early to Intermediate 1 Biology in order to take advantage of its holistic assessment format. This offered less-able pupils a greater chance of success since Standard Grade Biology had no Foundation level. In addition, pupils identified early as being

Table 52.1 Number of candidates sitting each course in Biology

Year	SG (F:M)	Int. 1	Int. 2	HB	HHB	AH
2005	22,213 (2.3)	3,295 (1.7)	5,336 (2.2)	8,943 (2.1)	3,609 (2.9)	1,693 (2.55)
2006	23,200 (2.3)	3,975 (1.6)	5,326 (2.2)	9,044 (2.0)	3,737 (2.7)	1,886 (2.16)
2007	22,787 (2.2)	5,146 (1.6)	6,612 (2.0)	9,169 (2.0)	3,712 (2.5)	1,929 (1.97)
2008	22,319 (2.0)	5,699 (1.6)	6,755 (1.9)	9,132 (1.9)	3,755 (2.5)	1,955 (2.14)
2009	21,029 (2.0)	5,750 (1.6)	6,927 (1.9)	9,107 (1.8)	3,992 (2.4)	2,095 (1.8)
2010	20,570 (2.0)	5,718 (1.7)	7,354 (1.8)	9,308 (1.8)	4,078 (2.2)	2,177 (1.88)
2011	20,315 (2.0)	5,873 (1.7)	7,490 (1.8)	9,767 (1.8)	4,226 (2.1)	2,288 (1.68)

Note: SG = Standard Grade, Int 1 = Intermediate 1, Int 2 = Intermediate 2, HB = Higher Biology, HHB = Higher Human Biology; AH = Advanced Higher Biology. Brackets indicate the female to male ratio of the course candidate population per year.

borderline candidates for Standard Grade in S2 (in those schools that do not offer Standard Grade Science) tended to be steered towards Intermediate 1.

Despite this apparent popularity, a number of issues persist with the Biology curriculum; it is content-heavy, for example, and does not allow sufficient time for the development of inquiry skills in practical terms, or for the developing of informed attitudes. At Standard Grade, it could be argued that the diversity of the course led to a lack of cohesion. At Higher Grade there are too many topics, which allows little time for consolidation and remediation in the time available. In addition, a considerable gap existed in the ability required for Standard Grade Credit level and Higher Grade. Traditionally, Biology has a gender bias, with the ratio of females to males being approximately 2:1 (see Table 52.1) but there is evidence that more males are now taking the subject. Furthermore, when one takes the Scottish Relevance of Science Education (ROSE) findings into account, it would seem that Biology content knowledge, at present, is losing relevance to today's pupil population since Biology topics figure prominently in six out of the ten least popular topics that pupils wish to study (Farmer et al., 2006).

BIOLOGY IN THE SECONDARY CURRICULUM

Lower Secondary Stage

The S1–S3 phase of Curriculum for Excellence (CfE) science contains sixty-nine experiences and outcomes (E&Os) covering both level 3 and level 4, of which twenty-four focus specifically on biology, eleven at level 3 (six relating to content knowledge and five to experimental skills) and thirteen at level 4 (six relating to content knowledge, five to experimental skills and two to socio-scientific discussion). These E&Os are organised under the strand headings: Planet Earth: *Biodiversity and Interdependence* (relating to biodiversity, photosynthesis and evolution); Biological Systems: *Body Systems and Cells* (relating to cell theory; biotechnology); and Inheritance (relating to reproduction, DNA and genetics). Teachers are encouraged to deploy various active learning approaches such as cooperative learning and inquiry-based learning to enhance pupil engagement and enjoyment.

Middle Secondary Stage

Currently (2011–13) the S3–S4 curriculum consists of Standard Grade, and Intermediate One and Two Biology courses. At present pupils must choose at least one Science course in S3–S4. However, this situation is set to change in 2013 when pupils will be free to pick any science course or opt out of science altogether. National 4 and 5 courses will replace and streamline the present suite of courses (see below).

Upper Secondary Stage

Currently S5 and S6 pupils dependent on their S4 grades can choose Intermediate 2 Biology, Higher Grade Biology or Higher Grade Human Biology. However, Intermediate 2 Biology is to be discontinued as of 2014. Higher Grade Biology, Higher Grade Human Biology and Advanced Higher Biology are to be revised to bring them into line with the expectations of CfE. At present, both Higher Biology and Higher Human Biology contain three units, the Higher units being Cell Biology; Genetics and Adaption; and Control and

Regulation, and Higher Human Biology units being Cell Function and Inheritance; the Continuation of Life; and Behaviour, Populations and Environment. It is fair to suggest that both the Higher Biology and Higher Human Biology courses are content heavy with little room for practical work relating to the content. Advanced Higher contains two core units, Cell and Molecular Biology, and Environmental Biology; one half-unit, the Investigation; and three free-choice half units from Animal Behaviour, Biotechnology and Physiology, and Health and Exercise.

THE MANAGEMENT OF BIOLOGY IN SCHOOLS

The role played by principal teachers of Biology in the management and development of the subject at school and local authority level is being undermined as their roles are subsumed by faculty heads. This move towards faculties of science is worrying (voiced regularly at some authority-level Biology coordinators' meetings) since many faculty heads are physical scientists and, as such, struggle to fully appreciate the philosophy of Biology and its complexity. An uncomfortable perspective would be that many Physics and (to a lesser extent) Chemistry teachers privately question Biology's place as a science and often see it as the least important of the three. Biology is a rapidly advancing subject that is as deep as it is broad and that naturally lies at the interface between science and society. This requires biologists with a clear view of how the subject at large is developing to be able to make decisions that allow for the future development of secondary school Biology over the coming years. Without effective autonomous leadership at local level, decisions about the future development of the subject risk being sidelined.

Interdisciplinary Learning

Many controversial socio-scientific issues are biological in nature, and biologists can potentially contribute to the interdisciplinary teaching of these issues. However, in the context of CfE, interdisciplinary learning (IDL) is conceptually ill-defined. For example, do teachers enacting IDL teach the multiple dimensions themselves in the class context, or does IDL require a team approach with each teacher contributing his or her particular specialism? The answer to this question is vital to the implementation of this element of CfE. Recent research into how science teachers can engage pupils in IDL using socio-scientific discussion is described in Day and Bryce (2011; 2012) under the premise that one teacher presents all the perspectives rather than using a team approach.

Fieldwork

There are many opportunities for fieldwork in Biology, particularly in the area of environmental monitoring. However, the opportunities to participate in practical activities in the newer areas of molecular biology are restricted by availability of equipment, cost of reagents and expertise. Many schools get around these concerns by making arrangements with Further Education colleges where pupils can visit and participate in experiments such as agarose gel electrophoresis, polymerase chain reaction (PCR) and enzyme-linked immunosorbent assays (ELISAs).

LOOKING TO THE FUTURE

Biology (National 4 and 5)

The Biology (National 4 and 5) course is designed to be practical and experiential, with the aim of developing scientific understanding of biological issues. The published rationale for these courses suggests that the course covers a range of topics, from molecular through to whole organism and beyond. The course, so the rationale claims, allows flexibility and personalisation by offering choice in the contexts studied. Furthermore, the course aims to develop (within a biological context) learners' scientific and analytical thinking skills; investigative, experimental and problem-solving skills; understanding of biological issues; the acquisition and application of knowledge and understanding of biological concepts; and the understanding of relevant applications of biology in society. Thus courses should provide opportunities for pupils to become scientifically literate citizens, whilst developing their literacy and numeracy skills. However, a number of questions emerge from this rationale: in what way will true flexibility and personalisation be achieved in practice? Who decides what these relevant applications of biology are and how is the decision made? In what way are these applications relevant to society as a whole?

In terms of content, Biology National 4 and 5 each have three units of study: Cell Biology; Multicellular Organisms; and Life on Earth. However, at present there is no detailed course documentation that outlines course content. All National 4 courses will be internally assessed, with National 5 courses being assessed internally and externally. The reliance on internal assessment as the only evidence of competence at National 4 has led some practitioners to question the value of this qualification to employers and Universities. In addition, both courses contain an added value unit where pupils are expected to draw on and extend the skills they have learned from across the other units, and demonstrate the breadth of knowledge and skills acquired in unfamiliar contexts and/or integrated ways. To achieve the Biology National 4 and 5 course, the pupils must pass all of the required units, including the added value unit. At present, there is insufficient detail surrounding the nature or 'value' of this component to judge at this time how this might be implemented in practice. One further question remains: do the curriculum planners intend these courses to stand alone or to be taught in a bi-level manner? This issue will need to be resolved since both Biology National 4 and 5 contain the same unit titles and the draft unit descriptors indicate that they contain similar content, albeit in a differentiated form. The answer to this question will undoubtedly have staffing and workload implications.

Environmental Science (National 4 and 5)

A new Environmental Science course, which developed out of the Intermediate 2 and Higher Managing Environmental Resources (MER) course, is soon to be introduced. As with all National 4 and 5 courses, it has three units: Earth's Resources (encompassing the study of Planet Earth, Earth's Materials and Energy); Living Environment (encompassing the study of Ecosystems, Inter-relationships and Biodiversity); and Sustainability (encompassing practical and other learning activities related to natural resources and the impact of human activities on them). In addition, this unit will cover the principles of sustainable development, resource use and abuse, and global environmental issues. It remains to be seen how popular this will be, particularly in the light of the Scottish ROSE survey and considering that the uptake of Higher MER only totalled 620 pupils between 2006 and 2010. It is possible that Environmental Science might grow but it is more likely that it will end up following Biotechnology (as a niche subject) and become non-viable over the longer term.

Revised Higher Biology and Human Biology

The new revised Higher Biology course contains three units: DNA and the Genome (which explores the molecular basis of evolution and biodiversity); Metabolism and Survival (which considers the central metabolic pathways in cells and how they are controlled as well as how cells are manipulated and modified in biotechnology); and Sustainability and Interdependence (which attempts to model and understand complex interactions between many interdependent entities such as the human population's dependence upon sufficient and sustainable food production from the harvest of a narrow range of crop and livestock species).

The revised Human Biology course contains three units: Human Cells (which introduces stem cells as being capable of dividing and differentiating into specialised cells and emphasises the central metabolic pathways and their control as well as the central role played by DNA to cell processes); Physiology and Health (which focuses on reproduction and the cardiovascular system); and Neurobiology and Communication (which emphasises the importance of the brain's structure to its function).

As the implementation of the senior phase of CfE approaches, there have been many complaints from practitioners centred on the lack of clarity as to the content and depth of National 4 and 5 Biology courses. This is all the more problematic since these courses are designed to underpin the new Highers in Biology and Human Biology. In addition, it could be argued that the construction of these courses has paid scant regard to the philosophy of biology, particularly in terms of biology's ability to provide a perspective on the interface between science and society.

REFERENCES

Day, S. P. and T. G. K. Bryce (2011) 'Does the discussion of socio-scientific issues require a paradigm shift in science teachers' thinking?', *International Journal of Science Education*, 33 (12): 1675–702.

Day, S. P. and T. G. K. Bryce (2012) 'The benefits of cooperative learning to socio-scientific discussion in secondary school science', *International Journal of Science Education*. DOI:10.1080/0950 0693.2011.642324.

Farmer, S., M. Finlayson, R. Kibble and A. Roach (2006) *The ROSE Survey in Scotland – An Initial Report: Views of Secondary 3 Pupils on the Relevance of Science Education*. Glasgow: STEM-ED Scotland.

Griffiths, P. (2008) 'Philosophy of Biology', *The Stanford Encyclopaedia of Philosophy*. Online at http://plato.stanford.edu/entries/biology-philosophy

Scottish Executive (2006) *A Curriculum for Excellence, Progress and Proposals: A Paper from the Curriculum Review Programme Board*. Edinburgh: Scottish Executive.

Slingsby, D. (2006) 'Biological education: Has it gone anywhere since 1875?' *Biologist*, 53 (6): 283–4.

Scottish Qualifications Authority (2010) *Annual Statistical Report*. Online at www.sqa.org.uk/sqa/57528.html

Scottish Qualifications Authority (2011a) *Biology (National 4) Draft Course Rationale and Summary*.

Scottish Qualifications Authority (2011b) *Environmental Biology (National 4) Draft Course Rationale and Summary*.

53

Business Education

Brian Reid and Anne Bradley

The Business Education curriculum consists of a portfolio of four individual business subjects – Accounting, Administration, Business Management and Economics. Each subject is available for certification, but it is unusual to find all four being taught in any one school. Historically, all four subjects have been taught in S3 through to S6. The certification pattern was first Ordinary Grade followed by Higher Grade, then Standard Grade followed by Higher Grade. This was further refined by the new national qualifications (NQs) which introduced certification at Intermediate 1 and Intermediate 2 level. Applying a product lifecycle analysis to each subject, we could say that Business Management is still in growth. Administration, having grown rapidly since its introduction, has now reached maturity/saturation. Accounting is well past maturity and is in decline, while Economics would appear to be nearing the end of its lifecycle. Having four separate subjects in one department might be considered unusual, if not problematical, but the multi-disciplinary approach has been the norm from the 1960s until the present day.

A DEVELOPING CURRICULUM

In 1960, the department teaching Business subjects was known as the Commerce department. The pupils were almost exclusively female and the subjects were chosen from a menu consisting of shorthand, commercial arithmetic, bookkeeping and commerce. These were clearly vocational subjects and, as her Majesty's Inspectorate of Education (HMIE) later commented, the impression was of subjects that are useful and practical but not appropriate for selection by the most able pupils. This impression is one that still niggles the modern-day Business Education teacher. One could argue that many of the initiatives and developments in the Business curriculum since the 1960s have been attempts not only to meet the needs of business and of young people, but also to raise the perceived status of the subject within the profession.

In the mid-1960s the Business subjects were reviewed and fresh aims, content and methods were introduced. The department was rebranded, becoming the Business Studies department, and the menu of subjects on offer was radically altered with Accounting, Economics and Secretarial Studies being introduced at both Ordinary and Higher Grade. Economics, although a social subject, was generally taught by Business Studies teachers, with teachers in some schools also offering Higher Economic History.

There was little change to this menu of subjects for the next twenty years but by the

1980s, with the general move to provide certification for all young people, Standard Grades (SG) gradually began to replace Ordinary Grades across the school curriculum. The Scottish Consultative Council on the Curriculum (SCCC) Business Review Group (1987) opted to maintain the multi-disciplinary approach and recommended that Accounting and Finance, Economics, and Office and Information studies (OIS) be introduced at Standard Grade.

By introducing the more Information and Communications Technology (ICT)-intensive SG OIS and most importantly a new Higher Grade subject known as Management and Information Studies (MIS), the review group determined that, in order to teach Business Studies in Scotland, prospective entrants would continue to require not only a broad-based business degree but one that additionally contained advanced ICT application skills. Many Business Studies teachers at the time had developed their own expertise, and were already teaching advanced ICT through the delivery of SCOTVEC modules to the senior school, employing state-of-the-art hardware and software (much of it funded through the national Technological, Vocational and Education Initiative, TVEI). The introduction of MIS provided a more general business course for the first time. It had links with all the Business Education subjects and drew upon them to varying degrees.

The introduction of MIS was a successful and popular initiative; it eventually evolved into Higher Business Management in 1999 and led directly to the introduction of SG Business Management in 1997. At the time, there had been a rapid growth of interest in the ideas, concepts and practice of management studies in education as well as in business, and the value of MIS was recognised by many senior managers in schools. This facilitated the introduction of the new Higher into the S5/S6 curriculum. The introduction of MIS provided a less specialist introduction to business for the first time and attracted young people who would not normally have considered choosing business subjects at school level, thus helping to raise the profile and status of Business Studies overall.

From the late 1990s, across the portfolio of business subjects there have been a number of other significant developments. The department was again rebranded, this time as the Business Education department. Secretarial Studies, after thirty years of service, was replaced with Higher Grade Administration in 2000. SG OIS was phased out in 2001 and replaced with the even more IT-intensive SG Administration. Standard Grades, Highers and Advanced Highers in Accounting and in Economics were revised, and Advanced Highers were introduced in Administration and Business Management.

CURRENT PROVISION

Business Education departments have long contributed their IT expertise to the broad general education programme in S1/S2 and many departments contribute their business knowledge to whole-school initiatives like Enterprise and Financial Education. The extent to which Business Studies departments are involved in the production and delivery of S1 and S2 courses varies. The most common involvement is in ICT courses. This is completely dependent on the school's chosen model for the curriculum. Previous S1/2 courses in Business Education were criticised by HMI for their lack of intrinsic value; they were often used to introduce pupils to Business Education and to encourage them to take some Business Education courses from S3 onwards. It could be argued that there was nothing wrong with this, but most Business Education departments realised that their courses should have had value in themselves, and not simply be used as an advertisement for the subject. With the introduction of Curriculum for Excellence, the structure, content, learning outcomes, and learning and teaching approaches of these courses will now be clear and of value. The following is an example of what a Business Education department in one secondary school is trying to achieve:

> We are changing our S1/2 ICT course to take account of Curriculum for Excellence . . . Our main focus is on learning and teaching, rather than major changes to the curriculum. The thinking in our school is that Formative Assessment ties in really well with developing the 4 capacities. We are trying to take each lesson in turn and really think about the way in which we are delivering it . . . what could we do to get pupils actively involved?

However, Business Education subjects are all optional. At the end of S1, S2 or S3 (depending on the curricular model chosen), young people can choose to study one or more of the four business subjects, usually at an introductory level. Many schools or authorities have abandoned Standard Grade courses and have either introduced them to earlier year groups or have introduced Intermediate courses in S3 and S4. Higher courses still tend to be followed by S5 and S6 pupils.

It is very unusual to find all four subjects on offer in any one school. Schools are being given more autonomy, and with the implementation of Curriculum for Excellence, the shape of the curriculum and of assessment in all subjects is dramatically changing. Fewer schools now offer Accounting and fewer still have Economics on offer. Economics, however, still attracts large numbers in some schools, particularly in the independent sector.

There are four Standard Grade courses at Foundation, General and Credit level, as seen in Figure 53.1. Intermediate 1, 2 and Higher courses have similar content, differentiation being contained in the level of knowledge and understanding required. Table 53.1 shows the number of entrants in each subject at each level in 2011.

While presentations in Administration at SG/Intermediate levels are only slightly lower than all other Business subjects together (12,501 and 12,523 respectively), Business Management at Higher level accounts for the largest number of presentations, being almost three times the number for Administration. This may be largely due to the popularity of Business Management being offered in many schools as a 'crash' Higher in sixth year.

SUBJECT BY SUBJECT

Courses in all four subjects have until recently been presented at Standard Grade, Intermediate 1, Intermediate 2, Higher and Advanced Higher. With the introduction of Curriculum for Excellence and new certification, the four separate subjects will still remain, but in the senior phase only. Initially it was thought that Business Education subjects would sit within the Technologies. However, as progress was made fleshing out the experiences and outcomes required by the initiative, it became clear that Business Education should be within the suite of courses that has been decided for the Social Studies curriculum area – Business. Table 53.2 shows the revised structure.

Business courses and Administration and IT courses will be offered at SCQF levels 3 to 4 (National 3 and National 4). Business Management, Administration and IT, Economics and Accounting will be developed as discrete subjects at SCQF level 5 (National 5). The existing courses at Higher and Advanced Higher will reflect the principles and practice of Curriculum for Excellence and provide smooth progression through and between the

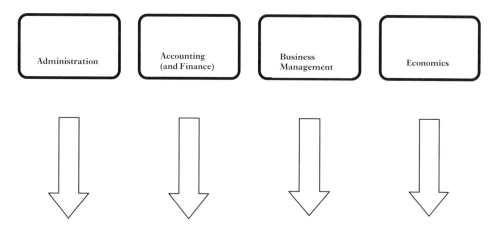

link to Intermediate 1, 2 and Higher level.

There are Access and Advanced Higher levels available too.

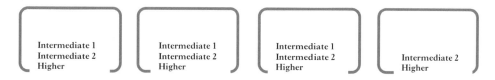

Figure 53.1   Number of candidates taking Business Education subjects in 2011

Table 53.1   Number of entrants by subject and level

	Administration	Business Management	Accounting	Economics
Standard Grade	5,890	5,302	1,601	101
Intermediate 1	2,720	1,088	99	0
Intermediate 2	3,981	3,732	282	318
Higher	2,608	6,932	1,204	576
Advanced Higher	17	197	39	74
TOTAL	15,216	17,251	3,225	1,069

Source: www.sqa.org.uk

Note: 2010 is the last year of Standard Grade certification and 2015 the last year of Intermediate Level certification. Advanced Higher Administration was scrapped in 2011 because of low numbers.

SCQF levels. These courses ought to provide seamless progression from the appropriate experiences and outcomes from the Social Studies curriculum area, and also from the Technologies curriculum area. The new courses do not provide direct replacement at National 4 level for existing National courses in Accounting and Economics. Aspects from both of these courses will be incorporated in the new National 4 in Business.

Table 53.2   The revised Business Education qualification suite

SCQF Level		Business Management	Accounting	Economics	Administration and IT
7	Advanced Higher	✓	✓	✓	
6	Higher	✓	✓	✓	✓
5	National 5	✓	✓	✓	✓
4	National 4		Business		✓
3	National 3		Business		✓

Table 53.3   Number of candidates taking Administration between 2006 and 2011

Level	2006	2007	2008	2009	2010	2011
Standard Grades	13,321	11,536	9,941	8,206	6,573	5,890
Intermediate 1	1,371	1,883	2,207	2,445	2,761	2,720
Intermediate 2	2,879	3,384	3,963	4,495	4,198	3,981
Higher	3,192	2,999	2,941	2,959	2,914	2,608
Total presentations	22,769	21,809	21,060	20,114	18,456	17,210

Source: www.sqa.org.uk

To give an indication of their relative importance with the trends affecting each subject Table 53.3 shows the total of all presentations (excluding Advanced Higher numbers which are not greatly significant) since 2006 when the SQA refined the NQs (i.e. Intermediate 1, 2 and Higher Grades).

Administration is the most vocational of the Business subjects and although numbers are falling it is still a popular subject choice in many departments. With its combination of a high ICT content and clear business context, Administration is unique to the Scottish school curriculum. Young people use industry-standard software packages to research, evaluate, communicate and summarise information in an effective manner. By doing so, they develop skills in problem solving and decision making with those who reach Higher Grade being well equipped to enter a career in business administration. Up until 2005, some universities refused to accept Higher Administration for entry into Higher Education. The Higher syllabus was revised in that year to include a degree of sophistication in the ICT content, which stretched many Business Education teachers as well as their S5 and S6 students. Advances in IT have necessitated a change in the content of Administration. It is being replaced by a more practical course entitled Administration and IT to overtake the more hands-on nature of Administration in the modern business world – reducing the previous emphasis on a theoretical approach.

Business Management continues to grow in popularity (see Table 53.4). Already it attracts significant numbers to Higher Grade. As the growth continues, Business Management has now become the key business subject of the future. SG Foundation and General and Intermediate 1 Business Management will be replaced by a 'common course' Business for National 3 and 4. This will allow departments to incorporate content from Business Management, Accounting and Economics depending on the choice/demand from pupils in their school. At National 5 level, Business Management will replace SG Credit and

Table 53.4   Number of candidates taking Business Management between 2006 and 2011

Level	2006	2007	2008	2009	2010	2011
Standard Grades	6,618	6,591	6,431	5,582	5,445	5,302
Intermediate 1	338	364	635	729	1,049	1,088
Intermediate 2	1,971	2,507	2,819	3,195	3,663	3,732
Higher	5,795	5,737	5,993	6,309	6,514	6,932
Total presentations	16,728	17,206	17,886	17,824	18,681	19,065

Source: www.sqa.org.uk

Table 53.5   Number of candidates taking Accounting (Accounting and Finance SG) between 2006 and 2011

Level	2006	2007	2008	2009	2010	2011
Standard Grades	2,363	2,273	2,003	1,932	1,630	1,601
Intermediate 1	119	84	100	76	96	99
Intermediate 2	365	372	361	348	335	282
Higher	1,630	1,459	1,465	1,345	1,220	1,204
Total presentations	6,483	6,195	5,937	5,710	5,291	5,197

Source: www.sqa.org.uk

Intermediate 2 Business Management. Business and Business Management provide a less specialist approach to the study of the business world. Business Enterprise is studied within the context of the key business decision-making areas – Marketing, Operations, Finance and Human Resources. At all levels young people acquire knowledge and understanding of the business world, develop analytical skills and are encouraged to apply them to make effective decisions.

The total number of presentations in Accounting continues to decline (see Table 53.5). The number of schools teaching it has also fallen. At times this has been the choice of the department (due perhaps to lack of staff expertise in this area), sometimes the choice of senior management in the school (to accommodate staffing levels and timetabling issues) and very occasionally the result of a local education authority taking an executive decision to remove the subject from all authority schools. Schools that do have the expertise and demand for Accounting will be able to tailor their Business course at National 4 to allow progression to National 5 Accounting.

The total number of presentations in Economics has fallen (see Table 53.6) and continues to decline. Competition with other Social subjects at the end of S2, the perception that Economics is a difficult subject and the introduction and popularity of Business Management have all had an impact. However, as for Accounting, schools that do have the expertise and demand for Economics will be able to tailor their Business course at National 4, to allow progression to National 5 Economics.

For departments faced with a range of subjects to offer and limited staffing, it might be expected that the future of Accounting and to a greater extent Economics will continue to be under threat. That Accounting and Economics still survive is down to the enthusiasm

Table 53.6   Number of candidates taking Economics between 2006 and 2011
Economics

Level	2006	2007	2008	2009	2010	2011
Standard Grades	289	244	182	138	89	101
Intermediate 1	10	42	11	7	10	0
Intermediate 2	307	344	294	340	362	318
Higher	686	649	620	633	633	576
Total presentations	3,298	3,286	3,115	3,127	3,104	3,006

Source: www.sqa.org.uk

of teachers in individual schools who are able to convince senior management of the value of these subjects in a crowded curriculum. Curriculum for Excellence recognises the importance of both of these subjects – as they have both been retained as separate subjects at National 5, Higher and Advanced Higher levels. Schools may now be able to offer either Accounting or Economics more readily and attract more pupil uptake at senior level, because of the foundation of knowledge and understanding created by the National 4 Business course content.

LEARNING AND TEACHING

All Business Education teachers have to be well versed in a range of business subjects and highly skilled in IT. Teachers often specialise in one or two subjects, but all have the benefit of being able to link their teaching with the real business world. The fact that young people perceive Business Education as relevant and practical helps to make learning and teaching both rewarding and stimulating. Business Education teachers are highly positive about their role and feel that they are teaching a subject that is both relevant and of value. In the HMIE report *Standards and Quality in Secondary Schools: Business Education 1996–2001*, the inspectorate commented that the ethos was good or very good in over 90 per cent of departments, and in almost all departments relationships between staff and pupils were good or very good. They also observed that almost all pupils showed enthusiasm when working in IT-related activity.

A lot of the work that young people do in Administration is IT-related with an increasing emphasis on practical understanding rather than theoretical fact-based learning. IT is also used widely to support learning and teaching across the Business curriculum with excellent support websites being specifically designed to assist both teachers and young people throughout the UK. Excellent support resources are also provided by the Business Education Network (BEN), Intelligent Resources and other new companies coming to the market. SQA and Education Scotland also support the demands of the modern curriculum through their website e-library of up-to-date resources and assessment exemplification. GLOW (Scottish Schools Digital Network), with its fully authenticated national education community, accommodates exciting possibilities in the use of IT to support learning and teaching in Business Education.

CONCERNS AND CHALLENGES

There are still concerns over the future of Accounting and Economics. As secondary school rolls continue to fall and Curriculum for Excellence, with its aim of reducing over-crowding in the curriculum, evolves, it is possible that Accounting and Economics might find their place under increasing threat. We have moved a step nearer to the idea of a more streamlined approach to Business Education by reducing the subject choice at level 4 of the curriculum. Business Education – although an 'optional' subject in Scottish schools – has survived the radical change imposed by Curriculum for Excellence. There are still four discrete subjects on offer, a testament to the content and relevance of the subjects taught in today's classrooms.

Curriculum for Excellence already poses significant challenges, with opportunities for some Business and IT input into the early years of the secondary school. Much of the subject content is relevant to the Social subjects suite of courses and the sophisticated IT skills of Business Education teachers can make a significant contribution in the Technologies. Business Education teachers also make a major contribution to the 'responsibility of all' areas identified under Curriculum for Excellence. For example, in Business Education young people develop their literacy, numeracy and communication skills in a variety of business contexts that they perceive as being relevant and of real value. They use IT to research the 'real world', solve problems, make decisions and communicate their findings to others, thereby developing their presentation skills and building their confidence in oral and written communication. Through learning and teaching in a real and relevant context, young people gain an insight into the economic and social dimensions of society and learn how they might, as successful learners, contribute to that society by becoming effective contributors and responsible citizens.

There is a growing trend for faculty arrangements of grouped subjects in schools leading to the appointment, for example, of a single faculty head to manage both Business Education and Computing. The principal teacher can be either a Computing or a Business specialist, with some who are dual-qualified. One of the effects of this trend is that the larger 'department' may have additional flexibility to offer courses identified within Curriculum for Excellence. Thus, the faculty arrangement might provide an advantage over the normal Business Education department, which has to compete with other subjects for a presence in the S1/S2 curriculum.

CONCLUSION

The future of Business Education is in the hands of those teachers who have successfully addressed the significant challenges of the past, supported by the skilled and enthusiastic teachers who are entering the profession. There are certain to be further challenges in the years ahead, not least the place of the subject in the Scottish secondary school. HMIE observed that 'Business and enterprise are at the heart of national growth and development and this is reflected in the important place that business education has in the post-school curriculum' (SOEID, 2002). Business Education teachers have worked hard since the 1960s to raise the status of Business Education in the school curriculum. With their renowned professionalism, commitment and enthusiasm they must continue to do so in the years to come.

REFERENCES

Scottish Office Education and Industry Department (1996) *Effective Learning and Teaching in Scottish Secondary Schools: Business Education and Economics.* Edinburgh: Her Majesty's Stationery Office.

Scottish Office Education and Industry Department (2002) *Standards and Quality in Secondary Schools: Business Education 1996–2001.* Edinburgh: Her Majesty's Stationery Office.

54

Career Education

Cathy Howieson and Sheila Semple

This chapter is being written at a time of major change for career information, advice and guidance in Scotland as Skills Development Scotland (SDS) launches its new service delivery model and its framework for career management skills. The changes to SDS provision combined with the implementation of Curriculum for Excellence (CfE) are likely to have a major impact on career education in schools, but this appears to be happening in an unplanned way as a consequence of these other changes. In this chapter we attempt to outline these developments and consider the possible impact on career education.

THE DEVELOPMENT OF CAREER EDUCATION IN SCOTTISH SCHOOLS

To understand the extent and implications of the likely changes to career education, it is necessary to consider its recent development in secondary schools. Career education first began to be given prominence in policy and practice in Scotland from the mid-1990s. The drivers for this were threefold: a realisation that the world of work was changing very rapidly and that young people and their parents needed to understand these changes and develop the skills to meet the resulting challenges; concern from employers and government that schools were not preparing young people adequately for their future working lives and thus to contribute to the country's economic performance; and a recognition from both parents and schools that career education was important. These concerns remain central to thinking on career education, indeed they have intensified as successive governments have placed increasing emphasis on the contribution that career work in schools can make to economic outcomes. Such expectations for career education have been considered in a number of research studies that have identified the positive contribution that well-designed career education can make to young people's career-related skills and in supporting their progression within and post-school (see Hughes and Gration, 2009, for an overview of this body of research).

The development of career education was taken forward by the Career Education Training Initiative (1995–8) under which the then Scottish Office provided money to all local authorities (LAs) to train teachers and librarians in the planning and delivery of career programmes in secondary schools. Despite resulting improvements in career education, it became clear that there remained inconsistencies in provision in secondary schools between and within LAs, and this recognition led in 2001 to the development of national curricular guidance on career education in Scottish schools (LTS, 2001).

Career Education in Scotland: A National Framework represented a significant advance in the position of career education in Scottish education: it extended the age range for career education to 3–18; it used the term 'career' in preference to 'careers' to indicate the need for a broader view of career development; and it set out learning outcomes for students to achieve at different stages (LTS, 2001). It is notable that the learning outcomes included content (i.e. the knowledge and understanding elements) as well as skills, since most teachers delivering career education would not have specialist career-related experience and knowledge to draw on to achieve the skill outcomes.

Between 2001 and 2004, the then newly established Careers Scotland worked with seconded teachers to design CareerBox, a national curriculum resource providing teaching materials to deliver the learning outcomes of the National Framework from 3 to 18. CareerBox led to increased consistency in provision across Scotland although in practice few schools used it in its entirety, instead 'mixing and matching' the new materials with tried and tested resources. Until 2009–10, this resource was regularly updated, and it continues to be used in many schools and colleges across Scotland.

Scottish education moved on, and other changes and initiatives had an impact on career education policy and practice including a greater focus on enterprise and more attention to the role of career education in the preparation and support for young people at risk of not achieving positive post-school outcomes. The most significant development has been the introduction of CfE (SE, 2004). While career education has always been a way to help pupils see purpose and relevance in their education and help them to link core skills to their future use, this has become even more significant in the context of CfE in which 'Relevance' is one of the stated principles for curriculum design, whereby 'Young people should understand the purposes of their activities. They should see the value of what they are learning and its relevance to their lives, present and future' (SE, 2004, p. 15).

CURRENT DEFINITION(S) OF CAREER EDUCATION

In the first edition of *Scottish Education* in 1999, we noted that there was no agreed definition of careers education; by the second edition, four years later, we were able to report that there was for the first time in Scotland an official definition of what was now to be termed 'career education'. But this has now been revised and the term 'career-related learning' is also being used. The most recent definition in policy documents (at the time of writing) is:

> Career Education, or career-related learning – is a process of learning, designed to help young people to develop the knowledge, confidence and skills they need to make well-informed, relevant choices and plans for their future, so they can progress smoothly into further learning and work. Successful career-related learning supports the acquisition of the whole range of knowledge, skills and attributes that contribute to the four capacities within CfE (SG, 2011a, p. 28).

The same document, however, also refers to 'Career Management Skills' (CMS) as does the Roe Review of post-16 education and vocational training in Scotland (SG, 2011b). CMS appear to encompass aspects that have previously been part of career education: 'Career Management Skills align with the experiences and outcomes of CfE and enable individuals to apply the skills to:

- develop personal awareness around likes, dislikes, strengths and weaknesses;
- gather, interpret and analyse career, learning and labour market information;

- explore options in learning and work and relate this to personal priorities and strengths; and
- take action to build a career pathway.' (SG, 2011a, p. 28; see also SG, 2011b, p. 79)

It appears that 'career-related learning' may be the term likely to be taken forward officially rather than 'career education' but, at time of writing, this is unclear and how this might differ in reality from 'career management skills', or what the relationship is between the two, is also not apparent.

AIMS, CONTENT AND ORGANISATION IN SCHOOLS

Regardless of how career education is defined or structured, its essential aims are consistent across the countries of the UK and internationally. Career education aims to support young people to:

- recognise preferences, strengths, weaknesses and motivators/values;
- learn about how the world of work and of post-school learning operates; the range of opportunities available; the skills and attitudes necessary to find work, training or a course and the likely challenges;
- develop skills to review, plan and adjust career ideas and to take decisions forward;
- understand the value and limitations of different information and advice sources including parents, family, friends, teachers, careers advisers and websites;
- practise the skills involved in job and course search.

Career education in secondary schools is generally still part of Personal, Social and Health Education (PSE) programmes although a small number of schools use a cross-curricular approach. Traditionally classroom work, including discussions, worksheets and, in some cases, DVD material, is used. ICT, in particular career websites, has played an increasing role in career education over the last decade or so, including programmes for self-assessment, career matching and transition skills (such as CV creation) and for the retrieval of occupational and educational information. The extent to which its use has been integrated into a career education programme has varied across schools and authorities; the embedding of ICT in career education programmes has been most likely in the authorities using the PlanIt Plus website partly because it has been developed in consultation with its funding LAs. The year 2011 saw the launch of Skill Development Scotland's MyWorldOfWork, an all-age career information and advice web service which among other aims, policy makers hope will provide useful content to support schools' career education programmes. However, it is still unclear whether or not career websites can have the same level of impact on career development as has been shown for more 'traditional' approaches (Howieson and Semple, 2011). MyWorldOfWork is expected by SDS to provide a national bank of career materials for schools, pupils, teachers and parents, replacing CareerBox.

Students may achieve career education outcomes with the support of specialist pastoral care or guidance staff teaching the group of students for whom they have responsibility, members of staff from a range of disciplines who have been allocated a role in the PSE programme as part of their timetable or, less commonly, non-specialist staff with a first-line tutorial role. The management of the overall programme is usually the responsibility of a member of the specialist pastoral care team.

CURRENT DEVELOPMENTS IN POLICY AND PRACTICE

As already noted, the situation is fluid and it is not yet clear what, if any, new guidance on career education will emerge. The 2001 National Framework, which provided specialist guidance on career education, is now generally perceived as outdated and is thus largely unused, but no new guidance and suggested structures for school career education programmes have been produced (nor do there appear at the time of writing to be any plans to do so). However, Skills Development Scotland has now published its *Career Management Skills Framework for Scotland* and, critically, this will not only guide the delivery of career advice, guidance and information services by career specialists but will also impact on career education in schools (SDS, 2012a). SDS expects schools to deliver lessons that develop career management skills (CMS) and that such lessons will 'be shaped' by SDS (p. 12; SDS, 2012b); it also expects that CMS will be built into lesson plans as part of CfE.

Building the Curriculum 4 (SG, 2009) signifies a clear intention that schools should deliver career education through the curriculum and as such represents a major shift from a largely discrete series of lessons as part of PSE, the approach used in all but a handful of Scottish secondary schools. Career education is likely to be delivered through experiences and outcomes in relation to Health and Wellbeing (under 'Planning for Choices and Changes') (SG, 2010), but also in relation to Literacy, Numeracy, Social Studies, Religious and Moral Education, Technology and others. It also links to Personal Learning Planning, and Enterprise and Employability, cross-cutting themes that are also the responsibility of all practitioners.

It is likely that delivery through the curriculum will be enhanced by immersion days, tutor inputs and perhaps a programme of visits and/or visiting speakers, often in collaboration with careers advisers and other specialist staff of SDS.

The planned change will alter how career education is taught, making all teaching staff responsible for the achievement of its outcomes; it is possible that the most common approach will be a tutor group model. It is likely that a specialist guidance or pastoral care manager will still be responsible for the design, planning and monitoring of career education (subject to LAs' decisions about the continuation of these posts).

KEY ISSUES

The present uncertainty in relation to terminology and definitions is an issue: the range of staff involved in career education means that they need to share a common terminology and a common understanding if they are to plan and carry out their roles effectively, otherwise there is a risk of confusion in expectations and overlap or gaps in provision. The change to delivery of career education through the curriculum presents considerable challenges for schools: effectively this means that all members of staff will be involved, more or less willingly. While there has always been an element of 'conscription' in relation to the teaching of PSE, this has been substantially reduced in recent years and only ever affected a proportion of staff: now all staff are potentially 'conscripts'.

Most teachers lack any specialist knowledge of career education on which they can draw to carry out their new role but it is unclear if there are plans to support and train them in this. There is no indication (to date) that the Scottish Government will fund a programme similar to the Career Education Training Initiative of the 1990s. While careers advisers have been increasingly encouraged to undertake capacity building with school staff, staff will need more systematic support and training than this: they receive almost no input on career education in their Initial Teacher Education, there appears to be little non-award bearing continuing professional development on this topic for serving teachers and there is now only one academic course for teachers that includes career education.

The cross-curricular delivery of career education has a number of positives, for example the potential to increase the perceived relevance of the curriculum to pupils and to increase the credibility of career education to higher-achieving pupils through its delivery in academic subjects. Nevertheless, the risks associated with cross-curricular delivery are substantial indeed. It requires good planning and monitoring of provision to avoid either duplication or gaps and, critically, to ensure consistency of provision. There is a hazard that delivery of outcomes through subjects makes career education dispensable when the subject curriculum hits pressure points.

The issue of consistency in provision for pupils across Scotland is a particular danger: no specialist national guidance on career education has been produced to replace the previous National Framework and the move to a cross-curricular approach is being combined with the freedom under CfE for schools to adopt different approaches, decide on different emphases and use different subject content. If a school, for example, decides to deliver career education through Religious and Moral Education, it is likely to have more focus on values and lifestyles than if delivered through Business Studies, in which case there may be more emphasis on labour market information, training opportunities and financial aspects. This freedom for schools also means that it will be very difficult to obtain a comprehensive picture of career education and its quality at LA and national level; an issue shared with other subject areas in CfE. There is a danger that the likely changes to career education will undermine the gains in consistency and quality made over the last decade and take career education back to the problems of the 1990s.

REFERENCES

Howieson C. and S. Semple (2011) 'Help yourself: Can career websites make a difference?' CES Briefing No 56. Online at www.ces.ed.ac.uk/PDF%20Files/Brief056.pdf

Hughes, D. and G. Gration (2009) *Evidence and Impact: Careers and Guidance-related Interventions – A Literature Review*. Reading: CfBT Education Trust.

Learning and Teaching Scotland (2001) *National Framework for Career Education 3–18 in Scotland*. Dundee: LTS.

Scottish Executive (2004) *A Curriculum for Excellence: The Curriculum Review Group*. Edinburgh: Scottish Executive.

Scottish Government (2009) *Curriculum for Excellence: Building the Curriculum 4: Skills for Learning, Skills for Life and Skills for Work*. Edinburgh: Scottish Government.

Scottish Government (2010) *Curriculum for Excellence: Health and Wellbeing: Experiences and Outcomes*. Online at www.ltscotland.org.uk/Images/health_wellbeing_experiences_outcomes_tcm4-540031.pdf

Scottish Government (2011a) *Career Information, Advice and Guidance in Scotland. A Framework for Service Redesign and Improvement*. Edinburgh: Scottish Government.

Scottish Government (2011b) *Review of Post-16 Education and Vocational Training in Scotland* (the Roe Review). Edinburgh: Scottish Government.

Skills Development Scotland (2012a) *Career Management Skills Framework for Scotland*. Glasgow: SDS.

Skills Development Scotland (2012b) *Corporate Strategy 2012/15*. Glasgow: SDS.

55

Chemistry Education

Douglas Buchanan

We live in interesting times! Since the introduction of Standard Grade in the 1980s, the waves of innovation that have been ongoing in Scottish chemistry education have led to imaginative use of courses in secondary schools as well as creative approaches to learning and teaching. Developments continue with Curriculum for Excellence (CfE), a major initiative that covers the entire 3–18 curriculum. Across the country, increased flexibility and choice is likely to lead to even greater variation in the student experience at the different levels. However, it would not be unfair to suggest that many secondary Chemistry teachers (like their colleagues in other subject areas) view this climate of ongoing change with varying degrees of apprehension.

THE 3–15 CURRICULUM

In the early years of most Scottish secondary schools, chemistry has always tended to form clearly identifiable sections of a science course that is predominantly based on national guidelines. Within CfE, as well as a set of 'content statements' that shape the 3–15 science curriculum (Education Scotland, 2010a) there is a Principles and Practice document that offers advice on planning (Education Scotland, 2010b). These publications provide a framework to support primary teachers with the introduction of aspects of chemistry to programmes of science work and, in turn, give secondary teachers the opportunity to consider learning and teaching of the subject within a broad general education and integrated context for students up to age 15.

COURSES AT NATIONAL 4 AND NATIONAL 5

At the time of writing, all existing provision, including the highly popular Standard Grade Chemistry course, attracting over 20,000 students, is being replaced by National 4 and National 5 courses that are designed to reflect CfE values, purposes and principles. Standard Grade is a two-year bi-level course, based on a core and extension model, with external assessment at both levels. Although there is much talk about 'raising the bar', National 4, a course that will be completely internally assessed, is likely to evolve from Standard Grade General Level, while National 5, which will have an external end-of-course examination as well as an internal unit assessment, is likely to be broadly in line with Standard Grade Credit Level. Not surprisingly, the perceived increase in workload associated with internal assessment is a matter of concern for teachers. Although these are one-year courses written for post-15 provision, there should be scope for increasing depth and specialisation in common areas in S1 to S3 and it is intended that attainment at national curriculum levels (relating to National 4 and National 5) will be recognised within the S3 profile.

HIGHER AND ADVANCED HIGHER

Progression from National 5 is to a one-year Higher course for students in S5 and then the Advanced Higher in S6. As with Standard Grade, the origins of these courses are well established and they have a healthy uptake with over 9,000 studying at Higher and just over 2,000 taking Advanced Higher, making chemistry at this level second in popularity only to Mathematics. For students in fifth and sixth year who are studying below Higher, the course at National 5 may be available when numbers permit viable class sizes.

THE IMPACT OF CFE

What can we expect for chemistry with the changes associated with the present initiative? The purposes of CfE are reflected in the four capacities: successful learners, confident individuals, effective contributors and responsible citizens. Consequently, there is a real emphasis on how teachers teach as well as what they teach, so that the introduction of CfE is as much to do with changes in methodology as changes in content.

Formative assessment techniques in combination with cooperative learning strategies are seen as vehicles to enable students to develop a deeper understanding of key ideas within a favourable classroom culture for interdependent learning. While these ideas have infiltrated many primary school classrooms, penetration into Chemistry/Science departments in secondary schools has been patchier. The system of external assessment, managed by the Scottish Qualifications Authority, is unhelpful to changes of this kind; teachers are trying, slowly and painfully, to move away from a rather traditional, largely recall-based, assessment regime to one that allows students to demonstrate real learning in terms of both knowledge and understanding and skills.

It is likely that a decluttered and less fragmented curriculum will be achieved by removing unnecessary detail and overlaps within Chemistry, and between Chemistry and other subjects. Here, while the opportunity to address content overload, to produce a more progressive curriculum and to explore issues relating to breadth versus depth of content will be welcomed by some, the workload implications of curricular changes are clear to all.

The content at 3–15 is described using much more broad-based statements, written in an 'I can do . . .' style, for example 'I can apply my knowledge of . . .'. This approach reverses recent trends by which outcomes have been specified in more and more detail and is still relatively contentious. While there are certainly strong arguments for encouraging diversity and the local ownership of content that is not going to be nationally examined, the lack of 'a typical framework' can present problems for teachers as well as students who have to move school. In addition, by addressing all the values, purposes and principles of Curriculum for Excellence, the outcomes are trying to be more than just assessment criteria. 'I can express an informed opinion on . . .' links social, ethical and moral issues to the outcomes and the likes of 'I can talk about . . .' and 'I can give a presentation to demonstrate . . .' are outcomes that touch on personal skills. While this opens up opportunities for interdisciplinary/

cross-curricular approaches, here again Chemistry/Science departments tend to be struggling with the implications of assessment.

KEY FEATURES OF COURSES

The following are central characteristics of courses at all levels:

- The acquisition of knowledge and understanding of essential chemical theory, processes and reactions is seen as an essential activity. However, considerable prominence is also given to problem solving, practical work and the development of core skills.
- Problem solving includes 'conventional' skills such as concluding and explaining, generalising and predicting, as well as 'related' skills like selecting, presenting and processing information. As a result, to develop these skills in the classroom, students engage in practical problem solving that is likely to involve designing and planning investigations and evaluating results as well as paper-and-pencil exercises that require students to decode written information about unfamiliar chemistry. Where appropriate, many students use problem-solving approaches to acquire the essential knowledge and understanding.
- A wide range of practical activities for a variety of purposes is seen as being important. Students are expected to engage in experiments in order to illustrate theory, e.g. prepare an ester, carry out a redox titration and develop practical skills such as producing and collecting a precipitate. Practical investigative work that offers a range of challenges is an important element of all courses.
- Theoretical chemical knowledge and understanding is made more relevant by giving prominence to social, economic, environmental and industrial applications. At National 4 and National 5, students are likely to study topics on fossil fuels, acid rain, corrosion, plastics and synthetic fibres and fertilisers while the new Higher course includes the chemistry of fruit flavours, cooking and the oxidation of food as well as covering design and production principles of the modern chemical industry.
- Chemistry teachers have always taken a commendable interest in their role in the development of core skills and each change in the curriculum tends to further sensitise this interest. It is expected that careful thought be given to communication skills as well as numerical work and opportunities to use information and communications technology (ICT). In addition, the increasing use of group methods is promoting the development of inter-personal skills.

APPROACHES TO LEARNING AND TEACHING

Thirty years ago, practical work by students tended to be limited and there was a heavy emphasis on theory combined with illustrative demonstrations by teachers. Copying from the blackboard, taking down dictated notes and memorising facts were common student activities. What now tends to be going on in a chemistry classroom?

To cope with the wide variety of student needs and abilities, Chemistry teachers recognise that effective learning and teaching requires judicious use of the complete range of methods. As a result, within the context of 'direct teaching', there is a place for exposition and whole-class question-and-answer sessions, accompanied by memorable demonstrations of illustrative practical work. However, more pupil-centred approaches are also used to deliver appropriate content and skills. Students, usually working in groups and guided by activity sheets, make regular use of textbooks, leaflets and posters, as well as experiments, models and video facilities to support their own learning. It says much for the drive and commitment of Chemistry teachers that a number of 'cottage industries' such as Chemcord, set up by teachers to produce and distribute a wide range of course resources, have become familiar features on the chemistry landscape. Increasing employment is being made of computers, including their use for PowerPoint presentations, to simulate experiments and show animations, to access the internet, for self-teaching programmes and to interface with scientific equipment, and a growing number of teachers are becoming proficient in the use of whiteboard technology. In this area also, teachers are demonstrating their ingenuity (see, for example, www.evans2chemweb, a site set up and managed by teachers).

QUALITY OF ATTAINMENT

The *Improving Achievement in Science* report (HMIE, 2005) points to well-designed Chemistry courses in S3 and S4, with students thoroughly prepared for the Standard Grade examination. An equally encouraging picture is painted by the results of examination awards with levels of attainment showing small but steady improvements over recent years. In 2011, for Standard Grade, 62 per cent of students taking the subject achieved an award at the Credit level with a further 37 per cent achieving an award at the General level, and the percentage of students achieving a Band A award and a 'pass' for Higher level was 29 per cent and 77 per cent respectively (based on pre-appeal data). It should also be noted that performance in Higher in Scotland generally exceeds performance in equivalent examinations elsewhere in the UK and levels of participation are considerably higher in Scotland. A comparison of the percentages of the 16-year-old population in Scotland with the 17-year-old population in England, Northern Ireland and Wales taking chemistry to A-level (average across 2000–7) shows 12 per cent taking the Scottish Higher compared with 5 per cent, 7 per cent and 4 per cent for the other countries respectively (Royal Society, 2007). Sound performances at the upper stages of secondary school are supported by the findings of Programme for International Student Assessment surveys of 15-year-olds in the principal industrialised countries. In part, this may reflect the fact that young people in Scotland have the opportunity to specialise in the separate sciences from age 14 and that Scotland has a healthier number of teachers who have a degree in Chemistry. That said, we cannot be complacent for, although the uptake has been steady in recent years, the beginning of the last decade saw a steady decline in the percentage of 16-year-olds choosing to study Chemistry.

It is hard to leave the subject of improved attainment in national exams without acknowledging that there are many unanswered questions surrounding this issue. Has the impact of continued change in content led to some of the 'more difficult chemistry' being moved to a higher level? Have questions been made more accessible for the students? Is there more successful 'coaching' towards the questions in the examinations? Or, perhaps, is it due to the greater use of more effective approaches to learning and teaching?

Moving to the lower years in secondary schools, Her Majesty's Inspectorate of Education's report (2005) is less positive about the quality of students' science education, indicating that for 12- to 14-year-olds, ways to raise achievement should be considered and weaknesses in both courses and assessment need to be tackled, for instance by taking account of students' prior experience at primary school and recent developments in the subject. There is also a clear message that many primary teachers lack both confidence and competence in the teaching of science. For some years now, these findings have been supported by the Trends in International Mathematics and Science Study that points to relatively disappointing performances from students in Scotland at ages 9 and 13.

CURRENT CHALLENGES

Investments provided for schools and councils through a response to the *Science Strategy for Scotland* (Scottish Executive Enterprise and Lifelong Learning Department, 2001) have been welcomed, but there is still much work to be done if significant numbers of students are to experience modern Chemistry courses delivered by well-prepared and enthusiastic teachers in a twenty-first-century environment. The following are among the challenges that stand out.

The chemistry community is anxious about the impact on chemistry education of the lack of subject leadership in both schools and local councils. The tone of responses to a survey of Chemistry teachers in every school in Scotland, carried out by the Royal Society of Chemistry Scottish Region Education Committee, was profoundly negative, with considerable scorn being heaped on the moves to replace principal teachers of science subjects with a new faculty system. Problem areas highlighted included the difficulty of managing and developing courses and assessment when there was a lack of subject expertise and the lack of promotion prospects for young teachers; there were also concerns about the fairness of budget allocation and the degree of direction as to how funds were to be allocated. Within councils, Science Advisors tend to have been replaced by non-subject Quality Improvement Officers who have a role in the inspection arena. The support of the subject specialist is being sorely missed.

Too many laboratories still present a dull and depressing learning environment and the use of outdated equipment is not uncommon. Indeed, many departments are poorly supplied with modern equipment for ICT, restricting opportunities for interfacing, simulating experiments and the development of subject knowledge, understanding and skills.

The almost exponential growth in knowledge means that much of the content of chemistry courses can go quickly out of date and a more responsive model for curriculum development is required. This in turn has serious implications for continuing professional development (CPD). Given the present age profile, many secondary Chemistry teachers would benefit from a more coherent approach to both Chemistry and pedagogical updating. Primary teachers recognise the need for higher levels of subject knowledge. *Science & Engineering 21 – An Action Plan for Education* (Scottish Government, 2011) recognises the need to 'build capacity and expertise of teachers' but, at a time when high quality CPD is urgently required, it is a matter of regret that the emphasis seems to be on 'plan' rather than 'action'.

New technologies have always been on the move in schools. Many Chemistry departments now use interactive whiteboards and the internet to support learning. The national internet learning initiative GLOW has been slow to take hold and in spite of the government push, not every school or teacher is GLOW-confident.

CONCLUSION

The many recent entries to the Chemistry teaching profession, with up-to-date experience of contemporary content, issues and pedagogy, consider that preparing for CfE is no more than part of the challenges associated with the start of a career. For the veterans of the previous initiatives, it is inevitable that there are some who will be relieved to find the escape hatch. Once seen as a golden opportunity for the subject, the present development is now viewed by many in the community as a dangerous experiment that is being thrust upon them without adequate assessment of risk like the impact of the current economic climate, changes to teachers' working conditions and levels of support and leadership. However, as always, it can be predicted with confidence that Chemistry teachers will be doing their best for the pupils in their care.

REFERENCES

Education Scotland (2010a) *Curriculum for Excellence: Sciences Experiences and Outcomes.* Online at www.educationscotland.gov.uk/Images/sciences_experiences_outcomes_tcm4-539890.pdf

Education Scotland (2010b) *Curriculum for Excellence: Sciences Principles and Practice.* Online at www.educationscotland.gov.uk/Images/sciences_principles_practice_tcm4-540396.pdf

Her Majesty's Inspectorate of Education (2005) *Improving Achievement in Science in Primary and Secondary Schools.* Livingston: HMIE.

Royal Society (2007) *The UK's Science and Mathematics Teaching Workforce.* London: Royal Society.

Scottish Executive Enterprise and Lifelong Learning Department (2001) *Science Strategy for Scotland.* Edinburgh: Scottish Executive.

Scottish Government (2011) *Science & Engineering 21 – An Action Plan for Education.* Edinburgh: Scottish Government.

56

Computing and Information Systems Education

Vic Lally

In the centenary year of Alan Turing's birth (2012), one of the important things to say about Computing and Information Systems education in Scottish schools is that it is on the cusp of change. Turing was the 'father' of modern computing – a little-known British genius who is commemorated in one of the leading schools of Informatics in the UK, at the University of Edinburgh (the Turing Room). Turing's contributions to the country's future, both as a computer scientist of genius and as a wartime code-breaker, are seminal. Yet, despite this, his reputation does not extend far beyond Computer Science. In a way, a similar fate has befallen Computer Science itself. As an area of study it has been somewhat neglected beyond the universities, yet there is no doubt that the skills of Computer Science and Informatics are of considerable and increasing importance for our economic and scientific futures. It is vital that the new curriculum developments in this field support and enhance the talents and abilities of Scotland's young people.

CURRENT PROVISION

One of the versions of Computer Science in Scottish schools is 'Computing'. As a subject it has been available at Intermediate 2 (SCQF level 5), Higher (SCQF level 6) and Advanced Higher (SCQF level 7) levels. This subject has focused on the study of Computer Science and its uses. Between them, these courses accounted for approximately 7,700 examination entries in 2011.

Computing has centred on developing problem-solving skills by encouraging learners to apply knowledge, understanding and practical skills. Computing has also included study of the professional, social, ethical and legal implications of its use, as well as the clear and concise communication of computing concepts using appropriate terminology. The course also offers options in Artificial Intelligence, Computer Networking and Multimedia Technology. The Higher qualification in Computing also encourages awareness of technological developments and progress, factors affecting system performance and issues of syntax and semantics. Topics of study include data representation, computer structure, peripherals, networking and software. Learners also acquire knowledge of and skills in developing software through the use of a high-level programming language. The course encourages them to make judgements, assess and compare ideas, and evaluate data. Advanced Higher

Computing extends these ideas and skills through investigation and analysis. It aims to equip learners with skills to design and implement a solution to a significant computing problem. The course focuses on the software development process, looking at software development languages and environments, high-level programming languages and standard algorithms. Students are assessed using both written and practical assessment instruments.

The second version of Computer Science has been through Computing Studies. This has been offered at Standard Grade (SCQF levels 3–5) and Intermediate 1 level (SCQF level 4). The key aim of this course is to provide knowledge and experience of 'the technology that lies at the heart of modern society'. It covers information technology concepts, the practical operation of hardware and software, and the awareness of how computers affect our work, home and leisure activities. The new subject currently being developed is called Computing Science. This has emerged in response to a build-up of concerns regarding both Computing and Computer Studies in Scottish schools (see below). It has been designed to combine the best aspects of both the current subjects. Computing Science will develop a range of computing and computational thinking skills, including skills in analysis and problem solving, design, and modelling, developing, implementing and testing digital solutions, across a range of contemporary contexts. In addition, the developers claim that it takes account of modern technologies and development methodologies related to software and information systems. In terms of assessment, one of the innovations will include elements that provide personalisation and choice in assignments at National 4, National 5 and Higher levels, with question papers also providing added value at National 5 and Higher levels. The next section will examine some of the concerns that have stimulated these developments.

COMPUTING AND COMPUTER STUDIES: THE PROBLEMS AND THE CHALLENGES

There is a developing consensus that courses in Computing and Computer Studies are in need of substantial revision to meet the needs of students and educators for the twenty-first century in Scotland. For example, one point that could be made is that the current suite of subjects has not concentrated enough on the main concepts of Computer Science, and has concentrated too much on hardware and systems that are outdated or rapidly becoming so. Similar issues have been raised about Scottish qualifications by the Computing at School Working Group (2012). In many ways both of these criticisms echo the more detailed range of concerns raised by the Royal Society about the state of Computing in schools across the UK (Royal Society, 2012). While the data and evidence presented in this report are based significantly on the English context, they also align with findings from interviews (conducted for this chapter) with other leading and informed figures in the field of Scottish education and teacher education.

Another of these challenges is the confusion between 'Computing' – the science discussed above – and the use of computers in a wide range of settings to manage a vast array of activities and communications, often referred to as 'Information and Communications Technology' (ICT). This is widespread among parents and pupils, schools, local authorities, teaching colleagues and government ministers. One of the consequences is that Computer Science itself may be often overlooked in this confusion. This has implications for policy, teacher education and pupils' future lives and careers. This confusion will need to be addressed as the new Computer Science qualifications are launched in Scotland. It is important to disaggregate the term 'Information and Communications Technology',

Table 56.1   First-year students on initial teacher training courses in Computing in Scotland

Year	Students
2007	66
2008	57
2009	38
2010	29
2011	22

Source: Royal Society, 2012, p. 74

so that 'Computer Science' can achieve some distinctive recognition as a central scientific discipline. This will require action by the Scottish Qualifications Authority (SQA), and the Scottish Government (see Royal Society report, 2012, Chapter 2). The teaching of Computer Science in Scotland may also be hampered by a lack of specialist teachers with up-to-date knowledge of developments in the field, and sufficient pedagogical subject knowledge to take advantage of the most recent curriculum innovations.

The General Teaching Council for Scotland (GTCS) maintains data on the teaching workforce in Scotland. It is important to note that GTCS data are self-reported. Accordingly, the number of Computing teachers registered in Scotland has increased from 771 in 2008–9 to 810 in 2010–11. These figures include provisionally registered teachers (that is, those who have not completed teacher training) whose numbers were reduced by 57 per cent during this period, from sixty-six to twenty-nine (see Table 56.1). The Scottish Government's census indicates that between 2007 and 2010 the numbers of publicly funded secondary school teachers teaching Computing as their 'main subject' dropped from 788 to 702, with a further 346 teachers who were teaching Computing but not as the main subject. During this period, the average age of teachers of Computing increased from 44 to 45 – among the highest average age of teachers in Scotland. In the same period the average age of Physics teachers dropped from 44 to 43 between 2007 and 2010, and that of biology teachers also fell, from 43 to 42. The average age of chemistry teachers remained steady at 44. The percentage of Computing teachers over the age of 55 increased from 14 per cent to 20 per cent. The indications are that the average age of Scotland's Computing teacher workforce looks set to increase further.

Addressing this problem will require action to increase recruitment of a new generation of Computer Science specialist teachers in Scotland. The Royal Society recommends that the Scottish Government should fully implement pupils' entitlement to third-level outcomes in Computer Science, requiring, as it will, the additional recruitment of specialist staff.

A lack of access to Computing-specific continuing professional development (CPD) opportunities in Scotland may impede teachers' attempts to keep up to date with developments in the field. For example, the new Curriculum for Excellence qualification in Computing Science has many more opportunities for pupils to develop their programming skills and acquire a more fundamental scientific understanding of the subject. This new qualification will provide opportunities for the use of 'Scratch' and other new programming tools and environments (Norton, 2012). For teachers in Scotland, additional CPD provision linked to this new emphasis on programming, and the role of ICT/Computing in delivering the aims of Curriculum for Excellence, is a priority (Royal Society, 2012, p. 82).

The Computer Science Inside Project (CSI) at the University of Glasgow (see http://csi.dcs.gla.ac.uk/index.php) has been developing a pedagogy to support the new Computer Science. It was designed to give students insight into programming without looking in detail at programming skills. This approach was influenced by the Computer Science Unplugged project in New Zealand (see http://csunplugged.org/) – a country that has taken the lead in innovative Computer Science pedagogy.

In a recent initiative in the United States conducted by the CSI team, students who participated in CSI workshops were involved not in writing programmes but in peer instruction techniques to help them to articulate what a piece of code is doing. Students involved in writing code often do not understand it, even if they can make it work. Educationally this can be a problem because, without an understanding of programming, pupils' fundamental grasp of the science itself cannot be built. After participating in the peer instruction students explained that they could now see that coding wasn't magic, but rather it was like opening a black box – they could see how the code worked and this had demystified it, giving them a better grasp of the underlying computer science. The need to provide suitable Computer Science CPD that focuses on such innovatory pedagogy, and thereby provide teachers with skills needed to make the new Computer Science a success in the classroom, is also highlighted in the Royal Society report (2012, p. 82).

LEARNING FROM INTERNATIONAL PERSPECTIVES

Looking at Computer Science teaching internationally, it is clear that other countries with a similar population size and GDP to Scotland have undertaken initiatives in the field of Computer Science school education from which Scotland might learn as it introduces its new Curriculum for Excellence. Israel, for example, undertook a major review of Computing in school in the 1990s. It now has one of the most rigorous Computer Science high school programmes in the world. Stephenson et al. (2005) consulted an international panel of Computer Science educators, including those in Scotland, Israel and Canada. They concluded that when a country is developing a new curriculum it is essential to ensure that it meets key criteria. These include making sure that there is a link between the outcomes required and the strategies used; that change is driven by 'real learning needs and not politically manufactured needs'; and that the context of larger social and economic forces is considered. Furthermore, stakeholder agreement, adequate resources and a long-term vision were also cited as being central to success in curriculum improvement. Hazzan et al. (2008) developed a model to encapsulate the current high school Computer Science curriculum in Israel that is built on these criteria. Their 'Four Key Elements' are:

> a well-defined curriculum (including written course text books and teaching guides); a requirement of a mandatory formal CS teaching license; teacher preparation programmes (including at least a Bachelors degree in CS and a CS teaching certificate study program); and research in CS education. (Hazzan et al., 2008, p. 281)

The new curriculum has been in place since 1995, and is taken by 10,000–20,000 students.

New Zealand is another successful Computer Science country with a population size and GDP comparable to those of Scotland. In 2008, two influential reports appeared (Grinsey et al., 2008; Carrell et al., 2008) that influenced a revamping of its school curriculum in Digital Technologies. The curriculum from 2011 has an explicit strand called Programming and Computer Science. Having established the importance of programming skills the curriculum designers are now shifting their focus to the infrastructural issues of creating suitable materials and developing teacher education. All seven of the major Computer Science departments have been involved in the process, as well as in the revised teacher education that will support it.

These examples help to provide a template for some of the issues and challenges that Scotland will face as it strives to implement and support its new Computer Science qualifications in Curriculum for Excellence.

CONCLUSIONS

As we pass the centenary of Turing's birth, Computer Science education is at a turning point in Scotland. There is good reason for optimism as the new Computing Science qualifications come on stream. The new emphasis on the rigour of the scientific aspects of the discipline will help young people to establish the foundations of successful careers. Educating a new generation of computer scientists will assist in developing Scotland's economy in changing and challenging global conditions. However, the challenges of meeting specialist teacher supply, developing suitable innovatory CPD with a pedagogical focus, and creating new and exciting teaching and learning materials will all need to be addressed if Scotland is to bring its Computing and Information Systems education onto the world stage in the twenty-first century.

ACKNOWLEDGEMENTS

I would like to thank all those experts in the Computer Science field in Scotland who gave their time to answer my questions about the current state of developments and future prospects. However, in interpreting and analysing their very helpful responses, errors and omissions may have occurred. These are entirely my own.

REFERENCES

Carrell, T., V. Gough-Jones and K. Fahy (2008) *The Future of Computer Science and Digital Technologies in New Zealand Secondary Schools: Issues of 21st Teaching and Learning, Senior Courses and Suitable Assessments.*

Computing at School Working Group (2012) *Challenges in Scotland.* Online at www.computingat-school.org.uk/index.php?id=cas-scotland

Grinsey, G. and M. Phillipps (2008) *Evaluation of Technology Achievement Standards for use in New Zealand Secondary School Computing Education.* Wellington: NZCS.

Hazzan, O., J. Gal-Ezer and L. Blum (2008) 'A model for high school computer science education: The four key elements that make it', *39th Technical Symposium on Computer Science Education, SIGCSE Bulletin,* 40 (1): 281–5. New York: ACM.

Norton, J. (2012) 'Why all our kids should be taught how to code', *The Guardian* (31 March). Online at www.guardian.co.uk/education/2012/mar/31/why-kids-should-be-taught-code

Royal Society of London (2012) *Shut Down or Restart? The Way Forward for Computing in UK Schools.* Online at http://royalsociety.org/education/policy/computing-in-schools/report/

Stephenson, C., J. Gal-Ezer, B. Haberman and A. Verno (2005) *The New Educational Imperative: Improving High School Computer Science Education, Final Report of the CSTA, Curriculum Improvement Task Force.* Online at http://csta.acm.org/Communications/sub/DocsPresentationFiles/NewImperativeIntl.pdf

57

Drama Education

Will Barlow

> The most valuable asset a nation has is the creativity of its children.
>
> Alan Plater (playwright)

Drama is part of Scotland's Curriculum for Excellence's (CfE's) Expressive Arts curriculum and aims to develop pupils' creative talent and artistic skills. The Expressive Arts help children to develop their understanding of self and others while advancing their social and cultural identity. Drama is offered at all stages in the 3–18 Curriculum, allowing pupils to engage in purposeful play. Ensemble playing offers pupils the opportunity to explore the themes and issues of a shared fictional context while developing their individual values, viewpoints and responsibilities as well as curricular knowledge and understanding. Drama offers a relevance to learning by adopting a fictional narrative to explain abstract curricular content and helps pupils relate what they have learned in the classroom to the real world. Therefore, Drama is a subject and a pedagogical approach that can transform learners' educational experiences.

NATIONAL QUALIFICATIONS RESULTS

Drama continues to grow in schools, with an increasing number of departments being established and pupils choosing the subject at certification level. In 2011, Standard Grade Drama, Intermediate 1 and 2 Drama and Higher Drama achieved a net increase in candidates from the previous year; Advanced Higher Drama saw a small net fall of candidates from 376 to 327 on the previous year. Examination results are also buoyant, with over 55 per cent of candidates achieving a Credit and 36 per cent gaining a General award at Standard Grade respectively; 88.6 per cent achieved a grade between A and C in Intermediate 1 Drama and 94.7 per cent achieved a grade between A and C in Intermediate 2 Drama; 87.7 per cent passed Higher Drama with a grade between A and C and 72.2 per cent achieved a pass at Advanced Higher Drama (SQA, 2011). Given the substantial nature and impact of these figures, it could be argued that drama education is prospering in terms of candidate numbers and attainment.

DRAMA PEDAGOGY

The four capacities of the CfE sit well with the ideals of drama education. If we consider that drama education helps to instil confidence (Maley and Duff, 2007), allows pupils to achieve success (Baldwin, 2009), develops citizenship (Neelands, 1998) and enables pupils to contribute to their and others' lives (Prendiville and Toye, 2007), it could be argued that drama education is an appropriate pedagogical approach focused on the experiences and outcomes of learners. CfE is constructed around the needs of the pupils by placing the child at the centre of the learning and teaching process. This is also true of drama education as the pupils are central to the construction of the unfolding dramatic narrative – they are the actors, playwrights and audience. The class works together as an ensemble sharing in the creating experience, constructing the drama together both within and outwith the fictional narrative. Therefore, pupils begin to reflect on their own lives and the lives of others through a process of creative exploration. Upon entering the secondary sector most pupils will have experienced some form of drama tuition up to and including Level 2 Drama experiences and outcomes. The pre-secondary school experiences and outcomes are designed to offer pupils the chance to learn through imaginary situations. These imagined situations provide pupils with the opportunity to engage in purposeful and spontaneous play. The aim of the drama teacher is to build on these skills while developing the pupils' enjoyment, knowledge and understanding of the drama process.

National 2 Performance Arts and National 3 Drama

National 2 and 3 have replaced the former Access 2 and 3 courses and are designed to be facilitated with pupils who may not cope with more challenging drama qualifications. In practice, National 2 and 3 are generally facilitated with pupils who have additional support needs and can be used across all year groups.

National 2 consists of one mandatory unit and two optional units. The mandatory unit aims to teach pupils basic skills in performing while developing their confidence and their understanding of the performing arts as a means of communication. The optional units, of which there are three, aim to develop the skills learned in the first unit within different contexts. National 3 aims to develop skills in creating and presenting drama over two mandatory units: Drama Skills and Production Skills. During the Drama Skills unit pupils will learn how to respond to stimuli and develop basic characters and an understanding of form and structure. The Production Skills unit aims to teach pupils a basic understanding of the production areas of lighting, sound, costume, props, make-up and set. The assessment criteria for both units require pupils to provide evidence of the knowledge of basic drama techniques, production skills and their reflections on their and others' work. The units are internally assessed by the class teacher.

Levels 3 and 4

Most pupils in S1–S3 will be working at Level 3 with more gifted pupils at Level 4. Pupils working at Level 3 are required to create drama from a range of stimuli, have the necessary skills in voice, movement and language to create realistic or stylised characters and reflect on their learning. In order to achieve the Level 3 experiences and outcomes, pupils are expected to work from a variety of stimuli, develop a range of characters and perform to an audience. The main difference between Level 3 and Level 4 is the depth of the investigation that the pupil achieves with characterisation, imaginative response, final presentation and evaluation. To achieve this differentiation some drama teachers may create units of work relating to the designated skills such as voice or movement, or offer a stimulus for the pupils to create a structured play and then present it to an audience. This approach teaches the performance skills that pupils require in the middle and senior phases of the curriculum, chiefly practical examinations of a scripted play.

National 4

In S4, pupils will either be presented at National 4 or National 5. The National 4 course consists of three internally assessed mandatory units: Drama Skills, Drama Production Skills and the Added Value Unit Drama Performance. The first unit, Drama Skills, provides pupils with the opportunity to develop a range of skills within the drama process. The second unit, Production Skills, aims for pupils to develop an understanding of a production team while developing their knowledge of script/scenario in preparation for a performance. The Added Value Unit offers pupils the chance to demonstrate their knowledge and understanding by creating, presenting and evaluating a drama performance in a chosen drama production role. The class teacher will examine pupils' performance in the production and their evidence documenting the creative process.

National 5

The National 5 Drama course has a similar structure to that of the National 4 course. However, the Course Assessment for National 5 Drama consists of two component parts: a question paper and a performance. Although the unit structures at National 4 and National 5 are similar, the level of pupil engagement and the quality of their work should become increasingly complex at National 5. The Course Assessment, Drama Performance Component Part One, will be in two sections: Section A, a written analysis of a performance the pupils have taken part in, and Section B, an assessment of pupils' drama knowledge and understanding in response to a text. Component Part Two assesses pupils in either acting or a production role along with a support log documenting their creative process. In order to pass the course, pupils must complete all of the units as well as the course assessment, and will be awarded on an A–D scale. The question paper will have a weighting of 40 per cent and the performance 60 per cent of the overall award. The drama performance is assessed on two separate criteria: a support log and a practical performance, with the presentation being marked out of fifty and the log out of ten.

Higher

The Higher Drama course aims to develop pupils' practical and theoretical knowledge and understanding in either acting or a production role. The recommended progression into this course is through completion of National 5 Drama. The course has two mandatory units, Drama Skills and Drama Production Skills, and culminates in the course assessment which has two component parts: a performance and a question paper.

The Drama Skills unit builds upon pupils' knowledge and understanding of the drama process through practical and theoretical responses to texts. Pupils will investigate the historical, social and cultural contexts of texts and communicate their ideas through acting or directing. Teachers are able to choose either to work on two texts from a prescribed list or to select one from the list and another suitable text of their own choosing. The Production Skills unit focuses on one text and its theatrical and historical context with pupils investigating its style, structure, form and staging. Pupils will be offered the choice to investigate from the perspective of an actor, director or designer in preparation for performance.

The course assessment consists of two components, a question paper and a performance, both of which have two sections. The question paper is marked out of forty, with Section A asking pupils to demonstrate their knowledge of a text they have studied and Section B requiring pupils to write an analysis of a performance that they have seen; both sections are marked out of twenty. Section A of the performance consists of a support log, which is marked out of ten, and section B a performance, which is marked out of fifty. Pupils assessed on acting are required to prepare two contrasting roles with one performance selected from a prescribed text, each lasting no longer than ten minutes. Directors can direct one of the actors in the aforementioned prescribed text(s) or they can facilitate a rehearsal lasting no more than twenty minutes. Designers will design a set for their chosen text and choose one additional production area to complement this. The set design is marked out of thirty and is assessed via a presentation lasting no more than twenty minutes. The elected production area chosen by the pupil can be in props, costume, make-up, lighting or sound.

Advanced Higher

The Advanced Higher Drama course provides progression from Higher Drama and follows the same course structure and unit titles as the Higher Drama course. The course will provide pupils with the choice of studying acting, directing or design via a mix of practical and theoretical studies. The Drama Skills unit requires pupils to create a devised drama through the interpretation and analysis of a complex text. The Production Skills unit aims to develop pupils' knowledge of two key theatre practitioners. The course assessment will consist of an Added Value performance and question paper.

TENSIONS

There has always been a debate in the field of drama education over the process of learning through drama or using drama to create a product. If we consider the CfE Drama experiences and outcomes alongside the National, Higher and Advanced Higher course structures, we find that they are based on three main elements – creating, presenting and evaluating. Therefore, it could be interpreted that the Scottish Qualifications Authority supports a view of drama education that is focused on the final product rather than the process that the pupils have experienced. Indeed, every CfE drama course is based on skills to be taught, leading to a presentation which, it could be argued, shifts the balance of intent from the needs of the participant to the needs of an audience. However, the problem with this view is that it can, as Neelands (1998) suggests, create an unnecessary divide between the two approaches that should be studied and practised in harmony; there will always be a problem with the drama curriculum if this imbalance continues.

The Drama curriculum should not ignore the contribution that drama education can have on the everyday life of pupils nor should it ignore the theatre tradition, as school is, for many, the only place where pupils develop an understanding of how theatre is created and appreciated. Instead, the CfE Drama course should strive to develop the connections between the process and product divide. Neelands (1998) suggests that there should be no justifiable reason why theatre skills cannot be taught within a process drama model and vice versa. Therefore, drama teachers should be encouraged by the opportunity that is afforded to them within the CfE to teach in innovative and creative ways. As such, drama teachers may wish to create a curriculum where they have an essential artistic function within the drama process working alongside the pupils. For example, drama teachers should consider the practice of working outside the fictional narrative that the children create, thus distancing them from the pupils' work, this being similar to what a theatre critic does when reviewing a performance. Research has shown that if the drama teacher does not work alongside the pupils within the fictional narrative, the pupils will only achieve a superficial level of understanding by reproducing their existing insights (O'Neill and Lambert, 1982).

THE DRAMA DEPARTMENT AND THE FACULTY

With the emergence of new Drama departments, and the managerial shift from principal teachers to faculty heads, drama teachers have found themselves on a new road of discovery. If we consider that drama is taught on average by the youngest teachers in schools (Scottish Government, 2009) it is reasonable to suggest that most new drama departments are staffed by relatively inexperienced teachers. With this in mind, a new drama department is usually placed within the folds of a faculty system, resulting in the drama teacher being the sole drama specialist within the school community and, more often than not, the teacher with the least practical experience as to how a department operates. Although the faculty head is there to guide staff on procedural matters relating to the day-to-day running of a department, they do not usually have subject-specific expertise. Inexperienced drama teachers can be expected to construct and facilitate a curriculum for the most part on their own. Therefore, the drama teacher will devise a curriculum, arrange assessments, set standards and, in some cases, write development and quality assurance plans – all of which was once the responsibility of the principal teacher. It is widely acknowledged that the faculty system has reduced the number of principal teacher posts. Scottish Government (2011) suggests that promotion opportunities for secondary teachers have also decreased because of the emergence of the faculty system. With this in mind, both old and new drama teachers sometimes find themselves within a faculty system undertaking the duties of a promoted member of staff without the rewards that come with promotion. Therefore, drama teachers must endeavour to ensure the extra responsibility that is usually placed on their shoulders does not hinder their 'artistry' within the classroom (Taylor, 2000).

INTERDISCIPLINARY LEARNING (IDL) AND DRAMA

Sommers (1994) indicates that although drama education has its own language and genres, its content must be derived through other means. With this in mind, other subjects are able to provide drama with relevant contexts for creating fictional narratives, while drama techniques can enrich the other curricular areas (O'Neill and Lambert, 1982). Neelands (1992, p. 39) offers a view of learning through drama and proposes the 'connection of teaching ideas and skills to real human activity'. Neelands (1992) believes joining curricular content with fictional contexts offers pupils the ability to re-create real life and provides a relevance to their learning as well as coherence within the curriculum. Drama provides children the unique opportunity to adopt roles and expertise of a particular occupation or community, whether in the present or in the past, which as O'Neill and Lambert (1982, p. 16) suggest, 'will give significance to the activity, strengthen the commitment and belief of the pupils and their willingness to work seriously and constructively'.

However, if drama is to be a central component of IDL it is important that it is applied as a means to scaffold a particular learning intention. For instance, if the IDL work is based on understanding the human experience, concepts, attitudes and real-life knowledge, then drama would be an appropriate approach to adopt.

THE FUTURE FOR DRAMA

There are still some schools in Scotland that have little or no drama provision. This is disheartening not only for the subject, but also for the missed educational opportunities for using drama to enhance learning and teaching. Local authorities (LAs) and headteachers should consider the positive effects drama has on our children's education, their social and emotional development and their ability to work with others in a constructive and empathetic way. Drama is a central component to the development of our understanding of who we are as a people, our culture and traditions. It is drama's unique ability to help young people develop the skills to live and work as a community within and outwith school that will help our nation and our schools prosper. The Secondary Head Association of England suggests that drama should become a vital component of every school and concludes that a school without a drama department is a school without a soul (SHA, 1998). Scottish LAs and headteachers may wish to consider the drama provision in their schools and seek to develop it as suggested by their English counterparts.

REFERENCES

Baldwin, P. (2009) *School Improvement through Drama: A Creative Whole Class, Whole School Approach.* London: Continuum.

Maley, A. and A. Duff (2007) *Drama Techniques: A Resource Book of Communication Activities for Language Teachers* (3rd edn). Cambridge: Cambridge University Press.

Neelands, J. (1992) *Learning Through Imagined Experience – Teaching English in the National Curriculum.* London: Hodder & Stoughton.

Neelands, J. (1998) *Beginning Drama 11–14.* London: David Fulton Publishing.

O'Neill, C. and A. Lambert (1982) *Drama Structures: A Practical Handbook for Teachers.* London: Century Hutchinson Ltd.

Prendiville, F. and N. Toye (2007) *Speaking and Listening Through Drama 7–11.* London: Paul Chapman Publishing.

Scottish Government (2009) *Teachers in Scotland, 2009.* Online at www.scotland.gov.uk/Resource/Doc/91982/0105432.pdf

Scottish Government (2011) *Advancing Professionalism in Teaching: The Report of the Review of Teacher Employment in Scotland.* Edinburgh: Scottish Government.

Scottish Qualifications Authority (2011) *External Assessment Report 2011 Drama.* Online at www.sqa.org.uk/sqa/2546.html

Secondary Heads Association (1998) *Drama sets you Free!* Leicester: SHA.

Sommers, J. (1994) *Drama in the Curriculum.* London: Cassell

Taylor, P. (2000) *The Drama Classroom: Action, Reflection, Transformation.* London: RoutledgeFalmer.

58

English Language and Literature Education

Hugh Gallagher and Linda Harris

When, in several public fora, a highly regarded and influential educational academic characterised teachers of English as those most likely to subvert school systems in the interests of
pupils and their learning, he touched on a central feature of life in many English classrooms.
After all, the subject lends itself to the pedagogical freedoms much vaunted in current
curricular discourses and policy initiatives. Scottish teachers of English may well feel
comfortable with that characterisation of their professional activity. They would recognise
themselves in a seminal survey as old as *Effective Learning and Teaching in Scottish Secondary
Schools: English* (1992) as innovative, imaginative and creative. Certainly, at least on paper,
the business of learning and teaching in the English classroom of a Scottish school has continued to change apace over a period of decades. The English classroom is perhaps a mis-
nomer and, certainly, what goes on there is more than learning about the English language.
Yet, when viewed dispassionately, it may be that the latest of those curricular changes
determined by Curriculum for Excellence – Brave New World or Armageddon, depending
on your perspective – could empower teachers of English in their efforts to develop Scottish
young people as literate, critical, analytical, linguistically aware and well-read. However,
they will do so in a learning environment in which the development of young people's
language skills has become, explicitly and unambiguously, the responsibility of *all* teachers.
Literacy Across Learning is a curricular thread that runs through the learning fabric of the
new curriculum; teachers of English will be expected to weave that in conjunction with all
of their colleagues, rather than being the service industry that supplies literate pupils for
others to teach.

HISTORICAL CURRICULAR JIGSAWS

From the introduction of Standard Grade in the early 1980s, what was taught in English
classrooms in Scotland was framed by a series of relatively unconnected curricular developments. Standard Grade English did lay enduring foundations. All English courses since
then have been built on the development of knowledge, skills and competence in talking,
listening, reading and writing, although the perception of the relative importance of these
has pendulumed over time. Generally studied in S3 and S4, it partially informed English
learning and teaching in S1 and S2 until the early 1990s, when the 5–14 programme
sought to provide a more prescriptive, linear, developmental continuum through primary
and up to S2. Sitting beyond Standard Grade were the evolving suites of courses for the

post-16 cohort. Higher English itself was subjected to major review and revision three times between 1986 and 2003 while Standard Grade and 5–14 went their separate, unreconstructed ways. Meanwhile, a parallel world of vocational English courses on offer in the 1980s and 90s focused largely on functional language development. The competing, even conflicting, assessment regimes of these curricula merely served to muddy already troubled waters, which Scottish teachers navigated skilfully.

LITERACY AND ENGLISH: LEARNING IN THE 3–15 CONTINUUM

The new curricular framework does try to address some of the most obvious flaws of earlier fragmented models. It is crucial to recognise the more prominent position accorded to literacy in the new framework. The development of the concept of literacy as a way of framing language development is, however, relatively recent in Scotland. Of the 137 Literacy and English Experience and Outcomes (Es and Os), only thirty-one are explicitly designated as 'English', and therefore, in secondary schools, exclusively the province of English teachers. In fact, these are restricted to learning about the specific features of spoken language; knowledge of language features in texts; stylistic devices used in texts; using stylistic devices to create texts and to influence readers; and conventions of creative texts. Developing the remaining skills described in the Es and Os is the responsibility of all teachers. Of course, teachers of English will continue to have the major role in supporting young people in their language development across these. Some fears have been expressed that English teachers are being reduced to the role of literacy support staff while some teachers of other subjects understandably balk at the thought of having responsibility for what has until recently been thought of as the province of the English specialist. Literacy Across Learning, as the manifestation of literacy as the responsibility of all has been termed, seems to be working well where the English teachers continue to do the job they always have done but where, in addition, they work in genuine partnership with other colleagues to consolidate generic literacy skills, often led by non-English specialists. Progress has also been evident in pupils' literacy where those colleagues identify and address context-specific and subject-specific literacy needs that pupils will have in their classrooms in order to access learning there. It is hardly a new idea: *Language Across the Curriculum*, a Scottish response to *A Language for Life* (1975), is over forty years old.

    The apparent newness of discourse and focus should not disguise the fact that much of what has been recognised and lauded historically as effective English teaching sits entirely comfortably with the principles and practice envisaged in Curriculum for Excellence: Literacy and English, as English is now called. The tensions and contradictions of the 'bolt-on' curricula of the past have been removed by the introduction of the 3–18 Curriculum which, at least in its intentions, maps a learning journey for developing knowledge, skills and competence in Literacy and English. In common with all other areas of learning, from nursery to S3, a series of Es and Os is offered to describe learning progression; in Literacy and English these cover what were four modes and are now three organisers, Talking and Listening; Reading; and Writing, and there is an acknowledgement that that *process* is central to learning. The development of understanding and skills and their application in increasingly complex language contexts characterises learning in English. Enjoyment and choice remains central to all of the experiences. Within each of the organisers, Es and Os are divided into 'sub-divisions' that do seem oddly arbitrary. All include 'Tools to help me to', covering technical knowledge and skills required to progress in each organiser. These have been criticised for being unspecific; it is not until senior phase course descriptors that particular knowledge of language requirements are specified as 'mandatory'. On the other hand, it has been argued that this approach allows teachers to shake off the manacles of age- and stage-related competence and to teach the technical elements of language as the context and the need arise. More generally, that freedom may enable pupils to enjoy learning about language and literature, culture and heritage in the relevant, contextualised and imaginative ways that they have in the best English classrooms for decades. Reading and Listening broadly focus on developing pupils' ability to find and use information, understand, analyse and evaluate. In Talking and Writing, the broadest focus is on creating texts, and organising and using information to create texts for different purposes. Each of these sub-divisions is then distilled further to describe more specifically what might be learned and how that will be built to ensure progression. It is envisaged that in the first three years of secondary school, most pupils will continue with the development of their learning in these areas until they reach level 4. In truth, there will still be the same challenges for English teachers that there always have been in progressing *all* pupils through the notional learning milestones represented by a framework of levels.

LITERACY AND ENGLISH: LEARNING IN THE SENIOR PHASE

From S4, pupils enter the senior phase where they will follow courses appropriate to their needs and progress. National 1–5 courses replace Standard Grade, Access and Intermediate courses, while revised versions of Higher and Advanced Higher complete the range. The emphasis on courses is important. While time is built into all of them for preparing pupils for the summative assessment phase, the emphasis is on pupils' learning that will subsequently be assessed, rather than on focusing only, or even mainly, on what is to be produced for summative assessment purposes. Course units are explicitly presented as 'statements of standards for assessment and not programmes of learning and teaching. They can be delivered in a number of ways.' Supportive documentation elsewhere highlights learning and teaching suggestions and it is to be hoped that these feature prominently in the process of writing course/syllabus plans if the trap of summative assessment-driven teaching is to be avoided. The key features of learning in the 3–15 Es and Os, and the language used to describe them, articulate well with those of the senior phase, focusing on: engaging pupils with a range of texts; literary and linguistic heritage; the diversity of language; how language works; and language as influence. Interestingly, there is a consistent focus on pupils at all levels developing strategic methodologies to enable them to access and create texts of increasing complexity.

Although debate has already begun about when in their school life pupils will take these courses – age and stage restrictions were lifted in the previous regime – it is intended that they should begin them in S4. At the time of writing, National 1 and 2 courses were still being written for pupils who formerly would have followed Access courses; National 3, for the same pupils, has been published. National 4, 5 and Higher have some common elements. They all contain two core units: Analysis and Evaluation, which covers learning about Reading and Listening, as receptive language modes; and Creation and Production, which covers learning about Writing and Talking, as productive language modes. Instantly recognisable knowledge, skills and processes feature in the Outcomes. In reading, for example, pupils will learn how to elicit main ideas and specific information, and how to use their knowledge of language to explain meaning and effect: this is the business of learning in English, going back to Standard Grade and beyond. There are no terrors here.

The differences in content of these three courses are largely qualitative. Key discriminatory terms can be easily detected. For example, 'straightforward' texts in National 4 become 'detailed' at 5 and 'depth' and 'complexity' feature in Higher. These semantic gymnastics are not new to English teachers. Those with long enough memories will remember the battlefields of the grade-related criteria wars when Standard Grade was introduced. The range of texts covered is expected to be greater. Specific mention is made in these courses of knowledge of language; at all levels, the main word classes, syntactical structures and writing conventions, including punctuation, are specified as mandatory learning targets. In National 5 and Higher, all pupils will have to study at least one Scottish text from a prescribed list, an echo from the 1980s that does not attract universal delight, at least with regard to the limitations inherent in what may be seen as arbitrary prescription. The choices that may populate such a list were exercising stakeholders at the time of writing and the preponderance of contemporary texts in some early drafts has prompted debate. It is also a feature of learning in the English classroom of today that the Scots language itself has begun to see regeneration, with children reading, writing and talking in Scots and seeing it as having parity of esteem with English.

ATTAINMENT AND ASSESSMENT

It seems reasonable to suggest that the Curriculum for Excellence curriculum and assessment system for Literacy and English should be taking account of attainment patterns in the literacy of the children of Scotland. The Scottish Government produced its aspirational Literacy Action Plan Scotland 2010 against a background of such attainment evidence. Scotland features in the Programme for International Student Assessment (PISA) study, a major three-yearly Organisation for Economic Cooperation and Development (OECD) international study of performance by 15-year-olds in reading, maths and science. Across three of these, 2003, 2006 and 2009, Scotland has remained in roughly the same position in comparison with other countries – only seven scored higher – and appeared in 2009 to have reversed a decline since the 2000 study, with a score higher than the OECD mean. However, it has been noted that this improvement is significantly attributable to the inclusion of new countries in the 2009 study; without them, no improvement would have been reported. Scotland's children also read less than their OECD counterparts. The most recent Scottish Survey of Achievement (2009) appears to support the PISA findings, with Reading attainment at broadly similar levels to those of 2005 and 2006. More worryingly, only a third of pupils in Scotland were assessed to be writing at the expected level in S2. Yet, the number of pupils attempting Higher English is now approaching 30,000 and the Scottish Qualifications Authority External Examiner's Report 2010 identifies poor examination preparation rather than deficiencies in literacy as being indicative of the inadequacies of weaker candidates.

Against that background, English teachers will be expected to use the now embedded principles of Assessment is for Learning (AifL) to inform professional judgements about pupils' attainment and progress through milestone learning levels in S1–S3, gathering evidence with and from pupils about how they are improving relative to their own previous performance and to the Outcomes. The new National Assessment Resource (NAR) offers support materials and exemplification of variable quality to assist English teachers in developing robust and supportive assessment procedures. There will be challenges in terms of consistency and the quality of evidence but, it could be argued, these have always existed, especially in S1 and S2. There are powerful voices who say that pupils will only be motivated to attain well if there is a summative assessment hurdle and a certificated reward at the end of the learning journey. Effective English teachers have given the lie to that for as long as English has been taught.

Attainment in the senior phase will be measured by internal unit assessment of reading, writing, talking and listening in all of the new National courses. It is exciting to note that evidence of attainment in these language areas can be gathered from integrated tasks and activities; the artificial separation of Close Reading, Textual Analysis, Writing and Critical Evaluation need never afflict learning in English again. Instead of a terminal examination, National 4 candidates will submit a piece of integrated work which will evidence what they have learned in the units. This way of assessing 'added value' is untried and there is some scepticism about its robustness. At National 5 and Higher, added value will be assessed by the submission of a Writing Portfolio; this was successfully reintroduced two years ago to the current National Qualifications courses and seems to have re-established the central-ity of writing, though these contributors remain baffled by the fact that this could only be achieved by increasing the external assessment weight it attracted. There will also be an examination that assesses the close reading of non-fiction – which includes what may be the much-welcomed return of summary writing – and critical reading of fiction, including 'context' questions on one of the set Scottish texts.

EFFECTIVE PEDAGOGY IN THE ENGLISH CLASSROOM

In a sense independently of the changing curricular landscape, Her Majesty's Inspectorate of Education's *Portrait of Practice in English* (published in 2008) and the *Curriculum for Excellence; English Excellence Group Report (2011)* revealed key aspects of what learning looks like in the current English classroom. Some of the features, like the need for a respect-ful ethos, dialogic teaching, the effective use of AifL strategies, could be found in any class-room. The most notable key specifics relating to the effective teaching of English included:

- developing pupils' language skills by exploring them in ways that showed their interconnect-edness, rather than by encouraging pupils to see them as discrete skill sets or knowledge areas such as Writer's Craft, Close Reading, Knowledge of Language;
- using a range of strategic approaches to develop pupils' writing, including exemplification, modelling, scaffolding, process *and* genrist approaches, real contexts and purposes for real audiences, and collaborative writing as a developmental stepping stone;
- using Directed Activities Related to Texts (DARTS) approaches to engage pupils actively and practically in the process of meaning-making;
- involving pupils wholly and actively in learning, using cooperative *and* collaborative *and* independent pedagogies.

THE WAY AHEAD

Scottish teachers of English face challenges. The teaching of language – grammar, syntax and punctuation – has always been seen as an important part of the classroom diet, but the lack of consistent, informed thinking about how best to teach that has bedevilled the process. Literacy standards will benefit from progress being made in that area; the recent work of Deborah Myhill (2007) could have a telling influence in this regard as it places learning about grammar firmly in the context of improving writing. Indeed, the re-establishment of writing itself at the heart of the curriculum, especially in the senior phase, should begin to address poor attainment in that aspect of English. The burgeoning sense of Scotland as a multilingual country affords challenges and opportunities for improving children's understanding of what language is and how it works. It also continues to offer major challenges to children whose first language is not English and to the teachers who support them.

There is much rhetoric in the air; neologisms pepper the new curriculum. Yet, the aspiration to develop connectedness in exploring and developing literacy skills may empower pupils to hone skills and acquire the knowledge that will lead them to be literate, critical, analytical, linguistically and culturally aware, well-read people. Perhaps more than anything, the English teachers of Scotland need to have the professional confidence and courage to believe that they can make that happen.

REFERENCES

Myhill, D. and S. Jones (2007) 'What works? Engaging in research to shape policy: The case of grammar', *English Teaching: Practice and Critique*, 6 (3): 61–75.
Organisation for Economic Cooperation and Development (2010) *PISA 2009 Results: Executive Summary*. Paris: OECD.
Scottish Government (2011) *Curriculum for Excellence: Excellence in English. A Report for the Scottish Government*. Edinburgh: Scottish Government.
Scottish Office Education Department (1992) *Effective Learning and Teaching in Scottish Secondary Schools: English*. Edinburgh: Her Majesty's Stationery Office.

59

Geography Education

Clare McAlister

WHY GEOGRAPHY?

Geography helps us to understand the world. Every day we experience geography in a new way as we engage with our environment and understand the limitations of how we might alter it. Geography develops our understanding of the world we live in and the challenges we face in the future; it helps to develop tolerance in learners and awareness of the difficulties faced by all life across the globe as it challenges stereotypes and supports citizenship education. It has been described as an 'awkward discipline' (Bonnet, 2008, reported in Roberts, 2011) because of the line it straddles between arts and science subjects. This unique perspective makes it an ideal subject for linking different areas of the curriculum through interdisciplinary study, bringing depth and breadth in understanding on issues and topics.

Areas of international concern such as sustainability permeate every aspect of the geography curriculum. Increasingly, geographical content and issues are in the news and featured in television programmes through the exploration of challenging environments, natural hazards, geological history and coastlines, and by explaining the causes and consequences of our changing climate. Many celebrities and media personalities journey to remote landscapes, bringing perceptions of these environments into our homes. This affects tourism as previously 'remote' or 'untouched' landscapes become areas that people want to visit, resulting in multiple benefits and problems for the local populations. The impact and importance of all these global issues are explored in classrooms throughout Scotland.

Young people in Scotland need to know what is happening in the world right now, what the planet's issues are and how we might address these for a sustainable future. Geography provides an opportunity to study this in a holistic way. With a focus on the need to improve the quality of life, challenge inequality and ensure justice for all the world's population, Geography develops values in learners as they begin to appreciate equity in the planet and how they might play their part as a global citizen. Eco schools education is embraced by many Geography departments and is an area that supports responsible citizenship in young people.

Geography is a subject that develops understanding of this planet and the life it supports. It assists in the refinement of skills necessary in other curriculum areas such as literacy and numeracy while allowing pupils to develop a healthy respect for life and landscape. No

Table 59.1   Curriculum for Excellence: People, Place and Environment in S1 and S2

Stage	S1 Curriculum for Excellence	S2 Curriculum for Excellence

Topic areas	Mapping (SOC 3-14a)
	Scotland (SOC 3-07a)
	Glasgow /River Clyde (SOC 2-10a)
	'Ancient' Scotland – Glaciation
	     (SOC 3-07a)
	Weather (SOC 2-12a)
	Transport (SOC 2-09a)
	Settlement (SOC 2-10a)
	Country/city studies (SOC 3-11a)
		Volcanoes/earthquakes (SOC 4-07a)
		Hurricanes (SOC 3-10a)
		Rainforests (SOC 4-10a)
		Seas and oceans (SOC 3-08a)
		Land use (SOC 4-08a, SOC 4-09b, SOC
		     4-10a, SOC 4-10a)

other subject does this in such a comprehensive way. Roberts (2011, p. 246) argues that Geography is an 'integral part of our lives' as not only do we experience it around us every day but by the choices we make in our daily lives, we also shape it.

GEOGRAPHY CURRICULUM: S1 TO S3

As Geography is such an engaging, evolving and fascinating subject, the curriculum aims to reflect this. The subject has an important place in the curriculum and at the time of writing, as Curriculum for Excellence is being rolled out, there are a number of subjects that are creating links to it. As a curriculum subject it utilises a variety of learning and teaching approaches, including fieldwork. Geography (People, Place and Environment at this stage) includes interdisciplinary approaches and a focus on the cross-cutting themes of global citizenship, sustainable development, creativity and enterprise. It is already well placed to deliver on global citizenship and sustainability as these themes permeate the curriculum. To deliver all of these core areas effectively a geographical input is essential.

The guidance for People, Place and Environment offers flexibility in the content covered and the stages learners move through. Practice varies, as does enthusiasm for the new curriculum, but a sample of the topic areas currently taught in geography departments in S1 and S2 is shown in Table 59.1. Many of the topics in the table could work well with interdisciplinary approaches. It is worth noting that the experiences and outcomes (Education Scotland, 2010) suggested here for each topic are merely a sample, not exhaustive, and many topics are relevant to more than one area. The content shown in the table will develop as the new curriculum moves into S3.

CURRENT S3 AND S4 PROVISION

In S3 and S4, schools have recently entered pupils for Standard Grade or Intermediate exams although the number of Standard Grade candidates has declined while Intermediate presentations have risen (SQA, 2011a). The relaxation of age and stage restrictions persuaded practitioners to engage with Intermediate examinations in S3/S4 as these courses articulate well with the current Higher course, thus presenting the opportunity to refresh areas of content. (For further information on Standard Grade and Intermediate, see Bairner, 2008.)

Table 59.2   National 4 and 5 areas of study

Physical environments	• Outline the effects of the physical landscape on weather in the UK and the nature of air masses and weather systems.
	• Describe and explain:
	  • the formation of two landscapes and features in the UK;
	  • the land uses of two landscapes and possible conflicts in the UK;
	  • the cause and management of land use conflicts in one landscape.
	  *Case studies from glaciated uplands and coastal landscapes or upland limestone and rivers and their valleys.

Human environments	• Explore social and economic indicators; global population distribution and birth and death rates in developed and developing countries. • Outline the characteristics of and developments in urban areas in the developed world and issues around shanty towns in the developing world. • Outline the changes in rural landscapes in the developed and developing world.
Global issues	• Study two global issues from: • Climate change • Impact of human activity on the natural environment • Environmental hazards • Trade and globalisation • Tourism • Health

S4 FROM 2013–14: NATIONAL 4 AND NATIONAL 5

National 4 and 5 courses in Geography bring a change in exam format. National 4 is internally assessed (pass/fail) and National 5 has an exam worth 75 per cent of the final mark and an assignment worth 25 per cent completed under exam conditions in school. 'Added Value' is a new term in Geography qualifications that at National 4 is achieved through an assignment and at National 5 through the external exam and assignment.

The areas of study at both levels are similar although expectations differ (SQA, 2012). A minimum of two case studies* should be explored in each unit and Table 59.2 provides a summary of the current course outline. National 3 is available at a more basic level to facilitate learning for a variety of pupil needs.

HIGHER 2014–15 ONWARDS

From August 2014, the Higher exam will consist of an exam paper worth 66 per cent and an assignment worth 33 per cent to be taken under exam conditions in school (SQA, 2012). This correlates well with the principles of the new curriculum. The units mirror those for National 4 and 5 so progression and links can be maintained. The new Higher course is outlined in Table 59.3 (SQA, 2012). For details pre-2014 see Bairner (2008).

The links between Intermediate and Higher Geography facilitate composite classes in the upper school. This is common in geography departments, which can be small, and may be why few offer Advanced Higher. Advanced Higher was reviewed in 2011 and consists of three units: geographical methods and techniques, the geographical study, and geographical issues (SQA, 2011b). This course develops candidates' analytical and critical thinking skills while exploring in depth geographical issues.

Table 59.3   Higher Geography from 2014

Higher	Human environments	Physical environments	Global issues (choose any two)
	Urban	Atmosphere	River basin management
	Population	Biosphere	Development and health
	Rural	Lithosphere	Global climate change
		Hydrosphere	Trade, aid and geopolitics
			Energy

GEOGRAPHY CANDIDATES AND ACHIEVEMENT

Given the interest through the media in environmental issues, it is surprising that Geography exam candidates have reduced in number since 2006 as other social subjects experienced a comparative increase. The reduction in Geography candidates is due, in part, to schools removing the subject from their curriculum. In 2010–11, of 411 possible present-ing centres, 383 presented pupils in Geography in S4 and 369 in S5 (SQA, 2011a). There is no evidence that achievement is a factor, however, as Geography has consistently achieved well in relation to the other social subjects.

In Scotland, achievement in Geography compares favourably with the other social subjects as results from the 2011 exams show. At Advanced Higher level, Modern Studies candidates achieved the largest percentage of 'A' passes and at Standard Grade History achieved a fractionally higher percentage of Credit level passes (51.2 per cent) compared to Geography (50.5 per cent). At every other level, Geography leads at 'A' grade passes with 26 per cent at Intermediate 1 (History 20 per cent, Modern Studies 25 per cent), 35 per cent at Intermediate 2 (History 26 per cent, Modern Studies 28 per cent) and 32 per cent at Higher (History 27 per cent, Modern Studies 23 per cent) (SQA, 2011a). This has been the pattern over the last few years and shows that despite a reduction in numbers the quality of learning and teaching in Geography continues to improve.

The lack of Geography in some schools means the 'broad general education' and choice (Scottish Government, 2008) that are pupil rights in the new curriculum could be difficult to deliver. It is encouraging that in Scotland's largest local authority Geography has recently been reinstated in two secondary schools where it had previously been removed from the curriculum. This is important to help maintain the numbers required to meet demand at university level.

LEARNING AND TEACHING

Geography delivers aspects of the four capacities of Curriculum for Excellence through its content, decision-making and evaluating exercises, and the consideration of opposing view-points. Greater routine use of active learning is required, however, and many departments are addressing this following concern that there was too much didactic teaching in the upper school (HMIE, 2008). This assists in the development of life and social skills.

Formative assessment strategies are now routine features in some classrooms and depart-ments can make constructive use of cooperative and collaborative learning. Thinking skills activities are a feature of lessons and although textbooks are still popular these rapidly become out of date as Geography is a highly visual and topical subject. Consequently, use is made of ICT and the internet in increasingly creative ways. Using these approaches enables pupils to become more discerning and critical of the media and what they source online. As geographical issues are a constant feature of our lives (tsunami, ash clouds, hurricanes, oil spills and so on) regular opportunities arise for interdisciplinary learning.

ICT in the Geography classroom helps engage learners in research through individual and group activities with pupils or generally as a teaching tool by the class teacher. GLOW is a resource that has been used well in some schools although there are many other excellent resources online. The combination of activities and content in the Geography curriculum facilitates engagement with the permeating skills of literacy, numeracy, and health and wellbeing.

Geography provides the opportunity for learners to apply their learning through the role it has in outdoor learning by fieldwork (LTS, 2010). Many departments zealously maintain fieldwork activities because of the advantages these bring to learners academically and socially. Other departments struggle to incorporate fieldwork, however, because of cover demands and timetable constraints. The opportunity to engage with fieldwork keeps Geography dynamic for pupils as they apply their skills and have memorable experiences. All of these activities develop learners socially as they learn life skills in respecting and working with others. Outdoor learning is an essential feature of the new curriculum and taking part in fieldwork increases learners' understanding of the human impact on the environment.

THE FUTURE

Geography is the present and the future as it addresses fundamental challenges that are experienced through the interaction of people and place across the globe. Its relevance to young people today cannot be underestimated as it teaches in a holistic way, bridges different areas of the curriculum, and develops understanding and critical thinking in pupils. Geography takes learners on a journey of discovery that explores how we deal with our present local, national and global issues and how these might be managed in the future. As our landscapes evolve, our weather patterns shift and our economies alter, Geography provides a lens to explore these changes. It is a subject that helps to shape thinking, to question what we see and to realise that there is no one correct answer to global issues.

Geography teachers need to be prepared for the challenges they face despite falling school budgets, subject choice pressure and faculty arrangements in schools (Scottish Government, 2001) which some specialists identify as a reason for the recent reduction in candidates. Geography teachers should maintain the integrity of their subject but be prepared to work across subject boundaries or through cross-curricular and interdisciplinary approaches. They need to ensure the subject maintains an important place in the curriculum as it is an essential component in delivering the core values of Curriculum for Excellence.

If working on an integrated faculty course, Geography teachers can support non-specialist colleagues in appropriate learning and teaching approaches. Geography is about interaction, change and process, and this can be used to the advantage of subject specialists. Fieldwork can be local, manageable and small scale, broaden pupils' awareness of global issues and maintain their enthusiasm for an international and insightful subject.

As 'traditional' global organisation is evolving, where resource access, changes in the world economy, global catastrophes and newly emerging countries alter our concept of place and our relation to it, Geography supports learners as they expand their understanding of

the world around them. As geographical issues and concerns become mainstream, departments bring to light for pupils the fact that geography is a part of everyday life.

REFERENCES

Bairner, J. (2008) 'Geography education', in T. G. K. Bryce and W. M. Humes (eds), *Scottish Education, Third Edition: Beyond Devolution*. Edinburgh: Edinburgh University Press, pp. 484–9.
Butt, G. (2011) 'Introduction', in G. Butt (ed.), *Geography, Education and the Future*. London: Continuum, pp. 1–11.
Education Scotland (2010) *Social Studies Experiences and Outcomes*. Online at www.ltscotland.org.uk/learningteachingandassessment/curriculumareas/socialstudies/eandos/index.asp
Her Majesty's Inspectorate of Education (2008) *Geography – A Portrait of Current Practice in Scottish Secondary Schools*. Online at www.educationscotland.gov.uk/Images/gpcp_tcm4-712867.pdf
Learning and Teaching Scotland (2010) *Curriculum for Excellence Through Outdoor Learning*. Online at www.ltscotland.org.uk/Images/cfeoutdoorlearningfinal_tcm4-596061.pdf
Roberts, M. (2011) 'Conclusion', in G. Butt (ed.), *Geography, Education and the Future*. London: Continuum, pp. 244–52.
Scottish Government (2001) *A Teaching Profession for the 21st Century. Agreement Reached Following Recommendations Made in the McCrone Report*. See at www.scotland.gov.uk/Publications/2001/01/7959/File-1
Scottish Government (2008) *Building the Curriculum 3*. Online at www.ltscotland.org.uk/Images/building_the_curriculum_3_jms3_tcm4-489454.pdf
Scottish Qualifications Authority (2011a) *Statistics*. Online at www.sqa.org.uk/sqa/57517.html
Scottish Qualifications Authority (2011b) *Advanced Higher Geography Arrangements Documents*. Online at www.sqa.org.uk/sqa/38867.html
Scottish Qualifications Authority (2012) *SQA Geography*. Online at www.sqa.org.uk/sqa/45627.html

60

Health and Wellbeing in Secondary Education

Monica Porciani

HEALTH THROUGH EDUCATION

During the last two decades there have been many initiatives introduced to help improve Scotland's health. Doing so through education has become a major focus for the nation's policy makers and leaders. Devolution in 1997 accelerated the process of highlighting health improvement as a key policy issue, since when it has undergone significant development and reappraisal. The Scottish Government has created a clear vision and strategic framework to address the nation's poor health record and, in particular, improve outcomes for children and young people. Tackling the gap in health inequalities remains a key challenge and requires new thinking on how to do this more effectively. Reducing this gap will be a complex process of improving wellbeing, changing attitudes and identifying effective interventions and pedagogies that develop health-enhancing life skills and behavioural change. In short, schools face a major challenge to ensure that health and wellbeing permeates the curriculum, and that all teaching staff can confidently contribute to teaching, learning and behavioural change in this area.

As awareness of health issues has grown, so too has media coverage concerned about the health of Scotland's young people and the pressures being placed on their mental, physical and social development. As a result, health education is now an extremely wide subject that embraces issues such as substance abuse, domestic violence, knife carrying, gang violence, body image, the sexualisation of children, internet safety and cyberbullying.

This chapter will examine the Health and Wellbeing agenda for Scottish secondary schools in light of recent research and theoretical perspectives, and in view of some of the more fundamental considerations for practitioners. Chapter 48 examines the development of health promotion in primary schools and, together, these chapters set the context for Health and Wellbeing from age 3 to 18 years.

HEALTH-PROMOTING SCHOOLS

Over the last thirty years the World Health Organisation (WHO) has led the development of health education and health promotion in schools. The key starting point was the publication of the Ottawa Charter (see WHO, *Ottawa Charter for Health Promotion*, 1986), which laid down the foundations for health promotion and defined the process of 'enabling people to increase control over, and to improve their health'. This process was not only concerned with strengthening the skills of individuals but was also directed at changing the social, economic and environmental conditions that impact on health.

Between 2002, when the Scottish Health Promoting Schools Unit (SHPSU) was established, and 2007, the date set by the Scottish Government for all schools to become health-promoting, the profile of health promotion in secondary schools in particular was raised significantly. In 2004, the SHPSU launched a National Framework document, *Being Well, Doing Well*. This publication provided schools and education authorities with a coherent structure to develop an integrated whole- school approach to health promotion. Chapter 48 in this volume highlights the key characteristics of *Being Well, Doing Well* as well as some of the key stages in developing the policy and support structure for schools. On the one hand, schools seemed to like the challenge, structure and support provided by the SHPSU and the accreditation process; on the other hand, there was increasing concern that the model was not necessarily translating into tangible improvements in young people's lifestyle choices. For example, schools working towards a gold award could often be seen with more children at the snack van across the road than in the school dining hall. However, by December 2007, the SHPSU was able to report to the Health Minister that all schools in Scotland were 'actively engaged' in health promotion, which set the scene for the introduction of Curriculum for Excellence (CfE) in 2010.

HEALTH AND WELLBEING ACROSS LEARNING

CfE introduced a new vision and ideology for improving health; building on the success of the Health Promoting Schools model, it has as a starting point an environment where health and wellbeing are at the centre of school life and learning. Essentially, the curriculum reform programme has created a new Health and Wellbeing framework bringing together three discrete curriculum areas – Personal and Social Education/Guidance, Food Education/Home Economics and Physical Education – as well as some of the more traditional health education topics. *Health and Wellbeing: Principles and Practice* (Scottish Government, 2009) provides an overview of the rationale and principles and is intended to complement an earlier document, *Guidance on the Schools (Health Promotion and Nutrition) (Scotland) Act 2007* (www.scotland.gov.uk/Topics/Education/Schools/HLivi/foodnutrition).

Together, these documents provide practitioners with guidance on how to start developing 'the statements of experiences and outcomes' for health and wellbeing, including some of the broad features of assessment, progression and links with other curricular areas. The guidance also highlights the four broad contexts for effective learning, namely ethos and life of the school; interdisciplinary learning; opportunities for personal achievement; and curriculum areas and subjects. The curriculum has been designed to enable young people to have experiences and outcomes that provide depth and progression in their learning from age 3 to 18 years. Additionally, curricular principles, such as personalisation, coherence and relevance, should help to ensure that learning meets individual needs, is relevant to the local community and links with other areas of the curriculum.

Overall the statements of experiences and outcomes are structured into the following six organisers, with the responsibilities of all staff written in italics:

- *Mental, Emotional, Social and Physical Wellbeing* (MESP);
- Physical Education, *Physical Activity and Sport*;
- *Planning for Choices and Changes*;
- *Relationships*, Sexual Health and Parenthood (RSHP);
- Food and Health;
- Substance Misuse.

Another document in the series, *Health and Wellbeing across Learning: Responsibilities for All Principles and Practice* (Scottish Government, 2009), provides specific guidance on the experiences and outcomes that are now the responsibility of all staff. The document explains that experiences and outcomes for health and wellbeing cover levels 3 and 4, which are defined as generally covering S2 and S3 of secondary education. Providing a broad general education is the key objective at this stage, and *Building the Curriculum 5* (2011) provides guidance to schools, particularly on aspects of interdisciplinary working and progression. The key focus is on developing life skills, capabilities and attributes that promote good health.

More significant is the shift in responsibility from secondary teachers who either have an interest in health, or who are Personal and Social Education (PSE) teachers or PE teachers, to all staff working with young people. Fundamental to this philosophy is the capacity to form and maintain good relationships, which can contribute to increased confidence and self-esteem, and help to develop resilience. This should include 'each practitioner's role in establishing open, positive, supportive relationships . . . where children and young people feel that they are listened to, and where they feel secure in their ability to discuss sensitive aspects of their lives' (Scottish Government, 2009, p. 3).

However, there does still appear to be a huge gap in terms of providing a robust approach or curriculum for the senior phase – only briefly mentioned in the documentation – and covering learning and teaching from S4 to S6. There does not seem to be any further guidance on what experiences and outcomes should continue into the senior phase or consideration of the teaching approaches that may be more effective and relevant for this age and stage.

IMPLEMENTATION

It would be extremely difficult to try and give an overview of the programmes, resources and initiatives used in the Health and Wellbeing curriculum as there are now very few national programmes, although this has been the subject of debate within the teaching profession. On the one hand teaching staff are looking for more guidance and ideas on which resources and programmes to use in terms of their effectiveness; on the other, national organisations are increasingly reluctant to recommend individual programmes or resources because there is now an expectation that school staff will work collaboratively to identify the needs of their own school community and develop approaches that best suit those needs.

Other chapters in this volume cover some of the topic-specific programmes and curriculum developments that now come under the general umbrella of Health and Wellbeing: see Chapter 40 (Personal Support and PSE in the Secondary School), Chapter 62 (Home Economics) and Chapter 69 (Physical Education and Sport).

In 2008, a consultation with key stakeholders highlighted key issues for local authorities and school management to consider. It was suggested that teachers would require targeted continuing professional development to build their knowledge and skills on substance misuse and RSHP, and particularly for non-specialists. While a faculty structure may facilitate cross-curricular work, there would have to be strong leadership to ensure that teaching staff were given time to plan and develop effective teaching approaches. A major concern was that in becoming the 'responsibility of all', health and wellbeing would still remain the domain of PSE, PE and Home Economics teachers, the key 'specialists' in this area. Unless there was serious investment in training, sharing practice and structures for effective collaboration, it would still be difficult for subject specialists to engage with health and wellbeing in a meaningful way.

RESEARCH AND PEDAGOGICAL ISSUES

Research shows that effective approaches to the learning and teaching of health promotion consistently advocate taking account of the complex circumstances of the communities in which young people live. Many of the life skills and competencies that health promotion can help to develop such as assertiveness and critical reflection are transferable skills shared with other curricular areas.

A recent international review of the evidence base examining effective health promotion practice is broadly supportive of the integrated whole- school approach and the four contexts for learning advocated in CfE. The review identifies a range of key features such as how 'good school management and leadership' are essential and, more importantly, asserts that 'young people who are connected to significant adults are less likely to undertake high risk behaviours' (St Leger et al., 2010, p. 1). Furthermore, building school connectedness for students is also associated with a 'reduction in sexual activity in adolescence'. Feeling good about school, being connected to significant adults, considering the social and environmental context, and acknowledging the emotional dimensions in learning are all identified as important features of a health-promoting school. More importantly, teaching staff who have a good understanding of mental health issues 'can achieve higher health and educational outcomes for the students'.

Again, recent research and emerging school practice indicate that CfE is offering new opportunities to reinvigorate Substance Misuse Education. Evidence suggests that secondary pupils enjoy drug education lessons when there is a focus on active learning, the use of participatory methods and the opportunity for discussion. A review of Substance Misuse Education carried out by Health Scotland (2009) stressed that this is also going to be more effective when it considers the students' own substance misuse, and places a greater emphasis on appropriate life skills that realistically help students to assess risk and minimise harm. Very often a holistic approach can offer support for innovative work in the curriculum. For instance, Fast Forward, an Edinburgh-based charity funded through central government to work with secondary schools on substance misuse, is developing and using a youth work approach. They offer one-to-one sessions targeted at developing risk plans for high-tariff young people, group work, drop-ins and peer education programmes that use a social norms approach.

Similarly, some alcohol and tobacco programmes have shifted away from classroom-based lessons which focus on teaching facts to supporting young people resist peer pressure using a social norms approach. A social norms approach helps young people to explore the difference between what they perceive 'to be the behaviour and attitudes' of their peers, which is often overestimated or exaggerated, and the reality of peer group behaviour (McAlaney et al., 2011). This is a new and emerging field of study for health promotion and as such only a few schools in Scotland have started to use it. If used with proper evaluation it could offer a fresh and more positive dimension to alcohol and drug education as it is focused on reducing 'misperceptions and social pressure', which will hopefully lead to a reduction in alcohol consumption and drug-related harm. Most notably, schools using it seem to be integrating new technologies as a medium for intervention and promotion to a much greater extent (websites to communicate and promote key messages, video clips, social networking and online surveys). Overall, this could offer a more cost-effective approach, be applied to other health topics such as sexual health, help to build teacher confidence and be a more effective and realistic way to engage senior pupils. Essentially, this is an 'asset-based approach' which builds on the positive and articulates with current research on wellbeing (see Chapter 48).

ASSESSMENT, MONITORING AND EVALUATION

Health and wellbeing will not be formally assessed by the SQA. However, it will be up to local authorities and schools to decide on appropriate forms of assessment. *Building the Curriculum 5* (2011) suggests that progress will be seen in the ways in which young people are 'developing and applying their knowledge' in key areas such as 'assessing risk and decision making'. Beyond S3, the SQA is currently developing a suite of new qualifications which will build on the experience and outcomes for health and wellbeing. A wide range of courses are under review and the SQA has produced a progress report for the 'next generation of National Qualifications' for Health and Wellbeing (2010). Some courses are vocational and offer routes into training and employment, such as Care (Health and Social), Early Education and Childcare. Additionally, the Skills for Work courses can be offered jointly by schools and colleges, and qualifications in Personal Development and Social and Vocational Skills offer customised learning in specific skills. On the other hand, some link more with curriculum subjects and offer awards at Higher level: Philosophy, Psychology, Sociology, Physical Education and Home Economics.

Beyond school assessment, local authorities have a responsibility to monitor and evaluate the impact of health and wellbeing programmes on young people's health outcomes. Policy makers and planners need to consider the short -term impact of improved health and wellbeing, which may improve school attendance or academic performance, as well as some of the more long-term, generational changes in meeting public health targets. Equally, the *Health Behaviour in School-Aged Children* survey (Currie et al., 2011) provides information on national trends and data from the 2010 cohort. Some improvements are showing, particularly in relation to eating habits. Encouragingly, levels of happiness and confidence for both boys and girls increased between 1994 and 2006. However, between 2006 and 2010 the happiness of boys and girls and the confidence of girls worryingly showed a marked decrease. Extensive information on the school environment has been collected and may help schools to plan and target health and wellbeing programmes more accurately. Additionally, strategies to tackle gender differences which are apparent for many of the health indicators would really start to embed some of the key principles discussed in *Building the Curriculum 5* (2011), namely relevance, coherence, personalisation and, above all, enjoyment.

FUTURE CONSIDERATIONS

Whilst strategy and tactics to improve health may have changed significantly in recent years, consensus on the pressing importance of the issue has not. Indeed, continuing to invest in health promotion has been one of the few areas in political and public life that continues to bring different groups together on a shared goal. Compared to the 1970s, Scotland is a healthier nation. Progress is clearly being made, but the pace of improvement remains slow and there are many entrenched problems. However, the outlook is very positive and in many respects Scotland is leading the world in the development of contemporary health promotion policies and strategies. CfE has placed schools in a strong position and has the potential as an 'asset -based approach' to create the conditions necessary for the health and wellbeing of young people to flourish in the twenty-first century.

REFERENCES

Currie, C., K. Levin, J. Kirby, D. Currie, W. van der Sluijs and J. Inchley (2011) *Health Behaviour in School-aged Children: World Health Organisation Collaborative Cross-national Study (HBSC): Findings from the 2010 HBSC Survey Scotland*. Edinburgh: University of Edinburgh Child and Adolescent Health Research Unit.

McAlaney, J., C. Hughes and B. Bewick (2011) 'The international development of the "social norms" approach to drug education and prevention', *Drugs: Education, Prevention and Policy*, 18 (2): 81–9.

NHS Health Scotland (2009) *School-based Substance Misuse Education: A Review of Resources*. Edinburgh: NHS Health Scotland.

Scottish Government (2009) *Curriculum for Excellence. Health and Wellbeing across Learning: Responsibilities for all Principles and Practice*. Edinburgh: Scottish Government.

Scottish Government (2011) *Curriculum for Excellence. Building the Curriculum 5: A Framework for Assessment*. Edinburgh: Scottish Government.

Scottish Qualifications Authority (2010) *Progress Report: Health and Wellbeing Curriculum Area*. Glasgow: SQA.

St Leger, L., I. Young, C. Blanchard and M. Perry (2010) *Promoting Health in Schools: From Evidence to Action*. Online at www.iuhpe.org/uploaded/Activities/Scientific_Affairs/CDC/School%20 Health/PHiS_EtA_EN_WEB.pdf

61

History Education

Neil McLennan

Writing a recent history of History education is no easy task in the seemingly ever-shifting Scottish education landscape. Those delving into education archives might think History has been a subject under relentless attack from marginalisation, curriculum decluttering, reduced class contact time and History departments being subsumed into social studies faculties. However, despite radical changes in Scottish education, History remains a popular, high-attaining subject.

Reports by HM Inspectors (now part of Education Scotland) and Scottish Government Excellence Group papers (Scottish Government, 2011) highlight numerous examples of excellent practice and how that good practice can be further disseminated. Many History teachers report having a higher Grade Point Average (GPA) in history departments than other departments in their school. Odd instances of History being dropped from senior phase student course choice options because of poor uptake or low attainment are in the minority. In the independent sector, too, History education remains strong. The changes, however, have sparked an important self-reflection and powerful reassessment of why we should teach history at all. Whilst defending their place in that ever-cluttered and competitive curriculum, History educators have had to think long and hard about why they are teaching young people about events from long ago and people about whom we often know little. This ongoing reflection and re-establishing of common core purposes is paying off. It would appear History is in the ascendancy.

PURPOSE

In the most recent discussions, the Royal Society of Edinburgh (RSE) History Working Group came up with a useful list of aims for History education. This list gives some answers as to why History should feature prominently in a twenty-first-century curriculum. The RSE Working Group stated that history should:

- enable learners to acquire breadth and depth in the knowledge and understanding of historical themes;
- develop learners' understanding of the place of change and continuity over time in the study of history;
- develop learners' skills in explaining historical developments and events, drawing conclusions and evaluating historical sources;

- develop learners' conceptual understanding and foster their ability to think independently;
- enable learners to detect bias and propaganda and to challenge prejudice;
- encourage learners to debate issues and, on the basis of evidence, form views and respect those of others;
- develop learners' imagination and empathy with people living in other periods;
- foster in learners an interest in history which will provide a life-long source of enjoyment. (RSE, 2011)

This list can be slightly amended, added to and debated, but the core essentials will be largely agreed by History educators. Foremost in the minds of History educators is that the study of History develops young people with the essential skills, knowledge, attributes and personal dispositions to succeed in learning, life and work.

RECENT DEVELOPMENTS

History teachers know better than anyone else in the profession about the causes and consequences of change and continuity. They know better than anyone the perils and opportunities change brings. After all, the themes of change and continuity play a large part in History teaching. For this reason history educators have been better prepared than most to overcome the challenges that educational change brings. Some are refreshed by the emerging curriculum whilst others still harbour understandable concerns. History itself is not monolithic but alters and changes according to research and new findings. In the same way, History education has also changed to adapt to new pedagogical approaches, curriculum structures and management structures within schools.

However, despite many educators sharing an understanding and acceptance of the value of History education, the positive impact of the subject is not fully embedded across all practice in Scotland. Students' experience of History education remains patchy. This is especially so in the early years, primary education and early years of secondary school. Students do cover historic studies but not always with a subject specialist teaching them and not always with the depth, breadth or application to which History teaching specialists would aspire. There is still work to be done to ensure consistent high standards of History education in the primary sector and to establish better curricular transitions. Some History teachers have been commended for their work in this area: a 'history walk' project in Stirling that combined history, heritage education and outdoor learning was featured prominently in a recent government report (Scottish Government, 2011).

History remains an option in the senior phase of secondary schools. The age-old debate as to whether or not History should be a compulsory subject throughout secondary education continues unabated although this is unlikely to be achieved in the near future. To help alleviate the problem both the Scottish Association of Teachers of History (SATH) and the Scottish Government History Excellence Group published a planning tool that aimed to ensure adequate coverage of the competing demands in a subject as complex as History. There are calls now to resurrect the use of that tool given that the whole curriculum will have been reformed once new Advanced Higher course, assessment and unit specifications are published in 2013.

CURRICULAR CHANGE: CURRICULUM FOR EXCELLENCE

The implementation phase of Curriculum for Excellence (CfE) understandably takes centre stage with regard to recent developments. CfE has seen broad, thematic experiences and outcomes provide a framework within which a degree of professional interpretation and local implementation, and a tapestry of different processes can be adapted. In CfE, History is not referred to by name. Instead the themes and skills we would associate with the discipline of History appear under the heading of Social Studies and under the sub-group of 'people, past events and societies'.

The ability to implement CfE experiences and outcomes in a range of different ways has sparked a major debate as to how History should be taught in our schools. Some have opted for a 'Plato to NATO' or 'Adam to Atom' approach. This particular approach was commended by the RSE Working Group on History in Scottish schools (RSE, 2011). However such an approach is often criticised for being 'a race' through history's main events and key figures. Critics argue that this dash does not offer any depth of understanding or real ability to learn or apply skills that can be developed through History education. Another approach can be described as 'local to global'. This model has younger years focusing on local history before building to geopolitical issues with educational maturity. Again this approach has its staunch advocates and critics. Some would argue that you remember best what you understand the most and, as such, memory of local history only taught in the early years is distant, vague and prone to marginalisation. Whatever the approach, the system-wide change of CfE has certainly provoked History educators into discussing and remodelling approaches to learning and teaching and course structures. There have been efforts to preserve a balance between local, Scottish, British, European and world history topics, alongside an awareness that students should be exposed to ancient, middle age and modern history. Furthermore, a balance must be struck between social, economic and military history if we are to give students a rounded experience in History education. During this reflection many History teachers are asking the question 'Why are we teaching this topic?' This remodelling applies not only to course content but also to pedagogy. History teachers have coped well with the pedagogical changes, increased emphasis on a range of formative assessment techniques, interdisciplinary learning and student-led learning. Discussions are ongoing as to the rigour of some of the more student-centred assessment devices. Many History teachers were practising the key principles of CfE before the green folders even arrived. They have continued to offer active learning and innovative and effective assessment techniques, and to inspire young people with challenging and enjoyable lessons.

During the early period of consultation around the new curriculum there were strong concerns that the sanctity of the subject might not be preserved. Early concerns that History was going to be sidelined as a discrete subject area seemed to be alleviated as CfE was implemented. Education Ministers now avoid that debate following Peter Peacock's dalliance with the potential for History not to appear in the curriculum. Despite that, many are still on their guard to preserve History as a key subject in the broad general education. This is especially the case as CfE documentation makes no explicit reference to 'History'. This is a point not lost on the RSE Working Group who suggest that 'history is in danger of being diluted under the CfE framework' (RSE, 2011). In defence of the new curriculum guidelines, the green folder does state: 'These organisers [people, past events and societies; people, place and environment; people in society, economy and business] recognise the special contribution made by each to the social subjects' (Education Scotland, 2010).

Children and young people are expected to participate in the following experiences and outcomes that are specific to the study of History:

- develop their understanding of history, heritage and culture of Scotland, and an appreciation of their local and national heritage within the world;
- broaden their understanding of the world by learning about human activities and achievements in the past and present;
- explore and evaluate different types of sources and evidence;
- learn how to locate, explore and link periods, people and events in time and place. (Education Scotland, 2010)

CURRICULAR CHANGE: NATIONAL QUALIFICATIONS

The final phase of curricular change came when the course specifications for National 3, 4, 5 and Higher were published in April 2012. Work is now ongoing consulting and reforming Advanced Higher provision. The new qualifications were to build on CfE principles by shifting pedagogy and raising the bar of expectation. Student choice has been broadened by adding a Value Added Unit. As part of the Value Added Unit students are expected to research and present on a topic of their choice. Some welcome the opportunity for student responsibility to investigate in depth an area of interest. Meanwhile, other, more experienced, History teachers dread a return to the time- consuming 'investigation' of the Standard Grade era when many criticised the potential for inherent unfairness through parental support.

In terms of topics there is a limited choice, although History remains the subject with the largest choice of topics to choose from. In National 5 and Higher the balance is set between Scottish, British, and European and World topics. There are five Scottish and British units to pick from respectively and a further nine (Higher)/ten (National 5) choices to cover a range of options in world history. This is a change from the Standard Grade thematic demarcation between Change and Continuity in Scotland and Britain, Conflict and Cooperation, and People and Power based topics.

National 3 and National 4 courses will be internally assessed with no external exam and no prescribed course content. The reality is that many will seek to align course content with the externally assessed National 5 course as bi-level teaching proves a necessity. National 5 students have a choice of topics to pick from under the broad sections of Historical Study: Scottish, British, and European and World. This is a major change from the Standard Grade units that went before. Under Standard Grade Scottish and British History appeared together under a thematic approach looking at change and continuity.

Perception and reality are two different things. Whilst there may appear to be a considerable degree of choice for students within the range of topics offered, the reality is that most students will be studying topics largely dictated by the availability of department resources and expertise and preference of the practitioner. However, students will have autonomy when choosing, studying and presenting their own research as part of the fourth assessable element, the Value Added Unit.

Topics appearing under the 'Scottish History' section of study and assessment include the Wars of Independence. The topics in this section are the same as those offered in the Higher Course for Paper 2. Critics have suggested this structure will lead to repetition and does not give a broad range of Scottish history to choose from, most notably pre-1286 history and more modern history including political history leading to the referendum on the question of Scottish Independence. The latter issue in particular is vitally important for students who will be exercising responsible citizenship when they engage in that process. Another issue has been raised in that having such similar topics at National 5 and Higher level may lead to repetition. However, centres have been informed that, where there are 'hierarchies', practitioners should make every effort to ensure there is no repetition. Indeed, there are strong voices trying to guide History departments to review their whole History curriculum to ensure the best fit for all students and one that avoids unnecessary repetition of topics or skills. In many regards the landscape is now clear for historians to develop strong progression paths in skills, knowledge and understanding.

At Higher level there have been no changes to the Scottish topic content. Significant changes were made to the topics and assessment of this course when the newly revised Higher Paper 2 was relaunched. The previous changes made were preserved and Paper 2 topics remained static after SATH made representation to the Scottish Qualifications Authority (SQA) concerning making too many changes at one time when there was not the resource or capacity to absorb such significant modifications.

In the British section, History departments will present students who have studied the following topics (the Higher topics appear in brackets after the National 5 topic): The Creation of the Medieval Kingdoms (Church, State and Feudal Society); War of the Three Kingdoms (The Century of Revolutions); The Atlantic Slave Trade (Atlantic Slave Trade); Changing Britain 1760–1900 (Britain 1851–1951), or, The Making of Modern Britain, 1880–1951 (Britain and Ireland 1900–1985).

National 5 students have a choice of ten topics whilst there are nine topics in Higher to pick from. The increased number of topics on offer reflects the size and scale of this area of history. The following topics are on offer at National 5 (again the Higher course is in brackets after the near equivalent course at the other level): The Cross and the Crescent (The Crusades); Tea and Freedom (The American Revolution); USA 1850–80 (at Higher the French Revolution up to 1799 is offered); Hitler and Nazi Germany (Germany 1815–1939); Red Flag, Lenin and the Russian Revolution 1894–1921 (Russia 1881–1921); Mussolini and Fascist Italy 1919–1939 (Italy 1815–1939); Free at Last? Civil Rights in the USA 1918–1968 (USA 1918–1968); Appeasement and the Road to War 1918–1939 (Appeasement and the Road to War 1919–1939); World War II (no equivalent course in Higher); The Cold War (The Cold War).

The last section of both the National 5 and Higher courses looks at the broad sweep of European and world history. Again, there has been criticism that there is not enough on offer. Whilst this has been rebutted by the argument that no qualification can offer every topic available or desired, it is a concern that students will only be able to focus on one specific area of history beyond their borders. However the lack of Far East or Middle East History gives it a strong 'western civilisations' feel, given it does not extend beyond Europe and America to any great degree. The absence of Chinese history has been cited as evidence of a lack of joined-up thinking at a time when Mandarin was being promoted in so many schools in Scotland as part of greater Scotland–China links (McLennan, 2012).

NATIONAL OR MULTINATIONAL?

Achieving a balance in National Qualifications between Scottish, British, and European and World, and the debates to maintain balance throughout the process of change, show

how History is vitally important for securing students an understanding of their nation and a developing global citizenship perspective. Scottish History education has been well represented internationally over the last few decades. Likewise, Scottish education has been receptive and welcoming of international inputs, thus demonstrating how integrated History education can and should be. Scottish History educators have presented at many overseas conferences and a number of high-profile History education conferences and continuing professional development events have been hosted in Scotland. At recent SATH Conferences, input from the Netherlands, Denmark, Wales, Northern Ireland and England has helped to broaden History educators' ideas and has opened up the sharing of good practice across borders.

Building on that very theme, the European organisation for history networks EUROCLIO is currently working on a resource that will bring together teaching and learning resources from across Europe. 'Historiana' will encourage learners and teachers to look at topics, themes, events and historical figures using 'multi-perspectivity'. It is hoped students will be encouraged to look at history from other time perspectives; the perspective of different places, different people's perspectives and the different perspectives between the eras. This approach offers lots of scope for the breadth, depth and application that is envisioned in CfE. Work is currently ongoing to ensure Scottish learners are linked in to this resource which offers opportunities to further expose history learners to the connected nature of our past (EUROCLIO, 2012).

Set against this multi-perspective European development were Scottish Government proposals for 'Scottish Studies' in the curriculum. Herein lies a major challenge that History teachers are faced with all the time. Not only do they have to balance out modern history with the ancient period, themes as wide-spanning as social, economic and military history, but they also have to ensure a geographic balance in learning. History educators know only too well the power of education. Hence a balance between nationalist curriculum developments and local history needs with wider British, European and world history coverage is sought at all times. One development that pleased many History educators was the successful launch of the revised Higher History courses in November 2009. The new structures ensured a balance by prescribing Scottish History units to Paper 2 (source-based) part of the exam. This balanced structure is maintained in the new National 5 and Higher qualifications. This gave national history its rightful protected place by prescribing that students must undertake study in Scottish History. These changes to Higher History saw a balance struck as History educators worked hard to eradicate an over-dominance of Bismarck and Nazi Germany in the Scottish History curriculum. Now History educators work hard to guard against any other dominance, including too much Scottish history. A balance of topics is in everyone's best interests. SATH has made representations at ministerial level, suggesting that further work needs to be undertaken to ensure there is adequate coverage of Scottish history and that the European and World History sections offer enough choice to ensure as complete a global coverage as is possible (McLennan, 2012).

Running alongside major changes to the curriculum, the Scottish Government initiated a working group to investigate the possibility of establishing 'Scottish Studies' in schools. The first mention of 'Scottish Studies' by Scottish Ministers was immediately interpreted as nationalist propaganda by opposition politicians. This claim was soon denounced as political point-scoring in what was essentially an education discussion. Other educators interpreted it as an effort to implement Social Studies 'through the back door'. Both of these claims were refuted by ministers and the debate fizzled out. However, the Scottish Studies

Ministerial Working Group progressed through the press storm and allegations of political expediency to produce a set of recommendations. These looked very different from the distinct Scottish Studies subject and qualification many thought would emerge. In essence, a guidance document was produced along with a web portal for bringing together the array of resources that can be used in any subject when studying Scotland (Education Scotland, 2012). For History teachers it will be business as usual as they aim to encourage learners to become more familiar with the history of their own country and at the same time widen their horizons to the wealth of European and world history from which comparisons can be drawn and lessons be learned in our own local area.

CONCLUSIONS: HISTORY EDUCATION ACHIEVING AND ATTAINING

Amidst all this change the most prevailing constant has been the consolidation of History being a well-taught subject that grows in popularity with students and in which they both attain academically and achieve personally. Changes to educational structures have not altered that trend. It would appear that learning lessons from history is true even in the case of the history of History education. The words of former American President Woodrow Wilson seem very apt looking back over this relentless period of reform: 'It is easier to change the location of a cemetery than to change the school curriculum'. Thankfully History is not, to quote one primary school student, 'just about dead people'. History education in Scotland, and beyond, is far more active than that.

REFERENCES

Education Scotland (2010) *Curriculum for Excellence: Social Studies Principles and Practice.* Online at www.educationscotland.gov.uk/Images/social_studies_principles_practice_tcm4-540398.pdf

Education Scotland (2012) *Studying Scotland.* Online at www.educationscotland.gov.uk/studying-scotland/index.asp

Education Scotland (2013) *Social Studies 3–18 Curriculum Impact Report.* Online at http://www.educationscotland.gov.uk/resources/0to9/genericresource_tcm4731946.asp?strReferringChannel=learningteachingandassessment&strReferringPageID=tcm:4-731910-64&class=ll+d157441

EUROCLIO (2012) *Historiana – Your Portal to the Past.* Online at www.euroclio.eu/new/index.php/work/historiana

McLennan, N. (2012) 'Historians, it's time to fight for the future of the past', *Times Educational Supplement Scotland* (11 May). Online at www.tes.co.uk/article.aspx?storycode=6225790

Royal Society of Edinburgh (2011) *Advice Paper (11-01), The Teaching of History in Scottish Schools* (Report of an RSE Working Group). Edinburgh: Royal Society of Edinburgh.

Scottish Government (2011) *History Excellence Group Report.* Edinburgh: Scottish Government.

Scottish Qualifications Authority (2012) *History Course Support Materials.* Glasgow: SQA.

62

Home Economics

Karen Bryce

> Home Economics in my view should be compulsory; it offers far more than basic cooking or kitchen management but more importantly vital life skills, self-confidence and knowledge essential for healthy living.
>
> Michel Roux Jr, Le Gavroche (2012)

> Home Economics teaches vital life skills and skills for work so should have an important place in everyone's school curriculum. Many of the people I meet in the hospitality industry have shown an early interest at school. The industry is crying out for good chefs and I think more professional chefs should be coming out to schools to work with young people interested in the hospitality industry.
>
> Andrew Fairlie, Gleneagles (2012)

These recent statements by two highly regarded Michelin star chefs draw attention to two reasons why Home Economics should figure in the Scottish secondary curriculum. First, they emphasise just how important the taught skills are in everyone's life and, second, they remind us that early exposure of the right kind to the subject at school has lasting benefits for work in the hospitality industry – a significant employer in Scotland and the rest of the UK. Both point to what modern Home Economics syllabuses should (and do) contain for the lower and upper years of secondary, the second point being particularly relevant to Hospitality courses at the new National levels.

Changes in society have shaped Home Economics courses. First, compared to a generation ago, more women now work and traditional family units are much less common. There is certainly more technology in the home and, though generally speaking there is more disposable income, debt and poverty are depressing features of many households, not helped by the present state of the UK economy. Second, eating patterns have changed. Despite the popularity of cooking programmes on TV such as *Masterchef*, people actually cook less than they used to. With respect to fast food, the 'McDonaldisation' of the world continues, catering for 68 million customers daily (it was 54 million five years ago when the third edition of this book was published). That said, there are increasing numbers of quality food outlets, with some sections of society – alas, only some – actually eating better. Courses need to reflect these changes and individual school departments must tailor their courses to suit their own pupils' needs.

Third, and as Scottish Government bluntly put it in a recent summary of statistics, 'Much of Scotland's poor health record can be attributed to its unhealthy eating habits'

(Scottish Government, 2011). This was first spelled out in the James Report (*Scotland's Health: A Challenge to Us All – The Scottish Diet*, 1993, Edinburgh: HMSO), with the Scottish Executive, and subsequently the Scottish Government, regularly surveying the nation's health and commenting on lifestyle choices. The Food Standards Agency (FSA) reported in 2012 that *none* of the Scottish dietary targets set in 1996, and expected to be reached by 2010, had been achieved. At best, another twenty-nine years would be required before the goal for consuming fruit and vegetables might be met; fat still makes up about 39 per cent of the Scottish diet and confectionery consumption has increased in the last ten years. And comparisons with England are worrying: research suggests that 1,647 fewer Scots would die each year if they followed the current English diet. Home Economics has an important role to play in this regard, not least in the teaching of Health and Wellbeing (HWB) as part of Curriculum for Excellence. Schools and local authorities are mandated by the Schools (Health Promotion and Nutrition) (Scotland) Act 2007 to provide wholesome food and drink. Much of the detail in the Act concerns 'school dinners', healthy snacks and free school meal entitlements, but the central point is that it 'places health promotion at the heart of a school's activities' (see www.scotland.gov.uk/Topics/Education/Schools/HLivi/foodnutrition).

Had Home Economics been made a core subject along with Physical Education, it would have been easier to address the chronic health problems in many parts of Scotland. A core location in the curriculum would have made Home Economics' contribution to HWB more significant and both subjects would have mutually benefited through joint endeavours.

HOME ECONOMICS AND CFE IN S1–S3

The active learning promoted by Curriculum for Excellence (CfE) was not new to Home Economics, though much work has been required of teachers to restructure courses in line with the four CfE capacities and the experiences and outcomes (E&Os) expressed in national documentation. Without subject advisors to organise working groups to create new courses, many departments have had to write their own. However, some authorities have appointed subject leaders/school-based development officers/lead principal teachers (the title varies depending on the authority), and part of their remit has been to help departments network across schools when devising courses. In its newest forms, the subject provides young people with learning that is challenging, engaging and motivating. It also provides a useful context for contributions to enterprise, citizenship and international education, with many schools organising whole-school events.

The E&Os in Home Economics draw from the areas of Technologies (TCH) including ICT, Health and Wellbeing (HWB), Literacy (LIT), Numeracy (MNU). Young people are given many opportunities while working in groups or carrying out peer assessment, self-assessment and sensory evaluations to contribute to HWB by:

- managing learning;
- encouraging learning and confidence in others;
- making friends;
- being part of a group in a range of situations;
- analysing and discussing elements of their own and others' work;
- identifying areas for improvement.

The use of subject dictionaries, highlighting words in recipes, note-taking while watching demonstrations, carrying out investigations and making presentations are a few of the ideas that contribute to the E&Os in Literacy across Learning. Weighing and measuring, recording survey results and comparative costing exercises are a few examples of the Numeracy tasks that are encountered in Home Economics.

Interdisciplinary Learning (IDL) forms an important part of CfE, and Hospitality lends itself to coordination with subjects such as Maths, ICT, Art, Technical, PE, Geography, Science and Modern Languages. Because of timetabling difficulties in various schools, some IDL is taught by one subject but it contributes to other subjects' E&Os.

Active learning strategies are also used to teach the 'theory' of Home Economics, for example in practical investigations; 'quiz, quiz, trade' tasks; 'think-pair-share' activities; 'show me' boards; 'stations'. Problem-solving tasks, such as 'design and make' and enterprise projects, where learners can create, devise, interpret and analyse, help progression to National levels 4 and 5. A number of teachers use Prezi (see www.prezi.com) on a smartboard to make presentations interactive. ICT is incorporated into many courses wherever the facilities make this possible.

NATIONAL LEVELS 4 AND 5

All the new and revised National courses reflect CfE values, purposes and principles. A course should provide learners with opportunities to continue to acquire and develop the attributes and capabilities of the four capacities as well as Skills for Learning, Skills for Life and Skills for Work. The most obvious change from Intermediate 1 and 2 is that the units in National 4 and 5 are the same. This means that the courses have to be differentiated in a way that allows progression without losing learners' interest. Some schools teach National 4 and 5 together over two years to avoid this. Schools can maximise class numbers by putting S4, S5 and S6 together. Also, the unit changes make it much easier to achieve the essence of CfE, which is that courses should provide smooth progression from S1–S6.

The new subject areas are: Food, Health and Wellbeing National 2; Hospitality Practical Cookery National 3, 4 and 5; Practical Cake Craft National 5; Health and Food Technology National 3, 4, 5, Higher and Advanced Higher; Fabric and Textile National 3, 4, 5 and Higher. There is also a Wellbeing award at National 3, 4 and 5, a two-year course taught by Home Economics, Physical Education and Science (see www.sqa.org.uk/newawards). The four subject areas taught at National 4 and 5 levels demand a wide range of expertise. If departments have adequate staff (this is often a problem), the strengths of the individual teachers should be used to provide the best learning and teaching in each subject area. Heads of department/faculties must draw attention to the important work carried out in these expensive courses through promoting their subject in a variety of ways, such as photographic displays, invitations to senior management teams (SMTs) to tasting sessions, subject flyers for parents, and so on. SMTs must be aware of the importance and relevance of the courses when funding and curriculum decisions are being made.

The most popular of the subjects taught under the umbrella of Home Economics is Hospitality: Practical Cookery. Its purpose is to provide young people with increased knowledge and skills which will not only lead to a better standard of personal life, but also allow them to make a focused decision about pursuing a career in the hospitality and tourism industries. In 2011, 6,439 pupils sat Intermediate 1 Practical Cookery (88 per cent pass rate) and 5,365 sat Intermediate 2 (94 per cent pass rate). It is a real success story.

The practical work is demanding for the teacher. Food is prepared for four people and presented as in hotels and restaurants; auxiliary help is therefore essential (but rarely available). This course is the most expensive as a wide variety of foods is used as well as the catering equipment and outfits needed to give a suitably 'real' experience. For the final exam the City of Glasgow College offers continuing professional development opportunities for teachers in all authorities by carrying out demonstrations of the exam dishes.

Glasgow's visionary and innovative Culinary Excellence Programme was integrated into Hospitality Intermediate 2 (soon National 5) and has been running for sixteen years. It gives pupils the experience of real-life hospitality contexts with the opportunity to be trained by top city chefs in their hotels and restaurants, half a day a week for twelve weeks, culminating in planning, making, hosting and serving a four-course fine-dining meal to invited guests. There are currently twelve schools each with their link hotel/restaurant involved in the programme and it has a high success rate for sending young people out into the industry, be it for further training or to start working. This is something that could be set up in any authority with a local hotel or restaurant.

Health and Food Technology (HFT) provides opportunities to study the relationships between health, nutrition, the functional properties of food, lifestyle choices and consumer issues. In 2011, 441 sat Intermediate 1 (93 per cent pass rate), 350 sat Intermediate 2 (69 per cent pass rate), 799 sat Higher (83 per cent pass rate) and 33 sat Advanced Higher (85 per cent pass rate). The course also provides practical and experiential opportunities. However, as pupils progress to Higher there is less practical work involved. Tight planners need to be written to try to introduce as much practical work as possible. This is only one of two subjects taught to Higher level (and only one to Advanced Higher) and is therefore important in raising the profile of the subject. In the Higher course, the use of exemplars, attending staff development sessions, good networking and acting as an SQA marker are the best ways to understand how to teach the Assignment (formerly the Technological Project).

In 2011, 623 sat the course previously known as Creative Cake Production Intermediate 2 (99 per cent pass rate). At National 5, Practical Cake Craft enables pupils to develop very specialised skills that will serve later in life as a leisure activity or could allow progression at college into Higher Professional Patisserie. There is a great shortage of bakers in Scotland and large supermarkets are sending their employees to the City of Glasgow College to train. Staff development courses have been available for teachers. National 5 Practical Cake Craft offers an excellent lateral progression from National 5 Hospitality. The pass rate is the way forward when persuading a school to put the subject into their curriculum. There are online galleries showing best practice for both Hospitality Practical Cake Craft (see www.sqa.org.uk/files_ccc/CfE_CourseUnitSupportNotes_N5_SocialStudies_HospitalityPracticalCakeCraft.pdf).

Fashion and Textile Technology (FTT) provides practical and experiential opportunities to apply skills relevant to, and develop knowledge and understanding of, the fashion and textile industry. In 2011, 484 pupils sat Intermediate 1 FTT (90 per cent pass rate), 182 sat Intermediate 2 (66 per cent pass rate) and 223 sat Higher (79 per cent pass rate). Although low numbers, these are rising. These figures may reflect the lack of training in the relevant skills of young teachers. In the meantime, some schools are losing the subject to Art departments. This could be a good IDL opportunity.

Skills for Work has not as yet had any changes made for CfE. These qualifications encourage young people to become familiar with the world of work. The four units – Working in the Hospitality Industry; Working in the Professional Kitchen; Working Front of House; and Introduction to Events – require schools to have links with a local college, a professional kitchen and a restaurant. It is a course that suits young people who would benefit from going into employment as soon as they can leave school.

The SQA's Skills Framework: Skills for Learning, Skills for Life and Skills for Work details the broad generic skills that learners are expected to develop through National 4 and 5. These must be built into courses. Unit Support Notes provide advice and guidance on the delivery, assessment approaches and development of Skills for Learning, Skills for Life and Skills for Work. Exemplification of standards is given in the National Assessment Resources (NARs).

KEEPING UP TO DATE

The opening quotation by Andrew Fairlie, as well as emphasising the importance of Home Economics, also indicates the significance of two-way links between work and school. That is, an important part of learning is to bring the hospitality industry into school or to take the young people out to it. The qualification in Hospitality: Practical Cookery fulfils this call. Chefs from local colleges and hotels will come out to schools to teach culinary knife skills and carry out demonstrations. Visits to the Braehead Cookery School (Kilmarnock) and Tennent's Training Academy and the Glasgow Cook School help young people get out into the real world of food. Projects with Seafood Scotland or Quality Meat Scotland, or involvement in competitions such as Springboard Scotland's Future Chef, encourage young people to progress in school and consider careers in hospitality. Springboard also runs summer schools for those interested in careers in the hospitality, leisure and tourism industries. The Royal Environmental Health Institute of Scotland (REHIS) supplies resources (often free of charge) to help pupils gain the REHIS (Food Hygiene) certificate. Using the BBC iPlayer to prepare dishes following celebrity chefs makes the experience more like 'real life' in the eyes of many learners. Some teachers deploy webcams set above a cooking unit so that demonstrations for food lessons can be shown on Smartboards while pupils stay at their work units. Given that young people watch a wide variety of cookery programmes, this keeps the subject up to date with their expectations. The British Nutrition Foundation (BNF) has a conference every year to update teachers. The BNF website has an abundance of useful resources including posters, leaflets, games, worksheets, podcasts and interactive websites. Their website www.foodafactoflife.org.uk provides a progressive approach to teaching about healthy eating, cooking, food and farming for 3- to 16-year-olds. Comic Resources supplies fun resources and games that help with differentiating courses.

SUBJECT LOCATION AND CURRICULUM STRUCTURE

Across the Scottish authorities, many Home Economics departments are discrete units and many are located in faculties, the latter varying in structure, for example one authority uses 'Health Improvement with Physical Education'. Currently, few faculty heads are Home Economics teachers and those who are not have difficulties in managing the subject. Many Home Economics departments have rotations in S1 and S2, so often there is not enough time to secure E&Os at level 3. An S3 pupil's experience should of course be based on the E&Os up to, and beyond, CfE level 4. At which stage in the curriculum subjects are chosen has an effect on how courses are structured, and this varies from authority to authority (or even school to school). At the time of writing, the 3+3 model was being adopted by many schools instead of the more traditional 2+2+2 model. In some schools, however, pupils choose their subjects at the end of S1. Other schools have rotations in S1 and, as a result of this, some S2 pupils have little practical experience of healthy eating. Headteachers need to be persuaded that all of S2 need some exposure to Home Economics, e.g. a slot in Personal, Social and Health Education (PSE) time, possibly for one period a week for ten weeks. However, there will still be young people who slip through the net. Senior management staff should not be allowed to forget the unique contribution that Home Economics makes to CfE.

ASSESSMENT AND RECORDING

This is the area where there is most change for Home Economics teachers. Each school will have its own ideas about how to map CfE achievement across the curriculum areas. Departmentally, each unit planner should identify the learning intentions for individual lessons in conjunction with the success criteria. These should be discussed with the class at the beginning of each lesson and a column in the Home Economics unit planner for 'Say, Write, Make, Do' used to note exactly what is being assessed. There should be breadth and challenge in assessments to allow all to achieve. In a practical class this can be the level of support given. The subject-specific HWB and TCH E&Os make it clear which areas should be assessed when carrying out practical work, and assessment recording sheets should reflect them. Profiling enables pupils to collect evidence of work and of their achievements. Profiles can include: tracking sheets, target cards, focus sheets (indicating areas for development), photographic evidence and certificates of achievement. At the end of each section of learning, a 'learning checklist' can be filled out where the traffic light colours are used. The teacher discusses this with each pupil and it is stored in the profile. There are excellent examples of these in the Active Home Economics level 3 and level 4 textbooks.

In S3+ the SQA provides unit assessments; however, there are no prescribed assessment methods, only assessment standards and evidence requirements. By combining unit assessments, the amount of assessment can be reduced. Evidence in S3 can be gathered and stored in an e-portfolio, for example. Assessment methods for 'Added Value' can be assignments, case studies, practical activities, performance portfolios, projects and question papers/tests. If a learner sits National 5 and fails, the National 4 Added Value Unit assures a pass at National 4. Work at pass, borderline pass and fail are kept for verification. Learning and teaching resources to assist teachers can be found online (see www.educationscotland.gov.uk/nq). In all courses a huge emphasis should be on preparing and enjoying eating a wide range of foods. When pupils enter the classroom the question should not be 'what are we making today?'; it should be 'what are we *learning* today?'.

CHALLENGES

Age and Gender Profile of the Subject

Recent statistics from government indicate that for the year 2009, the average age of the 1,001 Home Economics teachers in Scotland was 47 years, about one-quarter of them being over 55 years of age. Only twenty-one were male. The subject needs an injection of youth, in particular men. Increasing the number of boys in Home Economics is always a challenge. More male teachers should help achieve this. In 2011, the proportion of boys studying

Standard Grade Home Economics was 23 per cent; Intermediate 1 Hospitality 39 per cent, Intermediate 2 Hospitality 34 per cent and Higher Health and Food Technology 11 per cent.

Initial Teacher Education

The success of courses resulting in the overall increased uptake in the subject has caused problems owing to the continuing shortage of teachers. This is due to the limited number of teacher training places in the one-year PGDE course (offered by Strathclyde, Aberdeen and Dundee Universities) and the lack of a dedicated Home Economics degree. Students who initially take degrees in Nutrition and Consumer Science or Food and Health commonly do not intend to enter teaching. Many students and probationer teachers take extra courses in their own time to train in the skills they are lacking (for example, in cooking, basic sewing or creative textiles). The success and growth of the subject really depends on resolving these difficulties.

Name of the Subject

It will be apparent from what has been described in this chapter that the subject's name – Home Economics – is seriously out of date and many lament its continued use. Despite surveys and consultations, it seems that the subject areas involved in it are too wide to yield an agreed consensus. Though not ideal, perhaps the best solution is for each department (and school) to choose a name that best reflects the courses taught there. This takes us back to the diversity reflected in the quotations that preface the chapter. At present, some schools are resorting to the clutch of letters HFT (Health, Food and Textiles). Placing Health and Food first in this title certainly underlines the crucial part to be played by the subject given the serious societal concerns evident in modern Scotland.

REFERENCES

Scottish Government (2010) *Statistical Bulletin: Education Series: Teachers in Scotland (2009)* Online at www.scotland.gov.uk/Publications/2010/02/09090009/38
Scottish Government (2011) *High Level Summary of Statistics Trend.* Online at www.scotland.gov.uk/Topics/Statistics/Browse/Health/TrendDiet
Scottish Home and Health Department (1993) *Scotland's Health: A Challenge to Us All – The Scottish Diet* (the James Report). Edinburgh: HMSO.
Scottish Government (2007) The Schools (Health Promotion and Nutrition) (Scotland) Act 2007. Online at www.scotland.gov.uk/Topics/Education/Schools/HLivi/foodnutrition

63

Information and Communications Technology

Robert Munro

Information and Communications Technology (ICT) epitomises a state of flux, strikingly points up the disparity between desirable educational and societal uses and users of technology, and illustrates the accuracy of the adage that if you placed all educational experts in a line you would never reach a conclusion. Policies associated with the implementation of ICT-oriented strategies, questions and issues concerned with the classroom focus of ICT applications, and measures of ICT's impact on and value to education, have fuelled a contentious maelstrom for nigh on thirty years. Many different countries all over the globe, different educational bodies within these countries and even individual schools and teachers employed by these bodies have made widely differing decisions, adopted diverse ICT strategies and focused on implementations and uses of ICT which, for the most part, have proved abject failures or have contributed minimally to educational understanding. The killer ICT app for education still eludes us.

Considerable time and effort has gone into ICT wheel reinvention and refinement, has been spent floundering up and down blind alleys or has seen investment squandered on politically championed (and politically correct) flagship policies. Every so often these policies are jettisoned by a new tranche of politicians who envision a more effective educational system and future. In 2012, a rethink of educational policy in England heralded a new direction and focus for ICT. It proposed scrapping the existing curriculum and replacing it with new courses of study in Computer Science (and this ICT versus Computer Science debate is another contentious issue in many countries):

> Our school system has not prepared children for our new world. It has not prepared our students to work at the forefront of technological change. We want the creation of new high quality Computer Science GCSE and curricula encouraging schools to make use of the brilliant Computer Studies content available. Instead of children bored out of their minds being taught to use Word and Excel by bored teachers, eleven year olds should write simple 2D computer animations and by sixteen should be writing their own applications for smartphones. (Gove, 2012, referring to education in England)

Despite this fresh approach, reflected also in Australia and New Zealand, cynics might reasonably contend that the course of ICT in education is directed by people who know little about what it can be used for or what young consumers want to use it for. They might further suggest that educational usage will continue to lag behind technological development, valuable applications will be adopted too late (if ever) and ICT will continue to fail to achieve its alleged potential.

In sharp contrast to the situation in England, Australasia and most European countries, ICT in Scotland has never been a discrete subject in the Scottish secondary school curriculum – rather it is a pivotal, powerful and multi-faceted resource that can support and enhance, even potentially transform, any area of teaching and learning. This ubiquitous resource comprises sophisticated, powerful, yet increasingly easy-to-use learning tools. These can be applied in any subject area with the intention of naturally and fully embedding ICT effectively across and throughout the entire secondary curriculum. Teachers and pupils can use this sophisticated toolkit to identify, locate, access and collect all manner of digital information; manipulate, process and make sense of this garnered information to discern particular characteristics, trends, patterns and relationships; explore and establish concepts and build knowledge and understanding. ICT facilitates the effective presentation and communication of the conclusions of examination and assessment of the information and supports individual, paired, group and whole-class activity both within and between classrooms – right across the world. This pivotal resource holds the potential for realising the concept of anywhere-anytime learning.

Research (Condie and Munro, 2007) confirmed that ICT had an impact on teaching and learning, on attainment and, particularly, on motivation. However, it had not exercised as powerful an impact as expected, nor had the impact and influence always been sustained. Broad areas of the secondary curriculum had gained more than others, and the impact was always greatest where ICT was skilfully and thoughtfully embedded or integrated into everyday classroom experience. ICT had demonstrably enhanced pupil presentation skills, supported the development of basic literacy and numeracy, contributed to the development of problem-solving skills and allowed pupils to grasp more abstract and complex concepts. They found scant evidence of any appreciable increase in attainment resulting from the use of ICT.

The integral relevance and importance of ICT to the curriculum was evidenced by its inclusion as a core component of National Educational Guidelines (SCCC, 1999) and its central role in 'future-proofing' Curriculum for Excellence. ICT was at the heart of government strategies to create a digital society and was the raison d'être of the National Grid for Learning. Her Majesty's Inspectorate of Education regarded ICT as a natural part of good teaching and learning and considered that great progress had been made in capacity-building over recent years (HMIE, 2007). Education Scotland views digital literacy as the key to developing the skills for learning, life and work needed by young people in the modern world. It maintains schools must identify new ways of thinking about how they can place ICT at the heart of teaching and learning and, as technology becomes more pervasive and embedded in our culture, must provide learners with relevant and contemporary experiences that allow them to successfully engage with technology to prepare them for life after school. The quest over the years to exploit the alleged benefits of ICT has generated enormous expenditure on hardware provision, infrastructure development and in-service teacher training. Teachers are today expected to integrate ICT naturally in their classroom practice, and pupils (and parents) now expect unfettered access to ICT resources to further their learning.

CHARACTERISTICS AND CONSEQUENCES OF RAPID GROWTH

Secondary school pupils are digital natives who have grown up in the information age. Consequently most are thoroughly conversant with ICT – naturally and skilfully engaging with computers, laptops, tablets, smartphones and MP3 players, especially their social, entertainment and infotainment uses hosted on social media sites such as Flickr, Twitter and Facebook. Their teachers, often digital immigrants to whom ICT is not second nature, have struggled to assimilate and incorporate ICT into classroom practice, not necessarily to reap educational benefits but often simply to illustrate they are 'up to date', 'cool' or 'down with the kids'. Some have succeeded brilliantly, others have failed miserably; some have ICT-avoidance techniques down to a fine art while others have gladly departed the classroom scene. Teachers have had to cope with exceptionally rapid, wide-ranging change and development as ICT has been transformed from rarity status to everyday resource, dragging in its wake unprecedented attention, debate, activity and investment. Accelerating change has impacted on hardware, software, applications, and overall provision – every fresh developmental advance forcing teachers to reappraise teaching and learning strategies and ICT uses.

Rapid technological evolution has spawned a bewildering range of previously unimagined applications and processes – relatively recent and fundamentally innovative. Word processing, spreadsheets, simulations, databases, computer-aided design, email, multimedia, hypermedia, CD-ROMs, DVDs, videoconferencing, the internet, the World Wide Web, MP3/MP4 players, digital cameras, webcams, 3G/4G smartphones, avatars, learning platforms, laptops, tablets, iPods, iPads, broadband, wi-fi, podcasting, blogging, Facebook, e-readers, Kindles, Facetiming and wikis are commonplace terminology and convergent technologies now taken for granted. None of these powerful tools, all with great potential for teaching and learning, is more than twenty-five years old. Hardware platforms have morphed from desktops to laptops/notebooks/tablets. Computer systems are obsolete in less than three years. Memory and storage capacity, functionality, speed of program execution and multimedia capability drive remorselessly forward. Fast machines, enormous storage, internet access, multimedia functionality, unlimited connectivity and comprehensive digital data accessibility are now the norm. Software development, critically dependent on commercial rather than educational criteria, has constantly reflected an obsession with enhancing performance and expanding versatility. Development has been characterised by short-lived software cycles, rapidly outdated packages, software of limited educational value and the creation of ultra-sophisticated commercial applications overloaded with educationally irrelevant facilities. We now inhabit the age of the app – often free, certainly cheap – presenting a bewilderingly huge selection for our delectation. Generating appropriate educational software (even appropriate apps), however, has been massively problematic and extremely expensive, and has seriously impeded the successful educational deployment of ICT.

Unsurprisingly, most teachers have found it difficult to respond effectively to such rapid and far-reaching change. They have tried to incorporate and integrate the best aspects of ICT into their teaching and learning strategies – usually without the benefit of rigorous assessment of the potential of ICT in advance of its use, or evaluation of its impact and contribution after the event. Subject specialists have lacked support, guidance and advice on implementing ICT and have minimal software resources to deploy but often are so enthralled by ICT they enthusiastically promote its continued and expanding use despite supportive, conclusive research evidence that it enhances teaching and learning. Allegedly, ICT extends the range of teaching and learning strategies, enhances the flexibility of these strategies to accommodate pupils with diverse learning difficulties, stimulates the exploitation of distance and open learning opportunities and enriches the learning experience.

There is absolutely no evidence that many ICT-oriented experiences offered within the secondary curriculum have been enriching, that schools offer a full, judiciously integrated suite of experiences or that pupils have benefited much from their school-based ICT experiences. Many have questioned how long schools will retain twentieth-century teaching practices irrelevant to the needs of twenty-first-century learners and resist embracing the technological resources pupils use so extensively out of school. Increasing availability and widespread use of computers, ubiquitous broadband internet access and a communication-driven interactive lifestyle in the home and 'on the go' seldom complements ICT experiences in school. Rather it has exacerbated the digital divide and, in offering vastly superior, more socially enriching experiences, it has promoted pupil dissatisfaction with school provision. ICT use in Scottish schools, following the vanguard deployment of twenty microcomputers in 1979, has been uncoordinated, patchy, uninformed and frequently inappropriate. There has been scant evaluation of ICT let alone any assessment of successful use. The assumption has been that simply providing hardware and web access would magically trigger a learning revolution. The period has been a journey of radical, unplanned experimentation, regularly rocked by waves of innovation, and education has constantly been left flat-footed by change. The returns on Scotland's massive ICT investment look miserable. Teachers and pupils (innocent guinea pigs in the great ICT experiment) have been sadly short-changed.

THE SCENE TODAY – A MOSAIC OF DEVELOPMENT

The landscape of ICT in Scotland's secondary schools today is a messy collage where oases of plenty sit cheek by jowl with ravaged deserts. All schools have a considerable number of computers, a wide selection of associated peripheral equipment (especially interactive whiteboards (IWB)) and ubiquitous internet access. These essential resources vary widely in type, age and capability, are unevenly distributed, within and between schools, and are deployed inconsistently and to markedly different effect.

However, the post-millennium commitment to purchasing advanced computer hardware and reducing the computer–pupil ratio has paid dividends, particularly where school refurbishment and rebuilding initiatives have resulted in excellent provision of quality resources, open-access suites of advanced computers, flood-wired internet access and independently managed and maintained ICT resources. Some schools have explored widespread provision of personal computers or iPads. Some authorities have established interactive learning centres, comprehensively equipped community resources designed to support the development of digital media skills. One hot resource is the IWB, enjoying exponential growth despite the lack of conclusive research to illustrate that it does more than motivate less able pupils and facilitate understanding of visually oriented concepts in science and mathematics. Too often it is another boring presentation device teachers use to push information to pupils. No national coordination of these innovative, developmental activities occurs and no substantive research investigations into their efficacy have been commissioned.

Software availability, outwith provision of business-oriented and generic open-ended software, is limited, few teachers have comprehensive knowledge of subject specific software, departmental finances for software purchase are limited and local authority purchasing policy usually precludes the acquisition of anything other than tightly speci-fied licensed materials. Curriculum-specific resources are desperately needed but few exist as the Scottish software market is tiny and software development costs are not easily recouped. Education Scotland has developed the national schools digital network (GLOW), a web-delivered learning platform combining an integrated collaborative environment with a virtual teaching and learning environment. Designed to link every school, offer instant access to resources for teachers and learners, and facilitate personalised learning, it proved to have limited reliability, was difficult to use and actually offered teachers only limited resources. A new incarnation is promised but currently is delayed by in-fighting between politicians and educationalists (Richards-Hill, 2012).

Limited production of educational software principally results from the wide avail-ability of open-ended software packages such as PowerPoint and the pervasiveness of the Web. Teachers have been expected to exploit open-ended software to produce curriculum resources (ideally individualised) or involve pupils in creating presentations for display to other pupils – no cost resources. Teachers have generated curriculum-focused resources (usually lesson-support presentations) but few truly individualised materials exist as production is difficult and time-consuming. Pupils author indifferent reports, magazine/newspaper stories and multimedia shows which demonstrate ability to arrange and integrate text, graphics, sound and stilted animation into predictable templates but seldom illustrate acquisition of deep knowledge or an understanding of the issues, topics or concepts they present, let alone thoughtful appraisal and content redrafting.

The Web has become the Holy Grail. Every teacher wants to use it. So do their pupils although not for purely educational reasons. There are valuable resources teachers can integrate into teaching and learning but the Web is a classic example of how teachers were stampeded into using ICT without detailed consideration of how it might best be employed. Few teachers carefully formulated strategies to exploit the Web's educational potential and they lacked pedagogical vision and supportive guidance. Pupils, too frequently simply directed to particular sites and engaged in trivial tasks of elementary interpretation, need to know there is more to the Web than Google. They need to know how to search, know which search techniques produce the most effective results, read information with understanding (detecting bias and gauging authenticity) and identify patterns and conclusions from that information. These difficult and demanding skills take time to acquire. Nobody has decided when and how pupils should acquire these skills, who should teach them, and when and in what order they are best taught. Until these issues are resolved, Web usage will never transcend mere fact-gathering.

Despite its pivotal importance, ICT is simply one resource teachers are expected to master. Acquiring ICT expertise and deploying ICT effectively is difficult because of con-stant technological change and advancement, the bewildering range of applications, limited pedagogical advice, time pressures, cutbacks in the provision of continuing professional development and challenges posed by widespread curriculum reform. However, gaining expertise underpins informed decisions on whether or how they integrate ICT into their teaching and learning to the benefit of their pupils. Teachers get little detailed help and assistance from the education sector. While schools, local authorities and government bodies produce extensive, generalised policy documents on ICT their direct relevance to teachers wishing to use ICT to introduce, say, photosynthesis, to explore the role of pressure groups in environmental issues or to create a multimedia montage on cyberbullying is minimal. Teachers need imaginative, quality pre-service and in-service training and, critically, time to reflect on and develop related expertise. Pre-service courses provide insufficient guidance and direction on pedagogical aspects of ICT and trainee teachers are not specifically required to display ICT confidence or competence on school placement. Expensive national in-service activities have been failures and today ICT training is limited to local authority courses or 'in-school' gatherings illustrating local classroom successes.

TOWARDS THE BRAVE NEW WORLD?

The development of ICT in Scottish secondary schools has been nowhere near as successful as anticipated or predicted. Little of its alleged potential has been realised. ICT merely supports, occasionally enhances, but has yet to transform teaching and learning. Key issues, repeatedly articulated, remain inadequately addressed and unresolved.

- It is vital that a fresh, imaginative vision for ICT in education is formulated which embodies realisable results, is underpinned with comprehensive e-policy and incorporates emerging technological developments and convergence. To date development has been patchy, hasty, uninspired, reactive and safe. Education should articulate a progressive, coherent set of ICT skills and competences for secondary pupils together with a specific framework illustrating where, when and how they might be acquired and refined. Each school should determine a comprehensive, explicit e-strategy for whole-school development of ICT to complement the national policy (Condie and Munro, 2007; HMIE, 2007).
- Schools must create learning environments offering all pupils the opportunity of using ICT as and when desired. Pupils need not necessarily have their own computer, nor the schools' sophisticated learning platforms, but access to adequate, appropriate ICT resources throughout school must be available. Currently, investment disparity and inequitable resource provision favour particular departments, specific curricular areas and hotbeds (even hotheads) of innovative activity. Under-resourced departments require major investment, including intensive staff development.
- ICT-related staff development – enhancing pedagogic skills – is a priority for schools and teacher education institutions. The latter seldom illuminate best practice to students. Teachers (and teacher educators) should be encouraged to examine and evaluate ICT use rigorously, and be allocated time to reflect on uses and develop expertise.
- A national team within Education Scotland should identify the secondary sector's software and application needs and establish a development programme to create curriculum-appropriate educational resources. It is vital that GLOW matches its name in delivering resources to illuminate the curriculum.

Scottish education must realise the full potential of ICT. Failure so to do will mean that huge investment and years of teacher and pupil effort will have been wasted. Education will stand guilty of massive underachievement. Many pupils journey through school enjoying a minimal, trivial experience of ICT – yet in out-of-school time spend hours on technologically orientated activity that enhances their lives. Given unfettered access to appropriate technologies and sources of digital information, coupled with imaginative uses of ICT for teaching and learning within a curriculum guided by skilled ICT-adept teachers, pupils really could use ICT to acquire the gold of knowledge and transform their futures.

REFERENCES

Condie, R. and R. Munro (2007) *The Impact of ICT in Schools – A Landscape Review*. Online at http://dera.ioe.ac.uk/1627/1/becta_2007_landscapeimpactreview_report.pdf

Gove, M. (2012) Policy speech delivered at BETT. Online at www.education.gov.uk/inthenews/speeches/a00201868/michael-gove-speech-at-the-bett-show-2012

Her Majesty's Inspectorate of Education (2007) *Improving Scottish Education – ICT in Learning and Teaching*. Online at www.educationscotland.gov.uk/inspectionandreview/Images/iseicti-lat_tcm4-712782.pdf

Richards-Hill, J. (2012) *Glow Plight – Pride of Scotland or 'Zombie' Network?* Merlin John Online. Online at www.agent4change.net/grapevine/platform/1600-glow-plight-pride-of-scotland-or-a-zombie-network.html

Scottish Consultative Council on the Curriculum (1999) *Information and Communications Technology 5–14 National Guidelines*. Dundee: SCCC.

64

Mathematics Education

Ian Hulse

The development of Curriculum for Excellence (CfE) was governed by the following constraint: 'To face the challenges of the 21st century, each young person needs to have confidence in using mathematical skills, and Scotland needs both specialist mathematicians and a highly numerate population' (Scottish Executive, 2006, p. 18)

With the implementation of CfE well underway in secondary schools, this chapter considers central aspects of Mathematics provision, aiming to identify changes to, and challenges facing, secondary Mathematics education.

COURSES IN S1 TO S3

CfE views Mathematics as a rich and stimulating activity, vitally important in life, work and learning but also rewarding in itself. It splits Mathematics into successive levels, learning at each of which is described by a collection of experiences and outcomes. The organisers for these are 'Number, Money and Measure', 'Shape, Position and Movement' and 'Information Handling'. Some of the Mathematics experiences and outcomes are also used to describe learning in numeracy, which thus appears as something like a traditional subject. But, whereas traditional subjects in secondary education are delivered by subject specialists alone, in CfE 'all teachers have responsibility for promoting the development of numeracy' (Scottish Executive, 2006, p. 7).

CfE anticipates that pupils begin level 3 as they enter S1. However, the mathematics involved here is too advanced for a significant proportion of new pupils, so most S1 and S2 pupils are working through courses at level 2 or 3. In schools following the intended curricular model, pupils will progress through these courses (and, for some, courses at level 4) until their broad general education comes to a close at the end of S3. Unlike its predecessor, CfE is not complemented by a suite of national assessments with which to assess, record and report on pupil progress. Not only the experiences and outcomes, but also the standards and expectations associated with them, are to be interpreted by those delivering the new curriculum. This has led to worries that provision in mathematics and numeracy may not be adequately uniform and, in particular, that assessment methods will not embody a shared understanding of standards and expectations. Effective moderation will suffice for such an understanding to emerge, facilitated by the new National Assessment Resource, together with support and guidance offered by the Scottish Qualifications Authority (SQA) and Education Scotland; but time and training will be required to enable Mathematics teachers to make full use of these.

CURRENT COURSES IN S4 TO S6

At the time of writing, the majority of pupils in S4 were following Standard Grade courses. Begun in S3, these two-year courses were split into three levels, Foundation, General and Credit, which were continuously graded from 1 to 7 on the basis of external examinations taken towards the end of S4. Other courses pursued in S4 to S6 lead to national qualifications from the Higher Still suite: Access 3, Intermediate 1, Intermediate 2, Higher and Advanced Higher. National Qualifications are one-year modular courses. Save for Access 3, for which passing the units suffices for passing the course, they were graded A to D on the basis of external examinations.

The earlier Higher Still courses corresponded in challenge to the Standard Grade levels. Foundation/Access consists for the most part of number work and numeracy skills. General/Intermediate 1 introduces basic algebra, statistics, trigonometry and geometry. These were developed further in Credit/Intermediate 2, which also included material intended as preparation for the content of the Higher. The Higher addresses more advanced concepts and skills, requires a more formal presentation and introduces calculus. Advanced Higher anticipates the first year of Mathematics degree courses in both content and sophistication.

This range of Mathematics courses has led to various pathways for progression. Data available from the SQA show that National Qualifications in Mathematics are popular course choices in S5. Entries to Higher and Advanced Higher increased between 2006 and 2011. There was a significant decrease in entries at Standard Grade in S4 over the same period, though with more than compensating increases in entries to National Qualifications at the same stage. This trend has come about partly because Intermediates anticipated the modular structure of the Higher and partly because they scored more highly when measuring attainment on the unified points scale. However, in recent years the trend may also have been driven by anticipation of the new National Qualifications.

NEW NATIONAL QUALIFICATIONS IN MATHEMATICS

From 2013–14, new qualifications are being introduced in secondary schools. At the time of writing, all mathematical qualifications except the Advanced Highers for Mathematics have been formally published (SQA, 2012a). A sketch of the structure, content and administration of the new qualifications is thus possible for levels up to and including the new Higher.

The Mathematics curriculum area will be equipped with qualifications in Mathematics concentrating on the development of mathematical language and techniques and the exploration of mathematical concepts. Qualifications in Lifeskills Mathematics will also be available, to develop mathematical skills in applications arising in personal life and work. The new National Qualifications preserve the modular structure of the old ones. Updated Access 2 and 3 qualifications, renamed National 2 and 3, will be available in Lifeskills Mathematics. National 2 Lifeskills Mathematics consists of two compulsory units, 'Number and Number Processes' and 'Shape, Space and Data', and two optional units selected from 'Money', 'Time' and 'Measurement'. National 3 consists of three prescribed units, 'Manage Money and Data', 'Shape, Space and Measures' and 'Numeracy'. From 2013–14, National 3 Lifeskills Mathematics will replace Standard Grade Foundation and Access 3.

National 4 and 5 qualifications will be available in both Lifeskills Mathematics and Mathematics, and will consist of three prescribed units and a course assessment. For

Lifeskills Mathematics, the units at National 4 and National 5 will cover 'Managing Finance and Statistics', 'Geometry and Measures' and 'Numeracy'. For Mathematics, prescribed units will cover 'Expressions and Formulae', 'Relationships' and either 'Numeracy' (at National 4) or 'Applications' (at National 5). From 2013–14, National 4 and National 5 in these subjects will supersede General/Intermediate 1 and Credit/Intermediate 2 respectively. From 2014–15, the current Higher Mathematics will be superseded by the new Higher Mathematics. The units in this course will cover 'Expressions and Functions', 'Relationships and Calculus' and 'Applications'. There will be no Higher in Lifeskills Mathematics. Transition to the suite of new qualifications will be completed in 2015–16, when the new Advanced Highers for Mathematics will be introduced.

All new national qualifications will be certificated by the SQA. The Numeracy unit from National 5 Lifeskills Mathematics will be available as a free-standing unit for independent certification when required. Units will be internally assessed and externally verified. At National 4, the course assessment will consist of an examination, set and marked internally but along SQA guidelines (which stipulate inclusion of non-calculator items). These will be subject to internal verification by centres and external verification and certification by the SQA. National 4s will not be graded. At National 5 and Higher, course assessments will be external examinations consisting of two papers, in one of which a calculator may be used, and which will be set, marked and graded A to D by the SQA. It should be noted that the units in Lifeskills Mathematics from National 3 to National 5 occur in a hierarchy, as do the units in Mathematics from National 4 to Higher. This means that skills and knowledge are cumulatively built through these units so that successfully completed units from a higher level constitute (typically incomplete) evidence in favour of a course award at a lower level.

The new qualifications are perceived to have significant strengths, with Lifeskills Mathematics courses being welcomed as appropriate to some learners' needs and the broad content of Mathematics courses receiving general approval (SQA, 2012b). Discussion continues on many issues, for example how best to implement the new qualifications to allow for the possibility of a safety-net option, as dual presentation at Standard Grade currently does. Moreover, concerns have arisen, notably at the prospect of an increased assessment burden, the development of standards for assessment and verification, and the tight schedule for implementation (SQA, 2012b).

The question of whether or not adoption of the new Mathematics qualifications will secure intended gains can also be raised. One goal was simplification of a system of assessment that one critic described as 'impossibly difficult to understand' for members of the public and employers alike (Bryce, 2008, p. 59). With the prospect of separate qualifications in Mathematics, Lifeskills Mathematics and Numeracy, it is not clear that the system of assessment in Mathematics will be significantly more comprehensible to non-specialists than it was before. Another goal was to preserve strengths of the previous assessment system, such as the inclusiveness of Standard Grade and the modular structure of national qualifications. The latter has certainly been maintained but the systems of hierarchical units envisaged suggest distinct pathways of progression through Lifeskills Mathematics and Mathematics courses, respectively. This does not seem as inclusive in conception as Standard Grade, where everyone was entered on the same course, albeit at a level appropriate to his or her ability. Nevertheless, the new qualifications may yet be seen as inclusive if their introduction helps pupils to more fully realise their mathematical potential.

ATTAINMENT

Some years ago, the Organisation for Economic Cooperation and Development stated that 'Scotland performs at a consistently very high standard in the Programme for International Student Assessment (PISA). Few countries can be said with confidence to outperform it in mathematics, reading and science' (OECD, 2007, p. 16). More recently, international studies show that Scottish pupils continue to attain well in Mathematics in comparison to international norms; PISA 2009 has mean pupil performance at S4 significantly exceeding that of the rest of the UK and OECD, whilst the 2007 Trends in International Mathematics and Science Study (TIMSS) ranks Scotland seventeenth out of fifty-nine participating countries for mathematical attainment at S2. However, comparison of these studies with their predecessors shows that mathematical performance in Scotland has declined over recent years, that the gap between the highest and lowest attainers in Mathematics is getting wider and that there is a persistent gap in achievement in Mathematics between boys and girls at S4.

Some studies also provide data about attitudes to mathematics. TIMSS 2007 puts the proportion of S2 pupils enjoying Mathematics in Scotland at 33 per cent. Although the 2008 Scottish Survey of Achievement (SSA) shows that close to 80 per cent of S2 pupils want to do well at Mathematics, it reports the proportion to be less than 20 per cent for enjoyment of Mathematics and finding Mathematics interesting. These are sobering findings given that 'difficulties with literacy and numeracy and an apparent reluctance or inability to engage with demanding areas of learning such as mathematics . . . can become entrenched at these stages' (HMIE, 2009, p. 4).

The SSA also shows that the proportion of pupils exhibiting adequate skills at the expected level declines from 70 per cent in P7 to 55 per cent in S2. Despite calls to arrest the decline (HMIE, 2005), therefore, transitions from primary through early secondary are still associated with decreased mathematical attainment. Moreover, the survey shows that pupils from less deprived areas attain significantly more highly than pupils from the most deprived areas. This imbalance appears at all stages and levels but the biggest difference of 19 per cent is seen at the expected level in S2. A similar pattern emerges from data on attainment in numeracy.

From 2012, data on attainment has also been available from the Scottish Survey of Literacy and Numeracy (SSLN). These yearly surveys have been developed to complement CfE and will replace the SSA, monitoring performance in literacy and numeracy in alternate years. The SSLN 2011, which appraises numeracy, was published in March 2012. The study confirms that deprivation remains a significant factor for attainment in numeracy; pupils living with higher levels of deprivation were half as likely to be performing well or very well at the respective level than pupils with lower levels of deprivation. Gender imbalances were found at P4 and P7, though by S2 the difference between boys' performance and girls' performance was no longer significant. Attainment across transitions remains an issue, with 76 per cent of P7 pupils performing well or very well at the relevant level, in contrast to only 42 per cent of pupils in S2.

Not surprisingly, the findings of the SSLN 2011 have provoked criticism of CfE. In response, it has been argued that the results of the SSLN are not directly comparable to those of the SSA, which is true, though it hardly rules out all negative appraisals of the new curriculum's ability to deliver improved attainment in numeracy. It has also been noted that the S2 cohort tested in the SSLN 2011 were not following CfE, which does make the figures seem less discouraging, although this effect is somewhat diminished since the SSLN 2011 'assesses skills which pupils should be experiencing as part of good teaching and learning practice' (Scottish Government, 2012, p. 4). Nevertheless, with a curriculum that is barely two years old at secondary level, the politically unbiased stance must surely be that it is too early to assess the impact CfE has had on attainment in numeracy, at least in regard to these long-term trends. For initial evidence on this, we shall have to wait for publication of SSLN 2013, the next survey of its kind to assess numeracy.

Mathematics and numeracy attainment at secondary in Scotland thus presents a mixed picture, comparing well with international norms but exhibiting some decline and certain inequalities. Observers hope that the ongoing transition to CfE will address these issues for, where previous changes to curriculum and assessment raised attainment, 'by differentiating cognitive demand to reduce academic barriers', the new goal 'is to raise standards of achievement – that is, to increase demands on students' (OECD, 2007, p. 16). Doubt that this will in fact take place arises from the prospect of Lifeskills Mathematics courses which clearly could be used 'to reduce academic barriers', as Intermediates are when used for progression into S5 and S6. However, used effectively these courses will help to ensure that pupils have access to courses that are appropriate to their needs; the courses should thus support uptake of Mathematics and may also be useful 'to increase demands on students'.

PEDAGOGY

In 2005, Her Majesty's Inspectorate of Education (HMIE) reported that staff in most secondary schools 'had yet to consider the impact that different learning and teaching approaches and contexts for applying mathematical skills could have for developing pupils' learning skills, confidence, individual responsibility and effectiveness in contributing to group tasks and success' (HMIE, 2005, p.9). The underlying concern was that traditional Mathematics teaching was not being transformed into a kind of practice that would more effectively develop the four capacities of CfE.

Intervening years have seen a great deal of critical reflection on teaching approaches amongst Mathematics teachers. Opportunities in continuing professional development (CPD) have helped teachers build their knowledge of newer methods. Guidance and support has been made available through national bodies such as HMIE and Learning and Teaching Scotland (more recently, Education Scotland) and at local authority level. Moreover, new teachers have been trained in courses designed with more contemporary pedagogy in mind and this has been complemented by a 'world class' system of teacher induction (OECD, 2007, p.15).

This ongoing professional development has resulted in positive changes to mathematics pedagogy. HMIE (2010, p. 9) notes with approval certain teaching methods, which include Assessment is for Learning techniques and good use of ICT, that are 'presently contributing particularly well to successful learning in mathematics'. It also notes the presence of further 'strong characteristics of effective teaching' (p. 8) such as maximised learner-to-learner interactions, explicit drawing of cross-curricular links, responsive planning and the use of plenary sessions.

However, there remains a need for the effective use of such techniques to become more widespread. Not every teacher consistently invokes real-life contexts in which the Mathematics being taught can be used to solve problems, and 'relatively few' schools make sufficient use of cross-curricular contexts to enhance learning (HMIE, 2010, p. 8). Whilst there are teachers who are invigorating Mathematics teaching in secondary schools, 'in too many schools innovation has been insufficient and the outcomes for young people have not improved' (p. 2). Clearly, there is a need for further CPD in this regard.

LOOKING FORWARD

The foregoing review has identified significant challenges in key areas of secondary Mathematics education. Mathematics education must develop consistent and fair assessment strategies for implementation of the new curriculum and qualifications. It must continue to work to raise attainment and for a more equitable distribution of educational outcomes. It must increase the pace at which Mathematics pedagogy is being renewed. Meeting these challenges will require effective CPD for Mathematics teachers. Undeniably, 'We have to place professional development, covering both subject content and pedagogy, at the centre of our approach to change if we are to achieve better experiences and outcomes for learners' (HMIE, 2009, p. 2). The extent to which this will be possible in an era of cuts remains to be seen; testing times lie ahead.

REFERENCES

Her Majesty's Inspectorate of Education (2005) *Improving Achievement in Mathematics in Primary and Secondary Schools*. Livingston: HMIE.

Her Majesty's Inspectorate of Education (2009) *Improving Scottish Education: A Report by HMIE on Inspection and Review 2005–2008*. Livingston: HMIE.

Her Majesty's Inspectorate of Education (2010) *Learning Together: Mathematics*. Livingston: HMIE.

Organisation for Economic Cooperation and Development (2007) *Reviews of National Policies for Education: Quality and Equity of Schooling in Scotland*. Paris: OECD Publishing.

Scottish Executive (2006) *Building The Curriculum 1*. Edinburgh: Scottish Executive.

Scottish Government (2012) *Scottish Survey of Literacy and Numeracy 2011 (Numeracy)*. Online at www.scotland.gov.uk/Publications/2012/03/5285/0

Scottish Qualifications Authority (2012a) *Mathematics*. Online at www.sqa.org.uk/sqa/45750.html

Scottish Qualifications Authority (2012b) *Mathematics Feedback*. Online at www.sqa.org.uk/sqa/58366.html

65

Modern Foreign Languages Education

Dan Tierney

The late Professor Eric Hawkins said that teaching a language was like 'gardening in a gale'. The Scottish linguist may on occasion have agreed with him as Modern Languages education in Scotland has been blown from crisis to crisis, from new solution to new solution, and from working party to working party over the last fifty years.

FROM GRAMMAR TO THE AUDIOVISUAL APPROACH

In the 1960s, languages, usually French, were taught only to academic pupils in senior secondaries. The approach was based on grammar learning, analysis of language and translation. Able pupils could fill in blanks with the correct verb part and conjugate endless verbs, without any real communication taking place. Speaking was seldom encouraged, unless it was to read out loud round the class. The academic pupil would accept this diet, knowing that a language was a university entry requirement. He or she might travel to the country where the language was taught, only to be disappointed that the natives did not conjugate verbs, but wanted to engage in real conversations. When universities abandoned the need for a foreign language, there began a slow decline in language learning, although a language would still be considered a vital part of a rounded academic education.

In the late 1960s, as comprehensive schooling became the norm, the language teacher's situation of teaching only academic pupils was quickly challenged. The 'solution' lay in a move towards an audiovisual approach, with filmstrips, tapes and the coming of the language laboratories. In the 1970s, in the main course at the time, M. Marsaud would sit in his armchair reading his newspaper while Madame worked *dans la cuisine*. Behind each story, of course, lay a grammatical point which was the purpose of the story in the first place. Pupils would then practise endless drills in the language laboratory, not talking to each other, of course, but to the machine.

TOWARDS A COMMUNICATIVE APPROACH

With the audiovisual approach not finding favour with the whole ability range, new courses came into use. These would use cartoon strips and paired speaking cards. Much of the language would be transactional, such as choosing a flavour of ice cream. Although there was encouragement to move towards real communication, where there is an information gap and a real purpose in using the language, many of the activities remained practice activities.

Nevertheless, pupils were engaged in speaking and languages were probably more fun. The primary aim of language learning was redefined as an ability to communicate in line with recommendations coming out of the Council of Europe. A misunderstanding arose at this point, with many teachers believing that grammar was not to be taught. Some would claim that this is what was being encouraged by local authority language advisers at the time, although this was denied years later by some of those who were thought to have advocated that. However it came about, the pupils, denied the grammatical knowledge, were unable to manipulate language in other contexts. Universities, used to a grammar-based approach to prose and translation, began to complain about able pupils not knowing the fundamentals of grammar.

As the aims of language teaching in schools changed, the Scottish Education Department (SED) invited the Consultative Council on the Curriculum to set up a national project in 1975, which culminated in the course known as *Tour de France*. This was widely used, with the language set in real contexts. Learners were encouraged to speak to each other and the methods and approaches in S1 and S2 were more suited to a wider range of ability. However, there was a lack of coherence with approaches in the middle school, as O Grade examinations had not yet been revised and Standard Grade not implemented. Furthermore, language teachers began to criticise aspects of *Tour de France*, such as language about moving furniture in Stage 2 and mountaineering vocabulary such as crampons and ice axes in Stage 3.

LANGUAGES OUT OF THE CORE

The Munn Report (1977) did not include languages as a core subject for pupils in S3/S4, and at the end of S2 many pupils opted to leave the labs behind. In the 1980s, the old-style language laboratories were taken out and the new technology was the perimeter audio learning equipment (PALE) – cassette machines placed around the classroom which could be used for listening or speaking. At least with these the pupils could speak to each other and record their dialogues. Practice and even real communication could take place.

In 1985, the Scottish Central Committee on Modern Languages (SCCC) presented a report to the Consultative Committee on the Curriculum. This advocated the offering of languages other than French, and in 1988 the SCCC recommended more teaching of other languages. A policy of diversification was introduced in some parts of the country. Perhaps the 'solution' lay in offering either French or German, French or Spanish, or French or Italian, in S1. Where parents could choose a language, many chose French because that is what they had done. Where they were required to opt out from the language allocated, middle-class parents would often opt out of languages other than French. In one leafy suburb, there was a considerable backlash against Italian with comments that might be considered offensive at best, and racist at worst.

In spite of these new courses and approaches, languages were still not being continued beyond S2. The 1990 HMI Report, *Effective Teaching and Learning in Scottish Secondary Schools*, based on inspections from 1984 to 1988, noted that:

> the numbers of pupils continuing with a language in S3 have been declining almost to the point which was the norm before the introduction of the comprehensive school, when a modern language had been offered to 35–40% of the school population at most.

It also noted that in 1987, the proportion of pupils studying a language in S5 was under 20 per cent.

THE RETURN OF COMPULSORY LANGUAGES

In 1989, the SCCC argued that languages should remain an optional subject. The Scottish Association for Language Teaching (SALT) mounted a well-coordinated campaign to make a language a core subject, and tourist boards and industrialists, as well as teachers, lobbied the SED, although not all language teachers were in favour. The SED responded with a major policy shift, publishing *Circular 1178*. The Secretary of State wished to see that 'the study of at least one language other than English, and preferably a modern foreign language, should normally be pursued by all pupils through the third and fourth years of compulsory secondary school' (SED, 1989, para. 7). SALT and others had achieved what they had asked for, but there was also a surprise in the announcement with the reintroduction of primary languages and the vision of six years of language learning from P6 to S4. The Secretary of State also wished to see an increase in pupils continuing the study of modern foreign languages into S5 and S6 and more pupils studying German, Italian, Spanish and also Russian.

There was now a coherent approach from S1 to S4 and a political will in favour of languages. Many language teachers, using the target language more in the classroom for real communication, probably felt progress was being made. The 1992 SALT conference, coinciding with the Single European Market and with a fresh injection of new teachers to meet the demands of *Circular 1178*, had the confident title 'Modern Languages: Delivering the Goods'.

THE DECLINE AT S5

The Revised Higher was introduced and although the practical language skills developed to that point were encouraged, many teachers complained of the 'jump' from Standard Grade. Preparation for Higher was not being seen as a continuum from S1 to S5; instead there was a mad dash, with serious grammar cramming in S5. The Higher was seen as difficult and whereas compulsory languages had halted the decline up to S4, Higher presentations declined further. French had gone from 8,523 presentations in 1976 to 5,838 in 1986 and was down to 3,756 in 1996. Russian had almost disappeared, down to thirteen presentations in 1996, and Italian only had 106. German had also declined from 2,272 presentations to 1,640. Only Spanish bucked the trend, going from 295 in 1976 to 451 twenty years later. Research was conducted into the decline in four of the five languages and McPake et al. (1998) noted that even the students who did well at Standard Grade did not value the achievement. Although they had a good grade they did not feel able to use their foreign language for purposes they valued. The report also pointed to the lack of national motivation for language learning and the value of languages for higher education and employment. One further aspect in this climate of negativity was that among principal teachers there had been a 37 per cent swing away from support for Languages for All. Able pupils were not embracing languages and some of the less able were also resistant to compulsory languages and failing to be convinced of the purpose of modern languages.

ANOTHER CRITICAL REPORT AND 'ENTITLEMENT'

In 1998, HMI produced another report on Modern Languages, *Standards and Quality, Primary and Secondary Schools, 1994 – 1998: Modern Languages*. It recognised some of the progress made, but the Chief Inspector in his foreword stated:

> The report is not reassuring. It demonstrates quite clearly that, while there is some good learning and teaching in modern languages, the situation overall is far from satisfactory despite the extensive effort which has been put into transforming the teaching of modern languages in recent years and encouraging uptake by pupils. (SOEID, 1998, p. 3)

The SALT conference of that year was a depressing affair, held against a background of negative media coverage. Language teachers perhaps felt unfairly criticised, having tried to do what had been asked of them. This was articulated by Keir Bloomer, Director of Education for Clackmannan, who wrote 'what we have seen is a failure of policy far more than a failure of implementation' (Bloomer, 1998). The political response to the report was to set up a ministerial action group whose report, *Citizens of a Multilingual World* (2000), set out an ambitious rationale for Modern Languages which some described as unrealistic. Some of its recommendations were also seen as out of touch with the reality of the classroom: 'After a video-conferenced interaction with their partner abroad, for example, they may go over the recording by themselves or with their teacher and other students, including with their partners abroad' (Scottish Executive, 2000, p. 46). The report also outlined an 'entitlement' which was open to interpretation: 'However, we are not proposing that our recommended entitlement should be a legal requirement . . . we can see no reason for recommending that a requirement should be imposed' (p. 30). One common view was that pupils were entitled to learn a language but it was not compulsory. Some headteachers took languages out of the core curriculum based on this, and there was a general move towards more flexibility in the curriculum.

PRIMARY LANGUAGES AND THE PROBLEM OF TRANSITION

The language teacher, as well as trying to adopt new approaches for the whole ability range and for Standard Grade and Higher, also had to take account of another initiative, the reintroduction of primary languages. While a large amount of work, investment and planning went into this and achieved considerable success within the primary sector, there was perhaps insufficient planning and training within the secondary sector. Language teachers, so long used to a blank canvas, were faced with pupils who had different experiences in the last two years of primary. In some cases, there could be language mismatch due to placing requests. These and other problems of transition were identified (see Chapter 44).

CONTINUED DECLINE IN SECONDARY

At the upper end of the school most languages declined again. French Higher presentations went from 4,886 in 2003 to 4,499 in 2010 and German from 1,908 to 1,135, overtaken by Spanish which went up from 1,045 to 1,272. Italian went down from 263 to 213. A Baccalaureate was introduced for Science and for Languages, and the contrasting fortunes add to the depressing linguistic picture. While in 2011 there were 136 presentations for Science there were thirty-six for Languages.

In 2012, the Scottish Centre for Information on Language Teaching (SCILT) did an analysis of attainment levels at Higher Grade in comparison to the Social Sciences (SCILT, 2012). Spanish and French had the highest percentages of A grade passes (49 per cent and 43 per cent respectively). Geography (35 per cent) and German (32 per cent)were lower. The highest overall pass rates in 2012 were in Spanish (85 per cent), with French and Modern Studies both on 82 per cent. The overall pass rate in German at Higher compared to 2011 fell below that of any of the social sciences in 2012, contributing further to the gloomy picture for what was previously the second most commonly taught language in Scottish schools. In the middle school, there was still no clear position as to whether languages were optional or core. The 2009 analysis of trends by SCILT showed a decline in three of the major European languages (French, German and Italian).

In 2010, 67 per cent of S4 pupils were presented for qualifications in Languages. At a conference on languages where headteachers complained about the lack of a clear steer, Bill Maxwell of HMIE sought to clarify the position:

> Some schools are mistakenly making the study of modern languages optional, saying they want to reinforce the idea of personalisation of the curriculum. That should not be done at the expense of providing a broad general education and we see modern languages as part of that. (Buie, 2010)

CURRICULUM FOR EXCELLENCE

As part of the development of Curriculum for Excellence (CfE), excellence groups were set up and the Modern Languages Excellence Group Report argued the case for languages, expressed concern about decline and gave examples of good practice from different schools, exemplifying how, through CfE, the development of language skills can be achieved. The CfE Principles and Practice document reiterates many of the arguments for the importance of Modern Languages made in previous documents. It talks about languages and the nation's prosperity, and says that young people should be 'well equipped with the skills needed in the new Europe and in the global marketplace' (Education Scotland, 2010, p. 1). However, there is perhaps a shift in emphasis with more on language learning skills, on cultural aspects and on the links with literacy. The experiences and outcomes build on the communicative approach to Modern Languages developed to date. They reflect the talking, listening, writing and reading that one would expect in a current Modern Languages class-room. They encourage more group work, for example in preparing a presentation in the language, perhaps using ICT. The experiences and outcomes are also very specific about the Knowledge about Language to be developed, and the cultural aspect is also specified. The CfE levels have been linked to those being developed as part of the Common European Framework of Reference for Languages (CEFR) so that the level of competence achieved by learners will have a European-wide equivalence. The CEFR sets out what language learn-ers need to be able to use a language for communication. The levels of proficiency for each stage of learning are specified. That indicates that it is expected that Scottish students build up their competence in the same language, most likely to be French. Of course, one of the major problems for linguists here has been the dominance of English. On the continent, it is fairly easy to identify which language a pupil will need: English. In an English-speaking context like ours, it could be argued that fresh thinking is needed, that a more general lan-guage experience is needed with more emphasis on general language learning skills through a more basic level of two or more languages. The learner will have some knowledge of more than French and will be able to transfer the learning skills to whichever language might be identified at a later stage. At the time of writing, a new national Languages Working Group (LWG), involving key stakeholders, has been formed. Ministers are supportive of languages and wish to reverse the uptake trend. However, it remains to be seen whether or not CfE or the LWG offer the solution to the problems of Modern Language education.

REFERENCES

Bloomer, K. (1998) 'Translate concern into real policy change', *Times Educational Supplement Scotland* (27 November). Online at www.tes.co.uk/article.aspx?storycode=80905

Buie, E. (2010) 'Sideline Modern Languages at your peril, HMIE Chief warns secondaries', *Times Educational Supplement Scotland* (4 June). Online at www.tes.co.uk/article.aspx?storycode=6046379

Education Scotland (2010) *Curriculum for Excellence: Principles and Practice Modern Languages*. Online at www.educationscotland.gov.uk/learningteachingandassessment/curriculumareas/languages/modernlanguages/principlesandpractice/index.asp

McPake, J., R. Johnstone, L. Low and L. Lyall (1998) *Foreign Languages in the Upper Secondary School: A Study of the Causes of Decline*. Edinburgh: SCRE.

Ministerial Action Group on Languages (2000) *Citizens of a Multilingual World*. Edinburgh: Scottish Executive.

Scottish Centre for Information on Language Teaching (2012) 'Modern Languages vs. Social Sciences: A comparison of trends 2009–2012'. Online at www.scilt.org.uk/Portals/24/Library/statistics/ML%20vs%20Social%20Sciences%202009-2012.pdf

Scottish Consultative Committee on the Curriculum (1985) *The Diversification of Foreign Language Teaching in Scottish Secondary Schools*. Edinburgh: SCCC.

Scottish Consultative Committee on the Curriculum (1988) *The Provision of Languages other than English in Primary and Secondary Schools*. Edinburgh: SCCC.

Scottish Education Department (1977) *The Structure of the Curriculum in the Third and Fourth Years of the Secondary School* (the Munn Report). Edinburgh: HMSO.

Scottish Education Department (1989) Circular 1178.

Scottish Education Department (1990) *Effective Learning and Teaching in Scottish Secondary Schools: Modern Languages*. Edinburgh: SED.

Scottish Office Education and Industry Department (1998) *Standards and Quality, Primary and Secondary Schools, 1994–1998: Modern Languages*. Edinburgh: HMSO.

66

Modern Studies Education

Henry Maitles

In a relatively short time, some fifty years, Modern Studies has had a marked effect on the curriculum in most Scottish schools, being seen by educators, pupils and parents as a meaningful addition to social subjects. Indeed, it has in many schools and areas achieved parity with the two other major social subjects, History and Geography, and, taking further education college presentations into account, there are now similar presentations at Higher level in Modern Studies as in History or Geography. Although it is not yet taught as a discrete subject in all schools at S1/S2 (about 78 per cent in S1 and about 83 per cent in S2, according to the most recent survey), as far as Standard Grade, Higher Grade and university entrance are concerned, it is regarded as equal to the other social subjects. Curriculum for Excellence (CfE) made aspects of the subject area central, as well as ensuring that knowledge and understanding, skills and values in the area are being developed in the primary school.

WHAT IS MODERN STUDIES?

The subject was initially an amalgam of History and Geography, with some Politics thrown in, as the early exam papers showed. In the first O Grade in 1962, as well as questions of topical interest there were some on the Great Depression (of 1929), the rise of the Nazis, the Bolsheviks and map work questions. In its infancy, the subject was seen as being of most value for the less able as it related more directly to their immediate experiences, but fairly quickly the subject was seen as having value for all pupils. By the time of the first Higher Grade in 1968, the emphasis had shifted towards current affairs. The massive expansion of Politics and Sociology in the universities and the realisation that these subjects were central to an understanding of the complexities of modern societies meant that, since the 1988 Standard Grade arrangements, the subject has as its main aim the teaching and development of political literacy 'through a framework of analysis and a core of concepts adopted from the social sciences of politics and sociology'. Indeed, it was this aim of giving the pupils and students the tools to analyse complex societal questions that most Modern Studies departments saw as being particularly distinctive about the subject in a series of national consultation exercises organised by Her Majesty's Inspectorate (HMI) in 1994 and revisited in 2000 and 2007. The conclusions were that Modern Studies has a key role to play in the modern curriculum. It provides a sound context for learners to develop an awareness of the social and political issues they will meet in their lives. These reports suggested that the distinctive role of Modern Studies in the curriculum was to enable pupils to:

- develop social and political literacy;
- develop skills that will enable them to access, handle and evaluate information about the society and world in which they live;
- understand the society and world in which they live;
- promote citizenship, responsible participation in and respect for democracy;
- foster open-mindedness, participation and cooperation within society;
- develop an interest in and an understanding of current local community, national and international affairs;
- develop social skills;
- develop the ability to arrive at informed opinions and to reflect critically on society.

With these aims at its heart, Modern Studies has been seen as important by Scottish educationalists, particularly as there seems to be so much disaffection by young people towards politics as such, or at least organised democratic politics, despite a marked increase in involvement in single-issue campaigns. It is fair to say that the least apathetic, most politically interested young people in the school will be likely to be studying Modern Studies. That is not to say that there has been universal agreement over how political literacy should be taught in the schools, indeed whether it should be taught in the schools at all, as a glance at the debates of the early 1980s would show; there were those who believed that teaching political/sociological material would destroy democracy and others who believed that teaching it would bolster capitalism! Indeed, the whole area of bias is one that has led some to believe it should not be taught to younger children as there is left-wing bias inherent in the subject, although others have argued that areas of politics should be introduced as early as possible and that the problem of teachers 'sitting on the fence' when controversial issues are discussed (Ashton and Watson, 1998) must be tackled and that, particularly after the 9/11 events in New York and the 2005 suicide bombings in London, pupils should have the opportunity to discuss areas such as terrorism, Islamophobia, and the Iraq, Afghanistan and Libyan wars in a safe, constructive and non-threatening atmosphere. The Scottish Executive endorsed the importance of political education through the 5–14 Environmental Studies programme. Further, the decision to introduce education for citizenship (LTS, 2002) deepened the whole move towards political literacy teaching, and this has been further enhanced by the core strand of 'responsible citizenship' in CfE. The knowledge and skills associated with Modern Studies go much towards this important strand of citizenship. Additionally, there is the decision from the Scottish Government that in the devolution/ independence referundum in September 2014, voting will be extended to 16- and 17-year-olds. This would make discussion of the issues – a central one to the Modern Studies and citizenship area anyway – of even greater importance in the schools.

Modern Studies as presently organised is structured around a number of key concepts, seen as central to the development of the subject. These concepts – equality, rights and responsibilities, ideology, participation, need, power, representation – are believed to be the core of the subject and give the scope for analysing the subject and events in the real world. As pupils progress, there is a move from relatively simple to much more complex content. Nonetheless, although these concepts are clearly central, the list has been criticised as missing the crucial concept of 'class' and the consequent understandings from this. Whilst there is Scottish Qualifications Authority prescribed content at Standard Grade (although there will be more choice with National Qualifications 4 and 5) and Higher (albeit with choices at Higher), mainly of a sociological/political nature, a survey of departments shows a wide range of content in S1/S2, most of it now relating to CfE guidelines. Topics such as representation and laws; participating in society; media bias; human rights; multicultural society; the USA; the developing world; law and order; Europe; terrorism; a comparison of local area with another country or culture; and the United Nations Organisation are typical, and have an obvious relationship to both Standard Grade, National Qualifications 4 and 5 and Higher Grades, and are clear content areas in terms of the development of political literacy.

THE DEVELOPMENT OF SKILLS IN MODERN STUDIES

The skills developed in the subject are encapsulated in the term 'enquiry', involving both evaluating and investigating. Evaluating is the promotion of pupil ability in the critical appraisal and evaluation of information about social and political institutions, processes and issues through developing the ability to recognise lack of objectivity; to make comparisons and draw conclusions; and to express support for a personal or given point of view.

These are clearly central to the development of political literacy at any level; progression from S1 to S6 involves the use of increasingly complex, subtle and abstract sources. For the Higher, pupils are expected to analyse critically and evaluate complex sources and to show, through a decision-making exercise, how their evaluating skills can be applied to other specific contexts. Investigating involves the processes of planning, recording, analysing/synthesising and reporting and again is a vital skill for political literacy.

In addition, Modern Studies has a distinctive and important role in attempting to develop positive attitudes amongst pupils. This should include at all levels:

- respect for truth and reason;
- willingness to accept that other views and beliefs can have validity;
- willingness to accept the possibility of, and limits to, compromise;
- confidence and enterprise in pursuing information and communicating views.

These are often seen in pupil activities and course content towards issues such as poverty, the elderly, development issues and civil, human and equal rights. Where dealing with controversial issues, Modern Studies teachers should be allowing pupils to examine evidence relating to a range of views.

DYNAMISM IN THE CLASSROOM

This summary of what is taught in the subject misses out one of its central features – its dynamism in the classroom. The teaching and learning of Modern Studies has since its development as a distinctive sociological/political subject been characterised by the enthusiasm of the teachers and novel methodologies. Central to this has been the use of 'dialogue' in the classroom. Indeed, debate, role-play, dialogue, group work, stages work and the varied use of media and ICT have been central to its delivery in the classroom, especially around elections and civic participation. Modern Studies teachers are aware that the content of the subject means that many pupils will be coming to the classroom with some experience that they can input to the lesson. As HMI noted as early as 1992: 'Most teachers encouraged a classroom atmosphere in which open questioning and challenging of opinion was common-place' (HMI, 1992). The most recent full HMI report on Modern Studies (HMI, 2000) claims that in some 85 per cent of departments there was an ethos characterised by 'high expectations ... a brisk pace of work ... challenging tasks' and, further, that staff made a valuable contribution to the wider school and community 'through organising mock elections, debates, displays and excursions'.

ISSUES OF CONCERN AND DEVELOPMENT

The Real World and Change

What, then, of the future? The world is ever-changing and complex, and this provides tremendous opportunities and excitement for a subject like Modern Studies. It is a constant challenge to update content (although the Internet is of great use here) and, indeed, whole curricular areas depend on events in the real world. The fall of the dictatorships of Eastern Europe; the widening EU membership and euro crisis; New Labour and now Conservative–Liberal Democrat coalition politics in Westminster and the SNP in Scotland; youth disaffection and rioting in England; the evolving constitutional change in Britain, involving Scottish Parliament and Welsh and Northern Ireland assemblies and the independence referendum; new electoral systems; the ending of apartheid, but not inequalities, in South Africa; privatisations in the Welfare State; the events in the Middle East and the Gulf; the development of the euro; the events of 11 September 2001 and their aftermath; terrorism; the Iraq, Afghanistan and Libyan wars; and other political events all mean that Modern Studies teachers are having to revise course content regularly, something that adds greatly to workload but also keeps the subject relevant, dynamic and interesting and goes a long way to explain the popularity of the subject with S6 pupils and further education students. Nonetheless, there is a problem with content in the middle and upper school; for example, there is little space in either Standard Grade or Higher for the Iraq, Afghanistan and Libyan wars, any aspect of the relationship between Israel and the Palestinians or their neighbours or indeed any aspect of the Islamic world, such as the inspiring movements for democracy over recent years. Further, although China is an option in Higher, it is studied by a disappointingly small number of students. These are issues that Modern Studies teachers need to confront. How can the syllabus be opened up to allow the study of areas of conflict that develop? Otherwise, in what sense is the subject 'modern'? One suggestion could be to have an open area of the syllabus, perhaps dealing with an area of world conflict, that teachers can develop with pupils.

Curricular Developments

There are widespread curricular developments covering every area of schooling – the replacement of Standard Grade by new National Qualifications, the continuing development of the Higher Still programme and CfE. All of these offer great opportunities but also have potential difficulties.

The 5–14 syllabus and CfE gave the possibility of Modern Studies issues being taught from P1 to S2 and, in particular, those secondaries who have refused so far to implement Modern Studies in S1 and/or S2, whether for reasons of crowded curriculum, perceived unsuitability for young people or inertia to change, will now have to find ways of implementing learning around these issues. Modern Studies teachers and the Modern Studies Association are arguing hard that this should be done through the appointment of Modern Studies specialists where there are none at present, preferably organised in Social Studies departments or faculties, although there is a worry that in some of these schools there will be a temptation, for reasons of staffing, to deliver the Modern Studies elements through History and/or Geography.

CfE offers tremendous opportunities for Modern Studies. Apart from collaboration between feeder primaries and secondaries, which is in itself fruitful, Modern Studies sections in the secondaries will be able to expect pupils arriving with some experience and knowledge of the subject, hopefully meaning that planning and progression can be enhanced. There is the necessity of continually auditing courses, throwing out some parts and developing new units to fit CfE and the experiences of the students coming from the primaries, but, as argued earlier in the chapter, most schools are doing this and are ensuring that what is in the courses is relevant.

Thus, there is evidence that developments are well imbedded, although there are, in common with other subjects, worries over National Qualifications assessment, articulation with 'H', workload, content and the issue of more bi-level – or even multi-level – teaching and consequent poorer learning experiences for pupils.

Is Modern Studies Effective?

One of the central aims of Modern Studies, as shown above, is the development of political literacy. Is Modern Studies useful in terms of developing this body of knowledge and skills? There has been some research in this area. Mercer (1973) found little difference in terms of knowledge/understanding and values of pupils taking Modern Studies and those not. However, as has been pointed out, the nature of the subject in its early days (in particular its relationship to History and Geography) was perhaps central to these results. More recently, Maitles (2005; 2010) has found a marked difference in terms of knowledge, political interest and trust/cynicism levels between pupils studying Modern Studies and those not. This can be comforting for the subject, although as a caveat it must be noted that the 'better' Modern Studies scores can be explained by the fact that more politically knowledgeable and interested pupils may choose Modern Studies rather than the subject itself instilling the knowledge and interest. In terms of values/attitudes, the results suggest that there is not a marked difference, with Modern Studies students 'more positive' in some areas and History or Geography students 'more positive' in others.

Expansion and Limitations

Whilst it is undoubtedly true that Modern Studies is expanding in some areas and developing anew in some schools, there are a few schools where Modern Studies has been virtually eliminated as a subject in the middle school (S3 and S4). Indeed, this has also happened with regard to History and Geography. Worryingly, this has tended to be in schools with a larger percentage of lower-achieving pupils and is justified on the somewhat spurious educational basis of reducing choice and improving quality for these pupils by creating larger groupings in the other subjects. Fortunately, the practice is not widespread and, indeed, is being reversed in some areas.

Common Social Subjects Course in S1/S2

Another area of concern, in common with the other social subjects, although there are also some positive features, is the trend in some schools to have a Social Studies course in S1 (and sometimes in S2) where History, Geography and Modern Studies are taught by a single teacher, often uncertificated in one or two of these subjects. This can work well in situations where there has been full discussion, timetabled meetings and committed teachers with ownership of the course, and has the added advantage of reducing the number of teachers with whom each pupil has contact. Indeed the CfE proposals open up exciting possibilities for collaboration, leading to better and deeper learning; it seems obvious that if, for example, learning about and from the Holocaust can be developed in History, and through the diary of Anne Frank in English, with RME and Modern Studies doing work on values, genocide and racism, then the pupil experience will be much broader and more coordinated. And there is the exciting potential of adding in art, drama and music, for example, too. But, when staffing is the major consideration, there is often a lowest common denominator effect, leading consequently to poorer courses on offer.

HMIE FINDINGS

The detailed reports from Her Majesty's Inspectorate of Education (HMIE) outline many strengths in Modern Studies teaching, particularly in terms of methodology, as outlined earlier in this chapter. Further, the most recent full countrywide report (HMI, 2000) also notes 'pupils' enjoyment of Modern Studies and their good relationships with teachers' and 'high levels of commitment by teachers and good teamwork'. The reports also raised areas of concern that needed attention, such as the issue of progression in skills and content, planning in relation to assessment, and ensuring that pupils have a clear awareness of what is expected of them and are thus able to plan schemes for improvement. The 2007 report (HMIE, 2007) concluded that there were four key areas that needed further consideration and development:

- Are the learning experiences for learners imaginative, creative, stimulating and challenging?
- Do Modern Studies teachers promote independent learning using ICT and relevant interactive social scientific sources?
- Do Modern Studies teachers build learners' confidence by sharing the purposes of lessons and discussing with them key ideas which underpin the subject?
- Do Modern Studies teachers give learners enough practical opportunities to develop the aspects of citizenship which we teach in the subject?

At least part of the problem of these areas relates to an earlier concern – the fact that not all schools have Modern Studies principal teachers with the management time to deal with these weaker areas. Throughout Scotland there is clearly a preference by local authorities for faculty heads and whilst this opens up the possibilities of more joint and coherent work with the other social subjects, it needs to be monitored so that the weaknesses shown in the HMIE reports are not exacerbated.

INTO THE FUTURE

The future is thus one of optimism tempered by realism. The subject is tremendously popular with pupils, parents, further education students and professionals alike, and this is very important. The last twenty years have seen a rethinking of exactly how political literacy, one of the central areas of citizenship, can be developed within our education system, and within this perspective, Modern Studies clearly has an important central role.

REFERENCES

Ashton, E. and B. Watson (1998) 'Values education: A fresh look at procedural neutrality', *Educational Studies*, 24 (2): 183–93.

Dunlop, O. J. (ed.) (1977) *Modern Studies: Origins, Aims and Development*. London: Macmillan.

Her Majesty's Inspectorate (1992) *Effective Learning and Teaching in Scottish Secondary Schools: Modern Studies*. Edinburgh: SOED.

Her Majesty's Inspectorate (2000) *Standards and Quality in Secondary Schools: Modern Studies*. Edinburgh: SEED.

Her Majesty's Inspectorate of Education (2007) *Modern Studies – A Portrait of Current Practice in Scottish Secondary Schools*. Edinburgh: SEED.

Maitles, H. (2005) *Values in Education: We're Citizens Now*. Edinburgh: Dunedin Academic Press.

Maitles, H. (2010) '"They're out to line their own pockets!": Can the teaching of political literacy counter the democratic deficit?; the experience of Modern Studies in Scotland', *Scottish Educational Review*, 41 (2): 46–61.

Mercer, G. (1973) *Political Education and Socialization to Democratic Norms*. Glasgow: University of Strathclyde.

67

Music Education

Allan Hewitt

CONTEXT

Music has been a consistent presence within the Scottish educational system and current configurations are grounded in historical context. The mid- to late twentieth century was dominated by a curriculum that drew on the established division of music in the universities and conservatoires into performance, theory/rudiments and history. Pupils' ability to read and write musical notation was a given; performance repertoire was sourced from the Western classical tradition. Studies in music history and theory privileged pitch and rhythm perception, a knowledge of important composers and events, and the ability to deconstruct well-known items of the Western classical canon. Creative music-making and ensemble performances were almost entirely absent, though much excellent work took place in extra-curricular contexts. This was ideal preparation for entry to advanced study in the tertiary sector but, consequential to the emphasis on technical performance and notation skills, large numbers of young people were excluded who had a keen interest in music but lacked the traditional skills and expertise necessary to access the curriculum at certificated level.

The unpopularity of Music as a subject choice provided the context for its comprehensive overhaul within the secondary curriculum, stimulated by the publication of *Music in Scottish Schools* (SED, 1978). The impact of the philosophical and practical shift it represented was felt immediately in the development of the Standard Grade Music assessment documentation, followed in time by the content of the revised Higher Grade syllabus. The principles embodied in these developments were to shape the subsequent character of Music education in Scotland.

CHARACTERISTICS OF SECONDARY MUSIC EDUCATION

Three underlying philosophical imperatives have shaped Scottish Music education, informing curriculum development and having continued influence. These are broadly reflective of wider trends in music education, though Scotland can reasonably claim to have been at the forefront of innovation.

Accessible to all

First, formal Music education should be accessible to all. The threat to Music's continued place within the formal curriculum experienced in the 1980s inspired a concerted effort to remove any perceived barriers to study that were embedded in the existing curriculum. While accessibility may be a given at the early stages of secondary education, where Music was compulsory, it was applied also at the upper stages where studying Music was a choice. In the recent past, this ambition towards accessibility is most obvious in the progressive decrease of minimum requirements for performance in terms of technical difficulty and duration of recital. This makes it possible for pupils who do not possess relatively advanced levels of performing skill to take the subject.

Integrative

One of the aspects of Music education in Scotland that distinguishes praxis from other national contexts is the extent to which students engage in the full variety of musical activities rather than the class band ensemble-type activity that is the core of music education in some countries, but only a part of the experience in Scotland. The embrace of the three elements of performing, listening and creating music, and the deliberate attempt to transfer learning across these contexts, reflects an acceptance of a school of music education philosophy, notably Thomas Regelski's 'Comprehensive Musicianship' model (Regelski, 1981). The central tenet is that musical learning is achieved through application and experimentation in performance, composition and analysis, rather than simply 'playing music'.

Active Learning

Music education in Scotland is thus characterised by a focus on active learning, a belief that music education is about doing things – playing and creating music – rather than learning *about* music (Hewitt, 1995). Rooted in the Vygotskian concept of socially situated learning (Hewitt, 2008), emphasis is firmly on the practical aspects of music making and in particular a focus on developing pupils' conceptual learning rather than the abstractions of factual knowledge about music theory or history. The introduction of the concept list, which forms the basis of assessment in listening at Standard Grade and National Qualifications level and infuses learning across all three areas of music making, exemplifies this approach.

CURRICULUM

The curriculum is built around three basic activities: performing, listening and composing (termed 'inventing' at Standard Grade). No area dominates, though recent trends in assessment at the upper stages appear to downplay the importance of composition and privilege performance. In common with other creative arts subjects, Music is compulsory for pupils in S1 and S2 and subsequently offered as an option at S3–S6.

Performing

In S1 and S2 pupils encounter a variety of instruments including keyboard, guitar, drum kit and possibly voice, recorder and bass guitar. Developing a basic competence on at least one or two of these is expected, with a particular emphasis on performance in mixed-instrument groups. A range of resources is used to support this aspect of learning, including classroom-oriented ensemble arrangements and self-study material for individual practice.

At S3 and S4, pupils taking Standard Grade Music selected two instruments to study, one being identified as the 'solo' instrument (assessed by a short recital of 3–6 minutes at the end of the course) and the other as 'group' (assessed by a taped small-group performance). Instruments could be taught in class or by a specialist instrumental tutor and pupils aiming for a Credit-level award were expected to play repertoire of at least Associated Board Grade 3 standard.

Post Standard Grade, performance continues to be an important element of the curriculum. Unless they had selected the Music with Technology option (see below), candidates had to complete the Music: Performing unit that involves developing performance skills in either two instruments, one instrument and voice, or one instrument or voice and accompanying. Examination has been by recital in front of an external assessor, with requirements for recital duration and technical difficulty increasing with award level.

Composing

Composing activities at S1 and S2 vary widely between schools. It would be fair to say that this aspect of the curriculum generates the greatest diversity of practice and emphasis, and some schools are more imaginative and creative than others. Music technology provides an accessible and attractive platform for musical creativity, allowing pupils to explore different musical ideas and combinations that would otherwise be unavailable. More traditional approaches to composing, such as melody-writing and basic harmonisation, can be encountered alongside more contemporary activities like improvisation, songwriting and sound design.

In the middle and upper stages, composing is a mandatory part of the curriculum, though a reliance on internal assessment, where the class teacher rather than an external assessor assesses work, suggests that its place in the hierarchy sits below performance and listening. At Higher level, composition is assessed via the production of an audio folio lasting at least two minutes and containing two examples of creative work, supplemented with a programme note (detailing the compositional process and devices used) and a score/performance plan. Indeed, composition does not itself receive a grade at Higher level, only needing to be 'passed'.

Listening

Conceptual learning is a cornerstone of Music education and involves pupils developing an understanding of what a concept means and its practical application. So, for example, pupils at S1/2 would be expected both to *understand* the difference between 'ascending' and 'descending' tone sequences and to *identify* these when they occur in a piece of music. As noted above, this integration between theoretical understanding and practical application is an important underpinning feature of the Music curriculum. Listening work across all stages is often organised into a series of topical units that may derive from a musical style ('classical' or 'jazz') or another thematic aspect ('opera' or 'Scottish Music'). Teachers attempt to achieve the integrative aspect highlighted previously by linking performance, composition and listening activities within a unit, for example by having pupils perform a blues group performance, compose a blues improvisation and learn the historical and conceptual basis of blues music.

At the upper stages, the Music: Listening unit further extends candidates' conceptual understanding of music and supports learning within the composing and performance/technology units. At Higher level, this involves the detailed study of a number of prescribed works that encourage candidates to work at a broader/longer scale. Notably, there is a requirement to demonstrate understanding of musical notation within the formal assessment, which takes the form of a one-hour examination at the end of the unit.

NEW NATIONAL QUALIFICATIONS IN MUSIC

At the time of writing a set of National Qualifications (NQ) in Music has been prepared for introduction in 2012–13 to replace the existing NQ framework. The final examination diet for Standard Grade was 2013 and the existing National Qualifications will be phased out over a two-year period. While retaining much of the existing design and content and with some detail still to be published, it is useful to note some important modifications.

In common with other subject areas, the middle stages of secondary Music education will be divided into a Preparatory year (S3) and a Course year (S4), proceeding from the 'broad general education' in Expressive Arts in S1 and S2. The design and structure of the Preparatory year will be at the discretion of schools and colleges, facilitating the development of Music programmes that reflect localised strengths and expertise. In the Course year, students will study at one of three levels: National 3 (broadly equivalent to Foundation/Access under the existing structure), National 4 (General/Int 1) or National 5 (Credit/Int 2). Regardless of level, students will complete three units: Performing Skills, Composing Skills and Understanding Music. All will be internally assessed with external verification from the Scottish Qualifications Authority. On satisfactory completion of these modules students will proceed to assessment for the course award comprising a recital on one or more instruments in ensemble and/or solo context. Performance will be assessed by school music staff at National 3 and National 4 level, and by a visiting assessor at National 5. Notably, the performance examination will have a broader scope than has been the case and will include elements of reflection on repertoire and personal development. National 6, replacing the existing Higher level, retains the features of its predecessor. Additional minor developments include a revised concept list (forming the basis of the Understanding Music unit) and an emphasis of content over duration in the Composing Skills unit.

TRENDS IN UPTAKE AND ATTAINMENT

Uptake

One of the principal objectives of curriculum reform in Music in the 1980s was to arrest the significant decline in numbers taking the subject at S3–S6. Using candidate numbers as a criterion, the picture today is positive, suggesting that the aim has been achieved. Presentations at Standard Grade Music are strong: assuming the number of presentations in English is representative of the total Standard Grade population, in 2011 around 18 per cent ($n = 9,181$) were presented in Music. Numbers have been stable at Intermediate 1 level, rising from 798 in 2007 to 825 in 2011. Presentations peaked in 2008 at 887. Presentations at Intermediate 2 increased steadily from 3,095 in 2007 to 3,663 in 2011. Presentations at Higher level have also increased from 4,278 in 2007 to 4,585 in 2011. In 2011, 30,068 candidates were presented for Higher English, suggesting that around 15 per cent of pupils at this stage opted to study Music. Advanced Higher presentations have been stable, with 1,235 in 2007 and 1,299 in 2011.

Attainment

A review of grading distribution for the exam diets between 2007 and 2011 provides an interesting overview of attainment in Music. At Standard Grade, results improved during 2007–10 with the number of candidates being awarded the maximum grade increasing from 33.8 per cent in 2007 to 41.2 per cent in 2011. In general, this shift was achieved through a decreasing number of candidates being awarded grades in the middle bands.

At Intermediate 1, a B grade was the most common result in 2011 (31.4 per cent) compared to A (17.8 per cent) and C (27 per cent). A significant number (16.6 per cent, $n = 137$) of candidates received a 'no award' result. These patterns broadly reflect the trend in earlier presentations. At Intermediate 2, A grades were most common in 2011 (53.5 per cent) with 27.2 per cent receiving a B grade. 'No award' grades were less frequent at this level (4.4 per cent). This suggests a trend towards improved examination performance; in 2007 30.4 per cent received an A, 29.6 per cent a B and 21.8 per cent a C. In 2007, 12.3 per cent received a 'no award'.

In the 2011 Higher examination, 44.2 per cent achieved A, 30.4 per cent a B, 17.1 per cent a C and 3.8 per cent a D. 'No awards' were 4.5 per cent. As with the Intermediate 2, there appears to have been a trend towards the upper grade from 2007, when distribution was more even (28.4 per cent of pupils received A, 32 per cent received B and 23.4 received C). Only 1 per cent of pupils in 2007 received a 'no award'. At Advanced Higher, 60.5 per cent of candidates received an A grade in 2011, with 27.3 per cent receiving a B. This pattern of excellent performance at the most advanced stage has been consistent across the past six years.

CURRENT DEBATES AND CHALLENGES

Scotland boasts a rich and varied musical heritage with a proud record of producing world-class artists and composers across classical, jazz, rock, pop and traditional music. The accommodation of this diversity within a formal curriculum has been challenging, especially with a teaching profession whose background and expertise tended to be in the Western classical tradition. The desire to incorporate the rich diversity of musical experience within the classroom has stimulated some tension between delivering the building blocks of the classical tradition, such as notation, tonal harmony and technical skill in performance, and the desire (often from teachers themselves) to incorporate more contemporary approaches, or those drawn from a wider stylistic pool. Examples would include blues improvisation and the emphasis on the development of aural skills.

Similar challenges pertain to traditional Scottish music. The indigenous musical traditions of Scotland are now embedded into the formal Music curriculum, most noticeably in the requirement for pupils to develop their knowledge and understanding of concepts based in those traditions (particularly the vocal and instrumental types of repertoire) and in the ability of pupils to sit performance exams on traditional instruments such as the clarsach and bagpipes, and/or performing authentic repertoire. However, traditional music relics on a different form of pedagogy, one that is based on learning by ear, sharing repertoire and greater focus on the social aspects of music making. In this there is more commonality with rock, pop, jazz and world music than the Western classical tradition. The translation of these approaches in the formal Music curriculum is challenging if authenticity of practice is valued.

Technology and Training

The use of music technology, whether desktop-based or mobile, has transformed the creation and consumption of music. Young people have access to an unprecedented range of music and a multiplicity of platforms upon which to create their own music. In Scotland, Music educators have readily adopted technological innovation within their classrooms and there is general recognition of the advantages that it can bring, especially to creative work. There is a route at Higher level to allow pupils to focus on Music with Technology. However, this demands resource in terms of equipment and, more critically, in terms of training. There remains a key requirement for teachers to receive up-to-date, effective and classroom-focused training on contemporary technology. Otherwise, the danger is that classroom music and out-of-school musical experience will remain dichotomous for many young people in Scotland.

Instrumental Teaching

Finally, special mention should be made of the pivotal role of local authority-based instrumental teaching in Scotland. While the design of the curriculum was based on opening access to all pupils who wish to study Music, there can be no doubt that the support of peripatetic instrumental staff, who are usually responsible for delivering small-group instruction within a cognate instrumental family (such as woodwind), is vital. Such provision caters for pupils who wish to pursue the development of advanced skills that would simply be impossible within the classroom setting, and who lack the financial resources to access private instrumental tuition. Current threats to the funding of such services pose very real challenges to the continued high-quality provision of Music.

CONCLUSION

Music education in Scottish secondary schools has experienced a steady period of growth in numbers at S3–S6 and a positive trend in attainment. An explosion of innovation in curriculum and pedagogy in the early 1990s has produced a stable platform with a curriculum centred on a core philosophy of accessibility, integration and active learning. A range of issues continue to generate debate within the Music teaching community, and financial challenges pose a significant threat to the provision of instrumental teaching and extra-curricular activities upon which much that is positive about Music education depends.

REFERENCES

Hewitt, A. (1995) 'A review of the role of activity-based learning experiences in the music curriculum, and their current implementation in the Standard Grade Music course in Scotland', *British Journal of Music Education*, 12 (3): 203–14.

Hewitt, A. (2008) 'Children's creative collaboration during a computer-based music task', *International Journal of Educational Research*, 47 (1): 11–26.

Regelski, T. A. (1981) *Teaching General Music: Action Learning for Middle and Secondary Schools*. New York: Schirmer Books.

Scottish Education Department (1978) *Music in Scottish Secondary Schools, Curriculum Paper 16*. Edinburgh: HMSO.

68

Outdoor Education

Peter Higgins and Robbie Nicol

> The journey through education for any child in Scotland must include a series of planned, quality outdoor learning experiences. (Learning and Teaching Scotland, 2010, p. 6)

In the past five years the significant developments in Scottish education have been mirrored by those in outdoor education, and provision and interest in a wide range of aspects continues to grow in Scotland in ways not widespread in other parts of the UK or overseas. These changes have built upon a traditional Scottish empathy with outdoor education and a growing post-devolution policy interest. Recent policy changes have also been aided by an increasingly active research community and a broadening of the term 'outdoor education' towards 'outdoor learning' and its synonyms. This change has acted as a reminder that learning outside the classroom can be in the school grounds or locally based as well as in residential outdoor education settings. When documents are referred to in this chapter the original term (usually 'outdoor education' or 'outdoor learning') is used as there is no definitive distinction between these terms (see below, however). Whilst education outdoors can contribute to many curricular areas it is widely conceptualised as being based on three integrated areas of 'outdoor activities', 'environmental education' and 'personal and social development'. Whatever the focus, an experiential and adventurous approach to learning is a central pedagogical theme.

EARLY DEVELOPMENTS

The combination of variable climate, geological, social and cultural history and the resulting topography provide both the physical circumstances for outdoor recreation and the educational possibilities that enabled Scotland to become one of the first places in the world where outdoor education became formalised. The 1944 Education Act and the 1945 Education (Scotland) Act encouraged the use of the outdoors for environmental and nature studies, and councils to establish appropriate 'camps'. Many converted old mansions or purpose-built residential centres and by the 1970s, most councils offered extensive, progressive outdoor educational opportunities (Higgins, 2002). Training staff became a priority and the specialist courses in Scotland (Moray House and Dunfermline Colleges) offered in 1973 were amongst the first in the world (and still run today).

A DEFINITION?

As interest in 'outdoor education' has grown it has become an increasingly nuanced concept which, within Curriculum for Excellence (CfE), is considered to be an 'approach to learning' that is part of normal learning and teaching. Rather than discuss this in detail here we favour the statement on approach and content from the Learning and Teaching Scotland (LTS) document 'Curriculum for Excellence through Outdoor Learning' (2010). In terms of *approach*:

> The core values of *Curriculum for Excellence* resonate with long-standing key concepts of outdoor learning. Challenge, enjoyment, relevance, depth, development of the whole person and an adventurous approach to learning are at the core of outdoor pedagogy. The outdoor environment encourages staff and students to see each other in a different light, building positive relationships and improving self-awareness and understanding of others. (LTS, 2010, p. 7)

In terms of *content*, outdoor education might be considered as education 'in' (outdoor activities), 'through' (for example, personal and social education, therapy, rehabilitation, management development), 'about' (environmental education) and 'for' (sustainability) the natural heritage. It is usually interdisciplinary, integrated across these areas and often practical, interactive and reflective, with the role of the teacher being to encourage students to take responsibility for learning.

In terms of *location*, a concentric circles model describes five zones of outdoor learning with the school in the centre where outdoor learning opportunities are available in the immediate vicinity of the school grounds (Higgins and Nicol, 2002). As Beames et al. (2011, pp. 5–6) describe:

> beyond the school grounds is the local neighbourhood, which can be explored on foot or by using public transport. Day excursions ('field trips') often take place a little further away and usually require some kind of group transport. Residential outdoor centres, cultural visits, and expeditions that involve being away from home overnight comprise the fourth 'zone'.

The fifth zone is 'Planet Earth', which indicates the growing understanding attached to the importance of outdoor experiences in health, wellbeing and sustainability.

Learning outdoors contrasts with the 'classroom', as the environment is influenced by weather, the seasons, time of day and topography. The emphasis on 'outdoor learning' has stimulated scholars to rethink adventure as a concept. Traditionally adventurous experiences have been closely associated with physical outdoor activities. The emerging concept of outdoor learning accepts that most teachers do not have access to the training or equipment to provide such opportunities. The types of adventure that teachers are increasingly devising are essentially person-centred where the outdoors provides opportunities for learner discovery, creativity, curiosity, imagination and wonder to inspire learning. Consequently, a local urban environment can be as valuable as 'remote' or 'wild' areas.

POLICY AND CURRICULUM

Recent policy interest has been stimulated by reports suggesting children are increasingly separated from the natural environment; they have poor skills in risk management and exercise minimally (Gill, 2010). Outdoor learning can provide such learning opportunities, and policy support for outdoor education is growing in the UK. The 2005 Scottish Government's 'Outdoor Connections' programme (www.educationscotland.gov. uk/Images/OE%20Providers_tcm4-391133.pdf) has made 'connections across emerging outdoor education priorities and policies, programmes and people'; and has developed 'resources which will continue to improve the quality of outdoor learning' (LTS, 2007).

Building on these developments, government funding has been provided to employ specialist fixed-term contract Development Officers at Learning and Teaching Scotland (LTS) (now Education Scotland). Their work has been supported internally and by advisory groups, notably the Outdoor Learning Strategic Advisory Group which operated between 2008 and 2010. (This has now been replaced with other Education Scotland advisory and implementation arrangements.) Through this period considerable progress was made, culminating in 'Curriculum for Excellence through Outdoor Learning'. This was the first government document specifically to link a national curriculum with outdoor learning, and is a significant milestone. LTS, now in the guise of Education Scotland, has continued to build its documentary and web-based support for outdoor learning (see www.ltscotland. org.uk/learningteachingandassessment/approaches/outdoorlearning/index.asp) with this primarily to support teachers to deliver formal and informal curricula outdoors, but also to understand and communicate the reasons for doing so. In this initiative LTS has collaborated with other government agencies (such as Scottish Natural Heritage and Scottish National Parks), NGOs, universities and colleges, and the result is of considerable significance both nationally and internationally.

One of the most important recent policy developments has been the establishment of a 'One Planet Schools' Ministerial Advisory Group (One Planet Schools' Ministerial Advisory Group, 2012). Whilst the One Planet initiative has an overt focus on 'whole school approaches to sustainability in schools', it has an emphasis on outdoor learning with the intention of 'raising attainment, improving behaviour, inclusion and health and wellbeing' (see Chapter 31, Sustainable Development Education). This is significant as it recognises the interdisciplinary nature and broad relevance of outdoor learning. Another Ministerial Advisory Group on 'Scottish Studies' has prioritised culture, history and language, and here the role of the Scottish landscape will be central, with outdoor learning experiences providing a context for a deeper understanding of Scottish natural and cultural heritage (www.scotland.gov.uk/Topics/Education/Schools/curriculum/ACE/ScottishStudies).

RECENT RESEARCH

Building on recent research investment by the Scottish Government through LTS and Scottish Natural Heritage (see Nicol et al., 2007), more widespread research interest has developed amongst academics (primarily at Edinburgh and Stirling Universities) and also the number of Masters and Doctoral graduates with an outdoor education specialism continues to grow. This is mirrored by a growing funded research interest in related sectors, with organisations such as charities, National Parks, Sportscotland and the Forestry Commission looking at an increasingly diverse range of issues such as curricular relevance and educational attainment.

One rapidly developing new area of research is in the relationship between green space (areas such as urban parks, open countryside, woodlands, coastlines and so on) and health and wellbeing. Growing medical and social research literature indicates that young people are spending less time in green spaces and are physically less active than previous generations, and there is suggestive evidence that exposure to greenspaces affords both direct and indirect (by stimulating physical activity) benefits (see Sustainable Development Commission, 2008; Burns, 2011). Whilst some of this evidence relates specifically to the performance of children in schools, there are broader implications for outdoor education in terms of stimulating active lifestyle choices that may bring long-term health benefits.

PROVISION

Though the value of outdoor education is widely acknowledged, it is not consistently supported by Scottish councils, some increasing and others decreasing provision. Approaches to management vary within and between councils and may be cross-departmental (education, community, children's services); delivered by different people (teachers, rangers, instructors, youth workers); and take place in different settings (school grounds, field visits, centres). From a high point in the 1970s when many schools had dedicated outdoor education teachers (Higgins, 2002), there are now very few other than those who work with children with additional support needs in special schools.

Most council outdoor centres have seen substantial reductions in central funding and have become commercial businesses or charitable trusts, and independent external providers now deliver more pupil-days than council centres (Nicol et al., 2007). All have shown adaptability in responding to demanding financial circumstances, which seem likely to continue.

This 'mixed economy' lacks philosophical coherence, and provision (opportunity, duration, location) is variable (Nicol et al., 2007). Some school pupils may be taught regularly outside the classroom whilst others may experience (and pay significant charges for) a few residential days of outdoor education in their whole school career. This raises ethical issues associated with equity and opportunity in public education.

This cost/time issue may be a contributing factor to the growth of local school-based outdoor learning, and this may hold the greatest potential for development because of the new curricular importance attached to outdoor learning. A new vision for outdoor learning has begun to emerge as more teachers realise that it is not just about taking pupils to residential centres for specialist activities, but seeing the potential for teaching subjects in the school grounds or local neighbourhoods.

REPRESENTATION AND MANAGEMENT OF OUTDOOR PROVISION

There is no national framework for the management of outdoor education in Scotland although a number of bodies represent aspects of the sector. The situation is complex and mirrors some of the definitional issues identified earlier. The Scottish Advisory Panel for Outdoor Education is a forum for those who hold an advisory position within the thirty-two Scottish councils whilst the Association of Heads of Outdoor Education Centres is similar but for centre managers. The National Governing Bodies (NGBs) regulate outdoor instructional awards that have been adopted by the sector. There are a number of other agencies with a justifiable interest, such as NGOs (Field Studies Council, Royal Society for the Protection of Birds, John Muir Trust), and government agencies (Scottish Natural Heritage, Forestry Commission). 'Real World Learning' includes membership of some of the above organisations and others, but would not consider itself 'representative' – for example, there is no specific organisation for teachers who teach outdoors. Whilst this

demonstrates the breadth of the 'sector' it can be difficult for policy makers to gain an overview of provision, training needs or effectiveness of delivery (see below).

CURRENT ISSUES IN OUTDOOR EDUCATION

Cost, Time and Safety

In Mannion et al.'s (2007) study of Scottish schools, primary children's opportunities
were limited but generally greater than those of secondary pupils, as many of the latter had
no outdoor learning during the survey (summer term) and the average for those who did
was thirteen minutes per week. Other Scottish research (see Nicol et al., 2007) indicates
that teachers in primary, secondary, specialist and nursery schools perceive common and
specific barriers to outdoor learning, including financial costs to pupils and schools; time
involved in organising events; adult/pupil ratios required; and issues to do with safety, risk
and liability. Consequently, in deciding whether or not to organise outdoor study, teachers
weigh up effort and costs against benefits (perceived differently amongst teachers, parents
and pupils).

Despite perceptions of risk amongst parents, teachers and policy makers, accidents are
rare, especially in the wide range of outdoor educational activities taking place from schools
(Gill, 2010). This perception has generated anxiety over litigation, but recent concerns
amongst politicians and the public that children lack skills in risk awareness has led to
outdoor education being suggested as one way to teach these skills.

The potential for increased provision lies primarily in more teachers crossing the classroom threshold to take their classes outdoors, and local journeys do not incur high costs
(and sometimes none). Outdoor learning should not be seen as a demand on curricular
time but more an issue of the teacher choosing the most appropriate location. Beames et al.
(2011) make the point that some things are better taught indoors and some outdoors, and
it is for the teacher to choose locations based on what they are trying to achieve. Safety will
quite rightly remain a significant issue, but if the curricular potential of CfE is to be realised
then local authorities will need to adopt a more enabling approach to support teachers in
overcoming perceived barriers.

Licensing and Regulation

There is specific Health and Safety legislation pertaining to outdoor education: the
Activities Centres (Young Persons' Safety) Act (1995) and a dedicated inspection and
licensing agency – the Adventure Activities Licensing Service (see www.hse.gov.uk/aala/
aals.htm). The current UK government wishes to 'streamline' regulation and has proposed
that the licensing regime is replaced with a code of practice. For educational provision the
intention is to simplify the process that schools and similar organisations undertake before
conducting local outdoor learning activities or taking children on trips, and to change perceptions through a shift from a system of 'risk assessment' towards 'risk–benefit analysis'.
The review has led to different outcomes in the devolved administrations and, following an
extensive consultation period, the Scottish Government has decided that a statutory licensing scheme should be retained (www.scotland.gov.uk/Publications/2012/06/6153/0).
This was the widely held preference of local authorities and education professionals. The
government will work closely with stakeholders in maintaining an independent Scottish

licensing scheme, and to ensure that 'cross-border' activities are not compromised. In addition to licensing arrangements, schools, centres and other providers must of course comply with other national regulations such as the Disability Discrimination Act (2005).

Teaching Qualifications

There is no requirement for Teacher Education Institutes (TEIs) to deliver teacher training outdoors. Any such training is entirely at the discretion of individual TEIs (for example, the BEd and PGDE courses in Outdoor Learning at the University of Edinburgh are elective rather than required). Despite the absence of formal teaching qualifications in outdoor education in Scotland, the General Teaching Council for Scotland (GTCS) has included outdoor education as a recognised teaching subject (although registration is dependent on individual portfolios of experience) and also as a category in its professional recognition scheme.

The GTCS revision of the Professional Standards in 2012 was intended to contribute to a national framework for teachers' professional learning and development. Outdoor learning is seen as an important facet of 'learning for sustainability' and education professionals will be required to address this in their practice. This also reflects the Scottish Government's interest in Scottish Studies and 'One Planet Schools' noted above, both of which require teachers to understand the role of the outdoors in pupil development (see Chapter 31, Sustainable Development Education). Indeed, the report of the One Planet Schools Group (2012, p. 14) suggests that as part of 'learning for sustainability' there is an entitlement that 'outdoor learning should be a regular, progressive curriculum-led experience for all learners'. This will need to be integrated into curriculum design in schools, with teachers supporting pupils age 3–18 by providing opportunities to experience the zones of learning in the concentric circles model above. This of course has implications for teacher education programmes. It is also likely that the GTCS will encourage teachers committed to outdoor learning to apply for 'professional recognition' in the same way as for sustainable development education.

Similarly, lack of nationally coordinated in-service training for education outdoors leaves appropriate training/qualification open to interpretation. The widespread acceptance of outdoor activities qualifications seems inappropriate as these focus on safe and professional practice in skills development rather than 'education'. Similarly, specialist qualifications such as 'forest school leader' are unnecessary for most teachers to take their classes out to a local wood, beach and so on. Rather, what is needed is a means of helping teachers to be confident in local outdoor learning and aware of when they need specialist input.

Quality Assurance

Despite political support, the absence of a coherent understanding of the nature of outdoor learning and its benefits by education authorities and teachers continues to limit the quality and quantity of young people's outdoor learning experiences (Nicol et al., 2007). There remains no national policy, statutory requirements, regulatory mechanisms, formal teaching qualifications or quality assurance to encourage, establish and maintain standards of outdoor learning experiences. However, Her Majesty's Inspectorate of Education (HMIE) has increasingly reported on outdoor education where it has encountered it.

With outdoor learning receiving much greater curricular attention, teachers in schools, outdoor providers, local authority policy makers, TEIs and HMIE are currently working together to provide a national framework for outdoor learning that is policy-driven, empirically informed, supported by high-quality opportunities for continuing professional development and monitored through a robust but appropriate inspection process.

EDUCATION INDOORS?

The decisions taken by policy makers to support outdoor education since the establishment of the Scottish Parliament in 1999 have had both instrumental significance (through initiatives, resources, events and research) and presentational significance (it is clearly seen as important and mainstream). During the period under review the role of the LTS/ Education Scotland Development Officers (in Education Scotland and linked to the National Parks) has been crucial to the process of developing a national vision and provision for outdoor learning. In an uncertain financial climate it remains to be seen what priority will be given to supporting outdoor learning in the future, but clearly the growing curricular relevance provides a strong justification.

Nonetheless, it remains the case that one common implicit theme of most of Scottish 'education' is that it takes place 'indoors'. Outdoor educators have long considered this illogical as it ignores important learning opportunities to be found outside the classroom, and the principles of CfE have been central to outdoor education philosophy for some time. As Beames et al. (2009, p. 42) point out, as CfE

> aims to place the nature of the educated person at the centre of curricular purpose, and to reduce the amount of de-contextualised subject content, and to promote real world experience ... situated learning in the world outdoors looks exceptionally legitimised by CfE and exceptionally able to deliver CfE's purposes.

Whilst further practical capacity-building is required to promote outdoor learning in schools it is clear that such conceptual policy justification should inspire further 'education outdoors'.

REFERENCES

Beames, S., M. Atencio and H. Ross (2009) 'Taking excellence outdoors', *Scottish Educational Review*, 41 (2): 32–45.

Beames, S., P. Higgins and R. Nicol (2012) *Learning outside the Classroom: Theory and Guidelines for Practice*. New York: Routledge.

Burns, H. (2011) 'How supportive environments generate good health', in S. J. Marrs, S. Foster, C. Hendrie, E. C. Mackey and D. B. A. Thompson (eds), *The Changing Nature of Scotland*. Edinburgh: TSO Scotland, pp. 125–32.

Gill, T. (2010) *Nothing Ventured: Balancing Risks and Benefits in the Outdoors*. Online at www.eng lishoutdoorcouncil.org/wp-content/uploads/Nothing-Ventured.pdf

Higgins, P. (2002) 'Outdoor education in Scotland', *Journal of Adventure Education and Outdoor Learning*, 2 (2): 149–68.

Higgins, P. and R. Nicol (eds) (2002) *Outdoor Education: Authentic Learning in the Context of Landscapes (vol. 2)*. Kisa: Kinda Kunskapscentrum. Online at www.education.ed.ac.uk/out doored/research/oe_authentic_learning.pdf

Learning and Teaching Scotland. (2010) *Curriculum for Excellence through Outdoor Learning*. Glasgow: Learning and Teaching Scotland.

Mannion, G., L. Doyle, K. Sankey, L. Mattu and M. Wilson (2007) *Young People's Interaction with Natural Heritage through Outdoor Learning*. Perth: Scottish Natural Heritage.

Nicol, R., P. Higgins, H. Ross and G. Mannion (2007) *Outdoor Education in Scotland: A Summary of Recent Research*. Perth: Scottish Natural Heritage.

One Planet Schools' Ministerial Advisory Group (2012) *Learning for Sustainability*. Edinburgh: Scottish Government. Online at www.scotland.gov.uk/Topics/Education/Schools/curriculum/ACE/OnePlanetSchools/OnePlanetSchoolsReport

Sustainable Development Commission (2008) *Health, Place and Nature: How Outdoor Environments Influence Health and Well-being: A Knowledge Base*. Online at www.sd-commission.org.uk/publications/downloads/Outdoor_environments_and_health.pdf

69

Physical Education and Sport

Bob Brewer

This chapter presents a selective examination of the way Physical Education has been developed in Scotland and of how the constituent intentions, content and subject matter have been interpreted in alliance with sport and health to become a distinctive feature of current curriculum design in Curriculum for Excellence (CfE). In doing so, it anticipates a view that while there are often quoted claims to be heard about the contribution that Physical Education can make in the lives of children at school (and, increasingly, beyond that period), the ways in which these are embodied in curriculum practice are vulnerable to misinterpretation and misapplication, none more so than in the closely associated constructs of sport and health-related activity.

GETTING TO THIS POINT: A SEARCH FOR MEANING

Physical Education has never been short of attempts to state the significance of its place in the timetables for school-aged children. Quite where the emphasis and priorities have been directed for its presence in the Scottish curriculum have fluctuated between the broad scope afforded by Munn's reporting of the 'sixth mode' (physical activity), the diversity and rich-ness of its attributes demanding a 'firm place' for 14–16-year-olds, and later developments merely as one part of an expressive arts diet in the 5–14 Guidelines. A review of the associ-ated statements confirming Physical Education's position over the period of introduction of programmes that followed (1977–92) provides an indication of the variability of meanings curriculum writers were giving to it. Similarly, issues of definition were clearly such a matter of concern for observers of CfE (including politicians) that statements were added to the documentation for Health and Wellbeing to clarify distinctions between physical educa-tion, physical activity and sport. Such observations typify the 'struggle' in the texts claiming educational significance for Physical Education (McNamee, 2005). While to some extent this has been dominated by the legacy of the Peters-Hirst treatise about educational values, it is also clear that the currency of Physical Education as part of Health and Wellbeing (in CfE) reflects an attempt (at least) of justification beyond that of a narrowed interpretation of 'what counts'.

There are good reasons to dwell on the dilemmas raised here for physical educationists in Scotland, where the contest over rationale was encapsulated in the way the subject was to be adjudged in meriting examinable status. The form that certificated Physical Education took in its various guises – at Standard Grade (SGPE), Higher Grade (HGPE) and latterly in the Higher Still menu (HSPE) – appeared to rely on a 'new orthodoxy' characterised by an intellectualised evaluation of the knowledge arising out of practical-experiential learning and teaching. The manner and way these accounts of certificated Physical Education curricula have been shaped tend to indicate a path more akin to a view of education grounded in pupil–teacher permutations of facts and the analysis of these, relative to any authentic notion of 'practical knowledge'.

These trends indicating changes in emphasis for Physical Education have been borne out latterly in the statements allying it more explicitly to intentions associated with Health and Wellbeing as a critical area of CfE – what it suggests in relation to the meanings coupled with Physical Education accords with Kirk's regularly stated thesis that 'physical education is socially constructed, so that what takes place in the name of physical education at any given place at a given time is the product of struggles over *preferred* values and priorities between . . . coalitions of interested parties' (Kirk, 2010, p. 20: my emphasis).

HEALTH AND WELLBEING: CLARIFICATION OR CONSTERNATION FOR PHYSICAL EDUCATION?

Implicit in many previous statements about Physical Education has been the health welfare and fitness status of young people. However, the momentum created by seemingly compelling evidence in Scotland about levels of inactivity, concerns about dietary habits, weight gain and excess, along with lifestyle choices among school-aged children, began to make its mark with government and politicians as they calculated the costs of not dealing with the apparent 'obesity crisis' or the fall-out from alarmist headlines ('Schoolgirl waist size three inches bigger than in 1978', *Herald*, Thursday, 14 April 2011, p. 9). In Scotland it inspired a range of government reporting from health-related agencies (the evocatively entitled Physical Activity Task Force, for example), culminating in reporting from a Review Group on Physical Education (Scottish Executive, 2004) that encouraged, among many other things, a curriculum entitlement for every child of at least two hours of 'quality Physical Education' each week. Subsequent ministerial statements not only approved this two-hour timetabled allowance but legislated also for 400 additional PE teachers, as well as an explicit instruction that Health and Wellbeing was to be the concern of all schoolteachers. It fuelled the view that policy and practice were to be aligned.

The impetus from these events and from the interpretation of related worldwide research, formed, as Penney (2008) anticipates, a political opportunity for Physical Education to clarify and positively shape its development, but, conversely (as she also says), the potential for becoming sidetracked. As physical educationists gave scrutiny to the tone of CfE learning experiences and outcomes to be achieved ('I can, I am, I improve, I know') they would have been left in little doubt about the implications for PE practice – 'energetic play', 'developing and sustaining my levels of fitness' and 'my performance across all aspects of fitness' – while, in the allied strand of Physical activity and sport, the adjectives 'energetic' and 'vigorous' along with 'daily activity' (habits) pervade the expected nature of pupils' work in and beyond school time. All this, one must suspect, in the belief (and government hope) that the reported plight of the overweight, the obese and the slothful, or even the resentful, will be in some way diverted towards achievable beneficial health outcomes as the consequence of engagement in school-based programmes.

However, it is perhaps expedient to be watchful over such an expectation for Physical Education. A number of writers remind us of the sensitivities inherent in the promotion of health pedagogies, especially where these are based on perceptions of ideal body type and shape that are implicitly endorsed as medically and morally sound. Evans and Rich (2011) have summarised the trends in such a discourse that relate issues of 'fat' as some kind of moral failing – 'an outward sign of neglect of one's corporeal self' (p. 70) – to the demeaning effects of 'hierarchies of the body' on the identities of children. Similarly, Gard (2011) doubts the evidence relating to the efficacy of school-based physical activity interventions in sustaining anything like weight control (never mind the reduction of chronic disease). Indeed, any thought that the lifelong learning imperatives sought by CfE and elsewhere (Scottish Executive, 2004) can be demonstrated is invariably more objectively explained, Gard (2011, p.405) suggests, 'by the durability of economic, geographic and social factors that are conducive to being physically active'.

CERTIFICATION IN THE CFE ERA: WHERE NEXT FOR PHYSICAL EDUCATION?

Current undergraduates in current teacher education undergraduates in physical education may find it difficult to believe there is any dubiety about 'examinable', certificated Physical Education, conceding little to the anxieties that were felt by the profession during its introduction in Scotland from 1988. While teachers of that era were cautious about its implementation, the pupil uptake of certificated work has continued to swell (16,444 pupils at SGPE and 5,814 pupils at HSPE in 2010). It indicates a significant period of revision to the organisation and provision for teaching and learning in Physical Education in a period where explicit HMIE guidance and directive, along with specialist subject advisory support in the respective educational authorities, and an active Scottish Physical Education Association contributed to the leadership vibrancy of the time. But it was largely dominated by a concession that an examined curriculum, warranting various external reviews of pupil attainment, comes at a cost. The lauding of 'performance-led' and 'practical-experiential' pedagogical contexts that pervaded the various arrangements for SGPE (from 1988) and HSPE (2005 in its present format) have had to be tempered by actual teacher responses in coming to deal with the assessment protocols – more especially the weighting of practical, and knowledge and understanding forms of assessment. The constraining effects of this on the way Physical Education is conducted appear to put at risk the types of constructivist teacher–pupil environment that had been anticipated in guidance on pedagogy extolling 'practical workshops'. It further reminds the profession of the variable interpretation that will permeate attempts elsewhere in CfE to deliver whatever is meant by 'quality' teaching in two hours of Physical Education.

These consistently reported issues (HMIE, 2008; Thorburn and Gray, 2010) remain germane as the structures for examined courses are realigned in keeping with the rationale for CfE. With the diminution of the leadership agency seen in previous developments in Physical Education, Scottish Qualifications Authority appointees (sometimes teachers in a 'volunteer' writing role) appear to be the sole arbiters of ensuring that these new awards in Physical Education are meaningfully calculated. They might find considerable benefit from expanding the way pupil knowledge and understanding is nurtured and evaluated, more especially in the deployment of assessment modes that draw upon the use of electronic formats and applications that form an every day, every moment part of schoolchildren's lives. Physical Education's then innovative use of video assessment formats in the era of SGPE (despite resistance from the Scottish Examination Board) should give encouragement that such developments are possible and may enable pupils to demonstrate their understanding more fully and in context.

The case of certificated Physical Education may need further shrewd consideration as it must toil with the potential paradox posed by aligning principles endorsing a holistic account of Health and Wellbeing goals as part of CfE, with the performance orientations ('effective performance in challenging contexts') that have underpinned pupil engagement in previous versions of HSPE. The early drafts of the new awards ('works in progress' during 2011–12) tend to re-illustrate such parallel Physical Education universes, with pupil performance-driven knowledge targeted more explicitly than might have been anticipated in a culture promoting health and wellbeing. How becoming 'successful', 'confident', 'responsible' and 'effective' (the adjectives defining CfE 'capacities') is realised in the era of National Awards will be a challenging brief, particularly with regard to convincing teachers that changes are necessitated, when they, paradoxically perhaps, have become defensive about current courses that had initially been doubted.

SPORT AS PART OF SCHOOL LIFE: VARIOUS TALES OF LEGACY

Reference to sport *per se* in curriculum documentation in Scotland has been relatively sparse. It is present by implication, as in the performance improvement orientations of HSPE, but more merely as something that was assumed to occur in the extended curriculum, possibly as inter-school sport. The acknowledgement of sport and its place in Health and Wellbeing experiences and outcomes (although somewhat confusingly wrapped up with 'physical activity') may be welcome by Physical Education teachers whose background and philosophies tend inherently to reflect a sports tradition. Self-evidently, it also takes account of the very current engagement of the UK in hosting major World Championship, and Olympic and Commonwealth Games events such that it is hard to avoid the landscape of sport in the life and culture of these times – even the Queen's Christmas message of 2010 referred positively to the essential 'goodness' potentially involved in playing sports. In Scotland, the introduction of a Minister for Commonwealth Games and Sport sitting at the table of government is not without significance in fulfilling the 'transforming legacy' for youth sports participation envisioned and championed in the awarding of such major events. However, the notion that sport should be part of an active lifestyle for young people has been a continual clarion call from sports governing bodies to schools for over thirty years, the point in history at which teachers gradually began to withdraw from the volunteerism that supported extra-curricular school sport. With a review of teachers' contracted obligations (during 2011) unable to find formally for a return to such schoolteacher support of school sport, it leaves pupil sport uptake provision reliant on the additions government and local authority have initiated. This, since 2004, has largely centred on the Active Schools programme with Exchequer grant aid overseen by Sportscotland across thirty-two local authorities who, in turn, manage and deploy coordinators (in excess of 600) charged with fostering purposeful further school-based physical activity that befits context and situation ('more people, more places, more often'). Invariably it could embrace sports and the establishing of pathways to nurture participation, but also schemes promoting healthy eating, active travel (to school) and playtime/lunchtime activities. School sport participation itself has seen financial endorsement from banks, supermarket chains and the armed services, while national governing bodies of sport have been recently reminded that the claims for an enduring legacy must embrace their own efforts to nurture youth sport engagement in order to raise overall participation figures on which, significantly, their own funding future will be dependent.

The issues of 'legacy' arising out of the Olympic campaign (among others), so eloquently related in recent years, are thus complex for teachers and others to interpret. While some bold initiatives are evident (a 'school of sport', 'sports comprehensives' and Performance Schools in football) and innovative schemes have been lauded ('clubgolf', for example, which aims to introduce golf to every child in Scotland from the age of 9), a policy era of short-term financing invariably raises questions of priorities and the claims of benefit. Where such energies are placed for Active Schools is possibly such a case. As Reid's analysis of the programme details, the expertise and leadership required for the primary targets of the scheme (the inactive, the hard-to-reach groups, such as ethnic minorities, and girls), along with the nature of the activity that might draw children to it, might not be solved by just 'more sport' (Reid, 2009). Tales of an Olympic sport 'legacy' invite a policy balance to be had for those schoolchildren who are enthralled by it but which for others remains a distant and remote category of personal experience.

THINKING AHEAD: 'EYE ON THE BALL'?

Teachers of Physical Education may have been heartened by the government edict recommending the 'two hours for all' timetabled quotient. Practice indicates that it has been hard for local authorities to achieve this in anything like the envisaged timescales for implementation (scathingly reported on by the Scottish Parliament's education committee in 2009; in 2012, the authorities were given £6m in further forms of government funding to bolster the commitment). However, these are arguably minor considerations relative to the thinking that is now required for teachers in dealing with the expectancy, at least, that changes to the curriculum are to be enacted. As others have endorsed, this is a time of opportunity for Physical Education but also one of challenge, particularly in rationalising how such change might be fostered and responded to (Penney, 2008). This might be one reason why HMIE's (2008) portrayal of current practice depicting physical education's fulfilment of the various CfE 'capacities' is misplaced as it anticipates what Priestley (2010) describes as a 'business as usual' approach in dealing with change. Priestley's representation of how CfE might be audited, pitching existing practice against the prescriptions of experiences and outcomes, invokes what he describes as a 'tick-the-box approach, which will result only in changes to terminology, while (classroom) practices continue pretty much in their present form' (2010, p. 28). Whether or not this is the case for Physical Education will depend very much on the way Health and Wellbeing is to be developed, given that for many schools management under faculty arrangements will demand reviewed perspectives on how pupil content is organised, prepared for and assessed. For Physical Education teachers in schools genuinely committed to the holistic intentions associated with Health and Wellbeing agendas there will invariably be an issue of sharing content knowledge and appropriate pedagogies with other subject colleagues. As with the era of certification for Physical Education, it cannot be assumed that current teacher knowledge is sufficiently robust in adjusting to CfE experiences and outcomes of Health and Wellbeing. Cale and Harris (2011), in an overview of research into such school-based intervention programmes, pursue the point that pedagogy befitting such sensitive targets is not straightforwardly achieved. Their further observation that teachers of Physical Education tend to have a misguided judgement of their own knowledge of health-related fitness 'facts' stands as a stark reminder that, for the subject to thrive in a rapidly changing period of political and professional leadership, it will require a clarity of vision from its teachers to guarantee meaningful educational activity for schoolchildren.

ACKNOWLEDGEMENTS

The author acknowledges the counsel of his colleague Malcolm Thorburn in some earlier drafts of this work.

REFERENCES

Cale, L. and J. Harris (2011) 'Learning about health through physical education and youth sport', in K. Armour (ed.), *Sport Pedagogy – An Introduction for Teaching and Coaching*. Harlow: Pearson Education Limited, pp. 53–64.

Evans, J., E. Rich and B. Davies (2011) 'Critical health pedagogy: whose body is it anyway?', in K. Armour (ed.), *Sport Pedagogy – An Introduction for Teaching and Coaching*. Harlow: Pearson Education Limited, pp. 65–78.

Gard, M. (2011), 'A mediation in which consideration is given to the past and future engagement of social science generally and critical physical education and sports scholarship in particular with various scientific debates, including the so-called "obesity epidemic" and contemporary manifestations of biological determinism', *Sport Education and Society*, 16 (3): 399–412.

Her Majesty's Inspectorate of Education (2008) *Physical Education: A Portrait of Current Practice in Scottish Schools and Pre-school Centres*. Online at www.educationscotland.gov.uk/inspectionandreview/Images/pepcp_tcm4-712857.pdf

Kirk, D. (2010) 'The practice of physical education and the social construction of aims', in R. Bailey (ed.), *Physical Education for Learning: A Guide for Secondary Schools*. London: Continuum, pp. 15–25.

McNamee, M. (2005) 'The nature and values of physical education', in K. Green and K. Hardman (eds) *Physical Education: Essential Issues*. London: Sage, pp. 1–20.

Penney, D. (2008) 'Playing a political game and playing for position: Policy and curriculum development in health and physical education', *European Physical Education Review*, 14 (1): 33–49.

Priestley, M. (2010) 'Curriculum for Excellence: Transformational change or business as usual?', *Scottish Educational Review*, 42 (1): 23–36.

Reid, G. (2009) 'Delivering sustainable practice? A case study of the Scottish Active Schools programme', *Sport, Education and Society*, 14 (3): 353–70.

Scottish Executive (2004) *The Report of the Review Group on Physical Education*. Edinburgh: HMSO.

Thorburn, M. and S. Gray (eds) (2010) *Physical Education – Picking up the Baton*. Edinburgh: Dunedin Academic Press.

70

Physics Education

Kenneth MacMillan

THE CHANGING LANDSCAPE OF PHYSICS COURSES

In line with most other subjects, Physics qualifications in the upper years of Scottish secondary education are undergoing a process of unprecedented change. Standard Grade, Access 3, Intermediate 1 and Intermediate 2 qualifications are all being replaced. An altered Access 3 course (now entitled National 3) and newly created National 4 and National 5 exams are being introduced for S4 students in session 2013–14. The new Revised Higher course was made available for early adoption by centres during the 2011–12 academic year, but this will be dual-run with the pre-existing Higher course at least until the 2015 exam diet. At the time of writing, proposed amendments to the Advanced Higher course are at an early stage, with the new course due to commence in the 2015–16 academic year.

A SCIENCE STRATEGY FOR SCOTLAND

The Scottish Government's primary aims for science education in Scottish schools at the beginning of the twenty-first century were outlined in a document entitled *A Science Strategy for Scotland* (see www.scotland.gov.uk/Resource/Doc/158401/0042918.pdf). These were to lay the foundations for the development of Scotland's future scientists and to give everyone the skills and confidence to act as informed and questioning citizens in relation to scientific issues. The authors of the new National 4 and 5 courses and the Revised Higher and Advanced Higher courses in Physics would argue that these courses seek to achieve these aims. The extent to which this may be true will be examined in this chapter.

In 1988, Standard Grade Physics replaced the Ordinary Grade course, which was thought to be too abstract and difficult for many pupils. In essence, it was intended to inform pupils regarding the uses of Physics in the modern world and to make the subject more accessible to a wider audience through the introduction of an 'applications-led' approach and through bi-level assessment. The 'applications-led' approach sought to increase the appeal of Physics to pupils by emphasising its usefulness and the ways in which it impacted on their everyday lives.

The National Qualifications (NQs) were introduced in 1999, at which time the opportunity was taken to alter the content of both the Higher and the Certificate of Sixth Year Studies course (which was renamed as Advanced Higher). Some more up-to-date Physics was introduced into both syllabuses, but they remained intended primarily for the development of future scientists. The Intermediate 1 NQ course was originally designed as a basic course to allow pupils in S5 or S6 to pick up Physics if they had not studied it at Standard Grade, while the Intermediate 2 course was intended as a 'stepping-stone' between Standard Grade and Higher. However, since the content and style of the Intermediate 2 course mirrors that of the Higher course much more closely than the Standard Grade, increasing numbers of schools offered Intermediate 2 to their S3 and S4 pupils in the latter years of their availability (see below).

The National 4 and 5 exams replace the Standard Grade, Intermediate 1 and Intermediate 2 Physics courses, while the Access 3 course has been updated as National 3. Standard Grade will cease to be available after session 2012–13. Intermediate 1 and 2 will run alongside their replacement qualifications at least until the end of the 2015 exam diet.

The new National 3 and National 4 courses will be internally assessed by schools. The simpler National 3 course is comprised of three units and seeks to study everyday applications of Physics and its effect on society. The National 4 course provides a progression route from National 3, and is equivalent to a General level award at Standard Grade or an Intermediate 1 qualification, but with the extra requirement of an Added Value Unit consisting of a short project.

Like the Standard Grade Credit level and Intermediate 2 Physics courses that it replaces, the National 5 course utilises a final summative external exam. A new feature is an assignment that requires students to produce a report on an investigation for external assessment. A list of 'mandatory knowledge' statements (which have been widely criticised by teachers for a lack of sufficient detail) summarise the required learning outcomes for each of the three units in the new course. The content bears more similarity to the Intermediate 2 course than the Standard Grade, although some content has been dropped. For example, the content of the 'Waves and Radiations' unit does not include ray diagrams, the power of a lens equation and the operation of nuclear reactors from Intermediate 2. More controversially, some material has been moved down from the Higher, such as the gas laws and kinetic model which are included in the 'Electricity and Energy' unit. The third unit of the new syllabus, 'Dynamics and Space', mirrors much of the mechanics material from the Intermediate 2 course but momentum is no longer covered.

The transfer of material from the previous Higher was intended to increase the academic rigour of the National 5 course. However, the Intermediate 2 course was already perceived as being difficult by many of the S3 and S4 pupils who studied it. The introduction of conceptually demanding material, while replacing only some relatively straightforward content, runs the risk of making the new course too difficult. The addition of the new assignment also makes the new course more time-constrained than its predecessors.

In comparison with the pre-existing Higher Physics course (which will continue to be examined until at least session 2014–15) the Higher Physics (Revised) specifications have some additional content and an entirely new project-based unit called 'Researching Physics', bringing it into line with the National 4 and 5 requirements. The three taught units in the Revised course ('Electricity', 'Our Dynamic Universe' and 'Particles and Waves') introduce several new topics including Hubble's Law, the big bang theory, containment in nuclear fusion reactors and the Standard Model of fundamental particles. In addition, special relativity and the right-hand rule for charged particles in a magnetic field have been brought in from the Advanced Higher course, as has the Doppler Effect to explain the red-shift of galaxies. Lasers and analogue electronics have been removed from the previous Higher course, but given the new material that has been added, these changes almost certainly mean that the already crowded curriculum is now even more tightly packed.

The new content at Higher level is evidently intended to help students to appreciate some more up-to-date aspects of Physics. The recent newsworthy work at CERN has undoubtedly prompted the inclusion of some particle physics and the Standard Model. There has also been a clear attempt to satisfy students' appetite for astronomy which is being fuelled by the plethora of current television programmes that seek to discuss and popularise this field. However, given the lack of experimental work which is possible in the classroom concerning astronomy, particle physics and general relativity, this new content runs the risk of disengaging students. This is of concern because research by Sneddon et al. (2009) highlighted that Higher and Advanced Higher students broadly appreciated the practical aspects of Physics. Her Majesty's Inspectorate of Education (HMIE) (2008) also emphasised the importance of experimental work in nurturing successful learners at all stages of school education.

The Scottish Executive's 2006 progress report on *A Science Strategy for Scotland* outlined the Scottish Government's intentions to keep the curriculum updated and relevant. The introduction of the new National courses, along with the Revised Higher and Advanced Higher courses, appears to fulfil this aim. What remains to be seen is whether or not these additions prove to be capable of nurturing interest in the subject among upper secondary students or simply result in putting them off by confronting them with what they perceive to be overly complex and theoretical content.

An examination of the Curriculum for Excellence (CfE) experiences and outcomes, along with the content of the new courses, demonstrates progression of Physics ideas and concepts. Therefore, in relation to the government's stated aims for science education, the new courses are attempting to lay the foundations for the development of Scotland's future scientists. Whether the crowded content will allow Physics teachers the time to fulfil the second aim, that of giving their students the skills and confidence to act as informed, questioning citizens in relation to scientific issues, is perhaps less obvious.

UPTAKE AND SUCCESS RATES

The number of pupils who took Standard Grade Physics up until 2011 remained high despite the growth in Intermediate 2 (see below). The percentage of candidates gaining an overall Credit level award in the years 2007–11 was around 59 per cent (although it dipped to just 50 per cent in 2010) while the percentage awarded a General level award remained at about 30 per cent over the same period. However, a closer examination of the data reveals that while the grade boundary scores for the knowledge and understanding element were relatively static in the expected region of 70 per cent for a grade 1 and 50 per cent for a grade 2, those for the problem-solving element were more varied. In 2009, only 62 per cent was needed for a grade 1, and just 40 per cent for a grade 2. These figures suggest that students are continuing to find problem solving a particularly difficult skill to master.

The Access 3 course has attracted just over a thousand candidates annually in the period 2006–11. The Intermediate 1 uptake over the same period showed a continued steady increase. The pass rate for Access 3 increased to 83 per cent in both 2010 and 2011, having been around 71 per cent in the previous three years, and just 57 per cent in 2006. The pass rate for Intermediate 1 averaged around 70 per cent with a peak of 76 per cent in 2009 but a dip to just 55 per cent in 2007.

The figures in Table 70.1 below show that the number of pupils taking Intermediate 2

Table 70.1   Number of entries for examinations, at several levels in Physics, by year

Year	Int 1	S Grade	Int 2	Higher	Adv. Higher
2011	2,721	14,442	4,083	9,445	1,748
	(+4.3%)	(−0.9%)	(+4.6%)	(+4.8%)	(+1.0%)
2010	2,608	14,571	3,905	9,014	1,730
	(+2.0%)	(−1.4%)	(+2.9%)	(+0.1%)	(+13.4%)
2009	2,557	14,780	3,796	9,001	1,525
	(+7.5%)	(−3.3%)	(+8.8%)	(+2.7%)	(+8.7%)
2008	2,379	15,299	3,488	8,765	1,403
	(+13.7%)	(−4.0%)	(+4.1%)	(+2.1%)	(+1.7%)
2007	2,092	15,940	3,352	8,582	1,380
	(+13.4%)	(−6.6%)	(+26.7%)	(−0.4%)	(−4.0%)
2006	1,845	17,064	2645	8,617	1,437
	(+19%)	(+0.9%)	(+12.4%)	(−3.7%)	(+0.8%)

has been steadily increasing, primarily because of a rising preference for this over Standard Grade Physics. The overall pass rates have been around 70 per cent since 2007, having jumped up from a worrying figure of just 55 per cent in 2006, and peaking at 78 per cent in 2008. This suggests that teachers had made good use of the opportunity to deepen pupils' understanding afforded by spreading the course over two years. It is nonetheless concerning that around 20 per cent of each cohort failed to gain an award. It would therefore appear that the warning by HMIE (2005) that too many pupils are 'taking and failing NQ courses because they are at a level which is too demanding for them, based on their prior achievement' (p. 36) is still not being heeded carefully enough.

The number of students taking Higher Physics in the period 2001–6 was in decline. This trend continued until 2007, but was reversed in 2008 as the number of Higher Physics candidates increased each year thereafter until 2011, as shown below in Table 70.1. Note that the percentage change from the previous year is shown in brackets.

Along with a typical pass of rate of around 75 per cent, these figures are encouraging, although it is not clear what has caused this welcome change. It is possible that the subject has been popularised by the recent increased level of television exposure afforded by programmes such *Bang goes the Theory* and the numerous documentaries narrated by the youthful-looking Professor Brian Cox may be having a positive effect.

Between 2006 and 2011 uptake at Advanced Higher also improved, increasing each year apart from 2007. The pass rates remained encouraging throughout that time period with percentages all in the upper 70s. A report by the Higher Education Academy Physical Science Centre (2009) showed that the number of students entering Physics undergraduate courses throughout the UK had risen by around 1,000 over the seven years to 2007. Therefore it appears that the increasing uptake in Advanced Higher Physics is feeding through into the Higher Education sector after several years of concern about the uptake of Physics at UK universities.

LEARNING AND TEACHING

The most recent report on learning and teaching in the sciences by HMIE (2008) identified significant strengths. These included the finding that many secondary students were being exposed to a wide range of learning experiences in science which were appropriate to their needs. Teachers were also commended for ensuring that the pace and challenge of lessons was appropriate and that the relevance of the topics was emphasised to maintain the students' interest and motivation. The report also detailed several ways in which the learning and teaching process could be improved. Several of these details are particularly pertinent to the teaching of Physics.

Successive Scottish Qualifications Authority (SQA) External Assessment Reports for the different levels of Physics courses have continued to commend pupils for their ability to execute numerical calculations successfully. However, the feedback also highlights ongoing concerns about candidates' very poor proficiency in writing qualitative responses that demonstrate clear understanding, using technically correct terminology. Recent reports have warned that the need for candidates to give qualitative responses including descriptions and explanations is likely to become increasingly important in future assessments. Unfortunately, it still appears that insufficient classroom time is devoted to helping pupils to build up their understanding of Physics and to develop the ability to explain the concepts accurately. HMIE (2008) provided guidance on two strategies that could be of benefit in tackling this. First, it commended taking time to develop students' literacy skills. Second, the report emphasised the value of giving students opportunities to work collaboratively and to discuss their ideas, experiences and learning. However, the HMIE report noted that very often students were not given sufficient time to talk in groups or as individuals to hone these important skills. Teachers were therefore encouraged to use debates and discussions as a means of helping students to consider the social, moral and ethical impact of scientific endeavour.

The HMIE report also commented that secondary students were often relatively inactive in their learning and that teacher explanations tended to dominate in the classroom. The criticism that Physics teachers, in particular, have a tendency to utilise a highly transmissive pedagogy is not new, as the previous edition of this chapter commented on other similar findings. The advent of the new examinations, in their content-heavy form, is likely to exacerbate this problem and make the task of successfully addressing it all the more difficult.

The report sought to highlight strategies to address these concerns, without necessarily requiring extra classroom time. The use of more constructivistic pedagogies in teaching Physics, including making connections between Physics, other subjects and everyday experiences, was advocated. Teachers' use of questioning to consolidate learners' knowledge was commended, but the importance of good questioning to encourage greater thinking, understanding and reasoning was emphasised. A greater use of experimental work was also encouraged, particularly where this involved giving students greater responsibility for devising and carrying out experimental procedures to investigate and solve problems. This provides opportunities for students and teachers to discuss underlying Physics principles, but the pressure to simply 'get the results' and move on can mean that valuable opportunities to improve pupils' understanding are lost.

THE WAY AHEAD

The somewhat vague nature of the CfE experiences and outcomes in Science has been disconcerting for many teachers who have historically been familiar with a much more prescriptive curriculum. The supposedly less cluttered curriculum, with an increased emphasis on skills rather than knowledge, was intended to improve the way that Science, including Physics, is taught in lower secondary. This was argued to be a consequence of its more flexible, pupil-centred approach, with the stated intention of encouraging a greater depth of understanding. Given this rhetoric, it is ironic that the new National courses and Revised Higher are at least as prescriptive and more overcrowded than their predecessors. The level of prescription is partly an inevitable consequence of the need to produce a final examination which is accessible to all students throughout Scotland. However, the evident mismatch between the underlying teaching methodologies encouraged by the CfE approach in lower secondary and those required for the time-constrained, exam-driven courses in upper secondary is rather stark. Events over the next few years will determine whether or not the development of the new courses has missed an opportunity to deal with the significant issues that continue to be problematic in the teaching and learning of Physics.

REFERENCES

Her Majesty's Inspectorate of Education (2005) *Improving Achievement in Science in Primary and Secondary School.* Edinburgh: HMIE.

Her Majesty's Inspectorate of Education (2008) *Science. A Portrait of Current Practice in Scottish Schools.* Edinburgh: HMIE.

Higher Education Academy Physical Science Centre (2009) *Review of the Student Learning Experience in Physics 2008.* Online at www.heacademy.ac.uk/assets/ps/documents/subject_reviews/physrev_final.pdf

Sneddon, P., K. Slaughter and N. Reid (2009) 'Perceptions, views and opinions of university students about physics learning during practical work at school', *European Journal of Physics*, 30 (5): 1119–30.

71

Religious and Moral Education

Graeme Nixon

THE HISTORICAL BACKGROUND

The relationship between religion and education in Scotland imagined by John Knox in 1560, whereby reading was a means to salvation, may have led to the formation of parish schools and contributed much to the Scottish educational myth of egalitarian access to learning. One could even argue that the religious dynamism of the Protestant reformers produced an educational climate in which Scotland would more than punch above its weight throughout the Enlightenment and industrial revolution. However, throughout the nineteenth and twentieth centuries and in the early years of the twenty-first century, there have been social and educational changes in Scotland that have led to a diminishing of the role of religion in schools, and a metamorphosis of the subject area into something that would add velocity to Knox's already spinning coffin. The 1872 Education Act, which sought to preserve 'Religious Instruction', was designed to safeguard the Christian ethos of Scottish schools once education became the concern of the state and in the face of growing secular voices (Paterson, 2000). The primary legislation enshrined in 1872 continues to underlie Religious and Moral Education (RME), where the subject remains a legal requirement.

The move to a non-confessional, philosophical approach to RME gathered momentum in the 1970s and 1980s as teachers themselves sought credibility for RME in secondary schools by putting in place the same criteria for educational validity established for other subjects (Hannah, 2007). A new kind of religious literacy was advocated and argued for in policy documents in which RME could no longer be a superficial grasp of the phenomena of religion. Nor could it be an understanding of ritual and confession from the inside. In non-denominational RME since the publication of the Millar Report (SED, 1972), religious literacy has taken the form of recognition of the universality of certain questions about the nature of existence and meaning. To this extent religious literacy became a subset of philosophical literacy, an empathetic understanding in pupils of the ubiquity of these questions and a commitment to working out their own responses to them.

The individualistic emphasis on the personal quest or search required skills of discernment and criticality. The desire for educational credibility manifested itself primarily in a desire for national certification from the early 1980s onwards. At the same time the multicultural, increasingly secular and technological reality of life in Scotland was being reflected in the RME classroom. The multi-faith presentation of faiths and non-religious stances demanded the teaching of evaluative skills for pupils. In a way, as soon as RME became a non-confessional presentation of diverse views of reality (religious or otherwise) the subject would employ increasingly philosophical skills and content. As soon as Christianity was no longer taught as normative, philosophical skills would be a necessary component of RME pedagogy. The study of non-Semitic religion, particularly Buddhism, would offer exemplification that morality and supernaturalistic, theistic religion need not be conflated; a view that had increasing currency in an increasingly non-religious zeitgeist. In turn non-religious traditions would be recognised as areas to be included in the RME curriculum. The increasing emphasis on morality also demanded that teachers adopt the lexicon of moral philosophy, particularly as advances in technology represented challenges to traditional ways of moral decision making.

The move towards certification increasingly in statutory core time and not as an elective meant that the majority of departments were effectively engaging pupils in moral philosophy at a younger age. Into the 1990s and 2000s this process gained further momentum. The creation of Higher Still Religious, Moral and Philosophical Studies (RMPS) National Qualifications (1999) represented the formal recognition of philosophy in Religious Education. When in 2003 the Scottish Qualifications Authority (SQA) reviewed national qualifications in RMPS because of assessment anomalies, it also looked at the inclusion of philosophy in the subject. Consultation revealed that the majority of RME teachers were not only in favour of its inclusion, but that many described their approach to RME/RMPS as 'philosophical' from S1 to S6.

CURRENT PROVISION AND TRENDS

Research by Nixon (2011) reveals that typically in Scottish secondary schools in first to fourth years, pupils study a wide range of religious traditions, moral issues and units introducing RME as a subject area. Table 71.1 summarises this.

This research, which was based on 126 responses to a national survey by secondary RME departments, shows that in S1 and S2 of respondent schools, 710 units of work were offered. Of these units, 479 (67 per cent) were explicitly about religion with 136 about Christianity; 197 discrete units on each of the five other world religions outlined in the curricular guidelines; eighty-five thematic units on religious topics using material from a range of traditions; fifty-two introductory units; and nine units about other religious traditions not considered in the curricular guidance, such as primal religion and ancient Greek and Egyptian traditions.

The other units of work offered by departments in S1 and S2 included seventy-eight focused on a range of moral issues; fifty-two on philosophy and philosophy of religion; thirty-six on 'personal search' and sixty on a wide range of topics including the supernatural, life after death and critical thinking skills.

Table 71.1   S1–S4 Religious Education provision

Stage	Number of units, courses	Religion	Charity	Personal search	Ethics and moral philosophy	Philosophy	Other
S1/2	710	479 (67%)	5 (0.07%)	36 (5%)	78 (11%)	52 (7%)	60 (9%)
S3/4	367	68 (19%)	0	0	191 (52%)	53 (14%)	56 (15%)

SCOTTISH EDUCATION

In S3 and S4 of the respondent secondary schools, 367 units of work or courses were offered. Of these 188 were certificate courses offered within the Scottish Qualifications Authority (SQA); the remaining 179 courses were non-certificate. It should be stated that many schools offered a blend of certificate and non-certificate material as part of their S3–S4 curriculum.

In S3 and S4, sixty-eight units were discrete studies of particular religions as suggested by the SQA National Qualifications framework or non-certificate study of other religious traditions (for example Rastafarianism, New Religions and Wicca). Units on Ethics and Moral Philosophy numbered 191 of those studied in S3–S4. Of these, 106 were SQA certificate units in RMPS or Philosophy. The others contained courses looking at specific moral issues (for example, animal rights, racism and medical ethics) or philosophical issues (for example metaphysics, belief and science, and philosophy in the media).

From the 1980s, RME departments increasingly offered nationally certificated units in core time. This continued into the 1990s and 2000s. Although Higher Still (1999) was created as a post-16 framework of qualifications, many RME departments, quickly after its introduction, began to offer discrete intermediate RMPS units from the SQA National Qualifications suite at S3–S4 level rather than courses. In 2010, across Scotland 35,595 RMPS units were offered discretely in Scottish schools, predominantly in S3 and S4 core RME time, rather than as an elective (SQA, 2010b). The majority (25,503) of these concern morality and values. Only 4,820 of the total units concerned the study of a selected world religion. The remaining units (5,272) covered material such as the relationship between religion and science, the nature of belief and the existence of God. The prevalence of units dealing with moral philosophy, philosophy of religion and philosophy of science (30,775 out of 35,595), rather than the discrete study of a world religion, is marked.

During the SQA exam diet for session 2009–10, 3,203 pupils were presented for Higher RMPS (SQA, 2010b). Although this number is not yet close to those in comparable social subjects (in 2009–10 Higher Modern Studies had 7,385 candidates), it does represent a year-by-year increase in uptake. For example, there has been an increase of 1,097 pupils taking RMPS Higher since session 2007–8. This represents a 52 per cent increase in uptake over a period of three years.

Various views as to the growth of certificated RME have been posited. These have included those who argue for an enduring interest in religion and spirituality that may counter the apparent rise of the secular state (McKinney, quoted in Denholm, 2007). Other views, found in the Toledo guidelines for the teaching of Religious Education (OSCE, 2007), discuss unprecedented levels of public discourse about religious matters in the wake of 9/11; mass migration of peoples; environmental concerns; and increasing pluralism as factors that may explain the currency of RME at this time.

One aspect of Nixon's research (2011) is that there may be a correlation between the popularity of the subject and departments that have rebranded themselves 'RMPS'. Interestingly, of those departments who replied that they had no elective uptake, the majority (eighteen out of twenty-one) entitled themselves RE or RME. Perhaps, therefore, we should be careful in suggesting that increasing uptake represents enduring interest in religion *per se*; rather it may be indicative that the subject itself has evolved to accommodate the interests of a perhaps less religious, but no less questioning, pupil population. Indeed, in the author's research, RMPS is the title favoured by the largest group of respondent departments for the subject at all levels. These departments supported this title, stating that this mirrors what the subject has become: an inclusive, dialogic approach where religion represents but one amongst other approaches to morality, metaphysics and meaning.

CURRICULUM FOR EXCELLENCE

Curriculum for Excellence (CfE), in many ways, seems to support RME. The emphasis on exploring values, the development of critical thinking skills and the ongoing recognition of RME as one of the eight curricular areas all serve to protect the subject. CfE therefore seeks to elevate formally what has been central to effective RME practice to the level of the entire curriculum. This includes allowing pupils to rehearse moral decisions; address controversial issues; deal with different and apparently conflicting claims; and consider the nature of reliable knowledge in an age that is rich in information and perhaps poor in wisdom.

The non-denominational experiences and outcomes for RME (LTS, 2011), and the accompanying Principles and Practice paper, seek to continue these traditions in the subject. Significant developments also include outcomes at all levels relating to:

- Christianity as a line of development separate from other religious traditions to reflect the influence of Christianity on Scotland, thereby developing cultural literacy;
- the place of religion in Scottish society and the benefits and challenges of being religious in modern Scotland;
- the interface between belief and action, allowing pupils to examine and apply their ethical and/or religious beliefs in the school and its wider community;
- continued support for the personal search methodology, albeit as infused rather than as explicit as was the case in the 5–14 Guidelines.

Unsurprisingly, in the development of these experiences and outcomes, a number of issues of contention arose. Key issues related to the apparent privileging of Christianity in the RME curriculum and parochialism in confining study to the 'Scottish context' (and suspicions of politicisation). With regard to the first point, the response of the Scottish Interfaith Council, among others, to the proposed maintenance of the phrase '*other* world religions' (which was the strand in the 5–14 Curriculum) in the outcomes is perhaps most noteworthy. In their minds, this perpetuated a 'them and us' approach to the study of religion (conflating the educational provider with Christianity and giving Christianity a degree of narrative privilege).

Other responses to the consultation argued that setting Christianity apart in this manner is helpful neither to Christianity (in that many will reject such an emphasis) nor to the cause of RME which should be an open, philosophical study of religion and belief. Cultural literacy is irrelevant (or even counterproductive) to such a study or should perhaps reside in the History classroom. In any case, the outcome of these discussions was to drop the word 'other' from the curricular guidelines.

A further aspect of CfE is the attempt to develop interdisciplinary approaches, perhaps facilitated by the move towards faculty-style management structures. One issue this raises relates to the conscience clause and how to police it when pupil learning may, for example, in a thematic unit include geography, history, politics, and religious and moral beliefs. Hopefully this problem may hasten the view that the conscience clause is not only impractical, but also, in a non-confessional curriculum that is attempting to recognise the interrelated nature of knowledge and belief, an anachronism.

As stated previously, RME has evolved since the 1970s away from a confessional or pre-scriptive approach; this is perhaps best seen in the adoption of philosophy and philosophical approaches in the subject. In this regard, RME teachers are professionally conditioned to be wary of confessional approaches. Arguably CfE is guilty of this in its drive to create active citizens and uncritical assumption of certain pro-social values which, though wholly commendable, need to be arrived at by pupils rather than set in stone (or the parliamentary mace) from the outset.

The danger is perhaps therefore not institutional prejudice, but institutionalised moral-ity. Nowhere is this issue more apparent than in one of the bullet points associated with the active citizen capacity, where it states that pupils should 'develop ethical views of complex issues'. Many in the RME profession would regard this as pre-emptive and suggest that the development of 'complex views of ethical issues' is a more sound and desirable outcome that recognises the rational autonomy of the child and indirectly may lead to a deeper ethical understanding than a prescriptive approach would. Perhaps, therefore, RME has lessons for the wider curriculum as it attempts to infuse questions of value and ethics into all subject areas.

OTHER ISSUES

Other developments in RME include the introduction of faculty-style management struc-tures. Anderson and Nixon (2010) outline that RME typically resides in a humanities or social subject faculty and that 'faculty-isation' has taken place in approximately two-thirds of Scotland's local authorities. Responses to their questionnaire suggest that RME may be undergoing a process of marginalisation and that RME staff are feeling increasingly isolated, disenfranchised, overworked and unsupported. Arguments for faculties were principally that they would free up effective teachers to teach and involve them less in administrative tasks. In the CfE era the argument has also been that faculties would facilitate interdiscipli-nary learning. Anderson and Nixon (2010) address these claims thus:

> However, this is an argument that had little space in the key documents leading up to the crea-tion of faculties; where the main arguments given were in terms of giving effective teachers less management responsibilities. The irony here, outlined above, is that many unpromoted staff now have more management responsibilities. (p. 261)

In Anderson and Nixon's paper this contrasted with the experience of the majority of those working in a traditional principal teacher-led department. Only one of the forty-three facul-ties involved in their research was led by an RME specialist, perhaps lending weight to the view that marginalisation is taking place.

A further issue related to faculties is that of subject leadership not just in and between schools but in terms of the direction of RME at a national level. The types of policy evolu-tion in RME documented here would not have taken place but for the prominent role played by principal teachers who were sector-leading practitioners, heading up SQA developments and having a robust role to play in policy making for the subject area. This concern can perhaps be evidenced by the low levels of involvement in consultation being undertaken by the RME profession during the development of the RME experiences and outcomes for CfE. Despite there being nearly 400 secondary schools in Scotland and 2,045 secondary teachers registered in Religious Education, there were only fifty-five returns to the consultation, many of which were from faith groups or non-governmental organisations rather than RME practitioners or departments.

A further issue for schools to consider is that recently school inspectors have been suggesting that schools develop RME core inputs in the senior school, which, strictly speaking, is in line with the statutory position of the subject. For RME departments, deciding what to teach a conscript audience of 17- and 18-year-olds and how to engage them may be problematic. Nevertheless schools are beginning to explore a range of possible inputs in, for example, thinking skills, citizenship and community involvement.

CONCLUSION

These, as always, are interesting times for RME. Recognition and support from CfE, significant increase in uptake for certification and a growing recognition of the worth of RME internationally (as seen in the Council of Europe, Unicef and the Office for Security and Cooperation in Europe) need to be balanced against possible marginalisation and lack of leadership in the subject.

More than other subjects, perhaps, RME may be seen as a barometer of social change. The development towards RMPS evidences this. These developments certainly reflect a more secular and diverse Scotland, but they also perhaps reflect a more individualistic form of spirituality which may or may not be religious. For this reason it remains vital to the success and continued existence of RME that it seeks a more inclusive approach than narrowly to study religion. As stated in this chapter, this has certainly been happening, but nothing would signal this clearer for this writer than in the recognition of RMPS as the subject's title, root and branch, for the twenty-first century.

REFERENCES

Anderson, C. and G. Nixon (2010) 'The move to faculties in Scottish secondary schools: A case study', *School Leadership and Management*, 30 (3): 249–63.

Denholm, A. (2007) 'Resurrection of religion in Scots schools', *Herald Scotland*, 13 August. Online at www.heraldscotland.com/resurrection-of-religion-in-scots-schools-1.863086

Hannah, W. M. (2007) 'An analysis of the development of religious education within the secondary school curriculum and educational thinking, and its reception in the educational world'. Doctoral dissertation, University of Strathclyde.

Nixon, G. (2012) 'The emergence of philosophy in Scottish secondary school religious education'. Doctoral dissertation, University of Aberdeen.

Office for Security and Cooperation in Europe (2007) *Toledo Guiding Principles on Teaching about Religion and Belief in Public Schools*. Warsaw: Office for Democratic Institutions and Human Rights.

Paterson, L. (2000) *Education and the Scottish Parliament*. Edinburgh: Dunedin Academic Press.

Scottish Education Department (1972) *Moral and Religious Education in Scottish Schools* (the Millar Report). Edinburgh: HMSO.

Scottish Qualifications Authority (2010a) *Overview of Qualifications in the Religious and Moral Education Curriculum Area*. See at www.sqa.org.uk/files_ccc/Overview_of_quals_Religious_Moral_Education.pdf

Scottish Qualifications Authority (2010b) *Progress Report: Religious and Moral Education Curriculum Area*. Glasgow: SQA.

72

Science Education

Donald Gray

Science education is at a critical point in time: set in a context of significant global and climatic transformations, it is charged with a key role in preparing citizens and future scientists with the skills and new ways of thinking about techno-scientific innovations and our relationship with our environment. It has been proposed by Steffen et al. (2007) that we are living in a new epoch, the Anthropocene, an age that is characterised by the human impact on the planet and particularly the impact produced by the scale and speed of techno-scientific progress. Clearly there have been many benefits brought to humanity by scientific discoveries and technological progress, but this has been bought at a significant price both to human lives and to ecological stability. There is a growing call for a change to the way in which science is conducted and the values that underpin scientific thinking. Jane Lubchenco (1998), in her presidential address to the American Association for the Advancement of Science, said, 'the world at the close of the 20th century is a fundamentally different world from the one in which the current scientific enterprise has developed'. This statement was reiterated by Peter Raven (2002, p. 958), president four years later, who stated, 'We need new ways of thinking about our place in the world and the ways in which we relate to natural systems in order to be able to develop a sustainable world for our children and grandchildren'. The question is: does our current approach to science education in schools sufficiently prepare young people for a radically new and different way of thinking about science and its relationship with the natural world?

A HISTORICAL PERSPECTIVE

Science in secondary schools continues in the main to be taught as the three separate disciplines of Biology, Chemistry and Physics in the middle and upper stages, although general or integrated science as a discipline has been taught in the lower stages. It was also recognised as a certificate subject with the introduction of Standard Grade in the 1980s. This is, in part, determined and reinforced by the hegemonic control of content through the imposition of separate exams in the three main science areas with some acknowledgement of a general science given, primarily aimed at those who are deemed 'less able' to tackle the three main specialised sciences. There are a number of key stages which can be referred to as the precursors of the current science provision in Scottish schools.

The Scottish Education Department's publication *Primary Education in Scotland* (1965) had addressed the need for science education, but as the Scottish Committee on

Environmental Studies (SCES) report pointed out, 'It soon became clear . . . that most teachers required further guidance in recognising and exploiting good starting points for investigations' (1981, p. 3). Environmental Studies was established in primary schools to give pupils an introduction to the nature and language of science. It was also evident that science had a clear place in S1/S2. In 1969, the Scottish Education Department produced the influential *Curriculum Paper Number 7 – Science for General Education* which heralded a new approach to science in Scottish secondary schools. The S1/S2 course was presented as an integrated science course, an approach that proved to be controversial, not least because its introduction coincided with the establishment of separate science subject departments (HMI, 1994). Since then, integrated science in the first two years of secondary has been the norm rather than the exception. However, while science was recognised as an important component of both the primary and the early secondary curriculum, this focus also highlighted a continuing problem in providing a continuous, coherent and progressive curriculum from primary through to secondary.

Some initiatives did try to grapple with the problem of transition, for example the Science 5/13 Project in the 1970s, sponsored jointly by the Nuffield Foundation, the Schools Council (for England and Wales) and the Scottish Education Department. It was not until much later, however, that there was any attempt to coordinate children's experience of science in primary schools with that in secondary schools. In fact, there was little consideration given to coherent science education in primary schools until the 1980s when SCES published *Towards a Policy for Science in Scottish Primary Schools*. This was later built upon, and the S1/S2 Science curriculum was replaced by the science component of Environmental Studies 5–14s, first published in 1993 with the intention of providing a coherent, continuous and progressive approach to pupils' learning from P1 through to S2. Subsequent reviews of 5–14 were undertaken, and the HMI report *Improving Science Education 5–14* advised changes in the delivery of the science element' it was re-presented in the form of *5–14 National Guidelines – Environmental Studies* (SEED, 2000). The science component of Environmental Studies 5–14 was contained within three attainment outcomes: Living Things and the Processes of Life; Energy and Forces; and Earth and Space.

S3/S4 STANDARD GRADE

Standard Grade emerged from a complex, inter-related set of factors. Comprehensivisation, the raising of the school-leaving age in 1972 and the regrading of the O Grade awards resulted in a significant increase in the number of pupils being presented for the exam. However, that course, the O Grade, had always been designed for the top 30 per cent of the school population and so many who were presented for this exam were not suited for it. Thus, when the new Standard Grade exams came in with the call for 'certification for all', there was a need to re-examine the science courses that were available. Originally, the Standard Grade Science course was seen as an alternative to the three separate disciplines of Biology, Chemistry and Physics. It was the only science subject made available at Foundation, General and Credit levels. The other separate disciplines of Biology, Chemistry and Physics were (until the time of writing) available only at General and Credit levels until the planned cessation of Standard Grade in 2013 to be replaced by the new National Qualifications. Science was intended for those pupils who were considered unable to undertake the other sciences, either for those whose capabilities were deemed to be at

Foundation or General level, or for those whose main interests were in a non-science area but were deemed capable of working at Credit level. Since Science was the only science course that could be taken at Foundation level, it was often seen as the 'easy' option and was recommended for those pupils who found science in S1/2 difficult.

As the HMIE report on *Effective Learning and Teaching in Scottish Secondary Schools: Science* points out, all pupils in S3 and S4 were recommended to study a minimum of 160 hours of science during the two-year period, about 160 minutes per week. This minimum could be met by pupils studying Standard Grade Science or one of the three separate disciplines of Biology, Chemistry or Physics. While many schools have allowed pupils to study two separate sciences, and in some it is possible to study all three, the HMIE report stated that pupils studying Standard Grade Science should not combine this with one of the separate sciences. The reason given was that Standard Grade Science covers major themes drawn from Biology, Chemistry and Physics. Beyond Standard Grade, generic Science is only available at Access level, which is intended for those who found difficulty with Standard Grade but who may wish to consolidate their learning with the intention of proceeding to Scottish Vocational Qualification (SVQ) courses. The nature of the Standard Grade curriculum and the choices available have changed the profile of course choice in the sciences. The *Improving Achievement in Science* (HMIE, 2005) document pointed out that while entries in Standard Grade Biology had increased by 2 per cent from 2000 to 2004, entries in Chemistry, Physics and Science had declined by 7 per cent, 5 per cent and 46 per cent respectively. These decreases, particularly in Science, were accounted for by a substantial increase in numbers of S4 pupils presented for Access and Intermediate courses.

CURRENT DEVELOPMENTS: CURRICULUM FOR EXCELLENCE

Scottish education is in a phase of transition, some would say transformation, from a curriculum that is considered to be a disjointed progression through the older 5–14, Standard Grade and more recent National Qualifications, to one that has more coherence from 3 to 18 and attempts to address criticisms of current science provision in schools not catering for the needs of society, nor providing citizens with the knowledge, understanding and competences to engage with science-related issues in that society. The intention, as stated in the 2004 document *A Curriculum for Excellence*, is to produce 'for the first time ever, a single curriculum 3–18, supported by a simple and effective structure of assessment and qualifications' (p. 4). The ideals are sound but only time will tell whether or not the approach to science in the curriculum can succeed in fulfilling the aims of a coherent and progressive curriculum from 3 to 18 and also provide the kind of science education that can contribute to transforming society from its currently precarious and uncertain state to one which that offers a more sustainable future to new generations.

The science concepts of Curriculum for Excellence have been arranged using five organisers. These are:

- Planet Earth;
- Forces, Electricity and Waves;
- Biological Systems;
- Materials;
- Topical Science.

The finer detail of the content is provided as broadly stated experiences and outcomes. Thus, all the disciplinary science areas covered in the school science curriculum from 3 to 15 are encompassed within the one document. In some respects there has been an attempt at a more interdisciplinary science approach although the three main areas of biology, chemistry and physics are still clearly identifiable within the document. The *Sciences Principles and Practice* (LTS, 2010) document suggests that in the science curriculum a strong emphasis has been placed on the development of understanding and on critical evaluation, with expectations in some areas having been raised, although it does not specify directly what these are. However, the language used in this document betrays an emphasis on the preparation of young people for 'life and work' and the maximising of achievement. The experiences and outcomes of the specific content in the curriculum are set out as lines of development, and progression through these lines is indicated by curriculum levels: early; first; second; third and fourth; and senior phase.

However, it is interesting to note that while the curriculum was originally intended as a 3–18 curriculum, the experiences and outcomes are only specified up to the fourth level, at the end of S3, with no indication of the expectations across the five organisers for the senior phase of S4 to S6, yet the Scottish Qualifications Authority is currently in the process of finalising the new framework for National Qualifications, including those qualifications for the senior phase, without any content for this senior phase having yet been published. One cannot help but feel that, as far as curriculum and assessment is concerned, this is rather like the tail wagging the dog.

As well as the content specified in the curriculum, there is a clear intention to broaden the aims of science education to encompass scientific literacy and a lifelong interest in science. While there is no universal consensus as to what scientific literacy means, the Principles and Practice document provides some clarification by stating it encompasses the development of 'scientific values and respect for living things and the environment', being able to 'assess risk', 'making informed personal decisions and choices', 'expressing opinions', 'developing informed social, moral and ethical views of scientific, economic and environmental issues', being able to read and assess reports from a variety of sources and reflecting critically on these as well as being able to discuss and debate scientific ideas and issues. While there are many aspects of the new curriculum that can be clearly traced back to pre-existing ideas about science and the three separate areas of Biology, Chemistry and Physics, there has been an attempt to inject some new ideas with clearly stated interdisciplinary intentions, an expectation of more learning to take place outside the classroom and more focus on environmental concerns and awareness of socio-scientific issues through the organiser of *Topical Science*.

ASSESSMENT AND NATIONAL QUALIFICATIONS

As with other areas of the new curriculum there is an expectation that a variety of forms of assessment will be used with a greater emphasis on ongoing formative assessment that has a 'focus on children and young people's knowledge and understanding of key scientific concepts in the living, material and physical world, inquiry and investigative skills, scientific analytical and thinking skills, scientific literacy and general attributes' (*Principles and Practice*, p. 5).

Following on from the implementation of Curriculum for Excellence the framework for National Qualifications in Scotland has also been revised. In the proposed new framework

Standard Grade disappears to be replaced by new National Qualifications. General and Credit Standard Grades are replaced by National 4 and National 5 qualifications respectively. Foundation level Standard Grade is to be replaced with revised Access 3 qualifications, to be known as National 3.

In line with the previous conception of general science as a course to be offered to young people who are deemed to be unable to cope with the perceived more demanding disciplinary sciences of Biology, Chemistry and Physics, the new science qualification is to be offered only at SCQF levels 3 and 4, equivalent to the Standard Grade Foundation and General levels.

SUMMARY

In summary, the new Curriculum for Excellence provides an opportunity for a different approach to the teaching of science in schools. However, there are some concerns that the flexibility of the curriculum, alongside an examination system that will probably still be largely focused on the disciplinary sciences and content knowledge, will encourage teachers to do very much as before. There has been an opportunity to move science education in schools in a direction that will address some of the concerns relating to issues of critical concern to humanity's, and the environment's, long-term health and wellbeing, but unless there is a corresponding in-depth and sustained programme of professional development for science education aimed at educators at all levels, from pre-school through to tertiary level, there is a great danger that it will remain very much as the status quo, an opportunity missed.

REFERENCES

Committee on Primary Education (1981) *Towards a Policy for Science in Scottish Primary Schools.* Edinburgh: Moray House College, for the CCC.

Her Majesty's Inspectorate (1994) *Effective Teaching and Learning in Scottish Secondary Schools: The Sciences.* Edinburgh: SOED.

Her Majesty's Inspectorate (2000) *Improving Science Education 5–14.* Edinburgh: SEED.

Her Majesty's Inspectorate of Education (2005) *Improving Achievement in Science.* Edinburgh: Scottish Executive.

Learning and Teaching Scotland (2007) *Engagement Process: Science Experiences and Outcomes. Learning Teaching Scotland.*

Learning and Teaching Scotland (2010) Science: Principles and Practice. Online at www.education-scotland.gov.uk/Images/sciences_principles_practice_tcm4-540396.pdf

Lubchenco, J. (1998) 'Entering the century of the environment: a new social contract for science', *Science,* 279 (5350): 491–7.

Raven, P. H. (2002) 'Science, sustainability and the human prospect', *Science,* 297 (5583): 954–8.

Scottish Committee on Environmental Studies (1981) *Environmental Studies in the Primary School: The Development of a Policy.* Edinburgh: Committee on Primary Education.

Scottish Education Department (1965) *Primary Education in Scotland.* Edinburgh: HMSO.

Scottish Education Department (1969) *Curriculum Paper Number 7 – Science for General Education.* Edinburgh: SED.

Scottish Executive Education Department (2000) *5–14 National Guidelines – Environmental Studies.* Edinburgh: SEED.

Steffen, W., P. J. Crutzen and J. R. McNeill (2007) 'The anthropocene: are humans now overwhelming the great forces of nature?', *AMBIO: A Journal of the Human Environment,* 36 (8): 614–21.

73

Social Sciences Education

Vincent Oates

Since their introduction in 2000, more than 30,000 Higher and Intermediate candidates had, by the 2011 exam diet, been presented in the 'new' Social Science subjects of Psychology, Sociology and Politics. At a time of such dramatic political discourse we should not be surprised that a large number of young Scots, at both school and further education (FE) levels, intrigued perhaps by the concepts of identity, equality and power, have undertaken these 'new' subjects as they examine key issues in Scottish society. If we extend our range of new subjects to include Philosophy, the numbers presented soar beyond 40,000 (see Table 73.1).

DEFINING THE SOCIAL SCIENCES

Defining key terms is critical in this increasingly crowded curriculum area. The Social Sciences are not to be confused with the Social Subjects of History, Geography and Modern Studies. For the purpose of this chapter they are defined as including Psychology, Sociology, Politics and Philosophy, four of the twenty-four new subjects extending choice

Table 73.1 Number of awards in years 2001, 2005, 2006, 2010 and 2011 (pre-appeal)

Subject	Level	2001	2005	2006	2010	2011
w	Adv Higher		6			
	Higher	1,186	2,812	2,627	3,293	3,517
	Int.2		491	543	684	673
	Int.1		116	197		
Sociology	Adv Higher		8	4		
	Higher	378	635	617	895	982
	Int.2		156	183	179	233
	Int.1		21	23		
Politics	Adv Higher					
	Higher	8	76	75	202	302
	Int. 2					
	Int.1					
Philosophy	Adv Higher	5	15	17		
	Higher	446	800	797	914	912
	Int. 2	249	161	138	300	312
	Int.1					

which were introduced as Highers in 2000. Long established and successful in English schools and colleges, and immensely popular at undergraduate levels in Scottish universities, in twelve short years they have become well established and successful in Scotland. Hundreds of Scotland's teachers and lecturers present thousands of Social Science students each year for the Scottish Qualifications Authority (SQA) examinations. Given an almost total absence of professional support, this is a significant achievement. Many Modern Studies teachers, for example, well qualified academically, have played a dominant role in the expansion of Sociology at school level, though they have been slower to identify with and support developments in Politics. The impressive and sustained growth in Philosophy is almost entirely due to the enthusiastic commitment of schoolteachers of Religious and Moral Education. Psychology, on the other hand, owes its initial success to the expertise and support offered by FE colleagues. Many school students of Psychology travel to their local college, though in-school provision is growing. Tribute should be paid to the success, often overlooked, of the interface between schools and colleges which has characterised the growth of the Social Sciences. The contribution of colleagues in the FE sector in particular, as assessors, facilitators and teachers, cannot be overstated.

During this period of growth, quality assurance has been a source of concern for leading practitioners in each subject area as well as for the SQA. Initially, there was no scrutiny of teacher subject expertise. This legitimate concern was, to an extent, addressed by the publication in December 2005 of the *Framework on Professional Recognition* by the General Teaching Council for Scotland (GTCS). The impact of these new teaching pathways in the development of the Social Sciences has already been significant. Any registered teacher with eighty points in a Social Science subject can, with the support of their headteacher (who is their 'assessor of competence'), undertake an agreed programme of continuing professional development (CPD) and begin teaching that subject right away. A recent enquiry by an experienced teacher of English illustrates the new opportunities for any teacher. Her degree at Edinburgh University included two years' study in each of Psychology and Sociology. Since she took three subjects, each year being worth a total of 120 points, she has the necessary eighty points required to teach both Psychology and Philosophy under Professional Recognition. From August 2007, all new presenting centres in Psychology and Philosophy were required by the SQA to confirm that presenting teachers and lecturers met the GTCS approval criteria of eighty points, equivalent to SCQF level 8. Interestingly, under Professional Recognition, some FE lecturers of Psychology have already received accreditation and have now moved to local authorities and are employed as schoolteachers delivering Psychology to school clusters. The situation regarding verification in Sociology and Politics remains more indeterminate given the power that headteachers now have to initiate in-school developments. The fact that the adventurous spirit of Scotland's headteachers has been an important factor in driving the Social Sciences forward should be recognised (Oates, 2006). The issue of accreditation, however, is still of concern to professionals in the subject areas, especially Psychology. It should be noted that in all schools the headteacher is responsible for managing the introduction of a 'new' Social Science and for monitoring the integrity of subject delivery.

CURRICULAR PROVISION 2011–12

Modern Studies teachers easily identified with the Higher course structure for both Sociology and Politics. Sociology had three mandatory units. Studying Human Society analysed and evaluated sociological theories and research methods. Understanding Human Society was split into two parts covering a range of topics including the sociology of class stratification, of education, of the family, of welfare and poverty, of crime and deviance, and of the mass media. A similar approach in Politics covered Political Theory, Political Structures and Political Representation. A different weighting was evident in Philosophy. Here the four mandatory units related to Critical Thinking, Metaphysics, Epistemology and Moral Philosophy. Major aspects of the Higher Psychology course incorporated Understanding the Individual, and Cognitive and Physiological Psychology, while Investigating Behaviour incorporated research methods. The Individual in the Social Context was set within the domains of Social Psychology and the Psychology of Individual Differences. Advanced Higher is no longer an option for any Social Science. It was effectively withdrawn by the SQA in 2007. Low presentation numbers meant that no economic case could be made for its continuation.

CURRICULAR PROVISION POST-AUGUST 2012

Under Curriculum for Excellence (CfE), significant changes will affect each of the four subjects in terms of curriculum and assessment provision. Reflecting the aims, values and principles of CfE, the design of the new qualifications will incorporate a more skills-based, less prescriptive and more user-friendly approach. In Psychology, Philosophy and Sociology, all of which come under the aegis of 'Health and Wellbeing', courses will be offered at both National 5 and Higher levels, based on a notional 160 hours of study. To provide progression, units will be presented in each subject in hierarchies to reflect a common and sequential structure. The difference between National 5 and Higher normally lies in the degree of difficulty.

Psychology at National 5 comprises a three-unit structure related to Research, Mind and Behaviour, and The Social Context, where knowledge and understanding of Psychology and thinking and research skills are developed . Seventy-five per cent of marks are allocated to the final exam while 25 per cent go to an assignment. At Higher there will be a parallel three-unit structure with assessment based on a question paper worth 70 per cent and 30 per cent allocated to the assignment. Philosophy at both National 5 and Higher will have a similar three-unit structure related to Arguments in Action, The Nature of Knowledge and Moral Philosophy. With Sociology, the three units refer to Human Societies, Culture and Identity, and Social Issues. Assessment requirements in both subjects mirror the situation in Psychology. Politics, which comes under the aegis of Social Studies (Society), will only be offered at Higher level. Its three-nit specification requires study of Political Parties and Elections, Political Systems, and Political Theory.

CURRENT TEACHING PRIORITIES

Across the four subjects, teachers and lecturers identify two areas of concern. First, they require time and support to become familiar with the new curriculum and assessment arrangements. Fortunately effective organisations exist within the various subject communities to encourage networking and mutual support, such as the Association for the Teaching of Psychology in Scotland (see www.atps.org.uk). This is especially important for the many Social Science teachers who work in single-teacher departments. Second, and more urgently, those who teach seek regular and effective CPD to assist subject delivery in the context of CfE in three key areas:

- updated knowledge of current developments and thinking related to their subject;
- raised awareness of sharing good practice with regard to National 5 and Higher to enhance teaching and learning opportunities;
- improved professional practice and the opportunity to reflect critically on their work through personal study.

Such concerns are shared by colleagues in England. The call there is for more academic specialists to contribute to teachers' CPD (see www.pnarchive.org/docs/pdf/p20070312_issue41.pdf).

PRESENT TRENDS

Presentation figures in Sociology and Politics for 2011 show an increase and the expectation is for further growth in the future. The dramatic increase in Politics is due to the increasing popularity of the subject at S6 level for senior students. There is some concern that the figures for Psychology, though healthy and on an upward trend, might dip in the short term. Many schools that present Psychology students do so with the assistance of FE colleagues. Often there is no economic advantage for FE colleges in offering such support and there is evidence that more schools are seeking support from the SQA as FE colleges withdraw from this area of collaboration. Philosophy has maintained a stable trend. Nationally, debate has focused on the extent to which a whole range of philosophical initiatives can help individuals develop and discuss their own values and perspectives as citizens (Cassidy, 2008). For this reason the process of discussion and debate features in many areas of the curriculum, from P1 to S6. There is growing evidence too that other courses offered in the junior school have great potential. One interesting approach by Maitles and Gilchrist, promoting citizenship through a democratic approach to learning in Religious and Moral Education in S3, can be seen at www.leeds.ac.uk/educol/documents/00003459.htm

FUTURE PROSPECTS

Some view the Social Sciences as 'minority subjects', a term that a postmodern sociologist would deconstruct extensively for the power differential it portrays. Yet Scotland has a tradition of providing educational opportunities for its young people that encompass both breadth and depth. The need to educate the whole person is a key feature of Scottish educational philosophy. Citizenship is a national priority and global and international education are increasingly prominent, as evidenced in CfE. The Social Sciences encourage precisely that open and participatory ethos which assists active learning and teaching and helps ensure a commitment to values through discussion, debate and sometimes controversy. These dynamic approaches to learning and teaching are an integral part of contemporary educational theory, namely teaching contentious issues, media literacy, critical use of the internet, the case for adopting a more integrated approach to Social Studies (Priestley, 2009), global school partnerships, cooperative learning and the fostering of critical skills. Such laudable educational objectives lie at the heart of our seminal CfE programme. Indeed, from a Social Science perspective we might evaluate this initiative as a psychosocial model of educational development, referring as it does to self-esteem, confidence and citizenship.

All these are defining aspects of skills development in the Social Sciences. It is interesting, in the context of the Social Sciences, to note the current debate concerning the controversy developing around the teaching of Scottish Studies in our secondary schools. This topic, which looks likely to be embedded across the primary and secondary curriculum, may impact on the provision of the four Social Sciences and the related three Social Subjects (Denholm, 2012).

The late George Davie famously stressed the need to value the generalist tradition of education in Scotland. Within this tradition the encouragement of radical and critical thinking played a key role. A defining quality of Social Science provision is that it allows young Scots to engage in such radical discourse. It allows young citizens to compare key aspects of Scottish life, politically, economically, culturally and socially with aspects of social life in a wider social environment. The separateness of the Scottish system of education has been much commented on as a key aspect in defining Scottish identity. As McCrone observes, the curriculum we offer matters because 'people think of themselves as Scots because they have been educated, governed and embedded in the Scottish way . . . because of the micro contexts of their lives reinforced by, for example, the school system'. The provision of these new subjects has already given Scots the further opportunity to make greater sense of the society in which they live – a society increasingly complex and ideologically divisive. A society that faces the greatest constitutional issue in 2014 concerning our place within the United Kingdom.

In terms of policy delivery, the Social Sciences are crucial, for they encourage the skills development specifically sought in CfE. They assist young citizens to critically review their identity. They enable young Scots to expand and develop their own values and perspectives in a reasoned way and to reflect on values and perspectives that may be different to their own. They assist the 'democratic intellect' to engage in a reasoned and knowledgeable debate, the hallmark of a general liberal education. At a time of great national debate concerning our values and traditions, and our sense of national identity, the potential for the Social Sciences to encourage young Scots to develop and confidently express their own values and perspectives has never been more necessary.

REFERENCES

Cassidy, C. (2008) 'Philosophical citizens-a contradiction in terms?' *Critical & Creative Thinking*, 16 (2): 5–21.
Denholm, A. (2012) 'Call for our politicians to unite on Scottish Studies', *The Herald*, 19 March. Online at www.heraldscotland.com/news/education/call-for-our-politicians-to-unite-on-scottish-studies.17048256
McCrone, D. (2005) *The Same but Different: Why Scotland?* Talk given to the BSA Scottish Studies Group. Online at http://scottishaffairs.org/backiss/pdfs/sa55/Sa55_McCrone.pdf
Oates, V. (2006) Headlines, *Journal of Headteachers Association of Scotland*, 20 (1).
Priestley, M. (2009) 'Social studies in Scotland's school curriculum: a case for a more integrated approach', *Education in the North*, 17. Online at www.abdn.ac.uk/eitn/display.php?article_id=5
Staddon, G., A. Duffy and R. Cherrie (2005) *Psychology for Higher*. Paisley: Unity Publications.
Sweeney, T., J. Lewis and N. Etherington (eds) (2002) *Sociology and Scotland*. Paisley: Unity Publications.

74

Technology Education

Robert Doherty

Allied to Scotland's long-established engineering tradition, Technical Education is a strong aspect of the secondary curriculum across the third, fourth and senior phase. Technical Education in Scotland's secondary schools is provided through a range of courses that contribute to realising experiences and outcomes set out within the technologies aspect of Curriculum for Excellence (CfE). Technical Education draws its content from an engineering- and technology-related body of knowledge and range of generic and specific skills and capacities. It is characterised by courses of study involving craftwork, graphics, design and engineering. In addition, technical education seeks to contribute to the development of a broad range of skills and capacities including problem solving, creativity and communication. It provides experiences of work-related learning and looks to support the personal and social development of pupils as responsible, enterprising citizens who are conscious of their environment and the challenges of sustainable development.

In common with all the subject areas that provide aspects of the technologies curriculum, technical education seeks to support pupils in learning about the nature of technology and its complex relation to society. A second dimension that spans the technologies curricular framework is ICT, with a focus on the development of related skills to enhance learning. From the mid-1990s, courses offered in technical departments were linked together conceptually, and to national curricular frameworks, through the overarching concept of technological capability. Technological capability was defined at the time as 'understanding appropriate concepts and processes; the ability to apply knowledge and skills by thinking and acting confidently, imaginatively, creatively and with sensitivity; the ability to evaluate technological activities, artefacts and systems critically and constructively' (SCCC, 1996, p. 7). Interestingly, the concept of technological capability is absent from the language of Scotland's new curriculum. Nevertheless there is a detectible continuity with technological capability in terms of the experiences and outcomes mandated by the technologies framework of the new curriculum.

Contemporary arrangements for the first three years of secondary school are in flux under the implementation of CfE, moving from a general course in technology education for all pupils until the end of S2 to one in which choice for qualifications is being pushed back into S3. Departments of technical education are now required to provide a broader curriculum, defined by the technologies framework, across the first three years of secondary education. Under the new curriculum framework, at the third and fourth levels technical education will provide pupils with the opportunity to develop technological skills and knowledge in learning contexts organised around craft, design, engineering and graphics. There are clear demands being made within the contexts above, including the well-established manufacture of 3D projects, practical skills in wood, metal and plastics, design, opportunities for creativity and graphic skills and capacities. The new curriculum also requires the development of knowledge and skills related to the use of software applications, the application of scientific and mathematical knowledge, control technology and energy transfer. Technical departments will also be expected to contribute to generic areas of development across the technologies. In particular there is a focus on the interaction between the impact of science, engineering, technology and contemporary society.

The senior phase of Scotland's new curriculum allows for choice and pupils typically choose to study one or two technical subjects. The new curriculum framework presents the senior phase as the point of transition from a broad pattern of study to choice, personalisation and alignment with formal qualifications. Technical departments could in theory offer up to three courses (graphic communication, design and manufacture, and engineering science at SCQF levels 4–7), together with an additional three practical courses (woodworking, metalworking and electronics at SCQF levels 4 and 5). It would also be possible in some schools to offer Skills for Work courses (from a choice of five possible courses at SCQF levels 4 and 5). This array represents by far the broadest suite of potential courses available to any department in Scotland's secondary schools. In practice, departments, depending on school size, curriculum design and the socio–economic profile, will characteristically offer between two and four courses, with progression through the senior phase.

Courses in Design and Manufacture at National 5 develop pupils' knowledge of design, materials and manufacturing processes. It supports the development of design skills and the communication of design ideas and concepts. Students develop knowledge of manufacturing materials and develop design solutions through the production of product prototypes and models. Common design factors are engaged with, such as function, aesthetics, the economics of production and questions of environmental risk. Design and Manufacture provides openings for research and in particular provides pupils opportunities to be creative. Aligned to the field of product design, the course introduces common manufacturing processes and includes a 'cradle-to-grave' approach to the lifecycle of products. Students must achieve a pass in all of the course unit assessments. Summative assessment at National 5 has two components: a school-based design assignment and an external exam.

Graphic Communication courses at National 5 have a focus on communication through the medium of technical, manual and computer graphics. Students learn to present information using a range of drawings and graphics produced manually or using specialist software applications. In addition to skills, pupils develop knowledge and understanding associated with interpreting drawings and drawing conventions. The course provides opportunities for creativity around visual impact and clarity of communication. The content of courses reflects aspects of engineering and construction drawing, desktop publishing, drawing standards and conventions. Common areas of study include orthographic projection, computer-aided draughting and design, including views of sections and developments of forms based on partial prisms, cylinders, pyramids and cones. Students also learn about colour theory, layout and presentation techniques. They must successfully complete internal course unit assessments to move on to the summative assessment. At National 5 this comprises two equally weighted components: a school-based folio of work developed in response to a project brief, and an external exam.

The rationale for courses in Engineering Science at National 5 is overtly vocational in its concern that 'our society needs more engineers'. The content of Engineering Science draws upon familiar fields of knowledge, including mechanical, electrical and electronic engineering. Students study common engineering concepts and processes and are required to apply this knowledge to a range of contextualised engineering problems. Courses in Engineering Science provide the opportunity to develop skills in analysis, design, problem solving, evaluation and using specialised equipment. One of the three areas of study within the course is organised around the contexts and challenges of engineering and has a significant focus on providing a broad understanding of the relation between engineering, the environment, sustainable development and society. The second area, Electrical and Electronic Systems, involves pupils learning about analogue, digital and programmable systems, concepts and devices. The final area of study, Mechanical Systems, requires pupils to learn about structures, gear systems, pneumatics and concepts such as efficiency, force and energy. Across the three units of study there are opportunities for investigation and problem solving. In addition to success in internal course unit assessments, summative assessment for Engineering Science has two components: a school-based project and an external exam.

In addition to offering any combination of the three courses above, technical departments can opt to provide one or more distinctly 'practical' courses at National 4 and 5. Practical Woodworking, Practical Metalworking and Practical Electronics share a common focus on skills development, foundational concepts and knowledge, and manufacture or assembly tasks using tools and equipment. Notably the three practical courses are internally assessed and include a project or significant practical assignment.

COMMON PRACTICE IN TECHNICAL EDUCATION

Generally, teachers have access to dedicated specialised equipment, classrooms, computer labs and workshops. Approaches to teaching practical and skills-based content in technical education are characterised by whole-class teaching and teacher demonstration in combination with individual pupil practice and learning activities or projects. Such a mix of direct teaching, demonstration, activity and resource-based learning is evidenced across all stages of technical education. The use of collaborative approaches and group work has increased across the early years of secondary and within courses on design and manufacture. Differentiation within the technical curriculum is characterised by approaches focused on pupil product, on learning tasks and on extension materials. Prior to the senior phase, differentiation is commonly by product, with pupils across a range of abilities undertaking the same project or learning activities with differing levels of teacher support and pupil outcomes. Within the senior phase, strategies involve differential content, learning tasks, teacher support and outcomes distinguished by the SCQF levels of attainment. Within this framework, learning tasks and the content and product of project work are planned to meet the needs of individual pupils.

As part of a series of reports on effective learning and teaching in Scottish schools, Her Majesty's Inspectorate of Education (HMIE) published a report on technical education (SEED, 1999) drawing upon inspection evidence. The report linked positive pupil experiences to teaching styles, opportunities to be creative, levels of challenge and opportunities to work independently. It highlighted the predominance of craft in S1 and S2 courses and the need to broaden this stage of the curriculum as well as an overall growth in presentations for National Qualifications. The significant gender imbalance in favour of males across the middle and upper school technical curriculum was also noted. *Technical Education – A*

Portrait of Current Practice in Scottish Schools (HMIE, 2008) is the most recent publication from the inspectorate. This document aims to promote an improvement culture and stimulate reflection on learning and teaching within technical education. It devotes much of its focus to illustrating how technical education can contribute to the development of the four capacities desired by CfE.

CURRICULUM REFORM AND TECHNICAL EDUCATION

Attention to the technical curriculum and its subjects reveals a genealogy with clear roots in its industrial and vocationally oriented past (see Doherty and Canavan, 2006). A notable feature of the curricular history of technical education is an enduring tension over the optimum number of subjects and breadth of curriculum. The breadth and coverage of technical education's suite of courses following the review initiated by CfE maintained the wide range of courses, with the withdrawal of courses in Craft and Design being the exception. The content of contemporary courses in Graphic Communication can be traced back through antecedent courses in Engineering and Building Drawing. Discrete study of Woodworking and Metalworking merged over time and evolved into working with combined materials (Integrated Craft). The efforts of a movement of individuals and organisations advocating the inclusion of design education (Design Council, 1980) lead ultimately to Integrated Craft developing into courses in Craft and Design. The 'arranged' marriage of craft to design has not been without its tensions, with the long-established craft tradition having to make accommodations to its new partner. The teaching of design, its assessment and its integration with craft skills struggled to find an optimum balance. In 2004, Product Design was established as a course in its own right, although it has recently been revised as Design and Manufacture.

The introduction in 1988 of courses in Technological Studies (TS) stands as a marked curricular reform. This modernising turn produced a new course distinctive from its forerunners Applied Mechanics and Engineering Science, both historically marginal courses within the technical curriculum. The content of Technological Studies (for example, systems theory, electronics, pneumatics, computer control) and its emphasis on the integration of technologies, coupled with an approach towards supporting learning that gave emphasis to project work, resource-based learning and using technology in a problem-solving context, all combine to characterise the distinctiveness of this development. From its launch TS grew in popularity, supported in part by accessing funding made available through a UK-wide government programme: the Technical and Vocational Education Initiative. Presentations at Standard Grade in 1994 were running at 6,076; significantly, presentations had fallen to 3,649 by 1999.

Although the decline of TS cannot be explained by reference to a single causal factor, a number of contributing elements can be suggested: wider pressures on school managers to rationalise the curriculum, an uneven provision of professional development, an imprudent choice of equipment to support the resource-based learning aspects, delays by the Scottish Qualifications Authority (SQA) and its predecessor in updating its content and, importantly, competition in a crowded curriculum with more established courses such as Physics. The decline of TS, paradoxically in a period of concern over technologically mediated economic globalisation and a strategic focus on the knowledge economy (Peters, 2001), raised concerns among practitioner supporters and the inspectorate. TS was relaunched in 2003, available to pupils only at Credit and General level and with greater emphasis on theoretical knowledge at the expense of some of the practical, hands-on activity. This strategy ultimately proved to be impotent in halting its decline. The trend in presentations has continued downward, 2005 being notable as the number of presentation dipped below 2,000. It may be noted that the review of courses initiated by CfE has witnessed another relaunch for this area of study with a return to the antecedent course title of Engineering Science.

FUTURE PROSPECTS

The courses provided by technical departments within the technologies curriculum are advantageously positioned to offer rich learning opportunities and experiences, within what could be called the technology-learning continuum. While retaining comparatively recent design and engineering science innovations and reforms within its curricular reach, technical education has witnessed the reassertion of a skills tradition. The hyperbole around technology and design has been moderated by the resurgence of demand for practical courses and the strength of graphic communication. This has produced a less homogeneous provision of technical education with departments providing curricula that match the needs of pupils and the local curricular demands of their particular school. Questions and tensions around the identity of technology education are being resolved towards a broader and more diverse field of practice with all the challenges and demands that a wide-ranging curriculum brings. CfE has promoted interdisciplinary learning, or learning beyond subject boundaries, in the early years of secondary. This is a new obligation placed on secondary schools and its long-term impact or duration is an open question. Technical education is well placed to contribute to attempts to develop such experiences. Nonetheless, it is worth noting that providing interdisciplinary learning experiences across discrete areas of the technologies has not been without its difficulties, in particular attempts to provide learning experiences that integrate and make use of learning from across technical subjects in the early stage of secondary.

The most pressing concern facing technical education arises from the review of courses initiated by the development of CfE. The discontinuation of Craft and Design has for many departments created significant uncertainty. Following its introduction, Standard Grade Craft and Design has grown to average over 13,000 presentations each year, becoming the most familiar and popular qualification offered by many departments. Its removal marks a rationalisation that divides the study of design from that of craft; practical courses (at levels 4 and 5) and Design and Manufacture (at levels 4–7) are assumed by curriculum reviewers to provide an alternative. Departments with high numbers of presentations in Craft and Design face an uncomfortable transition; a decline in pupil numbers risks a reduction in subject teachers and a narrowing of the curriculum. Providing coherent new courses at the levels 3 and 4 is another area of challenge facing departments. Subject leaders are currently preoccupied with designing new courses that allow high-quality progression and support the new engineering aspects of learning while providing a focus on technology and society. However, curriculum leadership and development capacity has contracted in schools where departments are frequently led by non-subject specialists within a faculty structure of middle management.

It is an indictment to the place of technical education in the minds of decision makers that technical departments are not as yet being designed with multiple computer labs as standard. Arguably the demands of 3D modelling software used in technical departments require the highest specification of infrastructure of any application run in secondary schools. Engineering, design and, in particular, graphic communication provide an excellent context for the development of a range of contextualised ICT capacities and would benefit from an increase in the standard ICT provision of departments. At present the pedagogy and development of a progressive technical curriculum is arrested by the economic implications of providing pupils and teachers with appropriate levels of ICT infrastructure. Nonetheless, technology education enters the present period of curricular reform under the CfE programme with a strong uptake of the courses it contributes to secondary curricular provision and a noteworthy potential to provide the learning opportunities and experiences that are sought as part of Scotland's new curriculum.

REFERENCES

Design Council (1980) *Design Education at Secondary School Level*. London: Design Council.

Doherty, R. A. and B. Canavan (2006) 'Mapping reform in Scotland's technology education curriculum: change and curriculum policy in the compulsory sector', in M. J. de Vries and I. Mottier (eds) *International Handbook of Technology Education: The State of the Art*. Rotterdam: Sense Publishers, pp. 347–75.

Her Majesty's Inspectorate of Education (2008) *Technical Education – A Portrait of Current Practice in Scottish Schools*. Online at www.educationscotland.gov.uk/Images/TechnicalEducation CurrentPractice_tcm4-720948.pdf

Peters, M. (2001) 'National education policy constructions of the "knowledge economy": towards a critique', *Journal of Educational Enquiry*, 21 (1): 1–22.

Scottish Consultative Council on the Curriculum (1996) *Technology Education in Scottish Schools: A Statement of Position from Scottish CCC*. Dundee: SCCC.

Scottish Executive Education Department (1999) *Effective Learning and Teaching in Scottish Secondary Schools: Technical Education*. Edinburgh: SEED.

VIII

ASSESSMENT, CERTIFICATION AND ACHIEVEMENTS

Section VIII contains four chapters, all relating to assessment. The first one explores the several meanings of the expression as used educationally and where the conduct of assessment fits into the work of teachers. The second examines the activities of the Scottish Qualifications Authority (SQA), which handles the national assessment system, the text being written from an external perspective. The third looks at recent trends in attainment which are apparent in the annual rounds of examination results and the fourth looks at the wider system, at how pupils' learning has recently been, and currently is, monitored through national surveys and tests.

The starting point, as indicated in Chapter 75, is to recognise that assessment is multifunctional. It is used for different purposes, sometimes simultaneously, and therein lie the difficulties. The assessment that best serves learning (formative assessment) really needs to be different in kind from that which sums up the attainment of the learner at any particular point (summative assessment), yet often the pressures and the mechanisms with which practitioners comply roll these into one. Effective progress – for pupils and teachers – can suffer as a result and reporting mechanisms can be compromised to the detriment of the educational process overall. The chapter explores the many classroom strategies which have been advocated to improve formative assessment, noting the tendencies among researchers and providers of continuing professional development to somewhat neglect advice on how the substance of *what* is (or is not yet) being learned should remain the focus of ongoing assessment. Over the decades, thousands of hours of planning and deliberation (at national and school levels) have gone into explicating criteria by which educational judgements about grades and levels can be made. The nature and format of these have evolved with the changes made to national curricula, through Standard Grade, 5–14, (Higher Still) National Qualifications and now Curriculum for Excellence. The chapter looks critically at current thinking about assessment criteria and the reporting mechanisms associated with their use. It finishes by considering the practical realities of reconciling formative and summative forms of assessment.

Chapter 76 turns to the work of the SQA itself, an organisation whose main roles are concerned with awarding qualifications and with the accreditation (approval) of qualifications offered by other bodies, notably those concerned with workplace requirements. The functions, strategic priorities, and organisational management of the SQA are explored. The chapter then turns to the perennial concerns about pass rates in school examinations, looking at the stances taken by key players, including politicians, on the recent patterns of steadily improving figures nationally, as well as the new changes to the appeals procedures. An important matter of debate concerns the relationship between school qualifications and their use by higher and further education as metrics for decisions on course entry. The chapter highlights the growing concerns about the 'fit' between school and university, evidently exacerbated by the present years of austerity and the difficulties that young people experience in looking for a job (even those who are well qualified). In exploring the prospects ahead for the SQA, more imaginative forms of electronic assessment are looked at in some detail; their pros and cons are examined in the final section.

The third chapter in this section (77) reports on trends in the uptake and attainment figures for SQA qualifications from 2006 to 2011. Its figures graphically reveal the steady improvements that have taken place, the data being presented by 'qualification family' and by course type, as appropriate, including National Qualifications (NQs), Scottish Vocational Qualifications (SVQs) and Higher National Certificates and Diplomas (HNCs and HNDs). Some of the variability that seems due to gender, age and centre type (school vs college) is also discussed.

In addition to the comparisons over time that the Scottish Government can make of older pupils/students in NQ awards, efforts have been made to monitor the attainment of younger pupils in the 8–15 age range through sample-based surveys and tests. Chapter 78 examines these, tracing the practices of 'national testing' associated with the 5–14 Curriculum and the independent monitoring surveys that commenced with the Assessment of Achievement Programme (AAP) from 1983 to 2004, and which morphed in turn to the Scottish Survey of Attainment (SSA) from 2005. With Curriculum for Excellence these surveys have narrowed in character and now form the Scottish Survey of Literacy and Numeracy (SSLN), the 2011 numeracy survey results being reported in 2012 and the 2012 literacy survey results due to be published in 2013. The chapter explains the rationale for these successive waves of surveys, and describes their conduct and their centralised management. It concludes with some commentary upon the use of survey findings to reflect upon the learning that is taking place in schools.

75

Assessment in Scottish Schools

Tom Bryce

Assessment is *multifunctional*. It serves a number of purposes in education, the most important being argued here its influence upon learning. Hence the chapter begins with the nature and use of formative assessment, looking at strategies that teachers are encouraged to use, the research evidence favouring quality feedback to pupils (making it *feedforward*) and the importance of addressing the *substance* of pupils' thinking in what is assessed. Assessment is also required for summative purposes and at key points throughout schooling it is necessarily judgemental and used for a variety of predictive purposes, requiring care, assurances and comprehensible reporting. The chapter therefore looks at grades and qualification levels, tracking the changing nature of objectives and criteria through the recent major changes to the national school curriculum. Attention is paid to the new S3+ arrangements for certification which coincide with the publication of this edition. Finally, comments are made regarding the relationship between formative and summative aspects of assessment and the constraining (distorting?) effects of new reporting formats upon formative assessment.

FORMATIVE OR SUMMATIVE?

Assessment for teachers is conventionally thought of as something to be carried out *after* teaching has taken place. Simply put, it is to check on the learning that has taken place. For other professionals, however – in medicine, dentistry, social care and so on – assessment means something rather different. In the work of these professionals it is conventionally thought of as something to be carried out *before* treatment takes place. And, with ever-increasing public (as well as professional) scrutiny and accountability, the care with which such specialists carry out assessments tries to ensure that the treatments they pursue correspond closely and effectively: treatment leads to re-assessment and the resulting cyclic arrangement is beneficial to clients and professionals alike. There is some merit in teachers seeing comparisons in their own field and having equal concerns for rigour and *connection* in the relationship between teaching and assessment (and therefore being professionally accountable for it). Assessment should have, as its nature, a close and effective link with the teaching that led to its conduct: assessments that reveal inadequate learning should pointedly lead to the re-teaching required. The expression characterising the process in this way is *formative* assessment. To define it formally, 'all those activities undertaken by teachers, *and by their students in assessing themselves*, which provide information to be used as feedback to modify the teaching and learning activities in which they are engaged' (Black and Wiliam, 2001, p. 2, emphasis in the original).

For the best part of ten years, Scottish teachers have been persuaded through a national initiative to develop their practices in this way: to alter how they conduct assessment so that it has maximum impact on pupil learning, encouraging pupils to see how they can improve their current understandings and skills. The thrust of this Assessment is for Learning (AifL) movement has been to supply meaningful feedback *for* learning to occur, helping individuals to move forward from their current position. It contrasts with the traditional view of assessment, the assessment of the learning that has taken place: that is, looking backwards, checking what pupils have learned from their schoolwork. Its thrust is the grading *of* the learning that has or has not taken place and is usually said to be 'summative' in character, for it purports to summarise the pupil's learning, knowledge and capabilities up to that point. Summative assessment using predetermined criteria, often 'grade–related' (more of which later), is very much an established regime and gathered strength when the development of the Standard Grade curriculum in secondary schools in the 1980s began the idea of spelling out criteria nationally. However, it figures everywhere on the ladder of education, and assessment, whether formative or summative, is a preoccupation of teachers' lives, such are the demands it makes. There are positive and negative factors associated with the use of criteria to record grades as indications of assessment: positive in that it helps to ensure that everyone does the same thing and exercises judgements against the same standards; negative when everything and anything is considered 'grade-able', which invites the pejorative term Assessment is for Grading (AifG). An important issue is the relationship between formative assessments and those summative assessments that are used for key decisions such as permitting entry to a course (for example, in using S2 attainment results to allow pupils entry into particular courses in S3) or certificating exit from a course ('He got a B in his Higher English'). Whether it is possible to compromise constructively between assessing the learning that *has* occurred and assessing in the interests of *future* learning/re-learning will be considered later in the chapter. First, formative assessment itself will be looked at more closely.

ASSESSMENT IS FOR LEARNING

The AifL movement concentrated upon developing the quality of formative classroom assessment throughout the country. It derived considerable benefit from the impressive efforts by Dylan Wiliam of the London Institute of Education to disseminate the messages emanating from research on comparisons between summative and formative assessment in real classroom situations (see Black and Wiliam, 1998 and 2001; Black et al., 2002). These comparisons showed that where teachers, in the course of their assessment feedback, emphasise what pupils have done well and, more importantly, what they need to do to tackle the improvements required, the process is much more effective than simply grading the work. The argument turns on practicable, innovative strategies to change what teachers actually do. For many years, government, notably through Learning and Teaching Scotland (LTS), local authority continuing professional development (CPD) providers and schools who became convinced of the effectiveness of more formative versions of assessment all gave testimony to the benefits of *raising the quality of classroom interactions* in order to connect assessment and learning more explicitly. The emphasis was on the use by teachers of thoughtful questions, listening carefully to how pupils try to explain things and commenting reflectively on what they say or write; on helping pupils, staff and parents to be clear about what is to be learned and what success would be like; on giving timely feedback about the quality of pupils' work and how to make it better; and involving pupils in deciding the next steps in their learning. The AifL principles have been a central plank in Curriculum for Excellence developments nationally and their adoption has been evaluated during inspections of both schools and local authorities (Hutchinson and Young, 2011).

STRATEGIES FOR IMPROVING FORMATIVE ASSESSMENT

There is a fair amount of evidence in Wiliam's (and others') research to show that teachers can indeed be encouraged to give qualitatively better feedback, by instigating strategies such as:

- allowing longer 'wait' times during classroom questioning (to better ensure that pupils think about what is being pursued);
- adopting a 'no hands' strategy for that practice (to keep everyone alert and allow teachers to selectively target learners);
- incorporating 'traffic-light' systems to target help more readily (where pupils use coloured pens, cards, upturned paper cups, stickers, etc., to say what they are comfortable with and don't need going over (green); what they are rather uncertain about (amber); and what they can't do and need help with (red), all of which help teachers to better target their help);
- using 'two stars and a wish' strategies (where teachers try to ensure that they concentrate in a marking exercise on finding two things to comment favourably upon and one weakness (only) which needs addressing in such-and-such a way, thereby shifting the balance of demotivation/motivation that can arise from corrective feedback);
- making use of 'self- and peer-assessment' (pupils being trained to assess each other's work, enabling them to gain access to more reaction and discussion of their own efforts and understandings, rather than waiting on the teacher's feedback);
- adopting 'mini white boards' (hand-held boards to enable pupils to show their thinking to teachers during class sessions, allowing teachers to be selective about what or whom they need to address);
- bringing into play a 'secret student' strategy with a points-earning arrangement (where, from time to time, a pupil is chosen for close observation by the teacher/teachers for, say, a week and his or her contributions to class work monitored, the points thereby awarded contributing to the earning of the whole class towards a substantial and desirable end-of-session activity/ excursion/etc. – see www.aaia.org.uk/afl/the-classroom-experiment/);
- refraining from the use of grades when marking pupils' work (working with written comments instead) to prevent the 'What did you get?' phenomenon, which blinds learners to what the advice is.

EVIDENCE FOR THE EFFICACY OF GOOD FEEDBACK (MAKING IT *FEEDFORWARD*)

The last item is perhaps the most significant and demanding recommendation from researchers – actually *refraining* from the use of grades when marking. The argument here, borne out by a number of studies, is that pupils normally pay little or no attention to written feedback when grades are attached to their homework exercises, test results and so on. They simply engage in comparisons of grades with each other. Proponents of formative assessment urge teachers to take the uncomfortable step (given the prevailing regime) of *not* using grades and to operate with written comments only, these designed to focus upon what the pupil should do next and differently (and 'two stars and a wish' is predicated on this). The evidence that the quality of teacher feedback really matters does figure in research. For example, Hattie's scrutiny of the effects of various influences upon pupil (student) learning has involved him in determining 'effect sizes' in numerous studies of the relationships between a host of school variables and pupil attainment. 'Teacher feedback' tops the list of the score or more of potential variables built into these researches. Good feedback (according to Petty, commenting on Hattie's findings) includes:

> telling students what they have done well (positive reinforcement), and what they need to do to improve (corrective work, targets etc), but it also includes clarifying goals. This means that giving students assessment criteria for example would be included in 'feedback' . . . High quality feedback is always given against explicit criteria, and . . . as well as feedback on the task, Hattie believes that students can get feedback on the processes they have used to complete the task, and on their ability to self-regulate their own learning. All these have the capacity to increase achievement. Feedback on the 'self' such as 'well done you are good at this' is not helpful. The feedback must be informative rather than evaluative. (Petty, GeoffonHattie.doc at www.geoffpetty.com/research.html)

How big are the effect sizes in these meta-studies? For 'teacher feedback' it amounts to advancing a pupil's traditional grade at fourth year by two levels or so, or by advancing him or her by one year or more in attainment. The advocates of AifL do have something to say. However, it must be remembered that an important issue is that surface or rote learning (see Chapter 6) can yield effect sizes too and there should be concerns about the extent to which school and Scottish Qualifications Authority (SQA) assessments tap that kind of learning. The final chapter of Simpson's book on assessment is pessimistic. She argues that there is a fairly serious gap between authentic forms of assessment (really only suitable to internal, formative assessment) and the kinds of testing that figure in most forms of external certification (Simpson, 2006).

ASSESSING *WHAT* LEARNERS ARE THINKING

All of the advice listed above refers to *strategies* that teachers can use to make formative assessment better. They cut across topics, subject matter and the very substance of what learning is about. Wait time, no-hands-up, traffic lights and so on have in themselves nothing to say about what it is *in pupils' thinking* about the ideas at the core of learning to which teachers must pay attention. Some researchers have recently suggested that, important and successful though the movement to encourage more formative assessment has been, it has distracted researchers (and CPD providers) from focusing teachers' attention on *what* they should attend to in the process of formatively assessing. In the words of Coffey et al. (2011), looking at science teaching:

> By not delving into the specific substance of student thinking, the literature – and, subsequently, practice – misses and may undermine its fundamental objective . . . Strategies should be in the service of . . . what and how students are thinking and participating. (p. 4 of pdf)

From a research as well as a curriculum development perspective, the issue may be one of the relative balance in what researchers and practising teachers should concentrate on.

Coffey et al. readily concede the valuable emphasis there has been on how good descriptive feedback on pupils' work offers guidance on improvements to be made (*feedforward*), and on how it should be task-focused and timely. But they do stress that assessment should give more weight to the *substance* of what learners seem to be saying. Consistent with this is the literature on how people learn and change their ideas. Strike and Posner (1992) observe: 'If conceptual change theory suggests anything about instruction, it is that the handles to effective instruction are to be found in persistent attention to the argument and in less attention to right answers' (p. 171). This has practical classroom implications, as suggested by Coffey et al. (2011):

> we propose that it is essential for teachers to frame what is taking place in class [in terms of] students' ideas and reasoning . . . Formative assessment, then, becomes about engaging with and responding to the substance of those ideas and reasoning, assessing with discipline-relevant criteria, and, from ideas, recognizing possibilities along the disciplinary horizon. (p. 23 of pdf)

Similar concerns are raised by researchers concerned with the assessment of children's writing. Ellis (2012) found that Scottish primary teachers frequently determined success criteria before lessons took place rather than negotiating them with pupils. Often the criteria presented a narrow view of a successful piece of writing, focusing upon the technical/syntactic aspects of the work rather than the communicative purposes served by it. Headteachers did check that 'two stars and a wish' was being operated but did not monitor the content of the comments being noted by teachers. Interestingly, and of concern, a comparison of the comments given to pupils revealed that the more able writers were more likely to receive comments about what they had said, whereas less able writers were more likely to be given comments about technical and syntactic features. As Ellis notes:

> writing is about communicating ideas. If those who find it hardest to write fail to get feedback on *what* they have said, they may begin to view writing not as a means of communication, but as a task involving a set of rules and procedures to be applied correctly. The lack of intrinsic purpose will impact on the quantity of writing, on how they feel about it, on their understanding of why learning to write is important and on the potential that writing has to empower the writer. (p. 10)

With respect to CPD on formative assessment, the national evaluation of the AifL programme which was conducted in 2003 and 2004 (see Condie et al., 2005) reported the importance of the combined 'bottom–up' and 'top–down' forms of staff development activities in bringing about changes to assessment in teaching practice and, certainly at that time, the notably greater movement in primary schools over secondary schools. The report did emphasise that the impact and benefits of sustained efforts would be long-term. In this context it is puzzling to note that around 2010–11 in the LTS website (and therefore now the Education Scotland website) the expression 'Assessment is for Learning', along with pages devoted to advice and its encouragement, testimonies from practitioners and schools and so forth, rather disappointingly disappeared. This happened during the run-up to the introduction of the National 4 and 5 Qualifications (see below) and one wonders why there seemed to be a shying away from describing how teachers/schools might make the bridge from formative assessment (in the early years of secondary in particular) into the summative assessment necessary for certification forecasts and National Qualifications? Everyone has to do it, so what's wrong with careful advice on useful strategies and advice from successful practitioners. And recall that Wiliam himself, more than a decade ago, stated that 'we must refuse to accept the incompatibility of SA [Summative Assessment] and FA [Formative Assessment]. Instead we must find ways of mitigating the tension, by whatever means we can. Of course, this is a vast undertaking' (Wiliam, 2000, p. 16). Writing in 2011, he continued to press that a behavioural focus must be avoided and that feedback mechanisms need to take into account the wider circumstances of pupils' responses and the particular learning context in classrooms. Hutchinson and Young (2011) explicitly acknowledge that the AifL programme did *not* address the link with students aged 15–18 studying for National Qualifications. Citing the report of a pilot study by Hayward et al., they acknowledge that the mood among many secondary teachers meant reluctance 'to contemplate changes in their practice until arrangements for the senior phase and qualifications to support the new curriculum were clarified' (Hutchinson and Young, 2011, p. 66).

To explore this, it is worth considering the whole argument about SA and FA the other way round. One theoretician, Taras (2005), has argued that all assessment necessarily *begins* with SA, because it involves judgement, and that FA is SA plus feedback. She rationalises what happens educationally by distinguishing between the form and the function of assessment (the instructional process is the same for both but SA is multi-functional) stating that: 'Currently, FA is the antiseptic version of assessment and SA has come to represent all the negative social aspects' (Taras, 2005, p. 469). In other words, Taras recognises that beyond the place of assessment during learning, other factors figure in what may (or should) be done with the summarising judgements of assessment. These admittedly, and realistically, go way beyond scores and grades into how well schools can convince pupils, and their parents, that further progress is possible. Necessarily, teachers must find effective ways of encouraging young learners to believe in themselves that mid-term grades that fall short of those desired/required by the end of a course *are* improvable and that current judgements are not 'terminal'. Little of that is technical: much of it lies in the art of teaching and rests upon good working relationships between teachers and learners. A little more about this will be said later but a first consideration is to look briefly at how assessment criteria have developed in the Scottish system over recent decades and shape the operations of summative assessment.

GRADES, SUMMATIVE ASSESSMENT AND QUALIFICATION LEVELS

When teachers assess and report upon pupils' work they largely use criteria that have been articulated for them as part of whatever component of the (national) curriculum they teach. 'Good practice' and standardisation in assessment has been encouraged by government along with each of the recent major changes to the curriculum (in historical order): Standard Grade, SCOTVEC modules, 5–14, Higher Still (National Qualifications), then Curriculum for Excellence. Grade-related criteria began with the development of Standard Grade and their character and complexity has evolved over the years.

> **GRC: Conceived for Standard Grades (1–7, across three levels: Foundation, General and Credit)**

Two important developments took place in assessment during the 1980s. The first, which sought to replace norm-referencing (comparing pupils to each other, rank orders, using predetermined proportions to allocate proportions of grades about a mean), was initiated in response to the recommendations of the 1997 Dunning Report, *Assessment For All*, and produced assessment and certification strategies based on predetermined targets for learning. These were devised by subject groupings of teachers, led centrally by the Scottish Examination Board (the predecessor of the SQA). The second, related development was the allocation of grade levels to the outcomes of Standard Grade achievements (either in recognition that only limited progress had been made towards the certification of 'mastery learning', which was then aspired to, or, more plausibly, promoted as a political expedient to match the expectations of the givers and the users of future certificates). These developments built criteria, grades and grading into the heart of the assessment system. The groups of teachers who developed the criteria inevitably got bogged down in detail, since it is pretty nigh impossible to be both precise and terse. Rather than settle for description associated with a pass requirement for a Standard Grade subject, a compromise was struck to match more closely the traditional thinking of parents, of employers and of teachers, that is to preserve the notion of a scale of achievement from the most to the least able. What resulted was a system of grades 1 to 7, with 1 and 2 representing the Credit band, 3 and 4 the General band and 5 and 6 the Foundation band of Standard Grade (with 7 as 'no award'). Detailed criteria for what pupils should be able to do were distinguished by grade levels and were labelled extended grade-related criteria (E-GRC). Though not frequently used, the more general GRC were claimed to be meaningful to parents and employers. Criteria for assessment for certificate courses were contained in the SQA *Arrangements* document for each subject (the 'bibles', as many teachers described them). They generally took the form of 'Candidates should be able to . . .', or 'Candidates can . . .'. The differences between criteria for different grade levels were sometimes quantitative in character, sometimes qualitative; and there were instances where the distinction seemed forced and not particularly helpful to the classroom teacher. The thinking that lies behind criteria and targets is basically attuned to *behaviourist* thinking and instructional objectives. It is to some extent in conflict with current *constructivist* approaches to learning and mental growth (as used in Chapter 6).

GRC: Ignored for SCOTVEC modules (Pass all the Outcomes)

Also during the 1980s, developments in the FE sector led to the Scottish Technical and Vocational Education Council (SCOTVEC) specifying outcomes and criteria for its modules. The modular system did not take its cue from Standard Grade: it did not adopt grades for modules nor did it make distinctions between students. Instead, the sector opted for a set of outcomes per module, all to be mastered or non-mastered (thus taking no account of the reality of variations between students in possession of the same module). For a period, there were questions about the 'articulation' of the modules, that is the relationships between modules where sequence is important and some are prerequisites of others. Things were to change with the merger of SCOTVEC and the Scottish Examination Board (SEB) to form the SQA in 1997 but, chronologically, another big development was to take place in school curriculum and assessment.

GRC: Reconceived for 5–14 with an age and stage dimension (for levels A to E, with F added later)

When the idea of national curricula spanning the compulsory school years was introduced (and implicit in that was the idea of targets in ascending order), Scotland felt compelled to retain Standard Grade and confine its 'national curriculum' to 5–14, whereas the English curriculum spanned 5–16. This resulted in serious mismatches in attainment descriptors at different stages. Pupils moved upwards through 5–14 levels A to E (E being the 'highest') and were then switched to grades 1–7 (1 being the highest) for S3 and S4. Grades or levels then had rather different meanings. In Standard Grade, achieving a grade level 3, say, by the end of S4 was understood by scrutiny of the E-GRC so indicated; 3 was a position on a seven-point scale applied at the end of courses. In 5–14, a level was defined by a collection of the targets that should be attainable by a certain stage of schooling. Thus level B targets should have been met by most pupils in P4, level D by most pupils in P7, level E by most pupils in S2. While there were thousands of targets in the 5–14 Guidelines, it was intended that a teacher recognise the stage reached for any pupil through scrutiny of the numbers of targets reached.

The ambition for such assessment using grade levels was that parents should receive reports on their children that indicated their progress up the sequential rungs of the national curriculum ladder. However, it also allowed comparisons to be made to the achievements of the majority. Thus, for example, D was where most pupils should be by the end of primary school. In trying to steer national assessment through grades and levels, the consequences of some ambiguity of terminology must be lived with. Grades or levels are not easily or sharply defined entities. The 5–14 Curriculum developers opted to attach two years of schooling to each level through their selection of (initially) five levels for nine years of schooling (P1–S2). Two years usually constitutes a significant gain in a pupil's knowledge and skills. The many hundreds of targets associated with one grade varied greatly in their compass, difficulty and depth: grade levels such as D, therefore, cannot constitute some precise end-point. Terms adopted for targets and levels may appear attractively straightforward (and no doubt give some flexibility and freedom as far as curriculum guidelines are concerned). However, in practice, assessors, whether classroom teachers or as part of any system where standards are monitored, have much interpreting to do. While 5–14 documents offered curriculum guidelines, they did not present assessment blueprints.

> **GRC: Reconceived for National Qualifications with levels: Access, Int 1, Int 2, H, AdvH; outcomes (for the units) and grades A (high), B, C and D (fail) for the course achievements**

Higher Still, launched in 1999–2000, brought together academic and vocational qualifications into one multi-level framework for S5 and S6 and beyond into FE, essentially a big brother to Standard Grade. The range of qualifications (Access, Intermediate 1, Intermediate 2, Higher and Advanced Higher) extended the ability/attainment levels significantly and they became referred to as National Qualifications (NQs). In a very real sense NQs were made to reflect a combination of their predecessors (SEB courses, which were only ever externally assessed, and SCOTVEC modules, which were only internally assessed), for they were devised as courses made up of units, usually three in each, where the units were assessed internally and had to be passed prior to the candidate being permitted to sit the external examination. Assessment criteria for the NQ courses are similar in character to those evolved for Standard Grade. National Assessment Bank tests (NABs) were commonly used in schools and colleges to take the pass/fail decisions, either for a unit as an award in its own right, or as the requirement for external presentation. They were formally withdrawn in 2010, but at the time of writing (and before the start of National 4 and 5 courses, see below), many schools were still using them. Candidates who failed unit assessments could retake them, a consequence that added complexity to the considerable workload pressure upon subject departments as well as candidates. It takes little arithmetic to see that a pupil taking, say, five courses in S5 would be undertaking very many formal tests long before they reached the May diet of examinations, fifteen at least, with some schools requiring 'graded NABs' as well as 'prelim' examinations to be sat. A department had to fit in NABs for absentees and resits for those who failed them. Pupils and teachers were truly said to be 'NABed to death'.

The first decade or so of NQ developments saw little change in the operations of the system and virtually no lessening of the demands made upon teachers to carry out the assessments required. Chapter 71 of the third edition of this book gives an outline of the several official deliberations, public consultations and surveys conducted during this period, amidst fairly widespread concerns, both professionally and amongst the public, about the amount of assessment required to make things work. With regard to the basic structure of NQs, studies of the success of Higher Still by researchers at the Centre for Educational Sociology indicated that, in its first four years, the new system did extend opportunities for attainment, especially for middle- and lower-attaining 16-year-olds and for students with special needs (see Raffe et al., 2005).

GRC: Reconceived for Curriculum for Excellence with 'I can . . .' statements at levels 1–4, for pre-school up to 16 years; and with Access, National 4, National 5, H and AH courses for post-16 candidates

---

In 2004 a major overhaul of the whole-school curriculum was signalled in the government paper *Ambitious, Excellent Schools: Our Agenda for Action* (www.scotland.gov.uk/library5/education/aesaa-00.asp) and since then development activity in schools and authorities, as well as at national level, has been to evolve a 'Curriculum for Excellence' out of 5–14 (formally commenced nationally in session 2010–11). Other chapters of this book deal with the 'decluttering' of the curriculum, and the attempts to give schools more flexibility in what they teach children and give critical appraisals of the current state of play (particularly Chapters 3, 42 and 50). With regard to assessment criteria, a significant change in the way in which objectives are formulated took place. First, they now tend to emphasise skills rather than content. Second, the experiences and outcomes, or the Es and Os (or E&Os), take the form of 'I can . . .' statements, it being judged by the curriculum developers that expressing intentions in first-person, pupil terms would be clearer, more useful and understandable by those on the receiving end. Priestley and Humes have commented, however, that

> it does lead to a certain artificiality, when the language employed may not reflect the verbal skills of some pupils. In this sense, the 'subjectivity' of the experiences is misleading, an artifice devised by the planners rather than a true reflection of the learning process (Priestley and Humes, 2010).

Figures 75.1 and 75.2 illustrate, respectively, some examples for Science (the topic of electricity) and for Writing in English Language (the area of creating texts). Early refers to the pre-school years and P1. Levels 1 and 2 are those for lower and upper primary respectively; levels 3 and 4 are those for lower and middle secondary respectively (further details about levels follow later). It is too early to say whether teachers and pupils will behave very differently with criteria expressed in this way. However, an immediate impression is that by desiring such statements to express what should be experienced (the Es) *and* simultaneously what should be the outcomes (the Os), the latter seem diminished in detail. It will be for empirical research and fieldwork to ascertain whether assessment is blunted or not as a result.

Early

I know how to stay safe when using electricity. I have helped to make a display to show the importance of electricity in our daily lives.

Level 1

I can describe an electrical circuit as a continuous loop of conducting materials.

I can combine simple components in a series circuit to make a game or model.

Level 2

I have used a range of electrical components to help to make a variety of circuits for differing purposes. I can represent my circuit using symbols and describe the transfer of energy around the circuit.

Level 3

Having measured the current and voltage in series and parallel circuits, I can design a circuit to show the advantages of parallel circuits in an everyday application.

Level 4

Through investigation, I understand the relationship between current, voltage and resistance. I can apply this knowledge to solve practical problems.

Figure 75.1   CfE experiences and outcomes for Science (electricity)

Early

I enjoy exploring events and characters in stories and other texts and I use what I learn to invent my own, sharing these with others in imaginative ways.

Level 1

Having explored the elements writers use in different genres, I can use what I learn to create my own stories, poems and plays with interesting structures, characters and/or settings.

Level 2

Having explored the elements which writers use in different genres, I can use what I learn to create stories, poems and plays with an interesting and appropriate structure, interesting characters and/or settings which come to life.

Level 3

Having explored the elements which writers use, I can create texts in different genres by:

• integrating the conventions of my chosen genre successfully and/or;
• using convincing and appropriate structures and/or;
• creating interesting and convincing characters and/or;
• building convincing settings which come to life.

Level 4

Having explored and experimented with the narrative structures which writers use to create texts in different genres, I can:

• use the conventions of my chosen genre successfully and/or;
• create an appropriate mood or atmosphere and/or;
• create convincing relationships, actions and dialogue for my characters.

Figure 75. 2   CfE experiences and outcomes for Writing (creative texts)

Some commentary is due in respect of the four levels of attainment criteria, in particular their close match to the long-standing four levels used in England and Wales, as well as the more traditional Scottish terminology for ages and stages. Before 5–14, report after report throughout the twentieth century used traditional terms such as 'nursery and infant', 'lower primary' and 'upper primary', 'early secondary' and their correspondence to ages, actual

Scottish school stages	Scottish 5–14 levels	Scottish CfE levels	Age (years)	English Key Stages	School years
Pre-school and in Primary 1		early	3–5	Foundation	Pre-school to end of reception year
by end of P4 but earlier for some	A → B	first	5–7	1	1 and 2
by end of P7 but earlier for some	C/D	second	7–11	2	3, 4, 5, 6
in S1–S3 but earlier for some	E/F	third	11–14	3	7, 8, 9
		fourth	14–16	4	10, 11
[SCQF 4]*					
S4–S6		senior	16–18	sixth form	12, 13

Figure 75.3   Scottish CfE levels and English Key Stages

* Scottish Credit and Qualifications Framework (SCQF) level 4 matches up to National 4 Qualifications and the former Standard Grade, General or Intermediate1.

ages, was evidently the way that teachers think of pupils and the curriculum they address. CfE has such phrases in its language and the terms are all straightforward.

Figure 75.3 sets them out and the ages and stages for this Scottish initiative in the left-hand columns, where 5–14's A–F have been inserted in column two. Inevitably these overlap and bunch, given the reduction to four levels for CfE. But note the anglicisation apparent in the levels of the other columns and their age correspondences, where the terms are those in the national curriculum documentation for England and Wales. The boldened outline for columns three, four and five shows how closely the CfE levels correspond to the Key Stages of our southern neighbours – a step towards commonality across the countries of the UK, despite the proudly held distinctiveness of Scottish education?

BEYOND S2: NATIONAL AWARDS

Following a national consultation conducted in 2008, the Scottish Government announced in June 2009 that:

1. From 2013–14 onwards, there would be a new qualification at SCQF levels 4 and 5, called National 4 and National 5, to replace both Standard Grade (General and Credit) and Intermediate 1 and 2 whilst reflecting the best features of the then present arrangements (Standard Grade Foundation level would be removed, with Access 3 providing an appropriate replacement).
2. New qualifications in literacy and numeracy at SCQF levels 3, 4 and 5 would be introduced from 2012–13, to be called National Literacy and National Numeracy, based on a portfolio of work across the curriculum.* The literacy experiences and outcomes across learning can be found at www.ltscotland.org.uk/learningteachingandassessment/learningacrossthecur riculum/responsibilityofall/literacy/experiencesandoutcomes/index.asp

3. The existing Access, Higher and Advanced Higher qualifications would be retained as points of stability, and reviewed to ensure they fully reflect CfE.

* Note: This was changed in 2010 when the new Cabinet Secretary, Michael Russell, announced that these would be backed into English and Maths respectively in the form of tests.

The government was clearly pressurised by industry and commerce to put tests of literacy and numeracy in place, despite teaching unions, parents (the Scottish Parent Teacher Association) and several university Faculties of Education being against the proposal. A concession was granted that these be in S3, not S4, to allow more examinable subjects than five to be taken in S4. The plan was (and remains) that National 4 would be internally assessed, but not graded, i.e. coursework will be used with some quality assurance by SQA, and that National 5 would have both internal and external graded assessment (the latter an exam), something like the practice for the Intermediates. The external examinations would figure in S4+, clearly an attempt to revert to consistency across authorities. The government also stated that it might create a safety net for pupils who bypass S4 exams. NABs would be discontinued (in 2010) and replaced by National Assessment Resources (NARs), to be an online set of resources (see www.ltscotland.org.uk/learningteachingandassessment/ assessment/supportmaterials/nar/index.asp).

The new qualifications are being phased in between now and session 2015–16 (see www.sqa.org.uk/cfetimeline for details of the timeline). Following the introduction of CfE in session 2010–11, the last certification of Standard Grades took place in 2012–13, shortly before this text was published. Session 2013–14 was intended to see National 4 and National 5 being assessed in a dual run with current Access, and Intermediate Courses. A decision taken in the spring of 2012 followed representations from schools and authorities requesting a delay to the implementation of the National 4 and 5 level courses, and permitted individual schools to delay the start of their courses, providing they agreed to accept the offer of help from Education Scotland. The new Highers and Advanced Highers will be introduced in sessions 2014–15 and 2015–16 respectively. A representation of the new system in diagrammatic form is given in the two parts of Figure 75.4, the first showing the 3 + 3 model, the government's preferred option wherein a broad general education (BGE) continues for the first three secondary years, the second showing a 2 + 2 + 2 model, one reflecting the traditional pattern where pupils choose their subjects at the end of S2.

At the time of writing, the official advice given to teachers concerning assessment in CfE contained the following 'key ideas' (though it is to be hoped that more will follow):

1. Learner engagement in assessment is crucial.
2. Teachers need to use many approaches to assessment.
3. Assessment should focus on breadth, challenge and application.
4. Evidence of learners' progress can be gathered across the four contexts for learning.
5. Professional dialogue is central for agreeing standards.
6. Assessments should be reliable, valid and proportionate.
7. Curriculum for Excellence principles should underpin reporting.
8. Assessment needs to be quality assured.

See *Building the Curriculum 5: A Framework for Assessment* at www.ltscotland.org.uk/ publications/b/publication_tcm4617095.asp

A CfE '3 + 3' model for secondary

Level 4	S6	Higher	Adv Higher/Higher	3
	S5	National 4	Higher	National 2
	S4		National 5	1
Level 3	S3	Assessment of literacy and numeracy		*
	S2			
	S1			
Level 2	P7			
	P6			
	P5			
Level 1	P4			
	P3			
	P2			
	P1			

A CfE '2 + 2 +2' model for secondary

Level 4	S6	Higher	Advanced Higher	3
	S5	National 5	Higher	National 2
	S4	National 4	National 5	
Level 3	S3	Assessment of	literacy and numeracy	1
	S2			*
	S1			
Level 2	P7			
	P6			
	P5			
Level 1	P4			
	P3			
	P2			
	P1			

Figure 75.4   The educational ladder

* = point of subject choice
Note the change of terminology: In August 2013, Access 1 and 2 were replaced by National 1 and National 2. Access 3 and Standard Grade (Foundation level) were replaced by National 3.

RECONCILING FORMATIVE AND SUMMATIVE ASSESSMENTS: REPORTING

With regard to reporting assessment results to pupils and parents, for primaries, written comments are now being accompanied by CfE grades 1 and 2 (or 3+ as the case may be). For secondaries, written comments will now be accompanying CfE grades at levels 3–4 (or lower levels, as the case may be). At the time of writing, no further details have been published as to the anticipated use of traditional grades A–D (D fail) along with the broad CfE levels. The actual formats of current pupil reports vary by authority, the government having earlier decided not to insist upon a national format. However, a fair number have been capitalising on the electronic systems offered by SEEMiS Group PLC. These have the advantage that, as well as generating reports for pupils and parents, the system lets teachers/senior management teams carry out detailed monitoring of individual pupils, with user-friendly, visual formats of progress being made (or not). The very flexible electronic formats for monitoring pupils' progress also mean that senior management have increasingly powerful ways of monitoring subjects and teachers too. 'Could do betters' won't do! Nevertheless, grades dominate, everywhere, so 'aggregating' them sensibly is often problematic. Treating every recorded grade as if it was summative and somehow merited arithmetical averaging, when in fact it was earlier intended to be formative, will not advance the assessment process usefully. Much more subtle judgements are necessary in many cases, especially those where pupils are making steady gains and their earlier low grades should be ignored. The present context for teachers, one that is dominated by accountability and pressures to ensure that pupils will achieve the best possible final results, alas means that there is considerable pressure on them to treat recorded grades as if they were all summative. The system is in a predicament: genuinely formative assessment and grading are mutually contradictory and pupils and parents are part of the 'problem'. Not long into certificate courses they do ask how well they/their offspring are faring in respect of likely outcomes at the end of the course.

But some teachers do live with the grading regime and find it possible to get their pupils to take advice and improve their understandings. One has to reason that it all depends upon the integrity of the processes which teachers deploy, long-term, with their pupils and upon how genuine they are themselves (and can make themselves in the particular settings within which they teach). Teachers who turn pupils on to realistic prospects of advancement and how to make the best out of prevailing circumstances seem to be able to get pupils to face predictions as challenges, rather than as forecasts of certainty or defeat. As with everything in learning, it all turns on motivation. Good teachers know that the deep personal messages that they convey to pupils, day in and day out, through all their statements, both deliberate and casual, are crucial to what pupils take out of learning. In this sense the educational process is more important than the product. An effective process shifts the responsibility for learning from the teacher to the pupil. In recognition of this, some secondary schools have delayed the effects of grading, encouraging staff to use written commentary for assessment for a good part of a certificate course, only later combining comments and grades.

A rather different tack is taken in some secondary schools where departments use the summative data that they gather on their pupils in a formative way. They do this by looking at topic tests for a year group, highlighting areas of difficulty that arise from these tests and using that information to collectively reflect on ways to improve the teaching in the area concerned. Teachers then direct the development of teaching materials and activities to address any identified weaknesses in that area. This activity is being driven more because of accountability to headteachers for exam results than it ought to be.

Parent education and persuasion is a necessary aspect of any innovations in formative assessment. The use of electronic systems for reporting *with grades* as the main entries, desirable as it is, runs essentially counter to the main intention. Ironically, the technological advancements in reporting systems now permeating the system tend to be undermining all the efforts that have been made to improve the quality of formative assessment. Teachers *must* be effective assessors and convincing in the discharge of their duties to pupils and parents. The reporting system requires to be tailored accordingly.

ASSESSMENT AND THE TRANSITION BETWEEN PRIMARY AND SECONDARY

In concluding this chapter it is worth acknowledging a piece of recent research into how Scottish teachers have fared in assessing pupils' work against CfE's experiences and outcomes. The outstanding problems facing the education system as a whole at the present time pick up on many of the points argued in the preceding sections.

The *Assessment at Transition Report* (Hayward et al., 2012) contains the findings of a Scottish Government funded project carried out by a large team of researchers at Glasgow University. The project set out 'to explore how shared understandings of the purposes and potential of assessment at transition between primary and secondary might be developed most effectively'. The team looked at evidence from research, from national and local authority policy documentation, and from practice (interviewing pupils and teachers). Much good practice was reported to be in place. However, both primary and secondary teachers felt that it was difficult for secondary planning to use both broad 'levels' information and detailed information about the progress of individual pupils. CfE levels information was only used for setting, and secondary teachers expressed the need for more detail on content coverage, portfolios of pupil work and conversations with individual pupils prior to the start of S1. These points are consistent with what is apparent in the literature, difficulties in smoothing the transition being often reported as partly through lack of detailed information applicable to different subjects and partly because of differing priorities in the two sectors. The development of professional relationships and cross-visits between primary and secondary teachers is emphasised in the national and international literature as being helpful to promote understanding, as are formative approaches to learning and assessment. The practitioners interviewed in this Scottish research indeed valued professional interaction across the primary–secondary interface and want more of it in 'protected time'.

The Glasgow researchers found that, with respect to the recording of assessment information, there were significant variations – across and between school clusters and within secondary schools. Teachers want greater clarity about P7 profiles and reporting, for many believe that, in practice, the former merely duplicates the latter. The interpretation of standards evidently concerns teachers, there being uncertainty about how to come to a judgement about the CfE level reached by each pupil. The report states (on p. 13) that:

> Some teachers used an inappropriate 'grading' approach (grading each single task) rather than a 'best fit' judgement – this was in effect encouraged in some LAs by the requirement to record very frequently levels and 'Developing, Consolidating, Secure' within levels (for tracking individual

progress), despite teachers' expressed concerns that the information being recorded lacked validity and consistency across teachers and schools and was not helpful for planning future learning.

With such serious findings, the writers of the report conclude that there must be a better alignment between the policy aspirations for CfE and what is currently happening in schools. They consider that teachers (in both sectors) must be jointly involved in the design of the information gathering system, and the P7/S1 transition is pivotal. Exemplifications are much needed of how teachers can decide upon a level of attainment through scrutiny of the profile of a pupil's work to yield a 'best fit'. In intimating the publication of this report, the *Times Educational Supplement Scotland* of 3 August 2012 emphasised how fragile progress in the area of transition from primary to secondary has been under CfE.

REFERENCES

Black, P. and D. Wiliam (1998) 'Assessment and classroom learning', *Assessment in Education*, 5 (1): 7–74.

Black, P. and D. Wiliam (2001) *Inside the Black Box*. London: King's College.

Black, P., C. Harrison, C. Lee, B. Marshall and D. Wiliam (2002) *Working Inside the Black Box: Assessment for Learning in the Classroom*. Slough: NFER-Nelson.

Coffey, J. E., D. Hammer, D. M. Levin and T. Grant (2011) 'The missing disciplinary substance of formative assessment', *Journal of Research in Science Teaching*. Published online 7 September DOI.1002/tea.20220

Condie, R., K. Livingston and L. Seagraves (2005) *Evaluation of the Assessment is for Learning Programme: Final Report*. Glasgow: University of Strathclyde, Quality in Education Centre.

Ellis, S. (2012) 'Teaching Writing: Reconciling Policy and Pedagogy'. Paper presented at the American Educational Research Association annual conference (Non Satis Scire: To Know is Not Enough) held in Vancouver, British Columbia, 13–17 April.

Hayward, L., I. Menter, V. Baumfield, R. Daugherty, N. Akhtar, L. Doyle, D. Elliot, M. Hulme, C. Hutchinson, G. MacBride, M. McCulloch, F. Patrick, E. Spencer, G. Wardle, H. Blee and L. Arthur (2012) *Assessment at Transition Report*. Glasgow: University of Glasgow School of Education.

Priestley, M. and W. Humes (2010) 'The development of Scotland's Curriculum for Excellence: Amnesia and déjà vu', *Oxford Review of Education*, 36 (3): 345–61.

Raffe, D., C. Howieson and T. Tinklin (2005) 'The introduction of a unified system of post-compulsory education in Scotland', *Scottish Educational Review*, 37 (1): 46–57.

Scottish Qualifications Authority (2006) *Review of Estimates, Derived Grades and Appeals: Report and Recommendations*. Glasgow: SQA.

Simpson, M. (2006) *Assessment*. Edinburgh: Dunedin Academic Press.

Strike, K. A. and G. J. Posner (1992) 'A revisionist theory of conceptual change', in R. A. Duschl and R. J. Hamilton (eds), *Philosophy of Science, Cognitive Psychology and Educational Theory and Practice*. Albany, NY: State University of New York Press.

Taras, M. (2005) 'Assessment – summative and formative – some theoretical reflections', *British Journal of Educational Studies*, 53 (4): 466–78.

Wiliam, D. (2000) 'Integrating summative and formative functions of assessment. Keynote address to the European Association for Educational Assessment, Prague: Czech Republic, November 2000.

Wiliam, D. (2011) 'What is assessment for learning?' *Studies in Educational Evaluation*, 37: 3–14.

Website

Learning and Teaching Scotland, AifL website: www.ltscotland.org.uk/assess/

76

The Scottish Qualifications Authority

Tom Bryce and Walter Humes

THE SQA'S ORIGINS, ROLE AND FUNCTIONS

The Scottish Qualifications Authority (SQA) took over all the responsibilities of its predecessor bodies, the Scottish Examination Board (SEB) and the Scottish Vocational Education Council (SCOTVEC), on 1 April 1997, following the Education (Scotland) Act 1996 (later amended by the Scottish Qualifications Act 2002). The reasons for the merger had become apparent in the course of the preceding decade. Historically, the concerns of upper secondary education (the province of SEB) and further education (FE), vocational education and training (the province of SCOTVEC) had been fairly distinct. However, increasingly the separation of academic and vocational qualifications came to be regarded as inadequate to meet the needs of a society in which knowledge was expanding and changing rapidly, and in which the employment market was demanding new skills over and above traditional forms of understanding. The convergence of these pressures meant that the case for a unified qualifications framework and a single qualifications body was compelling.

The merger, however, was not straightforward. The SEB had established systems and structures geared mainly to the school sector, informed by the professional views of teachers and based on fairly conservative notions of worthwhile knowledge and the best means of assessing it. SCOTVEC, by contrast, had pursued an agenda that was strongly influenced by the expressed needs of employers in business and industry, and had developed a wide range of modular courses using innovative methods of assessment. There was, in other words, a significant culture gap between the two organisations, a culture gap that helps to explain some of the difficulties that subsequently arose. In the early years of the merger, a substantial amount of time was devoted to the question of how integration of SEB and SCOTVEC procedures could best be promoted. This took place at a time when Higher Still reforms were reaching a critical stage in their implementation. Instead of giving so much attention to internal matters such as structure, staffing, and terms and conditions of service, the SQA might have been wiser to concentrate on ensuring that service to its external clients could be delivered efficiently.

Matters came to a head in the summer of 2000 when thousands of students waiting for the outcome of their Higher and Standard Grade examinations received wrong results, late results or, in some cases, no results at all from the SQA. This precipitated a serious crisis in Scottish education, fuelled by sustained public concern and media attention. The event proved to be a critical test for the new Scottish Parliament and several investigations were mounted to discover what had gone wrong. Parliamentary committees conducted enquiries that sought to explain the educational dimensions of the debacle and to address questions of accountability: key players were subject to detailed questioning about their degree of responsibility for what had happened. A further enquiry conducted by management consultants Deloitte and Touche identified a number of weaknesses, including data mishandling and poor information systems. It also suggested that management had relied too heavily on structures and practices inherited from the predecessor organisations, the SEB and SCOTVEC, and had failed to develop an operational plan geared to the new challenges encountered in session 1999–2000 with the implementation of Higher Still. Emergency procedures were put in place to correct mistakes and omissions, including the replacement of senior staff at executive and board levels. A fuller account of the various measures is given in earlier editions of this book and Paterson (2000) offers a detailed analysis of the significance of the episode not only for the SQA but also for the reputation of Scottish education. The relationship between the (then) Scottish Executive and the SQA altered significantly, switching from an 'arms-length' approach by Ministers to what one observer at the time called Ministerial 'vice-like grip'. It will be suggested below that the current 'corporate' style of SQA management is partly explicable in terms of the aftermath of the crisis of 2000.

The SQA has two main roles: awarding qualifications (other than degrees) and accreditation. With regard to the first of these, the SQA devises a range of qualifications designed for school and college students as well as work-based learners. (A summary of the portfolio of qualifications is given at the start of Chapter 76.) These qualifications are subject to validation and review processes to ensure that they meet the needs of learners and are updated as required. The SQA, in liaison with the education and training establishments that enter students for qualifications, arranges for and carries out assessments and awards certificates to successful candidates. The second role – accreditation – is essentially a quality assurance function in relation to qualifications offered by other organisations and ensures that the awarding bodies meet certain standards. Bodies that have received SQA approval include the Engineering Construction Industry Training Board, the Chartered Management Institute, City and Guilds, the Mineral Products Qualifications Council and the Royal Academy of Dance.

STRATEGIC PRIORITIES

In its corporate plan for 2011–14, the SQA identifies eight strategic priorities:

- develop, deliver and maintain a portfolio of qualifications and services to support the needs and aspirations of Scotland, its people and the economy;
- be regarded as a leader in assessment and quality enhancement of learning, in Scotland, and recognised worldwide;
- enhance the role of qualifications and services in recognising the skills of individuals across the education and training system;
- ensure SQA activities support the Scottish Government's agenda to maximise the benefits to Scotland of international engagement;
- subject to demand and statutory requirement, accredit and assure the quality of qualifications, delivered in Scotland – other than those conferred by higher education institutions;
- ensure high quality, continually improving, efficient and responsive service delivery;
- continue to develop SQA as a leading public body;

- continue to develop a business model that maximises funding and efficiency to allow SQA to meet its statutory obligations in the changing economic and public sector environment. (SQA, 2011)

These strategic objectives are then elaborated in a series of 'corporate actions' which are intended to translate broad aims into specific objectives. While much of the document is expressed in the kind of generalised managerial discourse that is now standard in public bodies, certain key features stand out. First, the SQA is content to work to the agenda on education and training set by the Scottish Government. Given that a substantial proportion of its income comes from government, this is hardly surprising. Nevertheless, the explicitness of its commitment to official policy is striking: for example, part of the strategic plan involves mapping the SQA's priorities against national outcomes set by government. It would be interesting to know what kind of dialogue takes place between senior civil servants and SQA officials. Is it always a matter of the former saying, 'This is what government wants – it's your job to help to deliver it', or is there scope for the latter to make any substantive input into the policy process? There is a perception in some quarters that the SQA has been a more biddable organisation than, for example, Learning and Teaching Scotland, before it joined with the inspectorate to become Education Scotland (ES). This may in part be a legacy of the examinations crisis of 2000, indicating a desire to avoid any repetition of ministerial criticism, but it could also be viewed as sensible political positioning at a time of major curriculum reform.

Second, the economic context is a major driver of the SQA's strategic priorities. It is stated that the organisation will 'have a key role in helping to move Scotland towards sustained economic recovery by ensuring that employers and individuals can access the skills and learning to support them through recession and into growth'. Reference is made to the need for people to 're-skill' and 'up-skill' their qualifications to strengthen their employment and career prospects in difficult times. The Scottish Government's emphasis on the employability and skills agenda, involving not only further education colleges and employers but also schools and universities, is seen as giving the SQA a vital role in developing new qualifications in response to challenging circumstances. In other words, there is a market opportunity at home that sits well with another aspiration, namely the SQA's desire to generate income from commercial and international activities.

A third striking feature of the SQA's strategic plan is the emphasis it places on partnership – partnership not only with government but also with a wide range of other agencies, including local authorities, employers, sector skills councils, professional bodies, ES, the Scottish Funding Council, the Scottish Credit and Qualifications Framework, Scotland's Colleges and Universities Scotland. By the very nature of its work, the SQA has to negotiate and liaise with many organisations and clearly this requires strong networks of contacts and good lines of communication across the educational and training systems. Once again this is set in a political and economic context, with reference to the National Performance Framework, Public Services Reform (Scotland) Act 2010 and *Skills for Scotland: Accelerating the Recovery and Increasing Sustainable Economic Growth*, the last being a Scottish Government publication of 2010.

An important speculation concerning these points, particularly the first – the SQA's contribution to policy development – relates to how innovations actually take place. When major change is contemplated, considerable care combined with original thinking is required, as well as insight into what teachers can be persuaded to accept. For example, in the case of the upper school curriculum and the evolution of National Qualifications (NQs) in particular, where is the important planning done and by whom? Where does the balance of power lie between civil servants and SQA personnel? Who meets with whom on a regular basis, and at what level do they operate? How is the continuing 'intelligence' of any operation maintained? How would we know if important ideas and proposals originate within the SQA itself or if they have been driven by government officials at the behest of ministers? An understandable concern with confidentiality means that it is hard for 'outsiders' to gain a good understanding of the way assessment policy is initiated, developed and refined. This raises questions about the structure and management of the organisation.

ORGANISATIONAL STRUCTURE AND MANAGEMENT

The chief executive of the SQA since 2007 has been Dr Janet Brown, who was formerly Managing Director of Industries with Scottish Enterprise and before that worked in business management in the private sector. This background perhaps explains the strong 'corporate' character of the organisation. Dr Brown works with an executive team of six directors whose remits cover Finance, Business Systems, Business Development, Operations, Qualifications Development, and Human Resources and Organisational Development. Overall policy and strategy is determined by a Board of Management, which consists of ten members drawn from schools and colleges, and public and private sector organisations. Board minutes are available on the SQA website and suggest that the members engage in robust discussion of financial, strategic and educational issues. One of the criticisms of the examinations crisis of 2000 was that the board at that time had adopted a rather laissez-faire attitude and had not exercised sufficient oversight of operational matters which might have enabled them to anticipate some of the problems that arose. One consequence, which has had implications for the way many public bodies now operate, is that boards are now expected to take a more active role, subjecting executive officers to careful questioning about their reports and recommendations.

The SQA also has an advisory council. Its role is to advise the SQA on the needs and views of stakeholders in relation to qualifications and awards. The membership of sixteen includes representatives from schools, colleges, employers and trades unions, all of whom will have perspectives to offer on the fitness for purpose of the SQA's qualifications and the efficiency with which the processes of conducting examinations and awarding qualifications are carried out. As its name suggests, the advisory council does not have executive power to make decisions but, given the need to retain the confidence of clients, the SQA would be unwise to disregard the representations of council members. A parallel might be drawn with the private sector where company boards have had to respond to shareholder views expressed at annual general meetings.

Much of the day-to-day work of the SQA is carried out by teams working in particular areas of specialism. For example, there are forty-two Qualifications Design Teams (QDTs) working on the design and development of qualifications within particular subjects such as English, History, Maths and Chemistry. Membership is made up of subject experts drawn from local authorities, colleges, universities and employers. There is also a Curriculum for Excellence (CfE) Liaison Team, with dedicated staff serving different geographical areas, providing advice and support about the new qualifications being introduced to reflect the changes in curriculum. Between October 2012 and March 2013, a programme of subject implementation events, targeted at principal teachers and faculty heads, were held to prepare for the new National 2 to National 5 courses starting in session 2013–14. Reports of such events suggest that they are greatly valued by teachers. Lines of responsibility between specific continuing professional development (CPD) teams and the overall management structure are clearly defined. The QDTs, for example, work to strategic guidance from Curriculum Area Review Groups. Overall, the SQA emerges as an organisation which, in management terms, has moved on significantly from the events of 2000.

PASS RATES: 'GRADE INFLATION' AND 'DUMBING DOWN'?

In terms of carrying out the key function of marking the NQ examination papers and delivering certificates on time, the SQA has operated very successfully with no serious glitches whatsoever in the last dozen years. The controversies that have figured during these years affect all examination bodies, everywhere, and are more than technical in nature. They relate to standards and how marks are interpreted educationally; the ever-present concern with *pass rates*.

	2008	2009	2010	2011	2012	Change
Standard Grade	98.0%	98.5%	98.5%	98.5%	98.9%	0.4
Intermediate 1	71.9%	73.4%	72.7%	76.0%	76.1%	0.2
Intermediate 2	78.0%	78.1%	79.1%	80.3%	80.2%	−0.1
Higher	73.4%	74.2%	74.6%	75.2%	76.9%	1.8
Advanced Higher	75.8%	77.8%	77.5%	79.3%	80.1%	0.9
Baccalaureate	–	–	76.8%	80.5%	79.1%	−1.3

Figure 76.1 Pass rates in National Qualifications across the years 2008–12

In August each year, Scottish pupils receive the results of their efforts in the May/June NQ examinations. In 2012, 158,908 candidates received awards, the overall pass rates being as shown in Figure 76.1 along with those for the previous four years. The final column shows the change from 2011 to 2012. In the case of passes at Higher, the increase of 1.8 per cent against 2011 took the pass rate to nearly 77 per cent – the sixth year in a row it has risen. The national press publicise these annual figures and each year there is an almost identical spate of reactions to the rising pattern of pass rates:

- The SQA highlights 'the best-ever levels' of results and asserts that they demonstrate the value of qualifications.
- Government politicians congratulate pupils and teachers on their well-earned achievements.
- Opposition politicians also congratulate pupils and teachers but claim there is public suspicion about a lowering of standards.
- Newspapers express 'fresh concerns' that qualifications are being 'dumbed down'.
- Perhaps a little too defensively, teaching unions point to the robustness of the qualifications framework and state that results inevitably fluctuate a bit from year to year.
- Local authorities claim that the results vindicate their commitments to raising standards and aspirations (with, in 2012, the directors of education in Glasgow and Edinburgh both pointing to better attendance rates in their city schools).
- Many teachers concede that increases in pass rates reflect their growing familiarity with courses and the demands of particular examinations.

From time to time, some commentators concede the significance of the last of these points. Teachers do teach to the exams and they get better at it, so we should not be surprised about rising pass rates. However, exam passing does not guarantee being successful in later life, a matter painfully underlined by the current, and worsening, mismatch between exam proficiency and growing unemployment. The issue of precisely what form examinations should take and how different they need to be (compared to the past) in the interests of better serving individuals and society provokes lively debate. Ian Bell, in an article entitled 'Define achievement before berating our pupils' ability' in *The Herald* of 8 August 2012, contributes an interesting perspective. He points out that reported concerns about 'falling standards' constitute a repeated phenomenon; they were expressed in the 1960s, the 1980s and the 2000s as well as the present. What is different, he argues, is that rising pass rates at the end of secondary school now coincide with universities finding it necessary to provide remedial courses in basic subjects, e.g. Strathclyde's 'top-up' maths classes for first year students; several Scottish, and English, universities' provision of remedial English (yet the very same institutions turn out increasing numbers of graduates). As Bell states: 'Schools, it seems, have mastered the Higher, yet what is required for the Higher doesn't always suit the universities'. In his article, he therefore does not find fault with schools, for they are hitting their intended target; nor with universities, for they are turning out graduates with enviable degrees. Rather it is that all parties involved should be concerned about what we mean by 'achievement'. More than ever, it requires clarification and new forms of assessment must be created, attuned to what school leavers and university entrants *both* need. It is far from evident from CfE developments to date that we are making progress towards that target. The SQA has no jurisdiction over universities, of course, so it is interesting to speculate how any joint schools/universities/Government/SQA investigation into these matters might be instigated.

The political sensitivity of this issue should not be underestimated. No government (of whatever party) would like to concede that it may be presiding over a period of falling standards, particularly at a time when international comparisons of educational achievement attract considerable attention. Equally, the professionals involved (teachers, curriculum developers, lead examiners, senior bureaucrats) want to maintain that the quality of teaching and the rigour of the examination process ensure that levels of achievement are being maintained or improved (see also Chapter 75). Likewise, pupils (and their parents) wish to be assured that their results are a fair reflection of their efforts. In other words, there are many groups with a strong vested interest in arguing that there are few grounds for concern. What would be helpful would be some properly independent research comparing forms of assessment and patterns of results over an extended period. It would not be easy to construct such a research project – the methodological challenges would be considerable – but it might provide a better basis for informed judgement than the current exchanges of claim and counter-claim. However, the chances of such research being commissioned are remote, precisely because of the political risks that the findings might carry.

APPEALS

Related to the matter of pass rates is the procedure that enables candidates to challenge the decisions of the examiner, what for many candidates and their families is a vexed matter: appeals. It has to be said that the SQA has operated a commendably impressive appeals procedure for many years. Where a candidate does not perform as well in a national exam as the school or college expected, his or her teachers can submit an appeal whereby the examiners check alternative evidence (such as previously completed prelim exams) to consider if a grade can be raised. In 2011, the SQA received 64,309 appeals and of these 49 per cent were unsuccessful. Prior to 2006–7, a statistically based 'derived' grade procedure was also used (one that checked how accurately secondary departments in the school in question forecasted their results). That procedure ceased in 2007, the SQA's research favouring the predictiveness of appealed grades over derived grades. The decision was seen in terms of equity across schools and catchment areas, not least because the derived appeals procedure favoured large schools. Recently, the SQA has decided to streamline its appeal procedure following consultations and from session 2013–14 onward, two new services will operate. It is claimed (on the SQA website) that these will provide better support for candidates and make fewer demands on teachers and lecturers:

> The 'Exceptional Circumstances Consideration' which will ensure that candidates, who their school or college believe have suffered as a result of exceptional circumstances, such as bereavement or illness, will be able to submit alternative evidence of demonstrated attainment before results are published. This 'alternative evidence' will take the form of coursework, class assessments or prelims.

> The 'Post-Results Service' which will ensure that if, after results day in August, a school or college is concerned by a candidate's result they can request an administrative review of the script and/or a request to have the marking of the script checked. This could result in a candidate's grade going up or down.

This will mean that pre-existing evidence will be used and new evidence not required solely for the purpose of an appeal (the latter said to be common at the time of writing). Schools and colleges are charged for unsuccessful appeals – clearly one part of the pressure to prevent the ever-increasing spate of appeals that are made, half of which fail because there is no back-up evidence to support them. School Leaders Scotland's General Secretary, Ken Cunningham, welcomed the proposed simplification, stating that the new services 'will continue to strengthen what is recognised globally as a robust national qualifications body. It will be important, however, in the early days of the new appeals system that, as at present, a close watch is kept on how it works in practice.'

ADVANCED HIGHERS AND THE BACCALAUREATE

Qualifications at the senior levels of school have been the focus of concerns about how usefully they relate to university entrance. Advanced Highers (AHs) (level 7 in the Scottish Credit and Qualifications Framework, the highest level of certificate offered by the SQA) are sometimes taken by pupils (aged 16–18) in their sixth year of school or at college, these qualifications anticipating the first year of university work in the subjects concerned. Hence they sometimes enable candidates to gain direct entry into second year. AHs replaced the Certificate of Sixth Year Studies in 2001. They demand more independent work of candidates than do Highers and most subjects require the completion of a project, thus necessitating some research, analysis and extended essay-writing. Combining two AHs in languages or science subjects with an interdisciplinary project allows candidates to be eligible for the Scottish Baccalaureate.

The Advanced Higher and Baccalaureate figures in Table 76.1 are worthy of comment, not for the pass rates but for the numbers of candidates entered for the qualifications. The proportion of S6 pupils who take them is not as high as one might suspect, particularly in the case of the Baccalaureate where there were only 182 candidates nationally in 2012 (a rise of eight from the previous year) with another fifty pupils choosing to pursue the interdisciplinary project alone. That project is the defining feature of these subject group qualifications. Baccalaureates have recently been introduced in Social Science and Expressive Arts. Overall, the bulk of entrants come from the independent sector.

The role of AHs sometimes splits opinion. On the one hand, they are valued for what possessors of them are capable of doing at university and this is apparent at selection of Scottish candidates for places at *English* universities. As far back as 2006, the Director of Admissions for the Cambridge colleges commented favourably upon what they indicated about candidates:

> We are very happy with Advanced Highers. They have features we wish A-levels had. It is more difficult for candidates to get A grades at AH and the grades are more meaningful, so we are more likely to make offers to Scottish schools. (*The Sunday Times*, 10 December 2006)

In more recent years, both Oxford University and Cambridge University selection has depended upon three As at A Level for English candidates compared with two As + one B at AH Level for Scottish candidates. Some Scottish applicants possess three As at AH. Ironically Scottish AHs do not receive comparable recognition on their own home territory. Universities Scotland stands by the use of Highers, not Advanced Highers, for selection and this firmly relates to the four-year pattern of Honours degrees in Scotland. Nevertheless, headteachers frequently say that more account should be taken of Advanced Highers, amongst other things arguing that they help prevent pupils 'coasting' in S6, having achieved unconditional entry on the basis of their S5 Highers. What is rarely acknowledged in this debate are the very low numbers achieving Advanced Highers, nationally, in any year: it is only about 2 or 3 per cent of the cohort across all subjects. Overall numbers stand currently at about 21,000 entries per year nationally, the figures increasing by about 1,000 each year. Putting this another way, only about 12 per cent of S5 Higher candidates go on to take Advanced Highers the following year.

INNOVATION IN ASSESSMENT: E-ASSESSMENT

In the drive to make assessment more reliable and efficient, and also more responsive to the needs of users (whether candidates, presenting centres, employers or universities), the SQA has explored the possibilities of electronic resources. Recent estimates are that approximately one-third of the world's population now uses the internet, with digital technologies changing the way that texts are produced and displayed, and therefore how they are read by students. The impact on learning (and hence assessment) is considerable and educators at all ages and stages require to be familiar with the rapidly changing landscape around them. Electronic forms of assessment themselves constitute an important challenge for examination bodies in many countries at the present time. The SQA's *Annual Review 2009–2010* records that the organisation received £1.7 million from the European Social Fund 'to enhance the delivery of National Certificates, National Progression Awards (NPA), Skills for Work, and English for Speakers of Other Languages (ESOL) courses'. This followed the Scottish Government's investment of £95 million in 129 projects across Scotland 'to develop the national workforce, create and safeguard jobs, and regenerate communities'. The projects, which ran until May 2011, have focused on the development of innovative e-learning and e-assessment materials for new pre-vocational and professional qualifications. Currently, for example, the organisation offers training events and online support ('Deskspace Training Courses') for employers and providers concerned with Skills for Work.

Many claims are made for e-assessment, including:

- increases in teaching time with the automatic marking of questions and quick return of results to students;
- online analysis of learners' responses permitting feedback (tailored to an extent);
- the use of social software technology (blogs and wikis) by students to share views and information, leading to possibilities for group assessment streamlining/standardising marking; and
- the storage of extended response answers for later scrutiny by teachers.

Anyone familiar with closed test items of the standard fixed response kind (say the basic 'choose one from four alternatives' in a simple multiple-choice format) will appreciate that it is easy to work up their complexity to make guessing less likely, thus enhancing the quality of the test concerned overall. Modern forms of e-assessment easily lend themselves to attractive and interesting possibilities: drop-down lists with animations; combining different demands in the question stem in multimedia displays; drag and drop pictures or symbols in order to answer queries; 'connect' tasks where information has to be linked together by the examinee from two lists or a matrix of possibilities; and so forth.

However, open response questions can now be formatted electronically, simple versions requiring the student to type into designated sections of the computer screen ('free text' items), more complex ones incorporating simulations (generally called 'simulation items'). An 'experiment and respond' item, for example, would require the student to move icons on screen and respond to instructions and questions accordingly. On-screen diagnostics can be made adaptive, that is they can be made to change according to the responses given by the person undertaking the assessment. If test material is being used formatively, then a sophisticated e-assessment format can supply feedback item by item. If they are being used summatively, then summary screens can provide feedback overall, as well as scores and grades. The makers of e-assessment materials claim that a central advantage is that, since the speed of interacting with test content is learner-driven, the feedback that can be supplied is given exactly where and when it is needed – at the point of any cognitive conflict the learner is experiencing.

Private manufacturers of e-assessment materials, such as 'Surpass: The E-Assessment Platform' (the SQA is one of their clients), believe that their products hold out the prospect of transforming learning, not just assessment. It is pertinent to note that as part of the first national surveys of pupil attainment associated with the implementation of CfE (the Scottish Survey of Literacy and Numeracy (SSLN), numeracy being checked in odd-numbered years from 2011 and literacy in even-numbered years from 2012), the SQA was involved in a scoping exercise in 2011 to trial monitoring interactively. Its scoping report stated:

> introducing technology to assessment is not just about the transfer of paper to screen. It is as much about the general changes that are occurring in the way technology is impacting on learning, on the way young people interact and communicate with each other, on the way they research

and communicate information and about how they will use technologies as tools in the workplace of 2020. (See SSLN at www.scotland.gov.uk/Topics/Statistics/Browse/School-Education/SSLN)

'TAG Developments', another private company working on e-assessment (and currently investigating the use of social media as collaborative online learning tools in Singapore), is looking at how evidence-based assessment can be 'machine-marked', i.e. exploiting the internet so that authentic assessment of, for example, workplace-located tasks can be carried out. Clearly, this will open up the possibility of significant advances in the validity of qualifications as the technology develops. Employers do want evidence of real-life skills (such as collaboration). TAG is developing authoring tools to make criteria tagging of evidence easier for the teacher. In this, such a tool essentially selects or identifies parts of the student's work that may demonstrate meeting certain objectives, and thereby draws them to the attention of the teacher to confirm or override the suggestions picked out by the software.

Closer to home, certainly of greater familiarity to many teachers in Scotland, is the recent upgrading of the SCHOLAR forum. This is a partnership led by Heriot-Watt University and provides flexible, interactive educational resources online for many Higher and Advanced Higher subjects. The web-based learning allows teachers to set pupils work and track how they are managing it. That is, formative assessment is integrated within it, there being sophisticated interactivities and simulations to bring about the learning and ongoing diagnostic assessment of mistakes in thinking. A number of teachers attest to the very varied times at which pupils use this resource (which they may appraise by the submission times apparent on work that the teacher can closely monitor). Publicity material associated with SCHOLAR claims that 45 per cent of respondents in a survey reported they used the online materials out of school hours about once or twice per week. Enthusiasts speak well for the engagement that can be achieved. Carole Graham, a Modern Languages teacher at Tynecastle High School in Edinburgh, has spoken at CPD events and conferences attributing the success of her sixth year, tri-level teaching (pupils tackling AH, H and Intermediate 2 in the one class) to her use of SCHOLAR. See at http://scholar.hw.ac.uk

PROSPECTS

Notwithstanding the very great advantages which may accrue to these innovations in electronic assessment, they will not come without their own problems. Technology has many benefits and creates new possibilities but it also offers scope for misuse. The more that is transferred from paper to electronic forms of communication, and the more powerful the software and hardware available to young people, the greater the risk of plagiarism – increasingly complex and sophisticated forms of plagiarism. For teachers, the sources of original effort become increasingly difficult to ascertain and credit accordingly when it comes to assessment. And academics who study the phenomenon are quick to point out that students need considerable amounts of help to understand what is and what is not plagiarism. The 'cut and paste' mentality, drawing on material readily available on the internet, is widespread among the young. Carroll (2008), admittedly focusing more upon tertiary institutions and foreign students, but generalising it to home students, recommends that 'all students will need to know what is expected of them concerning plagiarism, most will need specific teaching of the necessary skills . . . before they can acceptably "do their own work"'. He states unequivocally that:

Staff and students will need safe contexts in which the concept of plagiarism, its complexity and how the rules are applied in practice, can be discussed. Perhaps this means rethinking the induction session to include this topic or making space in a module to cover what is expected. Students simply cannot grasp what is needed without some degree of experiential learning.

The SQA will necessarily address and re-address these matters in the years ahead.

Another issue that is likely to be high on the agenda in the immediate future is the relationship between the SQA and the new body ES. Clearly communication between them is still developing but it is critical that thinking about attainment (a prerogative of the SQA) and thinking about learning (a priority for ES) should be addressed jointly. *Attainment* and *learning* are not synonymous, whatever the layman's interpretation of these words, and energies should be focused upon how deep forms of useful learning can be better assessed than they are currently. At present attainments may be rising but, in themselves, existing forms of assessment fall short of convincing everyone that learning is getting better in schools. The solutions to such problems will be more than technical in nature; joined-up thinking and creativeness is required.

This kind of dialogue should not, however, be confined to in-house discussions between the SQA and ES. It should involve a wide range of stakeholders (practitioners, researchers, academics, employers) who have an interest in ensuring that qualifications genuinely reflect knowledge, skill and understanding. This relates to the point made earlier in the chapter about the desirability of greater openness regarding the processes involved in policy initiation and development. No single group has a monopoly of wisdom, and the thinking of government officials and senior SQA and ES staff is likely to benefit if informed by the perspectives of others who are equally concerned to ensure that curriculum and assessment policy is not only efficient in operational terms but also well grounded intellectually. Such an approach could only further enhance the credibility of the SQA.

As this chapter was being written, major political concerns about the standards of GCSE qualifications were taking place in England, with re-grading of the 2012 results being urged by politicians and public alike. These were accompanied by the English Education Minister Michael Gove proposing reforms to the curriculum and examination system – to many observers, taking a backward step to reinstating an O Level programme for more able pupils alone. The English situation is complicated by the existence of several examination boards rather than the single board that operates in Scotland. This is one aspect of the greater diversity that can be seen in the English system, evident for example in the variety of types of secondary school compared with the relative uniformity of the comprehensive system in Scotland. For a small nation such as Scotland, there are clearly good grounds for having a single national body overseeing all sub-degree level qualifications. It is vital, however, that it commands the respect of those who come into contact with it, whether as examinees, schools, universities or employers (see Paterson, 2012). Considerable efforts will continue to be devoted to monitoring standards and maintaining quality, not only to consolidate the reputation of the SQA but, more importantly, to serve the needs of the Scottish educational system as a whole.

REFERENCES

Carroll, J. (2008) 'Assessment issues for international students and for teachers of international students'. See at www.heacademy.ac.uk

Paterson, L. (2000) *Crisis in the Classroom*. Edinburgh: Mainstream.
Paterson, L. (2012) 'Gove's exams could shed light on our two traditions', *TESS*, 28 September, 35–6.
Scottish Qualifications Authority (2011) SQA Corporate Plan 2011–14. Online at www.sqa.org.uk/
    sqa/files_ccc/2011-14CorporatePlan.pdf

77

SQA Findings on Scottish Attainments

Rob van Krieken

The Scottish Qualifications Authority (SQA) develops, assesses and awards qualifications taken in workplaces, colleges and schools. It provides qualifications across Scotland, the UK and internationally. Separately, as SQA Accreditation, it authorises vocational qualifications (other than degrees) delivered in Scotland, including Scottish Vocational Qualifications, and approves awarding bodies that wish to award them. As an awarding body, the SQA works with schools, colleges, universities, industry and government, to provide high-quality, flexible and relevant qualifications. It strives to ensure that its qualifications are inclusive and accessible to all, that they recognise the achievements of learners and that they provide clear pathways to further learning or employment. It provides raw data to the Scottish Government which performs in-depth analyses for the benefit of schools and educational authorities and for policy. This chapter reports on trends in uptake and attainment of SQA qualifications from 2006 to 2011. Within the limits of available data and analyses, it also describes some of the variability of attainment across the population of candidates by gender, age and centre type. Finally, this chapter identifies some of the issues that were important in the last five years and which are expected to become important in the next. The chapter focuses on the number and types of SQA qualifications that have been undertaken and achieved by candidates in centres in Scotland. Overseas candidates learning at Scottish centres are included. Of course, more learning and more training has taken place in Scotland over the last five years than is certificated by the SQA. However, the discussion is restricted to certificated attainment of SQA qualifications, specifically Group Awards and National courses. It does not cover attainment in Scotland of qualifications offered by other awarding organisations, nor does it cover attainment of non-certificated learning and training, for instance in primary school, community centres or work. One also needs to keep in mind that the attainment reported here only reflects the awards that have been newly attained in a particular year, without taking into account all awards attained previously by that year's candidates, or indeed by the whole population. Chapter 77 reports on attainment as measured in national surveys.

THE SQA QUALIFICATIONS PORTFOLIO

The SQA offers several types of qualifications. They can be grouped in families as follows.

- *Standard Grades*: Standard Grades are the well-known National Qualifications developed since the 1980s to be taken at the end of compulsory education, in S4. There are three levels, Foundation, General and Credit. Most learners sit exams at two levels in up to seven courses.

- *National courses*: These were introduced in 1999. They are available at Access 1 to 3, Intermediate 1 and 2, Higher and Advanced Higher. Some schools offer Intermediate units and courses as alternatives to Standard Grade in second, third and fourth year. Courses at Intermediate levels are also suitable for those wishing to take up a new subject at school or college. Usually, learners progress from Intermediate to Higher levels in a selection of courses in fifth year, and increasingly to Advanced Higher in sixth year. Highers are normally needed for entry into university or college to study for degree or Higher National Certificate or Diploma courses (HNCs or HNDs). Advanced Highers are aimed at students who have passed Highers, and are usually taken in sixth year of school or at college. These courses extend the skills and knowledge gained at Higher level and are useful for entry to university or employment. As described in Chapter 74, Standard Grade and Intermediate Awards will be replaced by National 4 and 5 Awards. The analysis of the attainment data in the years 2006–11 which follows below therefore includes Standard Grade and Intermediate performance.
- *Higher National Certificates and Diplomas*: These are a preparation for a vocational career or for further study. They are normally delivered by further education colleges.
- *Scottish Vocational Qualifications*: Scottish Vocational Qualifications (SVQs) are based on national standards of competence, developed by representatives from industry, commerce and education. They are normally acquired on the job, in realistic working environments or as an apprenticeship. SVQs are offered by various awarding organisations accredited by the SQA. The figures in this chapter only show SVQs awarded by the SQA itself.
- *Other Group Awards*: These are more flexible combinations of units for vocational purposes, such as National Certificates and National Progression Awards. These are mostly delivered by further education colleges.
- *Professional Development Awards*: Professional Development Awards (PDAs) are designed to develop the skills of young people, graduates and other adult learners. They are ideal for continuing professional development (CPD) so that employers can use them to enhance the skills of their employees. PDAs are available for a wide range of skills and professions and are generally delivered by colleges.

Figure 77.1 shows that in 2011, the qualification families awarded to most learners were National courses and Standard Grades which together make up 90 per cent of all qualifications awarded.

The relative size of each of the main families within the total number of qualifications has changed over time. Figure 77.2 shows that the percentage of National courses awarded has increased, while that of Standard Grade awards has gone down. Although the number of successfully completed qualifications in other group awards and in PDAs has doubled, and that in HNC and HND qualifications has grown too, they still form just under 10 per cent of the total. The total number of awards has grown slightly, if anything, while the relevant age groups in the Scottish population showed signs of a slight decrease (General Register Office for Scotland, 2011). This seems to indicate that the same number of learners has attained slightly more qualifications.

The following figures present a survey of attainment over the period from 2006 to 2011 for each qualification family separately by presenting side by side the number of entries and successfully completed courses. Most entries that did not result in an award were not completed within the available time or were withdrawn. Only a few of them were because the candidates did not meet the standard. Spreadsheets with detailed information on entries and awards are accessible through the SQA Statistics Reports & Information web page

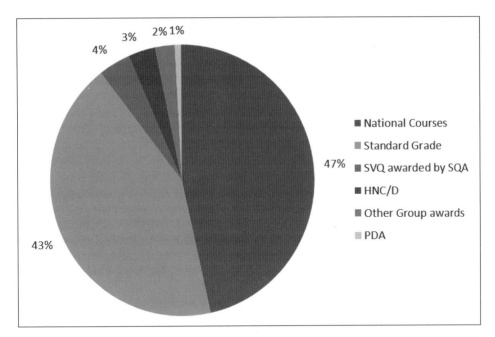

Figure 77.1   Qualifications awarded by qualification family in 2011

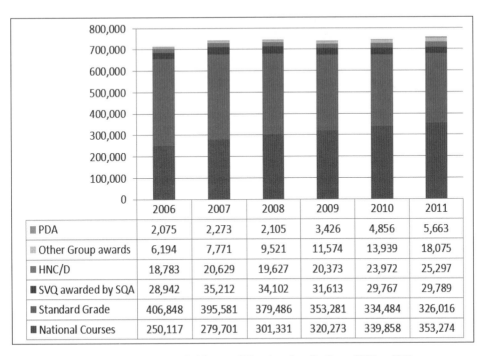

	2006	2007	2008	2009	2010	2011
PDA	2,075	2,273	2,105	3,426	4,856	5,663
Other Group awards	6,194	7,771	9,521	11,574	13,939	18,075
HNC/D	18,783	20,629	19,627	20,373	23,972	25,297
SVQ awarded by SQA	28,942	35,212	34,102	31,613	29,767	29,789
Standard Grade	406,848	395,581	379,486	353,281	334,484	326,016
National Courses	250,117	279,701	301,331	320,273	339,858	353,274

Figure 77.2   Qualifications awarded by qualification family from 2006 to 2011

(www.sqa.org.uk/sqa/48172.html). Numbers of awards and entries are those registered in the same year. In some cases it may have taken longer than one year to successfully complete a course that nominally takes one year of full-time study, and in other cases the course was not yet completed.

ATTAINMENT BY QUALIFICATION TYPE 2006–11

- *National courses*: National courses are usually made up of three National units and an external assessment (which could be an exam or a piece of coursework). They were originally developed as one-year courses for use in post-16 education, for those who had achieved a Standard Grade and for adults. There are National courses at various levels.
- *Access 1, 2 and 3*: Access 1 units are designed for students who require considerable support with their learning, while Access 2 and Access 3 courses consist of normally three units, designed for those with moderate support needs. There is no external course assessment; the course is successfully completed when all units have been passed. Access 3 is comparable with Standard Grade Foundation level.
- *Intermediate 1 and 2*: Intermediate 1 and 2 are often taken by learners who have completed either Standard Grades or courses at Access 3. For some students Intermediate 2 is a stepping stone to Higher. They are also suitable for those wishing to take up a new subject at school or college. Many schools now offer Intermediate units and courses as alternatives to Standard Grade in second, third and fourth year.
- *Higher*: Highers are aimed particularly at learners who have passed subjects at Standard Grade Credit level, or who have successfully completed a course at Intermediate 2. They can also be taken without having achieved a lower level, for instance by adults wishing to study Highers at college, or by learners in sixth year ('a crash Higher'). Highers are normally needed for entry into university or college to study for degree or HNC or HND courses.
- *Advanced Higher*: Advanced Highers (AH) are aimed at learners who have passed Highers, and are usually taken in sixth year of school or at college. The main purpose of AH courses is to allow learners to take the skills, knowledge and understanding they have already acquired from their previous study to a deeper and more challenging level. In doing AH courses, they will develop skills that include higher-order thinking skills, research and investigation skills and independent study skills and they will work with less supervision and more autonomy. These courses extend the skills and knowledge gained at Higher and are useful for entry to university or employment.
- *Skills for Work courses*: A specific group of National courses are the Skills for Work courses. These were introduced to develop employability skills and to encourage school students to become familiar with the world of work. They involve a strong element of learning through involvement in practical activities that are directly related to a particular vocational area, and they develop knowledge and skills that are important to employment. They are available at the same levels as other National courses and are often delivered and assessed by a school and college working in partnership. They do not involve a course assessment such as an exam. The qualifications are quality assured by SQA, as are other qualifications without course assessments, such as Higher National and Scottish Vocational Qualifications.

Figure 77.3 shows that at the four levels from Intermediate 1 and 2, through Higher to Advanced Higher, the numbers of courses entered and of those successfully completed have been steadily rising since 2006.

Figure 77.4 gives the number of courses awarded in a particular year as a percentage of the number of entries (pass percentage). It shows that except at Access 2 the success rate has generally been rising.

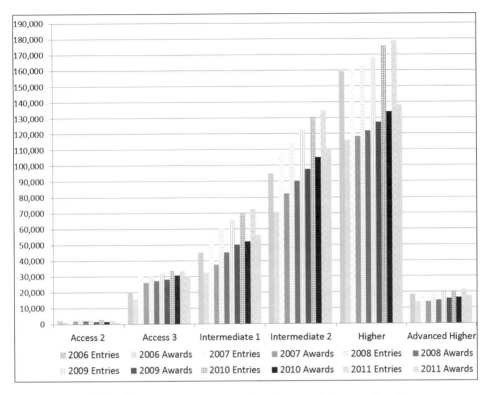

Figure 77.3   National courses: courses entered and successfully completed
from 2006 to 2011

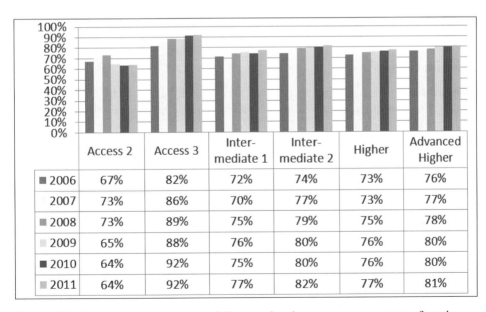

	Access 2	Access 3	Inter-mediate 1	Inter-mediate 2	Higher	Advanced Higher
■ 2006	67%	82%	72%	74%	73%	76%
2007	73%	86%	70%	77%	73%	77%
■ 2008	73%	89%	75%	79%	75%	78%
2009	65%	88%	76%	80%	76%	80%
■ 2010	64%	92%	75%	80%	76%	80%
2011	64%	92%	77%	82%	77%	81%

Figure 77.4   National courses: successfully completed courses as percentage of entries
from 2006 to 2011

Differences in pass percentages over time are often seen as an indication of a trend in standards (see also Chapter 75). This is, however, based on various assumptions, which may or may not be true. It is often assumed that learners undertaking courses and assessments in successive years are comparable, so that a rise in pass rates would indicate a drop in the standards set in assessments and exams. This assumption of constant ability may be reasonable when applied to whole-year groups of learners in schools, but it does not necessarily apply to smaller or varied groups taking qualifications in colleges and workplaces, especially not when learners switch from one qualification to another, for instance from Standard Grade to Intermediate.

In addition to its other quality assurance systems to ensure that national standards are maintained, the SQA monitors whether standards set by assessments and examinations are constant by regularly asking panels of experts to compare a sample of qualifications. Their reports are available on the SQA website (see references). They generally conclude that the standards are comparable. Changes in attainment, therefore, may have been caused by changes in the composition or application of groups of learners, or by other factors such as the quality, conditions or organisation of teaching and training. It is usually assumed that the context in which courses are offered, taught and learned remains the same, that is to say that learning materials, teaching time, time invested by learners, quality of teaching, practice with specifications and assessments, and also any changes in general knowledge or work practices that can have an important influence on the course remain the same over time.

As standards of exams are monitored and have not been shown to be dropping, the increase in attainment should be explained by other factors. Over the reported period, 2006–11, there were no major changes to the educational system, but slow developments such as the increasing move to self-evaluation frameworks cannot be excluded. Examples of other factors that may be responsible for a rise in the percentage of passes are an increasing familiarity with the standards, centres' increasing experience in entering at the level where learners have the best chance of success and possibly an increasing awareness of the importance of success rates amongst a range of stakeholders.

Standard Grades

Standard Grades have generally been taken over the third and fourth year at secondary schools. Learners often take seven or eight subjects including Mathematics and English. There are three levels in Standard Grade: Credit (grades 1 and 2), General (grades 3 and 4) and Foundation (grades 5 and 6). Learners usually take exams at two levels: Credit and General, or General and Foundation. This makes sure that learners have the best chance of achieving as high a grade as possible. Only the highest level a learner achieves is certificated. Figure 77.5 presents the levels achieved from 2006 to 2011. Practically all learners who were entered for Standard Grade (98 per cent) were awarded one of the three levels. Figure 77.5 shows that each level was awarded to a relatively stable percentage of the total number of awards, for instance just under 50 per cent of all awards was at Credit level in all years. The table shows, however, that the total number of awards decreased at every level from 2006 to 2011.

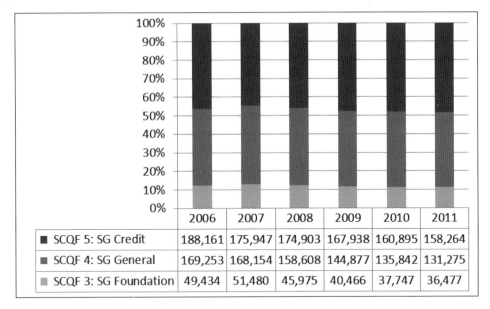

	2006	2007	2008	2009	2010	2011
■ SCQF 5: SG Credit	188,161	175,947	174,903	167,938	160,895	158,264
■ SCQF 4: SG General	169,253	168,154	158,608	144,877	135,842	131,275
▨ SCQF 3: SG Foundation	49,434	51,480	45,975	40,466	37,747	36,477

Figure 77.5   Awarded levels within Standard Grades from 2006 to 2011

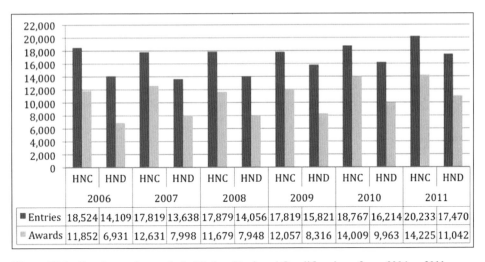

	HNC	HND	HNC	HND	HNC	HND	HNC	HND	HNC	HND	HNC	HND
	2006		2007		2008		2009		2010		2011	
■ Entries	18,524	14,109	17,819	13,638	17,879	14,056	17,819	15,821	18,767	16,214	20,233	17,470
▨ Awards	11,852	6,931	12,631	7,998	11,679	7,948	12,057	8,316	14,009	9,963	14,225	11,042

Figure 77.6   Entries and awards in Higher National Qualifications from 2006 to 2011

Higher National Qualifications

Higher National Certificates and Diplomas have a long and proud history as the leading higher education qualifications for technician, technologist and first-line management occupations. There are two types of Higher National Qualifications. These are HNCs at Scottish Credit and Qualifications Framework (SCQF) level 7 and HNDs at SCQF level 8. If taken as full-time study, HNCs usually take one year to complete and HNDs usually two years to complete.

HNCs and HNDs are developed by the SQA in partnership with further education colleges, universities and industry. They provide both the practical skills and the theoretical knowledge for employment. Many of the qualifications allow articulation to the second and third years of (Scottish four-year) degree programmes. Qualifications developers are advised that relating their design and structure to National Occupational Standards will ensure that the qualifications are fit for purpose and serve the needs of candidates, employers and the economy. There are around 300 HNCs and HNDs covering subject areas from the more traditional – accounting, business administration, childcare, computing, engineering, and hospitality – to the newer – creative industries, paralegal studies, sports and leisure. Figure 77.6 shows that both HNC and HND entries have increased slightly in 2010 and 2011. This continues the steady growth of the number of entries and awards for HNDs since 2007.

Scottish Vocational Qualifications

Scottish Vocational Qualifications are wholly based on National Occupational Standards (NOS) developed by Sector Skills Councils/Sector Skills Bodies. They assess the application of skills, knowledge and understanding as specified in the standards through performance evidence in the workplace or a realistic working environment (RWE) as appropriate. They also show how the content of the NOS refers to the relevant Core Skills. The SQA is accredited to offer over 400 SVQs. There are five levels of SVQs, from level 1 (SCQF 4, comparable in level with Standard Grade General) to level 5 (SCQF 11, comparable in level with a Master's degree). SVQs are increasingly being allocated SCQF level and credits points, with the SCQF level now included in the qualification title alongside the traditional SVQ/NVQ level 1 to 5. Entry numbers at the lowest and highest levels are small. Figure 77.7 presents totals over all five levels. It shows that since 2007 the number of entries has decreased by roughly 30 per cent, while the number of awards only declined by about 15 per cent.

Group Awards

National Qualification Group Awards include National Certificates (NCs), National Progression Awards (NPAs) and Awards (AWDs). Scottish Group Awards (SGAs) were discontinued in 2009. National Certificates and National Progression Awards are designed to prepare learners for employment, career development or progression to more advanced study at HNC/HND level. They also aim to develop a range of transferable knowledge including Core Skills. Each one has specific aims relating to a subject or occupational area. The qualifications are aimed at 16–18-year-olds or adults in full-time education. Over seventy qualifications have been developed at SCQF 5 and 6. They are aligned to National Occupational Standards or other professional or trade body standards, as appropriate to the Group Award. At SCQF level 2 and 3, a National Certificate requires fifty-four SCQF credit points while the higher levels require seventy-two SCQF credit points. National Progression Awards require a minimum of twelve SCQF credit points (see Endnote, p. 710). Figure 77.8 shows that numbers in Scottish Group Awards declined before their removal in 2009. The 'Awards' which were introduced in 2010 have more than equalled the Group Awards uptake by 2011. Entries and awards in National Certificates and National Progression Awards have increased strongly, with NPAs reaching a peak of entries in 2008. Since then the numbers of successfully completed NPAs have been closer to the numbers of entries.

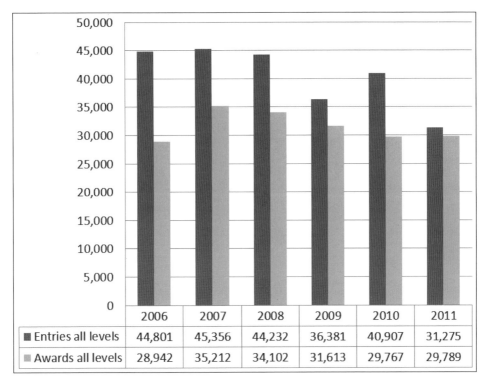

Figure 77.7   Entries and awards in Scottish Vocational Qualifications from 2006 to 2011

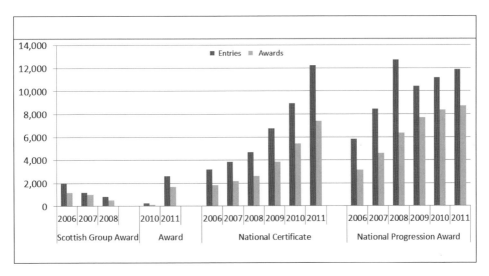

Figure 77.8   Entries and successfully completed Group Awards from 2006 to 2011

Professional Development Awards

PDAs are designed to develop the skills of young people, graduates and other adult learners. They are ideal for CPD so employers can use them to enhance the skills of their employees. PDAs are available for a wide range of skills and professions and are generally provided through colleges. PDAs are available at SCQF levels 6–12. At SCQF level 6 they have a minimum credit value of twelve SCQF credit points, while at SCQF levels 7–12 they have a minimum credit value of sixteen SCQF credit points. Although the numbers of entries for PDAs are relatively small, Figure 77.9 shows that they have more than doubled. The numbers of successfully completed PDAs have slightly lagged behind.

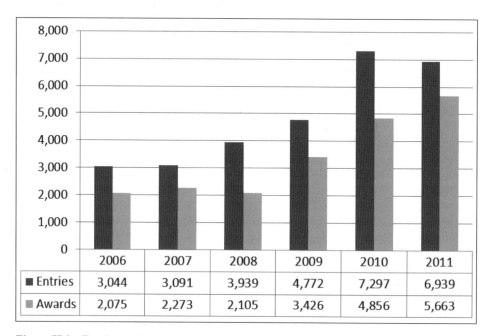

	2006	2007	2008	2009	2010	2011
■ Entries	3,044	3,091	3,939	4,772	7,297	6,939
■ Awards	2,075	2,273	2,105	3,426	4,856	5,663

Figure 77.9   Entries and awards in Personal Development Awards from 2006 to 2011

Candidates and Centres in 2011

This section will focus on attainment in relation to characteristics of candidates. SQA only collects direct information about candidates' characteristics by way of registering age and gender, and information about centres by registering the centre type. The following figures show attainment according to age groups, gender and centre type. The year 2011 is taken as the basis for this section.

Age Groups

Information about awards and age groups is shown separately for, on the one hand, Standard Grades and National courses, and, on the other hand, Higher National, Scottish Vocational Qualifications and National Certificates.

Standard Grades and National Courses

Figure 77.10 shows how each of the Standard Grades and National courses awards were distributed across age groups. Most (80 per cent) Standard Grades at General or Credit level in 2011 were completed at age 15, and the remaining at age 14. Intermediate 1, on the other hand, was taken by a greater range of learners, from 13 to 17, and even by some older than that. Advanced Higher was clearly limited to the 16–18 age group, while Highers started to be taken at 15 and continued to be taken in all age groups after that, like Intermediate 2.

The SQA's 2011 progression report (http://www.sqa.org.uk/sqa/files_ccc/ASR2011_Progression.xls) shows that, on average, of those entered for Intermediate 1, as many as 15 per cent had a Standard Grade award, and almost a third of Intermediate 2 candidates had previously attained a Standard Grade. The percentages varied by course. High percentages of Intermediate English candidates were reported to have previously attained a Standard Grade.

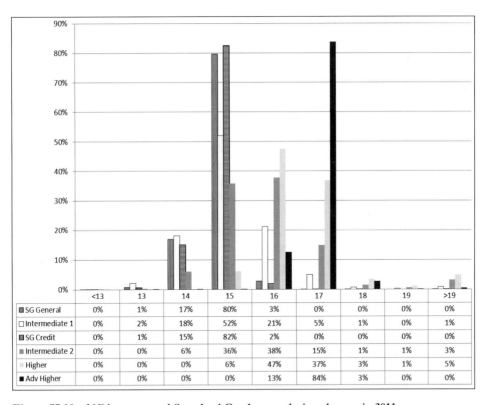

	<13	13	14	15	16	17	18	19	>19
SG General	0%	1%	17%	80%	3%	0%	0%	0%	0%
Intermediate 1	0%	2%	18%	52%	21%	5%	1%	0%	1%
SG Credit	0%	1%	15%	82%	2%	0%	0%	0%	0%
Intermediate 2	0%	0%	6%	36%	38%	15%	1%	1%	3%
Higher	0%	0%	0%	6%	47%	37%	3%	1%	5%
Adv Higher	0%	0%	0%	0%	13%	84%	3%	0%	0%

Figure 77.10   NC learners and Standard Grade completions by age in 2011

Note: As learners in Standard Grade courses usually enter for two levels, this graph uses their resulted (best) level. For National courses the available age-related data were for all learners who had taken a course assessment, whether successfully or not.

Higher National Qualifications

Figure 77.11 shows that Higher National Qualifications (HNCs and HNDs) attract a large number of entries from learners younger than 20 years old. Few of the HND entries in this age group (26 per cent) result in awards. In all other age groups, however, most entries are completed successfully (99 per cent, 71 per cent and 71 per cent respectively). HNDs are likely to have been started by learners just under 20, to be completed successfully and counted as awards in the next age group.

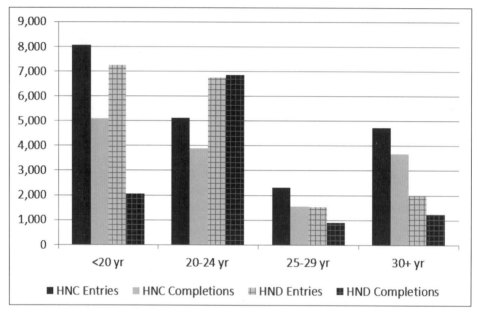

Figure 77.11   HNC and HND entries and successful completions by age group in 2011

Scottish Vocational Qualifications

Figure 77.12 shows how entries for each SVQ level are distributed over age groups. Predictably, the highest levels (levels 4 and 5) of these work-related qualifications are more frequently undertaken when learners are older and more experienced, while a large part of the uptake of the lowest three levels (levels 1 to 3) comes from learners younger than 20 years old, who are starting their working life. The 40- to 49-year-old age group shows a relatively keen interest in SVQs compared to younger and older age groups.

National Certificates

National Certificates are aimed at 16–18-year-olds or adults in full-time education. Figure 77.13 shows that more than half the entries did indeed come from these age ranges.

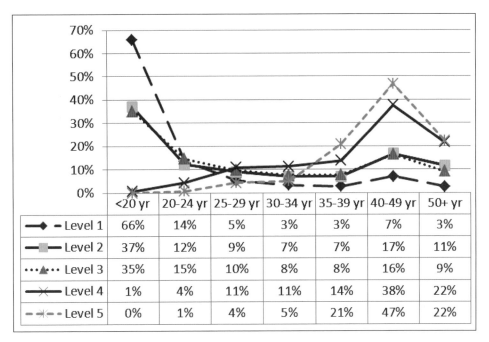

	<20 yr	20-24 yr	25-29 yr	30-34 yr	35-39 yr	40-49 yr	50+ yr
—◆— Level 1	66%	14%	5%	3%	3%	7%	3%
—■— Level 2	37%	12%	9%	7%	7%	17%	11%
··▲·· Level 3	35%	15%	10%	8%	8%	16%	9%
—✕— Level 4	1%	4%	11%	11%	14%	38%	22%
—✳— Level 5	0%	1%	4%	5%	21%	47%	22%

Figure 77.12   Entries for SVQ levels by age group in 2011

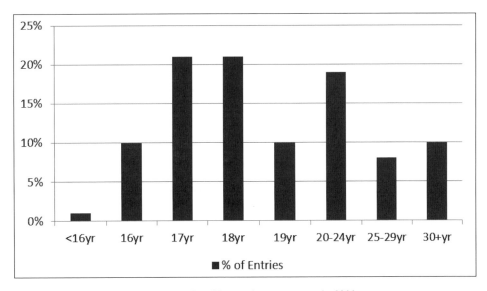

Figure 77.13   Entries in National Certificates by age group in 2011

Gender

National Courses and Standard Grades

The overall balance between male and female candidates entered for National courses and Standard Grades is equal. In 2011, as many male as female candidates attained an award for these qualifications. There were differences, however, in the level of awards attained. Figure 77.14 shows that at the lower levels, Intermediate 1 and 2, more female candidates than male candidates attained A grades. At Advanced Higher, however, the advantage of female learn-ers had moved to higher percentages of grades B and C. The percentage of males without a Pass was higher than the percentage of females without a Pass at all levels.

The same pattern occurred in the distribution of Standard Grade levels, as shown in Figure 77.15. More female than male candidates attained the highest two grades (grade 1 and 2 constitute a Credit).

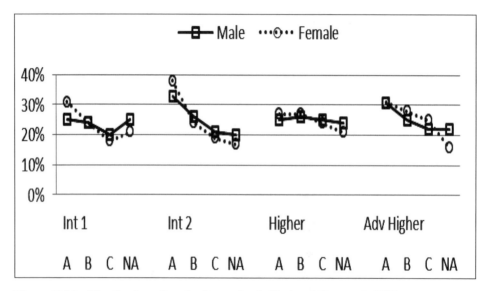

Figure 77.14 **Distribution of grades by gender in National Courses in 2011**

Note: NA = 'No Award', i.e. 'No Pass'. Ungraded National courses, such as Skills for Work, have been left out.

Higher National Qualifications

In HNCs, successful females outnumber males in every age group, except in their early 20s. In HNDs, male and female learners are equally successful in every age group except in their late 20s, when the number of successful females is slightly lower.

Centre Type

Schools and colleges increasingly worked together to provide a wide range of National courses and units to learners aged from 14 to 18. These are the parts of the National courses

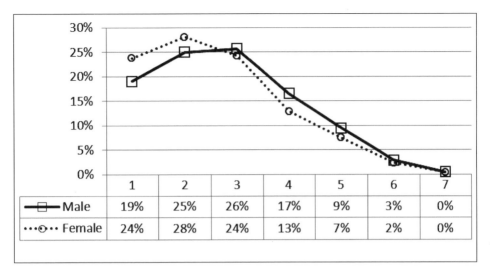

Figure 77.15   Distribution of levels by gender in Standard Grades in 2011

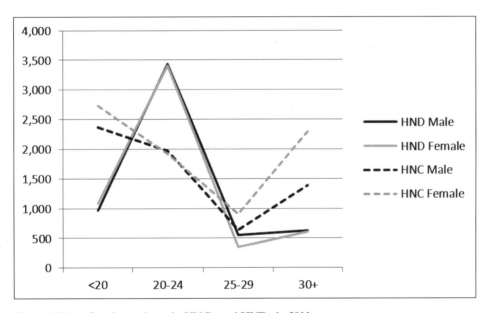

Figure 77.16   Gender and age in HNCs and HNDs in 2011

offered at levels Access 2 to Advanced Higher. It can be difficult to document which centre type contributes to award statistics, because school learners who take a course provided by a college may be awarded either through the school or through the college. Table 77.1 provides a detailed breakdown of 2011 entries for National course units. As many as 29 per cent of National units are awarded through colleges. In colleges, the average number of units taken by a learner is smaller than in schools (7.7 against 9.2), and relatively more learners take just one, two or three units.

Table 77.1   Units by learner and centre type in 2011

Number of units	All learners	FE learners	School learners	Workplace/ training provider	Other
1	34,013	18,365	12,627	1,449	1,572
2	18,728	10,900	6,197	685	946
3	21,867	6,267	13,022	1,663	915
4	11,951	4,406	7,190	163	192
5	10,229	3,163	6,714	215	137
6	11,814	2,759	8,886	65	104
7	9,857	2,362	7,458	20	17
8	11,522	2,696	8,773	11	42
9	10,724	2,291	8,374	0	59
10–14	68,905	14,094	54,661	101	49
15–19	33,634	11,290	22,275	19	50
20+	7,857	2,003	5,843	7	4
Total learners	251,101	80,596	162,020	4,398	4,087
Total Units	**2,144,382**	**623,865**	**1,492,723**	**13,983**	**13,811**
Units per learner	*8.5*	*7.7*	*9.2*	*3.2*	*3.4*
Percentage units per centre type	*100%*	*29%*	*70%*	*1%*	*1%*

DEVELOPMENTS AND OPPORTUNITIES

In the period from 2006 to 2011, the SQA has refreshed its qualifications portfolio. It replaced the Scottish Progression Award (SPA) and the Scottish Group Award (SGA) with National Progression Awards (NPAs) and National Certificates (NCs). It also introduced a range of new qualifications, such as Skills for Work courses and Scottish Baccalaureates while starting the development of a new generation of National Qualifications which will be introduced from 2014–15 on.

Skills for Work

It has been recognised for some time that there is a need for vocational courses for young people in the 14–16 age group. These should give them the opportunity to develop knowledge and skills that will help to prepare them for the world of work. In November 2004, the Scottish Executive Report *A Curriculum for Excellence* called for 'more skills-for-work options for young people, robustly assessed, to help them to progress into further qualifications and work'. Following a successful two-year pilot from 2005 to 2007, the SQA has made a range of Skills for Work courses available to centres. These courses are for pupils in third and fourth year of secondary school and above, and they focus on the world of work.

Skills for Work courses are different from other vocational provision because they focus on generic employability skills needed for success in the workplace. The courses offer opportunities for learners to acquire these critical generic employability skills through a variety of practical experiences that are linked to a particular vocational area such as construction, hairdressing, hospitality etc. Skills for Work courses help provide young people with good opportunities to develop their self-confidence. They also aim to provide a very positive learning experience. For many young people, an early chance to work on practical skills that relate directly to the world of work will provide real benefits to their overall educational programme. The courses are intended to provide progression pathways to further education, training and employment. Given their practical nature, experiential learning in appropriate learning environments is an essential feature of each course, although work placement is not essential. Young people taking one of them will normally spend some of their time at a local college, other training provider or employer. This will mean learning in a different environment, meeting new people and facing new challenges. By 2011, as many as 15,000 entries were made for Skills for Work courses, mostly at Access 3 and Intermediate 1 level.

Scottish Baccalaureates

The Scottish Baccalaureates in Science and Languages have been available for delivery since August 2009. The SQA has been encouraged by the uptake of the Baccalaureates, which has increased steadily. Enthusiasm for the awards has been shown by the HE sector; it welcomes the greater focus that the Baccalaureate provides for S6 pupils as well as the skills developed through the Interdisciplinary Project component that match well with the skills required for study at HE level.

As the Scottish Baccalaureates offer an excellent transition from school to HE, FE or employment, it is expected that learners are able to 'hit the ground running' at this important next stage of their lives and that retention rates would improve as a result. In 2010, directed by the Scottish Government, the SQA undertook a scoping exercise on the possible expansion of Scottish Baccalaureate provision. Based on this the existing two Baccalaureate awards are to be broadened to include additional subjects and two new Baccalaureates are being developed in the areas of Social Sciences and Expressive Arts. All current Advanced Higher subjects are to be included in a Scottish Baccalaureate award thus making the Scottish Baccalaureates accessible to a broader cohort of learners.

Wider Achievement

With the growing focus on developing fully rounded individuals and providing more options for students, the SQA has created a portfolio of qualifications that provide recognition for wider achievement activities. These qualifications help schools deliver Skills for Learning, Skills for Life and Skills for Work, and smooth the transition to Curriculum for Excellence delivery. See Table 77.2 for an overview.

Next

The next five years will no doubt see more changes as the new courses at National Levels 4 and 5 are introduced. The economic context and the increasing rate of young people staying on in education will affect entries.

ENDNOTE: SCQF CREDIT POINTS

The allocation of SCQF Credit Points does not refer to a perception of ability, nor is it based on age or experience but is worked out by those with an expert knowledge of the subject who

Table 77.2   Wider achievement awards from the SQA available in 2011

Work Skills	SCQF Level	Personal Skills
Employability Steps to Work Skills for Work	3	Personal Development Access 3 Volunteering Skills Award
Employability National Progression Award Enterprise & Employability Steps to Work Skills for Work Safe Road User Award Internet Safety	4	Personal Development Int 1 Personal Finance Award Safe Road User Award Internet Safety Volunteering Skills Award
Leadership Award NPA Enterprise & Employability Skills for Work	5	Personal Development Int 2 Leadership Award Volunteering Skills Award
Leadership Award NPA Enterprise & Business	6	Personal Development Higher Leadership Award

make a professional judgement on how many hours it would take the typical learner (not those who complete the learning outcomes quickly nor those who require additional time) to achieve the learning outcomes at a given level. This is described in the SCQF *Handbook: User Guide* (2009) as 'the time judged to be required for the "average learner" to achieve the learning outcomes and does not measure the time actually taken by any individual learner'. The estimation of the time required is referred to as notional learning hours. One SCQF Credit Point represents a notional ten hours of learning (SCQF, 2010).

ACKNOWLEDGEMENTS

The author is grateful to several colleagues for their helpful comments on the draft for this article, and especially to Marie McGhee, Susan Kirk and Noel Thomson for the data and ideas they provided. Most of the data presented in the figures in this chapter are derived from the spreadsheets available from the SQA website with statistical reports.

REFERENCES

General Register Office for Scotland (2012) 'Mid-year population estimates; Scotland and its council areas by single year of age and sex: 1981–2011'. See at www.gro-scotland.gov.uk/statistics/theme/population/estimates/mid-year/time-series.html

Scottish Credit and Qualifications Framework Partnership (2010) *SCQF Credit Points Explained: Notional Learning Hours*. Online at www.scqf.org.uk/content/files/resources/Notional%20Learning%20Hours.pdf

Scottish Executive (2004) *A Curriculum for Excellence*. Edinburgh: Scottish Executive.

Scottish Qualifications Authority (2006) *Monitoring Standards Digest 2006*. Online at www.sqa.org.uk/files_ccc/MonitoringStandardsDigest_2006.pdf

Scottish Qualifications Authority (2007) *Monitoring Standards Digest 2007*. Online at www.sqa.org.uk/files_ccc/MonitoringStandardsDigest2007.pdf

Scottish Qualifications Authority (2008) *Monitoring Standards Digest 2008*. Online at www.sqa.org.uk/files_ccc/MonitoringStandardsDigest2008.pdf

Scottish Qualifications Authority web page for Statistic Reports and Information. See at www.sqa.org.uk/statistics

Scottish Qualifications Authority (2013a) *Monitoring Standards over Time: National Qualifications, Higher National Units and Scottish Vocational Qualifications in 2011 compared with previous years.* Online at www.sqa.org.uk/files_ccc/MonitoringStandardsOverTime.doc

Scottish Qualifications Authority (2013b) *Monitoring Standards over Time 2011: SQA's response.* Online at www.sqa.org.uk/files_ccc/MonitoringStandardsOverTime2011SQAResponseActions.doc.

78

National Assessments: Improving Learning and Teaching through National Monitoring?

Ernie Spencer

The role of national monitoring of pupils' learning within the context of Curriculum for Excellence is consistent with key aspects of Scottish assessment policy that have been in place for some time. Monitoring in Curriculum for Excellence includes two main kinds of activity: gathering information about overall national performance of pupils in the 8–15 age range through sample-based surveys/tests; and comparison over time of the performance of older pupils in the Scottish Qualifications Authority (SQA) National Qualifications. Both these types of activity were features of the national scenario before the development of Curriculum for Excellence, contributing with other kinds of information to attempts to evaluate and improve educational provision at national, local authority and school levels. It is very likely that analysis of SQA results, adapted to the new National Qualifications arrangements currently under development, will continue to play an important part in evaluation and improvement activity in the Curriculum for Excellence context. In relation to the Curriculum for Excellence 'broad general education' stage (ages 3–15) a new approach to gathering sample-based test data in the Scottish Survey of Literacy and Numeracy (SSLN) takes monitoring of national performance in a new direction. This chapter seeks to demonstrate both the continuity of policy on monitoring as part of the wider national assessment system and the significant differences between current and previous approaches. It proceeds by summarising key aspects of where we were, describing where we are now and, finally, raising some discussion issues.

THE ROLE OF NATIONAL MONITORING IN ASSESSMENT POLICY: WHERE WE WERE

Monitoring 5–14 – National Assessments and Surveys

In the previous edition of *Scottish Education*, Condie (2008) described arrangements for 'National Assessment' of pupils' learning in the context of the 5–14 Curriculum (from 1991) in terms of two systems, National Assessments and Monitoring Surveys.

National Assessments

One system, the 5–14 National Assessments (originally called and commonly thought of as 'National Tests'), provided data on the performance of individual pupils in relation to the published 5–14 curricular 'targets' in English Language and Mathematics. These National Assessments had been intended to complement and, in some sense, confirm teachers' professional judgement of classwork to decide whether a 5–14 level (A, B, C, D, E or F) had been achieved. In practice, however, they had often come to replace, rather than support, professional judgement (see, for example, Hayward and Spencer, 2006, pp. 228–9, referring to a number of studies).

Monitoring Surveys

The other system described by Condie, national monitoring, aimed to determine the proportion of pupils achieving expected curricular standards at specified stages of their primary and early secondary school careers. She gives a succinct history of the two types of national sample-based testing 'surveys' used successively to provide this information at national level – the Assessment of Achievement Programme (AAP) from 1983 to 2004 and the Scottish Survey of Achievement (SSA) from 2005. The specific aims of both the AAP and the SSA surveys were to:

- determine what pupils knew and could do in agreed aspects of subject areas;
- measure performance in relation to 5–14 levels described in national curricular guidelines (in the case of AAP, this applied after the introduction of the 5–14 Curriculum in 1991);
- provide comparisons of the performance of pupils at each of the stages surveyed;
- provide comparisons by gender;
- provide comparisons over time.

Monitoring by Survey Only – the Scottish Survey of Achievement

From the start of the implementation of the 5–14 curriculum and assessment arrangements in the early 1990s until 2004, the first system, National Assessments (in English Language and Mathematics only), as well as providing individual pupil information, contributed to both local and national monitoring in parallel with the AAP surveys. Schools annually informed their local education authority and central government of the proportions of pupils at each stage judged to have achieved the various levels. A 'target-setting' initiative devised and promoted by Her Majesty's Inspectorate of Education (HMIE) in the 1990s sought, in principle, to enable schools, with the support of their education authority, to achieve a target (such as an increased proportion of pupils achieving 5–14 level D in Primary 7 or a Credit award at Standard Grade) by improving learning and teaching. However, in many cases, the initiative did not in fact result in the intended focus on improved learning and teaching. Sliwka and Spencer (2005) reported that many headteachers and classroom teachers held the view that target-setting encouraged them to focus on summative assessment, rather than assessment for learning. They noted also that some seemed to regard action to develop very good learning and teaching as separate from, or even inimical to, their need to improve results, which inevitably had 'high stakes' status when both education authorities and HMIE were monitoring progress towards individual schools' targets.

Assessment, Testing and Reporting 3–14: Consultation on Partnership Commitments (Maclellan, 2004), the last of a number of consultative reviews of assessment arrangements in the years 2000–4, made it clear that a large proportion of teachers and representatives of parents, local authorities and other educational agencies regarded the central collection of 5–14 National Assessment results as of limited use, because of doubts about the quality of the data derived solely from teachers' marking of the National Assessments. A large proportion also expressed opposition to the continuation of the national testing regime because it encouraged 'teaching to the test' and did not provide valid enough information about pupils' real attainments, accepted that teachers' professional judgement should be paramount in deciding when and how assessment should take place and agreed that a new Scottish Survey of Achievement, based on the AAP, should be introduced to provide national data on performance. (They did, however, wish to retain the testing materials – the National Assessment tasks – in an 'assessment bank' as support for teachers' own judgements. The concluding Discussion section of this chapter contains some comment on the extent to which this endorsement of the quality of the National Assessment tasks was really justified.) In response to the Maclellan Review, the government did introduce the SSA to replace both the previous types of monitoring activity, the gathering of 5–14 National Assessment information and the AAP. It was part of what was intended as a coherent national assessment system that also included 'assessment for learning', personal learning planning ('assessment as learning'), 'assessment of learning' based firmly on teachers' professional judgements and annual progress plans for each pupil.

By comparison with AAP, the SSA expanded the information available from the national monitoring survey in a number of ways. AAP surveys of performance in English Language, Mathematics and Science had been conducted in a three-year cycle at P4 (age 8–9), P7 (age 11–12) and S2 (age 13–14). The SSA extended the subject areas covered to four with the inclusion of Social Subjects and relevant enquiry skills (despite opposition to bringing in other subject areas from most teachers in the Maclellan Review) and included assessment of core skills such as reading and numeracy across differing curricular contexts, working together in groups, problem solving and ICT skills. A larger sample of pupils was included in each survey to enable some analysis of the data at local authority as well as national level. The stages involved in the surveys changed from P4, P7 and S2 to P3, P5, P7 and S2 and the cycle became a four-year one, to accommodate the new subject area. The sampling arrangements were designed so that it was possible to compare the performance of the same year group of pupils longitudinally (in P3 and P7 or P5 and S2) in the same curricular area. The SSA also included questionnaires for teachers and children in the sample, asking about their teaching and learning experiences in the particular subject area being assessed that year. It also collected information about the teacher's assessment of each sampled child's attainment, allowing comparison of teachers' assessments with performance in the monitoring tests.

In addition to national monitoring using the SSA, Scotland participated during the 1990s and up to 2006 in international studies of attainment, including the Progress in International Reading Literacy Study (PIRLS – age 10–11), the Trends in International Mathematics and Science Study (TIMSS – age 10–11 and 14–15) and the Organisation for Economic Cooperation and Development Programme for International Student Assessment (PISA – age 15–16) in reading, numeracy and science literacy.

Monitoring Through SQA National Qualifications

SQA examination results have for many years been used to track national performance trends in a straightforward way, comparing year-on-year proportions of pupils gaining the various grades in Standard Grade/Intermediate, Higher and Advanced Higher qualifications. In most subjects the number of examination candidates is high enough to make reliable statistical comparisons possible. There has been in recent years at national level a consistently upward trend in performance in key areas such as Higher English – leading to some political self-congratulation but also to questions about 'grade inflation' and consistency of standards over years. In other areas, for example sciences and modern languages, overall uptake and performance figures have raised questions about the appropriateness of strategies for engaging young people in the subjects and of learning and teaching approaches.

More detailed and sophisticated analysis of SQA results than simple comparison of overall national performance has typically been carried out at school level as part of self-evaluation and improvement planning and also in inspections by HMIE. This has been in effect a process of monitoring individual schools by enabling comparison with 'benchmarks' to raise questions about where and how improvement could occur. Support for this analysis of assessment data has been provided in the Standard Tables and Charts (STACs) jointly developed by the Scottish Government, HMIE and the SQA. They provide for each school overall and for each subject a range of indicators including two key measures:

- *National Comparison Decile*: this shows in which of ten decile (percentile) bands the school is placed in the rank order of all schools' performance over a period of five years. This is in effect a measure of comparison with the national average performance, as well as of rank, and shows any trend in performance;
- *Comparison with Comparator Schools*: this indicates the school's or subject department's ranking in a group of twenty schools with similar characteristics, identified using five factors for which robust data exist. Two principal components combining these factors explain most of the variance: degree of deprivation (73 per cent) and urban/rural location (15 per cent). Typically these comparisons are made over a three- or five-year period. (This measure exists because it is recognised that comparison of performance only with the national average does not take account of important factors affecting attainment. However, HMIE advises care in using it, because of other relevant factors for which no data are available.)

For each subject STACs provide two powerful additional measures, again given over a five-year period, so that trends are indicated:

- *Relative Value*: a measure of pupils' performance in a subject by comparison with their results in all their other subjects and the national average. Statistical significance is indicated by asterisks: * (90 per cent level); ** (95 per cent level) and *** (99 per cent level). This measure is particularly valuable because it identifies relatively high- and low-achieving departments *with the same pupils*, raising questions for reflection/discussion about successful pedagogical practice in high-achieving departments and about need for different pedagogical approaches (or other changes) in less successful ones.
- *Progression Value*: a measure of progress made by pupils in a subject compared to all their attainment in an earlier year, so similar to the Relative Value measure, but over time. A positive value indicates more progress made by this school's pupils than is typical nationally. Statistical significance is again indicated by asterisks: * (90 per cent level), ** (95 per cent level) and *** (99 per cent) level. This type of measure is regarded as the most rigorous to

apply, so long as appropriate data about the earlier levels of performance exist. In Scotland it provides information specifically about how effectively a subject department prepares pupils for Higher examinations in S5/S6.

Use of Monitoring Information

The Scottish Government reported nationally on attainment in the curriculum aspect involved in each SSA survey, using the 5–14 levels framework, and on the attainment of core skills. It also published on its website information on Scotland's performance in the international attainment studies. However, it is important to note that, in the context of the policy for a coherent national assessment system which emerged after the Maclellan Review (2004), the results of the national monitoring survey, of the international studies and even of the 'high stakes' SQA examinations are not the only factors taken into account in evaluating education – other elements in the system also come into play.

Condie (2008) quotes the 'assessment quadrant' from the Scottish Government *Circular 02* (2005), which set out the several kinds of information it was intended should come into play within a coherent assessment system to evaluate and improve Scottish education. It is reproduced in Table 78.1 in slightly expanded form to show the place within it of analysis of SQA National Qualifications results, as well as the 5–14-related assessment arrangements covered by *Circular 02*.

This diagrammatic representation of the assessment policy promoted by the 2005 Circular gives an indication of the sophisticated thinking underpinning it. A key characteristic of Scottish educational policy is that it is not informed solely by test/examination results (or teachers' internal summative assessments), though these types of evidence contribute

Table 78.1   Assessment quadrant

	Formative	
Internal	Formative assessment. Personal learning planning. Involving learners, and parents and other adults, in the learning process.	Local authorities' and schools' collection and analysis of information (including in-school and SQA assessment results) to inform evaluation and improvement. HMIE inspection feedback to schools and local authorities and follow-through activities; and reports on aspects of the whole education system.
	Teachers' judgements and reports; with local moderation and 5–14 National Assessments and SQA National Assessment Bank tasks for National Qualifications Units (if teachers wish to use them) as part of understanding and sharing standards.	Scottish Survey of Achievement P3, P5, P7, S2. International studies (PISA, PIRLS, TIMSS). Analysis of SQA results. HMIE inspections and reports on authorities and schools.	**External**
	Summative	

to policy making. All kinds of assessment information, formative and summative, internal and external, and including evaluations, in school and local authority self-evaluation and in inspections, not only of pupils' attainment but also of curriculum planning, learning and teaching, climate for learning and expectations, ethos, inclusiveness, recognition of pupils' achievements outwith academic study and partnership with parents, were viewed as contributing to one overriding purpose: to improve learning for each individual pupil. The role of the results of monitoring activities – the SSA, the international studies and the analysis of the results of SQA examination results – was to provide accountability information on trends in national performance, but, in principle, this information, in conjunction with evaluations of education by HMIE, was intended to inform policy making oriented to improvement. Its principal purpose was envisaged as the identification of issues for exploration and reflection in the process of school self-evaluation and improvement planning (and in inspections by HMIE). 'Intelligent Accountability' was a key idea: it requires much information/data; much reflection on it and on the factors that may underlie it; and improvement action that does not oversimplify the issues but recognises the complexity of effecting real change. (Ideas about the intended role of assessment and other data in evaluation and improvement processes are expounded in *How Good Is Our School? The Journey to Excellence*, HMIE, 2006, p. 91).

SSA results (including questionnaire data on learning/teaching), performance in 16+ and 17+ qualifications and HMIE evaluation of schools and the system contributed to curriculum policy action in the Curriculum for Excellence development. The new focus on literacy and numeracy across the curriculum resulted partly from HMIE evidence but also from a pattern of performance in SSA surveys suggesting that too few pupils at the end of primary school and in the early years of secondary achieve the relevant national levels of attainment. The development and implementation within Curriculum for Excellence of a national Science and Engineering Action Plan was influenced by SSA results and questionnaire data, uptake of and performance in Science National Qualifications and HMIE inspection evidence suggesting that pupils have a poor experience of investigative science in primary and early secondary education. Similar survey plus inspection evidence, along with, for example, comments from higher education teachers about students' limited capacity to think for themselves and apply knowledge influenced the general Curriculum for Excellence orientation to 'process', skills development and application, rather than factual knowledge.

THE ROLE OF NATIONAL MONITORING IN ASSESSMENT POLICY: WHERE WE ARE NOW

Same Overall Assessment Policy – but Changes in Monitoring Arrangements

The broad conception of how various kinds of assessment information should contribute to effective education described in the 'assessment quadrant' above remains very important in the development of assessment policy for Curriculum for Excellence. Though it is not yet clear how assessment of Curriculum for Excellence will be developed and implemented in practice, the national assessment guidance in *Building the Curriculum 5: A Framework for Assessment* (Scottish Government, 2011) and its associated documents maintain two key principles: that all assessment and evaluation activities should aim to provide information helpful to the improvement of learning for each pupil; and that a wide range of evidence should be taken into account, not simply test/examination results. In its essence, therefore, the 'quadrant' presentation remains entirely relevant to assessment and evaluation in Curriculum for Excellence. Adapted to take account of Curriculum for Excellence developments it would, for example, on the 'Internal' side include the P7 and S3 Pupil Profiles proposed in *Building the Curriculum 5* and exclude the references to using 5–14 National Assessments as support for teachers' judgements. On the 'External' side it would refer to use by schools of 'Senior Phase Benchmarking' (STACs material re-organised to match Curriculum for Excellence concerns, such as pupils' achievements outwith formal education and the forthcoming new National Qualifications) and to inspection as carried out by Education Scotland (following the merger of HMIE and Learning and Teaching Scotland). In the bottom right corner references would be updated to include the new SSLN and remove international studies in which Scotland will no longer participate (PIRLS and TIMSS).

It is in this bottom right-hand corner of the assessment quadrant, focusing on summative external assessment, that key changes have been made, specifically to arrangements for monitoring overall national performance.

Fewer International Surveys and a New Scottish Monitoring Tool

One significant change is the decision to 'rationalise' survey information to be gathered. Scotland will no longer take part in the PIRLS and TIMSS international surveys, though it will continue with PISA. This decision was made partly to reduce the burden of administering the surveys in schools – both PIRLS and TIMSS were due in 2011 and the next PISA survey was in 2012 – at a time when schools would be gearing up for new Scottish National Qualifications. A financial saving in a difficult time was also a factor in reaching the decision. The PISA survey was retained because there is a large and consistent group of countries that regard it as an important measure and because of its focus on 'skills for life', which were considered to relate well to the Curriculum for Excellence philosophy and aims.

The second significant change is in the nature of Scotland's own monitoring survey covering the period of 'broad general education' (ages 3–15) in the Curriculum for Excellence structure. The SSLN has replaced the SSA.

The Scottish Survey of Literacy and Numeracy

Fewer Stages Assessed and Narrower Curricular Focus

The SSLN aims to monitor performance in literacy and numeracy at P4, P7 and S2 in alternate years, starting with a numeracy survey in 2011 and a literacy one in 2012. (The results of the 2011 numeracy survey were published in March 2012.) The SSA covered four curricular areas plus core skills at P3, P5, P7 and S2. The change from four year groups to three is justified on the Scottish Government website as further reducing the assessment burden on schools (as is the dropping of the PIRLS and TIMSS international surveys).

The focus specifically on literacy and numeracy derives from the prominence given in Curriculum for Excellence guidance to the idea that all teachers should develop pupils' literacy and numeracy across all curricular areas and from concern at the level of the Cabinet Secretary for Education and Lifelong Learning that there should be regular updating of information about performance in these areas to inform policy development. (Curriculum for Excellence guidance also highlights consistently the duty of all teachers to develop pupils' Health and Wellbeing across all aspects of school life: however, no monitoring of understanding of or progress in Health and Wellbeing is planned by government survey, though the Scottish Schools Adolescent Lifestyle and Substance Use Survey (SALSUS) provides information on smoking, drinking and drug use by teenagers and on pupils' attitudes to substance misuse.)

The SSLN is starting afresh in providing comparative data over time. Because the new surveys relate to the Curriculum for Excellence experiences and outcomes (Es and Os) rather than the previous 5–14 curricular targets, it will not be possible to compare SSLN survey results with earlier SSA performance. New baselines for comparison will thus be established by the first SSLN survey in each of the two areas.

Gathering of broad performance information on literacy and numeracy to inform policy decisions is not the only major aim of the SSLN. In accordance with the thrust of the whole Curriculum for Excellence assessment policy and, in particular, the idea that all assessment, including monitoring activities, should lead directly to improvement of learning, a key element in the SSLN strategy is provision of CPD and learning/teaching resources designed to help teachers address areas of weak learning in literacy and numeracy identified in the surveys. In the past, publication of both AAP and SSA results was accompanied (or followed) by material intended for teachers' use that raised curricular or pedagogical issues and suggested areas for reflection. However, the SSLN strategy breaks new ground in that the intention is to provide a significant amount of quite specific guidance designed to promote reflection and facilitate learning and teaching action addressing particular aspects of literacy and numeracy. The current stage of development of this material is described below.

Sampling

There are changes, too, in the sampling methodology employed to identify the pupils who will take the survey. These changes are similarly justified in terms of reducing the pressure on schools. The changes to the method of sampling are such that it is no longer possible for local authorities to have a large enough number of pupils taking the survey to use the results as local accountability measures (which was possible with the SSA). The new sampling system includes a small number of pupils from every school: two from each of P4 and P7 and twelve from S2. The individual pupils are selected centrally by the Scottish Government's Education Analytical Services, using random sampling. The total number of pupils involved at each stage is approximately 4,000. Sampling only three stages and keeping overall numbers down to what is needed for just a national picture of performance (rather than also enabling local performance measures) have reduced the sample by some 75 per cent by comparison with the 2008 SSA survey. Individual pupils do not take all the survey tasks. For example, in the 2011 numeracy survey each pupil took three of ninety assessment booklets covering the whole range of numeracy Es and Os. Each of the ninety booklets was taken by a statistically appropriate sub-sample of some 300–400 pupils. The small number of pupils per school also allows practical and electronic assessments to be more manageable.

Questionnaires and Assessments

Each survey consists of questionnaires for pupils and teachers and written and practical assessments. (There is also a school feedback questionnaire, which asks participating schools to describe their experiences and perceptions.) The pupil questionnaire seeks information about factors likely to affect learning, such as attitudes and classroom experiences. The teacher questionnaire focuses on how Curriculum for Excellence has been implemented in the school and on the assessment approaches adopted. The assessment tasks are designed to sample quite fully the knowledge, skills, capabilities and attitudes identified in the Curriculum for Excellence Es and Os at each of the first, second and third levels in the curriculum framework. The focus is clearly on the appropriate level for most pupils at the relevant age (P4, P7 or S2), though in aspects of literacy such as Listening and Talking and Writing some pupils may be able to show in the survey task achievements matching the level above that identified as appropriate for most at their age.

The 2011 numeracy survey focused only on the Es and Os designated in the curriculum framework as 'Mathematics and Numeracy' (MNU); it did not assess performance in relation to those designated as 'Mathematics' (which include Shape, Position and Movement). Almost all the MNU Es and Os were included. (A small number were omitted because they do not lend themselves to a survey task – an example is an E and O relating to budgeting in everyday life.) There were several tasks relating to each of the 'organisers' within the Mathematics and Numeracy framework. Under Number, Money and Measurement, the organisers are: Estimation and Rounding; Number and Number Processes; Fractions; Decimal Fractions and Percentages; Money; Time; and Measurement. Under Information Handling, the organisers are Data and Analysis; and Ideas of Chance and Uncertainty.

The pupils taking part in the survey faced three types of task – 'atomistic', 'extended' and pupil–teacher interaction. Atomistic tasks are short and stand alone; they are designed to assess Knowing (facts, concepts and procedures), Applying (knowledge and understanding to solve problems and answer questions) and Reasoning (solve non-routine problems, analyse and justify). Extended tasks assess the Find (find, select and record information), Process (process, calculate and classify information) and Evaluate (evaluate information) skills. They comprise a data source and associated questions (eight in the tasks at the first level; twelve in the tasks at second and third levels). The contexts of the information in the data sources in extended tasks derive from numeracy across learning in school and from numeracy beyond the classroom and in everyday life. The pupil–teacher interaction element includes, for example, mental arithmetic tasks.

In reporting performance in the numeracy survey SSLN has adopted a cut-off score strategy to make judgements about how effectively pupils were achieving a particular Curriculum for Excellence level (first level for P4, second for P7 and third for S2). These cut-off scores for levels were set in consultation with Education Scotland, the SQA, teachers and an independent assessment expert, based on an analysis of the tasks involved in the assessment. Pupils scoring 75 per cent or more in the survey tests were considered to be 'performing very well at the level'; those scoring 50–75 per cent were 'performing well at the level'. The scores taken as indicating that pupils were 'working within the level' or 'not yet working within the level' varied with the stage the pupils were at. For S2, 34 per cent or less was regarded as representing the category 'not yet working within the level'; for P7 and P4 the relevant scores were respectively 19 per cent or less and 9 per cent or less. These figures were determined by estimating the number of marks that could potentially be obtained in the assessment using only skills acquired at the previous level. There were more tasks in S2 that used second-level skills and relatively few P4 tasks that used early-level skills. Pupils regarded as 'working within the level' at each stage were those whose scores fell between 50 per cent and the relevant lower score at that level representing 'not yet working within the level'. The 'survey design document' published along with the report on the Scottish Government website gives a full description of the 2011 numeracy survey (see www.scot-land.gov.uk/Publications/2012/03/5285/downloads#res390588).

Less detailed information is available about the nature of the 2012 literacy survey tasks – at the time of writing these are still in the process of development. The survey will assess Reading, Writing and Listening/Talking in English and (on request by a school) Gaelic. Reading tasks will be presented in two forms: a 'paper and pencil' booklet with four sections and thirty questions on a range of traditional print texts; and an online 'booklet' with four sections and twenty questions on non-print texts, including webpage and moving image texts. The survey thus aims to reflect the range of texts listed as appropriate for reading/ study in the Curriculum for Excellence English and Literacy guidelines and to engage pupils in reading in a range of cross-curricular contexts. Questions on the texts in both forms of assessment are categorised as 'Access and Retrieve', 'Integrate and Interpret' or 'Reflect and Evaluate', and they require both multiple choice and 'composed answer' types of response. Pupils in 50 per cent of schools will take part in the Listening/Talking tasks; those in the other 50 per cent will submit two representative pieces of class-based writing. Listening/ Talking tasks will involve group discussion based on topics and prompt cards supplied to the school by the SSLN team. The discussions will be recorded using the national GLOW Meet system, which schools will be able to access through an individual URL. The require-ment for Writing will be for the two pieces of work completed as part of classwork to address two different purposes and be taken from two different curricular areas. Guidance will be provided for schools on both the Listening/Talking and the Writing tasks.

Most of the actual survey tasks and the criteria used to mark them will not be publicly available. Clearly, it would be counterproductive to publish tasks that will be repeated in a later survey for comparison purposes. Another part of the reasoning here is that, as the policy set out in *Building the Curriculum 5: A Framework for Assessment* (Scottish Government, 2011) seeks to promote every teacher's assessment professionalism, including creation of appropriate tasks, specification of criteria and sharing of standards through moderation discussions with colleagues, publication of SSLN tasks and criteria could constrain this professional development by encouraging too narrow teacher assessment (restricted to what the SSLN tasks include) and by providing external 'benchmarking' for the Curriculum for Excellence levels. However, the SQA Academy site (www.sqaacademy.org.uk/login/index.php) contains exemplars of the types of task included in both the numeracy and the literacy surveys and a proportion of actual SSLN tasks will be released each year.

CPD and Learning/Teaching Support

Education Scotland is responsible for producing the CPD resources intended to enable teachers to improve pupils' learning in aspects of literacy and numeracy identified in the SSLN surveys as needing attention. The Reference Groups offering advice on the surveys also contribute to quality-assuring the associated CPD resources. Following the publica-tion of the 2011 numeracy survey findings in March 2012, the first set of materials became available on the Education Scotland website.

The aim is to develop and, over time, expand a 'dynamic resource' aimed directly at addressing pupils' relatively weak performance in particular areas of numeracy – identified in analysis of the survey results as 'Areas for Improvement' – and indeed weak performance on specific survey test items. The material invites teachers to review and reflect on the tasks that caused pupils difficulties and to think about their own teaching practice in these areas of work. The resource goes beyond previous AAP- or SSA-related encouragement to reflect on learning and teaching in that it provides in respect of each Area for Improvement a range of practical teaching strategies. These strategies are presented as a basis for teachers' consideration of how to improve their own teaching in very specific ways. One example relating to Fractions (identified as an Area for Improvement in the 2012 P7 survey) demonstrates two strategies for helping pupils to understand what is involved in working out 4/5 of 5,400. The teacher is invited to consider whether one is easier than the other and whether one might be better in one situation and the other for a different problem. The materials are presented in a technologically sophisticated way, enabling links to other Education Scotland resources, including material in the National Assessment Resource (NAR). They are intended to engage teachers not only in reflection on their own practice but also in interaction and discussion, for example within Education Scotland and local authority assessment networks. The resource aims to reinforce the idea that all assessment, whether classroom-based or part of a monitoring process, can and should contribute to improvement of learning and teaching and to increasing the relevance and usefulness of the SSLN for teachers.

Management of the SSLN

The SSLN surveys are the outcome of collaboration among a range of key bodies and people. The Scottish Government sets the policy for the surveys and, through its Education Analytical Services Division, has overall responsibility for the design, analysis, delivery and reporting of each. The SQA and Education Scotland collaborate with the Scottish Government in developing and implementing the surveys. The SQA is responsible for the operational aspects, including the development and trialling of assessment tasks, printing and distribution of the survey materials, administration of the survey in schools and recording the results. In collaboration with Education Scotland, the SQA also develops the success criteria for the assessment tasks. Education Scotland is responsible for developing and making available the learning and teaching resources for schools related to the SSLN findings. It also has a role in setting up the Reference Groups which provide curricular and assessment advice for each survey.

The practical decisions about each survey are taken by the SSLN Project Management Board, which includes representatives from each of the Scottish Government, the SQA, Education Scotland and the Association of Directors of Education. The Management Board receives advice from an Operational Group (comprising the Scottish Government, SQA and Education Scotland officers) and a Reference Group responsible for guidance on such matters as the content of the survey, the types of task to be used, the criteria to be applied, the weighting of tasks and so on. The Reference Group is chaired by an Education Scotland Officer and comprises teachers and representatives of the Scottish Government, SQA and Education Scotland (typically including someone from the inspection arm of the organisation). When the Operational Group has agreed the coverage and strategy for each survey, the SQA appoints teachers who develop the specific tasks to be included. The Reference Group and teacher reviewers (also appointed by the SQA) evaluate this work before the survey is implemented. There is also a formal trialling of assessment tasks built into the arrangements for each annual survey: in addition to pupils taking the survey that year, for example in numeracy, a small number of others in each school try out assessment tasks prepared for the following year's survey in literacy.

POINTS FOR DISCUSSION AND CONSIDERATION

The status of the former AAP and SSA surveys and of SQA National Qualifications data as evidence for a broadly accurate account of the overall educational performance of Scottish pupils has been consistently high over many years. It is likely that the new national survey system, the SSLN, will similarly be regarded as an important measure of national perform-ance. Though there are some reasons for questioning this high status of the evidence used in monitoring overall performance (see below), there is justification for it, too, in the large amount of high-quality professional collaboration that comes into play in developing, implementing, marking, analysing and reporting on the national surveys and the SQA examinations. There are, however, two key areas in which there may be room for reconsid-eration of current policy in respect of SSLN/monitoring.

The Potential of SSLN/Monitoring to Inform Effective Assessment for Curriculum for Excellence

We know from practical experience in Scotland – the discrepancy that existed between patterns of 5–14 attainment reported by schools on the one hand and the AAP patterns of performance and HMIE judgements about pupils' overall attainment on the other (see, for example, Hayward and Spencer, 2006, pp. 228–30) – and from research (for example, Harlen, 2004; Black et al., 2010; Black et al., 2011) that it is difficult to obtain valid and reliable evidence about overall attainment using only teachers' in-school assessments, unless there is very intensive support to develop and maintain their assessment profes-sionalism. Current development of teachers' assessment professionalism for Curriculum for Excellence, for example through the NAR, concentrates on reflection on and exemplifica-tion of assessment for learning and appropriate tasks and criteria for specific, separate learn-ing and/or assessment activities. There is at present little or no national (or local) guidance on the processes of deciding whether a pupil has achieved a Curriculum for Excellence level. National assessment policy (Scottish Government, 2010a) states a general expectation that a decision about a level should be based on professional teacher judgement of an individual pupil, using the Es and Os for the curricular area, quality assurance and moderation, with the NAR as a tool to support the judgement. However, the Es and Os specified for the curricular areas do not, on their own, constitute clearly defined standards or assessment rubrics: there is no indication in them, for example, of either the amount or the quality of work that would guarantee successful achievement, and some are worded identically across two or even three levels (covering six or seven years of school experience). Valid assessment of achievement of a level involves complex procedures for which at present no guidance is available. These include decisions about not only the nature of appropriate tasks but also the appropriate size of a sample of pupils' classwork and the application of a 'best fit' judgement in relation to a rubric for the level specifying criteria for success. At present, policy is keeping the SSLN and development of these aspects of teachers' assessment professionalism quite separate – the report on the 2011 numeracy survey, for example, explicitly states that the cut-off scores related to Curriculum for Excellence levels should not be used in numeracy assessment other than within the survey. There is, however, potential for the thinking of those involved in making levels decisions in the SSLN to contribute to the development of teachers' professionalism in making such judgements about pupils' work in school.

Apart from the need to find ways of helping teachers in this area, there is another important justification for use of the SSLN for this purpose. It is the fact that a large proportion of Scottish local authorities, under political pressure to provide 'accountability' evidence of pupils' progress, use commercial standardised tests, in the absence of effective teacher assessment of attainment of Curriculum for Excellence levels. This is wasted effort and money, since the standardised tests do not reflect the Es and Os specified in the Curriculum for Excellence guidance and have been shown in the past (for example in Hayward and Spencer, 2006) to come to replace rather than support teacher assessment. The SSLN, by contrast, has been designed specifically in relation to the Es and Os, and the follow-up provision of CPD materials by Education Scotland aims to promote effective teaching of the curriculum.

One other aspect of SSLN arrangements is also worthy of comment. Condie (2008) described the incorporation of former AAP tasks in the 5–14 assessment bank as helpful in promoting teachers' awareness of good assessment tasks; and the Maclellan Review (2004) reported that teachers, though they wanted the formal 5–14 testing system to end, had confidence in the quality of the tasks and wanted them to be available to support teacher assessments. In principle there is a potential for SSLN tasks to serve as models for some assessment tasks used in schools. However, in respect of Reading tasks at least, there is evidence that a high level of confidence in the quality of national monitoring tasks in the past may have been unjustified. Hayward and Spencer (2006) demonstrated that, in fact, many of the Reading tasks failed to assess important aspects of the reading process, including 'Integrating and Interpreting' and 'Reflecting and Evaluating': the nature of the questions and answer formats was such that very large proportions of the available marks could be obtained simply by recognising or finding and copying points from the Reading text. (The approach to designing SSLN literacy survey questions described above was developed partly in response to these findings.) Hayward and Spencer did, in fact, conduct their analysis not on national survey (AAP) tasks of the time but on 5–14 National Assessments, almost all of which had previously been used in AAP surveys. This raises an issue about the advisability (despite its obvious practical justification) of the SSLN policy to make publicly available only examples of the actual tasks and criteria used in monitoring surveys. Even though the system of advisory and quality assuring groups built in to SSLN arrangements is impressive, there would be further benefit if all the survey tasks and criteria could, in due course, be open also to academic critique. Such an arrangement would further strengthen the quality assurance and public accountability of the monitoring system.

Monitoring Too Little of Pupils' Learning?

It can be argued that the monitoring use of SQA examination results in the latter stages of secondary education provides overview information about a very wide range of pupils' learning and continued participation in PISA contributes additional information specifically on reading, numeracy and science. It is worth remembering, however, that within the various curricular areas, the nature and predictability of SQA examinations may narrow more severely than the public might suppose the range of learning on which they are providing evidence. It will be of great interest to see if and how the design of the emerging new National Qualifications addresses the issue of narrow and predictable coverage of curriculum knowledge and skills in examinations.

The justifications put forward for restricting monitoring surveys in the 3–15 age range to literacy and numeracy have validity – they are related to the reduction of burdens on schools and to cost, as well as to the importance of learning in these two areas to all the rest of pupils' progress. However, there is a danger that national monitoring focused only on these two areas may contribute to a perception among headteachers, teachers and local authority personnel (including elected councillors) that learning in other curricular areas does not really matter. If the education system does not succeed in the next few years in enabling teachers to make effective in-school assessments of achievements and progress in curricular areas other than literacy and numeracy, there will be no evidence available for the Scottish Government or Education Scotland to draw on in evaluating the success of much of the whole Curriculum for Excellence programme. There is a case for keeping open the possibility that national surveys might be designed from time to time to obtain evidence about learning in curricular areas such as Science, Technologies, Social Subjects and Expressive Arts, which have significant importance in the development of young people as educated Scots. Perhaps there is a potential too for surveys assessing the extent to which some of the broader aims of Curriculum for Excellence have been achieved. To obtain valid survey information about young people's general success as learners, individual confidence, effectiveness as contributors and commitments and action as responsible citizens would present significant challenges, but perhaps very worthwhile ones to meet.

ACKNOWLEDGEMENTS

The author wishes to express gratitude to several people who provided information to inform this chapter – Mal Cooke and Katherine McNab of the Scottish Government; Alexandra Bell, Barbara Hill and Lillian Munro of the Scottish Qualifications Authority; and Norman Emerson and Linda Rae of Education Scotland. Nevertheless, responsibility for the content is his alone.

REFERENCES

Black, P., C. Harrison, J. Hodgen, B. Marshall and N. Serret (2010) 'Validity in teachers' summative assessments', *Assessment in Education: Principles, Policy & Practice*, 17 (2): 215–32.
Black, P., C. Harrison, J. Hodgen, B. Marshall and N. Serret (2011) 'Can teachers' summative assessments produce dependable results and also enhance classroom learning?', *Assessment in Education*, 18 (4): 451–69.
Condie, R. (2008) 'National Assessment', in T. G. K. Bryce and W. Humes (eds), *Scottish Education, Third Edition: Beyond Devolution*. Edinburgh: Edinburgh University Press.
Harlen, W. (2004) *A Systematic Review of the Evidence of Reliability and Validity of Assessment by Teachers used for Summative Purposes*, in Research Evidence in Education Library. EPPI-Centre, Social Science Research Unit, Institute of Education, University of London.
Hayward, L. and E. Spencer (2006) 'There is no alternative . . . to trusting teachers', in M. Sainsbury, C. Harrison and A. Watts (eds), *Assessing Reading – From Theories to Classrooms*. Slough: National Foundation for Educational Research.
Her Majesty's Inspectorate of Education (2006) *How Good Is Our School? The Journey to Excellence*. Livingston: HMIE.

Maclellan, E. (2004) *Assessment, Testing and Reporting 3–14: Consultation on Partnership Commitments.* Final report for Scottish Executive Education Department.

Scottish Government (2005) *Circular No. 02: Assessment and Reporting 3–14.* Online at www.scotland. gov.uk/Publications/2005/06/2393450/34518

Scottish Government (2010a) *Curriculum for Excellence: Building the Curriculum: A Framework for Assessment: Understanding, Applying and Sharing Standards in Assessment for Curriculum for Excellence: Quality Assurance and Moderation.* Edinburgh: Scottish Government. Online at www. ltscotland.org.uk/Images/BtC5SharingStandards_tcm4-630057.pdf

Scottish Government (2010b) *Curriculum for Excellence: Building the Curriculum 5: A Framework for Assessment: Reporting.* Edinburgh: Scottish Government. Online at www.ltscotland.org.uk/ Images/CfEReportingdocument_tcm4-612845.pdf

Scottish Government (2010c) *Curriculum for Excellence: Building the Curriculum 5: A Framework for Assessment: Recognising Achievement, Profiling and Reporting.* Edinburgh: Scottish Government. Online at www.ltscotland.org.uk/Images/BtC5RecognisingAchievement_tcm4-641217.pdf

Scottish Government (2011) *Curriculum for Excellence: Building the Curriculum 5: A Framework for Assessment* (revised version). Edinburgh: Scottish Government. Online at www.ltscotland.org. uk/Images/BtC5Framework_tcm4-653230.pdf

Sliwka, A. and E. Spencer (2005) 'Scotland: Developing a coherent system of assessment', in Organisation for Economic Cooperation and Development, *Formative Assessment: Improving Learning in Secondary Classrooms.* Paris: OECD.

IX

FURTHER AND HIGHER EDUCATION

This section deals with post-school education, the period after compulsory schooling leading to a wide range of academic and vocational qualifications in further education colleges and universities, as well as to many types of informal learning. Two earlier chapters (7 and 8) provided an overview of further education and higher education provision. The chapters in the present section give a fuller account of the aims of further and higher education, the types of courses available, the teaching and learning methods employed and the policy pressures to which institutions have been subject. It has been a time of significant change, evident not only in the reshaping of the institutional structures of further education but also in the profile of the student population, with more mature students, more part-time students and the strengthening of links between the college and university sectors. Some people even argue that the rationale for the traditional division between 'further' and 'higher' education can no longer be sustained and that a common funding and policy framework should be put in place. While this is likely to be resisted, particularly by the 'elite' universities, arguments about the precise form that post-school provision should take are likely to continue.

Chapter 79 offers an interesting conceptual analysis of the differences between 'powerful' and 'useful' knowledge, drawing on historical and comparative accounts of academic, liberal and vocational education. It argues that while Scotland has a long and distinguished tradition in offering courses that are geared to employment, vocational education now needs to be reconceptualised in terms that emphasise not only its utility but also its empowering educational benefits. At the same time, the vocational value of subjects that have traditionally been seen as 'liberal' should be recognised. Chapter 80 examines a range of issues that affect the quality of learning in further and higher education: the spatial context in which learning takes place, including the impact of information technology and the growth of online learning; the various forms of training and professional development that are available for new and experienced lecturing staff; and the increasing attention that is given to the student experience, including support for those who may have a specific learning disability. The emergence of 'communities of practice', consisting of networks of professionals with particular interests, who share problems and insights, and discuss relevant research findings, is seen as one indication of the importance now given to the relationship between teaching methods, forms of assessment and learning outcomes.

Chapter 81 describes the diverse and evolving character of Scottish universities, drawing attention to the distinction between 'ancient' institutions, those established in the 1960s and more recent 'post-1992' creations. Questions of governance are explored, including the role of university courts and academic departments: as part of this, reference is made to the 2012 von Prondzynski Report which made recommendations for significant changes in governance, aimed at ensuring greater transparency and accountability. At the time of writing, it is not known whether the Scottish Government will implement these recommendations. The changing pattern of undergraduate and postgraduate courses is noted: while science, technology and engineering remain strong compared to other parts of the UK, some other subjects (such as modern languages) have declined. Among the challenges facing Scottish universities is the question of whether their distinctiveness will be subject to pressures deriving from the Bologna process of higher education convergence, agreed by European education ministers in 1999 and adopted formally by the European Union in 2010. Distinctiveness is also a theme in Chapter 82 which considers whether the concept of the 'democratic intellect', so powerfully articulated in George Davie's 1961 book, is still valid. Three specific challenges are identified. First, it is suggested that 'the general public and potential students have begun to question the validity, quality and cost of a university degree, as a result of the mass extension of higher education'. Second, the close relationship between the state and the university sector is subject to review because of the spiralling costs of expanding the system: the current policy of not charging fees to home-based students may not be sustainable in the long run. And third, 'the old idea of the university degree as a passport to social mobility has come under fire', both from the political left on the grounds that it is failing working-class students, and from the political right on the grounds that it has led to a 'dumbing-down' of standards. These challenges are explored using findings about the access and retention of working-class students, evidence relating to the effects of commercialisation of research and the variable success of attempts to promote the American model of fundraising from alumni.

Chapter 83 focuses on the work of the Open University (OU) in Scotland. It is a unique institution, now the largest university in Europe, which allows students to study at home, however geographically remote they may be, using learning materials that have been developed by expert course teams and supported by various forms of educational technology. The vision for the OU was announced in 1963 by the then Prime Minister, Harold Wilson, and it came into being in 1969. By any standards it has been a great success. It has shown itself to be highly innovative and responsive to student needs: in the national Student Experience Survey the OU regularly comes top in Scotland. The chapter describes the open-access policy of the OU, the range of undergraduate and postgraduate provision, and partnership arrangements with employers and local colleges. Not all post-school education leads to formal qualifications in the shape of certificates, diplomas and degrees. Chapter 84 looks at the diverse field of adult learning, tracing its history and development in Scotland and noting the significance in the shift of discourse to 'lifelong learning', the notion that the process is not time-limited or confined to formal institutions. People wish to learn for a variety of reasons, including a wish for personal fulfilment, a desire to become involved with and contribute to the community and a determination to acquire knowledge and skills that may bring economic benefits through employment. All of these are valid but the chapter notes the serious tensions that continue to exist between them.

79

Liberal, Academic and Vocational Knowledge Education

Roy Canning

In an interesting chapter in his book *Bringing Knowledge Back In* Michael Young asks an important and timely question: 'How can vocational knowledge be distinguished from academic knowledge?' Justifiably he claims that very few authors have attempted to answer this question by giving a coherent epistemological account of the type of knowledge that underpins vocational education (Young, 2008). This debate on the nature of vocational knowledge is long overdue, particularly within further and higher education. What is the type of knowledge that characterises the vocational and how is this knowledge different from other forms of knowledge? What is the role of knowledge within the vocational curriculum and can it be taught in an educationally meaningful way? This chapter will address these important questions through exploring both the meanings and the tensions associated with the concepts of 'powerful and useful knowledge' in the context of Scottish education. It will be argued that both forms of knowledge have a role to play, but that vocational education needs to be conceptualised in much broader terms to allow for a greater range of subjects to be taught within the post-compulsory education curriculum.

A PROCRUSTEAN ENTERPRISE

Interestingly, for many UK scholars the debate on what constitutes the vocational is often discussed with reference to other countries rather than their own. In international comparisons Germany is often held up as an exemplar of good practice with an emphasis on occupational structures (*Beruf*), a broader educational curriculum (*Bildung*) and a strong link between theory and practice (*Duales System*). Going further afield, the US invariably offers us the most rewarding comparisons in terms of vocational education and social justice and alongside Australia helps us to question the underlying social class divisions and gender bias that often characterise much of initial vocational education. However, rather intriguingly, there is little in the literature on how vocational knowledge has been conceptualised by academic writers in the UK. Perhaps this is not surprising, as the overwhelming desire of cultural commentators has been to elevate and privilege liberal knowledge within a paradigm that entraps and often denigrates the vocational. Indeed, this privileging of 'powerful knowledge' has a long and distinguished history.

Matthew Arnold's *Culture and Anarchy* offers one of the most celebrated accounts of

British society and the role of education and literature (Arnold, 1869). Writing in the middle of the nineteenth century he warns against the insularity, complacency and muddled-headedness of *practicality*. Instead he encourages us to stay aloof from the practical view of things by adopting a disinterested pursuit of perfection. This cultural inheritance of the best that has been thought and said is required in order to avoid rough and coarse action. This sweetness and light of intelligent thought is founded upon a liberal arts education. Here the distinction between Hellenism and Hebraism is made, where the former is characterised by beauty, knowledge and spontaneity, while the latter is concerned with duty, rules, subjugation and the self. Arnold's concern was to counter the British Protestant obsession with obedience and strictness of conscience with those who wish to avoid the trouble of thinking.

Arnold's concept of culture and the role of liberal arts education followed the publication of another canonical text that also privileged universal knowledge while disapproving of useful knowledge. Writing in 1852, Newman associates liberal education with a habit of the mind, freedom, equitableness and wisdom (Newman, 1907). Here the *utility* of knowledge is questioned, the need for the mechanical and particular that relies upon memory ridiculed. Universal knowledge in contrast refuses to be informed by an end as nothing accrues of consequence beyond the using. Useful knowledge and liberal knowledge are in opposition, as the latter cannot be gained through learning or acquirement, while the former has aimed low but fulfilled its aims.

Like Arnold, Oakeshott (Oakeshott, 1975) believed liberal education offered a place apart that enabled us to make the most and best of ourselves. This 'ordeal of consciousnesses' was concerned with conduct and not simply behaviour and could not be acquired through instrumental learning. The distinction here was made between work and play, with toilsome activity and the joy of pursuing a disinterested form of knowledge. Genuine learning was not concerned with the acquisition of vocational knowledge, with utility or a body of knowledge that does not look outside itself. This was seen as pantomime learning that maintained the current manner of living and rarely raised itself above the level of the practitioner. Vocational learning meant being able to read the literature but not think the literature. In contrast it is freedom from considerations of utility that characterises the liberality and joy of genuine learning.

Bernstein also argued that theoretical knowledge differs from the everyday knowledge of experience (Bernstein, 1999). Extending the work of Durkheim, he characterises abstract knowledge as a form of vertical discourse, while the everyday knowledge of practice could be seen as a form of horizontal discourse. The analogous comparison made by Durkheim is between the sacred and the profane. Here the mundane knowledge of the everyday is likely to be local, context dependent, tacit and specific. According to Young these knowledge structures can be seen as representative of the different forms of knowledge within the curriculum. The vertical forms of knowledge are theoretical, hierarchical and transcendent, while the horizontal forms of knowledge are practical, context dependent and imminent. Here we are told that knowledge embodied in the curriculum is objectively given and transcends the social conditions under which it is produced. It is socially constructed but not *purely* a social construction.

What is striking about this very British discourse of knowledge is the relentless privileging of a particular form of knowing. What counts is the sacred, vertical, abstract and transcendent. Not only does this count but it also constructs a paradigm within which every other form of knowledge is legitimised. This, according to Brandom (2008), can be seen as 'A Procrustean enterprise, which can proceed only by theoretically privileging some aspects of the use of a vocabulary that are not at all *practically* privileged, and spawning philosophical puzzlement about the intelligibility of the rest' (Brandom, 2008, p. 7).

Of course it is the everyday and mundane knowledge associated with the vocational that becomes the *other* within these discourses. Here practical knowledge exhibits a weak grammar, lacks coherence and structure, and is unable to transcend its conditions of production. It is characterised by concrete situations that are inextricably linked to a material base and thus unable to embody any principles of connectedness.

Since Newman introduced this debate about the value of 'useful knowledge' we have witnessed the gradual but important shift in what constitutes a liberal education. Newman, like Arnold, excluded professional education within this definition. Anything that had a useful purpose would have little to offer beyond its use. However, by the time we arrive at Oakeshott, liberal education embraces the scientific and with Bernstein encompasses the specialised languages of the social sciences. More recently, this extension to the project of powerful knowledge has gained a hold within the current debates surrounding competency-based education and pedagogies connected with social constructivism.

USEFUL KNOWLEDGE

The notion of useful knowledge has, rather interestingly, been debated for some considerable time. Its roots can be found in the philosophy of John Locke in his collection of essays entitled 'Some Thoughts Concerning Education'. Writing in the late seventeenth century Locke questioned the value of a classical education:

> I confess, containing one great Part of Wisdom, is not the Product of some superficial Thoughts, or much Reading; but the Effect of Experience and Observation in a Man who has liv'd in the World with his Eyes open, and convers'd with Men of all Sorts. (Locke, 1692, p. 74)

Here he argues that education has been confounded with learning. For him gainful knowledge was concerned with the 'internal perception of the mind' and with knowing as seeing. It is this proposition that Newman challenged in his *The Idea of a University*. A less well-known but equally important figure to defend the value of useful knowledge was Richard Edgeworth in his *Essays on Professional Education* in 1808. Here for the first time we have a detailed argument put forward for the establishment of a professional education curriculum, one based upon the usefulness of knowledge for those new professionals being educated in colleges and universities prior to embarking on careers in an ever-expanding British Empire. These professional studies, it was suggested, would include aspects of political economy, the practical sciences and philosophical history.

This emerging debate between powerful and useful knowledge intensified throughout the nineteenth century and, rather intriguingly for this new edition of *Scottish Education*, found its fullest expression in the articles contained within the *Edinburgh Review*. In fact it is in these reviews that Edgeworth questions the value of a classical education, where issues of gender and class in education are raised by scholars for the first time and, above all, where the utility and usefulness of powerful knowledge is questioned. These debates fill the pages of the *Edinburgh Review* for much of the century and come to represent and reflect the tensions arising between those advocating a liberal education based upon the classics and those championing a professional education based upon modern science and reason. Looking back, it can be argued that the notion of a liberal education came to rely less heavily on a classical education during this period. In this sense useful knowledge did win the day as utility emerged as the dominant theme of learning and education for the next century. However, it could also be argued that as powerful knowledge subsumes professional education within its rubric the debates surrounding the utilitarian aspects of learning simply shifted to another domain of education. The terrain now under scrutiny became vocational education. Yet the debates of the twentieth century would sound remarkably familiar to people of the nineteenth century, albeit incorporating a different language, as vocational knowledge attempts to gain a 'parity of esteem' with other forms of knowledge.

VOCATIONAL EDUCATION

Interestingly, what is often regarded as vocational education is frequently determined with reference to an industrial era where the vocational becomes synonymous with the crafts and trades and with particular intermediate levels of qualification. This quote from a recently commissioned review of the literature on vocational learning in Scotland demonstrates this point:

> For the purpose of this literature review, vocational learning is defined as education, training and/or learning intended to equip persons for a specific vocation in industry (broadly defined including traditional and creative), commerce, IT and/or that which specifically seeks to develop knowledge and skills in learners in order to operate successfully in the world of work. It encompasses apprenticeships and technical education where the learner directly develops expertise in a particular trade or group of techniques or technology, as well as Skills for Work qualifications and other similar courses. While we are aware that much of higher education is vocational, we have been asked to exclude from the scope of this review professional/vocational courses in subjects such as medicine or accountancy, entry for which normally requires prior attainment in non-vocational subjects. Higher level learning in specific vocational and technical areas (e.g. between SVQ level 4 and 5) may, however, come within the scope. The treatment of work-based and workplace learning and training in this report focuses on learning up to SVQ level 4 (HNDs). (Scottish Government Social Research, 2008, p. 2)

There is an acknowledgement here that the vocational can be represented at different qualification levels and across different occupational structures. Here it is possible to have foundational-, intermediate- and higher-level vocational awards and that these may also cover service-based industries and the public- and third-sector economies. Also hinted at are the different forms of knowledge that could be included within the notion of vocational: literary, scientific, artistic and aesthetic. However, the quote clearly highlights the confusion surrounding any attempt to narrowly define what in fact constitutes vocational education. What is missing here is a basic conceptual framework for determining the essential features of what counts as vocational learning.

CONCEPTUALISING VOCATIONAL KNOWLEDGE

The vocational requires us to replace concern with *meaning* by concern with *use* (Wittgenstein, 1958). Here it is important *to do* in order to count. This pragmatic turn towards embodied practices is not simply another dimension within the discourse of powerful knowledge. It is a radical challenge to it where everything is what it is and not another thing. Here we are invited to engage with a much more complex and broader notion of knowledge, one that has its own internal logic and grammar. This conception of knowledge extends beyond the 'perfection of the intellect' to other domains of knowing, including the sensorial, emotive, spatial and somatic. It is in essence a form and expression of knowledge that is characterised by a *difference in kind* and not simply a dimension of another property. There are similarities, of course, with other forms of knowledge as it prepares young people for life and requires foundational literacy and numeracy abilities. However, it is *different in kind* by being materialistic, discursive and normative in form and expressed through multiple and complex representations. It is where meaning has been written into things and not layered over them (Wittgenstein, 1958). It also acknowledges that the particular and universal can cohabit the same space and time. That one need not exist only in the absence of the other or, as Brandom (2008) would claim, a set of doings and sayings that reflect both use and meaning.

This is not to deny the existence of propositional knowledge but rather to recognise a particular type of *theoretical quietism* or low-level generalisation understood as concrete embodiments of extended and iterative practices. These understandings are more likely, in the initial stages of learning anyway, to be embodied and tacit and arrived at by constant rehearsal and repetition and, interestingly, often through the 'giving and asking for reason'. It will also involve the reiteration of norms or values transmitted within occupational groupings or modelled by teachers during practice-based learning activities. These values are not simply the neo-conservative ones of obedience and quiescence captured within an instrumental vocationalism, but rather come to represent a set of social practices. However, returning to Newman, it is important to acknowledge that vocationalism and liberal education are not necessarily opposed to one another:

> If then I am arguing, and shall argue, against Professional or Scientific knowledge as the sufficient end of a University Education, let me not be supposed . . . to be disrespectful towards particular studies, or arts, or vocations, and those who are engaged in them. In saying that Law or Medicine is not the end of a University course, I do not mean to imply that the University does not teach Law or Medicine. What indeed can it teach at all, if it does not teach something particular? It teaches all knowledge by teaching all branches of knowledge and in no other way. (Newman, 1907, p. 147)

For Newman a broad liberal education was always useful but a useful education was not always liberal. This is an interesting point and opens up the debate about the moral and ethical dimensions of vocational education. Within a number of European countries that have an upper-school based vocational education system 'useful knowledge' is often combined with the liberal arts. Indeed, within Scotland there is a strong argument for having a mixed-mode vocational curriculum in the senior school phase with the introduction of Curriculum for Excellence.

Any conceptual framework that attempts to encapsulate the essence of vocationalism needs to fully embrace the notion of useful knowledge. It is important here *to do* in order to count as saying something. This discursive aspect of the vocational also requires a language in order to interact, a language that often has to be acquired at the initial stages of development. This does not mean that *use* is devoid of *meaning* but rather that meaning and use can be mutually illuminating. We also have to acknowledge the essential materiality of the vocational, whether this is in terms of people, material objects or the manipulation of artefacts. These characteristics of vocationalism are represented at different levels of ability (foundational, intermediate and higher levels of vocational education) and across different occupational groupings (trades, crafts, technician, associate and professional occupations). This expansive interpretation of the meaning of vocationalism gives us a much broader and richer canvas to work upon when considering the further and higher education curriculum.

CONCLUSION

There has been a long and distinguished history of vocational education provision in further and higher education in Scotland. Indeed, the ancient universities north of the border differed significantly from those in England, relying less on the study of a classical education and more on the continental notion of a professional in the age of enlightenment. The very nature of what constitutes an education was relentlessly debated within the *Edinburgh Review*. Indeed, this often reflected the wider debates in the nineteenth and twentieth centuries on the nature of a liberal education. However, the notion of powerful knowledge evolved over time and place and came to embody many of the subjects associated with the age of science and reason, eventually also incorporating the new disciplines of the social sciences. It is difficult under these circumstances to argue that the project of powerful knowledge was socially constructed but not *purely* a social construction. In fact, a liberal education often came to represent the 'social imperatives and cultural needs of the time'. Gradually this derisive discourse about useful knowledge that positioned it 'narrowly and weakly' in comparison with powerful knowledge was eroded. However, this is not to deny the contribution made by Newman on liberal education. In the case of vocational education he would today have probably encouraged us to ask the important but simple question; what is educational about vocational education?

REFERENCES

Arnold, M. (1869) *Culture and Anarchy* (1st edn). Project Gutenberg Literary Archive Foundation.

Bernstein, B. (1999) 'Vertical and horizontal discourses: an essay', *British Journal of Sociology of Education*, 20 (2): 157–73.

Brandom, R. (2008) *Between Saying and Doing: Towards an Analytic Pragmatism*. Oxford: Oxford University Press.

Edgeworth, R. L. (1808) *Essays on Professional Education*. Memphis, TN: General Books.

Edinburgh Review (1835) *Selections from the Edinburgh Review*. Vol. III. Paris: Baudry's European Library.

Locke, J. (1692) *Some Thoughts Concerning Education*. Online at www.fordham.edu/halsall/mod/1692locke-education.asp

Newman, J. H. (1907) *The Idea of a University*. London: Longmans, Green, and Co.

Oakeshott, M. (1975) 'A place of learning', *Colorado College Studies*, 12, 6–29.

Scottish Government Social Research (2008) *Attitudes to Vocational Learning: A Literature Review*. Edinburgh: Scottish Government Social Research.

Wittgenstein, L. (1958) *Philosophical Investigations*. Trans. G. E. M. Anscombe. New York: Macmillan.

Young, M. (2008) *Bringing Knowledge Back In*. London: Routledge.

80

Teaching and Learning in Further and Higher Education

Christine Sinclair

A SHIFTING TERRAIN AND ITS PEOPLE

Scotland's distinctive physical geography has inevitably played a role in creating and sustaining its colleges and universities. Geography also provides a common metaphor in educational research, for example in discussions about academic landscapes, fields of study, learning spaces, borders and territories along with broader spatial metaphors such as student-centred learning. There is an increasing tendency in literature about teaching and learning in further education (FE) and higher education (HE) to recognise that both physical and metaphorical educational spaces have an impact on pedagogy. Digital technology has brought additional manifestations of the metaphor, for example virtual learning environments (VLEs). It is clear that a sense of place and space plays a big part in how we characterise education. This chapter reflects the complex interplay between physical, metaphorical and virtual spaces and the people who use them in Scottish tertiary-level teaching and learning.

Other chapters in this volume record mergers, divides, federal alliances and debates affecting FE and HE. These changing alliances are mirrored in the ways that Scotland researches, develops, supports and evaluates teaching and learning in the tertiary sector. The notion of what constitutes effective 'teaching and learning' is thus affected by changing institutional structures as well as by changing pedagogy. There is here an attempt to map the alignment between educational research and national and institutional structures, and to explore mechanisms for supporting teachers and learners at a time when their landscape is changing.

The relationship between research and teaching can be uneasy, particularly in universities, where the dominance of the Research Excellence Framework (REF) ensures that research in the academic disciplines is privileged over teaching. Although higher education teaching is now established as itself a worthy subject for research, academic staff are understandably more anxious to secure their own research outputs than to study those emerging from what some see as an unrelated field. Nevertheless, there have been UK and Scottish pressures to ensure that new university lecturers undertake some professional development in teaching and learning, which does involve reading the relevant literature. With increased fees in other parts of the UK, pressures for a 'licence to teach' in universities are likely to increase.

The pressures are arguably even stronger in FE, where the Scottish Government has taken a direct interest in programmes for FE teachers. Papers on professional development in FE frequently position lecturers themselves as adult learners (for example, Cornelius, Gordon and Ackland, 2009). This categorisation provides a link to a valuable literature for theorising what is happening in teaching and learning in the tertiary sector. It also draws attention to the complexity of trying to separate teaching and learning: teachers can be learners too. The next section takes a closer look at the courses they take.

Staff Development in Teaching and Learning

Probationary lecturers in (most) Scottish universities are currently expected to achieve at least part of a postgraduate qualification in higher education teaching, commonly known as a PGCert but having various titles and levels. This is normally undertaken after appointment within the participant's own institution – although there are exceptions to this. For FE lecturers, there is a named Teaching Qualification – TQ(FE) – provided by three Scottish universities: Aberdeen, Dundee and Stirling, in conjunction with participating colleges, and also normally taken after the participant has been appointed as a lecturer.

In both sectors, the programmes for new lecturers must be based on professional standards. The TQ(FE) course is defined in Scottish legislation and is accredited by the Scottish Government and the General Teaching Council. The professional standards were updated in 2012 (Morrison, 2012). In HE, the PGCerts are accredited by the UK Higher Education Academy and are expected to comply with its UK Professional Standards Framework, which delineates expected areas of activity, core knowledge and professional values.

Programmes in both sectors tend to be structured around three broad themes:

- professional development of academic staff;
- teaching, learning and assessment;
- student learning and identity.

Other (sometimes elective) topics might include: teaching and learning in the disciplines, supervision of postgraduates, teaching and learning online, equality and diversity in education, academic leadership and management, academic writing. The provision and balance of these topics varies across institutions and some programmes do not have elective elements. The programmes are delivered in a variety of modes from face-to-face workshops, through blended learning, to totally online.

The TQ(FE) is delivered through Schools of Education in the three universities, with local support in the participating colleges. The PGCerts in universities are delivered through centres with a variety of names. A generic term for those with responsibility for courses for new lecturers in universities is 'educational developer', though there are other titles, such as 'lecturer in academic practice'. For some, then, this is an academic position and such educational developers are likely to be involved in educational research and may be expected to participate in the REF. Educational developers have themselves been subject to the shifting terrain in most institutions, with resulting changes in structures, job titles, statuses and remits. Most of the centres that do this work in universities have been merged, split, disbanded or replaced in the past decade, and few of the titles of the centres remain the same.

Support for Student Learning

Some of the centres concerned with educational development also support the student learning aspect of teaching and learning. In some institutions, though, this is the responsibility of a separate unit or individual. A generic term for those who support student learning and writing in universities is 'effective learning adviser'. Although other terms might be found, the work of a strong network of practitioners – Scottish Effective Learning Advisers (Scot-ELAs) – has led to this term being adopted by many universities.

Similar study-support roles are also found in FE colleges, but with a wider range of titles and often with an emphasis on supporting dyslexic students or those for whom English is not their first language. There is much learning support for FE students within their courses: smaller class sizes and more informal staff–student relationships are characteristic of FE. Students moving from FE to HE frequently suggest that they may have been 'spoonfed' at college and are worried that they will now be on their own. Such students can be pleasantly surprised to discover that their university has effective learning advisers, although in some institutions the ground is shifting here too.

Helping students to learn is also an integral feature of FE provision to support students into HE through dedicated accredited courses. The spatial and geographical metaphor is present here as well, with the notion of wider access (see Chapter 29) with its routes into education, entry and exit points. Wider access is now a well-established link between FE and HE, promulgated through networks such as the Scottish Wider Access Programme (SWAP).

Professional Networks and Communities of Practice

The above description indicates a volatile environment for those whose job it is to support HE and FE teachers, students or both. Professional networks and communities of practice provide some sustaining structures and continuity, while jobs and centres change or disappear.

Scotland's geography permits ease of travel between many educational institutions. In the case of more remote institutions, Scotland was in the forefront of technological solutions to networking, especially through the links between colleges that are now part of the University of the Highlands and Islands. The country's size also leads to manageable numbers for representation at formal and informal gatherings, though some of the networks focus on regions rather than the whole of Scotland.

Scot-ELAs meet twice a year in each other's institutions and keep in touch between meetings. A network of Scottish Higher Educational Development (SHED) also meets regularly in each other's institutions to share and promote good practice in teaching and learning. As a sub-group of Universities Scotland, this network provides a link between university management and the educational development community, allowing the latter to feed into university strategy.

Both FE and HE receive support from networks associated with quality assurance of teaching and learning. HM Inspectorate of Education is part of a national body – Education Scotland – which provides resources and information for FE as well as quality assurance (see www.educationscotland.gov.uk/). The Quality Assurance Agency (QAA Scotland) uses a process of Enhancement Led Institutional Review (ELIR) for HE institutions, which offers a lighter touch than the quality inspections in the rest of the UK. In keeping with that ethos, QAA Scotland also supports a number of enhancement themes in Scottish universities, and runs an annual conference which provides opportunities for networking and knowledge exchange (www.qaa.ac.uk/Scotland).

There are many other networks that have an impact on teaching and learning, around specific areas of interest such as student employability, disability and e-learning. There are also many examples of 'communities of practice', especially in the FE sector as could until recently be seen from the website of Scotland's colleges (www.scotlandscolleges.ac.uk/). The communities of practice identified there emerged from forums of support staff with specific shared interests because of their role in their college. Again, the intention is that these groupings feed into strategy.

CHALLENGING THEMES FROM EDUCATIONAL RESEARCH

The expression 'communities of practice' came out of research into learning (Lave and Wenger, 1991) and offers yet another indication of the geographical metaphor, linking place and people. In its original use it was specifically not related to communities in educational establishments, but referred to a perspective based on the observation that learning is always situated and social. Communities of practice were not presented by the authors as a pedagogical tool, but were observed to offer explanations for how learning occurs. The term was rapidly taken up by business and education, however, to provide a label for groups of people with shared interests, and even to deliberately establish such groups as a way of promoting particular policies or strategy. This may illustrate a tendency of education to use theoretical constructs, sometimes inappropriately, 'to create general principles that become the basis for prescribing universal solutions' (Fenwick et al., 2011, p. 32), but the proliferation of the term 'communities of practice' does highlight a recognition of educational institutions as sites of social interaction.

Though the expression 'student-centred learning' continues to be in vogue, a shift in the literature from a focus on individual student learning may be indicated by the pervasive use of the word 'communities', for example communities of inquiry, of learning, of practice. The need for a move from an individual focus, especially in HE, has been provocatively highlighted by Haggis (2009) who argues that practitioners in adult, community and further education have in recent years been exposed to a wider pool of theoretical stances than those relying on the UK's main HE literature, which was until recently dominated by 'approaches to learning' themes. While these have their place, Haggis argues for consideration of other perspectives, such as academic literacies, complexity theory and actor network theory. Based in the University of Stirling, Haggis challenges the readers of one of the journals she critiques (*Studies in Higher Education*), who practise not only in Scotland but also in the rest of the UK and beyond. The expansion of theoretical influence she advocates does seem to be emerging in Scotland, through a more reflexive consideration of how groups or networks of people learn together, rather than a narrow focus on (deficits of) how individuals approach learning. The remainder of this chapter selectively presents literature and activities in FE and HE that negotiate this tension between the personal and the social in complex spaces and situations.

The three main themes of the PGCerts and the TQ(FE) highlighted in the previous section are underpinned by broad-based educational research and by scholarship of teaching and learning (SoTL) undertaken by practitioners themselves, including those in the Scottish context. By writing about their experiences, innovations and conceptualisation of what is happening in Scottish institutions, educational developers are contributing to global perspectives on professional development, teaching and assessment, and student learning and identity. These three themes provide sites for further exploration of the changing Scottish tertiary education environment in the subsections below.

Professional Development: Learning Activities in Communities of Practice

Educational developers face a number of challenges in supporting academics to find their academic 'place' in FE or HE. Academic staff have many other demands on their time, some of which may be at odds with precepts from professional standards for teaching. Time available for development activities is itself a major issue, and one that is not equitably distributed across participants undertaking a teaching qualification (Smith, 2011). Teaching qualifications thus need to be both flexible and relevant to an individual's situation, acknowledging personal contexts as well as developing members of an academic community (Cornelius et al., 2009). The educational developers themselves are facing increased demands on time and changes to their own communities, and these have led to creative approaches to professional development, frequently supported by technology.

The tension between personal and social learning is a recurring theme in this chapter. In a specific attempt to overcome this tension, Cornelius et al. report on the development, implementation and evaluation of a model of 'learning activities' for the TQ(FE) run by the University of Aberdeen. The adult learners on the TQ(FE) find their own route through their blended learning programme. They choose from a set of structured and resource-based activities that can be used in a variety of ways: independently, with peers, in tutor-led workshops, and in both face-to-face and online modes.

The developmental work reported by Cornelius et al. (2009) is predicated on the notion that learners construct their own learning. Constructivism is a dominant current philosophy underpinning course design in both FE and HE, especially where courses take place in digital environments. However, although the routes are individualised through learner choice, the context is still a social one. By working within the community of FE lecturers, participants gradually move from reflecting on their own specific professional issues to constructing shared meanings and conceptualisations of practice. As the authors say, 'in TQ(FE) they begin to speak like teachers' (Cornelius et al., 2009, p. 383).

In innovative programmes where participants create their own routes and construct their own learning, there is still a considerable role for tutor and peer support. The need to maintain effective tutor support at a time of structural change was faced by educational developers on another TQ(FE) programme based at the University of Dundee. Here the participants (over 200 a year) are all online. When the programme teaching team was reduced from eight to under five full-time equivalent employees, over a period of four years, the team had to find a way of maintaining high levels of support. A collaborative approach among the remaining team members resulted in a shared identity online – 'TQFE tutor', a single point of contact for all participants. The tutors have shared the work using a rota, and have centralised emails, a blog and microblogging (Twitter). Not only have the learners on the course benefited from peer interaction and collaboration, the teachers have too, reporting that they have learned from each other's practice. This creative response to a potential crisis forms part of a project supported by the Joint Information Systems Committee (JISC), the UK's organisation supporting information and digital technologies in education and research. Details of the project entitled *EFFECT: Evaluating Feedback for E-learning:*

Centralised Tutors can be found at www.jisc.ac.uk/whatwedo/programmes/elearning/ assessmentandfeedback/effect.aspx

Examples such as these might be recognised as educational developers practising innovative teaching initiatives and solutions to problems that are 'congruent' with their own messages to participants on their courses. Smith (2011) warns that lack of congruence may be a key issue for institutions promoting PGCerts. In other words, courses for teachers must themselves be models of good practice. Though she was based at the University of Strathclyde at the time of writing, Smith's (2011) study was a UK-wide one into the lives of probationary academic staff. It was distinctive in analysing the PGCert in its context as a requirement for probationary staff. It is salutary that Smith discovered that the PGCert is not necessarily uppermost in the minds of new staff in universities, some even being unaware that they are doing such a qualification. The lack of impact may in part be because small professional development workshops feel far removed from teaching practices in some academic disciplines. Smith notes: 'when more discursive activities are promoted, those who work with very large first-year classes . . . can feel disempowered rather than supported by the PGCert' (Smith, 2011, p. 77).

Nevertheless, there has been some interesting work by educational developers in Scottish universities to support academic staff with large classes. A description of one influential project – Re-engineering Assessment Practices in Higher Education (REAP) – follows below.

Teaching, Learning and Assessment: Extending the Classroom through Re-engineering, Self-regulation and Dialogue

The REAP project formed part of a major programme funded by the Scottish Funding Council between 2005 and 2007: the e-learning Transformation Programme. Three universities were involved in the project: Strathclyde, Glasgow and Glasgow Caledonian. The researchers specifically looked at the largest classes in these institutions and worked with academics in these departments to develop strategies for assessment and feedback that promote effective learning even with very large numbers of students. The work was grounded in well-established assessment and feedback principles and was widely disseminated to the sector in terms of evidence of its success. The researchers have been able to demonstrate that the combination of good quality research, an emphasis on students' responsibility for their own learning and thoughtful exploitation of the capabilities of new technologies can combine to bring about transformation in large classes.

It has long been recognised that assessment is a key driver for students. In his website on REAP, David Nicol suggests that assessment practices should build on this observation and ensure that assessment and feedback practices help higher education students to learn how to become self-regulated learners (see www.reap.ac.uk/). This website offers tools for teachers as well as suggestions for policy and commentary on research. There is evidence in tertiary education literature of wide take-up of the principles of good feedback practice, and the REAP project is frequently cited. The resources are then useful both for the teaching qualification programmes for probationary staff and also for anyone in universities concerned about the quality of teaching, learning and assessment.

Reflecting the concern in this chapter for the relationship between the personal and the social, the REAP website highlights both the need for students' self-regulation and the view that 'feedback is a dialogue'. When dealing with large classes, the notion of self-regulation might be a comforting one, shifting the responsibility from teacher to student. However, self-regulation is a curricular goal and not an exhortation to students; the move towards students being able to 'monitor, manage and self-direct' their own work means careful attention to course design and mechanisms for feedback.

One dialogic approach that has proved successful, developed further in a later project also discussed on the REAP website, is to use student peer review. This is now on the increase in universities and colleges, suggesting that not only is the teacher a learner, but the learner is now also a teacher. However, David Nicol warns against the confusion between peer review and peer assessment. He has discovered that many students dislike being asked to summatively assess other students' work but do see the benefits of reviewing other students' work and receiving reviews from fellow students.

While feedback is a dialogue, it is not always a comfortable one: feedback is consistently reported as the least satisfactory aspect of students' experience in the UK's National Student Survey (NSS). This annual survey, started in 2005, has a considerable impact on Scottish universities, who strive to get good rates of participation and to improve in areas where problems are highlighted. Scottish FE students do not participate in this survey, though their counterparts in England and Wales do. For details of this survey, see www. thestudentsurvey.com/

More opportunities for dialogue are encouraged through Student Participation in Quality Scotland (SPARQS). This organisation is run by the National Union of Students Scotland, and is funded by the SFC. Its aim is to involve students in both FE and HE in improving the quality of teaching and learning in Scotland. More details can be found at www.sparqs.ac.uk/

Initiatives such as the NSS and SPARQS perhaps ensure that students are seen as participants in education rather than passive recipients of it. An alternative perspective on this, however, is that students are now customers or consumers and these are their forums for registering their levels of satisfaction about the product. In this view, education has become just another commodity in a globalised marketplace. There are many academic papers and books on this topic; here, the main aim is to start to indicate potentially contested ways of defining the complex situations described in this chapter.

The question of students as customers or consumers leads into the third current major area of concern: who are the students and how do they learn?

Student Learning and Identity: Self-regulation on a Global Scale

For some decades now, educational developers and university teachers have wrestled with the problem of how to be student-centred in an era of mass higher education. The main teaching emphasis for student-centred learning in recent years in the UK (and other countries) has been to promote curriculum alignment: where activities aligning learning and teaching objectives, intended learning outcomes, assessment and content ensure that students take the appropriate approach to learning (Biggs and Tang, 2011). Prefaces to successive editions of Biggs's seminal work illustrate that there have been debates over the nature of outcomes-based education, some seeing it as a part of a managerialist agenda where universities are more like businesses than places of learning. While Biggs is keen to stress the pedagogic value of learning outcomes, this does not prevent the idea from being adopted for other purposes. There does indeed now seem to be a global marketplace for education, and this discourse may become entangled with discourses that focus on pedagogy.

The Biggs and Tang (2011) work is typical of educational literature in beginning by referring to increasing numbers of students from a wider range of backgrounds, and with a more diverse set of needs. Diverse needs may have their roots in physical geography: the customs and culture of international students' own countries' education systems are perhaps different from the Scottish/UK context. For others, the sense of place may be more metaphorical; some may feel 'out of place' at university or college.

There are more optimistic aspects to diversity too: many students look forward to becoming part of the new world they are entering, both physically and metaphorically. Technology has allowed students to explore that new world before they reach university or college though official and unofficial student websites. Technology also supports wider access to tertiary education in several ways. Assistive technologies create increased opportunities for disabled students; a range of modes of study makes it possible for students to attend university virtually rather than physically, thus enabling some who might not otherwise have benefited.

Student identity is indeed increasingly being linked to technology in more fundamental ways. The 'digital natives' trope suggests that students who have grown up with digital technology will be more comfortable in digital environments than their ('immigrant') teachers will, and many papers testify to the popularity of this expression. There seems now to be an additional notion that 'digital natives' have needs and expectations of the use of technology in their college and university courses based on their 'always-on' lifestyle. As Bayne and Ross (2011) observe, however, this may be a dangerous and problematic use of the geographical metaphor. The 'immigrant' teachers are unable to change because of their birth-date and yet are required to do so by an increasingly market-driven educational environment that extols technology. The natives/immigrants metaphor may fit our obsession with place in education; it also carries other – divisive and even racialised – connotations. Bayne and Ross argue for care to be taken over metaphors that end up being simplistic and limiting with respect to agency in the student–teacher relationship. In practice, students and teachers turn out to be less easy to categorise than the binary of native and immigrant would suggest.

It is necessary, though, to consider student identity and learning in the context of their 'virtual' learning environments as well as their physical and metaphorical ones. Digital media themselves provide new kinds of landscape. These include not only VLEs that initially provide 'transitional objects, enabling academics to work with the new and the old simultaneously' (Cousin, 2005, p. 128), but also kinds of spaces that are starting to move away from notions underpinning traditional academic environments, such as wikis and microblogging which can be used produce new kinds of academic texts.

Students then need to know how to 'be' in the rapidly changing environments of colleges and universities. Effective learning advisers are now more likely to find themselves supporting students in negotiating their new environments than doing remedial work to 'fix' skills deficits (although their role is still frequently regarded in this light by other people). This includes student production of academic texts and other forms of assignment in arenas that are contested, emergent and constantly changing. The expression 'literacies' is increasingly seen in research literature: students need information literacy, academic literacy and digital literacy.

GEOGRAPHY AND SPACE: A LOOSENING OF BOUNDARIES?

With physical as well as metaphorical and virtual learning environments undergoing a turbulent period in FE and HE, it is perhaps a good time to be taking a closer look at the implications for teaching and learning. In considering emerging approaches, educational researchers from the Universities of Stirling and Toronto – Fenwick et al. (2011) – take a closer look at the 'spatial framings of practice' and associated metaphors and analyse the rhetorical work that is going on. For example, they propose that the notion of student-centred learning can be associated with 'putting every aspect of the student under the spotlight and thereby more subject to surveillance' (Fenwick et al., 2011, p. 162), including some of the more intrusive demands for reflective practice. This provides an alternative slant on the expression's rhetorical effect of 'generating warm feelings among many educators' and suggests again that we should be vigilant about how metaphors are used.

Whether we are talking about digital natives, student-centred learning, alignment or communities of practice, the pervasive spatial and geographical metaphors surrounding our educational practices can both explain and constrain what we are able to do. It will be important to be aware when a metaphor's rhetorical power is determining or limiting educational options. Perhaps it is not necessary, for instance, to position teachers as de-centred from learning or non-native to digital spaces. Perhaps learners and teachers can choose or develop their own communities of practice. Perhaps, though, it is just important that we recognise the potential of language for limiting what we do as well as sustaining it.

The emphasis on geography and spatial theorising has been used here to illuminate ways that Scottish FE and HE practitioners conceptualise and practise teaching and learning. Looking to the newer 'sociomaterial' perspectives on education advocated by Fenwick et al. (2011) may be necessary for understanding what is happening in a distinctive education system in a small country in times of major change.

In 2012, a potential transformation or disruption to global higher education became a major topic of debate in the blogosphere: the Massive Open Online Course (MOOC). Originating in prestigious universities in North America, the MOOCs have offered free university education online to anyone in the world. In July 2012, the University of Edinburgh announced that it had become the first UK partner to join the Coursera consortium, enrolling thousands of students into free online short courses. Several such initiatives emerged almost simultaneously in 2012, a year that has been proposed as a turning point for education.

Whether MOOCs turn out to be truly transformative or a short-lived interesting experiment, some of the recent lessons in teaching and learning will be valuable. A learner engaged in a MOOC will certainly need to be able to self-regulate. Many of the MOOCs promote peer review as well, as the major way to scale up feedback. The tension between the individual and the network is likely to come to the fore. The roles of both teachers and learners in such environments are likely to be the subject of much research and debate. There will potentially be a new set of issues for educational developers and effective learning advisers: or a new set of roles, names, structures and places for them.

REFERENCES

Bayne, S. and J. Ross (2011) '"Digital native" and "digital immigrant" discourses: a critique', in R. Land and S. Bayne (eds), *Digital Difference: Perspectives on Online Learning*. Rotterdam: Sense.

Biggs, J. and C. Tang (2011) *Teaching for Quality Learning at University: What the Student Eoes* (4th edn). Maidenhead: Open University Press.

Cornelius, S., C. Gordon and A. Ackland (2009) 'Towards flexible learning for adult learners in professional contexts: an activity-focused course design', *Interactive Learning Environments*, 19 (4): 381–93.

Cousin, G. (2005) 'Learning from cyberspace', in R. Land and S. Bayne (eds), *Education in Cyberspace*. Abingdon: RoutledgeFalmer.

Fenwick, T., R. Edwards and P. Sawchuk (2011) *Emerging Approaches to Educational Research*. London: Routledge.

Haggis, T. (2009) 'What have we been thinking of? A critical overview of 40 years of student learning research in higher education', *Studies in Higher Education*, 34 (4): 377–90.

Lave, J. and E. Wenger (1991) *Situated Learning: Legitimate Peripheral Participation*. Cambridge: Cambridge University Press.

Smith, J. (2011) 'Beyond evaluative studies: perceptions of teaching qualifications from probationary lecturers in the UK', *International Journal of Academic Development*, 16 (1): 71–81.

81

Institutional and Curricular Structures in the Universities of Scotland

John Field

By 2012, there were fifteen universities in Scotland, including the newly designated University of the Highlands and Islands (UHI). There are also the Open University (OU), which is UK-wide and has national offices in Edinburgh, and three smaller higher education institutions (HEIs) offering specialist provision. Conventionally, they are often grouped into three broad classes: the 'ancient' universities, the 'chartered' universities and the 'new' universities. The ancient group comprises institutions with their roots in medieval Scotland: Aberdeen, St Andrews, Edinburgh and Glasgow were founded between 1411 and 1583. Although some of the next group – Dundee, Heriot-Watt, Stirling and Strathclyde – were based on older institutions, they were established as universities by royal charter during the expansion of higher education following Lord Robbins' review in 1963. The others were created under the 1992 Further and Higher Education (Scotland) Act, which gave university status to six former central institutions – University of Abertay Dundee, Glasgow Caledonian University (GCU), Edinburgh Napier University, Robert Gordon University, Queen Margaret University (QMU), and the University of the West of Scotland (UWS). In addition to these three groups, Glasgow School of Art, the Royal Conservatoire of Scotland and the Scottish Agricultural College all offer specialist provision and are funded as universities by the Scottish Funding Council (SFC).

This chapter will explore the institutional and curricular structures of the university sector. These structures are, of course, dynamic, reflecting the many factors that are helping to change the sector. As a result, the landscape is a changing one. The number of universities and other HEIs has fallen from twenty-three in 1994 to nineteen by 2012, usually as a result of mergers between small, specialist institutions and larger universities (Ramsden, 2012, p. 7). In 2011, for example, Edinburgh College of Art completed its merger – which many might see as more of a takeover – with the University of Edinburgh. In the same year, the Privy Council awarded university status to the UHI. As the Scottish Government has asked the SFC to consider greater collaboration between universities, including possible mergers, further changes are entirely possible (Scottish Government, 2011). The chapter will therefore present its analysis of structures against this background of change. It should be read alongside Chapters 8 and 15, which deal with the character, policy and funding of Scottish higher education.

STEERING THE SECTOR AND GOVERNING THE INSTITUTIONS

Scotland is, comparatively speaking, a small country, yet its higher education landscape is complex. Its universities draw their legal standing from a variety of legal instruments, including royal charters, parliamentary legislation at UK, European and Scottish levels, and – in the case of the ancient universities – papal bulls. While modern university constitutions are broadly shaped by the 1966 Universities (Scotland Act), which provided for the main officers and statutory committees of universities, each institution has interpreted these in the light of its own history and ambitions. Not only does each university have its own decision-making structures, shaped by its own traditions; other organisations – notably colleges – also offer a large number of higher education programmes. Moreover, each university is an independent corporate institution, with charitable status; its governing body, along with its senior managers, is responsible for the overall direction and strategy of the university.

Overall responsibility for steering the system lies with the SFC. Created in 2005 by a merger of the funding bodies for further and higher education, the SFC is formally a non-departmental public body of the Scottish Government, and its business is overseen by a Council Board of up to sixteen members who are appointed by the First Minister for Scotland. While universities are able to raise funds by various means, the SFC is by far the largest single funder. In 2012–13, it allocated some £1.02 billion for the nineteen HEIs, with further funding from the Scottish Government to support teaching in nursing and midwifery. The SFC issues an annual 'letter of guidance' to the institutions that it funds, the context of which is largely shaped by the overarching priorities of the Scottish Government for the sector; in turn, the SFC can advise ministers on all aspects of higher (and further) education. Its role is therefore largely that of a 'buffer' between the sector and the government. While it does not intervene directly in the organisation and management of individual HEIs, its senior officers meet frequently with the principals, and pay visits to institutions under the Funding Council's Strategic Dialogue programme, to discuss policy and other issues. Within this broader framework, each HEI enjoys considerable autonomy.

Each university has its own governing body, often known as the University Court. Its membership varies in size, currently standing between seventeen and twenty-eight members, the majority of whom are appointed from outside the university (Prondzynski, 2012, p. 9). Among its many tasks are the selection and appointment of new members, and at most universities it elects its own chair, normally from among the 'lay' members. At Stirling, for example, the current chair is Mr Alan Simpson, a retired consulting engineer; he in turn replaced Dr Doris Littlejohn, an employment lawyer. These are often eminent individuals with a record of civic leadership; Alan Simpson chairs the National Youth Orchestras of Scotland, while George Borthwick, chair of the Edinburgh Napier governing body, is a former chair of Scottish Business in the Community.

Matters are handled slightly differently in the ancient universities. Typically, the Court of the ancient universities is chaired by a Rector, elected by students (and, at Edinburgh, by students and staff), usually for a three-year period. This practice is rooted in the original papal bulls, issued when the older universities were founded, which allowed for the election of an academic head for each institution. Today, the post is often held by celebrities or other public figures, such as the actor Brian Cox, who was elected Rector of Dundee for the period 2010–13.

Formally, and legally, the governing body is responsible for overseeing the HEI's activities and setting its strategic direction; it must also account to the SFC and the Office of the Charities Regulator for its financial affairs. In addition, it appoints the principal. Overarching responsibility for academic matters, including the curriculum, rests with a separate academic board, chaired by the principal. These bodies vary enormously in size; some comprise all professors in the university while others have a smaller but representative membership of twenty to forty people. Their role includes maintenance of standards, granting of degrees and approval of new programmes.

Most day-to-day business, in teaching and research, is managed and delivered through some sort of departmental structure. Academics are often compared to tribal groups in their loyalties, based largely on shared commitment to the discipline. One widely cited study of 'academic tribes and territories' argues that these discipline-based collective identities have weakened in recent years, as higher education has expanded rapidly, and academics have been subjected to stronger external and managerial control, while many disciplines have sub-divided and new subjects have emerged; yet global academic alliances and the use of subject-based systems for managing accountability have helped to sustain this tribal feature of the sector (Becher and Trowler, 2001, pp. 16–19). While the precise arrangements vary from one university to another, most academics still belong to, and organise their teaching through, some sort of subject-based grouping.

These academic groupings have, though, been through a number of recent changes. Most universities have explored ways of controlling costs and improving efficiency, often seeing a reduction in the number of organisational sub-units as one way of achieving these goals. Stirling, for example, had twenty-one departments in 2000, organised into four faculties; by 2011, it had abolished faculties and merged the departments into seven schools. Edinburgh had nine faculties in 2002, which it then reorganised into three colleges (Humanities and Social Science; Science and Engineering; and Medicine and Veterinary Medicine). UWS moved in 2008–9 from a structure of seven schools, each of which had its own sub-units, to three faculties, responsible for eight schools.

Internal reorganisation was often partly a response to growth in student numbers and an attempt to handle organisational complexity. UWS, formed from the merger of Paisley University with Bell College in 2007, became the largest higher education partner on the Crichton campus in Dumfries, delivering some programmes through college partnerships. Some Scottish universities have sizeable operations overseas. Heriot-Watt, already a pioneer in distance teaching, offers a range of engineering, management and technology programmes in Dubai's Academic City, and through other local partners elsewhere. Abertay has delivered programmes since the 1980s through partners in China and Malaysia, while Strathclyde has 2+2 arrangements with institutions in China, Malaysia, India and South Korea. Where such arrangements lead to the award of a qualification from a Scottish HEI, the HEI is responsible for quality assurance, and its procedures and processes may then be audited by the Quality Assurance Agency (QAA, discussed further below).

Elsewhere, restructuring is seen as a way of breaking down disciplinary boundaries and encouraging collaboration in teaching and research. In research, Glasgow hoped to facilitate the formation of large, team-based research proposals for strategic bids and programme grants from UK and international bodies; in teaching, it planned to develop interdisciplinary provision that would appeal to international and postgraduate students. As at GCU, the university also hoped to achieve cost reductions and reduce delays in decision making. Tied as they were to reductions in academic staffing, these changes were highly controversial, spilling over into social media campaigns and public lobbying of the University Court.

CURRICULAR STRUCTURES

Full-time undergraduate degree programmes typically last for three years for an ordinary Bachelor's degree or four years for a Bachelor's degree with honours. This compares with the three-year Bachelor's programmes that are envisaged as the standard pattern across Europe; but most school leavers in Scotland enter university at 17, compared with 18 in most other European countries, and some Scottish universities offer three-year honours degrees for entrants from outside Scotland. Further, the ancient universities continue to award a Master of Arts at the end of undergraduate studies in the Humanities. Part-time undergraduates take longer, with most completing in four to six years. Within the UK, though, Scotland is distinctive in the low proportion of undergraduates who study part-time, particularly when compared with the English system (Universities UK, 2011, p. 55).

Particularly in the first two years of study, Scottish degree programmes encourage a degree of breadth, before students specialise in their final two years. This breadth is some-times constrained by professional regulatory bodies, who prescribe the curriculum in their field to a greater or lesser extent. Some students in Scottish universities therefore follow a highly prescribed curriculum, while others cover a wide range of subjects. Stirling in par-ticular has a reputation for breadth, with many of its students taking joint honours degrees, and being required to follow a range of subjects through a highly modularised curriculum. Typically, at Scottish universities, the number of hours of study is relatively low by inter-national standards (again, with the exception of subjects regulated by outside bodies), and there is a strong emphasis on independent learning.

Although study patterns are generally more varied and broader than elsewhere in the UK, Scottish universities otherwise offer the same range of subjects as elsewhere. Student numbers are proportionately higher in science and technology than in the other UK nations, with over half of all full-time undergraduates in Scotland registered for degrees in science, technology, engineering and maths (STEM) subjects, compared with fewer than half in England and Wales. This may be partly caused by the large numbers of higher education students in Scotland who take Higher Nationals in colleges, many in areas such as social studies or management that in England and Wales are taught in universities.

Some historically important subjects have declined in popularity in recent years. These include modern languages; in 2011, campaigners presented a 3,000-strong petition to the Scottish Parliament, calling for greater protection for modern language teaching in general, and for the smaller languages (including Russian) in particular in the universities. Some science subjects have also been hit by falling or static demand, combined with the rising costs of teaching lab-based subjects to small groups. According to the Universities and Colleges Union, the number of degree courses in single honours science and maths in Scotland declined by 10 per cent between 1998 and 2007.

Universities also offer a range of taught and research programmes at postgraduate level. Masters courses can be taken full-time, usually over one year (compared with the two years proposed as a European standard under Bologna) full-time, or two years part-time. Some universities also offer postgraduate certificate and diploma courses, either as modular ele-ments in a Masters programme or as taught courses in their own right. Most universities also offer research degrees. A PhD (Doctor of Philosophy) typically takes three years of full-time study, and is usually assessed through a dissertation of some 60,000–80,000 words in length, based on the student's original research. Several universities now group their postgraduate programmes together in a graduate school, while those with relatively large numbers of research students have created a graduate school within a faculty or college. Typically, graduate schools organise social events for postgraduate students, provide generic skills training for research students and serve as a clearing house for information on such matters as scholarships, careers and funding opportunities.

In addition, universities can and do collaborate at postgraduate level, though this is often due to external influences. The oldest, the Scottish graduate programme in economics, brings together eight universities who deliver a one-year (two-year part-time) MSc in Economics at Edinburgh, followed by a three-year doctorate at a participating university. The Scottish Graduate School for Physics was created in 2006 as part of a wider research collaboration, stimulated by start-up funding from the SFC. The Scottish Graduate School in Social Science began in 2011, as the biggest in the Economic and Social Research Council's (ESRC's) new UK-wide network of doctoral training centres. Usually, these collaborative graduate programmes are intended to improve access to training for students, and secure access to funding for the universities.

Study programmes at all Scottish universities are based on the Scottish Credit and Qualifications Framework (SCQF). It is often argued that credit frameworks encourage participation, mobility, flexibility and comparability between different study programmes, and this case has been generally accepted in Scotland, where most of the sector had adopted credit-based schemes before the introduction of the SCQF in 2002. The SCQF has adopted a currency of one credit point for, on average, ten hours of learning time. The number of credit points is then calibrated by the programme level, from level 1 for basic entry-level learning through to doctoral studies at level 12. Undergraduate higher education is represented by levels 7 for first year or Higher National Certificate studies through to level 10 for Honours level studies (some Scottish universities have chosen to rate most of their undergraduate teaching at levels 8, 9 and 10, with virtually none at level 7). Taught postgraduate programmes are largely rated at level 11.

While this scheme differs slightly from the European Credit Transfer System, it is largely compatible with it. And internationally, Scottish universities enjoy a strong reputation, reflected in their attractiveness to students from overseas. Among full-time students, some 44 per cent of postgraduates and 7 per cent of undergraduates come from outside the European Union, while 13 per cent of postgraduates and 8 per cent of undergraduates come from other EU countries. And, as noted above, a number of Scottish HEIs have international partnerships of different kinds. This thrust to internationalise the sector has been strongly supported by the Scottish Government, which views international higher education as a way of attracting new talent to Scotland and building international trading partnerships as well as raising Scotland's prestige and visibility overseas (Scottish Executive, 2007). Moreover, higher education is also a successful export industry; as well as fee income, one study estimated that foreign students spent some £15 million in Scotland's economy, a figure that some academics challenged as an underestimate (*Scotsman*, 12 August 2010).

MAINTAINING QUALITY AND STANDARDS

Quality assurance and responsibility for standards are first and foremost the responsibility of institutions. Universities largely set their own assessment tasks (though in some professional areas these are supplemented by assessments designed with or by outside regulatory bodies), and set out the regulations governing their courses. Each institution is also responsible for the appointment of external examiners, who normally serve on the examinations board for the degree concerned.

The QAA, sometimes perceived by academics as an outside body, is in fact owned and controlled by the sector. Much of its funding comes from subscriptions from universities and colleges or the funding councils, and its board is appointed by the national representative associations for universities across the UK. It convenes working groups of experienced academics to draft frameworks for higher education awards and benchmarks for subjects, and publishes a code of practice for the assurance of quality and standards. It is also charged with conducting institutional reviews of individual universities and other higher education providers, as well as with advising the Privy Council on applications for university status. Its reports carry real clout, so its influence should not be understated.

In Scotland, the QAA takes a slightly different approach from the rest of the UK. It has a national office in Glasgow; its Scotland Committee includes four senior academics, a college principal, the director of education of a major professional institute and a student representative. Two of the senior academics also sit on the QAA's UK board. The QAA's most visible and significant involvement in quality assurance is through regular institutional reviews, conducted on behalf of the funding council, as required under the 2005 Further and Higher Education (Scotland) Act. Under its agreement with the SFC, the QAA requires each university to undergo an Enhancement Led Institutional Review (ELIR), a title chosen to reflect an emphasis on developmental improvement. QAA Scotland is also expected to promote general quality development, through support for a programme of enhancement themes and international benchmarking. These themes, chosen jointly with the sector with a view to improving learning and teaching, have included such topics as flexible delivery, research-teaching linkages and integrative assessment.

Currently, each institution goes through an ELIR once in four years. The institution submits a reflective analysis of its own approach to improving learning and maintaining standards; it is then visited by a team of six reviewers, three of whom are UK academics; one of the others is a student reviewer, and one is an international reviewer, usually from an overseas HEI (and often, in practice, possessing close ties to Scotland). The reviewers initially visit for a two-day period to agree an agenda and identify useful documentation with senior managers, then return for three to five days to meet a range of students and staff. The review team then produces a report which, after receiving comment from the HEI, is revised and published. The main purpose of the process is said to be largely developmental, and focused on quality enhancement; but the report includes a judgement in the degree of confidence the review panel has in the institution's management of academic standards, and its assurance and enhancement of the student experience. This judgement can be expressed in terms of three standard forms: confidence, limited confidence and no confidence. In practice, it is normal for the panel to recommend confidence in the institution's procedures and processes, though in 2009 that judgement was in one instance expressed with some degree of conditionality.

However secure the procedures, inevitably some students will be dissatisfied. Each university has its own complaints system, which it must publish. Those who remain unsatisfied may then contact the Scottish Public Services Ombudsman. Out of 3,489 complaints received by the Ombudsman in 2010–11, eighty-six concerned higher education; most were rejected or deemed out of jurisdiction. The most common cause of complaint was over assessment outcomes, such as the class of a student's degree. Fourteen Scottish HEIs, and the OU, have chosen to participate in the National Student Survey commissioned by the

Higher Education Funding Council for England as part of its quality assurance procedures. In general, the results suggest that overall satisfaction levels are high, with slightly more students in Scotland expressing satisfaction than in England; however, this may reflect the low levels of part-time study in Scotland, as this was the most dissatisfied group.

INSTITUTIONAL DIFFERENTIATION

A number of commentators argue that the distinctiveness of Scottish higher education has increased following devolution. Keating suggests that one way in which devolution has increased distinctiveness is that it has reduced differentiation. Since 1999, he argues, institutions in Scotland have evolved in a relatively integral and egalitarian direction that has worked against competition and diversity (Keating, 2007). Yet there is still an important degree of differentiation. Even if we disregard the division between colleges and universities (and this is debatable, given the sheer scale of higher education provided in the college sector), the universities may be categorised in a number of different ways. The generally accepted distinction between 'ancient', 'chartered' and 'new' is simply one of these.

First, there are clear differences of size. Far the largest in terms of student numbers are Edinburgh, with almost 25,700 students in 2009–10, and Glasgow, with 25,600; Strathclyde is third, with just over 23,300. The largest 'new' universities are GCU, with nearly 17,700, and UWS, with 17,500. The specialist institutions have relatively small numbers; smallest by far is the Royal Conservatoire, with fewer than 800, while Glasgow School of Art has 1,750. Staffing levels vary rather more; Edinburgh is at the head with 3,010 academic staff, followed by Glasgow with 2,625 and Dundee a distant third with 1,480, just ahead of Strathclyde; largest among the new universities are Edinburgh Napier and GCU, with 830 academic staff each. The financial picture is even more asymmetrical, reflecting the balance of research income in institutional budgets. Far the largest was Edinburgh, with an income in 2010–11 of £650 million, while Glasgow's was £450m. This in turn contrasts with the larger 'new' universities; GCU's income was £112m, while UWS came in at just under £96m. So the differences in scale financially are much greater than the differences in student numbers.

Second, universities present themselves, and focus their strategic goals, in different ways. In particular, we can see a very broad division between those who aim to be world-leading in research and teaching, and those who focus on teaching, employability and inclusion; the following paragraph summarises the missions that the universities embraced in 2012. Edinburgh opens with the statement that its mission is to 'shape the future by attracting and developing the world's most promising students and outstanding staff'. St Andrews begins in similar fashion: 'to achieve the highest international standards of excellence in scholarship, manifested in the quality of its research and of its graduates'. Glasgow presents itself in a wider canvas, less focused on the internal landscape of academia: 'to undertake world-leading research and to provide an intellectually stimulating learning environment that benefits culture, society and the economy'. Others present themselves as more focused on teaching and a contribution to national wellbeing. Abertay's mission, for instance, is 'to provide a distinctive and high-quality university education that empowers our students intellectually, socially, culturally and economically, and to generate new knowledge and learning that reinforces national competitiveness'. Of course, these statements need to be seen as aspirational, but they provide an indication of how an HEI wishes itself to be seen.

Third, universities take very different approaches to recruitment. Some universities have difficulty recruiting the minimum numbers agreed with the SFC, while others have difficulty ensuring that they do not recruit over the SFC's maximum. This recruitment pattern is closely linked to HEIs' responses to wider participation policies. Both the Scottish Government and the SFC promote policies for wider participation in higher education, seeking to balance the strong current bias of recruitment towards the most advantaged sections of Scottish society. Under its Learning for All strategy, the SFC set out in 2005 a series of priorities for both further and higher education, and progress is monitored by its Access and Inclusion Committee. In the event, progress has been extremely uneven. In the case of articulation from further to higher education, for example, the Scottish Government has expressed concern over the extent to which the transfer of credit from Higher Nationals to degree study is limited to a small number of mostly post-92 universities. In 2011, the government announced that it was considering legislation to create a statutory framework guaranteeing articulation from college to university (Scottish Government, 2011, p. 19).

Fourth, and probably most obviously, the universities differ by their performance in research. While this chapter has concentrated on institutional and curricular structures, universities are often characterised externally by the extent to which they succeed in research. The clearest example of this is the importance attributed to research performance in the main international rankings. The influential world ranking carried out by Shanghai Jiao Tong University has Edinburgh in fifty-third place; Glasgow just makes it into the top 200, Aberdeen is in the top 300 and Dundee in the top 400. The *Times Higher Education* ranking, which excludes Nobel prizes, paints a rather more favourable portrait: it puts Edinburgh at thirty-sixth place, Glasgow at 102nd, Aberdeen at 151st and Dundee at 176th, while Stirling is between 301 and 350. This pattern is also reflected in the shares of postgraduate education, with Edinburgh by far the largest provider, accounting for roughly one in every eight postgraduates in Scottish HEIs.

Fifth, there are considerable differences in perceived status. One easy way of measuring this is through the league tables compiled by newspapers in the UK, or by expert panels such as the Shanghai Jiao Tong index. Some league tables, such as that compiled by the *Guardian*, lean more towards the quality of teaching, while others make more use of indicators of research quality. Each table will therefore measure different things; I remember Colin Bell, then principal at Stirling, joking that if you wait long enough, a league table will come along that is designed for you. While most university managers and senior academics publicly disparage the value of these indicators, they are also quick to publicise them when their own department or university shows up well, and they are routinely discussed in senior management meetings.

These differences are also reflected in different strategies for collaboration. Take, for example, the alliances that universities create within the sector. All of the Scottish HEIs belong to Universities Scotland, a representative organisation that promotes the sector's interests and provides a forum for policy discussion, and which is controlled by a board made up of the nineteen principals of Scottish HEIs. In addition, most Scottish institutions belong to specialised groupings within the UK and beyond. Edinburgh and Glasgow belong to the Russell Group, a grouping of twenty UK research-intensive universities, and also to Universitas21, a global alliance of twenty-three research-intensive institutions. St Andrews belongs to the 1994 group, which also presents itself as comprising research-intensive institutions. UWS, Abertay and Edinburgh Napier are members of Million+, an association of mostly large universities who pride themselves on their accessibility, while GCU and the

OU belong to the University Alliance, which positions itself as a group of business-engaged institutions. These groupings vary considerably in their roles, though they often share a common interest in benchmarking, lobbying and sharing experience; the international groupings are also often concerned with the development of cross-national opportunities for study.

FUTURE DEVELOPMENTS

Scotland's universities have changed considerably in recent years. Many of those changes have been driven by external forces, such as the rapid expansion in participation and global policy interest in the sector's contribution to innovation and growth. Others reflect the specific aspirations and policies that have emerged within Scotland, particularly since the re-establishment of the Scottish Parliament in 1999. Similar forces are reshaping higher education systems in many nations, leading to a growing degree of convergence; nevertheless, the Scottish system, while very much open to wider influences and models, retains many distinctive features and structures. How are these likely to fare in an increasingly global and ever more complex higher education marketplace?

In the past, many Scots have seen the distinctiveness of their education system as a key feature of national identity. Yet so far as higher education is concerned, this distinctiveness may be diminishing. Viewed within the wider European context, the Scottish system has adopted a number of policies that are designed to promote greater convergence between student experiences across Europe. The Scottish Government has embraced the Bologna process of higher education convergence, agreed by European education ministers in 1999, and adopted formally by the European Union in 2010 as a mechanism for creating a common European higher education area (EHEA) across the forty-seven nations who are taking part. The authors of a 'score card' noted that the Scottish system had achieved all the changes set out under the Bologna agreement, and indeed Scotland was the only country to have implemented the agreement in full (Rauhvargers et al., p. 121). As the aim of this process is to encourage comparability, coherence, consistency and mobility across the EHEA, it follows that the different national systems will increasingly converge, and that different degree structures and qualification frameworks will lose much of their distinctiveness.

Moreover, many of the features of the Bologna process – standardised degree structures, formal quality assurance procedures, credit-based qualifications frameworks – go with the grain of other developments within Scotland. Internationally, governments and institutions increasingly see these changes as helping them compare themselves with competitors elsewhere and improving their standing internationally. Nationally, the Scottish Government is actively encouraging the sector to use the SCQF as a way of increasing articulation from college, and introducing 'accelerated degrees', including direct entry to the second year of study. These are seen as increasing the system's efficiency and cost-effectiveness, both by shortening overall periods of study and by improving retention (Russell, 2011). So far, then, there are plenty of signs that Scotland's system will increasingly align itself with others internationally, and lose some of its distinctiveness in the process.

Yet there are also reasons for supposing that universities, and the higher education system more broadly, will continue to show many distinctive features. Even as part of the EHEA, many of the characteristics of the Scottish system are likely to remain, at least in the short and medium term. Compliance with Bologna can sometimes be rather mechanistic. For example, the Scottish Government has reported that it has increased its emphasis on the international dimensions of the higher education curriculum, and introduced an international dimension into the process of institutional review. According to the SFC guidance which the government cited in support of its claim, review teams should have an 'understanding of national and international good practice', and internal reviews should include more external members, one of whom may come from 'outside Scotland'. And while ELIR teams routinely include an overseas reviewer, they normally come from an English-speaking background, and often have personal ties to Scotland.

What is certain is that the sector will continue to develop and change. As in many countries, higher education is widely viewed in Scotland as an engine of economic competitiveness and a driver of social mobility. There are likely to be lively policy discussions over its funding, shape and size in the future, as the strains of maintaining a mass higher education system largely through public funding start to make themselves felt. The Scottish Government is considering proposals for the reform of higher education governance, as promised in the Scottish National Party's manifesto, and is planning to promote wider access, articulation and reductions in the number of HEIs, possibly through legislation, as well as increasing the concentration of research funding in a smaller number of universities, while ensuring that research activities are more closely aligned to the government's national priorities (Scottish Government, 2011, p. 36). Scottish HEIs are also affected by policies in the other UK nations, as well as by the more immediate impact of the recession on Scottish society and the economy. Social change, economic change and political pressures also make it likely that Scotland's universities will need to rethink the nature of their contract with Scottish society. They are not alone in these tasks, as comparable pressures and forces are at work elsewhere, but they will need to undertake these challenges in the unique context that is contemporary Scotland.

REFERENCES

Becher, T. and P. Trowler (2001) *Academic Tribes and Territories: Intellectual Enquiry and the Culture of Disciplines*. Buckingham: Open University Press.

Higher Education Statistics Agency (2011) Staff Data Tables. Online at www.hesa.ac.uk/index.php/component/option,com_datatables/Itemid,121/task,show_category/catdex,2/

Keating, M. (2007) 'Higher education in England and Scotland after devolution', *Regional and Federal Studies*, 15 (4): 423–35.

Prondzynski, F. (2012) *Report of the Review of Higher Education Governance in Scotland*. Edinburgh: Scottish Government.

Ramsden, B. (2012) *Institutional Diversity in UK Higher Education*, Oxford: Higher Education Policy Institute.

Rauhvargers, A., C. Deane and W. Pauwels (2009) *Bologna Process Stocktaking Report 2009*. Brussels: Vlaamse Overheid.

Russell, M. (2011) Letter of guidance to the Scottish Funding Council. Edinburgh: Scottish Government.

Scottish Executive (2007) *International Lifelong Learning: Scotland's Contribution*. Edinburgh: Scottish Executive.

Scottish Government (2011) *Putting Learners at the Centre: Delivering our Ambitions for Post-16 Education*. Edinburgh: Scottish Government.

Universities UK (2011) *Patterns and Trends in UK Higher Education*. London: UUK.

82

Democratic Intellect or Degree Factory? The Changing Civic and Cultural Place of the University in Scotland

George Kerevan

What does Scottish society want from its universities? To pass on the collective wisdom of humanity or to provide a passport to the best jobs? To act as the world's greatest research lab or to be an express lift to social mobility in a small country? And what happens if these demands – traditional and modern – find themselves in obvious conflict? Welcome to the precarious world of the contemporary Scottish university. A world suddenly made even more precarious by the advent of global economic downturn and long-term public austerity.

In 2007, just as the great millennium economic boom was peaking, two events occurred, separated by a few weeks, which provide a telling insight into the social role of higher education in Scottish culture in the twenty-first century.

In May, the first SNP administration was elected to the Scottish Parliament, with Alex Salmond as First Minister. All but one member of the new Cabinet had degrees from Scottish universities, and from no fewer than eight separate institutions of higher learning. Political ideology aside, this was a Cabinet whose intellectual horizons and social convictions had been shaped by those same universities. Indeed, with Professor Christopher Harvie, one of Scotland's foremost historians, elected as a new Nationalist MSP, professional academics were also well represented at the heart of government. Tellingly, one of the first symbolic actions of the new administration was to abolish the student graduate endowment fee – a tuition fee by any other name. In justification, the SNP invoked the Scottish tradition of open access to higher education as a means of promoting individual advancement and cultural solidarity. Later, in September 2012, as Alex Salmond kicked off the SNP's independence referendum campaign at a rally in Edinburgh, the very first example he would cite of Scotland wanting to take a different road from the rest of the United Kingdom was his administration's reintroduction of free university tuition.

The second event in 2007 was the death in March of the historian and philosopher George Davie, at the ripe old age of 95. In 1961, Davie published a now famous treatise, *The Democratic Intellect*, which more than any other work made the case for Scotland's universities being a unique motor force in the formation and retention of a distinctive Scottish national culture. Davie also purported to show how, starting in the nineteenth century, the anglicisation of traditional Scottish higher education, portending over-specialisation and middle-class elitism, had endangered a world-renowned university system and thereby seriously undermined Scottish identity. His book became a nationalist Bible, preaching of a lost golden age both of university education and of cultural independence. As a result of the book's success, the role of Scotland's universities in national life was to become a matter of profound political debate – much more so than in England. The long reach of *The Democratic Intellect* could be seen in the swift move by the SNP government to make university entrance free. In many respects it is possible to criticise Davie's analysis as romanticised, if not a sheer historical invention. But it is a potent, meritocratic myth and is now central to how the SNP government sees the role of Scotland's institutions of higher education. This chapter will examine the interplay between the myth and the reality, in order to chart the changing social role played by the universities in Scotland.

Courtesy of its Presbyterian culture, Scotland developed a more extensive university system earlier than England, which relied on the elitist Oxbridge duo until as late as the nineteenth century. Scotland's traditional universities – St Andrews (1411), Glasgow (1451), Aberdeen (1495) and post-Reformation latecomer Edinburgh (1583) – were originally hybrids of secondary school, adult education class and university. Adult, male skilled artisans routinely took non-graduating classes, diffusing what was essentially secondary school education much wider than in England. Davie's lamented nineteenth-century reforms actually changed this for the better, separating out higher education, raising teaching standards and professionalising research. This resulted in genuinely world-class academic institutions as we now know them. In fact, working-class participation in taking full degrees expanded after the reforms because philanthropist Andrew Carnegie funded a scheme that by 1910 covered much of the fees for half of all Scots undergraduates. The distinctive Scottish generalist MA degree grew in importance and demand only after the modernisation that Davie criticised (though Davie attributes this to a 'counter revolution' in 1917–27 against the Scottish Education Department and its fixation with specialisation).

Through the first half of the twentieth century, Scotland's universities supplied the trained staff of the Scottish professions – lawyers, teachers, doctors and ministers of religion – thereby maintaining, if not reinforcing, a distinct Scottish identity. Enrolments rose from 6,000 in 1900 to 10,000 on the eve of the Second World War. Most students were from the professional middle classes but children from working-class backgrounds made up around a third of university entrants – a healthy proportion for the time. It was largely the working-class students who took the three-year generalist MA degree so beloved by George Davie, basically as a route into the teaching profession. Yet this was a fiercely meritocratic system that respected the rigid caste differences between the middle-class professions served by the universities and the skilled working classes served by an elaborate apprenticeship network (backed up by highly effective technical colleges). Until the 1970s, the Scottish working class seemed to accept the universities as a promotional ladder to the middle class, not as a means for abolishing class differences *per se*. Indeed, there remained a conservative working-class allegiance to the notion of the university as an elite institution where their privileged sons and daughters could better themselves through hard work. As late as 1971, after students at the new University of Stirling greeted the Queen with a demonstration that degenerated into rowdy drunkenness, local bus drivers refused to stop at the campus as a way of showing their disapproval.

All this was about to alter, and Davie's book, published in the early 1960s, played its part in justifying the coming sea change – university expansion premised on the economic need for skilled manpower. Davie's accent on a generalist higher education open to the best from every class was to be transmuted into its antithesis: a mass vocationalism, which Scotland would take even further than England though clothed in the garb of allowing the working class unfettered access to higher education. Scotland began the 1960s with 18,500 students in four universities. No new university had been established for over half a millennium. It ended the decade with 38,000 students in eight universities. This proved the single most revolutionary institutional reform between World War Two and the advent of the Scottish Parliament. It initiated a continuous (if not accelerating) expansion of higher education that has continued till the present day. By 2010–11 there were 214,000 Scottish domiciled students enrolled in local higher education institutions and vocational colleges, plus another 76,000 from the rest of the UK and abroad studying in Scotland – an all-time record total despite the economic downturn. Of these, 150,000 were studying first degrees, an increase of 33,000 since only 2001–2. And, though the number of Scottish domiciled students dipped slightly in 2007–8 as a result of the financial crisis, it quickly recovered. Nothing, it seems, can halt the popularity of university education in the public's eye, especially in Scotland where the higher education participation rate in 2010–11 was an all-time high of 55.6 per cent (of 16–30-year-olds) compared to 47 per cent in England.

Davie's emphasis on a bogus democratic era of higher education, supposedly lost, has helped to justify this new university system. But this model, while socially worthy and economically justifiable, has bred its own frictions. The early years of the twenty-first century have seen an emerging cultural crisis in the civic role of the Scottish university. What might be called the 'consensus' of the mythic Davie model – the ideal of the Scottish university as the open, classless and independent guardian of the national culture – is threatened, just as the new SNP government seeks to revive it. Three major fissures have appeared:

1. Business, the general public and potential students have begun to question the validity, quality and cost of a university degree, as a result of the mass extension of higher education – something Scots of all classes in the first half of the twentieth century would find absurd. The argument that 'more is better' may have reached its limit. This is having an impact on enrolments and business hiring practices.
2. The close relationship between the state and the university sector fostered by mass vocationalism is being revised by the state itself, on cost grounds. In 2006, the Labour government at Westminster introduced university tuition fees in England, but referred to them as a 'top up' to direct state funding. Then, in 2010, the new Conservative–Liberal Democrat coalition raised the cap on what fees English universities could charge to £9,000 per year (incidentally causing a major loss of electoral support for the Lib Dems). At the same time the coalition made it clear that tuition fees were to start replacing direct grants to universities, as a means of cutting overall public expenditure.
3. The old idea of the university degree as a passport to social mobility has come under fire: from the left, who accuse the universities of failing working-class students; and from the right, who accuse the universities of dumbing down their standards precisely to encourage enrolments from those from disadvantaged backgrounds.

It was inevitable that the vast expansion of the university sector would alter the social and economic standing of higher education. But this shift is in danger of turning into a crisis of goals, financing and possibly academic standards – problems the global economic crisis has only intensified. The remainder of this chapter seeks to examine some of the issues that are emerging in this process.

REAL WORLD OR IVORY TOWER? VOCATIONALISM AND TEACHING QUALITY

At the beginning of the twenty-first century, universities play a pivotal role in the Scottish economy, more so than at any time in their long history and generating around 6 per cent of GDP. To the chagrin of traditionalists, they now also refer to themselves as 'businesses'. A standard charge is that vocationalism and the demand to bring in more funding from the private sector has threatened university standards. Today, some 30 per cent of Scottish students are studying business-related degrees (including law), certainly the most popular subject specialism. Is this proof of academic dumbing down? Or a sign that Scottish universities are robustly engaging with the real world?

To answer these questions it is important to grasp that Scottish universities have never suffered quite the separation from the commercial world originally found in England. The strength of Scotland's business and engineering tradition – a tradition that might be christened the Scottish Practical Intellect, as opposed to Davie's Democratic Intellect – rests on the unique links the traditional Scottish universities always maintained with the commercial and civil world, as distinct from the English Oxbridge ivory tower tradition. During the English industrial revolution and even after, classics and theology predominated over science and medicine at Oxbridge. Things, however, were different north of the border. Newton's ideas were taught in Scotland before Cambridge accepted them. As early as 1800, Edinburgh University had twelve chairs of science and medicine. At Glasgow University, Joseph Black, one of the most renowned chemists of the eighteenth century, concentrated on applied industrial research. His influence on the university's instrument maker – a certain James Watt – helped stimulate Watt's invention of the modern steam engine, the power source that created the industrial revolution. Indeed, the Enlightenment tradition of rationalist thinking that was the product of Scotland's universities in the eighteenth century served as the foundation for the growth in Scotland's scientific and technical progress in the nineteenth and twentieth centuries.

The Scottish Practical Intellect also inspired a generation of teaching and research institutions that would form the precursors of the four new Scottish universities of the 1960s: Strathclyde, Heriot-Watt, Dundee and Stirling. Today Strathclyde teaches some 29,000 full- and part-time students, plus another 34,000 people on distance learning, short courses and continuing professional development. That makes it probably the UK's largest provider of postgraduate and professional education. The tradition of the Practical Intellect is also central to Heriot-Watt, named after James Watt himself. It is consistently among the top UK universities in terms of industrial and commercial funding per member of academic staff. A pioneer Heriot-Watt spin-out company, the Interactive University, markets Scottish higher education courses over the internet throughout the globe. With over 60,000 students, it is one of the largest online learning communities in the world.

This suggests *per se* that there has been no overall dumbing down of academic rigour or innovation in order to accommodate vocational subjects. Indeed, three Scottish universities – Edinburgh (rank 21), Glasgow (rank 54) and St Andrews (rank 93) – make it into the prestigious QS global university rankings for 2012, on a par with the Netherlands and Canada and more than from Sweden, Denmark or Finland. There is much criticism in the business world – usually with little supporting analytical evidence – that universities are turning out graduates in 'soft' or non-essential subjects. A look at which subject areas have seen the largest increase in Scottish student numbers over the decade to 2010–11 indicates no Gadarene rush towards the ephemeral. Student numbers in medical subjects were up 16 per cent in the period 2001–11, in science and engineering up 20 per cent and in law up an astonishing 62.3 per cent, while total numbers were up 7.6 per cent. What Scottish universities teach today is very much in their own technical and commercial tradition.

A more realistic concern is whether the growing numbers of students being sucked into the higher education system can be taught adequately and then find a job when they graduate. In particular, given funding and teaching pressures, are marginal students from the former polytechnics being well served? When Scottish student numbers doubled over the decade of the 1990s, so did the staff–student ratio. This led to 'tutorials' of thirty students in some of Scotland's ex-polytechnic universities.

There is a constant refrain from Scottish employers that graduates lack practical skills, i.e. competency in communication, numeracy, and the use of information technology. One could argue that such general skills should be inculcated at secondary school. On the other hand, it is questionable how a student can complete a first degree course without them.

THE UNIVERSITY PLC? COMMERCIALISATION AND RESEARCH

Has the contemporary drive to make links with the business world perverted research interests? The most interesting – not to mention the most successful – model for developing research and funding collaboration has been the experience at Dundee University, which became independent of St Andrews University in 1967. Despite its location in a peripheral and declining industrial centre with high unemployment, Dundee University is now world-renowned for its medical and biological research. Three out of the twenty most cited academics in the UK are based at Dundee – Sir David Lane (cancer), Sir Philip Cohen (diabetes, cell signalling) and Peter Downes (cell signalling). In the decade from 2000 to 2010, Cohen ranked as the world's most cited biochemist. Dundee University's biomedical research has received top five star ranking ever since the UK national Research Assessment Exercise was introduced in 1986, producing almost the highest research income in the UK (£50 million per annum). Despite this emphasis on research, and with over 16,000 students, Dundee still ranked in the top ten UK institutions for teaching and learning quality, in the *Times Higher Education* student experience survey of 2010.

How did Dundee achieve this world quality? The key strategy has been a determination to bring the best research minds in the world to Dundee. The lynchpin was Sir Philip Cohen, who came to Dundee in the early 1970s by way of the University of Washington in Seattle. Cohen fell in love with Dundee and Tayside and determined it would become his research Eden. It was Cohen who courted the Wellcome Trust, one of the world's biggest research sponsors, to fund activities. In 1994, the Trust made a donation of £10 million towards a new, 70,000 sq. ft Medical Sciences Institute, then the largest single charitable donation ever given to a Scottish university. It was also Cohen who went after the top life sciences researchers in the world – never taking no for an answer – and eventually persuaded them to come to Dundee. He enticed Sir Alfred Cushieri, the pioneer of 'keyhole' surgery; and Sir David Lane, who was previously Principal Scientist at the Imperial Cancer Research Fund in London and discoverer of the p53 gene that controls the growth of tumours in many common cancers.

The Dundee example is proof that a rigorous commercial attitude does not mean the sacrifice of academic achievement. In 2011, data from the Higher Education Statistics Agency showed that Scottish universities won 14 per cent of competitive UK research funds (public and private) despite Scotland having 8.5 per cent of the UK population. But how far is it possible to escape reliance on state finance?

PUBLIC MONEY OR PRIVATE SPONSORSHIP? THE FUNDING DEBATE AND ALUMNI RELATIONS

Even if Scottish universities have managed to retain their teaching and research quality in this age of mass vocational study, they are still very much financial wards of the state. In 2010–11, they were receiving on average some 37 per cent of their funding from the basic state grant but nearer 50 per cent when public research grants are included. Three universities were particularly state-dependent: the University of the West of Scotland (70 per cent of income), Glasgow Caledonian University (58 per cent) and the University of Abertay Dundee (56 per cent). If all state tertiary education funding and private research money going to universities is added in (a standard benchmark of the Organisation for Economic Cooperation and Development), then spending on Scottish higher and further education exceeds the EU average. However, with an era of retrenchment in public spending now on the cards, it is clear that Scottish universities will struggle to find the resources to stay competitive in global terms.

There are four avenues to attaining greater independent income: pursuing commercial research contracts, attracting fee-paying foreign students, charging tuition fees to domestic students and expanding alumni giving (possibly to create an eventual endowment fund). While Scottish universities have heroically boosted their contract research, a combination of recession and competition from other institutions suggests this source of funding will not grow so fast in the future. As we have noted already, over a quarter of students at Scottish universities are non-domiciles. Again, with other universities and internet education offering competition, this source of funding must be reaching its limit. The option of increased student fees was rejected by Scottish universities at the time of the Cubie Report in 1999. This leaves alumni giving, pioneered in America.

Scotland has played an important role in the recent expansion of alumni giving in the UK. The seminal name here is the late Henry Drucker. Born in New Jersey, Drucker completed a doctorate in political philosophy at the London School of Economics before moving to Edinburgh University in 1967. In the 1980s, he set up Edinburgh's fledgling development office, drawing on the American model of structured alumni funding. On the basis of this early successful experiment, he was invited to become Director of Development at Oxford University in 1987. He launched the Campaign for Oxford in 1988 with the ambitious target (for then) of £220 million. It closed in 1994 having raised £341 million. Drucker introduced into British and Scottish staples of alumni relations features that now seem obvious: the database, the alumni magazine and dedicated staffing.

All Scottish universities now have structured giving projects. However, alumni and charitable giving, legacies and endowment income varies significantly between institutions – Edinburgh remains the most successful, following Drucker's lead. In 2010, the author JK Rowling made a £10m donation to Edinburgh University to set up a new research clinic for multiple sclerosis. As of 2011, only seven UK universities (including Glasgow and Edinburgh) have endowments of over £100 million – in the same year there were seventy-four in the United States with endowments exceeding $1bn (£640m). Partly this is due to the lack of a philanthropic culture in the UK. And partly it is the failure of universities to grasp the scale of effort needed to extract significant alumni giving on a sustainable basis.

Johns Hopkins University, for instance, has a team of 200 staff solely devoted to running its alumni giving department. The surprising thing is that in the five years to 2011, despite recession and austerity, UK universities actually increased their charitable and alumni income from £513m to £693m. This was in part thanks to a substantial increase in the number of donors (including companies and trusts), by over 50 per cent, from 132,000 to 204,000. As alumni and charitable giving to universities is a reasonable index of their social standing, this suggests higher education, despite tabloid moans about dumbing down, junk courses and verbally illiterate graduates, is still held in high regard.

On the downside, one dubious aspect of the new awareness of grooming alumni has been the explosion in granting honorary degrees to a much wider selection of former students – and sometimes just to the great, rich and famous with some tenuous connection to the local area. The once staid Glasgow University handed out thirty-two honorary degrees to celebrate its 550th anniversary in 2001. They included motor racing legend Sir Jackie Stewart and TV presenter Kirsty Wark. While these eclectic choices could be argued to have some individual validity, the decision of St Andrews in 2006 to award a Doctor of Letters to the Hollywood film star Michael Douglas provoked howls of derision. The same university had already awarded an honorary doctorate in music to Bob Dylan, who kept his eyes shut while the university choir sang *Blowin' In The Wind*. Neither of these celebrities had any prior association with St Andrews but the resulting publicity no doubt helped the university's American recruitment following the graduation of Prince William.

To some, this is just Davie's Democratic Intellect in a populist guise. To others, it is a crude attempt at public relations combined with a brazen pandering to rich celebrities who might open their wallets. Harry Reid, a distinguished former editor of the *Glasgow Herald*, with two merited honorary degrees to his credit, one from Glasgow University, the other from Edinburgh, commented, 'To receive one Honorary Degree is ostentatious. To receive two is vulgar.'

HOW BIG IS BIG? SOCIAL INCLUSION AND THE QUEST FOR STUDENT NUMBERS

In June 2000, Henry McLeish, Minister with Responsibility for Higher Education, took time to denounce Edinburgh, St Andrews and Aberdeen Universities for failing to take more students from 'lower social-income groups'. The class bias, or otherwise, of Scotland's university system has remained an extraordinarily sensitive topic and our higher education institutions remain the public whipping boys of politicians anxious for a headline. In June 2012, a dozen years after McLeish's outburst, the National Union of Students (NUS) in Scotland was still accusing Scotland's universities of having a 'truly awful' record when it came to admitting students from poorer backgrounds. According to the NUS, Scotland's older universities each typically recruited fewer than 100 students from 'deprived' backgrounds. (This is defined as those who grew up in one of the least affluent 20 per cent of postcode districts, in the Scottish Index of Multiple Deprivation, so-called MD20.) St Andrews University admitted that only thirteen of its students came from these areas. In response, Michael Russell, the Scottish Education Cabinet Secretary, said it would be necessary to 'step it up' on widening student access.

How valid is this complaint about lack of access? In truth it is hard to find compelling evidence that most Scottish universities, rooted in dense, industrial conurbations, have ever been anything but socially open. This has also been facilitated by the traditional, broader-based Highers system at secondary school. The inclusion policy has found an open door at university management level with the ready introduction of part-time courses, modular courses, and open and distance learning provision, as well as by running access initiatives such as summer schools, collaboration with schools, and further education and outreach programmes. We should also remember that in the era before the expansion of university places in the 1960s, secondary schools in working-class areas in Scotland still taught a fiercely 'classical' curriculum aimed at university entrance.

The real key to social inclusion – in the sense that higher education was now the expected norm for a majority of young Scots – came in 1992, when five new independent universities were created out of their former polytechnic chrysalises: Glasgow Caledonian University (GCU), Napier University in Edinburgh, the University of Abertay Dundee, Paisley University and the Robert Gordon University in Aberdeen. Size predominates in these veritable Peoples' Universities. GCU and Paisley (now merged with Bell College to create the University of the West of Scotland, UWS) have around 17,000 students each, Edinburgh Napier has 14,000 and Robert Gordon 13,000. These 1992 polyversities (with later additions such as Queen Margaret University and the University of the Highlands and Islands) today provide a quarter of the university places in Scotland. Servicing largely their own local labour markets, they have the theoretical ability to tailor degree courses to fast-moving local needs. For instance, the unexpected emergence of Scotland as an international base for designing computer games has spawned a serious research institute at Abertay and a degree course at UWS. But their main forte lies in the standard vocational primers of late-twentieth-century post-industrialism: business studies, communications, hospitality management, health studies and computing.

The result of these changes was to boost participation rates in higher and further education in Scotland to over 50 per cent by the start of the millennium – one of the highest in the EU and higher than in England (by 56 per cent to 47, in 2011) though participation south of the border has also expanded greatly since 1992. At first this seemed a confirmation of the success of mass vocationalism and even a return to Davie's vision of *The Democratic Intellect*. However, by the first decade of the twenty-first century doubts were beginning to creep in, prompting the sort of criticism initiated by Henry McLeish. For, despite higher overall student numbers, Scotland appeared to lag behind England in working-class participation. In 2006, as the great millennial economic boom was reaching its peak, only 29.3 per cent of young full-time degree entrants in Scotland were from classes 4 to 7, i.e. from outside professional middle-class families. While this was also the UK figure, many English regions had a better working-class participation rate, including the North East and North West, Yorkshire, the East and West Midlands, and London. In 2010–11, the Scottish figure was marginally better at 29.6 per cent from classes 4 to 7, but it was 30.7 in England. It remains to be seen what the impact of the different fee regimes north and south of the border will have on these numbers, but it is easy to see why Scots might feel something has gone wrong. When all is said and done, the proportion of working-class children in the student population in Scotland is scarcely any better than it was in the 1960s, even if the absolute numbers have soared. The mass vocational experiment might be providing more trained workers but it has not been delivering social mobility. In April 2005, a widely reported London School of Economics study argued that social mobility was actually declining in Britain. These findings seemed corroborated by another 2005 study, conducted at Edinburgh University, which surveyed 15,000 Scots born between 1937 and 1976. Total upward mobility – meaning moving into a higher social stratum – was found to have fallen from 52.8 per cent in the eldest group to 39.7 per cent in the youngest.

These findings were (crudely) explained by the theory that university expansion had overwhelmingly benefited the children of the middle classes, whose parents were better able to manipulate the system and who gave encouragement to their offspring. Politicians of all colours soon demanded that Scotland's universities devote more effort to encouraging enrolment from children from so-called deprived backgrounds, even to the point of positive discrimination. However, while middle-class children may have certain social advantages when it comes to parental encouragement to seek a university place, there is no evidence of deliberate class bias in university selection. Since 2001, every higher education institution in Scotland has signed up to a commitment to improving social inclusion in higher education, including valuing non-academic achievement in the selection process. In essence this has meant that the older Scottish universities, such as Edinburgh, actually tend to discriminate on the margins against students from independent schools. They could hardly do otherwise given their dependence on state financing. Then there is the Schools for Higher Education Programme, financed by the universities and the Scottish Funding Council. This aims to identify and encourage talented young pupils (S3–S6) in low progression schools, who usually have no family experience of higher education, to apply to university. In Lothians, between 2009 and 2011, this programme worked directly with 2,000 pupils, over 60 per cent of whom went on to university, a quarter of those going to the University of Edinburgh.

More likely, the failure of working-class children to take greater advantage of the mass expansion of university places from the 1990s onwards lies outside higher education altogether – at secondary level, where many students still fail to gain the necessary entry qualifications or learn the skills for advanced study. Only 10.5 per cent of pupils from the 20 per cent most deprived areas in Scotland obtain the normal minimum entry requirements for university compared to 48 per cent from the least deprived 20 per cent – something the NUS failed to note in its criticisms mentioned above. The improvements in English working-class student participation rates may be explained by the emphasis placed after 1997 on boosting literacy levels in schools in deprived areas. In fact, Scottish students from poor backgrounds who do achieve university entry-level qualifications are just as likely to go to university (if not more so) as their middle-class counterparts. Between 37 and 40 per cent of all pupils who satisfy entry criteria from MD20 areas go on to university, compared to an equivalent figure of only 30 to 33 per cent of all pupils from the most advantaged areas. All of which suggests the crude attack on Scottish universities for being elitist is misplaced – something George Davie would have appreciated.

We should also note a serious unintended consequence of the social inclusion policy and emphasis on maximising student numbers: the high drop-out rate. The student drop-out rate in Scotland rose through the first decade of the new millennium to nearly one in ten of first-year students. Scotland now has the worst drop-out rate in the UK. By 2010–11, it was 9.4 per cent compared with 8.6 per cent for the UK and 8.4 per cent in England. At the University of the Highlands and Islands, first year drop-out rates exceeded a third of students with only 48.6 per cent of students expected to graduate. A quarter of students at the University of the West of Scotland were reported to have dropped out. It is true that wastage rate also increased across the UK, but the relatively poor performance in Scotland needs explaining. The standard explanation is student poverty. On average, the retention rate for students from the most deprived backgrounds is 7 per cent lower than those for students overall. But another valid reason is that marginally performing students in a mass teaching environment will have particular learning difficulties. This ballooning of student numbers inside each university is in stark contrast to the political injunction in the primary and secondary schools for ever-lower class sizes.

Another problem is that degrees for marginal students do not automatically lead to good jobs or career satisfaction. The global economic downturn has complicated analysing the graduate jobs pattern, but the Scottish Funding Council (SFC) has produced interesting data on graduate perceptions of the usefulness of their degree course. Tracking the 2007 graduate cohort in 2010, the SFC found that 55 per cent would, in retrospect, change their university, subject or qualification. Nearly a third would have changed their subject area, while nearly a fifth would have decided not to go to university at all. This may suggest that prioritising university degrees over shorter, flexible HNCs or HNDs is not always the best way to go when it comes to meeting local labour market needs, especially in a period of economic crisis.

TO CHARGE OR NOT TO CHARGE? THE TOP-UP DEBATE

The social inclusion debate returned to the boil in 2006 when English universities started charging tuition fees. When such fees were first mooted, the Scottish higher education sector rejected the idea outright. David Caldwell, then Director of Universities Scotland, wrote in *The Scotsman* (20 November 2002):

> Wider participation will suffer unless students from poorer families continue to be exempted from payment for tuition. If they are not, the consequence will be that they are largely excluded from the universities charging the highest fees, creating a system that is more and not less socially divided.

This was the long arm of Davie's *Democratic Intellect* argument in contemporary guise: universities, as the cradle of citizenship, should be free to enter (if only theoretically). But the price exacted in the modern world is domination by the state and the loss of academic freedom – thus Caldwell was forced to end his article with the standard denunciation of Holyrood for underfunding the universities. There was also the suspicion that lurking in Caldwell's arguments was the fact that Scottish universities are loath to enter competition with each other. The significant thing about the early top-up debate was the fact that it produced little new thinking on the part of opponents in Scotland, barring asking for more taxpayers' cash.

Yet some were beginning to think the unthinkable. In late 2006, Professor Bernard King, Principal of the University of Abertay, suggested that Scotland's 'richer universities' should finance themselves from fees that would be used to cross-subsidise scholarships for poorer students. Sir Brian Lang, of St Andrews University, described the Scottish funding system as 'unsustainable' and urged a national debate on tuition fees. This debate was brought to a halt by the decision in 2007 of the SNP government to abolish the graduate endowment scheme, a £2,300 levy on graduates kept by the Scottish Government to fund bursaries for poorer students. Henceforth Scottish higher education would return to what Michael Russell called the 'traditional values' of free university tuition. Then the recession hit. The question became how to pay for free mass university education in an era of austerity. One alternative has not returned to the debate: fees. The re-election of an SNP administration at Holyrood, this time with an absolute majority, confirmed the popularity of the 'no fees' policy. Indeed, the Scottish Labour Party, which had introduced the graduate endowment, reversed its opposition to free tuition at the 2011 Holyrood election. Iain Gray, then the Scottish Labour leader, promised: 'A Labour government will not introduce any up-front fees or graduate contribution for access to higher education in the lifetime of the next Parliament. There will be no price tag on education.'

However, when rejecting the model of student tuition fees followed in the rest of the UK, the SNP government failed to grasp the anomalies that would result. An EU member (or devolved region) cannot charge students from other EU states more than local students. That led to the hardly fair situation where a student from England attending a Scottish university pays full fees but one from the EU does not. In another anomaly, students from Northern Ireland are eligible for dual Irish citizenship, meaning they can escape tuition fees at a Scottish university. The Scottish Government was forced to close this loophole by demanding that anyone seeking the fee exemption would have to show they had spent time in the other country for which they claim citizenship. But the biggest problem with Scotland's free university education remained: its cost. Plus the fact that English universities could now charge £9,000 per student per year while Scottish universities could not, giving institutions south of the border an implicit competitive advantage. Of course, as English tuition fees rise, Westminster will reduce – if not abolish – central government funding of higher education. So ultimately tuition fees in England cannot be regarded as additional funding. But the fees do give English institutions control over their own income, and that flexibility could prove decisive now higher education has become a globally competitive industry.

In the short run, the SNP government has endeavoured to maintain funding to Scotland's universities. But if the Treasury in London continues to hold the purse strings, Holyrood can only ensure that transfer of resources by cutting back elsewhere. That is precisely what has happened. At the end of 2011, John Swinney, the Finance Secretary, announced that the SFC's higher education budget would rise from £926 million in 2011–12 to £1,062 million in 2014–15, despite cash from Westminster shrinking by £3.3 billion (11 per cent) over the period. This was to be achieved by cutting the SFC's budget for further education colleges from £545 million in 2011–12 to only £471 million in 2014–15, by dint of merging college facilities and rationalising course provision. While college rationalising can be justified on grounds of over-provision, it is not a trick that can be performed twice. At some point in the coming decade, Holyrood will have to find more money for higher education, or the fees debate will make an unwelcome return, even if Scotland becomes independent.

It is possible to continue to fund Scottish universities by changing national budget priorities. But this will test the willingness of the electorate to back the universities as they did in an earlier era. Of the ten UK universities in greatest debt in 2011, three were Scottish: the University of Aberdeen (£7.6 million), Queen Margaret University (£159,000) and the Glasgow School of Art (£26,000). Queen Margaret had the highest borrowing levels of any UK university at 200 per cent of income. If the residue of the Davie myth remains popular, public funding might be forthcoming. After all, the Scottish Government can point to the success of its 'no fees' policy: in 2012, data from the Universities and Colleges Admissions Service showed that Scotland was the only part of the UK to see a rise in university admissions. But the jury is still out. It might be that the generation that has experienced the patchy record of mass vocationalism may be less willing to double university investment. In which case, the question of how to fund our universities will come back to haunt us.

CONCLUSIONS: THE 'SCOTTISHNESS' OF SCOTTISH UNIVERSITIES

George Davie saw the universities as a bulwark of Scottish culture under attack by anglicisation. In the late 1970s, only one Scottish institution opposed the principle of devolution
– the combined Scottish universities. So was Davie right?

Here was Davie's Democratic Intellect paradox writ large. The bastion of the Scottish
professions – lawyers, accountants, teachers, clerics – was opposing the very Scottish
Parliament designed to protect their separate Scottish fiefdoms. Indeed, the universities
actually succeeded in their campaign to be excluded from the remit of the ill-fated 1979
Assembly project. Why did the universities turn traitor, as some were wont to put it? More
to the point, why did they change their minds?

Some in the nationalist camp explained the paradox with disparaging references to the
influx of non-Scottish staff and students after the great university expansion of the 1960s.
On the Labour devolutionary left, the explanation was the supposed class elitism of the
universities. Neither argument held much water. In numerical terms, Scottish universities
were still dominated by Scots students and academics. And incoming academics showed
a pronounced tendency to go native, particularly in the social sciences. Professor Chris
Smout, at Edinburgh University, produced a seminal work, *A History of the Scottish People*
(1969), that signalled the renaissance of modern Scottish historiography and therefore of
views on national identity. The American Henry Drucker was the mentor of Gordon Brown
and a fierce polemicist for devolution.

The true explanation for the anti-devolution stance was money. The shift towards state
funding had begun in 1918 with the creation of the all-UK University Grants Committee.
In the era of expansion in the 1960s and 1970s, the Scottish universities opposed a separate
Scots funding body because they were concerned they would receive fewer resources than
their English counterparts. But come Mrs Thatcher, the entire Scottish establishment,
including the universities, decided that devolution was a better way of protecting local
interests than integration with UK bodies. Paradoxically, it would be the Conservative
government of John Major that finally devolved Scottish higher education (in 1992) with
the transformation of the Scottish polytechnics into universities and their merger with
the existing universities under the new Scottish Higher Education Funding Council
(SHEFC).

Aside from the narrow, mechanistic debates over social inclusion and job creation,
what evidence is there that the universities are playing a radical intellectual role in the new
Scotland as they did during the Enlightenment period? Again, the jury is still out. While the
Scottish universities have maintained a global presence in high technology research, their
international impact in the arts and social sciences has diminished. George Davie would
explain this as a reflection (and proof) of the abandonment of a uniquely Scottish approach
to education based on giving as wide as possible a part of the population a generalist understanding of learning.

For example, the technical revolution in economics of the past thirty years failed to
gain much of a local academic foothold, condemning the home of economic science to a
theoretical backwater. The Scottish history departments are influential at home – historians
such as Edinburgh University's Tom Devine have become almost household names – but
stand accused of a cosy parochialism that justifies a corporatist, self-satisfied view of the
nation, despite its low economic growth. The more radical voices – such as Tom Nairn on
the left and Michael Fry on the right – have never enjoyed a Scottish university chair. The

prominent political scientists, such as John Curtice at Strathclyde, are important for their technical work rather than in political philosophy.

Why this intellectual lacuna, particularly in the social sciences? Partly it is lack of funds to keep the best minds here in Scotland; partly it is a lack of critical academic mass; but some have speculated that the transformation of Scotland's universities into degree factories and industrial research engines has narrowed their ability to be critical of the culture and state that funds them. The issue here is not dumbing down but a loss of intellectual focus caused by instrumentalism. George Davie would take this as a vindication of his argument. The dilemma was summed up by Professor Duncan Rice of Aberdeen University, in a paper for the Policy Institute in 2005: 'Undervaluing non-vocational research and teaching will jeopardise our national intellectual and cultural life, and even our success as a humanely functioning democracy.'

George Davie's concept of the Democratic Intellect was a mythologising of the Scottish dream that an education was an infallible passport to the good life. But the Faustian bargain of mass university expansion has been a dependency on state financing and state educational targets. Post-devolution, the Scottish universities are being forced to rethink that bargain. Their ultimate choices will reshape not just themselves but the Scottish nation.

83

The Open University in Scotland

Pete Cannell and James Miller

The Open University (OU) is unique. It is the largest university in Europe, with more than a quarter of a million students, and the only one that has bases and functions within the four home nations of the United Kingdom. Established in 1969, it was regarded by Harold Wilson as one of his finest achievements. Scotland played a significant role on its route to implementation. It was Jennie Lee MP (Fife) who is largely credited with bringing the whole project to fruition. At the time Lee (who had been married to Nye Bevan and later became Baroness Lee) was the Joint Parliamentary Under-Secretary of State at the Department of Education and Science, and chair of the advisory committee which was asked by the Wilson government at the time to 'consider the educational functions and content of a University of the Air'. The formal announcement outlining the development of such an educational institution was made in a speech by Harold Wilson in Glasgow in 1963.

THE OPEN UNIVERSITY IN SCOTLAND

Within the UK the OU has bases within Scotland, Wales and Ireland with its headquarters situated in Milton Keynes, which in turn is supported by ten regional centres across England. The Open University in Scotland (OUiS) is one of the nineteen higher education institutions in Scotland and receives its public funding from the Scottish Funding Council (SFC). Following much debate, full time higher education (HE) remains free for students resident in Scotland. However, students studying at less than full-time intensity are responsible for their own university fees. This is a key differentiator between part- and full-time HE. Nevertheless, one in four undergraduate students study at less than full-time intensity and, of those, one in four study with the OUiS.

The OUiS contributes fully to the academic, civic and economic development of Scotland. The university is a full member of the body that represents HE in Scotland, Universities Scotland. In an economic evaluation of the impact of the OUiS it was concluded that for every £1 of recurring public funding received the university returned in excess of £5 to Scotland's economy (Biggar Economics, 2011).

QUALITY AND STANDARDS

From its inception, the OU has maintained a commitment to open access. Allowing individuals to enrol on university degrees without prior entry qualifications was highly controversial in the early days of the university and remains very unusual in the UK. However, despite the initial doubts that it would be a 'real' university, the quality of the OU curriculum and its graduates is now unquestioned. Its methods and materials have been adapted and adopted by many other institutions and it has come top for student experience in Scotland for each of the six years that it has been part of the National Student Survey. Open Universities have been established in more than fifty countries around the world.

Across the UK, the OU has managed its functions as a single entity, ensuring that the same standards, material and approach are available to students no matter where they are resident. However, as devolution has matured from its origins in the late twentieth and early twenty-first centuries, different education policies have developed, which means that different student support measures have had to be introduced to reflect the different approaches adopted by different governments in England, Scotland, Wales and Ireland. The academic standards remain absolute and are assured by the Quality Assurance Agency (QAA) for higher education.

SCOTLAND AND CURRICULUM

The population of Scotland is less than 10 per cent of the UK total but it is spread across a geographical area that is in excess of one-third of the UK's land mass. This presents particular challenges as well as many opportunities for the OU. The OUiS is the largest provider of part-time HE in Scotland, with 16,138 students enrolled in the academic year 2009–10. In the same year, 2,303 students in Scotland were awarded qualifications. Without the constraints of a campus, students can be found in every postcode district across the mainland and the islands, with the highest participation density on Shetland.

The university employs 500–600 Associate Lecturers (ALs) with the same geographical spread to support students through their study programmes. The number of ALs is flexed according to the number of students and their work is supported by academics based at the national centre in Edinburgh. Other administrative staff at the Edinburgh office ensure that a full range of support services are available to students. Academic members of staff are in turn part of a deanery covering seven individual faculties. The faculties are Arts; Business and Law; Education and Languages; Health and Social Care; Maths, Computing and Technology; Science; and Social Science. The curriculum is also delivered through this deanery. Across the four home nations courses are also developed which are specific to individual nations; for example, Law in Contemporary Scotland, Sustainable Scotland and Gaelic in Modern Scotland, which was developed specifically as an OpenLearn module. Although developed with Scotland-based students in mind, these are available and undertaken by students in other parts of the UK and beyond.

LEARNING AND TEACHING

Innovation in learning and teaching through 'supported open learning' has been critical to the success of the OU. At the heart of this system has been a rigorous system of module and curriculum design that is cost-effective because it is delivered at large scale, a Fordist approach to curriculum development and delivery. The design and development of the modules that comprise the curriculum starts with a course team. Such teams may involve full-time academics, educational technologists, part-time tutors and outside experts. Until recently this system meant that there was a sharp distinction between course production and course presentation. Course production was centralised and ceased once presentation began; course presentation had local delivery facilitated by ALs but was monitored and assessed through university-wide systems. New technology affords a different, more dynamic and long-term relationship between materials production and module presentation and as a result boundaries between production and presentation are being eroded and reshaped.

Almost all OU students are online for at least some part of their experience. Radio and late-night TV are things of the past and the multimedia mix of materials that supports their study is in continual evolution. Audioconferences are nowadays usually based on web telephony. Other synchronous communication methods, including desktop videoconferencing and the use of online virtual classrooms, are increasingly important. However, synchronous communication can never be the only solution for students who are mainly in work and studying in the context of busy lives. The OU's virtual learning environment, based on a Moodle platform, is accessed by more than 60,000 students every day and supports a variety of asynchronous collaborative learning tools. All students have access to Moodle forums. Students access all their study resources and support through a common and personalised portal known as StudentHome. The most recent development, and one that is exhibiting the fastest growth, is the use of mobile technologies; there were 26,910 unique visits to the StudentHome site through this medium in September 2011.

OPEN EDUCATIONAL RESOURCES

In 2006, with a grant from the William and Flora Hewett Foundation, the university established OpenLearn. The OpenLearn site is a portal for free educational resources across a wide variety of subject areas, ranging from access to postgraduate levels. These materials are available under a Creative Common Licence, allowing the material to be downloaded and used as long as the university is acknowledged and the usage is not for commercial gain. The site also includes social networking tools to encourage informal collaborative learning. In November 2011, there were around 11,000 hours of learning materials available on the website, including 6,697 hours taken from undergraduate and postgraduate modules. The site has had over 17.7 million visits since its launch in 2006 and now averages 285,000 unique visitors a month. In addition, the university was the first UK institution to join iTunes University (iTunes U). In 2011, the OU reached the milestone of 40 million downloads from iTunes U, making it the global leader in freely available online resources.

Collaboration with the BBC has been a key element of the university's identity. In the early days, OU material linked to courses of study and broadcast via both radio and television defined many people's image of the OU. More recently, however, this collaboration has been in relation to providing highly accessible programmes on a wide variety of subjects. These have become BAFTA-winning programmes with significant audiences. In 2009–10, there were 300 million viewers and listeners to OU/BBC co-productions. Collaborative outputs have included *Bang Goes the Theory*, *The Frozen Planet*, *History of Scotland*, *Child of Our Time* and *The Symphony*.

REDEFINING THE LEARNER JOURNEY

The OU's open admissions policy and its distinctive pedagogical approach have opened up study possibilities to many who would not have otherwise been able to participate.

However, as *Learning For All?* (SFC, 2005) pointed out, economic inequality and social deprivation continue to be important obstacles to access. Informed by the wider debate in Scotland and by experience from practice the OU has been proactive in the last decade in developing access partnerships and sustainable approaches to providing pathways into HE for 'non-traditional' learners. There is now a wide and diverse range of partnerships with community-based organisations, which made use of the university's suite of short access courses (*Openings*).

Another significant area of partnership aimed at widening access is the OU's work with Scotland's Colleges. As we write, the OU has twenty-three formal partnerships with colleges. As these partnerships mature they are beginning to develop a view of the combined college and OU curriculum that doesn't simply imply a linear 'progression' from college to university but instead shows a more nuanced view of a combined curriculum that affords more student-centred approaches. So, for example, some students may begin their HE experience with an OU Access course, study for a Higher National at college and then come back to study for a degree; or students may combine college study and OU study together to meet their personal goals.

A recent innovation is the development of the Young Applicant in School Scheme (YASS). Introduced in Scotland in 2008 following a pilot project with Highland Council in the previous year, the programme has in excess of seventy schools and 500 students. The scheme helps schools provide a broader and more diverse curriculum for pupils in sixth year. This is a particular challenge for smaller schools and schools in rural areas but the opportunity to study an OU module as part of the sixth year offering has also proved very popular in urban areas.

WORK-BASED AND WORKPLACE LEARNING

Working directly with employers is an important component of the OU's business, and 79 per cent of the FTSE 100 companies sponsor their employees to study with the OU. As a proportion of OU student numbers, however, the corporate sponsorship route is relatively small. In 2009–10 it stood at 9 per cent of undergraduates with over half of these from the public sector. The OU also has a continuing engagement with individuals in the workplace through their union structures, most notably in recent years with Unison. However, a new and dynamic area of partnership was initiated in Scotland in 2007 when the university made an important strategic partnership with the Scottish Trades Union Congress (STUC). The memorandum of understanding highlighted a mutual commitment to widening access and lifelong learning. Since 2007, joint work with the STUC's learning arm, Scottish Union Learning, has developed innovative approaches to bringing employees in to HE in collective ways. Some of these examples are very strongly vocational; for example, shopfloor workers in large engineering workplaces are studying on pathways to BEng qualifications. In other cases the subject of study is less immediately vocationally relevant but there are real and positive outcomes in confidence, 'soft' skills and propensity to take up further study opportunities. At the heart of some astonishingly successful student journeys supported through these partnerships lie two approaches that have been understood by the university for a long time but are not always possible to fully achieve: respect and recognition for lived experience and opportunity to reflect on that experience; and peer support. In the summer of 2011, the OU in Scotland began a three-year SFC funded programme aimed at generalising and building on the insights and experience gained through the STUC partnership with a view to contributing to a better understanding and more effective use of the synergies between HE and workplace training.

UNDERGRADUATE PROVISION

With the notable exception of the four-year honours degree in Social Work, OU under-graduate degrees are structured on a three-year honours framework. However, all modules are credit rated against the Scottish Credit and Qualifications Framework (SCQF), and alignment with the SCQF is built into the qualification design principles that course and programme teams must adhere to.

The Bachelor degree (ordinary and honours) is very similar to that which can be found in any traditional, campus-based university. A unique feature of the OU, however, is the Open Degree, BA/BSc (Open). The Open Programme gives students the freedom to choose the courses that make up a 'personalised' undergraduate qualification. Students are able to tailor their own qualification to meet their own individual requirements and can choose from over 300 modules. Most undergraduate degree pathways allow exit points at Certificate of Higher Education and Diploma of Higher Education (DipHE). A distinctive set of more than twenty work-based learning qualifications are presented as DipHEs in Scotland and Foundation Degrees in England.

POST-GRADUATE PROVISION

Again in a similar way to more traditional universities, the OU offers a postgraduate pro-gramme from certificate to diploma and up to higher degrees. Perhaps one of the most suc-cessful is the Masters in Business Administration (MBA) offered by the Faculty of Business and Law. It is an internationally renowned programme with more than 22,000 graduates active in eighty-eight countries. The programme is one of only two in Scotland that has achieved the much sought after triple accreditation for Business Schools.

RESEARCH

Research is a key feature of the university and central to the achievement of its mission. In the 2008 Research Assessment Exercise (RAE), the university climbed twenty-three places to forty-third, securing a place in the UK's top 50 higher education institutions. The results show that over 50 per cent of the university's research is 'internationally excellent' (3*) and 14 per cent is 'world-leading' (4*), as determined by the 2008 RAE's expert and peer review process. Its breadth matches the quality of research, with units submitted from all seven faculties. The research higher degrees are also provided across all faculties, including MPhil and PhD as well as more discipline-specific higher degrees (for example, Doctor of Education, DEd).

FUTURE DEVELOPMENTS

The use of technology to drive education and improve the student experience is where the university had its origins, and now its future in a new millennium is inextricably linked with technological advances. Supporting learning and teaching is so much more than simply turning documents into PDFs. Technology allows students to access e-books which have embedded video explanations, animations that demonstrate the unfolding and folding of DNA strands to improve understanding of the double helix, virtual microscopes to aid scientific advances, recreated historical scenes and 3D digital simulation to describe complex engine systems, all of which can be accessed by the student remotely at a time which is suitable to them. This will be a key demand of the twenty-first-century student. However, technology also affords opportunities for the development of social networks and human interaction. These have always been part of the OU experience and the Open University in Scotland will remain in the forefront of future development and provision.

REFERENCES

Biggar Economics (2011) *Economic Case for Part-Time Higher Education in Scotland: A Report to the OU in Scotland.* Roslin: Biggar Economics.
Scottish Funding Council (2005) *Learning for All?* Edinburgh: SFC.

84

From Adult Learning to Lifelong Learning in Scotland

Rob Mark

Until quite recently government policy and funding in the field of education has been focused almost exclusively on children and younger people. Much less funding has been available to support learning beyond the post-compulsory stage and adult learners have had to support their own learning or seek out support from employers or specially funded programmes. For this reason, those benefiting from adult learning have tended to be the better off and adult learning has consequently remained an activity for only certain sections of the population.

The Scottish Government has recognised the importance of widening participation in adult and lifelong learning, particularly in terms of its potential contribution to developing the economy and in assisting Scotland to compete in an increasingly competitive global market. It has also recognised the importance of adult education in contributing to personal development, as well as to improved health and wellbeing. The Scottish Government, in common with governments elsewhere in Europe, is committed to promoting high and inclusive levels of participation in adult learning.

As we deal with recession and its legacy, it is essential that the adult population have the necessary education and skills to contribute to economic recovery and that our education system be reformed to reflect the changing demographics which are likely to pose many challenges for Scotland in the future. An ageing population and a recent decline in participation in lifelong learning in Scotland (dropping from 38 per cent of the adult population in 1996 to 33 per cent in 2009) provides the Scottish Government with real challenges in a new era of economic austerity.

In this chapter, I briefly look at the development of adult and lifelong learning in Scotland. As in the rest of the UK, what adult learning might or might not be is at best vague and confusing and has been generally superseded by the term 'lifelong learning' when referring to the education of adults. To aid the reader in understanding this evolving field of practice, I will therefore examine the terminology in more detail and the implications for practice.

WHAT IS ADULT LEARNING?

Attempts to define adult learning have led to a plethora of definitions and varied understandings of what adult learning is about. The aims and goals of adult learning have also varied over time, as have the meanings of the words 'adult' and 'learning', which are highly contested terms in the academic literature. The term 'adult' itself can have numerous meanings, which can influence our understanding of adult learning. It can refer to a biological state (post-puberty), a legal state (such as the voting age of 18) or indeed a psychological state (where the individual's 'self-concept' is that of an 'adult'). Other interpretations have linked the meaning of adult with a type of behaviour (i.e. adulthood as being in touch with one's capacities whatever the context) or with social roles linked to adulthood (adulthood as the performance of certain roles such as working, raising children, etc.).

Adult educators have defined learning in many different ways. Some writers define it in terms of objectives or outcomes. Others, such as Kolb, argue that learning is best conceived as a continuous process grounded in experience, not in terms of outcomes: 'Learning is the process whereby knowledge is created through the transformation of experience.' (Kolb, 1984, p. 38). This approach has strongly influenced adult learning where experience and critical reflection are emphasised as an important part of the learning process.

Adult learning can also be said to be closely linked to those activities that we engage in during the post-compulsory education period of our lives. However, this interpretation is also fraught with difficulty and there is a confusing array of terminology that includes further, higher and community learning, all laying claim to particular aspects of learning in our adult lives.

EARLY DEVELOPMENT OF ADULT LEARNING IN SCOTLAND

According to Cooke (2006), adult education in the UK is generally thought to have developed from the earlier part of the twentieth century onwards. One of the early references was the Adult Education Committee of the British Ministry of Reconstruction, which concluded in 1919 that:

> adult education must not be regarded as a luxury for a few exceptional persons here and there, nor as a thing which concerns only a short span of early manhood, but that adult education is a permanent national necessity, an inseparable aspect of citizenship, and therefore should be both universal and lifelong.

Cooke (2006, p. 2) notes that many educational historians believe that until comparatively recently there has been relatively little adult education in Scotland. In support of this, he notes the 1919 Report of the Ministry of Reconstruction on adult education which contained a confident assertion by a Scottish educationalist that 'it would be wise to assume that non-vocational adult education of an organised nature is at present non-existent in Scotland'. Jacobsen (1992, p. 278), however, points out that the development of adult education in Scotland was more closely linked to a movement for popular enlightenment similar to that in the Scandinavian countries and Germany, rather than in England and Wales, and similarly the Committee of Inquiry on Adult Education, which reported in 1975, concluded that 'the inescapable fact is that Scotland was very much slower than England to develop adult education in an organised way' (SED, 1975, p. 3). This is demonstrated in the strength of independent working-class education in the west of Scotland and the Fife coalfields with their more radical vision of society and consequent distrust of collaboration between working-class organisations such as the Workers' Educational Association and other educational establishments (Cooke, 2006, pp. 267–77).

Cooke says that adult education developed to fulfil a variety of functions including remedial education, improving the skills of the workforce and education for citizenship. He also notes that that the classic form of adult education provision was evening classes, but there were many others, including day schools, summer school, mutual improvement societies and self-education, often linked to library provision. The courses and programmes that developed were part-time and fitted in on top of working life (Cooke, 2006, pp. 1–3).

THE ALEXANDER REPORT AND ADULT EDUCATION IN SCOTLAND

A landmark in the development of adult education is Scotland was the publication of the Alexander Report in 1975. The report of the Committee of Inquiry into Adult Education, otherwise known as the Alexander Report (1975), was given a remit to examine 'voluntary leisure time courses for adults that are educational, but not specifically vocational' (SED, 1975, p. vi). Thus adult education was clearly defined as 'non-vocational' education and adult learning was firmly placed in a particular social, cultural and economic context.

In many ways, the Alexander Report was remarkably far-sighted, arguing that education should no longer be concerned solely or primarily with the training of the intellect and that there should be a changed emphasis from teaching to learning. It forecast the massive expansion of higher education in Scotland and welcomed the growing trend for initial education to concentrate on key skills (SED, 1975, p. 24).

The report also viewed education as a lifelong process and learning as a basic characteristic of life. It identified four main aims for adult education: the reaffirmation of individuality; the effective use of the resources of society; fostering the pluralist society; and education for change. The report singled out groups that were particularly likely to be affected by this sense of isolation and alienation. They included the family, the elderly, the disadvantaged and the handicapped. It recommended that 'adult education should be regarded as an aspect of community education and should, with the youth and community service, be incorporated into a community education service' (HMSO, 1975, p. 35). The report recommended that adult education should participate increasingly in community development and that much more experimentation would be needed. As a result a numerically weak and underdeveloped adult education service was incorporated into a much better staffed and resourced youth and community service with very different ideological roots and cultural policies.

The Alexander Report signalled a significant change in how adult learning should be organised in Scotland. Prior to Alexander, adult learning had been the outcome of a largely voluntary movement, which had a focus on freedom and liberation that was both personal (in the sense of widening horizons) and social. There had been comparatively little of the 'learning for leisure' approach and a great deal of emphasis on striving and struggle by people who indeed had very little leisure time. It might also be argued that adult education had been reached out to by a minority of people and was characterised as an elite movement. The report noted the potential growth of leisure, which opened up exciting possibilities for expanding both the quality and the quantity of adult education (SED, 1975, p. 23).

Following the Alexander Report, most authorities in Scotland restructured their youth and community, and adult education services into community education services. Since then, there have been numerous debates as to what community education is and how it should be organised.

FORMAL, NON-FORMAL AND INFORMAL LEARNING

The Alexander Report, with its recognition that adult learning can take many different forms, also encouraged the development of new ways of thinking about education. Adult learning could be something that takes place not only in an institution but also in the community or through individuals engaging in their own learning outside of the formal system of education. It introduced a debate about contexts of learning, which were said to be formal, non-formal or informal.

Tight (1996, pp. 68–9) says that formal, non-formal and informal learning terminology developed quickly in the 1960s and 1970s. Formal learning, he notes, is generally thought of as what goes on within education and training systems, beginning in school, moving through to university and usually leading towards certification. In addition to general academic studies, it may include learning taking place in other institutions that focus on technical and professional training. It generally has top-down curriculum formation where the learning is prescribed and handed down to learners. Non-formal learning, he says, refers to organised educational activity outside the established formal system. It is not provided by an educational or training institution and takes place within organisations that do not need to mimic the more restrictive frameworks and accreditation systems of the formal sector. It is, however, structured to serve identifiable learning clienteles and learning objectives, although it generally does not lead to a qualification. An enduring theme of non-formal learning has been that education should be in the interests of the learners and that organisation and curriculum planning should preferably be undertaken by the learners themselves, i.e. that it should be a 'bottom-up' or negotiated curriculum. It is also often argued that it should empower learners to understand and if necessary change the social structure around them. In Scotland, it has had clear links with the practices of educators such as Paulo Freire whose ideas have influenced the development of community education and literacy learning. One example of this is the Gorgie-Dalry Adult Learning Project in Edinburgh (Kirkwood and Kirkwood, 2011) which used the radical ideas and approaches of Freire on reflection and action as a tool for change in adult learning.

Another way of engagement in learning is informal learning, which may be said to cover all forms of learning not included in formal and non-formal learning. Tight (1996, p. 69) notes that it refers to 'the lifelong process by which every individual acquires and accumulates knowledge, skills, and attitudes and insights from daily experiences and exposure to the environment – at home, at work, at play'. He states that informal education is unorganised, unsystematic and even unintentional at times, yet it accounts for the great bulk of any person's total lifetime learning, including that of even a highly 'schooled' person. It is not based on any curriculum and could be described as conversational in form. In Scotland as elsewhere informal learning occurs in the everyday lives of its citizens whether at home watching TV or through an array of educational, social and recreational activities that individuals engage in.

In summary, formal education has been linked with schools and training institutions, non-formal with community groups and other organisations, and informal with learning from other experiences such as interaction with friends, family and work colleagues. The distinguishing lines between one form of learning and another are nevertheless blurred and sometimes all three forms of learning can exist in the one place.

TOWARDS AN UNDERSTANDING OF ADULT LEARNING AS LIFELONG LEARNING

By the 1970s, lifelong learning was increasingly being cited internationally as a key issue for development, but there was no shared understanding of its usage at global level. The Faure Report, *Learning to Be* (1972), sought to institutionalise the concept of lifelong education by advocating the right and necessity of each individual to learn for his or her social, economic, political and cultural development. While acknowledging the existence of lifelong education practices in diverse cultures all over the world, the report emphasised that lifelong education should be enshrined as a basic concept in educational policies. It argued for lifelong education to be the 'master concept' for educational policies.

The concept of lifelong learning requires us to shift our thinking on learning away from one that focuses on learning as something that happens largely in schools towards one that goes on throughout life and includes learning both in formal educational institutions and in informal situations from the world around us. What seems clear from the literature is that in the process, little attention was paid to distinguishing 'education' and 'learning', which were often used interchangeably. Field (2000, p. 35) has argued that there has been a fundamental shift in the behaviour of adults who increasingly regard the day-to-day practice of adult learning as routine. Field suggested that many adults take part in organised learning throughout their lifespan and that 'non-formal' learning permeates daily life and is valued (2000, pp. 38–49). He notes that typical of the last of these has been a substantial increase in activities such as short residential courses, study tours, fitness centres, sports clubs, heritage centres, self-help therapy manuals, management gurus, electronic networks and self-instructional videos (2000, p. 45). The new adult learning is part of a much broader process. As individuals come to rely less on traditional institutions and the authority figures associated with them – church leaders, parents, aristocracy – to guide their behaviour, so they become more self-directed. At least in principle, they can select from a variety of possible role-models; traditional role models certainly do not disappear (indeed, they are an important if little-understood resource for fundamentalist movements), but to select any role model requires that individuals face up to an increasing range of biographical options (Field, 2000, p. 57).

FROM ADULT LEARNING TO COMMUNITY LEARNING AND SOCIAL INCLUSION

In Scotland, there has been a growing replacement of the notion of community education with that of community learning. The Scottish Executive (1999) report *Communities: Change Through Learning* set out a new vision for Scotland as a dynamic learning society and one where all of its citizens, particularly those who are socially excluded, should develop their potential to the full and engage in active and informed citizenship. Community education was seen as a key contributor to lifelong learning, playing a significant part in combating social exclusion. Adult learning in the community was seen as a way of helping people make a real contribution to their own communities and to participating in the local and national democratic processes. It was also seen as a way of developing skills applicable to any aspect of life and building the confidence and capacity to tackle wider social and economic issues, such as health and community engagement. It was envisaged that through community engagement, individuals could develop literacy or basic life skills to overcome social exclusion, and through community engagement some adults might progress into further and higher education or into employment.

While this presented a new challenge for community educators in promoting community learning, the report has been criticised for not paying enough attention to the conceptualisation of community learning and the extent to which the service should be promoting learning in the community for personal development and community learning where people engage with each other to bring about changes that enhance local life.

FACTORS INFLUENCING PARTICIPATION IN ADULT LEARNING

In 1997, the former Department for Education and Employment (DfEE) commissioned the first National Adult Learning Survey (NALS, 1997), which provided information on participation in 'lifelong' or 'adult' learning and in 2005, the Scottish Executive commissioned a follow-up survey with the aim of providing robust data representative of the Scottish adult population as a whole which could inform policy on adult learning in Scotland.

The study found that overall, participation in adult learning in Scotland was high, with 82 per cent of adults aged under 70 engaging in some form of adult learning. Although these figures are encouraging, there is still a substantial minority (18 per cent) not involved in any of the wide range of learning activities covered by NALS. Learning was also found to be strongly related to work, with participation in vocational learning significantly higher (74 per cent) than participation in non-vocational learning (28 per cent). Participation was also found to decline with age. While 93 per cent of those aged 16 to 39 were recent learners, this reduced to 83 per cent in the 40–59 age group and to 40 per cent among those over 60 years old. Men (87 per cent) were found to be more likely than women (78 per cent) to be involved in any type of learning. The number of years spent in full-time education, qualification levels and the level of parental education were all strongly associated with participation in adult learning.

The most commonly mentioned barrier to learning was lack of time because of work (45 per cent), followed by family-related time constraints (32 per cent) and preferring to spend time doing other things (32 per cent). However, in spite of citing wide-ranging barriers to participation in learning the vast majority of both learners (96 per cent) and non-learners (93 per cent) believed that learning is important to success at work (97 per cent) and that it is something people should participate in throughout their lives (89 per cent). In terms of incentives and measures to overcome barriers to learning, two-thirds of those for whom lack of time was a barrier said that they would consider learning from home via the internet. That said, learners tended to be more open than non-learners to learning in new ways, including via the internet (76 per cent of learners agreed that they liked this idea, compared with 50 per cent of non-learners).

THE DEVELOPING LIFELONG LEARNING POLICY CONTEXT IN SCOTLAND

Education has a long tradition of being socially valued in Scotland and has been high on the political agenda, falling within the remit of the Scottish Parliament. The Scottish Executive's understanding of lifelong learning has emphasised continuous development of skills, knowledge and understanding essential for employability and personal fulfilment. While economic competitiveness has been a major driving force in recent lifelong learning developments, social inclusion issues such as widening access for under-represented social groups has also been given a strong emphasis.

A number of Scottish Government documents relating to lifelong learning have been developed in recent years. The Green Paper 'Opportunity Scotland' (1998) was Scotland's first policy document on lifelong learning and emphasised the need for people at all levels to have access to work-based learning opportunities and to maintain Scotland's competitiveness in the global economy. In 2001–2, the Scottish Parliament Enterprise and Lifelong Learning Committee undertook an inquiry into lifelong learning in Scotland. Its final report was published in October 2002 and led to the Scottish Executive publishing its lifelong learning strategy for Scotland, *Life through Learning: Learning through Life* (2003). The strategy emphasised the importance of nurturing confident, knowledgeable and skilled people who can participate in economic, social and civic life.

In 2006, the Scottish Executive undertook a consultation *Lifelong Learning –Building on Success: A Discussion of Specific Issues related to Lifelong Learning in Scotland* which focused on the themes of engagement with employers; flexible learning opportunities; entitlement and discretionary support; information, advice and guidance; community learning and development; and journeys into and through learning.

In 2007, the earlier lifelong learning strategy was replaced by a new skills strategy. *Skills for Scotland: A Lifelong Skills Strategy* provided a new agenda for skills and learning in Scotland to include early years provision, schools, further and higher education, work-related learning and informal learning. The vision laid out was one of a smarter Scotland with a globally competitive economy based on high-value jobs with progressive and innovative business leadership.

Scottish Government policy has also been strongly committed to ensuring that access to education is based on ability to learn and not ability to pay. Removing barriers to accessing lifelong learning is a key element of this approach. All higher education institutions in Scotland have therefore been focused on having admission processes and support systems that ensure that everyone can take advantage of the opportunities offered by higher education regardless of their background or personal circumstances.

In December 2008, the Scottish Government launched a consultation paper on a fair student support package. Significant increases in funding, specifically towards the further education sector in Scotland, have also taken place. Such changes have coincided with changes in the labour market in Scotland; as manufacturing has declined and the services sector has grown, further education colleges have begun to offer a more diverse range of programmes.

In addition, an Individual Learning Account (Scotland) scheme (ILA Scotland) was launched in two phases in 2004 and 2005. ILAs were intended to widen participation in adult learning; introduce new learners to adult learning; provide an opportunity for those who had not recently participated in learning to do so; encourage individuals to invest in and take ownership of their own learning; and prioritise the learning needs of certain groups of learners (in particular those on low incomes). Premium funding was also paid to higher and further education institutions to encourage them to recruit students from under-represented groups (such as mature students, students from lower social classes, minority ethnic groups and disabled students). Each institution is also compared with a similar institution elsewhere in the UK in relation to the proportion of students from such under-represented groups.

A further issue arising from the expansion of lifelong learning was the need to provide a way to recognise diverse learning across the sector through a common credit framework. The Scottish Credit Qualifications Framework (SCQF) was launched in December 2001 and now provides a flexible training pathway by providing lifelong learning credits that allow for accumulation and transfer with other education and training sectors. The SCQF also recognises 'in-house training' and a range of employers' own learning programmes have been included in the framework, for example in the police and fire services, banking, social care and voluntary sectors. The system also provides a framework for the recognition of informal and non-formal learning.

More recently, in *Putting Learners at the Centre – Delivering our Ambitions for Post-16 Education*, the Scottish Government (2011) laid out its proposals to achieve sustainable economic growth. The document lays emphasis on the difficult economic circumstances of unemployment, particularly youth unemployment, and sets out proposals for wide-ranging reform of the full range of government-funded post-16 education in Scotland.

FUTURE TRENDS IN ADULT AND LIFELONG LEARNING IN SCOTLAND

A close analysis of policy and practice in adult learning shows a clear direction in understanding and engagement with adults to promote learning in Scotland. First, while the rhetoric about the goals of adult learning may be broadly conceived to include personal, social and employment-related motives, there is a clear shift and emphasis towards recognising adult learning as a lifetime activity (lifelong learning) and valuing vocational learning as particularly important. Second, lifelong learning is becoming more and more related to a wider education and skills agenda rather than simply supporting leisure activity or the engagement of hard-to-reach disadvantaged groups. A third discernible change is centred on encouraging participation of individuals in learning and encouraging them to be self-directed and to take responsibility for planning their own learning. This has been further encouraged though the growth of technology which allows adults who cannot for a variety of reasons attend classes to learn at their own pace and in their own choice of place.

In Scotland, lifelong learning policies share overall policy goals for lifelong learning that have been adopted elsewhere in the UK and in Europe. Such policies have focused on the twin aim of developing skills for employment and for social inclusion. Field (2009) argues that the Scottish Government policies for skills have identified employer demand for and utilisation of skills as an important policy area. He also notes that policies for community-based learning, which are part of a distinctive integrated youth work and community work service, sets out a more managerial and audit-led approach that is designed to concentrate attention on outcomes and emphasise the importance of community-based learning in promoting basic literacy and numeracy and English for speakers of other languages.

Another issue in the debate about lifelong learning in Scotland centres on social exclusion and widening participation. Cooke (2006) mentions that the debate about education and social cohesion is not a new one, but dates back to the nineteenth century. He shows how adult education movements in the twentieth century encouraged participation of adults lacking in basic education, though this was at best patchy and confined to specific industrial locations.

Since the Alexander Report in 1976, lifelong learning policy in Scotland has tended to highlight the need for adult and lifelong learning policies to reach out to excluded groups of adults. In a similar way to the European Commission's Memorandum on Lifelong Learning (2001), Scottish lifelong learning policy identifies social cohesion, active citizenship and positive tolerance of diversity as objectives. However, Field (2009) notes that current levels of inequality are incompatible with the current policy goals of the Scottish Government, which emphasise the importance of lifelong learning in contributing not only to economic development but also to achieving 'social justice, stronger communities and more engaged citizens' (Scottish Government, 2007, p. 6). Scottish policy consistently recognises the need to widen participation by providing second chances for adults, particularly in areas of social and economic deprivation.

A further issue facing Scotland is that it is an ageing society and this has implications for meeting the lifelong learning needs of this cohort group. Many people spend more than a third of their adult lives in retirement, and the number of people over 65 is set to accelerate rapidly over the next two decades. In 2007, the Scottish Government published a report, *All Our Futures: Planning for a Scotland with an Ageing Population*. The report deals with issues around the demographic ageing of the population in Scotland and sets out a vision for a future Scotland that values and benefits from the talents and experience of older people. The report identifies improving health and wellbeing, and providing learning opportunities in later life as two key priorities for action. While there have been some notable examples of projects that seek to engage older adults, the recent Scottish Government White Paper (2011) *Putting Learners at the Centre* has failed to take on board this challenge with its focus on meeting the needs of younger adults. Opportunities to engage older adults in employment in partnership with employers, and the potential to develop their skills and knowledge to promote personal, social and civic engagement are being undervalued.

CONCLUSION

In this chapter, I have sought to offer some insights into the growth and development of policy and practice in adult learning in Scotland. The Scottish Government has shown a very strong and proactive commitment to the promotion of lifelong learning. Scotland has pursued a separate stance to developments in education and training when compared with other UK systems, for example, through the range of financial incentives to encourage disadvantaged groups into education. Although Scotland has an adult participation rate in lifelong learning above the EU average, significant work remains to be done in several areas including the unequal participation of certain groups in lifelong learning.

The inquiry into the future for lifelong learning *Learning through Life* (Schuller and Watson, 2009, p. 1) proposed a vision of a society in which 'learning plays its full role in personal growth, and emancipation, prosperity, solidarity and global responsibility'. The right to learn throughout life is a human right and provides a new challenge for policy makers in Scotland.

An examination of adult learning policy and practice in Scotland shows that tensions continue to exist between promoting lifelong learning to meet the needs of the economy and promoting learning for personal development and to encourage community engagement and civic participation. In times of economic austerity the challenge becomes particularly pointed as governments focus on economic recovery. One of the greatest challenges facing the Scottish Government today is how to manage the competing needs of promoting skills for economic recovery and providing new routes into learning that take account of the needs of individuals, communities and society. It remains to be seen whether the Scottish Government can manage these sometimes competing needs for the benefit of all of Scotland's citizens.

REFERENCES

Cooke, A. (2006) *From Popular Enlightenment to Lifelong Learning: A History of Adult Education in Scotland 1707–2005.* Leicester: NIACE.

Field, J. (2000) *Lifelong Learning and the New Educational Order.* Stoke on Trent: Trentham Books.

Field, J. (2009) 'Lifelong learning in Scotland: cohesion, equity and participation', *Scottish Educational Review,* 41 (2): 4–19.

Jacobsen (1992) 'Denmark', in P. Jarvis (ed.), *Perspectives on Adult Education and Training in Europe.* Leicester: NIACE.

Kirkwood, C. and G. Kirkwood (2011) *Living Adult Education: Freire in Scotland.* Boston, MA: Sense Publishers.

Kolb, D. A. (1984) *Experiential Learning: Experience as the Source of Learning and Development.* Upper Saddle River, NJ: Prentice-Hall.

Schuller, T. and D. Watson (2009) *Learning Through Life: Inquiry into the Future for Lifelong Learning.* Leicester: Niace. Scottish Education Department (1975) *Adult Education: The Challenge of Change* (the Alexander Report). Edinburgh: HMSO.

Scottish Executive (1999) *Communities: Change through Learning.* Report of a Working Group on the Future of Community Education. Edinburgh: Scottish Office.

Scottish Government (2003) *Life Through Learning; Learning Through Life: The Lifelong Learning Strategy for Scotland.* Edinburgh: Scottish Office. Online at www.scotland.gov.uk/Publications/2003/02/16308/17752#1

Scottish Government (2007a) *National Adult Learning Survey.* Scottish Centre for Social Research. Edinburgh: Department of Enterprise, Transport and Lifelong Learning. Online at www.scotland.gov.uk/Publications/2007/03/16105856/1

Scottish Government (2007b) *All Our Futures: Planning for a Scotland with an Ageing Population.* Online at www.scotland.gov.uk/Topics/People/Equality/18501/Experience

Scottish Government (2011) *Putting Learners at the Centre – Delivering our Ambitions for Post-16 Education.* Edinburgh: Scottish Office. Online at www.scotland.gov.uk/Publications/2011/09/15103949/0

Tight, M. (1996) *Key Concepts in Adult Education and Training.* London: Routledge.

X

CHALLENGES AND RESPONSES: EDUCATION FOR ALL?

As its title indicates, this section deals with a number of disparate issues which can be seen as representing a challenge for the system. Some of these relate to various bodies and services with which some in education must, or should, liaise, some relate to the position of particular groups whose historical experience in the education system has been neither very positive nor beneficial, and, in the case of community education, one that represents a distinctly different model of educational provision from the statutory sectors. The 'inclusion agenda', central to this section, has embraced a wide variety of different interests over the past decade or so, and part of this has led to a stronger sense of integrated children's services in many council areas. Thus the chapters in this section that deal with psychological services, social work and multi-agency working are probably much less contentious or surprising than they once might have been. However, many perennial challenges for the education system remain unsurprising, some as stubbornly intractable as ever, and so there are also chapters here on disaffection, poverty, gender, sectarianism and race.

Chapter 85 provides a helpful foundation for this section by exploring the meaning and practical implications of 'inclusion', including a recent historical review of related policy developments. Welcome attention to the experiences of children and young people highlights some of the challenges for the future of inclusive practice, including pressure on resources, required professional development and the need for more 'joined-up' policy. Chapter 86 focuses on one of the most high-profile examples of inclusion, namely provision for those learners who require additional support. The chapter outlines the various changes in policy and approach over recent years, which has seen the discourse shift from 'special needs' to the concept of 'additional support needs'. Various associated guidelines and legislative frameworks are explained and a number of difficulties and anomalies identified. One of the biggest challenges is the risk of a 'postcode lottery' where provision varies markedly across the country.

Chapters 87 and 88 explore the respective roles of the psychological and social services in relation to education. Both note the changing landscape of such services where roles as external experts or advisers have shifted more towards roles in collaborative approaches. In the case of psychological services, also stressed is the emergence of more proactive roles such as in the development of nurture groups, literacy initiatives and in a whole range of issues around pastoral and learning support, now very much centred on the *Getting it Right for Every Child* (GIRFEC) agenda. In the case of social work, its key role in supporting the education of some of the most vulnerable and 'challenging' elements of society is duly recognised. The particular case of children in care is given detailed attention as a way of highlighting the central place of social workers, and so inter-professional working, in making a long overdue impact on improved provision. This issue of multi-agency, and interprofessional, working, especially in relation to GIRFEC, is addressed specifically in Chapter 90. Teachers can now expect to be engaged in far more of this at classroom level than was previously the case.

Chapter 89 considers the place of community education, positioned as it is outside the institutionalised forms of education in Scotland. The chapter surveys its evolution, including the recent shift in nomenclature that has also been mirrored in a much stronger emphasis on stipulated outcomes than was typically the case in the past where dialogue, trust and informal pedagogical relationships were central. The chapter shows the degree of pressure that has been experienced within the sector recently, where budgetary and staffing constraints have been matched by numerous changes in the pattern, and level, of provision across local authorities and communities in Scotland.

Chapter 91 considers disaffection with schooling, exploring a number of key factors that affect non-attendance and exclusion. Central to the debate are perspectives, with the various relevant groups and individuals often having quite different understandings of relevant causes and experiences. The chapter stresses the importance of relationships as being at once central to disaffection but, in an improved form, as vital to its being tackled effectively. The focus on pastoral responses in the conclusion reflects this, as well as perhaps indicating an emerging willingness of educational establishments to take responsibility for such disaffection more seriously. Educational responses to the challenge of poverty are much less likely to incite confidence. Chapter 92 presents a welter of evidence about the continuing negative impact of poverty on educational attainment, many decades after its significance was first identified. Given the impotence of educational professionals in tackling the socio-economic roots of the problem, what is left is a range of measures designed, at best, to alleviate some of its worst consequences. That poverty has such an early and damaging impact has led to increased focus on early years provision, as the chapter shows. Continued targeted, educational support is argued as the best professional means of minimising poverty's baleful effects. Chapter 93, while focused on gender, argues that this has also to be seen as interconnected with many other variables, such as poverty and race, in how it is manifested within education. The chapter also explores the place of women generally within the public sphere in Scotland, where statistics show that gender inequality is still a significant issue. The chapter stresses that while attention has been given to gender in respect of educational attainment, its role in many other aspects of its educational experience remains largely unexplored.

Chapter 94 addresses the issue of sectarianism, for many years an unaddressed, but pervasive, aspect of Scottish society. The chapter presents a comprehensive survey of the development and extent of sectarianism and its effects across Scotland. It concludes by acknowledging the number and range of educational responses which have been implemented in recent years, calls for the need now for rigorous evaluation of their effectiveness, while recognising that their reach can only be to limited numbers of youngsters and for the limited years of their schooling. The long history of racism is similarly adduced in Chapter 95 as background to the recent emphasis on 'race equality' in education. A range of related legislative and policy developments is examined as background to a review of the current situation and the consequent implications. The chapter argues that teachers, need a much fuller understanding of the issues involved and greater confidence in dealing with them.

85

Inclusion for All?

Julie Allan

The inclusion of all children in mainstream schools has been adopted as a key educational policy in Scotland. It is, however, a policy that has been experienced as challenging, not least of all because of uncertainty over its meaning, and one that has met with some resistance. This chapter addresses the question of what inclusion is and outlines the legislation and policy in Scotland relating to the children and young people for whom inclusion is intended. The chapter then considers who is included within Scottish education and details some of the barriers to inclusion that arise from current educational policy and legislative frameworks. The views of children and young people about the importance of inclusion – and the negative effects of exclusion – are reported and the chapter concludes with some thoughts on what changes might be necessary if inclusion is to succeed.

WHAT IS INCLUSION?

There is much uncertainty about what it means to include. Inclusion was introduced in the early 1990s to replace integration, which had been brought in with the Warnock Report (Department of Education, 1978) and subsequent legislation. Integration had come to be criticised for being overly concerned with the physical placement of children with special educational needs in mainstream schools and for a lack of regard for the quality of their educational experiences. Inclusion, formalised and to an extent mandated, by the Salamanca Statement and Framework for Action on Special Needs Education and adopted in 1994 by ninety-two countries and twenty-five international organisations, was presented as a two-fold activity of increasing participation and removing barriers to that participation (Barton, 1997). This meant that as well as seeking to involve children in schools, efforts had to be made by those schools to remove barriers. These barriers may be environmental, structural or attitudinal. Environmental barriers arise from features of the physical location or layout of the school which prevent access or make this difficult. Structural barriers are caused by the way an institution functions and in a school this may be, for example, forms of assessment or an emphasis on writing that excludes individuals with particular difficulties. According to disabled people, it is attitudinal barriers that are the most significant and these may include negative behaviour such as bullying or condescending expressions of pity or admiration.

Suspicions have been voiced that what takes place in the name of inclusion is no better than integration and that schools have failed to address the second part of the inclusion formula, that is removing the barriers to participation (Allan, 2008; Slee, 2011). Furthermore, concerns have been expressed about the continued uncertainty regarding what precisely it means to be inclusive and this provoked one of the UK's teaching unions, the National Association of Schoolmasters Union of Women Teachers (NASUWT), to place special educational needs at the top of its agenda for debate:

> Teachers welcome children with special needs into mainstream schools providing that the school can meet their needs and the motivation for the placement is in the best interests of the child rather than a drive by local authorities to save money on specialist provision and support. However, a lack of a clear shared, national definition of what inclusion means and the variation of provision across the country means pupils, parents and indeed teachers face a postcode lottery of support and provision. (NASUWT, 2009)

Questions and concerns about inclusion from teachers have stemmed from confusion about what it is supposed to do and for whom; frustration about being unable to undertake it because of pressures from competing policy demands, especially from drives to raise achievement; guilt about letting down children and parents; and exhaustion, feeling that things cannot continue as they are (Allan, 2008). Even Baroness Warnock, recognised as the 'architect' of inclusion in the UK, has weighed in with what is not so much questions about inclusion as a damning pronouncement on inclusion as 'disastrous' (Warnock, 2005, p. 22). In a pamphlet published by the Philosophy of Education Society of Great Britain, she declared it to have been a mistake to have thought that all children could succeed in mainstream schools and lamented that 'children are the casualties' (ibid., p. 14) of this mistake.

INCLUSION IN SCOTLAND: LEGISLATION AND POLICY

Under the terms of the Education (Additional Support for Learning) (Scotland) Act 2004 (amended 2009), responsibility for special needs lies with the education authority. This legislation introduced the new terminology 'additional support needs', which replaces 'special needs' and is intended to be a much broader concept. The term, however, has added some further confusion with a definition that is somewhat tautological:

> A child or young person has additional support needs for the purposes of this Act where, for whatever reason, the child or young person is, or is likely to be, unable without the provision of additional support to benefit from school education provided or to be provided for the child or young person. (www.legislation.gov.uk/asp/2004/4/section/1)

Additional support needs, then, are the needs of individual children for support over and above, or different from, that which is normally provided within a regular school. The additional support needs legislation ended a system of assessing and recording children with significant special educational needs that was tied to resource allocation for special educational needs. It was considered unfair because of the different patterns of assessment within different education authorities and a sense that there was a 'geographical lottery', with children more likely to be recorded in particular areas of Scotland because of the policy and practices of that authority.

Under the additional support needs legislation, where children's additional support needs are such that they require support that is external to the school (for example, physiotherapy, speech therapy or occupational therapy), education authorities have a legal duty to prepare a Coordinated Support Plan. This statutory document contains details of the child's additional support needs, the individuals required to provide this support and a nomination of the school to be attended by the child. The Coordinated Support Plan is reviewed annually by the education authority. Schools are expected to follow the procedures within staged intervention before seeking to have a Coordinated Support Plan opened for an individual child.

There is a 'presumption of mainstreaming' within the Standards in Scotland's Schools etc. Act 2000, whereby the education authority is expected to make provision for a child with additional support needs to be educated in a regular school unless there are 'exceptional circumstances'. Education authorities must also produce an 'accessibility strategy' indicating how they will increase children's participation in the school's curriculum, improve the physical environment of the school and improve communication with disabled pupils (Education (Disability Strategies and Pupils' Educational Records) (Scotland) Act, 2002).

The 'presumption of mainstreaming' has been embedded in the legislation in Scotland since the Education (Scotland) Act 1980, but has coexisted with the rights of parents to choose a school for their child. These two aspects are not always compatible, that is parents may seek a special, rather than a mainstream, placement. The coexistence of a mainstreaming presumption and parental choice within the legislation has led to a significant expansion of the population of children having additional support needs, as will be seen below with the examination of who is actually included.

WHO IS ACTUALLY INCLUDED? PATTERNS AND TRENDS

In Scotland, statistics show a continuing upward trend in the proportions of children with 'additional support needs' being placed in mainstream schools, but also an increase in the proportions identified as having additional support needs (Scottish Government, 2008; 2011). In 2011, 14.7 per cent of pupils in Scotland were identified as having additional support needs (98,523 pupils), compared with 6.5 per cent (44,177 pupils) in 2009 and 5.3 per cent (36,454 pupils) in 2007. Of those children identified as having additional support needs, 3 per cent were deemed to have emotional, social or behavioural difficulties, with boys making up approximately two-thirds of the overall proportion of children with identified additional support needs. According to the Scottish Government (2011), better recording practices and improved data capture, together with the requirement to list all reasons for support and not just the principal reason, explain some of the increases. Other explanations may lie in the resource implications of identifying additional support needs.

Patterns of placement among children with additional support needs have altered over recent years. In the years between 2004 and 2009, while the additional support needs population was gradually increasing, the numbers of children in special schools remained relatively steady, with a fairly modest decline, as the numbers of children with additional support needs in mainstream continued to increase. It is only in the last few years that we have seen a more substantial drop in the special school population, from 15 per cent in 2009, to 10 per cent in 2010, and to 7 per cent in 2011.

The introduction of the Education (Additional Support for Learning) (Scotland) Act, which established Coordinated Support Plans for children with significant needs, brought forward anxieties that it would replicate the 'geographical lottery' that was a feature of the Record of Needs system. The statistics certainly indicate some substantial regional variations, with some rural areas more likely to issue Coordinated Support Plans (Shetland

Islands and Eilean Siar), but with other rural areas (East Lothian, North Ayrshire and West Dunbartonshire) and Glasgow, an urban authority, issuing Coordinated Support Plans for around half of the local authority average. Oddly, the Scottish Government provides statistics on what it calls 'integration', by which it distinguishes different amounts of time spent in mainstream classes and produces figures for children with different levels of need. Thus it is possible to compare levels of participation between children who have a Record of Needs (the formal statutory system of assessing children with significant special educational needs which was in place until 2005); those who have a Coordinated Support Plan (which replaced the Record of Needs); and those with Individualised Educational Plans. This last group appears to spend more time in mainstream classes, with fewer spending no time at all, while children with Coordinated Support Plans spend less time in mainstream classes and more spend no time at all in mainstream.

BARRIERS TO INCLUSION

A number of shifts in the political and policy context appear to have created, at least perceptually, barriers to inclusion. The features of these policy contexts are not specific to Scotland but represent what Ozga and Jones (2006) refer to as 'travelling policy' (p. 2), migrating between countries and representing a relatively coherent set of policy concerns across Europe and beyond. They include a focus on economic need; emphasis on rapid reform; insistence on the national education system becoming 'world class', as evidenced through international league tables such as PISA and TIMMS; belief in the benefits of business involvement in state schooling; and the promotion of differentiation at the expense of equality of opportunity (Alexiadou, 2002). These policies are 'sedimented into institutions and operative networks' (Robertson, 2006) and given credence and acceptability through a careful process of reiteration, elaboration and inflection (Ball, 2007). However, these policies are recognised as undermining efforts, in Scotland as elsewhere, to promote a social inclusion agenda and as actively contributing to inequalities (Gillborn and Youdell, 2000).

Responsibilities for inclusion are often held across ministries (such as health, education and social welfare), that have little connection between them. At the same time, however, the language of public services is becoming infused with the prefixes 'inter-', 'multi-' and 'co-' and Hartley (2009) points out that this 'inter-regnum' (p. 127) disturbs accepted understandings about school and expectations of professionals, and blurs the distinction between consumer and provider. Inclusion, in this new configuration, is thus a shared responsibility among professionals and involving parents, and one where the lines of accountability are (even) less clear. The implication within policies on inclusion, especially those urging joined-up working, is that it can be achieved through improved governance and service delivery, but as Edwards et al. (2001) point out, this contradicts the idea that exclusion and inequality are actually created through 'the economic mode of production' (p. 420).

Watson (2009) notes how in Scotland there is a prevalence of deficit-oriented language in inclusion policy and an assumption that '"support" provides the necessary scaffold to make good this deficit' (p. 162). The paradox that the naming of deficits is instrumental in releasing resources remains. An increasing individualisation may be discerned in assessment processes, 'personalised learning' and, for those with special educational needs, Individualised Educational Programmes. In spite of the promise that 'special educational needs will be a thing of the past', issued by Mike Gibson of Her Majesty's Inspectorate of Education in heralding the new legislation, the Additional Support Needs (Education) (Scotland) Act 2005, the continued dominance in Scottish inclusion policy of deficit language sustains the notion that inclusion is about a discrete population of children who require special help (Allan, 2008).

Amid the conceptual confusion that exists around the meaning of inclusion, a strong and rigid special education paradigm, driven by a deficit or medical model, continues to dominate policies and, inevitably, classroom practice. One effect of this extremely powerful special education paradigm is the silencing of the pupils and their parents, making them mere recipients of provision. Another effect can be seen in the material resources for teachers, in the form of packages of advice and support produced commercially and by the government, which claim to offer remedies to the 'problem' of inclusion. Handbooks, containing promises such as '60 research-based teaching strategies that help special learners succeed' (McNary et al., 2005) construct inclusion as a technical matter and assail teachers with advice about *effective* inclusion. This amounts to lists of conditions required for inclusion, recommendations about strong leadership or platitudes, for example 'Inclusive schools will certainly be aiming for the highest possible levels of performance across the school' (HMIE, 2004). Most problematic is the medicalised orientation to children and their deficits, encouraging new teachers to look out for children who fit a particular diagnosis. Whilst these materials might offer the reassuring prospect of a practical way forward for teachers, they are likely to entrench teachers' sense of failure and cause concern when children inevitably do not match the neat diagnostic categories supplied. The absence of any discussion of values in these resources for teachers is also disconcerting and, furthermore, these guides offer no insights into how they and their institutions might undertake the significant cultural and political changes in thinking and practice in order to become inclusive.

At the same time as these policy shifts appear to be undermining inclusion, there are some powerful legal frameworks that uphold the rights of children to be included. The UN Convention on the Rights of the Child, endorsed and ratified across Europe, safeguards certain rights and provides a mandate for greater participation by children, although Lee (1999) describes Article 14, which refers explicitly to children's participation, as a mixture of potential toothlessness and bold intent. The European Convention on Human Rights protects human rights and freedoms within Europe and has been used successfully to challenge exclusion within the Czech Republic. Although this is a very particular example, it highlights the potency of the legislation. In 2007, the Czech Republic brought a case to the European Court of Human Rights challenging the practice of 'shunting' Roma children into special schools. In the case, presented on behalf of eighteen Roma children, it was argued that Roma children in the city of Ostrava were twenty-seven times more likely to be segregated than other similarly situated non-Roma children. The Court ruled that the practice of segregating Roma children amounted to unlawful discrimination in breach of Article 14 of the European Convention on Human Rights, having reached the decision that special schools had a 'prejudicial impact' (www.opensocietyfoundations.org/press-releases/europes-highest-court-finds-racial-discrimination-czech-schools), but importantly had embraced the principle of indirect discrimination, which allowed for a prima facie allegation of discrimination to shift the burden to the defendant state to prove that any difference in treatment was not discriminatory. This outcome was hailed as a 'Pathbreaking judgement' in relation to inclusion: 'Its ruling is particularly significant now, as Europe grapples with the implications of its rapidly growing ethnic, racial and religious diversity'.

Some strong challenges to exclusion have come from disability organisations and voluntary sector organisations. Disability groups, often run by disabled people for disabled people, have tended not to focus on education, but on the right of disabled people to be included in society more generally. However, the UK organisation People First adopted a highly successful and high-profile campaign for inclusive education, which it took to the government to guide its response to the House of Commons Select Committee Report (2006), which had been equivocal about inclusion. It sought to answer some of the questions about the viability of inclusion:

> Over the last few months we have seen the inclusion of our disabled children and young people being ATTACKED by teacher's unions, academics and by the Government. And on every occasion the voices of inclusion have been IGNORED – those of us who know that inclusion can work and does work . . . The Government's response to the Education and Skills Select Committee's report on SEN is due in October so we must DISPEL THE MYTHS in the report that inclusion isn't working and that disabled children and young people are better segregated from their communities. (www.allfie.org.uk/docs/We%20Know%20Inclusion%20Works.pdf)

People First's other current campaign – 'Not dead yet' – is focused on assisted dying and is extremely powerful, but People First argues, in calling for disabled people and parents to provide their stories of how inclusion has made a difference, that this campaign needs to be 'bigger than the inclusion movement' in order to succeed. Whilst the activism by the voluntary sector organisations and People First has been important, it does not seem to have led to wholehearted acceptance of inclusion. Some of the voluntary organisations that actively campaign for inclusion have been particularly effective in lobbying governments although they also provide an important role in supporting parents. Within the UK, the Alliance for Inclusion and Parents for Inclusion, and in Scotland, Equity in Education have been especially prominent and influential.

WHAT CHILDREN AND YOUNG PEOPLE SAY

The many children and young people I have encountered whilst undertaking research find inclusion such a simple concept and such an obvious right that they are mystified as to why adults experience it as a struggle. Inclusion, for children and young people, appears to be a matter of basic human rights:

> It doesn't matter what hair colour you have, what eye colour you have, what origin you have, what colour your skin is. It doesn't matter if a bit of your body doesn't work – you have the right to come to this school. (Allan et al., 2006)

In the study of children's rights from which the above quotation was taken a group of children were invited to look at inclusion in their school; they very quickly and easily understood this to be about both increasing participation and removing the barriers in the school. They readily identified the barriers as coming from the school environment, structures and attitudes but found themselves puzzled that the adults could not avoid displaying behaviours and attitudes that so obviously restricted participation. In research with young disabled students (Allan, 1999), it emerged that teachers represented the biggest barriers to their efforts to actively seek inclusion and both the disabled students and their non-disabled peers found this disappointing and frustrating. The disabled students themselves suggested that teachers' fear of difference made them act inappropriately, as the following comment from a visually impaired student suggests:

> [The teacher is] really nice, but she never says 'see' to me – she says 'I'll give you this and you can listen to it' and it's a sheet of paper and she never likes to use the word 'see', or anything to do with the eyes and you can tell when people are trying to avoid that. It puts you off. (p. 63)

Criticism of teachers from mainstream students also highlighted the inappropriateness of 'special treatment' of disabled students and the discomfort it produced, as this quote, specifically about one student, illustrates:

> I think they sometimes go out of their way to help [disabled student], but she doesn't like that, she likes to be treated normally . . . If anybody makes a fuss of her she gets really embarrassed. (p. 63)

Finally, at a recent seminar event for children and young people – to discuss diversity – teachers were again criticised for making too much of diversity by 'overprotecting' disabled students and standing in the way, literally, of social interaction (Allan et al., 2009). Although the children and young people struggled with the language of difference, they asserted the importance of having opportunities to talk together about it, to consider what it means to be different and to explore their relationships. They also articulated some very clear views about the right to be included and illustrated a sophisticated understanding of structural discrimination which prevented this from happening. They argued that disabled people needed to learn social skills and if they went to a 'disabled school', they would only learn from other disabled children. The inclusion of disabled students in mainstream schools was also, in their view, good for them: 'It also means that people begin to understand disabled people.' The clarity in the minds of children and young people about the right to be included in mainstream schools and the right to belong in society is salutary.

LOOKING FORWARD TO INCLUSION?

Oliver and Barnes (1998) offer a vision of what an inclusive world might look like:

> It will be a very different world from the one in which we now live. It will be a world that is truly democratic, characterised by genuine and meaningful equality of opportunity, with far greater equity in terms of wealth and income, with enhanced choice and freedom and with a proper regard for environmental and social continuity. (p. 102)

This vision contrasts with the world of the school in which the pressures and constraints have made it difficult for teachers to work inclusively and, indeed, have produced exclusion for the teachers themselves. Ballard (2001) suggests that inclusion starts with ourselves and it may be that before inclusion can move anywhere near Oliver and Barnes' vision, attention needs to be given to the conditions under which teachers currently work. Inclusion for all, then, means that those charged with delivering it as well as the recipients need to belong.

Looking ahead, it would seem that the current educational climate is a particularly challenging one, with inclusion appearring to be all the more difficult to achieve. The economically driven imperative to raise achievement and the fragmentation of provision threaten to undermine inclusion, whilst the emphasis on individualisation and the continued dominance of 'special needs' discourage approaches to inclusive practice that are about all children. At the same time, the power of legal frameworks, particularly the European Convention on Human Rights, to challenge exclusion and discrimination and the mandate for children's participation and inclusion set by the UN Convention on the Rights of the Child provides some grounds for optimism.

There are clearly some concerns about the capacity of the education system – and the teachers within it – to 'deliver' inclusion, and it is teachers and their unions who are expressing these concerns most volubly. It would be a mistake to interpret these concerns as a lack of commitment to providing the best educational opportunities for all. Rather, it is vital that their very real concerns, and those voiced by others such as researchers, parents and children, are heard and responded to. The most urgent issues to be addressed are the competing policy demands and problems associated with provision that is fragmented or not 'joined up'. An acceptance that there is no 'magic solution' for inclusion, nor any recipe book for teachers to follow when they have children with additional needs of whatever kind in their classrooms, will be an important step towards progress in inclusion. Children, young people and families with direct experiences of inclusion and exclusion can help to inform and shape practice, and research that seeks their perspectives will provide knowledge which will in turn help teachers to develop their own inclusive practice and will enable schools to become more inclusive. In addition, teacher education programmes that help teachers to understand and engage critically with the challenges of inclusion and diversity will do much to limit the emergence of further questions about inclusion and concerns about its future.

REFERENCES

Alexiadou, N. (2002) 'Social inclusion and social exclusion in England: Tensions in education policy', *Journal of Education Policy*, 17 (1): 71–86.

Allan, J. (2008) *Rethinking Inclusive Education: The Philosophers of Difference in Practice*. Dordrecht: Springer.

Allan, J. (1999) *Actively Seeking Inclusion: Pupils with Special Needs in Mainstream Schools*. London: Falmer.

Allan, J., J. I'Anson, S. Fisher and A. Priestley (2006) *Promising Rights: Introducing Children's Rights in School*. Edinburgh: Save the Children.

Allan, J., G. Smyth, J. I'Anson and J. Mott. (2009) 'Understanding disability with children's social capital', *Journal of Research in Special Educational Needs*, 9 (2): 115–21.

Ball, S. (2007) *Education plc: Understanding Private Sector Participation in Education*. London: Routledge.

Ballard, K. (2001) 'Including ourselves: teaching, trust, identity and community', in J. Allan (ed.), *Inclusion, Participation and Democracy: What is the Purpose?* Dordrecht: Kluwer.

Barton, L. (1997) 'Inclusive education: romantic, subversive or realistic?', *International Journal of Inclusive Education*, 1 (3): 231–42.

Department of Education (1978) *Report of the Committee of Enquiry into the Education of Handicapped Children and Young People* (the Warnock Report). London: HMSO.

Edwards, R., P. Armstrong and N. Miller (2001) 'Include me out: Critical readings of social exclusion, social inclusion and lifelong learning', *International Journal of Lifelong Education*, 20 (5): 417–28.

Gillborn, D. and D. Youdell (2000) *Rationing Education: Policy, Practice, Reform and Equity*. Buckingham: Open University Press.

Hartley, D. (2009) 'Education policy and the "inter" – regnum', in J. Forbes and C. Watson (eds), *Service Integration in Schools*. Rotterdam: Sense.

Her Majesty's Inspectorate of Education (2004) *How Good is our School? Quality Management in Education. Inclusion and Equality, Part 2: Evaluating Education for Pupils with Additional Support Needs in Mainstream Schools*. Online at www.educationscotland.gov.uk/Images/hgiosasnms_tcm4-712659.pdf

Lee, N. (1999) 'The challenge of childhood: Distributions of childhood's ambiguity in adult institutions', *Childhood*, 6 (4): 455–74.

McNary, S., N. Glasgow and C. Hicks (2005) *What Successful Teachers Do in Inclusive Classrooms: 60 Research-based Teaching Strategies That Help Special Learners*. London: Sage.

NASUWT (2009) Press Release: 'NASUWT calls for a fit for purpose, national definition of inclusion'. Online at www.epolitix.com/stakeholder-websites/press-releases/press-release-details/newsarticle/nasuwt-calls-for-a-fit-for-purpose-national-definition-of-inclusion-2///sites/nasuwt/

Oliver, M. and C. Barnes (1998) *Disabled People and Social Policy: From Exclusion to Inclusion*. Harlow: Addison Wesley Longman.

Ozga, J. and R. Jones (2006) 'Traveling and embedded policy: The case of knowledge transfer', *Journal of Education Policy*, 21 (1): 1–19.

Robertson, P. (2006) 'Innovation theorists downgrading importance of new technology'. *Canberra Times*, 3 June. See at http://ecite.utas.edu.au/49193

Scottish Government (2008) *Pupils in Scotland, 2007*. Statistical Bulletin. Education Series Edn/B1/2008/1.

Scottish Government (2011) *Pupils in Scotland, 2011*. Online at www.scotland.gov.uk/Resource/0038/00388991.xls

Slee, R. (2011) *The Irregular School: Exclusion, Schooling and Inclusive Education*. London: Routledge.

Warnock, M. (2005) *Special Educational Needs: A New Look*. Impact No 11. London: The Philosophy Society of Great Britain.

Watson, C. (2009) 'Mythical spaces and social imaginaries: Looking for the global in the local in narratives of (inter)professional identification', in J. Forbes and C. Watson (eds), *Service Integration in Schools: Research and Policy Discourses, Practices and Future Prospects*. Rotterdam: Sense.

86

Additional Support Needs

Lio Moscardini

The concept of additional support needs has provided a framework, in theory at least, for the recognition of all children who require additional support. Traditionally, responses to difference have been based on a medical model of identifying a deficit within individual children and categorising and segregating on the basis of this diagnosis. The adoption of the term 'additional support needs' represents a significant conceptual departure from the construct of special educational needs by taking into account the broader social and contextual factors that give rise to the need for support. If we are to avoid simply substituting one term for another then consideration should be given not only to underlying principles of support and their application in practice but also to an understanding of what constitutes additional support needs.

The move towards a broader interpretation of educational support should be seen within the context of the process of inclusion. Since its establishment in 1999, the Scottish Parliament has introduced laws relating to education that are concordant with the United Nations Conventions of the Right of the Child and with European Human Rights legislation. These developments reflect a shift from the needs-driven agenda of the latter decades of the twentieth century towards a recognition of the rights and entitlement of all children to a quality education. In Scotland, the construct of additional support needs is situated within legislative frameworks and socio-cultural contexts that are commensurate with a Scottish self-image of an egalitarian and socially just society in which all its members are seen to matter.

The Education (Additional Support for Learning) (Scotland) Act was passed in 2004 and the Code of Practice published the following year. Since the last publication of *Scottish Education* in 2008 there have been amendments to the Act in 2009 and revisions by the Scottish Government to the Code of Practice (Scottish Government, 2010). These revisions have seen educational support frameworks situated alongside Curriculum for Excellence and within the overarching national policy of *Getting it Right for Every Child* (GIRFEC). Through the legislative frameworks and related policies that have taken into consideration factors relating to disadvantage and social deprivation, Scotland has adopted a broad and inclusive stance in relation to educational support that reflects the position outlined by the Organisation for Economic Cooperation and Development (OECD). The development of policy and practice in this area is being keenly observed beyond Scotland. The extent to which the rhetoric of inclusion and the translation of policy into practice have been realised in the experiences of children who require additional support continues to engender debate.

A progress report on the implementation of the Act concluded that 'more needs to be done' for children from disadvantaged circumstances (Scottish Government, 2012, p. 26). The narrative of vulnerable and disadvantaged children in the educational system predates the establishment of compulsory education in 1872. The challenge presented by particular learners who stress the educational system and defy categorisation has existed since Victorian times, their underachievement even then being recognised as related to social deprivation. Once labelled as 'backward' children, the perceived requirements for these children at various times have included: treatment following a designation of handicap; education-based diagnosis; a response to an identified need; and, most recently, the recognition of the 'reasons for support'. There is an underlying pattern to their story which resonates with current issues and practices and which remains unresolved either by individual pathologising or by systemic approaches.

Outlined in this chapter are the developments that led to the adoption of the term 'additional support needs', the current legislative framework and its background, and unresolved issues relating to the identification and support of vulnerable children. This discussion is situated against a background of the ongoing narrative of children who, while recognised within the construct of additional support needs, are not generally recognised within the discrete category of disability.

THE CONCEPT OF ADDITIONAL SUPPORT NEEDS

In Scotland the term 'special educational needs' has been replaced by the term 'additional support needs' in legislation; the latter term is recognised as broader and more inclusive in scope and definition. The statutory definition set out in the Education (Additional Support for Learning) (Scotland) Act 2004, amended 2009, is as follows:

> A child or young person has additional support needs for the purposes of this Act where, for whatever reason, the young person is, or is likely to be, unable without the provision of additional support to benefit from school education provided or to be provided for the child or young person. (Section 1.1)

The new framework means that many children who may not have been identified within the previous framework of special educational needs are now recognised through statute as being entitled to additional support. The term applies to all children who 'for whatever reason' require additional support. It is noteworthy that this need for support may be short-term or long-term. Reasons for support may include:

- having motor or sensory impairments;
- being bullied;
- being particularly able or talented;
- having experienced a bereavement;
- experiencing interrupted learning;
- having a learning disability;
- being looked after by a local authority;
- having a learning difficulty (for example dyslexia);
- living with parents who are substance abusers;
- living with parents who have mental health problems;
- having English as an additional language;

- not attending school regularly;
- having emotional or social problems;
- being on the child protection register;
- being a young carer. (Scottish Government, 2010, p. 13)

This list, taken from the Code of Practice (ibid.), is not exhaustive nor are the circumstances assumed to mean that additional support will be necessary. For example, in the case of children who are looked after by a local authority, the education authority has a duty to establish whether a child who is looked after by the authority requires additional support in order to benefit from school education. The legislation imposes a duty on education authorities, delineated in the Code of Practice, to identify and keep under review any additional support needs of children and the adequacy of any support provided.

The term 'additional support' is defined in the 2009 legislation as something that is 'additional to, or otherwise different from provision (whether or not educational provision) made generally for children' (Section 1.3). This is an important point of law which helps to clarify a misconception expressed by some practitioners, that 'all children have additional support needs'. To suggest that all children require additional support implies that no child requires support that is in any way additional to or different from the support that all children receive.

THE LEGISLATIVE FRAMEWORK AND ITS BACKGROUND

The Education (Additional Support for Learning) (Scotland) Act 2004 as amended in 2009 was passed by the Scottish Parliament on 20 May 2009. The amendments that came into force on 14 November 2010 include:

- the broadening of the concept of 'additional support' to include support from services outwith the school and beyond education;
- the automatic assumption that children who are looked after by a local authority (LA) have additional support needs with an obligation for LAs to consider whether or not these children require a Coordinated Support Plan (CSP);
- an extension of the rights of parents to request a specific assessment at any time and to make out-of-area placing requests;
- following a successful out-of-area placing request parents should have access to mediation and dispute resolution from the host authority;
- increased parental rights in respect of access to the Additional Support Needs Tribunals for Scotland (ASNTS);
- the provision of a new ASNTS national advocacy service.

The 2004 Act, which took effect from November 2005, superseded the Education (Scotland) Act 1980 which was the main legislative framework concerned with the provision for children with special educational needs. The 1980 Act placed a duty on education authorities to open a statutory planning document known as a Record of Needs for those children with pronounced, complex or long-term special educational needs. Scottish Executive statistics show that in 2004, around 2 per cent of the school population had a Record of Needs. The Record of Needs system was a statutory procedure for assessing and recording children with special educational needs and was established following the recommendations of the Warnock Report. This was the final report of the Committee of Enquiry into the Education of Handicapped Children and Young People, chaired by Mary Warnock and presented in 1978. It was a landmark report largely responsible for putting in place the construct of special educational needs; it also recommended the abolition of statutory categories of handicap and the introduction of the term 'children with learning difficulties'. The report reinforced a move towards a more integrated approach and the recognition of the educability of all children. It was not until the Education (Scotland) (Mentally Handicapped Children) Act 1974 which, acting upon the recommendations of the Melville Committee Report (1973), recognised that all children were educable. The 1974 Act overturned the Education (Scotland) Act 1969 which had deemed some children to be 'unfit for education or training either by ordinary methods or by special methods'. Until 1974 responsibility for children deemed 'ineducable and untrainable' lay outwith education. The Warnock Report, which was a UK-wide report, famously recognised that about 'one in five' children could experience difficulties in learning at some point in their school career. In Scotland in the same year, 1978, a report led by Her Majesty's Inspectorate and published by the Scottish Education Department, *The Education of Pupils with Learning Difficulties in Primary and Secondary Schools in Scotland*, sometimes referred to as the Progress Report or the PWLD Report, stated that up to 50 per cent of children in the educational system might experience difficulties in learning at some point. Two fundamental themes emerged from the PWLD Report: the need to recognise educational support as a whole-school responsibility and the recognition of the curriculum as a barrier to learning. It is worth noting that over thirty years later we are still wrestling with the idea of the learning environment as a contributing factor to learning difficulties. The PWLD Report helped to highlight in Scotland the existence of a large group of children in all schools who, on account of the learning environment, would require additional support in their learning at some time. However, the extent to which all identified children might receive the necessary support was driven by the special educational needs apparatus; many children may not have been recognised within a discrete category of special educational need and so may not have received the required support.

A further development in the chronology of Scottish legislation was the Standards in Scotland's Schools etc. Act 2000. Section 15, which took effect in August 2003, set out the requirement of mainstream education for all children in what is frequently referred to as 'the presumption of mainstream'. Exception to this requirement can be made on the grounds of suitability of such placement on the basis of the child's ability or aptitude; unreasonable public expenditure; and any detrimental effect on other children with whom the child may be educated. In October 2002, the Disability Strategies and Pupils' Educational Records (Scotland) Act 2002 took effect, placing responsibility on education authorities and schools to recognise the rights of children with disabilities and to meet their needs effectively by developing better communication, increased participation of the child and improvements to the physical environment. These Acts underlined further the shift away from a recognition of need and towards the rights and entitlements of children.

The most significant piece of legislation in this field in the new millennium, the Education (Additional Support for Learning) (Scotland) Act 2004, came about following a period of consultation by the Scottish Executive. This process commenced in 2001 with the consultation document 'Assessing our children's educational needs – The Way Forward?' which invited comments on the current procedures and proposals for change. The consultation revealed two sets of opposing views: on one hand parents and voluntary organisations expressed a strong desire to maintain separate special educational needs legislation with a revision of the Record of Needs system, while on the other hand many local authorities argued against a separate special educational needs category and for the abolishment of the Record of Needs system on the basis of equity, claiming that the system served the socially advantaged (Riddell and Weedon, 2010, p. 118). The resultant recommendation was for a flexible system that would provide a statutory mechanism of support for those children with complex educational needs while being responsive to the additional support needs of a wide range of children through a process of staged intervention. The extent to which these aims have been fulfilled will be discussed further.

The outcome of the consultation was the 2003 policy paper *Moving Forward! Additional Support for Learning* which supported a legislative framework around the concept of additional support needs. The new framework was described as representing 'a more inclusive approach with a move away from the current negative connotations of SEN which has too much emphasis on weaknesses and problems' (ibid., p.11).

The proposed changes which consequently came into effect were:

- the replacement of the Record of Needs system for assessment and recording with a more streamlined process for intervention (Staged Intervention);
- the introduction of CSPs for those children experiencing long-term complex or multiple barriers to learning and who required access to a range of services from outwith education;
- a requirement for local authorities to have mediation services in place for early resolution of disputes;
- extended rights of appeal for parents of children with a CSP to allow them to challenge the level of provision proposed;
- the establishment of Additional Support Needs Tribunals Scotland (ASNTS) to hear appeals. (ibid., p. 11)

SUPPORTING CHILDREN'S LEARNING: CODE OF PRACTICE

The current Code of Practice (Scottish Government, 2010) replaces the 2005 version, taking account of the 2009 amendments to the Education (Additional Support for Learning) (Scotland) Act 2004; it provides guidance on the legislation and illustrates how this might be applied.

Factors Giving Rise to Additional Support Needs

The Code of Practice outlines factors that give rise to additional support needs; these four overlapping themes are the learning environment; family circumstances; disability or health need; and social and emotional factors. Additional support needs arising from the learning environment relate to barriers to learning created by, amongst other things, inflexible curricular arrangements and inappropriate approaches to learning and teaching. This reflects recommendations made in the 1978 PWLD Report. Family circumstances include a home life that is disrupted by poverty, domestic abuse, parental alcohol or drug misuse, homelessness or parental health problems. Issues relating to disability or health need are most closely related to previous special educational needs categories, for example sensory impairment, autism spectrum conditions, learning difficulties and mental health problems. Social and emotional factors may be related to behavioural difficulties as well as issues such as bullying or racial discrimination (Scottish Government, 2010, pp. 24–5).

This elaboration of factors that give rise to additional support needs takes into consideration social issues which arguably are less explicit in more traditional constructions of special educational needs. The broad concept of additional support needs as set out in the Code of Practice reflects the position taken by the OECD which cites UNESCO's statement in 1997 that in some countries

> the concept of 'children with special educational needs' extends beyond those who may be included in handicapped categories to cover those who are failing in school for a wide variety of other reasons that are known to be likely to impede a child's optimal progress. (OECD, 2007, p.12)

In order to facilitate cross-national comparisons the OECD set out operational definitions across three categories that permitted a broad range of 'special educational needs' to be represented. These categories were: (1) Disabilities viewed as 'organic disorders in relation to sensory, motor or neurological defects'; (2) Difficulties arising primarily from problems in 'the interaction between the student and the educational context' and (3) Disadvantages related primarily to 'socio-economic, cultural, and/or linguistic factors' (OECD, 2007, p. 20). Although an issue with the OECD categorisation is that these categories in themselves are not mutually exclusive, it is evident that the concept of additional support needs as promoted in Scotland recognises the broad range of factors that contribute to a need for additional support. Scottish legislation and policy have established frameworks that have striven to promote a collaborative and flexible model of support that is responsive to all these factors.

Support Frameworks

The Code of Practice does not prescribe a specific model for assessment and support procedures to be adopted by all authorities; instead it sets out guidance on the Act's provisions and a framework for a staged approach to identifying and supporting children with additional support needs that each of the thirty-two education authorities should develop. An argument offered in support of this approach is that it is respectful of the diversity and range of provision across Scotland; however, it has resulted in an inconsistency of practice and bewildering array of terminology relating to individualised support planning across education authorities.

The revised Code of Practice recognises Curriculum for Excellence as an inclusive and flexible curriculum for all learners. It also sets out a clear framework that connects the process of staged assessment and support to the integrated services approach outlined in the GIRFEC policy. GIRFEC is a national programme underpinned by the principles of the United Nations Conventions on the Right of the Child; it aims to ensure that all children receive the help they need when it is needed through a coordinated approach across all agencies. The following five questions are provided for practitioners in GIRFEC. These questions suggest a dynamic response and are relevant to any professional with a duty of care towards children. In the context of the classroom the first question compels an identification of barriers to learning.

- What is getting in the way of this child or young person's wellbeing?
- Do I have all the information I need to help this child or young person?
- What can I do now to help this child or young person?
- What can my agency do to help this child or young person?
- What additional help, if any, may be needed from others? (Scottish Government, 2010, p. 37)

Staged Intervention

All education authorities have put this staged approach in place. The number of discrete stages varies across authorities, with most authorities setting out between three and six stages. Parents and/or carers and the child should be involved in the process. In the various models the stages are conflated or expanded accordingly; nevertheless the fundamental model is that at the initial stage identification and support takes place within the classroom. At the next level, identification and support goes beyond the classroom but remains within the school, for example other members of staff may help in the assessment and support process. Beyond this level, identification and support goes outwith the school but remains within educational services, for example referral may be made to an educational psychologist. At the highest level, support is required from agencies outwith education, for example, social services or the health board. These stages are not necessarily sequential or hierarchical and some children may require high-tariff support to be put in place immediately on account of the nature of their additional support needs, for example looked-after children or children with complex support needs. Furthermore, the process of staged intervention is recognised within the context of the responsibility every teacher has in supporting learners. This reflects a recommendation of the 1978 PWLD Report.

Staged intervention begins in the classroom. This is detailed in most local authorities' guidelines. However, there is a lack of clarity surrounding the earliest phase of staged intervention, usually referred to as Stage 1. This classroom-based level of support could be viewed as something that occurs regularly within the context of the routine, ongoing support from the class teacher. If a child is deemed to require additional support within the classroom then it would seem appropriate that information about this child and the support processes involved should be communicated. The extent to which this should be formalised presents a dilemma. Formalisation may constrain the support process, on the other hand the assumption that communication will occur effectively through informal mechanisms may result in some children not receiving the support they need.

The problem is compounded further by the distinction between 'Universal Support' and 'Targeted Support' as set out by Education Scotland. It should be noted that the online definition of Universal Support provided by Education Scotland is not consistent with that set out in the Code of Practice which implies a more individualised response (Scottish Government, 2010, p. 38). At the time of writing, Education Scotland documentation states that every child is entitled to 'Universal Support' with all staff having a responsibility in this. 'Targeted Support' is described as 'additional focused support . . . usually co-ordinated by staff with additional training and expertise through a staged intervention process'. This raises the issue of the role and responsibility of the class teacher in providing support particularly through the process of staged intervention at the earliest stage (Stage 1). The distinction as set out by Education Scotland is problematic for two reasons. First, it undermines the teacher's role and responsibility in providing targeted support in the classroom by suggesting that this is the role of a more qualified 'expert' from outwith the classroom. This is not to suggest that deeper knowledge and understanding may not be required to support particular learners, however, it gives a misleading message regarding the class teacher's role in the process of staged intervention, particularly in the teacher's capacity to provide focused (targeted) and specific yet low-level support to individuals within the classroom. The second problem relates to the process of staged intervention. Most local authorities' guidelines make clear that at the earliest stage the process starts in the classroom with the class teacher. The Education Scotland account of targeted support seems to reflect a higher level of staged intervention, thus negating the purpose of Stage 1. This is a cause for concern particularly if one considers which children are at risk of being overlooked in this process. It does not seem unreasonable to suggest that appropriate pedagogical responses within the context of the learning environment of the classroom are an appropriate Stage 1 strategy within the scope of the class teacher.

Although the 'learning environment' is recognised within the Code of Practice as a factor that gives rise to additional support needs there is a worrying reluctance to recognise this as a significant barrier to learning for many children. Contrary to HMI recommendations in the 1978 PWLD Report, deficit indicators, redolent of remedial and within-child deficit models, continue to prevail. At the time of writing, information available online through Education Scotland continues to display this deficit model with barriers to learning being described in terms of within-child deficits. The process of staged intervention has been linked to GIRFEC (Scottish Government, 2010, p. 38); however, there is a concerning use of language where this process has been set out. At each level the need for further support is described as 'situation not resolved and need for further action identified'. For some children the need for ongoing support will be lifelong, some children in fact possibly requiring multi-agency support from birth. To view children and young people as 'situations to be resolved' flies in the face of fundamental principles of inclusion and support. It would be more appropriate to consider whether further additional support is required.

Coordinated Support Plans

The process of staged intervention requires appropriate planning to be in place. Depending on the support required this may be within regular group planning although some children may require an individualised education programme (IEP) to be developed. Each education authority has developed its own model of staged intervention along with its accompanying planning framework (and terminology). Regardless of the particular framework of staged intervention in place the highest tariff individual support plan relevant to all local authorities is the CSP. The CSP is the only statutory plan and was intended to replace the Record of Needs. It is for those children who require support from a range of different services, whose additional support needs arise from complex or multiple factors that are deemed to have a significant effect on the education of the child and for whom this support will be likely to continue for more than a year.

Within their staged intervention framework many local authorities have put in place high-level multi-agency support plans that are not statutory, the use of which has resulted in only 0.5 per cent of the state school population having CSPs. Scottish Government statistics for 2010 show that the highest recording authority has ten times more CSPs opened than the lowest recording authority. This practice highlights tensions created by the opposing interests of parents and education authorities identified by Riddell and Weedon (2010). Mike Gibson, the former head of Support for Learning Division, Scottish Government, has stated that 'we are in a worse position with CSPs than we were with Records of Needs' and is concerned that it may fall to parents and young people to ensure that effective provision is in place if education authorities fail to fulfil their statutory duties (Gibson, 2011). Gibson's argument is consistent with the position expressed in the Doran Report, *The Right Help at the right time in the right place* (September 2012), a strategic review of learning provision for children and young people with complex additional support needs, which stated that complex additional support needs should not be interpreted as 'referring solely to the needs of children with multiple physical, sensory and intellectual impairments' (p. 63). Complex additional support needs can arise from any of the four factors outlined in the in Code of Practice and 'complex' can refer to the complexity of support arrangements required. While education authorities may argue that higher tariff but non-statutory planning provides for effective support it does little to assuage parental concerns. A further related issue is that it may be only those parents and young people with the confidence and capacity to make representation, or who are represented by a lobbying group, who contest provision.

ADDITIONAL SUPPORT NEEDS TRIBUNALS FOR SCOTLAND

The Additional Support Needs Tribunals for Scotland (ASNTS) was established in November 2005 following the 2004 Act. The function of the ASNTS is to hear appeals, known as references, made by parents and young people against the decisions of education authorities relating to the provision of educational support. In March 2011, the jurisdiction of the ASNTS was extended and consequently it may also consider references relating to claims of disability discrimination within education. A requirement of the 2009 amendments to the 2004 Additional Support for Learning Act was a legal duty on the Scottish Government to provide a national advocacy service to parents and young people to support them through the ASNTS process. The providers of this service are known as 'Take Note', a partnership between Barnardo's Scotland and the Scottish Child Law Centre.

At the time of writing, the most recent annual report of the ASNTS (ASNTS, 2011) showed that half of all references concerned placing requests and half related to CSPs. In relation to the nature of the additional support needs of references received, most, at 37 per cent of all references, concerned children with autistic spectrum disorder. The second largest group was physical or motor impairment (20 per cent). The remaining references covered a range of eight categories, the largest being 'other moderate learning difficulty' at 9 per cent; learning disability represented 6 per cent; social, emotional and behavioural difficulties 5 per cent; and looked-after children 2 per cent. Twenty-five per cent of all references concerned one particular local authority. These data raise two issues that relate to Riddell and Weedon's analysis (2010): the first concerns issues of equity and the representation (or possible under-representation) of particularly vulnerable groups; the second relates to the classification of particular groups of children and how they come to be identified and accounted for within the system.

ISSUES OF CLASSIFICATION AND REPRESENTATION

In the landmark book *A Sociology of Special Education*, now thirty years old, Sally Tomlinson distinguished between normative and non-normative categories of disability (Tomlinson, 1982); normative categories are those conditions about which there is a general (normative) agreement, usually through diagnosis or known aetiology. The non-normative group is comprised of children whose difficulties have no known aetiology; it consists largely of children with general (as opposed to specific) learning difficulties and/or behavioural and emotional difficulties. Tomlinson considered the existence of the group from a sociological perspective, arguing that social class has a significant bearing on the identification and response to this particular group of learners. It is the largest group of children with additional support needs in the system and is characterised by disadvantage and low socio-economic status. This group has been recognised within the post-Warnock category of moderate learning difficulties (Norwich and Kelly, 2005) although the extent to which children within this group now come to be identified and supported through the process of staged intervention remains to be seen.

HMIE, now part of Education Scotland, identified a 'lack of clarity and consistency' in the collation of data around pupils with additional support needs (HMIE, 2010, p. 9). This places vulnerable children at risk of not securing the support they need. By definition the concept of additional support needs implies a fluctuating group, which presents a challenge in quantifying certain groups of learners, most notably those who would be considered with non-normative categories. This relates directly to how (and whether) these children are identified and recorded through a process of staged intervention and how any resultant data come to be inputted statistically. Arguably the children being counted are those who are most easily identified within what Tomlinson describes as normative categories. An analysis of Scottish Government *Statistical Bulletins, Pupils in Scotland* records from 2004 to 2011 suggests that this may be the case.

Data presented in the Statistical Bulletins are problematic in terms of providing a clear picture of the representation and proportionality of particular groups. This is not only because of the multiple counting involved (children may be recorded within various categories simultaneously), but also because of the lack of clarity that surrounds the recording and reporting procedures. The Scottish Government gives no specific guidance to local authorities on categories to be recorded and reported. The statisticians therefore work with the various and varied categories and terms presented by local authorities which have been gathered from schools. Within local authorities there is no clear picture of which groups of children are actually being recorded. For example, in one local authority schools only inform the authority of those children who are at the higher levels of staged intervention; children who are supported within the classroom and the wider school are not necessarily being recorded beyond the school. It would appear therefore that the figures are largely dependent on how schools and subsequently local authorities interpret and apply the recording processes. This may also explain why children who generally struggle in their learning, and who would be considered to have additional support needs, may be overlooked in the formal recording process, particularly at the earliest phase of staged intervention, while those children whose difficulties would be considered within normative categories are more readily quantifiable. The former group should not be lost in the process.

In its report HMIE found that education authorities 'are not always fully aware of the range of additional support needs among children and young people in schools' (ibid., p. 9). This lack of clarity does not only exist at local authority level; Scottish Government's Pupils in Scotland records contain a shift in categorisation, since 2006, which is problematic. The old categories of 'main difficulty of learning' have been replaced by new categories of 'reason for support'. Statistically the largest of the new categories is now the 'learning disability' category; the largest of the old categories was the 'moderate learning difficulty' group. This latter category has disappeared and it is not clear how the 'learning disability' group is accounted for. There is a category of 'other moderate learning difficulty' but this seems something of an anomaly given that there is no superior group to which this might be a subordinate.

A problem with the super-category of 'learning disability' as applied in statistical records is the lack of account of how this group is actually comprised. It appears to function as a catch-all category rather than to reflect a clearly defined group of learners. Furthermore, there appears to be no mechanism within data collection procedures for recognising the potentially large group of learners for whom the learning environment is the source of difficulty. Yet this is one of the four factors identified as giving rise to additional support needs. Although the enumeration of non-normative groups is problematic, the prominence of the learning disabled category is a cause for concern; it is regressive in both overlooking social and environmental factors and in situating the difficulty within the child.

TEACHER EDUCATION

The General Teaching Council for Scotland (GTCS) has responsibility for regulating the teaching profession in Scotland. This responsibility includes ensuring that required standards are met to achieve full registration into the profession. The Standard for Full Registration specifies that registered teachers must effectively identify and respond appropriately to pupils who require additional support. There is also a requirement under the Standard for Initial Teacher Education that programmes of initial teacher education (ITE) should prepare student teachers in their capacity to support all pupils. Under the Requirements for Teachers (Scotland) Regulations 2005, teachers working with children with visual impairment, hearing impairment or dual-sensory impairment are required to have an additional qualification. There is however no legal requirement for an additional qualification for teachers working with any other groups of children or young people with additional support needs. All of the Scottish teacher education institutions offer postgraduate course to Masters level in the area of inclusive education/educational support. This is within the context of teachers' career-long professional learning and is recognised as such by education authorities who identify a qualification in this area as desirable.

While universities have a duty to ensure that students undertaking courses in ITE learn about additional support needs, and this requirement is fulfilled, there are concerns that this aspect of teacher professional development is inadequately covered at both pre-service level by universities and post-service level by education authorities. In 2010, ENABLE Scotland investigated teacher professional development in the area of disability in all Scottish ITE institutions as well as across all thirty-two local authorities. ENABLE found that although all universities address additional support needs within core elements of ITE courses the content was basic and general. They also found that although most local authorities make 'training' (sic) available this is not mandatory. The 2010 report of the Donaldson Review team, *Teaching: Scotland's Future*, also identified a need for increased teacher professional development in the area of additional support needs. It is noteworthy that of the six explicit references to additional support needs within the document four are qualified by specific reference to dyslexia and autism. There are two issues related to these recommendations: the first is a concern with the notion of 'training' as something that is separate from the teachers' ongoing professional development; the second relates to a conceptualisation of additional support needs. If the call is for further teacher development in additional support needs then there is a need to be specific about what is meant by additional support needs – implicitly the call seems to be for teachers to know more about particular disabilities and impairments. Donaldson makes this explicit in relation to the two high-profile and important fields of dyslexia and autism. It is worth perhaps reflecting on the need for professional development that focuses on the development of teaching approaches that support the participation of all children.

The National Framework for Inclusion (available at www.frameworkforinclusion.org)

has been developed by the Scottish Government through the Scottish Teacher Education Committee (STEC). The Framework was designed by a working group of academics from each of the Scottish ITE institutions. It aims to support students and teachers in developing their knowledge and understanding of inclusive education and emphasises the need to focus on values and beliefs for inclusion in advance of considering professional knowledge and understanding and skills and abilities.

This relates to the findings of Norwich and Lewis's (2005) systematic review which found no evidence of distinct pedagogies for children with learning difficulties. The significance of this is that it challenges the notion that there are specific pedagogies for groups of learners in which teachers require 'training'. There are some areas in which specific pedagogies do exist, for example in the teaching of children of autistic spectrum conditions; however, this does not negate the view that by making the learning environment more accessible for particular children all children benefit. For many teachers it may be about recognising and extending what they are already doing and developing the kind of pedagogical content knowledge required to support all learners. For example, if teachers have a deep understanding of children's mathematical thinking, of how they develop an understanding of number and manipulate mathematical ideas, then they will be well placed to identify and support a learner in trouble. They will also have less need to seek out some kind of diagnosis that is unlikely to give them any indication of what to do pedagogically. Furthermore this deeper understanding will benefit every child in the class. This example could be applied to any curricular area. Rather than viewing teacher expertise in educational support as being primarily about individualistic responses to specific categories of disability, greater emphasis needs to be placed on the development of teachers' knowledge and understanding of inclusive pedagogy. This focuses on establishing a learning environment for all children rather than one that is for most children with individual responses to those identified as different.

FUTURE PRIORITIES

Scotland has much to be proud of in its adoption of the concept of additional support needs and the translation of this into policy. Legislation and policy frameworks underpin an educational support system designed to facilitate a dynamic response to identifying and responding to the needs of all children. Future priorities should lie in continuing to develop a consistent and equitable approach to ensure that all children receive the support to which they are entitled. This may require more careful consideration of how particular groups come to be identified and supported.

In considering the level of support required against the incidence rate within school populations, there is evidence that the low-incidence group of children who require high levels of support are not assured statutory CSPs with local authorities employing non-statutory additional support plans in their place – and there is an inconsistency of practice across education authorities. This is the realisation of a concern expressed by McKay and McLarty, the authors of the chapter equivalent to this one in the previous edition of *Scottish Education*. In relation to the high-incidence group of children who require lower levels of support, issues revolve around identification, recognition and ultimately agency.

This chapter began by outlining a concern about the high-incidence group of vulnerable and disadvantaged children recognised within the construct of additional support needs but in reality often overlooked in practice (Scottish Government, 2012). Given that many children are identified as requiring additional support for the first time in school, class teachers have a key responsibility in recognising and responding to children requiring support through a clear and coherent model of staged intervention. This support should be recognised as a dynamic process situated within the context of an inclusive learning environment. The development of inclusive pedagogical approaches provides a context for the support of all learners. In this way vulnerable children, who might be recognised in non-normative categories, come to be recognised and supported rather than being misrepresented within a disability category. The real concern is that a continued focus on normative categories fuels a persistence with individualised responses to difference ultimately resulting in the term 'additional support needs' becoming a proxy for special educational needs with those children who have been a source of tension in the educational system for over a century failing to receive the support to which they are entitled.

REFERENCES

Additional Support Needs Tribunals for Scotland (2011) *Sixth Annual Report of the President of the Additional Support Needs Tribunals for Scotland*. Glasgow: ASNTS. Online at www.asntscotland.gov.uk/asnts/files/Annual%20Report%202010-2011.pdf

Gibson, M. (2011) 'Just where are we with co-ordinated support plans?', *Times Educational Supplement Scotland* (11 November), 33.

Her Majesty's Inspectorate of Education (2010) 'Review of the Additional Support for Learning Act: Adding benefits for learners'. A report by HMIE to Scottish Ministers, November 2010. Online at www.educationscotland.gov.uk/inspectionandreview/Images/raslaabl_tcm4-712941.pdf

Norwich, B. and A. Lewis (2005) 'How specialized is teaching pupils with disabilities and difficulties?', in A. Lewis and B. Norwich (eds) *Special Teaching for Special Children? Pedagogies for Inclusion*. Maidenhead: Open University Press.

Organisation for Economic Cooperation and Development (2007) *Students with Disabilities, Learning Difficulties and Disadvantages: Policies, Statistics and Indicators*. Paris: OECD.

Norwich, B. and N. Kelly (2005) *Moderate Learning Difficulties and the Future of Inclusion*. London: Routledge-Falmer.

Riddell, S. and E. Weedon (2010) 'Reforming special education in Scotland: tensions between discourses of professionalism and rights', *Cambridge Journal of Education*, 40 (2): 113–30.

Scottish Government (2010) *Supporting Children's Learning: Code of Practice*. Online at www.scotland.gov.uk/Resource/Doc/348208/0116022.pdf

Scottish Government (2012) 'Supporting children's and young people's learning: A report on progress of implementation of the Education (Additional Support for Learning) (Scotland) Act 2004 (as amended)'. Online at www.scotland.gov.uk/Resource/0038/00387992.pdf

Tomlinson, S. (1982) *A Sociology of Special Education*. London: Routledge & Kegan Paul.

87

Psychological Services and their Impact

Tommy MacKay

Educational psychology services in Scotland are unique (Boyle and MacKay, 2010). In setting out their unique aspects, this chapter discusses the history of the profession from the early days of child guidance services, the effects of legislation, the qualifications and training of staff, the range and source of referrals and the contribution made to the Children's Hearings and social work. Consideration is also given to the impact of the profession on local and national policy, and to current issues and challenges, with a particular focus on the contribution of educational psychology to the mental and physical health of all children and young people. The uniqueness of Scottish educational psychology services may be demonstrated in relation to four aspects of their history and development: their statutory foundation; the role and functions of psychologists; the development of nationally agreed quality standards; and the establishment of post-school psychological services.

A UNIQUE STATUTORY FOUNDATION

The first aspect of the uniqueness of Scottish services is that they are built on a statutory foundation that is broader than for any other country in the world (MacKay, 1996). Their functions are prescribed in Section 4 of the Education (Scotland) Act 1980, with subsequent amendments, as follows:

> It shall be the duty of every education authority to provide for their area a psychological service in clinics or elsewhere, and the functions of that service shall include
> (a) the study of children with additional support needs;
> (b) the giving of advice to parents and teachers as to appropriate methods of education for such children;
> (c) in suitable cases, provision for the additional support needs of such children in clinics;
> (d) the giving of advice to a local authority within the meaning of the Social Work (Scotland) Act 1968 regarding the assessment of the needs of any child for the purposes of any of the provisions of that or any other enactment.

In a number of respects these duties will be seen as having much in common with the work done by psychologists elsewhere in the UK, but there are several important differences. First, while sharing many aspects of professional practice and development with services in England and Wales, Scottish services are fundamentally different in that all of the above duties are mandatory and not discretionary. While, for example, the contribution of the educational psychologist in England and Wales is generally wide-ranging, the duties that must be provided by law are narrow, and are limited to the assessment of children and young people in relation to the Statement of Needs.

Second, the term 'additional support needs' when used to describe the functions of psychological services is intended to be of very broad interpretation. It replaced the term 'special educational needs', which in its turn was a direct replacement for the older term 'handicapped, backward and difficult children', which it was an attempt to modernise. The population of children and young people embraced by this description has been defined in statutory instruments and official guidance, and includes the full range of psychological problems of childhood, whether educational, behavioural or developmental, and whether occurring in the context of school or elsewhere. Indeed, the single most important legislative statement that can be made about educational psychology in Scotland is that it is not a school psychological service, but provides such a service as part of a wider statutory remit.

Third, the statutes governing Scottish educational psychology require services to give advice not just to the education authority but to the 'local authority', that is, to the council as a whole, in relation to areas beyond schools and education. The breadth of that function beyond education is seen in the reference to the Social Work (Scotland) Act 1968, by which the psychologist has a duty to provide assessment and advice in relation to the Children's Hearing system.

DEVELOPMENT OF CHILD GUIDANCE SERVICES

Educational psychology is a relatively young profession, and its development in Scotland dates from the 1920s. The context in which it developed was set by its parent discipline child psychology, which had become an established subject in the universities by the end of the nineteenth century. In 1884, Francis Galton had opened in London his anthropometric laboratory for the study of individual differences, and had advocated the scientific study of children. James Sully, a founder member of the British Psychological Society and convenor of its first meeting in 1901, opened a psychological laboratory in 1896. In his classic *Studies of Childhood* (1896) he outlined the importance of 'the careful, methodic study of the individual child', and teachers and parents were invited to take difficult children to his laboratory for examination and advice on treatment. Sully paved the way for a new kind of specialist to work with children in the educational sphere, and in 1913 Cyril Burt became the first educational psychologist in the UK on his appointment to London County Council.

These events had a significant influence on the development of child guidance services in Scotland (Boyle and MacKay, 2010). In 1923, the first appointment of a child psychologist was made when David Kennedy Fraser was appointed jointly by Jordanhill College to train teachers for schools for the mentally handicapped and by Glasgow Education Committee as a psychological adviser. Meanwhile the Bachelor of Education degree (the EdB, not to be confused with the current pre-service degree qualification, BEd) was established in all four universities, and this provided the background to training in educational psychology for many years. In the late 1920s, Dr William Boyd established an 'educational clinic' at Glasgow University, while Professor James Drever set up a 'psychological clinic' at Edinburgh.

While these were the forerunners of the Scottish child guidance clinics, the first establishment to bear this name was the independent Notre Dame Child Guidance Clinic, founded in Glasgow in 1931. It was also the last to use such a description, since the term 'child guidance service' was replaced by 'psychological service' in subsequent educational legislation. The Notre Dame Clinic was established on an American model which favoured a three-member team of psychologist, psychiatrist and social worker, and its main focus was on the emotional and behavioural problems of childhood. Renamed the Notre Dame Centre in 1994, it continues to provide a therapeutic service to children and young people in cooperation with health, social work and education services.

THE EFFECTS OF LEGISLATION

The statutory period for child guidance began with the Education (Scotland) Act 1946. Glasgow had established the first education authority child guidance service in 1937, to which it appointed a full-time psychologist, and by the outbreak of the war several authorities had clinics in operation, mainly on a voluntary basis and operating on Saturday mornings. In recognition of these developments the 1946 Act empowered education authorities to provide child guidance services, with a range of functions expressed in almost identical terms to the present statutory duties. The Act also required the Secretary of State to make regulations defining the various categories of handicapped children, and these were set out in the Special Educational Treatment (Scotland) Regulations 1954. This had important implications for psychologists, who developed a central role in determining which of these children required special education.

The functions of the child guidance service became mandatory in 1969, while the Education (Mentally Handicapped Children) (Scotland) Act 1974, by bringing every child in Scotland under the care of the education authority, led to an extended role for psychologists in working with pupils with complex learning difficulties. The Record of Needs legislation in 1981 extended the psychologist's role further. The Record was discontinued with the passing of the Education (Additional Support for Learning) (Scotland) Act 2004, which gave parents a new right to request a psychological assessment of additional support needs.

In addition to the Education Acts, several other pieces of legislation have had important implications for the development of psychological services. Until the early 1970s, psychologists worked almost exclusively with children, the main thrust being with those of primary school age and to a lesser extent with pre-school children. During the 1970s there was a rapid development of the service provided to children of secondary age and to young people. The Record of Needs legislation in 1981 had dealt extensively with the position of young people over 16, and following the Disabled Persons (Services, Consultation and Representation) Act 1986 services were renamed as 'regional or island authority psychological services', with a remit for the population aged 0–19 years. This new term was also soon rendered obsolete, and following the Local Government (Scotland) Act 1994, psychological services faced a period of major reorganisation under the thirty-two new unitary authorities established in 1996. The Children (Scotland) Act 1995 again provided a changing context for the work of psychologists, and extended the rights of children (including those with additional support needs) to have their views taken into account in decisions regarding their education and care. Finally, the Standards in Scotland's Schools etc. Act 2000 made provisions for promoting social inclusion and raising attainments in core skills, and in doing so highlighted areas in which the future contribution of educational psychology would be vital.

QUALIFICATIONS, TRAINING AND STAFFING

The training of educational psychologists has changed dramatically over the years both in structure and in content. Prior to the 1960s, psychologists were first and foremost teachers. Indeed, they were frequently listed in education department records as 'teachers employed as psychologists', and it was usually recommended that they should have a minimum of two years' teaching experience. Entry to the profession was through the MEd Honours degree (formerly the EdB), specialising in Educational Psychology. In 1962, a postgraduate course in educational psychology was established for graduates with a first degree in psychology and, to meet the demands for recruitment following services becoming mandatory in 1969, postgraduate courses of this kind were soon operating in Aberdeen, Edinburgh, Glasgow, Stirling and Strathclyde Universities. They offered the degree of MSc or the Diploma in Educational Psychology (later MAppSci).

For a number of years there was considerable debate about whether teacher training and experience were to be viewed as necessary qualifications for entry to educational psychology, and for a period many employing authorities continued to demand full General Teaching Council (GTC) registration. It was the profession itself that moved away from this position and recommended new approaches to training. Now the only route into the profession is through an honours degree in psychology and a postgraduate degree in educational psychology. This training recognises that it is the study and practice of psychology itself that best informs the assessment and intervention strategies used by psychologists, and which best equips them to give appropriate advice to teachers, parents and others. A broader experience of the education system than was provided under the former teacher training arrangements is recognised as being an essential aspect of training, and this is provided for within the structure of the postgraduate programmes. Most entrants to the profession take the four-year single honours degree in Psychology at one of the Scottish universities and proceed to the two-year MSc in Educational Psychology at either Dundee or Strathclyde University. Trainees are required to spend at least two years following (or prior to) their first degree gaining additional qualifications or experience in fields relevant to educational psychology. This may be, for example, in children's homes, teaching, research or the voluntary sector. As a result, entrants to the profession have for many years been very highly qualified and experienced in their preparations for beginning work as educational psychologists. Practice tutors from the field are centrally involved in supervising placements in psychological services throughout the two postgraduate years.

The final steps in reaching independent professional status involve a probationary year working under the supervision of an appropriately qualified psychologist in a Scottish local authority psychological service, to meet British Psychological Society (BPS) requirements for eligibility to become a chartered psychologist and for registration with the Health Professions Council (HPC), a statutory requirement for all practitioner psychologists since 2009. Psychologists may proceed from there to undertake the degree of Doctor of Educational Psychology (DEdPsy), but their existing qualifications are already recognised as being at the doctoral level required for HPC registration. Quality and standards of training and induction into employment are monitored by the training committee of the BPS Scottish Division of Educational Psychology. For psychologists in service, local arrangements for further study and training are supplemented by a national programme of continuing professional development.

Staffing levels in educational psychology services in Scotland vary, but on average they provide a ratio of approximately one psychologist to 3,000 of the 0–19 population. Each of the thirty-two local authorities has its own psychological service, and in almost every case these are under the direction of a principal educational psychologist, supported by senior psychologists except in the smallest services. Psychologists in training previously received a trainee grant and had their fees paid by government funding, but this funding was withdrawn in 2012. Since trainees must now be self-funding, this has raised concerns in the profession about future recruitment, at a time when previous recruitment issues had only recently been addressed.

THE ROLE AND FUNCTIONS OF PSYCHOLOGISTS

The second aspect of the uniqueness of Scottish services relates to the role and functions of psychologists. These include research as a core function agreed at government level. MacKay defined three levels of work and five core functions for the profession, together with the quality standards that represent good practice (MacKay, 1999). Following a national review of educational psychology in Scotland, these were endorsed by the Scottish Ministers as the basis on which services would operate (Scottish Executive, 2002). The three levels are the level of the individual child or family, the level of the school or establishment and the level of the local authority. Psychologists have a key role in facilitating interactions between these levels. They also cover the entire age range of children and young people in both mainstream and special sectors in relation to a full spectrum of educational and clinical difficulties in learning, behaviour and development. In addition, they frequently occupy the central role in coordinating the work of a multi-disciplinary team from health, education and social work and from the voluntary agencies. The breadth of this work gives psychological services a pivotal role in assisting the local authority in the management and development of resources in the field of additional support needs.

In relation to each of the three levels of work, the five core functions are consultation, assessment, intervention, training and research. All of these functions operate within an interactive context in which the problems of individual children and young people are assessed as part of a wider environment such as classroom or school. While assessment and intervention therefore may involve the use of a wide range of techniques and strategies directly with the individual, including a range of standardised assessment instruments, a central part of the psychologist's role is in assisting parents and teachers in supporting children with difficulties. This leads to considerable involvement by psychological services in parenting skills, classroom management strategies and staff training, and in the development of new methodologies for helping young people who experience problems in their learning, behaviour or development.

Although acting frequently in a liaison capacity between the education authority, the school and the child or parent, the psychologist in giving advice and in making recommendations must always act in the best interests of the child or young person. This is required by the Code of Conduct and Ethics of the BPS and the Standards of Conduct, Performance and Ethics of the HPC, both of which bodies set nationally recognised professional standards in relation to psychological practice. One of the key skills of the psychologist therefore in giving independent advice is the ability to negotiate arrangements that will best meet children's needs, and to handle tensions that may arise from the perspective of the school or other agencies, or indeed between the child and the parent.

QUALITY STANDARDS

The third respect in which Scottish services are unique relates to quality standards. The profession in Scotland has been proactive in taking steps to ensure promotion of quality services and maintenance of professional standards. It has done this in three main ways. First, the performance indicators published by the Scottish Executive (MacKay, 1999) were the first nationally endorsed quality standards in the world for educational psychology services. They were fully supported and developed throughout the entire process by an extensive consultation exercise involving all staff in all services. These were developed further as a comprehensive self-evaluation toolkit in the standard format used by Her Majesty's Inspectorate (HMIE, 2007).

Second, through the BPS Scottish Division of Educational Psychology, psychologists campaigned for the establishment of a fully chartered profession, and became the only branch of UK psychology to be fully regulated in this way several years before regulation became a statutory requirement. Third, the profession requested that the education functions of psychological services should be included in the HMIE inspections of education authority services, so that they would be subject to the same process of scrutiny as other branches of education. This resulted in an inspection of all services, undertaken from 2006 to 2010 (HMIE, 2011).

RANGE AND SOURCE OF REFERRALS

The foundation of a psychological service and its predominant activity is casework. This is based on interactive assessment and intervention involving both the children or young people who are referred and the local contexts, such as school or family, in which they function. The range of problems referred is almost certainly wider than for any other branch of psychology. Reasons for referral include all of the traditional groupings within the field of additional support needs – moderate, severe and complex learning difficulties; visual and hearing impairments; physical disability; emotional and behavioural disorders; and language and communication disorders. Overall referral patterns reflect an increased interest in and concern with the areas of specific learning difficulties, attention deficit/hyperactivity disorder, mental health issues, the autistic spectrum and child abuse. Referrals may arise in discussion with a variety of agencies, and in some cases are made directly by parents. Older children and young people have a right to make a confidential self-referral, and this is treated in a way that takes account of age and maturity, and the nature of the problem referred. Nevertheless, since problems do not generally occur in isolation but within a family, social or educational context, the small group of self-referrals would normally be guided towards a position that encouraged liaison with other agencies.

It is the schools themselves, however, that have always accounted for perhaps 80 per cent of the referrals to psychological services across Scotland, and much of the backbone of the work arises from the referrals of pupils with educational difficulties or behaviour problems in the classroom. While this may be the most routine aspect of the work of the psychologist it is often the contribution that is most valued by teachers and others who are seeking to support children with difficulties.

CHILDREN'S HEARINGS AND SOCIAL WORK

The Children's Hearings in Scotland were developed as an alternative system to the juvenile courts for dealing with children and young people in trouble. Cases are heard by a panel which has a range of options including home or residential supervision orders, or in some instances referral to the sheriff. Since 1969, one of the statutory functions of psychological services has been to provide reports to the social work department or to the Reporter to the Children's Panel in cases where psychological assessment and advice may be helpful.

The pattern of referrals from the Reporter varies from one area to another, and in some services accounts for up to 12 per cent of the workload. The problems referred may occur mainly in relation to the home, the school or the community, and may centre on issues of child care and protection, criminal offences or school attendance issues. In addition to the cases that reach the Reporter, there is a large number of other situations calling for joint working between psychological services and social work, and the effect of more recent legislation has been to increase the involvement of the psychologist with social work and the Reporter in a wide range of child care issues.

POST-SCHOOL PSYCHOLOGICAL SERVICES

The fourth respect in which Scottish services are unique is in the provision of post-school psychological services (MacKay, 2009). The Beattie Report on post-school education and training for young people with special needs (Scottish Executive, 1999a) recommended that educational psychology services should be extended to provide a service to young people in the 16 to 24 age group who had left school. Following a period of preparatory work to develop a structure and role for such services, the Executive funded a pilot project in twelve Pathfinder authorities for the period 2004–6. On the basis of the evaluation of this initiative (MacKay, 2006) the government extended the provision of post-school psychological services to all thirty-two authorities.

The establishment of post-school services represented a significant challenge to educational psychology in terms of the structure and role of services, additional recruitment requirements, continuing professional development for staff, the curricula of university training programmes and finding field placements for trainee psychologists. It also required educational psychologists to provide services beyond education, and to work in partnership with agencies that have a national rather than a local authority structure, such as Careers Scotland. More fundamentally, provision of services to adult age groups raised issues regarding the nature and scope of educational psychology itself, as a profession with a focus on children and adolescents and on models drawn from developmental psychology.

IMPACT ON EDUCATIONAL POLICY AND DEVELOPMENT

As well as fulfilling their central task of assisting children and young people with additional support needs, educational psychology services have made a substantial impact on education authority policy and development. Their contribution has been significant not only in the field of additional support needs but also in relation to education in general. This may be illustrated by reference to four areas.

First, the role of psychologists in shaping policy for additional support needs at national and local authority level has been a crucial one. Most authorities have relied heavily on psychological services in planning and developing their provision, and in a national context psychologists have contributed substantially to government circulars and guidance in this area. Psychologists have also been the dominant force in promoting a philosophy of inclusive education, and in developing the context that enables pupils with additional needs to be educated along with their mainstream peers.

Second, through research, training, promotion of good practice and production of resources, educational psychologists have had a vast influence on classroom management strategies, anti-bullying policies, parent partnership, child protection procedures, learning support, and school organisation and ethos. It is probably the case that virtually every educational establishment in Scotland at nursery, primary, secondary and special level uses strategies or resources developed by psychological services. Individual psychologists have also made contributions to good practice that have had national and international impact (see, for example, McLean, 2003; 2009).

Third, psychologists have been central in highlighting the importance of socio-economic disadvantage as a major dimension in Scottish education. Through published research they have not only emphasised its significance as the principal correlate of educational underachievement but have also developed a range of interventions for tackling its effects. Recent examples include the research on nurture groups in fifty-eight Glasgow schools (Reynolds et al., 2009) and the development of resources to promote nurturing schools (Glasgow City Council, 2011). In addition, in many education authorities psychologists have been instrumental in developing a policy framework that targets additional resources on disadvantaged populations.

Fourth, the work of educational psychologists in Scotland in designing projects for improving children's achievement in literacy has been internationally recognised and has had a major impact on national practice in the setting up of the National Literacy Commission. This contribution has been acknowledged in the design and development of literacy initiatives in almost all of the education authorities in Scotland. Notable examples are the West Dunbartonshire Literacy Initiative (Burkhard, 2006) and the Read On project (Topping, 2001).

A number of consumer studies have been published in which the views of teachers, parents and others have been surveyed. These have acknowledged the impact of psychological services and their value within the education system.

CURRENT ISSUES: THE DEVELOPMENT OF 'UNIVERSAL PSYCHOLOGY SERVICES'

The national review of services (Scottish Executive, 2002) envisaged a future in which the educational psychologist would provide holistic services across the contexts of home, school and community, and would contribute to the 'well-being of all children and young people, and not only to those with special educational needs' (para. 2.30). The review emphasised opportunities for psychologists in relation to each of the five national priorities for education in Scotland: in raising standards of attainment in the core skills of literacy and numeracy; in supporting the skills of teachers and self-discipline of pupils, and enhancing school environments; in promoting equality and helping every pupil to benefit from education; in working with parents to teach pupils respect for self and one another; and in equipping pupils with the skills, attitudes and expectations necessary to prosper in a changing society. Many of the examples given in this chapter illustrate the ways in which such universal psychology services have already been developed in some of these areas.

The commitment of educational psychologists to a universal psychology aimed at addressing the wellbeing of all children and young people is necessary for the future of the profession as one that has central relevance to the needs of society. This is reflected in the theme of the 2012 annual conference for educational psychologists in Scotland – 'Building capacity in universal services'. Two areas are highlighted here as key priorities: the mental health agenda and the physical health agenda.

The Mental Health Agenda

For a number of years, there has been a well-documented rise in the prevalence of mental health problems in children and young people. This includes depression, suicide rates, anorexia nervosa and other serious eating disorders, alcohol problems, drug abuse, and emotional and behavioural difficulties in general. Addressing the mental health issues of children and young people has become a central political imperative to which public agencies in health, education and social services are expected to respond, and for more than a decade it has been a government priority (Scottish Executive, 1999b).

However, it has become increasingly clear that educational psychologists are a key therapeutic resource for young people, especially in educational contexts such as schools. They are the professionals most thoroughly embedded in educational systems; they have the widest training in child and adolescent psychology; and they are therefore best poised to be generic child psychologists. Appropriate and evidence-based educational psychology practice can play a crucial role in bringing about positive change in the lives of children and young people, not only through expert individual therapeutic work but also through preventative programmes at whole-school and authority level to build young people's resilience and to promote mental wellbeing. Psychologists have also led the development of resources and quality standards in this area, such as the self-evaluation tool *How Nurturing is our School?* (Glasgow City Council, 2011).

The Physical Health Agenda

The promotion of physical health is a central priority of the Scottish Government. Its *Better Health, Better Care: Action Plan* (NHS Scotland, 2007) commits it to supporting good health choices and behaviours amongst children and young people. It has determined that 'health promotion will permeate every aspect of school life' (p. 30). Through Curriculum for Excellence children will have opportunities to take part in physical activities and learn about health and wellbeing. The Active Schools initiative aims to promote healthy, active and well-motivated communities providing new opportunities to become involved in active pursuits. Meanwhile, in a UK context, the need for a vision for health promotion could hardly be more pressing. The government's policy document, *Healthy Lives, Healthy People* (Department of Health, 2010), while offering a radical new approach to public health in England, sets out a vision for the whole of the UK. It notes that Britain has become the most obese nation in Europe, has among the worst rates of sexually transmitted infections recorded, has a relatively large population of problem drug users, has rising levels of harm from alcohol and has over 80,000 deaths every year from smoking alone.

The subject of health and educational psychology is essentially a 'greenfield site' (MacKay, 2011, p. 7), but one in which educational psychologists are well positioned to play a central role, by drawing from health psychology models that focus on the links across awareness, attitudes, intentions and behaviour, and by applying these models to supporting schools in their health promotion agenda.

THE FUTURE

Educational psychology in Scotland is a vibrant and confident profession which has success-fully embraced major changes and challenges and which anticipates a positive future. At the same time the profession faces a range of pressures and challenges. Several of these lie in the continuing tensions between 'old' and 'new' models of educational psychology. The old model was of the expert working with the individual child and relying on the widespread use of psychometric tests, particularly the intelligence test. The new model was of the col-laborative professional working in consultation with schools and organisations at systemic level. These, of course, are caricatures, and the process of change towards wider and more dynamic ways of working has been of long duration. It has been marked, however, by vast diversity of philosophy and practice between individual psychologists and across services. The tensions may be seen, for example, in conflicting views on the place of psychometrics, on the extent to which there should be a focus on working directly with the individual child and on the position of the profession in relation to the 'medical model', with some services playing no central role, for example in autism diagnostic teams, while others are an integral part of the process.

Although facing these and other tensions and challenges, educational psychology, as an integral and vital element in the local authority structure, has made a significant impact on educational policy and practice nationally. The inspection of educational psychology by HMIE (2011) concluded that across Scotland services were meeting the needs of parents and families effectively, and that they were working to the benefit of individual children and young people through intervention programmes and therapeutic approaches. They had made important contributions to the implementation of key national priorities, including the Education (Additional Support for Learning) (Scotland) Act 2004 and its 2009 amend-ments, and the *Getting it Right for Every Child* (GIRFEC) agenda. The breadth of their work gave educational psychology services a pivotal position in assisting education authori-ties in the development and implementation of policies and practice to raise educational standards for Scotland's children and young people, and in improving their achievement and transition into education, training and the world of work.

It is not only in the national but also in the international arena that the profession in Scotland has established its place (Topping et al., 2006). In looking to the future, Scottish educational psychology is poised to provide an extended range of universal services in promoting physical and mental health in schools and in the community and in contributing to the national priorities for education in Scotland, not only for those who have additional support needs but for all children and young people.

REFERENCES

Boyle, J. M. and T. A. W. N. MacKay (2010) 'The distinctiveness of Scottish educational psychol-ogy services and early pathways into the profession', *History and Philosophy of Psychology*, 12 (2): 37–48.

Burkhard, T. (2006) *A World First for West Dunbartonshire – The Elimination of Reading Failure.* London: Centre for Policy Studies.

Glasgow City Council (2011) *How Nurturing is Our School?* Glasgow: Glasgow City Council.

Her Majesty's Inspectorate of Education (2007) *Quality Management in Local Authority Educational Psychology Services: Self-Evaluation for Quality Improvement.* Livingston: HMIE.

Her Majesty's Inspectorate of Education (2011) *Educational Psychology in Scotland: Making a Difference.* Livingston: HMIE.

MacKay, T. A. W. N. (1996) 'The statutory foundations of Scottish educational psychology services', *Educational Psychology in Scotland*, 3: 3–9.

MacKay, T. A. W. N. (1999) *Quality Assurance in Educational Psychology Services: Self-Evaluation Using Performance Indicators.* Edinburgh: Scottish Executive.

MacKay, T. A. W. N. (2006) *The Evaluation of Post-School Psychological Services Pathfinders in Scotland.* Edinburgh: Scottish Executive.

MacKay, T. A. W. N. (2009) 'Post-school educational psychology services: International perspectives on a distinctive Scottish development', *Educational and Child Psychology*, 26 (1): 8–21.

MacKay, T. A. W. N. (2011) 'The place of health interventions in educational psychology', *Educational and Child Psychology*, 28 (4): 7–13.

McLean, A. (2003) *The Motivated School.* London: Sage.

McLean, A. (2009), *Motivating Every Learner.* London: Sage.

Reynolds, S., T. MacKay and M. Kearney (2009) 'Nurture groups: A large-scale, controlled study of effects on development and academic attainment', *British Journal of Special Education*, 36 (4): 204–12.

Scottish Executive (1999a) *Implementing Inclusiveness – Realising Potential.* Edinburgh: Scottish Executive.

Scottish Executive (1999b) *Social Justice: A Scotland Where Everyone Matters.* Edinburgh: Scottish Executive.

Scottish Executive (2002) *Review of Provision of Educational Psychology Services in Scotland* (the Currie Report). Edinburgh: Scottish Executive.

Sully, J. (1896) *Studies of Childhood.* London: Longmans Green.

Topping, K. (2001) *Thinking, Reading, Writing – A Practical Guide to Paired Learning with Peers, Parents and Volunteers.* London: Continuum International.

Topping, K., E. Smith, W. Barrow, E. Hannah and C. Kerr (2007) 'Professional educational psychology in Scotland', in S. Jimerson, T. Oakland and P. Farrell (eds), *The Handbook of International School Psychology.* Thousand Oaks, CA: Sage, pp. 339–50.

88

The 'People' People: The Many Roles and Professional Relationships of Social Workers

Ian Milligan

A CONTROVERSIAL BUSINESS

This chapter will offer an introduction to the social work profession and an overview of some key principles and factors that shape social work practice – 'a controversial business' (Horner, 2006, p. 2). Social work is controversial perhaps because it involves highly sensitive areas of work and the exercise of power, such as intervening in family life to protect children, providing reports for courts and Children's Hearings, or assessing people who want to foster or adopt. In such situations it is self-evident that making the 'right' decision is a challenge and whichever decisions are made are likely to leave some people unhappy and liable to criticise the social workers involved or the system they represent. Indeed, according to Horner social work 'inevitably attracts opprobrium' because of its location 'at the interface between the rights of the individual and the responsibilities of the state towards its citizens' (Horner, 2006, p. 2). It is widely accepted that social work as a whole is complex and challenging: 'Social workers undertake some of the most demanding tasks society asks of any group of staff . . . Over many years, society has come to expect more of social work and has asked social work to do more' (Scottish Executive, 2006, p. 1).

So this chapter is written in order to promote inter-professional understanding; to help *other* professionals, especially education personnel, understand how social workers approach their work. Particular emphasis will be given to the relationship-based nature of professional social work. Social workers undertake their work through building relationships with the 'service users' they work with, and working with other professionals is also an important part of the job. In broad terms, social work is required to carry out two contrasting types of function: personal support and advocacy (the care function) on the one hand and 'social control' (the protection function) on the other: 'What is apparent is that society expects social workers – and their colleagues engaged in the broader related field of social care – to both protect and care for those citizens deemed in need of such protection and care' (Horner, 2006, p. 5).

PUBLIC CRITICISM OR SUPPORT

Social workers and their profession have been the target of a great deal of public criticism associated with the deaths of young children who were 'known' to social services. There has been a series of high-profile enquiries, starting with the death of Maria Colwell in 1973, where the decisions and practices of social workers have been examined in detail and with the benefit of hindsight (see Parton, 2004, for a critical review of the role of inquiries). Maria was seven years old when she was returned from foster care to her mother and subsequently murdered by her stepfather. Responses to two recent deaths, those of 'Baby P' (Peter Connelly) and Brandon Muir, display contrasting 'treatment' of social workers from respective UK and Scottish Ministers. This may reflect a more respectful view of social workers in Scotland and an 'official' recognition of the difficulties they face. Peter Connelly was 17 months old when he died in London in August 2007, and Brandon Muir was 23 months when he died in Dundee in March 2008. Both children had been severely assaulted by the partners of their mothers, and in both cases the social workers and health professionals were criticised for failing to act timeously or effectively. It is not the intention to examine these cases here but rather to consider the respective governmental responses in the immediate aftermath. In the 'Baby P' case, the UK Minister for Children, Ed Balls, made scathing criticisms of the social workers involved and the Director of the Children's Services Department was forced to resign. When Brandon Muir died in Dundee – only shortly after the highly publicised 'Baby P' case – there was no equivalent reaction from the Scottish Minister for Children, Adam Ingram. Rather, the response of the Scottish Government was to recognise the difficult nature of the social workers' job. Both governments did require the respective local authorities to take action to improve their child protection services and they also set in train various reviews. When the Scottish enquiries reported in August 2009 the Education Secretary, Fiona Hyslop, announced the creation of a new national centre to support local child protection activity and rejected calls for legislation to ensure that more children were taken into care, and instead emphasised the need for more support for 'front-line professionals' (Scottish Government, 2009).

SOCIAL WORK AS A PROBLEM-SOLVING PARTNERSHIP

Social work is commonly seen as a 'helping' profession, and social work departments have long been established in all local authorities to provide help to those in need or difficulty in one way or another, including people with disabilities. While social workers are indeed expected to offer 'support, guidance and assistance' – in the words of the Social Work (Scotland) Act 1968 – the question of *how* that help is offered is central to understanding the roles of social workers. Social workers are trained to engage, assess and intervene in people's lives but do not believe that they should have the answers, or access to all the resources required to solve people's problems. Rather, the emphasis is on respect for people as individuals, with their own strengths and qualities as well as difficulties, and social workers will always be keen to avoid 'dependency' of service users on them. This commitment to working *with* people rather than doing things *for* them or *to* them has been reinforced in recent years by changing terminology from 'client' to 'service user'. This term seems to have been universally adopted by social workers as the 'correct' or best term to use, and to be preferable to the older term 'client'. The adoption of the term has been associated with notions of not 'labelling' people and 'empowerment', which has become a central way of thinking about work with people who are often socially excluded or marginalised (Adams et al., 2009). Some writers have criticised the term as symptomatic of a 'managerialist' turn in social work in which complex individuals with difficulties are viewed as if they were consumers of services with a range of choices (Wilson et al., 2008, p. 7). On a more positive reading the aspiration behind its use is that people should not be categorised because of their disability, or addiction, or family problem – which could lead to disrespect or discrimination – but only by the fact that they are 'using services'. The international definition of social work, accepted by the British Association of Social Workers, prefers the term 'problem solving' to 'helping' and includes the promotion of the social justice function of social work: 'The social work profession promotes social change, problem solving in human relationships and the empowerment and liberation of people to enhance well-being . . . Principles of human rights and social justice are fundamental to social work' (International Federation of Social Workers, 2000).

This definition emphasises a wider, community-development function which may apply more in low-income or 'developing' countries than in wealthier countries. Nevertheless, wherever social work is practised the focus is on individuals in need, their family relationships and resources, *and* their social context.

Since the Regulation of Care Act (2001), social work is now a fully regulated profession with a 'protected title', meaning that someone can only be called a social worker if he or she is registered with the Scottish Social Services Council (SSSC) or its equivalent across the UK. Like nurses and teachers, social workers must adhere to professional codes of conduct and meet registration requirements. They may also be prevented from working as a social worker if, following an investigative process, they are found to have seriously breached the rules and ethics of their profession. The following extract from the Code of Conduct for workers gives an indication of the multiple responsibilities that social workers have and the strong emphasis on a 'rights-based' approach to practice. Part of the Code states that social service workers must:

- protect the rights and promote the interests of service users and carers;
- strive to establish and maintain the trust and confidence of service users and carers;
- promote the independence of service users while protecting them as far as possible from danger or harm;
- respect the rights of service users whilst seeking to ensure that their behaviour does not harm themselves or other people. (Scottish Social Services Council, 2009, p. 23)

RELATIONSHIP-BASED WORK

From the time of its growth and development as a generic service in the late 1960s (Hothersall, 2006), social work was described as a 'personal social service', and the main tool at the disposal of the social worker is their relationship with the 'service user'. This is a professional relationship oriented around addressing specific issues or problems. Sometimes the relationship will be very short-term, for example while carrying out an initial assessment. Where social workers have a longer-term relationship with their service users, the latter may sometimes refer to their social worker as a friend. Social workers are usually very uncomfortable about being described as a friend, and certainly do not think of themselves in that way – but nevertheless the notion of being a 'friendly professional' (Wilson et al., 2009, p. 2) is apposite to relationship-based practice. Social workers form relationships in order to gain a non-judgemental insight into their service user's situation with a view to carrying out assessments that include client strengths as well as difficulties. While always seeking to form empathic and respectful relationships with service users, social workers will nevertheless have working relationships with many people who are not happy to be 'working' with them. Social workers will still seek to understand difficult situations non-judgementally and assess needs professionally: 'relationship-based practice involves practitioners developing and sustaining supportive professional relationships in unique, complex and challenging situations' (Wilson et al., 2008, p. 8).

Social workers also have important roles as 'gatekeepers' to services. For example, they need to make the community care assessments which determine whether an older person receives care in his or her own home or a place in a residential home. In children's services, too, social workers make recommendations to courts and Children's Hearings as to when a child should be taken into care or returned home, and in relation to criminal justice social workers act as probation officers monitoring compliance with court decisions. So it is clear that social workers have statutory functions and act on behalf of society in challenging situations. Nevertheless in all these differing aspects – providing support, assessing eligibility for services or undertaking abuse investigations – the importance of relationship-based practice continues to be affirmed by many within the profession: 'it [social work] is above all about relationships. We see at the heart of social work the provision of a relationship to help people (children, young people and adults) negotiate complex and painful transitions and decisions in their lives' (Wilson et al., 2008, p. xiii).

Other public service professionals might take issue with the emphasis in this chapter on the relationship aspect of social work. After all, are not all public servants, notably teachers, nurses and doctors, involved in relationships with the public? While this cannot be denied, it is nevertheless a feature of social work that its practitioners are expected to develop purposeful relationships with especially vulnerable or troubled 'users and carers', and carry out sensitive interventions on behalf of the wider society.

Social workers also have to operate in multiple settings and the ability to initiate constructive relationships in many different contexts is another key aspect of the social work role. Other professionals generally operate in one main type of environment: the school, the clinic, or perhaps an office or centre of some kind. Social workers, while being office-based, are expected to engage alongside others in *their* domains; the service users' homes, the school, clinic, residential home and so on. Even in situations where they are the 'lead professional' with unique roles and statutory responsibilities, such as child protection investigations or community care assessments, social workers are usually working alongside others. In child protection investigations they will often work with the police and when making care assessments they have to draw on the contributions of various others, including the GP, service user and their family. Thus it is clear that establishing effective relationships with all sorts of people constitutes a large part of the social work role. In consequence, communicating effectively and honestly about sensitive personal matters, verbally and in writing, is a key skill.

GENERIC TRAINING FOR SPECIALIST TASKS

Social workers are trained to intervene on the basis of values including respect, empowerment, dignity, partnership and so on, and to avoid punitive or patronising approaches. To acquire these skills social workers now need to qualify through a degree-level training programme. It is important to note that this training is of a generic kind; it is intended to equip prospective social workers to operate in any of the areas mentioned above. Since the 1960s, the educational level of a social work qualification has progressed from a higher education 'certificate' to 'diploma', and since 2003 to honours degree level. A leading social work academic who examined the impact of the honours degree on the profession has claimed that the introduction of an honours degree 'is due recognition that social work requires not only practitioners who have skills in human relationships, but that these skills have to be underpinned by theory and knowledge about the complexity of these relationships' (Orme and Coulshed, 2006, p. 1).

In recent years there has been an increasing emphasis on involving service users and carers very directly in the training of social workers. The 'user and carer' formula denotes the fact that social workers usually have to engage with the subject of their intervention *and* the people who are that person's immediate carers. These carers have sometimes banded together and campaigned for better services and for their perspectives to be listened to. 'Carer' voices have been especially prominent in areas such as learning disabilities. Similarly, the 'user' voice has been particularly prominent among adults with physical disabilities and those with mental health problems. People in these situations have formed self-help groups and campaigning organisations seeking to influence social policy, and they are often critical of the way that social work services are provided, for example, Shaping Our Lives, 'a national network of service users and disabled people'. The influence of such voices can be seen in the fact that the regulations governing the training of social workers now require the involvement of 'users and carers' in all aspects of the training, from involvement in student selection to contributions to the curriculum (Scottish Executive, 2003). Social work training includes, of course, specific theories and practice skills related to work with people of all ages and with a wide range of difficulties, needs and rights. However, it also includes a considerable emphasis on inter-professional or collaborative working, which is considered further below. Knowledge of the law, human rights and the application of government guidance is also major focus of training. Other public sector professionals may be surprised by the extent to which social workers in their daily work will have familiarity with specific pieces of legalisation and will often be following specific policies and procedures: 'law and social policy affect practice at almost every turn' advises a recent textbook for social work students (Hothersall, 2006, p. 3).

INTER-PROFESSIONAL PRACTICE

As already noted, social workers often spend a considerable portion of their time interacting with other professionals, including police officers, housing officials and early years workers as well as school teachers and health personnel. While each profession has its distinct identity and focus of work, it is important for professionals to have a basic understanding of each other's roles so that shared work can be undertaken on the basis of up-to-date knowledge of the other and not just out-of-date impressions or even prejudices. Another reason for gaining an insight into the perspective and key tasks of other professional groups is that greater collaboration and the desire for 'joined-up working' has been a major theme of policy makers and governments for some time (Milligan and Stevens, 2006; Quinney, 2006). Governments have been pushing for more inter-professional collaboration because it is believed that no one department or service can successfully tackle some of the persistent and serious social problems such as drug and alcohol addiction and protecting children from parental neglect. Nevertheless despite the obvious appeal (to policy makers) of encouraging professionals to work together, there is less clarity about what this means in practice in the face of the continuing existence of separate professions with their own focus of work:

> While it is clear that a lack of collaborative working can lead to failures to protect vulnerable people, there is not yet a body of research evidence to demonstrate when and how learning and working together with other professionals leads to more effective and safer practice. (Quinney, 2006, p. 7)

Whether it is a first referral or an ongoing case, social workers are usually involved in a process of assessment, intervention and then re-assessment. To do this properly they need to get a rounded picture of a child or adult's difficulties and so typically they will be in phone contact with health visitors, where there is concern about a baby or toddler, or teachers in the case of older children. The health visitors and teachers may in fact have been the ones who raised the child welfare concern in the first place. Social workers often have two contrasting aspects to their engagement with school staff. On the one hand they will be seeking information – perhaps requesting a report – about the child's behaviour or educational progress; on the other hand they may be giving some information about the child's family situation or perhaps advocating for the child following a period of absence or exclusion.

However, there is one key difference between social work and health or education, in that the latter two are universal services – they actually serve the whole population and are for the most part valued. Generally speaking, using these services does not carry any stigma, apart perhaps from the mental health field. Social work, by contrast, is not a universal service. It is open to anyone who needs a service but its remit is a targeted or selective one. It is a service that protects vulnerable children and adults and channels services to them with the aim of helping them to the point where they no longer need assistance. Social work services also play an important role in other areas of child welfare such as the provision of long-term 'respite care' for children with serious or multiple disabilities. Services such as respite care, or 'short-break' services as they are now known, are generally popular with families and much in demand. However, when social workers intervene in family life there is usually considerable stigma associated with the process. Social workers are expected to counter stigma and discrimination and must show respect for, and offer support to, vulnerable, difficult and sometimes dangerous people. They bring this with them to the work of professional collaboration. While not denying for a moment that teachers and nurses too have professional obligations not to discriminate, it is often the social worker's job to advocate on behalf of people whom other professionals find difficult.

WORKING WITH CHILDREN AND FAMILIES

> At one level, the whole area of dealing with child abuse and neglect is a highly regulated and formalised state activity with formal mechanisms (broadly referred to as 'child protection procedures') in place, underpinned by legislation to be adhered to by all social workers, particularly those with statutory responsibilities. On the other hand, dealing with a child who has been abused or neglected, whose parents may deny involvement in this and who are angry and frightened is a very personal, 'in your face' experience which is fluid, subjective, messy and scary; something very difficult to regulate. (Hothersall, 2006, p. 73)

Where a child's wellbeing is the focus of concern the social worker will seek to work with the parent(s) to identify the issues that are leading to the child being neglected or abused, and the quotation above gives an excellent sense of what that involves for the social worker, and why it is such a demanding task. Many families will be affected by drug or alcohol addiction, mental illness or domestic violence. Other parents may be vulnerable because of a learning disability and lack of family or community support. Sometimes parents are willing to work voluntarily with a social worker, but often social workers have to compile reports which are submitted to the Children's Hearing system for consideration as to whether 'compulsory measures of supervision' may be required. In these situations the Children's Hearing may decide either to place a child in care or keep him or her at home but require the social worker to provide supervision, through regular visits that can range from monthly to much more frequently when there is a high level of concern about a child's wellbeing. Supervision orders imposed by the Children's Hearing will run for a maximum of one year though they can be, and often are, renewed. When working with a child and his or her family the social worker will aim to increase the capacity of the parent(s) to provide good enough care for their child. If parents are willing and able to acknowledge the problem the social worker tries to identify strengths and resources that the parents have and the network they might be able to draw on. So social work is always seeking to find a way to strengthen the family and when it is assessed that the child is safe and the family are providing appropriate levels of care, then social work will withdraw. They may help them access resources, such as drug counselling or benefits advice, or practical help in terms of replacing furniture and so on. Social workers can also provide service users with small cash payments in emergency situations. This is justified when the provision of a small payment – typically for food or electricity – can prevent an admission to care of a child or sibling group with all the disruption, distress and costs associated with even a short stay in care.

Although they have a child protection function and can in extreme cases take a child into care against the parents' wishes, the aim of social work intervention is to keep children within their birth family and to provide parents with the support that will enable them to keep their child safe. Thus social workers will usually try hard to keep families together, even when other professionals might feel that things are going seriously wrong and children are suffering the effects of neglect or inadequate parenting. While some children are relieved to be taken away from intolerable circumstances others often say that they want to remain with their parents and only for the abuse or neglect to stop.

Nevertheless it is important to note that significant numbers of children *are* taken into care or, in the official jargon, become 'looked after away from home'. In fact the numbers of children 'looked after' have been increasing steadily since the early 2000s and the most recent statistics show around 16,000 children in Scotland are 'looked after' at any one time, around 1.5 per cent of the population aged 0 to 18 (Scottish Government, 2012). Out of these children, 5,400, or 33.9 per cent, will be in the 'looked after at home' category. Of the remainder around 5,300 children are in foster care, with a further 4,000 or so placed, on the decision of the Children's Hearing, with family or friends (kinship care). There will be a further 1,500 children in residential care, either children's home or special residential school, and another small group of children are adopted each year. It is difficult to summarise the 'care journey' of these children. They are in fact a very heterogeneous group; some are young babies but many are teenagers. Some will only have a short period of time in care before being reunited with their family, while others will spend many years in care. For a small number of young children the local authority is faced with the difficult problem of finding a permanent placement when it is decided by the court that they are to be placed for adoption against their parents' wishes. Traditionally this option has been pursued for a small number of children, but in recent years, particularly with regard to the impact of heroin addiction on some parents with young children, it has been necessary to make more decisions to find permanent alternative families via adoption or long-term fostering.

THE EDUCATION OF CHILDREN IN CARE

Since the publication of the *Learning with Care* report (Her Majesty's Inspectors of Schools and Social Work Services Inspectorate, 2001) the education of 'looked-after children' has been a focus of policy making (Scottish Executive, 2007) and subsequently service innovation (Connelly et al., 2008) and practice development (Scottish Government, 2008). The fact that children who were under social work supervision, and may have spent considerable periods in foster or residential care, were doing so badly in terms of their educational attainment was seen as an indictment of both social work and education services. While getting precise data about the levels of educational attainment of 'looked-after children' is difficult, the Scottish Government has been requiring local authorities to report on these annually. Evidence from the annual 'Looked After Children' statistics supports professional experience that many children in care were falling well behind by their early secondary years (Scottish Government, 2004), few were taking Highers and one figure from 2008 suggested that only 2.6 per cent of looked-after children progressed directly to university compared to 35.5 per cent of peers (Scottish Government, 2008). (See Chapter 89 for a more detailed account of this topic.)

As a result the government decided that there must be improvement in this aspect of care, and published a report entitled *We Can and Must Do Better* (Scottish Executive, 2007). What was striking about this policy drive was that both social service workers and teachers were being addressed simultaneously. Social workers were told that they must have higher aspirations for the children in their care and not just write off their educational chances because they faced major personal and family problems. Social workers were now expected to monitor educational progress closely and understand how well a child was doing compared to other children of the same age. The residential and foster carers were also expected to do much more to provide 'educationally rich environments' in their homes and actively support homework and encourage children's learning through the provision of wider social and educational opportunities. Similarly, schools were told that they must not have low expectations of children simply because they were in care and had very difficult backgrounds. Rather, they were expected to know who the looked-after children were in school, and then to monitor their progress providing such additional support as might be needed. Indeed, new roles were created for schools – each school was to identify a 'designated manager' whose task was to be a 'champion' for the looked-after children in their school. However, there is little evidence yet about how effective this strategy is or whether it is simply that one more policy-driven responsibility has been added to the many others held by senior school staff.

These developments illustrate the way that social workers are expected to go beyond merely working with, or alongside, other professionals, and instead should really engage (on their child's behalf) with the education system. It is no longer sufficient simply to get a child to attend school, which might have been the emphasis in the past.

CONCLUSION

Social work is a challenging profession and commonly involves working with members of society who are affected by poverty and exclusion combined with significant health difficulties or serious personal or family problems. The UK continues to be a very unequal society and the effects of inequality confound policy makers in many fields including health, education, housing and social welfare. In recent years, central government has made the reduction in child poverty a priority but progress has been slow and targets are not being met. Many of the previous societal responses to disability, mental ill health and child maltreatment involved separation of people from the mainstream – in long-stay hospitals, day centres or special schools. These types of 'solution' have been rejected in favour of maintaining people within families and communities whenever possible and retaining only a small number of separate centres or institutions to deal with exceptional circumstances. There is widespread agreement that people with disabilities and disadvantages should not be segregated from society if at all possible and should have their needs for care and support, health and housing, education and employment met in 'normal' or mainstream environments. Even when children do need to be removed from their own home, the alternative is to be used for as limited a time as possible. Similarly, for older people the greatest emphasis is on developing services that allow people to remain in their own homes for as long as possible. While these trends present huge challenges for those such as community nurses and GPs, in the area of health, and for school staff in terms of the presumption of mainstreaming, the social work contribution is critical across both these professional domains. The social work role involves assessing need and acting both as a gatekeeper and a monitor of service delivery for some of the most disadvantaged or 'challenging' people in society.

In all these arenas professionals are likely to find that they expected to work together in the support of people in need and to provide services in an inclusive and non-stigmatising way. Wherever this is happening you will find social workers. They have a unique role, but they cannot usually achieve good results on their own and they are often accountable in diverse directions: to service users, to the State that employs them and to civil society. They are acting as agents of the local state, on behalf of society as a whole, to assess risk and meet crisis situations, while they are also seeking to help their service users to claim their rights and access services to which they are entitled. The job cannot be made easy but it can be made easier and more effective if other professionals take the time to understand their role and demonstrate a willingness to work collaboratively with them.

REFERENCES

Adams, R., L. Dominelli and M. Payne (2009) *Social Work: Themes, Issues and Critical Debates* (3rd edn). Basingstoke: Palgrave Macmillan.
Connelly, G., J. Forrest, J. Furnivall, L. Siebelt, I. Smith and L. Seagraves (2008) *The Educational Attainment of Looked After Children – Local Authority Pilot Projects: Final Research Report.* Edinburgh: Scottish Government.
Horner, N. (2006) *What is Social Work? Context and Perspectives* (2nd edn). Exeter: Learning Matters.
Hothersall, S. (2006) *Social Work with Children, Young People and their Families in Scotland.* Exeter: Learning Matters.
International Federation of Social Workers (2000) 'Definition of social work'. Online at ifsw.org/policies/definition-of-social-work/
Milligan, I. and I. Stevens (2006) *Residential Child Care: Collaborative Practice.* London: Sage.
Orme, J. and V. Coulshed (2006) *Social Work Theory and Practice* (4th edn). Basingstoke: Palgrave Macmillan/BASW.
Parton, N. (2004) 'From Maria Colwell to Victoria Climbie: Reflections on public inquiries on child abuse a generation apart', *Child Abuse Review*, 13 (2): 80–94.
Quinney, A. (2006) *Collaborative Social Work Practice.* Exeter: Learning Matters.

Scottish Executive (2003) *The Framework for Social Work Education in Scotland*. Edinburgh: Scottish Executive.

Scottish Executive (2006) *Scottish Executive Response to the 21st Century Social Work Review: Changing Lives*. Edinburgh: Scottish Executive.

Scottish Government (2004) *Children's Social Work Statistics 2003–04*. Online at www.scotland.gov.uk/Publications/2004/10/20121/45472

Scottish Government (2008) 'Destinations of leavers from Scottish schools 2007–08'. Online at www.scotland.gov.uk/Publications/2008/12/08090751/13

Scottish Government (2009) 'Death of Brandon Muir'. Press Release 19 August. Online at www.scotland.gov.uk/News/Releases/2009/08/19130947

Scottish Government (2012) 'Children's social work statistics Scotland'. Online at www.scotland.gov.uk/Resource/0038/00388582.pdf

Scottish Social Services Council (2009) 'SSSC Codes of Practice for Social Service Workers and Employers'. Online at www.sssc.uk.com/component/option,com_docman/Itemid,486/gid,1020/task,doc_details/

Wilson, K., G. Ruch, M. Lymbery and A. Cooper (2008) *Social Work: An Introduction to Contemporary Practice*. Harlow: Pearson.

Website

Shaping Our Lives: A National network of service users and disabled people at www.shapingourlives.org.uk

89

Community Education and Community Learning and Development

David Wallace and Janis McIntyre

This volume demonstrates the diverse history and aspirations for education in Scotland. Understandably, most of us readily equate 'education' with the experience of school and other institutionalised forms of further and higher education. Given this dominant experience and powerful discourse, very few of us, in thinking of education, would reflect on non-formal, informal and community-based education. Yet education takes powerful and diverse forms outwith the institutions. Community education as a field of practice systematically engages informal and non-formal education processes in the interests of achieving a wider social and democratic purpose. In this chapter, we explain the emergence of community education and subsequently community learning and development from founding principles. We set the analysis in the context of recent Scottish Government policy that, although largely taking forward programmes established by previous administrations, is emerging as a distinctive project of the two-term government of the Scottish National Party. Among contemporary developments have been the re-envisaging of the adult literacies strategy, a review of post-16 education, the development of a youth work strategy, a review of the further education college sector and the creation of a new strategy for community learning and development. Our aim here is to construct a critical portrayal of community education within this policy context and to portray a unique and vital facet of Scottish education that, at the point of writing, remains dynamic and highly relevant to aspirations for education in Scotland. Yet, as we will argue, community learning and development is in need of intellectual, material and political renewal.

LOCUS OF COMMUNITY EDUCATION AND THE SHIFT TO COMMUNITY LEARNING AND DEVELOPMENT

Founded on a canon of educational theory located predominantly in the works of Dewey, Gramsci and Freire, community education is informed by core and overlapping conceptions of community development, popular education, critical pedagogy, new literacies studies and informal education. Though these ideals in practice are countered by instrumental and economistic forms of learning, community-based education is seen as part of a broader democratic process in which education has a social purpose. An engagement with and extension of social practices, learning in community education at its purest is explicitly situated (located within the lives of participants) and socio-cultural (responsive to the cultural milieu of participants).

Social purpose democratic education is a founding principle for community education and, demonstrably, for its reincarnation as community learning and development. Successive developments in the profession and in government policy for community learning and development have reinforced ideals of social justice and self-determination – through strategies for collaborative participation and empowerment, dialogue as a foundation for practice and a concern to develop critically informed action by participants.

Representing an amalgam of discrete and loosely coupled practices in youth work, community-based adult learning and community development work, community education is organised largely through local authorities and third-sector voluntary and charitable organisations. A graduate profession since the early 1990s, it evolved from earlier professional qualifying courses in youth and community work offered by colleges of education from 1964 (notably at Moray House in Edinburgh and Jordanhill in Glasgow). Succeeding its predecessor organisation in 2009, the Community Learning and Development Standards Council for Scotland now oversees standards, training and registration for the profession. Though qualified practitioners predominantly hold professional qualifications in community education, the field of practice is now called community learning and development (CLD). The evolution of this new title grew in part from a government concern to bring together community education and community development approaches. Though the new term was first expressed in policy in Scotland in 2002, the UK-wide National Training Organisation for Community Learning and Development had been established earlier by the UK government in 1998.

No account of the evolution of community education in Scotland would be complete without reference to the influential report entitled *Adult Education – The Challenge of Change* (Scottish Education Department, 1975), which resulted from a committee of inquiry led by Professor Kenneth Alexander. Commonly referred to as the Alexander Report, it proposed the creation in Scotland of community education services bringing together for the first time adult education, youth work and community work under the one organisational and philosophical framework. Coinciding with the formation of nine new regional councils (that had strategic responsibility for education provision), the report provided the catalyst for the creation of local authority community education services in almost every corner of the country, continuing largely in this form until further local government reorganisation in 1996.

Following local authority reform in 1996 the regional councils were disbanded and thirty-two unitary authorities were created. Disaggregations, reductions in economies of scale and reprioritisations led to a period of some disruption and regrouping for community education staff, and consequently for the programmes for which they were responsible. In the new unitary authorities, community education services were no longer discrete and, impacting on continuity and identity, were often subsumed into new departments. Since then, community education has been subject to almost continual review in local authorities, has been renamed as community learning and development and is now managed and implemented across the country in a range of differing organisational forms – some retaining dedicated operational values around community education, others amalgamated into more loosely coupled community services and programmes. The social purpose and social justice locus, in the association with issues of inequality and priority groups, was initially retained but began to be dissipated by new priorities and demands of more generalised service departments and agencies.

Although non-statutory, there is a close association between community learning and development and government legislation for community planning, in which practitioners have a key role to support community participation and engagement with multi-agency strategies. Local authorities must each publish a community plan and a community learning and development strategy that are shaped by three national priorities: achievement through learning for adults; achievement through learning for young people; and achievement through building community capacity (Scottish Executive, 2004).

Working in teams or project groups, practitioners are often deployed to a particular geographical area (a locale) or have a particular catchment area (covering a number of locales). Like teachers or lecturers, they have expertise in adopting a range of educational approaches. Distinctively, however, the community educator will network in a community, develop a profile of interests and issues, seek to build working relationships and negotiate learning activities in partnership with its constituents. Practitioners are also involved routinely in partnership work with schools and learning communities and with other agencies such as housing associations, health boards and further education colleges. Normally there is engagement with forums established to ensure interdisciplinary practice and to coordinate local community and neighbourhood policy priorities. Further, practitioners network and engage at neighbourhood level with a wide range of volunteers and community leaders, supporting and resourcing community-based learning which is connected to forms of activism, to local needs assessment and to addressing the issues and interest of local residents. Practice may take place in community centres, in other public facilities such as libraries, in schools, in youth centres and in neighbourhood project bases – occasionally in purpose-built premises but more consistently in premises converted for open access or general community use. Although imbued with universal and egalitarian purposes, the work is not currently organised as a universal service. Rather, fieldwork practitioners are remitted to enact social justice priorities and engage with those for whom structural inequality and discrimination shape their lived experiences. Characteristically the confidence and knowledge gained from this process represents a transformational experience for participants, developing voice and agency that until involvement remained dormant or suppressed (Taylor, 2011, p. 210).

COMMUNITY EDUCATION AND COMMUNITY LEARNING AND DEVELOPMENT – IMPACT OF POLICY

A series of developments initiated immediately following the inception of the UK Labour givernment in 1997 and the Labour-led devolved government in 1999 suggested that community education was a central concern for government in Scotland (Scottish Office, 1998; Scottish Executive, 2004). Community education, in principle, resonated with New Labour priorities for lifelong learning, social inclusion and active citizenship. A high priority was consequently accorded to community education in policy discourse. Broadly, though nuanced by revised political relations between local and national government, these priorities have been retained through two successive periods of Scottish National Party government (from 2007). Although welcomed initially by those who had invested professionally in the field of practice, this renewed impetus, including the adoption of the new term 'community learning and development', also heralded subtle but far-reaching shifts in the narrative. These shifts embody a number of issues for the community education value base, and for the practice of CLD.

The first and perhaps most fundamental of these shifts grew out of a policy development in 1998 in which community education was promoted by the then Scottish Executive as an approach or way of working rather than a discrete sector of education. This reflected an urge to promote the wider development of community education principles and practices. However, a crucial if largely unplanned implication of this was that practitioners qualified as community educators saw claims being made to community-based approaches that were inconsistent with the values and principles of the profession. There were also those for whom such approaches were subsidiary to their core business and main agency functions. Therefore, community education became a method that could be adopted by others working with individuals and groups in communities, with no safeguards in place about preserving the value base or ensuring professional practice. Indeed, some employers no longer saw the professional qualification as essential to full-time posts in the field of community education. That this still resonates is evident in the need to clearly define CLD as a profession, as high-lighted by the Standards Council for CLD in its recent discussions related to the creation of a professional register of practitioners.

Further legislation introduced in 1999 required local authorities to publish community-learning plans for their area. A central aspect of this was that local residents were to be involved in the creation of the plans. A key role was identified for CLD practitioners to support individuals and groups to engage in the community planning process. Although contested as service-led rather than community-led (delivering participants to policy rather than the other way around), the close connection to community planning made a new and direct correlation between the practices of CLD and the more efficient coordination of local services. Existing staff resources, which were already fairly thinly spread, were not replenished to meet these new and additional commitments.

Since the establishment of community education, policy statements have continued to emphasise the importance of this area of work being community-based. There is a virtue in practice that may be expressed as *in* the community, *with* the community and *for* the community. However, Tett (2010) has noted that in recent CLD policy this definition of community is being more narrowly expressed as geographical neighbourhoods. The effect is to limit the focus, in policy and in practice, to local concerns, which are important but which can be inappropriately isolated from their more general or structural context (for example environmental issues, housing issues, economic issues). Ignoring other conceptions of community, such as communities of interest or online communities, also undervalues vital associational and shared concerns that transcend the locale. Concerns that may have regional, national or global dimensions – and which may sustain the yeast of education and democracy – are largely excluded from official CLD discourses and, axiomatically, from official practices.

In common with a number of related sectors, a further shift in policy has been a move away from the emphasis on the *process* of engaging with individuals and communities and a move towards a focus on measurable *outcomes* for programmes in which they engage. A consequence of this has been an increased interest in the use of a framework for inspection of CLD practice that emphasises the outcomes and impact of CLD work. Expected outcomes are described in detail, making CLD much more limited and open to scrutiny and regulation (Tett, 2010, p. 26). A consequence for CLD can be that some practitioners feel pressured to focus and report on quantifiable aspects of this work such as concentrating on what are seen as more accountable pre-packaged programmes (for example the upsurge in youth workers who are required to offer programmes such as the Duke of Edinburgh Awards and Prince's Trust schemes).

The problem here is that we observe service shifts that suggest a move away from more open-ended engagements founded on mutuality and trust, dialogue and informal education. If funding or inspection requires product (for example certification) it is difficult, if not impossible, for practitioners to justify other negotiated or critical practices on the grounds of principle. In such a scenario the crucial time spent in building and sustaining working relationships and networks in a particular community is underestimated and undervalued. This is a vital issue especially when appreciating that highly skilled practitioners engage with the most impoverished of social circumstances and in areas displaying greatest indices of deprivation.

The implementation of Curriculum for Excellence has become an overarching concern for educational practitioners in and out of school. The articulation of Curriculum for Excellence aspirations – young people developing capacities as successful learners, confident individuals, responsible citizens and effective contributors to society – closely aligns with CLD practices and principles. Coburn and Wallace (2011, p. 24) recorded that youth work practitioners and managers within CLD welcomed Curriculum for Excellence as validating work they were already engaging in. The practitioners' expertise in experiential, situated and informal forms of community-based education means they are well placed to advance Curriculum for Excellence priorities. Whether this becomes a nascent border pedagogy (Coburn and Wallace, 2011, p. 42), bridging formal and informal education, depends heavily on whether the confines and values of formal education are truly being made more permeable through Curriculum for Excellence.

COMMUNITY EDUCATION AND COMMUNITY LEARNING AND DEVELOPMENT – PRINCIPLES IN PRACTICE

In its contemporary manifestation the stated aim of CLD work is to support people to tackle issues that affect them, through community action and community learning (Scottish Executive, 2004). Practitioners are routinely identified with these ideals and though drawn from a wide range of backgrounds have often had prior experience as volunteers and activists, youth workers or tutors. However, outside policy, contrasting perspectives on the role and purpose of community education can be found. On the one hand the focus may be on the interests of the individual, while on the other, the work is centred on supporting the collective and working towards a democratic society. Tett (2010) identified three approaches to community education practice: universal, reformist and radical. In the universal model, the community educator provides learning and development opportunities open to the whole of the population. As we have seen, this approach has not been strongly evident in practice. Instead, the priority has been to ensure that scarce resources are targeted to particular disadvantaged and excluded groups, an approach supported in policy and characterised as reformist. Here, the role identified for community education is in supporting participants to develop skills and self-confidence in order to combat disadvantage or exclusion. The key purpose for community education in the reformist model is the provision of learning opportunities for individuals, families and groups with the aim of supporting personal development that may lead to personal, social or economic gains.

In the radical tradition, the practitioner holds a structural view of injustice and inequality and works with communities to take action for social change. From this perspective, the practitioner works with individuals and groups with the aim of developing critical consciousness in order to initiate action on inequality and to affect change in society. The radical tradition in community education has been strongly influenced by the work of Brazilian educator Paulo Freire, whose seminal empowering approach was to support learners to critically understand their world – developing new levels of consciousness in order to be able to change it (Freire, 1970). Freire's approach was to work alongside learners, building a curriculum that was rooted in their lived experience and on critically informed action. However, although a strong tradition, the numbers of practitioners working predominantly within the radical perspective in Scotland are relatively small. In terms of Taylor's classification (2011, p. 187) the core focus in practice may be expressed as the development of social capital (networks and norms established through building relational capacity) with an increasing emphasis on human capital (located in the development of individual skills and knowledge). Organisational capital (expressed through the habits of organising and the willingness to take action) appears to be a strong principle but is afforded least priority in CLD policy discourse and practice.

Whichever perspective is held, the approach in community education practice is underpinned by a theoretical analysis of informal education. Jeffs and Smith (2005) have argued that informal and formal educators share a common aim in that both seek to foster learning. They emphasise that whilst informal educators sometimes adopt formal methods in their work, their concern with fostering learning in everyday social situations (2005, p. 25) marks them out as informal educators. The purpose of informal education is defined as working with people to encourage them to learn from and build on their experiences. The emphasis here is on *working with* people, as opposed to *working on* them, calling for a core empathy and concomitant value base. Implicit in and central to these theories of informal education is a commitment to the sharing of power between educators and learners in order that 'they become jointly responsible for a process in which all grow' (Freire, 1970, p. 61).

CURRENT ISSUES AND CHALLENGES IN CLD

A CLD workforce survey undertaken by Lifelong Learning UK (LLUK) in 2010 provided information on 9,460 individuals involved in the implementation of CLD programmes in Scotland. Worryingly, the survey highlighted a 23 per cent decrease in paid local authority staff compared to a similar survey in 2008. LLUK has identified a potentially deleterious trend in which the sustainability of CLD provision nationally is in doubt. We must at least consider the potential effect of this and express concern about what may accumulate as a strategic running-down of provision. These apparent reductions in staffing levels have come at a time when an SNP government concordat with local authorities allows greater discretion on local funding priorities in return for agreement on national initiatives, such as a freeze on council tax and for planning around fifteen single-outcome agreements. The risk here is that CLD as a national entity will be susceptible to further local restructuring or reductions in a service that is vulnerable because of its non-statutory position.

Although there has never been a fully consistent pattern of CLD provision across the country, discontinuity of provision across neighbourhoods and across local authority areas is increasingly the norm. While diversity is to be welcomed where it leads to innovation and creativity in the development of learning opportunities, in some local authority areas reductions in funding and reorganisation have led to scarcity in provision with fewer full-time qualified staff spread more thinly across an authority area. Straining democratic accountability, and adding to growing sense of fragmentation, some CLD services are now structured in arm's-length charitable companies set up by local authorities (such as in Glasgow and Highland council areas). The voluntary sector, which makes a significant contribution, is under increasing strain and struggling to retain resources for community-based learning programmes.

The period of SNP governance has been characterised, therefore, by reorganisation of services and reductions or dissipation in staffing and other resources for CLD. The result has been the diminution of CLD, with the proportion of the workforce involved in com-munity capacity-building being reported as tremendously low at 7 per cent (LLUK, 2010, p. 14). In addition to these changes, Tett (2010) has identified a trend towards full-time qualified staff moving away from direct educational practice towards supporting practice through part-time and volunteer workers.

Yet despite such an apparent downturn and other cuts in public finances, the Scottish Government continues to prioritise CLD, affording this area of work a central role in a wide range of policies in lifelong learning, adult literacies, youth work, community safety, capacity building and regeneration (Scottish Government, 2007). An allocation of £3.4m in funding for continuous professional development for CLD staff, made in 2009, further underlines this commitment. Key drivers for CLD practice continue to relate to politically informed participation, empowerment, inclusion and equality, self-determination and part-nership (Scottish Executive, 2004).

THE FUTURE

As we noted at the outset there are a number of initiatives in education policy making that are emerging at the point of writing and that will have future implications for CLD practice. We cannot at this stage determine fully the specification and impact of these on CLD. A consultation has been initiated to inform the production of a new strategy for community learning and development. In order to reinvigorate this area of education and to ensure its sustainability into the future, the new strategy would do well to respond to the following issues that were identified by CLD practitioners in a recent series of nationwide conversations, facilitated and published by the CLD Standards Council in November 2011. Examining obstacles to their contribution to advancing Scotland as a learning society, they reported the following:

- a lack of visionary thinking and leadership, both from politicians and professionals;
- a political agenda driven by short-termism, quick fixes and a search for popular solutions;
- a lack of policy coherence; silo mentalities are too evident and there is little holistic thinking;
- a culture fixated on inspections and institutions; a competitive mindset purporting to promote cooperation;
- a focus on individualism – the 'me' before 'we' society – which is more destructive of aspira-tions the current financial challenge;
- learning is not valued. There is a lack of space, in daily life and increasingly physically, for opportunities to think creatively and reflect profoundly;
- no collective voice exists for the CLD approach and there is little understanding of its processes.

However, the limited time allocated to the production of the new strategy suggests that it is unlikely to be able to address these concerns in detail. Indeed, the focus may be the role for CLD in addressing the priorities identified in other policy areas such as the post-16 education strategy and the principles advanced in the Christie commission on the future development of public services in Scotland. This latter development offers a considerable opportunity for CLD in that it conveys a cluster of recommendations concerning areas in which CLD have a proven track record, namely:

- Public services are built around people and communities, their needs, aspirations, capacities and skills and work to build up their autonomy and resilience.
- Public service organisations work together effectively to achieve outcomes.
- Public service organisations prioritise prevention, reducing inequalities and promoting equality.
- All public services constantly seek to improve performance and reduce costs and are open, transparent and accountable.

One area of concern remains the sharp focus on performance and outcomes by local and national governments – on which there may yet be government legislation. That is not to say that a high quality of service is not important in CLD (any more than it is in any comparable area) but the creation of performance measures and specification of outcomes is a highly problematic and subjective enterprise. As the practitioners in the above identify, such measures often take forms that are essentially inimical to CLD principles for practice in that they fail to take account of the CLD process that may be participative, dialogical and democratic. Neither do they readily account for the context of structural inequality in which learning takes place and the complex demands of such practices. It remains to be seen whether the new CLD strategy will seek to rein in or amplify the movement towards regulation through increased scrutiny of performance and outcomes.

It will take very careful management and political direction to avoid repeating a scenario where CLD is given a high profile in policy initiatives but is afforded limited resources with which to develop the work. As Taylor (2011, p. 3) cautions, it is important to guard against a 'spray-on' solution that covers fault lines of economic decline and social fragmentation.

The review of community planning remains to be concluded. However, the emphasis by Christie on better coordination of public services and greater community participation in their design and implementation re-emphasises the core concern for community engagement that in recent years has been a dominant factor in CLD planning. It is hoped that the new CLD strategy will acknowledge the sterling effort of practitioners thus far and address the need for the development of CLD so that it can continue to make a key contribution to the Christie recommendations.

Our analysis is that the human resources required to develop the CLD project are in decline despite social and economic indicators that point to the increasing need for professionally qualified community educators and the programmes they develop. Certainly the decline in the number of full-time staff evidenced by the LLUK survey is worrying. This leads us to question whether the central roles ascribed to CLD in national policies for lifelong learning, adult literacies, youth work and capacity building are at risk of being undermined by a failure of strategic investment. Community learning and development managers characterised their response to the new strategy by seeking support and resources to deliver their action plans.

Further evidence of the need for joined-up governance to support this enterprise is exemplified in two other related areas concerning professional qualifications and the development of practice. Adult literacies has been a central priority for CLD throughout the implementation of the Adult Literacies and Numeracy in Scotland Strategy (ALNIS) since 2001. However, despite the intent in ALNIS and in the revised adult literacies strategy to 2020, there is as yet no sustainable funding for the Professional Graduate Diploma in Education (PGDE) (Adult Literacies). If the PGDE is to be the professional standard for literacies tutoring, as appears to be the case, then it should be centrally funded in the medium to longer term. Second, inconsistency in governance has been exemplified by the decision (taken within the university) to close one of the oldest professional qualifying courses in community education at the University of Strathclyde. The central and continuing role for qualified CLD staff in vital areas of social and educational policy appears not to have militated against this decision.

CONCLUSION

Learning for work is of course highly valued and it is clear that for many participants in community learning and development an outcome of their participation is an acquisition of useful learning and the building of a range of capabilities that may be transferable – to community and family life, to further education, to training or to employment. CLD, however, has a broader social purpose and should not be configured centrally around the demands of the workforce. Further, despite the aspiration for social and economic inclusion through education, the gap between the richest and the poorest in our society is growing. Social class continues to be the main indicator of success or failure in schools and the sense of failure following school for some is compounded by a profoundly deterministic message that learning is not for them. In these alienating circumstances the seeds for learning through life are likely to fall on stony ground. However, open, creative, informal and collaborative forms of community education can provide positive and engaging starting points in the interests of individuals and groups in the community. The development of assets in citizenship, lifelong learning and community education are initiated by the conversational and associational practices of people working and learning collaboratively. Community educators engage with learners, community leaders and activists. Though rooted in informal education their programmes are nevertheless reflective, methodical and systematic – pedagogically discrete but professionally parallel to the educational practices of teachers and lecturers. It is the retention and development of such principles and practices that provide the hope of a different and more progressive discourse in education – one that at its heart is concerned with social purpose democratic education.

There does appear to be growing recognition that really useful learning is not dependent on stratified, psychological and cognitive traditions of subject-based schooling. Keying directly into humanitarian concerns about structural inequality and discrimination, we must open up education to build a more socially just and inclusive vision. To realise this vision requires a firm reiteration of the values and ethics of social purpose democratic education through community education; it requires a greater level of staffing and resources to be in place and it requires an informed and proactive political leadership at national and local level. This is a vision in which participants engage in personal and collective development, in which educators capitalise on social and cultural practices that mediate and build participation. It is a vision in which there is a common pursuit of social purpose education whose key values are 'a commitment to social justice, greater social and economic equality, and a more participatory democracy' (Johnston, 2000, p. 14). We argue here that it is this that represents the distinctive and core value base of community education and its constituent domains of informal education practice in youth work, adult learning and community work. It is this value base that remains a crucial element of community learning and development.

REFERENCES

Coburn, A. and D. Wallace (2011) *Youth Work: In Communities, and School.* Edinburgh: Dunedin Academic Press.

Freire, P. (1970) *Pedagogy of the Oppressed.* New York: Penguin Books.

Jeffs, T. and M. K. Smith (2005) *Informal Education, Conversation, Democracy and Learning* (3rd edn) Derby: Education Now.

Johnston, R. (2000) 'Community education and lifelong learning: local spice for global fare', in J. Field and M. Leicester, *Lifelong Learning – Education Across the Lifespan.* London: RoutledgeFalmer.

Lifelong Learning UK (2010) *Profile for the Community Learning and Development Workforce in Scotland 2010.* Edinburgh: LLUK

Scottish Executive (2004) *Working and Learning Together to Build Stronger communities. Scottish Executive guidance for community learning and development.* Edinburgh: Scottish Executive.

Scottish Government (2007) *Skills for Scotland. A Lifelong Skills Strategy.* Edinburgh: Scottish Government.

Scottish Office (1998) *Communities: Change through Learning.* Edinburgh: HM Stationery Office.

Taylor, M. (2011) *Public Policy in the Community* (2nd edn) Basingstoke: Palgrave Macmillan.

Tett, L. (2010) *Community Learning and Development* (2nd edn). Edinburgh: Dunedin Academic Press.

90

Multi-agency Working

Graham Connelly

Setting out the Scottish Government's ambitions for children in the autumn of 2011, the then Minister for Children and Early Years, Angela Constance, said, '[children's] services need to be personalised and focused on what the child and family need – and agencies must find better ways to work together to meet these needs' (www.scotland.gov.uk/Topics/People/Young-People/legislation/minister/keynote-address).

The theme of this chapter, like that of the Minister's speech, is what is often referred to as 'joined-up' working, the concept of professionals collaborating to provide effective services for the most vulnerable children and their families. It considers the professional imperatives for collaboration between agencies and the barriers that present significant challenges to action. The chapter begins with an outline of the policy context. This is followed by a discussion of multi-agency working in the school context and the implications for practice in the more specific context of children and young people who are 'looked after' by local authorities (see also Chapter 88).

THE POLICY CONTEXT

The broader political context lies in the statutory requirements following from the Local Government in Scotland Act 2003 giving local authorities the 'power to do things which they consider will advance well-being'. The relevant sections of the Act, in relation to the governance of children's services, are contained in Part 2 which deals with community planning. The provisions of this part of the Act give local authorities and other public bodies, such as police authorities and health boards, statutory duties to participate in community planning. Local authorities can also invite other bodies like further education colleges, universities, business and voluntary organisations, and community groups to take part in community planning. Following the election of the SNP minority administration in 2007, the new Scottish Government agreed a 'concordat' with local government collectively, the effect of which was to make a requirement for a so-called 'single outcome agreement' between each local authority and the Holyrood government. The principle behind single outcome agreements (SOAs), maintained when the SNP formed a majority administration after the 2011 election, is that funding transferred to local authorities in the annual budget settlement should not be subject to 'ring-fencing' for specific projects; the SOAs set out the locally agreed priorities, with reference to national outcomes and indicators. From the 2009–10 budget year the agreements were effectively contracts between the Scottish

Table 90.1 Extract from 'Good Governance Principles for Partnership Working' (Audit Scotland, 2011)

Key principles	Features of partnerships when things are going well	Features of partnerships when things are not going well
Clearly defined outcomes for partnership activity	Understand the needs of their local communities and prioritise these	Prioritise their own objectives over those of the partnership
Partners agree what success looks like and indicators for measuring progress	Have a clear picture what success looks like and can articulate this	Be unable to identify what success looks like
	Have clearly defined outcomes, objectives, targets and milestones that they own collectively	Fail to deliver on their partnership commitments
Partners implement a system for managing and reporting on their performance	Have a system in place to monitor, report to stakeholders and improve their performance	Don't have agreed indicators for measuring each partner's contribution and overall performance or do not use monitoring information to improve performance
	Demonstrate that the actions they carry out produce the intended outcomes and objectives	Be unable to demonstrate what difference they are making

Source: www.audit-scotland.gov.uk

Government and local community planning partnerships, representing key public services. In devising the SOAs, community partnerships typically consulted stakeholders, such as local businesses, representative bodies and service users.

There are fifteen 'national outcomes', including, for example, the commitment to improve the life chances of children, young people and families at risk. The method of assessing progress against outcomes is to use data related to 'national indicators'. For example, Indicator 5.2.67 tracks the 'Percentage of Looked After Children school leavers in positive and sustained destinations'. (Information about outcome agreements, outcomes and indicators is available from the Improvement Service; see www.improvementservice. org.uk)

A report in 2011 by Audit Scotland examined the role of community planning partnerships specifically in relation to economic development but also made recommendations that are more generally applicable to the governance of partnership working. These include a set of 'good governance principles for partnership working' intended for use in auditing the performance of community planning partnerships. Table 90.1 shows, for illustration, principles for performance measurement and management, one of four aspects outlined in the report (the others being behaviours, processes and use of resources).

The area of government policy in relation to services for children which is most dependent upon these principles is what has become known as the *Getting it Right for Every Child* (GIRFEC) approach. This has several aims but one of these is particularly dependent on effective multi-agency working – the recognition of the importance of drawing help towards the child rather than passing the child from one service to another (see www.scotland.gov. uk/Publications/2010/07/19145422/0).

Achieving this aim, according to policy guidance, is facilitated by giving significant responsibilities for the overall wellbeing of children to the so-called 'universal services' of health and education. In essence, the GIRFEC approach intends to encourage professionals to view the child as part of a wider system comprising family and community, to be vigilant towards the child's broader developmental needs and to avoid a child at risk of neglect or abuse disappearing from the professional 'radar'. The GIRFEC system aims to do this, among other approaches, by appointing a 'named person', usually a health visitor for pre-school children and the headteacher or other senior manager in a school setting. The role of the named person includes ensuring that 'core' information, such as where the child lives and the details of the principal carers, is accurate and acting as a conduit or advocate to access additional support for the family. According to the authors of a report outlining the experience of a 'pathfinder' trial of the GIRFEC approach in the Highland Council area, the named person role allowed children's needs to be identified earlier, to be supported longer within universal services and consequently to need targeted help for shorter periods, and to be critical in supporting the transition from single to multi-agency support (Stradling et al., 2009). A second key role envisaged by GIRFEC is the 'lead professional', where more than one service is involved with the child. Both roles may be performed by the same professional, though government guidance suggests it may be appropriate to transfer the lead role to a specialist service, typically a social work agency. The rationale for not automatically transferring the role when specialist services become involved includes countering the assumption that responsibility for a child's welfare should always be passed to social workers when difficulties arise.

Similar approaches are in operation in other countries; what appears to be unusual, if not unique, about the Scottish approach is the provision for all children to have a named person. At the time of writing, GIRFEC had not been implemented in all local authorities, but the assumption that universal provision is a good thing has been challenged. The journalist Kenneth Roy, writing in a critique that spanned two issues of the online journal *Scottish Review* in 2010, argued that the purported virtues of GIRFEC 'have been swallowed whole without proper scrutiny of the claims or, more generally, of the underlying agenda' (see archive at www.scottishreview.net). Roy's main concerns relate to the 'intrusion into privacy' and the 'establishment of a vast database of personal information about our children' which he contends raise both practical and ethical concerns.

It is important to remember that the GIRFEC approach is a means to an end, an attempt to provide a framework, or set of systems, for professional practice in relation to the safety and wellbeing of children, and not an end in itself. The assumptions underlying such a systemic approach have important implications for the way in which professionals employed by different agencies, and influenced by different forms of training and workplace cultures, collaborate in the best interests of children and their families. Experience from the Learning in and for Interagency Working Study (LIW) suggests that two changes are demanded of professionals in doing inter-agency work. First, practitioners learnt that they needed to look beyond the boundaries of their organisations at what else was going on in children's lives and, at the very least, to develop some understanding of how other professionals interpreted specific children, their needs and strengths. Second, this outward-looking stance was accompanied by a revived focus on individual children with complex lives who were interconnected with their families and communities. The complexity of children's worlds was no longer hidden from practitioners by their looking at them using the narrow lenses of a tightly focused profession (Edwards et al., 2009, pp. 9–10). The implications of inter-agency working for schools are discussed in the following section.

MULTIPLE AGENCIES AND THE SCHOOL CONTEXT

There is a long history in Scotland of recognition of the importance of joint working between education, social work, health and other agencies. The Kilbrandon Report of 1964, famous for proposing what subsequently became the system of Children's Hearings (www.scotland.gov.uk/Publications/2003/10/18259/26875), envisaged a specialist 'social education department' within local authorities, bringing together all children's welfare services. Although this recommendation was not implemented, the principle of collaboration was established in youth strategies during the 1970s and 1980s, and more recently was the basis of New Community Schools (NCS). For a fuller account of the history of inter-agency collaboration in children's services in Scotland, see Cohen (2005). French (2007) says that multi-agency working involves partnership and integration. Partnerships, she says, are 'working relationships in which different groups of people work together to support the child and family' (pp. 47–8). This vision of joint working underlined the previous Labour–Liberal Democrat administration's plan to have all publicly funded schools designated as Integrated Community Schools (ICS), based on the experience of the NCS initiative. The official evaluation of the pilot programme was not encouraging, however, in relation to the initial success of NCS in promoting multi-agency working. Unsurprisingly, the researchers found that commitment by staff, managers and partners was an important success factor, but they also uncovered considerable barriers, including differences in working hours and holiday arrangements between professional groups, differences in understandings about professional matters such as confidentiality, and difficulties in finding time to meet to discuss different perceptions of practice and to plan joint strategies. Effective multi-agency staff development was regarded as contributing to improved collaborative working, but the evaluation pessimistically concluded that 'the overall extent to which NCS projects had contributed to multi-agency training for the specific needs of vulnerable children was reported as fairly limited' (Sammons et al., 2003). Baron (2001) has been critical of a tendency towards 'increasing professionalisation of the issues of deprivation' (p. 100). In contrast to an approach which Baron characterises as state centralisation of power, a more democratic account of the potential of multi-agency working in a community school context is outlined by Illsley and Redford (2005). The project they described, based in an NCS in Perth in central Scotland, was explicitly aimed at empowering families through building and sustaining relationships in very practical ways, such as phone calls and the use of humour. The authors report a resultant 'belief in the "ordinariness" of education' and evidence of equality of power in the 'growing number of occasions when parents have approached staff and included them in their social occasions' (p. 165).

In a review of inter-agency working conducted for the Irish government, Statham (2011) concludes that this practice is becoming increasingly common in children's services internationally and is widely regarded as improving the quality of services and support offered to children and their families. She cautions that there is so far limited evidence of improved outcomes for children and families resulting from this way of working, but that there is promising evidence from many countries on the benefits of a more joined-up approach in improving professional practice and providing better support at an earlier stage for children and families who need it.

As the NCS initiative in Scotland found, there are significant barriers to multi-agency working, but what are the factors that facilitate it? Two sources are helpful in this regard: Statham (2011) identified eleven 'enablers' of joint working in her review of the research literature; meanwhile Cassidy, in a study in four Scottish local authorities, constructed a set of seven pairs of factors capable of 'driving and shaping the scope, pace and progress of embedding integrated working in children's services' (2008, p. 9). Unsurprisingly, the two studies identified broadly similar characteristics. When the two lists are amalgamated, twelve conditions for effective multi-agency working emerge, as listed below.

- being clear about the purpose of multi-agency work;
- vision and leadership, with identified 'champions' and dedicated posts for developing capacity in collaborative working;
- having a commitment to joint working among managers and practitioners;
- experiencing a culture of collaboration and willingness to develop new professional identities;
- making efforts to develop strong personal relationships and trust between partners;
- achieving clarity about roles and responsibilities;
- putting efforts into maintaining good communication;
- providing opportunities for joint/multi-professional training;
- having good experiences of inter-professional working and opportunities to develop and practise the skills needed for this type of work;
- willingness to restructure and develop services in ways required to meet children's needs;
- having clear procedures for information sharing, including databases;
- providing opportunities for secondments between services, or having services co-located in one building.

These twelve conditions in general reflect the perspectives of practitioners and it is important to recognise that the perspectives of service users are paramount, and may be rather different. Some of these characteristics are discussed further in the next section in which multi-agency working is examined within the specific context of a group of children whose generally poor outcomes have become a major concern among politicians, policy makers and practitioners.

MULTI-AGENCY WORKING AND LOOKED-AFTER CHILDREN

Being 'looked after' typically means a child is provided with compulsory measures of 'supervision' as defined by the Children (Scotland) Act 1995, though some children become looked after under voluntary agreements. Compulsory measures are actions taken for the 'protection, guidance, treatment or control' of children under a set of conditions (such as lack of parental care, failure to attend school regularly, committing an offence) specified in Section 52 (2) of the Act. In Scotland in 2011, more than 16,000 children were looked after. This figure accounted for 1.5 per cent of all children up to the age of 18 across the country, although the proportions of looked-after children are higher in the larger cities (for example, 2.8 per cent in Glasgow). The process of becoming looked after involves a Children's Hearing, at which a panel of three volunteer members of the community considers background reports and listens to the views of the child, family members and professionals. If the panel concludes that compulsory measures of care are necessary it will specify whether these should be provided 'at home', i.e. with the child remaining in the usual family home (about 40 per cent of all looked-after children) or 'away from home'. Half of all children looked after away from home live in family-type settings, either with foster carers or potential adoptive parents, or in so-called 'kinship' settings where a member of the close or extended family is officially recognised as the main carer. A minority (about 10 per cent)

Table 90.2   Attendance of children continuously looked after for twelve months (June 2011)

Placement	Percentage attendance
Looked after at home	78.7
Residential care in local authority homes	84.0
Foster care by local authority	96.3
Foster care in independent or private sector placements	95.9
All children	93.2

Source: www.scotland.gov.uk/Publications/2011/06/23123831/0

lives in group settings, including residential homes in the community (also called 'units', young people's centres or children's houses), residential schools and secure care settings. This figure is an average, however, and when age is taken into account foster care is more common as a placement for younger children and residential care for older children. For example, 20 per cent of 12- to 15-year-old looked-after children live in residential settings, compared with less than 3 per cent of 5–11-year-olds and a negligible proportion of under-5s. The overall proportion of looked-after children cared for in group settings has been falling over a period of many years in comparison with increasing proportions of children living in foster and kinship placements. For example, in 1976, while 36 per cent of looked-after children lived in residential settings, 22 per cent were in foster care (see www.scotland.gov.uk/Topics/Statistics/Browse/Children).

Looked-after children are at risk of poor physical and mental health, low educational attainment and unemployment. One indicator of poor outcomes in the educational context is school attendance. Table 90.2 shows the percentage attendance of children who were looked after continuously for twelve months during 2010–11. What is evident is that children in foster care typically attend well (better than the average for all children) but that children in local authority children's homes have below average school attendance and those remaining with their families while on home supervision orders have considerably below average attendance. The attendance of looked-after children has improved in recent years, as has their attainment, though the gap in attainment between looked-after children and all children has not decreased. Concerns about the generally poor educational outcomes of looked-after children prompted the Education and Culture Committee of the Scottish Parliament to conduct an inquiry. (Interested readers can access the evidence presented to the Committee, among which the official SPICe Briefing by Camilla Kidner (26 October 2011) is particularly recommended, and the Inquiry report, at the Parliament website; see www.scottish.parliament.uk).

Among five implications for practice identified by the Committee was the need for greater joined-up working between agencies. Its members noted that while the necessary legislation and policies were in place, these needed to be better implemented. The key policies are contained in the 2007 government report, *Looked After Children: We Can and Must do Better* (www.scotland.gov.uk/Publications/2007/01/15084446/0). Multi-agency working, according to the report, means local authorities and their partners acting as 'good corporate parents', a term that implies that representatives of the state perform a quasi-parental role in their actions towards and on behalf of looked-after children. The expectations of corporate parents in different agencies are specified in the 2008 practice guide, *These are our Bairns* (www.scotland.gov.uk/Publications/2008/08/29115839/0) A number of factors appear to be critical in determining the effectiveness of corporate parenting, and, in consequence, successful multi-agency working. Three factors, drawn from the list of twelve outlined earlier in this chapter, are discussed here: good communication; clarity of roles; and procedures for information-sharing.

Good Communication

There is considerable evidence to suggest that schools are inhibited from fulfilling their duties as good corporate parents because they are not always clear which children are looked after. There are several possible reasons for problems in identifying children with accuracy. One has to do with confusion in schools about the different categories of looked-after children, particularly those in kinship care and those looked after at home. The difficulty in identifying children, for whom a school shares responsibilities, is highlighted in the field note quoted below, from pilot research conducted in 2008. The research report, *Supporting Looked After Children and Young People at School*, is online at http://strathprints.strath.ac.uk/6175/

> When we initially asked the high school to provide us with details of their looked-after children we received only six data sheets – all accommodated children (children in residential or foster care). Further discussion led to a concern that the group we were interested in might involve 'hundreds' of children. After further clarification we found that twenty-eight young people were looked after at home.

In another study, conducted between 2006 and 2008, University of Strathclyde researchers asked eighteen local authorities with pilot projects aimed at improving the educational outcomes of looked-after children to provide details of the attainment of young people targeted for special intervention (see www.scotland.gov.uk/Publications/2008/09/12095701/0).

More than half of the authorities experienced difficulties in supplying basic information which parents of all children would expect to be readily available, and one authority had still not supplied the information three months after the deadline. Difficulties in information transfer between local authorities and government, between departments within authorities and between agencies often have organisational causes, including the use of different databases, though considerable efforts have been put into improving information transfer in recent years. Scottish Government guidance, based on the research referred to above, highlighted the importance of personal contact and of not relying solely on formal – typically electronic – channels.

> It is good practice for a liaison professional (often this will be a social worker) to inform the school's designated senior manager for looked-after children and young people in person. In one pilot the social work database was amended to include a field to note the details of the school attended. This allowed the information to be sorted by school and for details to be provided monthly to relevant schools (www.scotland.gov.uk/Publications/2009/03/25142835/0).

Professional attitudes can also be a barrier. Teachers may believe the responsibility for initiating contacts in relation to looked-after children rests with social work services, and social workers may not always give sufficient emphasis to children's learning and attainment. One approach to overcoming these problems is a multi-agency one known in some areas as the Joint Assessment Team (JAT) which discusses support arrangements for individual children and their families. An important by-product of regular meetings is that professionals get to know and respect each other, and good working relations often flow from such personal contacts. Sometimes simple practical measures can produce significant benefits. For example, school managers complain about difficulties in making contact with social workers, though electronic media are helping to improve communication. The lack of a common language for planning and monitoring services has caused difficulties between agencies in the past, a difficulty that the GIRFEC principles are intended to counteract.

Clarity of Roles

The most basic rule in effective multi-agency working is to be clear about who does what. An important role in relation to supporting looked-after children in school is that of the designated manager (DM). The role is elaborated in the guide entitled *Core Tasks for Designated Managers in Educational and Residential Establishments in Scotland*, and is envisaged as having important functions in communicating with families and among professionals, making arrangements to meet the learning needs of individual children, acting as an advocate if necessary and organising relevant training for staff (www.scotland.gov.uk/ Publications/2008/09/09143710/0).

The role of DM is typically undertaken by a headteacher or depute head, and this will be only one of many roles performed by a school's senior manager. One experienced designated senior manager described her role to a University of Strathclyde researcher:

> I think it's about knowing who the children are and not being in their face but just knowing them and formally tracking them, but also informally tracking them . . . On a week-to-week basis I speak to pastoral care and I would maybe check in with the pupils as well if I felt that they needed a bit of extra support. (See http://strathprints.strath.ac.uk/6175/1/strathprints006175.pdf)

Achieving clarity of understanding of the role involves both a willingness to accept responsibility and also confidence in interacting with fellow professionals inside and outside of one's agency. In a report of a seminar entitled *Experience of Learning and Educational Outcomes for Looked After Children and Young People*, published by the Pupil Inclusion Network Scotland (PINS) in November 2011 (see www.pinscotland.org), it was noted that delegates 'emphasised the importance of each and every individual taking both professional and personal responsibility for each and every looked after child/young person'. One delegate commented that:

> Resources are important, as is funding, but it's about creating a culture of understanding and care so that those involved in supporting looked after children and young people offer support and challenge to one another but also take personal responsibility for their part in the support package.

Procedures for Information-sharing

Some years ago a DM told me that she did not know which children in her school were looked after because a social worker had insisted this information was confidential. The pupils' looked-after status only became clear when information about their attainment was requested by social work services for statistical reporting purposes, but this was clearly too late to be of any value in planning for the children's educational development. The social worker misunderstood the meaning of confidentiality and the school manager did not feel empowered to challenge an incorrect view. At the other end of the spectrum of privacy is the story told to me by a student about interviewing a DM who explained that information was shared only on a 'need to know' basis; the student later found details of looked-after children in a handbook for teachers which was given to students and visiting tutors. Confusion about what data can be shared between agencies and among professionals within the same agency is a common problem. There are real worries about ethical and legal considerations. Local authorities need to provide clear guidance to professionals who are expected to work together and professionals should also avoid hiding behind bureaucratic procedures instead of seeking clarity about safe mechanisms for sharing information. A 14-year-old boy came late to a first-period class. The teacher shouted at him and said he would be reported for a breach of school rules. The boy swore at the teacher and the incident escalated, resulting in exclusion from school. The teacher later learned that the boy was looked after 'at home' but instead of getting support he was in reality the main carer for a younger brother and their mother was addicted to heroin. The teacher felt guilty and questioned the school's 'need to know' policy. A DM of a secondary school told me that he had changed his views about sharing confidential information and that a child's looked-after status was now made available to all teachers who would have contact with the pupil on a secure intranet site accessible only to teachers. The DM maintained that the change in practice had averted exclusions and teachers had become more understanding and appreciated being treated as equal professionals. Differences of view remain in what is admittedly a difficult and sensitive issue. Nevertheless, the delegates attending the multi-professional PINS seminar referred to above tended to agree about the importance of sharing selective information with a teacher who has a looked-after child in his or her class.

A shared view was that teachers need to know if a child is looked after but they need more support and training to consider what this knowledge means to them and how it is applied to their interface with the learner. Training for teachers should ensure that they do not see 'being looked after' as the defining characteristic of the child.

CONCLUSION

The assumption that looked-after children can expect to have poor outcomes, in school and beyond, underplays the significant achievements of many adults with looked-after backgrounds (see, for example, Duncalf, 2010). The 2006 Social Work Inspection Agency report, *Celebrating Success* (www.scotland.gov.uk/Resource/Doc/129024/0030718.pdf), makes encouraging reading. The authors concluded from their interviews with thirty adults or young people who had been looked after that five factors are important for satisfying lives: having people in their lives who care about them; experiencing stability; being given high expectations; receiving encouragement and support; and being able to participate and achieve. These conditions are at least in part dependent on the multiple agencies involved in the care of looked-after children and young people working well together.

It is clear, therefore, that inter-professional and multi-agency collaboration will increasingly form an important part of the practice of all who work with children and families. This has important implications for their pre-service education and continuing professional development. For teachers in particular this will mean having opportunities to engage with other professionals in order to learn about their jobs, training and ways of working. Schools have traditionally been hierarchical in structure, and relationships with other agencies have tended to be part of the responsibilities of senior staff. These practices are changing as a result of greater integration of children's services. Teachers can expect that collaboration with other professionals will play a more central part in their work. They need the knowledge and skills to enable them to collaborate effectively and also, crucially, the encouragement of managers to gain experience to allow them to develop the necessary competence.

REFERENCES

Baron, S. (2001) 'New Scotland, New Labour, new community schools, new authoritarianism?', In S. Riddell and L. Tett (eds) *Education, Social Justice and Inter-agency Working: Joined-up or Fractured Policy*. London: Routledge.

Cassidy, J. (2008) *Locality-based Working in Integrated Children's Services in Scotland: Observation on Current Practice* (EMIE Report 93). Slough: EMIE at NFER.

Cohen, B. (2005) 'Inter-agency collaboration in context: The "joining-up" agenda', in A. Glaister and B. Glaister (eds), *Inter-agency Collaboration: Providing for Children*. Edinburgh: Dunedin Academic Press.

Duncalf, Z. (2010) *Listen up! Adult Care Leavers Speak Out: The Views of 310 Care Leavers Aged 17–78*. Manchester: Care Leavers' Association.

Edwards, A., H. Daniels, T. Gallagher, J. Leadbetter and P. Warmington (2009) *Improving Inter-professional Collaborations: Multi-agency Working for Children's Wellbeing*. London: Routledge.

French, J. (2007) 'Multi-agency working: The historical background', in I. Siraj-Blatchford, K. Clarke and M. Needham (eds), *The Team around the Child: Multi-agency Working in the Early Years*. Stoke-on-Trent: Trentham Books.

Illsley, P. and M. Redford (2005) '"Drop in for coffee": Working with parents in north Perth new community schools', *Support for Learning*, 20 (4): 162–6.

Sammons, P., S. Power, K. Elliot, P. Robertson, C. Campbell and G. Whitty (2003) *Key Findings from the National Evaluation of the New Community Schools Pilot Programme in Scotland*. Edinburgh: Insight 7. Online at http://www.scotland.gov.uk/library5/education/ins7-00.asp

Statham, J. (2011) *A Review of International Evidence on Interagency Working, to Inform the Development of Children's Services Committees in Ireland*. Online at www.effectiveservices. org/images/uploads/file/publications/Interagency%20Working_Evidence%20review%20 Final%20version.pdf

Stradling, B., M. MacNeil and H. Berry (2009) *Changing Professional Practice and Culture to Get it Right for Every Child: An Evaluation of the Development and Early Implementation Phases of Getting it Right for Every Child in Highland 2006–2009*. Online at www.scotland.gov.uk/ Publications/2009/11/20094407/0

91

Disaffection with Schooling

George Head

Disaffection, as far as it can be identified through non-attendance in schools, is problematic, to varying degrees, in all 'western' countries. In the UK, the US and most of Europe, for example, the state provides free education in nursery, primary and secondary schools. In common with the rest of the UK, in Scotland children between the ages of 5 years and 16 years are required by law to be in education, normally in schools, thereby entitled to eleven years of compulsory education. Disaffection with schooling is notoriously difficult to 'define' and is often associated with disengagement, which is equally complex, entailing notions of non-cooperation, non-participation and non-attendance. A number of studies in both Scotland and England have focused on pupils who were identified as disaffected by their teachers, usually on the basis of their (mis)behaviour in school. Almost inevitably, school disciplinary procedures lead to such behaviour resulting in exclusion or pupil self-withdrawal from school, referred to, in Scottish Government statistical publications, as unauthorised absence including truancy. Whilst truancy may be seen as a negative and irresponsible reaction to school and learning, exclusion is often seen as a socially and legally acceptable decision on the part of schools as a means of addressing pupil disruption and poor behaviour. Absence, truancy and poor behaviour (leading to exclusion) have, there-fore, been considered as markers of pupils' disaffection with schooling and, historically, the Scottish Government's published statistics on exclusions and unauthorised absence have been used to identify the extent of pupil disaffection in Scottish schools. This chapter explores the complexities of what is considered disaffection with schooling before going on to consider the extent of the problem, the factors that contribute to pupil disaffection and the measures historically chosen by schools and local authorities to address it.

DEFINITION AND TERMINOLOGY

Defining what exactly constitutes problematic non-attendance and hence disaffection in school is difficult, complex and complicated by a number of factors, some of which pertain to schools and others lying beyond the school. Consequently, this leads to difficulty in how levels of absence are calculated and how research and literature are interpreted. For example, some authorities and schools consider term-time holidays as absence which, whilst it can be considered non-attendance, is not necessarily a marker of disaffection.

In June 2003, the then Scottish Executive Education Department (SEED) issued a circular on non-attendance that included definitions of what constituted attendance, authorised absence and unauthorised absence in Scotland. Attendance was defined as 'participation in a programme of educational activities arranged by the school' (Scottish Executive Education Department, 2003, p. 2). In addition to attendance at school itself, this definition allowed for work experience, educational visits, study leave during exam times, other events organised in conjunction with the school and education through outreach services or hospital teachers.

Unauthorised absence in Scotland, therefore, remains simply any unexplained absence, truancy and family holidays during term time. The one context that remains within a 'grey' area is absence as a result of exclusion. Whilst it is recognised that exclusion is 'imposed by the school and not the action of a pupil or parent' (SEED, 2003, p. 4) and therefore does not constitute unauthorised absence, it nevertheless remains a contested area and is reported separately from other absence.

Within a schools context, Charlton et al. (2004) argue that there is a close relationship between exclusion and truancy and their negative impact on behaviour and the relationships among pupils and teachers. Hilton's (2006) Scottish study found similar relationships among long periods of truancy, exclusion from school and pupil disaffection. Truancy is described as 'unauthorised absence from school for any period as a result of premeditated or spontaneous action on the part of pupil, parent or both' (SEED, 2003, p. 4). This definition was confirmed in subsequent bulletins on attendance and absence statistics for Scottish schools up to and including December 2011.

The complex nature of non-attendance in schools is reflected in the range of terminology used to identify or describe young people who are not in school. Terminology can be as obvious and transparent as, for example, 'absentee' most likely to be used to described someone who is not at school for a short period. However, where unauthorised absence or periods of non-attendance are more persistent and long term, the terminology applied to young people becomes more sophisticated with connotations of deficit in social, psychological and learning aspects of their make-up.

Cooper and Mellors (1990) argue that the choice of term for young people who are persistently absent from school depends on how the problem of non-attendance is perceived and the way in which schools and teachers deal with the pupils concerned. They differentiate between teachers' perceptions of truants on the one hand and school refusers on the other, and their research indicates that teachers scored school refusers lower in terms of being hard-working and well-behaved, as having poor relationships with their peers, and lower in global self-esteem in comparison with truants. School refusers scored themselves higher than their teachers did in all categories, thereby suggesting a dichotomy in the understanding of and approaches to non-attendance among these groups of young people. The label assigned to students is not just a matter of semantics, as the explanations for and subsequent management of persistent absence is dependent on the perceptions that underpin the terminology.

The term 'school refuser' may be chosen in preference to other common usages such as 'truant' and 'school phobic' for two principal reasons. First, the terms 'truant' and 'phobic' carry with them connotations that can serve as distractions when considering the learning of the young people involved. Truants are often characterised as being disaffected or disengaged with schooling and the approach suggested is one of alternative, usually vocational, education. Consequently, young people considered in this way are likely to find themselves attending further education colleges for at least part of their education.

Phobic, on the other hand, carries connotations of a quasi-medico-psychological deficit.

Whilst there is a tendency in some of the literature to equate the terms 'phobic' and 'refuser', the latter does not carry the psychological weight of the former. The common experience of young people in Scotland considered phobic is referral to an educational psychologist and, in the most extreme cases, removal from mainstream to segregated education in a special school. In both cases, the student's problem is constructed as not belonging to the school, curriculum or pedagogy, and responsibility for creating the context in which the young person can learn is located outwith the mainstream classroom.

Second, the more general term, 'refuser', encompasses both truant and phobic but without the subjective element in the determination of the latter terms. All school refusers are simply that: they refuse, for whatever reason or none, to go to school. That is the commonality among them and the starting point for dealing with their learning. The decision on whether a student is described as phobic or truant, however, is subjective, dependent on the opinions of teachers and others who work with the pupil. The description may well be accurate but can limit the approach adopted and act as a distraction from the main goal of education, and prime focus of schools and teachers, that is, the young person's learning. In such cases, the terms 'truant' and 'phobic' suggest a deficit route, assuming that the disaffection or phobia has to be 'fixed' before learning can be addressed. School refuser, on the other hand, simply describes what happens and makes no social, psychological or moral judgement on the young person or his or her behaviour.

EXTENT AND VARIATION

As with any definition of absence, getting a clear picture of the extent of the problem and variations in its intensity is complex. The Scottish Government publishes annual statistics on school attendance that indicate that overall absence rates are around 7 per cent (the actual figure for 2010–11 being 6.8 per cent) based on the number of half-days attended over the school year as a percentage of possible school half-days for those pupils who were in school for six months or more (Scottish Government, 2011; 2008). These figures cover attendance at mainstream primary and secondary schools as well as special schools and whilst the overall average rate of absence is just under 7 per cent, there is considerable variation among the sectors. Scottish Government statistics indicate, for example, that the level of absence in primary schools is consistently lower than in other sectors. The figures for December 2008 show absence in primary schools at 4.9 per cent whilst the levels in secondary and special schools were 8.9 per cent and 8.4 per cent respectively. Whilst these percentages might seem low and possibly insignificant, they represent a number of around 45,000 pupils in Scotland who are absent from school in any one day. In addition, children with additional support needs, looked-after children, children whose first language is not English and children from urban areas of deprivation are over-represented in these statistics.

In Scotland, Hilton (2006) identified that in the years leading up to 2003, there had been a drop in the overall use of exclusion. This trend was complicated, however, by the fact that whilst there had been a noticeable decrease in temporary exclusions, the pattern of permanent removal from the register was more erratic and any fall in figures less marked than for temporary exclusion. Scottish Government figures for December 2011 indicate that there has been a significant (11 per cent) decrease in exclusions from school and that temporary exclusion accounts for only 0.1 per cent of absence, as it has done consistently over a number of years.

FACTORS AFFECTING DISAFFECTION

Research has highlighted the connections between poverty, deprivation, low socio-economic class and non-attendance at school. Relationships among attendance and a number of other general educational factors such as the negative correlation between absence and attainment have been suggested as significant, although no causal link has been established. It can also be argued, however, that reasons for absence and the main barriers to regular attendance depend on the individual perspectives of pupils, parents, teachers, social workers and para-professionals, and research has also established three sets of influences that encompass the range of reasons for non-attendance. These are home influences, school influences and pupil influences.

Home influences include family problems, attitudes towards school, and cultural and neighbourhood influences. Bimler and Kirkland (2001), Charlton et al. (2004) and Reid (2004a; 2004b) also identify home background as a crucial influence on attendance. Home contexts were seen to be the most influential factors by teachers and schools. In addition, Davies and Lee (2006) found that, depending on family history and academic performance, teachers held low expectations of some students. For example, Reid (2004a) found that the vast majority of unauthorised absences in primary schools were parentally condoned and that teachers believe that a pattern of parentally condoned absence, related to poor parenting skills and drug and alcohol abuse, is the reason behind most non-attending behaviour and disaffection.

School factors include the ethos, leadership, curriculum and systems. Perhaps surprisingly, however, whilst teachers may have considered the academic aspect of school as a factor precipitating truancy, it was not universally seen as being problematic by young people (Attwood and Croll, 2006; Davis and Lee, 2006). In those studies where school work was cited by pupils as an influencing factor, it was not so much the curriculum itself but how it was taught that was identified as being an issue. In these instances, pupils identified teaching as instruction and teachers' perceived lack of interest in them as individuals as contributing towards feelings of disaffection and subsequent truancy. Moreover, assessment-driven learning, league tables and lack of adequate support for learning were considered to be significant influencing factors (Hilton, 2006; Reid, 2006).

In Hilton's (2006) study, difficulties with school work included large class sizes, the formal academic nature of the curriculum and lack of support for learning. Moreover, she reported that the constant focus on assessment undermined enjoyment of practical and creative activities. In Reid's (2006) study of educational social workers, his participants also identified the inflexibility of the national curriculum in England and Wales and the consequent lack of an appropriate alternative curriculum with an emphasis on practical activities as significant.

Those school factors that were considered to have a strong influence on pupils' decisions to truant were mostly regarding the school ethos, management and systems which left pupils feeling alienated. In each of the studies discussed in this chapter, bullying (especially being bullied) was cited by pupils as a reason for absenting themselves from school. This appears to have been exacerbated by a perception that some schools' pastoral care systems were inadequate for dealing with issues between pupils. Closely related reasons given for non-attendance were illness (particularly in cases where the school was perceived to be unconcerned) and exclusion or suspension, which was equally interpreted as a sign of lack of concern on the school's part (Attwood and Croll, 2006; Charlton et al., 2004; Hilton, 2006;

Reid, 2006): 'At the heart of the disaffection the young people expressed was their sense of alienation from the key adults who embodied the values and priorities of mainstream school' (Hilton, 2006, p. 307).

Pupils with high levels of non-attendance acknowledge the school-based factors as influencing decisions to absent themselves from school, but from their perspective, other factors were more significant. For example, in Attwood and Croll's study, they found that there was little complaint about the nature of the curriculum, but the general school atmosphere and poor relationships with teachers were the main reasons for non-attendance (Attwood and Croll, 2006).

Relationships with other pupils were also cited as significant factors. Bullying, lack of friends, unruly behaviour and peer-group pressure were cited in a number of studies as having a strong influence on pupils' decisions to truant (Attwood and Croll, 2006; Bimler and Kirkland, 2001; Hilton, 2006). Indeed, the school as a social setting rather than its role as an academic institution would appear to be a much more noteworthy factor. The social nature of school was particularly highlighted in Davies and Lee's (2006) study. The young people involved in their research were clear that the social aspects of schooling were the major factors affecting their attendance and were able to project the impact of these factors on their lives beyond school. For them, their relationships with teachers depended on the professional stance and personal traits of individual teachers; how they taught and their attitudes towards young people. Appropriate classroom interaction for them was based on mutual respect and being treated in an adult fashion, and teaching was about generating insight and understanding rather than instruction. Neither the subject being taught nor the content of the curriculum was problematic for them.

Similarly, peer relations were powerful factors, especially for girls. As was the case in other studies, bullying, friendships and behaviour in classes and around the school were factors taken into consideration prior to absenting from school. For example, a significant number of participants in Attwood and Croll's (2006) study were able to identify a negative precipitating event or series of events such as bullying or behaviour in class prior to withdrawing from school. Similarly, the quality of friendships and peer relationships around the school was seen by pupils as strong influential factors in deciding whether or not to absent themselves from school. This is similar to Head and Jamieson's (2006) finding, where the 'perceived constant surveillance by school, teacher and peers' (p. 38) contributed towards the creation and reinforcing of an identity related to students' reasons for not attending school.

Hilton's (2006) study revealed a similar focus on relationship issues, especially those between pupils and teachers, rather than curricular matters. In addition, there was a perception among her participants that where relationships among pupils were difficult and problematic, teachers were unwilling to interfere. When pupil relationships were dealt with as a matter of school discipline, this was perceived as a mechanistic response that did not attempt to address the root of the problem and was considered symptomatic of teachers' and schools' lack of real concern for their pupils' welfare. Even when school was spoken of in educational terms, participants expressed dissatisfaction with the problems of obtaining adequate support. This led to a growing sense of isolation and not being valued, which in turn impacted on students' behaviour, including non-attendance. For these young people and those in other studies, there was a real sense of disappointment with school and school systems which they perceived to have failed them as people. For pupils, therefore, unlike the perceptions of their teachers and other professionals, it is school as a social setting and especially the relationships between pupils and teachers that are the most persuasive and powerful factors precipitating a decision not to attend school.

In addition to the set of three influences discussed above, Attwood and Croll (2006) also identified two sets of factors that impact on truancy: those that render young people vulnerable to truancy, mostly what could be described as environmental factors; and those that precipitate truancy, or what could be termed causal factors. Whilst Attwood and Croll assign factors to each of these categories, it may be that what constitutes environmental or causal factors depends on the perspective of the individuals involved. For example, most of the adults in each of the studies appear to have interpreted school-based factors such as curriculum, assessment and exams, and young people's 'failure' to perform to a high level as causal factors. Other factors such as school ethos, pedagogy and matters of pastoral care and support for learning would, almost by definition, be construed as environmental factors. The young people themselves, however, held an opposing view. Hinton's participants, for example, considered the academic challenge of schools as non-causal but the factors that precipitated truancy were related to school as a social setting, especially relationships with teachers and other pupils.

Moreover, there also appears to be a possible dichotomy between the views of parents and those held by teachers, social workers and other adults. Parents see the main causes of non-attendance as in-school matters including bullying and teachers' attitudes towards children. Teachers and other professionals, by way of contrast, appear to view the home environment and the influence of parents as having a greater influence on attendance (Davies and Lee, 2006).

Whilst non-attendance may be a problem for schools, however, self-withdrawal, that is, a pupil deliberately and possibly openly choosing not to attend school, may in fact be a solution for some non-attenders who find school difficult for a number of reasons, some of which are discussed below (Davies and Lee, 2006; Head and Jamieson, 2006). In these instances, Davies and Lee (2006) argue that the pupils' decisions to disengage with school amount to the articulation of a critique of school and the educational system. Similarly, Hilton (2006, p. 310) argues that in some instances, the problem may lie with teaching and the curriculum and not the pupil: 'the narrowed academic focus of the current curriculum and formalized pedagogy has led some scholars to interpret truancy as an entirely rational and understandable choice for pupils who see little relevance in it for their own working lives'.

Truancy is also a social problem with social costs and therefore cannot be considered in isolation. Reid (2004b, p. 57) cites evidence from the 1998 Social Inclusion Report in England which indicates that 65 per cent of crime committed in shopping centres during daytime can be attributed to young people who should otherwise have been at school. Bimler and Kirkland (2001) similarly associate truancy with other social issues such as drinking, minor crime and other forms of anti-social behaviour. Reid (2006) also points out that longitudinal studies indicate that there may be links between poor attendance and a range of social factors that have an impact on later adult life. Attwood and Croll (2006) also highlight that levels of truancy become more marked in secondary school. Truancy and attendance (Scottish Government, 2011) figures for Scotland reflect that trend and also suggest that additional support needs and social deprivation, such as that indicated by registration for free school meals and the Scottish Index of Multiple Deprivation, exacerbates the extent to which children and young people from disadvantaged backgrounds are likely to be absent from school.

ADDRESSING DISAFFECTION: PUNITIVE APPROACH

Within the four UK countries, parents can be prosecuted if their children do not attend compulsory education either in school or at home. In England and Wales, there is an emphasis on the regulation of parents' and young people's behaviour with regard to attendance at school: a range of procedures are followed beginning with the issue of an attendance order and, if parents do not make appropriate arrangements for their child's education, fines can be imposed or they can be sent to prison. In Scotland, local authorities have statutory responsibilities to provide appropriate education for children and young people. Pupils who do not attend school can be referred to a children's panel (the hearings system in Scotland for supporting children and young people at risk) and sent to segregated provision, for example a special school or unit. In addition, under the terms of the Education (Scotland) Act 1980, parents of children who do not attend school and who have not made other appropriate arrangements for their education can be reported to the Procurator Fiscal. Indeed, the regulatory philosophy may be so ingrained in approaches to dealing with attendance that even some measures intended to support rather than punish, such as guidance teams and support bases, have been nevertheless interpreted by young people as forms of punishment (Hilton, 2006).

However, issues of non-attendance at schools are complex and confusing, and measures taken to address pupil absence have been largely ineffective and lacking in coherence, coordination and a common understanding of the problem. The latest available figures from the

Table 91.1   Percentage attendance and absence by detailed reason, 2006–7 to 2010–11

	2006–7	2007–8	2008–9	2009–10	2010–11
Attendance	**93.3**	**93.2**	**93.3**	**93.2**	**93.1**
In school	91.4	91.4	91.4	91.3	91.1
Late	1.6	1.6	1.7	1.7	1.8
Work experience	0.2	0.2	0.2	0.2	0.2
Sickness with education provision	–	–	–	–	–
Authorised absence	**5.3**	**5.2**	**5.1**	**4.9**	**4.9**
Sickness without education provision	3.1	3.3	3.4	3.5	3.4
Very late	–	–	–	–	–
Authorised holidays	0.1	0.1	0.1	0.1	0.1
Exceptional domestic circumstances	0.1	0.1	0.1	0.1	0.1
Other authorised	1.9	1.7	1.5	1.2	1.2
Unauthorised absence	**1.4**	**1.5**	**1.5**	**1.8**	**1.9**
Unauthorised holidays	0.4	0.4	0.4	0.4	0.5
Unexplained absence, including truancy	0.8	0.9	0.9	1.2	1.3
Exceptional domestic circumstances (unauthorised)	–	–	–	–	–
Other unauthorised	0.2	0.1	0.1	0.1	0.1
All absences (authorised and unauthorised)	**6.7**	**6.7**	**6.6**	**6.7**	**6.8**
Temporary exclusion	**0.1**	**0.1**	**0.1**	**0.1**	**0.1**

Scottish Government. Online at www.scotland.gov.uk/stats/bulletins/00949

Note: The information in this table will be affected by differing reporting practices across local authorities and over time.

Scottish Government offer an example of the levels of attendance and absence and the range of reasons responsible.

Whilst on the whole the problem of truancy remains consistently at a relatively small level, there is nevertheless an enduring issue to be addressed for the small core of pupils responsible for most incidences of truancy. One appropriate way of addressing non-attendance for this group may be to consider the experiences of young people from the two perspectives suggested by the reasons cited for truancy: namely, environmental factors and causal factors, which relate closely to Attwood and Croll's (2006) duo of precipitating events and school as a social setting. The combination of people and setting has been highlighted as the crucial mix in considering matters of non-attendance. For example, Broadhurst et al. (2005, p. 106) argue:

> At the heart of debates about education and participation is the intractable debate around agency and structure . . . Who or what is at fault in relation to the persistent disengagement of children and young people from schooling? There is concern that discourses associated with The Third Way place greater emphasis on strategies to enhance individual agency and are more punitive than pupil-centred or family-centred methods (Blyth, 2001), failing to account for the deeply intractable nature of school disengagement and alienation from formal systems.

ADDRESSING DISAFFECTION: PASTORAL APPROACH

Punitive measures, however, have not been the sole means of addressing disaffection, behaviour and non-attendance; what could be described as a more welfarist approach (Macleod, 2006) has also been adopted. In the welfarist model, agency is not conceptualised as a citizen's responsibility to participate in a social contract, but is considered more in terms of a human capability to be nurtured and developed and an entitlement that is to be fostered and met. Welfarist approaches, therefore, mostly centre around measures aimed at reducing school exclusions and absences through addressing the educational and social needs of young people. For example, Charlton et al. (2004) evaluated an alternative curriculum approach and found that *inter alia* the young people involved appreciated and responded to being treated like adults, the more relaxed atmosphere, better relationships with teachers and, most importantly, having control over their lives. They reported that some participants in the scheme chose to start attending school again as a direct result of their experience on the programme. Davies and Lee (2006) similarly argue that responding to non-attendance would require addressing the quality of relationships between teachers and pupils.

The way in which disaffection and non-attendance in schools is addressed depends, therefore, on how absence is conceptualised. Bimler and Kirkland (2001) speculate that there may be eight 'styles' of truanting that accounted for each of the individual reasons that young people offered for their non-attendance. The reasons themselves were identified as belonging to five clusters of truanting, two of which were associated with parental influences and three related to delinquency. Regarding non-attendance in terms of these clusters in turn suggests interventions based on school factors, family factors and factors related to teenage rebellion and delinquency. Broadhurst et al. (2005) similarly identify the relationship between home and school as significant, but discriminate between 'enduring' and 'discontinuous' forms of disengagement with school. Whilst the former category is suggestive of the breakdown of social networks requiring intensive, long-term and probably multi- and inter-agency intervention, the latter implies disruption rather than breakdown and that short- to medium-term interventions would suffice.

However, regardless of the conceptualisation, certain factors emerge as common. These can be thought of as belonging to one or more of three strands: the relationships between home and school; what happens in school itself; and school as a social institution, especially the relationships between pupils and teachers. Each of these strands can be addressed in terms of systems, with, for example, schools having policy statements on dealing with learning, behaviour, non-attendance and sharing information, and working towards greater cohesion in multi- and inter-agency initiatives.

Consequently, in an overtly holistic and ecosystemic approach, some local authorities are encouraging better attendance at schools as part of strategies to address social inclusion (Reid, 2004a). However, the same author points out that his research reveals that where multi-disciplinary measures are in place, it is often the case that teachers are unaware of the other professionals involved and that headteachers may in fact prefer resources to be entirely school-based rather than belonging to the central authority (Reid, 2004a), and that the processes involved have come to be seen as problematic and frustrating (Reid, 2004b; 2006). In Scotland, initiatives to address behaviour in schools through Curriculum for Excellence and Getting it Right for Every Child, intended to develop greater coherence and collaboration among children's services, may also be taken into account when considering levels of absence, truancy and exclusion and hence indications of disaffection with school.

Addressing school disaffection in a holistic way entails, in the end, a pedagogical (in its widest sense) approach. It concerns the values and beliefs that teachers, schools and the wider community hold regarding young people, their learning and their place in society. Ultimately, it includes the values and beliefs held by young people themselves and how they play out in the complex relationships and interactions between teachers and pupils in schools. The foundations of children's and young people's development, learning and behaviour are laid by the environment in which they grow up, including school. Pastoral measures to address disaffection, therefore, recognise and affirm children and young people as members of the school community within the wider community with the rights, capabilities and entitlements that membership entails. Whilst in a punitive context disaffection and its manifestations are seen as obstacles and barriers to learning and participation in schooling, in a pastoral approach these same features form the conditions that allow for the exploration and nurturing of pupil identities related to their sense of themselves as learners. Thus, these same young people cease to be 'disaffected pupils' and become instead young people whose relationships, behaviour and attendance indicate that they might be experiencing disaffection with schooling.

REFERENCES

Attwood, G. and P. Croll (2006) 'Truancy in secondary school pupils: prevalence, trajectories and pupil perspectives', *Research Papers in Education*, 21 (4), 467–84.

Bimler, D. and J. Kirkland (2001) 'School truants and truancy motivation sorted out with multidimensional scaling', *Journal of Adolescent Research*, 16 (1): 75–102.

Broadhurst, K., H. Paton and C. May-Chahal (2005) 'Children missing from school systems: exploring divergent patterns of disengagement in the narrative accounts of parents, carers, children and young people', *British Journal of Sociology of Education*, 26 (1): 105–19.

Charlton, T., C. Panting and H. Willis (2004) 'Targeting exclusion, disaffection and truancy in secondary schools', *Emotional and Behavioural Difficulties*, 9 (4): 261–75.

Cooper, M. and M. Mellors (1990) 'Teachers' perceptions of school refusers and truants', *Educational Review*, 42 (3): 319–26.

Davies, J. D. and J. Lee (2006) 'To attend or not to attend? Why some students choose school and others reject it', *Support for Learning*, 21 (4): 204–9.

Head, G. and S. Jamieson (2006) 'Taking a line for a walk: including school refusers', *Pastoral Care in Education*, 24 (3), 32–40.

Hilton, Z. (2006) 'Disaffection and school exclusion: Why are inclusion policies still not working in Scotland?', *Research Papers in Education*, 21 (3): 295–314.

Macleod, G. (2006) 'Bad, mad or sad: Constructions of young people in trouble and implications for interventions', *Emotional and Behavioural Difficulties*, 11 (3), 155–67.

Reid, K. (2004a) 'The views of head teachers and teachers on attendance issues in primary schools', *Research in Education*, 72: 60–76.

Reid, K. (2004b) 'A long-term strategic approach to tackling truancy and absenteeism from schools: The SSTG scheme', *British Journal of Guidance & Counselling*, 32 (1), 57–74.

Reid, K. (2006) 'The views of education social workers on the management of truancy and other forms of non-attendance', *Research in Education* 75: 40–57.

Scottish Executive Education Department (2003) *Circular no. 5/03: School Attendance and Absence*. Edinburgh: Scottish Executive.

Scottish Government (2008) *Attendance and Absence in Scottish Schools 2007/08*. Edinburgh: Scottish Government.

Scottish Government (2011) *Summary Statistics for Schools in Scotland no. 2: 2011 Edition*. Edinburgh: Scottish Government.

92

Poverty and Schooling in Scotland

Daniela Sime

Currently in Scotland, one in four children live in poverty. Thousands of children suffer from poor health, live in unsuitable accommodation and have limited access to services because their families cannot afford to give them the opportunities that children from more affluent backgrounds have. Poverty has a devastating effect on children's wellbeing, education and life chances. Low income in the family is associated with delays in cognitive development, social skills and school readiness in children as young as 3. Later on, in school, the achievement gap between poor and non-poor children gets wider. This also means that poor children are more likely to leave school early and with no qualifications, which leads to the transmission of poverty over generations. Ending child poverty and socio-economic disadvantage, as well as addressing the educational underachievement of poor children, need to become priorities for all public services. This chapter examines the current situation of child poverty in Scotland. It first defines poverty and identifies the factors that contribute to child poverty. It then examines the current policy context and the impact of poverty on children's education and wellbeing, concluding with some implications for policy and practice.

POVERTY AND SOCIAL JUSTICE

The widely adopted definition of poverty is the one developed by Peter Townsend in 1979:

> Individuals, families and groups in the population can be said to be in poverty when they lack the resources to obtain the types of diet, participate in activities and have the living conditions and amenities which are customary, or at least widely encouraged and approved, in the societies in which they belong. (1979, p. 31)

Poverty is thus more than income and material deprivation, although it includes these. Lack of money plays a key role in how people participate in society, in relation to resources they can secure (such as food, fuel and housing), but also in relation to the level of access to services, leisure activities and political participation. Also, poverty needs to be seen as relative to the customary practices of each society, so poverty in Scotland may be qualitatively different from the poverty experienced by people in other countries.

Tackling poverty is an issue of social justice and equal opportunities. The UK has one of the highest associations between social class and educational performance and life opportunities among the countries in the Organisation for Economic Cooperation and Development

(OECD), according to the Programme for International Student Assessment survey. The 2007 UNICEF study on the wellbeing of children in twenty-one OECD countries also revealed that young people in the UK were among the most likely to adopt risky behaviours in teenage years (use of drugs or alcohol, or being sexually active), as well as reporting low levels of satisfaction with their relationships and happiness. In their book, *The Spirit Level*, Wilkinson and Prickett (2009) demonstrate that several health and social problems (such as obesity, teenage pregnancies, mental illness, low life expectancy) or social issues (such as educational performance, trust at community level, imprisonment rates) depend not on how wealthy a society is, but on how equal (or unequal) it is. In other words, societies such as the UK or the US, with their high levels of inequality, are more likely to be faced with social problems than more equal societies, such as Japan, Sweden or Spain. Tackling social disadvantage is thus a matter of addressing the wealth distribution to reduce the gaps between the rich and the poor, and increasing access to opportunities and representation of all groups.

MEASUREMENTS OF POVERTY

Low income is considered a clear indicator of poverty. Across Europe, a family's income is judged in line with a threshold value, which is agreed at 60 per cent of the median income. Using data from the Households Below Average Income (2012), a lone parent with two children living on less than £278 a week after housing costs (which is 60 per cent of the median of £431) or a couple with two children living on less than £349 a week after housing costs (median is £582) are considered to be living in poverty. These figures are adjusted yearly in line with inflation. Based on this measurement, almost one million people in Scotland are living in relative poverty and of these, 630,000 people are in absolute poverty, with limited access to basic resources, such as food, fuel and clothing (McKendrick et al., 2011). Children are at greater risk than adults, with one in four of Scotland's children – that is 260,000 children – currently living in poverty. Despite a misinformed general opinion that poor children live in workless households, more than half of children in poverty (57 per cent) live in households with at least one adult in work.

What are the implications of these measurements for schools? The fact that half of the children in poor families have one or both parents in work makes it very difficult to identify children in this group. Assuming that employment automatically means better resources may create the false impression that families can cope with their daily demands, when in reality their income may be limited. Using children's entitlement to free school meals or clothing grants as indicators of families' circumstances is often the best proxy that teachers have to identify children in this group. However, many families do not claim these even when entitled, to hide their circumstances out of embarrassment, which means that children's home circumstances are often unknown to their teachers.

WHAT CAUSES POVERTY AND WHO ARE THE CHILDREN MOST LIKELY TO BE POOR?

A range of factors contributes to people being in poverty (McKendrick *et al.*, 2011). *Individual factors* refer to people's choices and behaviours. Blaming individuals for not trying 'hard enough' to get out of their situation is often used as a political strategy, to distract from the wider socio-economic factors that shape people's lives. For example, not having work in the local area is a major barrier to people's employment, given added costs of childcare and transport when looking for work further away. There are, then, a range of *social factors* that may be a cause of poverty. For example, for lone parents, usually single mothers, the cost and availability of childcare and the gender pay gap are major barriers to employment and significant causes of poverty. Finally, *political and economical factors*, such as the strength of the economy and initiatives put in place to tackle poverty, are key factors impacting on poverty levels. It is important to see these factors as inter-related and to examine individuals' circumstances as a combination of their own agency and structural aspects that may be outside their control.

One key aspect of poverty in Scotland is its geographical distribution. Poverty is most prevalent in parts of Glasgow, where around half of all households are income deprived, according to the Scottish Index of Multiple Deprivation (SIMD). Furthermore, within the city, the distribution of poverty is unequal. Almost half of Glasgow's population live in the 20 per cent of the most deprived areas in Scotland (see www.understandingglasgow.com for more data on the city). Poverty is also affecting the local authorities around Glasgow, with West Dunbartonshire, Inverclyde, North Lanarkshire, Renfrewshire and South Lanarkshire having among the highest rates of poverty in Scotland (see McKendrick et al., 2011, for detailed figures). However, these areas are situated close to areas of relative affluence, such as East Dunbartonshire and East Renfrewshire, which suggests that geographical distribution is not the sole explanation for what affects people's opportunities.

Children are at a significantly higher risk than other groups of being poor. Based on the Households Below Average Income Data 2010–11, their risk of experiencing poverty is increased if they live in lone-parent households (41 per cent of children in these households are poor) and in households where no one works (68 per cent of children in these households are poor) or someone works part-time (64 per cent). In households with three or more children, 40 per cent of the children are poor, and households with young children are also at a higher risk. Children with disabilities and those of certain ethnicities are more likely to be poor. In Scotland, Asian children are twice as likely as white children to be poor (43 per cent of Asian households, as opposed to 21 per cent of white ethnic groups) and 34 per cent of children from 'other ethnic groups' live in poor households. These risk factors must be understood in the wider context and while acknowledging that belonging to one of these groups does not automatically place individuals in poverty. The fact that some groups are more at risk is significant, as it needs to inform anti-poverty initiatives and, in the context of education, alert those involved with children to the potential challenges they are faced with.

POLICY CONTEXT AND ANTI-POVERTY INITIATIVES

In 2008, the Labour-led UK government announced its intention to introduce a Child Poverty Bill, to legislate the commitment to eradicate child poverty by 2020. Given the high levels of child poverty, over 3.8 million children at the time, it meant that tackling child poverty became enshrined in law. The Child Poverty Act (2010) sets out a duty on the UK government to monitor targets to eradicate child poverty and on devolved governments to develop regional strategies. The Conservative–Lib-Dem government set out its planned approach in a document entitled *A New Approach to Tackling Child Poverty* in 2011, which reassuringly confirms the commitment to eradicate child poverty by 2020.

In Scotland, the main fiscal policy levers such as tax credits, taxation and social security benefits remain responsibilities reserved to the UK government, which makes it difficult to adopt a distinctive approach. However, provision of education and social services is devolved, which means that involvement of local authorities in tackling child poverty through services delivered locally is crucial. In 2011, the Scottish Government issued its *Child Poverty Strategy for Scotland*, which identifies three key principles:

- *early intervention and prevention*, with a focus on targeting effective interventions at early years and concentrating on preventing families falling into poverty;
- *an assets-based approach*, meaning that individuals' own skills, knowledge and views will be prioritised in any initiatives of support;
- *a child-centred approach*, promoting the rights of children to be involved and heard in decisions affecting their lives.

The child-centredness and multi-agency approach in tackling disadvantage are aligned with the principles promoted through another key document, *Getting it Right for Every Child* (GIRFEC), which aims to implement a clearer system of planning and delivering services for children by putting their views at the heart of the process. The Scottish Government is committed to the implementation of GIRFEC, ensuring that children's needs are prioritised and a multi-agency approach is adopted whenever several services need to be involved with the child.

In addition to the principles of GIRFEC, there are three inter-related frameworks seen as pivotal in providing a shared approach for the Scottish Government and its local partners (local authorities, the NHS, the third sector, community planning partners) in tackling poverty and inequality. The first one, *Achieving our Potential: A Framework to Tackle Poverty and Income Inequality in Scotland* (2008b) includes a concordat with local authorities, giving them responsibility for targeting anti-poverty strategies locally. The document includes a range of actions aimed at supporting people to find work and make work pay, tackle health inequalities and discrimination, improve children's life chances and ensure better housing. In line with the commitment to concentrate on preventive work, the *Early Years Framework* (2008a), also developed in the context of the concordat, calls for 'transformational change' in how early years provision and support for families with young children is delivered. It proposes a vision that establishes

> a new conceptualisation of early years – that children should be valued and provided for within communities; the importance of strong, sensitive relationships with parents and carers; the right to a high quality of life and access to play; the need to put children at the centre of service delivery; to provide more support through universal services when children need it; and that children should be able to achieve positive outcomes irrespective of race, disability or social background. (p. 4)

The *Early Years Framework* is a ten-year plan, aiming to deliver a 'radical improvement in outcomes', and actions suggested include a coherent approach to service delivery; better quality of pre-school provision; improved collaboration between agencies; and empowerment of families and children. These proposed actions may need further devolved powers to allow a direct investment in early years in Scotland. International evidence suggests that countries with low levels of poverty have the highest quality of early years settings, with fully integrated provision, early years educators trained to degree level and affordable universal entitlement (in Norway and Sweden, for example, children are entitled to full-time provision from the age of 1).

Finally, the third framework, entitled *Equally Well*, is the first Scottish policy that sets out the government's commitment to tackle social inequalities in health. It promotes new approaches such as early and targeted interventions, as well as universal services. Together, the above three frameworks, all launched in 2008, aim to provide the basis for tackling inequality and social disadvantage, despite the challenging current financial climate and the issues surrounding the limited autonomy in decisions on matters reserved to Westminster.

IMPACT OF POVERTY ON CHILDREN'S HEALTH AND WELLBEING

The limited access to resources, both material and social, has profound effects on children's health and wellbeing. *Growing Up in Scotland* is the first longitudinal study in Scotland, monitoring 14,000 children born here since 2005 and aiming to examine the factors that may impact on their development. Based on the data collected when the children were 3–4 years old, the study revealed that poverty has considerable effects on children's wellbeing from this young age. While some families can move in and out of poverty, being only temporarily poor, others stay in persistent poverty and their circumstances never chance. Persistently poor children had disproportionate development and language problems, as well as other difficulties (see Figure 92.1).

In terms of health, children from low-income families tend to have a poorer diet, given the constraints that limited budgets and restricted access to healthy foods put on parents' choices. Later on, in teenage years, mental illness is more prevalent in low-income households, especially among boys (Scottish Health Survey, 2009), with higher rates of depression, anxiety and suicide than other groups. These effects continue into adulthood, with higher rates of illness and disability among adults in low-income households and a much reduced life expectancy. For example, in Glasgow, adults in some of the affluent areas live on average almost thirty years longer than those in the most deprived areas.

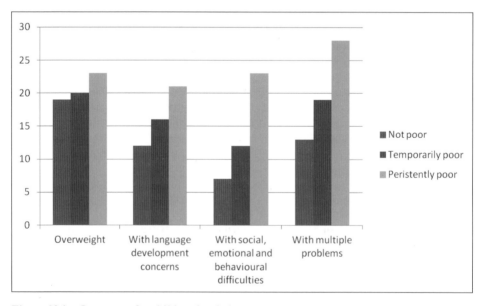

Figure 92.1   Outcomes for children by their poverty status

Source: *Growing Up in Scotland*

There are other damaging effects that poverty has on children, through the limited opportunities they may have to access good-quality housing and leisure activities. Bad housing is linked to increased health problems, such as asthma and mental illness, and many children live in overcrowded accommodation, with no space to study. The 2009 *Scottish Household Survey* has also revealed the impact that living in a deprived neighbourhood has on children's leisure activities. Overall, children had less access to playgrounds and parks and their parents were more likely to perceive their local area as unsafe. Other research has also shown that children from deprived areas may not be able to access leisure opportunities because of the high additional costs of transport or equipment required, even if activities may be offered as 'free' at the point of use.

THE IMPORTANCE OF EARLY YEARS

The *Growing up in Scotland* study and other research have shown that the early years are crucial to a child's development and readiness for school. However, class differences are already apparent even before children enter early years education. Research shows that there are big differences in the environments that children are exposed to from birth. Young children from poor families are significantly less likely to be read to every day (42 per cent) than children from the more affluent families (79 per cent) and less likely to engage in other formative activities, such as arts, sports or musical activities in the home or at local playgroups (Goodman and Gregg, 2010). This points to the importance of the quality of the home learning environment and parenting style in the first years of a child's life. The differences in parental approaches to caring for their children were found to account for some of the cognitive gaps at the age of 3. Other factors that impact on the chances of a positive home environment are the mother's age and education level, number of children in the family and father's employment status. The study of the data from the 1970 Birth Cohort Survey (BCS) conducted by Feinstein (2003) showed that around 10 per cent of children in the bottom group at 42 months are in the top quartile by the age of 10. This suggests that poor children can still catch up later, which highlights the importance of ensuring that children's early years experiences are in high-quality settings.

The Effective Provision of Pre-School Education (EPPE) study followed the progress of 3,000 children aged 3–11 to examine, among other things, if pre-school, primary and home learning could reduce social inequalities. The study found that families in which parents were engaged in activities with their children strongly promoted children's intellectual and social development. The behaviours identified as especially significant included reading together, playing with numbers, painting and drawing, singing and using rhymes. Attending pre-school was shown to be especially beneficial for children from disadvantaged backgrounds, especially if the early years settings were of a better quality. Although the parents' socio-economic status and education were important factors, the quality of the home learning environment was more important. This suggests that family poverty does not necessarily mean that children cannot have supportive and enriching home experiences to prepare them for learning and parents/carers have the biggest influence on children's outcomes. The implication for educators working with parents is thus to raise parents' awareness and skills in relation to the significant contribution that their caring behaviours in the early years have on children's achievement later on.

IMPACT OF POVERTY ON EDUCATION

Social class at birth is considered a good indicator of the educational input that children will receive throughout their childhood. This achievement gap is a major factor in perpetuating the social divide and the patterns of social mobility across society. Feinstein's analysis (2003) examined the extent to which children's social class is linked to their educational achievement. The survey included thousands of British children who were tested at four ages (22, 42, 60 and 120 months old). The analysis provided clear evidence that by the age of 22 months, children from lower socio-economic backgrounds are already behind their peers in terms of language, social and emotional development. Furthermore, the gap between children in the top and bottom social class is getting wider as children grow older. While at 22 months, children from the bottom social class groups are thirteen percentiles behind their peers, at 10 years old, the difference between the groups grows to twenty-eight percentiles. Another striking finding was that performance in early years can predict children's chances of achieving good qualifications by the age of 26. Based on results at 42 months, only 17 per cent from the bottom quartile will achieve A level qualifications or above, while 52 per cent from the top quartile will do so. These findings suggest that before children enter school, their chances of achieving well academically and securing well-paid employment later on in life are already substantially different, depending on the social class they were born in.

Studies have found that children's experiences of schooling also differ in relation to their socio-economic background. These discrepancies are often acknowledged by the young people themselves, who accept that they are not going to get the same quality of education or have the same outcomes as their non-deprived peers (Horgan, 2007). The hidden cost of schooling (Preston, 2008), including costs for uniforms and shoes, lunches, transport, school activities and trips, means that children are often in no position to take part in extra-curricular activities or self-exclude themselves from these activities, to buffer the effects of additional costs on their families (Ridge, 2002).

For children of school age, education also means access to extra-curricular activities after school hours or during holidays. Middle-class children are again at an advantage, being able to afford culturally and educationally enriching activities after school that provide a clear continuity with the curriculum. Support through private tutoring and parental involvement in completing homework are more common in middle-class families. At community level, the quality of services is also linked to the so-called postcode lottery, where areas of deprivation are often blighted by limited play spaces, unsafe parks and poor-quality services. These discrepancies in the quantity and quality of out-of-school activities that children can afford and that are available locally mean that educational opportunities children from different social backgrounds have outside school are remarkably different.

Access to good-quality services and diverse experiences is also linked to parental aspirations for their children's education. Parents' own experiences of education and educational achievement influence their expectations and confidence. Research shows that middle-class parents are more likely to demand good-quality services and participate in school activities, while lower-class parents feel less confident to do so (Crozier and Reay, 2005). This has led some authors to talk about 'elite participationists', represented mainly by middle-class mothers. While middle-class parents expect their children to 'stand out' and do well academically, working-class parents expect children to 'fit in' and 'stay out of trouble', and generally have lower expectations in terms of academic achievement. This is despite the fact

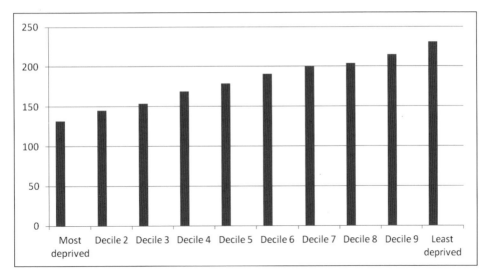

Figure 92.2   Average tariff scores of S4 pupils in Scotland, 2009/2010, by level of deprivation (SIMD rankings)

that parents and children of all social classes believe in the importance of education and the opportunities it offers.

Differences in parental expectations and type of involvement in children's learning at home and at school may be two of the reasons why, overall, children from lower socio-economic groups do less well academically. Figure 92.2 shows the relationship between the tariff scores recorded in 2009–10 for S4 children and the profiles of the areas in which they live, based on the SIMD, which combines several indicators to build up an area profile. The data shows that the tariff scores of children living in the most deprived areas (130) was almost half of the scores of children living in the least deprived areas (238). This clearly shows that children from more disadvantaged areas do less well academically and that poverty is for many children the source of their academic underachievement.

Low achievement has also an ethnic dimension, with certain ethnic groups (for example, black Caribbean and Gypsy Traveller) scoring considerably worse in exams than other ethnic groups. Gypsy Travellers are also more likely to report incidents of bullying and racism at school. However, other ethnic minority groups, like Indian and Chinese children, do much better than all other groups, including white children, which suggests that ethnicity on its own is not a risk factor.

The final aspect of inequality in educational achievement relates to the prospects young people have after leaving school. On average, poor children are more likely to leave school early and with no qualifications than their better-off peers (Scottish Government, 2011b). Within the OECD countries, Scotland has one of the highest proportions of young people in the 15–19 age group not in education, training or employment (the so-called NEET group), with most of them coming from deprived backgrounds and having no qualifications. This also means that in terms of access to higher education and better employment prospects, children from better-off families are again at an advantage.

TACKLING THE EDUCATIONAL UNDERACHIEVEMENT OF POOR CHILDREN: IMPLICATIONS FOR SCHOOLS AND EARLY YEARS EDUCATORS

The fact that the attainment gap between poor and non-poor children has remained unchanged over the last decade and is present even before the child's second birthday suggests that current policies of tackling underachievement in schools have not been successful and need to start much earlier.

In recent years, there has been a range of initiatives aimed at parents, often specifically targeting groups identified as vulnerable or 'at risk'. In Glasgow, the Triple P Positive Parenting Programme (www.triplep.net) aims to help 'every parent' to support their children's development. Evaluations of other similar initiatives targeted at disadvantaged families show a clear impact on children and parents' social and emotional wellbeing, but the outcomes in terms of children's cognitive development are less clear (Goodman and Gregg, 2010). Provision of this type of support is needed to ensure that parents from all backgrounds know how best to encourage their children's learning and development from birth.

Similarly, there needs to be more investment in early years provision, with extended entitlement for all children and highly trained staff. Currently, children in Scotland are entitled to free, part-time provision of up to twelve and a half hours a week (fifteen hours in some areas) after their third birthday. The current entitlement comes too late for many children and is still considerably less than the entitlements to childcare in other European countries. This also means that parents are often unable to return to work or education and become deskilled because of the crippling costs of childcare. Finally, the training of early years staff mentioned in the *Early Years Framework* (2008a) is key to increasing their ability to tackle educational disadvantage.

At school level, Curriculum for Excellence recognises the issue of underachievement and aims to offer a more holistic approach to children's education, by recognising that children may require different levels of support. Currently, there are no clear mechanisms to tackle underachievement through targeted support, especially when the underachievement is a result of children's socio-economic background. Teachers do not have access to information on pupils' family background, as home visits are not common practice, and rely on information volunteered by parents to gain a sense of the barriers to learning due to children's home circumstances. Schools need more explicit mechanisms to identify children at risk, including those in temporary poverty, in order to plan support needed and tackle academic underperformance. For many children, the cultural divide between home and school means that expectations from parents and teachers are so different that engagement with educational activities is seen as a betrayal of home and community values (Crozier and Reay, 2005). If school values are not in line with family values, children may not want to be in dissonance with family expectations of them.

Research shows that parents' own cognitive abilities and other childhood circumstances correlate with their children's academic performance (Goodman and Gregg, 2010). Parents with low qualifications will often talk about their limited confidence in engaging with school activities and helping their children learn. One key challenge for teachers is therefore to identify the best ways to raise family aspirations and to find genuine ways for parental engagement. Equally, raising children's aspirations can be a challenge, given the area effect on people's confidence. While in more affluent areas there may be a more consistent approach to encouraging children to 'aim high', with immediate role models, children from more disadvantaged areas can be drawn into a defeatist attitude, with statements such as 'no one in this area goes to university'. This is not to say that children or parents in deprived areas may not have high aspirations or the potential to succeed. However, inter-generational experiences of low achievement and other immediate pressures, for example having to gain employment and provide for the family, mean that academic achievement may be hindered by other factors, with long-term consequences for young people's opportunities.

FUTURE PRIORITIES

Anti-poverty initiatives and educational policies can arguably do more to reduce inequalities in Scotland and tackle the long-term effects of poverty on children's wellbeing and achievement. Poverty has a moral cost, as it allows children to grow up in deprivation, underachievement and with low opportunities for participation. It also has a real cost, estimated at around £25 billion a year across the UK to counter the effects of poverty later on, through services such as adult education and training, healthcare, and police and criminal justice (McKendrick et al., 2011). This makes it essential that anti-poverty initiatives, with explicit mechanisms to indicate progress, are continued at national level.

For education, the priorities are clearly in terms of identifying children at risk early and providing specialist support. Accessible, good-quality early years provision and well-trained staff are crucial to reducing the achievement gap early on. Targeted funding, through parental programmes and area-based initiatives, needs to be evidence-based and look at ways of skilling parents in supporting children's learning and development. Raising parents' and children's educational aspirations in terms of school leaving age and positive destinations afterwards, including higher education, is another key aspect. This needs to be done in the knowledge that many parents and children from deprived backgrounds have high expectations, but cannot afford to pursue these because of other pressures.

In schools, tackling educational underachievement early will only be possible with targeted support to help underachieving children. This may require specialist teachers and additional funding, perhaps through a pupil premium as campaigned by Save the Children, to support and incentivise schools. In times of economic downturn, it may be even more challenging to invest in tackling academic disadvantage, through schemes such as additional tutoring and mentoring which have been proved successful. However, given the long-term costs in support services required later by underachieving adults, the investment in education seems to have both an economic and a moral rationale.

In addition to aiming to improve universal provision and providing additional funding, area-based initiatives aiming to improving the quality of services need to be continued. This will ensure that high-quality services are available where they are most needed and delivered by experienced staff, aware of the challenges people in poverty are faced with. Well-trained and experienced staff are also needed when families with complex needs who have traditionally disengaged with services are targeted.

The approach to delivering services and tackling disadvantage is constantly changing, and teachers and other educators are expected to play a more central role in this. Teachers have a moral responsibility to support all children to perform to the best of their ability in their given circumstances and ensure that they do not adopt stigmatising or defeatist attitudes and behaviours. In order to do this, teachers need knowledge, skills and determination to ensure that children and families of all socio-economic backgrounds are benefiting from the educational opportunities available and that education will help tackle social inequalities, rather than perpetuate them.

REFERENCES

Crozier, G. and D. Reay (2005) *Activating Participation: Parents and Teachers Working Towards Partnership*. Stoke-on-Trent: Trentham Books.

Goodman, A. and P. Gregg (2008) *Poorer Children's Educational Attainment: How Important are Attitudes and Behaviour?* York: Joseph Rowntree Foundation. Online at www.jrf.org.uk/publications/educational-attainment-poor-children

Horgan, G. (2007) *The Impact of Poverty on Young People's Experience of School.* York: Joseph Rowntree Foundation.

Magadi, M. and S. Middleton (2007) *Severe Child Poverty in the UK*. London: Save the Children. Online at www.crsp.ac.uk/publications/severe_child_poverty_in_the_uk.htm

McKendrick, J. H., G. Mooney, J. Dickie and P. Kelly (2011) *Poverty in Scotland: Towards a More Equal Scotland?* London: Child Poverty Action Group.

Preston, G. (2008) *2 skint 4 school: Time to End the Classroom Divide*. London: Child Poverty Action Group.

Ridge, T. (2002) *Child Poverty and Social Exclusion: From a Child's Perspective*. Cambridge: Polity Press.

Scottish Government (2008a) *Early Years Framework*. Online at www.scotland.gov.uk/Resource/Doc/257007/0076309.pdf

Scottish Government (2008b) *Achieving our Potential: A Framework to Tackle Poverty and Income Inequality in Scotland*. Online at www.scotland.gov.uk/Resource/Doc/246055/0069426.pdf

Scottish Government (2011a) *Child Poverty Strategy for Scotland*. Online at www.scotland.gov.uk/Resource/Doc/344949/0114783.pdf

Scottish Government (2011b) *Summary Statistics for Attainment, Leaver Destinations and School Meals*. Online at www.scotland.gov.uk/Resource/Doc/920/0119410.pdf

Wilkinson, R. and K. Pickett (2010) *The Spirit Level: Why Equality is Better for Everyone*. London: Penguin Books.

Websites

Child Poverty Action Group at www.cpag.org.uk
Joseph Rowntree Foundation at www.jrf.org.uk
Poverty Alliance at www.povertyalliance.org
Save the Children at www.savethechildren.org.uk
Understanding Glasgow at www.understandingglasgow.com

93

Gender and Scottish Education

Sheila Riddell

More than two decades ago, Paterson and Fewell argued that gender inequality was 'embedded within the structure and texture of Scottish education' (Paterson and Fewell, 1990, p. 2). The male domination of educational space was so much part of the fabric of Scottish education that it was almost invisible and was therefore unchallenged. This chapter considers the extent to which gender is still a neglected area within Scottish education. It is argued that in some respects, gender has attained a higher profile over recent years, featuring, for example, in the Scottish Government's analysis of high-level equality statistics (Scottish Government, 2006). However, many social and cultural aspects of girls' and boys' educational experiences, which play an important part in shaping adult identity, remain unexplored. Indeed, the focus on school attainment, and the lack of qualitative research on pupils' experiences of Scottish education, has sometimes contributed to the conclusion that girls are doing very well in the education system and the main issue to be addressed is the problem of boys' underachievement.

This chapter attempts to offer a more nuanced analysis, rejecting the view that girls and boys can be conceived of as homogeneous social groups and that the only challenge for educators is to tackle the issue of 'failing boys'. Analysis of the intersection between gender and social class in relation to attainment, identification of additional support needs (ASN) and school exclusions points to the existence of major within-group differences. Middle-class boys and girls perform very well within the education system, whilst boys and girls from socially disadvantaged backgrounds encounter major educational difficulties. Furthermore, whilst some girls are performing better than their male peers in school, this advantage is not fully translated into labour market advantage. Analysis of data on the position of women and men in the public sphere in Scotland shows that the position of women in high-profile roles in Scottish society, including education, has improved only slowly and has actually deteriorated in some areas since the establishment of the Scottish Parliament in 1999. The chapter concludes by suggesting that there is a need for a much greater focus on equality within Scottish education policy and practice, with intersectional analysis contributing to a deeper understanding of the part played by education in reproducing social advantage and disadvantage. Analysis of educational outcomes is important because of the link between school attainment, future life chances and the distribution of economic resources. However, this type of analysis provides only part of the picture. There is also a need for research that investigates pupils' social and cultural experiences within formal and informal school settings, which play a critical role in shaping identity.

UNPACKING THE NOTION OF EQUALITY

Discussion of educational equality needs to be informed by an understanding of the types of equality that are possible and desirable. Equality of outcome, framed within a discourse of (re)distribution, suggests that, in the interests of social justice, there is a need to break the link between educational attainment, social background and individual pupil characteristics such as gender. Whilst it is not possible to create a system in which all pupils achieve similar outcomes, it is important to identify and reduce disproportionalities in school attainment linked to variables such as gender and social class. By way of contrast, other accounts of educational equality, framed within a discourse of recognition, emphasise the importance of individual and group diversity. Within this discourse, far from blurring difference, the central goal is to celebrate cultural identity and difference. A key question here is to what extent attainment differences between social groups may be tolerated if these are linked to cultural identity. Some commentators focus on the tensions between the politics of redistribution and the politics of recognition, whilst others maintain that it is not only possible but also desirable for education policy to address different types of inequality, since these are often interlinked. In education, for example, this would involve making efforts to equalise the attainment of girls and boys from different social classes, whilst at the same time tackling racism and sexism. A central argument of this chapter is that since the 1970s, considerable emphasis has been placed on improving girls' academic attainment, with positive results, but there has been less focus on the way in which masculinities and femininities are produced within school, which may be damaging for both sexes.

GENDER, SOCIAL CLASS AND ATTAINMENT IN SCOTTISH EDUCATION

A major change within the Scottish education system over the past half-century has been the shift in the overall attainment levels of girls and boys. The Scottish Young People's Survey, conducted by the Centre for Educational Sociology (CES) at Edinburgh University from 1972 to 1992, provides longitudinal data on the educational outcomes and attitudes of Scottish school leavers. Comparisons of girls' and boys' examination performance over time revealed that whereas in the early 1970s there were no gender differences, by 1984 there was a considerable female advantage. Explaining these changes, CES researchers maintained that comprehensive reorganisation in Scotland was associated with a general improvement in standards of attainment, with girls, and pupils of low socio-economic status, being the main beneficiaries. It is also the case that the improvement in girls' relative attainment is linked to the influence of second-wave feminism, which emphasised the importance of women's participation in the public sphere of the labour market as well as the private sphere of the home. Second-wave feminism coincided with major economic changes in the late 1970s associated with the rapid increase in the price of oil. The disappearance of many jobs in areas such as shipbuilding, coal mining and manufacturing had an extremely negative impact on young working-class men, since these were the sectors where they had traditionally found employment. The expansion of the service sector, which occurred during the 1980s, led to an increase in female employment, although the jobs on offer in areas such as social care, beauty and call centres were often poorly paid and insecure. Households increasingly depended on women's as well as men's wages to cover expenditure. As a result, the confluence of feminist ideology and labour market changes contributed to a much greater emphasis on girls' educational attainment and labour market participation.

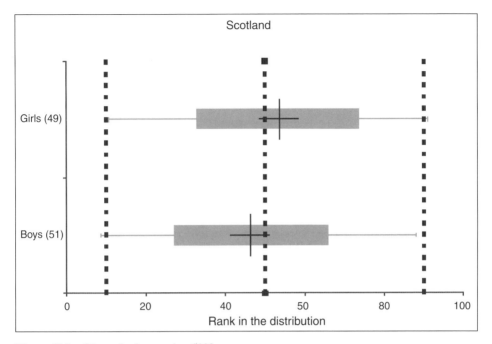

Figure 93.1   S4 results by gender, 2008

Source: Hills et al., 2010

Note: For each group, the black cross marks the group median. The thin horizontal bar shows the range between the 10th and 90th percentiles. The thicker bar shows the range between the 30th and the 70th percentiles. The three vertical lines running from the top of the chart to the bottom show the 10th, 50th (median) and 90th percentiles of the overall population.

The higher educational attainment of girls relative to boys has continued since the trend was first noted in the 1970s. Croxford et al. (2001) showed that in 1999, girls gained more Standard Grade awards than boys and the largest differences in performance were found at the highest levels of attainment, with more girls than boys gaining five or more awards at 1–2 (Credit level) and 1–4 (General and Credit level). A similar pattern was found at Higher Grade. In 1999, 55 per cent of young men compared with 61 per cent of young women completed S5 and S6 with three or more Higher Grade passes at A–C. Scottish Qualifications Authority (SQA) data from 1999 showed that female candidates performed better than males in every subject they entered, apart from PE, Economics and General Science. A decade later, Scottish Government data for 2010 showed a similar pattern, with girls doing better than boys throughout the distribution (see Figure 93.1). At the same time, as shown in Figure 93.2, differences in attainment associated with social disadvantage are much larger than those associated with social class. As noted by Hills et al., the differences between median results in the most and least deprived neighbourhoods in Scotland were equivalent to crossing half of the overall range of achievement.

A number of points are suggested by these data. First, it is evident that the relative difference in the performance of the most advantaged and least advantaged social groups is considerable and has not significantly eroded over time. Whilst gender differences persist,

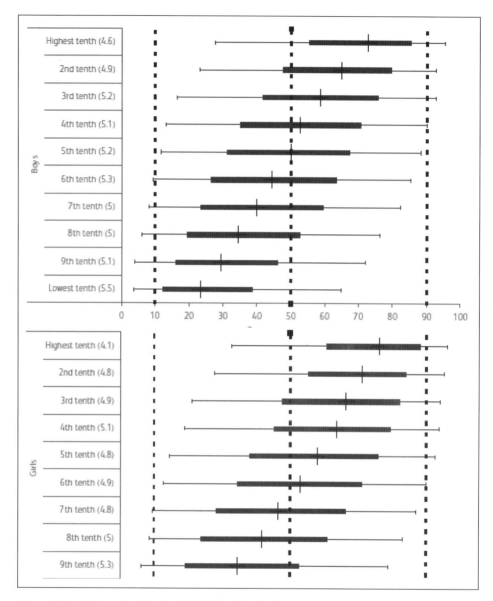

Figure 93.2 S4 results, Scotland, 2008, by deprivation level of neighbourhood (tenths of Scottish Index of Multiple Deprivation)

Source: Hills et al., 2010

Note: For each group, the black cross marks the group median. The thin horizontal bar shows the range between the 10th and 90th percentiles. The thicker bar shows the range between the 30th and the 70th percentiles. The three vertical lines running from the top of the chart to the bottom show the 10th, 50th (median) and 90th percentiles of the overall population.

social class differences are much greater, so a major concern of Scottish educators should be to narrow the attainment gap between those from more and less socially advantaged backgrounds. These differences in attainment are strongly associated with inequality in household income and, as noted by Hills et al. (2010), relative to other European countries both the UK and Scotland have high levels of economic inequality that act as a brake on social mobility. Despite the commitment of successive Scottish governments to tackle inequality, levels of economic and educational inequality in Scotland and England are broadly similar and highly problematic because of their association with many other social problems, including diminished life chances and adverse social problems ranging from domestic violence to drug and alcohol abuse (Hills et al., 2010).

Since inequalities related to social class are clearly much greater than those related to gender, the question arises as to whether gender issues still require attention. As argued below, it is essential to understand the ways in which gender intersects with social class at all levels and in subtly different ways. In order to illustrate aspects of this intersection, I discuss gender and the curriculum, ASN and post-school outcomes.

GENDER AND THE CURRICULUM

It is evident that gender differences in subject uptake have proved remarkably resistant to change, with major implications for the labour market position of women and men. Croxford et al. (2001) noted gender differences in subjects within curriculum modes. Since science is such an important subject in an increasingly technological age, it is worth looking closely at male and female participation in this area. Croxford (1997) analysed such patterns over a fifteen-year period in the context of the introduction of the common curriculum in the 1980s and the implementation of equal opportunities legislation. The proportion of girls aged 14–16 studying Physics slowly but steadily climbed from 10 per cent in 1976 to just over 20 per cent in 1990. In Biology, the proportion of boys studying the subject has also increased, from 12 per cent in 1976 to 28 per cent in 1990, although the pattern here is less smooth, with small declines in 1986 and 1988. Croxford concluded that even though the common curriculum in Scotland is presented in gender-neutral terms, the opportunities for choice within it result in girls and boys opting for different routes, with their attendant messages about appropriate concerns and future occupations for males and females. This, she suggests, may be attributed to 'deep-seated attitudes that some subjects are more appropriate for girls or boys'. She commented, 'Gender differences in post-compulsory courses and careers would be reduced if there was a larger common entitlement and less choice of subjects for the final two years of each national curriculum' (Croxford, 2000).

To what extent has the curriculum become more gender-neutral over the past ten years? In 2008–9, as illustrated by Table 93.1, gender differences in science subject awards are still very much in evidence. With regard to passes at SCQF level 5 (Standard Grade) in Physics, boys outnumber girls by two to one, whilst in Biology the reverse pattern is evident. Croxford's argument for deferring choice continues to be relevant, since decisions made at age 14 shape later options. In 2009, Kathleen Lynch and Maggie Feeley published a European comparative report on gender and education, examining, amongst other things, international differences in girls' and boys' representation in diverse subject areas (www. nesse.fr/nesse/activities/reports/gender-report-pdf). Some European countries, such as Sweden, where subject choice is deferred until upper secondary stage, have less marked gender divisions in science compared with Scotland. The strongly gendered curriculum in

Table 93.1   Qualifications of Scottish school leavers in Science and Maths by gender, 2008–9

Total qualifications attained by leavers at SCQF level 3 to 5, by subject gender: 2008/09

	SCQF Level 5		SCQF Level 4		SCQF Level 3		SCQF Levels 3 to 5	
	Male	Female	Male	Female	Male	Female	All	% of all leavers
Mathematics	7,542	7,993	10,290	9,951	8,158	7,874	51,808	94.0
Biology	3,621	7,676	3,180	6,168	1,525	2,865	25,035	45.4
Chemistry	5,646	5,770	3,902	3,700	1,243	1,223	21,484	39.0
Physics	6,278	2,798	4,081	1,124	1,495	402	16,178	29.4

Total qualifications attained by leavers at SCQF level 6 (Higher), by subject, grade and gender: 2008/09

	Male			Female			All Passes	
	A	B	C	A	B	C	All	% of all leavers
Mathematics	2,032	2,099	1,603	1,761	2,002	1,727	11,224	20.4
Chemistry	1,170	1,023	923	993	973	910	5,992	10.9
Physics	1,468	1,408	1,009	618	516	418	5,437	9.9
Biology	569	629	596	1,016	1,248	1,197	5,255	9.9

Source: Scottish Qualifications Agency

Scotland continues to send out clear messages to girls and boys about appropriate construc-tions of masculinity and femininity. Becky Francis (in Jackson et al., 2010) argues that girls, including those who are higher-achieving, may be reluctant to focus on science rather than arts subjects because of their fear of being perceived as unfeminine 'boffins'. This explains the well-established pattern of gender-specific subject choice, and helps to explain why girls and boys are complicit in decisions that may be against their long-term interests. The ongoing gendering of the curriculum in Scottish schools underlines the central point of this chapter: that it is far too simplistic to assume the only problem remaining to be solved is that of boys' underachievement.

GENDER AND ADDITIONAL SUPPORT NEEDS

A further persistent issue in Scottish education is the association between gender and ASN, which again cannot be understood in the absence of intersectional analysis. Table 93.2 shows the number of pupils identified as having additional support needs by gender and reasons for support.

Overall, two-thirds of pupils identified as having ASN are boys and they outnumber girls in every category of difficulty. Gender differences are greatest in the areas of social, emo-tional and behavioural difficulties (SEBD) (76 per cent male), autistic spectrum disorder (86 per cent male) and specific learning difficulties (such as dyslexia) (69 per cent male). Genetic and physiological differences between males and females are likely to account for some of these differences. However, the fact that the largest gender differences occur in areas that are dependent on professional judgement as well as pupil behaviour suggests that it is also nec-essary to look at the performance of masculinity by (some) groups of boys and the way this

Table 93.2   Pupils with additional support needs: reasons for support by gender, 2010
Occurrences. Pupils with more than one reason for support will appear in each row.

				Rate per 1,000 pupils		
	Female	Male	Total	Female	Male	Total
Pupils for whom reason for support is reported[1]	23,322	45,492	68,814	70.6	132.6	102.2
Learning disability	4,004	7,530	11,534	12.1	22.0	17.1
Dyslexia	2,722	5,841	8,563	8.2	17.0	12.7
Other specific learning difficulty (e.g. numeric)	2,131	4,093	6,224	6.5	11.9	9.2
Other moderate learning difficulty	3,816	6,647	10,463	11.6	19.4	15.5
Visual impairment	833	1,172	2,005	2.5	3.4	3.0
Hearing impairment	688	867	1,555	2.1	2.5	2.3
Deafblind	27	25	52	0.1	0.1	0.1
Physical or motor impairment	1,666	2,851	4,517	5.0	8.3	6.7
Language or speech disorder	2,169	5,031	7,200	6.6	14.7	10.7
Autistic spectrum disorder	920	5,586	6,506	2.8	16.3	9.7
Social, emotional and behavioural difficulty	3,551	11,187	14,738	10.8	32.6	21.9
Physical health problem	1,647	2,298	3,945	5.0	6.7	5.9
Mental health problem	212	442	654	0.6	1.3	1.0
Interrupted learning	475	652	1,127	1.4	1.9	1.7
English as an additional language	2,764	3,289	6,053	8.4	9.6	9.0
Looked after	1,067	1,327	2,394	3.2	3.9	3.6
More able pupil	376	400	776	1.1	1.2	1.2
Other	2,105	3,743	5,848	6.4	10.9	8.7

[1] The number of pupils for whom a reason for support is recorded was amended on 3 February 2011.

Source: Scottish Government, 2011

is understood by teachers. Intersectional analysis is particularly important in understanding the social processes involved in the construction and identification of SEBD. Whilst all types of ASN are more likely to occur amongst pupils living in socially deprived neighbourhoods, this discrepancy is particularly marked in relation to the large group of pupils identified as having SEBD. This is a particularly stigmatised category of difficulty which is used by professionals to label children, but is rarely sought by parents, unlike categories such as attention deficit and hyperactivity disorder, autistic spectrum disorder or dyslexia, which have been described by Roger Slee (1995) as 'labels of forgiveness' since they imply that neither parent nor child is to blame for the educational difficulties that have arisen.

As with pupils identified as having SEBD, it is clear that exclusions are not randomly distributed amongst the pupil population but are socially structured. Table 93.3 shows that boys and pupils who have ASN (mainly SEBD and learning disabilities) are much more likely to be excluded than others. Pupils who are looked after by the local authority are nine times more likely to be excluded than others, whilst pupils living in the 20 per cent most deprived areas are seven times more likely to be excluded than those living in the 20 per cent least deprived areas as defined by the Scottish Index of Multiple Deprivation. Despite the clarity of these patterns, gender and social class analyses have been almost invisible in the world of education for children with ASN, which tends to focus on the needs of the individual pupil in isolation from his or her social context.

Table 93.3   Cases of exclusion and rate per 1,000 pupils by gender, looked-after status, disability, additional support needs and Scottish Index of Multiple Deprivation (SIMD, 2009) 2009–10

	Cases of exclusions	Rate per 1,000 pupils
Boys	24,168	70
Girls	6,043	18
Assessed or declared disabled	798	70
Not assessed or declared disabled	29,114	44
Looked after by local authorities	3,875	355
Not looked after by local authorities	26,336	40
Pupils with additional support needs	7,651	174
Pupils with no additional support needs	22,261	35
Lowest 20% of SIMD (Most deprived)	13,076	91
Highest 20% of SIMD (Least deprived)	1,614	12

Source: Scottish Government, 2011

Disproportionalities in the field of ASN and exclusions highlight the social and educational marginalisation of boys from disadvantaged backgrounds. Scottish Government statistics on the prison population (one of the highest in western Europe at 153 per 100,000 population) show that 95 per cent of prisoners are men aged under 25 from socially disadvantaged backgrounds. Half were previously excluded from school and the majority have literacy and numeracy skills below the level that would be expected for an 11-year-old child. Given the 'school to prison pipeline' also identified in other developed countries, there is clearly an economic as well as a social imperative to address the educational failure of economically and socially disadvantaged young men. However, this is not to imply that girls from socially disadvantaged backgrounds are 'doing fine'. Osler (2006) has drawn attention to the negative experiences of girls who are excluded, or who absent themselves, from school, often finding themselves allocated to units where staff are used to dealing with the problems of violent young men rather than depressed young women. As noted above, two-thirds of pupils identified as having learning difficulties in Scottish schools are young men who also have behavioural problems. As a result, the difficulties of girls who may hide their problems by withdrawing from social interaction in the classroom may easily be overlooked. In addition, as discussed in the section below, irrespective of their level of achievement at school, young women generally do worse than their male counterparts, as indicated by their post-school outcomes.

GENDER AND POST-SCHOOL OUTCOMES

Girls' performance in Highers has improved more rapidly than that of boys since the late 1970s, and this is reflected in the fact that they now make up the majority of students in higher education, as shown in Table 93. 4.

The difference is particularly marked in the university sector, where 57 per cent of undergraduate students are female. In further education colleges, which account for about 20 per cent of all higher education in Scotland, the gender difference is much less marked, with women making up 51 per cent of all higher education students in further education colleges. Despite the numerical dominance of women in higher education, gender dif-

Table 93.4 Students by headcount and per cent in colleges and universities by level of education and gender in Scotland, 2009–10

	Colleges HE level		Colleges FE level		Universities HE level	
Men	22,853	49%	138,627	45%	107,988	43%
Women	23,757	51%	169,848	55%	143,341	57%
Total	46,609	100%	308,476	100%	251,330	100%

Source: Scottish Funding Council

ferentiation of the higher education curriculum remains strong, reflecting and amplifying gender differences in the school curriculum. It is also the case that women do not translate their success in school and higher education into the labour market. Hills et al. note that women are paid 21 per cent less in terms of median hourly pay for all employees and 13 per cent less than men for those working full time. Allowing for shorter working hours, weekly earnings of women in full-time employment are 22 per cent less than those of men. For women in their 20s, the gap is much smaller, but within four years of graduation, nearly twice as many men have earnings over £30,000 as women. Hourly wages for women, far from growing with experience, are highest for those in their early 30s and lower for each subsequent age group. Unlike men, career progression in wages is only seen for women with higher qualifications employed in the public sector. Women's pay relative to men's declines at the moment of first becoming a mother, and continues to decline throughout most of the first child's childhood. Gender inequalities in the labour market are not only experienced by well-qualified women. Howieson and Iannelli (2010) demonstrated that girls with low levels of qualification at school have much worse labour market outcomes than their male peers. Overall, then, although girls are outperforming boys in school, they are certainly not garnering the benefits of this early success later in the world of work which lies beyond the school gates.

WOMEN AND MEN IN PUBLIC LIFE IN SCOTLAND

Given the emphasis on equality in the Scotland Act 1998, it is worth considering the extent to which the Scottish Parliament, established in 1999, has succeeded in delivering greater gender equality. As noted by Phillips (1998), the fair representation of women in the public sphere is extremely important because of the messages that reverberate across society, including into schools and workplaces, about whose voices should be heard and which agendas should be addressed. The data presented in Table 93.5 on the percentage of women in top jobs in Scotland allow us to identify trends in different areas from 2003 to 2011. Women are clearly under-represented in elected office, and now make up a quarter of Scottish Westminster MPs. In other areas, however, there has been a worrying decline. Around 35 per cent of MSPs are women, a lower proportion than was the case in 2003, and only 16.7 per cent of Scottish MEPs are women. The proportion of women acting as local authority council leaders has fallen by half and is now only 16.7 per cent of the total. Women are now better represented in top jobs in education, accounting for 30.9 per cent of second-ary school headteachers, 28.6 per cent of further education college principals and 28.6 per cent of university principals. Given the preponderance of female staff in many parts of the

Table 93.5   Percentage of top jobs in Scotland held by women since 2003

	2003	2004	2005	2006	2007/8	2011
Politics						
MPs with Scotland constituencies	15.3	15.3	15.3	13.6	13.6	22.4
Ministers in the Scottish Parliament	22.2	27.8	27.8	27.8	31.3	31.6
Members of the Scottish Parliament	39.5	39.5	39.5	38.8	34.1	34.9
Local authority council leaders	18.8	18.8	18.8	18.8	18.8	9.4
Scottish Members of the European Parliament	25.0	28.6	28.6	28.6	28.6	16.7
Public sector						
Public appointments	32.2	33.6	34.7	34.7	32.4	32.2
Local authority chief executives	9.4	12.5	12.5	12.5	12.5	28.1
Senior police officers	6.9	7.1	7.1	10.7	7.4	14.8
Judges of the Court of Session	9.4	9.4	12.5	11.8	11.8	15.2
Headteachers of secondary schools	17.6	17.6	21.0	23.2	25.9	30.9
Further education college principals	22.9	26.1	22.7	27.3	29.5	28.6
University principals	14.3	14.3	14.3	21.4	21.4	28.6
Health service chief executives	23.8	23.8	19.0	23.8	23.8	36.4
Trade union general secretaries	No data	No data	No data	18.6	20.6	25.7

Source: Equality and Human Rights Commission, 2011

education system, there is clearly a need to ensure fair representation at the highest levels. Furthermore, schools have a very important job to do in encouraging girls as well as boys to develop the confidence that will enable them to engage in politics and the public sphere.

FUTURE ISSUES FOR POLICY MAKERS AND PRACTITIONERS

As a preliminary to this section, it is worth noting the rapid changes that have happened in the position of women in society over the past two decades and the perils of predicting the future. From a position of performing worse than boys at Higher Grade in the mid-1970s, girls of all social classes are now performing better than boys of similar social class in all subject areas, although gender differentiation in the curriculum remains stubbornly in place. In the late 1970s, however, this was not what was predicted. Noting the way in which post-war education reports and legislation had tended to reinforce the provision of different education for boys and girls, Deem predicted that after a brief period of liberalism in the 1970s which saw the introduction of equal opportunities legislation, the advent of Thatcherism was about to herald:

> A gradual return to the education of women for domestic labour, emphasis on the importance of motherhood to the economy and the reproduction of 'suitable' labour power (i.e. that which is prepared to accept low wages and discipline) as the need for women's paid work outside the family evaporates. In many areas, girls leaving school will have little possibility of entering employment at all; if they do find jobs, especially in manufacturing, clerical or secretarial work, it is likely that the microchip will soon begin to eat away at that work. (Deem, 1981, p. 141)

Such analysis assumed that women's position in the labour market was more tenuous than that of men, that male labour would be preferred to that of women and that motherhood was foisted on women to serve the needs of the economy rather than something they chose them-selves. For the past twenty years, jobs in manufacturing, where men predominated, have disappeared, whilst the service sector, employing more women than men, has expanded. More women with young children are in employment and girls' education is based on the assumption that they will be economically active for most of their lives, as well as shoulder-ing the major responsibility for home making and child-rearing. So, whilst avoiding the pitfalls of prediction, it is worth concluding with some of the questions for research, policy and practice that demand to be addressed over the coming decade.

Over the next decade, it is likely that devolution will progress further or that Scotland will attain full independence. In either case, there is likely to be considerable reflection on the nature of Scottish identity and the type of country Scotland aspires to be. This could involve further moves in the direction of economic liberalisation, with low taxation, a minimal welfare state and growing levels of inequality. Alternatively, Scotland might choose to adopt a Nordic form of social democracy with high taxes, a strong welfare state and a marked emphasis on equality. Given existing anxieties about boys' performance and their vulnerability to school failure and exclusion, it will be important for schools to use the new focus on the development of a positive Scottish identity to foster new versions of mas-culinity that reject macho posturing and place greater value on emotional development in all children. Tackling male disaffection and violence requires a critical look at popular male culture, rather than seeing the male as the norm and the female as in some way deficient. Male teachers clearly have an immensely important role to play here (though the increasing feminisation of the teaching force runs counter to this). Some attempts to assist boys, such as establishing single-sex classes, may actually do more harm than good by perpetuating the idea that boys are essentially different from girls and therefore require an entirely different approach to the curriculum, pedagogy and assessment. Interestingly, Murphy ('Equity, assessment and gender', in Salisbury and Riddell, 2000) has shown that there is no form of assessment that disproportionately favours girls (girls do better, no matter how they are assessed).

Paying attention to the problems of socially disadvantaged boys does not mean that girls can now be ignored. In addition to enjoying far less teacher attention than boys, young women may well be the victims of male violence both inside and outside the school. High achieving middle-class girls may experience fear of failure, becoming the custodians of middle-class awareness of risk and danger. The rate of teenage pregnancy is higher in Scotland than in the rest of the UK, and yet there is still reticence about the discussion of sexual health in some schools. Issues that have a gender dimension, such as discipline, violence and bullying, are still often seen in gender-neutral terms, despite the evidence that these are perpetrated and experienced differently by boys and girls (see Riddell et al., 2010).

Finally, the gendered impact of a range of policy innovations needs to be explored. These include policies of privatisation and marketisation, currently being strongly promoted by the coalition government at Westminster but with knock-on effects for the Scottish educa-tion system. In the wake of the international financial crisis, local authorities will continue to experience year-on-year budgetary reductions leading to inevitable cuts in education spending. Responses to the crisis have to date included a demonisation of welfare claimants and a renewed emphasis on the redemptive power of work in the absence of jobs. Over the coming years, it will be important to analyse the gendered impact of policies relating to the privatisation of education, public spending cuts and welfare reform.

Throughout this chapter, an attempt has been made to draw out the interaction of a range of variables, for it is impossible to understand the effects of gender without also paying attention to the multiple identities that people occupy, based on nationality, ethnicity, age, social class, sexual orientation and disability. In particular, intersectional analysis is essential to understand the way in which gender and social class interact. Exploring these interactions, whilst continuing to promote the idea of greater social equality based on the principles of both redistribution and recognition, will provide much work for researchers and practitioners well into the next decade.

REFERENCES

Croxford, L. (1997) 'Participation in science subjects: The effects of the Scottish Curriculum Framework', *Research Papers in Education*, 12 (1): 69–89.

Croxford, L. (2000) 'Gender and national curricula', in J. Salisbury and S. Riddell (eds), *Gender, Policy and Educational Change: Shifting Agendas in the UK and Europe*. London: Routledge.

Croxford, L., T. Tinklin, A. Ducklin and B. Frame (2001) *Gender and Pupil Performance Interchange 70*. Edinburgh: Scottish Executive.

Deem, R. (1981) 'State policy and ideology in the education of women, 1944–1980', *British Journal of Sociology of Education*, 2 (2): 131–43.

Equality and Human Rights Commission (2011) *Sex and Power 2011 Scotland*. Glasgow: Equality and Human Rights Commission.

Hills, J., M. Brewer, S. Jenkins, R. Lister, R. Lupton, S. Machin, C. Mills, T. Modood, T. Rees and S. Riddell (2010) *An Anatomy of Inequality in the UK*. London: London School of Economics.

Howieson, C. and C. Iannelli (2010) 'The effects of low attainment on young people's outcomes at age 22–23', *British Education Research Journal*, 34 (2): 269–90.

Jackson, C., C. Paechter and E. Renold (eds) (2010) *Girls and Education 3–16: Continuing Concerns, New Agendas*. Maidenhead: Open University Press.

Murphy, P. (2000) 'Equity, assessment and gender', in J. Salisbury and S. Riddell (eds), *Gender, Policy and Educational Change: Shifting Agendas in the UK and Europe*. London: Routledge.

Osler, A. (2006) 'Excluded girls: interpersonal, institutional and structural violence in schooling', *Gender and Education*, 18 (6): 571–91.

Paterson, F. and J. Fewell (eds) (1990) *Girls in their Prime: Scottish Education Revisited*. Edinburgh: Scottish Academic Press.

Phillips, A. (1998) *The Politics of Presence*. Oxford: Oxford University Press.

Riddell, S., J. Kane, G. Lloyd, G. McCluskey, J. Stead and E. Weedon (2010) 'Gender and the new discipline agenda in Scottish schools', in C. Jackson, C. Paechter and E. Renold (eds), *Girls and Education 3–16: Continuing Concerns, New Agendas*. Maidenhead: Open University Press.

Salisbury, J. and S. Riddell (eds) (2000) *Gender, Policy and Educational Change: Shifting Agendas in the UK and Europe*. London: Routledge.

Slee, R. (1995) *Changing Theories and Practices of School Discipline*. London: Routledge.

94

Religious Intolerance: Sectarianism

Stephen J. McKinney

One of the catalysts for the contemporary debate about sectarianism in Scotland and the related discussion about sectarianism and education is the lecture delivered at the Edinburgh International Festival by the composer James MacMillan in August 1999. He described sectarianism and the continued existence of anti-Catholicism in Scottish life as Scotland's shame. This provoked a series of strong reactions of condemnation or support from politicians, Christian Churches and academics in an extended aftermath that received considerable media attention. Perhaps the most significant outcome of the MacMillan lecture was that it prompted a growing realisation that the debate on the history and continued existence of sectarianism was complex, but was characterised by vague conceptualisation and imprecise use of terminology and, often, when presented in the media, denigrated into stereotype and superficial argumentation. It became clear that this was a debate about serious anti-social attitudes and behaviour that impinged on many of the important spheres of Scottish life: public discourse; family life; the media; academia; sport; religion; education; law; and politics. Further, this widely publicised contemporary debate created an uncomfortable disjuncture with the more positive and optimistic academic and political discussions on Scottish identity and culture prompted by the opening of the new devolved Scottish Parliament in 1999. The Labour–Liberal Democrat coalition Scottish Executive (1999–2007) pressed for social change. They challenged the Old Firm (Celtic and Rangers football clubs) and other football clubs to publicly act against sectarianism. They hosted a major summit on sectarianism (2005), published subsequent action plans (2006), proposed changes to legislation and initiated and approved anti-sectarian education. In 2008, the Scottish SNP Scottish Government (2007–) was initially criticised by Jack McConnell, the previous First Minister, for allowing the anti-sectarian impetus to stall but the SNP continued the work and introduced anti-sectarianism legislation. This chapter will touch on many of these aspects of the sectarianism debate but is concerned primarily with sectarianism and education, particularly school education. The chapter will begin with a discussion of terminology and continue with a brief overview of the history of sectarianism and the contemporary debate in the twenty-first century. It will then explore Catholic schools and sectarianism, and educational initiatives to combat sectarianism.

TERMINOLOGY

As has been suggested above, the definition or description of the terms used in the debate about sectarianism is of crucial importance. What is sectarianism? It is not a word that is exclusive to Scotland, nor is it a word that refers exclusively to interdenominational Christian hostility. It is closely related to prejudice, discrimination and bigotry. Pious (2003) points out that most social scientists agree that prejudice 'involves a prejudgement, usually negative, about a group or its members'. He adds that this is not confined to a 'statement of opinion or belief, but an attitude that includes feelings such as contempt, dislike or loathing' and states that discrimination occurs when members of a group are put at a disadvantage or treated unfairly because of their membership of the group. My understanding of the word 'bigotry' is that it refers to a narrow-minded intolerance of others, especially directed at those of other races or religions. Contemporary sectarianism refers to intolerance between a number of different groups within the same religious faith that could lead to hostility and possibly even violence.

In the Scottish context, the historical Catholic–Protestant divide has become almost synonymous with sectarianism – sometimes configured as anti-Irishness or anti-Catholicism, though these terms can limit the focus of the debate to a form of racial discrimination or a one-sided form of religious bigotry. It has emerged that forms of sectarianism exist within other faith groups in twenty-first-century Scotland, such as sectarianism between different Muslim groups in Glasgow. Because of limited space, this chapter will be restricted to the commonly perceived Catholic–Protestant divide. Once again, terminology is very important. The words 'Catholic' and 'Protestant' appear to be used in the sectarianism debate as sociological labels with little acknowledgement or understanding of the wide variety of types of interpretation of Catholic and Protestant identity that exist in contemporary Scotland. The words 'commonly perceived' have been chosen carefully as, despite recent legislation and convictions for sectarian offences, there is little systematic social science evidence about the scope and extent of sectarianism in contemporary Scotland (for some useful insights, see Bruce et al., 2004; Deuchar and Holligan, 2008; Raab and Holligan, 2012).

Trying to establish a more detailed definition of sectarianism for the contemporary Scottish scene is problematic, but I have constructed the following as a working definition that can be applied to the different manifestations of sectarianism in contemporary Scotland (adapted from Leichty and Clegg, 2001; Bruce et al., 2004; Scottish Government, 2012). Sectarianism consists of intolerant and anti-social beliefs and attitudes that may be translated into actions. These can be expressed in inter-personal, communal and possibly institutional ways. Sectarianism involves some exclusivist and intransigent understanding of religious beliefs and attitudes and typically is in the form of a shared or group identity that fosters a sense of belonging. This is sometimes more of a quasi or nominal religious identity, with very loose connections to mainstream religion. Sectarian groups tend to claim that their identity is founded on authentic historical roots and shared memory – roots and memory that may be selective, self-serving or semi-mythical. The group is configured such that other groups that hold contrasting beliefs and attitudes can be perceived to threaten the identity and history of the group and are stigmatised as the 'others'. In a sense it is a claim for belonging and communal identity that is defined partly by affirming an authentic identity but partly by opposition to the threat of the inauthentic – the 'others'. Sectarianism, therefore, justifies the marginalisation, alienation and possible demonisation of the 'others'. This can lead to hostility, verbal abuse, intimidation and even violence.

HISTORY OF SECTARIANISM IN SCOTLAND

The academic discussion of the history of sectarianism in Scotland is fraught with conceptual and methodological challenges. McAspurren (2005) highlighted the academic tensions between historians, social scientists and educationalists and the dispute about the reliability of the types of evidence used in each discipline. There can also be a common assumption that sectarianism in Scotland is somehow unique, and consequently there have been few attempts to frame the history in wider conceptual debates about migrants and typologies of migrant experience. The concise history of sectarianism below is an introduction to this topic and the references provide more extensive sources.

Contemporary sectarianism has its roots in the Scottish Reformation and the radical rejection of Catholicism by Calvinist Protestantism. The extent and enforcement of this Reformation was widespread, though Catholicism continued to be practised in some parts of the North and some of the Western Islands. The Catholic population diminished and Scotland was perceived to be missionary territory by the Vatican. The Presbyterian Church of Scotland became a national institution. This national institution was to gain even more importance after the Union of Parliaments of Scotland and England in 1707 and became a significant marker of Scottish identity in the absence of Scottish self-government. The small Catholic community in Scotland (emancipated in 1829) was to be increased in the nineteenth and twentieth centuries by the arrival of immigrant Catholic Lithuanians, Poles and Italians, but the arrival of the Irish Catholic immigrants was to have the greatest impact (McKinney, 2008).

Irish Catholics had been migrating gradually to Scotland for work from the late eighteenth century and the numbers grew from 25,000 in the 1820s to 126,321 in 1840. The series of famines in Ireland from 1845 to 1849 led to a large-scale exodus and by the 1850s there were about a quarter of a million (predominantly Catholic) Irish-born in Scotland (Devine, 2006). The growth of the Catholic community aided the restoration of the Roman Catholic hierarchy in 1878. This immigrant group was fleeing destitution and possible death and arrived in great number, with few resources, to cities like Glasgow which were already overpopulated. As with the sudden arrival of any large group of impoverished immigrants, this caused resentment in the 'host' population. The Irish Catholics were perceived to be competitors for unskilled work and a drain on social services. Further, they were Catholic – a challenge not just to the Presbyterian vision of Christianity that rejected Catholicism, but also to the role of the Church of Scotland as surrogate Parliament.

There are allegations of discrimination against Catholics in the labour market. It is often claimed that institutional sectarianism (discriminatory employment practices) was a feature of Scottish industrial life up to the post Second World War period and possibly beyond. This is difficult to assess as the evidence for this is often anecdotal or based on oral histories. There are also suspicions that some Catholic communities engaged in introversion and self-isolation and Catholics were stereotyped as strike breakers. Mitchell (2008, pp. 3–19) challenges these accounts as exaggerated with evidence of recurring patterns of mixed marriage and, while acknowledging some incidences of strike breaking, evidence of wide participation in industrial action by those of Irish Catholic extraction from the mid-nineteenth century.

Three important aspects of the history of sectarianism in the nineteenth and twentieth centuries continue to impact on contemporary debate in Scotland. These are the Orange Order; the establishment of football clubs associated with 'Catholic' or 'Protestant' support; and anti-Catholic activity between the two World Wars. The Orange Order is a Protestant fraternity, founded in Ireland in 1795 and committed to the maintenance of the 'Protestant Constitution and Christian heritage of the United Kingdom' (Grand Orange Lodge of Scotland, online at www.orangeorderscotland.com/). Irish immigration to Scotland in the nineteenth century had not been restricted to Catholics. Irish Protestants had also immigrated, although they were fewer in number. These Irish Protestants have been presumed to be Presbyterians but they were, in fact, Presbyterians and Church of Ireland (Meredith, in Mitchell, 2008). Both denominations of Irish Protestant were to have strong links with the Orange Order in Scotland and helped the Order to grow in Scotland in the nineteenth century. The Order and the traditional Orange Walks have been linked with anti-Catholic sentiments and have been the focus of tension and outbreaks of violence in the past. The official stance of the Orange Order in the twenty-first century is a more moderate pro-Protestantism, and the behaviour of the largely working-class rank and file is internally monitored (Kaufman, in Mitchell, 2008). The Order in Scotland takes a strong stance against paramilitary sympathies, and unruly bands have been banned from participating in marches. In the last thirty years, the Orange Order has diminished in size and has become increasingly secular and marginalised from mainstream Protestantism (Bruce et al., 2004; Kaufman, 2008). The question of the rights of the Orange Order to march in public is hotly debated each year, with little sympathy for the marches from the press and media.

Catholic male religious and Irish immigrants, or those of Irish descent, founded a number of football clubs in three major cities: Glasgow (Celtic, 1888); Edinburgh (Hibernian, 1875) and Dundee (Dundee United, originally Dundee Hibernian, 1909). Historically, these clubs drew on a predominantly 'Catholic' support and are all matched with rival teams drawing on 'Protestant' support: Celtic and Rangers (1872); Hibernian and Hearts (1874), and Dundee United and Dundee (1893). The local derbies in the three cities have, at times, been flash-points for 'Catholic/Protestant' divisions which, fuelled by consumption of alcohol, have had the potential to erupt into hostility and violence – most notably in the Celtic–Rangers fixtures.

Anti-Catholicism and the activities of anti-Catholic campaigners such as Alexander Radcliffe, John Cormack and John White in the early to mid-twentieth century are dis-cussed in some detail in the previous editions of this book (see Finn, 1999, 2003; Conroy, 2008) and in works such as Brown (1991), Bruce et al. (2004) and Devine (2006). Academic opinion, however, is divided on the extent of popular support for sectarianism in this period and the longevity of the effects. Perhaps it is more instructive to observe that many of these campaigners came to prominence in the economic depression between the two World Wars. They were often extremists who preyed on widespread anxieties about unemployment and social insecurity, and used the rhetoric of racism, religious difference and, crucially, economic threat posed by the Catholics of Irish descent to galvanise support. This support tended to be short-lived but this anti-Catholic activity has had a strong impact on historical and cultural memory.

There were a number of important sociological and ecclesiastical developments in the post Second World War era leading up to the millennium. The multinational companies that became established in this period are credited with open employment practices. The introduction of comprehensive schooling and grants for higher education meant that a greater percentage of Catholics were able to enter the professions and higher-level employ-ment (Devine, 2006). The later stages of this period are also marked by a significant decrease in Church of Scotland attendance and also attendance in the Catholic Church. Academics such as Brown (2001) and Bruce et al. (2004) interpret this as the inevitable result of secu-larisation. The decrease in Church attendance may be the result of a number of factors: secularisation, indifference or increasing affluence but it raises serious questions about quasi-religious or nominal religious identity distanced from the influence of mainstream churches.

Research by Deuchar and Holligan (2008) on territoriality and sectarianism in Glasgow suggests that within the scope of the sample, most of the young people had no interest in religion but were conscious of issues related to religious divisions. They noted that the biggest influence on any sectarian attitudes came from the family. This detachment from the mainstream Christian Churches is highly relevant because it is a detachment from a potentially alternative, or even corrective, influence. These Christian Churches have been engaged in sustained ecumenical dialogue and shared activities since the 1960s (the Orange Order expresses its anxieties about the 'Romeward tendencies' of the Church of Scotland from the 1970s, www.orangeorderscotland.com). Brown (2000) claims that this ecumenical dialogue has brought an end to any explicit sectarian or anti-Catholic discourse in the institutional Church of Scotland. Brown's comment can be substantiated by a series of symbolic historic events and actions. Archbishop (later Cardinal) Winning addressed the Church of Scotland Assembly in 1975. The moderators of the Church of Scotland of 1982 and 2010 met Popes John Paul II and Benedict XVI when they visited Scotland. The Church of Scotland dissociated from anti-Catholic statements in the Westminster Confession of Faith and publicly apologised for attacks on the Irish Catholics in the early twentieth century.

SECTARIANISM: THE TWENTY-FIRST CENTURY

The James MacMillan lecture may have been one of the catalysts for the contemporary debate but increased hostility between some supporters of Celtic and Rangers football clubs was to prompt Jack McConnell into organising a highly publicised Summit on Sectarianism on 14 February 2005. Participants included representatives from the Catholic Church, the Church of Scotland, the media, the police, the Orange Order, industry, local authorities, football clubs and supporters' clubs, educational organisations and anti-sectarian organisations, but very limited academic representation. Ironically *The Record of the Summit on Sectarianism* (Scottish Executive, 2005) fails to express any clear definition of sectarianism, but it does identify and discuss 'four key themes central to tackling bigoted and sectarian attitudes and behaviours'. These are: interfaith work; education; sport; and marches and parades. These would later become distilled to three: football-related violence; marches and parades; and education. The Scottish Executive also published *Action Plan on Tackling Sectarianism in Scotland* (2006) and *Building Friendships and Strengthening Communities: A Guide to Twinning between Denominational and Non-Denominational Schools* (2006). Both documents highlighted the importance of education. Education, then, has been consistent as one of the fundamental components of the Scottish Government's strategy to address sectarianism in contemporary Scotland.

Further football-related hostility led to First Minister Alex Salmond calling a meeting for police and representatives of football clubs and associations to be held on 8 March 2011. A joint statement was produced condemning violence, bigotry and alcohol misuse in relation to football-related activity. Concurrent with this joint statement, the Scottish Government invested over half a million pounds in a number of key public organisations that are committed to tackling sectarianism (and racism), including Sense over Sectarianism; Nil by Mouth; Show Racism/Bigotry the Red Card; the Youth Community Support Agency, which promotes religious tolerance; and the Iona Community, which runs anti-sectarian courses in Scottish prisons (Scottish Government news release, 2011). Subsequent funding of £272,000 to eradicate bigotry was shared among Sense over Sectarianism, Nil by

Mouth, Show Bigotry the Red Card and the Iona Community for 2012 to 2013 (Scottish Government news release, 2012). Some of these organisations will be discussed in sections below. The Scottish Government also commissioned a sectarianism poll, published on 2 September 2011. The results indicated that 89 per cent of Scots agree that sectarianism is offensive; 89 per cent agree that sectarianism is unacceptable in Scottish football; 85 per cent agree that sectarianism should be a criminal offence; and 91 per cent agree that stronger action should be taken to tackle sectarianism and offensive behaviour associated with football (Sectarianism Poll Data Tabulations, 2011, TNS BMRB. Online at www.scotland.gov. uk/Topics/Justice/law/sectarianism-action-1/publications).

It was stated that these statistics represented the opinion of 'an overwhelming majority' of the Scottish people and they were used to expedite the progress of the Offensive Behaviour at Football and Threatening Communications (Scotland) Act. This Act was passed by the Scottish Parliament on 14 December 2011 and came into force on 1 March 2012. The Act includes coverage of sectarian chanting and threatening behaviour related to football matches.

CATHOLIC SCHOOLS IN SCOTLAND AND SECTARIANISM

Scottish Executive and Scottish Government documentation in the contemporary debate on sectarianism has never stated that Catholic schools in Scotland cause or promote sectarianism. The *Record of the Summit* (2005) contains a very brief and bland reference to denominational schools – 'the role of denominational and non-denominational schools was discussed'. It is also emphasised that denominational and non-denominational schools do not teach sectarianism or intolerance, but the reverse. This position is maintained in the *Action Plan* (2006), *Building Friendships* (2006) and subsequent Scottish Government documentation. However, the question of possible links between state-funded denominational schools and sectarianism lingers in public perception and the media and needs to be discussed (McKinney, 2008). State-funded denominational schools in Scotland are synonymous with Catholic schools (bar one Jewish primary school and a small number of Episcopalian schools). The issue, therefore, is focused on the possible links between state-funded Catholic schools and sectarianism.

This focus may appear to be consistent with some debates in Northern Ireland; however, great care needs to be taken in such comparisons as Catholic schools in Scotland are not inextricably bound to (in some places, rigid) territorial divisions, as many Catholic schools are in Northern Ireland. Nor are there easy comparisons in funding arrangements. Similarly, it can be problematic to locate the Scottish debate within the wider debates on faith schools in England and Wales. These wider debates include a greater variety of faith schools, e.g. Church of England, Catholic, Jewish and, to a lesser extent, Muslim, Hindu, Sikh, Orthodox Christian, Evangelical Christian and other Christian denominations. These debates focus on contesting state funding for faith schools; divisiveness of faith schools; faith schools as selective (on grounds other than religious); faith schools inhibiting social cohesion; faith schools as instruments of indoctrination or inhibiting rational autonomy; and faith schools denying the rights of the child. The issue about Catholic schools and sectarianism could, arguably, be configured somewhere between debates about the divisiveness of faith schools and faith schools inhibiting social cohesion, though with some qualifications (see Chapter 27). The question of divisiveness is not normally constructed along the lines of destructive anti-social attitudes and behaviour that are endemic to sectarianism. Allegations of the inhibition of social cohesion *are* centred on the perception of an intentional religious and cultural exclusivism. It is interesting to note that these allegations are usually focused on Muslim, Jewish and Emmanuel Christian schools in England, not Catholic schools (McKinney, 2008).

There are further complications. The inevitable focus on Catholic schools in the faith school debate in Scotland can create a culture of suspicion that opponents to Catholic schools in Scotland are anti-Catholic, rather than opposed to faith schools *per se*. It is important to acknowledge that secularists, humanists and some academics and politicians are consistently opposed to state funding for faith schools and perceive Catholic schools in Scotland as a local manifestation of a wider UK problem.

Are state-funded Catholic schools linked to sectarianism? At least three possibilities emerge from the debates: Catholic schools are one of the causes of sectarianism; Catholic schools contribute to sectarianism; and Catholic schools are linked to sectarianism by association. The argument that Catholic schools are one of the causes of sectarianism has no historical foundation as sectarian attitudes and behaviour pre-date the establishment of post-Reformation Catholic schools in Scotland. It would also seem illogical and irresponsible for the government of 1918 to welcome such schools into the national state-funded school system and allow them to retain their religious identity if they were the root cause of sectarianism. If Catholic schools are perceived to be a contemporary root cause, this would have to be substantiated with evidence.

The second possibility is that Catholic schools contribute to sectarianism. On 21 January 2007, the *Sunday Times* reported on a commissioned poll that revealed that 70 per cent of Scottish voters believed that denominational schools contribute to sectarianism and should no longer be state-funded (details of the questions and demographics of the sample of 1,005 voters were not provided). The *Sunday Times* published an accompanying commentary article by Alex Salmond, which praised Catholic schools and refuted any links with sectarianism, presumably to balance the discussion. The poll seemed to indicate that some members of the Scottish electorate think that Catholic schools contribute to sectarianism. It is difficult to conceive of Catholic schools intentionally contributing to sectarian attitudes or behaviour, as this would be inauthentic and incoherent – directly and radically antithetical to their publicly espoused rationale to foster Christian values and build a Christian community within the Catholic school. It is of course possible, but such attitudes or behaviours discerned in a Catholic school would seriously endanger the Catholic identity and, if sustained, would threaten its continued existence. It is also very difficult to conceive that a serving government would not take punitive action against any state-funded school that contributed to anti-social attitudes and behaviours that are viewed so seriously.

Perhaps the possibility that is most likely is that Catholic schools may be linked to sectarianism by association, but this can apply equally to the non-denominational schools. The Catholic school as an institution does not condone sectarianism; nor does the non-denominational school. It may be that some individuals associated with Catholic schools, or non-denominational schools, harbour or even articulate sectarian attitudes, and, in extreme cases, demonstrate sectarian behaviour, in their private or public lives. This can be interpreted as naive, ill-informed or rooted in misguided versions of Christian or quasi-Christian identity, but remains resolutely socially unacceptable and unacceptable to mainstream Christianity. These are people who have some association with the school system, and where these attitudes and behaviours are actually manifested in Catholic or non-denominational schools corrective action would be taken.

ANTI-SECTARIAN INITIATIVES AND RESOURCES IN SCHOOL EDUCATION

The *Record of the Summit on Sectarianism* (2005) is a useful starting point as it identified education – both school education and education outside schools – as one of the four key themes in tackling sectarianism. The *Record* praises the good work undertaken in anti-sectarian education and the creation of resources for use in school. It suggests that sectarianism can be addressed across the curriculum and that young people require a greater understanding of history. Pupils from different schools should meet, and joint campuses and initiatives such as twinning are helpful. Consequently, the section on 'work to be taken forward' recommends that good practice and positive experiences should be identified and shared, and good practice should be rewarded through awards schemes or other incentives. This work to be taken forward was progressed in the *Action Plan on Tackling Sectarianism in Scotland* (2006). This document outlined some successes such as the launch of the web-based education resource Don't Give It, Don't Take It. This resource was accompanied by seminars and a national conference for teachers. Plans included greater use of drama in schools and greater opportunities for twinning. The then Scottish Executive pledged to fund anti-sectarian project work in schools.

In 2006, the Scottish Executive also published *Building Friendships and Strengthening Communities: A Guide to Twinning between Denominational and Non-Denominational Schools.* The document recommended that denominational and non-denominational schools work together to provide opportunities for the pupils to meet each other. Successful twinning often includes a specific focus (a shared task or study), but does not necessarily have to be explicitly focused on sectarianism. The document advises that a member of senior staff champions the process and it should involve other staff too. Parents should be kept informed and, where possible, external agencies or bodies, such as Nil by Mouth, could be invited to support the activities. Examples of good practice cited were shared assemblies, S6 conferences, joint drama workshops and performances. These initiatives and documents represented a concerted approach to profile and promote anti-sectarian education. As stated above, there was criticism that the anti-sectarian initiative had stalled under the SNP administration and this criticism was consolidated by some research. Deuchar and Holligan (2008) state that the young people they interviewed in their study claimed that they had no input on sectarian issues in school. Consequently, their report recommended that anti-sectarian initiatives and education be 'put back on the political agenda' (p. 19). The SNP government's response to this recommendation (and others) was to re-prioritise anti-sectarianism education and provide some supportive funding to a number of key local and national organisations engaged in anti-sectarian education.

Sense over Sectarianism (SOS) is a partnership between Glasgow City Council, Nil by Mouth, Celtic FC, Rangers FC, the Glasgow Presbytery of the Church of Scotland and the Catholic Archdiocese of Glasgow. The aim is to challenge sectarianism in the greater Glasgow area and provide support and free resources for Glasgow schools. SOS has produced a short document that outlines how anti-sectarian education for primary schools can be aligned to experiences and outcomes of Curriculum for Excellence. These experiences and outcomes are mostly drawn from Health and Wellbeing, and Literacy but some are drawn from Religious and Moral Education, Social Studies and Expressive Arts. Interestingly, none is drawn from Religious Education (Roman Catholic schools) but this may be an oversight. Resource packs include 'Beyond a Culture of Two Halves' to assist youth workers, an SOS drama pack and 'Divided City' (based on the novel by Teresa Breslin) that is mainly used by P7 pupils. 'Divided City' has been used to great effect in Glasgow schools, for example in the ten denominational and non-denominational primaries associated with Knightswood and St Thomas Aquinas secondary schools (*TESS*, 24 June 2011). Each denominational primary was twinned with a non-denominational primary and all of the P7 pupils read the book. One headteacher stated that the twinning had a positive impact on the relationships between the pupils and led to further collaboration such as joint trips and sporting events.

Nil by Mouth is a registered charity that was established in Scotland in 1999 by Cara Henderson in response to the sectarian murder of her friend Mark Scott in 1995. This charity aims to achieve a 'society free from sectarianism where cultural and religious diversity is respected and celebrated by everyone'. Nil by Mouth provides interactive workshops and training programmes for schools and youth groups. These are designed to draw on the attitudes and experiences of the young people and to encourage them to challenge sectarianism in their lives and in society. In October 2011, Nil by Mouth launched its 'Champions for Change' School Accreditation Scheme. The scheme is an opportunity for schools to celebrate their anti-sectarianism work and earn recognition for their best practice. Duncanrig secondary school in East Kilbride was the first school to achieve accredited status in June 2012. The school organised anti-sectarian workshops and an inter-faith football tournament. The pupils in the school created a code of conduct that did not permit sectarian words, jokes, songs or negative behaviour towards others on religious grounds. If the code was broken, the pupil would be asked for an explanation and a letter sent home.

Show Bigotry the Red Card is a strand of the anti-racism charity Show Racism the Red Card that was founded in 1996 and predominantly uses football players and teams as role models (www.theredcardscotland.org/home). They work closely with football teams for young people providing interactive anti-sectarian workshops alongside football sessions (for example, in North Ayrshire). They adopt a similar approach with youth organisations, targeting the 'hard to reach' 16–19 age group across the west of Scotland. Education Scotland highlights 'challenging sectarianism' on their website and provides information on sectarianism and examples of anti-sectarian resources and shared practice. There is a helpful link between the themes of challenging sectarianism and religious bigotry with Curriculum for Excellence and the UN Rights of the Child legislation.

CONCLUDING REMARKS

'Scotland's shame' has become Scotland's public, and highly publicised, shame. Sectarianism and anti-sectarianism have become the focus of continued debate and concerted intervention as Scotland has progressed into the twenty-first century. There is now greater clarity about the history, nature and locus of sectarianism and sectarian activity. Within Scottish society a strong emphasis on anti-sectarianism policies and strategies has been developed and progressed. Residual sectarian attitudes can remain and are difficult to monitor and regulate, but legislation has been introduced to tackle offensive behaviour and the government is determined to check and punish any manifestations of sectarianism. This includes sectarian statements posted on fan websites and social networking sites. The major football clubs have publicly opposed sectarianism though initiatives such as Bhoys against Bigotry and later Youth against Bigotry (Celtic) and Follow with Pride (Rangers). All football clubs have clear statements of unacceptable conduct. The Orange Order continues to project a more moderate public profile.

Major Scottish institutions – the Scottish Government, local authorities, mainstream Christian Churches and charitable organisations – demonstrate steadfast commitment to anti-sectarianism and supporting anti-sectarian education in schools and youth work. The next stage of the strategy should be to evaluate the long-term effects of anti-sectarian education and the potential benefits for Scottish society. This could be initiated with those young people who have participated in projects such as the twinning of primary schools in Glasgow (SOS), Champions for Change (Nil by Mouth) and the workshops provided by Show Bigotry the Red Card. The evaluation could measure their attitudes as they mature into young adults and, critically, move beyond the influence of school education or youth groups. Perhaps one of the deeper issues is how the anti-sectarian message and anti-sectarian education continues for some young people who, once they have left school education and youth groups, appear to be outside the realms of many societal influences.

REFERENCES

Brown, C. G. (2001) *The Death of Christian Britain*. London: Routledge.

Brown, S. J. (1991) 'Outside the covenant: The Scottish Presbyterian churches and Irish immigration, 1922–1938', *The Innes Review*, 42 (1): 19–45.

Brown, S. J. (2000) 'Presbyterians and Catholics in twentieth-century Scotland', in S. J. Brown and G. Newlands (eds), *Scottish Christianity in the Modern World*. Edinburgh: T. & T. Clark.

Bruce, S., T. Glendinning, I. Paterson and M. Rosie (2004) *Sectarianism in Scotland*. Edinburgh: Edinburgh University Press.

Deuchar, R. and C. Holligan (2008) *Territoriality and Sectarianism in Glasgow: A Qualitative Study*. Glasgow: University of Stratchclyde and University of the West of Scotland. Online at www.educationscotland.gov.uk/images/Territoriality_and_Sectarianism_in_Glasgow_-_Report_tcm4-584986.pdf

Devine, T. M. (ed.) (2000) *Scotland's Shame? Bigotry and Sectarianism in Modern Scotland*. Edinburgh: Mainstream.

Devine, T. M. (2006) *The Scottish Nation 1700–2007*. London: Penguin Books.

Education Scotland (2010) *Challenging Sectarianism*. Online at www.ltscotland.org.uk/supportinglearners/positivelearningenvironments/inclusionandequality/challengingsectarianism/index.asp

Leichty, J. and C. Clegg (2001) *Moving beyond Sectarianism*. Dublin: The Columba Press.

McAspurren, L. (2005) *Religious Discrimination and Sectarianism in Scotland: A Brief Review of Evidence (2002–2004)*. Edinburgh: Scottish Executive Social Research.

McKinney, S. J. (2008) 'Do Catholic schools in Scotland cause or promote sectarianism?', in S. J. McKinney (ed.), *Faith Schools in the 21st Century*. Edinburgh: Dunedin Academic Press.

Mitchell, M. J. (ed.) (2008) *New Perspectives on the Irish in Scotland*. Edinburgh: John Donald.

Pious, S. (2003) 'The psychology of prejudice, stereotyping and discrimination: an overview', in S. Pious (ed.), *Understanding Prejudice and Discrimination*. New York: McGraw-Hill.

Raab, G. and C. Holligan (2012) 'Sectarianism: myth or social reality? Inter sectarian partnerships in Scotland, evidence from the Scottish longitudinal study', *Ethnic and Racial Studies*, 35 (11): 1934–54.

Scottish Government publications referred to in this chapter are downloaded from: www.scotland.gov.uk/Topics/Justice/law/sectarianism-action-1/publications

95

'Race' Equality in Scottish Education

Rowena Arshad

In the title of this chapter, the word 'race' is in inverted commas as an acknowledgement that this is a discredited term with no scientific basis. The term however continues to be enshrined in legislation and used in common parlance. Some policy makers, researchers and writers prefer to use the term 'ethnicity' rather than 'race'. This is in part an attempt to move away from the term 'race' and its connotations with historical abuses such as slavery but also an attempt, at least in the UK, to try and acknowledge the differences in people as defined by the House of Lords (*Mandla* v. *Dowell Lee*, 1983). The House of Lords defined ethnic groups as people who have some long shared history (ancestral or geographical) and characteristics arising from a range of factors that include social and cultural conventions, a common language, literature and religious observance. Both terms are sometimes used synonymously, leading to hybrid terms such as 'race/ethnicity' which can cause confusion.

For educators, it is important to be aware of the different cultural factors such as language, diet, religion, family origins and social conventions which contribute to the make-up of the ethnicity of a learner. It should be remembered that the characteristics of ethnicity can also be fluid and imprecise, which is why self-identification of ethnicity is favoured in data collection exercises. However, as educators we also educate and act against racial prejudice, racial discrimination and racism, and these can be triggered by a combination of factors, including those related to ethnicity but also by skin colour, nationality and migrant status.

It is perhaps helpful to attempt to define how 'race' equality has been used in education. Robin Richardson (2003), an experienced adviser in equalities work, suggests the term has largely been used in two ways. The first is as a measurable outcome. Achieving 'race' equality in education would mean reducing any gaps in attainment and achievement between different ethnic groups. The second is as a moral value, aspiration and principle, so we would educate people not to discriminate. The two are connected concepts and there is a need to be mindful of both definitions.

The demography of Scotland in terms of ethnic diversity has been changing in direction and at a pace that has not been witnessed since the migration of Irish people to the west of Scotland in the latter half of the nineteenth century. The in-migration upturn in recent times is evident from the Scottish Government's *High Level Summary of Statistics* (Scottish Government, 2011) where the previous trend of net out-migration began to reverse in the late 1980s, to be replaced in the early to mid-2000s by a net in-migration trend, a situation that has lasted up to the time of writing this chapter, with net gains of at least 19,000 people per annum since 2004. Most recorded in-migrants are young people in their late teens or young adults up to the age of 30, including those of school age and students in further and higher education. In-migrants have come from within the United Kingdom, the European Union and overseas. Scotland's school pupil population has consequently witnessed an increase in ethnic and linguistic diversity in the past decade. In 2007, there were 138 different languages reported as being the main home language from pupils attending Scottish schools, with 15,411 pupils identified as having English as an Additional Language (EAL). This figure rose to 24,555 in 2011 (*Summary Statistics for Schools in Scotland*, 2, 7 December 2011; online at www.scotland.gov.uk/Publications/2011/12/06114834/16). The spread of languages spoken covers all local authorities in Scotland The last known figure published by the Scottish Government was in 2009 (see www.scotland.gov.uk/Publications/2009/11/05112711/70).

In terms of ethnicity, of the 670,235 pupils whose ethnic backgrounds were known, nearly 93 per cent recorded themselves as White (Scottish, Other British, Gypsy/Traveller or Other). Approximately 5.1 per cent of pupils recorded themselves as from a minority ethnic group (including the category Mixed) with the largest group being of Asian Pakistani background (1.6 per cent) followed by Mixed (1 per cent). In contrast, the teaching workforce in Scotland remains predominantly white, female and monolingual and this profile has remained fairly constant over the years. The latest Scottish Government statistics for teachers record that 95 per cent were White UK or White Other, 2 per cent Minority Ethnic and 3 per cent Not Disclosed with little variation among sectors (see www.scotland.gov.uk/Publications/2011/12/06114834/9).

An obvious question arises then about whether the Scottish teaching workforce is 'fit for purpose' for twenty-first-century diversity in Scottish schools. It is impossible to say whether a more diverse teaching workforce would assist the promotion of 'race' equality, but what it would do is raise the profile of ethnic and linguistic diversity far more than is the case at the moment. The key to promoting 'race' equality and challenging racism is for the Scottish teaching workforce as a whole to become knowledgeable and aware of 'race'-related issues and to work with such diversity. Research has shown that a considerable number of teachers in Scotland remain uncomfortable engaging with issues related to 'race' differences and racism (Scottish Executive, 2005) and that pupils find that teachers have an under-appreciation of the impact of everyday racism on pupils (Caulfield et al., 2005). Therefore there is a need for those who educate and mentor teachers to develop understanding and confidence in engaging with matters related to 'race'. Part of the development of such confidence is to have knowledge about the debates around 'race' equality in education and to consider strategies for engaging with increased diversity at the chalkface.

The first part of this chapter traces key developments in the discourses on multicultural and anti-racist education (MCARE) up to the establishment of the Scottish Parliament in 1999. Next, it critically reflects on developments since 1999, touching briefly on the impact of legislation. It then moves on to discuss some issues that teachers need to be mindful of as they take forward 'race' equality in their work. Finally, the chapter identifies some of the challenges as we work through this current age of austerity.

'RACE' EQUALITY PRE-DEVOLUTION

The dominant approach in Scottish education in the 1970s could be characterised as 'assimilationist': the emphasis was on assisting children for whom English was a second language (designated 'ESL children') to 'catch up' with indigenous English-speaking peers in their adopted country. The response in many Scottish regions was the establishment of language centres to which children could be withdrawn from mainstream schools for full- or part-time education. Community languages such as Punjabi, Urdu and Cantonese were deemed of less value and indeed potentially harmful to the cognitive development of the 'ESL child'. Eager for their children to achieve in their 'adopted' country, minority ethnic parents listened in good faith to teachers, crediting them with knowing best; and, as English was to be given priority, they often refrained from speaking their mother tongue to their children at home. The change in direction to multicultural education, which was being introduced in England, was yet to be reflected in Scotland, where the emphasis was still on the assimilation of minority ethnic children into a white English-speaking Scottish culture.

Multicultural education, when it was introduced, concentrated on celebrating exotic aspects of minority cultural traditions with the aim of promoting understanding and toler-ance, while ignoring discriminatory barriers in institutional policies and practices. The most significant initiative to prompt the shift to MCARE was the Swann Report, *Education for All* (DES, 1985). Originally set up to investigate the problems of minority ethnic children, it concluded by drawing attention to the growing underachievement of African-Caribbean pupils in mainstream schools and highlighted the impact of social and economic factors. It was the first government report to mention 'institutional racism' as a problem in British society and urged all schools, irrespective of ethnic composition, to confront the issue of racism as part of political education. The MCARE approach recognised the value of cultural diversity but went further, embracing an analysis of issues of power and social justice and arguing for basic changes in the social structures of society, a view that was consistent with the legal frameworks of the day, including the Race Relations Act 1976. This period saw a plethora of courses on MCARE offered to teachers and the production of policies and guidelines for permeation of MCARE into curricula. The prevalence and effectiveness of these discourses have remained contentious and problematic in Scotland, where the educa-tion community is still divided on whether to adopt multicultural education or anti-racist education, or both, and on whether to incorporate MCARE within a generic equal oppor-tunities policy or to retain discrete policies for each equality dimension. The consultations undertaken by the Centre for Education for Racial Equality in Scotland (CERES) in 1999 led to the following conclusions:

- Schools (particularly primary schools) tended to verge on playing 'safe' rather than challeng-ing racism; their curriculum approach reflected multiculturalism in the choice of resources and an emphasis on festivals and global-development education.
- Compartmentalisation and 'bolt-on' approaches predominated, particularly in the second-ary sector, where the responsibility for MCARE in the curriculum was often located within specific subject areas and mainly within social subjects.
- Visible minority ethnic pupils were still viewed as 'incomers'/'foreigners' or alternatively were endowed with an assimilated 'Scots' or 'New Scots' identity; how they defined them-selves was not given much attention by the curriculum developers and researchers.
- Bilingualism, apart from Gaelic, was perceived as a problem by teachers; the provision of community language teaching (for example, Urdu, Punjabi, Bengali, Cantonese or Arabic) was sparse, despite the well-documented research evidence on the cognitive benefits of bilin-gualism and the maintenance of mother tongue. This was further aggravated by the shortage of bilingual teachers in general and, in particular, as members of what was then known as English as a Second Language (ESL) services in Scotland.

- Few authorities had effective policies for dealing with racial harassment, despite the evidence of racial bullying; some appeared to be reluctant to see the relevance of such policies, particularly for early years or special education sectors.
- The rhetoric of 'parental power, choice and diversity' promulgated by the Conservative government had remained marginal to the interests of minority ethnic parents, who were invisible in many of the policy documents in Scottish education and, more seriously, in decisions about their children's education.

Meanwhile, at general and education-policy level, it was widely assumed that Scotland had 'good race relations' and that there was 'no problem' here. Consequently, racism did not become an issue in Scottish political and policy discourse or, by extension, in teacher education institutions or schools. Later, there was a shift from a stance of total complacency to one that accepted, albeit grudgingly, that racism was a phenomenon not confined to urban areas where high numbers of minority ethnic people resided, such as Birmingham. The research by three Central Region primary teachers, Donald, Gosling and Hamilton, *'No problem here'? Children's Attitudes to Race in a Mainly White Area* (SCRE, 1995) remains a very useful example of the kind of study that starkly addresses the importance of pursuing an active anti-racist agenda, particularly for schools with low numbers of minority ethnic pupils.

'RACE' EQUALITY SINCE SCOTTISH DEVOLUTION

Around the time of devolution, two events occurred in the United Kingdom that signalled a step-change in how those in power in Scotland responded to issues related to 'race'. The first was the publication of the Stephen Lawrence Inquiry Report (Macpherson, 1999). This report challenged those in power to address the matter of institutional racism, a concept previously not acknowledged in any real sense in Scotland. The report discussed the central importance of organisational culture and suggested that norms, assumptions, expectations and culture were powerful influences in shaping the ethos of a workplace. The second was the enactment of the Race Relations (Amendment) Act (RR(A)A) 2000, which is discussed further later in this chapter. The then Scottish Executive responded by publishing *An Action Plan for Scotland* in 2000 and creating two Scotland-wide groups to take forward its recommendations. One of these groups, the Race Equality Advisory Forum (REAF), prepared a 'race' equality strategy for Scotland, which included a section on education. The REAF education sub-group consulted widely with education practitioners and came forward with fifty-six recommendations covering all levels of Scottish education. Among the key recommendations were:

- the introduction of a presumption that all data collection and reporting should be done on an ethnically disaggregated basis and, where appropriate, by religious affiliation, belief and languages used;
- the development and publication of a strategy in which English as an Additional Language (EAL – this term replaced the previous expression, English as a Second Language, ESL) and bilingual provision could be maintained, developed and resourced in Scotland;
- providers of continuing professional development courses for teachers should include 'race' equality issues as both permeative and discrete strands;
- the upcoming review of initial teacher education should incorporate an analysis of equality issues, including 'race' equality; the General Teaching Council for Scotland to ensure that consideration of 'race' equality issues form part of the quality control during validation reviews of teacher education courses/institutions and in the setting of teacher competences.

The Scottish Executive responded by commissioning a website and staff development materials for teachers including a self-evaluation resource to complement the HMIE publication *How Good Is Our School?* These materials were all placed on the Learning and Teaching Scotland (now Education Scotland) website but unfortunately most of them are no longer available following a change of government and an updating of the site. A key resource that has been retained is *Learning in 2(+) Languages* (LTS, 2005). This document helps classroom teachers better support children who are accessing the curriculum through EAL. It examines the strengths and development needs of bilingual learners and how to address them more effectively within the mainstream classroom. The Scottish Executive Central Research Unit (CRU) commissioned an audit of research on 'race'-related issues within Scotland in the past ten years. The CRU report by Netto et al. (2001) also included an education chapter. That chapter documents over 100 pieces of research related to 'race' and education. HMIE (2005) conducted an inspection of how 'race' equality was being taken forward in Scottish schools.

The Scottish Executive also commissioned the first study on the experiences of minority ethnic pupils in Scottish schools. The Minority Ethnic Pupils' Experiences of School in Scotland (MEPESS) research (Scottish Executive, 2005) involved interviews with ninety-four pupils, eighty-two teachers and thirty-eight parents across four authorities. The report found that many teachers identified the promotion of 'race' equality as working with minority ethnic pupils, particularly regarding how well the school was supporting bilingual pupils through its interaction with the EAL service; and with schools having a strong stance on tackling racist incidents, plus the promotion of multiculturalism through the celebration of faiths and festivals. Few teachers focused on how they might use the curriculum to take forward anti-racist issues or on what the benefits of 'race' equality work might be for majority ethnic pupils or for themselves as teachers. Unlike many of the teachers interviewed, parents did not equate 'race' equality only with bilingualism or tackling racist incidents. 'Race' equality was perceived in broader terms: the need to recognise individual and collective identities, to foster a positive self-image in children, to create and maintain a socially just environment and to challenge deficit and tokenistic models of awareness. On the whole, parents and pupils appeared comfortable with the terms 'race equality' and 'anti-racism', even though their interpretations varied. In contrast, many teachers acknowledged unease with the vocabulary of race. There was a marked avoidance of terms such as 'anti-racist' or 'race equality'; instead, teachers tended to use words such as 'inclusion' and 'diversity'.

Though the MEPESS findings in this area contrast with the findings of Caulfield et al. (2005) that, overall, young people in Glasgow schools felt that their teachers did show respect for different customs and religious practices, the study did demonstrate that, for some respondents, the experience of racism was a daily reality. Such findings corresponded with those of Caulfield et al., who also found that nearly all of the fifty-six minority ethnic young people interviewed in Glasgow had either encountered or witnessed racist behaviour. Caulfield et al. found that the incidence of racism tended to peak in secondary schools, increasing after S2. From the MEPESS study, it would appear that there existed a gap between the reality of pupils' lives and those of their teachers, whom pupils considered to be generally unaware or ignorant of such issues. Teachers, in the main, interpreted the infrequency of witnessed racist incidents as a sign that there were no problems, and the central and valuable role of authority EAL or Bilingual Support Services were singled out for special praise as problem-sorters. The MEPESS study concluded that the perceptions by the three groups regarding the meaning of 'inclusion' and its relationship with 'race' equality varied considerably. Well-founded education initiatives must address such divides, or they fail to engage the joint commitment of pupils, parents and teachers.

In the period since 2007, the funding for 'race' equality work in education has seen a significant decrease. In the education sector, challenging racism has largely been through the funding of Show Racism the Red Card, which works with schools through workshops on prejudice reduction and challenging Islamophobia. The reduction in funding for 'race' equality work can be attributed in part to the banking crisis of 2008 which saw public-sector spending reduced; however, other factors have also contributed, namely the government's belief that things are improving in Scotland and that 'race' equality work in schools will be taken forward as part of the Additional Support for Learning Act 2004 and through main-streaming 'race' in general educational initiatives such as Getting it Right for Every Child.

THE IMPLICATIONS OF LEGISLATION

The first major piece of legislation for education since 1980, the Standards in Scotland's Schools etc. Act 2000, included equal opportunities in its schedules. It required each edu-cation authority to include an account 'of the ways in which they will, in providing school education, encourage equal opportunities and in particular the observance of the equal opportunity requirements' (Section 5.2b). However, the key legislation that was to bring the most wide-ranging change in 'race' equality in Scotland was the RR(A)A 2000. This pioneering Act was introduced to strengthen the framework for ensuring that all public authorities provide services in a way that is fair, accessible and non-discriminatory on the grounds of 'race', ethnicity or colour. It introduced three key provisions:

- It widened and strengthened the anti-discrimination provisions within the Race Relations Act 1976 to include all public functions.
- It extended the range and number of public authorities covered by the Act.
- It introduced a new and enforceable duty on key public authorities to promote 'race' equality in all that they do.

As a result of the RR(A)A 2000, Scottish pupil attainment is now disaggregated according to ethnicity. In 2006, the Scottish Executive published *High-Level Summary of Equality Statistics: Key Trends for Scotland*, Chapter 6 of which covers school education. In rela-tion to pupil attainment, there is now a national picture of how different ethnic groups are performing in schools. These latest statistics show that minority ethnic female pupils are attaining more Standard Grades at Credit level than minority ethnic male pupils, and overall minority ethnic pupils are attaining more Credit grades than white pupils. Of the minority ethnic pupils, Chinese pupils are attaining the highest; the lowest attainment is for pupils whose ethnic groups are not known/disclosed, and then African pupils. Attainment patterns would appear to have remained fairly consistent across all ethnic groups since 2002–3. While pupil attainment results have been published since 2006, there has unfor-tunately been no further update on the ethnicity breakdown since the 2006 statistics. The RR(A)A 2000 was replaced by the Equality Act 2010. The Equality Act, which has its home in the Westminster Parliament, brought together a range of older equality-related legisla-tion relating to 'race', gender and disability with the addition of three new areas – sexual orientation, religion and belief, and age – into a single framework. At the time of writing this chapter, the Equality and Human Rights Commission has indicated that there will not be a statutory code of practice for schools but that a guidance document would be published instead. The only guidance available at present is one released by the Department for Education for schools in England and Wales (see www.education.gov.uk/aboutdfe/ policiesandprocedures/equalityanddiversity/a0064570/the-equality-act-2010).

In Scotland, the Additional Support for Learning (ASL) Act 2004 is viewed by many politicians, education policy makers and practitioners as an important piece of legislation to support the diversities of pupils within Scottish schools. The implementation and maintenance of the ASL Act has had huge support and funding from the Scottish Government and is often cited by schools, local authorities and the Scottish Government as a key vehicle for promoting inclusion (and 'race' equality) for all pupils. This Act, developed within the Scottish Parliament, places a duty on every education authority in Scotland to meet the 'additional need' of any pupil in its care. 'Needs' as defined by the Act are wide-ranging and cover pupils who are being bullied and those with different ability or learning needs (gifted, with learning difficulty, those who require EAL support) as well as particular categories of pupils such as those from gypsy traveller backgrounds.

However, anyone engaging with 'race' equality work in Scottish schools needs to interrogate the possibilities and limitations of the Additional Support for Learning Act (2004) in relation to addressing and promoting 'race' equality. It can be argued that the ASL Act, by focusing attention on individual pupil needs, has enabled Scottish education to disengage from considering institutional forms of discrimination as suggested by the Stephen Lawrence Inquiry report (Macpherson, 1999). The ASL Act's main focus is to ensure that learning and teaching provision is adjusted to ensure every child is included. This may or may not require adjustments at institutional level. The Lawrence Inquiry report emphasised the need for institutional change, which required vigorous promotion of the ethical/ ideological values of 'race' equality within services and institutions, to recognise the existence of racism at different levels (personal, cultural and institutional) and to make changes accordingly. The ASL Act falls short of meeting these requirements.

TAKING 'RACE' EQUALITY FORWARD IN SCOTTISH SCHOOLS

There are some key questions which those who are taking forward 'race' equality work in schools could usefully reflect upon:

Do Teachers and Pupils Understand that 'Race' Equality Work is for All?

As already mentioned, the MEPESS study found that very few teachers interviewed recognised that 'race' equality work is of benefit to all pupils and should be taken forward regardless of the numbers of minority ethnic pupils in a school. It is still common for 'race' equality work to be perceived to be largely of benefit to minority ethnic pupils. It is not uncommon for teachers and pupils to equate multicultural education with teaching about 'international' cultures rather than the diverse cultures within Scotland (majority and minority).

Do Staff Appreciate how Racism can Occur in Everyday School Life?

Racism in its overt forms such as racist graffiti, racist name-calling or bullying is largely recognised and understood by teachers and certainly by senior pupils. No teachers or schools in Scotland would tolerate overt forms of racism, and most would find a way to address any such incidents. However, everyday forms of racism can go unnoticed and unchallenged. Subtle and everyday racism is rarely recognised or understood by those who are not on the receiving end and when such examples are pointed out, a common reaction is disbelief that racism can happen in this day and age. It is difficult to fully explain everyday racism but examples could include the telling of a racist joke in jest being seen as acceptable as it is 'not meant to hurt'; the question 'where do you come from?' being largely asked only of those who 'look different'; and operating 'colour-blindness' ('we don't see black or white, we treat everyone the same') in the mistaken belief that overlooking racial, ethnic or cultural differences promotes racial harmony and that identification of difference is discriminatory. Yet it is rare to hear of a minority ethnic person who would say that they do not see difference. Other examples could include bias by omissions and commissions in teaching resources and the systematic failure to offer first-language assessment as part of the initial/profiling assessment of bilingual pupils to determine appropriate educational provision. School leaders in particular would be well-advised to read Chapter 6 of the Stephen Lawrence Inquiry Report to see how institutional racism might apply to the organisational ethos of schools and local authorities.

Is 'Race' Equality Being Promoted at all Levels – that is, at the Classroom as well as School Level?

It is often easier to work at individual levels, promoting multicultural topics and celebrating festivals and faiths. However, if the capacities of Curriculum for Excellence are to be fully met, teachers will need to be bold and engage with challenging topics such as prejudice and discrimination. For example:

- *Confident Individuals* would include valuing diversity, offering insights into other lives, developing a sense of belonging for all (not making the assumption that there is an average pupil, that is a white, English-speaking, able-bodied, middle-class, Christian boy, living in a house with his biological, heterosexual parents).
- *Successful Learners* would include providing learners with an understanding and analysis of discrimination. Learners might be taught to explore what people have in common and where they differ, to look beyond labels and stereotypes, to develop an understanding of complex identity and to consider how discrimination manifests itself at a personal, cultural, institutional and structural level and within different contexts, for example in the world of work.
- *Responsible Citizens* would include building learner capacity to challenge discrimination against themselves and others. Learners would be given insight into the experience of being discriminated against, practising standing up for themselves, each other and unknown others and engaging in learning activities directly related to injustice, inequality, prejudice, discrimination and human rights. They would explore how people have resisted injustices locally and globally and how collectively people have shown solidarity with each other and achieved justice.
- *Effective Contributors* would include providing learners with opportunities to take action against discrimination. Learners would have a part in decision-making processes in school or institutional initiatives related to equity and anti-discrimination, for example against bullying, welcoming refugees, challenging gender stereotypes. They might become allies against discrimination through developing peer support skills, mentoring skills and campaigning skills, and they may carry out research to extend their own knowledge and understanding of discrimination and become familiar with legislation and political systems that uphold rights and responsibilities. (This framework was developed by Judith Mackinlay for CERES in 2007.)

CONCLUSION

The Scottish Government and local authorities have continued to declare their support for implementing the Equality Act 2010 and taking forward equality and fairness particularly via the Getting it Right for Every Child initiative, the ASL Act and the development of Curriculum for Excellence. Audit Scotland, evaluating the impact of RR(A)A 2000, found that local authorities needed to give 'race' equality higher priority. Their report recommended that public bodies needed to embed 'race' equality more effectively into improvement programmes and stated that more was required to identify and share good practice. It is therefore disappointing that some of the more recent government-commissioned reports aimed at modernising provision, such as the Calman Commission's 2009 report of its examination of Scottish devolution (*The Commission on Scottish Devolution*), the 2010 Christie Report on local authority reorganisation (*Commission on the Future Delivery of Public Services in Scotland*), which refers mainly to socio-economic inequality and the Donaldson Review of Initial Teacher Education (*Teaching Scotland's Future*, 2010) which makes no recommendation at all regarding the equalities field as a whole, collectively provide no mention of addressing 'race' equality in twenty-first-century Scotland.

Several key individuals who have worked in the field of promoting equality in Scottish education have expressed their views on achievements, hopes and fears. There was some optimism about the appointment of a senior inspector within HMIE with special responsibility for implementing the Equality Act 2010, an initiative that might help focus the Inspectorate's attention on evaluating local authority and school performance and confidence in equalities issues. The merger of HMIE and Learning and Teaching Scotland into one body, Education Scotland, has the potential of bringing equalities policy, evaluation, resource production and distribution into better alignment. It was also hoped that the Equality Act 2010, when it becomes fully operational, can have a significant impact in mainstreaming 'race' and the other equality areas into policy and practice dimensions of Scottish schools.

A senior local authority officer said that newly qualified teachers are increasingly less informed about issues to do with equality and inclusion. Others said that with the cuts in posts that used to support equalities work in local authorities and the cessation of funding for networks and organisations that used to link practitioners and support 'race' equality work across Scotland, the reality is that no one has an overall picture of how 'race' equality or anti-racist work is currently being taken forward in schools. Moreover, many resources developed in the first six years after devolution on multicultural and anti-racist education have not been updated or are no longer accessible.

Too much is still left to the individual teacher, headteacher, school or local authority officer to take forward. In this age of austerity, there is now an even greater need for those in charge of school education in the Scottish Government to be proactive in promoting 'race' equality in education. A laissez-faire approach to equalities and the setting of equality targets is not good enough in a context where many decision makers and practitioners at best still do not fully understand what 'race' equality means or at worst are under the naive impression that we have achieved 'race' equality in Scotland.

No one in Scottish education will argue that 'race' equality is an area that should not be taken seriously. However, the challenge to Scottish education is whether it is prepared to loosen its conservatism and to be bold enough to address key concepts of power, discrimination, racism and oppression instead of hiding behind more palatable terms like 'inclusion', 'diversity' and 'equal opportunities'. However, to do this, we need to provide opportunities for teachers and other education practitioners to discuss and debate sensitive and difficult issues without fear of being accused of being a 'racist'. In the current climate of cutbacks, opportunities for such spaces for discussion are being lost.

The current moves at education policy and planning levels to engage with issues of difference under the generic umbrella of equality, diversity and fairness is pragmatic. However, in so doing, care has to be taken not to lose the specific areas of equality such as race, gender, sexual orientation, social class and so on, particularly the areas the majority populus might perceive to be either irrelevant, too intimidating or simply no longer as important. This requires all involved in Scottish education from the government, providers of initial teacher education, those who quality assure and those who write curriculum to those who register teachers to critically reflect on how they are promoting 'race' equality and proactively challenging racism at all levels.

ACKNOWLEDGEMENTS

The author would like to thank Alan Bell, CERES Research Associate, for assisting in fieldwork interviews, analysis of documentation and advice about the content of this chapter.

REFERENCES

Caulfield, C., M. Hill and A. Shelton (2005) *The Experiences of Black and Minority Ethnic Young People following the Transition to Secondary School*. Glasgow: SCRE. Online at www.strath.ac.uk/media/departments/glasgowschoolofsocialwork/gccs/media_42667_en.pdf

Fanshawe, S. and D. Sriskandarajah (2010), *You Can't Put Me in a Box*. London: Institute for Public Policy Research. Online at www.ippr.org/images/media/files/publication/2011/05/you_cant_put_me_in_a_box_1749.pdf

Learning and Teaching Scotland (2005) *Learning in 2(+) Languages: Ensuring Effective Inclusion for Bilingual Learners*. Dundee: Learning and Teaching Scotland. Online at www.ltscotland.org.uk/Images/LearningInTwoPlusLanguages_tcm4-306089.pdf

Macpherson of Cluny, Sir William (1999) *The Stephen Lawrence Inquiry: Report of an Inquiry by Sir William Macpherson of Cluny*. London: The Stationery Office. Online at www.archive.official-documents.co.uk/document/cm42/4262/4262.htm

Moray Council (2005) *Race Equality*. Online at www.moray.gov.uk/moray_standard/page_43019.html

Netto, G., R. Arshad, P. de Lima, F. Almeida Diniz, M. MacEwen, V. Patel and R. Syed (2001) *Audit of Research on Minority Ethnic Issues in Scotland from a 'Race' Perspective*. Edinburgh: SECRU.

Richardson, R. (2003) 'Removing the barriers to race equality in education: ten points to think and talk about'. Paper presented at 'Steps for Promoting Race Equality in Education' conference, Brunei Gallery, London, 10 June. Online at www.teacherworld.org.uk/Articles/Robin-1.htm

Scottish Executive (2005) *Insight 16: Minority Ethnic Pupils' Experiences of School in Scotland (MEPESS)*. Edinburgh: Scottish Executive. Online at www.scotland.gov.uk/Publications/2005/03/Insight16/1 and (full report) www.scotland.gov.uk/Publications/2005/03/mepess/1

Scottish Government (2011) 'High level summary of statistics (HLSoS), population and migration' (updated August 2011). Online at www.gro-scotland.gov.uk/Statistics/at-a-glance/high-level-summary-of-statistics-trends/index.html

XI

SCOTTISH TEACHERS, TEACHER EDUCATION AND PROFESSIONALISM

This section deals with a wide range of issues relating to teachers: their professional preparation and subsequent development; their self-regulating professional body and trade union affiliations; research about them and by them, as well as the national research association to which a number subscribe; and the journals (both academic and professional) concerned with what they do.

The distinctive history and current provision of teacher education in Scotland is described in Chapter 96. Initial teacher education (ITE) was originally provided by monotechnic colleges of education for much of the nineteenth and twentieth centuries, universities being initially slow to accept education as an undergraduate subject, thereafter only developing postgraduate diplomas and higher degrees for teachers, as distinct from initial preparation for the classroom. The end of 'the binary divide' across the UK occurred in 1992 and the termination of the Council for National Academic Awards (which had validated many of the qualifying degrees and diplomas awarded by colleges and polytechnics) signalled the end of the college of education sector in Scotland. Mergers between colleges of education and universities took place thereafter and ITE moved wholly into the university sector. The chapter traces the chequered developments of that decade and the 2000s resulting in the present seven university Schools of Education, all with reduced levels of staffing and circumscribed activities. The two chapters following this look in depth at what takes place within ITE (Chapter 97) and in professional development beyond (Chapter 98). Both chapters scrutinise the complex governmental and professional politics relating to how teachers are, or should be, trained, Chapter 97 concentrating on the undergraduate four-year BEd Primary qualification and the one-year postgraduate (PGDE) qualification (where graduates in various disciplines can qualify to enter either primary or secondary teaching), Chapter 98 analysing the framework and standards of professional development and the shifts in its terminology and character over the last fifteen years or so (from 'in-service education' (I/S) to 'continuing professional development' (CPD), to 'professional learning'). The chapters have much to say about the extensive examination carried out during 2010 for the government by former Senior Chief Inspector Graham Donaldson and published in January 2011. His report recommended a wholesale review of the suite of professional standards. The development work required to operationalise its many recommendations was carried out by a National Partnership Group and its findings were accepted by the Scottish Government by the end of 2012. Efforts are currently underway to strengthen both the undergraduate degree route and the postgraduate qualification-plus-induction pathway, in particular and different ways. The former will see the move from dedicated BEd (Primary) degrees to joint honours degrees combining subject disciplines and educational preparation; the latter will see strengthened partnerships between university Schools of Education and induction placement schools. Some aspects of the deliberations have proved challenging to all of the parties involved. A government review of teacher employment was also published in 2011 (the McCormac Report) and, while its main focus was on teachers' pay and conditions, issues relating to ongoing professional learning (and therefore matters dealt with by Donaldson) also came under consideration, as explained in Chapter 98.

The relationship between educational research on teachers and teaching and what happens in classroom practice is the subject of Chapter 99. The author tracks something of 'the ebb and flow [across the last 150 years] that has characterised and continues to characterise deliberation between practitioners, researchers and policy makers in this contentious area'. Ambitions for evidence-informed professional practice and the dictation of national priorities by government have dominated the twenty-first-century orientation to research, and researchers themselves have become much committed to the idea of 'communities of practice'. The successes as well as the disappointments of these inter-related endeavours are considered carefully in this chapter.

In the third edition of this book, the late John Nisbet documented the first thirty years of the work of the Scottish Educational Research Association (SERA). Here, in Chapter 100, attention is paid to the last ten years of SERA's operations. The discussion concentrates on the organisation's membership, its activities and liaison with central government, together with the several serious challenges to its successful continuation during a period of austerity. As the author of Chapter 101 notes, the keynote addresses given at the annual SERA conferences are published in the *Scottish Educational Review* (*SER*), an important outlet for academics working in the Scottish universities and dealing with matters of national policy and practice. *SER* is not formally affiliated to SERA (in the way that *BERJ* is to BERA), but the links between the two are close. Chapter 101 describes all of the professional educational journals available in Scotland, noting their differing contents and emphases.

Teachers' professional organisations are the subject of Chapters 102 and 103. The former deals with trade union associations and is written by the General Secretary of the largest union, the Educational Institute for Scotland (EIS). The latter describes the work of the General Teaching Council for Scotland (GTCS), the now independent, self-regulating national professional body for teachers, and is jointly written by its Chief Executive and Director of Education and Professional Learning. In the present climate, and for rather different reasons, both kinds of bodies perform important functions in a modern democracy. The GTCS provides safeguards, a point not lost on the authors who note that GTCS gained its full independence from the Scottish Government in the same year, 2011, as the General Teaching Council for England was disbanded by the UK government. The final chapter in this section, Chapter 104, is a robust description of Scottish teachers by the late Bill Gatherer and, as stated in the opening section to the whole book (Chapter 1), was contained in the third edition of *Scottish Education* and has been repeated here as a tribute to him.

96

The Evolution of Teacher Education and the Scottish Universities

Moira Hulme and Ian Menter

Teacher education in Scotland has a distinctive history. Although current provision of initial teacher education (ITE) is led from seven university Schools of Education, the shifting pattern of provision through the nineteenth and twentieth centuries has been a fascinating story, with colleges and universities being key players but the government, local authorities, churches and the inspectorate all playing roles. The existing picture is not necessarily a stable one, with continuing desires to modernise the teaching profession, connecting with provision for teacher learning and development and the universities being challenged to contribute in new ways. The underlying economics of teacher supply and demand have also been a continuing factor in shaping provision.

In this chapter we take a generally historical narrative approach to examine the origins of teacher education and how it is that universities became so centrally involved, not only in ITE but in several aspects of teacher development. The first section starts in the nineteenth century and takes us through to the middle of the twentieth century, when universities were beginning to consolidate their involvement. The second section looks at the process of universitisation that occurred towards the end of the century. We then consider some of the stresses and strains that were involved in these processes, before concluding by considering very recent developments that, yet again, provide significant challenges as well as opportunities for the universities in their engagement with teacher education.

FROM THE NINETEENTH TO THE TWENTIETH CENTURY – COLLEGES OR UNIVERSITIES?

Between 1835 and 1907, teacher training was provided by denominational colleges while universities provided general education in the arts and sciences. Proposals for Education as a university subject, the establishment of Faculties of Education and the creation of a Scottish 'teacher's degree' did not receive serious attention until the last quarter of the nineteenth century. A foundation was laid by an early proposal for university Chairs in Education by Professor James Pillans of Edinburgh University in 1834. From its establishment in 1847, the Educational Institute of Scotland (EIS) lobbied for professors of Education as part of a long campaign to elevate teaching to the status of a graduate and self-governing profession. By 1864, the Argyll Commission recommended combining normal school training with university training for prospective teachers. Whilst the Education (Scotland) Act (1872) transferred parochial and burgh schools to local authorities (excluding Catholic schools) it did not introduce a unified system for teacher training. Separate roles for the universities and the training colleges became established in state-financed 'concurrent' modes of attendance by advanced (male) scholars in the Scotch Code of 1873. Cruickshank (1970) notes that this settlement was made possible by comparatively low university fees, the availability of residential accommodation provided by the training colleges and the close proximity of the colleges to the universities.

From the outset the place of teacher education in universities was contested. The Free and Established Churches sent deputations to London in 1875 to oppose the founding of chairs in Education. Denominational colleges feared that a university contribution might reduce the number and calibre of candidates entering the training colleges. The first chairs of Education – J. M. D. Meiklejohn at St Andrews and Simon Somerville Laurie (previously an assistant to Pillans) at Edinburgh – were financed in 1876 by endowments from the Bell bequest, supplemented by a precarious (and short-lived) government grant. A deputation to London by the four ancient universities in August 1877, to expand university interest in teacher education, was unsuccessful. Laurie's proposal for a direct role for St Andrews University in teacher training, with Madras College as a practising school was rejected in favour of maintaining distinct (and cost-effective) roles (Cruickshank, 1970, p. 99). In 1888, with the incentive of a government grant for every student teacher who successfully completed training, the Scottish universities (with the exception of Glasgow) again sought a role in teacher education. The Scottish Education Inquiry Committee declared in favour of maintaining the status quo. Bell (1990, pp. 91–2) notes how, by limiting the role of universities to teaching 'the theory and science of teaching', the first chairs were restricted to offering non-credit carrying courses to volunteer enthusiasts.

It was argued that universities could not guarantee practical training, instruction in certain elementary subjects or moral and religious instruction. In addition, university entrance requirements restricted the number of prospective teachers eligible for university classes at a time of increasing demand. Issues of academic freedom, control over appointments and curricula, and supervision of courses were potential sources of tension. The Scottish Education Department (SED), with the inspectorate (HMI), was able to exert close control over the colleges and had no such precedent of inspection and regulation in the universities. The Department (from 1885) was influenced by the firm leadership of the Permanent Secretaries Sir Henry Craik and then Sir John Struthers (from 1904), neither of whom was inclined to transfer responsibility for teacher education to universities. Universities were not concerned with teacher supply or the equitable distribution of high-quality teachers across Scotland's schools. A compromise was achieved with the extension of SED support for a third year of university study for college students, which made graduation a possibility for prospective teachers undertaking concurrent study at the training colleges. From 1889, universities included the theory and history of education as a credit-worthy 'subject' eligible for inclusion in the award of a Masters degree. The art or craft of teaching remained the preserve of masters or mistresses of method employed by the training colleges and modelled in attached practising or demonstration schools.

At the start of the twentieth century, teacher training was governed through an established partnership between the Education Department (as dominant partner), HMI and the training colleges. The consolidation of state responsibility for teacher education came with the creation of four Provincial Committees in 1905 (Glasgow, Edinburgh, Aberdeen and St Andrews-Dundee). The Presbyterian Church transferred control of its six colleges to the Provincial Committees. The anomaly of national responsibility for schooling alongside denominational control of teacher training was partially resolved, precipitated by further division within the Free Church (Bell, 1990, p. 95). The formation of the National Committee for the Training of Teachers in 1920 (to coordinate the work of the Provincial Committees) saw the incorporation of the remaining training colleges, demonstration schools and residential hostels within one national system. There was now a statutory involvement of elected education authorities in ITE and accountability could not be conceded to university authorities. Strong central control over finance, staffing, student numbers and the types of course provided by the training colleges prevailed from 1905 until the late 1950s (Marker, 1994, p. 13). Undeterred, after sustained deliberation on different schemes for a Scottish degree in Education, the BEd/EdB degree was introduced by Aberdeen, Edinburgh and Glasgow Universities after the First World War (and by St Andrews in 1949). After the Second World War, this 'second first degree', combining research and taught courses in education and psychology, became highly regarded as a route to promotion in Scottish education (Nisbet, 2003).

Despite tight control over teacher education and the different ordinances regulating the work of universities, there is evidence of local cooperation and mobility of staff between the universities and the colleges in the first half of the twentieth century. In Glasgow, John Adams (Rector of the Free Church Training College) and David Ross (Rector of the Church of Scotland College) both later became university lecturers in Education. Adams lobbied for graduation for all trained men teachers before his appointment as Professor of Education of London University/London Day Training College in 1902. Professor Alexander Darroch, Edinburgh University (a student of Laurie and his successor), was honorary Director of Studies at Moray House in the early months of the Edinburgh Provincial Committee. William Boyd, of the University of Glasgow, acted as part-time Principal Lecturer in Education at the Glasgow training college from 1909 to 1923, and did much to promote the development of research partnerships with teachers (Brett et al., 2010). Lecturers at Aberdeen University and University College Dundee gave lectures in education and psychology at the provincial training colleges. University chairs in Education held dual roles from 1925 until 1951 – a move considered desirable on both educational and economic grounds. Godfrey Thomson held the role of Director of Studies at Moray House teacher training centre (and its demonstration school) whilst also fulfilling the role of research Professor of Education at Edinburgh; at St Andrews, the Directorship of the Training Centre was combined with the Bell Chair of Education, with William McClelland acting as Director of Studies at the Dundee Training Centre.

SED regulations for teacher training were amended in 1924 and 1931. The change in regulations in 1931 produced an increase in non-graduate applications. Whilst retaining a focus on the principles of teaching, a stronger focus was placed in the colleges on the professional dimensions of training: physical training; school management (discipline organisation and general method); methods for teaching school subjects (Cruickshank, 1970, p. 176). The 1935 *Report of the Advisory Council to the Scottish Education Department on the Training of the Woman Primary School Teacher* recommended that courses emphasise the 'practical work of schools rather than a university degree' (cited by Cruickshank, 1970, p. 172). The Report of the Advisory Council on Education in Scotland, *Training of Teachers* (1946), once more demurred against transferring responsibility for teacher education to the universities, concluding that teacher training would be 'to the detriment of the higher scholarship which has thriven so well under their guardianship' (p. 58).

THE SECOND HALF OF THE TWENTIETH CENTURY – THE UNIVERSITIES TAKE CONTROL

In 1958, the influential Scottish Council for the Training of Teachers (SCTT) replaced the National Committee as the coordinating and advisory body for teacher education. In acquiring independent governing bodies the colleges had greater autonomy to develop their individual character. However, as Marker (1994, p. 14) notes, 'this move towards greater independence for the colleges was still within a framework of central coordination'. Among the standing committees advising the SCTT, the Committee of Principals (which met monthly) exerted considerable influence on policy (composed of the seven college principals, with greater power held by the four city colleges and the SED assessor team). During the late 1950s and 1960s, the relationship between the principals and the SED was close, consolidated by a shared understanding of aims and regular consultation. The SED team consisted of representatives of the inspectorate (some of whom were former college staff), career civil servants and politicians.

In the post-war period, the issue of teacher supply attracted most attention. Shortages were particularly acute in west central Scotland. Between 1959 and 1968, the SED supported the modernisation of existing colleges, the relocation of others (Aberdeen 1968, Dunfermline 1966, and Notre Dame 1967) and the building of three new colleges (Callendar Park and Craigie in 1964, Hamilton in 1966). Central policy discussion focused on the number and location of colleges, and the range of courses available at different sites. By the time the SCTT was disbanded in 1967, the training colleges were operating as a two-tier system with four large city colleges – Aberdeen, Dundee, Jordanhill (Glasgow), Moray House (Edinburgh) – and six smaller 'second division' female colleges – Dunfermline College (women's, PE); Hamilton, Craigie (Ayr) and Callendar Park (Falkirk) (primary only); and Notre Dame (Glasgow) and Craiglockhart (Edinburgh) (Catholic colleges). This pattern of provision emerged in response to pragmatic concerns about teacher supply, alongside resistance to any 'dilution' of entry qualifications. Following the Robbins Report on higher education (1963), four university-validated but college-based undergraduate BEd courses for intending primary teachers were created: Aberdeen in 1965, Jordanhill and Moray House in 1966 and Dundee in 1967. With the establishment of these distinctive 'professional' degrees, the university EdB degrees were remodelled as two-year full-time MEd courses (with the first year leading to a Diploma in Education) or three years part-time.

From the mid-1960s, the composition of the policy community changed as new partners entered and new bodies such as the Open University and the Council for National Academic Awards (CNAA) began to operate in Scotland. The General Teaching Council of Scotland (GTCS) was founded in 1966 (which also ensured the continued involvement of key figures prominent in the SCTT). In 1967, the college monopoly on pre-service teacher training was broken with the establishment of the University of Stirling BA/BSc with secondary teaching qualification (funded through the Higher Education Grants Committee, rather than the SED). The expansion of the BEd degree in the late 1970s reduced perceptions of a two-tier system among the training colleges. With the end of the SCTT, the influence of the Committee of Principals diminished and their role shifted from one of policy formation to reaction to proposals and reports prepared by the SED and the GTCS.

The financial crisis of the late 1970s contributed to pressures for contraction of college provision. The publication of *Teacher Training from 1977 Onwards* (SED, 1977) heralded the end of the ten-college system with a number of forced mergers and closures. The proposed closures were temporarily reprieved in the face of organised resistance. Facing an uncertain future, the colleges responded by expanding in-service provision. Following a change in UK government, the postponed college closures were announced in *The Future of the College of Education System in Scotland* (SED, 1980). Whilst primarily tackling surplus capacity through the closure of Callendar Park and Hamilton Colleges and the merger of Craiglockhart with Notre Dame in 1981 (and the later creation of Northern College from the merger of Dundee and Aberdeen Colleges of Education in 1987), the SED document also contained concessionary mention of moves towards an all-graduate profession and the development of research in colleges. The persistence of monotechnic provision in specialist colleges of higher education outside universities was in part influenced by enduring issues of control. Universities were accountable to a UK minister whilst the colleges remained under the control of the Secretary of State for Scotland (Kirk, 1999, p. 101). Financial constraints and institutional rivalry over research limited cooperation. Locally negotiated mergers of the remaining colleges with the universities eventually came in the 1990s, following the closure of the CNAA (which had validated the BEd degree in some centres from 1983) and the 'repatriation' of the Scottish universities in 1992 (Further and Higher Education (Scotland) Act). Moves towards full universitisation were finally realised as a result of political and economic drivers, as much as the case for research-informed teacher education.

THE PROS AND CONS OF 'UNIVERSITISATION'

So it was that by the end of the twentieth century all of the provision for ITE in Scotland was or was about to be led from universities. This was a movement that certainly distinguished Scotland from England, where the mergers of colleges with universities (or polytechnics) had happened mainly in the 1970s and 1980s, but where, more recently, provision for teacher education was increasingly being made outside of the university sector. So what gave rise to this pattern in Scotland?

The colleges of education were seen to play a distinctive and significant role in the education system. College principals were among the 'movers and shakers' of education policy. Indeed, there was not universal joy from within the colleges of education about the prospect of the moves into universities. The principals were concerned that their influence not only over teacher education but also over the wider education system would be diminished. Many of the staff within the colleges felt anxious about transferring into universities, where they feared their distinctive professional expertise would not be fully recognised and that they would be working under new terms and conditions, including, in many cases, expectations about undertaking research.

However, there were also those who saw the move as a necessary development in raising the societal and intellectual standing of teacher education. The move towards an all-degree profession was taken as an indication that the proper location for teacher education was indeed in these bastions of the academy, the home of the renowned Scottish 'democratic intellect' (Davie, 1960). Since that time there has been a consolidation of the higher education base for ITE, as we shall see shortly.

Developments since these amalgamations have tended to prove both the doubters and the enthusiasts right. Teacher education is now operated by seven university Schools of Education across Scotland (see Table 96.1). Whereas the first university home for this provision was typically a 'Faculty of Education', often led initially by the relevant former College principal, we have now reached a point where most provision is within a 'School

Table 96.1   Seven providers of initial teacher education in Scotland

University	Old or new?	Former colleges	Current unit	Within
Aberdeen	Pre-92	Northern College	School of Education	College of Arts and Social Sciences
Dundee	Pre-92	Northern College	School of Education, Social Work and Community Education	College of Arts and Social Sciences
Edinburgh	Pre-92	Moray House	Moray House School of Education	College of Humanities and Social Science
Glasgow	Pre-92	St Andrew's (Catholic)	School of Education	College of Social Sciences
Stirling	Pre-92	N/A	School of Education (formerly Stirling Institute of Education)	
Strathclyde	Pre-92	Jordanhill	School of Education	Faculty of Humanities and Social Sciences
West of Scotland (formerly Paisley)	Post-92	Craigie	School of Education	Faculty of Education, Health and Social Sciences

of Education', led by a head of school, and where the School is but one part of a larger College or 'Super-faculty'. Very often the Head of the School of Education has very little budgetary power, including over staffing. In many of these Schools, there have also been pressures on education staff to become research active, so that a strong education submission may be made to the Research Assessment Exercise, or now the Research Excellence Framework (see Chapter 99). Institutions have dealt with these tensions in different ways, but in several Schools of Education, much of the teaching on ITE is done by staff on 'teaching-only' contracts or by visiting lecturers, sometimes called Teaching Fellows. Such staff do not have research expectations thrust upon them. The staffing profiles of university Schools of Education are now quite varied, but tend to include (at least) four distinctive groups – long-standing university staff, former College of Education staff, newly appointed university staff and temporary appointees of various sorts (Menter, 2011).

At the time of college mergers, a new grouping of Deans of Education was established. This was the Scottish Teacher Education Committee (STEC), which effectively replaced the former SCTT as the body that would meet with government and discuss policy issues in teacher education. In addition to its consultative activities, STEC now holds an annual conference which focuses each year on a particular current theme in teacher education.

There were some significant developments in the nature of the provision made by universities during the first decade of the twenty-first century. In ITE, there was a major innovative scheme at the University of Aberdeen, called Scottish Teachers for a New Era (STNE). This was a research and development project, co-funded by the university itself, the Scottish Executive and the Hunter Foundation (a philanthropic organisation funded by entrepreneur Tom Hunter). The STNE was modelled on the USA-based scheme Teachers for a New Era, which was funded by the Carnegie Foundation of New York, and the Ford and Annenberg Foundations. The STNE involved a redesign of the four-year BEd programme for primary teachers and introduced enhanced subject study into the first two years as well as developing a more 'clinical' approach to placement experience in schools. The model of the teacher underlying the approach was that of an enquiring professional, advanced in Scotland through the early work of William Boyd and later across the UK by Lawrence Stenhouse. Similar models were invoked elsewhere as other BEd programmes were revamped. Additionally, the University of Glasgow introduced Masters-level credits into its one-year Professional Graduate Diploma in Education (PGDE) programme for primary and secondary teachers, and indeed brought the separate programmes for primary and secondary closer together, so that much of the programme was common for both. Since 2011, beginning teachers who complete the Glasgow PGDE have had the opportunity to complete a Masters in Professional Practice with PGDE at an early career stage by extending systematic professional enquiry beyond ITE into the induction period.

In provision for post-qualifying teachers, the universities also had a very significant part in the provision of the Scottish Qualification for Headship (SQH) as well as for the Chartered Teacher (CT) Scheme. The SQH was devised as a means of ensuring adequate preparation for intending headteachers and was expected to become a mandatory requirement prior to appointment to a headship. The universities and local authorities formed three regional consortia across the country to provide the SQH programme. There was a strong enquiry element in the programme and a focus on whole-school development. The Chartered Teacher Scheme arose from the 2001 teachers' agreement *A Teaching Profession for the 21st Century* (TP21), widely known as 'McCrone', that being the name of the chairperson of the committee that reported to the Scottish Executive on teachers' pay and conditions (SEED, 2001). Although the scheme has been discontinued, nevertheless it was a very innovative programme that gave experienced classroom teachers an opportunity to develop their professionalism and to be awarded a significant increase in salary upon successful completion. Both the SQH and the CT Scheme are discussed in more detail elsewhere in this volume (see Chapter 98) but it is because of the central contribution that the universities made to both of these that they are mentioned here.

One of the key factors that has been shaping the university Schools of Education over the past fifteen years is the allocation of ITE numbers. The government carries out an annual school workforce planning exercise, which leads to a decision about the numbers of ITE places that will be funded across the country. Any rise or fall in allocations is usually evenly distributed across the providers, on a proportional basis. There have been occasions in the recent past when there have been very rapid rises and falls in these numbers, which has led to some real volatility in the resources allocated to universities for this provision. Table 96.2 shows the sudden reduction in numbers between 2009–10 and 2010–11.

Table 96.2   Changes in ITE funded places 2009–10 to 2010–11

	2010–11 intakes	2009–10 intakes	Change from 2009–10 to 2010–11	Percentage change
BEd Primary	700	1,200	−500	−42
BEd Secondary	202	202	0	0
PGDE Primary	405	1,355	−950	−70
PGDE Secondary	805	905	−100	−11
Combined degree	195	195	0	0
Total	2,307	3,857	−1550	−40

Source: SFC Circular SFC/05/2010

The sudden drop in 2010–11 led to major staffing reductions in most of the Schools of Education. This was followed in many cases by university-wide staff reduction schemes (through voluntary severance), so that many Schools of Education, as well as being 'reshaped', as discussed above, have also been drastically downsized. All in all, the years around the end of the first decade of the twenty-first century were very turbulent for university Schools of Education.

WHERE ARE WE NOW? DONALDSON AND BEYOND

Since devolution there have actually been three national reviews of teacher education, although only the first two of these considered ITE in any detail. These two were both outcomes of the McCrone report in 2001 (SEED, 2001), referred to above. TP21 included a two-stage review of ITE. These actually emerged as distinct reviews. The first was carried out swiftly by a consultancy firm, Deloitte and Touche. It led to a report that summarised ITE provision across the country and made some recommendations about areas that were judged to be in need of further development. These included training for support for learning and provision in science for primary teachers. It was also recommended that there should be further development in relations between universities, local authorities and schools in ITE provision.

This theme of partnership between contributors was picked up again by the second-stage review. This was carried out by a committee established by the Education Minister and took somewhat longer over its deliberations, eventually reporting in 2005. One outcome of this report was the establishment of new practical arrangements between universities and local authorities, with the latter each identifying an officer who would become the placement coordinator for the authority. This did help to ensure that there was a more planned approach to the allocation of places to universities for their students' school experience. However, other than this development, very little else of lasting significance emerged from either of these reviews.

However, in late 2009, the then Cabinet Secretary for Education, Fiona Hyslop, invited Graham Donaldson to undertake a wide-ranging review of teacher education in Scotland. Donaldson had just retired from the position of Senior Chief Inspector within Her Majesty's Inspectorate of Education (HMIE). The review was undertaken during 2010 and gathered a range of evidence from many sources. These included questionnaires, consultation meetings, overseas visits and a specially commissioned literature review. Donaldson's report, *Teaching Scotland's Future*, was published early in 2011 (Donaldson, 2011). The report contained fifty recommendations which, within weeks, and prior to an upcoming Scottish Parliamentary election, were accepted in full or in part by the Cabinet Secretary for Education, Michael Russell.

The report is undoubtedly the most wide-ranging on its topic within living memory. It has a vision for teacher education that is based on an understanding of teaching as a complex and challenging professional occupation. It places the universities at the heart of teacher learning and development and calls for much more continuity between the phases of a teacher's development. It also emphasises the significance of leadership as something that is the responsibility of all teachers.

A National Partnership Group (NPG) was established, co-chaired by the Scottish Government, STEC and the Convention of Scottish Local Authorities (COSLA). Also represented are other key bodies such as Education Scotland and the General Teaching

Council. The NPG established three sub-groups, respectively focusing on the early phase; learning through the career; and leadership. Subsequently an implementation plan was drawn up which is now being implemented.

In propounding the notion of a continuum of professional learning throughout the career, Donaldson notes that induction is currently a key phase which is apparently largely detached from the universities. This apparent anomaly has existed since the introduction of the salaried Teacher Induction Scheme (TIS), which was another outcome of the TP21 settlement and which affords a level of professional support that has been much admired by educationists from other countries. Revisiting the organisational structure of the TIS may create an opportunity for the universities to play a fuller part in ensuring greater continuity between ITE and the first year of teaching.

Later in 2011, another significant report was published following a review of teachers' pay and conditions. This revisiting of the ground covered by McCrone was carried out by a committee chaired by Gerry McCormac, Principal of the University of Stirling. One member of this committee was Graham Donaldson. The report was entitled *Advancing Teacher Professionalism*. In its references to teacher learning and development, it is by and large consistent with the vision set out in *Teaching Scotland's Future* and certainly acknowledges the importance of provision for continuing professional development and leadership development. However, it does call into question the continuing existence of the Chartered Teacher Scheme. There had been earlier questioning of the CT Scheme (see, for example, Scottish Government, 2008, *Report of the Chartered Teacher Review Group*, and the 2009 HMIE report *Learning Together: Improving Teaching, Improving Learning*), not so much for the learning that it offered, more for the lack of connection with school management structures.

Donaldson himself has made clear how he sees teacher professionalism being redefined through three major policy initiatives – his own report, the McCormac Report and the 'flagship' education policy of Curriculum for Excellence (CfE). At its inception CfE was seen very much as a curriculum that would enable teachers themselves to re-engage with curriculum development, with more opportunities for local adaptation as well as opportunities for teacher enquiry and research. As CfE was first trialled across the system, there was some anxiety among teachers that it provided only a vague framework. In the version that eventually emerged in 2009, there was a great deal of 'exemplification' of what might be offered as appropriate experiences for learners and so some of this anxiety has diminished. However, while the Donaldson and McCormac Reports do create a space for the development of a new form of teacher professionalism, there seems to be little systematic support either from the universities or from the government to ensure that enquiry and development are integral features of teachers' work across the career course.

CONCLUSION – SOME NEW CHALLENGES FOR THE UNIVERSITIES

The major challenges now facing the universities will include responding to the implementation plan from the NPG and this is likely to include a major rethinking around the degree entry route into primary teaching, the four-year BEd. Concurrent degree courses such as those provided at the University of Stirling as well as for secondary teachers in some subjects elsewhere, including Glasgow, may well become a model for all four-year entry programmes into teaching. This is likely to mean an increase in the subject study element, something that *Teaching Scotland's Future* suggested was currently underplayed in spite of the opportunities that universitisation had created.

There may be continuing volatility in ITE numbers as the politics of teacher supply and demand continue to be a significant element in media coverage of education – ranging from stories about the number of teachers on the job seekers' register through to stories about severe shortages in particular subject areas in some regions. But there will also be pressure arising from changed funding regimes for teacher education places. The government has proposed significantly reducing the funds available for ITE. This may make ITE provision less attractive to hard-pressed universities, many of whom are increasingly concerned with ensuring the highest possible achievement in research rankings – which are unlikely to be helped by significant numbers of staff having to invest so much of their time into 'delivering' poorly resourced ITE programmes.

On a more positive note, there are some indications that the universities will continue to innovate and ensure a changing culture in the provision of teacher education, so that schools and local authorities are drawn more fully into communities of practice with the universities. The only possible way that universities can play a full part in the agenda of rethinking teacher professionalism is likely to involve significant changes in the roles undertaken by university-based teacher educators and a significant development in the skills and confidence of those contributing from within the schools. Indeed *Teaching Scotland's Future* calls for every teacher to be a teacher educator and it is only through a radical rethinking along these lines that the distinctive contribution of universities as sources of research, curriculum development and support for the development of teacher enquiry is likely to be sustained.

REFERENCES

Bell, R. E. (1990) 'The Scottish universities and educational studies', in J. B. Thomas (ed.), *British Universities and Teacher Education. A Century of Change.* Lewes: Falmer Press, pp. 87–105.

Brett, C. E., M. Lawn, D. J. Bartholomew and I. J. Deary (2010) 'Help will be welcomed from every quarter: the work of William Boyd and the Educational Institute of Scotland's Research Committee in the 1920s', *History of Education*, 39 (5): 589–611.

Cruickshank, M. (1970) *History of the Training of Teachers in Scotland.* Edinburgh: Scottish Council for Research in Education.

Davie, G. (1960) *The Democratic Intellect – Scotland and her Universities in the Nineteenth Century.* Edinburgh: University of Edinburgh.

Donaldson, G. (2011) *Teaching Scotland's Future: Report of a Review of Teacher Education in Scotland.* Edinburgh: Scottish Government.

Kirk, G. (1999) 'The passing of monotechnic teacher education in Scotland', *Scottish Educational Review*, 31 (2): 100–11.

Marker, W. B. (1994) *The Spider's Web: Policy Making in Teacher Education in Scotland, 1959–81.* Glasgow: Strathclyde University.

Menter, I. (2011) 'Four "academic sub-tribes" but one territory? Teacher educators and teacher education in Scotland', *Journal of Education for Teaching*, 37 (3): 293–308.

Nisbet, J. (2003) 'A forlorn aspiration? The story of SUCSE', *Scottish Educational Review*, 35 (1): 60–4.

Scottish Executive Education Department (2001) *A Teaching Profession for the 21st Century.* Edinburgh: SEED.

97

Initial Teacher Education

Ian Smith

This chapter focuses on initial teacher education (ITE) in Scotland. However, ITE is increasingly seen as the first phase of a continuum of career-long teacher education stretching from ITE through Induction (the one-year post guaranteed to all Scottish ITE graduates, successful completion of which leads to full registration with the General Teaching Council for Scotland) into continuing professional development (CPD). The need to consider this continuum is a central emphasis in *Teaching Scotland's Future*, the Report of the Donaldson Review of Teacher Education in Scotland, published for the Scottish Government in January 2011 (Scottish Government, 2011a). At the time of writing, a National Partnership Group and its various sub-groups, drawn from key stakeholders, is taking forward the implementation of the Donaldson Report, based on *Continuing To Build Excellence In Teaching: The Scottish Government Response To Teaching Scotland's Future* (Scottish Government, 2011b), which accepts almost all of the Donaldson Report's recommendations in full, and the others in part or in principle. In considering the full continuum of teacher education, both the Donaldson Report and the Scottish Government's response specifically address ITE. Although focusing on ITE, this chapter also gives some consideration to the connections between ITE and later phases of the teacher education continuum. Similarly, while much of the discussion of ITE will be framed by the Donaldson Report, the broader context of Scottish ITE is established, including critical perspectives on the Donaldson Report where appropriate. (See also Chapters 96, 98 and 99 for other aspects of the broader context for Scottish teacher education.)

ITE IN SCOTLAND ENTERING THE SECOND DECADE OF THE TWENTY-FIRST CENTURY

An Established, Positive System?

In important respects, Scottish ITE entering the second decade of the twenty-first century could be described as a securely established, successful part of the Scottish education system. ITE was being delivered by the Schools of Education within seven Scottish universities (Aberdeen, Dundee, Edinburgh, Glasgow, Stirling, Strathclyde and the West of Scotland), with some additional small, part-time secondary provision from the Open University in Scotland (see Chapter 96). The merger of former monotechnic Colleges of Education with the universities had been completed earlier, and ITE was now fully integrated into the university sector. In contrast to other jurisdictions such as England, the delivery of ITE as a partnership between universities, local authorities and schools had not been challenged by the establishment of School-Centred Initial Teacher Training (SCITT) and employment-based routes that do not necessarily involve universities. This could be presented as protecting Scottish ITE from the practically oriented, technicist and apprenticeship approaches that many English teacher educators criticised as the failings of their own system (see Smith, 2010, p. 39). In contrast, Scotland could be seen as retaining a more balanced integration of theory with practice. The case could also be made that this applied to Scotland's comparative position on related professional standards, such as the Standard for Initial Teacher Education (GTCS and QAA Scotland 2006), with its expectation that student teachers know how to 'access and apply relevant findings from educational research' and 'engage appropriately in the systematic investigation of practice' (p.10) (see also Menter and Hulme, 2008, pp. 322–3, and Menter and Hulme, 2011, p. 388 on positive comparison of the Scottish standards with other parts of the UK; also Chapter 94 of *Scottish Education, Third Edition* for a fuller account of the development of the Scottish standards). At a more operational level, partnership between the universities and local authorities specifically had been strengthened by the development of regional consortia involving university staff and local authority placement coordinators working together to secure ITE student school placements, using the innovative Practicum online system.

Recent Constraints on Further Innovation?

On the other hand, Scottish ITE could be presented as constrained in its engagement with innovation in the first decade of the twenty-first century. The decade was largely spent responding to major fluctuations in the controlled subject intakes expected by the Scottish Government. For example, the intakes originally planned for session 2009–10 represented a five-fold increase from 2000–1 levels for the Professional Graduate Diploma in Education (PGDE) Primary, a 65 per cent increase for BEd Primary, while at their peak in 2005–6 PGDE Secondary intakes had been 61 per cent above 2000–1 levels. In successfully meeting such demanding increases in ITE intakes, it could be argued that ITE universities were under such severe pressures simply to deliver existing programmes to these increased intakes that the potential to engage in genuine programme innovation was severely restricted. After their success in meeting intake increases, ITE universities were then asked to reverse their position and severely reduce intakes, with late cuts requested for the 2009–10 intake. There were then much deeper cuts from 2010–11 onwards, notably 70 per cent in PGDE Primary intakes and 42 per cent in BEd Primary intakes. Although some increase in 2012–13 PGDE intakes is now planned, these cuts from 2009 required ITE universities to plan for severe medium-term contraction, rather than anticipated sustained expansion, with a consequent destabilising impact on planning for innovation based on growth.

Within this context, the overall Scottish framework for ITE qualifications has remained static for many years, based for the school sector on either generalist primary qualifications (to an extent covering the pre-school sector), or a fairly restricted range of subject-specific secondary qualifications (from a subject list which itself has not changed for some time). ITE qualifications are generally available as four-year undergraduate degrees or one-year PGDEs. Beginning from 2004, Curriculum for Excellence (CfE) has planned for five curriculum levels which encompass 3–18 education: early level (pre-school and P1); first level (to the end of P4); second level (to the end of P7); third, fourth levels (S1 to S3); senior phase (S4 to S6) (see Chapter 3). However, CfE has not so far led to new ITE programmes structured in different innovative ways around these levels. Potential innovations could include an early level educator qualification (such as the European pedagogue model), possibly providing the basis for the pre-school workforce to become an all-graduate teaching profession. New qualifications could be based upon a particular curricular area specialism at second, third and fourth levels, producing teachers able to work across the current primary/secondary divide. Other new qualifications could be developed at third and fourth levels and the senior phase, producing teachers/educators able to work in new ways at the secondary stage, for example by broadening the curricular area covered in a third and fourth level qualification, or defining new specialisms at senior phase, including approaches drawn from the current college sector, especially vocational education areas. None of these possibilities has been developed to date.

On partnership, a strong case can be made (see Smith, 2010, pp. 41–5) that Scottish ITE has largely remained trapped in a 'duplication' model of partnership, where university tutors have continued to spend a great deal of time on roles and responsibilities that could more appropriately be assumed by teachers within partner schools, such as providing practical preparation for student teachers' placement teaching, and observing and assessing the classroom practice of student teachers. This has constrained the development of genuinely collaborative partnership in Scottish ITE, which would maximise the distinctive contributions university staff and partner school staff can make to the professional development of student teachers, with university staff providing 'research and theory-based knowledge and perspectives' and partner school staff providing 'situated knowledge of teaching and schooling and practical perspectives' (Smith, 2010, p. 42, quoting D. McIntyre (ed.), *Teacher Education Research in a New Context: The Oxford Internship Scheme*, London: Paul Chapman Publishing, 1997, p. 5). Adopting the analysis on the relationship between knowledge and practice of Cochran-Smith and Lytle, such collaborative partnership would progress a form of teacher knowledge known as 'knowledge of practice', a synergy between the 'knowledge for practice' generated by researchers within universities and the 'knowledge in practice' that experienced teachers produce through their own practice and reflection on their practice. 'Knowledge of practice' can be progressed through inquiry communities involving new kinds of collaboration between universities and teachers in schools. (See Smith 2010, p. 38, drawing upon M. Cochran-Smith and S .L. Lytle, 1999, 'Relationships of Knowledge and Practice: Teacher Learning in Communities', *Review of Research in Education*, 24, 249–305.) In Scotland, ITE partnership between universities and schools has not yet been grounded within such broader collaborations.

As mentioned earlier, the priority for much of the first decade of the twenty-first century was simply to secure placements for the greatly increased numbers of ITE students. The pressure to achieve this was so great that it would have been inappropriate for universities to risk destabilising partner school acceptance of students by pushing for collaborative innovations in partnership, when these could have been rejected by school staff as involving an additional role for themselves. In particular, this has to be placed in the context of historical issues with school staff attitudinal resistance to such enhanced roles, and difficult questions on where the resources for the additional activities associated with collaborative partnership would come from (Smith, 2010, pp. 44–5; Smith, 2011, pp. 20–1).

Another issue for Scottish ITE entering the second decade of the twenty-first century was the extent to which it engaged with any developing European trends to establish school teaching as a Masters-level profession. For example, the much-praised Finnish ITE system is based on all teachers achieving a Masters degree over five years. Although one university had designed a five-year Masters undergraduate ITE degree for secondary science, and partial Masters-level credit had been granted by some universities within their PGDE programmes, there had been no general move to benchmarking ITE programmes as full Masters programmes, or even to suggesting that all school teachers should be required to achieve Masters status through CPD (for coverage of these issues, see Smith, 2010, pp. 47, 51; Smith, 2011, pp. 31–2).

In 2005, the Scottish Government had launched what was presented as a major national reform initiative in ITE. This was the Scottish Teachers for a New Era (STNE) programme, funded by the Scottish Government, the Hunter Foundation and Aberdeen University, and designed as a six-year programme to produce an innovative BEd (Primary), essentially as a national pilot. This drew heavily upon US thinking, which emphasised such approaches as ITE students studying subjects outwith education (see Chapter 95 of *Scottish Education, Third Edition* for more detail on the STNE programme). Although the STNE project had been given the difficult task of disseminating its developments across the other Scottish teacher education universities, it is not clear that this happened to any great extent. A reasonable conclusion may be that STNE remained an interesting development within one programme at one university, rather than the basis for innovation across the national system.

Certainly, Scottish ITE was the object of considerable Scottish Government review in the first decade of the twenty-first century. A 'first-stage' review of ITE, commissioned from the external consultants Deloitte and Touche, was completed in 2001. A 'second-stage' review, undertaken by an appointed Review Group of senior stakeholders, reported in 2005. At various times Her Majesty's Inspectorate of Education (HMIE) also completed Aspect Reviews of ITE, such as the report on student teacher placements in 2005. However, those involved in Scottish teacher education have emphasised that these reviews were not as broad or deep as certain reviews of teacher education undertaken in other countries, and had limited impact in stimulating fundamental and creative innovation (see Smith, 2010, pp. 33–4; Menter and Hulme, 2008, pp. 325–6; and Menter and Hulme, 2011, p. 389).

Therefore, entering the second decade of the twenty-first century, Scottish ITE could be presented as a generally strong system, which had successfully completed the challenging integration into the university sector and delivered fully on demanding targets to increase the numbers of student teachers for Scotland's schools. On the other hand, teacher educators keen for further, more fundamental innovations, especially perhaps on ITE partnership, were experiencing some frustration. Indeed, the central need to increase intakes to existing ITE programmes for most of the first decade of the twenty-first century had significantly constrained opportunities to innovate on the structure and delivery of programmes.

THE DONALDSON REVIEW OF TEACHER EDUCATION

Any current discussion of ITE in Scotland must be framed around the Donaldson Review of teacher education. At the request of Scottish Government, Graham Donaldson, the former Senior Chief Inspector at HMIE, led a review of teacher education in Scotland during 2010. The reasons for Scottish Government establishing this Review were not completely clear, and it was certainly not suggested as originating from any deep concerns about fundamental weaknesses in ITE. In the Review, Graham Donaldson was supported by an appointed Review Team and Review Reference Group, generally drawn from fairly traditional 'leadership class' sources (see Smith, 2010, p. 34). However, aspects of the Review appeared to be more inclusive than previous reviews. For example, online techniques were used, inviting all interested individuals and organisations to submit formal responses and contribute to interactive debates. An academic research team was commissioned to inform the Review by completing a comparative literature review of approaches to teacher education in the twenty-first century (Menter et al., 2010), although one area of debate is the extent to which the final Report drew on the academic review as an evidence base for its main recommendations. Crucially, the Review was asked to consider the full continuum of teacher education from ITE through Induction to CPD, in contrast to the previous reviews which had concentrated exclusively on ITE. The Donaldson Report, *Teaching Scotland's Future: Report of a Review of Teacher Education in Scotland*, was published in January 2011 (Scottish Government, 2011a). By March 2011, the Scottish Government had published its response, *Continuing To Build Excellence In Teaching: The Scottish Government's Response To Teaching Scotland's Future* (Scottish Government, 2011b). The Scottish Government's response accepted almost all the Report's recommendations in full, and the others in part or in principle. The Scottish Government established a National Partnership Group, with associated sub-groups, to take forward implementation of the Report's recommendations. The National Partnership Group comprises representatives from the Scottish Government, the teacher education universities, the Association of Directors of Education in Scotland (ADES) for local education authorities, Education Scotland (the new body bringing together the work of HMIE and Learning and Teaching Scotland), the General Teaching Council for Scotland (GTCS), headteachers and teachers. There is a sub-group for the early phase of professional learning, which will specifically cover ITE. In addition, there are sub-groups for career-long professional learning and professional learning for leadership. At the time of writing, the sub-groups are working on detailed implementation plans to be reported to the National Partnership Group by June 2012 (see Scottish Government, 2011c).

EVALUATING DONALDSON

As indicated, the Scottish Government has accepted almost all of the Donaldson Report, and the implementation groups have essentially been tasked with ensuring that the Report's recommendations take effect. Therefore, any discussion of the future development of Scottish ITE involves evaluating the appropriateness of the Donaldson Report.

Positive Commitment to the Principles of Collaborative Partnership Involving Universities

Certainly, the Report is broader, and in some senses deeper, than previous reviews. It contains fifty recommendations, covers the full continuum from ITE through Induction to CPD, and provides some references and a selected bibliography which at least partly reflect the commissioned academic literature review. Specifically relating to key themes for ITE, the Report calls for further developing and strengthening collaborative partnership between universities and schools, local authorities and the teaching profession (Scottish Government, 2011a, p. 48 and Recommendations 3, 15 and 16). The Report emphasises the need to avoid a divide where 'exploration of theory is most often considered to reside within the on-campus delivery, with "practice" residing within placements'. Instead, the campus-based and school-based components 'should be seen as interlinked, with connections being the means of developing educational theory through practice' (p. 42). More specifically within partnership, the Report advocates formalising an enhanced role for school staff in supporting and assessing student teachers on ITE placements (pp. 5, 7, 8, 46, 73 and Recommendations 20, 28 and 39). The proposal to pursue 'hub teaching schools' as a possible approach can also be seen as an attempt to achieve greater depth to collaborative partnership (pp. 7–8, 45 and Appendix 2). The Report recommends a more integrated approach to ITE and Induction within the early phase of teacher education, including a role for universities in the Induction year (pp. 8, 47 and Recommendations 25 and 30).

A further positive perspective on the Donaldson Report's position over collaborative partnerships involving universities can be found in Hulme and Menter (2011), who compare the Report favourably with the recent English Schools White Paper, *The Importance of Teaching*. In contrast to the English White Paper's 'significant omissions' of 'the value of university-based teacher education and the professional knowledge base of teacher education' (p. 77), Hulme and Menter argue that the Donaldson Report avoids the 'discourses of derision' and 'distrust' towards teacher education which are found in England, and presents the development of teacher education positively as a collaborative partnership with key stakeholders, including the universities (p. 80).

While the Donaldson Report has been generally welcomed as a positive contribution to the future development of Scottish teacher education, there are a number of reasons for arguing that it does not yet provide the fullest basis for ongoing innovation in ITE, and that significant work remains to be done by teacher education stakeholders if long-term creative innovation is to be secured.

An Early Narrowing of Focus on the Quality of ITE Students

Much public debate immediately after the publication of the Report focused narrowly on sections suggesting that a significant number of ITE students 'lack some of the fundamental attributes to become good teachers, including . . . literacy and numeracy' (Scottish Government, 2011a, p. 27). The Report recommended that ITE candidates should undertake diagnostic competence assessment in literacy and numeracy, with the implication that some below a certain threshold will be rejected for entry, and others below a higher threshold may be admitted, but will be required to raise their competence levels before completing ITE (p. 27 and Recommendation 5). These approaches to selection for ITE entry illustrate some of the weaknesses in the Report's use of evidence. Approaches are proposed on the basis of evidence that the Report concedes is 'largely impressionistic' (p. 27). However, the commissioned academic literature review had concluded that 'research on the impact of testing as a means of regulating entry to the profession is inconclusive' (Menter et al., 2010, p. 27). Certainly in the short term, the Report's approach to selection for entry generated some negative press and public perceptions that ITE student intakes had significant weaknesses in literacy and numeracy. This is not consistent with the general perception of the teacher education community, which must now reassure the wider public on the quality of ITE students. In addition, the teacher education community now faces the challenging implementation task of translating the Report's general calls for diagnostic assessment of literacy and numeracy competence into specific practice. More generally, it is to be hoped that time devoted to these narrower issues of student quality does not distract from the need to engage with more fundamental ITE reform.

Continuing Challenges in Achieving Collaborative Partnership

As discussed, the most fundamental need for ITE reform relates to partnership, and the Report supports the development of collaborative partnership in a number of ways. However, the Report could have engaged more robustly with a number of persistent challenges which continue to threaten the full implementation of collaborative partnership in Scotland, and which must be addressed by all stakeholders (see Smith, 2011, pp. 20–1; Smith, 2010, pp. 40, 44–5). The Report does not directly address the likely continuing challenge from school staff attitudes which resist an enhanced role in assessing and supporting ITE students on placements. There has been a very significant history of this staff resistance in Scotland. The Report could support its call for an enhanced school staff role more robustly by explicitly recognising these conservative school staff attitudes and the need to challenge them. Similarly, the Report does not directly address the resource issues associated with an enhanced school role within ITE partnership. These issues are complex and challenging, involving not only aspects of school and local authority funding, but also university funding. The Report does not explicitly explore which funding streams may provide the resources for enhanced collaborative partnership activities.

There would be particular challenges in implementing a partnership model based on hub teaching schools. The Scottish teaching profession has traditionally resisted the identification of elite schools within teacher education. Again, the Report could have commented more directly on this. Presumably, hub teaching schools would also require enhanced resourcing, but once more the Report does not demonstrate a model for this. Of course, although the Report suggests that hub teaching schools would contribute to collaborative partnership, there is no actual Recommendation on hub teaching schools, and the Government's response to the Report specifically asks the National Partnership Group to consider the concerns expressed by a number of organisations over hub schools (Scottish Government,2011b, p. 7).

A Continuing Problem with Curricular Overload in ITE, Especially for Primary Generalists

The Report has some difficulty in dealing with what it describes as the 'quart into pint pot' issue, the potential overload in ITE because of 'the ever-expanding set of expectations of what should be included, particularly in primary education' (Scottish Government, 2011a, p. 8). While the Report accepts 'it is neither necessary nor feasible for a teacher to be a subject expert in all areas of the primary curriculum', it does emphasise that teachers must have 'sufficient understanding to stretch and progress children's learning' (p. 89). However, in addition to 'subject matter', the Report repeats a familiar list of other items that new teachers 'should be confident in their ability to address' (ibid.). These include underachievement; additional support needs; assessment in the context of deep learning; and the management of challenging behaviour. The Report partially recognises the underlying tensions in generalist primary teachers being expected to master a wide range of subject areas, in addition to these more generic issues. However, the assumption seems to be that Scottish school teaching will still be based on 'the generalist teacher . . . at the heart of primary education' (ibid.), with the implication that the relevant teaching qualification will remain primary and generalist. The Report is not completely convincing in addressing the tensions associated with this.

Nor is the Report fully clear on some proposed solutions to the 'quart into pint pot' problem. It suggests identifying core components for ITE 'and so reducing or rephasing expectations of how much will be covered and when'; 'increasing the available time'; 'expecting more of students themselves' (p. 89). While stressing the importance of core components, the Report makes no attempt to specify 'subject matter' core components (in contrast, for example, see the suggestion in Smith, 2010, pp. 48–9 for a focus on English and Literacy, and Mathematics and Numeracy as core subject components in primary ITE). In part, the reference to increasing available time can be linked to the emphasis elsewhere in the Report on the integration of ITE with Induction to create a 'five-year experience for undergraduates' and a 'two-year experience' for postgraduates (Scottish Government, 2011a, pp. 87–8, including Recommendation 10). However, the Report does not specify what could be moved from ITE to Induction within this integrated experience. Beyond this, while there is some reference to 'extending the PGDE beyond the current September to June (10 month) pattern' (p. 41), the Report makes no formal recommendation on lengthening the PGDE (for example to a fully funded eighteen-month programme). Rather, the Report seems to be referring to time outwith formal terms, and linking this with increasing expectations on students, especially before entry to ITE. Recommendation 13 states that 'clear expectations about the necessary prior learning for teacher education courses should be developed together with diagnostic assessments and online resources to allow students to reach that baseline in advance of formally embarking on a course'. These suggestions contain unclear dimensions. For example, it is not clear how reasonable it is to expect ITE students to be able to engage in significant course-related work prior to entry. Such potential issues seem to suggest that it is more appropriate for the teacher education community to re-emphasise the fundamental principle of filtering ITE content down to key aspects, rather than attempting unclear approaches to covering more content without formally extending the length of fully funded programmes.

Lack of Innovation in the Framework of Teaching Qualifications

The Report does not explicitly explore the possibilities for innovation in the framework for Scottish teaching qualifications, for example those discussed earlier on CfE levels. It will be important for the teacher education community to explore such possibilities. Innovation in teaching qualifications could be a way of dealing with the tensions around overload for the primary generalist. Primary ITE teaching qualifications could be specific to particular curricular area specialisms. These could cover the full primary stages (CfE early, first and second levels), cross the traditional primary/secondary divide (CfE second, third and fourth levels) or focus on a particular stage (for example, CfE early level and first level). Similarly, the Report does not consider the use of GTCS Professional Recognition in this respect. Professional Recognition enables the GTCS to confirm a teacher's expertise in a curricular area. This could be used specifically as a mechanism for achieving primary subject specialism through CPD (see Smith, 2011, p. 23; and Smith, 2010, pp. 46–9 for suggestions on this). Instead of such approaches, all the Report offers is the rather vague suggestion that 'existing moves to develop specialisms within each school should be encouraged' (Scottish Government, 2011a, p. 89).

In addition to these primary-related issues, the Report does not address explicitly any possibilities for other innovation in the framework of Scottish secondary teaching qualifications, again including those discussed earlier on CfE levels. For example, these include

additions of new subjects to the current list of secondary qualifications; possible differentiation between qualifications covering CfE third and fourth levels from those covering the
senior phase, such as third and fourth level qualifications covering broader curricular areas
than senior phase qualifications; possible widening of the range of secondary qualifications
to include vocational areas currently covered in the college sector.

Replacing the BEd Primary with Concurrent Degrees

The Report recommends the replacement of the existing Primary BEd degree with new
concurrent degrees which 'combine in-depth academic study in areas beyond education
with professional studies and development' and which 'involve staff and departments
beyond those in schools of education' (pp. 6, 24–5, 39–40 and Recommendations 7 and 11).
This recommendation appears to be based on a number of arguments. There is the suggestion that BEd students essentially seek 'narrow training of immediate and direct relevance to
life in the classroom', and do not sufficiently 'extend their own scholarship' into 'the values
and intellectual challenges which underpin academic study' (p. 6). There is the general
argument that 'Undergraduate student teachers should engage with staff and their peers in
other faculties much more directly as part of their general intellectual and social development' (ibid.), and also the more specific suggestion that 'opportunities should be created for
joint study with colleagues in cognate professions such as social work' (ibid.). The Report
also argues that concurrent degrees will enhance the marketability of education degrees
beyond the education sector (pp. 24–5).

The recommendation to replace the existing BEd with concurrent degrees was an unexpected aspect of the Report, and certainly could not have been anticipated from the commissioned academic literature review. The recommendation was endorsed in the Government
Response, and appears to have been accepted by the relevant implementation groups. All
involved in Scottish teacher education would support the general argument that undergraduate primary ITE should be a fully intellectually demanding, genuine university experience
(see Menter and Hulme, 2011, p. 393). However, there are some who have concerns that
the Report's approach to future degree structure is based more on impressionistic evidence
than the fullest consideration of research and theoretical perspectives on the nature of ITE.

Smith (2011, especially pp. 21–31) argues that the proposal to move to concurrent
degrees threatens a new prescriptive narrowness in undergraduate primary ITE. Research
and theoretical perspectives suggest the importance of not being dogmatic about ITE
programme structure (ibid., pp. 25–6). These perspectives also identify general criteria
for producing appropriate, high-quality ITE programmes, such as the need for coherence,
which could be more difficult for concurrent degree programmes to meet but arguably met
more fully by some form of continually innovating BEd programme (ibid., pp. 29–31).
Such critiques are concerned with the limitations of the Report's arguments for concurrent
degrees, relative to wider research and theoretical perspectives on ITE. It is not clear exactly
why the Report thinks BEd degrees cannot provide primary ITE students with 'the values
and intellectual challenges which underpin academic study'. There are many existing education studies courses within BEd programmes that explicitly address broader and deeper
academic issues, and there are those who will strongly defend the status of education studies
as an academic discipline (ibid., pp. 24, 26). For example, some argue specifically that the
study of curriculum theory can be a vehicle for engaging with wider areas of academic study,
through courses delivered from schools of education that achieve exciting interdisciplinary

connections (ibid., p. 27). On subject studies for primary ITE students, there is also the argument that it may be more appropriate to undertake courses in the subject disciplines, possibly within schools of education, which are explicitly structured to relate to the subsequent primary school applications of the discipline (rather than courses presented in other parts of the university where no attempt has necessarily been made to connect with primary school applications) (ibid., pp. 28–9).

The Report does not specify which subjects outwith education should be studied. It is not clear whether the Report is saying that the study of any other discipline is appropriate, regardless of the extent of the discipline's connection to the primary school curriculum (or, indeed, if it has any connection), or whether only certain other disciplines are relevant, for example those in cognate professions such as social work, or those that prepare for teaching in the secondary sector as well as the primary sector.

Discussion of the possible relationship between teaching and associated professions such as social work opens up another fundamental debate about the Donaldson Report. Forbes and McCartney (2011) argue that the Report risks teacher education policy in Scotland 'becoming mobilised around the notion of mono-professional education' (p. 39). They stress the crucial importance of inter/professional collaboration, suggesting the Report conceptualises inter/professional co-working in a limited way that does not connect to wider children's sector policies. Forbes and McCartney urge those involved in the implementation groups to 're-form teacher education within a programme of "joined-up" initial professional preparation for the wider children's sector workforce' (p. 51).

It is not clear that the Report has made its case fully for the marketability of concurrent degrees beyond teaching. The Report itself states 'representatives of the business community have indicated that a teaching qualification is not necessarily seen as an asset in a prospective employee in other employment sectors' (Scottish Government, 2011a, p. 25). Such employers may continue to see concurrent degrees as essentially 'teaching qualifications' because they include a specific focus on education.

Continuing Issues with Workforce Planning

Questions over the wider marketability of concurrent degrees are important because they relate to the broader issue of teacher workforce planning. As already discussed, the current approach to workforce planning has led to severe fluctuations in ITE intakes, destabilising future programme and staff planning in teacher education universities. Unresolved tensions over this issue have again been evident in recent Scottish Government moves for some increase to 2012–13 intakes, which have been resisted by other stakeholders such as the teachers' professional associations, concerned over continuing lack of full-time, permanent posts for newly and recently qualified teachers. The Donaldson Report hopes that concurrent degrees 'might also prove more marketable for students who do not find employment in teaching' (p. 88). Beyond concurrent degrees, the Report only offers general recommendations on improving 'the accuracy of the workforce planning model' (Recommendation 6, and pp. 24–5). The Report may not be breaking sufficient new ground here. As already indicated, there are questions over the extent to which concurrent degrees will actually increase the transferable marketability of teacher education qualifications. In the future, more fundamental questions may have to be addressed on teacher workforce planning and ITE intakes in Scotland. It may be necessary to widen the margins in workforce planning by consciously recruiting more student teachers than the system can guarantee full-time permanent posts for (preferable to the alternative of facing teacher shortages in the future). Such an approach would clearly require stakeholders to move beyond the simple reaction that this will be training teachers for unemployment. A new public discourse may be required to recognise that it will be perfectly acceptable for ITE graduates to take their transferable skills into other forms of employment, or that teachers moving outwith Scotland to find jobs can be viewed positively as the export of talent from a small nation with a particularly strong higher education system. More specifically, questions may have to be asked about the continuation of ITE as a controlled subject within higher education funding and planning, or even about the continued guarantee of an Induction post to all ITE graduates.

No Masters-level Profession

Although not exclusively an ITE-related issue, the Donaldson Report makes clear it is 'not advocating a "Masters profession" as a key policy driver' (p. 10), and is not suggesting 'an immediate policy of requiring all teachers to be educated to Masters level' (p. 75). Rather, the Report simply gives some encouragement to increasing the number of Scottish teachers who may achieve Masters qualifications. For example, it is suggested that Masters level credits can be built into ITE, Induction and CPD, with teachers having 'Masters accounts' (pp. 10, 75–6 and Recommendation 44). However, apart from leaving Scotland adrift of any increasingly general European benchmark on an all-Masters profession, this approach fails to establish a clear, consistent position on ITE and Masters qualifications. The implication is probably that such qualifications will finally be completed within CPD. However, while there will certainly be no general move to full undergraduate Masters ITE qualifications, there is no prohibition on individual universities taking this approach. Similarly, there is no suggestion that there should be a standard number of Masters-level credit points available within either undergraduate or PGDE ITE programmes. While this leaves scope for innovative flexibility within ITE, it also threatens a potentially confusing inconsistency, especially on the relationship between ITE and CPD over Masters qualifications.

CONCLUSIONS

At the time of writing, the short- to medium-term development of Scottish ITE will clearly be dominated by the moves to implement the Donaldson Report. As discussed, there is much that is positive in the Report's recommendations, especially its commitment to the principles of collaborative partnership over ITE, involving a guaranteed role for the universities. However, if the ultimate aim is to secure the most appropriate framework for long-term creative innovation in ITE, no system should rely exclusively upon one report. Any report carries the risks of being over-prescriptive in narrowing certain options, and cannot be the complete answer for future developments. In these respects, the Donaldson Report is no exception. The Scottish teacher education community must avoid spending a disproportionate amount of time on narrow issues implying an exaggerated deficit in the quality of ITE entrants. All stakeholders must overcome major attitudinal and resource challenges if the principles of collaborative partnership are actually to be implemented in practice. Hard issues must be addressed on the content and structure of ITE programmes to ensure that content overload is prevented, and there can be genuine innovation in the framework of teaching qualifications over time. A new prescriptive narrowness in undergraduate primary ITE should be avoided. Scottish ITE should consider fully how it prepares its graduates for inter-professional working. It will be essential to move forward from recent destabilising approaches to teacher workforce and ITE intake planning, and this may require a new public discourse on such matters. As part of a continuum of teacher education, Scottish ITE should be clearly linked to a coherent national position on progressing Scottish school teaching towards a Masters-level profession.

REFERENCES

Forbes, J. and E. McCartney (2011) 'Educating Scotland's future together? Inter/professional preparation for schools and children's services', *Scottish Educational Review*, 43 (2): 39–54.

General Teaching Council for Scotland and Quality Assurance Agency Scotland (2006) *Guidelines and Standards: The Standard for Initial Teacher Education*. Edinburgh: General Teaching Council for Scotland.

Hulme, M. and I. Menter (2011) 'South and North – Teacher Education Policy in England and Scotland: A comparative textual analysis', *Scottish Educational Review*, 43 (2): 70–90.

Menter, I. and M. Hulme (2008) 'Is small beautiful? Policy-making in teacher education in Scotland', *Teachers and Teaching*, 14 (4): 319–30.

Menter, I. and Hulme, M. (2011) 'Teacher education reform in Scotland: national and global influences', *Journal of Education for Teaching*, 37 (4): 387–97.

Menter, I., M. Hulme, D. Elliot and J. Lewin (2010) *Literature Review on Teacher Education in the 21st Century*. Edinburgh: Scottish Government. Online at www.scotland.gov.uk/Resource/Doc/325663/0105011.pdf

Scottish Government (2011a) *Teaching Scotland's Future: Report of a Review of Teacher Education in Scotland*. Edinburgh: Scottish Government.

Scottish Government (2011b) *Continuing To Build Excellence In Teaching: The Scottish Government's Response To Teaching Scotland's Future*. Edinburgh: Scottish Government. Online at www.scotland.gov.uk/Resource/Doc/920/0114570.pdf

Scottish Government (2011c) *Teaching Scotland's Future National Partnership Group*. Online at www.scotland.gov.uk/About/NationalPartnershipGroup/

Smith, I. (2010) 'Reviewing Scottish Teacher Education for the 21st Century: Let Collaborative Partnership Flourish', *Scottish Educational Review*, 42 (2): 33–56.

Smith, I. (2011) 'Re-visiting the Donaldson Review of Teacher Education: Is Creative Innovation Secured?', *Scottish Educational Review*, 43 (2): 17–38.

98

Teacher Professional Learning

Aileen Kennedy

THE GLOBAL CONTEXT OF TEACHER PROFESSIONAL LEARNING

Since the first edition of *Scottish Education* was published in 1999, the world of professional learning for teachers in Scotland has changed considerably, and terminology has evolved alongside the changing policy and practice. What was originally seen in rather simplistic terms as 'in-service education' became known as 'continuing professional development' (CPD), but is now gradually becoming referred to as 'professional learning' as the purpose becomes more explicitly focused on teacher learning rather than development in a more general sense. This change in terminology also helps to shift the focus conceptually from something that can be 'provided' for a teacher: CPD, to something that the teacher owns: learning. However, the term CPD is still used regularly, and will be used in this chapter where it reflects current common usage or historical terminology. These changes in terminology reflect the ongoing debate about teacher professional learning across the globe. Indeed, the trajectory of many professional learning policies worldwide can be seen to reflect ideas promoted in globally influential documents such as those produced by the Organisation for Economic Cooperation and Development (OECD). This global move is driven by increasing competitiveness as nation states seek to improve their own economies by improving the educational attainment of their citizens. Thus, global measures of pupil attainment such as the Programme for International Student Assessment (PISA), the Trends in International Mathematics and Science Study (TIMSS) and the Programme for International Reading Literacy Survey (PIRLS) have become indicators of the success of nation states' school systems. Indeed, Stronach (2010, p. 10) contends that deference to such measures of 'cultural performance' is resulting in a 'global homogenizing effect'. This competitive environment has resulted in nation states seeking to replicate the policies and practices of the countries seen to be the best 'performers', and organisations such as the OECD have played their part in this by sharing evidence of 'what works'. At the root of this is the influential pronouncement in the 2005 OECD report *Teachers Matter*, which stated that 'raising teacher quality is perhaps the policy direction most likely to lead to substantial gains in school performance' (p. 23).

Scotland, of course, has responded in its own way to this global context and this chapter begins by giving an overview of the current Scottish policy context. Thereafter it outlines the current structure of what is known as the 'CPD framework' before drawing to a close with discussion of some key tensions and challenges.

THE POLICY CONTEXT OF TEACHER PROFESSIONAL LEARNING IN SCOTLAND

Following a fundamental review of career-long teacher education in Scotland, the 'Donaldson Report' (Donaldson, 2011) was published. The Donaldson Report, together with the report of the review of teacher employment in Scotland – the 'McCormac Report' (Scottish Government, 2011) – has had, and will continue to have, significant influence on the shape of teacher professional learning policy in Scotland. This section outlines the current structure of professional learning policy, but it must be recognised that the operationalisation of the recommendations in the Donaldson and McCormac Reports will continue to have influence beyond the date at which the text for this chapter was finalised.

Before going on to consider the detail of the current structure for professional learning it is worth noting that the 'system' as a whole is very much built on a standards-based conception of professional learning. This reflects an international trend, although it should be recognised that in many ways Scotland was seen internationally to be ahead of the game in its adoption of such an approach. Such an approach is not without its critics, however, and the challenges to such an approach will be considered later in the chapter.

The formalisation of CPD for teachers in Scotland can be traced back to a recommendation in the 'Sutherland Report' in 1997 and the resulting Scottish Office consultation on the establishment of a national framework of CPD in 1998; it became formalised in legislative and policy terms through the Standards for Scotland's Schools etc. Act in 2000, which made statutory provision for the General Teaching Council for Scotland (GTCS) to expand its remit to consider 'career development'; and the McCrone Agreement (*A Teaching Profession for the 21st Century*) in 2001 in which improved opportunities for career-long professional development were to be seen as part of a package of measures designed to enhance the teaching profession in terms of both its own esteem and capabilities and its public perception. The McCrone Agreement addressed a number of issues relating to pay and conditions, but also set out a number of changes to policy relating to 'professional development'. These included:

- introduction of the Teacher Induction Scheme, which guaranteed new teachers a one-year training contract with a maximum class commitment of 0.7 full-time equivalent (FTE), the remaining time to be used for professional development. Significantly, it also made provision for mentoring;
- an additional contractual thirty-five hours per year of CPD for all teachers, with CPD seen as a condition of service that was to be applicable and accessible to everyone;
- the requirement for all teachers to have an annual professional review, resulting in a CPD plan;
- the expectation that teachers would maintain a CPD portfolio – a prerequisite for entry to the Chartered Teacher Programme;
- establishment of the Chartered Teacher Programme, designed to recognise and reward good classroom practice, ensuring that teachers would not have to choose between class teaching and management in order to progress their careers.

There is still limited research evidence as to the impact of the McCrone Agreement, although a number of evaluative studies were undertaken, including a report by Audit Scotland in 2006 into the value delivered to date through the Agreement, a report by Her Majesty's Inspectorate of Education (HMIE) in 2007 into the implementation of the

Agreement and the publication of a parliamentary report on the same topic in May 2007. The Audit Scotland report acknowledged that progress had been made in a number of areas but raised questions about how the then Scottish Executive Education Department (SEED) could possibly know whether the policies had been effective, given that very few measurable targets had been associated with the implementation plan. The HMIE report also acknowledged that considerable progress had been made, particularly in relation to the development of more constructive relationships between teachers, their employers and SEED. However, the report cautioned that there was, as yet, very limited evidence of any impact on children's learning. While it might seem reasonable to expect evidence of impact on children's learning, such evidence of cause and effect is notoriously difficult to identify, given the wide range of factors impacting on pupil learning. The parliamentary report, drawing on the Audit Scotland and HMIE reports together with oral evidence from a number of stakeholders, reported that some of the more positive aspects of the implementation included the success of the Teacher Induction Scheme and better CPD provision. So, the general consensus was that things were progressing well, but with little real evidence of impact on pupil learning gains or on any other identifiable measures.

However, in late 2009, the Scottish Government announced that it was commissioning a review 'to examine the current system of educating teachers both at initial student stage and during their professional career to meet the needs of pupils in the 21st century and Curriculum for Excellence' (Scottish Government Press Release, 20 November 2009). The review was to be led by Graham Donaldson, former Senior Chief Inspector of HMIE. Shortly after the Donaldson Review reported, the Scottish Government announced that it was inviting Professor Gerry McCormac, Principal of the University of Stirling, to conduct a review on the impact of the McCrone Agreement and the current state of teacher employment (Scottish Government Press Release, 28 January 2011). Both the Donaldson and McCormac Reviews have been carried out explicitly within the context of the current curriculum reform, Curriculum for Excellence (CfE), which demands teachers who are autonomous, confident and knowledgeable about pedagogy, individual pupils and local contexts.

The Donaldson Report (Donaldson, 2011) was on the whole fairly positive about many aspects of teachers' professional learning, and acknowledged the international praise for the Teacher Induction Scheme, for the contractual requirement for teachers to undertake CPD and for the Chartered Teacher scheme. In his report, Donaldson made fifty recommendations, all of which were accepted in full, in part or in principle, by the Scottish Government. The government set up a National Partnership Group (the NPG) to take forward the recommendations, the detailed work of which was carried out by four sub-groups, one of which focused on career-long professional learning. Sixteen of the fifty recommendations in the report appeared under the section entitled 'Career-long learning for teachers and leaders'. These recommendations include:

- a proposed new standard for active registration and a review of the overall standards framework;
- a move towards more local, collaborative approaches to teacher professional learning;
- greater focus on evaluating the impact of teacher professional learning on pupil achievement;
- all teachers seeing themselves as teacher educators, having had training in mentoring;
- increased opportunities for online CPD and also for accredited learning at Masters level;
- national professional learning strategies being informed by needs identified by evidence such as international benchmarking;

- greater local authority control over who enters the Chartered Teacher Programme;
- a new leadership pathway being developed, including appropriate ongoing professional learning for established headteachers.

All of these recommendations should be set in the wider context of the Report, which promotes a more integrated partnership approach to teacher education across the career spectrum, involving schools, local authorities and universities. Subsequent to the report of the National Partnership Group being published in 2012, a National Implementation Board has been established to take developments forward.

Interestingly, although the Donaldson Report advocates a research-informed approach to teacher professional learning at all levels, this does not form a part of the recommendations in relation to career-long learning. Another key issue discussed, but not appearing in the recommendations, is the acknowledgement that supply teachers tend to find it very difficult to access and engage in appropriate professional learning opportunities.

In September 2011, the report of the Review of Teacher Employment in Scotland, commonly known as the 'McCormac Report' (Scottish Government, 2011), was published. While the central focus of this review was on teachers' pay and conditions, issues of ongoing professional learning inevitably came into the mix. This report echoed and supported some of the recommendations made in the Donaldson Report, but it also contained some departures from previous direction. In particular, the McCormac Report recommended discontinuation of the Chartered Teacher Scheme, despite a lack of evidence to support this move in educational terms. Although the official title of the McCormac Report is *Advancing Professionalism in Teaching* there is evidence that much of the direction of the recommendations is driven primarily by financial concerns rather than a central concern to enhance professionalism.

Other recommendations in the McCormac Report which have a bearing on teacher professional learning policy include:

- the development of a 'revitalised process of Professional Review and Personal Development [PRPD]' (p. 16);
- the GTCS and/or universities devising a form of professional recognition for teachers who have engaged in sustained innovative and collaborative practice, or who have engaged in sustained mentoring or research, this recommendation appearing to be some acknowledgement of the role of Chartered Teachers;
- supply teachers being entitled to 'high quality CPD' and participation in the PRPD process.

At the time of writing final agreement on the detailed implementation of the McCormac recommendations is still to be agreed, the Cabinet Minister for Education, Michael Russell, has announced his acceptance of the proposal that the Chartered Teacher Programme be discontinued (Scottish Government Press Release, 9 February 2012).

Teacher professional learning policy will also be impacted on by the Public Services Reform (General Teaching Council for Scotland) Order 2011, which granted the GTCS full independence of Scottish Ministers with effect from 2 April 2012. The associated legislation placed a duty on the GTCS to bring forward a system of 're-accreditation', termed 'professional update' by the GTCS. Professional update will require all registered teachers to provide evidence of continued professional learning tied in to the new PRD process, and requiring teachers to be explicit in their engagement with career-long professional learning.

THE CPD FRAMEWORK AND THE PROFESSIONAL STANDARDS

Notwithstanding the caveat that policy in this area is currently undergoing significant change, the following section outlines the development of the various components of what is commonly referred to as the 'CPD framework': sets of standards and procedures covering initial teacher education (ITE), induction, ongoing professional learning and headship as well as arrangements for ongoing professional review and development. This chapter gives an overview of the structure as a whole and its historical development; it does not go into detail about the content of individual standards and associated processes. Such information can be accessed through the GTCS website at www.gtcs.org.uk

In November 1999, in the wake of the national consultation on CPD, SEED announced that it was going to create a new framework for the continuing professional development of teachers, and that a Ministerial Strategy Committee for CPD would be established to oversee the development and implementation of a national strategy. The Committee drew its membership from a variety of stakeholders in education and business, and had a number of sub-groups charged with particular responsibilities, including the development of the Chartered Teacher Programme; procedures for professional review and development; education inclusion; and leadership and management. However, while the Ministerial Strategy Committee for CPD was charged with overseeing the development of the CPD strategy, it should be noted that many of the constituent parts were well underway prior to its establishment.

Chronologically in terms of teachers' careers, the first standard that teachers have to meet is the Standard for Provisional Registration (formerly the Standard for Initial Teacher Education); however, ITE is dealt with elsewhere in this volume so will not be considered in any detail here. The next stage in a teacher's professional education is induction, an area which in the late 1990s was acknowledged as being long overdue for review. The Standard for Full Registration (SFR) was officially launched in June 2002 (with revised versions published in 2006 and 2013) as a result of the McCrone Agreement, with guidance about the implementation of the Teacher Induction Scheme being issued by the GTCS shortly thereafter. However, work on the development of a standard and a new framework for induction had begun in 1998. The Teacher Induction Project, funded jointly by the GTCS and SEED, initially envisioned a standard based on the list of competences detailed in the *Guidelines for Initial Teacher Education Courses in Scotland*, which were published by the Scottish Office in 1998. As it became evident that there would be a new Standard for ITE, the remit of the Teacher Induction Project changed to accommodate this, the justification being that the profession would expect coherence, and that the SFR would need to be based on the equivalent ITE standard.

The same coherence argument was not initially articulated for the Standard for Chartered Teacher, where the standard was developed in a quite different way. Rather than employing a development officer, answerable to individual officers in the employing bodies (SEED and the GTCS in the case of the development of the SFR), the Chartered Teacher Project was put out to tender. The tender was awarded to a consortium from Arthur Andersen consultants together with the Universities of Edinburgh and Strathclyde, the project team being directly responsible to the Ministerial Strategy Committee for CPD. The brief in developing the Standard for Chartered Teacher was to start with the identification of the qualities and characteristics of the chartered teacher and to develop a standard based on this evidence. This approach contrasts markedly with the equivalent brief in the induction phase where the key focus was to build on an existing standard. Indeed, not only were the approaches to developing standards for full registration and chartered teacher quite different, but the processes used to develop the related programmes were also contrasting. The development of the Chartered Teacher Programme was subject to wide and varied consultation by the project team and was debated rigorously in the educational press. In marked contrast, the framework for the implementation of the new induction requirements was developed by the GTCS, and was put out to schools and employers as a *fait accompli*. And while arguably all stakeholders were invited to respond to the consultation on its revision in 2006, the proposed revisions were fairly superficial.

The third standard in the framework was the Standard for Chartered Teacher, which formed a central core of the Chartered Teacher Programme. The development of what became known as the Chartered Teacher Programme was not entirely straightforward, however. Its origins can be traced back to questions in the 1998 consultation on CPD surrounding issues of 'standards to give recognition to very good classroom teachers', which became labelled as 'the expert teacher'. In early 2000, the Arthur Andersen consortium was awarded the tender, the main brief of which was to develop a standard and associated programme for the award of 'expert teacher'. However, with the publication of the McCrone Report in May 2000, and the subsequent McCrone Agreement in 2001, the brief of the project team changed, and 'chartered teacher' developed a specific definition of its own, allied not only to CPD but also to salary and conditions: chartered teachers earn nearly £8,000 more than classroom teachers at the top of the main grade scale.

This complex nature of chartered teacher status, in terms of CPD, pay and conditions, led to significant debate about the role, purpose and rewards attributable to chartered teachers and aspiring chartered teachers. One of the more public debates concerned the nature of the Chartered Teacher Programme itself and the extent to which it should be seen as either a 'professional' or an 'academic' programme, polarising the two concepts in a rather unhelpful way. It was acknowledged that in the early days of the programme there would need to be a route for experienced teachers to make claims for chartered teacher status based on their experience, but this 'accreditation' route was time limited and closed in 2008. Another high-profile debate related to the financial aspect of the programme: teachers were required to self-fund. Five years into its development, the Chartered Teacher Programme was reviewed. The review made recommendations on closing the accreditation route, the duties and roles of chartered teachers, and the requirement to ensure that chartered teachers made an impact beyond their own classrooms. More recently, however, despite the Donaldson Report recommending some minor changes to the scheme, therefore supporting its continuation, the McCormac Report recommended its discontinuation, and it was this recommendation that was accepted by the Cabinet Minister for Education.

The Ministerial Strategy Committee for CPD recognised that while chartered teacher status would be attractive to many teachers who wished to remain in the classroom and be recognised and awarded accordingly, there would be others who aspired to management roles in schools. It therefore established the Leadership and Management Pathways Sub-Group (LAMPS) to look at a parallel route of CPD for such teachers. It is interesting to note, however, that there has never been any directly corresponding recognition in terms of pay and conditions for teachers following this route – other than the enhanced likelihood of eventually securing a management position. This route ultimately lead to the Standard for Headship, which could be achieved either through the Scottish Qualification for Headship (SQH) or through what has been known as 'the flexible route'.

The Donaldson Report, however, recommended a wholesale review of the suite of professional standards, a task led by the GTCS. The revised suite of standards (to be implemented from August 2013) is based around the three phases established through the sub-groups of the National Partnership Group (early phase; career-long professional learning; leadership) and has adopted the following structure:

- Standards for Registration (encompassing provisional and full registration);
- Standard for Career-Long Professional Learning;
- Standards for Leadership and Management (encompassing middle leadership and headship).

While the above stages and associated standards mark significant aspects of a teacher's career it is recognised that not all teachers will seek promoted positions after attaining full registration, and that others, while perhaps aspiring to a middle leadership post or headship at some point in the future, will be happy to teach as a main grade teacher for some time. These teachers make up a significant percentage of the teaching workforce, and if the philosophy of CPD as a commitment to lifelong learning is to be truly meaningful then the professional learning of these teachers must also be considered within the framework. The Ministerial Strategy Committee for CPD considered this aspect through its review of the existing Staff Development and Review guidelines, which were modified to take account of the McCrone Agreement, and became known as Professional Review and Development. Under the McCrone Agreement, every teacher teaching in a Scottish school was required to participate in the Professional Review and Development process, taking part in a professional review with his or her line manager on an annual basis. The McCormac Report has suggested, however, that the PRD process as it currently stands is inadequate and has recommended the development of a revised professional review and personal development process (PRPD). The development of this process is currently being considered by a National Working Group in conjunction with GTCS plans for Professional Update.

Within the CPD framework as it now stands there are two particular foci: one is concerned with individual standards appropriate to particular stages of a teacher's career, the other relates to career-long concerns such as the need for all teachers to engage in the PRD/PRPD process and the recognition of the SFR as the baseline against which teacher competence is judged in relation to the teacher's right to be registered with the GTCS. In 2005, another aspect of the CPD framework was introduced which is not allied to any one particular standard: there had been a growing emphasis, perhaps exacerbated by the need of teachers to account for their annual thirty-five hours of CPD, on the desirability of accreditation or recognition of CPD undertaken. In response to this, the GTCS launched its Framework of Professional Recognition and Accreditation in December 2005. This framework allows teachers to work towards gaining GTCS recognition in particular subjects, cross-curricular areas such as literacy or ICT, or generic areas such as mentoring; this provides a halfway house between formal qualifications and achievement of standards, and informal or ad hoc CPD. This will arguably become a more prominent aspect of the framework as details emerge of the requirements for Professional Update with the GTCS.

In the early post-McCrone days, much of the development of the framework was driven by SEED, with HMIE and the GTCS playing significant roles, and the Ministerial Strategy Committee being charged with overseeing the process. As the original remit of the Ministerial Strategy Committee became fulfilled, structures for overseeing the implementation of the CPD framework were reconsidered. This resulted in the appointment of a National CPD Coordinator in 2004, and the subsequent development of a National CPD Team working originally under the auspices of COSLA, then based in Learning and Teaching Scotland. While the team no longer exists in name, its functions have been incorporated within Education Scotland.

TENSIONS AND CHALLENGES

Differing Conceptions of Professionalism

In advocating changes to teacher professional learning policy, both the Donaldson Report and the McCormac Report appeal to notions of 'advanced' or 'enhanced' or 'twenty-first century' professionalism, suggesting that this will improve teacher performance and, ultimately, pupil achievement. However, what is not made explicit in either report, or in most professional discourse, is what professionalism actually means, despite significant resources being invested in the development of professionals and their professional learning. In reviewing the literature on professionalism it is evident that there exist numerous interpretations of what professionalism entails, each with its own underpinning educational/political ideology. The work of Judyth Sachs has been seminal in identifying differing conceptualisations of professionalism. She contrasts democratic professionalism with managerial professionalism (Sachs, 2003), contending that the dynamic nature of the concept of professionalism reflects a response to 'changing social, economic and political conditions' (Sachs, 2003, p. 6). Democratic professionalism implies a commitment to social justice through collaborative working and the demystification of professional work. Managerial professionalism, on the other hand, privileges compliance with policy directives, efficiency and individual accountability. Sachs (ibid.) cautions that the focus on accountability within the managerial conception serves to limit teachers' capacity to articulate their own conceptions of professionalism, claiming that:

> managerialist professionalism is being reinforced by employing authorities through their policies on teacher professional development with their emphasis on accountability and effectiveness. The purpose of these is to shape the way teachers think, talk and act in relation to themselves as teachers individually and collectively. (p. 122)

It is easy, then, to see how these two conceptions of professionalism might be in conflict, and also how the two might infer different models of professional learning policy. For example, the standards-based CPD framework now in place in Scotland is supported by a managerial conception of professionalism, providing, as it does, a means of accounting for individual teachers' competence. However, the emphasis on collegiality in the McCrone Agreement, on collaborative professional learning in the Donaldson Report, on professional autonomy in CfE, as well as the increasing emphasis on inter-professional working in social policy more generally, leans much more readily towards a democratic conception of professionalism. Indeed, Whitty (2008) outlines a four-fold typology of professionalism, in which he categorises 'democratic' and 'collaborative' professionalism as distinct entities (the other two categories being 'traditional' and 'managerial' professionalism), therefore suggesting even greater prominence of conceptions of professionalism outwith the managerial perspective.

Crucially, contemporary critical analyses of professionalism (for example, Evetts, 2009;

Evans, 2011) tend towards the view that professionalism is principally an ideology linked to matters of control. The discourse of professionalism is therefore not neutral; rather it is a powerful political tool through which ideological notions of society and education can serve to influence practice. Teacher professional learning policy and practice arguably therefore acts as a powerful channel for political control. In contemporary Scotland, particularly in the context of CfE, it is worth questioning the extent to which teacher agency is either promoted or stifled through current teacher professional learning policy: if a culture of autonomy, collegiality and collaboration is genuinely seen as desirable, then explicit consideration must be given to processes of change and reform. How do we exert a shift in balance between different forms of professionalism underpinning teacher professional learning policy so as to support a more collaborative, collegiate and potentially democratic approach?

Collaboration vs Individualism

The tension between collegiate, collaborative working espoused in much current education policy and the individualistic way in which standards for teachers are written and used is an important one for Scottish education. When teachers are encouraged to view professionalism in individual terms, resulting in individual as opposed to collective accountability, the opportunities for, and desirability of, a collaborative concept of professionalism become limited. This is despite the fact that some of the rhetoric, and arguably some of the intentions outlined in, for example, the Standard for Chartered Teacher call for collaborative action and a 'shared collegial undertaking'. Nonetheless, both culture and structure must support this ideal, and the current privileging of individual teacher accountability through professional learning policy militates against more collegiate forms of accountability that emanate from the profession rather than being imposed on them from above. The increased teacher autonomy so central to CfE requires a shift in culture in terms of how teachers expect, and are expected, to account for their own professional learning. That is not to say that standards should be abandoned, rather that their formation and use need to be appropriate to the desired outcome. This is particularly important as we embark on a new system of reaccreditation tied to registration with the GTCS, which has the capacity to further entrench the view that professional learning and accountability is an individual pursuit. Therefore, if autonomous, collegiate teachers are required, then individualistic, narrowly defined and narrowly interpreted standards will not support the kind of professional learning necessary to fulfil the objectives.

   On the other hand, there is evidence of collaborative moves from within the profession, aided significantly by the development of social networking technologies. For example, Twitter has enabled educators at all levels in the system to communicate with each other outwith the traditional sectoral and hierarchical boundaries, and TeachMeets are another increasingly popular means by which teachers engage in professional dialogue with colleagues outwith formal established structures. While these developments have the potential to enhance collaborative professional learning, we must be careful about assuming that such collaborative communication necessarily promotes quality learning. This will undoubtedly be an area of enormous growth in the coming years, and it is likely that the current fairly limited body of research evidence will grow apace.

Evaluating the Impact of Professional Learning

The Donaldson Report recommends that evaluation of teacher learning needs to move away from simple evaluation of the learning activity to more systematic evaluation of impact on pupil achievement. It has long been acknowledged, however, that this is a very complex aspiration, as isolating the factors contributing to any individual pupil's development is extremely challenging given the vast range of influences on pupils, both within and outwith school. Nonetheless, this is an area of increasing interest internationally, and, indeed, in some places, teachers are evaluated in direct relation to how well their students perform in summative tests, the so-called 'value-added' approach (see Chetty et al., 2011). However, even if this measure of teacher effectiveness were to be seen as unproblematic, it still does not allow us to identify how particular professional learning events or activities relate directly to improvements in pupil achievement. It would be easy, however, to dismiss attempts at measuring the impact of teacher professional learning on pupil achievement as manifestations of a managerial culture, but the real challenge, it seems, is to find ways of identifying impact that do not distort reality or result in unintended consequences such as teaching to the test.

THE FUTURE

Taking into account both national and international trends, it looks as though a standards-based framework of professional learning will remain dominant for some time to come. However, what is not set in stone is the way in which the standards are used, by both the system and the individual. There is a possibility that if the intended culture of teacher autonomy and creativity espoused in CfE really comes to pass, then teachers will be able to use the standards as an aid, rather than a prescription, to support their professional learning. It will be important, however, to ensure that we do not allow our policies on teacher learning to be viewed in a deficit way, based purely on 'needs' that are translated as weaknesses to be remedied. Indeed, Hoekstra and Korthagen (2011) suggest that while professional learning is 'often triggered by a problematic, troublesome, or otherwise negative situation . . . reflection on one's successes and finding explanations for positive experiences might be much more beneficial to professional learning' (p. 78).

REFERENCES

Chetty, R., J. Friedman and J. Rockoff (2011) *The Long-term Impacts of Teachers: Teacher Value-added and Student Outcomes in Adulthood*. National Bureau of Economic Research. Working Paper No. 17699. Cambridge, MA. Online at http://obs.rc.fas.harvard.edu/chetty/value_added.pdf

Donaldson, G. (2011) *Teaching Scotland's Future: Report of a Review of Teacher Education in Scotland*. Edinburgh: Scottish Government.

Evans, L. (2011) 'The "shape" of teacher professionalism in England: Professional standards, performance management, professional development and the changes proposed in the 2010 White Paper', *British Educational Research Journal*, 37 (5): 851–70.

Evetts, J. (2009) 'The management of professionalism: A contemporary paradox', in S. Gewirtz, P. Mahony, I. Hextall and A. Cribb (eds), *Changing Teacher Professionalism: International Trends, Challenges and Ways Forward*. London: Routledge.

Hoekstra, A. and F. Korthagen (2011) 'Teacher learning in a context of educational change: informal learning versus systematically supported learning', *Journal of Teacher Education*, 62 (1): 76–92.

Sachs, J. (2003) *The Activist Teaching Profession*. Buckingham: Open University Press.

Scottish Government (2011) *Advancing Professionalism in Teaching: The Report of the Review of Teacher Employment in Scotland*. Edinburgh: Scottish Government.

Stronach, I. (2010) *Globalizing Education, Educating the Local: How Method Made us Mad*. Abingdon: Routledge.

Whitty, G. (2008) 'Changing modes of teacher professionalism: traditional, managerial, collaborative and democratic', in B. Cunningham (ed.), *Exploring Professionalism*. London: Institute of Education, University of London.

99

Research and Practice

Moira Hulme

This chapter examines the relationship between research on teachers and teaching and what takes place in classrooms. Such consideration necessarily entails discussion of the tensions among professionals – teachers and other school professionals, university and school-based teacher educators, and education researchers. Each generation of educationists and policy makers has grappled with the vexing issue of 'impact'. This is not a new debate. The relationship between research-based knowledge, professional preparation and teachers' practice has been struggled over for around a century. It cannot be reduced to a technical or communication issue as is sometimes implied in accounts that bemoan a lack of 'knowledge transfer'. How educational research is commissioned, the topics that are identified as problems worthy of enquiry at particular junctures, how research is conducted, by whom, for whom, and to what end requires consideration of the politics of knowledge and action. Foremost in this debate is the politics of professionalisation – the development of specialist fields of knowledge and expertise and the work of professionals in securing jurisdiction over these emergent fields.

Scottish education provides an interesting case in the interweaving of the educational sciences and the professional preparation and continuing development of teachers. The contemporary relationship between professional practice and multifarious forms of educational research reflects long-standing tensions between the academic enterprise and professional mission of university Schools of Education. These debates date back to before universitisation (that is, the integration of the monotechnic colleges of education within universities from the 1990s; see Chapter 96), and occupy a significant place in deliberation on the site, content and locus of control of teacher education in the second decade of the twenty-first century.

This chapter is organised in four sections. First, the early movement to professionalise and mobilise the teaching workforce is outlined. Second, a bifurcation of research and practice fields is noted with the professional advance of educationists within the academy. Renewed interest in systematic enquiry by teachers is considered alongside policy inclinations to render curriculum material, assessment practice and pedagogical strategies 'teacher proof'. Third, the emergence of hybrid models of research engagement is outlined that carry forward the challenges and counterclaims of the past to new sets of circumstances. Finally, the limits and affordances of the current discourse of 'research-informed professionalism' are considered. The confines of the chapter necessarily evoke an over-simplification of complex issues and contain many omissions. However, it is hoped to convey something of the ebb and flow that has characterised and continues to characterise deliberation between practitioners, researchers and policy makers in this contentious area.

PROFESSIONAL KNOWLEDGE: BEGINNINGS

The professional knowledge base of teaching – often reduced to 'what teachers should know and should be able to do' – has been the focus of sustained debate. The history of the professions is a history of struggle to claim jurisdiction over specific fields through the assertion of a specialist (and exclusive) knowledge base. The development of specialist knowledge in the study of education is evident in the founding of chairs/academic appointments, the formation of associations/learned societies, the establishment of academic and professional journals (and through publication rates therein), through academic credentials and professional qualifications, and regulation of membership. In the applied field of teacher education it is further evident in the development of professional standards and curricula that aim to set out the 'essential' knowledge bases that inform professional practice.

From its establishment in 1847, the Educational Institute of Scotland (EIS) lobbied for university involvement in teacher education. Representing the organised interests of teachers, in part trades union and in part learned society, the EIS leadership saw links with universities and the development of a specialised knowledge base as integral to teachers' claim to professional status. Robert Burton used his presidential address to the EIS congress in 1858 to call for professors of 'pedeutics'. The EIS petitioned Universities Commissioners for chairs in education and maintained a constant lobby as the national system developed following the 1872 Education (Scotland) Act. Speaking at the EIS General Meeting in 1873, William Jolly, HM Inspector of schools, called for 'systematic training in the Theory and Practice of Teaching, by means of a University Course of instruction'. Jolly (1874) argued for the creation of chairs and lectureships in education, the establishment of 'practising' or 'experimental' schools organised by universities and the creation of an 'educational museum' or 'consulting room' for serving teachers. At the same meeting, EIS President William MacDonald argued that 'every nerve must be strained to place the whole profession beside the other learned professions'. A Chair Committee was formed with the aim of 'rousing teachers to practical effort on this important matter, to obtain subscriptions for the establishment of Chairs of Education in the Scotch Universities' (Glasgow, 1875).

The first chairs were endowed in 1876 through the bequest of Andrew Bell: Simon Somerville Laurie at Edinburgh and John Miller Dow Meiklejohn at St Andrews. It was a further seventeen years before they were joined by the first lecturers in Education – Joseph Ogilvie in Aberdeen (appointed 1893) and David Ross in Glasgow (appointed 1894); and considerably longer until the first professors in Education were appointed in Glasgow and Aberdeen – Stanley Nisbet (1951) and his brother John Nisbet (1963). The new class of academics advancing Education as a university subject in the late nineteenth century (eligible for inclusion in a Masters degree from 1889) operated in a competitive academic environment and sought uneasy alliances with ecclesiastical factions (denominational training colleges) and the administrative bodies of the local and national education state. Preparation for elementary school teaching remained concentrated in local training colleges. Although after 1895, provision existed to support concurrent attendance at training college and university classes the demands of this mode of attendance were considerable. Whilst securing a place for Education in the university calendar and promoting a degree of collaboration with the colleges (including mobility of staff), clear demarcations were sustained between pedagogical training provided by the 'masters and mistresses of method' of the training colleges and their demonstration schools, and the higher education function of university lecturers. Different types of knowledge (academic and practical) and different credentials (MA, diploma, teacher certification) worked to produce different categories of teacher for working lives in different types of school. Differentiation and specialisation increased barriers between an emerging discipline of Education (as a university subject and field of research) and the workaday lives of many teachers in the expanding school system.

Publication is an important tactic in advancing knowledge claims and marking profes-sional jurisdiction. During the late nineteenth and early twentieth centuries, teacher educa-tion was developing as a nascent field of knowledge in Scotland with the publication of a number of 'methods manuals' authored by normal school/training college principals. These included David Stow's celebrated *Training System* (1854), and James Currie's *The Principles and Practice of Early and Infant School Education* (1857) and *The Principles and Practice of Common School Education* (1861). Within the universities, principles broadly drawn from psychology found expression in the work of Alexander Bain, University of Aberdeen, who was influenced by the German educationist Johann Herbart. Bain was influential in the Society for the Development of the Science of Education founded in 1876 and published *Education as a Science* in 1892. However, it was not until the first two decades of the twenti-eth century that a distinctive 'education science' began to emerge strongly. The uneasy place occupied by Education within universities (with its association with state control and a low-status, largely feminised occupation), and the perception among some that its presence in the university calendar was not justified, accelerated drives to render education progressively more 'scientific'. James Drever did much to advance experimental psychology in Scotland, influenced by developments in the laboratories of Leipzig, Jena and Berlin, particularly the investigations of William Wundt (1832–1920) and Ernst Meumann (1862–1915) on percep-tion, memory and intelligence. Through the work of Alfred Binet (1857–1911), Edward Thorndike (1884–1949) and Guy Montrose Whipple (1876–1941), the new technology of intelligence testing (or 'mental measurement') gained ground. The borderland between psy-chology and pedagogy was being occupied by European scholars such as Jean-Ovide Decroly (1871–1932) in Belgium and Edouard Clarapede (1874–1940) in Switzerland to create a new field of 'experimental pedagogy' (Nisbet, 1999). Alexander Darroch (Laurie's successor as Edinburgh Bell Chair) published *The Place of Psychology in the Training of the Teacher* in 1911, quickly followed by Robert R. Rusk's *Introduction to Experimental Education* in 1912.

Whilst a small number of pioneer educationists in Scottish universities moved further from the professional field in a drive to professionalise education research, teachers' associa-tions continued to use research engagement in their strategies to raise the status of teaching. Formed in 1919, the EIS Research Committee sought to promote teachers' involvement in research studies through invitations published in the *Scottish Educational Journal* (*SEJ*). The Research Committee achieved some success in eliciting the cooperation of teachers in work conducted by William Boyd at the University of Glasgow, but less success in fulfilling the aspiration that teachers might routinely engage independently in small-scale studies of their own classroom practice (Brett et al., 2010). It is telling that the first 'experimental' enquiries prioritised by the Research Committee in the early 1920s focused on establishing common assessment standards in the core subjects of elementary teaching, that is, were concerned with 'standard tests' as 'measuring devices'. Teacher control over systems for examination and pupil assessment, the currency of schooling, was seen as central to self-determination. Boyd's Code of Professional Etiquette for Teachers (1917) was adopted as the EIS Code of Conduct, an early manifesto for self-government. Higher education and engagement with research were seen as hallmarks of professionalism, necessary in the struggle for professional status enjoyed by medicine and law. However, at this juncture the EIS Research Committee overestimated the capacity and willingness of a large proportion of the teacher workforce to engage in, as well as with, research.

Debate on the purpose and content of the first 'teachers' degree' in the second decade of the twentieth century highlights ever-present tensions between the academy, the profession, and the needs and priorities of the education state. Research training, initially only acquired in psychology laboratories through the medium of German, became available to an elite cadre of teacher candidates undertaking the two-year 'EdB' (a 'second first degree' for teachers with a first degree in arts or science and a course of professional training at a training college). This programme was available at the four ancient universities from the 1920s (with greater uptake after the Second World War). This settlement (for 'super Bachelors' rather than a Masters degree) offered a pathway for progression that reconciled demand for large numbers of teachers, high turnover and shortages in some areas, with the ambitions of some teachers for higher academic status and occupational rewards derived from specialisation. The developing science of education and allied fields of public administration created new opportunities for a minority of enterprising researchers and practitioners. The application of psychology to the educational issues of the day led to the development of the schools psychological service. A Psychological Clinic for Children and Juveniles was established in Edinburgh in 1925, followed by Child Guidance Clinics in Glasgow, Aberdeen and Dundee in the 1930s. The EdB was later redesignated MEd (Hons) to distinguish the award from the newly created BEd (Primary Education) courses at Aberdeen (1965), Jordanhill and Moray House (1966), and Dundee (1967). The BEd in turn has been the focus of deliberation and will be replaced from 2014 by concurrent BA, BSc or MA in Education programmes in response to the changing demands of teaching and the changing position of Schools of Education in universities.

PROFESSIONALISATION AND DIVERSIFICATION OF RESEARCH

The Scottish Council for Research in Education (SCRE) was founded in 1928, funded in part by the EIS and in part by the Association of Directors of Education, with the intention of conducting large-scale systematic investigations that would overcome some of the limitations in scope, method and resource of experiments undertaken by the EIS Research Committee. Nisbet (1999, p. 8) has argued that the appointment of Rusk, then Head of Education at Jordanhill Training College, as the first (part-time) Director of the SCRE marked the dominance of 'scientific' approaches to educational research over the 'school-based curriculum-centred style of Boyd'. The development of the SCRE (now the SCRE Centre at the University of Glasgow) as a collaborative research network has been documented by Lawn (2004). A commitment to applied research is reflected in the composition of the management board. Representatives were drawn from the Association of Local Education Authorities, EIS, Association of Directors of Education, National Committee for the Training of Teachers, Universities of Scotland, the Scottish branch of the British Psychological Association and the Association of School Medical Officers in Scotland. The role of the SCRE in contributing to the International Examinations Inquiry (IEI) of the 1930s did much to position Scotland at the forefront of educational research internationally during this period. Lawn et al. (2008) have charted the development of an influential

Scottish School of Education Research (1925–50). The SCRE developed specialisms in survey research and large-scale educational assessment, contributing to the Scottish Mental Surveys (1932, 1947) led by Godfrey Thomson (Edinburgh Bell Chair 1925–51), and by William McClelland's work on *Selection for Secondary Education* (1942). Whilst the SCRE enjoyed close connections with the teaching community and education policy makers, the engagement of teachers in original research was not fully supported. Contract research undertaken by full-time researchers replaced projects that relied on the voluntary efforts of university and college staff collaborating with teachers. The absence of teacher voices or accounts of teacher research is noted by Brown (1988) in the edited collection *Education in Transition*, which celebrated sixty years of research by the SCRE.

By 1950, discipline-focused educational research was established as a specialist field requiring advanced statistical and psychological training. When Godfrey Thomson retired in 1951, the dominance of psychology in university Education Departments in Scotland was subject to challenge from emergent sub-divisions within educational research. The first issues of the *British Journal of Sociology* and the *British Journal of Educational Studies* were published in 1950 and 1952 respectively. With the appointment of Liam Hudson as Bell Professor (1968–77), and his successor Noel Entwistle (1978–2003), the primacy of testing, pioneered in Room 70 Moray House, was contested. The contribution of David Hamilton and Malcolm Parlett, also Edinburgh based, were significant in pioneering alternative approaches to curriculum research. The 'methodolatry' of experimental psychology waned as alternative paradigms competed for attention. Disillusionment with 'arithmetic' paradigms focused on measurement, control and prediction were challenged by renewed emphasis on the complex social settings of schools and classrooms. Drawing on social anthropology and the new sociology of education, attention turned from a dominant focus on attainment to concern with processes and relations of schooling. Parlett and Hamilton used a theatre metaphor to critique conventional technocratic (or 'outsider') evaluation.

> An agricultural-botany evaluator is rather like a critic who reviews a production on the basis of a script and audience applause-meter readings, having missed the performance. There is no play that is director-proof, any more than an educational innovation is teacher-proof or student-proof. If this is acknowledged, then it becomes imperative to study an innovation through the medium of its performance and to adopt a research style and performance that is appropriate. (Parlett and Hamilton, 1972, cited in Hamilton, 2004, p. 193)

The 1960s and 1970s was a period of significant growth for higher education and educational studies. Innovation in teacher education included Donald McIntyre's work on micro-teaching at the University of Stirling (1969–76). From the 1960s, the sociology of education grew rapidly, emphasising barriers to educational opportunity. Closer alignment was sought between research, policy and practice, as research commissioning by public bodies emphasised 'relevance'. The Educational Research Board of the Social Science Research Council was established in 1965 (renamed the Economic and Social Research Council in 1983 in a further dispute over 'scientific' knowledge). Research-based evidence, alongside other sources, was included in the Crowther (1959), Newsom (1963), Robbins (1963) and Plowden (1967) Reports. The number of UK societies and journals grew, including the Philosophy of Education Society of Great Britain (founded 1964); the History of Education Society (1967); the British and Scottish Educational Research Associations (1974); the British Comparative Education Society (1979); and the *British Journal of Sociology of Education* (launched 1980). By the 1980s, it was the Department of Sociology at Edinburgh, through the work of the Centre for Educational Sociology (CES), that had achieved a strong track record in research council grants for school-related studies. From the mid-1980s, policy interest in how schools make a difference (within-school effects) gave rise to the development of 'school effectiveness' as a new research modality.

In contrast, the explicit professional orientation of the colleges, their regulatory role and the need to assert a distinct place for monotechnic colleges in the higher education landscape did not support the prioritisation of research activity, although a National Inter-College Committee on Educational Research (NICCER) was established to coordinate efforts. The position of the colleges outside the universities, and subject to policy frameworks that prioritised teacher supply, inhibited research use to inform programme design and the involvement in research of college staff. The integration of college staff within university Faculties of Education from the 1990s (with the exception of Stirling University which was established with a Department of Education in 1967) created diverse micro-communities or sub-tribes that differed in terms of professional identity, training and mission. Institutional mergers and restructuring produced a shifting power base. However, the location of pre-service teacher education within universities did present new opportunities for creative interchange and synergy between professional education and educational research.

RECENT MODELS OF RESEARCH ENGAGEMENT

This section focuses on the aspirations for evidence-informed professional practice in the twenty-first century. Research council thematic priorities have sought to align research agenda with national priorities (notably the closer coupling of research to the pursuit of national economic competitiveness). User engagement and attention to processes of knowledge exchange are now expected features of research design. The extent to which these aspirations might be realised depends, of course, on political expedience and policy makers and practitioners' receptiveness to learning and capacity to adapt. There are dangers in the 'evidence turn', not least where research starts from the premise that problems in practice can be 'repaired' through the application of 'usable' knowledge generated elsewhere.

At a national level there have been a number of strategic developments to generate and apply insights from educational research (Pollard and Oancea, 2010). Between 1999 and 2009, the UK Teaching and Learning Research Programme (TLRP) received Economic and Social Research Council (ESRC) funding totalling £43 million, a key outcome of which was the production of evidence-informed principles for effective pedagogy. In Scotland, the Applied Educational Research Scheme (AERS) received £2 million from the Scottish Funding Council and the Scottish Executive Education Department between 2005 and 2009 to improve the infrastructure of educational research across Scottish higher education institutions (HEIs). Stronger links were sought between researchers, policy makers and practitioners in addressing the country's long-term educational needs. 'Entry level' engagement allowed interested users, observers and potential participants to learn about developments in the AERS thematic networks: Learners, Learning and Teaching; School Management and Governance; and Schools and Social Capital. Other attempts to broker research knowledge include the activities of the Assessment Reform Group (1989–2010), funded by the Nuffield Foundation, which exerted a strong influence on the Assessment is for Learning Development Programme in Scotland (2002–4); and the work of the Scottish Teacher Education Committee (STEC) in developing a National Framework for Inclusion funded by the Scottish Government in 2009. These initiatives have contributed to an understanding of knowledge mobilisation as a complex and contingent process. There are considerable cultural and resource implications in developing research partnerships that extend beyond linear (one-way) models of knowledge adoption.

School-level initiatives that have emphasised local ownership include the Schools of Ambition Programme (2006–10), a collaboration between fifty-two schools, a consortium of the Universities of Glasgow, Aberdeen and Strathclyde, and the Scottish Government Schools' Directorate. The programme was distinctive in promoting action research within a national programme for school change. Nominated schools were encouraged to explore flexible, creative and innovative approaches to school improvement. Each school submitted a 'transformational plan' outlining priorities for change and received additional funding of around £100,000 per annum for three years. Common themes included community engagement, curriculum flexibility and leadership development. A commitment to self-evaluation was a condition of the award (drawing on approaches to school self-evaluation first developed from the work of John MacBeath in the late 1980s). Each school undertook to map the 'distance travelled' towards locally defined goals with support from a university mentor and Scottish Government adviser. Whilst a bold attempt to devolve responsibility for curriculum innovation to schools, many struggled to reconcile espoused support for creativity and managed risk-taking with the challenge of demonstrating positive outcomes – 'transformation' – within an ambitious timescale in challenging circumstances.

The experiences of the Schools of Ambition lend force to Stenhouse's call for the concurrent pursuit of teacher development and curriculum development. The model of the 'teacher-as-researcher' continues to appeal to those who seek to democratise research relations (reducing barriers between researchers and researched) and those advancing the notion of the knowledge-creating school. Although research-mindedness is embedded in the professional standards framework for teachers in Scotland there remain few opportunities to participate in sponsored forms of collaborative research with external partners and few sources of funding for teacher-led enquiry. The Chartered Teacher (CT) Programme, one of the flagship policies to result from the 2001 Teachers' Agreement, *A Teaching Profession for the 21st Century*, closed in February 2012. The introduction of the chartered teacher grade was broadly welcomed as an attempt to recognise pedagogical expertise. Participation was elective with eligible teachers self-nominating and self-funding progression through a part-time Masters programme (see Chapter 98). Salary increments were achieved for modules completed. Despite initial optimism participation fell below the forecast rate of 25–30 per cent of eligible teachers. Donaldson (2011, p. 76) reported that 'only around 2% of the profession or 1,107 teachers in Scotland have become chartered teachers . . . a further 2,912 have partially completed modules on chartered teacher courses, gaining additional salary payments'. Decision makers expressed concern about the contribution of CTs to school improvement given the considerable role ambiguity of this non-promoted post. Recruitment to and progression through the programme was frozen in June 2011. The McCormac Review of Teacher Employment, which emphasised affordability and impact, recommended closure of the programme in September 2011. Some support for teacher research is available through a small-scale scheme managed by the General Teaching Council for Scotland (GTCS) (2003–), which provides funding for expenses and up to ten days' release from school. Research reports on the GTCS website indicate take-up of two scholarships per annum. There are limitations and dangers in approaches to practitioner enquiry based on the lone scholar. The challenges involved in fostering cultures of enquiry are considerable, difficulties that are all the more acute in hierarchical and performative work settings.

Effective mediation of research knowledge is critical in strengthening research-practice links. Progress has been uneven and is threatened by the closure of brokerage agencies in the UK government's 'bonfire of the quangos' from 2010. Many research resources for teachers are frozen, no longer available or await archiving. These include digests, such as *Research for Teachers* commissioned by the General Teaching Council for England (abolished in April 2012), and resources produced by the Teacher Training Resource Bank (TTRB), the British Educational Communications and Technology Agency (BECTA) and the UK Department for Education's Research Informed Practice Digests (TRIPS). In Scotland, the Scottish Educational Research Association (SERA) launched the *Researching Education Bulletin* for practitioner researchers in 2011. A promising Emerging Researchers' Network, launched in 2007, has struggled to sustain an active membership. The Aberdeen based journal *Education in the North*, established in 1965, moved to an online format with one issue per annum in 2008. Education Scotland offers the bi-monthly *Research Round-Up* and attempts have been made to use GLOW, the national schools intranet, to support dialogue and knowledge exchange. It is noteworthy that GLOW currently excludes members of the academic community whilst academic publishing excludes many practitioners. The current debate on open-access publishing may lead to knowledge sharing, but it will not preclude a continuing need for mediation.

The relationship between research and practice occupies an important place in the applied field of teacher education. The interface of research and practice is navigated by university Schools of Education through research institutes, graduate schools and programmes of undergraduate and postgraduate professional education. Research-active teacher educators routinely work across professional, institutional and sectoral borders. Cooperation and collaboration has produced a body of research on curriculum, pedagogy and assessment, and social justice and equity issues. This work has a high profile at SERA conferences and is reported through the SERA journal, *Scottish Educational Research (SER)*. Educational researchers who participate in teacher education can fulfil a brokerage role. Knowledge of practice produced by 'hybrid educators' may speak more directly to the concerns of practitioners. Knowledge of context may help collaborative researchers' ideas to gain traction in policy circles such as Education Scotland and the Scottish Qualifications Authority.

Aspirations for research-informed professional practice appear in proposals to develop teaching schools, loosely informed by the idea of teaching hospitals, as 'hubs of learning'. *Teaching Scotland's Future* (Donaldson, 2011) recommends 'hub teaching schools as a focal point for research, learning and teaching' (pp. 91, 111–12).

> The creation of a network of such 'hub school' partnerships across all authorities and also involving national agencies would enable much more direct engagement of university staff in school practice, with research as an integral part of this strengthened partnership rather than as something that sits apart. (Donaldson 2011, p. 8)

A clinical approach to teacher education is not without precedent in Scotland. The Scottish Teachers for a New Era (STNE) project at Aberdeen University sought to promote teaching as a clinical and evidence-based profession. Since 2010–11 the University of Glasgow and Glasgow City Council has trialled a new approach to teacher education for intending primary and secondary teachers. The Glasgow West Teacher Education Initiative (GWTEI) involves cohort placements in clustered partner schools. Pre-service teachers attend weekly school-based seminars (with school staff and a university tutor) and participate in learning rounds that aim to challenge cultures of privacy. A university tutor works closely with school staff in each learning community. Joint work includes co-assessment of student teaching and mentoring, marking a break from the traditional 'crit lesson'. Two sets of staff contribute to the programme – school-based and university-based educators – in an attempt to promote better integration of university and school work. Three issues have proven difficult: integration of initial teacher education with the early career phase; greater involvement of experienced teachers in the programme; and development of action research by university tutors to support programme development. Other challenges include issues of resource and governance; building capacity (in mentoring, coaching and enquiry); communication; contractual and status issues (including different conditions of service, recognition and reward structures between university and school staff); and challenges of impact assessment. Introducing change alongside coexisting 'traditional' models of (university-led) teacher education is difficult. The Glasgow initiative has challenged deeply held professional identities and disturbed established ways of working, particularly the role of the secondary subject specialist (university) tutor. It is not surprising that innovation in partnership development is generating both heat and light.

CONCLUSION

Rusk (1952), writing in the inaugural issue of the *British Journal of Educational Studies*, argues that Scotland was well placed at the start of the twentieth century to lead the development of research-informed professional practice. His account expresses considerable optimism with regard to capacity for teacher education research and the cultivation of researcherly dispositions among Scottish teachers. From the first decade of the century, training college students were familiarised with the procedures and made acquainted with the results of research; thus a supply of qualified workers in research was provided and an influx of teachers favourably disposed to research was annually entering school (Rusk, 1952, p. 39). Writing at the close of the twentieth century, Nisbet (1999, p. 9) strikes a less optimistic note.

> The Educational Institute of Scotland, in supporting research in 1917, had hoped that it would confer on teaching the status of a profession, like other professions based on specialist knowledge. Research has not met this aspiration: neither teachers nor researchers have the autonomy of a professional activity, and Boyd's idea of teacher involvement, revived by Stenhouse in the 1960s, has still to fight for general acceptance.

One hundred years after the promotion of collaborative enquiry by Boyd, and following the attainment of full independence by the General Teaching Council, the most recent review of teacher education in Scotland carries a familiar refrain and reasserts a strong association between evidence use and improvement action.

> If we are to achieve the aspiration of teachers being leaders of educational improvement, they need to develop expertise in using research, inquiry and reflection as part of their daily skill set. (Donaldson 2011, p. 70)

The prospects for the research-practice interface in the second decade of the twenty-first century are uncertain. In times of austerity, with cuts to public expenditure and concern with maintaining frontline services, the relationship between research and practice is under strain. Funding for government-commissioned research has contracted and education does not occupy a prominent place in UK and European research funding streams (Christie et al., 2012). Knowledge exchange, consultancy and research-informed CPD activities compete with other pressing local authority spending priorities. Education budgets are no longer ring-fenced. Significant fluctuation in student places for initial teacher education in Scotland from 2010 has had a destabilising impact on many Schools of Education. Reductions in staffing have intensified workloads with implications for research and researcher development, especially for early career academics. There are consequences for those labelled 'research inactive' in terms of career advancement, networking opportunities and professional development. This is especially the case for staff employed by research-intensive universities with an eye on world rankings. Greater selectivity and concentration of funds are likely to result from research policy and technologies to audit research performance such as the Research Excellence Framework (REF). The increased significance of research metrics (journal impact rankings and citations per paper) directs researchers' attention towards an international rather than a local audience. Less weight is attached to co-authored outputs generated through joint work in calculations of impact.

This direction of travel stands in contrast to the collaborative and inclusive 'social practices' approach to research capacity-building advocated by Christie and Menter (2009). Christie et al. (2012, p. 35) call for greater collaboration between research networks, more opportunities for academic interchange and mobility, and enhanced interdisciplinary and trans-professional collaboration. Economic pressures may create a pull towards retrenchment rather than innovation and boundary crossing. A number of studies have noted greater differentiation in the kinds of research undertaken by Schools of Education. Higher-rated HEIs are more likely to concentrate on disciplinary enquiry, and large-scale quantitative and longitudinal studies, rather than teacher development and co-enquiry (Christie et al., 2012, pp. 30–1). It is likely that the current climate of university funding, research commissioning and research assessment will increase the bifurcation of teaching and research activities in the fragmented field of educational studies. Funding challenges may support further specialisation that distances the research activities of some university Schools of Education from the professional field and diminishes the capacity of others to engage in high-quality research. Alternatively there are opportunities to generate a collaborative dividend through the reinvigoration of practice-based, professionally orientated and multidisciplinary studies. Now, as before, the relationship between educational research and teachers' practice will depend on the autonomy and capability of researchers and practitioners, and on the development of school–university partnerships that position both as producers of knowledge.

REFERENCES

Brett, C. E., M. Lawn, D. J. Bartholomew and I. J. Deary (2010) 'Help will be welcomed from every quarter: The work of William Boyd and the Educational Institute of Scotland's Research Committee in the 1920s', *History of Education*, 39 (5): 589–611.

Christie, D., M. Donoghue, G. Kirk, M. McNamara, I. Menter, G. Moss, J. Noble-Rogers, A. Oancea, C. Rogers, P. Thomson and G. Whitty (2012) BERA-UCET Working Group on Education Research. Prospects for Education Research in Education Departments in Higher Education Institutions in the UK. Online at www.bera.ac.uk/news/bera-ucet-report

Christie, D. and I. Menter (2009) 'Research capacity building in teacher education: Scottish collaborative approaches', *Journal of Education for Teaching*, 35 (4): 337–54.

Donaldson, G. (2011) *Teaching Scotland's Future: Report of a Review of Teacher Education in Scotland*. Edinburgh: Scottish Government. Online at www.scotland.gov.uk/Resource/Doc/337626/0110852.pdf

Glasgow, W. (1875) 'The training of teachers'. Paper read before the Ayrshire branch of the Educational Institute and at the Educational Congress in the Corporation Galleries Glasgow in December 1874. Glasgow: Robert Forrester.

Hamilton, D. (2004) 'Illuminative evaluation', in S. Mathison (ed.), *Encyclopaedia of Evaluation*. London: Sage, pp.191–4.

Jolly, W. (1874) 'The professional training of teachers', *Fortnightly Review*, 16 (93): 353.

Lawn, M. (2004) 'The institute as network: The Scottish Council for Research in Education as a local and international phenomenon in the 1930s', *Paedagogica Historica*, 40 (5–6): 719–32.

Lawn, M. (ed.) (2008) *An Atlantic Crossing? The Work of the International Examination Inquiry, its Researchers, Methods and Influence*. Oxford: Symposium.

Nisbet, J. (1999) 'How it all began: Educational research 1880–1930', *Scottish Educational Review*, 31 (1): 3–9.

Pollard, A. and A. Oancea (2010) *Unlocking Learning? Towards Evidence-informed Policy and Practice in Education*. Final report of the UK Strategic Forum for Research in Education. London: SFRE. Online at www.sfre.ac.uk/wp-content/uploads/2008/05/final-report.pdf

Rusk, R. R. (1952) 'The Scottish Council for Research in Education', *British Journal of Educational Studies*, 1 (1): 39–42.

100

The Scottish Educational Research Association

Fran Payne

The first thirty years of the existence of the Scottish Educational Research Association (SERA), founded in 1974, is well documented by Nisbet (2005). The chapter he wrote for the third edition of *Scottish Education* draws on this work. In this fourth edition, although reference is made to historical data, the chapter concentrates on SERA in the first decade of the twenty-first century.

DEVELOPMENTS IN THE TWENTY-FIRST CENTURY

SERA's overall purpose is 'Working for the improvement of education through promoting and sustaining high quality educational research' (SERA, 2006, p. 1). This translates into five specific aims:

- raising the quality of educational research through supporting and encouraging innovation, rigour and relevance;
- encouraging the development of a research infrastructure to ensure sustainability of the activity;
- improving knowledge transfer/exchange and influencing education policy and practice as well as policy on educational research;
- providing a forum for all individual researchers, through arranging conferences, seminars, networks and the website;
- promoting the use of educational research across the wider community (schools, colleges, community groups, governmental and non-governmental organisations, as well as parents, students and the general public) through effective educational and awareness-raising activities. (SERA, 2006, p. 3)

These aims mirror the objectives of SERA's updated 2005 constitution (available at www. sera.ac.uk) and guide its strategic five-year plan for 2006–11 following a review and reassessment of SERA's activities in response to the rapidly changing context in educational research whereby quality, capacity and sustainability came to the fore. Following the performance of Scottish University Schools of Education in the 2001 Research Assessment Exercise (RAE) and concerns about the quality of educational research, the 2004–09 Applied Educational Research Scheme (AERS) funded by the then Scottish Executive

Education Department (SEED) and Scottish Higher Education Funding Council (SHEFC) was established (see Chapter 98). One of its main aims was to increase research capacity in Scotland through a programme of activities delivered in collaboration by three major Scottish universities. Some Scottish researchers were included in the UK-wide Economic and Social Research Council (ESRC) Teaching and Learning Research Programme, which also aimed to build research capacity. Moreover, as a founding member of the European Educational Research Association (EERA) with representation on EERA Council, SERA was aware of the increasing importance of the international context of educational research. Similarly, SERA established closer links with the British Educational Research Association (BERA) in 2001 and has representation on BERA Council, and was a founding member of the World Educational Research Association (WERA) in 2009. Recently, SERA established closer collaboration with the Nordic Educational Research Association (NERA). Thus the plan was used as a framework to steer its strategic activities (SERA, 2006, p. 3) in pursuance of its aims. These aims are achieved through a number of priorities:

- strengthening SERA's organisational infrastructure including the development of the membership base and of membership services;
- raising the profile of SERA in Europe and beyond through further development of links with other educational research organisations;
- developing a press and media strategy designed to raise awareness in Scotland (and beyond) of the significance of educational research and of SERA;
- development of the annual conference, supporting it as an international forum, with Scottish educational research at its core;
- ensuring the achievements of AERS are sustained and are expanded beyond schools' research;
- developing SERA networks and their activities, including provision for postgraduate students and new researchers;
- further development of the relationship between research, policy and practice through strengthening our liaisons with Scottish stakeholder bodies.

ACTIVITIES

To fulfil its priorities SERA's activities are managed by an executive committee elected at its annual conference. Co-opted members include a postgraduate student and representatives of the stakeholder education community, that is Scotland's Colleges, the Association of Chartered Teachers, the General Teaching Council for Scotland (GTCS) and the former Learning and Teaching Scotland (LTS). Furthermore, SERA maintains links with other organisations or associations relevant to education or educational research, sometimes no more than sharing information about events. Similarly, with co-opted members these links have been stronger at some times than at others. One long-standing association is with the journal *Scottish Educational Review* (*SER*) with subscription included in the membership fee, and SERA represented on its board.

In addition to the office bearer roles, executive members take responsibility for particular areas of operation: membership services; conference organisation; communications; the website; and overseeing the networks. The networks bring together academic staff, practitioners and policy makers with an interest in a particular area of study. Networks are a means of building membership but principally act as the focus for member activities. Each network organises its own activities, for example seminars, and presents a symposium at the conference. The first network established in 2001 was the policy network, followed by the high-ability and early years networks in 2004. When AERS ended in 2009, SERA set up the citizenship and democracy, emerging researchers and social capital networks in support of its commitment to sustain AERS' work. Furthermore, to recognise the excellence and promise of early career researchers SERA has awarded the Brisard prize annually since 2007 for the best research paper written by an early career researcher based in Scotland, in memoriam of a colleague who served on the executive in 2004–5.

SERA expects members to adhere to its ethical guidelines, and *Starting Points for Research in Schools*, produced in collaboration with SEED, teachers and local authority representatives, provides guiding principles for good practice for stakeholder groups, but is also aimed at encouraging and supporting novice practitioner researchers. To further encourage researchers, including teacher practitioners, to publish their research findings, SERA initiated the biannual online *Researching Education Bulletin* in 2011.

MEMBERSHIP

SERA is a membership association 'open to all individuals with a professional or academic interest in research in education in Scotland' (SERA, 2005, p. 2). Its membership base consists of university and college staff, research staff, teachers in schools, administration/policy staff, including representatives from the GTCS, Her Majesty's Inspectorate of Education (HMIE) and local authorities and has fluctuated over the years (Nisbet, 2005, p. 72). The numbers of university and college staff members have risen and now represent almost two-thirds of the membership. Simultaneously, teacher numbers have steadily declined to less than 10 per cent. In recent years, SERA has been faced not only with a falling membership (200+ in the 1970s to 126 in 2010), but also an ageing population of researchers. Attempts are being made to attract more postgraduate and early career researchers using initiatives such as social networking sites and online blogs.

Membership has been mainly among those with an interest in teacher education. However, SERA has aimed in recent years for a broader appeal and the conference has drawn in social work and community education staff from universities as well as further education college staff. The majority are individual members but there is also institutional affiliation, and honorary and life membership. Communication with members is principally via the website (www.sera.ac.uk) which has member-only and executive-only areas in addition to public access. Members receive email alerts such as the conference call for papers and information about events. A new logo was produced in 2005, and later updated in 2010 to include the strapline 'improving education through research' to explain its purpose.

ANNUAL CONFERENCE

The annual conference, held in various locations since 2010, is the main event in SERA's calendar. The two-and-a-half-day programme previously included a Saturday, with the latter primarily aimed at practitioners. However, with declining Saturday attendance a decision was made in 2010 to only hold a two-day event on weekdays. In 2010 and 2011, the organisers resurrected the SERA debate to follow the keynote lecture, an important mainstay of the programme delivered by an eminent academic usually from outwith Scotland, and to conclude the conference on a high note.

From 2004, the conference has reverted to a specific theme which has revolved around topical issues and government initiatives, for example, in 2010, 'Integrating for

Impact – Educational Research, Policy and Practices' and, in 2011, 'Educational Research in an Age of Austerity'. The papers presented comprise a range of empirical and theoretical research including commissioned and practitioner research. Although delegates are mainly from Scotland the conference attracts a regular following from elsewhere in the UK and overseas. The numbers attending remain fairly static and in 2011, 134 delegates presented a total of sixty-seven individual papers and seven symposia. A significant number of presenters are not SERA members and it has been noticeable in recent years that many delegates only attend to give their presentation and do not engage for the whole day, far less the whole conference.

LIAISON WITH THE SCOTTISH GOVERNMENT

An important feature in SERA's existence has been its relations with government education officials which have 'blown hot and cold over the years' (Nisbet, 2005, p. 57). In 2001, to progress discussions at meetings, a joint memorandum was produced which formed the basis of agenda items, including national policy and strategy for educational research; shaping priorities for funded research; horizon scanning and future directions; dissemination; building research capacity, including practitioner research and enquiry; ethics; research governance; and contractual arrangements. This agreement marked a period of successful working relations with SEED.

The new government in 2007 resulted in reorganisation within the Scottish Government Education and Analytical Services department and changes in SERA's relations with the Scottish Government. Since 2009, at the request of the Scottish Government, SERA representation at meetings with the Scottish Government is now limited to the president and a few others, with a new agenda and terms of engagement set by the Scottish Government. The focus has been on collaboration between research funders, users and researchers which has included events such as a Scottish Government organised summit entitled 'Improving Engagement', followed by a SERA organised forum in 2010, 'Impact through Collaboration in Educational Research' with speakers and an audience of policy makers, practitioners and researchers. The latter explored the nature of educational research in Scotland, ideas for more strategic approaches to collaborative research and the necessary infrastructure to support clearer links between research and its impact on policy and practice, including dissemination in a more widely accessible form to the policy and practice communities. These events were concurrent with the UK Strategic Forum for Research in Education (SFRE) which examined research creation, mediation, application and impact in the four constituent nations, with SERA and the Scottish Government contributing stakeholders. SERA considered the 2010 forum key to re-establishing dialogue with the Scottish Government. However, collaboration since then has been minimal, with the 2011 conference the first time in memory that no Scottish Government official attended. Ongoing disquiet about SERA's relations with the Scottish Government was discussed at the 2011 AGM as the business plan for 2011–14 stated diplomatically that 'Over the last four years the erstwhile strong collaboration that the SERA Executive enjoyed with the Scottish Government . . . has declined somewhat . . . it may be helpful to enter into wider discussions with the newly formed Education Scotland' (SERA, 2011, p. 5).

CONCERNS AND FUTURE CHALLENGES

The devolved financial settlement to local authorities under terms of the 2007 Scottish Government local government concordat resulted in fewer funds held centrally for direct commissioning of research, and simultaneously a change of direction in Scottish Government research interests and priorities with a greater focus on quantitative research and its outcomes, for example the Programme for International Student Assessment (PISA) study. Moreover, funding of the sponsored research scheme ceased. This had offered awards of up to £10,000 to early career researchers. Since then, there has been growing unease within SERA, expressed in presentations and the SERA 2011 conference debate, about the current direction of government funding for educational research in Scotland, both in terms of the reduction in funding and consequential number of projects commissioned, and emphasis on quantitative research. These issues were discussed further in the *Times Educational Supplement Scotland* (9 December, 2011, pp. 12–15) by the incoming SERA president, past presidents and noted academics; all expressed disquiet about the lack of high-quality innovative research commissioned by the Scottish Government on school education, but particularly empirical studies and theoretically based curriculum development research underpinning Curriculum for Excellence (CfE), the major policy driving change in schools. While the Scottish Government points towards its involvement in a range of research on CfE, working with the Association of Directors of Education in Scotland, Scotland's Colleges, Skills Development Scotland, the Scottish Qualifications Authority and so on, academic researchers remain sceptical of the scale and depth of this type of research and its reliance on mainly quantitative data. Similarly, as well as the dearth of Scottish Government commissioned major research projects on education, SERA is concerned that contracts are increasingly awarded to private consultancies at the expense of higher education staff. However, not all SERA members rely on government funding which can bring with it added pressure and loss of academic freedom.

These developments seem to indicate a reluctance on the part of the Scottish Government to engage with the higher education community. It has been suggested that the direction for SERA to follow in its future relations with government might be to liaise with the recently formed Education Scotland, the former LTS and HMIE. However, there is a need for caution and while not wishing to prejudice future relations, it will be interesting to see how this unfolds and develops from when LTS was a co-opted member on the SERA executive and actively involved with SERA activities. Similarly, this suggested closer liaison appears somewhat surprising considering that Education Scotland is currently commissioning little research from within Scotland. Moreover, Education Scotland in its bi-monthly *Research Round-Up* appears to actively promote more research from outwith than from within Scotland. However, it will be important that SERA considers all options to increase research opportunities including small-scale qualitative research for its members. Concerns about the lack of engagement between academic researchers and politicians are not new in SERA. The November 2004 newsletter reported that:

> SERA should take a more proactive approach and raise the profile of the role of educational research among the political community in Scotland. This could be a two strand approach, the first simply raising the awareness of MSPs by an improved general communications strategy to include a wider email list including politicians . . . A second approach would be a more targeted strategic attempt to influence key individuals in relation to specific themes or issues, by identifying potential implications of policy developments.

Perhaps it now more important than ever for SERA to lobby on behalf of its membership and put these words into action to protect its interests at a time when the outlook for educational research is also bleak beyond Scotland. The exclusion of the social sciences and humanities from the European Framework Programme Horizon 2020 is of concern, and it would be important for SERA to lobby against this in alliance with BERA and EERA.

SERA has expressed commitment to increase its early stage career researcher, postgraduate student and practitioner researcher members. The Donaldson Report (2010) argued for the teaching profession to be a more evidence-informed profession and for greater integration between universities and schools. There could be opportunities whereby the government provides financial support for university education staff to support practitioners conducting research, similar to the model of the SEED/Scottish Government Schools of Ambition programme (2006–9), and which may ultimately impact on increasing teacher numbers in SERA.

In an age of austerity, as a small member association SERA is facing financial challenges. One source of income is from membership subscriptions but with numbers remaining static over recent years it relies heavily on income generated from its conferences to sustain its activities. University Heads of Schools of Education have supported the work of SERA through allowing time for executive members to attend meetings and in some instances financial support for travel. They could assist further by encouraging more staff to join SERA.

The challenge for SERA will not only be to remain financially viable through increasing its membership, but also to have a stronger voice on issues of educational research policy and funding. Thus it can continue to play an important role not only in improving education in Scotland, but in supporting researchers who, Deuchar (2011, p. 8) asserts, have to contend with 'a new set of challenges in terms of building further capacity, sustaining collaboration and demonstrating impact'.

REFERENCES

Deuchar, R. (2011) 'Scottish educational research: Past, present and future challenges', *Research Intelligence*, 115, 8–9.
Donaldson, G. (2010) *Teaching Scotland's Future: Report of a Review of Teacher Education in Scotland.* Edinburgh: Scottish Government.
Nisbet, J. (2005) *Thirty Years On: The Scottish Educational Research Association.* Aberdeen: SERA.
Scottish Educational Research Association (2006) *Strategic Plan 2006–2011.* Online at www.sera.ac.uk/docs/Publications/SERA%20strategic%20plan%200108%20revision.doc
Scottish Educational Research Association (2011) *SERA Business Plan 2011–2014.* Presented at the AGM, SERA Conference, Stirling.

101

Education Journals

Walter Humes

Education journals have several purposes: to communicate information about government policies and new legislation; to report on events of professional interest; to offer in-depth analysis of topical subjects; to provide a forum for comment and debate; to alert teachers to resources they may wish to use; to encourage career development; to present the findings of research. The journals that will be described below give variable emphasis to this range of purposes.

The *Times Educational Supplement Scotland* (*TESS*) is a weekly publication and probably the major source of news and informed opinion for teachers, lecturers in further education (FE) and teacher educators working in universities. A separate publication, *Times Higher Education* (*THE*), covers UK and international developments in higher education (see below). *TESS* dates from 1965 but until 2006 Scottish material had to be accommodated within a format that was determined by the parent English edition of the journal. Various ways of doing this were tried: for example, as well as Scottish news pages at the front, there was for a time a separate Scottish supplement for features and comment. However, this was never entirely satisfactory and the creation of the Scottish Parliament in 1999 strengthened the case for a publication that better reflected the separate identity of the Scottish educational system. Following a change of ownership, a separate thirty-two-page Scottish newspaper was published, complemented by a colour feature magazine common to the English, Welsh and Scottish editions. The most recent reformatting of the publication took place in February 2011, with a switch to an entirely Scottish forty-eight-page full-colour magazine.

Based in Edinburgh, *TESS* employs five journalists who provide balanced reports not only of policy initiatives at central and local government but also of what is happening in bodies responsible for assessment and curriculum development and of interesting work in schools and colleges. The paper has a website which provides extended news coverage and allows readers to exchange views. The post-school sector, represented by Scotland's self-governing FE colleges, also features in pages of *TESS*, with a particular emphasis on skills and training, and their contribution to economic development.

The editorial stance of *TESS* does not support a particular union or political line. This independence gives it an authority and strength, though it sometimes means that parts of the Scottish educational establishment are not entirely pleased with the coverage they receive. Several pages of the paper are taken up with opinion pieces written by education professionals (teachers, lecturers, researchers, administrators and so on) rather than journalists. These reflect a variety of perspectives on education, once again ensuring that no single 'party line' is being promoted. A lively letters page offers further scope for a robust exchange of views. The paper also carries job advertisements.

The current circulation is over 6,000 but the readership is likely to be significantly larger as copies are provided in many school staffrooms and other places where education professionals meet (estimated at over 44,000 in 2012). *TESS* undoubtedly makes a significant contribution to their understanding of issues and developments in Scottish education.

A publication that has a larger circulation than *TESS* but which cannot claim the same degree of neutrality in its coverage is the *Scottish Educational Journal (SEJ)*, the magazine of the Educational Institute of Scotland (EIS), the largest teachers' organisation. Unsurprisingly, its aim is to communicate with the EIS membership, inform them of current issues and seek support for union policies. There is a 'campaigning' quality to many of the articles, particularly when parliamentary elections are imminent and the lobbying of political parties is seen as an important part of union activity. Matters relating to salaries and conditions of service also feature prominently, though a range of other topics of interest to both school and FE members are covered too. The *SEJ* appears as a thirty-two-page colour magazine six times a year (including a special issue reporting on the union's annual general meeting, where motions are debated and voted on, and policies approved).

The EIS journal has been around for a long time. It dates back to 1852, only five years after the founding of the Institute. In 1918, it merged with another publication, the *Educational News*. Its character has been subject to change as the educational and political climate has shifted. In the 1920s, for example, it became an important vehicle for promoting educational research, encouraging teachers to contribute to projects led by Dr William Boyd, Head of the Education Department at Glasgow University (see Chapter 95). At other times it has taken on the character of a union news sheet, rallying the troops, especially when the Institute has been in dispute with government and the possibility of industrial action has arisen (notably in the mid-1980s). However, simply informing members of significant developments in Scottish education, such as Curriculum for Excellence or the introduction of new National Qualifications, has been a recurring theme throughout the *SEJ*'s history.

Similar in format to the *SEJ* is *Teaching Scotland*, the magazine of the General Teaching Council for Scotland (GTCS), the professional body with which all teachers working in state schools in Scotland must be registered. All registered teachers receive a copy and the magazine can also be accessed online. It contains a range of articles, informing readers of the activities of the Council, highlighting topics that are attracting particular interest at any given time (such as health and wellbeing or citizenship education) and celebrating successes by both teachers and pupils. The tone is generally upbeat and there is an absence of articles that engage in a sustained and critical way with some of the harder issues in Scottish education. Some articles come across as rather boastful about the achievements of GTCS, though perhaps this is unsurprising since it is effectively a 'house' magazine rather than a forum for independent comment. In recent years, the balance between text and photographs seems to have shifted in favour of the latter: in this it is merely following a trend evident elsewhere (such as in some inspectorate publications).

Both the EIS and the GTCS are fortunate in being able to finance the cost of their publications from members' subscriptions and registration fees. Other, less well-resourced organisations rely on electronic newsletters to keep members up to date with developments. This has been the route followed by the Association of Chartered Teachers in Scotland (ACTS) and the Scottish Educational Research Association (SERA), though, as noted below, SERA members receive a copy of the twice-yearly academic publication *Scottish*

Educational Review. A similar trend can be seen in the FE sector. *Broadcast*, a quarterly magazine for FE staff, published by Scotland's Colleges (incorporating the Scottish Further Education Unit) ran to more than eighty issues but was put on hold in 2010, pending a review of policy on publications. Now an electronic monthly newsletter, *The Brief*, goes out to all staff in the FE sector.

Another journal, the future of which is also under review, is *Connected*, which was published from 2000 to 2010, running to twenty-seven issues. With a particular focus on information and communications technology, it was produced by Learning and Teaching Scotland (LTS) and appeared three times a year as a thirty-six-page magazine (also available online). It was aimed at a broad readership – students, parents and communities as well as education professionals – and drew attention to the vast range of electronic material that could enhance learning. Special features were devoted to the annual Scottish Learning Festival, which serves as a showcase for innovative technologies, and to the potential of GLOW, a virtual learning environment developed exclusively for Scotland's educational community. With the restructuring of LTS and its amalgamation in 2011 with Her Majesty's Inspectorate of Education under the new name of Education Scotland, *Connection* was discontinued though, at the time of writing, no final decision has been taken about its future.

Scottish Educational Review (*SER*), which started in 1968 (originally under the title *Scottish Educational Studies*), provides an important outlet for serious research-based articles relating to educational policy and practice, though many academics working in Scottish universities aim to have their work published in UK and international journals which, in terms of research reputation, are often regarded as more prestigious. *SER* is published twice a year, in May and November, and articles are subject to systematic peer review by two academic referees. A useful feature of the journal is its regular reports on educational debates and legislation in the Scottish Parliament. It also publishes the text of keynote addresses given at the annual conference of the Scottish Educational Research Association (SERA) (see Chapter 100). Although not formally affiliated to SERA, *SER* enjoys close links to the association and SERA members receive copies of *SER* as part of their annual subscription. A member of the SERA Executive serves on the editorial board of *SER*. Abstracts of the two most recent issues can be accessed on the *SER* website, as well as the full text of older issues dating back to 1997. At the time of writing, consideration is being given to switching completely to electronic publication, as the cost of producing hard copies for a limited print run is becoming difficult to sustain. The number of subscribers in recent years has rarely exceeded 400.

Education in the North, launched in 1964 but with a gap in publication between 1988 and 1994, is an annual journal produced by the School of Education of the University of Aberdeen, originally available in hard copy but now in electronic format. The aim of the journal is to provide 'information, comment and research findings in a way that will have broad appeal to teachers in primary and secondary schools, to lecturers in further and higher education and to other professionals including community education workers, educational psychologists and educational administrators'. This breadth of appeal is reflected in the types of material published. As well as academic articles subject to peer review, there is a features section consisting of shorter, less formal pieces, and a section reviewing recent publications.

Two publications focusing on youth and community education have already made the switch from hard copy to electronic format only. From 2009, *A Journal of Youth Work*, with the subtitle 'Research and Positive Practices in Work with Young People', has appeared online three times a year, superseding its paper-based predecessor, *Scottish Youth Issues Journal*. It is published by YouthLink Scotland in association with Strathclyde University. However, the decision to close the Department of Community Education at Strathclyde may lead to an alternative institutional connection. Another journal, *Concept*, based at Edinburgh University, also moved to online publication (retaining the same name), following a decision by its previous publisher to review its list of publications. *Concept* describes itself as a 'journal of contemporary community education practice and theory'. It too appears three times a year.

The commercial pressures to which academic journals are subject are well illustrated by the history of the *Journal of Adult and Continuing Education* which started as the *Scottish Journal of Adult and Continuing Education* in 1973, dropping the word 'Scottish' in 1994. The editorial team is led by staff at the University of Glasgow but the journal is currently published by Manchester University Press. In contrast to *TESS*, which has asserted its distinctive Scottishness with increasing vigour, in the internationally competitive world of higher education a journal with a 'Scottish' label runs the risk of seeming parochial.

An interesting angle on the competing pressures from local, national and international sources can be seen in a relatively new journal, *The Journal of Teacher Education and Teachers' Work*. This arose out of the activities of a joint research group of the Universities of Glasgow and Strathclyde, which included projects on teacher professionalism and teacher identity as well as teacher education. The first issue appeared in 2009 and, in the main, featured articles from staff at Glasgow and Strathclyde. However, the editorial board includes representatives from England and overseas, and subsequent issues have been much more international in character. This reflects the desire of major universities to see themselves as global players, not confined in their interests to local communities.

The field of higher education is well covered by *THE*, founded in 1971, a weekly publication of some eighty pages which provides detailed reports of a wide range of matters of interest to academic staff and university leaders: political and financial pressures; research awards; international league tables; academic controversies; senior appointments. There are also extended opinion pieces and substantial book reviews. Although *THE* is not specifically Scottish, universities north of the border regularly feature in reports, reflecting the fact that higher education across the UK is subject to common concerns deriving from the need to respond to national expectations about teaching and research quality. The Scottish school sector, by contrast, is relatively insulated from developments elsewhere in the UK.

Probably the most popular item in *THE*, to which many readers turn first, is a long-running satirical column on the back page written by the broadcaster and former professor of sociology Laurie Taylor. Using a fictitious institution, the University of Poppleton, as the backdrop for his observations, Taylor turns a penetrating eye on the absurdities of academic life, drawing attention to the gap between rhetoric and reality, the increasingly oppressive nature of university bureaucracy and the farcical contortions of university senior managers in seeking to justify policies that seem to undermine academic values. For many lecturers, the Taylor column provides a much-needed tonic at the end of the week.

There are other publications which provide some coverage of education but which have a wider remit. *Holyrood Magazine* includes reports of policy debates that have relevance to the work of the Scottish Parliament, and *Scottish Affairs*, produced by Edinburgh University, publishes a range of articles on topics of social, political and cultural significance. Broadsheet newspapers, notably the *Herald* and the *Scotsman*, have specialist education journalists, though editorial demands usually mean that they concentrate on matters of controversy rather than seek to provide balanced coverage.

It is difficult to assess the impact of the publications that have been reviewed. Of the specialist education journals, only the *SEJ* and *Teaching Scotland* reach a mass market and there is no way of knowing whether the teachers who receive them read them carefully, skim them cursorily or set them aside for later perusal or early recycling. The material in *TESS* is likely to have greater influence on senior staff (headteachers, administrators, teacher educators) than on the wider profession. Again, the number of classroom teachers who read the 'heavy' academic articles in *Scottish Educational Review* is likely to be small – hardly surprising, given the daily pressures and demands of most schools.

The printed word has undergone massive changes in recent years because of regular advances in technology and this trend is likely to continue. Journal editors have to be constantly on the alert and willing to adapt as readers' expectations change and technological innovation renders older forms of communication obsolete. An additional challenge is that new modes of advertising, utilising electronic methods, mean that sources of income on which some publications have traditionally depended can no longer be guaranteed. For certain publications, the continuing availability of hard copies remains important but the trend is towards online access, either as an additional or an exclusive format. What remains constant is the need for teachers to keep up to date with changes that affect their professional lives and to engage with ideas that can inform their thinking and practice. Educational journals make a valuable contribution towards these ends.

102

Teachers' Professional Organisations

Larry Flanagan

Over the past two decades, general membership of trade unions has fallen in both the public and the private sectors; education, however, has a higher density of trade union membership and this is unlikely to change in the foreseeable future.

Part of the reason for this historically high level of organised representation lies in the fact that Scotland is home to the oldest teacher organisation in the world – the Educational Institute of Scotland (EIS). Since 1847, Scottish education and Scottish teachers have been served by this organisation (granted a Royal Charter in 1851 by Queen Victoria). Even today it remains the largest and most influential of the Scottish teacher trade unions and professional associations, of which there are several.

The EIS recruits education professionals from all grades of post in all sectors of education: nursery, primary, special and secondary, as well as having networks for special categories such as Instrumental Music teachers, Quality Improvement Officers (QIOs) and educational psychologists. It also has self–governing associations for both further and higher education: the Further Education Lecturers' Association (FELA) and the University Lecturers' Association (ULA). Overall membership of the Institute, based on its affiliation to the Scottish Trades Union Congress (STUC), is just under 60,000. The EIS is also affiliated to the Trades Union Congress (TUC).

Whilst the EIS is the largest organisation, in the secondary sector there is also the Scottish Secondary Teachers' Association (SSTA), which was founded in 1944. Originally predicated on the premise of secondary teachers requiring to be organised separately when primary teaching was not a graduate profession, the SSTA has continued to attract some teachers in the secondary sector for a variety of reasons. During the industrial dispute of the 1980s, it was seen as being less militant than the EIS and accordingly attracted some support from those who wished to limit their involvement in industrial action. Ironically, it has recently adopted a more belligerent tone on a number of issues, notably Curriculum for Excellence (CfE). The SSTA affiliates to the STUC on the basis of 7,800 members but does not affiliate to the TUC.

The third trade union is NASUWT (the name being derived from its antecedent organisations the National Association of Schoolmasters and the Union of Women Teachers), a UK-wide body which has recently claimed to increase its presence in Scotland, affiliating to the STUC on 7,000 members. Unlike the SSTA it recruits from primary as well as secondary and also recruits non-teaching staff. In England it has gone from being a minor player in the membership stakes to now rivalling in size the National Union of Teachers, as a result of a fairly aggressive recruitment drive over more than a decade. Unfortunately, most neutral observers of the scene in England would conclude that the trade unions are actually weakened by being divided in the way that they are, as inter-union rivalry affords management an opportunity to undermine the impact of teacher action.

Previous discussions in Scotland about uniting the teacher trade unions – at least the two main bodies of the EIS and the SSTA – have, however, made little progress. This is perhaps surprising given the general trend towards amalgamation and merger amongst many other unions and the relatively few major policy differences that exist between the Scottish-based organisations.

Outwith the three STUC-affiliated teacher trade unions there exist a further four bodies worthy of note: the Association of Teachers and Lecturers (ATL), Voice, the Association of Headteachers and Deputes in Scotland (AHDS) and School Leaders Scotland (SLS). The ATL is a UK-wide union affiliated to the TUC which recruits on a limited basis in Scotland, mainly in the independent sector. Voice developed from the Professional Association of Teachers, which expanded into Scotland in the 1980s as a non-striking alternative to both the EIS and the SSTA, and it remains as such. Voice accepts membership from others involved in education such as nursery nurses. The AHDS and SLS represent headteachers in their respective sectors, primary and secondary, and have close links with similar bodies in England and Wales. Both recently opened their ranks to include depute heads and principal teachers as a means of boosting their membership. School Leaders Scotland (previously known as HAS) in particular sees itself as primarily a professional association and indeed it has been developing its profile along similar lines to the Association of Directors of Education in Scotland, seeking to influence government policy and acting as a forum for consultation. There is some evidence that both national and local government are keen to support this particular profile.

It is perhaps significant that when, in 2004, the SLS and AHDS chose to walk out from membership of the Teachers' Panel of the national negotiating forum, the Scottish Negotiating Committee for Teachers (SNCT), they promptly sought to act as advisers to the Convention of Scottish Local Authorities (COSLA), the management side of that body. Indeed, at local negotiating level, the two Associations often sit as advisors to management. A significant number of headteachers maintain dual membership of their headteacher association and one of the teacher trade unions.

The final organisation to mention is the University and College Union (UCU), which was formed in 2006 following a merger between the Association of University Teachers (AUT) and the college lecturers' union NATFHE. In Scotland, UCU is a predominantly higher education organisation, having only a relative handful of college lecturers in membership, as the EIS represents the vast majority (96 per cent) of this group of educators.

Most teacher organisations see themselves as having a dual function – to act in the traditional sense of a trade union in protecting their members and advocating on their behalf on employment issues such as conditions of service and salaries; but also to contribute, as a professional voice, to debate and the development of policy in the broader interests of Scottish education. This dual responsibility is not always evenly discharged as the political affairs of the day often create the context for union activity.

The trade union nature of teachers' organisations was shaped by the major disputes of the 1970s and the mid-1980s, when the EIS in particular, and to a lesser extent the SSTA and NASUWT, were engaged in industrial action around conditions of service and salaries. The successful resolution of the two main campaigns of these periods created a legacy of loyalty from members which has helped to sustain the high level of unionisation prevalent in the profession.

A major consequence of the agreement entitled *A Teaching Profession for the 21st Century* (often called the McCrone Agreement, although the final negotiated arrangements differed substantially in some areas from the McCrone recommendations) was an established consensus on the importance of continuing professional development (CPD) for teachers, and this opened the door for the development of the professional aspect of the work of the teaching unions. The EIS, in particular, has been keen to involve itself in this area of work. It works in partnership with a number of universities, for example to deliver professional development courses (see also Chapter 99). It was involved heavily with the University of the West of Scotland around the development of the Chartered Teacher Programme and it has ongoing partnerships with Edinburgh, Glasgow, Aberdeen and Stirling Universities around leadership training and other CPD opportunities.

A fairly recent development within the EIS, since 2003, but not pursued by other unions, has been the creation of Learning Representatives in support of the previous Labour government's lifelong learning agenda. Learning Reps, as they are known, can be school-based or multi-establishment and are trained by the EIS, in conjunction with higher education partners, to develop an expertise in supporting colleagues in the pursuit of professional development. Where they have been established, they work cooperatively with local authority education departments to help deliver desired outcomes around the CPD agenda; over one hundred joint EIS/local authority events have been organised, for example, in support of a more collegiate approach to the delivery of professional development. This area of activity bears testimony to the professional nature of teacher organisations in Scotland.

Fortunately, the refocusing on professional development afforded by the *Teachers' Agreement for the 21st Century* followed on from the timely establishment of the Scottish Parliament in 1999. The fact that education is a devolved matter has shaped the more consensual nature of education policy debate in Scotland than elsewhere in the UK, notably England. The previous Labour and Labour–Lib Dem Executives and the current SNP-led government have all been supportive of a process of engagement with the teaching profession, rather than one of confrontation which had certainly been the hallmark of the previous decade. However, the more straitened financial period in which we exist may well test the notion of collegial approaches more generally.

The key forum for negotiations on salary and conditions of service for teachers and associated professionals is the tripartite Scottish Negotiating Committee for Teachers, which involves COSLA (eight seats), as the umbrella organisation for local authority employers, Scottish Government (three seats) and the teachers' side (eleven seats), where the EIS holds a majority position. As a result of its predominance over the teachers' side, in reality the EIS is the key decision maker for potential agreements, a position that can be exploited by the other trade unions who are free to agitate on sensitive matters without having to take responsibility for the eventual success or failure of negotiations.

The current Teachers' Panel composition, from 2011, is based on respective memberships relating to those who are covered by SNCT arrangements: thirteen EIS; three SSTA; two NASUWT; one Voice. From this the negotiating team comprises eight EIS; one SSTA; one NASUWT; and one seat shared in rotation between Voice and the SSTA.

The Scottish Government, which is represented by civil servants at the SNCT, maintains bilateral contacts with all the teacher organisations and is generally keen to work in a constructive manner on matters of policy. It is significant, for example, that the professional associations (the EIS, SLS, AHDS and SSTA, later replaced with NASUWT) were all invited to take up places on the CfE Management Board and have played a key role in shaping the direction and detail of this major programme, notwithstanding growing tension around the resourcing and rate of implementation that has been developing recently.

Relationships between COSLA and the trade unions tend to be more fraught as there is a direct employer/employee function in play. This is apparent from the COSLA evidence submitted to the McCormac Review, set up to review teachers' conditions of service, which was largely fuelled by economic considerations on the part of local government. Within the SNCT, COSLA is represented by elected councillors.

Within each local authority there exists a Local Negotiating Committee for Teachers (LNCT) operating under the general umbrella of the national body and certain specifically delegated areas of responsibility, for example agreeing job-sizing arrangements for promoted posts. In some LNCTs elected councillors meet directly with union representatives but in most the management side is staffed by senior directorate members. LNCT agreements are co-signed and publicised as negotiated policy statements. In some authorities the remit has been broadened so that the LNCT acts as a general consultative forum. Some LNCTs have a more collegiate approach than others but generally speaking from a trade union perspective they are seen as important, effective bodies which help to maintain a constructive working relationship between teachers and their employers.

Following a period of relative calm in terms of industrial relations the financial crisis has precipitated a number of areas of dispute that threaten that stability, and indeed the issue of pensions sparked the first nationwide teachers' strike in over twenty-five years on 30 November 2011.

There has, of course, been a significant level of industrial action in the further education sector, primarily involving the EIS which has a substantial membership there, organised through FELA. The independent status of colleges, which have been faced with major financial challenges, led at times to an unfettered approach to industrial relations on the part of some college managements, and the 'plant' based negotiations that arise in such scenarios can become quite intense. A return to national negotiations on salaries and conditions, a possibility under the current government's proposals for reorganising the further education sector, might address some of these issues.

Although unions organise matters slightly differently, a key aspect of the service offered to members is individual support to those who find themselves in difficulty in their employment. For many teachers the main motivation to join a trade union remains the need to guarantee advice and support if things go wrong. All the teacher organisations, however, have been forced to broaden the range of services they provide to members to include areas such as insurance offers, discount purchases and professional development opportunities; the EIS, for example, is the principal shareholder of a company called EIS Financial Services.

An increasing pressure on the unions has been the volume of litigation they are now involved in, which is a costly demand on their resources. Tribunals and court proceedings are a staple aspect of modern union activity. However, despite the expansion of ancillary services by unions it seems certain that over the forthcoming decade teachers will have a renewed focus on protecting their conditions of service and salary levels which will see a greater focus bearing on the trade union function of their representative bodies. Given the financial pressures that have arisen in the public sector and the consequent attacks on teachers' salaries and conditions, it seems certain that teacher trade unions will continue to be centre stage in the landscape of Scottish education.

103

The General Teaching Council for Scotland: An Independent Professional Body

Anthony Finn and Tom Hamilton

The General Teaching Council for Scotland (GTCS) became the world's first independent self-regulating professional body for teaching on 2 April 2012. Although there has been a clear international trend towards the introduction of teaching councils over the last fifteen years, some countries do not have councils, not all councils have the same powers or status as the GTCS and the General Teaching Council for England (GTCE) ceased to function on 31 March 2012. What factors cause some teaching councils to thrive, while others fail to survive? What will be the role of professional bodies for teaching in the twenty-first century? And what are the implications of the GTCS's independence for teaching in Scotland?

GTCS AS A PROFESSIONAL BODY

The GTCS, the oldest teaching council in the world, was established by the Teaching Council (Scotland) Act 1965 and met for the first time on 11 March 1966. Its initial focus was on ensuring that teachers working in Scottish schools were suitably qualified for that purpose. At that time, problems of teacher shortage were routinely solved by the employment of 'uncertificated' teachers, many of whom had limited qualifications. Consequently, while the establishment of a council with a requirement for teachers to be registered was controversial in the late 1960s, its mission to ensure that all those working as teachers were qualified was supported by the educational community.

Today, local authorities in Scotland can only employ registered teachers with appropriate academic and teaching qualifications, a standard that has not yet been achieved in many other countries, including elsewhere in the UK. The GTCS is also responsible for the regulation of cases of teacher misconduct, conviction or competence and, most notably, oversees not only entry standards for teaching but also a suite of professional standards that govern teaching careers. In April 2012, the GTCS became responsible for the introduction of a system of 're-accreditation' of teachers, which is intended to confirm that high standards are being maintained by teachers. As a result of these developments, it seems reasonable to assert that the GTCS is no longer simply a regulator, having now become a professional body, 'which maintains and enhances teaching standards and promotes and regulates the teaching profession in Scotland' (GTCS, 2011).

TEACHING AND PROFESSIONALISM

Traditionally, the 'grand' professions (medicine, law, divinity) were considered to have special professional status, largely based on the training, qualifications and ethics required of those who practised in these areas. To legitimise a claim for professional status for teaching in Scotland, it is necessary to consider what professionalism is and how this might be applied to teaching. Of course teaching is frequently described as a profession and claims are frequently made that specific educational reports and agreements promote teacher professionalism (for example, Donaldson, 2011; McCormac, 2011 and the Scottish Negotiating Committee for Teachers, 2001). There has, however, perhaps been insufficient study of what this means in practice. Indeed, the overuse of the word 'professional' in other contexts – the receipt of payment in sport, the description of a level of performance or service and the rather contrived concept of a 'professional foul' in football all offer confusion rather than clarification.

Professionalism in teaching, as in other professions, is often defined by reference to the specific practice of individuals or establishments. And yet, there is guidance that can help us both to define professionalism and to apply this to teaching. Perhaps the most widely used generic definition of professionalism is offered by the Australian Council of Professions:

> A profession is a disciplined group of individuals who adhere to ethical standards and uphold themselves to, and are accepted by, the public as possessing special knowledge and skills in a widely recognised body of learning derived from research, education and training at a high level, and who are prepared to exercise this knowledge and these skills in the interest of others.

Despite this good starting point, there appear to have been relatively few fully developed definitions of professionalism within teaching, although a number of bodies have attempted to describe standards of professionalism for teachers (for example, the GTCS's professional standards; California Standards for the Teaching Profession).

In addressing this dilemma, we have chosen to amend Burbules and Denison's helpful definition of professionalism in teaching (1991) as the basis for a modern statement of the expectation of teaching as a profession. The original statement was broadly consistent with the Australian generic model in its emphasis on learning, qualification, the promotion of the public interest and the concept of individual autonomy. We argue, however, that there is a related need for self-evaluation, professional development and improving standards of practice. We have therefore added three additional elements and refined others (our changes in italics). Our view is that it is not sufficient simply to reach an early professional standard; there is also a requirement to maintain and improve standards throughout a career. Finally, we anticipate an explicit requirement, observed routinely in the practice of good teachers, to do the best job possible, taking account of the context in which you conduct your professional duties and any constraints which these might place on your practice.

- clearly defined practical and theoretical knowledge;
- systematic education;
- certification of practitioners;
- professional autonomy *and accountability*;
- prioritisation of service to others before economic benefits;
- *commitment to keep learning and improving throughout a career*;
- *aspiration towards optimal performance*;
- *collaboration with other professionals.* (amended from Burbules and Densmore, 1991)

Related to this is an expectation that teachers will seek to improve by learning skills necessary to address change or refine teaching approaches. This is mirrored in Donaldson (2011) who argues that teachers should become:

> Increasingly expert practitioners whose professional practice and relationships are rooted in strong values, who take responsibility for their own development and who are developing their capacity both to use and contribute to the collective understanding of the teaching and learning process.

THE ROLE OF TEACHING COUNCILS IN PROMOTING PROFESSIONALISM: DEVELOPMENTS IN DIFFERENT JURISDICTIONS

The GTCS has developed and strengthened its role within the Scottish educational community in recent years and is now a key player in discussions about the direction of educational policy and practice in Scotland. As its reputation has grown, the work of the GTCS has attracted considerable interest from other countries seeking to develop profession-led regulation in teaching.

Teaching councils (or equivalent bodies) have now been established in a large number of countries, although this trend is most evident in English-speaking countries. For example, councils have been established in and across the UK and Ireland, in New Zealand, in all Australian states and in some parts of Canada; there is a growing number in Africa (notably in South Africa and Nigeria) and across the Caribbean; and there has been recent interest in the Middle East and in Scandinavia. In many of these countries, local practices have been partly shaped by experience in Scotland. As a result, some quite robust councils have now been formed. In others, powers are still developing (for example, the General Teaching Council for Northern Ireland has yet to be granted final powers to regulate, while Teaching Council Ireland, despite the recent publication of an impressive range of policies on teacher education, does not yet have the power to insist that all teachers are required to register).

The recent history of teaching councils offers interesting perspectives on factors that assist or constrain their effective operation. It is, for example, evident that governments have a strong political interest in the quality of the teaching profession and will, prior to giving power to a teacher-led body, wish to be reassured that the public interest will be upheld, that professional standards will be maintained and improved and that councils can be trusted to address difficult professional issues, most notably the sensitive and appropriate handling of teacher competence and conduct.

Some recent examples may be instructive here. In Scotland, the government conducted a careful review of the future of the GTCS in 2009 and was ultimately satisfied that it was a reliable and trusted body that could be given further powers and responsibilities. In its conclusions (Scottish Government, 2010), the government reported that there was considerable confidence across all stakeholders in the GTCS. For example, the employers' body, the Convention of Scottish Local Authorities, stated that 'the GTCS is an effective and well-respected regulatory body for the teaching profession in Scotland'. This confidence justified the GTCS being granted an enhanced, independent status: 'Consultees demonstrated considerable support for giving the GTCS a more explicit responsibility in relation to the standards.'

The reputation of the GTCS has been earned during many years of attention to detail and of close and careful partnership with stakeholders in Scottish education. And yet, even in Scotland, and particularly in the new independent Council, it is important to emphasise that members, whatever their background, must speak on behalf of the teaching profession rather than represent any organisation that might have sponsored or nominated their membership. In addition, Council processes require to be open and accountable, reflecting the interests of the profession and recognising the significant responsibility of the Council to protect the public interest.

In countries where councils have been formed successfully, this Scottish partnership model has been replicated and, indeed, Scottish approaches have often influenced initial Council structures. Two recent examples, however, show the vulnerability of teaching councils when consensus is not fully achieved.

It is arguable that the GTCE, established in 2001, had not gained widespread support across the profession. Like all councils it faced some concern about the level of its fee and its role beyond a narrow interpretation of regulation. More importantly, it also had difficult relations with at least one large trade union which regularly sought its abolition or restriction of its activities (NASUWT, 2010); in addition, it lost some public credibility when a case taken against a teacher member of the BNP did not lead to his removal from the register (*GTCE* v. *Walker*, 2010). Nonetheless, the GTCE was still broadly respected and it was therefore very surprising when an Education Minister with a political preference for deregulation quickly decided, just weeks after the election of a coalition government in Westminster in May 2010, that this Council should be abolished. On 2 June 2010, Michael Gove informed the House of Commons: 'The GTCE does not improve classroom practice, does not help professionals develop, does not help children learn – in short it does not earn its keep – so it must go.'

If the demise of the GTCE can be understood as reflecting political volatility fed by a lack of overall consensus across stakeholders, recent developments in British Columbia are more attributable to disputes and tensions within the Council itself. They provide strong evidence of the need for Councils to be seen to promote the public interest and to be independent of outside groups. The Avison Report (2010) on the British Columbia College of Teachers commended the quality of work undertaken by staff but exposed what it described as 'an imbalance between the interest of members and the public interest' and 'a lack of common purpose due to opposing philosophies of the primary groups'. Perhaps more worryingly, it also highlighted the presence in the College of members who 'intrude upon the capacity of BCCT to be . . . an independent entity responsible for self-regulation of teaching'. Avison argued that the main teaching union in British Columbia operated as a group within the College, although these criticisms were strongly rejected by the British Columbia Teachers' Federation. Following the publication of the Avison report, however, the provincial government decided to restructure regulation in the province by dissolving the existing College in January 2012 and establishing a smaller British Columbia Teachers' Council that represents all members of the education community. The new council sets standards for teachers with respect to conduct, competency and certification.

Overall, therefore, it is clear that successful teaching councils need to ensure that they maintain close contact with the profession and operate effectively, consensually and credibly within acceptable professional parameters. Where these aspirations have been achieved, as in Scotland and Australasia, they become not only accepted but also valued bodies.

THE QUALITY OF TEACHING AND LEARNING

As argued above, the GTCS has moved from being a regulatory body to a more rounded, professional body with a strong central place in Scottish education. Its original role of stopping 'uncertificated' teaching has now become the more ambitious target of further raising the already generally high quality of teaching and learning for pupils and students.

The Legislative Order that grants the GTCS its new independent status (Scottish Government, 2011) states that the GTCS's principal aims are to contribute to improving the quality of teaching and learning, and to maintain and improve teachers' professional standards. Taking the second of these, Article 28 of the Order specifies that as one of its general functions the independent GTCS has the power 'to establish (and to review and change as necessary) the standards of education and training appropriate to school teachers'. However, before establishing new standards or changing existing ones the GTCS must consult teachers, employers and other interested persons – and have regard to their views.

The existing teacher education Standards have been widely accepted. This acceptance is largely built on the Standards offering a coherent statement of what constitutes being a successful teacher: professional knowledge and understanding, professional skills and abilities, and professional values and personal commitment. However, acceptance is also partly constructed on the professional consensus built up through the consultation processes used in their development and review, so the new legislation's injunction to consult simply reinforces existing good practice. If teachers' professional standards are to be maintained and improved, it is vital that teachers recognise and support the Standards that they must address.

The Donaldson Report (Donaldson, 2011) recommends a 'reconceptualised model of teacher professionalism'. The Report also supports the idea of Standards being 'challenging and aspirational'. The GTCS concurs with these sentiments and in its guardianship of the Standards endeavours to support such ideas. The requirement that the GTCS contributes to improving the quality of teaching and learning also accords with the role and rationale of the GTCS.

Various pieces of international research have placed considerable emphasis on the importance of teacher quality for the eventual success of educational systems. The oft-repeated mantra from Barber and Mourshed (2007) that 'the quality of an education system cannot exceed the quality of its teachers' is one example of how teacher quality has become a focus of research, particularly in a time of international comparisons between national systems.

However, the Organisation for Economic Cooperation and Development (OECD) (2005) counsels that 'there are substantial challenges in ensuring that all teachers – and not only the most motivated ones – are lifelong learners, and in linking individual teacher development to school needs'. So what is the role of the GTCS in meeting this challenge? Donaldson (2011) states: 'The GTCS is pivotal in supporting and assuring teacher quality. It is the guardian of twenty-first century professionalism.' This is certainly complimentary but what is the GTCS doing to ensure that this is sustained? The GTCS recognises the complexity of being a contemporary teacher (see, for example, Niemi, 2009) and is aware of research that points at approaches that encourage educational systems to get the best out of their teachers. Scotland is building on the strong foundation of having an all-graduate teaching profession, teachers holding appropriate academic and teaching qualifications, and having a commitment to professionalism through GTCS registration – but it cannot rest there. It is important that teachers are lifelong learners and there needs to be an awareness of how careers develop. Sammons et al. (2007) identify the concept of Professional Life Phases and point out that within these phases consideration needs to be given to resilience, commitment and effectiveness.

As well as pedagogic knowledge, content knowledge and pedagogic content knowledge (Shulman, 1986), teachers also need to know about and have expertise in the emotional and motivational aspects of learning. Niemi (2009) writes of the importance of teachers encouraging resilience and self-efficacy in learners. It follows that if teachers are going to be lifelong learners, they too need these qualities, and this is confirmed by other educational research.

The OECD (2009) states the following:

> Reports of self-efficacy have been shown to be linked to productivity and influence people's actions in the workplace. When teachers envisage effective teaching as a skill that can be acquired, this feeling of self-efficacy can help them better analyse and solve problems. Conversely, those teachers confronting a low feeling of self-efficacy can experience self-doubt and become preoccupied with evaluative concerns if efforts proved unsuccessful.

The report continues:

> The Teaching and Learning International Survey (TALIS) identifies close associations between factors such as a positive school climate, teaching beliefs, co-operation between teachers, teacher job satisfaction, professional development, and the adoption of different teaching techniques. For all of these factors, much of the variation identified was in differences among individual teachers rather than among schools or countries. The implication is that by addressing teachers' attitudes, beliefs and practices as a whole, there is scope for considerable improvement in teaching and learning, but that this may require individualised support for teachers rather than just whole-school or system-wide interventions.

System-level change is important. However, the need for individual teachers to focus on their own improvement must not be overlooked. Sammons et al. (2007) state that:

> CPD [continuing professional development] alone is unlikely to exert a major impact on teacher effectiveness. It needs to take place within professional, situated and personal contexts which support rather than erode teachers' sense of positive identity and which contribute, in each Professional Life Phase, to their capacities to maintain upward trajectories of commitment.

In language somewhat redolent of Star Trek, a more recent McKinsey Report (Mourshed et al., 2010) suggests that:

> In the final frontier of school improvement, the journey from great to excellent, systems focus on creating an environment that will unleash the creativity and innovation of its educators and other stakeholder groups. At this point in the improvement journey, system educators are highly skilled and have a body of agreed routines and practices that have become innate to how they work. The intervention cluster for the journey from great to excellent serves further to enhance the educators' responsibility for looking after each other's development; the systems give their teachers the time, resources, and flexibility to reflect upon and try out new ideas to better support student learning.

Two key points from these last two quotations are about education systems facilitating an ethos that allows time, space and support for teacher development and having teachers who are proactive in advancing their development. The GTCS would wish to play a leading part in encouraging these two approaches within the Scottish education system. GTCS accreditation of Initial Teacher Education programmes, GTCS involvement with the Teacher Induction Scheme and GTCS guardianship of the teacher education Standards all support the development within Scotland of the system envisaged above. The GTCS also encourages work towards enhanced professionalism for all teachers in Scotland.

One aspect of the work of the GTCS is its Teacher Researcher Programme. This encourages teachers to undertake small-scale research into aspects of professional practice. Relatively small amounts of funding allow teacher researchers to take time out of class to conduct this research. GTCS staff offer support and advice on presenting findings which are normally published as research reports on the GTCS website. Some teacher researchers have also presented at conferences such as that of the Scottish Educational Research Association (see Chapter 100). While the GTCS is keen to ensure that findings reach a wider audience, for those directly involved in the programme there is clearly an effect on their own learning and practice, perhaps on their own self-perceptions and self-efficacy.

The same is true of the Framework for Professional Recognition/Registration which has two purposes. The first is to encourage greater flexibility in registration and hence teaching. Teachers can use the Framework to gain registration for other sectors or subjects. The second purpose is that of Recognition, in essence 'a professional pat on the back' from the GTCS. Teachers can claim Recognition for work in specific areas of expertise in teaching or wider professional practice. The Recognition process involves teachers making a claim within their school, often through Professional Review and Development. Each teacher has to demonstrate expertise, show how professional reading has contributed and, importantly, illustrate how they have disseminated good practice to colleagues. There are no monetary rewards. Having Professional Recognition might add to a teacher's CV but for most teachers the principal reward has been the simple recognition from their peers that they are doing something in a meritorious fashion that has been recognised by the GTCS. Cynically, Professional Recognition could be viewed as just a certificate, but feedback from teachers shows how much it has been valued, boosting confidence, resilience and self-efficacy.

At the time of writing, a third plank of the GTCS's work in encouraging system improvement and individual teacher personal development is mired in uncertainty by a recommendation from the McCormac Report (2011) that the Chartered Teacher Programme be 'discontinued'. The GTCS accredits the university Chartered Teacher Programme and arranged the Accreditation Route for experienced teachers to claim Chartered Teacher status. It is not the purpose of this chapter to explore the Chartered Teacher Programme's difficulties but it is ironic that the programme being considered for closure has encouraged teachers to take on Masters level study; study which has at its heart professional action and accomplished teaching and which has been completed by many teachers who are the personification of enhanced professionalism.

Another irony is that the Chartered Teacher Programme is exactly the kind of professional development programme which research suggests has the greatest impact on classroom practice. Meeting the Standard for Chartered Teacher requires programmes to produce teachers who engage in 'critical reflection, practitioner enquiry and collaborative discussion' (Scottish Government, 2009) and the OECD (2011) states that:

> Results from TALIS show that, across countries, relatively few teachers participate in the kinds of professional development that they believe has the largest impact on their work, namely

qualification programs and individual and collaborative research, even if those who do commit considerable time and money to these courses consider them effective.

Further to the proposed closure of the Chartered Teacher Programme, the GTCS has been working with various partners, including internationally, to develop ideas of accomplished teaching which may offer a way forward if McCormac's recommendation is accepted. Accomplished teaching could have a wider currency within the teaching profession and perhaps offer a solution to Donaldson's recommendation of a Standard for Active Registration, a Standard to which teachers could aspire as their careers develop. While Donaldson's terminology does not gain widespread support, the concept is worth exploring by GTCS during its reviews of Standards.

Rounding off this section, it is worth noting that the GTCS is currently developing a system of professional update for all registered teachers in Scotland. New legislation imposes on the GTCS a 'duty to make a re-accreditation scheme', a scheme which the GTCS has designated more positively as 'Professional Update'. The Order does indeed refer to the scheme allowing the GTCS to keep itself informed about the standards of education and training of registered teachers but the GTCS's principal reason for developing Professional Update is the more positive one of it contributing to improving the quality of teaching and learning and maintaining and improving teachers' professional standards.

Other education systems have already planned or implemented programmes of re-accreditation, some successfully, some less so. In Australia, for example, the Victorian Institute of Teaching has a Renewal of Registration process requiring teachers to undertake set amounts of professional development over a specified period. This seems to work well and has earned the support of teachers, politicians and the public. However, in Canada, the *Ontario College of Teachers'* Professional Learning Program, which endeavoured to follow a similar format, ran into opposition and was described as 'divisive' by the Ontario Minister of Education when he revised the legislation in 2004. More recently, in Japan, a Teacher Licence Renewal system has run into the sand. It has been reported to the GTCS that this was mainly because it was a top-down, bureaucratic system, portrayed by the Japanese mass media as a means of removing incompetent teachers – thus, instead of attracting the support of teachers, it simply gained opposition to its imposition. Similarly the English White Paper *Your Child, Your Schools, Our Future* (2009) proposed a 'licence to teach' which was damaged by the Secretary of State's assertion that it would 'weed out weak teachers'.

Clearly, GTCS recognises those elements that have encouraged success in Australia and those that have caused difficulties in Canada, Japan and England – and lessons have been learned. Professional Update should be a force for good in Scottish education, encouraging teachers to be proactive in their own professional development, and giving a valid reason for arguing for space, time and resources to devote to professional development. Professional Update should help to engender a positive ethos in Scottish teacher education in line with the type of systemic development encouraged by such international heavyweights as the OECD and McKinsey. For Professional Update to work and to have the positive benefits envisaged it must be non-bureaucratic, have teacher support, be meaningful for those within the system and deliver tangible results in improving the quality of teaching and learning in Scottish education.

CONCLUSION

If teaching councils are to survive and thrive, we would argue that they must be, or become, independent professional bodies engaged in activities relevant to teachers and to teaching. In practice, their approach should be to ensure that

- teaching is seen as a complex, high-order profession;
- professional expectations are high;
- regulatory processes are fair and equitable;
- they act with credible authority in pursuit of the public interest.

Good teaching councils must be willing to stand up for and promote teaching as a profession but they must be wary of adopting stances more appropriate to a trade union or other interest group.

It will therefore be important that an *independent* GTCS maintains and extends the consensus on which it has built its success over the last forty-six years. This does not mean that it cannot have opinions, even strong opinions, on professional issues but these should be both formed and expressed in a measured way. This approach is consistent with the assertion of Sutherland in the 1999 edition of this book that the GTCS 'is not a lapdog and it is certainly more than a watchdog'. Of course, the Council's independence has developed significantly over the last twelve years but it has gained and retained respect because its professional policies and practices have been valued and supported. However, having now won the right to formal independence, the Council should remain conscious of the lessons of recent experience in other jurisdictions and continue to seek consensus for its approach to teacher professionalism. By gaining trust and acting sensibly in the public interest, professional decisions will be supported, or at least respected, by the profession and by the public at large. Hard-won rights may be taken away if the council, or its members, act inappropriately or unprofessionally.

The influence of Scotland in the development of teacher professionalism across the world has been further enhanced by the Scottish Government's decision to grant independence to the GTCS. In the future, as in the past, teaching councils and regulators are likely to look to Scotland for an example of a mature, self-regulating professional body with both regulatory and professional powers. They should, like the GTCS, aim to use their powers carefully and to develop operational standards that will provide positive examples of independence, thus offering safeguards against the whim and volatility of any other bodies, including government.

REFERENCES

Avison, D. (2010) *A College Divided: Report of the Fact Finder on the BC College of Teachers.* Vancouver: Completed for BC State Government.

Barber, M. and M. Mourshed (2007) *How the World's Best-performing School Systems Come out on Top.* London: McKinsey and Company.

Burbules, N. and K. Densmore (1991) 'The limits of making teaching a profession', *Educational Policy*, 5 (1), 44–63.

Donaldson, G. (2011) *Teaching Scotland's Future. Report of a Review of Teacher Education in Scotland.* Edinburgh: Scottish Government.

General Teaching Council for England (2010) *Report of Disciplinary Findings.*

McCormac, G. (2011) *Advancing Professionalism in Scottish Teaching. Report of the Review of Teacher Employment in Scotland*. Edinburgh: Scottish Government.

Mourshed, M., C. Chijioke and M. Barber (2010) *How the World's Most Improved School Systems Keep Getting Better*. London: McKinsey and Company.

NASUWT (2010) 'Conference resolutions 2010'. Online at www.thedigitalpublisher.co.uk/nasuwt-conf-resolutions2010

Niemi, H. (2009) 'Why from teaching to learning?', *European Educational Research Journal*, 8 (1): 1–17.

Organisation for Economic Cooperation and Development (2005) *Teachers Matter: Attracting, Developing and Retaining Effective Teachers*. Paris: OECD.

Organisation for Economic Cooperation and Development (2009) *Creating Effective Teaching and Learning Environments: First Results from TALIS* (Executive Summary). Paris: OECD.

Organisation for Economic Cooperation and Development (2011) *Building a High-Quality Teaching Profession: Lessons from Around the World*. Paris: OECD.

Sammons, P., C. Day, A. Kington, Q. Gu, G. Stobart and R. Smees (2007) 'Exploring variations in teachers' work, lives and their effects on pupils', *British Educational Research Journal*, 33 (5): 681–701.

Scottish Government (2010) *Towards an Independent General Teaching Council for Scotland: Consultation on the Future status of the GTCS*. Edinburgh: Scottish Government.

Scottish Government (2011) *Public Services Reform (General Teaching Council for Scotland) Order 2011*. Edinburgh: Scottish Government.

Scottish Negotiating Committee for Teachers (2001) *A Teaching Profession for the 21st Century*. Edinburgh: Scottish Government.

Shulman, L. S. (1986) 'Those who understand: Knowledge growth in teaching', *Educational Researcher*, 15 (4): 4–14.

Sutherland, I. M. (1999) *The General Teaching Council in Scottish Education*. Edinburgh: Edinburgh University Press.

104

Scottish Teachers

Bill Gatherer

IMAGES AND MYTHS

The Scots are famously proud of their education system, but its vaunted superiority is not often attributed to the teachers themselves. Yet since the Reformation, with its strong social and religious emphasis on learning, teachers have been entrusted with the important functions of promoting literacy and character formation, and for centuries the schools have been strongly supported by both the authorities and the ordinary people. Teaching has always been regarded as a worthy occupation, albeit not endowed with much social prestige.

The pictures we have of teachers in the eighteenth and early nineteenth centuries fall into three main categories. The local parish schoolmasters, educated at university and appointed by the ministers and the heritors (landowners), were selected for their moral as well as their educational qualifications. These were the respected dominies who abound in biographies and novels as the inspirers of the 'lads o' pairts', the clever boys from poor homes who became successful in later life, carrying throughout the world the image of pragmatic intellectual power which is still cherished as a national characteristic. Scots writers are generous in their praise of their teachers. Robert Burns, Thomas Carlyle, David Livingstone, Hugh Miller, Ramsay MacDonald (himself a pupil teacher until he was 18) and countless others testify to the beneficent influences of their schoolmasters: hard-working men of integrity and scholarship, well enough versed in the classics to equip their pupils for higher learning, able to introduce them to the glories of literature and philosophy, powerful role models and religious mentors but themselves as poorly paid and badly housed as the people whose children they served.

Then there were the schoolmasters in the burgh schools and academies in the large towns: men of genuine scholarship, with higher social status and comfortable stipends, able to mingle with their pupils' affluent parents. They could teach Latin and Greek, Mathematics, Philosophy; they wrote scholarly papers and delivered them in the numerous field clubs and literary and scientific societies that met throughout the country; they wrote books; many were doctors of law or philosophy; some became Professors of the University. These schoolmasters were an elite that transmitted an educational heritage and also preserved much of what was best in the national culture.

Then there were the women. In the eighteenth century many parishes had dame schools, run by any decent widow or spinster who could read and write and teach knitting, spinning, sewing and any other accomplishment valued by the parents, and who could put the girls and boys through the agony of scripture lessons. By the mid-nineteenth century the academies and high schools were appointing ladies to teach the womanly crafts and 'deportment'; but it was not until the large-scale feminisation of the profession in the later nineteenth century that women were perceived seriously as teachers and acknowledged as worthy of training and able to teach important subjects. Many tributes are paid in biographical literature to the women (mostly remembered as 'old') who taught in elementary schools and gave the great majority of Scots the only learning they knew. Hugh Miller fondly remembered Miss Bond in the little school in Cromarty, an accomplished and refined lady who wrote *Letters of a Village Governess*. Another Victorian autobiographer told of old Janet setting aside her pipe and taking up the 'ABC card' and likening it to a key that opens the door to knowledge and shuts it to ignorance. And William Adamson, a leading Labour politician in the 1920s, gave a moving account in one of his last parliamentary speeches of his schooldays in a mining village, with about a hundred pupils of all ages in a single room, and a lone heroic woman in charge. Of course there has been an accretion of myth around the testimonies recorded. The 'lad o' pairts' himself was largely mythic: for every poor, hard-working, intellectually gifted boy who was made into a scholar or a pioneer of empire by the free and thorough schooling he got at the local school there were thousands whose schooling was as threadbare as their breeks, who ended up as half-starved peasants or miners or factory workers. And for every inspiring dominie celebrated in the reminiscences of successful Scots there were hundreds of pedestrian drudges.

But the myths were to some extent true, and though their apotheoses in the tales of the so-called Kailyard writers in Victorian times were larger than life, they were sincerely believed in, and their power has been attested in the great educational charities of such figures as James Dick and Andrew Carnegie. As McPherson points out, the myths, as folk stories celebrating dearly held values, have lived on in many public statements about equality, tradition and dedication to learning in Scottish education (McPherson, in Humes and Paterson, 1983).

Modern Scottish writers seldom draw teachers with much sympathy. The only great masterpiece is Muriel Sparks' Miss Jean Brodie, a brilliant portrayal of the teacher's charismatic centrality in the lives of intelligent girls. Alasdair Gray's character Duncan Thaw finds his teachers both daunting and ridiculous. James Kelman's Patrick Doyle (in *A Disaffection*) is a teacher at the end of his tether, but his plight has little to do with his job: Kelman wanted to create a character whose working-class origins combined with a high educational and cultural consciousness. Schools and teachers seem to have no intrinsic dramatic potential such as can be found in the professional worlds of doctors and police officers. This is true also of ephemeral writing, where teachers are seldom drawn with respect. An exception was the 1950s television series *This Man Craig*, which recounted the adventures of a sensitive teacher at a time when Scottish schools were taking on greater pastoral responsibilities. Craig was a 'housemaster' in a city comprehensive school, and each episode dealt with a social problem connected with one of his pupils; he was unconventional, wore a tweed jacket rather than a suit, and he was frequently in conflict with authority because of his commitment to his pupils' needs. That Scottish teachers do not feature often in television fiction is no doubt mainly due to the absence of a commercial market; but there is no reason to doubt that they would be perceived as pompous fools or petty tyrants, as are most of the teachers who feature in British films. Scottish teachers themselves have been entertained for many years by John Mitchell's comic anti-hero Morris Simpson, whose hapless career is described in regular chapters in *The Times Educational Supplement*. Here is the secondary school brought to life with quiet satire, the recurring educational issues of the day seen through the eyes of a variety of truer-than-life members of staff.

THE DARK IMAGE

There is a sinister aspect to the story of Scottish teachers. Partly because they were virtually second-hand clergymen, expected to bring their pupils to the milk of the Calvinist doctrine by teaching and preaching and chastisement, the parish schoolmasters wielded a harsh discipline. The tawse, or belt, described by George MacDonald as a 'long, thick strap of horsehide, prepared by steeping in brine, black and supple with constant use, and cut into fingers at one end', was openly used on children from 5 years old and upwards. The teacher has frequently been portrayed as a cruel tyrant, ever ready to administer brutal 'justice' for sins as varied as playing truant and forgetting parts of the Shorter Catechism. This continual abuse was sanctioned by supervisors and parents alike in the belief that sparing the rod would spoil the child. MacDonald remembered his teacher in Aberdeenshire in the 1830s as a grim sadist. A hundred years later, in Mallaig, John Alexander MacKenzie's schooling was 'a continual battle with the teacher'; the strap was in daily use and vigorously applied at the slightest excuse (from *A Mallaig Boyhood*, 1996). In *A Scottish Childhood* (1985), Peter Brodie, a Moderator of the General Assembly of the Church of Scotland, remembers a kindly woman teacher in the 1920s, still however armed with the belt and ready to dole out 'three of the best' from a keen sense of duty. In the same book, the journalist Magnus Linklater remembers his teacher's strap in the 1950s as 'a weapon of vengeance, black with age and hardened by constant use'.

Many Scots remember their teachers with a mixture of fearful loathing and reluctant respect. Naturally those who did well at school recall their teachers with more gratitude than those whose schooldays were more painful. But despite the scourge of the belt the majority of the less academically successful pupils seem to have considered their teachers fair and considerate, as we learn from the work of researchers such as McPherson and Gow in the 1970s. In *Tell Them from Me* (1980), they report that the belt was used in about a quarter of Scottish secondary schools, and despite the urgings of government officials to use it sparingly and 'as a last resort', in a large minority of schools a large minority of pupils were belted. Despite that, the majority of the pupils surveyed believed that although some teachers were capricious punishers most of them were kind-hearted and forced to use the belt by their circumstances – large classes, bored and resentful pupils and irrelevant curricula.

By 1980, there was a growing groundswell of belief among Scottish teachers that the belt was both demeaning and ineffectual, and some of the local authorities set up panels of teachers to discuss alternative forms of discipline. Advisers and inspectors encouraged schools to dispense with corporal punishment altogether. Hugh MacKenzie tells in his book *Craigroyston Days* (1996) how a 'new atmosphere' and a 'more appropriate curriculum' led to a gradual decline in belting, until in 1981–2 the staff (with only two dissenters) agreed to ban corporal punishment. By the time the government legislated against the use of the belt most Scottish schools had virtually abandoned it, and the vast majority of the teachers welcomed its disappearance.

The ethos of Scottish schools today is kindlier than ever before; inspectors write of a pleasant and purposeful atmosphere, conducive to effective learning. Time and again in their reports they refer to 'the school's ethos' and the 'commitment and teamwork' of the staff as 'key strengths'.

THE GROWTH OF PROFESSIONALISM

With the formation of the Educational Institute of Scotland (EIS) in 1847, Scottish teachers acquired a formal means of expressing a long-felt desire for a true professional voice. They had long been accorded what amounted to official status: they held their jobs *ad vitam aut culpam*, an enviable security enjoyed by the clergy themselves; they had been officially recognised in government acts and regulations as important functionaries; but they had always been – at any rate at parish level – under the dominance of the ministers. With the rapid industrialisation and urbanisation of the nineteenth century they saw the destruction of their cosy, if modest, authority. The parish schools could not cope; town schools were built hastily and badly staffed; many thousands of city children could not attend school at all. The interventionist legislation enacted in London and applied to Scotland as well as England and Wales introduced new systems of control that diminished their autonomy: pupil-teacher schemes, inspection, regulation of teaching content. The EIS soon became a vigorous lobby and forum, yet its efforts were unsuccessful in winning either goal of professional authority or political influence (Humes and Paterson, 1983, p. 75 ff). This was because the occupation of teaching was changing radically and irreversibly.

The new city schools had little or no connection with the parish schools of a former age. There was developing a deep historic shift from a world in which teachers were important figures in Scotland's religious culture to a society that was controlled by the state and in which teachers were a secular workforce (Anderson, 1995, p. 296). By the end of the nineteenth century, teaching covered a wide range of occupational categories, the schoolmasters giving way to massed ranks of public employees, predominantly female. Mid-century, men made up 65 per cent of the teaching profession; by the end of the century, they constituted 41 per cent; now they are less than a third.

The feminisation of the teaching profession has been one of the most important factors in its development (Humes and Paterson, 1983, p. 137 ff). In the nineteenth century, women's main entry was through the teacher training institutions, which offered them one of the few available paths to a professional career. The government treated them as cheaper, subordinate teachers well into the twentieth century. The employment of large numbers of women was initially forced by a high demand for teachers. When, during the 1920s and 1930s, there was a surplus of qualified persons, men teachers were nearly always given precedence and women teachers were paid less, had less chance of promotion and were required to leave when they married. Women could find jobs in secondary schools but it was common for less qualified men to be their heads of department. During the last fifty years, however, women's presence in the profession has rapidly become more powerful, and they have achieved both financial parity and equality of esteem. But even now the majority of headships and other management positions are held by men. While there is little or no evidence of overt discrimination, women can still fairly claim that the gender bias has not wholly disappeared. At the same time, women teachers are now clearly in the majority: 94 per cent of primary teachers and 60 per cent of secondary teachers are women.

Teachers' march towards genuine professionalism met with increasing success. Better qualifications and training helped. By 1940, the great majority of teachers had training certificates. The unions worked hard to eliminate uncertificated teachers and this was at last accomplished in the 1970s. Teaching in Scotland is now an all-graduate profession.

Teachers' capacity to participate in policy formation has also increased greatly in recent decades. From the 1920s onwards, the Scottish Education Department (SED) included teachers in various advisory councils and negotiating committees; increasingly after 1918 the unions were able to represent their views to government with growing expectation of being listened to; after 1945 their voices were both more powerful and more constructive. The rise of 'experts' in the training colleges and universities, nearly all of them trained teachers with practical experience in classrooms, greatly enhanced the profession's authority: although their claim to a unique professional knowledge was often questioned by civil servants, teachers came to be acknowledged as practitioners of a special kind of craft and the exponents of specialised professional theory. The foundation of the Scottish Council for Research in Education (SCRE) in 1928 (see Chapter 99) created a powerful new partnership between practising teachers and their professional allies (McPherson and Raab, 1988, p. 256 ff). It was the strength of this partnership, sustained by an impressive corpus of research and exposition, that led eventually to a recognition that teachers could efficiently control professional organisations such as a national examination board, teacher training institutions and a General Teaching Council (GTC – see Chapter 103) that administers regulations for professional accreditation, discipline and the maintenance of standards.

The establishment of the Scottish Parliament in 1999 has made governmental policies more reflective of the views of ordinary people, but it has subjected teachers and their managers to closer public scrutiny. Through their unions and professional associations, and in the press, teachers' voices have become more prominent and influential. One of the Parliament's first acts was to set up the McCrone Committee to inquire how teachers' pay, promotion structures and conditions of service should be changed to ensure 'a committed, professional and flexible teaching force which will secure high and improving standards of school education for all children in Scotland into the new Millennium'. The implementation of the McCrone Report has significantly enhanced the public perception of Scottish teachers: in terms of remuneration, professional respect and policy-making powers their status is now higher than ever before.

IN DEFENCE OF EDUCATIONAL VALUES

During the last forty years there has been a rapid growth of teachers' influence in the development of new educational approaches. At both national and local levels they have been heavily represented in consultative bodies. Their influence was crucial in the 1965 review of the primary school curriculum, and the Memorandum it produced provided a reasoned, detailed rationale for the conduct of primary schooling which has long been admired throughout the world. When in 1965 the SED set up the Consultative Committee on the Curriculum (CCC), charged with leading a comprehensive reform of the content and methods of all teaching at primary and secondary levels, teachers were members of the main committee and leading members of its many national development committees (McPherson and Raab, 1988, p. 243 ff). While it is certainly the case that none of these arrangements has come near to realising the claims for true democracy and egalitarianism that are characteristic of Scottish educational rhetoric, the fact remains that teachers gained unprecedented responsibilities and powers.

A wide range of progressive approaches continues to be a prominent feature in all Scottish schools. The curricula are now wider and more varied, and teachers can readily introduce new methods and materials. The 'mission statements' of primary schools indicate that children's personal interests as well as their educational needs are of prime concern to the staff. Secondary schools in Scotland are by any standard well staffed, with teachers specially trained in a very wide variety of disciplines and activities. Since the establishment of the new Scottish Parliament there has been an important advance in the political influence of teachers. The organisation Learning and Teaching Scotland (LTS), the successor to the erstwhile SCCC, is almost wholly staffed by teachers – some seconded for a period from their schools and others who have gained permanent posts in management and curriculum development. LTS is now acknowledged as the Scottish Government's principal source of guidance on curricular matters and works with the civil service (including a new model of Her Majesty's Inspectorate of Education). (Editors' note: LTS and HMIE were combined in 2011 to form Education Scotland (ES).)

Teachers are always subject to control from external authorities; but although they can recognise the right of politicians to prescribe general educational policies, they have professional values that they are obliged to protect. The first of these is that children's needs and interests must take precedence in any consideration of what should be taught. Another important value is that teachers need a degree of autonomy in determining an individual pupil's educational needs and the best ways of meeting them. Modern teachers are well informed about the psychological characteristics of children and how learning most effectively proceeds, and they demand acknowledgement of their ability to diagnose and prescribe for their students' learning requirements. Unfortunately they are frequently attacked by politicians and journalists who have only subjective prejudice and personal memories of school experience to substitute for professional knowledge. The main planks of the case against modern teaching are crudely simple: education is a service bought by parents; private schools give the best service but are unavailable to the majority, so state-provided schools should be made as like private ones as possible; parents and the providers of schools (the government), not teachers, should stipulate what they want pupils to learn. Successive governments have introduced and maintained arrangements to increase control mechanisms devised by national authorities: performance measurements; the publication of league tables of schools' performance; more control by school boards and governors, giving them power to hire and fire staff; and the introduction of the language of market forces, such as 'development management', 'consumer choice' and 'market power'. In England and Wales, these policies were all enshrined in the Education Reform Act of 1988. In Scotland, where no government could flout the tradition of consultation and debate, the government issued a paper, 'Curriculum and Assessment in Scotland: A Policy for the 1990s', which proposed national prescriptions for the curriculum and making schools more accountable to parents through new school boards, including national testing schemes and the publication of results. The so-called consultation process soon demonstrated a deep and widespread dismay throughout the teaching profession (Roger and Hartley, 1990). It was argued that the curriculum depended almost wholly on the skills and energies of highly trained teachers, and the government's clumsy attempts to invade their autonomy would dangerously impede the development of teachers' professionalism. In the event, some of the more radical proposals were watered down, but the determined reactionary policies of the Minister, Michael (now Lord) Forsyth, constituted sore anxiety for the profession. With devolution, the Scottish education service has largely freed itself from the dominance of Westminster politicians and the expectation that every innovation designed for English institutions must be adapted to fit Scottish conditions. A number of far-reaching reforms have been planned, mostly still to be fully realised. But Scottish teachers are still wary of attacks on their professional values. It is no wonder that many deplore the 'de-professionalisation' and the 'de-skilling' that come from treating teachers as mere technicians rather than experienced professional educators.

Scottish teachers have deservedly won a central role in the management of what and how they teach. The schemes of development produced in the last three decades of last century, the products of working parties staffed by teachers and development officers, have been evaluated and modified in the classrooms. A new integrated curriculum and assessment structure for the whole schooling process is now being developed to cater for the needs of the young people of the twenty-first century . It can now be claimed with confidence that whatever the politicians and their disciples propose, it will be teachers who finally determine the content and methods best suited for Scottish pupils.

TEACHERS, 'GAMEKEEPERS' AND 'REFUGEES'

Generalisations about teachers are inevitably weakened by the immense variety of types contained in the profession. The categories of certificated teachers in Scotland range from nursery teachers who are assisted by nursery nurses (qualified and trained but not teachers), to primary school, special school and secondary school teachers. All of these are formally attested and certificated by the GTC. In the tiny number of recognised private schools there may be a few untrained and uncertificated teachers, but this is now rare, as parents and governors put a high value on proper qualifications. In further education colleges the majority of the teachers – given the title of 'lecturers' – are formally trained or under part-time training. Only in the universities are there many untrained teachers, and the provision of training and accreditation for university staff is now an agreed priority.

Scottish authorities strongly emphasise the need for formal leadership throughout the education system. Every school and college has a headteacher or principal, and the staff are ranked and functionally labelled; this of course is a universal feature in education systems, but in Scotland there has been an unusual emphasis on hierarchy. The implementation of the McCrone Report will flatten out the structures, but only partially. It is characteristic, too, that outside of schools and colleges there is a large number of people who have left regular school teaching to assume other jobs. These are variously described as 'leaders', or 'poachers turned gamekeepers', or 'hangers-on', or 'refugees from the chalkface'. As in all workforces, those who remain at the basic levels of provision look askance at those who have moved away – especially if, as is usually the case, moving away means more power and more autonomy and more pay. The McCrone reforms give successful class teachers a welcome boost in status and remuneration.

Humes' percipient account of the powers and values of educational leaders in Scotland assigns little authority to teachers at large, except of course in so far as officials such as directors of education, inspectors and advisers are deemed to be teachers; it is evident that, regardless of their professional beginnings, these officials become somewhat removed in their perceptions as well as their functions from the daily tasks of teaching pupils in classrooms. Even leaders of teachers' unions, whose main mission is supposed to be to represent teachers' interests, occasionally assume values and purposes that conflict with those of their rank-and-file members.

The terms invoked by the 'leaders' – 'partnership', 'cooperation', 'consensus', 'participation' – can often be exposed as rhetoric at best and, at worst, mere pretence. Humes argues that classroom teaching is regarded as a 'modest rung on the ladder of career advancement', and that success may be partly defined in relation to the ability to secure non-teaching jobs: teachers themselves have endorsed a hierarchical career structure that creates 'a situation in which the more specialist opportunities that arise, the less prestige the unpromoted teacher enjoys' (Humes, 1986, p. 22).

There is a case to be made, however, in defence of those whose jobs are designed to support the teachers by giving them advice, encouragement and in-service training. From the point of view of planners and administrators there are certain constraints on teachers' work that make support services essential. Teachers are relatively stationary: they spend nearly all their time in classrooms, and they have relatively little experience of other schools, so they are less able than professional advisers and supervisors to form impressions and generalisations about the conditions that need to be assessed in order to facilitate change. Teachers, too, are naturally preoccupied by the needs of their own pupils, and they are less able to formulate hypotheses and propositions about young people in general. It is true that reflective teachers can, over time, build up the wisdom of experience that makes them unequalled as advisors on many aspects of education. But that activity requires time, and lack of time is teachers' greatest constraint. They face classes for several hours each day, every day, coping with the multifarious problems that children bring to them, and they put in many hours every week marking work, preparing lessons and meeting a host of bureaucratic demands. And because teachers are increasingly playing greater roles in the formulation of guidance to all concerned, they need time to do the essential work of researching, describing, devising proposals, consulting others and so on. Guidance and advice must be written and issued; schools must be visited; teachers must be given training and encouragement.

The advisory and support services built up by the regional education authorities between 1975 and 1996 were ultimately accepted by the great majority of teachers as useful and necessary. But the governments led by Thatcher and Major were never enthusiastic about that form of collaborative management. Believing that the education system should be run like a large business, they relied on published regulations and enforced compliance, and they expected the government inspectorates to 'monitor' and 'evaluate' the effectiveness of the workforce in the implementation of the managers' instructions. Her Majesty's Inspectors (HMI) were required to carry out government's policies, and unavoidably they were compelled to apply objectives that had little to do with teachers' professional values. The creation of the Office for Standards in Education (Ofsted) brought, in England and Wales, a system of commercially contracted inspectors whose carefully stipulated functions are almost wholly monitorial, with the few remaining HMIs supervising the system and preparing reports for the politicians and the public. In Scotland. the inspectors' jobs have become much more concerned with formal school inspections and the implementation of government policies. Despite these constraints they have remained essentially loyal to the most central values and concerns of Scottish teachers, as their many published school reports can testify.

The new governmental insistence on control by regulation and overt appraisal has malignly affected Scottish local authorities: in the larger education authorities during the 1980s, advisers were to a significant extent replaced by 'adspectors', former advisory officers charged with functions described as 'quality control' and 'assessment'. When, in 1996, the government abolished the regions and set up smaller unitary authorities, a large number of advisory posts disappeared for wholly economic reasons, and ad hoc 'quality control' teams are now struggling to provide some measure of advisory support to teachers along with monitoring and evaluation services to the directors. Fortunately the professional expertise of practising teachers is now great enough to promise a new resurgence of development activity and teacher support. A highly effective device is the secondment of skilled experienced teachers to act as 'development officers': both at national and local level these have spent their time – periods varying from two or three months to two or three years – working on innovative programmes, devising teaching schemes and materials, and visiting schools to support teachers in their classrooms. This arrangement has been successful in the teacher training institutions, in government projects and in the schools themselves, and the new Scottish administration has warmly endorsed the idea. Despite the ever-present danger that teachers and lecturers on short-term contracts will be badly treated in terms of pay and conditions of service, and the recurrent suspicion that the authorities will try to use them to reduce costs rather than enhance services, teachers given time out will always prove a blessing to the profession at large.

The truth is that teaching, as a profession, lends itself to constant variety and adaptability. There can surely be no other professional body so full of various talents, so rich in such a wide range of specialist skills, creative ability and versatility. In other professions there are a few specific academic disciplines that yield the knowledge their members need; in education there are dozens of disciplines represented even in the basic jobs. Perhaps that is why teachers so frequently leave the profession – not simply because they may dislike it but because they have talents that allow them to do other things. In Scotland it is possible to list hundreds of politicians, writers, painters, musicians, administrators and businesspeople who have all at one time been teachers – and not always unsuccessful ones. This may reflect the hardships of the job, but it may well also reflect the vitality of the practitioners.

REFERENCES

Anderson, R. D. (1995) *Education and the Scottish People*. Oxford: Clarendon Press.

Humes, W. M. (1986) *The Leadership Class in Scottish Education*. Edinburgh: John Donald.

Humes, W. M. and H. M. Paterson (eds) (1983) *Scottish Culture and Scottish Education 1800–1980*. Edinburgh: John Donald.

McPherson, A. and C. D. Raab (1988) *Governing Education*. Edinburgh: Edinburgh University Press.

Roger, A. and D. Hartley (eds) (1990) *Curriculum and Assessment in Scotland*. Edinburgh: Scottish Academic Press.

XII

FUTURE

The concluding section offers a number of perspectives on possible future developments in Scottish education. While these are partly speculative, they are informed by the substantial body of evidence and analysis presented in the previous sections. No one can foretell the future with accuracy, but there are certain recognisable features of the educational landscape that policy makers and practitioners will have to negotiate in the years ahead: the full implementation of Curriculum for Excellence; international league tables of achievement, on which Scotland's position will be scrutinised closely; the implications of rapid technological advance for learning processes and teaching methods; the restructuring of further education and its articulation with a mass system of higher education. All of this will take place within a political context that could lead to a changed relationship between Scotland and the rest of the United Kingdom, to be tested in the referendum on independence in 2014. Scottish education is, therefore, at an interesting point in its historical development: the chapters that follow attempt to sketch some of the directions it might take.

A major determinant of educational policy is finance, and Chapter 105 explains how education in Scotland is funded, tracing the process from the spending reviews carried out at UK level to budget allocations by the Scottish Government and decisions taken by local authorities. The economics of Scottish education is a subject that is not well understood and the chapter offers informed insight into the budgetary process, drawing attention to the importance of power relationships between the various agencies involved. It shows how central government and local authorities use their control over funding to promote their favoured educational objectives, though in a period of budgetary constraint the room for manoeuvre is limited. Teachers' salaries are the largest element in the education budgets of local authorities, amounting to nearly 70 per cent of the total. An increased focus on not only the comparative levels of funding allocated to particular sectors of the educational system (e.g. early years compared to higher education), but also on the educational outcomes achieved is detected. It is pointed out, however, that a crude investment/return model is limited, since well-funded initiatives can have unintended consequences and 'value' is a contested concept. By giving detailed figures for the various forms of educational expenditure, and by comparing the per capita spending in Scotland with that in other parts of the UK, the chapter helps to raise awareness of this very important aspect of educational provision.

Chapter 106 looks at the difficult question of the relationship between central and local government in the administration of education. Starting from an historical perspective, and taking account of both earlier reorganisations of local government and the effects of devolution, it draws attention to some of the inconsistencies in current arrangements. The role of local government has become problematic, partly because of the centralising tendencies of national government and partly because of pressure to give more autonomy to schools. Add to that financial constraints deriving from the freeze on council taxes and the scene is set for a reduction in services and/or the sharing of services between two or more authorities (also rehearsed in Chapter 16). The chapter considers three main options and identifies the central problem as 'reconciling economies of scale with local accountability'.

In a wide-ranging survey of innovative experiments in education, Chapter 107 examines some of the ways in which schools might be encouraged to change. It draws attention to the fact that a great deal of worthwhile learning takes place outside formal classrooms. Very different future scenarios are considered, ranging from attempts to make the existing system more effective, through market models that may produce more diversity but also more inequality, to the development of independent learner networks that would push in the direction of de-schooling. The difficulty of bringing about effective change in highly institutionalised and bureaucratic educational systems, which are generally risk-averse, is shown to be considerable. At the same time, the vital role of school as a 'critical social, moral and political agency' is acknowledged.

Post-16 educational provision has been a major strand of educational policy for the Scottish Government, motivated by a desire to strengthen the skills of employees as part of the strategy to promote economic growth. Chapter 108 examines six main 'drivers of change': structural reform, evident in the merger of colleges as part of 'regionalisation'; a move to funding based on increased efficiencies and outcome agreements; the development of clearer 'learner journeys'; pressure to achieve improved coherence in post-16 provision; greater organisational and educational autonomy; and an emphasis on 'purposeful partnership working'. Relations between central government and the college sector have been going through a difficult phase, partly because of a disappointing funding settlement in 2012–13 and partly because of the uncertainties associated with mergers and rationalisation of provision. Perhaps more than any other sector, further education faces the prospect of major changes in its governance, management and operating arrangements in the period to 2020.

Chapter 109 addresses the question of what is distinctive about universities in an age when higher education is no longer the preserve of an elite but is widely available on a mass scale. It acknowledges that all sorts of other institutions are in the business of producing knowledge, but claims that 'universities are uniquely required, and in a position, to cast all their activities against the backdrop of the search for truth'. The chapter then goes on to discuss a series of more practical concerns: the effect of differential funding streams in Scotland compared to the rest of the UK; global pressures on universities in terms of the recruitment of students and competition coming from major new players in the higher education market (such as India and China); the importance of producing high-quality research output to maintain Scotland's position in international rankings. Preserving Scotland's 'unique attachment to education as a democratising and public good' is seen as a difficult but worthy aspiration.

As this book was going to press, the Cabinet Secretary for Education, Michael Russell, published his draft Post-16 Education (Scotland) Bill which, among other things, contains new powers that will allow ministers to set priorities for universities and colleges in return for the financial support they receive – powers that relate both to widening access and to rules on governance. Unsurprisingly, immediate expressions of concern from universities, colleges, unions and opposition politicians about political interference in institutional autonomy were forthcoming in the press.

The international character of much policy discourse in education is the subject of Chapter 110. It draws an important distinction between 'Europeanisation and Globalisation', and questions the common assumption that 'the global, transnational agenda of education policy making is of greater significance and has more impact than the European Education Policy Space (EEPS)'. Drawing on recent research evidence, the chapter illustrates the nature and extent of Scottish involvement in European discussions about the direction of educational policy and practice. It suggests that Scottish policy makers have succeeded in gaining status and distinctiveness within Europe and that there is growing understanding of the differences between Scottish education and other systems within the UK. Given the debate about Scotland's constitutional future, Europe has become an important point of reference, with the educational systems of small countries such as Finland and Denmark assuming greater comparative significance than provision in England.

The final chapter (Chapter 111), written by the four general editors, emphasises the importance of the political and economic context within which future policy decisions will be taken. It suggests that there may be increasing tension over the allocation of resources between the various sectors of education (pre-school, primary, secondary, further, higher, adult and community). Areas where further research is needed are identified and the question of whether the existing policy community in Scotland is capable of generating the new ideas that may be required is raised. Competing pressures leading in different directions are noted: the global dimension of educational reform tends towards convergence of educational systems, while the desire to celebrate distinctive Scottish values and traditions encourages divergence, particularly from the rest of the UK. The hope is expressed that, whatever the outcome of the constitutional debate, education will remain high on the policy agenda of all political parties.

105

The Funding of Scottish Education

David Bell

INTRODUCTION

This chapter explains how education in Scotland is funded. It focuses primarily on school education, but also discusses the funding of early years, college and university education. Power and finance are inevitably closely linked. The aphorism 'he who pays the piper calls the tune' is as true in education as in other walks of life. National governments and local authorities use their control over funding to regulate and provide incentives intended to further their educational priorities. By following the financial trail, this chapter therefore traces key power relationships within the Scottish education system.

Politicians know that ultimately they will be judged by the outcomes of their policies. However, though they control the input (cash) to the education system, they cannot directly control outcomes. An increasingly sophisticated electorate is less impressed with the amount of resource allocated to education and more with the outcomes that this cash achieves (e.g. school performance). Realising this, politicians have increasingly sought to link education budgets to quantifiable outcomes that can demonstrate how effectively money is being spent. There are advantages with this approach because it focuses attention on the effectiveness and efficiency of the educational system. There are also disadvantages, since it is almost impossible to design top-down targets that do not have unintended consequences.

The tradition of private payment for education disappeared from Scotland many years ago. It lingers on in Scotland's relatively few private schools. In 2012, there were around 31,000 pupils attending private schools in Scotland, representing only 4.5 per cent of Scotland's total pupil population, which just exceeds 700,000. Scotland has a much lower level of private support for education than most countries in the Organisation for Economic Cooperation and Development (OECD). On average, public funding accounts for 84 per cent of all funds for educational institutions across OECD countries – the remaining 16 per cent comes from private contributions, notably parents. Thus, Scots are more willing than citizens in many other countries to trust the state to act as their agent in the delivery of education. Education is a 'merit' good which yields both private and public benefits. The public benefit provides a rationale for state support. Systems that rely more on private funding rely less on the agency of the state, but also tend to favour those with the ability to pay, reducing equality of opportunity among potential consumers of education.

There is also a growing divide between the Scottish and English responses to the balance between private and public support for resource provision in education. This is at its most stark in relation to the balance between public and private support for higher education, with Scotland providing free university tuition while English universities can now charge up to £9,000 per annum.

Understanding how public funds are disbursed is therefore key to understanding how resources are allocated within Scottish education. This chapter starts by explaining how these are determined. In particular, it explains the processes by which taxes received by HM Treasury in Westminster eventually help fund Scottish education.

FROM UK TAXATION TO SCOTTISH EDUCATION

The UK is a highly centralised state. Compared with most other democracies, particularly federations, it allows sub-national levels of government meagre control over finance. Technically, this is described as vertical fiscal imbalance. In practice, it means that the funding of Scottish education to a large extent depends on decisions made at Westminster. And, in turn, local autonomy over education within Scotland is limited by the way in which funds are distributed to educational institutions within Scotland by the Scottish Government. Where power is more widely distributed, education is much more open to local influences. Switzerland, one of the highest-income countries in the world, has a very decentralised system of taxation, where it is not uncommon for communities to vote on whether to raise taxes to pay for an educational development such as a new school.

On a regular basis, the UK government carries out a Spending Review. This is a crucial exercise for all spending departments, since it largely determines their funding for the next two to three years. Its main outcome is a budget showing the resources that each department (including the Scottish Government) will receive. The two-to-three-year horizon means that departmental planning can be made on a medium-term basis, rather than from year to year. The Spending Review is managed by HM Treasury. Each department – health, transport, local government and so on – makes its bid for resources. The Treasury weighs up the strategic importance of the arguments and considers how the spending proposals balance up against likely future revenues from income tax, national insurance, VAT and so on. There is, of course, political input reflecting government priorities and commitments that have been made to the electorate.

The most recent Spending Review was conducted shortly after the coalition government came to power in 2010. It faced a chronic imbalance between revenue generation and spending commitments. The Spending Review therefore charted a course towards a budget that is closer to fiscal balance – where tax revenue equals the amount of government spending. In terms of direction, this did not differ from the course taken by the previous Labour administration, though the pace at which budget balance was intended to be achieved was significantly quicker under the coalition. In December 2012, it was clear that the coalition had not been able to follow its original deficit reduction plan because of weaker than expected economic growth. This implies that for at least the next five years, successive Chancellors will have little option but to continue to cut public spending – and this is likely to have an adverse effect on the funding of education in both Scotland and the UK as a whole.

The Spending Review sets Departmental Expenditure Limits (DELs) for each spending department. The DEL allocations provide the medium-term budgets used for planning purposes. DEL allocations are subdivided between current and capital expenditure. Departments can vire from current to capital spending but not from capital to current.

THE FUNDING OF SCOTTISH EDUCATION

This prevents departments from using monies allocated to, say, the building of roads and hospitals, to meet short-term wage demands.

The Scottish Government also receives a DEL allocation as part of the Spending Review process. Its size is determined by the Barnett Formula. The effect is to increment Scotland's baseline budget by its population share of any change in DEL allocations in those English spending departments that have responsibilities under the control of the Scottish Government in Scotland – such as health or education. Therefore, once decisions about allocations to English departments have been made, the Barnett Formula is applied to determine Scotland's Barnett 'consequentials'. So if, in the Spending Review, the English Department for Education's DEL increases by £100m, the Scottish DEL will increase by £100m multiplied by the ratio of Scotland's population to England's. Since Scotland's population is currently equivalent to 10 per cent of the English population, Scotland's DEL budget will increase by a 'consequential' of £10m. The Scottish Government is under no obligation to spend this additional cash on education. Though seemingly complex, the Barnett Formula has many advantages for the Treasury, the principal of which is that it avoids direct negotiation between the Scottish and Westminster governments over the allocation of funding to Scotland.

While most public spending by the Scottish Government is encompassed by the DEL framework, it also receives an allocation of Annually Managed Expenditure (AME) from the Treasury. AME comprises those elements of spending that are relatively difficult to manage other than on an annual basis. In general, this type of spending is not relevant to direct spending on education though AME is used to balance teachers' pensions if the value of pension contributions from employed teachers and from their employers falls short of payments to retired teachers.

Recent and planned DEL aggregates for the Scottish Budget from 2011–12 and 2014–15 are shown in Table 105.1. The entries relevant to education are shaded. The Education and Lifelong Learning portfolio includes college and university education, which together account for about £1.6bn of the Scottish Government's budget. These are channelled through the Scottish Funding Council, an arm's-length body, which carries out Scottish Government policy in relation to colleges and universities. It also includes spending on another non-departmental governmental body – the Student Awards Agency (SAA). By 2015–16, more than £850m will be spent by the SAA on grants and bursaries for students attending higher education. The Education and Lifelong Learning budget also supports activities relating to employability, skills and lifelong learning. Though each of these bodies has external representatives on its governing body, they are charged with implementing Scottish Government policy in relation to education.

The second main budget line supporting education is that allocated to local government. Education is the largest component of local authority expenditure in Scotland. Therefore the size of the local authority budget is of vital interest as far as school education is concerned. The share of local authority budgets in total Scottish Government spend has been declining and is expected to continue to decline – from 35 per cent of the overall Scottish budget in 2008–9 to 29.2 per cent in 2014–15. This inevitably means that local authorities find their financial position increasingly difficult. Over the same period of time, health spending is expected to increase its share of the Scottish Budget from 32.8 to 34.5 per cent.

In recent years, the Scottish Government's total budget has increased or decreased at broadly the same rate as that of the overall UK public sector budget. This is because the main drivers of the change in the UK budget have been in policy areas for which the

Table 105.1   Scottish Government Spending Review 2011: departmental expenditure limits

	2011–12 Budget £m	2012–13 Draft Budget £m	2013–14 Plans £m	2014–15 Plans £m
Health	11,268.7	11,483.0	11,703.0	11,845.5
Other Health, Wellbeing & Cities Strategy	97.6	104.9	163.8	238.9
Total Health, Wellbeing & Cities Strategy	11,366.3	11,587.9	11,866.8	12,084.4
Finance, Employment & Sustainable Growth	467.9	483.4	466.2	460.5
Education and Lifelong Learning	2,501.7	2,544.1	2,569.1	2,613.5
Justice	1,264.3	1,344.1	1,294.8	1,243.9
Rural Affairs & the Environment	540.6	530.9	511.5	513.5
Culture & External Affairs	245.6	237.8	232.5	221.4
Infrastructure & Capital Investment	2,126.1	2,225.0	2,300.3	2,387.8
Administration	236.0	214.7	202.6	193.5
Parliamentary Business & Government Strategy	8.2	6.5	6.3	6.0
Crown Office & Procurator Fiscal	108.2	108.1	108.1	108.7
Local Government	9,046.5	8,881.8	8,664.1	8,677.5
Scottish Parliament and Audit Scotland	95.9	95.5	95.5	95.5
Total	28,007.3	28,259.8	28,317.8	28,606.2

Source: Scottish Spending Review 2011 and Draft Budget 2012–13

Scottish Government has responsibility, such as health, local government and transport. As a result, because of the operation of the Barnett Formula, growth in Scotland's budget has followed that in the UK as a whole. Health spending in Scotland has grown at almost exactly the same rate as that in the UK as a whole because successive Scottish Governments have opted to change the health budget in line with growth south of the border. This was not imposed by Westminster: it has been a policy choice of successive Scottish administrations. Choosing to increase (or decrease) spending at the same rate as the rest of the UK is perhaps the least politically contentious option. For example, not increasing health spending in Scotland at the same rate as England would undoubtedly draw down a great deal of criticism on the Scottish Government.

However, because spending per head in Scotland was higher than that in England when the Barnett Formula was first introduced, the level of spending per head across most public services is higher in Scotland than in England. This is shown for education spending in Table 105.2, which is drawn from the Public Expenditure Statistical Analysis (PESA) carried out by HM Treasury.

These data are presented in per capita terms – not per pupil or per student. The average spend per pupil depends on the number of children relative to adults in the population. Scotland has slightly fewer children relative to its population due to its slightly lower birth rate, implying the gap in spend per pupil would be even greater than Table 105.2 implies. The table shows increasing levels of spending on education in cash terms in all of the UK nations from 2005–6 to 2009–10. In 2010–11, spending per head in cash terms fell in both England and Wales while it continued to rise in both Scotland and Northern Ireland. This implies an even larger cut in real terms. These differences between countries might be explained by differential response to recent austerity budgets in the devolved territories – particularly in the extent to which local authority budgets were squeezed. Over the period,

Table 105.2   Education spending per capita

	2005–6	2006–7	2008–8	2008–9	2009–10	2010–11
England	£1,137	£1,177	£1,259	£1,330	£1,409	£1,356
Scotland	£1,289	£1,394	£1,431	£1,462	£1,489	£1,547
Wales	£1,180	£1,244	£1,324	£1,390	£1,446	£1,436
Northern Ireland	£1,298	£1,327	£1,382	£1,424	£1,497	£1,526
UK identifiable expenditure	£1,157	£1,203	£1,280	£1,347	£1,420	£1,381
Ratio: Scotland/UK	111%	116%	112%	109%	105%	112%

Source: Public Expenditure Statistical Analysis, HM Treasury

per capita spending on education in Scotland consistently exceeded that in the UK as a whole, with the margin varying from 16 per cent in 2006–7 to 5 per cent in 2009–10.

Some of this difference can be attributed to real differences in costs. These include costs of transport and also the running costs of relatively small schools. Other differences may arise from the extra costs of educating children in highly deprived areas – though the extent of the differences in deprivation levels between Scotland and England is not clear-cut, with comparisons being sensitive to how deprivation is measured. It is not clear whether these explanations fully account for the differences in spending, or whether there are also differences in efficiency and/or the quality of educational provision between England and Scotland. These are extremely difficult to measure, particularly as qualification systems differ radically. One comparison that can be made legitimately is the relative success of those joining the UK labour market from the Scottish and English educational systems. Although this comparison provides a legitimate test of the relative efficiency of the two systems, it is generally eschewed by the educational establishment. Economic success is one attribute among many that one might wish the educational system to deliver: but it is particularly vital since most economists would agree that human capital is the principal driver of economic growth, and therefore of the ability to pay for continuing improvements in public services.

Another approach to measuring comparative efficiency is the use of international testing standards. Economists interested in the outcomes of the educational process frequently analyse national performance using the OECD Programme for International Student Assessment (PISA) tests, where the form of the test is internationally consistent. Clearly, there is a danger of excessive focus on the measurable impacts of education. But there is also a danger of dismissing such analyses as not measuring what the education establishment views as key outcomes. In a world where living standards are declining and may not recover for a considerable period, the dismissal of measurable economic metrics may be perceived as complacent. There is no doubt that attempts to measure the quality of educational provision will continue, driven by politicians, by taxpayers and by parents who wish to be assured that the educational process delivers value for money. They will inevitably disagree, however, on what constitutes 'value'.

As a result of the Spending Review process, the Scottish Government receives a DEL allocation, for both current and capital spending. As mentioned previously, there are no restrictions on how the Scottish Government spends that money; it is free to allocate among its own policy priorities. So the higher level of spending per head in education in Scotland partly reflects choices made by successive Scottish administrations. However, decisions about spending on schools are mostly taken by local authorities. Higher education spending per head also reflects their choices. Nevertheless, because responsibility for schools lies with local authorities, post-devolution administrations may have been more willing to squeeze local authority budgets than, say, health. Cuts to budgets can then be blamed on local authority choices rather than on reductions in grant from the Scottish Government.

Local authorities are not entirely dependent on Scottish Government funding. In principle, local authorities control council tax and non-domestic (business) rates. One might expect that this would give them greater leverage over local education issues. However, in 2010–11, revenue for the whole of Scotland from council tax was £1.9bn, while revenue from non-domestic rates was £2.1bn. These contributions are small by comparison with the local authority grant income from the Scottish Government of £11.1bn. And, as in almost any other situation, small players cannot expect to control the game.

Even where local authorities are in principle able to control their own revenues, the reality may be different. Using their large central grant as leverage, the Scottish Government has been able to persuade local politicians to freeze council tax for the last five years. Though this has cost more than £700m, the Scottish Government's judgement is that this measure is popular with the voters. Some councils might have preferred instead to increase council tax and maintain or increase service provision. However, councils that refused to accept the council tax freeze faced the possibility of a reduced grant from the Scottish Government, effectively blocking any such action.

How does the Scottish Government decide how much grant to allocate to each of Scotland's thirty-two local authorities? Successive Scottish administrations have wrestled with this problem. The answer that they have come up with, which is transparent and obviates the need for extensive negotiations with local authorities, is to drive the allocations by formula. In the next section, we examine the basis of this formula.

ALLOCATING EDUCATION FUNDING TO LOCAL GOVERNMENT

The mechanism for allocating grants to individual local authorities is known as the Grant Aided Expenditure (GAE) system. GAE is determined by the 'client group' approach. This means that the funding allocation to each local authority is largely determined by the size of the population (number of clients) to whom the service is relevant. Thus, the provision to Clackmannan for secondary education is largely determined by the number of pupils of secondary school age in Clackmannan. Figure 105.1 shows the quite dramatic falls in pupil numbers in each of the local authorities across the past decade, 2000–11, averaging in the region of 10–15 per cent. However, there are important 'tweaks' which mean that the provision is not simply determined by pupil numbers. For example, island authorities receive significantly larger provisions because of the greater cost of delivering education in these areas. Second, various adjustments are made to increase provision in deprived areas because of the higher costs of education where there are a large number of non–native English speakers, where families may be dysfunctional and so on. Such adjustments are contestable in the sense that the size of the required adjustment is difficult to measure precisely. However, in general, and unlike the situation in England, allocations in Scotland have tended not to cause significant discord between local authorities.

The GAE system allocates more resources to an authority as the volume of 'needs' in that area increases. So it is in the local authority's interest to paint as black a picture as possible of its circumstances. Clearly, this weakens any incentive to improve, since there are relatively few cash rewards for improved performance, though local authorities can be

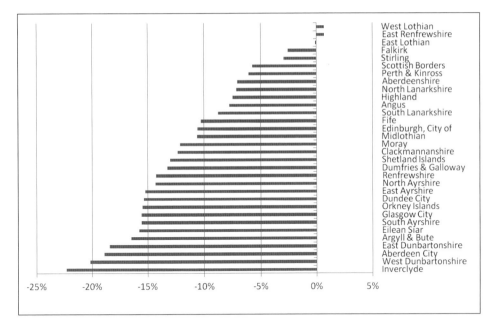

West Lothian
East Renfrewshire
East Lothian
Falkirk
Stirling
Scottish Borders
Perth & Kinross
Aberdeenshire
North Lanarkshire
Highland
Angus
South Lanarkshire
Fife
Edinburgh, City of
Midlothian
Moray
Clackmannanshire
Shetland Islands
Dumfries & Galloway
Renfrewshire
North Ayrshire
East Ayrshire
Dundee City
Orkney Islands
Glasgow City
South Ayrshire
Eilean Siar
Argyll & Bute
East Dunbartonshire
Aberdeen City
West Dunbartonshire
Inverclyde

Figure 105.1   Change in pupil numbers 2000–11

sanctioned if they fail to meet their statutory obligations. Setting a minimally acceptable floor on performance does not seem a particularly strong way to drive improvements in educational quality.

English local authorities also receive funding allocations that are driven by a 'client group' formula. Perhaps it is frustration with the lack of incentive for quality improvement inherent in this approach that has led both the previous and current English administrations to experiment with the direct funding of schools, thus seriously weakening the role of local authorities in school education.

The GAE does not directly provide a stream of cash to local authorities. Rather it represents what is known as a spending *provision*. This is an estimate of the overall cost of providing a particular service. The GAE is the basis for calculating the Scottish Government grant but is not the amount provided to the local authority by the Scottish Government. The simple reason that GAE does not represent actual funding is that not all cash support for local authority services comes from the Scottish Government. As mentioned earlier, some funding derives from council tax receipts and from non-domestic rates. The cash provided by the Scottish Government takes the estimated revenues from these other sources into account. Table 105.3 gives the GAE provision for local authority education budgets aggregated across Scotland for the fiscal year 2010–11. Implicitly, the table shows the relative priorities that the Scottish Government assigns to different types of education and to different aspects of the educational process. These aggregate amounts are then divided between the local authorities, programme by programme.

This allocation gives an implicit picture of Scottish Government educational priorities. Thus, though there is relatively strong empirical evidence of the effectiveness of investment in early years education (see, for example, the work of Nobel-laureate James Heckman), it is allocated a relatively small amount of funding compared with primary and secondary

Table 105.3   Grant Aided Expenditure 2010–11 (£000s)

Nursery Teaching Staff	£26,215
Primary Teaching Staff	£902,523
Secondary Teaching Staff	£1,141,745
Special Education	£243,588
School Transport	£54,853
School Meals	£74,691
School Non-Teaching Costs inc Property	£859,543
School Hostels & Clothing	£26,998
School Security	£15,173
Gaelic Education	£5,570
Teachers for Ethnic Minorities	£8,317
Education Deprivation Assessment	£59,005
Community Education	£122,207
Residual FE	£2,317
Residual FE Travel & Bursaries	£5,492
Childcare Strategy	£44,556
Sure Start Strategy	£59,912
Adult Literacy & Numeracy	£12,482
National Priority Action Fund	£248,828
Former Excellence Fund	£66,600
Pre-School Education	£162,695
Teacher Pensions	£113,774
TOTAL	**£4,257,085**

Source: Grant Aided Expenditure 2012–13 (Scottish Government)

schooling. Notwithstanding the fact that there has recently been an increase in spending on early years, the total spend on nursery teachers, SureStart, childcare and pre-school education combined amounts to less than 7 per cent of total GAE provision for education. Provision for the salaries of secondary teachers alone accounts for almost 27 per cent of GAE allocations. This indicates the extent to which *inertia* drives funding allocations in Scottish education. On the basis of the evidence and starting from a zero baseline, the amount of resource devoted to early years education would surely be greater. But since spending patterns in Scottish education tend to change very slowly, radical changes in the structure of provision are almost unprecedented.

Overall financial support for local authorities from the Scottish Government covers a number of services other than education. Social care, transport, local amenities and refuse collection all place demands on local government budgets. Once it receives its allocation, a local authority is in principle free to spend it as it sees fit. However, in practice, its freedom to act is tightly constrained, partly because it must first use its budget to meet its statutory obligations. This includes school education, but it has other statutory responsibilities in relation to children, adults and older people.

However, even though local authorities are tightly constrained, *actual* spending on education generally exceeds the relevant GAE allocation. The position can be seen in Figure 105.2 which shows the percentage difference between actual expenditure on education and the GAE allocation by Scottish local authorities in 2010–11. Some local authorities, particularly island authorities, spend substantially in excess of their GAE allocations. Larger local authorities, particularly the cities, adhere more closely to their allocations.

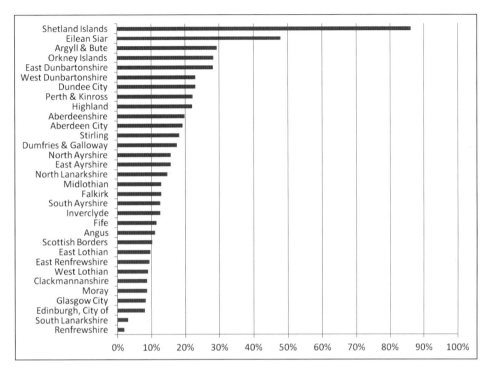

Figure 105.2   Difference between GAE allocation and local authority spending in 2010–11

Source: Scottish Government

Does this imply that GAE allocations do not put sufficient weight on the costs associated with delivery of education in the islands? Not necessarily – island authorities may be choosing to redirect spending into education because their allocation is over-generous in other areas for which it has responsibility and it is possible to redirect funds into education. Or they may have quite legitimately taken the view that the value implicitly placed on education by the GAE is less than they would wish. Assuming they meet their legal obligations, they have a democratic mandate to vary the weight given to education from that of the Scottish Government. In the next section, we examine these costs more closely.

THE COSTS OF SCHOOL EDUCATION

Total education expenditure by Scottish local authorities in 2010–11 is shown in Table 105.4. This amounted to £4.9bn. Secondary education cost £150m more than primary education. The costs of specialised instruction in secondary schools offset the economies of scale associated with the larger size of secondary schools.

Over 69 per cent of spending on schools is allocated to employee costs. This proportion is broadly the same across pre-primary education, primary education and secondary education. Only with special education and community learning is the share of employee costs significantly less. This is due to their greater need for specialised equipment and transport. Overall operating costs for schools totalled over £1.3bn, with secondary education accounting for the largest single share.

Table 105.4 Local authority expenditure on education 2010–11 (£m)

	Education	Pre-primary education	Primary education	Secondary education	Special education	Community Learning	Other non-school funding
Employee costs	£3,368	£223	£1,303	£1,400	£338	£85	£20
Operating costs	£1,336	£85	£475	£515	£184	£57	£20
Support service costs	£150	£8	£54	£57	£13	£7	£12
Other	£2	£3	−£6	£13	−£8	£2	−£3
Total Expenditure	£4,857	£318	£1,827	£1,985	£527	£152	£48

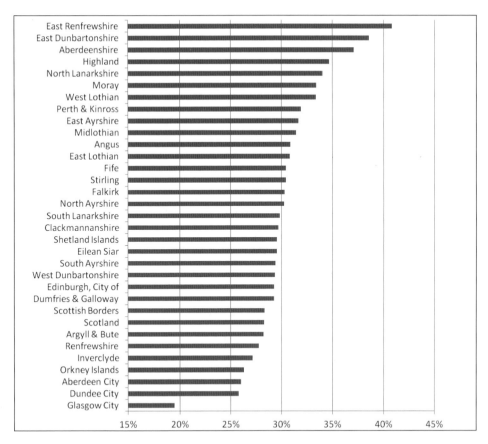

Figure 105.3 Education spending as share of local authority spending

Source: Scottish Government

The data in Table 105.4 are for Scotland as a whole. Differences in expenditure by local authority largely reflect differences in the circumstances of local authorities. Nevertheless, it is possible to calculate the proportion of its total budget that each local authority allocates to education. These shares for 2010–11 are shown in Figure 105.3. Top of the list, and the only authority to spend more than 40 per cent of its budget on education, is East Renfrewshire. Though physically its neighbour, Glasgow City is at the other end of the distribution of education spending. Indeed, the cities typically spend less than other parts of Scotland. This may reflect their greater ability to realise economies of scale through larger schools, lower transport costs and so on. It may also indicate requirements to allocate a greater share of their budgets to providing services for a wider hinterland and/or particular socio-economic problems associated with our larger cities.

SALARY COSTS

Salaries account for 69 per cent of spending on education by local authorities. Given that their overall budgets are fixed and they have a variety of obligations outside education,

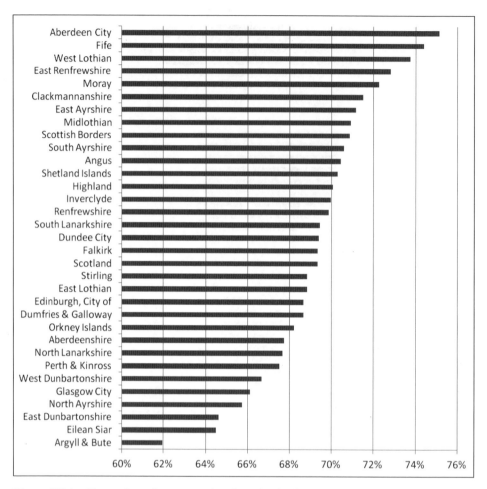

Figure 105.4 Share of employee costs in education budget

local authorities have limited latitude to vary their salary bills. However, the share of wages in total education spending does vary considerably by local authority, as shown in Figure 105.4.

The share varies from around 75 per cent in Aberdeen City to 62 per cent in Argyll and Bute. This again reflects differences in other costs, such as transport, which is likely to account for a much larger proportion of the education budget in Argyll and Bute than in Aberdeen. Other factors, such as local labour market conditions, may force local authorities to pay somewhat higher salaries to attract teachers to areas where, for example, housing costs are relatively high. However, Figure 105.4 does not show a consistent overall pattern that might explain the variation in the share of salary costs in total educational costs, suggesting that some of the variation may be due to unpredictable differences in local authority policies and/or in the efficiency of delivery.

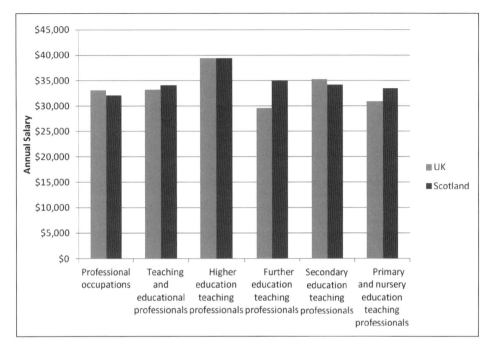

Figure 105.5   Annual salary by professional occupation 2012

TEACHER REMUNERATION

Since teachers account for a substantial majority of the educational workforce, teachers' pay dominates local authority education budgets. Hence local authorities are particularly sensitive to changes in teachers' pay and conditions. On the one hand, they need to maintain a well-motivated and efficient teaching workforce. On the other, they need to contain teachers' remuneration in order to stay within their budgets.

In recent years, the average nominal (and real) weekly pay of Scottish teachers has increased broadly in line with teachers in the rest of the UK. Rapid increases in the middle of the last decade have been offset by successive pay freezes in pay as a result of the downward pressure on local authority budgets which, in turn, reflect government attempts to reduce the UK's budget deficit. These have particularly affected those at the top of pay scales, who have not benefited from annual incremental increases. The 2012 estimates for annual pay amongst professionals, including those employed full-time in education, is shown in Figure 105.5.

Differences in the annual salary of education professionals between Scotland and the UK are generally relatively small. For professional occupations as a whole, including education, annual earnings in the UK are somewhat higher than in Scotland. This reflects the relative strength of the private sector outside Scotland, where professional earnings are somewhat higher than in the public sector. Higher education professionals earned just less than £40,000 on average, while other education professionals in Scotland average between £30,000 and £35,000.

For most groups, differences in annual earnings between Scotland and the UK as a whole are not statistically significant, though the differential in favour of educational professionals compared with all professionals seems slightly larger in Scotland than in the rest of the UK (RUK). This suggests that teaching is relatively more attractive in Scotland compared with other professions, at least as far as pay is concerned.

The groups that do seem to fare relatively well in Scotland are primary teachers and, in particular, teachers in further education. This may reflect differences in bargaining outcomes. These groups may have successfully argued for greater comparability with secondary teachers in Scotland compared with RUK. It may also reflect differences in the arrangement of these services (primary schools and further education colleges) between Scotland and England.

Are education professionals better paid in Scotland? Clearly, in terms of their nominal pay, there is little difference between Scotland and the UK as a whole. However, their real pay may differ because they face different costs. In particular, housing costs are typically lower in Scotland. One possible corollary is that higher real pay rates in Scotland would attract higher quality recruits into teaching in Scotland. However, Scottish teachers, with a median age of 44, compared with 42 in the rest of the UK, might expect to be paid more than their counterparts in RUK. This is because the structure of teachers' pay typically rewards seniority. Age is one of a number of factors that complicates simple comparisons of mean or median pay levels for teachers in Scotland with other professional groups.

The distribution of earnings among Scottish teachers is more concentrated than that among non-teaching professionals. This means that the pay gap between the top and bottom of the teaching profession is smaller than the gap for other professionals. This is not surprising given that 'other professionals' comprise a wide range of different occupations. What is perhaps more unexpected is that teachers' pay in Scotland is also less widely spread than is teachers' pay in RUK. This might indicate that the rewards for taking greater responsibility in the teaching profession are higher in England than in Scotland.

Nevertheless, what is clear is that because of the overall size of the pay bill, teachers' remuneration is a major issue for both local and national government in Scotland. Similarly teachers' pensions are a source of financial concern to government since, as with many other public-sector pension schemes, government bears the risk should such schemes become insolvent.

CAPITAL COSTS

Another important component of education spending is that allocated to school building. Many new schools around Scotland have been built recently under Private Finance Initiative (PFI) or Public Private Partnership (PPP) contracts. Payments on these contracts typically extend over a twenty-five year period, and are funded from current budgets, implying that they represent yet another claim on already stretched local authority resources. In 2012–13, the Scottish Government will pay £963m for all of its PFI/PPP contractual obligations. This amounts to 2.8 per cent of its total budget. The Education and Lifelong Learning portfolio (colleges and universities) account for £326m of this total, while payments from the Finance, Employment and Sustainable Growth portfolio (which includes local government) will be around £140m. These commitments will clearly constrain budgets for the foreseeable future and there is a widening debate on whether they really deliver value for money.

SPENDING ON OTHER FORMS OF EDUCATION

School education is the most important, but not the only form of expenditure on education in Scotland. Nursery education, colleges and universities all play a role in providing education to a different and broader set of age groups. They also account for a significant set of costs, almost all of which are met from public funds.

It is unusual for large shifts to occur in relative spending on these components of the Scottish education system. This is partly because of incumbent advantage in resource disputes. In general, individuals value losses higher than they value gains. Hence incumbents can always make the powerful argument that the political cost of reducing spending on some service will be greater than the political gain from expanding some other service, even though the balance of evidence suggests that this is an appropriate course of action.

This argument is particularly relevant in the case of early years education. As mentioned earlier, there is a wide international literature that demonstrates that investment in early years yields much higher rates of social return than educational investments later in the life course. The Scottish Government argues that 'a failure to intervene effectively to address the complex needs in the early years of an individual's life can result in a nine-fold increase in direct public costs over the long term' (Scottish Government, 2012, Scottish Budget: Draft Budget 2013–14). Part of its preventative spend strategy has been increasing the resources allocated to early years intervention, including the establishment of a 'change fund' designed to provide increased focus on early years. This is a complex strategy, involving contributions from departments other than education. Nevertheless, in relation to the total budget of the relevant departments, the amounts involved are small. Seismic changes to the Scottish education budget are about as common as significant seismic activity in Scotland.

Further and higher education provides a further significant call on public resources. The colleges are almost completely dependent on government funding, while universities have significant sources of funding from teaching and research over which the Scottish Government has no control. Both colleges and universities receive public funding through the Scottish Funding Council, which in 2013–14 will have a budget of around £1.6bn. Just over £1bn of this goes to the higher education sector; colleges will receive £471m in running costs. However, the higher education budget does not include the £300m contained in the Scottish budget to cover both student tuition fees and student support. This amount has increased rapidly, partly to compensate universities for not having been given the power to charge tuition fees, while comparable English institutions can charge each student up to £9,000 per year.

College funding has been cut more sharply than other parts of the education budget. The government has embarked on a programme of reform and centralisation of college provision. This involves a significant amount of new building as existing colleges merge. The Scottish Government will expect to realise cost savings as a result of this rationalisation. But it also may have taken the view that, given the overall constraints on its budget, reductions in college funding would meet less political opposition than would cuts in university funding, given the storm caused by the increase in tuition fees in England.

Colleges are perhaps closer to the needs of employers than are other parts of the education system: it has always proved difficult to ensure that college provision and employer needs are aligned, in the way that occurs, say, in Germany. Initiatives such as Scotland's Colleges Energy Skills Partnership attempt to ensure that the immediate needs of employers are being met. Anticipating employers' needs is also extremely difficult, given that the current demands that employers register may not be relevant in the future.

CONCLUSIONS

The allocation of resources to the education system is highly complex. Governments have to balance the needs of education against other priorities. Ultimately the electorate determines the kind of government that is in power and the policies that they deliver. Education is always reliant on an altruistic electorate because the benefits from education are rarely realised within the lifetime of a parliament and often not within a generation.

There is also a danger that education spending is like an oil tanker, difficult to redirect. As evidence piles up on what kinds of intervention are, or are not, effective, pressures to change the ways that Scotland allocates funding to education inevitably gain some traction. However, perhaps Scots suffer more acutely from aversion to change than those in other parts of the UK because, since devolution, the reforms in the Scottish educational system have been much less radical than in, say, England. Ultimately, such change is controlled by shifts in budget allocations. Without the control of funding, it is difficult to envisage any stakeholder effecting substantive change in Scotland's education system.

106

Tensions between Central and Local Government in the Administration of Scottish Education

Keir Bloomer

BACKGROUND

Scotland has a very long tradition of government encouragement of education. More than half a century before John Knox's famous Book of Discipline, an Act of Parliament in the reign of James IV had encouraged the establishment of schools. It was not, however, until well into the second half of the nineteenth century that the idea of a national system of education took root. A variety of considerations – concern about foreign economic competitors and the need to educate the citizens of an emerging democracy among them – caused parliament to legislate to ensure that elementary education would become universally available and that, as it did so, attendance would become compulsory.

The new schools were not built by central government but by parish school boards. These boards were, nevertheless, public bodies. As the Victorian state expanded its activities, it was assumed that funding by the state necessarily involved management by the state, although not at national level.

Scotland's state education system has always been managed at three levels: national, local and school. The national level has been responsible for legislation and has always had an inspectorial or quality assurance function, although the significance of this has grown greatly in recent years. The intermediate level originally comprised ad hoc bodies in the shape of the parish school boards, the functions of which were subsequently transferred to local authorities. Over the years, it has been largely concerned with organisational matters (such as the provision of resources, buildings and staff). Decisions about day-to-day management issues, however, have always been taken at school level.

The national level of governance has always been to a significant extent Scottish. The 1707 Act of Union established a United Kingdom national government and a free trade area. This national government was not, however, concerned to any great extent with culture and social policy. Thus, in common with the church and the law, Scotland's education system remained separate from that of England. In due course, it became the responsibility of the Scottish Office. This system of administrative but not political devolution remained in place until the establishment of the Scottish Parliament in 1999.

Over the years these arrangements have probably been seen as working reasonably well. Indeed, they have largely been taken for granted. Recently, however, several factors have contributed to a growing feeling that they perhaps need to be reviewed. As educational management has become increasingly a matter of conscious policy making rather than merely administration, the relationships among the three tiers of management have become more uneasy. Traditional models of local and central government have been criticised as bureaucratic and inefficient. Devolution has created a new context in which different arrangements might be possible.

THE CURRENT CONTEXT

The new arrangements put in place by the devolution settlement raise important questions about the future management not merely of Scottish education but of the whole of the Scottish public sector. The existence of a Scottish Parliament and Scottish Government ought logically to lead to a reconsideration of how public affairs are run at a sub-national level. To date, this has happened only in a piecemeal and limited fashion. At some point, however, the issues will have to be addressed.

In the first place, it is difficult to justify (or even understand) the complexity of the governance structure of the public sector in what is, after all, a small country. Why should the division of Scotland into fourteen areas be seen as appropriate for health but six be regarded as more effective for justice or seven for transport? Policing is currently provided by eight forces but these will shortly become just one. At a time when collaboration among public bodies is seen as of increasing importance, how are these structures expected to relate to the thirty-two local authorities? Why are some services, such as planning, social housing and school education, managed by multi-purpose, democratically accountable councils, while others, such as health, have ad hoc boards answerable to the Scottish Government?

To these important questions of structure and accountability can be added a more fundamental concern. In a country of only five million people, with a devolved government responsible mainly for local authority and health functions, is there a need for a second elected tier of government at all? If there is, what functions should it fulfil and what size should the units be? The criticism often made of Scottish local government – perhaps particularly by those interested in education – is that there are currently too many councils and that they are too small to be effective. Why does Scotland need thirty-two directors of education or thirty-two quality improvement teams?

Yet it is possible to make out a very different argument. Maybe one of the key functions of local government is to build grassroots democracy. Maybe it is not local enough. Perhaps there are too few councils. But the logic of this argument would not lead to a requirement for even more education directors. Rather, it would suggest that local government should be concerned with only small-scale local services and that education should be run in some other way.

The drive for greater efficiency in public services, however, could bring about a rather different solution. Much attention has been focused on the possibility of reducing the cost of central support services. Thus, the then Scottish Executive's discussion paper 'Transforming Public Services', published in 2006, saw merit in the option of 'shared services' that would provide back-office support to several councils and/or other public bodies. A single service centre could provide human resources support, payroll services and information technology back-up to a group of local authorities and other agencies.

Somewhat surprisingly, the idea was not extended to services dealing directly with the public, such as education. Furthermore, remarkably little progress has been made despite the investment of large sums of money. However, in the course of 2011, two examples of pairs of councils seeking to set up jointly managed education services were announced. In a less ambitious version of a plan to share all services conceived some years earlier, Clackmannanshire and Stirling Councils took advantage of vacancies in senior positions to enter into a partnership for the delivery of education and social work services. Stirling leads on education and Clackmannanshire on social work. A similar partnership between East and Midlothian Councils did not reach fruition.

If such approaches prove successful, it may well be that education will come to be managed by federations of councils, thus (at least to an extent) reconciling economies of scale with local accountability. While such an approach would retain local government control of schools, it would probably reduce the influence of councillors, giving greater autonomy to the senior officers of the joint services. An additional pressure to adopt measures of this kind lies in the gloomy economic situation that has prevailed since 2008. In contrast with the early years of devolution when resources increased substantially, all levels of government now face the need to make major savings.

THE DECLINE OF LOCAL GOVERNMENT

Other signs of the diminishing significance of this middle tier of management have been evident for some time. An obvious instance would be loss of responsibility for particular areas of service provision. Thus, local government ceased to have any responsibility for the management of further education in 1994 when colleges became autonomous incorporated bodies. Similarly, the Careers Service became part of Scottish Enterprise in 2002. Although further organisational changes took place later, the idea of returning the service to local government control was not seriously considered. There have, however, been two even more important developments that have reduced further the importance of the local authority level of educational management.

The Centralising Role of Policy

The first of these concerns the growing importance of policy making and its centralising effect. Central government has, of course, always exercised the right to legislate in relation to Scottish education. In addition, government has issued 'advice' and 'guidance' that have lacked the force of law but have substantially directed the educational activities of councils.

Sometimes this advice has concerned controversial matters such as the introduction of comprehensive secondary schooling in the 1960s. However, relatively little of it related to the curriculum or to pedagogy. In this respect, the setting up in 1974 of the Munn and Dunning Committees to look at curriculum and assessment in the middle years of secondary schooling can probably be seen as a milestone. Since that time central government, whether at Westminster or more recently at Holyrood, has issued a stream of policy pronouncements that intimately influence what is taught, which methods should be employed and how progress should be measured.

For perhaps twenty-five years, these policies were developed in a somewhat ad hoc fashion. The committees mentioned above were established in response to particular perceived problems. In the same way, at later dates, committees were established to look at provision in the years 10 to 14 and in the later years of secondary education. Various smaller working groups developed policy on less significant issues.

By the later 1990s, however, a more ambitious notion of policy making had begun to take hold. The new Scottish Parliament determined that one of its first major pieces of legislation would concern school education. The consultation document that was issued in advance canvassed the suggestion that the new Act should set out certain broad objectives for school education in Scotland, in effect comprising some kind of 'mission statement'. This idea received considerable public support, not least from teachers who felt that greater coherence in policy making was required. Nevertheless, no such mission statement was incorporated in the final Act, largely, it is understood, for technical legal reasons. The Act did, however, give the Minister power to determine 'national priorities', thus accomplishing much the same aim by a different route. Indeed, the fact that the policy-making power was delegated to the Minister rather than being incorporated in the primary legislation could be seen as an even more emphatic growth in centralised authority.

It is worth noting that this more ambitious phase of national policy making has taken place at a time when the policy-making capacity of local authorities has diminished. In part, this is a consequence of the structural changes made in 1995–6. At that time, while the three Islands authorities continued, twenty-nine new unitary councils took over the educational responsibilities of the previous nine regions. None of the new councils would rank as more than medium-sized in English terms. The largest, Glasgow and Edinburgh, were comparable only with the previous Grampian and Tayside regions. No council was in a position to operate on the same scale as Lothian, still less Strathclyde.

Strathclyde can, indeed, be regarded as a pioneer in the field of what came to be called during the Blair era 'joined-up policy'. Its 'Social Strategy for the 80s' offered an ambitious vision of the council corporately pursuing ends that lay far beyond the scope of any single service. Thus, for example, it indicated how school education could be expected to contribute towards broad social and economic objectives. After 1996, however, it was clear that the locus for policy making of this kind lay firmly at Holyrood (or, perhaps more accurately, Victoria Quay), not with the local tier of governance.

Even setting aside more ambitious, cross-disciplinary policy making, the ability of local authorities with an average population of only 150,000 or so to formulate genuinely independent educational strategies has to be in doubt. The policy role of local authorities has thus, for the most part, come to be more focused on developing local approaches for the implementation of national strategies rather than fully autonomous policy making. This trend has, of course, reinforced the view widely held by teachers that they are members of a national service who are employed, more for reasons of administrative convenience than anything else, by local authorities.

A further aspect of the centralising effect of the increasing emphasis on policy has been the growing influence of the Inspectorate. There have, of course, been inspectors for as long as there have been state schools. Furthermore, they have always played a role in the development of educational policy. That role has, however, changed and developed in recent decades.

The decision of the then Conservative government in 1983 to publish reports on school inspections represents an important milestone. The basic concept of inspection had, from the outset, been about guaranteeing minimum standards of performance. However, the idea behind publication was that of creating a kind of quasi-market in education with a view to improving standards. On the whole, there is little evidence that parents have used inspection reports in the way the government anticipated. Nevertheless, the notion of actively using inspection as a tool for improving standards rather than merely eliminating the unacceptable has proved very influential.

That influence has not, however, been made effective through the operation of the market but rather by encouraging compliance with centrally determined policy. Fear of unfavourable comment in inspection reports is widely seen as giving added force to national policy pronouncements. This influence of inspection is evident at both school and local authority level. Indeed, the introduction of a system of inspecting the councils' discharge of their education functions is in itself a demonstration of the diminishing significance of the local authority tier of management. Where agents of one level of government inspect the activities of another, there can be no pretence of equality or even genuine partnership. The value of inspection as a mechanism for quality improvement can obviously be debated. What would be hard to dispute is that, despite recent attempts on the part of the Inspectorate to encourage flexibility and diversity, inspection has served to encourage conformity with national policy.

School Autonomy: A Force for Decentralisation

The second major trend tending to reduce the influence of local authorities has been a steadily increasing emphasis on the autonomy of the individual school. Running in parallel with this is the importance attached to the leadership qualities of the head teacher.

It has always been taken for granted that day-to-day decisions regarding the running of the school are made by the headteacher or by other staff on authority delegated by the headteacher. So far as the individual pupil or parent was concerned, the head was, for most practical purposes, the ultimate authority figure.

There were, however, many decisions affecting the running of the school that were taken by officers of the local authority. They decided how many teachers the school should have. Very often, they were responsible for their appointment. Almost all matters relating to buildings were decided by them. Important aspects of curriculum organisation or timetabling were in their hands. Over a period of, perhaps, the past twenty-five years, the trend has been to decentralise much of this decision making to school level. The former Inner London Education Authority had experimented in the 1970s with delegating a significant measure of budgetary control to headteachers. This idea was taken up by the Conservative government during the 1980s and became a statutory requirement in England and Wales.

At the end of the 1980s, the education department of the then Strathclyde Regional Council underwent a far-reaching reorganisation, which foreshadowed a number of significant developments in Scottish education in the 1990s. It saw, for example, the introduction of a formal quality assurance system with indicators of good practice of the kind that would later be introduced nationally through *How Good is our School?* Amongst the most significant of these developments was the establishment of Scotland's first scheme for devolving some measure of financial control to school level. The thinking behind the introduction of this scheme was partly that, wherever possible, decisions should be made close to where they had practical effect, and partly that the best way of avoiding prescriptive legislation of the kind that had been enacted in England and Wales was to take a positive initiative and demonstrate that local authorities did not require to be coerced into this kind of decentralisation.

At much the same time, schools became largely responsible for appointing their own teaching staff. In part, this was the result of a further Strathclyde initiative under which schools were empowered to appoint staff to un-promoted and junior promoted positions. In part, however, it resulted from the 1988 School Boards Act which gave parents limited powers in relation to the running of schools through the establishment of bodies akin to the Boards of Governors which had existed south of the border for decades. Probably the most significant of the Boards' powers concerned appointments of senior promoted staff. It is perhaps symptomatic of the distrust then prevailing between national and local government that it was felt necessary to prescribe in detail in primary legislation what should be the composition of an interview panel involved in the appointment of, say, an assistant headteacher.

The School Boards Act and, even more so, its short-lived successor, the Self-Governing Schools Act, represented a phase of government action that was concerned not merely to decentralise power to school level but to see that power exercised by parents rather than by staff of the local authority. Subsequent events demonstrated that Scottish parents did not aspire to be school managers in this way. The Self Governing Schools Act was virtually unused and was abolished shortly after a new Labour government took power in 1997. Even the introduction of School Boards enjoyed only limited success with many parents preferring the informality of Parent Teacher Associations to the legalism of the School Board legislation. (This preference later caused Boards to be replaced in legislation by Parent Councils – see Chapter 21.) In retrospect, it is clear that the Conservative government not only misinterpreted public opinion but also failed to act coherently in terms of its own free market doctrines. In a more marketised education system, the place of the parent was surely as consumer rather than manager.

Although the measures enacted in the late 1980s have now disappeared, the idea of involving parents (and other stakeholders) more actively in the running of schools has not gone away. The idea of setting up local trusts to manage clusters of schools that was canvassed by East Lothian Council in 2010–11 had this aim. However, the idea was not taken forward following the local government elections in 2012.

SCENARIOS FOR THE FUTURE

The new century thus sees the balance of power and influence among the three traditional levels of management changed radically. On the one hand, individual schools have achieved much greater levels of autonomy. Increasingly they see themselves as units within a national education system, encouraged certainly to collaborate more closely with other public services but with no strong sense of commitment to a particular local authority. For policy direction, they look increasingly to the Scottish Government. While in terms of operational management they are answerable to the director of education, a more powerful line of accountability lies through inspection to the national level.

Furthermore, it seems certain that the process of devolving authority to school level will continue. There seems to be a political consensus to this effect. The Cameron Report on Devolved School Management (as the system of delegating budgets to schools is now known) remains to be implemented but would increase the financial powers of schools significantly.

An obstacle to increasing decision-making powers at school level is the belief that small schools (especially in the primary sector) simply do not have the management capacity to cope. However, there is an increasing tendency to see the 'cluster' of associated schools as a unit of organisation. How far this process will go remains to be seen. So far, there has been no successful attempt to replace the post of school headteacher by cluster principal (although joint headships of primary schools have become quite common). It is also quite possible that schools may join together in larger federations on the basis of shared interests.

At the same time, the significance of the national level has also grown enormously. Its powers have been explicitly increased by legislation. Its own ambitions as well as the modest scale of operation of the great majority of local councils have given it an effective monopoly in relation to policy direction. The Scottish Parliament and Scottish Government have adopted increasingly hands-on approaches to major services such as education.

In 2011, a significant reorganisation of national agencies took place. Learning and Teaching Scotland and Her Majesty's Inspectorate of Education were brought together to form Education Scotland with a more powerful remit than any previous national agency (see Chapters 19 and 20). This took place at a time of severe resource constraints and it is unclear how well positioned the new body will be to play a serious role in educational development and simultaneously maintain an extensive inspection programme. In short, it is uncertain whether the formation of this body will represent a further stage in the centralisation of strategic decision making or not.

In a sense, Curriculum for Excellence perfectly exemplifies these trends. It is at one and the same time both a centralising and a decentralising programme. Central government has clearly enunciated what it sees as the fundamental purposes of education. Schools (and other education providers) exist to help young people become 'successful learners, confident individuals, effective contributors and responsible citizens'. Seven principles of curriculum design are also set out in policy. The experiences and outcomes state in some detail what learners should be able to achieve. In other words, government has prescribed the *ends* of education.

However, it takes a much more relaxed view of the *means*. Teachers are encouraged to exercise their imagination and creativity. The experiences and outcomes do not specify how the desired objectives are to be achieved or, in most instances, even what content should be used. Schools are free to introduce new structures and to innovate. To an extent that was not true of any previous initiative, Curriculum for Excellence sets out to empower the teaching profession. The significant point is that these new freedoms are designed to be exercised at school, not local authority, level.

Given the flight of power and influence from the middle to the two outer tiers of governance, it is difficult to imagine that the current arrangements will remain unchanged for long. This chapter, therefore, concludes with some speculation on possible directions for change.

Shedding the Middle Tier

The most obvious possibility is the disappearance of the middle tier of management, with its functions transferring either to the Scottish Government or to school level. Most people see little reason why schooling should vary from county to county on the basis of local politics. In any event, in recent times little consideration seems to have been given to formulating and articulating a case for local government involvement. With the advent of new technology, it is difficult to argue that schools should be managed on the basis of geography when physical proximity to those responsible for staffing or finance is no longer a necessity.

An argument can, however, be developed that decisions about resource allocation, especially if factors such as social deprivation are to be taken into account as well as more mechanistic variables such as pupil numbers, are better made at a level where the circumstances of individual schools are likely to be known and understood. For the same reason, schools can be both more critically challenged and more effectively supported from a comparatively local level. Arguments based on local policy preferences are more difficult to sustain. As services become increasingly personalised and choice dominates the political agenda, it becomes more difficult to justify local authority-wide differences arising from political decision rather than the exercise of personal preference.

Without local authority involvement, however, the national tier of management would have a monopoly on strategy and policy making. It is the existence of thirty-two councils with some capacity for research, policy development and support for schools that gives Scottish education the modest level of diversity that it possesses. Without this middle tier, important local initiatives such as cooperative learning in North Lanarkshire or synthetic phonics in Clackmannanshire would not have enriched the educational scene. Despite the relative lack of capacity of generally small local authorities, this argument based on pluralism in policy making is probably the strongest available to proponents of local government involvement.

There is, however, another argument that might come to be seen as important. The idea that some issues are essentially cross-cutting and can only be effectively tackled by agencies acting in collaboration has given rise to an emphasis by the Scottish Government on collaborative planning and joint action. These concepts are enshrined in the notion of 'community planning'. As yet, its achievements have been modest and there is little evidence that the school sector has played a significant role. However, were community planning to begin to fulfil its promise, local authorities, operating at the right level to promote collaboration among separate services and agencies, could find a renewed sense of purpose.

Modernising the Local Government Role

A second possibility for the future would see this capacity for pluralism enhanced through partnership working among local authorities. Both the Scottish Government and the Westminster government are keen to see the public sector achieve greater efficiency and cost-effectiveness through this type of approach. Two examples of jointly managed education services, created in 2011, were mentioned earlier.

There are, however, other models that could be explored. An obvious instance would be the creation of joint boards to manage unified education services. This model goes beyond the existing examples which see two separate services with a common senior management structure being accountable to two (or more) councils. Instead, the services would be fully combined and accountability would be to a joint board similar to those in charge of police and fire and rescue services in some parts of the country.

There is another, less radical, possibility that could also be considered. One of the criticisms often made by teachers of the 1995–6 local government reorganisation is that the new smaller authorities are unable to maintain an extensive range of specialisms within their educational development and quality improvement services. In the same way, psychological services have had difficulty in maintaining more than a basic provision. Similar arguments can be made in relation to more mundane support activities such as the processing of footwear and clothing grants, the organisation of school crossing patrols or the recruitment of supply staff. These criticisms could perhaps be met (at the same time as achieving economies of scale) by amalgamating some or all of the support services provided by a group local authorities for their schools.

It is thus possible to envisage several means by which a modernised local authority level of management could be created. Potentially, it could be at one and the same time less costly and more able to exercise genuinely strategic responsibilities. In other words, it is possible – in theory at least – to conceive of a way in which the middle tier of educational management might reassert its independence and purposefulness without sacrificing the local political accountability inherent in the thirty-two council structure.

Embracing the Notion of Choice

A third and more radical approach, at odds with the statist ethos that has prevailed in post-devolution Scotland to date, would question the assumption made in Victorian times that state funding and state management of schools need necessarily go together. In essence, a voucher system would introduce genuine customer choice and thus significantly reduce the policy-making function of government at whatever level.

There would, of course, be no place for a middle tier of management. However, it would be possible – indeed, the experience of the Scottish Council of Independent Schools and that of the Specialist Schools and Academies Trust in England suggests that it would be probable – for groups of schools to create their own education authorities from the bottom up. A national inspectorate would be likely to remain in place but more as a guarantor of minimum standards than as an agency with influence over policy.

An advantage of this kind of arrangement that has not often been noted is that it would allow a state-funded education system to benefit from 'early adopters'. In a politically driven system, change takes place only when there is a sufficient consensus to reduce political risk to acceptable levels. In an epoch in which change in the outside world is rapid and accelerating, it is questionable whether this can generate a sufficiently speedy response from the education service. Private enterprise, by contrast, benefits from individual customers who are prepared to lead change, thus generating innovation. It may well be that this is a clinching argument in the fluid circumstances of the twenty-first century.

There are, of course, many variations on these three options and, no doubt, other possibilities altogether. What does seem certain, however, is that the tensions now apparent in the traditional three-tier model are sufficiently great to ensure that the status quo is unsustainable. The future may be uncertain but it will certainly be different.

107

Scenarios for the Future of Schooling and Education

John MacBeath

At a Cambridge University seminar in early 2012, David Istance of the Organisation for Economic Cooperation and Development (OECD) presented MEd students (most of them practising teachers) with six scenarios for the future of schools. As the author of these now seminal hypotheses of the future he was interested in how classroom teachers would view the probability and the desirability of each of the six potential forecasts. Would teachers opt for 'business as usual' – 'the robust bureaucratic system' – which posits a continuing and perhaps even further tightening of schools' conventions as we have come to know them? Or would they opt for the deschooling scenarios which describe learner networks and schools in which learning spills over into communities beyond containing school walls? While the first of these, the *reschooling* scenarios, were seen as probable they were viewed as less desirable, while the *deschooling* scenarios were seen as more desirable but less probable.

'Learner networks and a network society' envisages new forms of cooperative networks in which there is a proliferation of sites for learning and schools enjoy less of a monopoly on learning and act less as a curriculum delivery service. In 2010, at a conference in the United Arab Emirates, the Oxford scholar Baroness Greenfield reported on her research into how 11-year-olds spent their time. Nine hundred hours in school were overshadowed by 1,277 hours spent out of school and 1,934 hours in the virtual world. Not only is it a question of relative amounts of time, but her findings point to the nature of the activity as schools struggle to compete with the interactive and personalised nature of learning offered through the medium of new technologies.

In the United States the Khan Academy, an online tutorial centre which claims thousands of new adherents on a daily basis, 'inverts the normal rhythms of school' so that 'lectures' (the predominant teacher mode in classrooms) are viewed in the students' own time while homework is done at school. Initially the 2,500 short online 'lectures' were created as a complement to classroom teaching, but in effect these have largely replaced direct teaching so that teachers, freed from lecturing and marking, attend to individuals or groups who require help. Teachers benefit from a sophisticated 'dashboard' system which provides ongoing information as to how students are progressing, where they are stuck and, crucially, their methods of attacking and trying to resolve problems. Students can engage with these videos at home or in the classroom, reviewing, pausing and repeating without censure, embarrassment or a feeling of guilt for wasting the teacher's time. Once they're answering questions without making mistakes, Khan's site automatically recommends next steps, new challenges to confront (see www.wired.com/magazine/2011/07/ff_khan/all/1).

There are obvious parallels here with developments in the Highlands and Islands in Scotland where the long and sometimes hazardous journey to school may become less ritual as 'lessons' and homework tasks are already made available online. As Graham Leicester and colleagues of the Scottish-based Futures Forum argue, 'latent innovation is already there'. It is not always easy to recognise, they write, because it is tempered by the power of the status quo, 'hindered at least in part because they [change agents] have not reckoned with the power of the sunk infrastructure to constrain innovation' (Leicester et al., 2009, p. 38) even in the face of evidence that education systems in their current form are not fit for purpose.

LEARNING FROM THE PAST

Nowhere is this more clearly illustrated than in radical innovations that have enjoyed a brief life, too much on the edge to be mainstreamed. Parkway, the school without walls in Philadelphia with offshoots in some other American cities, was an exciting but ultimately unsustainable adventure. It was replicated in Renfrewshire in Scotland in the early 1970s in an experimental programme with disaffected 15-year-olds in which, for an eleven-week period, 'school' was the city. While it was a huge success during its all too brief life, far exceeding the expectations of teachers, students and the director of education, for the latter the potential risks involved had provided too many sleepless nights for the venture to be continued.

Letting students loose in the city on their own initiative on a trust basis was indeed a risky business. Who could have predicted that a disaffected 15-year-old would get himself out of bed to catch an eight o'clock bus to take him forty-five minutes west across the city to Robertson's jam factory where he would put in an eight-hour day, while on the next day travel for over an hour east to study biology in Calderpark Zoo on the very outskirts of the city? Each individual student had his or her own tailor-made week structured around places and events that could be found in the telephone directory and Yellow Pages. For the entire period, these young people never touched down in their school. Their daily timetable took them to learning sites such as hospitals, museums, art galleries, zoos, observatories, hotels, restaurants, department stores, supermarkets, factories, train and bus stations, garages, court houses, police stations, the Ambulance Service, the Automobile Association, the Royal Navy, the Scottish National Orchestra and the Glasgow University Observatory. As in Philadelphia, Rochester and Boston, teachers met with individual students or groups in cafés, parks or in the workplace to discuss, extend and evaluate their learning.

While it was a one-off event never to be repeated in that adventurous form, a great deal had been learned about the initiative, resilience and unseen capabilities of young people and the consequent need to take stock of where failure lay, not in the potential of the young but in the limitations of curriculum and assessment. *The Child in the City*, written by Colin Ward in 1978, offers valuable insights into the nature of intellectual adventuring in urban areas:

> The city is in itself an environmental education, and can be used to provide one, whether we are thinking of learning through the city, learning about the city, learning to use the city, to control the city or to change the city. (p. 3)

Half a century earlier, Henry Morris, Chief Education Officer for Cambridgeshire, began creating village colleges to realise his vision of learning for all in one cultural learning centre. It would, he planned, take all the various vital but isolated activities in village life – the school, the village hall and reading room, the evening classes, the Agricultural Education courses, the Women's Institute, the British Legion, Boy Scouts and Girl Guides, the recreation ground, the branch of the county rural library, the athletic and recreation clubs – and, bringing them together into relation, create a new institution for the English countryside. It would create out of discrete elements an organic whole, in which the whole would be greater than the mere sum of the parts. It would be a true social synthesis – it would take existing and live elements and bring them into a new and unique relationship. The village college, said Morris, would 'provide for the whole man, and abolish the duality of education and ordinary life':

> It would not only be the training ground for the art of living, but the place in which life is lived, the environment of a genuine corporate life. The dismal dispute of vocational and non-vocational education would not arise in it. It would be a visible demonstration in stone of the continuity and never ceasingness of education. There would be no 'leaving school'! – the child would enter at three and leave the college only in extreme old age (Morris, 1925).

The attempt to transfer Morris's rural idyll to a council house scheme on the fringes of Edinburgh may go down in history as a glorious failure – but the creation of the Wester Hailes Education Centre in the late 1970s and its counterparts in Livingston were imaginative attempts in Scotland to transform a school into a learning centre for a whole community. Their essential failing was perhaps in going too far and too fast in trying to realise their transformational vision, failing to meet people's expectations of what a school should look like and what learning should be about.

EXTENDING THE MARKET MODEL

The sixth OECD scenario – Extending the Market Model – suggests a future far removed from the collaborative networked scenario, yet there is a meeting point with the networked society as learning and teaching sites become more diversified. With a more open educational market, it is suggested, new providers would seize opportunities to offer their services, encouraged by fundamental reforms of funding structures, incentives and regulation. This scenario would gain its greatest impetus in countries where schooling is viewed as a private as well as a public good, where the most valued learning is determined by the consumer, by choice and by demand, 'buying' educational services from a variety of competing providers. Such a scenario is bound to run against the grain in Scotland where democratic values, comprehensive schools, equality of access and positive discrimination have long been distinguishing hallmarks of national and local authority policies. As the deschooling scenarios become more probable, however, the challenge for the Scottish educational community will be to attenuate the incursions of a market ideology while daring to 'boldly go' where we haven't gone before.

Sir Ken Robinson, formerly chair of the Blair government's Creativity Committee, offers evidence to support such a contention. Addressing an educational conference in Glasgow in 1999, he confronted the paradox of trying to create the future by doing what we did in the past. A system rooted in the intellectual culture of the enlightenment and the economic circumstances of the industrial revolution has, he argued, built into it a whole set of assumptions about social structure and capacity and an intellectual model of the mind which has long outlived its usefulness – too deeply embedded in the 'gene pool' where the Platonic myth of gold, silver and base metal abilities continues to flourish.

In a study of 1,500 children given tests on divergent thinking, 98 per cent of 5-year-olds scored at 'genius' level. Tested again five years later at 8 to 10, and again at 13 to 15, at each stage their 'genius score' dropped progressively to below 50 per cent. Robinson adds:

> Our children are living in the most intensely stimulating period of the earth. They are being besieged with information and calls for attention from every platform, computers, iPhones, advertising, from hundreds of television channels and we penalise them now for getting distracted, from what? Boring stuff at school. (Robinson, 2010)

MOVING EDUCATIONAL HORIZONS

In travelling towards an educational future we would surely not have started from here, but with the weight of history behind us, what is the path to a future more in tune with a twenty-first-century society? The Futures Forum (Leicester et al., 2009) offers its own scenarios, differing from the OECD models by offering a more process-orientated model of how a system may move from 'business as usual' (akin to the first OECD scenario) to a more visionary future. Three possible 'horizons' are posited by the Futures Forum, comprising 'a useful framework both for understanding the deeper processes of long term societal change, and for designing more effective policy interventions' (p. 3).

The first horizon (H1) is represented by 'standards-based systematic reform'. This highly influential model – 'more of the same but better' – has considerable appeal to politicians and policy makers as its purpose is to get the most out of the system as it exists without disturbing public opinion, vested interests or straying too far from the comfort of 'the way we do things round here'. The consequence is, argue the authors, being condemned to 'go on measuring the wrong things as a misleading proxy for the right ones' (p. 18). As this dissonance becomes more apparent, however, the 'business as usual' model will be gradually superseded by new ways of doing things. So, as the shortcomings of the first horizon system become more and more conspicuous, a second horizon is formed – 'a moving border between past and future'.

The second horizon (H2) is the 'Cinderella zone', struggling for recognition as it moves away from the comfortable familiarity of H1. It will inevitably be judged by the conservative standards of the first horizon and so carries within it inherent risk: 'It is clear that the challenge lies in the transition zone, the second horizon. This is the risky space. It can be chaotic and confusing with so many ideas competing for attention' (p. 26).

In response to threats to the status quo, even if only temporarily, the system will, it is conjectured, respond with a 'capture and extend' scenario in which 'innovations in H2 are mainstreamed' in order to prolong the life of the existing system against the grain of a changing world' (p. 4). To move to the third horizon (H3) – 'the ideal system we desire' – requires a distinction to be made between innovations that are essentially technical, serving to prolong the status quo and those that are transformative and help to bring the third horizon vision closer to reality. H3 represents a 'mature perspective' in which 'we can identify elements in the present that give us encouragement and inspiration' (p. 5), addressing the challenges to the first horizon *and* nurturing. the seeds of the third. There is a need to

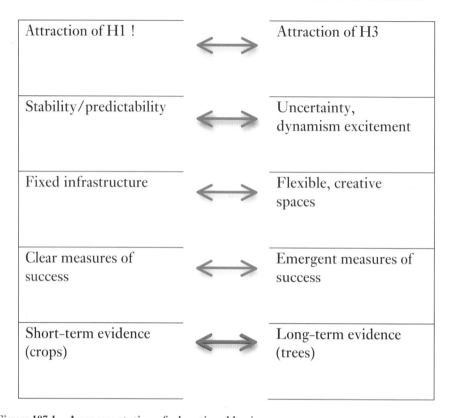

Figure 107.1   A representation of educational horizons

'keep the lights on' today and to find a way of keeping them on a generation from now in very different circumstances' (p. 5).

This is the work of 'pragmatic visionaries', teacher leaders and teacher organisations who understand the nature of the bridge between the present and future, and between the probable and the desirable. It implies knowing where the levers of change lie and how to address both strengths and limitations of the present, and how to play a part in shaping the future.

In Figure 107.1, the essential characteristics of the first and third horizons are depicted while the arrows represent the push and pull that occurs in the second horizon. These both push back to a need for stability while also pushing forward, learning to embrace uncertainty, and holding on to comfortable and familiar measures of success while opening the door to new and more challenging measures.

This movement from H1 to H3 cannot happen, it is argued, as long as there are dichotomies, paradigm wars, claims and counter claims. Pursuing synergy implies a refusal to compromise, getting the best out of both worlds.

The questions it leaves us with are the assumptions that underpin the third horizon – both questions of probability and desirability. To what extent will the future be defined by uncertainty, flexible and creative spaces and on what evidence does such a scenario rest? Is such a future desirable and by whom and in what context?

A THIRD FUTURES VISION

Like the Leicester et al. model, the two-dimensional axis proposed by Jean-Michel Saussois (2009) provides a frame for understanding the processes by which a system moves from status quo to a more desirable future. It confronts a series of questions. What are the internal and external forces that push politicians and policy makers from change to conservation, from vision to survival? International benchmarking? Scarcity of resources? Pressure groups and special interest groups? The recurring demand for back to basics? What forces drive the change from the transformational models towards a more market-orientated system? Political ideology? Parent lobbies? Service providers? Employer groups? Mass media?

Saussois' four quadrants, as seen in Figure 107.2, are defined by a north–south axis from social to individual, and a west–east axis from closed to open. North–south deals with normative contents and expectations about schooling and is labelled the 'value line'. The east–west dimension is the socio-technical aspect of schooling – the 'supply line' – in which the school is considered as a system, closed and held in place by convention or, alternatively, challenged by a more open set of social and economic forces.

From North to South

Schools are embedded within societies that value social and individual orientations differently and place the purposes of schools somewhere between those two extreme poles. To the north, education is socially oriented and schools are aimed at cohesion, equity and reproduction (close to OECD scenario 1). The south is individualistically oriented, with schooling increasingly geared to its clients as individual consumers (OECD scenario 6). These two poles express a range of values as to how people are bound together in social arrangements in which schools are an integral part. The teacher plays an active, if implicit, part in the transmission of values as the school is a key expression of the social fabric.

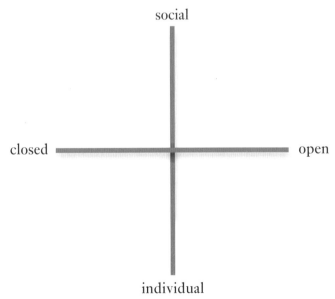

Figure 107.2   Saussois' four quadrants

The individual teacher becomes the provider of services, and parents expect from the school a service delivery to fulfil their child's needs while at the same time meeting the demands of curricular and assessment mandates defined increasingly at an international remove from the classroom. The increasing use of the word 'delivery' in English is symptomatic of a change in the conception of a teacher's authority, as an intermediary 'delivery service' rather than defined morally, socially or within the subject expertise where teachers' authority has traditionally been located.

However, when a global move occurs towards the southern pole of the value line, the institutional authority of the school diminishes and the knowledge authority of the teacher decreases because

> individuals are making decisions and acquiring knowledge through different networks, through newspapers or the television, or the internet. Opinions are formed through informal discussion with parents and friends rather than recourse to an external scientific authority: *my opinion is as worthwhile as the teacher's* (p. 9).

From West to East

The move along the west-to-east axis can be seen as a re-engineering of the central administrative procedures through decentralisation, shifts in decision-making processes, redesigned to accommodate new and differing modes of coordination, workforce remodelling and changes in the recruitment of teachers with differing profiles. These change forces, which impel a more open and market-orientated system, are made possible, argues Saussois, where there are weak teachers' unions, lacking in voice, without public support or lacking the internal solidarity to resist change or propose viable alternatives.

When schools operate as *closed systems* it means they are sufficiently independent as the reference point for what they offer, defined in terms of internal structures, timetables, subjects, standard operating procedures, and distribution of rewards and punishments through specific rules and internal committees. Teachers are certified by their specialised knowledge – knowing why, knowing what and knowing how – the last named being the most difficult to acquire and indicative of a 'good teacher'. Schools' tight integration, coordination and control 'aim to ensure stability, which become ends in themselves rather than means to an end' with concentration on the principles of internal organisational functioning (p. 11).

As schools move towards more *open systems*, there are more ways than one of producing a given outcome. As the variety of demands grow, these have to be matched by a variety of initiatives coming from both the inside and without the constraints of controls from a central authority. Options or electives come less and less from the supply side (that is, teachers deciding what is taught in the discipline they are familiar with) but are determined by stakeholders in a more market-driven system. Teachers are then obliged to shift or widen their role from 'delivery' to collaboration in emerging networks and inter-agency initiatives.

Saussois' thesis offers Scottish teachers a model for collaborative reflection, discussing where their school might be placed within those four quadrants (the actual) and where they would like it to be (the desirable). Such a conversation would inevitably generate a list of obstacles, but perhaps also possibilities, and lead to a consideration of what teachers and school senior leaders might do to make the desirable future happen.

A Scottish headteacher writing about the improvement agenda has urged teachers to challenge the rhetoric, to create a new discourse within and beyond their schools, to be in the vanguard of reinventing schools.

> It is the wrong agenda because the main shift needed is not to 'improve' but to learn in a rapidly changing conditions and circumstances. At such a time we need a new discourse of intrinsic motivation . . . shaping an educational system suitable for a 21st century. (MacKinnon, 2009)

A PLACE CALLED SCHOOL

In all of these hypothetical scenarios, the school plays a role from occupying centre stage at one extreme to a place in the supporting cast on the other. Whether or not knowledge and skills may be gained in sites other than school, the powerful social and moral role of schooling should not be omitted from the equation. In Von Hentig's series of letters from a kindly uncle to his nephew Tobias, he mounts a series of arguments explaining why Tobias should attend school. Perhaps the most powerful of these is the social and moral case.

> In school, you meet people different from yourself from different backgrounds, children you can observe, talk to, ask questions, for example, someone from Turkey or Vietnam, a devout Catholic or an out-and-out atheist, boys and girls, a mathematical whiz kid, a child in a wheelchair . . . I believe wholeheartedly that the open school is there first and foremost to bring young people together and to help them to learn to live in a way that our political society so badly needs. (Von Hentig, 1995, p. 47)

This argument for school as a critical social, moral and political agency does, of course, rest on a vision and purpose that teachers and students may strive to keep alive in the face of reductionist policies and competitive pressures. Such a future may defy the most beautifully designed models and most learned predictions.

The three scenarios from the OECD, the Scottish Futures Forum and the Saussois matrix are all speculative as to futures that are more or less likely and more or less desirable but beg the question of how we might get there from here. While it is the Scottish Futures Forum that addresses the issue of change, moving the horizon of thinking and doing is a daunting challenge. A recent Scottish study (MacBeath et al., 2009) sheds light on the power of the status quo and the phenomenon of 'lock in' where each component of the machine is so interlocked that it is impossible to move without the risk of meltdown.

The 2009 study revealed that, in many respects, 'lock in' is more in evidence in Scotland than in some other countries because of the vaunted 'vertical relationship' of schools, local authorities and national government. This is both a strength and a weakness of the system. Its strength is in tempering the worst excesses of a market system in which schools compete, sometimes ruthlessly and unethically, for customers. Its weakness is in constraining initiative and innovation.

In interviews with Scottish heads there were descriptions of 'walking the tightrope of complex and multiple accountabilities'. One third of Scottish headteachers surveyed claimed that they had 'very little autonomy'. Nearly half (45 per cent) agreed that they had 'some autonomy'. References were made to the proportion of time spent in reacting to a 'constant stream' of authority requests, 'serving the bureaucracy'. 'You [the local authority] are there to service me, not the other way round', said one head who talked about the 'fault line' between school and local authority priorities. It was in respect of accountability that the fault line appeared most acutely, and was described as 'one way traffic' of pressure down and accountability up. While internal accountability to staff, and to pupils and their parents was keenly felt and positively embraced, being held accountable 'for criteria not your own' was widely regarded as disempowering. For a newly appointed head continually 'watching your back' was described as a new and 'scary' experience, and in tension with the immediate and 'direct accountability' to pupils and staff.

As one secondary headteacher put it: 'You spend most of your time reacting', describing the range of reviews and inspections including biannual performance review, mid-cycle inspections, intensive local authority pre-inspection quality assurance visits, unannounced Care Commission visits, hygiene inspections, health and safety inspections and fire inspections, for which she had to undertake two days of training out of school. Lack of opportunity to innovate was inhibited by requirements to use authority-designated suppliers, for example, who could be expensive, inefficient and slow to respond. What were seen as spurious health and safety and 'political correctness' issues could, it was said, simply hamper efforts to implement change. The 'bureaucratic ceiling', the burden of directives from above and the concomitant lack of latitude for decision making were widely shared sources of frustration, described by more than one head as evidence of 'managing not leading'.

A few headteachers interviewed had had experience of headship in other countries, including England. These heads made unfavourable comparisons with the scope and flexibility they believed they enjoyed there to innovate and to solve problems without having to seek permission for what were seen as trivial matters – such as fixing a broken window, painting over graffiti, planting daffodils, changing in-service days or departing from a standardised authority PowerPoint presentation. The interplay among those three loci of decision making in Scotland – school, local authority and government – was where 'dutiful compliance' and 'assertive rule breaking' met and where adventurous headteachers and leading-edge local authorities were able to look ahead rather than in the rear-view mirror.

IN PRAISE OF RULE BREAKING

'Every rule is an arbitrary border waiting to be crossed by adventurous people'. This aphorism from an anonymous author (The Mafia Manager, V, 1996) captures the essence of a category of heads who were self-confessed risk-takers and rule-breakers. They were happy to go their own way in full knowledge of the risks and consequences of what they could and could not get away with. They thrived on challenges with a belief that, whatever the problems they confronted, they were unfazed by those in positions of authority external to their schools. There was a sense of fulfilment in rising to the challenge and expressing deeply held educational values. The latitude for going your own way depended to some extent on a weighing up of permission and sanction, and being 'brave enough', as one headteacher put it, to navigate around the structures and strictures. 'I like to sail pretty close to the wind' said one highly experienced primary head who confessed to deploying a range of subversive strategies developed over a lifetime in headship. There was a regretful note of counsel for their employers: 'It would be nice to have greater bravery by the local authority'.

'Rules are for fools,' says one of Scotland's most successful entrepreneurs, Chris Van der Kuyl, quoted in *GC* magazine as saying 'All successful entrepreneurs have broken the rules of their business'. Of Winston Churchill it was said, 'He was a young man in a hurry who always broke the rules. That was the secret behind his greatness' (Roberts, 1994). The name Rosa Parks may be forgotten but her decision to sit in a whites-only Memphis bus seat sparked a year-long boycott and was a catalyst for the civil rights movement in America.

It raises the question of whether schools' obsession with rules is actually counterproductive to initiative, to learning and to leadership. From the earliest encounter with school and with 'the way we do things round here', conformity has become the most valued property of the school and of the educational system, and the greatest brake on 'futures thinking'. Avolio and colleagues write:

> Breaking rules is in our view critical to how the child develops a sense of agency for doing what is not only expected later in life, but also going beyond expectations to do what the individual believes is right. We suggest these experiences will predict ascension into leadership roles later in life above and beyond one's personality and heritability'. (Avolio et al., 2009)

LOOKING IN THE WRONG PLACES

There is an apocryphal story of the drunk man looking for his keys under the lamppost, not near to where he actually dropped them but because that was where the light was. Policy solutions have consistently looked in the wrong place, to more testing, more targets, more, earlier, and longer time in the classroom and increased pressure.

> If the way we think of change is limited by imagining things very much like the ones we know (even if 'better'), or by confining ourselves to doing what we know how to implement, then we deprive ourselves of participation in the evolution of the future. It will creep up on us and take us unawares. (Papert, 2002)

Those words, written a decade ago, are a reminder of the limitations and sterility of so much education policy. They are also a reminder of the disjunction between the context of classroom teaching and contexts of growing up, between the desirable and the probable. David Hargreaves' counsel to school leaders and to classroom teachers to learn to 'fly below the radar' – with a little help from their friends – is where the journey from the past to the future begins.

REFERENCES

Avolio, B. J., M. Rotundo and F. O. Walumbwa (2009) 'Early life experiences as determinants of leadership role occupancy: The importance of parental influence and rule breaking behavior', *The Leadership Quarterly*, 20 (3): 329–42.

Leicester, G., K. Bloomer and D. Stewart (2009) *Transformative Innovation In Education: A Playbook for Pragmatic Visionaries*, International Futures Forum, Triarchic Press Ltd. See at http://triarchypress.co.uk/pages/book21.htm

MacBeath, J., P. Gronn, D. Opfer, K. Louden, C. Forde, M. Cowie and J. O'Brien (2009) *The Recruitment and Retention of Headteachers in Scotland*. Edinburgh: Scottish Executive.

MacKinnon, N. (2009) 'Inspection at the end of time: The need for a new lexicon, ethos and method of school evaluation'. Unpublished paper (July 2009).

Morris, H. (1925) *The Village College. Being a Memorandum on the Provision of Educations and Social Facilities for the Countryside, with Special Reference to Cambridgeshire*. Cambridge: Cambridge University Press.

Organisation for Economic Cooperation and Development, Centre for Educational Research and Innovation (CERI) *The OECD Schooling Scenarios*. Online at www.oecd.org/document/10/0,37 46,en_2649_39263231_2078922_1_1_1_1,00.html

Papert, S. (2002) *The Children's Machine: Rethinking Schools in the Age of the Computer*. New York: Basic Books.

Roberts, A. (1994) *Eminent Churchillians*. London: Weidenfeld & Nicolson.

Robinson, K. (2010) 'Changing education paradigms'. Lecture to the Royal Society for the Encouragement of Arts (January 2010).

Saussois, J. (2009) 'Scenarios, international comparisons, and key variables for educational scenario analysis', in B. Hoffman, E. S. Mardis and A. Marcia, *A Decade of Promises: Discourses on Twenty-first-Century Schools Policy and Research*, Baltimore, MD: Johns Hopkins University Press.

Von Hentig, H. (1995) *Warum muss ich in die Schule gehen?*, Berlin: dtv-Taschenbücher.

108

The Future of Colleges in Scotland

Craig Thomson

As colleges in Scotland moved into the second decade of the twenty-first century, they found themselves at the centre of a significant programme of reform. Elsewhere in this volume, in Chapter 7, the beginning of the 2012–13 academic year was described as a key time in this journey. It was at that point that colleges reached a watershed. An era of continuous development stretching back for two decades came to an end. Radical change began based on reform proposals that had been debated, discussed and planned for some time. As these wide reforms to the purpose, structure and operation of the sector began to be implemented, colleges were already working in a turbulent context and facing significant challenges. In particular, these resulted from the changing and intensifying requirements of learners and government in a period of serious economic downturn. Associated with this downturn, deep cuts in government funding continued to be implemented.

This chapter takes the watershed as a point from which to look into the future and to endeavour to anticipate the sector that will develop as challenges are faced and significant change unfolds. This includes reflection on the structure and funding of the college sector and the development of the wider tertiary system in Scotland. Rather than simply using this as an opportunity to compare a past that has already been described in this volume with a future that is, at best, uncertain, the opportunity is also taken to consider the general direction of change in the wider international context.

THE DIRECTION OF CHANGE

The main driver of significant change at the time of the watershed was the proposals set out in *Putting Learners at the Centre: Delivering Our Ambitions for Post-16 Education* (hereafter referred to as PLC), a Scottish Government policy consultation document published in the second half of 2011 (Scottish Government, 2011). Following the conclusion of a three-month consultation exercise and the unfolding of a parallel review of governance (Scottish Government, 2012a) the Scottish Government put forward plans for the reshaping of the sector (Scottish Government, 2012b). These were set within the context of wider change to the full post-16 sector, the stated objective of the reform programme. However, the focus of reform was firmly on the college sector. It was here that reform would be most wide-reaching and change would be most fundamental.

THE REFORM PROPOSALS

Following consideration of the responses to the PLC consultation, the main strands of reform were presented in a parliamentary statement (Scottish Parliament, 2012) as:

- regionalisation;
- redistribution of funding according to need;
- a move to funding based on outcome agreements;
- additional focus on the needs of learners;
- clearer pathways and links between different parts of the post-16 system;
- the development of stronger partnerships between schools, colleges, community learning and development, universities and business;
- an enhanced role for the Scottish Credit and Qualifications Framework (SCQF);
- more sophisticated arrangements to enable learners to pursue non-linear pathways;
- improved articulation;
- fair and affordable support arrangements;
- local discretion of colleges to deliver tailored support and to improve support for part-time learners;
- recognition and development of part-time learning;
- revised, collaborative knowledge exchange arrangements;
- strong and purposeful partnership working.

In considering the future development of the college sector towards 2020, the main lines of intended change can be drawn from these points. Table 108.1 focuses on the six that are most likely to shape the sector as it moves through the middle of the decade. The remainder of this chapter considers each in turn.

In focusing on these points it is important to emphasise that while these will drive key elements of reform in the sector, this will unfold in a wider context of change. In particular, the broad economic and resulting financial context within which the college sector will develop will be a challenging one. The economy and the labour markets that will emerge as the UK moves out of a period of zero and low economic growth will be different from those in place when recession began to bite in 2009 and 2010. As the economy shifts and develops, the college sector will respond. The most predictable changes associated with this include a shift at the margins from full-time to part-time programmes through the middle of the decade as the economy recovers. This will repeat the experience of the sector as the UK economy emerged from recession in the 1980s and in the 1990s. Also, as labour markets tighten, demands will be placed on colleges to help marginal groups re-enter the workforce. As part of this, as the economy moves forward, colleges will find themselves charged with helping those left behind, in particular those who failed to find work during the period of severe economic difficulty.

This is familiar territory, part of the corporate memory of the college sector. Colleges will change and flex as they meet these challenges. However, achieving this will prove more difficult than in previous post-recession periods. The changes discussed under the six headings in Table 108.1 will take place in a period in which public funding available for colleges is severely restricted. Public spending is unlikely to be reinstated to the levels experienced in the first decade of the century. Colleges will continue to experience severe financial pressures and, if the spending trajectory in place at the time of the watershed remains in place, they will find themselves having to operate as the poor relation in Scotland's educational family. The Cinderella sector will be back in the kitchen.

Table 108.1   The future of colleges in Scotland: Six drivers of change

Structure	Implementation of regionalisation
Funding	A move to funding based on outcome agreements and inter-regional redistribution of funding
Learner focus	The development of clearer 'learner journeys' and additional focus on the needs of learners
Coherence	The development of a more straightforward and coherent post-16 system
Autonomy	Organisational and educational autonomy
Partnership	Strong and purposeful partnership working

STRUCTURE

The structure being planned and brought into place at the watershed as the 2012–13 session began was quite different from that which had been in place during the era described in Chapter 7. Previously, the dominant structural unit was the individual incorporated college with the number of units remaining at just over forty throughout the 1993–2012 period (albeit configured in slightly different ways). Under the new arrangements, the dominant unit became the region. Changes underway or in prospect at the time made it likely that the sector would move into the medium- and longer-term future with a national structure based on around twelve regional units.

As the implementation of serious reform began, merger plans were well under way in a number of regions, and large regional colleges were being created. However, in other regions, plans stopped short of merging all of the colleges in the area into a single corporate entity. Largest among the mergers, three colleges in Edinburgh came together formally early in the 2012–13 academic year to create a single unit. Merger was also moving towards conclusion in the west region. In Glasgow, while merger plans were being taken forward, the aim was to produce larger units in the Glasgow region but not a single unit at that stage. The intention was that Glasgow region should retain three 'sub-regional' colleges. Other regions such as Lanarkshire also envisaged a future in which elements of sub-regional college autonomy would be retained.

Despite this variation in approach and the vigorous debate taking place at the time, it was clear that it was the region that would become the primary unit. Indeed those colleges that held onto their independence in the early stages of regionalisation could be viewed as embracing an illusion. As this new world began to unfold, the political tide was running in favour of single regional colleges and it was clear that merger into single college regions would ultimately be the order of the day for many if not all regions. It would be the role of the region, for example, to enter into a regional outcome agreement with the Scottish Funding Council (SFC). This would define the priorities and outcomes to be delivered either by the single regional college or by the several colleges in the region.

It would be at regional level that planning would take place and decisions would be made on the distribution of funding. It was here that the key point of accountability to and through the SFC would be located. As part of this, decisions would also be taken at regional level on the overall location of courses; the ways in which resources should be deployed to achieve effectiveness; and, very importantly at the time, how colleges would deliver the significant efficiencies and cost reduction required by government. Furthermore, it was

Table 108.2   Planned regions and the subordinate colleges

	Region	Subordinate college(s)
Major regions	Aberdeen and Aberdeenshire	Aberdeen and Banff and Buchan Colleges
	Ayrshire	Ayr, Kilmarnock plus James Watt College (Kilwinning Campus)
	Central	Forth Valley
	Edinburgh	Jewel and Esk, Stevenson and Telford Colleges
	Fife	Adam Smith and Carnegie Colleges, and the non land-based provision at Elmwood College
	Glasgow	Anniesland, North Glasgow, Stow, John Wheatley, Cardonald, Langside, City of Glasgow
	Lanarkshire	Coatbridge, Cumbernauld, Motherwell and South Lanarkshire Colleges
	Tayside	Dundee & Angus Colleges
	West	Reid Kerr and Clydebank Colleges, and the James Watt College (Inverclyde Campus)
Minor regions	Dumfries and Galloway	Dumfries and Galloway College
	Borders	Borders College
	West Lothian	West Lothian College
Special region	Highlands and Islands	Perth, Lews Castle, Orkney, Shetland, Inverness, Moray, North Highland, Argyll and West Highland Colleges

at regional level that the college sector would forge its most important partnerships with employers, community planning partners and others.

Table 108.2 shows the planned regions and the subordinate colleges in each at the time of the watershed. This shape suggested that, with the possible exception of Glasgow Region, all major regions would move to single-college status by the second half of the decade. Future arrangements for the three minor regions created as a result of geography and political expediency were less clear. However, if these were to continue as separate entities, strong alignment with larger neighbours would be required.

The colleges making up the University of the Highlands and Islands (UHI) offered a continuing anomaly. On the one hand, drawing further education provision more closely into the UHI offered a possible test bed for the creation of a dual-sector, comprehensive tertiary institution encompassing both further and higher education. On the other hand, development of college provision in uneasy alignment with an institution embracing a purer university model would threaten to leave further education as a subordinate or feeder element of its work.

FUNDING

From the point of the watershed, arrangements were progressively brought in by the SFC to distribute funding to colleges through the regional body. The basis for this was outcome agreements setting out the activities that would be undertaken. While the focus was primarily on the region, regional bodies were also asked to include description of their contribution to nationally agreed outcomes. Implementation in 2012–13 included delivering the

Table 108.3   The SFC's five regional outcomes

1	Efficient regional structures	To deliver efficient regional structures to meet the needs of the region
2	Right learning in the right place	To contribute to meeting the national guarantee for young people, meeting the demands of the region, and where appropriate the nation
3	High quality and efficient learning	To ensure that learners are qualified to progress through the system in both an efficient and a flexible manner
4	A developed workforce	To ensure learners are qualified and prepared for work and to improve and adapt the skills of the regional workforce
5	Sustainable institutions	To secure, well-managed and financially and environmentally sustainable colleges

changes required to move regionalisation of the sector to the next stage. The five regional outcomes defined by the SFC for 2012–13 are shown in Table 108.3.

In effect, outcome agreements were framed across these areas based on measurable objectives stretching from the macro to the micro. They included targets for high-level structural change including college mergers. They also specified targets for improvements in key performance indicators to do with completion and achievement; articulation to university; and volume of engagement with schools.

In defining the nature and purpose of outcome agreements, SFC guidance also took the first steps in the development of a narrower and more prescriptive specification of the role and purpose of colleges (a point that had been central to the debate around the reform proposals). Guidance on the implementation of outcome agreements made it clear that the primary role of colleges was to meet the needs of a particular region; to be able to demonstrate return on SFC/Scottish Government investment; and to meet regional vocational education and training needs. The voice of employers should be listened to closely and the needs of the economy considered carefully, ensuring that there was adequate supply of appropriate labour for the region.

The SFC also specified that, in fulfilling this purpose, colleges should be able to demonstrate that their work and outcomes were complementary to those of other stakeholders including Skills Development Scotland (SDS), Scotland's Enterprise Network and Community Planning Partnerships (CPP). In particular, closer alignment with SDS appeared to be strongly in prospect and the future was one in which colleges would be involved in deeper engagement including joint planning with, or as part of, CPPs.

The SFC also indicated that outcome agreements would cover three years but that within this period performance would be reviewed annually with the outcome of reviews used to determine future funding. It was clear that funding mechanisms for colleges were going to change fundamentally, with decisions on the distribution and redistribution of funding to regions and between regions, strongly controlled by SFC management, as opposed to adhering to a universally applied model as had been the case over the previous two decades.

In addition to making it clear that colleges were moving into a more centrally controlled future, this set of arrangements and requirements helped to highlight the fact that the future would not necessarily free them from the complexities of the past. The intention of the reform proposals had been that the role and lines of accountability of colleges should be clearer and more coherent. However, as colleges moved through the second decade of the twenty-first century it was much more likely that their position would continue to be characterised by ambiguity as they endeavoured to balance priorities and to face in several directions at once reaching out regionally towards CPPs; nationally towards a managerial SFC; and both regionally and nationally towards employers and other powerful stakeholder groups.

LEARNER FOCUS

In the early stages of discussion and development of the programme of reform to the college sector, debate around achieving greater learner focus was imprecise and unhelpful. Strong statements from politicians and policy makers about the need for greater learner focus can be argued to have lacked substance and, of more concern to the sector, to have been used as lightly coded proxy attacks on colleges for acting as self-serving institutions. Fortunately, these early skirmishes were relatively quickly replaced by a more helpful debate around how the concept of learner focus should be understood and what could be done on a practical level to improve the experience of learners making their way through Scotland's complex and often confusing post-16 education system.

A central element of this was consideration of 'the learner journey' with the challenge being to make it easier for learners to enter and move through the system successfully. It is here that the main areas of change to this aspect of the work of colleges began to coalesce. Five core areas of change can be identified that will continue to shape the work of the college sector and the context within which it operates in the period towards 2020:

- information, advice and guidance;
- qualifications;
- articulation from college to university;
- transition from school to college;
- learner engagement.

The first of these, information, advice and guidance (IAG), had been in a period of almost continuous change and uncertainty for well over a decade. The service had moved from local authority control to operation as autonomous 'careers companies', had then shifted to 'alignment' with Scottish Enterprise, before completing its migration and becoming part of SDS. As part of this, the various elements of the service (careers guidance in schools, engagement with colleges and the provision of adult guidance) had all been subject to major change.

The emergence of regional colleges in the first half of the decade can be viewed as likely to have a positive impact in this area through, for example, clearer and broader partnerships with SDS at regional and national level. This should improve consistency in the ways in which IAG are understood and delivered. The way in which these developments play out in colleges will be shaped by two key factors. First, Curriculum for Excellence (CfE) will increasingly frame understanding of the content and purpose of the curriculum in, and at the interface between, schools and colleges. Skills for Learning, Skills for Life and Skills for Work are central to this. Second, the Scottish Government IAG strategy (Scottish Government, 2011) will shape the understanding of how IAG is delivered across the post-16 landscape, with the majority of learners managing their own engagement with information and advice while more intensive, face-to-face support is made available to those requiring specific help.

As wider reform unfolds, changes and developments in qualifications are going to play an important part in shaping the future for colleges. This will be important both at colleges' points of interaction with other parts of Scotland's post-16 sector and also, fundamentally, at the core of their operations, helping to define the role that they play and the ways in which they operate.

In a very challenging period, colleges will continue work to develop their programmes and to ensure that qualifications remain relevant and also to assess and recognise achievement appropriately. This will be underpinned by the SCQF and by the development of new units in literacy and numeracy which will transcend specific vocational programmes and will also play an important part in enabling seamless progression for learners.

As colleges move through the middle of the decade, a number of lines of change to qualifications are likely to prove particularly important in defining the future. In particular, the final stages of the implementation of new qualifications in support of CfE, review of the non-advanced qualifications offered by colleges and changes to the apprenticeship system will all have an impact. The development of self-validation and awarding powers for colleges is also likely to emerge from the middle of the decade as regional colleges gain confidence and turn their attention to the ownership and costs associated with their qualifications.

In addition to shaping the understanding of the purpose of the curriculum, changes associated with CfE will alter the nature of the qualifications presented and the skills and expectations of learners at the point of transition from school to college. This will be most evident in the first half of the decade. The final diet of Standard Grade examinations will take place in the early summer of 2013 and will be followed two years later by the end of Intermediate 1 and 2, Higher and Advanced Higher qualifications. In their place, from 2013–14 learners in schools and in colleges will be preparing for and taking National 4 and 5 qualifications (at SCQF levels 4 and 5) and, from 2014–15, Revised Highers (effectively National 6).

In parallel with these changes, from around the middle of the decade, it is likely that developments in the apprenticeship system and the customisation of qualifications by colleges (as they assert control over these) will lead to further variations in the location of learning with more workplace or work-based learning in evidence. This point is touched on further, in the section on college autonomy, in later stages of this chapter.

The role of colleges in the provision of higher education in Scotland is covered in some detail in Chapter 7. An important element of this is articulation from college to university. This will continue to be a major issue as regional colleges develop and as other aspects of the reform programme are managed into place. An intensifying focus on flexible learning and part-time study will increase the importance placed on the delivery of higher education in colleges, particularly at SCQF levels 7 and 8. In parallel, work will continue to improve articulation from higher education courses in colleges into degree-level study in university. The size of the larger regional colleges will help to introduce more parity into the relationship between colleges and universities. The wider scope of operation of regional colleges should help to move the Scottish post-16 system onto a landscape characterised by large-scale regional and national articulation arrangements as opposed to relying in large part (as was the case at the time of the watershed) on narrow faculty-to-faculty or course-to-course agreements.

Changes associated with CfE have the potential to help to smooth transition from school to college. While CfE has at times proved a controversial development in schools, colleges tended to embrace it more enthusiastically and more easily given the consistency of large elements of CfE with practice already in place in the college sector. The development of a deeper shared understanding of the curriculum between schools and colleges and the revision of qualifications will help to remove some of the barriers or inconsistencies experienced by learners as they move through an important and often difficult transition from one sector to the other.

On a very practical level, the further development and implementation of Skills for Work programmes and qualifications and the wider delivery of college programmes in schools will also help to bring the two sectors closer together. However, as colleges move towards and through the middle of the decade, overlap with schools at SCQF levels 5, 6 and 7 will continue and, more broadly in the post-16 debate, the question of the purpose of year 6 in Scotland's secondary sector will remain.

The period leading up to and through the reform programme was one in which learner engagement enjoyed a high profile. In particular, planning and delivery of programmes increasingly involved consideration of ways in which learners could and should be able to influence their learning experience. Reviews of colleges by HMIE paid close attention to this point. As colleges change and develop through the reform period, the influence and scope of this will increase and extend significantly. In addition to influencing the development and delivery of courses and programmes, student input will play a part in the wider (including strategic) development of colleges. Student associations will be funded more generously and will also experience economies of scale as part of larger institutions. This will help them to develop the expertise and capacity required to engage more successfully as autonomous and sustainable elements of the college landscape.

COHERENCE

The move to a regional structure can be viewed as central to the objectives of the reform programme and the creation of a more coherent post-16 education system in Scotland. This is one of the keys to achieving clearer, more straightforward learner journeys. However, it is open to question whether radical change in one part of the post-16 structural terrain will be sufficient to achieve overall coherence and clarity. Further action involving the university sector and other parts of the post-16 landscape will also be required. Unfortunately, despite suggestion on the part of policy makers that they have an appetite for this wider agenda, the early stages of reform were almost exclusively focused on the college sector.

In reflecting on whether comprehensive change in Scotland is likely, it is worth considering international trends in this area. These do not provide grounds for optimism. Indeed, taking this perspective tends to suggest that Scotland's overall post-16 or tertiary system will remain complex and multi-faceted. In making international comparisons, an element of caution is necessary. The language of debate in Scotland includes all of post-school education under the 'tertiary' heading. However, international definitions would tend to view the work of colleges as being split between 'upper secondary provision' (most further education in colleges) and tertiary provision (largely the higher education work that colleges carry out). For the purpose of this chapter, Scotland's college sector is argued to be most appropriately viewed through the tertiary lens, given that the broad context of the PLC changes is presented by government as one that does encompass all of tertiary education.

This position can also be accommodated by viewing tertiary education in Scotland as being composed of three 'tiers', in contrast to countries with less diverse systems based on unitary or binary systems. In the former, all or the great majority of provision is concentrated in universities while in the latter, non-university institutions play important roles.

In spite of the abolition of the formal divide between universities and what were formally known as central (polytechnic equivalent) institutions, the divide remains in Scotland between older/higher status (tier 1) and newer (tier 2) universities with the latter group characterised by less orientation towards research and by lower research funding and overall levels of wealth. Colleges make up tier 3, and the primary point of articulation from college to university is from tier 3 to tier 2. As tertiary education in Scotland moves towards 2020, issues of equity and parity will remain with learner journeys on Scotland's tertiary train line, remaining subject to first-, second- and third-class travel.

Patterns of provision in other parts of the world suggest that this is a deep-seated and widely applied model with issues of equity and fairness in funding for students and institutions generally set to one side as the tertiary train moves on. Looking around the world, Australia can be identified as hosting a similar system to Scotland with a top tier made up of the 'Group of Eight' research-intensive universities while a second is composed of less prestigious universities. The third tier in Australia is made up of Technical and Further Education (TAFE) institutions which perform a role that is roughly equivalent to colleges in Scotland. In the USA, community colleges make up tier three of a basic three-tier structure with elite and less prestigious universities making up each of the other two (internally diverse) tiers.

Generally, the move internationally appears to be towards more diversity and an increase to or towards three tiers. This has been apparent in, for example, the Scandinavian countries where the largely unitary systems in Sweden and Denmark have shifted at the margins. Advanced vocational training (*kvalificerad yrkesutbildning*) courses have been increasingly offered in second- and third-tier institutions including vocational colleges. In Denmark, technical institutions can be viewed as covering tiers two and three, as do Norway's university colleges, Finland's polytechnics and the *Hogescholen* (technical institutions) in the Netherlands.

Both history and international comparisons make it clear that coherence is never going to be achieved by way of a move to a single system or single tier of tertiary institutions. The focus therefore has to be on arrangements at the margins at points of articulation and transfer of students and credit between tiers. It is here, in the area of articulation, that most stands to be gained in terms of simplification and support for learner journeys. This highlights the importance of the role that the SCQF will play in the future of colleges and of tertiary education and, associated with this, the importance to colleges of the range and coherence of the qualifications that they offer.

AUTONOMY

Institutional autonomy was one of the most closely guarded aspects of the college sector in the twenty-year period from incorporation in 1993 to the watershed at the start of the 2012–13 academic year. The return to a model based on more central control was a clear and explicit part of the programme of reform. The implementation of a regional structure and increased levels of intervention from the SFC provided the broadest and most fundamental indication of this. Also on a broad scale, changes were ushered in to governance arrangements making it clear that the levers of power rested firmly at the centre. Other smaller but significant changes included the stated intention to move control of capital projects more into the direct control of the SFC and to establish a national forum through which 'the Scottish Government . . . would drive the sector forward and constantly review and evolve the sector in terms of fitness for purpose in a changing educational and economic world' (Scottish Government, 2012).

The extent to which the strong tightening of central control is a permanent change will become apparent as colleges move through the middle of the decade towards 2020. On the one hand, very strong central control can be viewed as a necessary but temporary position allowing fundamental reorientation of the sector to be managed into place quickly and effectively. Within this view, central control will be gradually relaxed in the middle of the decade as tested and trusted arrangements and relationships develop. On the other hand, the move to tight central control can be interpreted within a model apparent at Westminster and Holyrood for some time in which ministers take more direct control of significant elements of government activity. In this view, the tightening of the central grip is unlikely to be reversed in the foreseeable future.

Changes to autonomy are also likely to unfold in other, more specific aspects of college activity as larger regional colleges gain confidence and exert their influence. This is likely to lead to an increase in the educational freedoms that they enjoy as they assume more control over the qualifications that they offer and the systems within which they assess and improve the quality of their work. Relationships with employers and the economy are likely to prove particularly influential in framing the context within which colleges assume more control of the range and level of the courses and qualifications offered.

This will play out in part through developments in work-based and closely work-related programmes. As part of the reform agenda, it was announced that the apprenticeship landscape would change, with new Technical Apprenticeships being brought in at levels 8 and 9 and Professional Apprenticeships being introduced at level 10 (Scottish Government, 2012b). The titles of these awards will no doubt be subject to debate. However, the general intention is clear and, although changes associated with this are likely to be delayed by the sheer volume of activity in the early stages of reform, it is likely that activity in this area will begin in the 2013–14 academic year.

This part of the reform agenda has the potential to change the relationship between colleges and apprenticeships with more of the learning involved being located in the college sector based on improved and extended relationships between colleges and employers. It will have the potential to develop relationships between colleges and private-sector providers as colleges move through a period in which larger elements of vocational education shift to private providers and successful private/public alliances become increasingly important.

Although Skills Development Scotland is likely to hold the reins on these changes in the short term, opportunities will develop for colleges increasingly to work more directly with employers in shaping and delivering these qualifications. By the middle of the decade, a landscape populated by around a dozen large regional institutions will offer fertile ground for strategic alliances between employers and colleges at regional, national and UK levels.

PARTNERSHIP

The need to improve and extend partnerships has been part of the rhetoric of the public sector in Scotland for some considerable time with CPPs firmly established as the main model within which aspirations in this area have been pursued. Two elements of the Scottish Government description of CPPs (Scottish Government, 2010) provide a clear indication of how new regional colleges will find their place in Scotland's public-sector landscape. The first of these describes community planning as the mechanism at regional level which should provide 'the key over-arching partnership framework helping to co-ordinate other initiatives and partnerships and where necessary acting to rationalise and simplify a cluttered landscape'. The second describes how community planning is intended to 'improve the connection between national priorities and those at regional, local and neighbourhood levels'.

It is at the CPP table that regional colleges will increasingly determine their priorities and plans in conjunction with health boards, local authorities, the voluntary sector and other players. This will also help to frame the context in which they manage other key partnerships with employers and with local communities. As indicated in the previous section, partnerships with employers will be critical to the future success of the college sector. In the case of local communities, specific groups will be established separately by colleges, in conjunction with other public-sector partners and, critically, in conjunction with the voluntary sector, to ensure that local communities have formal lines of input and influence in the development of college strategy and engagement in college activities.

CONCLUSION

The second decade of the twenty-first century is a time of change and challenge for colleges in Scotland. In addition to dealing with the ebbs and flows of the economy and the associated needs of individuals and communities, colleges have embarked on a major period of reform. As the decade progresses, the economy, governments and key players in and around the sector will all be subject to change. However, the momentum of reform will continue.

On the one hand, the sector will continue to be shaped by reform as it is propelled towards 2020 in a revised structure and working within different governance, management and general operating arrangements. On the other, colleges will be characterised by strong points of continuity as underlying values to do with access, equity and opportunity are sustained and as work goes on in classrooms, workshops, labs and learning centres.

REFERENCES

Scottish Government (2010) 'Public sector reform'. Online at www.scotland.gov.uk/Topics/Government/PublicServiceReform

Scottish Government (2011) 'Career information, advice and guidance in Scotland. A framework for service redesign and improvement'. Edinburgh: Scottish Government.

Scottish Government (2012a) 'Report of the review of further education governance in Scotland'. Edinburgh: Scottish Government.

Scottish Government (2012b) 'Reinvigorating college governance: The Scottish Government response to the report of the review of further education governance in Scotland'. Edinburgh: Scottish Government.

Scottish Parliament (2012) *Official Report Debate Contributions: Meeting of the Parliament 29 February 2012*. Edinburgh: Scottish Parliament.

109

The Future of Higher Education

James C. Conroy and Anton Muscatelli

Ex Umbris et imaginibus in veritatem

These words, translated as 'out of the shadows and phantasms into the truth', are inscribed on the tomb of John Henry Newman, perhaps the most articulate proponent of the modern 'idea' of the university. Newman wished these thoughts to be so written as a testament to the enduring claim that the university is, at its very core, centrally concerned with the search for truth. In a world much changed from that experienced and, no doubt, envisaged by Newman, such a sentiment may seem out of place in the contemporary university. However, as we shall suggest, the future of Scottish higher education is ineluctably tied to such a claim precisely because universities differ in important respects from a wide range of public and private institutions that might rely on, or be devoted to, the production of knowledge or its manifold and complex uses.

To answer the question, 'What is the future of Scottish higher education?' entails some speculation given the substantial uncertainty that surrounds the evolution of institutions of higher education not only in Scotland and the UK but internationally. The challenges include, but are not exhausted by shifts in the balance of power (away from Europe and North America and towards a much wider distribution of economic and cultural goods); changes to funding mechanisms; growing numbers of countries teaching undergraduate and postgraduate programmes in English; continuing debates about the balance of private and public benefit; the professional advantages to be accrued from entering higher education; and increasing, often conflicted, forms of internal and external accountability.

The challenges that lie before Scottish education are substantial and the threats significant but without some continuity with the historic entailments of a university, as evinced not only in Newman's epitaph but in his totemic claims to a liberal education, in 'The Idea of the University', it may be hard to discern what distinctive resources a university brings to civic society. If no such continuity exists then it might well be difficult to know what would distinguish the activities of the university from other social practices such as training centres, consultancies, think tanks, research institutes and the like; organisations that might just as easily be private and for profit as public and charitable. It is perfectly possible, indeed in some circumstances it may be highly desirable, that all kinds of organisations carry out particular knowledge generation and use functions in economies which, like Scotland, increasingly consider themselves to be dependent on the generation of utility knowledge. But, as we shall suggest below, that they should and, increasingly, will do so, opens up some fairly demanding territory for Scottish universities.

While there may be overlap across civic (public and private) institutions, universities are uniquely required, and in a position, to cast all their activities against the backdrop of the search for truth. Universities do occupy quite distinctive terrain from other kinds of knowledge producers. The university is required to attend to the meaning of scientific, social, economic and cultural activities. Students may well enter universities in search of certain positional advantages that arise from the acquisition of professional qualifications, or from the acquisition of cultural capital, or from the developed capacity to read the contents and meanings of the world more effectively. In addition, however, the twenty-first-century university remains a space where students come to make sense of who they are and what kinds of human activities are significant for them. A university is a place where they negotiate and renegotiate themselves into a new space (Giddens, 1991). These negotiations and renegotiations may entail entry into what is perceived as full adulthood or it may be into professional or personal identities. Over the next decade, as the full magnitude of the task facing Scotland (and indeed most advanced economies) of reimagining and renegotiating its position economically and politically, the role of the university as a resource for the young (and not-so-young) makes increasing sense. To argue persuasively for the comprehensive view of the activities of the university is not in any sense to underplay the imperative that Scotland's universities will be drivers of skills, engines of innovation and providers of opportunities for all who can benefit from them. Scotland needs its universities to play an increasingly proactive role in securing its economic and cultural future. In their study for the Organisation for Economic Cooperation and Development (OECD), Machin and McNally (2007) point out that the expansion of a graduate skills employment culture has been on the rise for several decades and that, in recent years, this trend appears to have accelerated as a consequence of 'skills-biased' technical change. Moreover, there is no evidence that this trend towards skills-biased technical change is likely to slow down in the coming decades.

It would be churlish and foolish in equal measure not to attend to the need for Scotland to develop a robust economic life. After all, many of those civic goods and services we enjoy depend on a complex coupling of wealth creation and wealth utilisation across health, welfare, civic participation, infrastructure and culture. Of course many of the non-university learning and research institutions denoted above can arguably do similar things for and in society. Indeed some of the key protagonists in the private educational and consultancy sector, such as Julie Mercer, Head of Education at Deloitte, have argued (see *Times Higher Educational Supplement*, November 2011, pp. 16, 24–30) that shifting legislative and funding patterns presage the dissolution of institutional differences as between the public and the private, the for-profit and the not-for-profit, as the higher education sector across the UK becomes more market-sensitive and consequently undergoes market segmentation. She further argues that universities consider themselves as commercial organisations driven by retaining and growing market share. Such a claim is only valid up to a point. The evidence so indicates to a remarkable resilience in the traditional model of the university: institutions are oriented towards producing education as a public good, driven not by financial return, but by the wish to maximise the dissemination of knowledge. Most academics in our universities share this objective, and their influence on the day-to-day activities of teaching, learning and research will remain central. Moreover, while it may be the case that strictly commercial firms and universities alike may collaborate for a range of strategic reasons, academics themselves continue to form cross-institutional alliances and partnerships for reasons of intellectual affinity and curiosity. Into the future it is this particular energy that is likely to sustain universities as vital public assets.

In what follows we explore tentatively a number of key issues that are likely to shape the future of Scottish higher education across the main areas of current and impending concern.

FUNDING STREAMS

In 2011, there was considerable anxiety that Scotland might not be able to retain its international competitiveness in higher education. The anxiety was compounded by the raising of the fee cap in England to £9,000, which would potentially have seen universities south of the border gain additional resources in real terms. In response to these expressed fears, following the 2011 election, the Scottish Government announced a settlement for higher education which, despite a challenging fiscal climate, raised the resources coming into universities in real terms. The 2011 spending review settlement in Scotland matched the resourcing of universities in England, whilst maintaining access to universities in Scotland free to Scottish (and European Union) students. In essence, two completely different visions for higher education have emerged in Scotland and England. In England, we have seen a drive to invert the post-war attachment to higher education as a public good and, in the process, transform it into a private good. Hence individuals would adopt a more calculating or actuarially rational approach to the personal investments they were prepared to make in themselves and their personal and professional development. In its decision to maintain state funding, the Scottish Government has continued to see higher education as a public good with its commitments to widening participation, and research and scholarly excellence. Clearly the intention is to continue to see education as serving these social imperatives. Prior to the financial crisis, and as a consequence of heavily constrained public funding, countries such as the USA and England witnessed a major increase in the real cost of higher education and this could ultimately have a very serious impact on widening participation, equity and social justice. The political furore over the appointment of Les Ebdon as the Head of the Office of Fair Access in England highlights the gulf opening up between it and Scotland. Whereas in England the battle rages over the priority to be afforded to access relative to excellence, this concern has much less resonance in Scotland. In an echo of the rhetorical attachment to the democratic intellect in Scotland, access to university for those who are able but suffering from social disadvantages is likely to remain a priority. This may well be fostered by ever-closer links with schools and would be furthered by an enhanced involvement of universities in the ongoing development of the curriculum and examination system.

According to Biggar Economics' independent analysis (in the Universities Scotland response to the Green Paper), Scottish universities contribute c. £6.2bn in gross added value to the Scottish economy. The sector directly employs some 35,000 people and indirectly supports 149,000 (7.6 per cent of the Scottish workforce). Consequently its financial health and success into the future is critical to the success and strength of civil, political and economic life in Scotland.

An ongoing consideration is the extent to which this increased level of public investment might result in a desire for greater control by society, and its elected representatives, of the outputs that universities produce (see Aghion et al., 2007; Estermann et al., 2011). To do so would follow something of an established pattern as there is some evidence that as government monies become more squeezed, and as the proportion of GDP given to universities from the public purse reduces, there is a concomitant growth in government regulation and control (cf. the experience of publicly funded universities in the US). Yet, as the work of Aghion et al. (2010) suggests, given that there is a significant causal link between the degree of autonomy granted to universities in states and countries and their performance (as judged by innovation measures such as patents, or universities' reputation indicators such as citations or positions in international league tables), the temptation to greater regulation should be resisted. As Aghion demonstrates, the best publicly funded university systems (in Europe as exemplified by countries such as Scotland, England, Switzerland and Holland; in the USA by states such as Massachusetts, California and New York) are those where universities are able to determine their own strategic direction, and respond autonomously to the incentive structure set by government and other funding agencies for research and teaching funding.

But, as core funding across the UK and beyond experiences heavy constraints, and as Research Council funding gets increasingly concentrated in large-scale projects and competition for that funding increases, Scottish universities will have to become increasingly creative and imaginative in accessing new sources of income to support scholarship. We would expect to see a refocusing of these efforts on European and extra-UK sources of funding. Perhaps success here can be enhanced by more attention to the cultivation of university partnerships with a concomitant distribution of expertise. This suggests that, in the future, universities may have to cultivate more extensive partnerships with a careful redistribution of effort. It is certainly clear from the Cabinet Secretary's letter of guidance to the Scottish Funding Council (SFC) that funding (especially research and horizon funding) will be directed increasingly towards those projects and activities deemed to be internationally excellent and economically important. From the funding decisions taken last year by the SFC it is already clear that research funding will be more aligned with higher quality outputs and outcomes and that lower quality outputs and outcomes will attract lower funding. So with higher levels of public funding comes greater responsibility for the sector to maximise the output of public goods. In any event, accountability is unlikely to diminish. Some of these domestic constraints are likely to be somewhat ameliorated by the continued emphasis on internationally generated income as part of the globalisation of Scottish universities.

GLOBALISATION

Despite the likelihood of increasing government control of universities, the future of Scotland's universities is not entirely in the hands of either the Scottish Government or the universities themselves. Changes to both the UK and the international landscape of higher education have had, and will continue to have, a significant impact on the identity and priorities of Scottish education. This is partly because universities have always been rather more internationally connected and focused than the communities in which they are located, and such connectedness simultaneously enhances opportunity and increases exposure, given that one of their core aims is the pursuit of knowledge. As Marginson and van der Vende put it, in a 2006 report to the OECD on globalisation and higher education,

> Higher education was always more internationally open than most sectors because of its immersion in knowledge, which never showed much respect for juridical boundaries. Higher education has now become central to the changes sweeping through the OECD and emerging nations, in which worldwide networking and exchange are reshaping social, economic and cultural life. (2006, p.4)

Over recent years, Scotland's universities have increased the number of international students (from both within and outwith the EU), and from the rest of the UK. These increases have been important to the gradually shifting identity of Scottish universities as international institutions. The most significant league tables such as Thomson-Reuters/ *Times Higher Education Supplement* and QS World University Rankings consider the numbers of overseas staff and students to be important proxies for international quality. Whatever the merits of such equivalence, Scottish universities must compete on an international stage, and currently they do, with five of them (Aberdeen, Dundee, Edinburgh, Glasgow and St Andrews) cited in the top 200, and three (Edinburgh, Glasgow and St. Andrews) in the top 100. When taken with its total research output and the citations count for publications, which is particularly significant for science, technology, engineering and mathematics (STEM) subjects, and proportionately to its population, Scotland outperforms most countries in the world.

As noted above, the international success of Scotland's universities and that of some other university systems is linked to the way in which they have responded and adapted to the funding environment. There appears to be a clear causal link between strong university autonomy and performance of university systems. It might therefore serve Scotland better to resist the understandable allure of direct control and enhance the autonomy of its universities. This, of course, may appear counter-intuitive given that at times of stress in public funding it is understandable that government would like to take more direct control of such matters as quality, access, salaries, internal apportioning of income, hiring policies and so forth. But, if we are to accept the data, the hoped for, and varied and complex contributions that universities can and need to make to Scottish public life in general and economic well-being in particular, are more likely to be well served by securing their autonomy.

Lest this be considered special pleading, all statistical analyses of the outputs of universities in Europe and the USA demonstrate a strong positive association with their institutional 'autonomy' and 'competitiveness'. Further, Aghion and his colleagues' work would suggest that exogenous increases in expenditures of US universities generate more patents if the public universities in question are more autonomous and where they face more local competition (for resources, faculty and students) from private universities. This in turn generates economic growth.

Note that this does not mean that publicly funded institutions should not be accountable, and should not maximise the outcomes in terms of public goods (economic, cultural, and social) from investment. What the work of Aghion et al. demonstrates is that optimising public welfare is most likely to happen if universities are autonomous, if incentives are set to pursue those outcomes and if universities are then asked to compete for those public funds. Autonomy and competition maximises the output of public goods. These conclusions also emerge from other recent studies (Salmi, 2007; 2009; 2011).

For a country with a small population and a depleted industrial and commercial infrastructure, Scottish higher education represents an internationally recognisable brand that, if it is to thrive, must exploit its educational traditions. This reputation has been used to create a substantial income stream to ameliorate real-terms freezes and decreases in state funding over the period from the early 1970s to 1997.

More recently, the number of universities establishing overseas campuses and transnational education has expanded considerably. Most Scottish universities now operate transnational programmes in countries such as China and India. A smaller number of Scottish universities (such as Heriot-Watt in Dubai and Malaysia) have actually developed fully fledged overseas campuses. Historically, institutions in the United States, Australia and Britain have dominated such overseas activities. This is changing rapidly and, perhaps more intriguingly, Chinese universities have been developing their own international presence. The dynamics of overseas activities are changing and are likely to change much further. As countries with a pattern of sending students overseas develop their internal capacity, Scottish universities will need to develop ever more sophisticated partnerships in order to retain both income streams and reputation. These will include increasing numbers of research partnerships as well as jointly badged and partner degrees with all the quality assurance complexity that this entails. Markets are likely to become more differentiated and segmented with respect not only to overseas institutional partnerships but also to target populations. It is also worth stressing, as we noted in the introduction, that increasingly, and unlike the pattern in the 1970s and 1980s, the drive towards internationalisation is not simply dictated by financial imperatives. In most cases, public universities around the world see maximising their impact, or reputation, as being the major driver. The wish to maximise the dissemination of knowledge and education is a motive in itself, and remains something that sustains universities in their own domestic educational missions.

Perhaps most significantly, in what is likely to become a hyper-competitive market, Scottish universities will need to re-imagine their curriculum to address international audiences with sometimes quite different social, economic and structural conditions. The imperative to rethink the curriculum is part of the need to continually refresh the kind of institutions we are in the service of our students.

STUDENTS

The increasing economic and positional pressures on students would suggest that, if Scottish universities are to support effectively those who directly or indirectly pay for them to flourish then they, the universities, will have to become increasingly responsive. There are many in the academy who consider that the best way to serve students is to 'educate' them, and that such education needs to be flexible and versatile, creative and imaginative, resourceful and robust, based on a hierarchy of knowledge and meaning and of knowledge and meaning producers. If there were ever an occasion when the transmission model of knowledge exchange was wholly dominant it was only in closed communities and was consequently and invariably doomed to ultimate failure. As Menocal illustrates, in her study of the great centres of Andalusian learning during the early Middle Ages, the relationship between teacher and student, between those who have acquired knowledge and those who desire to understand more, has never been merely a question of transmission. While the claims to the co-construction of knowledge in universities, often seen as an unequivocal good in the pages of the *Times Higher Education Supplement*, may be a little overwrought, it is undoubtedly the case that we will have to be, and be seen to be, increasingly responsive to the view that students are partners in knowledge acquisition. After all, it would be strange indeed to consider that knowledge itself somehow sat outside its embodied form in the life and mind of the student. The danger here is that the elision of traditional hierarchies further reinforces the drift towards 'seeing' students simply as customers or consumers.

The decision by the Scottish Government to move away from the much more general impulse towards the direct imposition of fees on students may appear to ease this particular pressure. But it would be a mistake to see this as a move likely to maintain the status quo. Scottish students are no less cosmopolitan than their counterparts elsewhere in the

United Kingdom and beyond, and they will have similar expectations with respect to the quality of their education including assessment, feedback, professional preparation and so forth. Indeed the expansion of expectation may see student career services and the range of support on offer continue to expand. Moreover, university programmes of all kinds are likely to see additional provision for the development of soft skills and dispositions which give some kind of positional advantage to their students. At one level this can appear to be a nil sum game given that all Scottish universities are likely to similarly expand their provision in these areas. However, the ever present danger for Scottish universities is that they fail to keep abreast of developments elsewhere and witness a haemorrhaging of able students from other parts of the UK. This is unlikely and Scottish universities will continue to develop support services of some sophistication.

More intriguingly, the shape and contours of the student experience are likely to continue to change with the increasing use of technologies but, for Scottish universities which wish to maintain their positional advantages, the embrace of technology should be accommodated in more subtle ways than might be currently the case, as institutions rush to expand their 'territory' technologically through the use of overseas locations and via virtual learning environments (VLEs) and blended learning. Here it is worth considering the role of the Scottish university as a site for teaching. Historically the lecture theatre or auditorium both actually and symbolically represented the centre of the 'teaching' experience. It was the location wherein the student was called to attention, to join with other students in attending to the plot lines established by the professor. This traditional way of considering the teaching function of universities has witnessed enormous displacement with the virtualisation and digitalisation of the auditorium. As lectures give way to workshops and problem-based learning, and as the taking of notes is replaced by surfing the inexhaustible data available online and elsewhere, the traditional signifiers of higher education give way to new constructions and descriptions of the activity of the university (see De Bie, 2011). Hence students are no longer primarily 'taught'; instead they 'learn', and such learning requires that they constantly negotiate an avalanche of often undifferentiated data. Under a previous dispensation students were invited to pursue those plot lines established and articulated by the professor with the requirement that they concentrate on particular features of a defined area of study and exclude from consideration certain other lines of enquiry. While the knowledge on 'display' was mediated, it was also public and relational. Here students were brought into a communal space even when they considered their performance and attainment individually. Some would argue that these pedagogical entailments represented forms of political and epistemological as well as pedagogical control and that new technologically enhanced learning, based on the principles of the co-construction of knowledge, offers both liberation and opportunity. With its emphasis on the exploratory, the problem-based and the provisional, 'learning', it is claimed, releases the student from the false obligations of an artificially constructed canon and reflects more fully the putative democratising impulses of late modern education. The arts, humanities and social sciences would appear to be more conducive territory for the triumph of 'learning' over 'teaching' with their emphases on the provisional and partial. Certainly this is the case with regard to the substance of the learning experience. However, it would be a mistake to underestimate the impact and future impact of the postmodern and post-structuralist turn on the sciences. Admittedly this impact is primarily to be seen in the development of pedagogies such as problem-based learning, but it is increasingly evident in the evolution of hybrid postgraduate courses, which are being developed across the traditional disciplinary boundaries. These courses are predicated on a recognition that the understanding of and responses to complex social, cultural and scientific challenges are to be found in the synoptic perspective that embraces both the different fields of enquiry and their interstices. All of this appears to signpost a promising way forward for Scottish universities. We should, the conventional argument goes, continue to embrace these epistemological and pedagogical shifts and produce courses and programmes that are ever more indebted to the complexification of both substance and pedagogical processes. In doing so we should increasingly adopt democratising technologies, open learning, negotiated curricula and flexibility of provision and qualifications.

Matters, however, may not be so simple. The advent of communicative technologies and flexibility has opened up the traditional university to increasing competition from non-traditional, for-profit and not-for-profit providers. It is likely that this competition will intensify as deregulation gradually opens up current 'learning' provision to a growing number of providers. And all of this does not touch on the, as yet, uncharted territory of Massive Open Online Courses (MOOCs). Some of this new provision, most especially in professionally oriented learning, is likely to be an expansion of the kind of extant partnerships that exist between public and private providers and professional bodies – in this sense universities have always been more flexible than is sometimes acknowledged in the political and popular rhetoric in which they are located (see Watson, 2009). Many such partnerships are themselves the product of a lack of real competition where Scottish universities (in common with other British universities) have enjoyed a near monopoly with regard to credentials. Degree-awarding powers have largely been the jealous preserve of universities hitherto but this situation is changing with regard to the English legislature and, if one reads carefully, a briefing paper for MPs authored by Sue Hubble and issued on 8 December 2011 (see www.parliament.uk/briefing-papers/SN06155.pdf), it is clear that the 2011 White Paper for England, *Students at the Heart of the System*, is but the opening salvo in a strategy to rethink the nature of education as a social good. It might be comforting for those involved in Scottish higher education to imagine that the policy changes emerging in England are unlikely to have much resonance in Scotland given the Scottish Government's decision to continue to fully meet the costs of higher education from the Exchequer but, as we have already pointed out, internationalisation is already making students more mobile and, under European competition law, it will be difficult to see how, once ensconced in the UK, such providers will not seek to expand their markets north of the border. Given that many of these 'private' providers operate with relatively low infrastructure costs (certainly significantly lower than those incurred in traditional Scottish universities) and the deployment of distance and blended learning, part-time tutors and so forth they are likely, in the medium term, to make some inroads into Scottish provision. Moreover, they will, as has already been seen in England, expressly target the arts, humanities and social sciences. This has the potential to undermine the provision of such subjects in the university. As yet, they are not in the position of offering 'learning' in the sciences given the very substantial front-end costs of setting up laboratories and that online and related learning is not conducive to student-conducted scientific experimentation. However, as virtual technologies become ever more sophisticated, entry into these fields should not be ruled out.

So, what have these matters to do with the future? As privatisation increases, as new providers enter the market and as technology becomes ever more sophisticated, private providers in the UK will compete on price. Traditional, publicly funded universities cannot respond purely in this dimension. If a university is to remain a university it does have to retain some significant breadth, and price alone cannot determine this. If price were the sole determinant of curriculum we would offer only those programmes and courses that produced the highest surplus. Consequently we would have to ask what actually distinguishes a publicly funded university from other providers. Perhaps more significantly, universities will have to offer additionality; given the two streams of funding students in Scottish and English universities will be what they currently are (but in different proportions), UK universities are going to be increasingly required to demonstrate that their students are in receipt of quality staff contact as well as substantial professional and personal support. Paradoxically, this will entail the recuperation of the auditorium as a place where professors and lecturers teach, though the nature of this teaching is likely to change. For example, Carl Gombrich at University College London offers an interesting vision of the lecture as sited on a VLE with students required to read it prior to the public meeting. The auditorium would then become the site for the interrogation of questions led by the professor. In any event, in the future, universities will have to return to considering the quality of their teaching.

RESEARCH

> To ensure that Scotland's research remains internationally competitive you should continue to focus on world-leading and internationally excellent research. Additionally, I would wish to see our funding of research concentrated in those institutions where Scottish Government funding will lever in the greatest resources from the Research Councils, the European Commission and other major research funders (2011).

Paragraph 19 of the letter from the Cabinet Secretary for Education and Lifelong Learning, dated 21 September 2011, to the Chair of the Scottish Funding Council offers a fairly clear pointer to the trajectory of government-supported research spend in Scottish universities over the next few years and, most likely, beyond. Of course the full detail of future research funding will depend significantly on the outcomes of the 2014 Research Excellence Framework but already it is clear that submitting institutions are unlikely to receive any funding for research falling below the threshold of work recognised to be internationally excellent. While the swing towards impact may have some effect on the distribution of resources this is likely to be at the margin and those institutions with substantial research of high quality, able to demonstrate significant impact, are likely to be the recipients of a concentration of funding. While this will not preclude particular institutions from making strategic decisions, it is likely that such potential concentration will lead to some significant market differentiation, with institutions becoming both highly selective in the areas where they concentrate their research energies and with some focusing more on translation activities and less on generating research findings. In Scotland, the actuarial rationality, which suggests that each pound spent in a particular kind of institution, for example one that is heavily research intensive, and likely to produce higher productivity and better research outcomes, is nevertheless apt to be tempered by other social imperatives that remain integral to the Scottish educational psyche. In particular the impulse towards the maintenance of diversity, rationality, and access and ever-wider participation is likely to play a significant role in any future distribution of resources.

In the future there may be a way to square the circle between producing high-quality research outputs and maintaining certain socially desirable imperatives (including diversity and perceived equity) but this would require that universities expand their already highly successful research pooling initiatives. Universities might voluntarily consider creating more extensive pools in social sciences, arts and humanities and where the division of labour might be between institutions that concentrate on scholarship and those that focus on translation activities. We acknowledge that such a move might be considered controversial but it is not, in fact, so very far from the current de facto situation. If Scotland's institutions of higher education were to choose to realign their research and translation activities, and the funding followed the successful output of the partners, this might well produce higher-quality research with a greater impact. Building on this, it might then be possible to conceive of scholars in research-intensive institutions working closely with others in both higher and further education to develop a more coherent sense of the kinds of abilities, capacities, dispositions and skills that need to be nurtured in an advanced technologically mobile and culturally sophisticated polity. Moreover, they might well be able to identify with greater precision the kinds of technological facilities necessary to develop such abilities. None of this need preclude the pursuance of the more abstract, theoretical or blue-sky forms of research and scholarly activity – indeed it is likely to, and should, create a more conducive space for such work. Such collaboration should not, however, preclude an element of competition in view of the evidence that competition for research funding (Aghion et al., 2010) appears to generate additional research productivity.

Given the very substantial investment in Scottish universities by the government it is likely that, in the future, the sharing of research findings and intellectual property with industry, commerce and the public sector will become more systematic and substantial and that this will shape more fluid partnerships with those who depend on knowledge generation to further their work. This entails some quite real dangers with universities becoming dominated by functional knowledge production and consequently losing the will and obscuring the imperative to think, reflect, hypothesise, experiment, test and so forth, simply because that is what human beings do. While recognising its complicated and always provisional nature universities must nonetheless continue to act in the pursuit of understanding, meaning and truth without fear or favour. This central theme in the life of the university will demand of both government and university the exercise of substantial trust. Despite the very real pressure on government to fund the useful (as if we knew what that was before we unearthed it) they should resist the understandable temptation to command and control and over-hypothecate income streams, trusting that universities work in the interest of an overarching public good. Similarly Scottish universities must demonstrate that scholarly activity does not slip into narcissism, nostalgia and self-indulgence but maintain openness to new possibilities.

CONCLUSIONS

In common with systems across the world, the future for Scottish higher education remains uncertain but it is clear that in recent days some important markers have been put down, markers that try to maintain Scotland's unique attachment to education as a democratising and public good, markers that will push funding towards excellence, markers that will continue to see the move towards greater involvement with the private sector and markers that will see some further growth in competition as well as collaboration. It is likely that as we move forward there will be perceptions of relative winners and losers. What is most important is that we retain the health of the whole and that is likely to require some readjustment by all.

REFERENCES

Aghion, P., M. Dewatripont, C. Hoxby, A. Mas-Colell and A. Sapir (2007) *Why Reform Europe's Universities? Policy Briefs 34.* Brussels: Bruegel Institute.

Aghion, P., M. Dewatripont, C. Hoxby, A. Mas-Colell and A. Sapir (2010) 'The governance and performance of universities: Evidence from Europe and the US', *Economic Policy*, 25 (1): 7–59.

De Bie, S. (2011) 'The auditorium in times of digitalisation and virtualisation', in M. Simmons, M. Decuypere, J. Vileghe and J. Masschelein (eds), *Curating the European University, Exposition and Public Debate.* Leuven: Unversity of Leuven Press.

Estermann, T., T. Nokkala and M. Steinel (2011) *University Autonomy in Europe II: The Scorecard.* Brussels: European University Association.

Giddens, A. (1991) *Modernity and Self-Identity: Self and Society in the Late Modern Age.* Cambridge: Polity Press.

Machin, S. and S. McNally (2007) 'Tertiary education systems and labour markets'. OECD. Online at www.oecd.org/dataoecd/55/31/38006954.pdf

Marginson, S. and M. van der Vende (2006) 'Globalisation and higher education'. OECD. Online at www.oecd.org/dataoecd/20/4/37552729.pdf

Salmi, J. (2007) 'Autonomy from the state versus responsiveness to market', *Higher Education Policy*, 20: 223–42.

Salmi, J. (2009) *The Challenge of Establishing World-Class Universities.* Washington, DC: World Bank.

Salmi, J. (2011) 'The road to academic excellence: Lessons of experience', in P. G. Altbach and J. Salmi (eds), *The Road to Academic Excellence: The Making of World-Class Universities.* Washington, DC: World Bank.

Watson, D. (2009) *The Question of Morale: Managing Happiness and Unhappiness in University Life.* Maidenhead: Open University Press.

110

Scottish Education from a European Perspective

Sotiria Grek

This chapter looks at Scottish education policy from the perspective of Europe. It places this discussion within the wider framework of Europeanisation of education, itself part and parcel of the emergent global education policy field (Ozga and Lingard, 2007). In order to understand and place Scotland within this international context, the chapter engages with two sets of dominant assumptions in the academic literature on education policy. The first is that the global, transnational agenda of education policy making is of greater significance and has more impact than the European Education Policy Space (EEPS) does. It suggests that the significance of EEPS is often obscured by ideas about policy that relate to subsidiarity and formal law making, and by its modes of operation through networks, negotiations and benchmarking. Research in the areas of governance and regulation in Europe is developing rapidly and is ambitious and wide-ranging in scope, but it is not yet very much engaged with the policy field of education and its distinctive operation as a means of regulation and governance (Walters and Haahr, 2005). In part this is because the dominant disciplines in European Studies – politics and law – may adopt frameworks that do not pick up the significance of education in developing Europe, because they often focus exclusively on formal powers and authorities. Thus the less formal policy instruments and processes that characterise emergent European education policy are less visible (Lawn and Grek, 2012). As argued elsewhere, there is a need for attention to education/learning policy in Europe that documents and analyses both its informal 'networking' forms and its reliance on such policy technologies as benchmarks, indicators and the circulation of data (Lawn and Grek, 2012).

The second dominant assumption with which the chapter takes issue is that the UK should be understood primarily as a unitary state in relation to international developments in education and that the UK government is the only point of reference in talking about education policy upon the global stage. This assumption is largely implicit in the education policy literature, which often uses the terms 'Britain', 'England' and 'the UK' interchangeably (though there are honourable exceptions – for example Jones, 2003). In the mainstream academic literature on education policy published in the UK, there is either an absence of recognition of the complexity of the education systems here, or passing reference to difference in the 'other' regions or sub-national systems. This is a long-standing problem; however, since political devolution in 1999, there has been a growth of interest in charting policy convergence and divergence (see, for example, Arnott and Menter, 2007; see also

Chapter 13 in this volume). The changed political situation in Scotland, following the election of a minority Scottish National Party (SNP) government in May 2007, and especially the strong electoral result with the SNP's sweeping victory in 2011 with an agenda that seeks independence for Scotland, not only has strengthened the possibility of divergence, but also in some ways reflects the increasing recognition and high status of Scottish education policy making in Europe.

In order to support this argument, the chapter draws on research undertaken as part of two Economic and Social Research Council (ESRC)-funded projects[1]: the now finished 'Governing by Numbers' project (2006–9) and the more recent and currently running 'Governing by Inspection' (2010–13). Both projects are comparative, seeking to establish connections and relationships not only within the UK and between England and Scotland in particular but also within Europe, as they mostly draw on comparisons with the Nordic states. This comparative orientation reflects an attention to context, and a desire to capture the possibilities of simultaneously 'local' and global development, and reflect the influence of historically embedded assumptions and beliefs on the mediation of global policy pressures. Both projects build on an exploration of education policy making at the international/ national/local/school interface and at the school level. Data collection methods have included document analysis of key policy texts as well as semi-structured interviews with key policy makers and stakeholders at all of these different levels – here, the chapter draws specifically on interviews with Scottish personnel who have been engaged in international activities. In selecting these interviewees and defining them as 'key informants', people were identified who operated at the interface between the transnational organisations and the national, and between the national and the local: these were members of what Lawn and Lingard (2002) define as a 'magistrature of influence'.

In the next section of the chapter this research agenda's approach to Europe and Europeanisation is explained and located in the wider context of globalisation and the influence of transnational agencies. This discussion is necessary because it provides the context within which Scottish education can be viewed from a European perspective.

EUROPEANISATION AND GLOBALISATION

It can be argued that a European education policy space has been in existence for many years, that indeed it is as old as the European Union. However, education as a policy space has been acknowledged only recently as an element of the European integration project. The publication of *The History of European Cooperation in Education and Training* by the European Commission (2006) demonstrates the uses of education in 'making' Europe. This refers to the propagation of a conception of Europe not merely as a geographical entity, but as a space of meaning, constructed around common cultural and educational values, ordering schemas and, more recently, shared governing tools. Indeed, from the 1960s onwards, the discourse of a common culture and shared histories was being circulated as a cluster of myths contributing to a European 'imagined community' rising from the ashes of the destructive Second World War. Education policy making for the 'people's Europe' took the form of cultural cooperation, student mobility, harmonisation of qualification systems and vocational training (European Commission, 2006). It was not a purely discursive construct but was pursued through Community programmes, such as Comett, Erasmus and later PETRA, FORCE and Lingua, that involved large numbers of mobile people and travelling ideas (European Commission, 2006). France and Germany led the project from the start, the former ceding governmental autonomy in exchange for greater predominance in Europe, the latter as part of a project of post-war rehabilitation.

In contrast, the UK imagined itself to have retained imperial status and looked on the choice of a European 'project' as one of many possibilities (Spiering, 2004). The UK could either engage with Europe, continue its association with the Commonwealth or build on its 'special relationship' with the USA – and the last was the preferred option. 'Delusions of grandeur' (Spiering, 2004, p. 140) and even traces of Germanophobia enhanced British 'difference' and an Anglo-Saxon identity as distinct from a European one. The UK was dragged into reluctant partnership in Europe, a role which it has sustained, as indicated in its relatively recent opt-outs from the European Monetary Union and the new Social Charter. In fact, the Treaty of Amsterdam of 1997, which suggested greater flexibility and a 'constructive abstention' approach for the member states, illustrates the UK's influence in the project of retaining political powers within the nation states.

In terms of education policy making, that attention to American, rather than European, models continues to distinguish policy in England, perhaps especially in the period since 1997, and the landscape of education provision in England is closer to that of the USA than to continental Europe. This is reflected in the extent to which 'ideologies of the market' along with adherence to the principles of new institutional economics have driven policy initiatives such as diversity in school provision, the adoption of parental choice, the adherence to competition as the basis of improvement and the extent of private-sector involvement in education (Ball, 2006, pp. 70–1). As the data from both projects cited above illustrate, continental European practices receive little attention in policy talk in England. In contrast, Europe is, and continues to be, an important reference point for Scottish policy, and its significance is increasing. There is, therefore, the possibility of interaction between the European project and UK political devolution, which may be played out in education policy and which could have an impact on the dynamics of policy development within the UK.

Thus the chapter suggests that the concept of Europe is not only present in the education policy narratives of stakeholders in Scotland but that, in fact, it is continually and strategically utilised as part of the current government's aspirations to independence. Europe's new governing tools, such as indicators, benchmarking and the open method of coordination, express what the European education project is now about: the creation of an arena of interdependent actors/nations, sharing knowledge and risk in a constantly changing world. In reporting the interview data below, the chapter shows the ways that Scottish policy makers see Europe as offering a fruitful policy space not only for learning but also for achieving recognition and international acclaim, often capitalising on the English retreat and disinterest in Europe as a point of reference. Quotations are taken from respondents interviewed as part of the two projects cited above and include inspectors, government officials and senior staff in national educational organisations.

SCOTTISH POLICY MAKERS OF 'EUROPE': GAINING DISTINCTIVENESS AND STATUS

> The Scottish inspectorate is looked upon as one of the leading if not THE leading inspectorate in Europe. (interviewee A)

The issue of the distinctiveness of Scottish education policy from that of the rest of the UK emerges strongly in all interviews with the Scottish officials who engage in international work. In fact, the most common ice-breaker in meetings in Europe is the encouragement to see Scotland 'differently'; the bold claim 'everything you know about England, forget!' (interviewee A) has become almost the motto of Scottish education actors abroad. Here an Inspector from Scotland compares English and Scottish inspectorate inputs to a conference:

> the subject was very much self-evaluation and I gave a presentation and talked about the Scottish context and the fact that we don't collect [. . .] data at national level in the way that we would have done against 5–14 in our main approaches. And our English counterpart gave a presentation and talked about the PANDA system. And this incredible sort of complex . . . machine and they were able to tell by the age of 11½ how youngsters will perform when they are X, Y and Z. (interviewee B)

As shown elsewhere (Croxford et al., 2009), the travelling of self-evaluation as a uniquely Scottish product of a progressive and bottom–up policy community has received recognition across Europe, with a great number of countries not only translating the *How Good is our School?'* proclaimed self-evaluation bible, but also travelling back and forth to Scotland to receive first-hand experience of it. This compares to the numerous visits to Finland following that country's success indicated by Programme for International Student Assessment (PISA) findings. As a result, the Scottish school inspectorate emphasises its role in explaining the 'distinctiveness of Scotland' to Europe, and uses this opportunity to promote Scotland's approach as 'ahead of the game' but in line with evolving European-wide models of quality assurance across public–sector services and business (interviewee C). Indeed, the interviewees seem eager to portray Europe and their interactions with Europe as a network of people and ideas that travel and connect in unexpected and interesting ways. They construct the European education policy arena as an area of exchange of experience and good practice. Interviewees describe a policy community, operating through more informal rather than formal relationships of policy dialogue, learning and trust:

> We're talking about things which almost develop into friendships and good collegiate working . . . It's constant . . . and likely to become more [so]. And it seems to me having discussed it with colleagues at various meetings over in Europe, as more and more accession countries come in that a lot of the countries that are coming are actually seeking assistance and advice and support. And they see particularly the European network policy makers group as a vehicle for that. (interviewee B)

> So, that happens across Europe, with Inspectorates visiting us, or us visiting them. And then there are some joint initiatives which relate specifically to developing practice [for example] . . . we produced a common point of reference of a framework for self-evaluation and external evaluation of ICT, which is now widely available. Although I think none of us actually use the evaluation in our own national context, we all take account of it in developing our own thinking nationally . . . If there is something that emerges as a consensus across a number of specialist European bodies, then you would be ill advised to pay no attention to it in your own practice. (interviewee D)

The data from interviewees in Scotland suggest that participating in the shared construction of a European education space is a working reality rather than, or as much as, a formal policy imperative; indeed they focus on the ways that they can contribute:

> If you think about the Barcelona agreement and so on that's not about an opt in or opt out . . . And this commitment to, you know, the particular areas that were identified as areas for improve-

ment. So we . . . I mean I don't think it was any . . . ever been a discussion as will we participate or not. I think the question would really be how can we best participate. What can we contribute? Or what do we give back? (interviewee E)

Returning to self-evaluation and the specific influence of the Scottish inspectorate through its involvement with the Standing International Conference of Inspectorates (SICI) (Croxford et al., 2009; Grek and Shaik, 2009; Lawn and Grek, 2012), Scottish inspectors appear as increasingly spending more and more of their time and attention on these international activities; indeed, this work has gained a momentum that they themselves often seem surprised by. For example:

> Here in Scotland HMIE has an overwhelming range of requests to engage in bilateral work, get visitors to go out and do training. The Scottish inspectorate has actually for example done a three-year project to train the Czech inspectorate wanting to move from the way it had perceived and had operated when it had a Communist government and now wanting to move to a different kind of inspection. We've done quite a lot of work with Portugal and other countries training inspectors. The Dutch tend to do work of that kind. Ofsted come and go a bit. (interviewee A)

Indeed, the fact that the inspectorate now engages in many outward and inward visits for the purpose of exchanging and often simply training other European inspectors is quite interesting in itself. For once, when asked about European exchanges, Scottish officials have lists of travel itineraries to report:

> We have made inputs to training events on self-evaluation for example – now those can be either at a SICI workshop or a general assembly or in some cases for example in Romania where SICI are effectively contracting us along with other inspectorates from Europe to do support training in different countries. Romania has been the most recent . . . But the money for Serbia is coming in from the World Bank . . . One of the most interesting ones was a Dutch inspector over for about a month as a kind of internship – they were very keen to see how we operated within Scotland. (interviewee E)

In fact, training events are now organised and follow specific formats. They are not one-off events – their frequency requires that specific inspectors are in charge of these international activities, which are very often led from ex-senior inspectors who have now moved on to occupy key positions at SICI, such as at its 'Academy'; the SICI Academy has precisely the specific remit to organise the teaching and learning of inspectorates across Europe. Teaching the Scottish inspection system not just in Europe but also beyond is not at all an add-on to the usual work of the former HMIE, and not even an area of international activity that simply covers a growing need to appear international; it has become routinised, everyday labour:

> There's a more general presentation – the 'bog standard' presentation if you like – that we tend to give in the place of self-evaluation in particular – the Scottish approach to school improvement . . . and then there's another one here which is more specifically delivered by one of the local authorities . . . And then this document here which we produced about 2 or 3 years ago about improving the curriculum through self evaluation – there's been quite a lot of interest in that, so that document has been spoken to in some of these events as well, about how you use self-evaluation in order to bring about curriculum improvement. (interviewee E)

Another aspect of this international activity which also to some extent has become routine is describing the Scottish HMIE in contradistinction to its English counterpart:

> And one of the first things I always say to visitors or visiting inspectorates coming to Scotland is, 'You'll have heard about Ofsted, we are very different to Ofsted' and I've said that to colleagues in Ofsted as well – and they acknowledge that. (interviewee E)

In fact, it appears that, at least during the last decade, the more Ofsted has become introverted and less active and interested in the SICI work or other exchanges, the more the Scottish inspectorate has been gaining ground. And although *How Good is our School?* has been translated into all sorts of languages, including Finnish, English policy actors have become more and more solitary and isolated at home: '[They] particularly resented the Scottish building of self-evaluation as [they] were very clear of the view that self-evaluation was not part of the solution but part of the problem' (interviewee A).

Finally, an interesting theme that continually emerges in discussions about the Scottish inspectors' work abroad is not only what they offer to their foreign colleagues but also the learning that they receive:

> I think they [Swedes] are, in some ways, closer to our way of thinking than Ofsted would be, say. The Skandics actually, we're quite interested in. Norway has spent some time with us. They had an OECD review in Norway last December. They have a directorate of education and training in Norway which is an organisation, an agency of government very like ours, actually – there's a sense in which we feel we're almost evolving towards similar territory from different starting points . . . Holland's another – and we talk to Holland quite a lot and we've done joint work with them. (interviewee F)

DISCUSSION

As shown above, and as others have shown in far greater analytical depth (see, for example, Ozga, 2009), the UK/England governance of education is characterised by emphasis on policy outcomes and is not congruent with the practices and processes of the European education policy discourse which works through the horizontal setting of agendas and the joint formulation of problems. Kingdon (1984) describes the processes of policy making and networking in the European scene as a 'policy soup' in which specialists/experts/epistemic communities/policy makers try out their ideas in a variety of ways. Some proposals 'float' longer than others and may be revised and combined with others to increase their viability. The proposals that survive over a series of meetings, that meet several criteria, that are technically feasible and fit with dominant values, are translated into the domestic policy in order to test their relevance to the national mood, their budgetary workability and the support they will receive. Thus, this characterisation may help to explain why Scottish policy makers seem to be much more aware of and at home with such policy processes that work through finding common meanings and sharing ideas and practices.

In searching for theoretical resources that help to make sense of the Scottish case, Beyers and Trondal's (2003) concept of 'ambiguous representation' is particularly useful in explaining the divergence of the policy approach to Europe of the English and Scottish officials:

> The ambiguous representation takes into account that actors are embedded in multiple institutional settings. Accordingly, the emergence of supranational or intergovernmental roles is not

only a matter of organisational contingencies at the EU-level. Bureaucrats are faced with at least dual allegiances; they are national officials working part-time at the European level. Multiple embeddedness implies dilemmas regarding what authority actors actually possess, whose interests are represented and how conflicting views are reconciled . . . Under these ambiguities actors may either fall back on familiar and traditional roles or, under certain conditions search for new roles like the supranational one. (Beyers and Trondal, 2003)

This argument suggests some explanations of the reasons for Scottish policy stakeholders being more open to policy exchange and learning, even under conditions of fluidity and negotiation. In fact, according to Beyers and Trondal's research (2003), 'bureaucrats from federal polities are more likely to adopt a supranational role than those coming from unitary policies'. When working groups are organised at a European level according to the principle of a specific purpose or sector, it is easier for them to transcend territorial representation and adopt an intergovernmental role. Although Scottish policy makers are eager to present a Scottish agenda, they seem also more willing to learn from their peers and exchange knowledge.

As well as being more at home with interdependencies, another element of the explanation may lie in the way in which Euroscepticism in Scotland was replaced by support for Europe as a means of encouraging the devolution agenda. Europe became an alternative point of reference for Scotland: UK policy developments could be challenged or mediated through reference to the EU. As Brown et al. (1998) argue, the growing significance of the EU was an important factor in the politics of Scottish self-government between 1979 and 1999. They point to four aspects. First, Europe was attractive to the SNP as an alternative framework of external security and trading opportunities. Second, the EU favoured subsidiarity, an argument that could be used in favour of devolution in the UK. Third, Europe – and especially small social democratic states – became the source of modernising and progressive ideas, rather than England. And lastly, in the years of the Conservative government's 'rolling back the state', Europe seemed to favour a social partnership model that had been rejected in Westminster. Hearn suggests that Scottish nationalism was reinforced by Europeanisation because 'the steady growth of the European Union has both eaten into the sovereignty of the British state, and made the viability within the EU seem more plausible, and Scottish independence less isolationist' (Hearn, 2000, p. 5). This is not to imply that the Scottish policy figures quoted here are Nationalists in a party political sense: rather that Europe offers Scotland a resource for the recognition of its difference from the larger, more powerful and more visible UK system of England. In fact, as indicated above, while the UK is the EU's 'reluctant partner', Scotland is arguably building an identity between two unions, one in the UK and one in Europe (Dardanelli, 2005).

Here it is also worth noting that education in Scotland has played a particularly strong role historically in the shaping and support of national identity, as one of the 'holy trinity' of institutions – law and the Church being the others – that encapsulated Scotland's 'stateless nationhood' from 1707 to 1999. Since the election of a Nationalist government in 2007, and the end of shared party political control across the UK and Scottish governments, there are strong incentives for the Scottish Government to signal positions (including on Europe) that are independent of policy direction in England, and that do not take England or the UK as the natural reference point but instead highlight Scotland's similarities to small, continental European countries like Denmark and Finland within Europe.

CONCLUSION

This chapter set out to challenge two assumptions that arguably are quite widely illustrated in the literature on education policy making . The first concerned the emphasis on global, transnational agendas promoted by organisations such as the Organisation for Economic Cooperation and Development (OECD) and the World Bank, and the relative neglect of EEPS. The pressure towards standardisation and conformity exercised by transnational agencies such as the OECD has increased. At the same time there is a desire to promote individualised, responsible learners. It is also important to direct attention to the working practices and processes of Europe, in particular its capacity to steer policy through the open method of coordination (OMC) and to drive convergence through indicators and benchmarks. Such attention should include recognition of the policy work of 'making' Europe that is done through informal networks, negotiations and learning. The second dominant assumption with which the chapter took issue is that of taking an undifferentiated UK or 'Britain' as the point of reference in talking about education at the international stage. Through the material presented here, it is clear that more consideration has to be given to the complexity of the UK policy arena, not least in its interactions with, and contrasting uses of, Europe.

ACKNOWLEDGEMENTS

The author would like to acknowledge the ESRC for supporting this research through the following project grants: 'Governing by numbers: Data and education governance in Scotland and England' (2006–9) (RES-00-23-1385); 'Transnational policy learning: A comparative study of OECD and EU education policy in constructing the skills and competencies agenda' (2010–12) (RES-000-22-3429); and 'Governing by inspection: School inspection and education governance in Scotland, England and Sweden' (2010–13) (RES-062-23-2241).

REFERENCES

Arnott, M. and I. Menter (2007) 'The same but different? Post-devolution regulation and control in education in Scotland and England', *European Educational Research Journal* 6 (3): 250–65.

Ball, S. (2006) *Education Policy and Social Class*. London: Routledge.

Beyers, J. and J. Trondal (2003) 'How nation-states "hit" Europe – ambiguity and representation in the European Union', *European Integration Online Papers*, 7 (5). Online at http://eiop.or.at/eiop/texte/2003-005a.htm

Brown, A., D. McCrone and L. Paterson (1998) *Politics and Society in Scotland*. Basingstoke: Macmillan.

Croxford, L., S. Grek and F. Shaik (2009) 'Quality Assurance and Evaluation (QAE) in Scotland: Promoting self-evaluation within and beyond the country', *Journal of Education Policy*, 24 (2): 179–93.

European Commission (2006) *The History of European Cooperation in Education and Training: Europe in the Making – an Example*. Luxembourg: European Communities.

Hearn, J. (2000) *Claiming Scotland*. Edinburgh: Polygon.

Jones, K. (2003) *Education in Britain*. Cambridge: Polity Press.

Kingdon, J. (1984) *Agendas, Alternatives and Public Policies*. New York: HarperCollins.

Lawn, M. and S. Grek (2012) *Europeanising Education: Governing a New Policy Space*. Oxford: Symposium Books.

Lawn, M. and R. Lingard (2002) 'Constructing a European policy space in educational governance: The role of transnational policy actors', *European Education Research Journal*, 1 (2): 290–307.

Ozga, J. (2009) 'Governing education through data in England: From regulation to self-evaluation', *Journal of Education Policy*, 24 (2), 149–62.

Ozga, J. and B. Lingard (2007) 'Globalisation, education policy and politics', in B. Lingard and J. Ozga (eds), *The RoutledgeFalmer Reader in Education Policy and Politics*. London: RoutledgeFalmer.

Ozga J., P. Dahler-Larsen, H. Simola and C. Segerholm (2011) *Fabricating Quality in Europe: Data and Education Governance*, London: Routledge.

Spiering, M. (2004) 'British Euroscepticism', in R. Harmsen and M. Spiering (eds), *Euroscepticism: Party Politics, National Identity and European Integration*. Amsterdam and New York: Rodopi, pp. 127–49.

Walters, W. and J. Haahr (2005) *Governing Europe. Discourse, Governmentality and European Integration*. London: Routledge.

111

The Future of Scottish Education

Walter Humes, Tom Bryce, Donald Gillies and Aileen Kennedy

The subtitle of this edition of *Scottish Education* is 'Referendum', referring to the opportunity Scots will have in 2014 to make an historic decision about the nation's future – whether to vote for political independence, ending the constitutional arrangements that have prevailed since the union of the Scottish and English parliaments in 1707, or to remain part of the United Kingdom, albeit with considerable powers devolved to the Scottish Parliament established in 1999. It will be a simple Yes/No vote, an earlier possibility of including a so-called 'devo-max' option, allowing for an even greater range of powers for the Scottish Parliament, having been ruled out. However, at the time of writing, political thinking in Scotland, as reflected in the views of the main parties and of media commentators, indicates that even if independence is rejected, the possibility of more radical constitutional change within the UK would still be a distinct possibility. Certainly, the SNP would push for 'devo-max', especially if the vote is close, and Labour, following its own policy review on the subject, is likely to pursue a similar course. The Scottish Liberal Democrats' commission on home rule argues that 'A rejection of independence will enable Scotland to continue down the track towards a modern, pluralist and federal relationship with the other parts of the United Kingdom' (*Federalism: The Best Future for Scotland*, 2012).

The Conservatives, more strongly committed to the union than any of the other main parties, will probably wish to see how planned changes that have already been agreed for 2016 onwards bed in, before considering more radical steps (2016 is the year when the next elections to the Scottish Parliament will take place).

How might all this affect Scottish education? Increased devolution (short of independence), and even federalism across the UK, would not pose any threat to the distinctive identity of the Scottish educational system: indeed, the 'educational home rule' which Scottish people have been used to for a very long time could only be strengthened. The determination of the education leadership in Scotland to pursue its own agenda would continue, probably with even greater resolution and confidence. In one sense that would also be true if the referendum vote is in favour of independence. But there would be other implications that might have far-reaching consequences for the way in which the educational system is financed, structured and managed. As Chapter 105 has shown, at present the financing of public services in Scotland is heavily dependent on a block grant from the UK government under the Barnett Formula, which some commentators believe is advantageous for Scotland. An independent Scotland would have to provide for education and other services from tax revenues generated in Scotland. This might necessitate economies, especially in

the short term while the recession continues, and could lead to disputes about budget allocations between different services.

A further possibility is that the present structure of local government, consisting of
thirty-two authorities, might be deemed unwieldy within an independent Scotland.
Questions have already been raised about its fitness for purpose in times of austerity, when
smaller authorities lack the resources to provide for services that were previously taken for
granted. It is the local authorities that are legally responsible for the provision of schooling
and the employment of teachers. In a future independent Scotland, a major reconfiguration
of educational structures is not an impossibility – either as a result of the amalgamation
of existing local authorities, or by removing education from local government altogether
through the setting-up of a regional system of education boards to disburse funds, with
much greater responsibility devolved to individual schools. The authors of Chapters 16 and
106 have set out in some detail possible changes to the present form of local governance.
Thus, while the distinctiveness of Scottish education will not be affected whatever the vote
in the referendum turns out to be, a 'Yes' vote could be the precursor to significant structural changes driven principally by economic factors.

INTER-SECTORAL TENSIONS

Economic factors will also be central to debates about the relative importance given to different sectors of education (pre-school, primary, secondary, further, higher, community
learning and development). Throughout 2012, there were tensions between further and
higher education over differential funding. To placate the universities over the decision
not to introduce student fees for home-based students, the Scottish Government reached
a financial settlement that was perceived as benefiting higher education at the expense of
further education. One newspaper leader detected an element of 'robbing Peter to pay
Paul' in the policy. This came at a particularly difficult time for the further education sector
which was under pressure to rationalise provision through mergers and staff reductions. By
late 2012, it was apparent that there was a large waiting list of over 20,000 students seeking
entry to courses, this at a time of skill shortages and economic stagnation. The Cabinet
Secretary for Education, Michael Russell, sought to defend the Scottish Government's
position, questioning the accuracy of the figures and reaffirming a commitment to ensuring
that every 16- to 19-year-old in Scotland who was not in education, training or employment
would be offered a place on a suitable course.

Other questions about investment priorities in Scottish education have been raised.
Perhaps the most intractable problem facing the system has been the failure to make much
headway with the significant minority of youngsters who do not gain much benefit from
their years of compulsory schooling. A substantial body of evidence now suggests that major
developmental damage can occur in the very early years through poverty, poor parenting
and the absence of the kind of stimulation (social, verbal, psycho-motor) that prepares
youngsters for the experience of schooling. This leads to the suggestion that, instead of
devoting so much attention to remedial measures (in literacy and numeracy, for example) at
a later stage, it makes more sense to invest in the early years so that children at risk can have
a better start to life. Curriculum for Excellence (CfE) does, of course, include the 3–5 age
range but some of the evidence points to the need for even earlier intervention (see Chapter
32). For critics, this raises the prospect of a 'nanny state' which is in danger of becoming
too intrusive in the lives of citizens, seeking to impose officially approved learning from the

cradle to the grave. Although still a tiny minority, the number of parents who now opt to educate their children at home because they are unhappy with state provision is increasing.

Yet another sector that has claims on the education budget is community learning and development (CLD). Sometimes called 'the Cinderella service' because it is easily forgotten amidst the emphasis on formal learning in primary and secondary schools, CLD covers a wide range of more informal types of learning provided through community activities and voluntary organisations. YouthLink Scotland is a national agency that supports the work of more than a hundred organisations engaged in diverse forms of engagement with young people, but it should be noted that CLD embraces the concept of lifelong learning and makes provision for learners of all ages. The aim is not just to benefit individuals but to improve the capacity of communities to work in partnership, tackling disadvantage and building a better future. In a guidance document published in June 2012, it is stated: 'CLD is an essential means of delivering Scottish Government priorities, in particular CfE, GIRFEC [Getting it Right for Every Child] and the government's social policy frameworks for combating poverty, tackling health inequalities and prioritising early years'. As the authors of Chapter 89 state: 'There does appear to be growing recognition that really useful learning is not dependent on stratified, psychological and cognitive traditions of subject-based schooling'. In the past many CLD courses have not been accredited and, as a consequence, have tended to be accorded low value. In an attempt to remedy this, CLD providers are now being encouraged to seek recognition for their courses under the Scottish Credit and Qualifications Framework.

There is no easy answer to the question of which sector should be given the biggest share of the education budget. All can reasonably claim that their contribution is important and any attempt to redistribute resources in a way that radically challenges historical allocations is likely to be strongly resisted by the sector(s) seen to be disadvantaged. Moreover, quite apart from internal rivalries within the field of education, there are always competing claims being advanced by other policy areas (health, transport, environment and so on). It is safe to predict that disputes about the relative social benefits to be obtained from different forms of public investment, both within education and across the range of public services, will continue unabated.

RESEARCH AND POLICY PRIORITIES

Knowing how to judge the relative costs and benefits of investment in different sectors of education requires an informed constituency of people who have a good understanding of the economics of education. In all three of the previous editions of *Scottish Education* a plea has been made by the editors for more research in this field, so far to limited effect. The chapter by David Bell in the present edition makes a most useful contribution but much more is needed. A specialist centre for the study of the economics of Scottish education would be highly desirable and could serve as a valuable resource for policy makers. There is such a centre in England (at the London School of Economics, with links to the Institute of Education) but there are currently no moves to set one up in Scotland. It is worth asking why this should be so. It is not because Scottish economists are uninterested in public-sector finance, as a substantial amount of work is carried out in other fields, such as health economics. Education perhaps seems dull in comparison, though its social value is undisputed. Professionals within education in most cases will have had little or no training in economics, though senior staff in local authorities have to advise councillors on major budget decisions.

The bulk of research in university schools and faculties of education focuses on curriculum, assessment and pedagogy and those conducting it are likely to feel ill-qualified to embark on work that is outside their comfort zone. Central government can draw on the expertise of statistical and economic specialists within the civil service: politicians may prefer to rely on them rather than encourage external sources of analysis which might cast doubt on the wisdom of certain policy decisions. But if policy is to be genuinely evidence-informed – as politicians so often claim is their intention – then the need for an enhanced body of expertise is self-evident.

Political considerations may also come into play in relation to research into CfE, which will remain a 'flagship' policy over the next few years. Although its development has been somewhat chequered, the fact remains that it is central to the immediate future of Scottish education. CfE is a 'high stakes' policy in the sense that political and professional reputations – and indeed the reputation of Scottish education as a whole – depend on it being perceived as reasonably successful. This arises partly from the scope and ambition of the project, indicated by its application to the 3–18 age range, as well as by the pervasive discourse of 'excellence'. As noted in Chapter 5, any major educational change needs to be evaluated independently over an extended period of some years. A worrying feature of CfE is that no large-scale research programme to assess its impact has been commissioned by the Scottish Government and, so far, the amount of independent academic research has been limited, perhaps reflecting caution in relation to a policy that that has so much political weight behind it. Any internal evaluation – for example, one carried out by the staff within Education Scotland – would lack credibility, since those conducting it would in effect be passing judgement on a policy that they had helped to initiate and promote. A healthy educational system needs to be prepared to interrogate the full range of evidence available, whether it is positive, negative or inconclusive.

There is widespread agreement that educational systems need to respond more quickly and effectively to the pressures for change coming from the external environment, whether technological, economic, social or cultural. This does not mean that such pressures should be accepted uncritically but it does mean that their educational implications have to be thought through carefully and a coherent position adopted. Failure to do so could lead to schools becoming viewed as archaic institutions, out of touch with what is happening outside their gates. The pace of technological development presents a particular challenge. There are concerns about the general levels of computing skills and continuing debates about the most suitable form of intranet provision, with some favouring a centrally control-led system while others prefer a more open environment with freer access to portable ICT devices (see *TESS*, 16 November 2012).

Issues of this sort raise important questions about the quality of thinking within the edu-cational system. How far is it capable of asking the right research questions and generating policy ideas that represent an adequate response to the external pressures? Critics some-times suggest that Scottish education is over-managed in bureaucratic terms and under-led in intellectual terms. How justified is this criticism?

Most educational debate in Scotland is initiated, and to a large extent controlled, by politicians, officials and education professionals. Although the bureaucratic infrastructure that sustains the system has been reconfigured from time to time (for example, the bringing together in 2011 of Her Majesty's Inspectorate of Education, and Learning and Teaching Scotland to form Education Scotland), membership of the policy community shows remarkable continuity. It is true that there are opportunities for other stakeholders (parents, employers, students) to express views on new policy proposals, but their input rarely makes a significant difference to what finally emerges. Against this background, the setting up in November 2011 of a Commission on School Reform by two 'think tanks', Reform Scotland and the Centre for Scottish Public Policy, was an interesting development. Both of these 'think tanks' describe themselves as 'independent' and, while this self-designation might be questioned, they are certainly not as politically committed as a number of similar bodies south of the border. Some members of the Commission could be considered as education 'insiders', but they were not there to represent a particular organisation, rather to explore ideas in an open-minded way. The focus of the Commission was on the longer-term needs of Scottish education, rather than on more immediate issues. Its objectives were:

- to form a fair and objective view of Scotland's educational performance compared to what is provided elsewhere;
- to consider the challenges that Scottish education is likely to face in the next fifty years and how likely it is to meet those challenges;
- to identify any problems within the current school system in Scotland and try and analyse the root causes of them;
- to develop proposals that will enable young people, whatever their background, to fulfil their potential and meet the unprecedented challenges of the modern world.

In its interim report, published in June 2012, the Commission highlighted a number of concerns. It suggested that while the general quality of Scottish education was 'good', it was 'not world leading'. The uniformity of the system, which from some perspectives could be seen as a strength, had limitations. Perhaps there was a need to 'encourage greater innovation and diversity'. Successive policies had failed to break 'the link between socio-economic disadvantage and educational success'. Among the other areas highlighted were the importance of development in the very early years; the need to make better use of new technology 'to free schools from current organisational constraints'; and more effective strategies for the management of change, including building leadership capacity.

The final report of the Commission will not be published until after this book goes to press but it is safe to predict the form that some of the recommendations might take. Scotland's record of managing educational change will come in for criticism: it will be argued that all the major national programmes (from Standard Grade onwards) have achieved less than was originally claimed and taken longer than envisaged, thus causing disillusion among some teachers. A case will be made for greater variation in types of school and for giving individual schools much more autonomy. Furthermore, it will be argued that while CfE has merit in terms of providing a sense of direction, it should not be seen as offering a definitive blueprint for the future: the scale of technological advance and global change will call for regular updating of curricular content, teaching and learning approaches, and skill development. Promoting advanced cognitive skills for the most able and improving outcomes for underachievers will both be given high priority.

These recommendations, if accepted, would have significant implications for both future schools and future teachers. Allowing for greater variety of types of school might be seen as compromising the principle of equality that has been so fundamental to the Scottish educational tradition. But it could be argued that it is a mistake to interpret 'equality' as meaning 'sameness'. Indeed, in some circumstances it would be unfair to treat all children in exactly the same way, without taking account of their differing interests, abilities and potential. A more subtle sense of equality would be 'equality of consideration', which recognises the unique character of each individual learner and makes educational provision accordingly. This would be quite different from the 'high status'/'low status' classifications based on perceptions of ability that used to apply in the pre-comprehensive days. It would be an attempt to move towards a more genuinely individualised form of educational provision than that which is currently offered. Nevertheless, such a reconfiguration of schooling provision is problematic: as learners are so significantly shaped by their backgrounds, tailoring schooling in this way carries the risk of merely reproducing social divisions. Certainly, any such reform would require teachers to be educated and deployed in different ways. The Donaldson Report, and the recommendations of the National Partnership Group which followed, represents a modest step in that direction by requiring prospective teachers to engage with forms of thinking outside traditional 'educational' subjects. The recommendations also set the bar higher for standards of literacy and numeracy among prospective teachers, require headteachers to gain a leadership qualification and encourage more teachers to study for a Masters level qualification (following the phasing out of the Chartered Teacher Scheme). Donaldson views these developments as indicators of 'enhanced professionalism'.

Having greater expectations in relation to tailored, individualised provision for pupils would also require more specialist teachers equipped to deal with the range of learning disabilities now encountered in mainstream schools. A report published in November 2012, entitled *The Right Help at the Right Time in the Right Place*, reviewing provision for children with complex additional support needs, presented a very mixed picture, with a significant number of parents reporting less than satisfactory experiences. New research in the fields of genetics and neuroscience (such as those referred to in Chapter 6) is adding to our knowledge of individual differences in ways that could revolutionise our understanding of how people learn, the obstacles they encounter and the best means of supporting their development. The number of people within Scottish education who are addressing questions of this sort is, at present, disappointingly small. In making this point, it is not being argued that the familiar items on the research and policy agenda – curriculum, assessment and pedagogy – should be disregarded, but it is to suggest that there is also a need to engage in 'horizon scanning' in order to identify those issues that may begin to reshape our approach to educational provision in fundamental ways.

SCOTTISH EDUCATION IN A GLOBAL CONTEXT

Part of the 'horizon scanning' has to take account of what is happening in other educational systems. As the world becomes more and more interdependent, it is necessary for countries to steer a course that not only respects the distinctive identity and traditions of their own educational systems but also takes account of international developments. Thus the decision about independence in 2014 is not the only factor that will affect the future shape of Scottish education.

There are global pressures, affecting all developed nations, that tend to push educational systems in the direction of greater convergence. These derive from a variety of sources. International studies of educational achievement, particularly those conducted by the Organisation for Economic Cooperation and Development (OECD), make political leaders extremely sensitive about their country's position on tables comparing results in language, science and mathematics. Global economic pressures, linked to technological developments and changes in patterns of employment, have led to an international emphasis on skills, enterprise and adaptability. Pasi Sahlberg, a Finn who describes himself as an activist for educational change, has referred to a Global Education Reform Movement influencing the thinking of politicians in many countries and driving policy in uniform directions. Traditional conceptions of knowledge are seen as too narrow and rigid to cope with the demands of rapidly changing work environments. Any country that does not take account of this perspective runs the risk of placing its young people at a disadvantage in a highly competitive world. New approaches to management in the public sector, emphasising improved efficiency, defined targets and clear lines of accountability, also tend in the direction of convergence across educational systems. Scottish education is, therefore, trying to set its distinctive agenda during a period when there are countervailing forces tending to push educational systems in a uniform direction. CfE has arrived on the scene at a moment when it has to negotiate tricky political and ideological terrain which is, at the same time, both national and international. In order to understand these tensions, it is necessary to say a little about the ideological background and, in particular, about the influence of neo-liberal thinking on educational systems. Although Scotland has been less directly affected by this than many other countries (particularly England), some of the discourse is evident in policy initiatives.

Neo-liberalism has achieved a dominant ideological position in Western democracies and in many instances it has had a profound effect on the nature of the school system. This is true of such countries as politically disparate as Australia, England, Sweden and the USA. Neo-liberalism can be summarised as comprised of five main principles: the primacy of the market and commitment to its expansion; reduction in public spending; privatisation of public services; deregulation, especially in respect of business practices; and a supreme focus on the individual in terms of freedom and responsibility, so eclipsing notions of community or public good. Its influence within education globally has had its most striking realisation in respect of school governance where institutions have been founded, or encouraged to become, independent of state control, so creating a quasi-market. Examples would be the Academy programme in England, where local authority control has been removed, and the 'free schools' movement which, again, allows for independence, private sector sponsorship and, at least in theory, greater parental influence.

So far in Scotland, the system has been resistant to such changes. While Michael Russell, the Cabinet Secretary for Education, was at one time interested in the Swedish free schools experiment, that interest has declined and more recent pronouncements show a closer affinity to the Finnish model of largely self-regulating comprehensive state education. However, there are still pressures which can, and will, exact strain on this position: one is from a number of UK non-governmental bodies, more avowedly right-wing than the Scottish 'think-tanks' referred to above, which are pressing for a reduction in central control and increased devolution, if not independence, to individual schools. The absence of a crisis narrative in Scottish education has largely kept such voices isolated and muted; there does not appear to be the same raucous public angst about state education as exists in England, for example – particularly in London, and reflected in the media. However, there are other challenges that may serve to increase such pressure on the system: principal among these are the regular PISA surveys, due to report next in 2015. Should Scotland's relative international position be shown to have declined, then pressure will be increased for changes to school governance in response. Of course, as with the case of the world rankings of universities, the rise of the Asian economy and improvements in performance of the countries of 'new Europe' inevitably mean that Scotland's position will face challenges but, regardless of these mitigating factors, calls for systemic change will be raised.

A second challenge relates to the fundamental inequalities inherent in the Scottish comprehensive model: in most urban areas, segregated social housing and the vagaries of catchment areas create highly socially stratified school compositions. The OECD has already highlighted how such social divisiveness compounds inequities in school outcomes and entrenches stagnant social mobility. Nevertheless, history suggests that while educational inequality troubles consciences, it rarely results in determined counteraction. In any event, the most likely response to this is the targeting of ameliorative resources towards those deemed in need, rather than a focus on the culpability of the system itself. Perhaps a more likely force for change will come from the continuance of years of frozen council tax levels which will put increased pressure on local authorities to review, and almost certainly reduce, existing levels of service provision. Disabling challenges to the comprehensive system may well prove to be not so much ideological as financial. The love of money may be the root of all evil, but the lack of it can be the root of much else.

REFERENDUM AND AFTERMATH

Since 1872, the state has assumed the main responsibility for the form and direction of Scottish education. In this sense education is inevitably political and periodic calls to 'keep politics out of education' are unlikely to have much effect. What underlies such calls is often a feeling that if the debate becomes too *party* political there is a risk that children's experience of schooling will become a battleground for the exchange of tribal slogans of a kind that will not contribute to genuine improvement of the system. What is striking about Scottish education in the post-devolution period is that, although there have certainly been differences of emphasis among the main political parties, there has also been a high measure of agreement about the fundamental principles involved. Education is seen as a public good which is an essential part of citizenship in a democracy. It has personal, social and economic benefits that justify the resources devoted to it. Furthermore, there is an honourable tradition in Scotland of regarding education as a means of promoting equality of opportunity, so that children from modest backgrounds can progress to advanced levels of study. Although this aspiration has never been fully achieved in practice, and there remains an intractable minority of pupils who underachieve, as well as a disturbing gap between the attainments of youngsters from advantaged and disadvantaged backgrounds, the ideal of equality of opportunity persists. It is an important part of the dominant narrative of Scottish education and one to which all political parties pay tribute, even though they may differ over the details.

But how adequate is this account in 2013 and how might it be subject to change in the light of the referendum result in 2014? Has there perhaps been too much consensus and insufficient critical interrogation of prevailing assumptions? Are there any post-referendum scenarios that might lead to greater diversity in the educational policies of the main political parties? Consider first the Scottish National Party (SNP). Its failure to win the devolution referendum of 1979 – not reaching the required 40 per cent threshold – led to a period of sharp decline and internecine strife. A clear rejection of independence in 2014 would be momentous for the SNP position. And anything worse than a narrow referendum defeat would be likely to open up profound fissures within the party once again. It could mean the pragmatic acknowledgement that independence is off the agenda for decades, an acceptance of devolution as the fixed situation, and so to an entire repositioning of the party. For some within the party, the so-called fundamentalists, this would be unacceptable and some kind of split might be inevitable, perhaps leading to a form of populist nationalism in the wake of the failure of its political counterpart. This might be characterised by an appeal to ethnic or cultural distinctiveness which could well have some distasteful ramifications if allowed to affect curriculum and schooling to any extent. Even if a major split were to be prevented, the party's status as referendum 'losers' could well affect its electoral prospects. Sections of the Scottish electorate might still see advantages in having an SNP government in Edinburgh as a counterweight to whatever party held power at Westminster, but a more likely outcome would be a Labour-led coalition in Scotland following the 2015 elections. Already the Labour leader, Johann Lamont, has sought to reposition the party in relation to free public services and this might lead to a further tightening of the education budget with inevitable cutbacks in existing provision. The debate would then be about protecting the services that were absolutely essential rather than about launching costly new initiatives. CfE would be on a 'steady maintenance' trajectory rather than a showcase development, with the risk of failing to keep up with countries that manage to respond more proactively to the need for change. The scene would be set for a rather sharper exchange of political views about priorities. The Conservatives might argue that the relative consensus around the state system was no longer sustainable and that experiments along English lines, allowing for more variation, were at least worth trying. The Liberal Democrats might emphasise their European credentials by arguing that we should look to countries in Northern Europe as the most suitable comparators against which to judge the Scottish system: in this they would be continuing a thread of SNP policy.

If current poll predictions prove inaccurate and the referendum results in a 'Yes' vote for independence, we enter territory of a kind that the former US Secretary of Defence Donald Rumsfeld famously called a world of 'unknown unknowns'. An extended limbo period would result as the various ramifications of a move to independence unravelled, with much depending on the scale of the victory. The legal and constitutional implications would be far-reaching, involving extensive financial, contractual and institutional negotiations. Substantive policy issues might have to take second place until these were resolved. For the education system, as for other aspects of Scottish life, lengthy uncertainty would be the inevitable consequence until the actual configuration of separate statehood emerged. The world thereafter, should this scenario occur, can be left to the next edition of *Scottish Education* to review.

GLOSSARY OF ABBREVIATIONS

AAC	Arts Across the Curriculum
AAG	Assessment Action Group
AALA	Adventure Activities Licensing Authority
AAP	Assessment of Achievement Programme
AB	Associated Board
ACCAC	Qualifications, Curriculum and Assessment Authority for Wales
ACDP	Advanced Courses Development Programme
ACET	Australian Council for Education through Technology
ACfE	*A Curriculum for Excellence* (also CfE)
ACOT	Apple Classroom of Tomorrow
ADES	Association of Directors of Education in Scotland
ADHD	Attention Deficit Hyperactivity Disorder
ADSW	Association of Directors of Social Work
AEAS	Association of Educational Advisers in Scotland
AEDIPS	Association of Educational Development and Improvement Professionals in Scotland
AEF	Aggregate External Finance
AERS	Applied Educational Research Scheme
AGL	Action Group on Languages
AGM	Annual General Meeting
AH	Advanced Higher (NQ level)
AHDS	Association of Headteachers and Deputes in Scotland
AHT	Assistant Headteacher
AHTS	Association of Headteachers in Scotland
AifG	Assessment is for Grading (pejorative)
AifL	Assessment is for Learning
AIM	Advanced Institute of Management
AL	Associate Lecturer
ALN	Adult Literacy and Numeracy
ALNIS	Adult Literacies and Numeracy in Scotland Strategy
AME	Annually Managed Expenditure
APEL	Accreditation of Prior Experiential Learning
APFL	Accreditation of Prior Formal Learning
API	Age Participation Index
APL	Accreditation of Prior Learning
APS	Assisted Places Scheme

APT	Assistant Principal Teacher
APT&C	Administrative, Professional, Technical and Clerical
APU	Assessment of Performance Unit
ARTEN	Anti-Racist Teacher Education Network
AS	Advanced Subsidiary (level)
ASBO	Anti-Social Behaviour Order
ASC	Association of Scotland's Colleges
ASCETT	Advisory Scottish Council for Education and Training Targets
ASDAN	Award Scheme Development and Accreditation Network
ASfL	Additional Support for Learning (also ASL)
ASG	Area Support Group
ASL	Additional Support for Learning (also ASfL)
ASLS	Association of Scottish Literary Studies
ASN	Additional Support Need
ASNTS	Additional Support Needs Tribunals for Scotland
ASP	Additional Support Plan(s)
ASPECT	Association of Professionals in Education and Children's Trusts
ASPEP	Association of Scottish Principal Educational Psychologists
AST	Advanced Skills Teacher
ASTER	Assisting Small-group Teaching through Electronic Resources
ATL	Association of Teachers and Lecturers
ATQ	Additional Teaching Qualification
ATQRE	Advanced Teaching Qualification in Religious Education
AUT	Association of University Teachers
AWBL	Assessment of Work-Based Learning
BA	Bachelor of Arts
BBBL	*Better Behaviour, Better Learning*
BBC	British Broadcasting Corporation
BCS	Birth Cohort Survey
BEAS	British Educational Administration Society
BECTA	British Education and Communications Technology Agency
BEd	Bachelor of Education
BELMAS	British Educational Leadership, Management and Administration Society
BEMAS	British Educational Management and Administration Society
BEN	Business Education Network
BERA	British Educational Research Association
BGE	Broad General Education
BPS	British Psychological Society
BSc	Bachelor of Science
BSCS	Biological Sciences Curriculum Study
C	Credit level (of Standard Grade)
CA	Classroom Assistant
CAA	Computer-Assisted Assessment
CABE	Commission for Architecture and the Built Environment
CAD	Computer-Aided Drawing
CAL	Computer-Assisted Learning

CAS	Computer Algebra System
CAST	Curriculum Advice and Support Team
CAT	College of Advanced Technology
CBEVE	Central Bureau for Educational Visits and Exchanges
CBI	Confederation of British Industry
CCC	Consultative Committee on the Curriculum
CCEA	(1) Council for the Curriculum, Examinations and Assessment *(Northern Ireland)* (2) The Commonwealth Council on Educational Administration
CCETSW	Central Council for Education and Training in Social Work
C&D	Craft and Design
CD-ROM	Compact Disc Read-only Memory
CE	College of Education
CEC	Catholic Education Commission
CEFR	Common European Framework of Reference for Languages
CEHR	Commission for Equality and Human Rights
CERES	Centre for Education for Racial Equality in Scotland
CERN	European Organisation for Nuclear Research
CES	Centre for Educational Sociology
CeVe	Community Education Validation and Endorsement
CfE	Curriculum for Excellence (also ACfE)
CGLI	City and Guilds of London Institute
CI	Central Institutions
CiC	Community Interest Company
CIDREE	Consortium of Institutions for Development and Research in Education in Europe
CILT	Centre for Information on Language Teaching
CIPFA	Chartered Institute of Public Finance and Accountancy
C&IT	Communications and Information Technology
CITB	Construction Industry Training Board
CLA	College Lecturers' Association
CLAS	The Association of Secondary Gaelic Teachers
CLASS	Committee for Language Awareness in Scottish Schools
CLD	Community Learning and Development
CLG	Company Limited by Guarantee
CLS	Community Learning Scotland
CMP	Contemporary Music Project
CMS	Career Management Skills
CNAA	Council for National Academic Awards
CNAG	Comunn na Gàidhlig (also CnaG)
CNSA	Comhairle nan Sgoiltean Araich
COLEG	Colleges Open Learning Exchange Group
COPE	Committee on Primary Education
COSHEP	Committee of Scottish Higher Education Principals
COSLA	Convention of Scottish Local Authorities (also CoSLA)
COSPEN	Committee on Special Educational Needs
COT	Committee on Technology

CP7	Curriculum Paper 7
CPAG	Child Poverty Action Group
CPD	Continuing Professional Development
CPPs	Community Planning Partnerships
CRE	Commission for Racial Equality
CRU	Central Research Unit
CS	Computer Science
CSI	Computer Science Inside
CSP	Coordinated Support Plan
CSR	Comprehensive Spending Review
CSU	Central Support Unit
CSUP	Committee of Scottish University Principals
CSYS	Certificate of Sixth Year Studies
CT	Chartered Teacher
CTC	City Technology College
CTI	Computers in Teaching Initiative
CtOG	Closing the Opportunity Gap
CV	Curriculum Vitae
CVCP	Committee of Vice-Chancellors and Principals
CYMS	Catholic Young Men's Society
DARTS	Directed Activities Related To Texts
DASH	Dumbarton Academy Seniors against Harassment
DCSF	Department for Children, Schools and Families
DEdPsych	Doctor of Educational Psychology
DEL	Departmental Expenditure Limit
DENI	Department of Education in Northern Ireland
DES	Department of Education and Science
DfEE	Department for Education and Employment
DfES	Department for Education and Skills
DHT	Depute Headteacher
DIA	Developing Informed Attitudes
DIUS	Department for Innovation, Universities and Skills
DM	(1) Department Meeting (2) Designated Manager
DMR	Devolved Management of Resources
DNA	Deoxyribonucleic Acid
DSM	(1) Designated Senior Manager (2) Devolved School Management (3) Diagnostic and Statistical Manual (of the American Psychiatric Association)
DTI	Department for Trade and Industry
DTTO	Drug Treatment and Testing Orders
DVD	Digital Versatile Disc; Digital Video Disc
EA	Education Authority
EAL	English as an Additional Language
EBP	Education Business Partnership
EC	(1) Educational Computing (2) European Community
E&CC	Enterprise and Culture Committee
ECEC	Early Childhood Education and Care

ECER	European Conference on Educational Research
ECITB	Engineering Construction Industry Training Board
EC&SC	Education Culture and Sport Committee
ED	Education Department
EdB	Bachelor of Education
EdD	Doctor of Education
EDRU	Education Department Research Unit
EDSI	Education Departments' Superhighways Initiative
EEC	European Economic Community
EECERA	European Early Childhood Education Research Association
EEPS	European Education Policy Space
EERA	European Educational Research Association
EFTRE	European Forum for Teachers in Religious Education
EfW	Education for Work
EGRC	Extended Grade Related Criteria
EHEA	European Higher Education Area
EIL	Education-Industry Links
EIP	Early Intervention Programme
EIS	Educational Institute of Scotland
EISP	Education for the Industrial Society Project
ELISAs	Enzyme-Linked Immunosorbent Assays
ELIR	Enhancement-Led Institutional Review
E&LLC	Enterprise and Lifelong Learning Committee (also ELLC)
ELLD	Enterprise and Lifelong Learning Department
ELLL	Education and Lifelong Learning
ELTR	Effective Learning and Teaching Report
EMA	Educational Maintenance Allowances
ENHPS	European Network of Health Promoting Schools
E&Os	Experiences and Outcomes (of CfE) (also Es & Os)
EPPE	Effective Provision of Pre-School Education
EPSD	Education for Personal and Social Development (also PSD)
EPSEN	Effective Provision for Pupils with Special Educational Needs
ERSDAT	Educational Research in Scotland Database
ES	(1) Education Scotland (formed from the merging of HMIE and LTS) (2) Environmental Studies (3) Enquiry Skills
ESD	Education for Sustainable Development
ESDG	Education for Sustainable Development Group
ESL	English as a Second Language
ESO	Education Support Officer
ESOL	English for Speakers of Other Languages
ESRC	Economic and Social Research Council
ETLLD	Enterprise, Transport and Lifelong Learning Department
EU	European Union
EUROCLIO	European Association of History Teachers
F	Foundation level (of Standard Grade)
FE	Further Education
FEC	Full Economic Cost

FEDA	Further Education Development Agency
FEFC	Further Education Funding Council
FELA	Further Education Lecturers' Association
FITLS	Flexibility in Teaching and Learning Scheme
FL	Foreign Language
FMRG	Funding Methodology Review Group
FT	Full Time
FTE	Full-Time Equivalent
FTLS	Flexibility in Teaching and Learning Scheme
G	General level (of Standard Grade)
GAE	Grand Aided Expenditure
GARA	Glasgow Anti-Racist Alliance
GC	Graphic Communication
GCE	General Certificate of Education
GCSE	General Certificate of Secondary Education
GCU	Glasgow Caledonian University
GDP	Gross Domestic Product
GIRFEC	*Getting it Right for Every Child*
GIST	Generic Issues and Strategies for Teaching
GLOW	Scottish Schools Digital Network (also SSDN)
GLPS	Gaelic Learners in the Primary School
GMC	General Medical Council
GNVQ	General National Vocational Qualification
GPA	Grade Point Average
GRC	Grade-Related Criteria
GSVQ	General Scottish Vocational Qualification
GTCE	General Teaching Council for England
GTCNI	General Teaching for Northern Ireland
GTCS	General Teaching Council for Scotland
GTTR	Graduate Teacher Training Registry
GUS	*Growing Up in Scotland*
H	Higher (NQ level)
HAS	Headteachers' Association of Scotland (now School Leaders Scotland)
HASAS	*Having A Say At School*
HBSC	*Health Behaviour in School-aged Children*
HE	Higher Education
HEA	Higher Education Academy
HEFCE	Higher Education Funding Council for England
HEFCW	Higher Education Funding Council for Wales
HEI	Higher Education Institution
HELP	Health Education for Living Project
HEQC	Higher Education Quality Council
HESA	Higher Education Statistics Agency
HF	Hunter Foundation
HGIOS	*How Good is Our School?*
HGPE	Higher Grade Physical Education
HIE	Highlands and Islands Enterprise

HMCI	Her Majesty's Chief Inspector
HMDSCI	Her Majesty's Depute Senior Chief Inspector
HMI	Her Majesty's Inspectorate
HMIE	Her Majesty's Inspectorate of Education (also HMIe)
HMSCI	Her Majesty's Senior Chief Inspector
HMSO	Her Majesty's Stationery Office
HN	Higher National
HNC	Higher National Certificate
HND	Higher National Diploma
HPC	Health Professions Council
HS	Higher Still
HSAP	Happy, Safe and Achieving their Potential
HSDP	Higher Still Development Programme
HSDU	Higher Still Development Unit
HSPE	Higher Still Physical Education
HT	Headteacher
HTML	Hyper Text Mark-up Language
H&W	Health and Wellbeing
HWB	Health and Wellbeing
IAPS	Independent Association of Preparatory Schools
IASG	Inter-Authority Standing Group for Gaelic
ICS	Integrated Community School
ICT	Information and Communications Technology
IDES	International Design Technology and Enterprise Support Network
IDL	Interdisciplinary Learning
IEA	International Association for the Evaluation of Educational Achievement
IEP	Individualised (or Individual) Educational (or Education) Plan (or Programme)
IFE	Informal Further Education
ILA	Individual Learning Account
ILB	Industry Lead Body
ILP	Independent Labour Party
ILT	Institute for Learning and Teaching (now the Higher Education Academy)
INEA	Inspection of Education Functions of Local Authorities
InSEA	International Society for Education through Art
INSET	In-service Education and Training
Int	Intermediate (NQ levels, Int 1 and Int 2)
IP	Innovation Platform
IQ	Intelligence Quotient
IRB	International Relations Branch (Scottish Office)
IRU	International Relations Unit
ISC	(1) Integrated Science Course (2) Independent Schools Council
ISCED	International Standard Classification of Education
ISEP	Improving School Effectiveness Project
ISES	Institute for the Study of Education and Society
IT	Information Technology

ITE	Initial Teacher Education
ITQ	Infant Teaching Qualification
ITV	Independent Television
IWB	Interactive Whiteboard
JANET	Joint Academic Network
JAT	Joint Assessment Team
JISC	Joint Information Systems Committee
JLLG	Joint Lifelong Learning Group
JTETW	*Journal of Teacher Education and Teachers' Work*
JWP	Joint Working Party
KAL	Knowledge about Language
KE	Knowledge Economy
KT	Knowledge Transfer
KU	Knowledge and Understanding
LA	Local Authority
LAC	Looked-After Children
LACE	Local Authority Current Expenditure
LAMPS	Leadership and Management Pathways Sub-Group
LAN	Local Area Network
LASFE	Local Authority Self-Financed Expenditure
LEA	Local Education Authority
LEC	Local Enterprise Company
LIW	*Learning in and for Interagency Working*
LLUK	Lifelong Learning United Kingdom
LMS	Local Management of Schools
LS	(1) Learning Schools (2) Learning Support
LSDA	Learning and Skills Development Agency
LTS	Learning and Teaching Scotland
LTSN	Learning and Teaching Subject Network
LWG	Languages Working Group
MA	(1) Master of Arts (2) Modern Apprenticeship
MAN	Metropolitan Area Network
MAppSci	Master of Applied Science
MBA	Master of Business Administration
MCARE	Multicultural and Anti-Racist Education
MCI	Management Charter Initiative
MEC	Multicultural Education Centre
MEd	Master of Education
MEDC	Micro-electronics Development Centre
MEP	Member of the European Parliament
MEPESS	Minority Ethnic Pupils' Experiences of School in Scotland
MER	Managing Environmental Resources
MERU	Management of Educational Resources Unit
MESP	Mental, Emotional, Social and Physical Wellbeing
META	Minority Ethnic Teachers' Association
MFL	Modern Foreign Language
MI	Multiple Intelligences

MIE	Minimally Invasive Education
MIS	Management and Information Studies
MLPS	Modern Languages in Primary Schools
MOOC	Massive Open Online Course
MP	Member of Parliament
MPhil	Master of Philosophy
MSA	Modern Studies Association
MSC	Manpower Services Commission
MSc	Master of Science
MSP	Member of the Scottish Parliament
MTHT	Management Training for Headteachers
NAB	National Assessment Bank
NAEIAC	National Association for Educational Inspectors, Advisors and Consultants
NALS	National Adult Learning Survey
NAME	National Anti-racist Movement in Education
NAR	National Assessment Resource
NASUWT	National Association of Schoolmasters Union of Women Teachers
NATFHE	National Association of Teachers in Further and Higher Education
NATO	North Atlantic Treaty Organisation
NC	National Certificate
NCC	National Curriculum Council
NCET	National Council for Educational Technology
NCH	National Children's Homes (Scotland)
NCIHE	National Committee of Inquiry into Higher Education
NCITT	National Committee for the Inservice Training of Teachers
NCS	New Community School (now Integrated Community School)
NCVQ	National Council for Vocational Qualifications
n.d.	No date
NDPB	Non-Departmental Public Body
NEET	Not in Education, Employment or Training (sometimes Not in Employment, Education or Training)
NFER	National Foundation for Educational Research
NGB	National Governing Body
NGfL	National Grid for Learning
NGO	Non-Governmental Organisation
NHS	National Health Service
NIACE	National Institute for Adult and Continuing Education
NOF	New Opportunities Funding
NOS	(1) National Occupational Standards (2) National Objectives and Standards
NPA	National Progression Awards
NQ	National Qualification
NQT	Newly Qualified Teacher
NQTG	National Qualifications Task Group
NRA	National Record of Achievement
NS-SEC	National Statistics Socio-Economic Classification

NTO	National Training Organisation
NUT	National Union of Teachers
NVQ	National Vocational Qualifications
ODL	Open and Distance Learning
OECD	Organisation for Economic Cooperation and Development
OED	Oxford English Dictionary
OFDL	Open, Flexible and Distance Learning
OfSTED	Office for Standards in Education (also Ofsted)
OIS	Office and Information Studies
OMC	Open Method of Coordination
ONC	Ordinary National Certificate
OND	Ordinary National Diploma
OSCE	Organisation for Security and Cooperation in Europe
OSCR	Office of the Scottish Charity Register
OSIC	Office of the Scottish Information Commissioner
OST	Office of Science and Technology
OU	Open University
OUVS	Open University Validation Services
PA	(1) Parent Associations (2) Practical Abilities
PALE	Perimeter Audio Learning Equipment
PAT	(1) Professional Association of Teachers (2) Planned Activity Time
PAU	Primary Assessment Unit
PBL	Problem-based Learning
PC	(1) Personal Computer (2) Parent Council
PCR	Polymerase Chain Reaction
PCS	Practical Craft Skills
PD	Product Design
PDA	(1) Professional Development Awards (2) Personal Digital Assistant (Handheld Computer)
PE	Physical Education
PEDP	Primary Education Development Project
PFI	Private Finance Initiative
PGCE	Postgraduate Certificate in Education
PGCE(P)	Postgraduate Certificate in Education (Primary)
PGCert	Postgraduate qualification in higher education teaching
PGCE(S)	Postgraduate Certificate in Education (Secondary)
PGDE(P)	Professional Graduate Diploma in Education (Primary)
PGDE(S)	Professional Graduate Diploma in Education (Secondary)
PhD	Doctor of Philosophy
PINS	Pupil Inclusion Network Scotland
PIPS	Performance Indicators in Primary Schools
PIRLS	Progress in International Reading Literacy Study
PISA	Programme for International Student Assessment
PLC	Putting Learners at the Centre
PLP	Personal Learning Plan
PPLS	Philosophy, Psychology and Language Sciences
PPP	Public Private Partnership

PS	(1) Primary School (2) Problem Solving (3) Pupil Support
PSBR	Public Sector Borrowing Requirement
PSC	Public Sector Comparator
PSD	Personal and Social Development
PSE	Personal and Social Education
PSHE	Personal, Social and Health Education
PSPC	Pupil Support/Pastoral Care
PT	(1) Part Time (2) Principal Teacher
PTA	Parent Teacher Association
PVG	Protection of Vulnerable Groups
PWLD	Pupils With Learning Difficulties
QAA(HE)	Quality Assurance Agency (for Higher Education)
QCA	Qualifications and Curriculum Authority
QDT	Qualifications Design Team
QIE	Quality in Education
QIO	Quality Improvement Officer
QMIE	Quality Management in Education
QR	Quality-related Research funding
QTS	Qualified Teacher Status
QuAC	Qualifications, Assessment and Curriculum
QUANGO	Quasi-Autonomous Non Governmental Organisation
RAE	Research Assessment Exercise
RBL	Resource Based Learning
R&D	Research and Development
RDG	Review and Development Group
RE	(1) Reasoning and Enquiry (2) Religious Education
REAF	Race Equality Advisory Forum
REF	Research Excellence Framework
REHIS	Royal Environmental Health Institute of Scotland
RET	Record of Education and Training
RI	Religious Instruction
RIF	Record of Inspection Findings
RIU	Research and Intelligence Unit
RME	Religious and Moral Education
RMPS	Religious, Moral and Philosophical Studies
ROSE	Relevance of Science Education
ROSLA	Raising of the School Leaving Age
RP	Received Pronunciation
RPs	Restorative Practices
RRAA	Race Relations Amendment Act
RS	Religious Studies
RSA	Royal Society of Arts
RSAMD	Royal Scottish Academy of Music and Drama
RSE	Royal Society of Edinburgh
RSHP	Relationships, Sexual Health and Parenthood
RUK	Rest of the UK
SAA	Student Awards Agency

SAAS	Student Awards Agency for Scotland
SAC	Scottish Arts Council
SACCA	Scottish Advisory Committee for Credit and Access
SAGT	Scottish Association of Geography Teachers
SALT	Scottish Association for Language Teaching
SATH	Scottish Association of Teachers of History
SATRO	Science and Technology Regional Organisations
SCAA	School Curriculum and Assessment Authority
SCAMP	Scottish Computer Administration and Management Programme
SCCC	Scottish Consultative Council on the Curriculum
SCCE	Scottish Council for Commercial Education
SCCM	Scottish Central Committee on Music
SCCOPE	Scottish Central Committee on Primary Education
SCCORE	Scottish Central Committee on Religious Education
SCCSS	Scottish Central Committee on Social Subjects
SCDS	Scottish Curriculum Development Services
SCE	Scottish Certificate of Education
SCEC	Scottish Community Education Council
SCEEB	Scottish Certificate of Education Examination Board
SCES	(1) Scottish Catholic Education Service (2) Scottish Committee on Environmental Studies
SCET	Scottish Council for Educational Technology
SCETDEX	SCET Indexing system
SCF	Scottish Council Foundation
SCI	(1) Scotland's Colleges International (2) School Characteristics Index
SCIS	Scottish Council of Independent Schools
SCOLA	Scottish Committee on Language Arts
SCOSDE	Scottish Committee for Staff Development in Education
SCOTBAC	Scottish Baccalaureate
SCOTBEC	Scottish Business Education Council
SCOTCAT	Scottish Credit Accumulation and Transfer
SCOTCERT	Scottish Certificate
SCOTEC	Scottish Technical Education Council
SCOTVEC	Scottish Vocational Education Council
SCPHRP	Scottish Collaboration for Public Health Research and Policy
SCQAITE	Standing Committee on Quality Assurance in Initial Teacher Education
SCQF	Scottish Credit and Qualifications Framework (see also SQF)
SCRA	Scottish Children's Reporter Administration
SCRE	Scottish Council for Research in Education
SCSWIS	Social Care and Social Work Improvement Scotland (Care Inspectorate)
SCT	Standard for Chartered Teacher
SD	Sustainable Development
SDE	Sustainable Development Education
SDELG	Sustainable Development Education Liaison Group
SDS	Skills Development Scotland
SE	(1) Scottish Enterprise (2) Scottish Executive
SEB	Scottish Examination Board

SEBD	Social, Emotional and Behavioural Difficulties
SED	Scottish Education Department
SEEC	Scottish Environmental Education Council
SEED	Scottish Executive Education Department
SEELLD	Scottish Executive Education and Lifelong Learning Department
SEETLLD	Scottish Executive Enterprise, Transport and Lifelong Learning Department
SEJ	*Scottish Educational Journal*
SEMRU	Scottish Ethnic Minorities Research Unit
SEN	Special Educational Needs
SENCO	Special Educational Needs Coordinator
SEQIA	Scottish Education Quality and Improvement Agency (now Education Scotland)
SER	*Scottish Educational Review*
SERA	Scottish Educational Research Association
SERAD	Scottish Executive Rural Affairs Department
SES	Socio-economic Status
SESEF	Scottish Earth Science Education Forum
SE/SI	School Effectiveness/School Improvement
SESS	Scottish Employers Skill Survey
SETT	Scottish Education and Teaching with Technology Conference (now the Scottish Learning Festival)
SFC	(1) Scottish Funding Council (formerly SHEFC) (2) Scottish Film Council
SFEFC	Scottish Further Education Funding Council
SFEU	Scottish Further Education Unit
SFH	Standard for Headship
SFHEA	Scottish Further and Higher Education Association
SFIS	School-focused Inservice
SFL	Support for Learning
SFR	Standard for Full Registration
SfW	Skills for Work
SG	(1) Scottish Government (2) Standard Grade
SGAs	Scottish Group Awards
SGCS	Standard Grade Computing Studies
SGDP	Standard Grade Development Programme
SGPE	Standard Grade Physical Education
SHA	Secondary Heads Association
SHEFC	Scottish Higher Education Funding Council
SHPSU	Scottish Health Promoting Schools Unit
SIMD	Scottish Index of Multiple Deprivation
SIMON	School Initiated Monitoring of Needs
SINA	Scottish Independent Nurseries Association
SITE	Standard for Initial Teacher Education
SJNC	Scottish Joint Negotiating Committee
SLC	Scottish Leaving Certificate
SLD	Scottish Languages Dictionary

SLS	School Leaders Scotland (formerly the Headteachers' Association of Scotland)
SLT	Speech and Language Therapist
SM	Scottish Masters
SMC	Scottish Mathematical Council
SMEA	Scottish Muslim Educationists' Association
SMT	Senior Management Team
SNAG	Schools Nutrition Action Groups
SNAP	(1) Scottish Network for Able Pupils (2) Scottish Network for Access and Participation
SNCT	Scottish Negotiating Committee for Teachers
SNH	Scottish Natural Heritage
SNP	Scottish National Party
SOAs	Single Outcome Agreements
SOED	Scottish Office Education Department
SOEID	Scottish Office Education and Industry Department
SOHHD	Scottish Office Home and Health Department
SOS	Sense Over Sectarianism
SOSB	*Scottish Office Statistical Bulletin*
SoTL	Scholarship of Teaching and Learning
SPA	Scottish Progression Awards
SPAG	Southside Parents' Action Group
SPARQS	Scottish Participation in Quality Scotland
SPEA	Scottish Physical Education Association
SPI	Statutory Performance Indicators
SPIE	Specify, Plan, Implement and Evaluate
SPMG	Scottish Primary Mathematics Group
SPPA	Scottish Pre-school Playgroup Association
SPRinG	Social Pedagogic Research into Group-work (project of TLRP)
SPSO	Scottish Public Services Ombudsman
SPTC	Scottish Parent-Teacher Council
SQA	Scottish Qualifications Authority
SQF	Scottish Qualifications Framework (see also SCQF)
SQH	Scottish Qualification for Headship
SSA	(1) Scottish Schoolmasters' Association (2) Scottish Survey of Achievement (3) School Support Assistant
SSB	Standard Setting Body
SSBA	Scottish School Board Association
SSC	Sector Skills Council
SSDN	Scottish Schools Digital Network (now called GLOW)
SSE	Scottish Standard English
SSEN	Scottish Schools Ethos Network
SSFE	Scottish School of Further Education
SSLN	Scottish Survey of Literacy and Numeracy
SSLS	Scottish School Leavers Survey
SSR	Strategic Spending Review
SSRC	Social Science Research Council

SSSC	Scottish Social Services Council
SSSERC	Scottish Schools Science Equipment Research Centre
SSTA	Scottish Secondary Teachers' Association
STACS	Standard Tables and Charts
STARS	Superhighways Teams Across Rural Schools
STEAC	Scottish Tertiary Education Advisory Council
STEC	Scottish Teacher Education Committee
STEG	Scottish Teacher Education Group
STEP	Scottish Traveller Education Programme
STNE	Scottish Teachers for a New Era
STSC	Scottish Teachers Salaries Committee
STSCC	Scottish Teachers Service and Conditions Committee
STUC	Scottish Trades Union Congress
SUCE	Scottish Universities Council on Entrance
SUfI	Scottish University for Industry
SUM	Student Unit of Measurement
SVQ	Scottish Vocational Qualification
SWAP	Scottish Wider Access Programme
SWIA	Social Work Inspection Agency
SWSI	Social Work Services Inspectorate
SYPS	Scottish Young People's Survey
TAC	Teachers Agreement Communications Team
TACADE	The Advisory Council on Alcohol and Drug Education
TAPS	Techniques for the Assessment of Practical Skills (in Science)
TDP	Teacher Development Partnership
TEI	Teacher Education Institution
TENET	Traveller Education Network
TES	*Times Educational Supplement*
TESS	*Times Educational Supplement Scotland*
TfW	Training for Work
THE	*Times Higher Education*
TIMSS	Third International Mathematics and Science Study
TLRP	Teaching and Learning Research Programme
TLTP	Teaching and Learning Technology Programme
TQ	Teaching Qualification
TQA	Teaching Quality Assessment
TQFE	Teaching Qualification Further Education
TQM	Total Quality Management
TRIPS	Research Informed Practice Digests (Department for Education, UK)
TS	Technological Studies
TSB	Technology Strategy Board
TSF	*Teaching Scotland's Future* (The Donaldson Report)
TSSE	Teachers Side School Education
TTA	Teacher Training Agency
TTRB	Teacher Training Resource Bank
TUFL	Trade Union Fund for Learning
TUWPL	Trade Union Working Party on Lifelong Learning

TVEI	Technical and Vocational Education Initiative
UCAS	Universities and Colleges Admission System
UCU	University and College Union
UFC	Universities Funding Council
UGC	University Grants Committee
UHI	University of the Highlands and Islands
UHIMI	University of the Highlands and Islands Millennium Institute
UK	United Kingdom
UKERNA	UK Education and Research Network Association
UKTI	United Kingdom Trade and Investment
ULA	University Lecturers' Association
UN	United Nations
UNDESD	United Nations Decade of Education for Sustainable Development
UNESCO	United Nations Educational Scientific and Cultural Organisation
UNICEF	United Nations Children's Fund
UPS	Unified Points Score Scale
US	(1) Universities Scotland (2) United States
USA	United States of America
USW	Understanding Standards Website
VAK	Visual, auditory or kinaesthetic (preferences in learning styles)
VLE	Virtual Learning Environment
VQ	Vocational Qualification
VRE	Virtual Research Environment
WARFs	Wider Access Regional Forums
WARP	Widening Access Retention Programme
WB	World Bank
WEA	Workers' Educational Association
WHO	World Health Organisation
WIC	Work Introduction Courses
WPD	Work and Pensions Department
WTA	Working Time Agreement
WTE	Whole-Time Equivalent
www	World Wide Web
YMCA	Young Men's Christian Association
YOP	Youth Opportunities Programme
YTS	Youth Training Scheme

INDEX